Some Useful Formulas

1. **Discount factor (Chapter 2, equation 2.3)**
   Value of $1 to be received at time T, disco...

$$DF_{T,k} = \frac{\$1}{(1+k)^T} = \left(\frac{\$1}{1+k}\right)$$

2. **Present value (Chapter 2)**
   Value today of a T-year cash-flow stream discounted at rate k

$$PV = [CF_1 \times DF_{1,k}] + \dots [CF_t \times DF_{t,k}] + \dots + [CF_T \times DF_{T,k}]$$

3. **Present value of a perpetuity (Chapter 2, equation 2.6)**
   The present value of an infinite stream of identical cash flows discounted at rate k

$$PV = \frac{CF}{k}$$

4. **Present value of a constant growing perpetuity (Chapter 2, equation 2.9)**
   Present value, at rate k, of a perpetuity growing at the constant rate g where the cash flow at the end of the first year is CF_1

$$PV = \frac{CF_1}{k-g} \text{ with } k > g$$

5. **Present value of an annuity (Chapter 2, equation 2.11)**
   Present value of a T-year annuity at a rate k with a cash flow CF

$$PV = CF \times ADF_{T,k} \text{ with}$$

$$ADF_{T,k} = \frac{1}{k}\left[1 - \frac{1}{(1+k)^T}\right]$$

6. **Sharpe ratio of asset i (Chapter 3, equation 3.8)**

$$\text{Sharpe ratio of asset i} = \frac{E(R_i) - R_F}{\sigma_i}$$

7. **Beta coefficient of stock i (Chapter 3, equation 3.11)**

$$\beta_i = \frac{Cov(R_i, R_M)}{Var(R_M)} = \frac{\rho_{iM}\sigma_i\sigma_M}{\sigma_M^2} = \rho_{iM}\left(\frac{\sigma_i}{\sigma_M}\right)$$

8. **Capital asset pricing model (Chapter 3, equation 3.13a, Chapter 10, equation 10.11a and Chapter 12, equation 12.10)**

$$E(R_i) = R_F + [E(R_M) - R_F]\beta_i$$

9. **Invested capital (Chapter 4, equation 4.5)**

   Invested capital = Cash + Working capital requirement + Net fixed assets

10. **Capital employed (Chapter 4, equation 4.6)**

   Capital employed = Short-term debt + Long-term debt + Owners' equity

FINANCE FOR EXECUTIVES

Managing for Value Creation

FINANCE FOR EXECUTIVES

Managing for Value Creation

SIXTH EDITION

Gabriel Hawawini

INSEAD

Claude Viallet

INSEAD

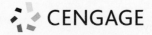

Australia • Brazil • Mexico • Singapore • United Kingdom • United States

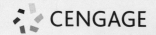
CENGAGE

Finance for Executives: Managing for Value Creation, Sixth Edition
Gabriel Hawawini & Claude Viallet

Publisher: Annabel Ainscow

List Manager: Jenny Grene

Marketing Manager: Sophie Clarke

Senior Content Project Manager:
  Sue Povey

Manufacturing Manager: Eyvett Davis

Typesetter: SPi Global

Cover Design: Elisabeth Heissler

Cover Images: Sebastian Kaulitzki/
Shutterstock; WHYFRAME/Shutterstock;
one line man/Shutterstock

For product information and technology assistance, contact us at
emea.info@cengage.com

For permission to use material from this text or product and for permission queries, email **emea.permissions@cengage.com**

British Library Cataloguing-in-Publication Data

A catalogue record for this book is available from the British Library.

ISBN: 978-1-4737-4924-5

Cengage Learning, EMEA
Cheriton House, North Way
Andover, Hampshire, SP10 5BE
United Kingdom

Cengage Learning is a leading provider of customized learning solutions with employees residing in nearly 40 different countries and sales in more than 125 countries around the world. Find your local representative at: **www.cengage.co.uk**.

Cengage Learning products are represented in Canada by Nelson Education, Ltd.

For your course and learning solutions, visit **www.cengage.co.uk**.

Purchase any of our products at your local college store or at our preferred online store **www.cengagebrain.com**.

Printed in China by RR Donnelley
Print Number: 01   Print Year: 2019

To our spouses, children and grandchildren, with love and gratitude.

GH and CV, 2018

This edition of Finance for Executives is dedicated to the memory of Claude Viallet, my friend, colleague and co-author.

Gabriel Hawawini, 2019

Brief Contents

CONTENTS

PART IV   MAKING FINANCING DECISIONS   315

PREFACE

Finance is an essential and exciting area of management that many executives want to learn or explore in more depth. Most finance textbooks, however, are either too advanced or too simplistic for many nonfinancial managers. Our challenge was to write an introductory text that is specifically addressed to executives, and that is both practical and rigorous.

The target audience includes executives directly and indirectly involved with financial matters and financial management, which is just about every executive. Over the past few years, several thousand managers around the world have used most of the material in this book. The text works well in executive-development programs – including executive masters of business administration (EMBA) programs – and corporate finance courses for an undergraduate or MBA audience either as a core text, where a more practical and applied emphasis is desired, or as a companion to a theoretical text to translate theory into practice.

Finance for Executives has a number of important features:

- **The book is based on the principle that managers should manage their firm's resources with the objective of increasing their firm's value.**

Managers must make decisions that are expected to raise their firm's market value. This fundamental principle underlies our approach to management. This book is designed to improve managers' ability to make decisions that create value, including decisions to restructure existing operations, launch new products, buy new assets, acquire other companies, and finance the firm's investments.

- **The book fills the gap between introductory accounting and finance manuals for nonfinancial managers and advanced texts in corporate finance.**

Finance for Executives is based on modern finance principles. It emphasizes rigorous analysis but avoids formulas that have no direct application to decision making. Whenever a formula is used in the text, the logic behind it is explained and numerical examples are provided. Mathematical derivations of the formulas are given in the appendices that follow the chapter in which they first appear. Recognizing that executives often approach financial problems from a financial accounting perspective, we begin with a solid review of the financial accounting system. We then show how this framework can be extended and used to make sound financial decisions that enhance the firm's value.

- **The chapters are self-contained.**

Each chapter can be read without prior reading of the others. When knowledge of a previous chapter would enhance comprehension of a specific section, we direct the reader to that previously-developed material. Further advice on this score is provided in the section titled "How to Read This Book."

- **The book can be read in its entirety or used as a reference.**

The book can be used as a quick reference whenever readers need to brush up on a specific topic or close a gap in their financial management knowledge. A comprehensive glossary and the index at the end of the book help the reader determine which chapters deal with the desired issue or topic. Most financial terms are explained when first introduced in the text; they appear in boldface type and are defined in the glossary.

- **Data from the same companies are used throughout the book to illustrate diagnostic techniques and valuation methods.**

We focus on the same set of firms to illustrate most of the topics covered in this book. This approach provides a common thread that reinforces understanding.

- **Spreadsheet solutions and formulas are included in the text.**

Recognizing that spreadsheets have become part of most executives' tool kit, the text shows the spreadsheet solutions to all the examples, cases, and self-test questions, when applicable. Formulas used in the spreadsheets are shown at the bottom of the tables for an immediate understanding of the solutions and for reproduction of the spreadsheets for personal use.

- **Each chapter is followed by self-test and review questions.**

The self-test questions that appear at the end of each chapter allow the readers to assess their knowledge of the subject. Most of the questions require the use of a financial calculator or a spreadsheet. Detailed, step-by-step solutions to the self-test questions can be found at the end of the book.

The review questions, which follow the self-test questions at the end of each chapter, provide the readers with the opportunity to challenge their knowledge of the subject and give the instructors relevant material to test the student's grasp of the concepts and techniques presented in the chapter. Solutions to review questions are available online only to instructors.

MAJOR CHANGES IN THE SIXTH EDITION

As was the case with the previous editions of *Finance for Executives*, we have incorporated in the sixth edition recommendations received from our colleagues at INSEAD and other schools and from a large number of students and executives who have attended courses and seminars in which the book was assigned. Here are the major changes from the last edition:

- We have written an entirely new chapter (Chapter 16) entitled Understanding Forward, Futures, and Options and Their Contribution to Corporate Finance.
- We have moved the presentation on currency risk from Chapter 15 (Managing Corporate Risk) to Chapter 17 (Making International Business Decisions).
- We use a new set of international companies from the pharmaceutical industry, GlaxoSmithKline and Sanofi, to illustrate how to perform a financial analysis using the concepts and techniques presented in Chapters 4 through 6.

- We have updated all chapters with the latest available financial information.
- We have introduced spreadsheets throughout the chapters to illustrate the valuation of bonds, stocks, and companies.
- We have prepared a new set of professionally designed PowerPoint slides to accompany the book.

WHAT IS IN THIS BOOK?

Although the book consists of self-contained chapters, those chapters follow a logical sequence built around the idea of value creation. The overall structure of the book is summarized in a diagram on the following page that illustrates the value-based business model. Managers must raise cash (the right side) to finance investments (the left side) that are expected to increase the firm's value and the wealth of its owners.

Part I, Financial Concepts and Techniques, begins with a chapter that surveys the principles and tools executives need to know to manage for value creation. Chapter 2 presents the concept of time value of money and reviews the mechanics of calculating present values for different streams of cash flows. Chapter 3 explains the relationship between the risk of a financial asset and its expected return, and examines the implications for financial investment management and the valuation of financial assets.

Part II, Assessing Business Performance, reviews the techniques that executives should use to assess a firm's financial health, evaluate and plan its future development, and make decisions that enhance its chances of survival and success. The chapters in this part examine in detail a number of financial diagnostics and managerial tools that were introduced in Chapter 1. Chapter 4 explains and illustrates how balance sheets, income statements, and statements of cash flows are constructed and interpreted. As an application, the appendix includes the financial statements of GlaxoSmithKline, an international pharmaceutical company. Chapter 5 shows how to evaluate a firm's operational efficiency and its liquidity position. Chapter 6 identifies the factors that drive a firm's profitability, analyzes the extent of its exposure to business and financial risks, and evaluates its capacity to finance its activities and achieve sustainable growth. The financial analysis tools presented in these chapters are applied to GlaxoSmithKline, whose financial statements are presented in Chapter 4. The analyses appear in the appendices to Chapters 5 and 6, including a comparative analysis of GlaxoSmithKline and one of its major competitors, Sanofi.

Part III, Making Investment Decisions, demonstrates how managers should make investment decisions that maximize the firm's value. Chapter 7 examines the net present value (NPV) rule in detail and shows how to apply this rule to make value-creating investment decisions. Chapter 8 reviews a number of alternative approaches to the NPV rule, including the internal rate of return (IRR) and the payback period rules, and compares them with the NPV rule. Chapter 9 shows how to identify and estimate the cash flows generated by an investment proposal and assess the proposal's capacity to create value.

Part IV, Making Financing Decisions, explains how managers should make financing decisions that maximize value. Chapter 10 shows how to value bonds and common stocks. Chapter 11 explains how firms raise fresh capital from financial markets policy and share buybacks. Chapter 12 shows how to estimate the cost of capital for a particu-

WHAT IS IN THIS BOOK?

PART I: FINANCIAL CONCEPTS AND TECHNIQUES

Chapter 1:
What does managing for value creation mean?

Chapter 2:
How to convert a stream of future cash flows into their present value.

Chapter 3:
What is the relationship between the risk of a financial asset and its expected return, and what are the implications for financial and investment management and the valuation of financial assets?

PART II: ASSESSING BUSINESS PERFORMANCE

Chapters 4 to 6:
How to interpret financial information to assess performance (Chapter 4), and how do financial structure and operational efficiency affect a firm's liquidity (Chapter 5), profitability, risk, and capacity to grow (Chapter 6)?

PART IV: MAKING FINANCING DECISIONS

Chapter 10:
How to value the securities that firms issue to raise funds?

Chapter 11:
How do firms raise the funds needed to finance their investments and return cash to shareholders?

Chapter 12:
What is the cost of the funds the firm raises?

Chapter 13:
What is the best mix of owners' funds and borrowed funds?

PART III: MAKING INVESTMENT DECISIONS

Chapters 7 to 9:
How should firms evaluate investment proposals and select value-creating projects?

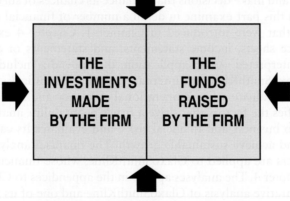

PART V: MAKING BUSINESS DECISIONS

Chapter 14:
How is a firm valued?

Chapter 15:
How risky is the firm?

Chapter 16:
How to use forward, futures and option contracts to control risk.

Chapter 17:
How do international activities affect the firm's value?

Chapter 18:
Is the firm using its resources efficiently to create value?

lar project as well as an entire firm. Chapter 13 explains how a firm should make value-creating financing decisions by designing a capital structure (the mix of owners' funds and borrowed funds) that maximizes its market value and minimizes its cost of capital.

Part V, Making Business Decisions, concludes with five chapters on making value-creating business decisions. Chapter 14 reviews various models and techniques used to value firms in the context of an acquisition. Chapter 15 provides a comprehensive framework to identify, measure, and manage the risks a firm faces. Chapter 16 shows how forward, futures, and option contracts can be used to control risk. Chapter 17 looks at financial management and value creation in an international environment where currency and country risks must be taken into account. Chapter 18 summarizes the analytical framework underlying the process of value creation and examines some of the related empirical evidence.

HOW TO USE THIS BOOK

Depending on your background and your needs, you may want to use this book in different ways. Below are a few guidelines. Also, refer to the exhibit on the next page for suggested sequences of chapters to cover depending on the type of program taken.

- If you are unfamiliar with financial management and financial accounting, you may want to begin by reading Chapter 1. It provides an overview of these subjects and will help you understand the fundamental objective of modern corporate finance and the logical relationships among the various issues and topics that make up that field. Although reading the first chapter will facilitate the understanding of those that follow it, it is not necessary to read it to comprehend the rest of the book – the chapters are self-contained.

- If you are not familiar with the basic concept of discounting and the calculation of present values, you should read Chapter 2. The chapter also shows you how to perform present value calculations with a financial calculator and spreadsheets. If you skip Chapter 2, you will find a review of these concepts in Chapter 7.

- If you wish to familiarize yourself with the concept of portfolio diversification and financial investment management you should read Chapter 3, but you do not need to read that chapter to understand any of the other chapters in the book.

- If you are not familiar with financial statements, it would be helpful, but not essential, to read Chapter 4 before you continue with the chapters in Part II. The chapter explains how to read a balance sheet, an income statement, and a statement of cash flows, and how to restructure these statements to interpret the information they provide.

- If you are unfamiliar with the functioning of financial markets, you should read the first five sections of Chapter 11 before you continue with the rest of Part IV. These sections provide an overview of the structure, organization, and role of financial markets.

- Last, if you have a basic knowledge of accounting and finance, you can go directly to the chapter dealing with the issue you wish to explore. Because the chapters are self-contained, you will not have to review the preceding chapters to fully understand your chosen chapter.

RECOMMENDED CHAPTERS ACCORDING TO TYPE OF PROGRAM

Chapter/Topic	Executive Education		MBA Program	
	1st course	2nd course	1st course	2nd course
1. Overview	✓		✓	
2. The time value of money	✓		✓	
3. Risk, return, and portfolio analysis			✓	
4. Financial statements analysis	✓		✓	
5. Operational efficiency and liquidity management	✓		✓	
6. Profitability and risk management	✓		✓	
7. Capital budgeting: NPV	✓		✓	
8. Capital budgeting: IRR & other methods	✓		✓	
9. Capital budgeting: Cash flow analysis	✓		✓	
10. Bond valuation		✓	✓	
10. Common stock valuation		✓	✓	
11. Financial markets and raising capital		✓	✓	
11. Dividend policy and share buybacks		✓		✓
12. Estimation of the cost of capital		✓		✓
13. Designing a capital structure		✓		✓
14. Valuing and acquiring a business		✓		✓
15. Corporate risk management		✓		✓
16. Forward, futures, and option contracts		✓		✓
17. International capital budgeting		✓		✓
18. Managing for value creation		✓		✓

ABOUT THE AUTHORS

Gabriel Hawawini (Ph.D., New York University) is emeritus professor of finance at INSEAD where he served as dean and held the Henry Grunfeld Chair in Investment Banking. He taught finance at New York University, Baruch College, Columbia University, and the Wharton School of the University of Pennsylvania where he received the Helen Kardon Moss Anvil Award for Excellence in Teaching.

Professor Hawawini is the author of 12 books and more than 70 research papers on financial markets and corporate finance. He teaches value-based management seminars around the world and sits on the board of several companies.

Claude Viallet (Ph.D., Northwestern University) was emeritus professor of finance at INSEAD. He was visiting professor of finance at Kellogg School of Management, Northwestern University. Before joining INSEAD, he worked as a project manager at a major oil company and as chief financial officer of a service company in Paris.

Professor Viallet was president of the European Finance Association and published widely in leading academic and professional journals. He also organized, directed, and taught management-development programs in Europe, the United States, Asia, and Latin America and provided consulting services to companies around the world.

ACKNOWLEDGMENTS

A number of colleagues and friends have been most generous with the time they spent reading parts of the manuscript for the previous editions and providing specific comments and suggestions. We also have received many useful comments from students and executives to whom the book was assigned.

We want to thank in particular our colleague Professor Pierre Michel who reviewed the first draft of many chapters, and made numerous insightful comments. We also want to thank Dr. Chittima Silberzahn for helping us update some of the exhibits, and Mr. Bennett Stewart of ISS Corporate Solutions who kindly provided us with the data in Chapter 18.

Below is the list of individuals who made comments and suggestions to some of the chapters in the current and previous editions of the book. We thank them all for their feedback.

José Benzinho *(ISCAC Coimvria Business School, Portugal)*

Tomasz S. Berent *(Capital Markets Department, Warsaw School of Economics, Poland)*

Hugh-Joel Bessis *(HEC Paris, France)*

Soren Bjerre-Nielsen *(Chairman of MT Hojgaard, Denmark)*

John Boquist *(Indiana University)*

David Borst *(Concordia University)*

Jay T. Brandi *(University of Louisville)*

Dave Brunn *(Carthage College)*

Adrian Buss *(INSEAD)*

Bruno Chaintron *(INSEAD)*

David Champion *(Harvard Business Review)*

Sudip Datta *(Wayne State University)*

Jean Dermine *(INSEAD)*

Helene Dore *(Crédit Agricole-CIB)*

Stephen Doukas *(Montreat College)*

Bernard Dumas *(INSEAD)*

Theodoros Evgeniou *(INSEAD)*

Paolo Fulghieri *(University of North Carolina)*

Marco Garro *(Bocconi University, Italy)*

Federico Gavazzoni *(INSEAD)*

Sergei Glebkin *(INSEAD)*

Adam Golinski, *(University of York)*

Dwight Grant *(University of New Mexico)*

Denis Gromb *(HEC Paris, France)*

George Hachey *(Bentley College)*

Alfred Hawawini *(Mirakl)*

Pekka Hietala *(INSEAD)*

Pierre Hillion *(INSEAD)*

A. Can Inci *(Bryant University)*

Laurent Jacque *(Tufts University)*

Donald Keim *(The Wharton School)*

Paul Kleindorfer (deceased) *(The Wharton School)*

Pascal Maenhout *(INSEAD)*

Sophie Manigart *(Vlerick Business School, Belgium)*

Kenneth J. Martin *(New Mexico State University)*

Pedro Verga Matos *(ISEG School of Economics and Management, Technical University of Lisbon, Portugal)*

Roger Mesznik *(Columbia University)*

Pierre Michel *(University of Liège and the Free University of Brussels)*

Arjen Mulder *(Department of Finance, Rotterdam School of Management, Erasmus University, The Netherlands)*
John Muth *(Regis University)*
Robert Obermaier *(Faculty of Business Administration and Economics, University of Passau, Germany)*
Jerome Osreryoung *(Florida State University)*
Joel Peress *(INSEAD)*
Urs Peyer *(INSEAD)*
Art Raviv *(Northwestern University)*
Lee Remmers *(INSEAD)*
Maryanne Rouse *(University of South Florida)*
Niels Sandalgaard *(Department of Business and Management, Aalborg University, Denmark)*
José Miguel Pinto dos Santos *(AESE Business School)*
Antonio Sanvicente *(IBEC Sao Paulo)*
Ravi Shukla *(Syracuse University)*

K. P. Sridharan *(Delta State University)*
Sascha Steffen *(European School of Management and Technology, Germany)*
Aris Stouraitis *(City University of Hong Kong)*
John Strong *(College of William & Mary)*
Matti Suominen *(Aalto University School of Economics)*
Lucie Tepla *(INSEAD)*
Andy Terry *(University of Arkansas at Little Rock)*
Nikhil P. Varaiya *(San Diego State University)*
Maria Vassalou *(Columbia University)*
Theo Vermaelen *(INSEAD)*
Ingo Walter *(New York University)*
Clement Wong *(University of Hong Kong)*
David Young *(INSEAD)*
A. Burcin Yurtoglu *(Corporate Finance, WHU – Otto Beisheim School of Management, Germany)*

Finally, we thank all the staff at Cengage Learning for their help and support in all the phases of development and production.

Gabriel Hawawini
Claude Viallet
January 2019

CENGAGE

Teaching & Learning Support Resources

Cengage's peer reviewed content for higher and further education courses is accompanied by a range of digital teaching and learning support resources. The resources are carefully tailored to the specific needs of the instructor, student and the course. Examples of the kind of resources provided include:

- A password protected area for instructors with, for example, a testbank, PowerPoint slides and an instructor's manual.

- An open-access area for students including, for example, useful weblinks and glossary terms.

Lecturers: to discover the dedicated lecturer digital support resources accompanying this textbook please register here for access: login.cengage.com.

Students: to discover the dedicated student digital support resources accompanying this textbook, please search for MANAGERIAL ECONOMICS on: cengagebrain.co.uk.

BE UNSTOPPABLE

FINANCIAL MANAGEMENT AND VALUE CREATION: AN OVERVIEW

An executive cannot be an effective manager without a clear understanding of the principles and practices of modern finance. The good news is that these principles and practices can be communicated simply, without sacrificing thoroughness or rigor. Indeed, you will discover that most of the concepts and methods underlying modern corporate finance are based on business common sense. But translating business common sense into an effective management system can be a real challenge. It requires, in addition to a solid understanding of fundamental principles, the determination and the discipline to manage a business according to the precepts of modern finance. Consider, for example, one of financial management's most useful guiding principles:

> Managers should manage their firm's resources with the objective of increasing the firm's value.

This may seem to be an obvious statement. But you probably know a number of companies that are not managed to their full potential value. You may even know well-intentioned managers who are value destroyers. Their misguided actions, or lack of actions, actually reduce the value of their firms.

How do you manage for value creation? This book should help you find the answer. Our main objective is to present and explain the methods and tools that will help you determine whether the firm's current investments are creating value and, if they are not, what remedial actions should be taken to improve operations. We also show you how to determine whether a business proposal – such as the decision to buy a piece of equipment, launch a new product, acquire another firm, or restructure existing operations – has the potential to raise the firm's value. Finally, we show you that managing with the goal of raising the firm's value provides the basis for an integrated financial management system that helps you not only evaluate actual business performance and make sound business decisions, but also design effective management compensation packages – compensation packages that align the interests of the firm's managers with those of the firm's owners.

This introductory chapter reviews some of the most challenging issues and questions raised by modern corporate finance and gives a general but comprehensive overview. Although the topics surveyed here are examined later in detail, many of the important terms and concepts are introduced and defined in this introduction with a clear indication of the relevant chapters you need to consult to get a complete presentation of each topic. After reading this chapter, you should have a broad and clear understanding of the following:

- The meaning of managing a business for value creation
- How to measure the value that may be created by a business proposal, such as an investment project, a change in the firm's financial structure, a business acquisition, or the decision to invest in a foreign country
- The significance of the firm's cost of capital and how it is measured
- Why some firms pay out cash dividends to their shareholders and buy back their own shares in the open market
- The function of financial markets as a source of corporate funds and the role they play in the value-creation process
- A firm's business cycle and how it determines the firm's capacity to grow
- The basic structure and the logic behind a firm's balance sheet, income statement, and cash-flow statement
- What is risk and how to define it, and how it affects the firm's cost of capital
- How to measure a firm's profitability
- How to determine if a firm is creating value

THE KEY QUESTION: WILL YOUR DECISION CREATE VALUE?

Suppose you have identified a need in the marketplace for a new product. You believe the product can be manufactured cheaply and rapidly. You are even confident it can be sold for a tidy profit. Should you go ahead? Before you make this decision, you should check the project's *long-term financial viability*. How will your firm finance the project? Where will the money come from? Will the project be sufficiently profitable to cover the cost of the funds required to finance it? More to the point, will the firm be more valuable with the project than without it? You should answer these questions before making a final decision.

The proposed venture will be financed by the firm's owners, its **shareholders** (you may be one of them), and by those who lend money to the firm, the **debt holders** (a bank, for example). Cash contributed by shareholders is called **equity capital**; cash contributed by lenders is **debt capital**. As with any other resource, capital is not free. It has a cost. Let's assume that the firm's annual **cost of capital** is 12 percent of the total amount of **capital employed**, the sum of equity and debt capital. The firm's owners will find the venture attractive only if its *operating profitability exceeds* 12 percent, that is, only if its profitability *before financing* the venture is higher than the cost of capital of 12 percent. Why? Because a project whose operating profitability *exceeds* its cost of capital should generate *more* cash than is required to pay for the cost of capital. It is that excess cash that makes the firm more valuable. (We will explain this in more detail throughout the book.) In other words, before deciding to go ahead with a business proposal, you should ask yourself the Key Question:

Will the proposal create value?

If, in light of existing information and proper analysis, you can confidently answer "yes", then go ahead with the project. Otherwise, you should abandon it.

The Key Question applies not only to a business proposal but also to current operations. If some existing **assets** are destroying rather than creating value, you should take immediate corrective actions. If these actions fail to improve performance, you should seriously consider selling those assets.

THE IMPORTANCE OF MANAGING FOR VALUE CREATION

We realize, of course, that the Key Question is much easier asked than answered. The next section describes how to apply the **fundamental finance principle** to help you answer the Key Question. Before introducing that principle, we want to explain why management's paramount objective should be the creation of value for the firm's owners. This objective makes business common sense if you think about a firm whose recent management decisions *reduced* the firm's value. What would happen in this case? The firm may be unable to attract the equity capital it needs to fund its activities. And without equity capital, no firm can survive.

You may rightly ask whether we are forgetting the contributions of employees, customers and suppliers. No firm can succeed without them. Great companies have not only satisfied owners, but also loyal customers, motivated employees, and reliable suppliers. The point, of course, is not to neglect customers, squeeze suppliers, or ignore the interest of employees for the benefit of owners: more value for shareholders does not mean less value for employees, customers, or suppliers. On the contrary, firms managed with a focus on creating value for their owners are among those that have built durable and valuable relationships with their customers, employees, and suppliers. They know that dealing successfully with employees, customers, and suppliers is an important element in achieving their ultimate objective of creating value for their owners.

Indeed, evidence supports the fact that firms that take care of their customers and employees also deliver value to their owners. Consider the results of an annual survey that asked executives, outside directors, and financial analysts to rate the ten largest companies in their industry according to the following criteria: (1) quality of management; (2) quality of products or services; (3) ability to attract, develop, and keep talented people; (4) company's value as a long-term investment; (5) use of corporate assets; (6) financial soundness; (7) capacity to innovate; and (8) community and environmental responsibilities.[1] The companies with the *highest* scores across all industries significantly outperformed the Standard & Poor's market index (an average of 500 companies) during the ten-year period that preceded the ranking. What was the stock market performance of the companies with the *lowest* scores? They were value destroyers. They delivered a *negative* return to their shareholders during the ten-year period that preceded the ranking. An analysis based on only the three criteria that relate to the way companies treat their customers (the second criterion), their employees (the third criterion), and their community (the last criterion) showed similar results.[2]

These results clearly indicate that the *ability of firms to create value for their shareholders is related to the way they treat their customers, employees, and community.* But you should not conclude that the guaranteed recipe for value creation consists of delighting customers, establishing durable relations with suppliers, and motivating employees. Some firms that deal successfully with their customers, employees, and suppliers are unable to translate this goodwill into a higher firm value.

---

[1] See *fortune.com/worlds-most-admired-companies*.

[2] See Edmans (2011) and (2012). For international evidence, see Edmans, Li, and Zhang (2014).

What should the firm's managers do in this case? They must revise the firm's current business strategy because their shareholders will eventually question the relevance of a strategy that does not allow the firm to produce a satisfactory return on the equity capital they have invested in it. Dissatisfied shareholders, particularly those holding a significant portion of the firm's equity capital, may try to force the firm's management to change course or may try to oust the existing management team. Or, they may simply withdraw their support by selling their holdings to others who might force changes.

Whether shareholders will be successful in getting management to change its strategy, or even be replaced, depends on a number of factors, including the institutional and legal frameworks that govern the relationship between management and shareholders, and the structure and organization of the country's equity markets in which the firm's shares are listed and traded. We simply suggest that *no firm can afford to have delighted customers, motivated employees, and devoted suppliers for too long if it does not also have satisfied shareholders.*

When asked in whose interest corporations are run, Mr. Jack Welch, the former chief executive officer of General Electric, replied, "A proper balance between shareholders, employees, and communities is what we all try to achieve. But it is a tough balancing act because, in the end, if you don't satisfy shareholders, you don't have the flexibility to do the things you have to do to take care of employees or communities. In our society, whether we like it or not, we have to satisfy shareholders."[3]

THE SATURN STORY

In the early 1980s, General Motors (GM), then the world's largest vehicle manufacturer, faced strong competition from foreign producers of small, efficient, reliable, and inexpensive cars. In response to this challenge, in 1985, GM set up a separate company to build an entirely new car, the Saturn. The car was designed, produced, and sold according to the best practices available at the time. Workers were highly motivated, car dealers could not keep up with demand, and customers were extremely satisfied with their cars. According to these criteria, Saturn was an undeniable success story.

The first car rolled off the assembly line in 1990. The project, however, never delivered the rise in the value of GM's shares that management had hoped would occur.[4] Why?

According to knowledgeable consultants, the $6 billion spent developing, manufacturing, and marketing the Saturn line of models was already so high that for GM to earn an acceptable return for its shareholders it would have had "to operate existing facilities at full capacity forever, earn more than double standard profit margins, and keep 40 percent of the dealers' sticker price as net cash flow."[5]

In 2009 GM stopped producing its line of Saturn cars, and in 2010 it discontinued the Saturn brand after acknowledging that it had lost about $20 billion on the project.[6]

---

[3] *Fortune*, May 29, 1995, p. 75.

[4] *Fortune*, December 13, 2004, "GM's Saturn Problem," pp. 119–127.

[5] McTaggart, Kontes, and Mankins (1994), p. 16.

[6] See the *New York Times*, October 1, 2009, "GM to Close Saturn After Deal Fails," and "Saturn Corporation" in Wikipedia.org.

Our question is: how long should a firm fund a project that delights its customers, pleases its distributors, and satisfies its employees, but fails to deliver value to its shareholders? Obviously, not very long if it wishes to survive. So what can we conclude about the ultimate purpose of a business enterprise? Is it exclusively about shareholder wealth creation, or is it about a **"stakeholders' approach"** that tries to balance the interests of all the parties associated with the firm (its customers, employees, suppliers, and owners)? We believe that this is a false debate. The focus should be on making decisions that raise the value of the firm, *and in doing so, the firm ultimately creates value for its stakeholders and society as a whole*.[7]

THE FUNDAMENTAL FINANCE PRINCIPLE

Recall the Key Question you should ask before making a business decision: will the decision create value? The Key Question can be answered with the help of the fundamental finance principle:

> A business proposal – such as a new investment, the acquisition of another company, or a restructuring plan – will create value only if the present value of the future stream of net cash benefits the proposal is expected to generate exceeds the initial cash outlay required to carry out the proposal.

The **present value** of the future stream of expected net cash benefits is the amount of dollars that makes the firm's owners *indifferent* to whether they receive that sum today or get the expected future cash-flow stream. For example, if the firm's owners are indifferent to whether they receive a **cash dividend** of $100,000 today or get an expected cash dividend of $110,000 next year, then $100,000 is the present value of $110,000 expected next year. (See Chapter 2 for a review of how present values are calculated.)

MEASURING VALUE CREATION WITH NET PRESENT VALUE

The difference between a proposal's present value and the initial cash outlay required to implement the proposal is the proposal's **net present value** or **NPV**:

Net present value = −Initial cash outlay + Present value of future net cash benefits

For example, if a firm's owners are indifferent between $100,000 today and $110,000 in one year, then a project that requires $105,000 today to buy a machine that is expected to generate a net cash flow of $110,000 next year, has a *negative* NPV of $5,000 because next year's cash flow is worth $100,000 today, which is $5,000 less than the initial cash outlay:

$$\text{NPV} = -\$105,000 + \$100,000 = -\$5,000$$

If the project is undertaken, it would reduce the value of the firm by $5,000.

We can use the NPV concept to restate the fundamental finance principle more succinctly:

> A business proposal creates value if its NPV is positive and destroys value if its NPV is negative.

---

[7] For a discussion on whether creating value for owners also creates value for all the firm's stakeholders, see John Martin, William Petty, and James Wallace (2009).

The proposal's NPV goes to the investors who *own* the project – in other words, to the shareholders of the firm that undertakes the project. This means that the shareholders should be able to sell their equity stake in the company that announced the project for *more* than they could sell it for if the project were not undertaken, and the difference should be equal to the project's NPV.

The firm's ability to identify the project, and the market expectation that the firm will carry out the project successfully, create an immediate increase in the firm's value and in the wealth of its owners. More precisely, if the shares of the firm are listed and traded on a stock exchange, the market value of the firm (the share price multiplied by the number of shares outstanding) should rise by an amount equal to the project's NPV on the day the project is announced, assuming the announcement is *unanticipated*, and the market agrees with the firm's analysis of the project's profitability. We return to this point later in the chapter when we examine the role played by financial markets in the process of value creation.

ONLY CASH MATTERS

The fundamental finance principle requires that the initial investment needed to undertake a proposal, as well as the stream of net future benefits it is expected to generate, be measured in cash. As Exhibit 1.1 shows, the investors who are financing the proposal – the firm's shareholders and debt holders – have invested *cash* in the firm and thus are interested only in *cash* returns. Note that the cash benefits of a project must not be confused with the increase in the firm's net profit expected from the project because profits are accounting measures of benefits, not of cash returns.

Chapter 4 identifies the differences between a firm's cash flows, its revenues, its expenses, and its net profit, and Chapter 9 shows how to estimate the cash flows that are relevant to an investment decision.

DISCOUNT RATES

Consider an investment proposal that requires shareholders to invest $100,000 today in order to generate an expected $110,000 of cash at the end of the year. Suppose that the present value of the $110,000 is $100,000. Recall that the present value is the value that makes the firm's owners indifferent to whether they receive $100,000

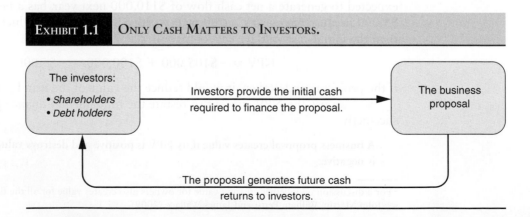

| EXHIBIT 1.1 | ONLY CASH MATTERS TO INVESTORS. |

The investors:
• *Shareholders*
• *Debt holders*

Investors provide the initial cash required to finance the proposal.

The business proposal

The proposal generates future cash returns to investors.

today or receive the expected $110,000 in one year. This is the same as saying that the firm's owners expect to receive a return of 10 percent from the project because $100,000 invested at 10 percent will yield $110,000 in one year. The 10 percent is called the **discount rate**: it is the rate at which the future cash flow must be *discounted* to find its present value. In other words, $100,000 is the *discounted value* at 10 percent of $110,000 to be received in one year.

If we want to estimate the NPV of a proposal, we must first discount its future cash-flow stream to find its present value and then deduct from that present value the initial cash outlay required to carry out the proposal. Chapter 2 examines the **discounting** mechanism in detail and explains how to calculate present values and how to estimate a project's NPV when the project has an expected cash-flow stream that is longer than one year.

In our example, we know the discount rate (10 percent) because we already know the expected future cash flow ($110,000) and its present value ($100,000). However, this is not usually the case. In general, a proposal's future cash flow must be estimated, and the discount rate must be determined. But what discount rate should be used? *A proposal's appropriate discount rate is the cost of financing the proposal.*

In the example, the return expected from the project must be at least 10 percent to induce shareholders to invest in the project. In other words, because 10 percent is the rate of return required by shareholders to fund the project, it is also the project's **cost of equity** capital. It represents the cost of using shareholders' cash to finance the investment proposal.

A PROPOSAL'S COST OF CAPITAL

In the previous example, the project was funded only with equity capital. Firms, however, typically finance their investment proposals with a combination of equity capital and debt capital, and both shareholders and debt holders require a return from their contribution to the financing of the proposal. When a project is funded with both equity and debt capital, the cost of capital is no longer equal to just the cost of equity. It is the weighted average of the project's cost of equity and its **after-tax cost of debt**,[8] where the weights are the proportions of equity and debt financing in the total capital used to fund the project.

To illustrate, suppose a project will be financed 50 percent with equity and 50 percent with debt. Also, assume the project has an estimated after-tax cost of debt of 4 percent and a cost of equity of 12 percent. Then, the project's **weighted average cost of capital** or **WACC** is equal to 8 percent:

$$\text{Project cost of capital (WACC)} = (4\% \times 50\%) + (12\% \times 50\%)$$
$$= 2\% + 6\%$$
$$= 8\%$$

In other words, the contribution of debt financing to the project's cost of capital is 2 percent (50 percent of 4 percent) and that of equity financing is 6 percent (50 percent of 12 percent) as shown in Exhibit 1.2.

If the proportions of equity and debt financing are modified, the WACC will be affected, not only because the financing proportions have changed but also because the **cost of debt** and the cost of equity change when the financing proportions are

---

[8] We explain in Chapter 12 why the cost of debt must be taken after tax.

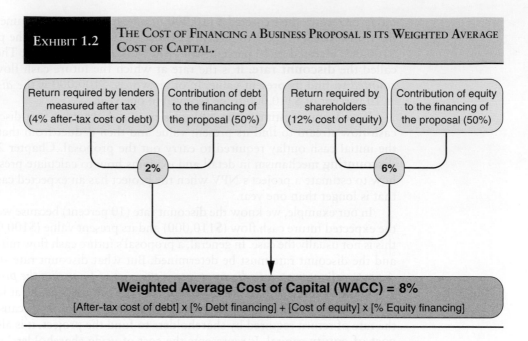

EXHIBIT 1.2   THE COST OF FINANCING A BUSINESS PROPOSAL IS ITS WEIGHTED AVERAGE COST OF CAPITAL.

Return required by lenders measured after tax (4% after-tax cost of debt)

Contribution of debt to the financing of the proposal (50%)

Return required by shareholders (12% cost of equity)

Contribution of equity to the financing of the proposal (50%)

2%

6%

Weighted Average Cost of Capital (WACC) = 8%

[After-tax cost of debt] x [% Debt financing] + [Cost of equity] x [% Equity financing]

altered. Chapter 12 shows how to estimate a project's cost of debt as well as its cost of equity and WACC. Chapter 13 demonstrates how the WACC is affected when the financing proportions change.

APPLYING THE FUNDAMENTAL FINANCE PRINCIPLE

The fundamental finance principle has widespread applications in major areas of corporate decision-making. In this book, we address the capital budgeting decision (whether an investment project should be accepted or rejected), the payout policy (when and how much cash the firm should distribute to its shareholders through cash dividends and/or by buying back its own shares in the open market), the capital structure decision (how much of the firm's assets should be financed with equity and how much with debt), the business acquisition decision (how much should be paid to acquire another company), and the foreign investment decision (how to account for multiple-currency cash flows and for the different risks of operating in a foreign country). The capital budgeting decision is covered in Chapters 7 through 9, the payout policy in Chapter 11, the capital structure decision in Chapter 13, the acquisition decision in Chapter 14, and the management of cross-border operations in Chapter 17. This section provides an overview of these corporate decisions.

THE CAPITAL BUDGETING DECISION

The **capital budgeting decision**, also called the **capital expenditure decision**, is primarily concerned with the acquisition of fixed assets, such as plant and equipment. This is a major corporate decision because it typically affects the firm's business performance for a long period of time. The decision criteria used in capital budgeting, such as the **NPV rule** and the **internal rate of return (IRR) rule,** are direct applications of the fundamental finance principle.

THE NET PRESENT VALUE RULE

The NPV rule is a direct application of the fundamental finance principle because it says that a project should be undertaken only if it does not destroy value. A project does not destroy value when its NPV is positive or zero. It destroys value when its NPV is negative.

A project with a positive NPV creates value because the present value of its expected future cash benefits is *greater* than the initial cash outlay required to launch the project. A project with a negative NPV destroys value because the present value of its expected future cash benefits is *less* than the initial cash outlay required to launch the project. A project with a zero NPV neither creates nor destroys value: it breaks even and should be undertaken because it covers all its costs. In general, the NPV rule can be stated as follows:

A project should be undertaken if its NPV is positive or zero and should be rejected if its NPV is negative.

The properties of the NPV rule are examined in detail in Chapter 7.

THE INTERNAL RATE OF RETURN RULE

One of the most commonly used alternatives to the NPV rule, especially in the analysis of capital expenditures, is the IRR rule. A project's IRR is a measure of its *operating* profitability, meaning that it *excludes* the cost of *financing* the project. Thus, to find out if a project creates value, you must compare the project's IRR to the cost of financing the project. Recall that the cost of financing a project is its WACC.

Suppose that a firm has a project whose IRR is 15 percent. The project can be financed at an estimated WACC of 10 percent. Should the firm invest in this project? The answer is yes because its operating profitability, measured by its IRR (which excludes the cost of funding the project), *exceeds* the cost of financing the project, measured by its estimated WACC. If a project's IRR is *lower* than its WACC, the project cannot be financed profitably and should be rejected. If the IRR is equal to the WACC, the project breaks even and should be undertaken because it covers all its costs. In general, the IRR rule can be stated as follows:

A project should be undertaken if its IRR is higher than, or equal to, its cost of capital, and should be rejected if its IRR is lower than its cost of capital.

Chapter 8 examines the properties of the IRR rule as well as other capital budgeting rules and compares them with the NPV criterion.

SOURCES OF VALUE CREATION IN A BUSINESS PROPOSAL

We have seen that firms with positive NPV proposals are expected to generate excess cash profits – that is, cash profits above the level required to remunerate the firm's shareholders. However, there is nothing more powerful than excess cash profits to attract a horde of eager competitors into a new market. Clearly, the challenge for firms with *recurrent* positive NPV businesses is to keep competitors at bay and prevent them from entering their markets. They must erect **entry barriers** that are costly enough to discourage potential competitors. These entry barriers must be costly enough to make the NPV of their competitors' proposals to enter the market negative, but not so costly as to wipe out their own positive NPV.

What are these entry barriers? Some of the most effective barriers are patents or trademarks on products that competitors are legally prevented from copying or imitating. For example, the pharmaceutical companies that own the patent for some of the world's best-selling drugs create considerable value for their owners during the period of time competitors are legally prohibited from producing the same medicine. But legal protection is not the only type of entry barrier. Some companies are able to create value for their shareholders without patent protection. Examples include companies such as Coca-Cola that use their superior marketing and advertising expertise to build a powerful brand name that is the source of value creation, or companies such as Apple that produce innovative and attractively designed products that cannot be easily imitated by competitors and that lead to strong sales at premium prices. Entry barriers can also be erected by creating a unique distribution channel. For example, Dell Computers has thrived for many years by selling directly to customers, over the phone and via the Internet, computers that are practically manufactured to order and shipped directly to the buyer.

Some firms also create value for their owners even without the benefit of a powerful brand name, an innovative and attractive product, or a unique distribution channel. These firms are able to erect entry barriers around markets for standard products that, in principle, could be reproduced easily and legally. How do they do it? They have simply managed to become their market's lowest-cost producer or service provider. Their market is protected because no one else is capable of producing the goods or services as cheaply as they can.

The point we want to make is that positive NPV businesses are not easily created, discovered, or protected. Firms that have developed or found positive NPV businesses have to prevent competitors from entering their markets and reducing their excess profit to zero. This is the essence of strategic management.

THE PAYOUT POLICY

A firm with $50 million of cash must decide whether to use it to fund a project with an IRR of 10 percent or distribute the $50 million to its shareholders. There are two methods the firm can use to distribute the cash to its shareholders: one is to pay them a cash dividend of $50 million; the other is to use the $50 million to buy back the firm's shares from its shareholders in the open market. The decision regarding when and how much cash the firm should distribute to its shareholders in the form of cash dividends or **share repurchases** is called the firm's **payout policy**.

We can apply the IRR rule to find out whether the firm should invest its $50 million in the project whose IRR is 10 percent or distribute the $50 million to its shareholders. As you may have guessed, the decision depends on the firm's WACC. If the WACC is lower than the 10 percent IRR, the project creates value and should be undertaken. If the WACC is *higher* than the 10 percent IRR, the project destroys value and should not be undertaken; in this case the cash should be paid out to shareholders either in the form of a cash dividend or through a **share buyback**. In Chapter 11 we examine in detail how firms should make these payout decisions in order to maximize the firm's market value.

THE CAPITAL STRUCTURE DECISION

Why would a firm want to modify its **capital structure**? We show in Chapter 13 that a firm's capital structure usually affects its value. And there is a particular capital structure for which the firm's value is the highest. The fundamental finance principle can help you determine the **optimal capital structure**, the one that maximizes the firm's value.

Contrary to an investment decision, the decision to change the firm's capital structure is not accompanied by an initial cash outlay. For example, if a firm decides to replace $100 million of equity with $100 million of debt, the net effect on the firm's cash position will be zero. (We ignore the transaction costs required to carry out this capital restructuring, also called **recapitalization**.) Thus, to apply the fundamental finance principle to the capital structure decision, we need to find out whether the value of the firm will increase or decrease as a result of the decision to change the structure of the capital used to finance the firm's assets.

To illustrate, suppose $100 million is borrowed at 5 percent and the corporate tax rate is 40 percent. Interest expenses are $5 million (5 percent of $100 million) and the firm's pre-tax profits are thus reduced by $5 million. The $5 million reduction in pre-tax profits means that the firm's owners will pay less tax. They will save $2 million in taxes *every year* (40 percent of $5 million). Conclusion: *everything else remaining the same*, the new capital structure should raise the value of the firm to reflect all the tax savings the firm is expected to receive in the future.

Unfortunately for shareholders, other things usually do not remain the same. As the firm replaces increasing amounts of equity with borrowed funds, the **risk** that it may be unable to *service* its debt (that is, pay the interest on the loan and repay the loan in full and on time) will rise. This rising risk, which accompanies increasing borrowing, generates **financial distress costs** that reduce the firm's value, thus offsetting the value created by the tax benefits of debt financing. Examples of financial distress costs include the loss of sales caused by customers' reluctance to buy products from a firm that soon may experience financial difficulties, as well as the inability to obtain supplies from companies that are reluctant to provide goods and services to a firm that may be unable to pay for them. Clearly, *as long as the present value of the expected tax savings from debt financing is higher than the present value of the expected costs of financial distress, additional borrowing will increase the firm's value.* When the present value of the expected tax advantage of debt financing is exactly offset by the present value of the expected costs of financial distress, the firm has reached its optimal capital structure. This **trade-off model of capital structure** is examined in detail in Chapter 13 along with a review of a number of other factors managers must consider when designing their firm's capital structure.

THE BUSINESS ACQUISITION DECISION

The acquisition of a company is just another type of investment, often a large one. It will create value for the shareholders of the acquiring firm only if the present value of the *incremental* future net cash flows that the combined assets of the merged firms are expected to generate after the acquisition, *exceeds* the *premium* paid to acquire the target company's assets (which is the price paid to acquire the target's assets less their pre-merger value). Applying the fundamental finance principle, we can write the following:

$$\text{NPV(acquisition)} = - \text{Premium paid to acquire the target company's assets}$$
$$+ \text{Present value of the post-acquisition } \textit{incremental}$$
$$\text{net cash flows from the merged assets}$$

If this NPV is positive, the acquisition is a value-creating investment. If it is negative, the acquisition is a value-destroying investment. Chapter 14 shows how the post-acquisition cash flows can be estimated, depending on the type of acquisition envisioned. For a pure **conglomerate merger**, one in which the business to be acquired is unrelated to the business of the acquiring firm, the relevant cash flows are those generated by the assets of the target company as "**stand-alone**" assets or "**as-is**."

Sometimes, an acquisition is expected to generate **synergies** that will raise sales or reduce costs *beyond the sum of the two companies' pre-acquisition sales and costs*. In this case, we have to estimate the amounts by which the cash flows of the combined assets are expected to increase when the acquisition is achieved, taking into account any synergistic effects. The discount rate that should be used to estimate the present value of these cash flows, and the various steps required to determine whether an acquisition proposal will create value, are the subjects of Chapter 14.

The Foreign Investment Decision

As with any other type of investment, investing abroad requires spending cash now with the expectation that the present value of the future net cash flows generated by the investment will be higher than the amount poured into the investment.

Again, the fundamental finance principle is applicable to that situation. The implementation of the principle is somewhat more complicated than for a domestic investment, however, because the cash flows from a cross-border investment are usually denominated in a different currency from the home currency and are exposed to additional risks, such as **currency risk** and **country risk**.

"Currency risk" refers to the risk associated with *unanticipated changes* in the value of the currency in which the investment cash flows are denominated; "country risk" refers to the risk associated with *unexpected events*, such as expropriation and exchange controls, that may adversely affect the project's future cash-flow stream. Chapter 17 examines these risks in detail and shows how they should be taken into account when analyzing a cross-border investment project.

After an investment project is undertaken, currency and political risks must be managed on a day-to-day basis. Chapter 17 describes how managers can reduce their firm's exposure to these risks. In particular, it explains how managers can use foreign exchange instruments, such as forward, futures, and options contracts, as well as currency swaps, to reduce the effect of currency movements on the cash flows generated by a foreign project.

THE ROLE OF FINANCIAL MARKETS

Financial markets play a key role in the process of business growth and value creation by performing two fundamental functions (see Exhibit 1.3). As **primary markets**, they provide the financing required to fund new business ventures and sustain business growth. They perform this function by acting as intermediaries between individuals and institutions that have a cash surplus they wish to invest and companies that have a cash deficit they wish to eliminate by raising new capital through the issuance of securities (certificates that recognize the rights of the holder). As **secondary markets**, they provide an efficient mechanism for trading **outstanding** (already issued) **securities** and translating the value-creating (or value-destroying) decisions of firms into increases (or decreases) in shareholders' wealth via higher (or lower) security prices.

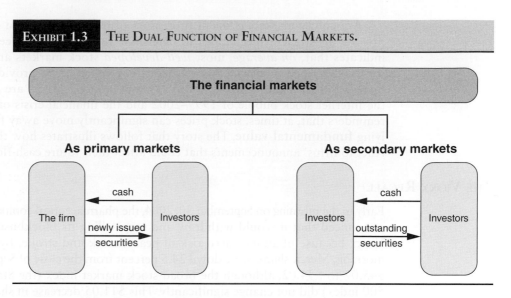

Exhibit 1.3   The Dual Function of Financial Markets.

These two functions are not independent of each other. The price of securities in the secondary markets is determined by the buying and selling carried out by traders in these markets. The price observed in the secondary market is then used by **investment bankers** as a benchmark against which they can set the price of newly issued securities in the primary market. (Investment bankers are financial intermediaries who help companies issue securities in financial markets to raise funds; see Chapter 11). Thus, a well-functioning secondary market facilitates the pricing of new securities issued in the primary market. As a consequence, the two markets are closely related. The structure and organization of financial markets and the role played by investment bankers are reviewed in Chapter 11. The determination of the price of the securities traded in these markets is examined in detail in Chapter 10. The section below provides an overview of the functions of financial markets as a source of capital and the role they play in the process of value creation.

The Equity Market

In an **efficient equity market**, the share price of firms adjusts instantly to new and relevant information as soon as it becomes available to market participants. Relevant information is any piece of news that is expected to affect a firm's future cash-flow stream. In an efficient equity market, stock prices should rise instantly on favorable news and drop instantly on unfavorable news (assuming, of course, that the piece of news was unanticipated). You can see why efficient equity markets play a key role in the process of value creation. As soon as a company announces a business decision that market participants interpret as having a positive NPV, the company's market value should increase by an amount equal to the market's estimation of that decision's positive NPV. Shareholders who wish to cash in do not have to wait for the firm to actually carry out its business decision. All they have to do is sell their shares to immediately receive their part of the value created by the firm's positive announcement. The opposite is also true. If market participants believe the decision has a negative NPV, the company's aggregate market value should fall by an amount equal to the market's estimation of that decision's negative NPV, and shareholders will suffer an immediate loss.

Are equity markets efficient processors of information? And do they actually provide an efficient mechanism to determine reliable stock prices? The evidence indicates that, *on average*, most *well-developed* stock markets around the world can be described as sufficiently efficient to be relied on to provide unbiased estimates of share prices. This is not to say that equity markets are *always* efficient: the Internet stock bubble of 1999–2002 and the financial crisis of 2007–2009 are reminders that, at times, stock prices can significantly move away from their underlying **fundamental value**. The story that follows illustrates how the stock markets react to firms' announcements that could affect their future cash-flow streams.

THE VIOXX RECALL

Early in the morning on September 30, 2004, the pharmaceutical company Merck & Co. announced that it would withdraw and stop selling its blockbuster arthritis drug Vioxx because of an increased risk of heart attack and stroke. By 10 o'clock that morning, Merck shares were down 24.5 percent from the close of September 29, from $45.07 to $34.02, although the broad stock market index (the Standard & Poor's 500 index) did not change significantly. This $11.05 decrease in share price applied to the 2.22 billion of Merck's outstanding shares represented $24.5 billion of value destruction ($11.05 times 2.22 billion). In other words, at that time, the market anticipated a decrease of $24.5 billion in the present value of Merck's expected future net cash flows, following the decision to retire Vioxx.[9]

It could have been expected that the withdrawal of Vioxx would benefit Pfizer Inc., which makes Celebrex, another arthritis drug belonging to the same class as Vioxx called COX-2 drugs. More precisely, it would have made sense that patients using Vioxx would now use Celebrex, thus increasing the future cash flows of Pfizer by an amount of the same order of magnitude as the decrease in Merck's cash flows. Indeed, by the time Merck's stock price was down to $34.02, shares of Pfizer were trading at $31.50, or $1.32 above the close on September 29. With 7.55 billion shares outstanding, this represents a $9.97 billion ($1.32 times 7.55 billion) increase in the **market capitalization** of Pfizer compared with the $24.5 billion decrease in that of Merck.

At that point, we could conclude, mistakenly, that the market was not functioning properly because Pfizer's share price increase was far from reflecting the expected transfer of cash flows from Merck. However, the withdrawal of Vioxx immediately raised questions about the safety of COX-2 drugs. For example, less than a couple of hours after the Vioxx recall, the US Food and Drug Administration issued a public health advisory hinting that the agency would require longer-term studies for COX-2 drugs. The lower-than-expected increase in Pfizer's market capitalization, relative to the decrease in that of Merck's, reflected the market expectation that many patients using Vioxx would be reluctant to switch to Celebrex.

Late on October 6, 2004, the *New England Journal of Medicine* published two reports from researchers who suggested that the side effects that caused the withdrawal of Vioxx were likely to affect all drugs belonging to the same COX-2 class. From the close of October 5 to the close of October 7, 2004, shares of Pfizer went down from $31.29 to $29.99, a decrease of $1.30, or 4.2 percent, while the Standard & Poor's index decreased insignificantly. This represents a decrease of $9.82 billion in the market capitalization of Pfizer.

---

[9] Merck's shareholders sued in 2004 and the company agreed in 2007 to a $4.85 billion settlement in the United States. And the court ordered Merck to appoint a chief medical officer to monitor product marketing and safety, which it did in December 2009. See the *New York Times*, April 4, 2010.

The Vioxx recall illustrates the role played by the stock markets as instant processors of news and as translators of relevant information about companies into value creation when the news is favorable and value destruction when it is unfavorable.

EXTERNAL VERSUS INTERNAL FINANCING

We now consider how financial markets function as primary markets. In this role, they act as a source of external financing to companies. Firms can raise equity capital by issuing shares of common stock in the equity market, or they can borrow by issuing debt securities in the debt markets. As mentioned earlier, to carry out this fund-raising task, they use the services of investment bankers (as opposed to **commercial bankers**, who extend loans). Short-term funds can be raised by issuing **commercial paper (CP)** in the **money market**, and long-term funds can be raised by issuing **bonds** in the corporate bond market. These markets, and the securities that are traded in them, are described in Chapter 11. Debt financing is necessarily external. Firms either borrow from financial institutions, such as banks and insurance companies, or issue debt securities, such as commercial paper and corporate bonds, in debt markets. Equity financing, however, can be either external (in the form of a new equity issue) or internal. **Internal equity financing** refers to **retained earnings**, the part of a firm's profits that the firm's owners have decided to invest back into their company instead of withdrawing it in the form of a cash dividend. The percentage of profits retained within the firm is called the **profit retention rate**. The percentage paid out in the form of a cash dividend is known as the **dividend payout ratio**.

As pointed out earlier, a firm may retain part of its profits to fund new projects. Funding projects with retained earnings makes business sense because most firms do not have *regular* access to external equity financing. And when external equity financing is available, it is more expensive than retained earnings because fees must be paid to investment bankers, and numerous costs are incurred to comply with the rules and regulations that govern external **equity funding**. Hence, calling on existing and new shareholders to raise external equity through a new share issue is usually an infrequent event in the life of a company. Most firms rely primarily on internal equity financing, through profit retention, to build up their equity capital. We show in the next section that *profit retention is the fuel of sustainable business expansion*. No business can travel the road of long-term growth without retaining some of its profit on a continual basis.

THE BUSINESS CYCLE

Suppose you decide to start a firm that you will call New Manufacturing Company (NMC), and you want to understand the financial implications of this decision. The following dialogue explains the system that ties the various drivers of your new business to the financial implications of your decision:

- "Why does NMC need capital (cash)?"
- "It has to purchase assets. Without the cash provided by investors in the form of equity and debt capital, NMC would not be able to buy assets."
- "Of course, but why does NMC need assets?"
- "It has to generate sales. Without productive assets, such as plant and equipment, NMC would not be able to manufacture goods for sale."
- "Surely, but then why does NMC need sales?"
- "It has to make profits. Without sales revenues, how could NMC generate any profits?"

- "True, but then why does NMC need profits?"
- "It must reward its owners (you and your partners in the business) in the form of dividend payments and must build up its capital base. By retaining part of its profits, NMC will be able to increase its equity capital, which, in turn, will allow it to increase the amount of cash it can borrow from **creditors**. For example, with a **debt-to-equity ratio** equal to one, NMC needs one dollar of additional equity to be able to borrow one extra dollar."
- "I understand. One last question: why does NMC need more capital?"
- "To purchase more assets, to generate more sales, to produce higher profits, to pay dividends, to increase retained earnings, to build up equity capital, to raise new debt, and to grow the business."

This sequence of events is called the firm's **business cycle**. It is illustrated in Exhibit 1.4. With an initial capital made up of equity and debt, NMC can finance an equal amount of assets. These assets will be used by NMC to generate sales. The amount of sales will depend on the efficiency with which NMC manages its assets. Efficient asset management means that NMC is able to produce a planned amount of sales using the *least* amount of assets.

Sales eventually will generate a profit. What will NMC do with that profit? Part will be reinvested in the business in the form of retained earnings, and the rest will be distributed to shareholders in the form of dividends. With additional equity capital (in the form of retained earnings), NMC will be able to borrow an amount that will depend on the firm's debt-to-equity ratio. With this added capital, NMC will start a

| EXHIBIT 1.4 | THE BUSINESS CYCLE. |

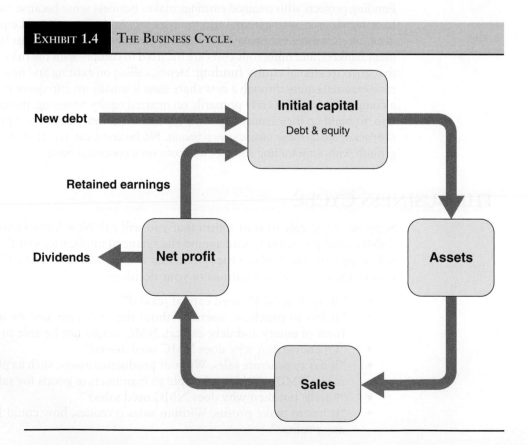

new cycle with more capital to fund more assets, which will produce more sales. The rate at which a company's sales can grow under those circumstances, that is, *without issuing new equity capital*, is called the **self-sustainable growth rate** (SGR).

The SGR is an important indicator of business performance and an important component of a firm's financial strategy. Chapter 6 shows how a firm can increase its SGR, and Chapter 18 shows how the SGR concept can be used to formulate an optimal financial strategy.

HLC'S FINANCIAL STATEMENTS

Financial statements, such as **balance sheets** and **income statements**, are the products of the financial accounting process. This process, shown in Exhibit 1.5, records financial transactions between the firm and the rest of the world.

THE BALANCE SHEET

The balance sheet is a statement that shows what a firm's shareholders own, called **assets** (such as cash, inventories, and buildings), and what they owe, called **liabilities** (such as money owed to banks and suppliers), at a specific date (usually at the end

EXHIBIT 1.5	A SIMPLIFIED VIEW OF THE FINANCIAL ACCOUNTING PROCESS.

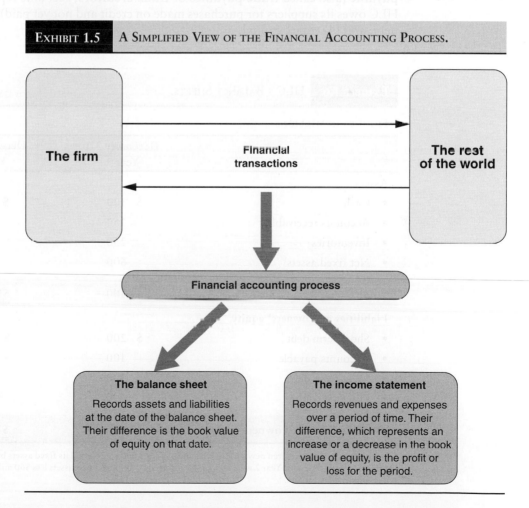

of a year or a quarter). The difference between a firm's assets and its liabilities is an accounting estimate of the equity shareholders have invested in their firm, called **owners' equity** or **book value of equity**.

As an introduction to the balance sheet, which is analyzed in detail in Chapter 4, we show in Exhibit 1.6 a simplified version of the balance sheet of the Hologram Lighting Company (HLC) – a fictitious firm – on December 31, Year 1 and Year 2.

The upper part of the exhibit lists the firm's assets with their corresponding accounting values at the date of the statement. The lower part lists the firm's liabilities and shareholders' equity with their corresponding accounting values at the same date.

The assets include (1) **cash**; (2) **accounts receivable** (also called **trade receivables** or **trade debtors**), which represent cash owed to HLC by customers who bought goods from HLC but have not yet paid for them; (3) **inventories** (raw materials, work in process, and finished goods not yet sold); and (4) **net fixed assets** (long-term assets such as plant, equipment, and buildings). When estimating the net value of fixed assets, an accountant deducts from the purchase price of the assets the **accumulated depreciation** expense to account for the loss in value caused by the wear and tear of the assets or their obsolescence (more on this in Chapter 4).

How were these assets financed? According to the lower part of the balance sheet, they were financed with (1) short-term borrowing from banks; (2) **accounts payable** (also called **trade payables** or **trade creditors**, accounts representing cash HLC owes its suppliers for purchases made on credit and not yet paid); (3) long-term debt; and (4) equity capital.

EXHIBIT 1.6	HLC's BALANCE SHEETS.

FIGURES IN MILLIONS

	December 31, Year 1	December 31, Year 2
Assets		
• Cash	$ 100	$ 110
• Accounts receivable	150	165
• Inventories	250	275
• Net fixed assets[1]	600	660
Total assets	**$1,100**	**$1,210**
Liabilities and owners' equity		
• Short-term debt	$ 200	$ 220
• Accounts payable	100	110
• Long-term debt	300	330
• Owners' equity	500	550
Total liabilities and owners' equity	**$1,100**	**$1,210**

[1] During Year 2, HLC acquired new assets worth $120 million and depreciated its fixed assets by $60 million. Thus, net fixed assets at the end of Year 2 were $600 million plus $120 million of new assets less $60 million of depreciation, which equals $660 million.

A Variant of the Standard Balance Sheet: The Managerial Balance Sheet

Note that HLC's balance sheet shows accounts receivable and inventories as assets, and accounts payable as liabilities. Although this presentation makes sense from an accounting point of view, it does not fit well with the traditional organization of a business for which these three accounts are managed together by operating managers. For this reason, we often will work with a variant of the traditional balance sheet, which we call the **managerial balance sheet**.

The Net Investment Required to Operate a Firm's Fixed Assets

HLC must hold both trade receivables and inventories because sales are not paid immediately by customers, and goods must be manufactured and stored before they can be sold. Without inventories and receivables, HLC would be unable to produce goods and sell them. However, these accounts represent required investments that HLC must finance. This financing is partly provided by trade payables because HLC does not have to pay its suppliers immediately. As a result, the *net* investment that HLC must make to support its production and sales activities is equal to the sum of its trade receivables and inventories *less* its trade payables. This net investment in operations, which is required to generate sales and profits from the firm's fixed assets, is called **operating working capital** or **working capital requirement (WCR)**.

HLC's WCR on December 31, Year 1, was equal to $300 million ($150 million of receivables plus $250 million of inventories less $100 million of payables). A year later it was up 10 percent to $330 million. Is this rise in WCR justified by the firm's operations? We answer this question in Chapter 5 where we also discuss the optimal management of a firm's WCR and show that it is one of the most effective ways to create value through improved efficiency.

HLC's Managerial Balance Sheet

Exhibit 1.7 shows HLC's managerial balance sheets on December 31, Year 1 and Year 2. The upper part of the managerial balance sheet lists the firm's **invested capital**: cash, WCR, and net fixed assets. Note that it is invested capital, not the assets in the standard balance sheet that must be financed by debt and equity capital. To finance its invested capital, HLC uses the capital listed on the lower part of the managerial balance sheet: short-term debt, long-term debt, and equity capital. Note also that HLC's invested capital is lower than its total assets ($1,000 million versus $1,100 million on December 31, Year 1 and $1,100 million versus $1,210 million on December 31, Year 2). The difference ($100 million at the end of Year 1 and $110 million at the end of Year 2) is the amount of accounts payable, which, in the managerial balance sheet, is recognized as a source of financing generated by the firm's operations and is accounted for in the WCR.

The managerial balance sheet gives a clearer picture than a standard balance sheet of the structure of the firm's investments and the capital it uses to finance them. Capital invested in cash, operations, and net fixed assets is reported under the heading "invested capital." And the sources of capital used to fund these investments are reported under the heading "capital employed." Chapter 5 shows why the managerial balance sheet is a better starting point for analyzing, interpreting, and evaluating the firm's investing, operating, and financing strategies.

HLC's debt-to-equity ratio is equal to one at the end of Year 2 ($550 million of total debt divided by $550 million of owners' equity). Is this capital structure the right

EXHIBIT 1.7	HLC's MANAGERIAL BALANCE SHEETS.

ALL DATA FROM THE BALANCE SHEETS IN EXHIBIT 1.6. FIGURES IN MILLIONS

	December 31, Year 1	December 31, Year 2
Invested capital		
• Cash	$ 100	$ 110
• Working capital requirement (WCR)[1]	300	330
• Net fixed assets	600	660
Total invested capital	$1,000	$1,100
Capital employed		
• Short-term debt	$ 200	$ 220
• Long-term debt	300	330
• Owners' equity	500	550
Total capital employed	$1,000	$1,100

[1] WCR = (Accounts receivable + Inventories) − Accounts payable. These are given in Exhibit 1.6.

one for HLC? How a firm should design an optimal capital structure is the topic of Chapter 13. At the end of Year 2, HLC had $220 million of short-term debt and $330 million of long-term debt. Is this the best combination of short-term and long-term debt for HLC? This question is addressed in Chapter 5.

THE INCOME STATEMENT

The purpose of the income statement, also called the **profit and loss (P&L) statement,** is to determine the amount of **net profits** (or **net loss**) the firm has generated during the accounting period. It is the difference between the firm's **revenues** and its **expenses** during that period.

A detailed analysis of a firm's income statement is presented in Chapter 4. In this section, we present a simplified version of HLC's income statement for Year 2, shown in Exhibit 1.8, and use it to show how this statement can provide valuable information about a firm's financial performance.

To generate sales revenue, HLC had to incur several types of expenses: first are the **operating expenses** (such as the cost of raw materials used in the manufacturing of the firm's products, and production costs, including **depreciation expense**); second is the interest expense (the amount of interest HLC must pay to its debt holders); and third is the tax expense the firm must pay the tax authorities on its pre-tax profits.

The difference between sales and operating expenses is called **earnings before interest and tax** or **EBIT** (also called **pre-tax operating profit** or **trading profit**). What is left of EBIT after interest expenses are paid is called **earnings before tax** or **EBT.** After accounting further for the tax expense, the remaining profit, which

EXHIBIT 1.8	HLC'S INCOME STATEMENT FOR YEAR 2.

FIGURES IN MILLIONS

	Year 2
Sales	**$1,000**
less operating expenses (including $60 of depreciation expense)[1]	(760)
Earnings before interest and tax (EBIT)	**$ 240**
less interest expense	(40)
Earnings before tax (EBT)	**$ 200**
less tax expense[2]	(100)
Earnings after tax (EAT)	**$ 100**
less dividend payment	(50)
Addition to retained earnings	$ 50

[1] See footnote 1 at the bottom of Exhibit 1.6.
[2] The corporate tax rate is 50 percent of earnings before tax.

belongs to the firm's shareholders, is referred to as **earnings after tax** or **EAT** (net profits). Finally, a portion of EAT is paid as dividends to the firm's shareholders, with the remaining being reinvested in the business as retained earnings. Think of EBIT as profit from HLC's operations that will be shared by three categories of claimants in accordance with a legally established order: first come the debt holders, then the tax authorities, and finally the owners. Debt holders, the first claimants, are entitled to interest payments. They are followed by the tax authorities that are entitled to a tax payment. Finally, the owners or shareholders are entitled to whatever is left. They, in effect, have a *residual ownership* of the firm's pre-tax operating profit. Note that during Year 2 HLC paid $50 million of cash dividend to its shareholders, an amount equal to half its net profits. Why is the dividend payment equal to 50 percent of net profits and not higher or lower? We answer this question in Chapter 11 where we review the firm's dividend policy.

HOW PROFITABLE IS THE FIRM?

Information provided in a firm's balance sheets and income statements can be combined to evaluate its financial performance, in particular the profitability of its equity capital and the profitability of its invested capital.

THE PROFITABILITY OF EQUITY CAPITAL

How profitable is a firm to its owners? The cumulative amount of the investment made by shareholders in the firm is reported as owners' equity on the firm's balance sheet (see Exhibit 1.7). It is also called equity capital. Because EAT represent the shareholders' claim on the firm's profits, the return on their equity investment is equal to EAT divided by owners' equity. This return is called **return on equity (ROE)**:

$$ROE = \frac{EAT}{Owners'\ equity}$$

In the case of HLC, EAT is $100 million in Year 2 (see Exhibit 1.8). Dividing this figure by $550 million of owners' equity at the end of that year (see Exhibit 1.7) gives an ROE of 18.2 percent.[10]

THE PROFITABILITY OF INVESTED CAPITAL

To measure the after-tax profitability of HLC's invested capital, we must use the after-tax profits generated by that investment. This is the firm's *after-tax operating profit*, which is equal to EBIT (1 − tax rate). The tax rate is applied *before* the interest expense is deducted from earnings because we want to measure the profitability of the firm's total capital, which is provided by both shareholders and debt holders. We thus need a measure of earnings *before* payments are made to debt holders and shareholders but after tax. This is after-tax operating profit. Dividing the after-tax operating profit by the amount of capital that was used to generate that profit gives a measure of the firm's **return on invested capital (ROIC)**.

$$ROIC = \frac{After\text{-}tax\ operating\ profit}{Invested\ capital}$$

ROIC is the same as **return on capital employed (ROCE)**, because invested capital is equal to capital employed, as indicated in the managerial balance sheet shown in Exhibit 1.7. What is the ROIC for HLC? After-tax EBIT is $120 million (50 percent of $240 million; see Exhibit 1.8) and year-end invested capital is $1,100 million. HLC's ROIC is thus 10.9 percent ($120 million divided by $1,100 million).[11]

Chapter 6 examines the relationship between a firm's ROE and its ROIC and analyzes in detail how managerial decisions can improve these two measures of profitability.

HOW MUCH CASH HAS THE FIRM GENERATED?

The cash flows expected from a business proposal are a key factor in deciding whether the proposal will create or destroy value. Measuring the cash flows generated by the firm's activities on a continuous basis is essential to verify that these activities indeed create value. We now show how to estimate the amount of cash a firm's activities generate using information in the firm's balance sheets and income statement. Chapters 4 and 5 answer this question in detail and examine the managerial implications of running a business with a focus on generating cash and creating value. In this section, we provide some insights on the issue of estimating cash flows from financial statements.

---

[10] If we divide EAT by owners' equity at the end of Year 1 ($500 million), we get an ROE of 20 percent. Because the amount of equity that generates the year's profit is closer to the average amount of owners' equity ($525 million), the least distorted measure of ROE is EAT divided by average owners' equity, that is 19.1 percent ($100 million divided by $525 million).

[11] If we take the initial invested capital, ROIC is 12 percent ($120 million divided by $1,000 million). If we take the average invested capital, ROIC is 11.43 percent ($120 million divided by $1,050 million).

Note that profits generated by a firm such as EBIT, or EAT, do not represent cash. To illustrate this point, consider an increase in sales. Both EBIT and EAT will increase immediately, but the firm's cash holdings will not increase until the customers pay for what they have bought. We want to know how much *cash* there is behind EBIT and EAT during the year in which these profits are recorded.

SOURCES AND USES OF CASH

A firm gets cash from three sources: (1) from its operations when customers pay the invoices that were sent to them; (2) from selling assets (an investment decision or, more precisely, a divestment or asset disposal decision); and (3) from borrowing or issuing new shares (a financing decision). A firm also spends cash on operating, investing, and financing activities: (1) on operating activities when it pays its suppliers, its employees, and the tax authorities; (2) on investing activities when it makes **capital expenditures** (also called **capex**), such as investments in new equipment; and finally (3) on financing activities when it reimburses debt and pays dividends. We show in Chapter 4 how data from balance sheets and income statements can be used to measure the respective contributions of operating, investing, and financing activities to the firm's total net cash flow. Of particular interest is the cash flow from operating activities, because operations are at the heart of the business. *A firm that does not generate sufficient cash from its operations over a period of time may destroy value and be headed for trouble.* It can buy time by borrowing or selling assets, but these sources of cash will eventually dry up.

THE STATEMENT OF CASH FLOWS

A firm's cash transactions over the reporting period can be summarized in a statement of cash flows. As an example, we show in Exhibit 1.9 a statement of cash flows for HLC for Year 2.

Note that the statement breaks down the firm's total net cash flows into the three main corporate activities we mentioned earlier: operating, investing, and financing activities. HLC has generated a positive net cash inflow from operations of $130 million (we explain in Chapter 4 *why* this operating cash flow is calculated as indicated in Exhibit 1.9). Investing activities generated a negative net cash outflow of $120 million (see Note 1 in Exhibit 1.6), and financing activities were neutral (new borrowings were exactly offset by dividend payments). Total net cash flow is thus $10 million ($130 million less $120 million). Conclusion: HLC began the year with $100 million of cash, generated $10 million of additional cash during the year, and hence ended the year with $110 million ($100 million plus $10 million) as indicated in the balance sheets in Exhibit 1.7.

Like balance sheets and income statements, the statement of cash flows is an integral part of a company's annual report. Information from annual reports is analyzed in the appendices of Chapters 4, 5, and 6.

HOW RISKY IS THE FIRM?

A firm does not know for certain whether its projected sales figures will actually be achieved. The firm may sell more or less than what it expected to sell. This is risk. It originates from uncertain sales figures and works itself through the firm's income statement until it finally hits the **bottom line**, that is, the firm's net profits.

EXHIBIT 1.9	HLC's Statement of Cash Flows for Year 2.

Based on the income statement in Exhibit 1.8 and the balance sheets in Exhibit 1.7. Figures in millions

	Year 2
Cash flows from operating activities	
Earnings after tax	$100
plus depreciation expense[1]	60
less cash used to finance the growth of working capital requirement[2]	(30)
A. Net cash flow from operating activities	**$130**
Cash flows from investing activities	
Capital expenditures and acquisitions[3]	(120)
B. Net cash flow from investing activities	(120)
Cash flows from financing activities	
New borrowings[4]	50
less dividend payments	(50)
C. Net cash flow from financing activities	**($0)**
D. Total net cash flow (A + B + C)	**$ 10**
E. Opening cash	**$100**
F. Closing cash (E + D)	**$110**

[1] Depreciation expense is a noncash expense that does not affect pre-tax operating cash flow. It is thus added back to earnings after tax in order to *cancel* the $60 million of depreciation expense included in earnings after tax.
[2] This is the difference between the working capital requirement at the end Year 2 ($330 million) and at the end of Year 1 ($300 million).
[3] During Year 2, HLC acquired new assets worth $120 million. See footnote 1 in Exhibit 1.6.
[4] This is the difference between total borrowing (short-term debt and long-term debt) at the end of Year 2 ($550 million) and at the end of Year 1 ($500 million).

How risk is transmitted from sales to profits is illustrated in Exhibit 1.10. First, sales fluctuate because of the uncertain economic, political, social, and competitive environments in which firms operate. These fluctuations are then transmitted to EBIT. This is **business risk**. Business risk is further magnified by the presence of fixed interest expenses that create a **financial risk**. The cumulative effect of business risk and financial risk is transmitted to the firm's earnings after tax, whose resulting fluctuations reflect the total risk. How a firm should measure and manage the risks it faces will be discussed in several chapters particularly in Chapters 15, 16, and 17.

Total risk is borne by the firm's *owners*. Owners have a claim on the firm's residual gains (the firm's net profits), but they must bear any residual losses. Whereas the remuneration of HLC's lenders is fixed, the remuneration of HLC's owners is the firm's uncertain profits. Thus, equity capital, the owners' investment in the firm, is riskier than debt capital, the lenders' investment in the firm. For this reason, HLC's

EXHIBIT 1.10	SOURCES OF RISK THAT AFFECT PROFIT.

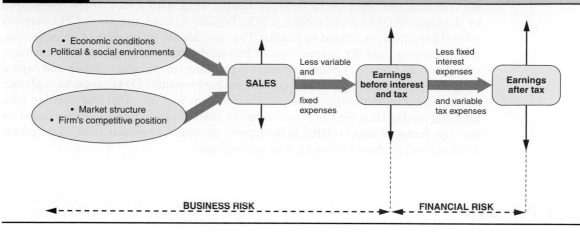

owners require a higher rate of return on their equity investment than the return required by HLC's lenders. Most shareholders dislike risk – they are **risk-averse** – and they require a higher rate of return to compensate them for the higher level of risk attached to equity capital. Shareholders' attitude toward risk is examined in Chapter 3. The effect of risk on the firm's profitability is analyzed in Chapter 6. The relationship between risk and the rate of return required by the suppliers of capital is explored in Chapters 12 and 13.

HAS THE FIRM CREATED VALUE?

The ultimate success of a firm is not measured by its capacity to grow its sales or produce profits. In the final analysis, what really matters is whether the firm's activities are making the firm more valuable. How can we find out whether a firm is creating value?

Consider the case of HLC. Has it created value during Year 2? We can answer that question by comparing the *return* HLC earned on its invested capital (ROIC) in Year 2 to the *cost* of that capital (which is HLC's WACC). If ROIC is higher than WACC, then we can conclude that HLC has *created* value *that year* because the return on capital *exceeds* its cost. If ROIC is *lower* than WACC, then we can conclude that HLC has *destroyed* value *that year* because the return on capital is *lower* than its cost. We can write the following:

If ROIC > WACC, there is value creation that year
If ROIC < WACC, there is value destruction that year

We have seen earlier that HLC's ROIC is 10.9 percent in Year 2. Assume that its WACC is 8 percent. Has HLC created or destroyed value that year? Given that its ROIC of 10.9 percent exceeded its WACC of 8 percent, we can conclude that HLC has created value that year. Chapter 18 examines in detail how value creation should be measured and how managers should manage their firm with the objective of creating value.

THE ROLE OF THE CHIEF FINANCIAL OFFICER

We conclude this overview of financial management with a look at the role played by the firm's chief financial officer (CFO). Broadly defined, the firm's CFO oversees several key functions related to finance. They include (1) accounting (data collection, record keeping, and the preparation of financial statements); (2) treasury management (cash and currency management); (3) planning (preparation of cash and capital budgets); (4) monitoring risk and controlling performance; (5) taxation (compliance and tax optimization); (6) communication (relations with investors and meetings with financial analysts); as well as (7) advising the head of the company and the board on strategic financial issues related to investment decisions, long-term funding decisions, dividend policy, share buybacks, and acquisitions.

KEY POINTS

1. The objective of financial management is value creation. This simply means that before making a decision, managers should always ask themselves the Key Question: *will the decision create value*? If in light of existing information and proper analysis they can confidently answer yes, then they should go ahead with the project.

2. The Key Question can be answered with the help of the fundamental finance principle. This principle says that a business proposal, such as a new investment, the acquisition of another company, or a restructuring plan, will create value only if the present value of its expected future cash benefits exceeds the initial cash outlay required to undertake the proposal. In other words, a business proposal creates value only if its net present value (NPV) is positive.

3. The fundamental finance principle can be applied to major corporate decisions, such as whether or not to invest in a new project, modify the firm's capital structure, acquire another company, invest abroad, or pay a dividend. The implementation of the principle requires the estimation of (1) the future cash-flow stream the decision is expected to generate and (2) the cost of financing the proposal. In general, neither input is easy to determine. Several chapters in this book are devoted to the issue of how these two inputs can be estimated, because they lie at the heart of all sound financial management systems.

4. Financial markets are not only a source of capital to finance corporate growth but also a processor of information about firms and an indicator of value creation. Firms, however, do not go to the financial markets to raise fresh equity every time they need additional equity capital to finance their growth. They can retain a portion of their profits and use it to meet their funding needs. Profit retention is necessary for a firm to sustain long-term growth.

5. Despite the fact that a firm's financial statements are prepared according to accounting conventions that generally do not reflect market values, these statements are a useful source of information when evaluating a firm's financial performance. The example of Hologram Lighting Company provides preliminary answers to the following six questions:

   (i) How profitable is the firm? Look at ROE and ROIC (more on this in Chapter 6).

   (ii) How fast can a firm grow without raising new equity? Look at the SGR (more on this in Chapter 6).

(iii) How much cash is the firm generating? Look at net operating cash flow (more on this in Chapter 4).

(iv) How risky is the firm? Look at business and financial risks (more on this in Chapters 6 and 15).

(v) What is the firm's cost of capital? Look at the WACC (more on this in Chapter 12).

(vi) Has the firm created value during the year? Check whether the ROIC exceeds the WACC (more on this in Chapter 18).

6. Managers should be able to answer other important questions: how should they manage their firm's assets? (Chapter 5); how should they make value-creating investment decisions? (Chapters 7 to 9, and Chapter 17 for decisions in an international context); how much cash should they distribute to their shareholders? (Chapter 11); how should they finance their firm's investments? (Chapters 11 and 13); how should they value their firm? (Chapter 14). In Chapter 18 we show that these various issues, together with the fundamental finance principle, form the basis of a comprehensive **value-based management system**.

FURTHER READING

1. Edmans, Alex. "Does the Stock Market Fully Value Intangibles? Employee Satisfaction and Equity Prices." *Journal of Financial Economics* 101 (September 2011).

2. Edmans, Alex. "The Link between Job Satisfaction and Firm Value, with Implications for Corporate Social Responsibility." *Academy of Management Perspectives* 26 (November 2012).

3. Edmans, Alex, Lucius Li, and Chendi Zhang. "Employee Satisfaction, Labor Market Flexibility, and Stock Returns Around the World." *ECGI Working Paper Series in Finance*, Working Paper No. 433/2014 (July 2014).

4. Jensen, Michael C. "Value Maximization and the Corporate Objective Function." In *Unfolding Stakeholder Thinking*, edited by Joerg Andriof, Sandra Waddock, Sandra Rahman, and Bryan Husted. Greenleaf Publishing, 2002.

5. Kaiser, Kevin, and David Young. *The Blue Line Imperative: What Managing for Value Really Means.* John Wiley & Sons, 2013.

6. Martin, John, William Petty, and James Wallace. "Shareholder Value Maximization – Is There a Role for Corporate Social Responsibility?" *Journal of Applied Corporate Finance* 21 (Spring 2009).

7. McTaggart, James, Peter Kontes, and Michael Mankins. *The Value Imperative.* The Free Press, 1994. See Chapters 2, 3, and 4.

8. Rappaport, Alfred. *Creating Shareholder Value.* The Free Press, 2000. See Chapter 1.

9. Stewart, Bennett. *Best-Practice EVA: The Definitive Guide to Measuring and Maximizing Shareholder Value.* John Wiley & Sons, 2013.

SELF-TEST QUESTIONS

1.1 Working capital requirement and managerial balance sheets.
Below are the balance sheets of the National Machinery Company (NMC) at the end of Year 1 and Year 2 as well as its income statement for Year 2. All figures are in millions of dollars.

Balance sheets			Income statement	
	December 31, Year 1	December 31, Year 2		
Cash	$ 100	$ 105	Sales	$1,500
Accounts receivable	200	210	Operating expenses	1,160
Inventories	300	315	Depreciation expense	100
Net fixed assets[1]	600	630	**Earnings before interest & tax**	240
Total assets	**$1,200**	**$1,260**	Interest expense at 8%[2]	32
			Earnings before tax	208
Short-term debt	$ 100	$ 105	Tax expense at 25%	52
Accounts payable	200	210	**Earnings after tax**	**$ 156**
Long-term debt	300	315		
Owners' equity[3]	600	630		
Total liabilities and owners' equity	**$1,200**	**$1,260**		

[1] During Year 2, NMC acquired new fixed assets worth $130 million and depreciated its fixed assets by $100 million.
[2] Interest expense is 8 percent of total debt at the end of Year 1 ($100 million plus $300 million).
[3] NMC has not issued new equity capital during Year 2.

Answer the following questions:

a. What is NMC's working capital requirement at the end of Year 1 and Year 2?
b. What are NMC's managerial balance sheets at the end of Year 1 and Year 2?
c. How much dividend has NMC paid out in Year 2?
d. What is NMC's sustainable growth rate?

1.2 **Weighted average cost of capital, profitability, and value creation.**

a. What is NMC's weighted average cost of capital based on its capital structure shown in its balance sheets in question 1.1? NMC's cost of equity is 15 percent. Its cost of debt is 8 percent and its pre-tax profits are taxed at 25 percent.
b. What is NMC's return on invested capital based on capital in Year 1?
c. What is NMC's return on equity based on capital in Year 1?
d. Has NMC created any value during Year 2?

1.3 **Statement of cash flows.**
Prepare NMC's Statement of Cash Flows for Year 2 based on the accounting information given in question 1.1. (Use the same format as the one shown in Exhibit 1.9.)

1.4 **Net present value and internal rate of return.**
NMC is considering a $95 million investment that is expected to generate a net cash flow of $111.4 million in one year. Answer the following questions:

a. What is the investment's net present value based on the weighted average cost of capital you found in question 1.2?
b. What is the investment's internal rate of return?
c. Should NMC undertake the investment?

d. NMC's share price before the announcement was $40. Assuming everything else is the same, what should be NMC's share price immediately after the investment is announced? NMC has 50 million shares outstanding.

1.5 The net present value of an acquisition.

Allied Eastern Corporation (AEC), whose market value is $100 million, is acquiring Home Target Services (HTS) for $12 million. Before the announcement of the acquisition HTS was worth $10 million. The estimated present value of the post-acquisition combined cash flows of the two firms is $115 million.

a. What is the net present value of the acquisition?
b. Is the acquisition value-creating?

The Time Value of Money

The rate of interest offered on a guaranteed one-year bank deposit is 10 percent: would you rather have $1,000 now or $1,000 in one year? You must have chosen $1,000 now because you can deposit $1,000 now and receive a sure $1,100 in one year (your initial $1,000 plus $100 of interest income).[1] This is a larger amount than getting $1,000 in one year. Thus, $1,000 today is more valuable than $1,000 in one year. We refer to this phenomenon as *the time value of money* because, as the example illustrates, the value of one dollar today depends on *when* you will receive it.

Note that at 10 percent, you are *indifferent* between receiving $1,000 now or $1,100 in one year. The two options are *equivalent*. If you have $1,000 now but rather have $1,100 in one year, you can deposit the $1,000 for one year at 10 percent and end up with $1,100 in a year, which is the same as getting $1,100 in a year. Conversely, if you know you will receive $1,100 in a year but rather have $1,000 today, you can borrow $1,000 now at 10 percent and pay back $1,100 in one year with the $1,100 you will receive one year from now, which is the same as having $1,000 today (we assume that you can borrow at 10 percent, the same rate as the one-year deposit rate). In other words, at 10 percent, $1,000 today is worth $1,100 in one year and $1,100 in one year is worth $1,000 today.[2]

Most financial decisions are affected by the time value of money because they typically involve spending money today with the expectation of receiving more money tomorrow. Consider the following example. The rate of interest is still 10 percent.

---

[1] In this chapter we assume that all future cash flows are riskless and that interest rates are guaranteed. Risky cash flows and risky rates are dealt with in subsequent chapters.

[2] What if the rate of interest is zero and the price of goods and services does not change? You should still prefer $1,000 today to $1,000 in one year because $1,000 now allows you to consume today a basket of goods and services worth $1,000 instead of waiting one year to consume the same basket (the assumption is that most people prefer immediate consumption to delayed consumption). What if there is price inflation? Price inflation would strengthen the case of immediate consumption because the basket of goods and services worth $1,000 today will be more expensive to buy in one year. What if there is price deflation? This is a case where you *might* prefer $1,000 in one year to $1,000 now. Why? Because the $1,000 will buy *more* goods and services in one year than they would today (goods and services will be cheaper next year because of price deflation) but the magnitude of the drop in price must be steep enough to compensate you for your delayed consumption.

Should a firm invest $101,000 in a project that will generate $110,000 in one year with no risk? Even though $110,000 is higher than $101,000 the answer is *no* because $110,000 in one year is worth *today* $100,000 at 10 percent, which is *less* than the $101,000 cost (or price) of the investment. In other words, the *value today* of the investment ($100,000) *is lower than the price* the firm has to pay today for that investment ($101,000).

One way of expressing this result is to calculate the net present value (NPV) of the investment:

$$\text{NPV(investment)} = \text{Value today of the investment} - \text{Cost (or price)}$$
$$\text{today of the investment}$$
$$\text{NPV(investment)} = \$100,000 - \$101,000 = -\$1,000$$

The investment should *not* be undertaken because its NPV is negative.

Another way to answer the question is to calculate the project's internal rate of return (IRR) and compare it to the interest rate of 10 percent. The project's IRR is the return the project will generate. It is equal to $\dfrac{\$110,000 - \$101,000}{\$101,000} = 8.91\%$.

The project should *not* be undertaken because its IRR is *lower* than the 10 percent the firm would earn on a bank deposit.

This chapter presents a number of formulas that allow you to estimate the value today of a future stream of cash flows and make financial decisions that take into account the time value of money using both the NPV rule and the IRR rule. Chapter 7 examines the NPV rule in more detail while Chapter 8 looks at the IRR rule. After reading this chapter, you should understand the following:

- What compounding and discounting mean
- What the difference is between the nominal and the effective rate of return
- What the difference is between the nominal and the real rate of return
- How to calculate the present value of a cash-flow stream
- How to use a financial calculator to get future and present values
- How to use a spreadsheet to get the present value of a future cash-flow stream
- What a perpetual cash-flow stream is and how to calculate its present value
- What an annuity is and how to calculate its present and future values

PRESENT VALUES AND FUTURE VALUES

We have shown that $1,000 now is worth $1,100 in one year if the annual rate of interest is 10 percent. We refer to the $1,100 as the **Future Value (FV)** in one year of $1,000 at 10 percent. And we refer to the $1,000 as the **Present Value (PV)**, at 10 percent, of $1,100 to be received a year from now. We use the capital letter T to refer to the number of years in the future (T for Time) and the lower case letter k to refer to the *annual* rate of interest. In our case $T = 1$ and $k = 0.10$. We can write:

$$FV = \$1,100 = \$1,000 + (\$1,000 \times 0.10) = \$1,000 \times (1 + 0.10) = PV(1 + k)$$
$$PV = \$1,000 = \frac{\$1,100}{(1 + 0.10)} = \frac{FV}{(1 + k)}$$

COMPOUNDING

Compounding refers to the growth of an amount of money that earns interest year after year, *including additional interest earned on the interest received in the preceding years.* Let's illustrate this phenomenon by examining what happens if you deposit $1,000 for *two* years at 10 percent. You know that the future value of $1,000 in one year at 10 percent is $1,100. If you deposit the $1,100 for an additional year at 10 percent, it will grow to $1,210 which is equal to the $1,100 deposit plus $110 of interest on that deposit (10 percent of $1,100). You can break down the $1,210 as follows: the initial $1,000, plus $100 of interest at the end of the first year, plus another $100 of interest at the end of the second year, plus $10 of interest at the end of the second year on the first-year interest of $100. We can write:

$$FV = \$1,100 \times (1 + 0.10) = \$1,000 \times (1 + 0.10) \times (1 + 0.10) = \$1,000 \times (1 + 0.10)^2 = \$1,210$$

$$FV = \$1,000 \times (1 + 0.10)^2 = PV \times (1 + k)^2$$

We can now generalize the above equation to get the future value of PV at the rate k in T years:

$$FV_{T,k} = PV \times (1 + k)^T \tag{2.1}$$

Because of the compounding effect, the future value $FV_{T,k}$ in T years at the rate k is also called the **compounded value** of PV at the **compound rate** k. And the magnifying term $(1 + k)^T$ is called the **compound factor**.

To illustrate, let's find out the future value of $1,000 in five years at a rate of 10 percent:

$$FV(\$1,000)_{5,10\%} = \$1,000 \times (1 + 0.10)^5 = \$1,000 \times (1.10)^5 = \$1,000 \times 1.6105 = \$1,610.50$$

Here is a table that gives you the compound factor for combinations of different years and compound rates, rounded to four digits after the decimal point:

	T = 1 year	T = 3 years	T = 5 years	T = 10 years	T = 15 years	T = 20 years
k = 3%	1.0300	1.0927	1.1593	1.3439	1.5580	1.8061
k = 6%	1.0600	1.1910	1.3382	1.7908	2.3966	3.2071
k = 10%	1.1000	1.3310	1.6105	2.5937	4.1772	6.7275
k = 15%	1.1500	1.5209	2.0114	4.0456	8.1371	16.3665

Note that *the compound factor is higher than one*. It increases when: (a) the rate k goes up (look at the columns) and (b) the number of years T rises (look at the rows). A question: how long will it take for an investment to double in value at 15 percent? A look at the table indicates that it will take slightly less than five years (the compound factor is about 2.01). Another question: the value of a house has quadrupled in ten years. What is the average annual rate of return? About 15 percent (the compound factor is about 4.05).

DISCOUNTING

Discounting is the reverse of compounding. Whereas compounding is the mechanism that provides the *future* value of a *current* amount of money (compounding converts present values into future values), discounting is the mechanism that provides the *present* value of a *future* amount of money (discounting converts future values into present values). We can get the present value (PV) at the annual rate of interest k of a future value (FV) to be received in T years by rewriting formula 2.1 as:

$$PV_{T,k} = \frac{FV}{(1 + k)^T} = FV \times \frac{1}{(1 + k)^T} \tag{2.2}$$

where PV is also called the **discounted value** of FV at the **discount rate** k discounted to the present over a period of T years. One divided by $(1 + k)^T$ is called the **discount factor (DF)**. It can be expressed as:

$$DF_{T,k} = \frac{1}{(1 + k)^T} = \left(\frac{1}{1 + k}\right)^T = (1 + k)^{-T} \tag{2.3}$$

As shown in formula 2.3 above, there are three different ways to calculate the discount factor (DF) with a calculator. For example, the five-year discount factor at 10 percent can be calculated as follows:

$$DF_{5,10\%} = \frac{1}{(1.10)^5} = \frac{1}{1.6105} = 0.6209$$

$$DF_{5,10\%} = \left(\frac{1}{1.10}\right)^5 = (0.9091)^5 = 0.6209$$

$$DF_{5,10\%} = (1.10)^{-5} = 0.6209$$

Note that the discount factor $DF_{T,k}$ is the value today of one dollar to be received in T years discounted to the present at the rate k. In our case, one dollar in five years is worth today 0.6209 dollar at 10 percent. What is the value today of $1,500 to be received in five years at 10 percent?

$$PV(\$1,500)_{5,10\%} = \$1,500 \times DF_{5,10\%} = \$1,500 \times 0.6209 = \$931.35$$

Here is a table that gives you the discount factor for combinations of different years and discount rates, rounded to four digits after the decimal point:

	T = 1 year	T = 3 years	T = 5 years	T = 10 years	T = 15 years	T = 20 years
k = 3%	0.9709	0.9151	0.8626	0.7441	0.6419	0.5537
k = 6%	0.9434	0.8396	0.7473	0.5584	0.4173	0.3118
k = 10%	0.9091	0.7513	0.6209	0.3855	0.2394	0.1486
k = 15%	0.8696	0.6575	0.4972	0.2472	0.1229	0.0611

Note that the *discount factor is less than one* because a dollar tomorrow is worth less than a dollar today. The discount factor decreases when: (a) the rate k goes up (look at the columns) and (b) the number of years T rises (look at the rows). In other words, *the farther away is a dollar in the future and the higher the discount rate, the smaller its present value.* Look at the table: it indicates that one dollar in one year is worth today about 97 cents at 3 percent but one dollar in 20 years at 15 percent is only worth today slightly more than 6 cents.

USING A FINANCIAL CALCULATOR TO SOLVE TIME VALUE OF MONEY PROBLEMS

Most financial calculators have a row of keys that provide the future and present values when the annual rate of interest and the number of years are entered into the calculator. The row of relevant keys usually looks as follows:

N is the number of years,[3] I/YR is the interest rate per year (without the percentage sign), PV is the present value, PMT is a periodic payment (which is zero for the moment; we will use this key later), and FV is the future value.

You can use the calculator keys to get any of the five variables shown on the keys if you know the other four.[4] Let's illustrate this with the following examples:[5]

(1) *Example 1: Finding the future value (when you know the present value, the number of years and the rate of interest).* A house is currently worth $200,000. Its value is expected to rise over the next ten years at the annual rate of 3 percent. What is the expected value of the house in ten years? Enter the number 10 in the calculator (it will appear on the screen) and press the N key; enter the number 3 in the calculator and press the I/YR key; enter the number 200,000 in the calculator and press the PV key; enter zero and press the PMT key; finally press the FV key: the calculator screen shows −268,783. The estimated value of the house in ten years is thus $268,783. The negative sign indicates that if you receive $200,000 today (a cash inflow) you will have to pay back $268,783 in ten years (a cash outflow). Had you entered −200,000 (an outflow) for PV, you would have found 268,783 for FV (an inflow). Finally, note that if you want to get the compound factors shown in the table in the section on compounding, just enter the number of years T in the N key, the rate k in the I/YR key, 1 in the PV key, zero in the PMT key and then press the FV key to get the corresponding compound factor.

(2) *Example 2: Finding the present value (when you know the future value, the number of years and the discount rate).* Should a firm invest $190,000 in a project that would be worth $300,000 in five years if the firm wants to earn a return of at least 12 percent on an investment of this type? Enter 5 for N, 12 for I/YR, zero for PMT, 300,000 for FV and then press the PV key: the calculator screen shows −170,228. The firm should not invest in this project because the present value of the investment ($170,228) is lower than the required initial cash outlay of $190,000. Note that the project's internal rate of return (IRR) is 9.57 percent, which is less than the required return of 12 percent (Enter 5 for N, −190,000 for PV, zero for PMT, 300,000 for FV and then press the I/YR key: the calculator screen shows 9.5654). Finally, note that if you want to get the discount factors shown in the table in the section on discounting, just enter the number of years T in the N key, the rate k in the I/YR key, zero in the PMT key, 1 in the FV key and then press the PV key to get the corresponding discount factor.

(3) *Example 3: Finding the number of years (when you know the present and future values and the rate of interest).* How long will it take for an investment to double in

---

[3] We use T (for time) to indicate the number of years; financial calculators usually use the letter N.

[4] We use an HP 10B business calculator to answer the questions in the chapter. Some financial calculators may require additional steps to get the answer. You should consult your calculator's manual.

[5] Make sure that your calculator is set up to calculate the interest rate on an annual basis (one period per year). Always clear your calculator of all the preceding inputs before starting a new calculation.

value if the interest rate is 8 percent? Enter 8 for I/YR, –1 for PV, zero for PMT, 2 for FV and then press the N key: the calculator screen shows 9.0065 (slightly more than 9 years).

(4) *Example 4: Finding the rate of interest (when you know the present and future values and the number of years).* What is the interest rate that will increase the value of an investment by 50 percent in six years? Enter 6 for N, –1 for PV, zero for PMT, 1.5 for FV and then press the I/YR key: the calculator screen shows 6.9913 (slightly less than 7 percent).

USING A SPREADSHEET TO SOLVE TIME VALUE OF MONEY PROBLEMS

The above four numerical examples can also be solved with a financial spreadsheet as shown below. NPER is the number of periods (years in our case) and RATE is the interest rate. The first column in the spreadsheet indicates the example's number and the last column provides the corresponding Excel formula.

	A	B	C	D	E	F	G
		NPER	RATE	PMT	PV	FV	Formulas
2	Example 1	10	3%	0	200,000	?	• *The formula in cell F3 is*
3	*Solve for FV*					–268,783	=FV(C2,B2,D2,E2)
4	Example 2	5	12%	0	?	300,000	• *The formula in cell E5 is*
5	*Solve for PV*				–170,228		=PV(C4,B4,D4,F4)
6	Example 3	?	8%	0	–1	2	• *The formula in cell B7 is*
7	*Solve for NPER*	9.0065					=NPER(C6,D6,E6,F6)
8	Example 4	6	?	0	–1	1.5	• *The formula in cell C9 is*
9	*Solve for RATE*		6.9913%				=RATE(B8,D8,E8,F8)

INTEREST RATE QUOTATION AND CALCULATION

There are a number of conventions regarding how the rate of interest is quoted and calculated. *Rates are quoted on a per-year basis,* meaning that if someone tells you the interest rate is 12 percent without any additional information, you should assume it is an annual rate. If the annual rate is 12 percent then the monthly rate would be quoted as '1 percent *per month*'. Note that if you receive 1 percent per month, your **effective annual interest return** will be higher than 12 percent because of compounding: you will earn monthly interest on the interest earned the previous month. We discuss this phenomenon in the next section.

Changes in interest rates are often quoted in terms of **basis points**. One basis point is equal to one-hundredth of 1 percent, that is, 0.0001, which is one unit of the fourth decimal point. For example, if the interest rate rises from 5.60 percent to 5.65 percent, we say that the rate is up 5 basis points or 5 **bps** (pronounced 'beeps').

Finally, rates are usually quoted on a nominal basis, meaning that they are not adjusted for the rate of inflation. A quoted rate of 12 percent means that you will receive in one year a return of 12 percent on your money regardless of what the inflation rate will be next year. We discuss below the difference between **nominal rates** (which are not adjusted for inflation) and **real rates** (which are adjusted for inflation).

THE ANNUAL PERCENTAGE RATE VERSUS THE EFFECTIVE ANNUAL RATE

Suppose you wish to borrow money from a bank. The bank quotes you a rate of 12 percent but says it will charge you 1 percent per month (12 percent divided by 12 months). The 12 percent rate the bank quotes you is called the **annual percentage rate or APR**: it is the simple one-year rate of interest that does *not* take into account the effect of compounding over shorter periods within one year (in our case, it ignores monthly compounding). The annual rate that takes into account the effect of monthly compounding is called the effective annual rate (k_{eff}); it is the annual rate you are paying if you are charged 1 percent per month. It is calculated as follows:

$$(1 + k_{eff}) = \left(1 + \frac{APR}{12}\right)^{12} = (1 + 0.01)^{12} = (1.01)^{12} = 1.1268$$

from which you get k_{eff} = 12.68 percent. In other words, because of monthly compounding the effective annual rate you are paying is 68 basis points higher than the 12 percent APR.

In general, if the letter 'n' indicates the number of sub-periods within a year, we have:

$$k_{eff} = \left(1 + \frac{APR}{n}\right)^{n} - 1 \tag{2.4}$$

The table below gives you the effective annual rate (k_{eff}) for different sub-periods with an annual percentage rate of 12 percent:

Compounding Sub-periods	n	Corresponding effective annual rate (k_{eff})
Semi-annual	2	$k_{eff} = \left(1 + \frac{0.12}{2}\right)^{2} - 1 = 0.12360 = 12.360\%$
Monthly	12	$k_{eff} = \left(1 + \frac{0.12}{12}\right)^{12} - 1 = 0.12683 = 12.683\%$
Weekly	52	$k_{eff} = \left(1 + \frac{0.12}{52}\right)^{52} - 1 = 0.12734 = 12.734\%$
Daily	360	$k_{eff} = \left(1 + \frac{0.12}{360}\right)^{360} - 1 = 0.12747 = 12.747\%$
Continuous	infinity	$k_{eff} = e^{0.12} - 1 = (2.7183)^{0.12} - 1 = 0.12750 = 12.750\%$

Note that the effective annual rate rises as the number of sub-periods increases but the effect is more pronounced for longer sub-periods (going from one year to six months raises the rate by 36 basis points, whereas going from one month to one week raises the rate by only 5.1 basis points). When the sub-period becomes infinitely small – meaning that interest is earned *continuously* – the effective annual rate reaches its highest value. It is found by raising the number e = 2.7183 to a power equal to the annual interest rate. The effective annual rate in this case is 75 basis points higher than the annual percentage rate.

(5) *Example 5: Discounting over periods shorter than a year.* You will receive $5,000 in 18 months. What is the present value at 6 percent with monthly and semi-annual discounting? With monthly discounting enter 18 for N, 0.5 for I/YR (6 divided by 12), zero for PMT, –5,000 for FV and then press the PV key: the calculator screen shows $4,570.68. With semi-annual discounting enter 3 for N, 3 for I/YR (6 divided by 2), zero for PMT, –5,000 for FV and then press the PV key: the calculator screen shows $4,575.71.

NOMINAL VERSUS REAL RATES

As pointed out earlier, the **nominal rate of interest** (k_{nom}) is a rate that is unadjusted for inflation. If the nominal rate was 10 percent last year and last year's inflation rate (r_{inf}) was 6 percent, what is the **real rate of interest** (k_{real}), that is, the rate of interest *without* inflation? A first answer is 4 percent, which is the nominal rate of 10 percent less the inflation rate of 6 percent. But this is only an approximate estimation of the real rate of interest. The precise real rate of interest is given by the following equation:

$$(1 + k_{nom}) = (1 + k_{real}) \times (1 + r_{inf})$$

where $(1 + k_{real})$ is the *real* value of a dollar in one year that has grown by a factor $(1 + r_{inf})$ to reflect price inflation (r_{inf} is the inflation rate). From the above equation, we can infer the correct real rate of interest as follows:

$$k_{real} = \frac{(1 + k_{nom})}{(1 + r_{inf})} - 1 \qquad (2.5)$$

In our case the nominal rate (k_{nom}) is 10 percent and the inflation rate (r_{inf}) is 6 percent. Applying the above formula you get a real rate (k_{real}) of 3.77 percent (check this). Note that the approximate real rate of 4 percent overestimates the correct rate by 23 basis points.

THE PRESENT VALUE OF A STREAM OF FUTURE CASH FLOWS

A stream of future cash flows can be represented by a **cash-flow timeline** which shows the *year* the cash flow will occur, its *size* and whether it is *positive* (a cash inflow) or *negative* (a cash outflow). Consider, for example, the following three-year timeline with cash flows measured in thousands of dollars:

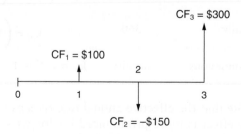

CF_1 is a cash inflow ($100) occurring at the *end* of Year 1, CF_2 a cash outflow (–$150) occurring at the *end* of Year 2, and CF_3 is a cash inflow ($300) occurring at the *end* of Year 3. Note the conventions: (1) point zero on the timeline is the present (now), point 1 is the *end* of the first year, point 2 is the *end* of the second year, etc.; (2) cash flows are assumed to occur at the *end* of the year; and (3) cash inflows (money received) are indicated by an upward arrow whereas cash outflows (money paid out) are indicated by a downward arrow. The above cash-flow stream could represent an industrial project that is expected to generate positive cash flows at the end of Year 1 and Year 3 but necessitates an investment at the end of Year 2 to expand the facilities.

What is the present value of this stream of cash flows at a discount rate of 10 percent? The first cash flow must be discounted at 10 percent for one year using the one-year, 10-percent discount factor ($DF_{1,10\%}$), the second cash flow must be discounted at 10 percent for two years using the two-year, 10-percent discount factor ($DF_{2,10\%}$), and the third cash flow must be discounted at 10 percent for three years using the three-year, 10-percent discount factor ($DF_{3,10\%}$). We can write:

$$PV(\text{cash-flow stream}) = [CF_1 \times DF_{1,10\%}] + [CF_2 \times DF_{2,10\%}] + [CF_3 \times DF_{3,10\%}]$$

$$PV(\text{cash-flow stream}) = [\$100 \times 0.9091] + [-\$150 \times 0.8264] + [\$300 \times 0.7513 = \$192.34$$

The present value of the cash-flow stream at 10 percent is thus \$192,340. You can find this present value faster using the cash-flow key in your financial calculator. Enter the following sequence of cash flows: $CF_0 = 0$; $CF_1 = 100$; $CF_2 = -150$; and $CF_3 = 300$. Enter 10 in the interest rate key for the 10 percent discount rate. Press the NPV key. The calculator screen shows 192.34. Alternatively, you can use the following spreadsheet:

	A	B	C	D	E
		Now	**1**	**2**	**3**
1	Timeline	Now	1	2	3
2	Cash-flow stream	$0	$100	−$150	$300
3	Discount rate	10%			
4	Present value	**$192.34**			

- B1 is now and the following cells indicate the end of years 1 to 3
- The formula in cell B4 is = NPV(B3,C2:E2)

THE NET PRESENT VALUE (NPV) RULE

Would you undertake the project described in the previous section if you had to invest today \$160,000? The answer is yes because the project's present value of \$192,340 exceeds the \$160,000 initial cash outlay. To put it another way, the project should be undertaken because its **net present value** is a positive \$32,340, the difference between the *value* today of the project's future cash-flow stream (\$192,340) and the initial expenditure of \$160,000 (think of this as the price of the project):

$$NPV(\text{project}) = -\text{Project's Price} + \text{Project's Value} = -\$160,000 + \$192,340 = \$32,340$$

THE INTERNAL RATE OF RETURN (IRR) RULE

What is your expected return on the project given that you spent today \$160,000 to acquire the future cash-flow stream? This rate, called the project's **internal rate of return,** can only be found with a financial calculator or a spreadsheet (we discuss this point in detail in Chapter 8).

Using a financial calculator:
Enter the following sequence of cash flows: $CF_0 = -160$; $CF_1 = 100$; $CF_2 = -150$; and $CF_3 = 300$. Look for the IRR key. Press that key and the calculator screen shows 17.89.
Using a spreadsheet:

	A	B	C	D	E
1	Timeline	Now	1	2	3
2	Cash-flow stream	−$160	$100	−$150	$300
3	IRR	<u>17.89%</u>			

- B1 is now and the following cells indicate the end of years 1 to 3
- The formula in cell B3 is = IRR(B2:E2)

The project is expected to generate a return of 17.89 percent, which is higher than the discount rate of 10 percent. In other words, the project is worth undertaking. Note that the IRR and NPV rules usually reach the same conclusion but there are cases when they do not. We examine this issue in Chapter 8.

THE PRESENT VALUE OF A PERPETUAL CASH-FLOW STREAM

A perpetual cash-flow stream, also called a **perpetuity**, has *identical* periodic cash flows that repeat themselves to infinity ($CF_1 = CF_2 = CF_3 = \ldots$). This is illustrated on the following timeline where the identical cash flows are equal to $100:

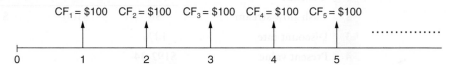

The present value of the above perpetuity at 10 percent is $1,000. Why? Here is the explanation: if you deposit $1,000 in a bank account that pays 10 percent per year, you will receive $100 every year *forever*, with the first payment one year from now. In other words, a perpetual stream of $100 per year is worth today $1,000. We can write: $1,000 \times 10\% = $100; dividing both sides by 10%, we have $1,000 = \dfrac{\$100}{10\%}$. We can generalize this relationship as follows (for a formal proof see Appendix 2.1):

$$PV(\text{perpetuity}) = \frac{CF}{k} \tag{2.6}$$

In our case we have CF = $100 (the perpetual annual interest payment) and k = 10 percent (the annual interest rate). Dividing CF by k yields a present value of $1,000. Note that even though there is an *infinite* number of future cash flows to discount, the perpetuity has a *finite* present value because the discounting process makes the present value of future cash flows smaller and smaller the farther out they occur.

The perpetuities discussed so far are called *standard* perpetuities because they start one year from now. There are nonstandard perpetuities such as *immediate* perpetuities (also called perpetuity *due* because the first cash flow occurs now) and *deferred* perpetuities (the first cash flow occurs after the first year).

Consider the case of the immediate perpetuity shown on the following timeline:

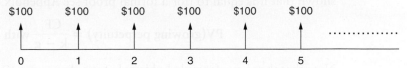

The present value of this immediate perpetuity is simply $1,100: it is the present value of a standard perpetuity ($1,000) plus the immediate cash flow of $100. In general, if CF is the perpetual annual interest payment, we can write:

$$PV(\text{immediate perpetuity}) = CF + \frac{CF}{k} \tag{2.7}$$

Consider now the *deferred* perpetuity shown below where the first cash flow begins at the end of the fourth year:

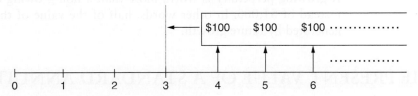

The present value of this deferred perpetuity can be calculated in two steps. First get the present value of the standard perpetuity at the end of the *third* year, that is, $\left(\dfrac{CF_4}{k}\right)$, which at 10 percent is $1,000, and then get the present value of $1,000 for T = 3 and k = 10 percent. We have:

$$PV(\text{deferred perpetuity}) = \frac{\left(\dfrac{CF_4}{k}\right)}{(1+k)^3} = \frac{\left(\dfrac{\$100}{0.10}\right)}{(1+0.10)^3} = \frac{\$1,000}{(1.10)^3} = \frac{\$1,000}{1.3310} = \$751.31$$

In general, if CF is the perpetual annual cash flow starting at the end of year T, we can write:

$$PV(\text{deferred perpetuity}) = \frac{CF_1/k}{(1+k)^{T-1}} \tag{2.8}$$

Clearly, a deferred perpetuity whose cash flow begins in four years is less valuable than a standard perpetuity whose cash flow begins next year. In our example the deferred perpetuity is worth $751.31 whereas the standard one is worth $1,000. The difference of $248.69 represents the present value of the first three cash flows of $100. Check this on your financial calculator.

THE PRESENT VALUE OF A GROWING PERPETUITY

A *growing* perpetuity has cash flows that grow at a *constant* rate forever. Suppose that the constant growth rate (g) is equal to 5 percent and that the first cash flow one year from now, CF_1, is equal to $100. The second cash flow (CF_2) will be $105($100 × 1.05), the third cash flow (CF_3) will be $110.25($105 × 1.05) and each subsequent cash flow will be 5 percent higher than the preceding one. What is the present value of this constant growth perpetuity at the discount rate k? It can be shown that it is equal to (for a formal proof see Appendix 2.1):

$$PV(\text{growing perpetuity}) = \frac{CF_1}{k - g} \text{ with } k > g \qquad (2.9)$$

Note that the above formula holds only for a discount rate (k) that is higher than the growth rate (g).[6] Also, note that setting the growth rate (g) to zero gives the present value of the standard perpetuity (see formula 2.6). In other words, formula 2.6 is a special case of formula 2.9.

Applying formula 2.9 to the case where CF_1 is $100, k is 10 percent, and g is 5 percent, we get:

$$PV(\text{growing perpetuity}) = \frac{\$100}{0.10 - 0.05} = \frac{\$100}{0.05} = \$2,000$$

A growing perpetuity is worth more than a non-growing one; in our case $2,000 instead of $1,000. In other words, half of the value of the growing perpetuity is generated by future growth.

THE PRESENT VALUE OF A STANDARD ANNUITY

A *standard* **annuity** is a cash-flow stream with *identical* cash flows ($CF_1 = CF_2 = CF_3 = \ldots = CF_T$) for T consecutive years as shown on the following timeline in the case of a $100 annuity:

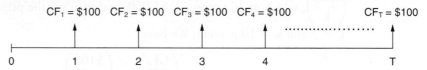

The formula for the present value of a T-year annuity at a discount rate k with a cash flow CF is (a proof is provided below):

$$PV(\text{annuity}) = \frac{CF}{k}\left[1 - \frac{1}{(1 + k)^T}\right] \qquad (2.10)$$

Note that the second term in the brackets is the T-year discount factor. When the number of years T goes to infinity, the discount factor goes to zero and formula 2.10 provides the value of a standard perpetuity (see formula 2.6).

What is the present value of a five-year annuity with a recurrent cash flow of $100 at a 10 percent discount rate? Applying formula 2.10, we get:

$$PV(\text{annuity}) = \frac{\$100}{0.10}\times\left[1 - \frac{1}{(1.10)^5}\right] = \$1,1000\times[1 - 0.6209] = \$1,000\times[0.3791] = \$379.10$$

Note that at 10 percent, the value of the five-year annuity of $100 is equal to only 37.91 percent of the value of a perpetuity of $100 (which is worth $1,000). You can easily get the present value of an annuity with your financial calculator. To illustrate, go through the following steps: (1) Enter 5 and press the N key (the number of years);

---

[6] Note that discounting *reduces* the size of the cash flows while growth *inflates* them. With a discount rate higher than the growth rate, cash flows shrink faster than they grow. As a result, the growing perpetuity has a finite value (instead of being infinitely large).

(2) Enter 10 and press the I/YR key (the 10 percent interest rate); (3) Enter 100 and press the PMT key (the annual recurrent cash flow); (4) Enter zero and press the FV key. To get the present value of the annuity press the PV key. The calculator screen shows -379.08.

You can find the formula for the present value of a T-year annuity by taking the difference between the present value of a standard perpetuity (shown with cash-flow arrows pointing upward on the timeline below) and the present value of a deferred perpetuity that begins in $(T + 1)$ years (shown with cash-flow arrows pointing downward on the timeline below):

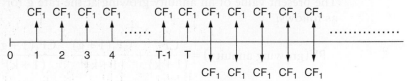

$$PV[\text{T-year annuity}] = PV[\text{standard perpetuity}] - PV[\text{deferred perpetuity starting in year } (T + 1)]$$

The present value of a T-year annuity at the discount rate k is thus:

$$PV(\text{annuity}) = \frac{CF_1}{k} - \frac{\dfrac{CF_1}{k}}{(1 + k)^T} = \frac{CF_1}{k}\left[1 - \frac{1}{(1 + k)^T}\right]$$

If we define the **annuity discount factor (ADF)** as the present value of a *one* dollar annuity for T years at the discount rate k, then the present value of the above annuity can be expressed as follows:

$$PV(\text{annuity}) = CF_1 \times ADF \text{ } with \text{ } ADF_{T,k} = \frac{1}{k}\left[1 - \frac{1}{(1 + k)^T}\right] \qquad (2.11)$$

Applying formula 2.11 to the previous example of a five-year annuity of $100 at a 10 percent rate, you find an ADF of 3.7908. The present value of the annuity is thus $PV = \$100 \times 3.7908 = \$379.08$. To get the ADF with your calculator, enter 5 for N, 10 for I/YR, 1 for PMT, zero for FV and then press the PV key. The calculator screen shows -3.7908.

(6) *Example 6: A mortgage loan.* You borrow $100,000 at 6 percent for 25 years to fund part of the purchase of a house. You repay this mortgage loan with equal monthly installments over 25 years. What is your monthly loan repayment? How much interest payment and how much loan repayment are in your first monthly installment? How much interest will you be paying over the entire life of the mortgage loan? This is an annuity problem. You know the annuity's present value ($100,000, which is the mortgage loan), the number of periods (T = 25 years × 12 months = 300 months), and the rate of interest per period (k = 0.06/12 = 0.50 percent). You are looking for the recurrent monthly annuity. According to formula 2.11, the annuity discount factor and the monthly annuity, CF, are:

$$ADF_{300,0.50\%} = \frac{1}{0.005} \times \left[1 - \frac{1}{(1 + 0.005)^{300}}\right] = 155.2069$$

$$CF = \frac{PV}{ADF} = \frac{\$100,000}{155.2069} = \$644.30$$

To get the same with your calculator, enter 300 for N, 0.50 for I/YR, $-100,000$ for PV, and zero for FV. Press the PMT key and you get your monthly payment of $644.30. Your interest payment in the first monthly installment is 0.50 percent of

$100,000, that is, $500. The balance of $144.30 is your first loan reimbursement. Over the life of the loan you make 300 payments of $644.30, that is, $193,290. The total amount of interest you paid over the life of the loan is thus $93,290 (the difference between your total payment of $193,290 and the $100,000 you borrowed).

THE PRESENT VALUE OF A GROWING ANNUITY

The present value of an annuity growing at the rate g for T years can be expressed as follows:

$$PV(\text{growing annuity}) = \frac{CF_1}{(1+k)} + \frac{CF_1(1+g)}{(1+k)^2} + \frac{CF_1(1+g)^2}{(1+k)^3} + \ldots + \frac{CF_1(1+g)^{T-1}}{(1+k)^T}$$

To find a formula to calculate this present value we can use the same method we employed to get the present value of a standard annuity: we take the difference between the present value of a growing perpetuity that begins in one year and the present value of a growing perpetuity that begins (T + 1) years from now. The present value of the growing annuity for T years is thus:

$$PV(\text{growing annuity}) = \frac{CF_1}{k-g} - \frac{\dfrac{CF_{T+1}}{k-g}}{(1+k)^T} = \frac{CF_1}{k-g} - \frac{\dfrac{CF_1(1+g)^T}{k-g}}{(1+k)^T}$$

Factoring out the common term $\dfrac{CF_1}{k-g}$ you get:

$$PV(\text{growing annuity}) = \frac{CF_1}{k-g}\left[1 - \left(\frac{1+g}{1+k}\right)^T\right] \tag{2.12}$$

To illustrate, assume $CF_1 = \$100$, T = 5 years, k = 10 percent, and g = 5 percent. In this case:

$$PV(\text{growing annuity}) = \frac{\$100}{0.10 - 0.05} \times \left[1 - \left(\frac{1.05}{1.10}\right)^5\right]$$

$$PV(\text{growing annuity}) = \$2,000 \times [1 - 0.7925] = \$2,000 \times [0.2075] = \$415$$

Note that the formula for a growing annuity also works when the growth rate g is *higher* than the discount rate k.[7] For example, assume that g is now 15 percent. In this case we have:

$$PV(\text{growing annuity}) = \frac{\$100}{0.10 - 0.15} \times \left[1 - \left(\frac{1.15}{1.10}\right)^5\right]$$

$$= -\$2,000 \times [1 - 1.2489] = -\$2,000 \times [-0.2489]$$

$$= \$497.79$$

---

[7] The formula does not work when the growth rate (g) is equal to the discount rate (k). When 'g' equals 'k' we have: $PV = \dfrac{CF_1}{(1+k)} + \dfrac{CF_1(1+g)}{(1+k)^2} + \ldots = \dfrac{CF_1}{1+k} + \dfrac{CF_1}{1+k} + \ldots = \dfrac{T \times CF_1}{1+k}$. In our example, if the growth is 10 percent (the same as the discount rate) then $PV = \dfrac{T \times CF_1}{1+k} = \dfrac{5 \times 100}{1.10} = 454.55$.

CF_1 CF_2 CF_3 CF_n CF_9

S^o

(7) *Example 7: Valuing a growing company.* Let's apply the growth formulas 2.12 and 2.9 to value a company that is expected to generate *next year* a cash flow of $80 million ($CF_1$ = $80 million) that will grow at 7 percent for the following four years (from the end of year one until the end of year five) and at 3 percent in perpetuity beyond year five. The discount rate is 10 percent.

Because there are two growth rates, the valuation is carried out in several steps:

Step one. Get the present value of the first five cash flows (CF_1 to CF_5) that grow at 7 percent. We have CF_1 = $80 million, T = 5, k = 10% and g = 7%. Applying formula 2.12 we get:

$$PV(CF_1 \text{ to } CF_5) = \frac{\$80m}{0.10 - 0.07} \times \left[1 - \left(\frac{1.07}{1.10} \right)^5 \right] = \$344 \text{ million}$$

Step two. Get the value, at the end of year five, of the perpetual cash-flow stream that grows at 3 percent. That value is called the company's **terminal value** at the end of year five (TV_5) because it is the value (in five years) of the last (terminal) stage of growth. Applying formula 2.9 we have:

$$TV_5 = \frac{CF_6}{10\% - 3\%} = \frac{CF_5 \times 1.03}{0.07}$$

What is the value of CF_5? It is the value of CF_1 growing at 7 percent for four years:

$$CF_5 = CF_1 \times (1 + 0.07)^4 = \$80m \times 1.3108 = \$104.86 \text{ million}$$

The terminal value at the end of year five is thus:

$$(TV_5) = \frac{CF_6}{10\% - 3\%} = \frac{CF_5 \times 1.03}{0.07} = \frac{\$104.86m \times 1.03}{0.07} = \frac{\$108.01m}{0.07} = \$1,543 \text{ million}$$

Step three. Get the present value of the terminal value at the 10 percent discount rate:

$$PV(TV_5) = \frac{TV_5}{(1 + 0.10)^5} = \frac{\$1,543m}{1.6105} = \$958 \text{ million}$$

Step four. The estimated value of the company is the sum of the two present values:

$$\text{Company Value} = PV(CF_1 \text{ to } CF_5) + PV(TV_5) = \$344m + \$958m = \$1,302 \text{ million}$$

The company's value can be also calculated with a spreadsheet as shown below. Row 1 indicates the cash-flow timeline. Row 2 provides the growth rates with which the annual cash flows are calculated. Cell G5 provides the terminal value at the end of year five. Cell B6 gives the present value of the first five cash flows at 10 percent and cell B7 the present value of the terminal value. The value of the company is in cell B8.

	A	B	C	D	E	F	G	H
1	Timeline	Now	1	2	3	4	5	6
2	Growth rates		7%	7%	7%	7%	7%	3%
3	Cash flows in million		$80.00	$85.60	$91.59	$98.00	$104.86	$108.01
4	Discount rate	10%						
5	Terminal value (TV$_5$) in million						$ 1,543	
6	PV(CF$_1$ to CF$_5$) in million	$ 344						
7	PV(TV$_5$) in million	$ 958						
8	PV(all CFs) in million	**$1,302**						

- B1 is now and the following cells indicate the end of years 1 to 6
- Formula in cell D3 is = C3*(1 + C2). Then copy cell D3 to next cells in the row
- Formula in cell G5 is = H3/(B4 − H2) to get the terminal value at the end of year 5
- Formula in cell B6 is = NPV(B4,C3:G3)
- Formula in cell B7 is = G5/(1 + B4)^5 to get the present value of the terminal value
- Formula in cell B8 is = B6 + B7 to get the value of the firm

THE FUTURE VALUE OF AN ANNUITY

At one time in your life you will retire and you may want to know how much you have to save annually in order to secure a specific amount of annual income during your retirement. To answer this question, note that the pre-retirement annual savings is an annuity and the value of your pension when you retire is the future value of this annuity. Example 8 below shows you how to calculate the amount of your pre-retirement annual savings to achieve a specific annual retirement income. Before we do this, we first need a formula to get the future value of an annuity.

To find the future value of an annuity for T consecutive years, we need to calculate the *future* value of the *present* value of the annuity using formulas 2.1 and 2.10, respectively, as follows:

$$FV(\text{annuity}) = PV(\text{annuity}) \times (1 + k)^T = \frac{CF_1}{k}\left[1 - \frac{1}{(1 + k)^T} \right] \times (1 + k)^T$$

$$FV(\text{annuity}) = \frac{CF_1}{k}\left[(1 + k)^T - 1\right] \qquad (2.13)$$

To illustrate, what is the future value of a five-year, $100-annuity at 10 percent?

$$FV(\text{annuity}) = \frac{\$100}{0.10} \times [(1.10)^5 - 1] = \$1,000 \times [1.61051 - 1] = \$610.51$$

In your calculator, enter 5 for N, 10 for I/YR, zero for PV, 100 for PMT and then press the FV key. The calculator screen shows −610.51.

(8) *Example 8: A retirement problem.* Let's apply the annuity formulas 2.10 and 2.13 to solve the following retirement problem. An individual expects to retire in 30 years and live for the following 25 years. If the person wishes to have an annual income

of $100,000 during his 25 years of retirement (starting at the end of his first year of retirement), how much should the person save annually over the next 30 years to achieve this goal if the rate of interest is 5 percent?

The present value at the end of year 30 of a 25-year annuity of $100,000 is given by formula 2.10:

$$PV_{30} = \frac{\$100,000}{0.05} \times \left[1 - \frac{1}{(1.05)^{25}} \right] = \$2,000,000 \times [1 - 0.2953] = \$1,409,394$$

With your calculator, enter 25 for N, 5 for I/YR, 100,000 for PMT, zero for FV and then press PV to get −1,409,394.

The future value, at the end of year 30, of a 30-year annuity of S dollars per year (where S is the annual saving we are looking for) is given by formula 2.13:

$$FV_{30} = \frac{S}{0.05} \times [(1.05)^{30} - 1] = S \times \left[\frac{(1.05)^{30} - 1}{0.05} \right] = S \times \left[\frac{4.32194 - 1}{0.05} \right] = S \times [66.44]$$

The PV of the annual retirement income at the end of year 30 (PV_{30}) must be equal to the future value of the annual saving at the end of year 30 (PV_{30}), thus:

$$\$1,409,394 = S \times 66.44$$

from which we get:

$$S = \text{Annual Saving} = \frac{\$1,409,394}{66.44} = \$21,213$$

The individual has to save $21,213 every year to retire in 30 years and collect an annual income of $100,000 every year during his 25 years of expected retirement period.

KEY POINTS

1. You cannot compare cash flows that occur at different dates in the future. If you want to know which of two cash flows is more valuable you must first calculate their present values by discounting them at an appropriate discount rate. The one with the highest present value is the most valuable.
2. When compounding occurs annually, the annual rate of interest is called the annual percentage rate (APR). When compounding occurs over periods shorter than one year (for example, a day, a week, a month, etc.), the corresponding annual rate of interest that takes into account compounding over the shorter periods is called the effective annual rate. The relationship between the APR and the effective annual rate is given by formula 2.4.
3. The discount rate is always stated on an annual nominal basis, meaning that it does not adjust for the inflation rate. To get a rate that excludes inflation, the nominal rate must be converted into a real rate using formula 2.5.
4. There are a number of formulas that allow you to convert specific cash-flow streams into their present value. They are summarized in Exhibit 2.1. The first row gives the present values of a standard annuity and a growing annuity. The second row gives the present value of a standard perpetuity and a growing perpetuity. Numerical examples are given for $CF_1 = \$100, T = 5$ years, $k = 10$ percent, and $g = 5$ percent.

5. The present value formulas reported in Exhibit 2.1 assume that the first cash flow occurs at the end of the first year. Any cash flow received now is not taken into account in the present value formulas.

6. The present value of a growing annuity is "the mother of all formulas" because it gives you all the other formulas as special cases (refer to Exhibit 2.1). The formula for a standard annuity is found by setting the growth rate (g) to zero. The formula for a standard perpetuity is found by setting the growth rate (g) to zero and taking the number of years (T) to infinity. And the formula for a growing perpetuity is found by taking the number of years (T) to infinity.

EXHIBIT 2.1	SUMMARY OF PRESENT VALUE FORMULAS.

THE FIRST CASH FLOW OCCURS AT THE END OF THE FIRST YEAR: $CF_1 = 100$
THE DISCOUNT RATE IS 10 PERCENT

	No growth	Growth rate of 5 percent
T = 5 years	**STANDARD ANNUITY**[1] $$PV = \frac{CF_1}{k}\left[1 - \frac{1}{(1 + k)^T}\right]$$ PV = \$379.10	**GROWING ANNUITY** $$PV = \frac{CF_1}{k - g}\left[1 - \left(\frac{1 + g}{1 + k}\right)^T\right]$$ (with k different from g) PV = \$415.06
Perpetuity	**STANDARD PERPETUITY**[2, 3] $$PV = \frac{CF_1}{k}$$ PV = \$1,000	**GROWING PERPETUITY** $$PV = \frac{CF_1}{k - g}$$ (with k > g) PV = \$2,000

[1] Annuity discount factor: $ADF = \frac{1}{k}\left[1 - \frac{1}{(1 + k)^T}\right]$

[2] Immediate perpetuity: $PV = CF + \frac{CF}{k}$

[3] Deferred perpetuity (first CF occurs at the end of year T): $PV = \frac{CF_T/k}{(1 + k)^{T-1}}$

PROOF OF FORMULA 2.9 AND FORMULA 2.6

We provide below a proof of formula 2.9 for a growing perpetuity. The proof of formula 2.6 for a standard perpetuity is identical and can be found by simply setting the growth rate (g) to zero.

$$PV(\text{growing perpetuity}) = \frac{CF_1}{(1 + k)} + \frac{CF_1(1 + g)}{(1 + k)^2} + \frac{CF_1(1 + g)^2}{(1 + k)^3} + \cdots$$

$$= \frac{CF_1}{(1 + k)} + \left(\frac{1 + g}{1 + k}\right)\left[\frac{CF_1}{(1 + k)} + \frac{CF_1(1 + g)}{(1 + k)^2} + \cdots\right]$$

The sequence in brackets is PV(growing perpetuity) and thus:

$$PV(\text{growing perpetuity}) = \frac{CF_1}{(1 + k)} + \left(\frac{1 + g}{1 + k}\right)[PV(\text{growing perpetuity})]$$

Multiplying both sides of the above equation by $(1 + k)$ and solving for PV (growing perpetuity), you get formula 2.9.

FURTHER READING

Drake, Pamela, and Frank Fabozzi. *Foundations and Applications of the Time Value of Money*. John Wiley & Sons, 2009. See the first six chapters and the appendices.

SELF-TEST QUESTIONS

2.1 **Present value, future value and discount rates.**
You borrowed $10,000 and will have to repay $15,000 in five years.

a. What is the present value of the loan?
b. What is the future value of the loan?
c. What annual rate of interest are you paying?
d. If the expected annual inflation rate is 3 percent, what is the real rate of interest you are paying?
e. What is the lender's effective rate of return with monthly compounding?

2.2 **Evaluating alternative strategies.**
A firm is evaluating two mutually exclusive strategies, a domestic expansion or an international expansion. The annual net cash flows of the two strategies are

given below in millions. The two strategies require the same initial investment of $100 million. The firm uses a discount rate of 8 percent for domestic projects and 12 percent for international projects. Which strategy should the firm adopt?

	CF_1	CF_2	CF_3	CF_4	CF_5
Domestic strategy	$25	$25	$30	$30	$30
International strategy	$20	$30	$40	$50	$40

2.3   **Making an investment decision.**
A company is considering buying a machine for $2 million that would reduce its annual net operating costs by $275,000 over the next ten years. The machine would be worthless after ten years. The company applies a discount rate of 7 percent for this type of investment.

a. Should the company purchase the machine?
b. What is your answer to question (a) if the annual reduction in costs rises by 7 percent per year?
c. What is the *minimum* reduction in annual net operating costs that would justify the investment?
d. What is the *highest* discount rate that would justify the investment?

2.4   **Retirement plan.**
A company's retirement plan requires a regular annual contribution of $8,000 from age 30 to the age of 60 (inclusive). The discount rate is 5 percent.

a. What is the 31-year annuity discount factor?
b. What is the plan's present value for an employee on his 26th birthday?
c. What is the plan's future value for an employee on his 29th birthday?
d. How long will the 29-year-old employee be able to draw an annual retirement income of $40,000 starting one year after he retires at age 60?

2.5   **Valuing a company.**
A company's current cash flow of $12 million is expected to grow at 15 percent for the next five years, then at 10 percent for the following five years and finally at 5 percent in perpetuity. The discount rate is 10 percent.

a. What is the company's value? Show your answer using (1) a spreadsheet and (2) the relevant time-value-of-money formulas.
b. What is the company's value if it did not grow at all?
c. Based on your answers to the previous two questions, what is the value of future growth opportunities? What is the value of future growth opportunities as a percentage of the company's value?

REVIEW QUESTIONS

1. **Finding the implicit interest rate.**
What is the interest rate that makes you indifferent between $1,000 in one year and $1,180 in three years?

2. **APR versus effective interest rate.**

   A bank is charging you an annual interest rate that is compounded monthly. If the effective interest rate you are paying is 6.17 percent, what is the annual percentage rate (APR)?

3. **Compounded value and compounded rate.**

   a. What would be the compounded value of one dollar in three years if the annual interest rate is 3 percent in Year 1 and is expected to rise to 5 percent in Year 2 and 6 percent in Year 3?

   b. What constant annual interest rate would produce the same compounded value over three years?

4. **Alternative financing plans.**

   You can purchase a car with one of the following two financing plans. You make a down payment of $12,000 and 36 monthly payments of $400 starting immediately. Alternatively, you can make 60 monthly payments of $492 starting next month without any down payment. Which plan offers a better deal if the interest rate is 6 percent?

5. **Annuity versus perpetuity.**

   You have just read an advertisement stating, "Pay us $100 a year for the next ten years and we will pay you $100 a year thereafter in perpetuity." If this is a fair deal, what is the implied rate of interest?

6. **Valuing a loan.**

   A company borrowed $10 million for five years from Atlantic Bank. The company pays Atlantic Bank a fixed annual rate of 8 percent and must pay back the $10 million loan at the end of the borrowing period. A year has passed since the loan was made and Atlantic Bank wants to sell the loan to Pacific Bank.

   a. If the interest rate is now 7 percent, what is the value of the loan?

   b. What would be the value of the loan if the company was paying the bank 4 percent every six months instead of 8 percent per year?

7. **Perpetual cash flows.**

   You are currently a member of a club whose annual membership fee is $2,000. The fee is expected to increase by 3 percent per year.

   a. Would you buy for $65,000 a lifelong family membership to the club that can be passed down to your descendants? You can earn 6 percent on a long-term bank deposit.

   b. What discount rate would make you indifferent?

   c. What annual membership fees would make you indifferent?

   d. What lifelong membership price would make you indifferent?

8. **Growing annuities versus growing perpetuities.**

   The municipal government has imposed a temporary, five-year tax increase on the value of property that will raise $80 million at the end of the first year. Property values are estimated to grow at a rate of 3 percent per year.

   a. What is the present value of the total amount of tax the proposal will raise if the discount rate is 8 percent?

   b. What is the present value of the total amount of tax the municipal government could raise if the tax is permanent and the discount rate is still 8 percent?

9. **Mortgage loan.**

   You borrowed $80,000 to finance the purchase of a property through a standard, 30-year fixed rate mortgage with an annual interest rate of 8 percent, compounded monthly.

   a. What is your monthly mortgage payment?

   b. How much interest and how much principal repayment are in your first monthly mortgage payment?

   c. How much interest will you pay over the full life of the mortgage?

10. **Retirement planning.**

    A junior employee, who just turned 25, decides to set up a personal retirement fund to supplement her government-funded pension plan during her first 20 years of retirement. She wants to have an annual income of $50,000 starting when she turns 65 and ending on her 84th birthday.

    a. What lump sum must she invest today at 6 percent in order to achieve her retirement plan?

    b. How much must she invest each month at 6 percent starting now until she retires in order to achieve her retirement plan?

RISK AND RETURN

The shares of two companies – Advanced Technologies and Best Beverages – are expected to return 10 percent. The shares of Advanced Technologies are riskier than those of Best Beverages. If you have to invest in only one company, which one would you select? Like most investors, you must have chosen the shares of Best Beverages because they have the *same* expected return as the shares of Advanced Technologies but are *less* risky.

This is the usual choice because individuals are typically risk-averse: they dislike risk and hold shares of riskier companies only if those shares are expected to generate higher returns to compensate them for the higher risk. To put it differently, if investors want higher expected returns, they will have to accept more risk because there is no reward without risk-taking.

In this chapter we examine the relationship between the expected return and the risk of financial assets. This relationship should be positive because investors are risk-averse: the riskier a financial asset, the higher its expected return. But how is risk measured and what is the exact relationship between expected return and risk? We answer these fundamental questions in this chapter. We show that the risk of a financial asset depends on whether it is held as a single asset or held in a portfolio of assets. Combining shares of many companies into a portfolio allows investors to reduce the risk of the individual companies held in the portfolio. We explain how this risk-reduction works and examine the implications for (1) the pricing of financial assets, (2) the estimation of a firm's cost of capital, (3) the evaluation of a portfolio's investment performance, and (4) the empirical analysis of share prices to find out if they react efficiently to new information. After reading this chapter, you should understand the following:

- How to measure the expected return and the risk of a financial asset
- How to measure the expected return and the risk of a portfolio of assets
- How the risk of a portfolio can be reduced through diversification
- Why the risk of an asset held alone differs from its risk if it is held in a portfolio
- How to invest your savings in an optimal manner, that is, how to invest your savings in order to earn the highest possible expected return for a given level of risk

- How the expected return of a portfolio of assets is related to its risk
- How the expected return of a financial asset is related to its risk
- How to evaluate the investment performance of a portfolio
- How to test whether stock market prices react efficiently to new information

MEASURES OF RETURN

In order to make investment decisions you need estimates of the expected return and risk of the financial assets available for investment (we use the words financial assets, assets, **securities**, and **stocks** interchangeably in this chapter). In this section we show how to estimate a stock's expected return based on its *historical* distribution of returns. The estimation of risk is covered in the following section.

REALIZED RETURNS

Suppose you bought shares of Alto Water Supplies (Alto) at the end of December at $46.92 a share. Three weeks later you received a **dividend per share (DPS)** of $0.62. At the end of January the price of Alto shares increased to $47.36. What is your **realized return** for the month of January (also called the **holding period return**)? It is the sum of (1) the change in share price over the period $(P_t - P_{t-1})$ and (2) any dividend per share received during that period (DPS_t), divided by the share price at the beginning of the period (P_{t-1}):

$$R_t = \frac{(P_t - P_{t-1}) + DPS_t}{P_{t-1}} = \frac{(P_t - P_{t-1})}{P_{t-1}} + \frac{DPS_t}{P_{t-1}} \qquad (3.1)$$

In the case of Alto shares, the return for the month of January (R_1) is:

$$R_1 = \frac{(\$47.36 - \$46.92) + \$0.62}{\$46.92} = \frac{\$47.36 - \$46.92}{\$46.92} + \frac{\$0.62}{\$46.92} = 0.94\% + 1.32\% = 2.26\%$$

Alto's total return for the month of January is 2.26 percent. It can be broken down into a **capital gain** (the change in share price) of 0.94 percent (the first term in equation 3.1) and a **dividend yield** (the dividend divided by the share price) of 1.32 percent (the second term in equation 3.1).

Suppose you collected the following 12 monthly returns for Alto shares over the previous year:

JAN	FEB	MAR	APR	MAY	JUNE	JULY	AUG	SEPT	OCT	NOV	DEC
2.26%	3.24%	5.96%	−3.90%	4.30%	−4.13%	3.51%	−5.09%	3.31%	3.61%	1.63%	−6.70%

This sequence of 12 monthly returns represents a *sample* of the true, *unobservable* distribution of Alto returns. From this sample distribution we can calculate Alto's **average arithmetic return** over the 12 months $(\overline{R}_{Alto})$ by adding the 12 observations and dividing them by 12:

$$\overline{R}_{Alto} = \frac{R_1 + R_2 + \ldots + R_{11} + R_{12}}{12} = \frac{2.26\% + 3.24\% + \ldots + 1.63\% - 6.70\%}{12} = 0.6667\%$$

EXPECTED RETURN

As mentioned earlier, in order to make investment decisions we need an estimate of the return we can expect from holding Alto shares. If Alto's return distribution is *stationary*, that is, if it remains the same over time, then the average return of its sample distribution would provide a reliable estimate of Alto's **expected return**, written $E(R_{Alto})$. But we would need to collect more than a year of monthly returns to obtain a reliable estimate of expected return. We only took 12 monthly observations to simplify the calculation. We will look at return distributions constructed with a larger number of observations later in this chapter.

ANNUALIZED RETURNS

If you want to convert a monthly average return into its annual equivalent, all you have to do is multiply the monthly return by 12. In the case of Alto, we have an annualized average return of 8 percent:

$$\overline{R}_{Alto}(annual) = 12 \times \overline{R}_{Alto}(monthly) = 12 \times 0.6667\% = 8.00\%$$

MEASURES OF RISK

Notice the significant amount of variations in Alto's monthly returns. They range from a high of 5.96 percent in March to a low of -6.70 percent in December compared to an average that is less than 1 percent (0.67 percent). These *unexpected* variations in Alto's historical returns indicate that Alto shares are risky. How is that risk measured? It is typically measured with summary statistics called the **variance** and the **standard deviation** of the distribution of stock returns.

MEASURING RISK WITH THE VARIANCE OF RETURNS

To measure the variance of returns you have to go through the following steps. First calculate the *deviation* of each monthly return (R_t) from the average return $(\overline{R})$, then square these deviations to get monthly squared deviations, $(R_t - \overline{R})^2$, and finally take the *average* of these squared deviations to get the variance. Applying this procedure to calculate the variance of Alto returns over the sample of 12 months – written $Var(R)$ or σ^2 (pronounced "sigma squared") – we find:[1]

$$Var(R_{Alto}) = \sigma^2_{Alto} = \frac{(R_1 - \overline{R})^2 + (R_2 - \overline{R})^2 + \ldots + (R_{12} - \overline{R})^2}{11}$$

$$Var(R_{Alto}) = \frac{(2.26\% - 0.67\%)^2 + (3.24\% - 0.67\%)^2 + \ldots + (-6.70\% - 0.67\%)^2}{11} = 0.1876\%$$

---

[1] Note that the average is calculated by dividing the squared deviations by 11 observations (the total number of observations less one). We do this because the 12 *sample* deviations are calculated using the *average* return instead of the true, unobservable, *expected* return. When we use the average return instead of the expected return we *lose* one independent data point because the average return is calculated using the 12 observations. Had we divided by 12, we would have produced a downward-biased estimate.

The variance of the distribution of Alto's 12 monthly returns is 0.1876 percent. It is also called the **variability** of Alto returns. Note that squaring the deviations makes them all positive. We do this to prevent negative deviations from canceling positive deviations. This is important because we want to measure "absolute" deviations, that is, deviations from the average return irrespective of whether returns are above or below their average value. *Think of risk as not knowing what the next period return will be*; it could be either above the average or below the average – you should not think that risk occurs only when returns are below their average value.

MEASURING RISK WITH THE STANDARD DEVIATION OF RETURNS

Because of squaring, the variance of Alto returns is not directly comparable to its average return. To measure risk with the same dimension as returns, we need to "undo" the squaring by taking the square root of the variance, called the standard deviation of returns or σ (pronounced "sigma"):

$$\sqrt{\text{Var}(R_{\text{Alto}})} = \sigma_{\text{Alto}} = \sqrt{0.001876} = 4.33\%$$

The standard deviation of the distribution of Alto's 12 monthly returns is 4.33 percent. It is also called the **volatility** of Alto returns. As pointed out earlier, you should think of risk as the unexpected deviations of returns from their average value. Alto shares are risky because their returns deviate from their average value and these deviations are unexpected: they can be large or small and they can be positive (above the mean) or negative (below the mean). Finally, recall that we are calculating the variance and standard deviation of a *sample* distribution of returns. These sample statistics are reliable measures of the future risk of Alto only if they are calculated with a large number of observations and if Alto's return distribution is stationary over time.

VARIANCE VERSUS STANDARD DEVIATION

You can measure the risk of an investment – such as Alto shares – either with the variance of the investment's returns (its return variability) or the standard deviation of its returns (its return volatility).[2] An asset that has no risk has zero variance and zero standard deviation. As the risk of an asset increases, both the variance and the standard deviation of its returns rise. And the higher the variance and standard deviation, the riskier the investment. For example, if the Bell InfoTech Company has a monthly return volatility of 5.77 percent, then its shares are *riskier* than those of Alto whose monthly return volatility is 4.33 percent.

ANNUALIZED MEASURES OF RISK

If you want to annualize the monthly variance, all you have to do is multiply the monthly variance by 12. In the case of Alto shares, we have an annual variance of 2.25 percent:

$$\text{Var}_{\text{Alto}}(\text{annual}) = 12 \times \text{Var}_{\text{Alto}}(\text{monthly}) = 12 \times 0.1876\% = 2.25\%$$

---

[2] Note that the terms "variance" and "standard deviation" are statistics terms. In finance we use the term "variability" to mean "variance" and the term "volatility" to mean "standard deviation."

To annualize the monthly volatility, you have to multiply it by the *square root* of 12 because volatility is the square root of variance. In the case of Alto shares, we have an annual volatility of 15 percent:

$$\sigma_{Alto}(\text{annual}) = \sqrt{12} \times \sigma_{Alto}(\text{monthly}) = 3.4641 \times 4.33\% = 15\%$$

RETURN DISTRIBUTIONS

We pointed out earlier that we cannot observe the true distribution of Alto's monthly returns. We can only get an **empirical return distribution** based on a *sample* of historical monthly returns. Unfortunately, the 12 monthly return observations reported in the first section are not sufficient to construct a statistically reliable empirical distribution. Hundreds of return observations are usually needed in order to produce a statistically reliable distribution.

In order to see what the distribution of a large sample of monthly returns looks like, refer to Exhibit 3.1 in which we report the monthly return distributions of two stock market indices: (1) the Standard and Poor's (S&P) 500 Composite Index, an index of 500 large US companies from 1926 to 2018, a period that covers more than 1,000 monthly returns, and (2) the EURO STOXX 50 Index, an index of 50 of the largest companies from 12 Eurozone countries, from 1987 to 2018. The European index, being more recent, has much fewer observations than the S&P 500. You will find in Exhibit 3.1, for each index, the average monthly return, the standard deviation of monthly returns as well as the magnitude and the month of the highest and lowest returns of each index.

The monthly return distributions in Exhibit 3.1 are called **histograms**. They are graphical representations of the return distributions that show the number of monthly returns that fall into equal ranges of one percentage point. As you can see on the exhibit, the distributions are almost bell-shaped. They come close to a so-called **normal distribution,** which is drawn on the histograms. Note, however, the returns at both ends of the distributions: they are higher than expected for a normal distribution. We usually refer to this phenomenon by saying that the empirical distribution of returns has "**fat tails.**" Even though return distributions are only approximately normal, we assume that individuals make investment decisions *as if* stock returns were normally distributed. The reason we do this is that the normal distribution provides a good approximation of the actual return distributions of portfolios containing a large number of stocks. Normal distributions also display a convenient property: they are fully described by their mean and standard deviation, which means that if you know the average return and volatility of a company's shares, you can draw the entire distribution of that company's returns based just on that information. In other words, if returns are normally distributed, you can compare the attractiveness of alternative single-stock investments only on the basis of their average return and volatility without missing any information.

MEAN-VARIANCE ANALYSIS

Comparing the attractiveness of alternative investments is what we do when we perform a so-called **mean-variance analysis**. Refer to the graph shown on the upper left side of Exhibit 3.2.

EXHIBIT 3.1	HISTORICAL DISTRIBUTIONS OF MONTHLY RETURNS OF THE STANDARD AND POOR'S 500 FROM 1926 TO 2018[1] AND THE EURO STOXX 50 FROM 1987 TO 2018.[2]

THE DISTRIBUTIONS OF HISTORICAL RETURNS IS CLOSE TO A NORMAL DISTRIBUTION

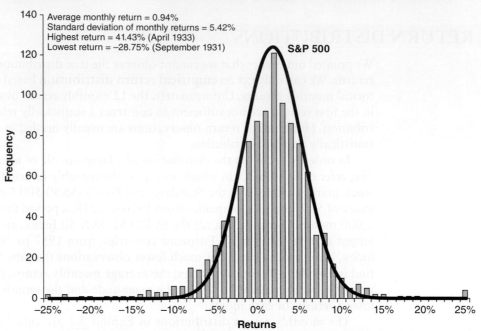

Average monthly return = 0.94%
Standard deviation of monthly returns = 5.42%
Highest return = 41.43% (April 1933)
Lowest return = −28.75% (September 1931)

S&P 500

1. Standard and Poor's 500 Composite Index (S&P 500) is a value-weighted index of 500 large US companies, with dividends reinvested. The monthly returns from 1957 to the present are those of the S&P 500. Returns prior to 1957 are those of the S&P 90.

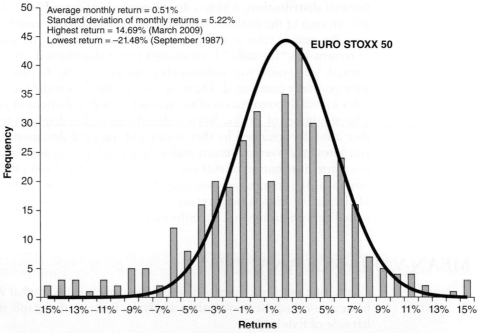

Average monthly return = 0.51%
Standard deviation of monthly returns = 5.22%
Highest return = 14.69% (March 2009)
Lowest return = −21.48% (September 1987)

EURO STOXX 50

2. The EURO STOXX 50 is a value-weighted index of the stocks of 50 large European companies from 12 Eurozone countries that captures approximately 60 percent of the free float market capitalization of these countries' stock markets.

EXHIBIT 3.2	STOCK SELECTION WITH INDIFFERENCE CURVES.

INDIFFERENCE CURVES SHOW INVESTORS' ATTITUDES TOWARD RISK

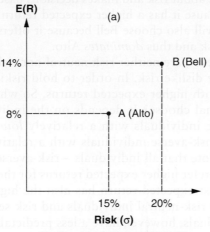

Position of Alto (A) and Bell (B)
shares on the risk-return plane

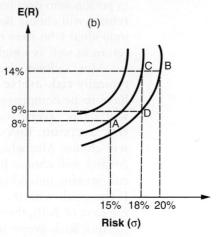

Mr. Martins's indifference curves

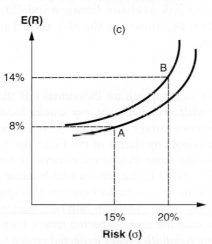

Mrs Lim's indifference curves

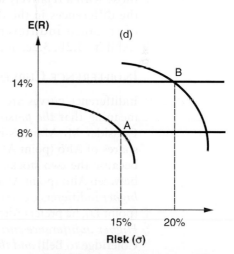

The indifference curves of risk-neutral
(flat) and risk-seeking (curved) investors

The vertical axis indicates the expected annual returns, $E(R)$, of financial assets, and the horizontal axis indicates their risk measured with annual volatilities. Recall that if the distributions of returns are stable, then the expected return of an asset can be estimated by calculating its historical average return, and its risk can be estimated by calculating the standard deviation of its historical returns. The stocks of two companies are shown on the **risk-return plane**: Alto Water Supplies (Alto), at point A, with its expected return of 8 percent and its return volatility of 15 percent (we found these numbers in the previous sections), and Bell InfoTech (Bell), at point B, with a higher expected return of 14 percent and a higher volatility of 20 percent (given).

ATTITUDES TOWARD RISK

Suppose you have to choose either Alto shares or Bell shares. Which one would you prefer? The answer depends on your *attitude* toward risk. A **risk-neutral** individual (a person who does not care about risk and makes decisions based only on expected return) will choose Bell because it has a higher expected return. A **risk-seeker** (an individual who likes risk) will also choose Bell because it offers a higher expected return as well as a higher risk and thus *dominates* Alto.

Most individuals, however, are neither risk neutral nor risk seekers. They are typically **risk-averse**. They dislike risk. In order to hold riskier assets, they will have to be compensated with higher expected returns. So which of Alto or Bell will a risk- averse individual choose? It depends on the individual's **degree of risk aversion**. Risk-averse individuals with a relatively *low tolerance for risk* will choose Alto whereas risk-averse individuals with a relatively *high tolerance for risk* will choose Bell. Note that all individuals – risk-averse, risk-neutral, and risk-seeking individuals – prefer higher expected returns for the *same level of risk*. If the stock with the highest expected return has also the highest risk (which is the case of Bell), then both risk-neutral individuals and risk-seekers will prefer it to Alto. Risk-averse individuals, however, have a less predictable behavior in this case. Those with a relatively high degree of risk aversion may prefer Alto whereas those with a relatively low degree of risk aversion may prefer Bell. We can capture the differences in the degree of risk aversion between individuals with the help of so-called **indifference curves**, drawn in the risk-return plane as shown in Exhibits 3.2b, 3.2c, and 3.2d.

INDIFFERENCE CURVES

Indifference curves are curves along which an individual has the same preference, meaning that *the person is indifferent between any stocks located on that curve*. Consider Mr Martin's indifference curves in Exhibit 3.2b. He is as happy holding shares of Alto (point A) as he is holding shares of the Coleridge Company (point C) because the two stocks are on the same indifference curve. But if he has to choose between Alto (point A) and Bell (point B), he prefers Alto because Alto puts him on a *higher* indifference curve. And if he has to choose between Alto (point A) and Dalcom (point D), he prefers Alto because, again, Alto puts him on a higher indifference curve. *Higher indifference curves provide the same expected return with less risk* (compare Coleridge to Bell) *and the same risk with higher expected return* (compare Coleridge to Dalcom).

Consider now Mrs Lim's indifference curves in Exhibit 3.2c. She prefers Bell to Alto because Bell is now located on a higher indifference curve than Alto. Notice that Mrs Lim's indifference curves are *flatter* than those of Mr Martin. *The flatter an individual's indifference curves, the less risk-averse the individual is* (he requires less expected return to compensate him for one additional unit of risk). In other words, Mrs Lim, being less risk-averse than Mr Martin, prefers shares of Bell, the higher-risk, higher-expected return company, while Mr Martin, being more risk-averse than Mrs Lim, prefers shares of Alto, the lower-risk, lower-expected return company.

Exhibit 3.2d shows the indifference curves of a risk-neutral individual, which are flat (because the person is indifferent to risk), and those of a risk-seeker, which curve downward (because the person is willing to give up some expected return in order to get more risk).

EVIDENCE FROM FINANCIAL MARKETS

We have noted earlier that riskier assets should offer higher returns because investors are risk-averse. If this principle prevails in financial markets around the world, *assets with higher historical volatility should also produce higher average returns.* Consider three types of financial assets: common stocks (shares of companies listed in the stock market), long-term government bonds (government debt for a period of at least 10 years), and short-term government bills (government debt for a period of up to one year).[3] Stocks should be riskier than long-term government bonds (because investing in a company is riskier than lending money to the government), and long-term government bonds should be riskier than short-term government bills (because the longer the duration of the loan, the riskier the lending). If this is the case, then stock returns should be more volatile than bond returns, and bond returns should be more volatile than bill returns. And if investors are risk-averse then the riskier assets should generate, on average, higher returns. This is exactly what is shown in Exhibit 3.3, which reports the risk (volatility) and the average arithmetic return of stock market indices, government bonds, and government bills in 23 countries calculated with annual returns from 1900 to 2017.

Look first at the three left columns that provide the volatility of each type of asset. As expected, in all the countries, stock returns are more volatile than bond returns, which in turn are more volatile than bill returns. Look now at the three right columns that give the average return of each type of asset in each country. Again, as expected, in each country, higher average returns are associated with higher volatility: stocks provide, on average, higher returns than bonds, and bonds provide, on average, higher returns than bills. Note that the magnitudes of average returns and volatilities vary significantly across the 23 countries. This can be partly explained by the fact that these countries have experienced significantly different rates of inflation over the period 1900 to 2017.

There is additional information in Exhibit 3.3 regarding stocks traded in the US markets: we have risk-return data on shares of large companies and shares of small companies. Because smaller firms are generally riskier than large, well-established companies, we should expect the stock returns of smaller companies to be more volatile than those of larger companies and, consequently, smaller firms should generate, on average, higher returns than larger companies to compensate investors for their higher risk. The data reported in Exhibit 3.3 are consistent with our expectations: the shares of smaller companies are significantly more volatile than those of large companies and, not surprisingly, generate a much higher average return. Similar results are observed in most stock markets around the world.[4]

COMBINING TWO STOCKS INTO A PORTFOLIO

In our analysis so far, investors could only hold shares in a single company. In this section we examine the case where investors can combine shares of two companies into a portfolio. In the following sections we analyze portfolios that contain more than two stocks.

---

[3] See Chapters 10 and 11 for a description and analysis of common stocks, bonds, and bills.
[4] See Hawawini and Keim (1995).

| | Exhibit 3.3 | Risk and Return in Capital Markets around the World for the Period 1900 to 2017.[1] |

The higher the risk, the higher the return

	Volatility (Risk)			Average Return		
Country	Stocks	Bonds	Bills	Stocks	Bonds	Bills
Australia	17.3%	11.4%	3.9%	12.2%	6.1%	4.5%
Austria	120.5%	75.7%	7.6%	28.9%	18.5%	4.1%
Belgium	24.2%	10.0%	3.1%	10.2%	5.9%	4.7%
Canada	16.9%	8.8%	3.6%	10.2%	5.6%	4.5%
China[2]	37.1%	9.4%	2.8%	8.5%	6.3%	4.4%
Denmark	21.9%	10.5%	3.6%	11.4%	7.5%	5.9%
Finland	30.8%	6.2%	3.4%	16.4%	7.4%	6.5%
France	24.7%	8.8%	3.5%	13.0%	7.4%	4.7%
Germany[3]	33.1%	13.5%	9.4%	13.4%	5.3%	3.4%
Ireland	23.0%	12.9%	4.1%	11.0%	6.5%	4.8%
Italy	32.9%	10.1%	3.3%	14.2%	7.3%	4.3%
Japan	28.9%	14.0%	2.6%	14.5%	6.7%	4.7%
Netherlands	22.6%	8.2%	2.4%	10.3%	4.9%	3.4%
New Zealand	20.2%	8.2%	4.2%	11.8%	6.2%	5.4%
Norway	27.6%	8.8%	3.5%	11.0%	5.9%	4.8%
Portugal	38.8%	15.9%	5.5%	16.3%	6.6%	6.3%
Russia[4]	89.5%	59.6%	31.6%	43.6%	33.3%	20.6%
South Africa	22.7%	9.6%	5.5%	14.7%	7.3%	6.1%
Spain	22.5%	11.1%	4.1%	11.5%	8.0%	5.9%
Sweden	21.5%	9.7%	3.3%	11.5%	6.6%	5.2%
Switzerland	18.7%	6.0%	1.9%	8.4%	4.7%	2.9%
United Kingdom	21.2%	11.9%	3.8%	11.2%	6.2%	4.8%
United States	19.7%	9.0%	2.9%	11.5%	5.3%	3.8%
Small stocks[5]	31.9%	–	–	16.6%	–	–
Large stocks[5]	19.9%	–	–	12.03%	–	–
World (in USD)[6]	17.0%	9.4%	2.9%	9.6%	5.3%	3.8%
World ex-USA (in USD)[6]	18.7%	13.2%	2.9%	9.1%	5.4%	3.8%
Europe (in USD)[6]	19.5%	14.8%	2.9%	9.1%	5.2%	3.8%

[1] Credit Suisse Global Investment Returns Yearbook 2018. All returns are nominal (unadjusted for inflation).
[2] 1993–2017.
[3] Excluding 1922–1923.
[4] 1995–2015.
[5] 1926–2016. Ibbotson, Roger. *Stocks, Bonds, Bills, and Inflation Yearbook, 2017.*
[6] Return data are weighted by the starting year equity market capitalization of each country.

Go back to the shares of Alto Water Supplies (Alto) and Bell InfoTech (Bell). Their characteristics are summarized below:

	Alto Water Supplies	Bell InfoTech
Expected Return (E(R))	8%	14%
Risk as volatility (σ)	15%	20%
Risk as variance (σ^2)	2.25%	4%

Based on the above information we want to calculate the expected return and the risk of a portfolio that combines Alto and Bell shares in different proportions.

PORTFOLIO EXPECTED RETURN

Suppose you have $10,000 to invest and decide to buy $6,000 worth of Alto shares and $4,000 worth of Bell shares. What is the expected return of your portfolio? In general, the expected return of a two-stock portfolio, $E(R_P)$, is the *value-weighted* average of the expected returns of the stocks in the portfolio:

$$E(R_P) = \left[w_1 \times E(R_1)\right] + \left[w_2 \times E(R_2)\right] \tag{3.2}$$

where the weights w_1 and w_2 are the proportions of money invested in stock 1 and stock 2, and $E(R_1)$ and $E(R_2)$ are the expected returns of the two stocks, respectively. In your case you have 60 percent of $10,000 invested in Alto ($w_A = 0.60$) and 40 percent invested in Bell ($w_B = 0.40$). The expected return of this portfolio, let's call it P_1, is thus:

$$E(R_{P_1}) = \left[0.60 \times 8\%\right] + \left[0.40 \times 14\%\right] = 10.40\%$$

Portfolio P_1 has an expected return of 10.40 percent. What is its risk?

PORTFOLIO RISK AND CORRELATIONS

Let's measure the risk of portfolio P_1 by calculating its variance. The variance of portfolio P_1 is determined by the following inputs:

1. The variances and the standard deviations of Alto returns ($\sigma_A^2 = 2.25\%$ and $\sigma_A = 15\%$) and Bell returns ($\sigma_B^2 = 4.00\%$ and $\sigma_B = 20\%$).
2. The proportions of funds invested in Alto ($w_1 = 60\%$) and Bell ($w_2 = 40\%$).
3. The *co-movements* of Alto returns with Bell returns. *When two stocks are combined into a portfolio, the risk of the portfolio is affected by the way the returns of the two stocks move in relation to one another.* They may have a tendency to move in the *same* direction (for example, when Alto returns are lower than their expected value, Bell returns are *likely* to also be lower than their expected value) or a tendency to move in *opposite* directions (for example, when Alto returns are lower than their expected value, Bell returns are *likely* to be higher than their expected value). These co-movements are measured with the **correlation coefficient** between the returns of the two stocks (written ρ_{AB} and pronounced 'rho'). The correlation coefficient goes from a maximum value of one ($\rho_{AB} = +1$) to a minimum value of minus one ($\rho_{AB} = -1$):

3.1   If the correlation coefficient is $+1$, the returns are said to be *perfectly positively correlated*, meaning that the returns are *always* moving in the *same* direction. For example, if Alto is down 2 percent then Bell *must* also be down. But you cannot tell by how *much* because the correlation coefficient says nothing about the *magnitude* of the drop in Bell returns; it only indicates the *direction* and the *likelihood* of the co-movements.

3.2   If the correlation coefficient is between $+1$ and zero, there is a *tendency* for the returns of Bell and Alto to move *together* and the *likelihood* that they are up or down together depends on the *size* of the correlation coefficient: the higher the correlation coefficient, the more likely that the returns of Alto and Bell will move together.

3.3   If the correlation coefficient is zero, Alto returns are unrelated to Bell returns. If Alto is up 2 percent, no information can be inferred on the direction and magnitude of Bell's movements.

3.4   If the correlation coefficient is between zero and -1, there is a *tendency* for the returns of Bell and Alto to move in *opposite* directions: the lower the negative correlation coefficient, the more *likely* that the returns of Alto and Bell will move in opposite directions.

3.5   If the correlation coefficient is -1, the returns are said to be *perfectly negatively correlated,* meaning that the returns are *always* moving in *opposite* directions. For example, if Alto is down 2 percent then Bell *must* be up but the correlation coefficient does not indicate by how much.

Suppose that the correlation coefficient between Alto returns and those of Bell is 0.40 ($\rho_{AB} = +0.40$), indicating that they have a tendency to move together. *This is usually the case for the shares of most companies listed on a stock market*: they tend, on average, to move up and down together in response to changes in the economic environment, but the relationship is not perfect, that is, there are days when they may move in opposite directions but there are a lot more days when they move together.

The formula for the variance, $\text{Var}(R_P)$, of a two-stock portfolio is:

$$\text{Var}(R_P) = \sigma_P^2 = w_1^2 \sigma_1^2 + w_2^2 \sigma_2^2 + 2w_1 w_2 \rho_{12} \sigma_1 \sigma_2 \qquad (3.3a)$$

Look at the structure of the formula: it has three terms; the first and second terms capture the contribution (to the risk of the portfolio) of the risk of the two stocks in the portfolio, and the third term captures the contribution (to the risk of the portfolio) of their co-movements through their correlation coefficient. The first two terms are always positive. The third, however, can be negative if the correlation coefficient is negative. Note that *the lower the correlation coefficient, the lower the portfolio variance and the less risky is the portfolio* (everything else in the formula is the same). We will return to this observation later in this chapter.

You can now calculate the risk of portfolio P_1 by plugging in the variance formula 3.3a the following seven inputs:

$$\sigma_A^2 = 2.25\%; \ \sigma_A = 15\%; \ \sigma_B^2 = 4\%; \ \sigma_B = 20\%; \ w_A = 60\%; \ w_B = 40\%; \ \text{and} \ \rho_{AB} = +0.40$$

We have:

$$\sigma_{P_1}^2 = [(0.6)^2 \times 0.0225] + [(0.4)^2 \times 0.04] + [2 \times 0.60 \times 0.40 \times 0.40 \times 0.15 \times 0.20] = 2.0260\%$$

To get the risk of portfolio P_1 measured by its standard deviation or volatility, you must take the square root of its variance:

$$\sigma_{P_1} = \sqrt{\sigma_{P_1}^2} = \sqrt{0.020260} = 14.23\%$$

COVARIANCE

We can simplify the formula for the variance of a portfolio by using a statistic called the **covariance** between the returns of the two stocks (written $Cov(R_1,R_2)$ or, simply, σ_{12}). It is equal to their correlation coefficient multiplied by the volatility of each stock:

$$Cov(R_1,R_2) \equiv \sigma_{12} = \rho_{12}\sigma_1\sigma_2 \qquad (3.4)$$

In our case, the covariance between the returns of Alto and those of Bell is:

$$\sigma_{AB} = 0.40 \times 0.15 \times 0.20 = 0.0120$$

And the risk (variance) of the two-stock portfolio given in formula 3.3a can now be written as:

$$Var(R_P) = \sigma_P^2 = w_1^2\sigma_1^2 + w_2^2\sigma_2^2 + 2w_1w_2\sigma_{12} \qquad (3.3b)$$

Enter the relevant inputs in the above formula and you will find that the variance of portfolio P_1 is indeed equal to 2.0260 percent.

Note that the covariance is just another statistic we use to measure the co-movement between the returns of two stocks. If covariance is positive, returns have a *tendency* to move together. If it is negative, returns have a *tendency* to move in opposite directions. If covariance is zero, returns are unrelated to one another. Finally, note that if you know the volatility of two stocks and their correlation coefficient, you can get their covariance using equation 3.4. And if you know their covariance and the volatility of the two stocks, you can get their correlation coefficient using the same equation.

DIVERSIFICATION CAN REDUCE RISK AND RAISE RETURN

Where is portfolio P_1 located in the risk-return plane? Its expected return is 10.40 percent and its volatility is 14.23 percent. It is shown in Exhibit 3.4 with Alto and Bell. Have you noticed something remarkable about the risk-return characteristics of portfolio P_1 compared to those of Alto? Look again at Exhibit 3.4 and think of the answer before reading on.

Portfolio P_1 has *less* risk than Alto (14.23 percent versus 15 percent) but a *higher* expected return (10.40 percent versus 8 percent). The portfolio is clearly a better investment than Alto shares. We show below that this is always the case: *risk-averse investors are always better off diversifying by combining shares of companies into a portfolio rather than investing in a single company.* To prove this, we first need to explain what an **opportunity set** is.

THE OPPORTUNITY SET OF A TWO-STOCK PORTFOLIO

How many different portfolios of shares of Alto and Bell can you construct? An infinite number. All you have to do is simply change the proportions of money invested

---

EXHIBIT 3.4   RISK-RETURN CHARACTERISTICS OF TWO STOCKS AND THEIR PORTFOLIO.

THE PORTFOLIO HAS A HIGHER EXPECTED RETURN AND A LOWER RISK THAN ALTO SHARES

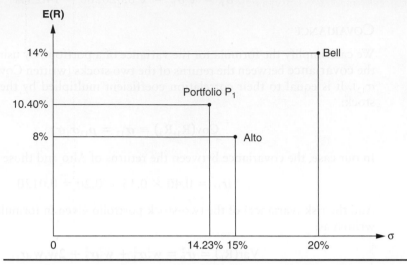

---

in each company. All these portfolios are shown in Exhibit 3.5. They are located on the curve starting at point A (where 100 percent of the money is invested in shares of Alto) and ending at point B (where 100 percent of the money is invested in shares of Bell).

The curve is called the opportunity set because it shows all the possible portfolios you can invest in by allocating your money between these two stocks. From point A you can "travel" on the opportunity set toward point B. As you move away from point A, you reduce the proportion of money invested in Alto shares and increase the proportion invested in Bell shares.

EFFICIENT AND INEFFICIENT INVESTMENT SETS

Look at portfolio P_{MRP} in Exhibit 3.5. It is called the **minimum-risk portfolio (MRP)** because no other portfolio on the opportunity set has a lower risk. Note that all the portfolios located between Alto (at point A) and the minimum-risk portfolio P_{MRP} are *less* desirable than the portfolios located between portfolio P_{MRP} and portfolio P_2 because they have the *same* risk as the portfolios located between Alto and P_{MRP} but offer a *higher* expected return. For example, an investor with a target volatility of 15 percent will never hold *only* shares of Alto (which have an expected return of 8 percent) because she can combine Alto shares with Bell shares to form portfolio P_2 which has a *higher* expected return of 11.27 percent with *same* 15 percent volatility.

The segment of the opportunity set from Alto to the minimum-risk portfolio – that contains all the dominated, undesirable portfolios – is called the **inefficient investment set**. And the segment from the minimum-risk portfolio to Bell at point B – that contains all the desirable portfolios – is called the **efficient investment set**. Portfolios located on the efficient set (which includes portfolio P_1 described earlier) are called **efficient portfolios**. And portfolios located on the inefficient set are called **inefficient portfolios**.

EXHIBIT 3.5	OPPORTUNITY SET AND PORTFOLIO SELECTION WITH $\rho_{AB} = +0.40$ AND RISK-AVERSE INDIFFERENCE CURVES.

RISK-AVERSE INVESTORS ALWAYS DIVERSIFY

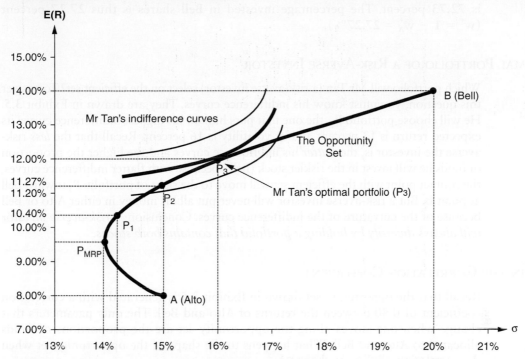

	E(R)	σ	w_A	w_B
Alto	8%	15%	100%	0%
Portfolio P_{MRP}	9.64%	14%	72.73%	27.27%
Portfolio P_1	10.40%	14.23%	60%	40%
Portfolio P_2	11.27%	15%	45.50%	54.50%
Portfolio P_3	12%	16%	33.33%	66.67%
Bell	14%	20%	0%	100%

P_{MRP} = Minimum-Risk Portfolio

What are the proportions of funds invested in Alto and Bell (w_A^* and w_B^*) in the minimum-risk portfolio (P_{MRP})? It can be shown that these weights can be calculated as follows:[5]

$$w_A^* = \frac{\sigma_B^2 - \sigma_{AB}}{\sigma_A^2 + \sigma_B^2 - 2\sigma_{AB}} \qquad (3.5)$$

---

[5] If you are familiar with differential calculus, replace w_1 with w_A and w_2 with $(1 - w_A)$ in equation 3.3b, then take its derivative with respect to w_A and set it to zero. You get: $2w_A\sigma_A^2 - 2(1 - w_A)\sigma_B^2 + 2\sigma_{AB} - 4w_A\sigma_{AB} = 0$. Solving for the optimal percentage in Alto shares (w_A^*), you find equation 3.5.

$$w_A^* = \frac{0.040-0.012}{0.0225+0.040-0.024} = \frac{0.028}{0.0385} = 0.7273 = 72.73\%$$

The percentage of funds invested in Alto shares in the minimum-risk portfolio is 72.73 percent. The percentage invested in Bell shares is thus 27.27 percent $(w^* = 1 - w_A^* = 27.27\%)$.

THE OPTIMAL PORTFOLIO OF A RISK-AVERSE INVESTOR

Which portfolio will Mr Tan (a risk-averse investor) select on the efficient set? To answer this question, you must know his indifference curves. They are drawn in Exhibit 3.5. He will choose portfolio P_3, the one that puts him on his highest indifference curve; its expected return is 12 percent and its volatility is 16 percent. Recall that the *less* risk-averse the investor is, the *flatter* his indifference curves and the higher the proportion of funds he will invest in the riskier stock (Bell), because with flatter indifference curves, the contact point with the efficient set will move to the right of portfolio P_3 toward Bell at point B. But a risk-averse investor will never put all his money in either Alto or Bell because of the curvature of the indifference curves. Conclusion: *a risk-averse investor will always diversify by holding a portfolio that contains both stocks.*

CHANGES IN THE CORRELATION COEFFICIENT

Recall that the opportunity set drawn in Exhibit 3.5 is generated with a correlation coefficient of 0.40 between the returns of Alto and Bell. The only parameters that change when one moves along the opportunity set are the proportions of funds allocated to Alto and Bell. What happens to the shape of the opportunity set when the correlation coefficient changes?

We pointed out earlier that the risk of a portfolio is reduced when the correlation coefficient decreases. This is shown in Exhibit 3.6. When the correlation coefficient between asset A and asset B decreases, the opportunity set moves to the left, that is, it becomes less risky for the same expected return. To illustrate, look at the horizontal line with an expected return of 12 percent and compare any two opportunity sets: the one on the left has a less risky portfolio for the same 12 percent expected return. When the returns of the two assets are perfectly positively correlated $(\rho_{AB} = +1)$, the opportunity set is a straight line joining asset A and asset B. Note that when the returns are perfectly negatively correlated $(\rho_{AB} = -1)$, the opportunity set has a minimum-risk portfolio that is riskless $(\sigma = 0)$. This happens because in this case there is a portfolio composition such that the risks of the two stocks offset each other exactly.[6]

COMBINING MORE THAN TWO STOCKS INTO A PORTFOLIO

We now turn to the examination of the characteristics of portfolios with more than two stocks. The expected return is in this case a straightforward extension of the

---

[6] You can find the proportion of wealth invested in the riskless portfolio by applying formula 3.5 with $\rho_{AB} = -1$. In this case $\sigma_{AB} = -\sigma_A \times \sigma_B$ and $w_A^* = \frac{\sigma_B}{\sigma_A + \sigma_B}$. With $\sigma_A = 25\%$ and $\sigma_B = 32\%$ you get $w_A^* = 56.14\%$ and $w_B^* = 43.86\%$.

EXHIBIT 3.6	THE SHAPE OF THE OPPORTUNITY SET WHEN CORRELATION CHANGES.

THE LOWER THE CORRELATION, THE LESS RISKY THE PORTFOLIO AS THE OPPORTUNITY
SET MOVES TO THE LEFT

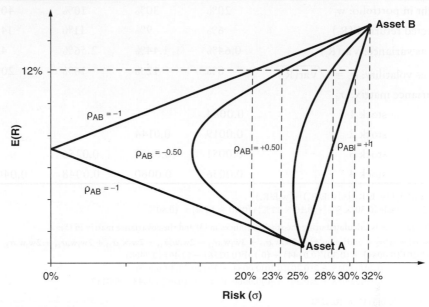

two-asset case given in equation 3.2. The formula for the portfolio risk, however, is
more complex as you will discover in this section.

PORTFOLIO EXPECTED RETURN

Suppose there are N stocks in the portfolio. The portfolio expected return is found
by expanding equation 3.2 to the case of N stocks:

$$E(R_P) = [w_1 \times E(R_1)] + [w_2 \times E(R_2)] + \ldots + [w_N \times E(R_N)] \qquad (3.6)$$

The case of four stocks is illustrated in the first two rows in Exhibit 3.7. Applying
equation 3.6 to the investment proportions (row 1) and expected returns (row 2)
given in the exhibit, you get an expected return of 10.60 percent for the portfolio
(see the calculation in the first note at the bottom of the exhibit).

PORTFOLIO RISK AND DIVERSIFICATION

What is the risk (variance) of a portfolio with N assets? Recall the structure of equation 3.3b that gives the risk of a two-stock portfolio. The first two terms capture the
contributions (to the risk of the portfolio) of the risk of each of the two stocks (σ_1 and
σ_2), and the third term captures the contribution of their covariance (σ_{12}). For portfolios with N assets, the structure of the formula remains the same: there are N terms
that capture the contributions of the risk of each of the N stocks ($\sigma_1, \sigma_2, \ldots, \sigma_N$)
followed by terms that capture the contributions of the correlations between *every*

EXHIBIT 3.7	CALCULATION OF THE RETURN AND RISK OF A PORTFOLIO WITH FOUR STOCKS.

	Stock 1	Stock 2	Stock 3	Stock 4	Portfolio
(1) Weight in portfolio: w_i	20%	30%	10%	40%	100%
(2) Expected return: $E(R_i)$	6%	9%	11%	14%	10.60%[1]
(3) Risk as variance: $Var(R_i)$	0.64%	1.44%	2.56%	4%	1.17%[2]
(4) Risk as volatility: $\sigma_i = \sqrt{Var(R_i)}$	8%	12%	16%	20%	10.82%[3]
(5) Covariance matrix: σ_{ij}					
stock 1	0.0064				
stock 2	0.0019	0.0144			
stock 3	0.0051	0.0058	0.0256		
stock 4	0.0056	0.0060	0.0048	0.0400	

[1] $E(R_P) = [w_1E(R_1)]+[w_2E(R_2)]+[w_3E(R_3)]+[w_4E(R_4)]$
$E(R_P) = [0.20 \times 6\%]+[0.30 \times 9\%]+[0.10 \times 11\%]+[0.40 \times 14\%] = 10.60\%$

[2] The portfolio variance is calculated using the stock variances in (3) and the covariance matrix in (5):
$Var(R_P) = w_1^2\sigma_1^2 + w_2^2\sigma_2^2 + w_3^2\sigma_3^2 + w_4^2\sigma_4^2 + 2w_1w_2\sigma_{12} + 2w_1w_3\sigma_{13} + 2w_1w_4\sigma_{14} + 2w_2w_3\sigma_{23} + 2w_2w_4\sigma_{24} + 2w_3w_4\sigma_{34}$
$Var(R_P) = (0.20)^2(0.0064) + (0.30)^2(0.0144) + (0.10)^2(0.0256) + (0.40)^2(0.0400)$
$\qquad + 2(0.20)(0.30)0.0019 + 2(0.20)(0.10)0.0051 + 2(0.20)(0.40)0.0056$
$\qquad + 2(0.30)(0.10)0.0058 + 2(0.30)(0.40)0.0060 + 2(0.10)(0.40)0.0048 = 0.0117$

[3] $\sigma_P = \sqrt{Var(R_P)} = \sqrt{0.0117} = 10.82\%$

pair of stocks. How many pairwise correlation coefficients are there in an N-stock portfolio? The answer is provided in Exhibit 3.8.

With two stocks there is one distinct (unique) correlation coefficient.[7] With three stocks there are three distinct correlation coefficients. With four stocks there are six distinct correlation coefficients (you can count the six lines connecting the four stocks). With five stocks there are ten distinct correlation coefficients. As you have noticed, the number of correlation coefficients increases faster than the number of stocks in the portfolio. *In general, if there are N stocks in a portfolio the number of distinct correlation coefficients is equal to $N(N-1)/2$.* The portfolio variance thus has N variance terms (one for each stock, shown below in the first set of brackets) followed by $N(N-1)/2$ distinct covariance terms shown in the second set of brackets:

$$Var(R_p) = \underbrace{[w_1^2\sigma_1^2 + \ldots + w_N^2\sigma_N^2]}_{N \text{ variance terms}} + 2\underbrace{[w_1w_2\sigma_{12} + \ldots + w_iw_j\sigma_{ij} + \ldots + w_{N-1}w_N\sigma_{N-1,N}]}_{\frac{N(N-1)}{2} \text{ distinct covariance terms}}$$

The calculation of the variance of a four-stock portfolio is shown in Exhibit 3.7. With four stocks, we have the six distinct covariances $[(4 \times 3)/2]$ shown in the lower part

---

[7] Note that two stocks have one *distinct* correlation coefficient but two *identical* correlation coefficients: one between stock 1 and stock 2 and an identical one between stock 2 and stock 1, that is, $\rho_{12} = \rho_{21}$. This is why there is a number 2 that multiplies the third term in equations 3.3a and 3.3b.

EXHIBIT 3.8	THE NUMBER OF DISTINCT CORRELATIONS IN A PORTFOLIO WITH MANY STOCKS.

THE NUMBER OF DISTINCT CORRELATIONS IN A PORTFOLIO RISES MUCH FASTER THAN THE NUMBER OF STOCKS IN THE PORTFOLIO

Number (N) of stocks in the portfolio	Geometric illustration	Number of distinct correlations in the portfolio
2		1
3		3
4		6
5		10
N	- - - -	$\dfrac{N(N-1)}{2}$

of the exhibit. The variance of this four-stock portfolio is 1.17 percent (see the second note at the bottom of the exhibit) and its volatility is 10.82 percent (see the third note at the bottom of the exhibit).

COVARIANCE AS A MEASURE OF RISK

When the number of stocks in the portfolio is high, the number of distinct covariances becomes very large. For example, with 100 stocks, the number of distinct covariances is 4,950 ($100 \times 99/2$). The implication is clear: *when the number of stocks in a portfolio increases, the contribution of the covariances to the risk of the portfolio becomes more and more dominant and the contribution of the variances of the individual stocks becomes less and less relevant. In other words, when a stock is in a very large portfolio, its relevant contribution to the risk of the portfolio is its average covariance with the other assets, not its volatility.* This, in turn, implies that *the relevant measure of the risk of any asset in a large portfolio is its average covariance with the other assets in the portfolio.*

To illustrate this phenomenon let's calculate the risk of a portfolio of 100 stocks. To simplify the calculation, let's assume that the same amount of money is invested in each stock. In other words, the proportion (w) invested in each stock is 1 percent (1 divided by 100). Let's further assume that each stock has a variance of 4 percent. Finally, let's assume that all pairwise correlation coefficients are equal to +0.50.

According to equation 3.4, the covariances are in this case all equal to 0.02 (Cov = 0.50 × 0.20 × 0.20). What is the risk of this portfolio? Note that there are 100 variance terms (one for each stock) and 4,950 distinct covariances. The risk of the portfolio is thus:

$$\text{Var }(R_P) = 100 \times [(1\%)^2 \times 4\%] + 4,950 \times [2 \times 1\% \times 1\% \times 0.02] = 0.0004 + 0.0198 = 0.0202$$

The individual risks of the 100 stocks (their variances) contribute less than 2 percent to the portfolio risk (0.0004 divided by 0.0202) while the 4,950 distinct covariances contribute more than 98 percent (0.0198 divided by 0.0202). The above example shows clearly that it is covariance that drives portfolio risk, not the volatility of the individual assets in the portfolio, as pointed out earlier. Actually, as the number of assets in the portfolio becomes very large, the risk of the portfolio converges to the average portfolio covariance (for a formal proof of this result, see self-test question 3.4). And the lower the average covariance, the lower the portfolio risk. Note that – as in the case of a two-asset portfolio – portfolio diversification reduces risk when correlations are less than one. In the above example, the volatility of a single stock is 20 percent (the square root of 4 percent) whereas the volatility of the 100-stock portfolio is 14.2 percent (the square root of 0.0202), a reduction in volatility of 29 percent.

PORTFOLIO DIVERSIFICATION IN PRACTICE

We have just shown how portfolio diversification reduces risk. This observation raises a practical question: how much risk-reduction can be achieved through portfolio diversification and how many different stocks do we need to get the most risk-reduction? We can only answer the question empirically by performing the following test. We start with a large sample of shares of different companies, measure their individual volatility, and calculate the average volatility (this gives us the average volatility of a single stock). We then form a large number of portfolios with shares of two companies, measure their volatility and calculate the average volatility (this gives us the average volatility of a two-stock portfolio). We keep repeating this procedure for portfolios up to, say, 50 companies. We then draw the graph in Exhibit 3.9.

The vertical axis indicates the risk of a portfolio *measured as a percentage of the average volatility of a single stock*. The horizontal axis indicates the size of the portfolio. Look at the graph: *as the number of stocks in the portfolio increases along the horizontal axis, the risk of the portfolio on the vertical axis declines*.

Initially, the risk-reduction is fairly steep. It then levels off when the size of the portfolio reaches about 25 stocks. At that point, on average, the risk (volatility) of the 25-stock portfolio is equal to about 40 percent of the risk of a single stock, meaning that 60 percent of the portfolio risk has been eliminated through diversification. The remaining 40 percent, however, is undiversifiable no matter how large the portfolio is. In other words, the risk of a portfolio has two components: a *diversifiable* component called **diversifiable risk** (also referred to as **unsystematic risk** or **firm-specific risk**) and an *undiversifiable* component called **undiversifiable risk** (also referred to as **systematic risk** or **market risk**). The practical implication of this observation is clear: *you need to hold a portfolio containing about 25 stocks to eliminate most of its diversifiable risk*, with the condition that the 25 stocks come from different sectors of the economy. This is a robust result that occurs in all stock markets around the world.

EXHIBIT 3.9	INCREASING THE SIZE OF A PORTFOLIO REDUCES ITS RISK.

ONLY A FRACTION OF A PORTFOLIO RISK IS DIVERSIFIABLE

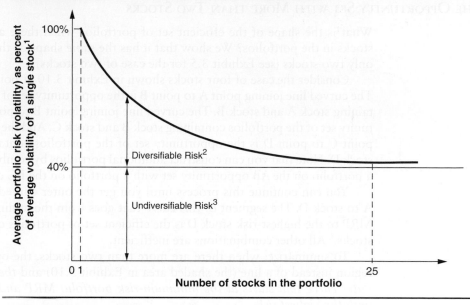

[1] The average return volatility of single stocks is 49.2%.
[2] Diversifiable risk is also called firm-specific risk or unsystematic risk.
[3] Undiversifiable risk is also called market risk or systematic risk.
Source: See Statman, Meier (1987).

FIRM-SPECIFIC RISK VERSUS MARKET RISK

Why is some of the risk of a portfolio undiversifiable? Because correlations between stock returns are usually always positive. In other words, because stock returns have a *tendency* to move in the *same* direction, some risk will remain in the portfolio no matter how large the portfolio is. But why are correlations usually positive? Because share prices react to *broad market* news *in the same fashion*. Suppose, for example, that the central bank announces a policy of low interest rates. Lower borrowing rates are good news for companies. As a result, their share prices move up together (not by the same magnitude, however; some companies are more sensitive to changes in interest rates than others).

And why is a portion of the risk of a portfolio diversifiable? Because share prices do not react to *firm-specific* news in the same fashion. Firm-specific news can be either "good news," pushing prices up, or "bad news," pushing prices down. These firm-specific price movements offset one another and reduce the overall portfolio risk. For example, a company may announce that it has won a contract that will raise its future profits, while on the same day another company may announce an unexpected labor strike that will lower its future profits. If the shares of the two companies are in the same portfolio, the rise in the price of the first will offset the drop in the price of the second, thus reducing the overall risk of the portfolio.

To summarize: *portfolio diversification works through the elimination of firm-specific risk, because the firm-specific risks of the individual stocks in the portfolio cancel out (bad news is offset, on average, by good news). But portfolio diversification cannot reduce systematic market risk because all shares are exposed to market* risk in the same fashion and hence the market risks of the individual stocks in the portfolio do not cancel out.

THE OPPORTUNITY SET WITH MORE THAN TWO STOCKS

What is the shape of the efficient set of portfolios when there are more than two stocks in the portfolios? We show that it has the *same* shape as the efficient set with only two stocks (see Exhibit 3.5 for the case of two stocks).

Consider the case of four stocks shown in Exhibit 3.10 at points A, B, C, and D. The curved line joining point A to point B is the opportunity set of the portfolios containing stock A and stock B. The curved line joining point B to point C is the opportunity set of the portfolios containing stock B and stock C. And the curved line joining point C to point D is the opportunity set of the portfolios containing stock C and stock D. Note that you can construct additional portfolios by combining, for example, a portfolio on the AB opportunity set with a portfolio on the BC opportunity set.

You can continue this process until you get the outer curved line joining stock A to stock D. The segment of this curve that goes from the minimum-risk portfolio MRP to the highest-risk stock D is the efficient set of portfolios containing the four stocks.[8] All other combinations are inefficient.

To summarize: when there are more than two stocks, the opportunity set is a region instead of a line (the shaded area in Exhibit 3.10) and *the efficient set is the outer curve that starts at the minimum-risk portfolio MRP and ends at the stock with the highest risk.*

Which efficient portfolio will a risk-averse investor choose? It depends on their degree of risk-aversion (which is reflected in the shape of their indifference curves). As indicated in Exhibit 3.10, the investor whose indifference curves are shown in the exhibit will select portfolio P.

EXHIBIT 3.10	THE SHAPE OF THE OPPORTUNITY SET WITH FOUR STOCKS.

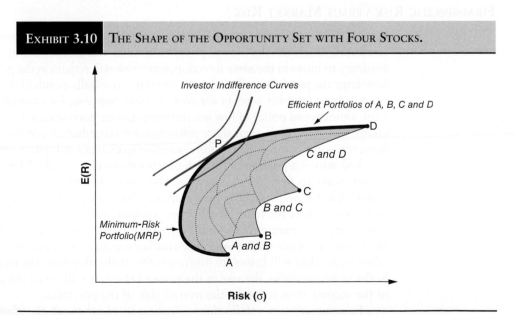

---

[8] A computer program will generate this efficient set by finding out all the portfolios with the highest returns for any given level of risk.

OPTIMAL PORTFOLIOS WHEN THERE IS A RISKLESS ASSET

Up to now, investment choices were limited to portfolios of only risky stocks. What would happen to the shape of the efficient set if investors are now allowed to deposit part of their funds in a bank account that offers a **risk-free rate** (R_F)? Before we answer that question, we should first find out if investors would be better off holding a portfolio in which there is a riskless asset with zero volatility ($\sigma_F = 0$) and zero correlation with the risky stocks ($\rho_{F,i} = 0$). A zero correlation between risky stocks and the **riskless asset** should *lower* the overall portfolio risk (recall that correlations between stocks are typically positive; thus, the introduction of a new asset with a zero correlation should reduce portfolio risk further). If this new opportunity set (the one with the riskless asset) dominates the curved one that contains only risky stocks, then investors would be better off if a riskless asset is available.

THE EFFICIENT INVESTMENT LINE

Refer to Exhibit 3.11. The dashed curve is the opportunity set of portfolios containing only risky stocks. The risk-free rate is 4 percent. It is located at point F on the vertical axis because it has no risk. Suppose you wish to invest part of your funds in the risk-free asset and the remaining balance in a risky portfolio located on the curved opportunity set. We show below that combinations of the riskless asset F with a risky portfolio on the curved opportunity set – such as P_1, T, and P_2 – are found on the *straight lines* joining point F to point P_1, point F to point T, and point F to point P_2, respectively. Which one of the three risky portfolios (P_1, T, or P_2) offers the highest return when combined with the risk-free asset? Exhibit 3.11 shows that it is the **tangent portfolio** T, the one on the line that has the *steepest* slope. All the other combinations (such as combinations of the riskless asset F with portfolio P_1 or portfolio P_2) are less desirable because they are located *below* the one joining the riskless asset F with the tangent portfolio T.

Let's call this superior opportunity set the **Efficient Investment Line (EIL)**. Refer to Exhibit 3.11. The EIL is a straight line starting at F and passing through point T: it has an intercept equal to R_F and a slope equal to $\left[\dfrac{E(R_T) - R_F}{\sigma_T} \right]$. The equation describing the expected return of each portfolio on this line is thus:[9]

$$E(R_P) = R_F + \left[\frac{E(R_T) - R_F}{\sigma_T} \right] \sigma_P \qquad (3.7a)$$

With the data in Exhibit 3.11, we have:

$$E(R_P) = 4\% + \left[\frac{12\% - 4\%}{16\%} \right] \sigma_P = 4\% + 0.50\sigma_P \qquad (3.7b)$$

---

[9] Consider a portfolio P on the EIL in which w_T percent of funds is invested in the tangent portfolio T and the balance $(1 - w_T)$ in the risk-free bank deposit. The expected return $E(R_P)$ and risk (σ_P) of portfolio P are:

$$E(R_P) = w_T E(R_T) + (1 - w_T)R_F = R_F + (E(R_T) - R_F)w_T$$

$$\sigma_P = \sqrt{Var[w_T R_T + (1 - w_T)R_F]} = \sqrt{Var[w_T R_T]} = \sqrt{w_T^2 Var(R_T)} = w_T \sqrt{Var(R_T)} = w_T \sigma_T \text{ because } Var(R_F) = 0.$$

From the second equation you get $w_T = \dfrac{\sigma_P}{\sigma_T}$. Substituting the value of w_T in the first equation, you obtain the equation of EIL.

| EXHIBIT 3.11 | THE EFFICIENT INVESTMENT LINE (EIL). |

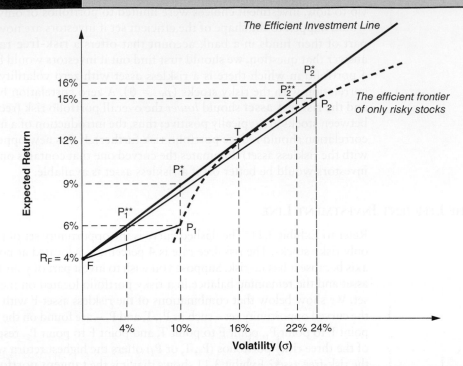

Portfolio	P_1	P_1^*	P_1^{**}	P_2	P_2^*	P_2^{**}	T
Expected Return E(R)	6%	9%	6%	15%	16%	15%	12%
Volatility (σ)	10%	10%	4%	24%	24%	22%	16%
Sharpe ratio	0.2	0.5	0.5	0.46	0.5	0.5	0.5

Equation 3.7b gives the expected return of any efficient portfolio P if you know its volatility and – by rearranging the equation – its volatility if you know its expected return. For example, an efficient portfolio with a volatility of 14 percent has an expected return of 11 percent:

$$E(R_P) = 4\% + (0.50 \times 14\%) = 4\% + 7\% = 11\%$$

and an efficient portfolio with an expected return of 10 percent has a volatility of 12 percent:

$$\sigma_P = \frac{E(R_P) - 4\%}{0.50} = \frac{10\% - 4\%}{0.50} = 12\%$$

THE SHARPE RATIO

The **Sharpe ratio** is a measure of an investment's expected return per unit of risk. *The higher the Sharpe ratio, the more attractive the investment is.* The investment's expected return is measured in *excess* of the risk-free rate, that is, as $[E(R_i) - R_F]$, and risk is measured with the volatility of investment's returns (σ_i). The **Sharpe ratio** of investment (i) is thus written as:

$$\text{Sharpe ratio} = \frac{E(R_i) - R_F}{\sigma_i} \qquad (3.8)$$

You may have noticed that the slope of the EIL (see equation 3.7a) is the Sharpe ratio of all the investments located on that line. Consider the tangent portfolio T. According to equation 3.8, its Sharpe ratio is equal to:

$$\left[\frac{12\% - 4\%}{16\%} \right] = 0.50$$

which is indeed the slope of the EIL shown in equation 3.7b.

Look at Exhibit 3.11. The EIL has the highest Sharpe ratio because it has the steepest slope of any of the lines joining the risk-free rate to a portfolio on the curved opportunity set. In other words, *if you want to find the tangent portfolio, all you have to do is identify the portfolio with the highest Sharpe ratio on the curved efficient set.*

MAKING OPTIMAL INVESTMENT CHOICES

Suppose for a moment that there is no risk-free asset. Refer to Exhibit 3.11 and assume that you are holding the optimal portfolio P_1 located on the curved efficient set of risky assets. Your expected return is 6 percent with a volatility of 10 percent. Assume now that a 4 percent risk-free asset becomes available. What should you do? Now that there is a risk-free asset, portfolio P_1 is no longer optimal. There is another portfolio, P_1^*, on the EIL, above portfolio P_1, that has the same risk as P but offers a higher expected return of 9 percent. You can find this return using the equation of the EIL (see equation 3.7b):

$$E(R_{P_1^*}) = 4\% + (0.50 \times 10\%) = 9\%$$

Portfolio P_1^* dominates portfolio P_1 because they have the same risk but portfolio P_1^* offers a higher expected return (9 percent instead of 6 percent). Because P_1^* is located on the EIL, *you can be certain that there is no other portfolio with an expected return of 9 percent that has a volatility that is lower than 10 percent.* Conclusion: you are better off selling portfolio P_1 and buying portfolio P_1^*, which is the optimal (best) portfolio when there is a risk-free asset. How are you going to do this?

The optimal portfolio P_1^* on the EIL combines a risk-free deposit earning 4 percent and the tangent portfolio that has an expected return of 12 percent with a volatility of 16 percent. Suppose you sold portfolio P_1 and netted $10,000. How are you going to allocate the $10,000 to the risk-free deposit and portfolio T in order to construct portfolio P_1^*? Let's say that w_T is the percentage of the $10,000 invested in the tangent portfolio with an expected return of 12 percent and $w_F = (1 - w_T)$ is the percentage in the 4 percent riskless deposit. The combination must offer 9 percent, which is the expected return of portfolio P_1^*. We can thus write:

$$9\% = 12\%w_T + 4\%w_F = 12\%w_T + 4\%(1 - w_T) = 8\%w_T + 4\%$$

from which you get $w_T = 62.50\%$. Conclusion: if you allocate $6,250 to portfolio T (62.50 percent of $10,000) and deposit the balance of $3,750 in the risk-free account (37.50 percent of $10,000) you will be holding portfolio P_1^*.

Alternatively, you could have opted to keep the same expected return as portfolio P_1 (6 percent) and reduce your risk by holding portfolio P_1^{**} on the EIL as shown in Exhibit 3.11. Your risk would in this case drop to 4 percent (check it out using the EIL equation 3.7b). What is the composition of portfolio P_1^{**} in this case? Using the same method as in the previous case, you will find that $7,500 is in the risk-free deposit and $2,500 in the tangent portfolio.

Let's now examine the case of portfolio P_2 located on the curved opportunity set of only risky stocks and compare it to portfolio P_2^* located on the EIL. Portfolio P_2^* has the same 24 percent volatility as portfolio P_2. What is its expected return? According to the EIL equation 3.7b, it is 16 percent (check this out). What is its composition? Applying the same method we used earlier to find the composition of portfolio P_1^*, we can write:

$$16\% = [12\% \times w_T] + [4\% \times w_F] = [12\% \times w_T] + [4\% \times (1 - w_T)] = [8\% \times w_T] + 4\%$$

from which we get $w_T = 1.50$ (150 percent). Notice that the percentage of funds invested in the tangent portfolio is higher than 1. What does this mean? It means that *more* than your available funds is invested in the tangent portfolio. For example, if you have $10,000, then $w_T = 1.50$ means that $15,000 must be invested in the tangent portfolio. Where are the extra $5,000 coming from? They are borrowed from the bank at 4 percent. In other words, to reach portfolio P_2^* you must borrow $5,000, add them to your initial $10,000 and invest the total of $15,000 in the tangent portfolio. Notice that w_F, the percentage of funds in the risk-free deposit, is negative to indicate that the amount is *borrowed* at 4 percent rather than *deposited* at 4 percent:

$$w_F = (1 - w_T) = (1 - 150\%) = -50\%.$$

Alternatively, you could have opted to keep the same expected return as portfolio P_2 (15 percent) and reduce your risk by holding portfolio P_2^{**} on the EIL as shown in Exhibit 3.11. Your volatility would in this case drop to 22 percent (check it out using the EIL equation 3.7b). What is the composition of portfolio P_2^{**} in this case? Using the same method as in the previous cases, you will find that $3,750 is borrowed and $13,750 is in the tangent portfolio.

What if the borrowing rate is higher than the deposit rate? If the borrowing rate is higher than the deposit rate (the rate at which investors lend their money to the bank) then the EIL is no longer a straight line. In practice, however, investors buy and sell stocks by opening an account with a stockbroker. And they can borrow money from their stockbroker at rates that are close to the risk-free rate to purchase stocks.[10]

Let's summarize our results so far:

1. When there is a risk-free rate and investors can borrow and lend (deposit their funds) at that rate, then the optimal portfolios are on the EIL, the straight line joining the risk-free rate to the tangent portfolio. The portfolios on the EIL are optimal because they offer the highest expected return for any desired level of risk and the lowest level of risk for any desired expected return.

---

[10] This scheme is called buying stocks on **margin**. It works this way: you open an account with a stockbroker by depositing, say, $10,000. Your broker may let you borrow up to, say, $10,000 to buy stocks as long as they are kept in the account. If their value drops below $10,000 you will have to replenish your account with fresh cash.

They dominate any portfolios on the curved opportunity set of risky stocks (except, of course, the tangent portfolio that is on both the curved opportunity set and the EIL).

2. To reach the segment of the EIL between the risk-free rate and the tangent portfolio, investors must allocate a fraction of their investments to the tangent portfolio and invest the balance in a risk-free asset (this is the same as saying that investors must *lend* their funds at the risk-free rate). In this case, the expected return and risk of their portfolio will be lower than those of the tangent portfolio but the Sharpe ratio of their portfolio will be the same as the Sharpe ratio of the tangent portfolio.

3. To reach the segment of the EIL beyond the tangent portfolio, investors must *borrow* at the risk-free rate and invest their initial funds plus the borrowed money in the tangent portfolio. In this case, the expected return and risk of their portfolio will be higher than those of the tangent portfolio, but the Sharpe ratio of their portfolio will be the same as the Sharpe ratio of the tangent portfolio.

THE MARKET PORTFOLIO AND THE CAPITAL MARKET LINE

What if all investors behave as summarized in the previous section? They *all* invest by choosing an efficient portfolio on the EIL. If, furthermore, they all have the *same* estimates of the expected return and risk of stocks, they will all be facing the *same* EIL and holding the *same* tangent portfolio. Do investors actually have the same estimates of the expected return and risk of stocks? Certainly not, but it is an acceptable and useful simplifying assumption in a world where information about companies and financial markets is freely available to most investors. Under this assumption, what would be the tangent portfolio? It must be *a portfolio that contains the shares of all companies held in proportion to their market value.* This unique and comprehensive tangent portfolio is called the **market portfolio** because it contains all the stocks available in the market.

THE EXPECTED RETURN OF THE MARKET PORTFOLIO

To illustrate the properties of the market portfolio in a manageable way, let's assume that the entire stock market consists of shares of only five companies: Atco, Bilco, Carco, Delco, and Enco. Their share price, number of shares outstanding, and stock market values are shown in Exhibit 3.12.

A company's stock market value (also called its **market capitalization**), shown in row 3, is equal to its share price (row 1) multiplied by its number of shares outstanding (row 2). Its weight in the market portfolio (row 4) is equal to its market value (row 3) divided by the market value of the entire stock market ($500 billion in our case). The expected return of the market portfolio is thus:

$$E(R_M) = [18\% \times 5.80\%] + [12\% \times 7\%] + [18\% \times 9.40\%] + [28\% \times 11.80\%] + [24\% \times 13\%] = 10\%$$

In general, if there are N risky assets in the market portfolio, its return is:

$$E(R_M) = [w_1 \times E(R_1)] + \ldots + [w_i \times E(R_i)] + \ldots + [w_N \times E(R_N)]$$

where w_i is the market value of asset i divided by the value of the market portfolio and $E(R_i)$ is the expected return of asset i.

	EXHIBIT 3.12	THE CHARACTERISTICS OF THE MARKET PORTFOLIO.

THE MARKET PORTFOLIO CONTAINS ALL ASSETS IN PROPORTION TO THEIR MARKET VALUE

	Atco	Bilco	Carco	Delco	Enco	Market Portfolio
1. Share price[1]	$10	$30	$18	$20	$24	–
2. Number of shares[1] (in millions)	9,000	2,000	5,000	7,000	5,000	–
3. Market value[2] (in millions)	$90,000	$60,000	$90,000	$140,000	$120,000	$500,000[3]
4. Weight[4]	18%	12%	18%	28%	24%	100%
5. Expected Return[1]	5.8%	7%	9.4%	11.8%	13%	10%[5]
6. Risk: Volatility[1]	15%	25%	30%	40%	50%	20%
7. Sharpe ratio[6] (Risk-free rate = 4%)	0.120	0.120	0.180	0.195	0.180	0.300

[1] The figures for the five stocks are given.

[2] Market value = Price (row 1) × number of shares (row 2).

[3] The market value of the market portfolio is equal to the sum of the five companies' market values.

[4] $\text{Weight} = \dfrac{\text{Market value (row 3)}}{\text{Market value of market portfolio}} = \dfrac{\text{Market value (row 3)}}{\$500,000}$

[5] The expected return of the market portfolio is the weighted average of the expected returns of the five stocks in row 5 using the weights in row 4:

$$E(R_M) = (18\% \times 5.8\%) + (12\% \times 7\%) + (18\% \times 9.4\%) + (28\% \times 11.8\%) + (24\% \times 13\%) = 10\%$$

[6] $\text{Sharpe ratio} = \dfrac{[\text{Expected return (row 5)} - 4\%]}{\text{Volatility(row 6)}}$

PROXIES FOR THE MARKET PORTFOLIO

In practice, no investor actually holds every single risky asset available in the market. But many do invest in market indices that are good substitutes or proxies for the unobservable market portfolio. Indeed, investors can buy indices that track the movements of the stock market. These indices are well-diversified portfolios that are likely to be very highly correlated with the market portfolio.

THE SHARPE RATIO AND THE EFFICIENCY OF THE MARKET PORTFOLIO

The Sharpe ratios of the five stocks are reported in Exhibit 3.12, row 7. Atco and Bilco have the lowest ratio (0.120) and Delco the highest (0.195). The market portfolio, however, is the most efficient investment because it has the highest Sharpe ratio, equal to 0.300.

THE CAPITAL MARKET LINE

What is the equation of the EIL when the tangent portfolio is the market portfolio? It is the same equation as that of the EIL (see equation 3.7a) in which the tangent portfolio is replaced with the market portfolio. If we use the subscript E to designate efficient portfolios, the expected return of these efficient portfolios is given by the following equation:

$$E(R_E) = R_F + \left[\frac{E(R_M) - R_F}{\sigma_M} \right] \times \sigma_E \qquad (3.9a)$$

This efficient investment line is called the **Capital Market Line (CML)**. It is the *unique* efficient investment line that *all* investors would use to make their investment decisions. Its slope is the Sharpe ratio of the market portfolio.

The CML is drawn in Exhibit 3.13 using the data in Exhibit 3.12. The risk-free rate is 4 percent and the market portfolio is at point M. Its expected return is 10 percent and its volatility is 20 percent. The equation of the CML is thus:

$$E(R_E) = 4\% + \left[\frac{10\% - 4\%}{20\%} \right] \times \sigma_E = 4\% + 0.30\sigma_E \qquad (3.9b)$$

The five companies are also shown in Exhibit 3.13 based on their expected returns and volatilities reported in Exhibit 3.12.

EXHIBIT 3.13   THE CAPITAL MARKET LINE (CML).

THE CML GIVES THE EXPECTED RETURNS OF EFFICIENT PORTFOLIOS WHICH COMBINE THE MARKET PORTFOLIO AND THE RISK-FREE ASSET

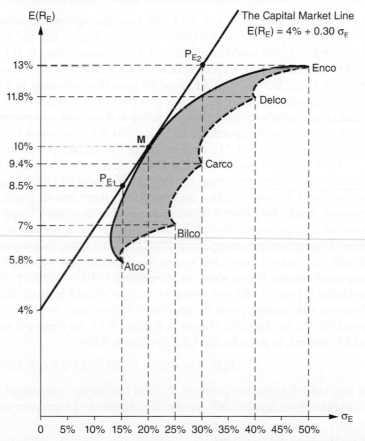

ASSUMPTIONS UNDERLINING THE CML

We have made a number of assumptions throughout the chapter without which we could not have obtained the equation of the CML. Let's summarize them here:

1. *Investors are risk-averse*; they will take on more risk only if they expect higher returns.
2. *Investors only care about the mean and the standard deviation of returns*; alternatively, we can assume that returns are normally distributed and are thus completely described by their mean and standard deviation.
3. *All investors have the same information*; they have the same estimates of expected returns, volatilities, and correlations (we say that they have **homogeneous expectations**) which allow them to compute the efficient set and make optimal investment decisions *without incurring any transaction costs*.
4. *Investors can borrow and lend at the risk-free rate.*

These assumptions are quite restrictive and you could rightly claim that they do not hold in the real world. The answer is that they hold as a first approximation. What matters ultimately is whether the risk-return model that comes out of these assumptions provides a useful framework for making investment decisions. If the model is useful and supported by empirical evidence, which is generally the case,[11] then we shouldn't be too concerned if the assumptions underlying it are a bit restrictive.

MODERN INVESTMENT MANAGEMENT: ALLOCATION BEATS SELECTION

Let's see how you could use the CML to make optimal investment decisions. Suppose you want to invest $10,000 in the stock that has the lowest volatility (see Exhibit 3.12). You could buy shares of Atco whose volatility is 15 percent (see row 6 in Exhibit 3.12). Your expected return will in this case be 5.8 percent (see row 5 in Exhibit 3.12). But you should know by now that investing in a single stock is not a wise investment decision. You know that the best investments are combinations of the market portfolio with either some lending at 4 percent (the portfolios on the CML to the left of the market portfolio M in Exhibit 3.13), or some borrowing at 4 percent (the portfolios on the CML to the right of the market portfolio M).

Look at Atco's position in Exhibit 3.13. It is located below the CML because it has a lower Sharpe ratio than the market portfolio (0.120 versus 0.300 as indicated in Exhibit 3.12, row 7). As a matter of fact, *there are no single stocks or combinations of stocks that have a Sharpe ratio higher than the Sharpe ratio of the market portfolio*. Conclusion: *the only efficient investment is the market portfolio held with some lending or borrowing along the CML*. Any other investment is inferior because it will have a lower expected return for the same risk or a higher risk for the same expected return. If you want an investment with a volatility of 15 percent (Atco's volatility), you should *not* select Atco; you should instead *allocate* your $10,000 between the market portfolio and the risk-free asset in order to reach the efficient portfolio P_{E1} on the CML shown in Exhibit 3.13. Its expected return, for a volatility of 15 percent, is given by the CML equation 3.9b:

$$E(R_{E1}) = 4\% + (0.30 \times 15\%) = 8.50\%$$

If you hold the efficient portfolio P_{E1} you can expect a return of 8.50 percent, which is higher than Atco's 5.80 percent for the same 15 percent volatility. What is its

[11] See Hawawini and Keim (1995).

composition? If w_M is the percentage of $10,000 invested in the market portfolio with an expected return of 10 percent and $w_E = (1 - w_M)$ is the percentage in the riskless asset that offers 4 percent, then the combination offering 8.50 percent (which is the efficient portfolio P_{E1}) must satisfy the following relationship:

$$8.50\% = [10\% \times w_M] + [4\% \times w_F] = [10\% \times w_M] + [4\% \times (1 - w_M)] = [6\% \times w_M] + 4\%$$

from which you find $w_M = 75$ percent. Conclusion: if you allocate $7,500 to the market portfolio (75 percent of $10,000) and deposit the balance of $2,500 in the risk-free account, you will be holding the efficient portfolio P_{E1} on the CML as shown in Exhibit 3.13. *You can be sure that there is no other investment with an expected return of 8.50 percent that has a volatility lower than 15 percent.*

What if you wanted a higher expected return than 8.50 percent? You could buy shares of Enco that have an expected return of 13 percent and a volatility of 50 percent (see rows 5 and 6 in Exhibit 3.12), but, again, selecting a single stock is not the right investment decision. You should hold instead the efficient portfolio P_{E2} located to the right of the market portfolio on the CML (note that any investment with a higher volatility than the market must be located to the right of the market portfolio). It has an expected return of 13 percent with a lower volatility than Enco (30 percent instead of 50 percent; check it out using equation 3.9b). What is its composition? Applying the same procedure as in the case of Atco, you will find that $w_M = 150$ percent and $w_F = -50$ percent, meaning that $15,000 is invested in the market portfolio: your initial $10,000 plus $5,000 borrowed at 4 percent.

The above examples clearly illustrate that modern investment management is about the *allocation of funds* to the market portfolio with lending or borrowing in order to hold portfolios located on the CML. It is not about the *selection of particular shares* based on the attractiveness of their individual risk-return characteristics. To put it succinctly, *allocation beats selection.* This approach greatly simplifies the investment process: *all risk-averse investors should hold the market portfolio, no matter what their degree of risk aversion is,* and then find the optimal combination of the market portfolio with borrowing or lending that puts them on their highest indifference curve.

This fundamental investment rule is known as the **separation principle** because the investment process is carried out in two separate steps. For investors, the first step is to identify a broad market index that is a good proxy for the market portfolio. The second step is to decide how to allocate their funds between the market index and the risk-free asset in order to reach their highest indifference curve consistent with their degree of risk aversion. Those with a high degree of risk aversion will tilt their allocation toward the risk-free asset (they will lend some of their funds by placing them in a risk-free deposit) whereas those with a low degree of risk aversion will tilt their allocation toward the market index (and those with a high tolerance for risk may borrow and invest more than their initial funds in the market index).

A CLOSER LOOK AT SYSTEMATIC RISK

We showed earlier that the risk of a stock has two components: a *diversifiable* component called firm-specific risk or unsystematic risk and an *undiversifiable* component called market risk or systematic risk. In this section we show how to measure a stock's undiversifiable risk with the help of the **Market Model** (also called the **Index Model**).[12]

---

[12] See Sharpe (1963) and chapter 8 in Bodie, Kane, and Marcus (2011).

BETA AND THE MARKET MODEL

The Market Model expresses the returns of a stock i ($\tilde{R}_i$) as a function of the returns of a broad stock market index ($\tilde{R}_M$) and a firm-specific or unsystematic return ($\tilde{U}_i$) as follows:

$$\tilde{R}_i = a_i + \beta_i\tilde{R}_M + \tilde{U}_i \qquad (3.10)$$

The tilde above returns indicates that the return is random. The first term on the right of the equation (a_i) is a fixed intercept. The **beta** of stock i (β_i) in the second term captures the *sensitivity* of the stock's returns ($\tilde{R}_i$) to changes in the stock market returns ($\tilde{R}_M$). Recall our earlier observation: because correlation coefficients are positive, the returns of an individual stock have a tendency to move with the market returns, but *the magnitude of the move is not the same for all stocks; some stocks are more sensitive to market movements than others.* Beta measures that sensitivity. Specifically, *beta tells you by how much the returns of a stock are expected to change, on average, when the market return changes by 1 percent.* For example, suppose that the General Engines Company (GEC) has a beta of 1.25. What does this beta indicate? It says that if the market goes up 1 percent or down 1 percent, GEC shares will, on average, go up 1.25 percent or down 1.25 percent.

CALCULATING BETA

In footnote 13 we show how to use the Market Model (equation 3.10) to come up with a formula to calculate the beta of a company's shares. It is equal to the covariance of the share returns with those of the market divided by the variance of the market returns:[13]

$$\beta_i = \frac{\text{Cov}(R_i, R_M)}{\text{Var}(R_M)} = \frac{\sigma_{iM}}{\sigma_M^2} \qquad (3.11a)$$

We can use the definition of covariance given in equation 3.4 to express beta as follows:

$$\beta_i = \frac{\rho_{iM}\sigma_i\sigma_M}{\sigma_M^2} = \rho_{iM}\left(\frac{\sigma_i}{\sigma_M}\right) \qquad (3.11b)$$

In other words, a stock beta is equal to the correlation of its returns with those of the market (ρ_{iM}) multiplied by the ratio of the stock volatility to the market volatility $\left(\frac{\sigma_i}{\sigma_M}\right)$. For example, if the market volatility is 20 percent, the beta of a stock with a volatility of 18 percent and a correlation of 0.60 with the market has a beta of 0.54 ($\beta = 0.60 \times \frac{18\%}{20\%} = 0.54$).

---

[13] Calculate $\text{Cov}[\tilde{R}_i, \tilde{R}_M]$ in which $\tilde{R}_i$ is replaced by its Market Model formulation given by equation 3.10. You get:

$$\text{Cov}[\tilde{R}_i, \tilde{R}_M] = \text{Cov}[(a_i + \beta_i\tilde{R}_M + \tilde{U}_i), \tilde{R}_M] = \beta_i \times \text{Cov}[\tilde{R}_M, \tilde{R}_M]$$

because $\text{Cov}[\beta_i\tilde{R}_M, \tilde{U}_i] = 0$ (the market returns $\tilde{R}_M$ are uncorrelated with unsystematic returns $\tilde{U}_i$) and 'a_i' is a constant. Rearranging the terms, you get the following expression for beta:

$$\beta_i = \frac{\text{Cov}(\tilde{R}_i, \tilde{R}_M)}{\text{Cov}(\tilde{R}_M, \tilde{R}_M)} = \frac{\sigma_{iM}}{\sigma_M^2}$$

THE PROPERTIES OF BETA

We can now use the beta formulas 3.11a and 3.11b to infer some important characteristics of a stock's beta.

1. Beta is a measure of the systematic risk or market risk of a stock because it is directly related to the covariance of the stock returns with those of the market. As explained earlier, this covariance risk *is the only relevant measure of the risk of a stock when the stock is held in a well-diversified portfolio*. Recall that the total risk of a stock has two components: one that can be diversified away by holding the stock in a portfolio (the stock's firm-specific risk), and one that is undiversifiable (the stock's systematic market risk). *Beta is a measure of the undiversifiable, systematic market risk and thus the only part of the risk of a stock that matters to risk-averse investors* (because risk-averse investors always diversify).

2. The beta of the market portfolio (β_M) is equal to 1 because the correlation coefficient (ρ_{IM}) is in this case equal to 1 and the stock volatility (σ_i) is equal to the market volatility (σ_M).

3. The beta of the riskless asset (β_F) is equal to zero because its volatility (σ_F) is zero.

4. Beta has the same sign as the correlation coefficient. If the correlation between a stock return and those of the market is negative, beta is negative. If it is positive, beta is positive. Because the correlations between stock returns and market returns are usually always positive, stock betas are usually always positive (in the next subsection we report the estimated betas of a number of companies around the world).

5. Beta measures the risk of a stock relative to the risk of the market. Stocks with a beta higher than 1 have more systematic risk than the market, and the higher the beta the riskier the stock. And stocks with a beta lower than 1 have less systematic risk than the market, and the lower the beta the less risky the stock.

6. When comparing two stocks, the one with the higher volatility (total risk) could have a lower beta (systematic risk). To illustrate, consider stock A with a 30 percent volatility and a correlation with the market of 0.80 and stock B with a 40 percent volatility and a correlation with the market of 0.55. If the market volatility is 20 percent, the beta of stock A is 1.20 and that of stock B is 1.10 (check this out). Even though stock B has a higher volatility than stock A, it is less risky when held in a portfolio because its beta is lower.

ESTIMATED STOCK BETAS

A company's beta can be estimated by regressing its stock's historical returns against those of the market. We show in Chapter 12 how to apply this statistical technique to estimate the beta of the shares of a company. Exhibit 3.14 reports the estimated betas of a sample of companies in different industries whose shares are traded on various stock markets around the world.

As pointed out earlier, betas are positive, ranging from a high of 1.81 to a low of 0.34. Notice that companies in the same industry have similar betas because they face similar risks. And industries that are considered riskier than the market average – such as motor vehicle manufacturing and internet services – have higher betas than companies in industries that are considered less risky than the market average, such as soft drinks and telecom services.

EXHIBIT 3.14	ESTIMATION OF THE BETA OF A SAMPLE OF COMPANIES IN DIFFERENT STOCK EXCHANGES AND INDUSTRIES[1].		
Company	**Stock Exchange**	**Industry**	**Estimated Beta**
Peugeot S.A.	Euronext Paris	Motor vehicle manufacturing	1.81
General Motors	New York Stock Exchange	Motor vehicle manufacturing	1.55
Honda Motor	Tokyo Stock Exchange	Motor vehicle manufacturing	1.28
Amazon.com Inc.	Nasdaq (New York)	Online distribution	1.71
Microsoft Corporation	Nasdaq (New York)	Software and services	1.28
Alphabet (Google)	Nasdaq (New York)	Internet information	1.27
Hewlett-Packard	New York Stock Exchange	Electronic equipment	1.72
Nokia	Helsinki Stock Exchange	Electronic equipment	1.55
Cisco Systems	Nasdaq (New York)	Electronic equipment	1.22
Morgan Stanley	New York Stock Exchange	Banking	1.49
Citigroup	New York Stock Exchange	Banking	1.49
Goldman Sachs Group	New York Stock Exchange	Banking	1.29
Groupe Casino	Euronext Paris	Distribution – discount	1.25
Costco Wholesale	Nasdaq (New York)	Distribution – discount	1.06
Carrefour	Euronext Paris	Distribution – discount	1.01
Chevron Corporation	New York Stock Exchange	Major oil and gas	1.21
Total	Euronext Paris	Major oil and gas	0.89
Exxon Mobil	New York Stock Exchange	Major oil and gas	0.82
Unilever	Euronext Amsterdam	Personal products	1.01
Nestlé	SIX-Swiss Exchange	Personal products	0.80
Delta Airlines	New York Stock Exchange	Major airlines	0.97
Air France–KLM	Euronext Paris	Major airlines	0.72
Pepsico, Inc.	New York Stock Exchange	Beverages – soft drinks	0.64
Coca-Cola Company	New York Stock Exchange	Beverages – soft drinks	0.57
Verizon Communications	New York Stock Exchange	Telecom services	0.70
ATT	New York Stock Exchange	Telecom services	0.34

[1] Source: Datastream April 2018.

PORTFOLIO BETA

The beta of a portfolio is the weighted average of the betas of the stocks that make up the portfolio. If w_i represents the percentage of the value of the portfolio invested in stock i whose beta is β_i, the beta of a portfolio (β_P) containing N stocks is:

$$\beta_P = w_1\beta_1 + w_2\beta_2 + \ldots + w_i\beta_i + \ldots + w_N\beta_N \qquad (3.12)$$

For example, consider a $10,000 portfolio with $6,000 invested in a stock with a beta of 1.30 and $4,000 in a stock with a beta of 0.90. The portfolio beta is in this case:

$$\beta_P = (60\% \times 1.30) + (40\% \times 0.90) = 1.14$$

Let's return to our earlier example of a market in which there are only five stocks. Exhibit 3.15 reports the betas of the five stocks and their weights in the market portfolio. We know that the market portfolio has a beta equal to 1. You can verify that this is indeed the case by plugging into equation 3.12 the data shown in Exhibit 3.15:

$$\beta_M = (18\% \times 0.30) + (12\% \times 0.50) + (18\% \times 0.90) + (28\% \times 1.30) + (24\% \times 1.50) = 1.00$$

THE CAPITAL ASSET PRICING MODEL

We have shown earlier that the CML gives you the expected return of an *efficient* portfolio ($E(R_E)$) if you know its volatility (σ_E). These are the portfolios located along the CML in Exhibit 3.13. The question we want to answer in this section is: what is the expected return of an *inefficient* investment and, in particular, of an *individual* stock which is the most inefficient of all investments? You cannot use the CML equation to get the expected return of an individual stock because, as shown in the previous section, the total risk of an individual stock (its volatility σ_i) is not the correct measure of its risk when the stock is held in a portfolio.

THE EXPECTED RETURN OF AN INDIVIDUAL STOCK

Recall from the previous section that the relevant measure of the risk of a stock is its beta coefficient – not its volatility or total risk – because the assumption is that investors are risk-averse and thus hold well-diversified portfolios. In other words,

---

EXHIBIT 3.15 THE BETAS AND EXPECTED RETURNS OF INDIVIDUAL STOCKS.

THE EXPECTED RETURN OF AN INDIVIDUAL STOCK IS GIVEN BY THE SECURITY MARKET LINE:
$E(R_I) = R_F + [E(R_M) - R_F]\beta_I$

	Atco	Bilco	Carco	Delco	Enco	Market Portfolio
1. Beta	0.30	0.50	0.90	1.30	1.50	1.00[1]
2. Weight in market[2]	18%	12%	18%	28%	24%	100%
3. Expected Return[3] (*Risk-free rate = 4%*)	5.8%	7%	9.4%	11.8%	13%	10%[4]
4. Volatility	15%	25%	30%	40%	50%	20%

[1] The market beta is the weighted average of the betas of the stocks in row 1 using the weights in row 2:
$$\beta_M = (18\% \times 0.30) + (12\% \times 0.50) + (18\% \times 0.90) + (28\% \times 1.30) + (24\% \times 1.50) = 1.00.$$
[2] See Exhibit 3.12, row 4.
[3] For example, the expected return of Atco is $E(R_A) = 4\% + [(10\% - 4\%) \times 0.30] = 5.80\%$.
[4] The market expected return is the weighted average of the expected returns of the stocks in row 3 using the weights in row 2:
$$E(R_M) = (18\% \times 5.8\%) + (12\% \times 7\%) + (18\% \times 9.4\%) + (28\% \times 11.8\%) + (24\% \times 13\%) = 10\%.$$

risk-averse investors only hold stocks in portfolios, never alone. Thus, *if stocks are held in a well-diversified portfolio their unsystematic, firm-specific risk is eliminated through diversification and the only risk that matters to an investor is beta, the systematic market risk.* Put differently, you should think of the risk of an individual stock as its portfolio risk (its beta), not as its stand-alone risk (its volatility). The implication of this observation is crucial to the determination of the return an investor should expect from holding a stock: because only beta risk matters, *the expected return of an individual stock* $(E(R_i))$ *will be related to its beta* (β_i), *not its volatility.* The specific equation that gives $E(R_i)$ as a function of β_i is:

$$E(R_i) = R_F + [E(R_M) - R_F]\beta_i \qquad (3.13a)$$

It is referred to as the **Security Market Line (SML)** and the model underlying its derivation is called the **Capital Asset Pricing Model (CAPM)**.[14] A mathematical derivation of the SML is provided in the appendix to this chapter. The CAPM states that a security's expected return is equal to the risk-free rate (the first term in the SML equation) plus a **risk premium** equal to the *excess* return of the market portfolio over the risk-free rate multiplied by the beta of that security (the second term in the SML equation).

What the CAPM says is that investors cannot expect to earn a return on the portion of a security's risk that has been diversified away at no cost (the unsystematic risk); they can expect to earn a return only on the portion of risk that they cannot eliminate through diversification (the systematic risk measured by the security's beta coefficient).

What is the equation of the SML based on the data in Exhibit 3.15? The risk-free rate of 4 percent and a market expected return of 10 percent. The excess return of the market portfolio, called the **market risk premium,** is thus 6 percent (10 percent minus 4 percent) and the SML equation is:

$$E(R_i) = 4\% + 6\%\beta_i \qquad (3.13b)$$

Look at the graph on the right side of Exhibit 3.16. It shows the SML (equation 3.13b) which gives the expected returns of Atco (point A), Bilco (point B), Carco (point C), Delco (point D), and Enco (point E) based on their beta coefficients given in the first row of Exhibit 3.15. For example, in the case of Carco, the expected return is:

$$E(R_{Carco}) = 4\% + (6\% \times \beta_{Carco}) = 4\% + (6\% \times 0.90) = 4\% + 5.40\% = 9.40\%$$

Note that the horizontal axis on the SML graph on the right of Exhibit 3.16 indicates beta, the correct measure of an individual security's risk. Look now at the graph on the left of Exhibit 3.16. The horizontal risk axis indicates volatility, the correct measure of an efficient portfolio's risk.

USING THE **CAPM** TO ESTIMATE A **COMPANY'S** COST OF **EQUITY** CAPITAL

We will show in Chapter 12 how to use the CAPM to estimate a company's cost of equity capital. In Chapter 1 we defined a company's cost of equity as the return shareholders expect to earn on their investment in the company. In other words, you

---

[14] The model was developed by Sharpe (1964).

| EXHIBIT 3.16 | THE CAPITAL MARKET LINE AND THE SECURITY MARKET LINE. |

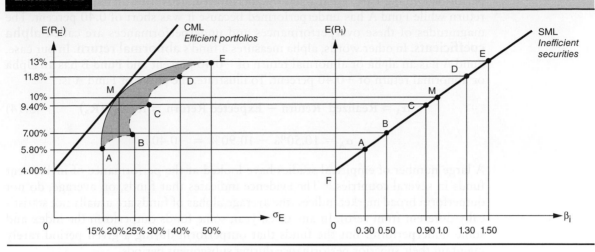

can estimate that cost using the SML equation because the SML gives you the return expected by stockholders if you know the company's beta. The estimated cost of equity of the five companies listed in Exhibit 3.15 is their expected return according to the SML, reported in row 3.

USING THE CAPM TO EVALUATE INVESTMENT PERFORMANCE

You can also use the SML equation to evaluate the performance of a diversified investment fund. Suppose Investment Fund A produced last year a return of 10.50 percent while Investment Fund B produced a return of 9.50 percent. Fund A has a beta of 1.15 and Fund B a beta of 0.85. Last year, a broad market index produced a return of 10 percent. The risk-free rate is 4 percent. Which fund underperformed and which overperformed compared to the market index?

You might be tempted to conclude that Fund A overperformed the market index because its return of 10.50 percent exceeds the 10 percent market return. Likewise, Fund B underperformed because its return of 9.50 percent is lower than the 10 percent market return. But these comparisons are incorrect because they do not take into account the risk of the funds. According to the CAPM, Fund A *should* have returned 10.90 percent and Fund B should have returned 9.10 percent because:

$$E(R_A) = 4\% + (6\% \times 1.15) = 10.90\%$$

$$E(R_B) = 4\% + (6\% \times 0.85) = 9.10\%$$

The proper measure of a fund's performance is the difference between its *realized* return and its *expected* return. Fund A has actually *underperformed* because its realized return of 10.50 percent is *lower* than the 10.90 percent the fund *should* have delivered given its beta of 1.15. And Fund B has actually *overperformed* because its realized return of 9.50 percent is *higher* than the 9.10 percent the fund *should* have delivered given its beta of 0.85.

To summarize: in order to properly measure the performance of alternative investments, their returns must be first adjusted for risk. We can then compare these

risk-adjusted returns to find out if the investment has overperformed or underperformed. In our case, Fund B has overperformed, delivering an extra 0.40 percent return while Fund A has underperformed because it was short of 0.40 percent. The magnitudes of these overperformances and underperformances are called **alpha coefficients**. In other words, alpha measures a fund's **abnormal return**. In our case, Fund A has an alpha or abnormal return of −0.40 percent and Fund B has an alpha or abnormal return of +0.40 percent. To illustrate, the alpha of Fund A is:

$$\alpha_A = \text{Realized Return} - \text{Expected Return} = R_A - E(R_A) \qquad (3.14)$$

$$\alpha_A = 10.50\% - 10.90\% = -0.40\%$$

A large number of empirical studies have looked at the performance of investment funds in several countries.[15] The evidence indicates that funds, on average, do not outperform broad market indices (the average alphas of funds are usually not statistically different from zero). In any given year, some funds outperform the index and some underperform. But the funds that outperform during a given period rarely maintain their superior performance during subsequent periods.

USING THE CAPM TO TEST THE INFORMATIONAL EFFICIENCY OF STOCK MARKETS

How fast does new information about a company get reflected into its stock price? Consider the example of a public announcement of a takeover. Typically, the share price of the **target company** rises significantly on the day the takeover is announced by the **bidding company**. In an efficient market, the price should adjust instantly and fully on that day. If, for example, prices continued to rise days *after* the announcement is made then investors could earn abnormal return days after the takeover is public news, which would indicate that the market is not informationally efficient.

How is the speed of price adjustment measured? The standard method is to calculate the daily alphas of a large sample of target companies a few days before the announcement and a few days after (note that the announcement day is different for the companies in the sample). Positive average daily alphas (calculated across the companies in the sample) would indicate that investors are able to earn abnormal returns (returns in excess of those predicted by the SML equation). If the market processes information efficiently, then the average daily alphas should be zero before the announcement. On the day of the announcement the average alphas should be positive. And on the days following the announcement the average daily alphas should be zero again if the stock market has fully adjusted to the news on the day of the announcement.

Look at Exhibit 3.17 where you see a plot of *cumulative* average daily alphas days before and days after the announcements of a takeover for a sample of US listed companies. The market seems to anticipate the takeover announcements two weeks before they are made public, but on the day of the announcement the price adjusts instantly and completely. There are no further adjustments on the days following the announcements. This is evidence of market efficiency to public announcements. One cannot tell if the rise in price *prior* to the announcements is a reflection of market expectation or an indication of trading gains based on inside information.

---

[15] See chapter 24 in Bodie, Kane and Markus (2011), Malkiel (1995), and Fama and French (2010).

EXHIBIT 3.17	ABNORMAL RETURNS OF TARGET COMPANIES 120 DAYS BEFORE AND 30 DAYS AFTER THE ANNOUNCEMENT OF A TAKEOVER.

SHARE PRICES ADJUST INSTANTLY AND FULLY TO THE TAKEOVER ANNOUNCEMENTS

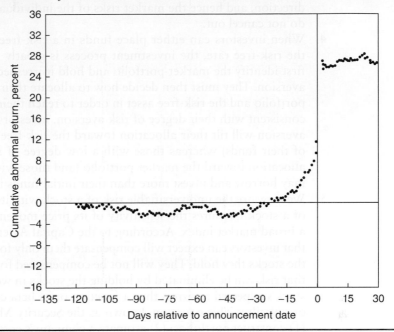

Source: "Merger Announcement and Insider Trading Activity," A. Keown and J. Pinkerton, *Journal of Finance*, September 1981.

KEY POINTS

1. We developed in this chapter a framework that helps investors make investment decisions based on the expected return and risk of stocks. If the empirical distributions of stock returns are stationary, then the arithmetic averages of historical returns are good estimators of the stocks' expected return, and the standard deviation of their historical returns can be used to measure their risk.

2. Investors are typically risk-averse. They dislike risk and will buy a riskier asset only if they can expect a higher return to compensate them for the higher risk. Even though investors are risk-averse, they do not have the same degree of risk aversion. Some are more risk-averse than others. This degree of risk aversion is captured graphically by drawing an investor's indifference curves on the risk-return plane. The higher the indifference curve, the better off the investor is. And the steeper the indifference curves, the more risk-averse the investor is.

3. Investors can reduce the risk of their investment through diversification by combining stocks into a portfolio. As the number of stocks in a portfolio increases, the risk of the portfolio declines, but it cannot be eliminated completely because stock returns are positively correlated. Risk-reduction through diversification works as follows. The total risk of a company's shares has two components: one that is diversifiable (called firm-specific risk) and one that is undiversifiable

(called market risk). Some of the risk of a portfolio is diversified away because the firm-specific risks of the individual securities in the portfolio cancel out (good news is offset, on average, by bad news). But portfolio diversification cannot reduce market risk because all shares are exposed to market risk in the same direction, and hence the market risks of the individual securities in the portfolio do not cancel out.

4. When investors can either place funds in a risk-free asset or borrow funds at the risk-free rate, the investment process is greatly simplified. Investors must first identify the market portfolio and hold it irrespective of their degree of risk aversion. They must then decide how to allocate their funds between the market portfolio and the risk-free asset in order to reach their highest indifference curve consistent with their degree of risk aversion. Investors with a high degree of risk aversion will tilt their allocation toward the risk-free asset (they will lend some of their funds) whereas those with a low degree of risk aversion will tilt their allocation toward the market portfolio (and those with a high tolerance for risk may borrow and invest more than their initial funds in the market portfolio).

5. We measure the undiversifiable risk of a stock with its beta coefficient. The beta of a stock measures the sensitivity of its price movements to the movements of a broad market index. According to the Capital Asset Pricing Model, the return that investors can expect will compensate them only for the undiversifiable risk of the stocks they hold. They will not be compensated for firm-specific risk because that risk can be eliminated by holding the stocks in well-diversified portfolios. A stock's expected return is thus a function of its beta coefficient, not its total risk or volatility. This equation, known as the Security Market Line, can be used to (1) construct portfolios; (2) estimate a company's cost of equity; (3) evaluate the performance of an investment fund; and (4) test the informational efficiency of a stock market.

FURTHER READING

1. Bodie, Zvi, Alex Kane, and Alan Marcus. *Investments*, 10th ed. McGraw-Hill, 2014.
2. *Credit Suisse Global Investment Returns Yearbook 2018.*
3. Fama, Eugene, and Kenneth French. "Luck versus Skill in the Cross-Section of Mutual Fund Returns." *Journal of Finance* 65 (October 2010).
4. Hawawini, Gabriel, and Donald Keim. "On the Predictability of Common Stock Returns: World-Wide Evidence." In *Handbooks in Operations Research and Management Science – Finance Volume*, edited by R.A. Jarrow, V. Maksimovic, and W.T. Ziemba, North Holland: Amsterdam, 1995, chapter 17, pp. 494–544.
5. Ibbotson, Roger. *Stocks, Bonds, Bills, and Inflation Yearbook, 2017.*
6. Keown, Arthur, and John Pinkerton. "Merger Announcements and Insider Trading Activity." *Journal of Finance* 36 (September 1981).
7. Malkiel, Burton. "Returns from Investing in Equity Mutual Funds 1971–1991." *Journal of Finance* 50 (June 1995).
8. Sharpe, William. "A Simplified Model of Portfolio Analysis." *Management Science* 9 (January 1963).
9. Sharpe, William. "Capital Asset Prices: A Theory of Market Equilibrium under Conditions of Risk." *Journal of Finance* 19 (September 1964).
10. Statman, Meier. "How Many Stocks Make a Diversified Portfolio?" *Journal of Financial and Quantitative Analysis* 22 (September 1987).

How to Get the SML Equation

The SML equation (3.13a) gives you the expected return of asset i ($E(R_i)$) if you know its beta (β_i) and the excess return of market portfolio ($[E(R_M) - R_F]$):

$$E(R_i) = R_F + [E(R_M) - R_F]\beta_i \qquad (3.13a)$$

To obtain this equation, we need to measure the contribution of security i to: (1) the risk (variance) of the market portfolio (σ_M^2), and (2) the market excess return ($[E(R_M) - R_F]$):

(1) Contribution to $\sigma_M^2 = w_i[w_1\text{Cov}(R_1;R_i) + w_2\text{Cov}(R_2;R_i) + \ldots$

$$+ w_i\text{Cov}(R_i;R_i) + \ldots + w_N\text{Cov}(R_N;R_i)]$$

$$= w_i\text{Cov}(w_1R_1 + w_2R_2 + \ldots + w_NR_N;R_i) = w_i\text{Cov}(R_M;R_i)$$

(2) Contribution to $[E(R_M) - R_F] = w_i[E(R_i) - R_F]$

Using (1) and (2), we can now get the Sharpe ratio of the contribution of asset i to the risk and excess return of the market portfolio:

$$\text{Sharpe ratio of contribution of security i} = \frac{\text{Contribution of i to } [E(R_M) - R_F]}{\text{Contribution of i to } \sigma_M^2} = \frac{w_i[E(R_i) - R_F]}{w_i\text{Cov}(R_M;R_i)}$$

$$\text{Sharpe ratio of contribution of security i} = \frac{[E(R_i) - R_F]}{\text{Cov}(R_M;R_i)}$$

In equilibrium, the Sharpe ratio of the contribution of security i must be the same as the Sharpe ratio of the market portfolio:

$$\frac{[E(R_i) - R_F]}{\text{Cov}(R_M; R_i)} = \frac{[E(R_M) - R_F]}{\text{Cov}(R_M; R_M)}$$

Multiplying both sides of the above equation by $\text{Cov}(R_M; R_i)$ and recalling that $\text{Cov}(R_M; R_M) = \sigma_M^2$:

$$E(R_i) - R_F = [E(R_M) - R_F]\frac{\text{Cov}(R_M;R_i)}{\sigma_M^2} = [E(R_M) - R_F]\beta_i$$

which is the SML equation 3.13a.

SELF-TEST QUESTIONS

3.1 Arithmetic versus geometric average returns.
Go to the first section in the chapter where the 12 monthly returns of Alto Water Supplies (AWS) are given in the subsection "Holding Period Returns".

a. Assume that you invested one dollar in AWS at the beginning of January. What is the dollar value of your investment at the end of December?
b. What is your average monthly return over the 12-month period based on the terminal investment value you found above? It is called the geometric average return.
c. Compare the arithmetic average return of 0.6667 percent reported in the chapter to the geometric average return you found in your answer to the previous question. When should you use the geometric average and when should you use the arithmetic average?

3.2 Investors' attitudes toward risk.
Consider an investor holding stock A with a 10 percent expected return and a 20 percent volatility. There are eight other stocks with the following risk-return characteristics:

	Stock B	Stock C	Stock D	Stock E	Stock F	Stock G	Stock H	Stock I
E(R)	15%	15%	15%	10%	5%	5%	5%	10%
Volatility	12%	20%	28%	28%	28%	20%	12%	12%

a. If the investor is risk-averse, indicate whether she prefers stock A to stock B, stock B to stock A or if she is indifferent between stock A and stock B. Answer the same question for stock A versus stock C, stock D, stock E, stock F, stock G, stock H and stock I.
b. Answer the same question if the investor is risk neutral.
c. Answer the same question if the investor is a risk seeker.

3.3 The characteristics of a two-stock portfolio.
Answer the following questions based on the information provided in Exhibit 3.5.

a. Given that portfolio P_3 has an expected return of 12 percent, show the calculation that provides its composition (one-third invested in Alto and two-thirds in Bell).
b. Calculate the volatility of portfolio P_3.
c. Consider a portfolio P_4 with 90 percent of funds invested in Alto shares. What is its expected return? Is it an efficient portfolio? Explain.
d. Show that the efficient portfolio that has the same volatility as portfolio P_4 is 55.45 percent invested in Alto shares. What is its expected return?

3.4 The risk of a diversified portfolio when the number of stocks is very large.
Consider a portfolio containing equal proportions of n stocks. Assume that all stocks have the same variance (Var) and that all pairwise covariances are the same (Cov).

a. Show that the variance of the portfolio (Var_P) can be written:

$$Var_P = \frac{1}{N}Var + \left(1 - \frac{1}{N}\right)Cov$$

b. Show that when the number of stocks n becomes infinitely large the variance of the portfolio is equal to the average covariance in the portfolio. What is the significance of this result?

3.5 **The capital asset pricing model.**
Answer the following questions based on the information provided in Exhibit 3.12.

a. An investor with $100,000 has a target expected return of 7 percent. Should he invest his funds in Bilco shares whose expected return is 7 percent? If not, what is his optimal investment decision? Provide the dollar amounts invested in each asset in his optimal portfolio and the number of shares the investor should buy.

b. What are the volatility and the beta of the optimal portfolio in the previous question? Explain the size of beta compared to the market beta.

c. An investor with $100,000 has a target volatility of 40 percent. Should she invest her funds in Delco shares whose volatility is 40 percent? If not, what is her optimal investment decision? Provide the dollar amounts invested in each asset in her optimal portfolio.

d. What are the Sharpe ratio and the beta of the optimal portfolio in the previous question? Explain the size of beta compared to the market beta.

e. What is the beta of an equally-weighted portfolio of Bilco and Delco shares?

f. What are the correlation coefficient and the covariance between the returns of Enco shares and those of the market portfolio?

REVIEW QUESTIONS

1. **Attitudes toward risk.**
Stock A has an expected return of 13 percent and a 25 percent volatility. Stock B has an expected return of 9 percent and a 30 percent volatility. An investor can only purchase one of the two stocks.

a. An investor bought stock A. What is her attitude toward risk?

b. An investor bought stock B. What is his attitude toward risk?

c. What is the expected return on stock B that would make a risk-neutral investor buy it?

d. What is the volatility of stock B that would make a risk-averse investor buy it?

2. **Characteristics of a two-stock portfolio.**
Stock A has an expected return of 8 percent and an 18 percent volatility. Stock B has an expected return of 16 percent and a 30 percent volatility. The correlation coefficient between the returns of stock A and stock B is 0.30.

a. What is the expected return of portfolio P_1 with 25 percent of funds in stock A and the balance in stock B?

b. What is the covariance between the returns of stock A and those of stock B?

c. What is the volatility of the portfolio P_1?

d. What are the expected return and volatility of the minimum-risk portfolio?

e. Portfolio P_2 has an expected return of 14 percent and a 25 percent volatility. Is it an efficient portfolio? Explain. What expected return should portfolio P_2 offer to be efficient?

3. **Risk reduction through diversification.**
   You invest one-third of your wealth in each of three stocks. The expected return and standard deviation of each individual stock is 10 percent and 20 percent, respectively. Each stock has a pairwise correlation of 0.50 with the returns of the two other stocks.

   a. What is the expected return of the portfolio?
   b. What is the risk reduction of investing in the portfolio containing the three stocks relative to investing in only one stock?

4. **Correlations, covariances and betas.**
   Refer to the data in Exhibit 3.12 to answer the following questions.

   a. What are the beta coefficients of the five stocks?
   b. What are the covariances and the correlation coefficients of the five stocks' returns with those of the market portfolio?
   c. Show that the correlation coefficient between the returns of stock A and stock B is equal to the product of their respective correlations with the market. Calculate the correlation coefficient between the returns of stock A and stock B.
   d. What is the beta of an equally-weighted portfolio of the five stocks? Compare it to the beta of the market portfolio.

5. **Negative betas.**
   The market portfolio has an expected return of 9 percent with a 10 percent volatility. The risk-free rate is 4 percent. A stock has a 20 percent volatility and a correlation coefficient of minus 0.10 with the market.

   a. What is the stock's beta? What does its sign indicate?
   b. What is the stock's expected return? Explain why it is lower than the risk-free rate.

6. **The CML versus the SML.**

   a. You hold an efficient portfolio. Which of the CML or the SML gives you the expected return on your portfolio? What could its composition be?
   b. You hold an inefficient portfolio. Which of the CML or the SML gives you the expected return on your portfolio? What could its composition be?
   c. Show that any portfolio on the CML is perfectly positively correlated with the market portfolio.
   d. Use the answer to the previous question to show that the SML reduces to the CML when an investment is efficient.

7. **The Capital Asset Pricing Model and investment allocation.**
   The market portfolio has an expected return of 11 percent with a 25 percent volatility. The risk-free rate is 5 percent.

   a. Investor A with $180,000 has a target expected return of 9 percent. How should he invest his $180,000?
   b. What are the volatility and beta of investor A's portfolio?
   c. Investor B with $200,000 has a target volatility of 30 percent. How should she invest her $200,000?
   d. What is the beta of investor B's portfolio?

8. **Estimating a firm's cost of capital.**
   Shares of the Pacific Electric Corporation (PEC) have an estimated beta of 1.10. PEC funds its assets with 50 percent debt at an average after-tax cost of debt of 6 percent.

The excess return on the market portfolio is 5 percent and the risk-free rate is 3 percent.

a. What is PEC's estimated cost of equity according to the CAPM?
b. What is PEC's estimated weighted average cost of capital?

9. **Evaluating portfolio performance.**
   Below are the recent performances of four investment funds, a market index (M), and a risk-free asset (F):

Investment Fund	A	B	C	D	M	F
Average return	7.90%	10.10%	9.80%	7.20%	9.20%	3.20%
Average volatility	35%	40%	32%	28%	30%	
Average beta	0.88	1.20	1.04	0.90		

a. Fill in the empty cells in the table above.
b. What are the alphas of the above portfolios? How did the investment funds perform?

10. **Testing for informational efficiency.**
    You want to test the speed with which stock market prices adjust to positive earnings' announcements. Company A makes its earnings announcement on May 20 and Company B on June 16. You collected for each company daily share price returns two days before the event day and two days after the event day, as reported below. Company A has a beta of 1 and Company B a beta of 2.

Company A	18 May	19 May	20 May	21 May	22 May
(1) Excess return on stock A	−1.99%	0.19%	1.00%	−1.27%	−0.45%
(2) Excess return on the market	−2.00%	0.50%	0.50%	−1.00%	−0.50%

Company B	14 June	15 June	16 June	17 June	18 June
(1) Excess return on stock B	2.25%	1.01%	−0.50%	−1.01%	2.00%
(2) Excess return on the market	1.00%	0.50%	−2.00%	−0.50%	1.00%

a. Calculate the alphas of each company for each of the five days.
b. Calculate the average alphas of the two companies for each of the five days (note that in practice you will need to collect data for a larger number of companies to get reliable averages).
c. Calculate the cumulative average alphas from day one to day five.
d. Plot the cumulative average alphas on a graph similar to the one shown in Exhibit 3.17. Interpret the data: is the market informationally efficient or not?

INTERPRETING FINANCIAL STATEMENTS

Firms are required by regulatory authorities and the stock markets in which their shares are traded – if they are listed on a stock exchange – to provide financial information about their business transactions. The purpose of financial accounting is to systematically collect, organize, and present financial information according to standard rules known as accounting principles or accounting standards. The formal outputs of the financial accounting process are the financial statements.

This chapter presents an overview of the principal financial statements: the balance sheet, the income statement, also called the profit and loss statement (P&L statement) or the statement of income, and the statement of cash flows. The chapter defines the words and expressions that are commonly used in financial accounting and explains the logic of – as well as the relationship between – the three statements. We also show how the statements can be amended, or supplemented, so that managers can better use accounting data to measure the financial performance of their firm or business units. After reading this chapter, you should understand the following:

- The terminology generally used in financial accounting
- How balance sheets, income statements, and statements of cash flows are prepared and how they are interrelated
- The most important accounting principles used to prepare financial statements
- How business and financial decisions affect the financial statements
- How to restructure a balance sheet into a managerial balance sheet
- Measures of performance, such as earnings before interest, tax, depreciation and amortization (EBITDA), and free cash flow

FINANCIAL ACCOUNTING STATEMENTS

Financial statements are formal documents issued by firms to provide financial information about their business and financial transactions. Firms must regularly issue at least three primary statements: a **balance sheet**, an **income statement**, and a **statement of cash flows**. Those statements can be found in the **annual report** that firms publish every year.[1]

The fundamental objective of the balance sheet is to determine the value of the net investment made by the firm's owners (the **shareholders**) in their firm at a specific date. The principal objective of the income statement is to measure the net profit (or loss) generated by the firm's activities during a period of time referred to as the **accounting period** (usually a year). Net profit (or loss) is a measure of the *change* in the value of the owners' investment in their firm during that period. In other words, a profit increases the value of the owners' investment reported in the balance sheet, whereas a loss reduces it. The main objective of the statement of cash flows is to explain how the different activities of the firm generated or consumed cash during the accounting period.

The balance sheet has information about what shareholders collectively own and what they owe at the date of the statement. The income statement has information about the firm's activities that resulted in increases and decreases in the value of the owners' investment in the firm during a period of time, while the statement of cash flows has information about the firm's activities that resulted in increases and decreases in the amount of *cash* held by the firm during the same period. In addition, notes are usually added to the financial statements. They provide more information about the statements' accounts, such as their nature and how they have been valued. Financial statements are prepared according to **accounting standards** and **principles**. Accountants in the US follow two prevailing systems of accounting standards: the US standards known as **Generally Accepted Accounting Principles**, or **US GAAP**, and the international standards known as **International Financial Reporting Standards**, or **IFRS Standards**.[2] Accountants have some leeway in implementing these standards, mostly in the valuation of some items in the balance sheet and income statement. Thus, to make meaningful comparisons between financial statements over time and across firms, it is necessary to check that the standards used, and their implementation, are identical from one period to another and from one firm to another. If they are not, adjustments need to be made.

To illustrate how business transactions are recorded in the financial statements, and to facilitate the understanding of the logic behind these statements, we use the fictitious company called Office Supplies (OS) Distributors. OS Distributors is a distributor of office equipment and supplies.

THE BALANCE SHEET

The main purpose of the balance sheet is to provide an estimate of the cumulative investment made by the firm's owners at a given point in time, generally at the end of the accounting period. This investment is known as **owners' equity**. It is the difference, at a particular date, between what a firm's equity holders collectively own,

---

[1] In many countries, publicly held companies are required to provide additional information and reports. For example, in the United States, publicly held companies are required to provide another report, called the 10-K, if the company is a US one and the 20-F if it is a foreign company listed on a US Exchange.

[2] The world's two most influential accounting standard-setting bodies, the US Financial Accounting Standards Board (FASB) and the International Accounting Standards Board (IASB), are currently working on reducing the differences between US GAAP and IFRS Standards. A summary of the key differences between the two standards can be found in Julie Santoro and Paul Munter (2017).

called **assets** (such as cash, inventories, equipment, and buildings), and what they collectively owe, called **liabilities** (such as debts owed to banks and suppliers):

$$\text{Owners' equity} = \text{Assets} - \text{Liabilities} \tag{4.1}$$

Many other terms are used to refer to owners' equity, including **shareholders' equity, shareholders' funds, book value of equity, equity capital, net worth**, and **net asset value**.

Exhibit 4.1 presents OS Distributors' balance sheets at year-end two years ago (Year –2), one year ago (Year –1), and this year (Year 0). A year-end balance sheet is the *closing*, or *ending*, balance sheet of that year. It is also the *beginning* balance sheet of the next year. Notes at the bottom of the balance sheets provide detailed information about some of the statements' accounts. OS Distributors' balance sheet in Exhibit 4.1 does not follow the format shown in equation 4.1. In the exhibit, assets are listed in one section and liabilities and owners' equity are listed in a different section. The dollar value of assets, however, is equal to the sum of the dollar value of liabilities and owners' equity because equation 4.1 can also be written as follows:

$$\text{Assets} = \text{Liabilities} + \text{Owners' equity} \tag{4.2}$$

According to equation 4.2, a firm's total assets must have the same value as the sum of its liabilities and owners' equity. In general, balance sheets follow the format of Exhibit 4.1 and equation 4.2.

For companies following US GAAP accounting rules, assets are usually listed on the balance sheet in *decreasing* order of liquidity, where **liquidity** is a measure of the speed with which assets can be converted into cash. Cash, the most liquid of all assets, is listed first, and land, the least liquid of all assets, is shown last. Assets are divided into two categories: **current** (or **short-term**) **assets** and **noncurrent** (or **fixed**) **assets**. Current assets are assets that are expected to be converted into cash within one year, whereas fixed assets have a life that is longer than one year.

Liabilities are listed in *increasing* order of **maturity**. **Current** or **short-term liabilities**, which are obligations that must be paid within one year, are listed first. Noncurrent or **long-term liabilities**, which are not due until after one year, are shown last. Liabilities are followed by owners' equity, which does not have to be repaid because it represents the owners' investment in their firm.

Assets and liabilities are usually recorded according to the **conservatism principle**. According to this principle, when in doubt, assets and liabilities should be reported at a value that would be *least* likely to overstate assets or to understate liabilities.

OS Distributors' owners' equity was $64 million, $70 million, and $77 million at the end of Year –2, Year –1, and Year 0, respectively. At each of these dates, owners' equity was equal to the difference between the firm's total assets and its total liabilities. For example, on December 31, Year –1, owners' equity was equal to the difference between total assets of $170 million and total liabilities of $100 million ($66 million of current liabilities plus $34 million of long-term debt). Note that owners' equity is a **residual value**. It is equal to whatever dollar amount is left after deducting all the firm's liabilities from the total amount of its assets. If total liabilities *exceed* total assets, owners' equity is negative and the firm is technically bankrupt. The following sections present a detailed analysis of the balance sheet structure.

CURRENT OR SHORT-TERM ASSETS

Current assets include cash and cash equivalents, accounts receivable, inventories, and prepaid expenses.

EXHIBIT 4.1	OS DISTRIBUTORS' BALANCE SHEETS.

FIGURES IN MILLIONS

	December 31, Year –2 (Two years ago)	December 31, Year –1 (One year ago)	December 31, Year 0 (This year)
Assets			
• **Current assets**			
Cash[1]	$ 6.0	$ 12.0	$ 8.0
Accounts receivable	44.0	48.0	56.0
Inventories	52.0	57.0	72.0
Prepaid expenses[2]	2.0	2.0	1.0
Total current assets	104.0	119.0	137.0
• **Noncurrent assets**			
Financial assets and intangibles	0.0	0.0	0.0
Property, plant, and equipment			
Gross value[3]	$90.0	$90.0	$93.0
less accumulated depreciation	(34.0) 56.0	(39.0) 51.0	(40.0) 53.0
Total noncurrent assets	56.0	51.0	53.0
Total assets	**$160.0**	**$170.0**	**$190.0**
Liabilities and owners' equity			
• **Current liabilities**			
Short-term debt	$ 15.0	$ 22.0	$ 23.0
Owed to banks	$7.0	$14.0	$15.0
Current portion of long-term debt	8.0	8.0	8.0
Accounts payable	37.0	40.0	48.0
Accrued expenses[4]	2.0	4.0	4.0
Total current liabilities	54.0	66.0	75.0
• **Noncurrent liabilities**			
Long-term debt[5]	42.0	34.0	38.0
Total noncurrent liabilities	42.0	34.0	38.0
• **Owners' equity[6]**	64.0	70.0	77.0
Total liabilities and owners' equity	**$160.0**	**$170.0**	**$190.0**

[1] Consists of cash in hand and checking accounts held to facilitate operating activities on which the firm earns no interest.
[2] Prepaid expenses comprises rent paid in advance (when recognized in the income statement, rent is included in selling, general, and administrative expenses).
[3] In Year –1, there was no disposal of existing fixed assets or acquisition of new fixed assets. However, during Year 0, a warehouse was enlarged at a cost of $12 million and existing fixed assets, bought for $9 million in the past, were sold at their net book value of $2 million.
[4] Accrued expenses consists of wages and taxes payable.
[5] Long-term debt is repaid at the rate of $8 million per year. No new long-term debt was incurred during Year –1, but during Year 0, a mortgage loan was obtained from the bank to finance the extension of a warehouse (see note 3).
[6] During the three years, no new shares were issued and none were repurchased.

CASH AND CASH EQUIVALENTS

Cash and cash equivalents include cash in hand and on deposit with banks and short-term investments with a maturity not exceeding one year. These short-term investments are usually referred to as **marketable securities**. They carry little risk and are highly liquid, meaning that they can be easily sold (converted into cash) with minimal change in value, that is, with relatively small capital gain or loss.

Examples of marketable securities are **certificates of deposit (CD)** issued by banks, shares in **money market funds,** short-term **government bills,** and **commercial paper (CP)** issued by corporations with good credit ratings. These securities are described in Chapter 11.

OS Distributors held $6 million in cash at the end of Year –2 This amount rose to $12 million at the end of Year –1 and then fell to $8 million at the end of Year 0 (see Exhibit 4.1). Note that OS Distributors did not hold any marketable securities at the dates of the balance sheets.

ACCOUNTS RECEIVABLE

Most firms do not receive immediate cash payments for the goods or services they sell. They usually let their customers pay their invoices at a later date. The invoices that have not yet been paid by customers at the date of the balance sheet are recorded as **accounts receivable**, also called **trade receivables** or, simply, **receivables**. Accounts receivable are debts owed to the firm by its customers and, for this reason, are also known as **trade debtors**. These assets will be converted into cash when customers pay their bills. The amount is usually reported net of **allowances for doubtful accounts**. Doubtful accounts arise when management expects that some customers may not meet their payment obligations.

OS Distributors' receivables have grown steadily during the three-year period, rising from $44 million at the end of Year –2 to $56 million at the end of Year 0 (see Exhibit 4.1). Chapter 5 examines whether this phenomenon should be cause for concern or is justified by the firm's activity.

INVENTORIES

Inventories are goods held by the firm for future sales (finished goods) or for use in the manufacturing of goods to be sold at a later date (raw materials and work in process). Thus, a manufacturing firm normally has three inventory accounts: one for raw materials, a second for work in process, and a third for finished goods. Inventories are reported in the balance sheet at cost, unless their market value has fallen below their cost. If, for example, some inventories have become obsolete and have an estimated liquidation value lower than their cost, then the firm should report them at their (lower) estimated value. This method, called the **lower-of-cost-or-market**, is an example of the conservatism principle mentioned earlier.

The cost assigned to materials that have not yet entered the production process at the date of the balance sheet is reported as **raw materials inventory**. In addition, some of the units in production may not yet have been completed. The cost of the raw materials that were used in the production of these units plus the labor and other costs applicable to these unfinished units make up the **work in process inventory**. Finally, the cost of completed units not yet sold at the date of the balance sheet constitutes the **finished goods inventory**.

Inventories for OS Distributors consist of goods purchased from manufacturers and stored in its warehouses until sold to retail stores. Like receivables, inventories have grown during the period Year –2 to Year 0, rising from $52 million at the end of Year –2 to $72 million at the end of Year 0. Again, Chapter 5 examines whether this growth should be worrisome or is justified by the firm's operations.

The growth in inventories could be caused by an increase in the price of the items purchased by OS Distributors from its suppliers for resale to its customers. Suppose it paid $100 for an item purchased two weeks ago, $101 for the same item purchased last week, and $102 for the same item purchased this week. OS Distributors holds three identical items in its inventory but paid a different price for each of them. When it sells one of these items to a customer, a question arises: which one has it sold? The first ($100), the second ($101), or the third ($102)?

If OS Distributors uses the **first-in, first-out** (or **FIFO) method** to measure the cost of its inventories, it will assume that it sold the first item it acquired ($100). If it uses the **last-in, first-out** (or **LIFO) method**, it will assume it sold the last item it acquired ($102). Alternatively, OS Distributors could use the **average cost method**. In this case, it will assume it sold an item at the average of the three prices ($101). The implication is clear: the firm's financial statements will be different, depending on which of the three valuation methods is adopted. After the sale of one item, two are left in inventories. With FIFO, the reported value of the remaining two items is $203 ($101 plus $102); with LIFO, the value is $201 ($100 plus $101); and with averaging, the value is $202 ($101 plus $101). Furthermore, if we assume that the item was sold to a customer for $110, the reported gross profit will be $10 with FIFO ($110 less $100), $8 with LIFO ($110 less $102), and $9 with the average cost method ($110 less $101). Compared with LIFO, FIFO *overstates* both the value of inventories ($203 instead of $201) and reported gross profit ($10 instead of $8) when prices are rising. Note that, under IFRS Standards, companies are not permitted to use the LIFO method, but they can under US GAAP and indeed most US companies do so.

PREPAID EXPENSES

Prepaid expenses recorded on a balance sheet are payments made by the firm for goods or services it will receive *after* the date of the balance sheet. A typical example is the payment for an insurance policy that will provide protection for a period of time that extends beyond the date of the balance sheet. It is recorded as a prepaid expense because the payment is made before the firm can benefit from the insurance coverage. Other common prepaid expenses include prepaid rent and leases. OS Distributors' balance sheets in Exhibit 4.1 indicate that the firm had $2 million of prepaid expenses at the end of Year –2 and Year –1 and $1 million at the end of Year 0.

The way prepaid expenses are accounted for illustrates a key accounting principle, known as the **matching principle**. This principle says that expenses are recognized (in the income statement) not when they are paid but during the period when they effectively contribute to the firm's revenues. Expenses *prepaid* by the firm must be carried in its balance sheet as an asset until they become a recognized expense in its (future) income statement.

Suppose, for example, that on January 1, Year –3, OS Distributors paid rent for three years, including rent for Year –3. The rent for the first year (Year –3) would be recorded as an expense in the Year –3 income statement. The remaining two-thirds of the total rent paid on January 1, Year –3, and not "consumed" during the year, would be reported as prepaid expenses in the balance sheet at the end of Year –3.

In the balance sheet at the end of Year –2, prepaid rent would represent only one-third of the total rent payment. On December 31, Year –1, the total rent payment would be completely "consumed" and no prepaid rent would appear in the balance sheet on that date assuming the firm had not entered into a new rental agreement for Year 0 and beyond.

NONCURRENT OR FIXED ASSETS

Noncurrent assets, also called fixed or **capital assets**, are assets that are expected to produce economic benefits for more than one year. These assets are of two types: tangible and intangible. **Tangible assets** are items such as land, buildings, machines, and furniture, collectively called **property, plant, and equipment**. They also include long-term financial assets, such as shares in other companies and loans extended to other firms. **Intangible assets** are items such as patents, trademarks, copyrights, and goodwill.

TANGIBLE ASSETS

Nonfinancial tangible assets are generally reported at their **historical cost**, which is the price the firm paid for them. As time passes, the value of these assets is expected to decrease. To account for this loss of value, their purchase price, reported in the balance sheet as the **gross value** of fixed assets, is systematically reduced (or written down) over their expected useful life.[3] This periodic and systematic value-reduction process is called **depreciation**. If depreciation is done on a yearly basis, the dollar amount by which the gross value of fixed assets is reduced every year is called an annual **depreciation charge** or **expense**. This dollar amount is determined by the length of the period over which the asset is depreciated and the speed with which depreciation takes place.

Several methods are used to determine the annual depreciation charge. The most commonly used is the **straight-line depreciation method**. When this method is used, the firm's assets are depreciated by an equal amount each year. According to the less frequently used **accelerated depreciation method**, the depreciation charge is higher in the early years of the asset's life and lower in the later years. The *total* amount that is depreciated is the same regardless of the depreciation method used; it is equal to the acquisition cost of the asset, assuming that the asset will be worthless at the end of the period over which it is depreciated.

To illustrate the effect of different depreciation methods, consider a firm that paid $300,000 at the beginning of the year for a machine that will be fully depreciated over a period of three years. Although the $300,000 was paid during the year the asset was bought, this amount is not recognized as an expense for that year. If a straight-line depreciation schedule is applied, one-third of the equipment cost is depreciated every year, and the annual depreciation charge is equal to one-third of $300,000, that is, $100,000. An accelerated depreciation schedule might call for half the cost of the equipment to be depreciated in the first year, one-third in the second year, and one-sixth in the third year.

The annual depreciation charges would then be $150,000 in the first year (half of $300,000), $100,000 in the second year (one-third of $300,000), and $50,000 in the third year (one-sixth of $300,000).

---

[3] Note that plant and equipment are systematically depreciated, but not land. It is assumed that the value of land does not decline with the passage of time.

EXHIBIT 4.2	COMPUTATION OF NET BOOK VALUE FOR TWO DEPRECIATION METHODS.

FIGURES IN MILLIONS

	Straight-Line Method			Accelerated Method		
	Year 1	Year 2	Year 3	Year 1	Year 2	Year 3
Gross value (acquisition cost)	$300	$300	$300	$300	$300	$300
Annual depreciation charge	($100)	($100)	($100)	($150)	($100)	($50)
Accumulated depreciation	(100)	(200)	(300)	(150)	(250)	(300)
Net book value	$200	$100	$ 0	$150	$ 50	$ 0

The value at which a fixed asset is reported in the balance sheet is its **net book value**. If the firm applies the **historical** or **acquisition cost principle** to value its fixed assets, then the net book value of a fixed asset is equal to its acquisition price less the **accumulated depreciation** since that asset was bought. In the above example, the net book value of the equipment at the end of each year after the asset was bought is computed as shown in Exhibit 4.2 for the two depreciation methods.

This example clearly illustrates that fixed asset values reported in the balance sheet can differ considerably, depending on the depreciation method applied. It is therefore important to keep this in mind before comparing the financial performance of different firms on the basis of their financial statements.

INTANGIBLE ASSETS

Intangible assets include patents, copyrights, trademarks, property rights, franchises, and licenses. When one firm acquires the assets of another for a price higher than the net book value in the acquired firm's balance sheet, this difference is **goodwill**. For example, suppose Firm A pays $10 million for the assets of Firm B, and the net book value of those assets on Firm B's balance sheet is $7 million. This transaction creates $3 million of goodwill on the balance sheet of Firm A.

Intangible assets are recorded at cost. As in the case of tangible assets, their value is usually gradually reduced as time passes. This cost-reduction process, called **amortization**, follows the same principles as depreciation for tangible assets. An exception is goodwill, which does not have to be amortized. Instead, firms must conduct an annual **impairment test**. If the estimated **fair market value**[4] of the acquired assets, including goodwill, falls below their net book value, goodwill must be reduced by the amount of the difference, called an **impairment loss**. That impairment loss is then reported in the firm's income statement as a reduction in revenues. In the previous example, if Firm A estimates two years after the acquisition of Firm B's assets that the fair market value of these assets is $9 million, it will have to recognize an impairment loss of $1 million by reducing goodwill from $3 million to $2 million ($3 million less $1 million).

---

[4] Fair market value is usually estimated using a discounted cash-flow technique, explained in Chapter 10.

OS DISTRIBUTORS' NONCURRENT ASSETS

We can now examine the structure of OS Distributors' fixed assets, as reported in Exhibit 4.1. They include only property, plant, and equipment. Their net book value was $56 million at the end of Year –2, $51 million at the end of Year –1, and $53 million at the end of Year 0. Annual depreciation charges, recorded as expenses in OS Distributors' income statements in Exhibit 4.7, were $5 million, $5 million, and $8 million, respectively.

At the end of Year –2, the **book value** of OS Distributors' fixed assets before depreciation (their gross value) was $90 million. This was the price paid when these assets were acquired. Accumulated depreciation was $34 million, so the net book value of the firm's fixed assets was $56 million, which was the difference between their gross value ($90 million) and accumulated depreciation ($34 million).

During Year –1, fixed assets did not change, so their gross value remained at $90 million (see note 3 in Exhibit 4.1). **Net fixed assets**, however, dropped to $51 million because accumulated depreciation increased to $39 million, the sum of accumulated depreciation at the end of Year –2 ($34 million) and the additional depreciation charge in Year –1 ($5 million).

During Year 0, OS Distributors enlarged its warehouse at a cost of $12 million. That same year, the firm sold a piece of equipment it no longer needed at its net book value of $2 million. (The equipment was bought some time ago for $9 million and had been depreciated by $7 million.) What was the effect of these two transactions on the value of net fixed assets at the end of Year 0? The gross value of the fixed assets increased by $12 million when the warehouse was enlarged and decreased by $9 million when the equipment no longer needed was sold. Together, these two transactions increased the gross value of the fixed assets from $90 million at the end of Year –1 to $93 million at the end of Year 0 ($90 million plus $12 million less $9 million), as shown in Exhibit 4.1. At the same time, accumulated depreciation increased by $8 million (the Year 0 depreciation charge) and decreased by $7 million (the recorded accumulated depreciation of the piece of equipment that was sold the same year). Thus, accumulated depreciation increased to $40 million ($39 million of initial accumulated depreciation plus $8 million less $7 million). Consequently, the net book value of OS Distributors' fixed assets at the end of Year 0 was equal to $53 million ($93 million less $40 million).

You could have obtained the same net book value of $53 million in a different way: start with the $51 million of net fixed assets at the end of Year –1, add the $12 million cost of the warehouse extension, and subtract both the net book value of the piece of equipment that was sold ($2 million) and the Year 0 depreciation charge of $8 million ($51 million plus $12 million less $2 million less $8 million equals $53 million). More generally:

Net fixed assets at the end of a period =
Net fixed assets at the beginning of the period
+ Gross value of fixed assets acquired during the period
− Net book value of fixed assets sold during the period
− Depreciation charges for the period   (4.3)

CURRENT OR SHORT-TERM LIABILITIES

Current liabilities include short-term debt, accounts payable, and accrued expenses.

SHORT-TERM DEBT

Short-term debt includes **notes payable**, bank **overdrafts**, drawings on **credit lines (lines of credit)**, and short-term **promissory notes**. The portion of any long-term debt due within a year is also a short-term obligation and is recorded in the balance sheet as a short-term borrowing.

OS Distributors' short-term borrowings consist of debt owed to banks and the portion of long-term debt being repaid by the firm at the rate of $8 million per year from Year –2 to Year 0. In total, short-term borrowing grew from $15 million at the end of Year –2 to $23 million at the end of Year 0.

ACCOUNTS PAYABLE

Accounts payable, also called **trade payables** or, simply, **payables**, are liabilities to the firm's suppliers of goods and services. Payables arise because the firm does not usually pay its suppliers immediately for the goods and services received from them. As a result, there is a time lag between the receipt of goods or services and payment for them. Until payment is made, the firm must recognize in its balance sheet the credit extended by its suppliers. (For this reason, payables are also known as **trade creditors**.) Accounts payable are equal to the dollar value of the invoices the firm has received from its suppliers but has not yet paid at the date of the balance sheet.

The balance sheets in Exhibit 4.1 show that OS Distributors' payables have increased from $37 million at the end of Year –2 to $48 million at the end of Year 0. Is that increase justified? This question is examined in the next chapter.

ACCRUED EXPENSES

Accrued expenses are liabilities other than short-term debt and accounts payable that are associated with the firm's operations. They arise from the lag between the date at which these expenses have been incurred and the date at which they are paid. Examples are wages and payroll taxes that are due but have not yet been paid on the date of the balance sheet. Note that the allocation of expenses to the accrued expenses account in the balance sheet is another application of the matching principle.

OS Distributors' accrued expenses were $2 million at year-end Year –2 and $4 million at year-ends Year –1 and Year 0. They consist of wages and taxes payable. **Wages payable** represent compensation for vacation days owed to OS Distributors' employees that had not yet been taken at the date of the balance sheets. OS Distributors must recognize its "debt" to its employees as wages payable in its balance sheet. Similarly, **taxes payable** is the amount of taxes owed at the date of the balance sheets. They are a debt to the tax collection agency and are recognized as taxes payable in the balance sheet until the firm pays its tax bill.

NONCURRENT LIABILITIES

Long-term liabilities reported on the balance sheet are liabilities with a maturity longer than one year at the date of the balance sheet. Examples of long-term liabilities are **long-term debt** owed to lenders, **pension liabilities** owed to employees (to be paid to them when they retire), and **deferred taxes** owed to the government's tax collection agency.

Deferred taxes originate from temporary differences between the amount of tax due reported in the income statement and the amount of tax claimed by the tax authorities. These two measures of tax expenses may differ because firms usually depreciate their fixed assets on a straight-line basis in their financial statements while the tax authorities apply accelerated depreciation schedules to some of these assets. As a result, the amount of depreciation that is effectively taxable during a given accounting period is different from the amount reported in the income statement. Using the same tax rate, the two approaches can produce different taxable income and thus different tax expenses.[5]

Consider a firm with $1,000,000 of revenues and $700,000 of expenses *before* depreciation charges are deducted. If depreciation charges are $100,000 on the basis of a straight-line depreciation schedule and $150,000 on the basis of an accelerated depreciation schedule, then profit before tax is $200,000 in the first case ($1,000,000 less $700,000 less $100,000) and $150,000 in the second ($1,000,000 less $700,000 less $150,000). If the tax rate is 40 percent, the amount of tax is $80,000 (40 percent of $200,000) when straight-line depreciation is used and $60,000 (40 percent of $150,000) when accelerated depreciation is used. In other words, the firm reports a tax expense of $80,000 in its income statement but actually owes only $60,000 in taxes. The difference of $20,000 between the two tax estimates represents a *postponement*, not an *elimination* of the tax owed to the collecting agency. The amount that is depreciated (the asset acquisition price) and the total amount that is deductible are the same in both cases; hence, the $20,000 must be recognized as a liability in the firm's balance sheet.[6]

OS Distributors had an outstanding (not yet repaid) long-term debt of $50 million at the end of Year −2. However, the firm repays $8 million of this debt every year, and this amount is recorded as a short-term borrowing (current portion of long-term debt). As a result, the long-term debt in the Year −2 balance sheet was equal to only $42 million ($50 million less $8 million due within a year). At the end of Year −1, the firm had repaid $8 million of its outstanding debt, but it still owed $42 million, $8 million of which was due in Year 0. Consequently, its long-term debt at that date was $34 million ($42 million less $8 million) and the current portion of its long-term debt was $8 million.

In Year 0, the firm borrowed $12 million to finance the extension of its warehouse (see note 5 in Exhibit 4.1). As a consequence, long-term debt increased by $12 million in Year 0, while still decreasing by the annual repayment of $8 million. Therefore, the long-term debt at the end of Year 0 was equal to $38 million (the initial $34 million less $8 million due within a year plus $12 million of new debt). In general:

Long-term debt at the end of a period =
Long-term debt at the beginning of the period
− Portion of long-term debt due during the period
+ New long-term debt issued during the period   (4.4)

---

[5] Note that the depreciation tax credit is the same for the two approaches; it is equal to the acquisition price of the asset times the tax rate. The difference is in the way this credit is distributed over the asset's life.

[6] Compared with the straight-line depreciation method, accelerated depreciation schedules overestimate depreciation expenses (underestimate profit before tax) during the beginning of the life of an asset, and likewise underestimate depreciation expenses (overestimate profit before tax) toward the end of the asset's life. Accordingly, the firm pays fewer taxes during the early years and more taxes during the later years of the asset's life.

OWNERS' EQUITY

As shown in equation 4.1, owners' equity at the date of the balance sheet is simply the difference between the book value of the firm's assets and liabilities at that same date. The book value of the investment made in the firm by OS Distributors' owners is reported at the bottom of the balance sheets in Exhibit 4.1. Owners' equity has grown from $64 million at the end of Year –2 to $77 million at the end of Year 0.

In most balance sheets, the owners' equity account shows several components, each representing a source of equity. Because one of these sources is the firm's reinvested profit, we postpone the presentation of the components of owners' equity (and the reason for the growth of OS Distributors' equity) until after the firm's income statement is discussed.

THE MANAGERIAL BALANCE SHEET

For managers of a firm's operating activities, the standard balance sheet as shown in Exhibit 4.1 for OS Distributors may not be the most appropriate tool for assessing their contribution to the firm's financial performance. To illustrate this point, consider trade payables. They are correctly recorded in the balance sheet as a liability because they represent cash owed to suppliers. Most operating managers, however, would consider trade payables an account under their full responsibility, much like trade receivables (cash owed to the firm by its customers) and inventories, both of which are recorded on the asset side of the balance sheet. It makes more *managerial* sense to associate trade payables with trade receivables and inventories than to combine them with other liabilities – such as short-term borrowings and long-term debt – that are primarily the responsibility of the financial manager. Keeping in mind the concerns of operating managers as well as those of financial managers, we restructure the standard balance sheet into a new one, called the **managerial balance sheet**, as shown in Exhibit 4.3.

On the left side of the managerial balance sheet, three items are grouped under the heading **invested capital**. These are cash and cash-equivalent holdings, **working capital requirement** (the difference between the firm's **operating assets** and its **operating liabilities**), and net fixed assets:

$$\text{Invested capital} = \text{Cash} + \text{Working capital requirement} + \text{Net fixed assets} \quad (4.5)$$

On the right side of the managerial balance sheet, two items are grouped under the heading **capital employed**. These are short-term debt and long-term financing, the latter consisting of long-term debt and owners' equity (we use the terms *financing, funding,* and *capital* interchangeably):[7,8]

$$\text{Capital employed} = \text{Short-term debt} + \text{Long-term debt} + \text{Owners' equity} \quad (4.6)$$

---

[7] For simplification purposes we assume that there are no other long-term liabilities. If there are any, they should be added to long-term debt. Similarly, short-term provisions, if any, should be included in capital employed. See Appendix 4.1.

[8] In practice, many companies and financial analysts define capital employed as the amount of capital used to finance a firm's core activities. Because many firms, especially large ones, hold cash far in excess of what is needed to run the cash transactions associated with their fundamental activities, capital employed is then defined as the sum of equity capital and net debt, the *difference* between debt (short- and long-term) and the amount of cash held by the firm. Some analysts and companies go as far as excluding noninterest-bearing debt, such as pension fund liabilities, from capital employed, on the basis that no (accounting) costs are associated with their use in financing the firm's activities.

EXHIBIT 4.3	FROM THE STANDARD BALANCE SHEET TO THE MANAGERIAL BALANCE SHEET.

The Standard Balance Sheet

Assets	Liabilities and owners' equity
Cash	**Short-term debt**
Operating assets *Accounts receivable* *plus* *Inventories* *plus* *Prepaid expenses*	**Operating liabilities** *Accounts payable* *plus* *Accrued expenses*
	Long-term financing *Long-term debt* *plus* *Owners' equity*
Net fixed assets	

The Managerial Balance Sheet

Invested capital	Capital employed
Cash	**Short-term debt**
Working capital requirement (WCR) *Operating assets* *less* *Operating liabilities*	**Long-term financing** *Long-term debt* *plus* *Owners' equity*
Net fixed assets	

Except for working capital requirement, which is examined in the following section, all the other accounts are the same in both balance sheets.

WORKING CAPITAL REQUIREMENT

Fixed assets alone cannot generate sales and profits. The managerial activities required to operate these assets in order to generate sales and profit are referred to

EXHIBIT 4.4   THE FIRM'S OPERATING CYCLE AND ITS EFFECT ON THE FIRM'S BALANCE SHEET.

Δ = CHANGE IN THE BALANCE SHEET ACCOUNT

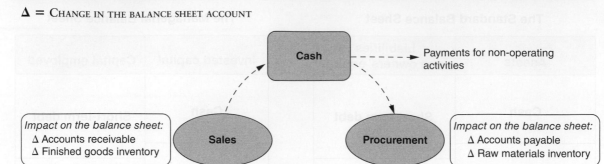

as the firm's **operating activities**. These activities require investments in the form of inventories and trade receivables as shown in the firm's **operating cycle**, described in Exhibit 4.4 for a manufacturing company.

The cycle starts on the right side with *procurement*, the act of acquiring raw materials. It is followed by *production*, during which the raw materials are transformed into finished goods. The cycle continues with the *sales* of these goods, ending when cash is collected from customers. The cycle repeats itself as long as the firm's production activity continues.

Each stage in the operating cycle affects the firm's balance sheet. Exhibit 4.4 shows the balance sheet accounts that change at each stage of the cycle. For example, when the firm buys raw materials (procurement), both inventories and accounts payable increase by the same amount – the former to reflect the purchase of the raw materials and the latter to acknowledge a debt to the firm's suppliers.

An alternative way to describe the operating cycle is shown in Exhibit 4.5. In this case, the firm pays its suppliers before receiving cash from its customers because it holds inventories (of raw materials, work in process, and finished goods) and accounts receivable over a period of time that is *longer* than its payment period. The period between the date the firm pays its suppliers and the date it collects its invoices is called the **cash-to-cash period** (or **cycle**) or the **cash conversion period** (or **cycle**).

What is the *net* investment (at the date of the balance sheet) that the firm must make to support its operating cycle? It is simply the sum of its inventories and accounts receivable less its accounts payable. If prepaid expenses are included in the firm's operating assets and accrued expenses are included in its operating liabilities, then the firm's net investment in its operating cycle is measured (at the date of the balance sheet) by the difference between its operating assets and operating liabilities.

EXHIBIT 4.5	THE FIRM'S OPERATING CYCLE, SHOWING THE CASH-TO-CASH PERIOD.

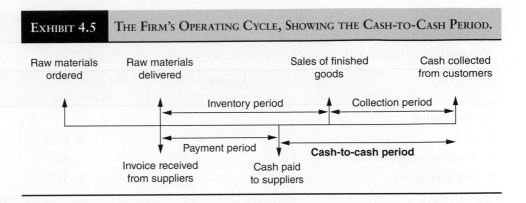

This difference is the working capital requirement (**WCR**), or **operating working capital**:

Working capital requirement (WCR) =
[Operating assets − Operating liabilities] =
[Accounts receivable + Inventories + Prepaid expenses]
− [Accounts payable + Accrued expenses]   (4.7)

WCR does not include the firm's cash holdings. There are two reasons for this. First, a company holds cash not only to support its operating activities but also to meet future cash expenses that are not related to its operations, such as the payment of dividends and the purchase of fixed assets. Second, operating cash is a separate investment held for precautionary reasons to meet payment obligations resulting from unexpected short-term changes in components of the WCR.

Finally, WCR does not include the firm's short-term debt. Short-term debt is used to finance the firm's investments, including its WCR. It may contribute to the financing of the firm's operating cycle, but it is not a component of it.[9]

With the information in the balance sheets in Exhibit 4.1, we can calculate OS Distributors' working capital requirement on December 31, Year −2, Year −1, and Year 0, using equation 4.7:

$$WCR_{12/31/Year\ -2} = \$44\ million + \$52\ million + \$2\ million$$
$$- \$37\ million - \$2\ million = \$59\ million$$
$$WCR_{12/31/Year\ -1} = \$48\ million + \$57\ million + \$2\ million$$
$$- \$40\ million - \$4\ million = \$63\ million$$
$$WCR_{12/31/Year\ 0} = \$56\ million + \$72\ million + \$1\ million$$
$$- \$48\ million - \$4\ million = \$77\ million$$

These are the figures reported in OS Distributors' managerial balance sheets shown in Exhibit 4.6. OS Distributors' WCR has risen from $59 million in Year −2 to $77 million in Year 0. How can we explain this growth? We examine this issue in the next chapter.

---

[9] Note that WCR can be negative. This happens when operating liabilities (accounts payable and accrued expenses) exceed operating assets (accounts receivable, inventories, and prepaid expenses). We examine this situation in Chapter 5.

EXHIBIT 4.6	OS DISTRIBUTORS' MANAGERIAL BALANCE SHEETS.

ALL DATA FROM THE BALANCE SHEETS IN EXHIBIT 4.1. FIGURES IN MILLIONS

	December 31, Year –2		December 31, Year –1		December 31, Year 0	
Invested capital						
• Cash	$ 6.0		$ 12.0		$ 8.0	
• Working capital requirement (WCR)[1]	59.0		63.0		77.0	
• Net fixed assets	56.0		51.0		53.0	
Total invested capital	**$121.0**		**$126.0**		**$138.0**	
Capital employed						
• Short-term debt	$ 15.0		$ 22.0		$ 23.0	
• Long-term financing						
Long-term debt	$42.0		$34.0		$38.0	
Owners' equity	64.0	106.0	70.0	104.0	77.0	115.0
Total capital employed	**$121.0**		**$126.0**		**$138.0**	

[1] WCR = (Accounts receivable + Inventories + Prepaid expenses) − (Accounts payable + Accrued expenses).

The managerial balance sheet provides a snapshot of the total capital used by the firm at a point in time (the capital employed shown in the bottom half) and the way that capital is invested (the invested capital shown in the top half). When we analyze business decisions in the remaining chapters, we will systematically refer to the managerial balance sheet as a relevant alternative to the standard balance sheet.

THE INCOME STATEMENT

The purpose of the income statement, also called the **profit and loss** or **P&L statement**, is to present a summary of the operating and financial transactions that have contributed to the change in the firm's owners' equity during the accounting period.[10] The accounting period is usually one year, but limited versions of the income statement can be produced more frequently, as often as quarterly.

We define **revenues** as the transactions that increase owners' equity and **expenses** as the transactions that decrease owners' equity during the accounting period. It follows that the net change in owners' equity during that period, known as **net income**, **net profit**, or, as shown in Exhibit 4.7, **earnings after tax (EAT)**, is simply

$$\text{Earnings after tax} = \text{Revenues} - \text{Expenses} \qquad (4.8)$$

This relationship is the model used to construct a firm's income statement. The firm's revenues are recorded first. They originate from many sources, including the sales

[10] There is one exception to these definitions. The issuance of new owners' equity increases it, and the repurchase of outstanding shares decreases it. These transactions, however, are not recorded in the firm's income statement as revenues or expenses.

EXHIBIT 4.7	OS DISTRIBUTORS' INCOME STATEMENTS.

FIGURES IN MILLIONS

	Year −2		Year −1		Year 0	
• Net sales	$390.0	100.0%	$420.0	100.0%	$480.0	100.0%
Cost of goods sold	328.0		353.0		400.0	
• Gross profit	62.0	15.9%	67.0	16.0%	80.0	16.7%
Selling, general, and administrative expenses	39.8		43.7		48.0	
Depreciation expense	5.0		5.0		8.0	
• Operating profit	17.2	4.4%	18.3	4.4%	24.0	5.0%
Special items	0.0		0.0		0.0	
• Earnings before interest and tax (EBIT)	17.2	4.4%	18.3	4.4%	24.0	5.0%
Net interest expense[1]	5.5		5.0		7.0	
• Earnings before tax (EBT)	11.7	3.0%	13.3	3.2%	17.0	3.5%
Income tax expense	4.7		5.3		6.8	
• Earnings after tax (EAT)	$ 7.0	1.8%	$ 8.0	1.9%	$ 10.2	2.1%
Dividends	$ 2.0		$ 2.0		$ 3.2	
Addition to retained earnings	$ 5.0		$ 6.0		$ 7.0	

[1] There is no interest income, so net interest expense is equal to interest expense.

of goods and services and the collection of fees and rental income. Then the firm's expenses are listed. They include material costs, depreciation charges, salaries, wages, administrative and marketing expenses, and interest and tax expenses. Expenses are deducted from revenues in a multiple-step procedure to measure the contribution of different activities to the firm's earnings after tax (see Exhibit 4.7).

The revenues and expenses related to the firm's operating activities are shown first, followed by those related to nonoperating activities, that is financing activities. Finally, the tax expense is reported. A detailed explanation of the structure of a firm's income statement is given in the following sections.

Among the many accounting principles used to construct financial statements, two are of particular importance in understanding the income statement. First is the **realization principle**, which says that revenue is recognized during the period in which the transaction generating the revenue takes place, *not when the cash from the transaction is received*. In other words, the firm's revenues increase when a product it sells or a service it renders is invoiced or sent to the customer, not when the cash payment takes place. Revenues are unaffected when payment is made. When the payment is received, the firm adjusts its balance sheet accordingly: cash rises by the amount received, and accounts receivable decrease by the same amount.

The second principle is the matching principle, which was explained in the discussion of the valuation of prepaid expenses. According to this principle, expenses associated with a product or service are recognized when the product is sold or the service rendered, *not when the expense is actually paid*. For example, consider a distribution company that purchases an item from a wholesaler, stocks it, and then sells it. Expenses will increase during the period when the item is sold, not when it was purchased and not when the company paid for it.

The realization and matching principles form the basis of what is known as **accrual accounting**. A consequence of accrual accounting is that a firm's earnings after tax are *not* equal to the difference between the firm's cash inflows and outflows that occurred during the accounting period (the firm's **total net cash flow**). For example, the fact that OS Distributors realized a net profit of $10.2 million in Year 0 does not mean that the firm has generated $10.2 million of cash during that year.

NET SALES OR TURNOVER

For most firms, sales are the main source of revenues. The revenues of the accounting period, net of any discounts and allowances for defective merchandise, make up the **net sales** or **turnover** account. OS Distributors' sales grew 7.7 percent during Year –1, from $390 million in Year –2 to $420 million in Year –1. Sales rose to $480 million in Year 0. Thus, the growth rate in Year 0 was 14.3 percent, almost double the Year –1 growth rate. The next chapter examines the consequences of this acceleration in the growth rate in sales on the firm's income statement and balance sheet.

COST OF GOODS SOLD

The **cost of goods sold (COGS),** sometimes called **cost of sales**, represents the cost of the goods the firm has sold during the accounting period. For a distribution company such as OS Distributors, the COGS is the acquisition price of the items sold from inventory plus any direct costs related to these items. In a manufacturing firm, goods incur various costs in the process of transformation from raw material to finished product, such as labor and other direct manufacturing costs. These costs make up the value of the finished goods inventory. They become COGS when the goods are released from inventory for sale. Depreciation expense on plant and equipment is often included in the COGS, although some firms report depreciation as a separate account in their income statement.

OS Distributors' COGS consists of goods purchased from manufacturers for resale to retailers. (Depreciation expense on the firm's warehouses is shown separately.) COGS rose from $328 million in Year –2 to $400 million in Year 0.

GROSS PROFIT

Gross profit is the first and broadest measure of the firm's profit shown in its income statement. It is the difference between the firm's net sales and its cost of goods sold. OS Distributors' gross profit was $62 million in Year –2, $67 million in Year –1, and $80 million in Year 0. Gross profit rose from 15.9 percent of sales in Year –2 to 16.7 percent of sales in Year 0 because the firm's COGS grew at a slightly slower rate than sales.

SELLING, GENERAL, AND ADMINISTRATIVE EXPENSES

Selling, general, and administrative (SG&A) expenses, sometimes referred to as **overhead expenses** or simply overhead, are the expenses incurred by the firm that relate to the sale of its products and the running of its operations during the accounting period. Expenses related to the training of sales people are an example of overhead. For OS Distributors, SG&A amounted to $39.8 million in Year –2, $43.7 million in Year –1, and $48.0 million in Year 0.

DEPRECIATION EXPENSE

Depreciation expense is the depreciation charge defined in the discussion of the balance sheet. It represents the portion of the cost of fixed assets that is expensed during the accounting period. When a fixed asset is purchased, the firm incurs a cost equal to the purchase price. This cost is recorded in the balance sheet as the gross value of the fixed asset. It is then charged or "expensed" (according to a depreciation schedule) over the years during which the asset is expected to generate some benefits. The amount expensed during each accounting period is recorded in the income statement in the depreciation expense account.[11] If the firm expensed the full cost of a fixed asset the same year it acquired it, the matching principle would be violated. A fixed asset, by definition, generates benefits beyond the year in which it was purchased. Thus, allocating its full cost to the purchase year would cause a mismatch between expenses and revenues for a number of years.

OPERATING PROFIT

Operating profit is a measure of the firm's profit from continuing operations that takes into account all of the firm's recorded expenses related to its operating activities: its cost of goods sold, its SG&A, and its depreciation expense. It is the difference between the firm's gross profit and the sum of the SG&A and depreciation expense. It measures the profit generated by the firm's normal and recurrent business activities before interest expense, nonrecurring gains and losses, and taxes. OS Distributors generated an operating profit of $17.2 million in Year –2, $18.3 million in Year –1, and $24 million in Year 0. Operating profit, measured as a percentage of sales, rose from 4.4 percent of sales in Year –2 to 5 percent of sales in Year 0.

SPECIAL ITEMS

Special items are transactions which are unusual or infrequent, such as extraordinary and exceptional losses and gains, nonrecurring items, losses and gains related to discontinued operations, and impairment losses resulting from a reduction in the value of goodwill. OS Distributors had no special items to report in its income statements. Note that, under IFRS Standards, special items are prohibited. The related transactions are recorded like any other revenue or expense.

EARNINGS BEFORE INTEREST AND TAX (EBIT)

Earnings before interest and tax, or **EBIT,** is the firm's operating profit less any special items such as earnings, capital gains, or losses from businesses or other investments that were sold during the accounting period. Because OS Distributors has not reported any special items in Year –2, Year –1, and Year 0 (see the company's income statements in Exhibit 4.7), its earnings before interest and tax in each of these three years are the same as its operating profits. Chapter 6 shows that EBIT

---

[11] Note that a "cost" can be either "capitalized" (meaning that it is recorded in the balance sheet) or "expensed" (meaning that it is recorded in the income statement).

plays an important role in the analysis of a firm's profitability because it enables the comparison of profitability for firms with different debt policies and tax obligations.

NET INTEREST EXPENSE

Net interest expense is the interest expense incurred by the firm on its borrowings less any income it received from its financial investments during the accounting period. OS Distributors has no interest income (see note 1 of the company's income statements); hence, the firm's net interest expense is equal to its total interest expense.

EARNINGS BEFORE TAX (EBT)

Earnings before tax, or **EBT,** is the difference between the firm's EBIT and its net interest expense. It is a measure of a firm's profits before taking taxation into account. OS Distributors' EBT was $11.7 million in Year –2, $13.3 million in Year –1, and $17 million in Year 0. Expressed as a percentage of sales, EBT grew from 3 percent of sales in Year –2 to 3.5 percent of sales in Year 0. This improvement in the firm's pre-tax profits in comparison to its sales is analyzed in detail in Chapter 6.

INCOME TAX EXPENSE

The income tax expense account is a tax provision computed in accordance with the firm's accounting rules. As mentioned earlier, this tax provision frequently differs from the actual income tax that the firm must pay. The difference is accounted for in the deferred tax account in the balance sheet. OS Distributors has no deferred taxes. Tax expense is thus equal to 40 percent of the firm's pre-tax profits.

EARNINGS AFTER TAX (EAT)

Earnings after tax, or **EAT,** are obtained by deducting the firm's income tax expense from its reported pre-tax profits, or EBT. It is also called the firm's **net earnings, net profit,** or **net income,** and often is referred to as the firm's **bottom line.** When earnings after tax are positive, the firm has generated a profit and is said to be **in the black.** When its earnings after tax are negative, the firm has generated a loss and is said to be **in the red.** More precisely, earnings after tax are a measure of the net change in owners' equity resulting from the transactions recorded in the income statement during the accounting period.

OS Distributors' earnings after tax were $7 million in Year –2, $8 million in Year –1, and $10.2 million in Year 0. As a percentage of sales, they grew from 1.8 percent in Year –2 to 2.1 percent in Year 0. Are the levels and growth rates of OS Distributors' earnings after tax adequate? The answer to this important question is the topic of Chapter 6.

EARNINGS BEFORE INTEREST, TAX, DEPRECIATION, AND AMORTIZATION (EBITDA)

Earnings before interest, tax, depreciation, and amortization (EBITDA) is a popular performance indicator among financial analysts. It is defined as follows:

Earnings before interest, tax, depreciation, and amortization (EBITDA) =
Revenues − Expenses excluding interest, tax, depreciation, and amortization   (4.9)

where revenues and expenses are from the income statement. Note the difference between EBITDA and EBIT: they differ by the amount of depreciation and amortization expenses (in the case of OS Distributors there is no amortization expense, so the difference comes only from depreciation expense). Thus, we can write:

$$\text{EBITDA} = \text{EBIT} + \text{Depreciation expense} + \text{Amortization expense} \qquad (4.10)$$

For OS Distributors, EBITDA in Year −2 was $22.2 million ($17.2 million of EBIT plus $5 million of depreciation expense). It was $23.3 million in Year −1 ($18.3 million plus $5 million), and $32 million in Year 0 ($24 million plus $8 million).

EBITDA is a relevant measure of operating profit when comparing operating profitability between companies in the same industry because it is not affected by the firms' financing decisions (interest expenses, a direct consequence of financing some assets by debt, are excluded from EBITDA), nor by their decision to use different depreciation or amortization schedules for fixed and intangible assets. EBITDA is also often used as a measure of performance when valuing companies using earnings multiples (see Chapters 10 and 14). But you should be aware that EBITDA alone cannot be an indicator of value creation. Take two firms generating the same EBITDA. Would you infer that their ability to create value is the same if one is using twice as much invested capital than the other one?

RECONCILING BALANCE SHEETS AND INCOME STATEMENTS

Transactions other than those recorded in the income statement can also affect owners' equity. For example, when a firm declares a **cash dividend** to be paid to its owners, the book value of owners' equity in the firm's balance sheet decreases by the amount of the declared **dividend**. Thus, the *net* increase in owners' equity is the difference between net earnings and dividends. This difference is called *addition to retained earnings*. When a firm sells (issues) new shares during the accounting period, the amount raised, less issuance costs, increases the firm's owners' equity. Conversely, when a firm repurchases some of its own shares, the amount paid to the shareholders who tender their shares, less transaction costs, decreases the firm's owners' equity. In general:

> Net change in owners' equity = Earnings after tax
> − Dividends + Amount raised by new share issuance
> − Amount paid for share repurchase $\qquad (4.11)$

OS Distributors did not issue or repurchase shares during the three-year period from Year −2 to Year 0 (see note 6 in Exhibit 4.1). As a result, each year's change in owners' equity was exactly equal to the addition to retained earnings from that year. Additions to retained earnings are reported at the bottom of Exhibit 4.7. OS Distributors retained $5 million of its net earnings at the end of Year −2, $6 million at the end of Year −1, and $7 million at the end of Year 0. Therefore, owners' equity at the end of Year −1 was equal to $70 million, the sum of owners' equity at the end of Year −2 ($64 million) and earnings retained in Year −1 ($6 million). At the end of Year 0, owners' equity had grown to $77 million, the sum of owners' equity at the end of Year −1 ($70 million) and earnings retained in Year 0 ($7 million).

The link between a firm's managerial balance sheets and its income statements is illustrated in Exhibit 4.8 for OS Distributors.

On the left side of this exhibit is OS Distributors' managerial balance sheet on December 31, Year −1, and on the right side is its managerial balance sheet on

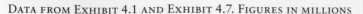

> **EXHIBIT 4.8**   OS DISTRIBUTORS: THE LINK BETWEEN THE MANAGERIAL BALANCE SHEETS AND THE INCOME STATEMENT.

DATA FROM EXHIBIT 4.1 AND EXHIBIT 4.7. FIGURES IN MILLIONS

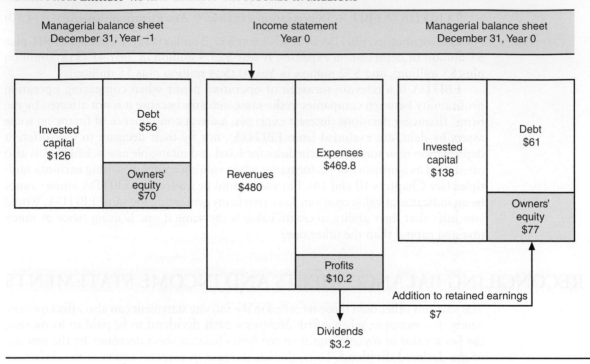

December 31, Year 0. Between the two balance sheets is the income statement for Year 0. The balance sheets show the book value of the firm's invested capital on the left side and the sum of its liabilities and owners' equity on the other side (capital employed). The income statement shows the firm's revenues on the left side and the sum of its expenses and its profits on the right side.

OS Distributors generated $480 million of sales revenues during Year 0. To get those sales, it used $126 million of invested capital (as indicated on the managerial balance sheet at the end of Year –1). After deducting $469.8 million of total expenses from its sales, OS Distributors reported a net profit of $10.2 million in Year 0. It declared a dividend of $3.2 million and retained the rest ($7 million). Because it had not raised new equity in Year 0, the firm's owners' equity increased at the end of Year 0 to $77 million, the sum of its original owners' equity of $70 million at year-end Year –1 and the retained earnings of $7 million.

Firms usually report changes in owners' equity, such as cash dividends, and stock issued and repurchased, in the **statement of shareholders' equity**.

THE STRUCTURE OF THE OWNERS' EQUITY ACCOUNT

Our analysis of owners' equity has shown that the *changes* in owners' equity come from earnings that are retained, net of any new issues of equity or any share repurchases that occurred during the accounting period. The owners' equity account in the balance sheet represents the accumulated contribution of these changes over many accounting periods, from the date at which the firm was created until the date of the balance sheet.

To clarify the origin of their equity, most firms provide a breakdown of their owners' equity into separate accounts that identify the different sources of equity. The most common items making up the owners' equity account are shown in Exhibit 4.9, which presents a detailed account of OS Distributors' owners' equity at year-end Year 0.

The first source of equity shown is **common stock**. The dollar amount is the number of shares the firm has issued since its creation multiplied by the **par value**, or **stated value**, of the shares. The par value of a common stock is an *arbitrary* fixed value assigned to each share of stock that is unrelated to its *market* price. The par value was set by those who created the firm and is stated in the firm's charter. It represents the maximum liability of the owner of the share in the event of the firm's liquidation. OS Distributors had 10 million shares outstanding at the end of Year 0, and each of the firm's shares has a par value of $1. Thus, the firm's common stock was recorded at $10 million at the end of Year 0.

The second source of equity shown is **paid-in capital in excess of par** or **share premium**. This is the difference between the cumulative amount of cash that the firm received from shares issued up to the date of the balance sheet and the cash it would have received if those shares had been issued at par value. The paid-in capital of OS Distributors was $20 million at the end of Year 0, indicating that the firm issued shares in the past that were sold for more than $1. Suppose, for example, that 1 million shares were sold five years ago for $5 each. That year, OS Distributors' paid-in capital in excess of par increased by $4 million, 1 million shares multiplied by the difference between $5 and a par value of $1.

The third source of equity, **retained earnings** or **reserves**, is the total amount of retained earnings since the creation of the firm. For OS Distributors, this "earned" capital amounted to $47 million at the end of Year 0.

The last account, **treasury stock**, is subtracted from the previous accounts. It represents the amount the firm spent to repurchase its shares up to the date of the balance sheet. OS Distributors has not repurchased any of its shares, so this account remains equal to zero.

THE STATEMENT OF CASH FLOWS

The purpose of the statement of cash flows is to present a summary of the cash flows from different activities of the firm that explains the *change* in the firm's amount of cash over the accounting period.

EXHIBIT 4.9	OS DISTRIBUTORS: OWNERS' EQUITY ON DECEMBER 31, YEAR 0.

FIGURES IN MILLIONS

	December 31, Year 0
Common stock	$10
10,000,000 shares at par value of $1	
Paid-in capital in excess of par	20
Retained earnings	47
(Treasury stocks)	(0)
Owners' equity	**$77**

The amount of cash held by a firm at a particular moment in time is found in the cash account on the asset side of its balance sheet. OS Distributors' balance sheets in Exhibit 4.1 show that the firm had $6 million in cash at the end of Year –2, $12 million at the end of Year –1, and $8 million at the end of Year 0. Define **total net cash flow** as the difference between the total amount of dollars received (**cash inflows**) and the total amount of dollars paid out (**cash outflows**). When OS Distributors received a dollar, its cash account increased by a dollar; each time it spent a dollar, its cash account decreased by a dollar. The amount of cash held by OS Distributors increased from $6 million to $12 million between December 31, Year –2, and December 31, Year –1. Therefore, during Year –1, its activities must have generated a *positive* total net cash flow of $6 million, the difference between $12 million and $6 million. During Year 0, the firm generated a *negative* total net cash flow of $4 million, because cash decreased from $12 million to $8 million during that year. Thus, a firm's total net cash flow is equal to the *change* in the firm's cash position during a period of time.

Total net cash flow, which accounts for *all* transactions the firm undertakes during a period of time, does not tell which particular activity has generated a cash surplus or a cash deficit during the period over which it is measured. For that purpose, the statement of cash flows breaks down a firm's net cash flows into three types of activities: **cash flows from operating activities, cash flows from investing activities**, and **cash flows from financing activities**. A typical cash inflow from operating activities is cash received from a customer, while a typical cash outflow is cash paid to a supplier. Examples of cash outflows from investing activities are payments for capital expenditures or for the acquisition of another company's assets, while examples of cash inflows are payments received from the sale of noncurrent assets, including financial assets. Cash outflows from financing activities include repayment of short-term or long-term debt or payments of cash dividends to shareholders, while cash inflows include the proceeds for short-term or long-term borrowings.

Exhibit 4.10 presents OS Distributors' statement of cash flows for the two years ending December 31, Year -1 and December 31, Year 0. It shows the contribution of the operating, investing and financing activities to the firm's change in cash during each of the two periods, measured by the **net cash flow** (the difference between the cash inflows and cash outflows) each one of these activities has generated during these periods. For a given year, the sum of the **net cash flow from operating activities**, the **net cash flow from investing activities**, and the **net cash flow from financing activities** is the firm's total net cash flow for that year, which, as we have shown, must be equal to the firm's change in cash position during the same period. To ensure that this is the case, the reconciliation between the cash position at the beginning of each year, the total net cash flow during the year, and the cash position at the end of the year are provided at the bottom of the statements.

PREPARING A STATEMENT OF CASH FLOWS

The cash inflows and outflows for the operating, investing, and financing activities are derived from year-end balance sheets and the income statements. In the case of OS Distributors, the cash flows in Exhibit 4.10 were calculated from the firm's balance sheets at year-ends Year –2, Year –1, and Year 0 and its income statements for the years Year –1 and Year 0.

The next sections explain how we did the calculations.

EXHIBIT 4.10	OS DISTRIBUTORS' STATEMENTS OF CASH FLOWS.

FIGURES IN MILLIONS

	Year –1	Year 0
• **Cash Flows from Operating Activities**		
Earnings after tax	$8.0	$10.2
Depreciation expense	5.0	8.0
Change in working capital requirement	(4.0)	(14.0)
Net cash flow from operating activities (A)	$9.0	$4.2
• **Cash Flows from Investing Activities**		
Sale of fixed assets	$0.0	$ 2.0
Acquisition of fixed assets	0.0	(12.0)
Net cash flow from investing activities (B)	($0.0)	($10.0)
• **Cash Flows from Financing Activities**		
Increase in long-term borrowing	$0.0	$12.0
Increase in short-term borrowing	7.0	1.0
Long-term debt repaid	(8.0)	(8.0)
Dividend payments	(2.0)	(3.2)
Net cash flow from financing activities (C)	($3.0)	$ 1.8
• Total Net Cash Flow (A + B + C)	$ 6.0	($ 4.0)
Cash, beginning of year	$ 6.0	$12.0
Cash, end of year	$12.0	$8.0

NET CASH FLOW FROM OPERATING ACTIVITIES

The **International Accounting Standards Board (IASB)** and the **Financial Accounting Standards Board (FASB)**, the major international and US accounting organizations, provide guidelines that firms have to follow when preparing their statement of cash flows. For the FASB, cash flows from operating activities are the cash impact of transactions that enter in the determination of earnings after tax (EAT). Thus, the sources of cash *inflows* from operating activities include the sale of goods or services, but also revenues from financial investments, such as dividends received from equity investments. The sources of cash *outflows* from operating activities include the purchase of materials for the manufacture of goods, the salaries and other compensation paid to employees, taxes, and also interest paid to debt holders. Note that the operating activities at the source of the cash flows from operating activities differ from those we defined earlier (see the section on working capital requirement). For us, operating activities are limited to the activities required to operate the firm's invested capital in order to generate sales, *excluding* any financial transactions such as interest paid or dividends received. For the IASB, financial income and expenses may be classified as operating, investing, or financing cash flows, provided they are classified consistently from period to period.

Not all revenues or expenses recorded in the income statement and related to operating activities generate or consume cash. A typical example is depreciation. There is no one to whom the firm pays depreciation.[12] Consequently, depreciation is excluded from the calculation of the net cash flow from operating activities. Furthermore, even though revenues and expenses eventually end up as cash inflows or outflows, they are not recorded as such in the income statement. As discussed in the section about the income statement, revenues (sales) are shown in the income statement only when recognized, that is, when customers are invoiced, not when cash changes hands. Thus, an increase in revenues does not necessarily imply a corresponding cash inflow.

Similarly, some expenses are *not* recorded in the income statement when payment is made, but only when they generate revenue. For example, expenses related to the purchase of merchandise by a distributor are recorded in the income statement as cost of goods sold only when merchandise is sold, not when payment is made.[13] Thus, an increase in expenses related to sales does not necessarily imply a corresponding cash outflow. How then can we measure the cash flows from operating revenues and operating expenses?

We first consider the cash inflows from operations that originate from the sale of goods and services. Each time a customer is invoiced, the firm's accountant records the sale by increasing both the firm's net sales account and its accounts receivable by the amount of the sale. Cash comes in later when the customer pays. At that time, the accountant records the transaction by increasing the firm's cash account and decreasing its accounts receivable by the amount paid. Therefore, by following what happens to receivables over a period of time, we can calculate the cash inflow from sales during that period. Starting at the beginning of the period, receivables increase each time a sale is made and decrease each time a bill is paid. We can write the following:

$$\text{Accounts receivable}_{end} = \text{Accounts receivable}_{beginning}$$
$$+ \text{Sales} - \text{Cash inflow from sales}$$

Rearranging the terms of the above equation gives us this:

$$\text{Cash inflow from sales} = \text{Sales} - [\text{Accounts receivable}_{end}$$
$$- \text{Accounts receivable}_{beginning}]$$

This equation can be written as follows:

$$\text{Cash inflow from sales} = \text{Sales} - \Delta \text{Accounts receivable}$$

where ΔAccounts receivable is the change in receivables during the accounting period.

If accounts receivable increase, ΔAccounts receivable is positive; if they decrease, ΔAccounts receivable is negative.

When accounts receivable *increase* during a period of time (ΔAccounts receivable *positive*), the cash inflow from sales is *less* than the sales revenue during that period of time. When they *decrease* (ΔAccounts receivable *negative*), the corresponding cash inflow from sales is *more* than the sales revenue during that period of time.

---

[12] When a fixed asset is acquired, the cash outflow is equal to the acquisition price of the asset. When that asset is subsequently depreciated over a period of time, the firm no longer experiences any cash movements related to the purchase of the asset.

[13] This is an application of the realization and matching principles, which we discussed earlier.

The procedure for estimating the cash inflow from sales over a period of time can be applied to all the operating expenses that involve cash transactions. As shown in Appendix 4.1, the related cash outflow is obtained by adjusting the dollar amount of an income statement account with the change in the corresponding balance sheet account during the accounting period. The result is a simple formula for obtaining the net cash flows from operating activities:

Net cash flow from operating activities = EAT + Depreciation expense − ΔWCR[14]

(4.12)

where EAT (earnings after tax) and the depreciation expense are from the income statement and ΔWCR, the change in the working capital requirement, (positive if it is an increase, negative if it is a decrease), is calculated from the managerial balance sheets.

Here is an intuitive interpretation of equation 4.12. The firm generates revenues and expenses that are captured in EAT. Depreciation expense, which is *not* a cash outflow but is an expense that reduces EAT, is added to EAT in order to cancel out its effect (a $1 increase in depreciation expense will decrease EAT by $1, but will not change EAT *plus* depreciation expense). Assuming that the firm's operating activities are growing, the firm must invest more in its operating cycle. This increased investment is measured by ΔWCR. To understand this, note that working capital requirement increases with the increase in the amount of cash due to the firm by its customers and with the increase in its inventories; it decreases with the increase in the amount of cash the firm owes to its suppliers and other creditors. That is, ΔWCR represents the *net* amount of cash the firm uses to finance the growth of its investment in the operating cycle during the accounting period. Because this cash is unavailable to the firm, it reduces its cash flow from operating activities.

Using the data in Exhibit 4.6, we can compute the change in OS Distributors' working capital requirement in Year −1 and Year 0 as follows:

ΔWCR$_{Year-1}$ = WCR$_{12/31/Year-1}$ − WCR$_{12/31/Year-2}$ − $63 million − $59 million = $4 million

ΔWCR$_{Year\ 0}$ = WCR$_{12/31/Year\ 0}$ − WCR$_{12/31/Year-1}$ = $77 million − $63 million = $14 million

and using equation 4.12 and data from the income statements in Exhibit 4.7, we can write:

Net cash flow from operating activities$_{Year-1}$ =
$8 million + $5 million − $4 million = $9 million

Net cash flow from operating activities$_{Year\ 0}$ =
$10.2 million + $8 million − $14 million = $4.2 million

These net cash flows are shown on the upper part of OS Distributors' statements of cash flows in Exhibit 4.10.

NET CASH FLOW FROM INVESTING ACTIVITIES

The firm's investments during the accounting period are not directly reported in its balance sheet or income statement. The balance sheet reports only the net book value of all the firm's fixed assets, and the income statement reports only the depreciation expense for the accounting period. Fortunately, firms usually provide supplementary

---

[14] If there is any amortization expense, it must be added to the depreciation expense.

information in the form of notes to their financial statements from which it is possible to calculate the cash flows related to the firm's investing activities during the accounting period.

For example, note 3 at the bottom of OS Distributor's balance sheets in Exhibit 4.1 explains that the firm did not sell or acquire fixed assets during Year –1. However, during Year 0, a warehouse was enlarged at a cost of $12 million and existing assets were sold at their book value of $2 million. Because OS Distributors does not hold any long-term financial assets, the cash flows from its investing activities are related only to the acquisition and sale of fixed assets. They are shown in the second part of the statement of cash flows in Exhibit 4.10. The net effect of the firm's investment decisions is a net cash flow of zero in Year –1 and a net outflow of $10 million in Year 0.

You can check that the net fixed assets accounts in the balance sheets are consistent with this information. Note that, over a period of time, these accounts increase when the firm acquires fixed assets and decrease when the firm deducts depreciation expense and sells fixed assets. Thus:

$$\text{Net fixed assets}_{\text{end}} = \text{Net fixed assets}_{\text{beginning}} + \text{Fixed assets acquisitions}$$
$$- \text{Depreciation expense} - \text{Fixed assets sales} \qquad (4.13)$$

OS Distributors had no fixed assets acquisitions or disposals during Year –1. The Year –1 income statement shows depreciation expense of $5 million, and the Year –2 balance sheet indicates $56 million of net fixed assets at the end of Year –2. As a result:

$$\text{Net fixed assets}_{12/31/\text{Year}-1} = \$56 \text{ million} + \$0 - \$5 \text{ million} - \$0 = \$51 \text{ million}$$

This is the same amount of net fixed assets reported in the balance sheet at the end of Year –1. In Year 0, OS Distributors acquired $12 million of new assets, sold $2 million of old assets, and had depreciation expense of $8 million. Given that net fixed assets at the end of Year –1 were $51 million, we have the following:

$$\text{Net fixed assets}_{12/31/\text{Year}0} = \$51 \text{ million} + \$12 \text{ million} - \$8 \text{ million}$$
$$- \$2 \text{ million} = \$53 \text{ million}[15]$$

NET CASH FLOW FROM FINANCING ACTIVITIES

Most firms carry out a large number of financing transactions over the accounting period. Some add cash to the firm, while others absorb cash. They are reported in the third part of the statements of cash flows for OS Distributors shown in Exhibit 4.10. Using data from the firm's balance sheets in Exhibit 4.1 and the total of dividends paid in Exhibit 4.7, you can identify and calculate the cash flows related to its financing decisions in Year –1 and Year 0.

The balance sheets in Exhibit 4.1 show that the firm's long-term debt in Year 0 increased by the $12 million used to finance the extension of its warehouse (see note 5). Short-term borrowings increased by $7 million in Year –1 as shown by the increase in its short-term bank debt from $7 million to $14 million. They increased again by $1 million in Year 0 from $14 million to $15 million. In Year –1 and Year 0, the firm repaid $8 million each year of its long-term debt (see note 5). Finally, as indicated

---

[15] The value of disposed assets in equation 4.13 is the net book value of the assets. If the sale price is different, the difference is either an extraordinary gain (the sale price is higher than the net book value) or an extraordinary loss (the asset is sold at a lower price than the net book value). These gains or losses are accounted for in the income statement and affect the firm's earnings after tax.

in Exhibit 4.7, the firm paid $2 million of dividends in Year –1 and $3.2 million in Year 0.[16]

In total, net cash flow from financing activities was a negative $3 million in Year –1 and a positive $1.8 million in Year 0, as shown in the third part of Exhibit 4.10. Note that payments of interest expenses do not appear among the cash outflows from financing activities. This is because, as mentioned earlier, they are included in the net cash flows from operating activities.

THE STATEMENT OF CASH FLOWS

The firm's total net cash flow is the balance of the firm's cash flows related to its operating, investing, and financing activities during a period of time. Recall that this net cash flow must be equal to the firm's change in its cash position during the period. We can now reconcile the cash flows from OS Distributors' activities in Year –1 and Year 0 with the changes in its cash position during these two years. This is done at the bottom of the statement of cash flows.

The firm's cash position at the beginning of Year –1 was $6 million. This is the amount of cash shown in the firm's balance sheet at year-end Year –2 in Exhibit 4.1. During Year –1, the firm's total net cash flow was $6 million so its cash position at year-end Year –1 must be $12 million (the initial $6 million plus the $6 million generated during the year). This is the amount shown in the firm's balance sheet at the same date. During Year 0, the total net cash outflow was $4 million. OS Distributors began the year with $12 million in cash, so it ended the year with $8 million (the initial $12 million less the $4 million consumed during the year).

We have pointed out that OS Distributors' statements of cash flows are not needed to learn that the firm generated $6 million in cash in Year –1 and consumed $4 million in Year 0. This information is available in the balance sheets given in Exhibit 4.1. OS Distributors' cash position was $6 million at the end of Year –2, $12 million at the end of Year –1, and $8 million at the end of Year 0. Hence, total net cash flow is $6 million in Year –1 ($12 million less $6 million) and a negative $4 million in Year 0 ($8 million less $12 million). If this information is readily available, what is the usefulness of a **statement of cash flows**?

The statement of cash flows tells you *how* and *why* the firm's cash position has changed during a particular period of time. It tells you *which* of the firm's decisions have generated cash and *which* have consumed cash. A sequence of historical cash-flow statements indicates whether and how a firm's cash flow is improving or deteriorating over time and thus whether the firm is in a sound financial position or heading toward troubled times.

PROBLEMS WITH THE STATEMENT OF CASH FLOWS

Recall that the FASB considers interest paid and financial income received as cash flows from operating activities. However, interest paid to the firm's debt holders is the result of the decision to use debt to finance some of its invested capital; similarly, financial income, which is the return from financial assets the firm holds, is the result of the decision to invest in financial instruments. Interest paid should, therefore, be

---

[16] Dividend payments are equal to the figures shown in the income statements because OS Distributors does not have any accrued dividends payable. At the end of both years (Year –1 and Year 0), the firm had paid its dividends for the year.

classified as part of the firm's financing activities and financial income received as part of its investing activities. Having those financial transactions included in the firm's operating activities makes it difficult to identify the specific impact of operating, investing, and financing decisions on the firm's cash flows. As mentioned earlier, the IASB lets companies decide where to allocate financial income and expenses but, unfortunately, only a few companies among those presenting their financial statements according to IFRS Standards exclude them from the cash flow from operating activities. Further, some items in the statement of cash flows do not show actual cash inflows and outflows. It shows them indirectly. Just look at the way the net cash flow from operating activities is arrived at. It is reconstructed from earnings after tax, not from the actual transactions related to specific operating activities, such as the sale of products and services or the purchase of materials to manufacture goods. Unfortunately, although firms have the choice to present their cash flows as actual cash flows, most of them choose not to do it and prefer an indirect method to report them.

FREE CASH FLOW

An often used measure of a firm's cash flow is the cash flow generated by the firm's invested capital. It is a measure of the cash flow available to those who *finance* the firm's activities, that is, the firm's lenders and the firm's shareholders. We show in Chapters 9, 10, and 14 that **free cash flow**[17] is a key input to value investment projects and businesses.

Since free cash flow is cash flow available to the suppliers of capital as a whole, it is not affected by the firm's capital structure decision. Whether the firm decides to use only equity capital or a mixture of equity capital and debt to finance its invested capital, its free cash flow will always be the same. Therefore, one simple way to obtain the free cash flow of any firm is to start by *assuming that its invested capital is entirely financed with equity capital*. Using this approach, we get the following from the firm's statement of cash flows in Exhibit 4.10:

$$\text{Free cash flow} = \text{Net cash flow from operating activities}_{\text{all equity financed}}$$
$$+ \text{ Net cash flow from investing activities} \qquad (4.14)$$

where net cash flow from operating activities$_{\text{all equity financed}}$ is the firm's net cash flow from operating activities as if its invested capital were all equity financed.

From equation 4.12, we can write the following:

$$\text{Net cash flow from operating activities}_{\text{all equity financed}} =$$
$$\text{EAT}_{\text{all equity financed}} + \text{Depreciation expense} - \Delta \text{WCR}$$

Given that an all-equity firm does not pay any interest, its earnings before tax are equal to EBIT. If T_C is the corporate tax rate, income tax expense is then equal to $T_C \times \text{EBIT}$. Factoring EBIT, we have the following:

$$\text{EAT}_{\text{all equity financed}} = \text{EBIT}\,(1 - T_C)$$

and equation 4.14 becomes:

$$\text{Free cash flow} = \text{EBIT}\,(1 - T_C) + \text{Depreciation expense} - \Delta \text{WCR}$$
$$+ \text{ Net cash flow from investing activities}$$

---

[17] Also called **cash flow from assets (CFA)**.

or:

$$\text{Free cash flow} = \text{EBIT}\,(1 - T_C) + \text{Depreciation expense}$$
$$- \Delta\text{WCR} - \text{Net capital expenditure}^{18} \qquad (4.15)$$

where "net capital expenditure" is the same as "net cash flow from investing activities" (the negative sign indicates that capital expenditures represent cash outflows).

In this equation, the term $\text{EBIT}(1 - T_C)$ is often referred to as **net operating profit after tax (NOPAT)** or **net operating profit less adjusted taxes (NOPLAT)**.

Applied to the case of OS Distributors (whose tax rate is 40 percent), we get this:

$$\text{Free cash flow}_{\text{Year}-1} = \$18.3 \text{ million} \times (1 - .40) + \$5 \text{ million}$$
$$- \$4 \text{ million} - \$0 = \$12 \text{ million}$$

$$\text{Free cash flow}_{\text{Year}\,0} = \$24 \text{ million} \times (1 - .40) + \$8 \text{ million}$$
$$- \$14 \text{ million} - \$10 \text{ million} = -\$1.6 \text{ million}$$

During Year –1, OS Distributors generated from its assets a free cash flow of $12 million whereas net cash flow from operating activities was $9 million (see Exhibit 4.10). How can we account for the $3 million difference given that net capital expenditures were zero in Year –1? Free cash flow is $3 million higher because it excludes net interest expense of $5 million and the tax reduction that goes with it, called the **interest tax shield**. In Year –1, this tax shield is equal to 40 percent of the net interest expense of $5 million, that is, $2 million (0.40 × $5million). In total, the difference is $3 million ($5 million less $2 million).

Equation 4.14 is the formula we will use in Chapter 9 to value an investment and in subsequent chapters to estimate the market value of a firm's assets.

KEY POINTS

1. This chapter explains how a firm's balance sheet, income statement, and statement of cash flows are prepared, what type of information they provide, and how they are related to each other. It also shows how the statements can be amended and supplemented for a better use of accounting data to assess the financial performance of a firm or a business unit. For example, the balance sheet can be restructured into the managerial balance sheet for the purpose of identifying the three components of a firm's invested capital: (1) cash; (2) working capital requirement (WCR); (3) net fixed assets, and the three sources of capital employed to finance the invested capital: (1) short-term debt; (2) long-term debt; and (3) equity capital. WCR, which measures the firm's investment in the operating cycle, is equal to the difference between operating assets (accounts receivable, inventories, and prepaid expenses) and operating liabilities (accounts payable and accrued expenses).

2. Two measures of performance typically supplement information provided by the income statement and the statement of cash flows. Earnings before interest, tax, depreciation, and amortization (EBITDA) is a relevant measure of operating profit when comparing firms with different methods of depreciating and amortizing fixed assets. Free cash flow is the cash flow generated by the firm's

---

18 Again, if there is any amortization expense, it must be added to the depreciation expense.

invested capital. It is a measure of the cash flow available to the firm's lenders and the firm's shareholders. Both measures can be obtained directly from the three financial statements.

3. The usefulness of financial statements is often limited by the relative quality of the information they contain. Financial statements are prepared according to principles and rules that are not necessarily applied in the same fashion and with the same rigor by all firms. Furthermore, despite the nearly universal adoption of the International Financial Reporting Standards (IFRS), accounting rules may differ between some countries and even between industries within the same country. Thus, to make meaningful comparisons between financial statements over time and between firms, it is necessary to check that the standards that are used and the way they are implemented are identical from one period to another and from one firm to another. If they are not, adjustments need to be made. For these reasons, a firm's financial statements should be interpreted with a critical eye. You should never take for granted a firm's reported profit figures or asset values. Always ask yourself how they were generated and which rules were used to estimate them. This point is clearly illustrated in Exhibit 4.11 with the case of the Singer Company. The following two chapters show how accounting information is used to assess firms' business and financial performance.

EXHIBIT 4.11	SINGER CO.: THE BOTTOM LINE

The Singer Corporation (first established as I. M. Singer & Co.) is well-known for its sewing machines. For financial accountants, however, Singer Co. is an interesting example of a different story: the need to check the story behind the figures.

Owing to an unforeseen series of events that left the Singer Co prey to an unexpected takeover, Paul Bilzerian became chairman of the company and proceeded to sell it piecemeal in 1988. A Chinese-American businessman named James Ting took over Singer as CEO in 1989. By September 1999, Singer was in Chapter 11 bankruptcy, together with Ting's Canadian holding company.

Bilzerian was convicted that year for securities and tax law violations over unsuccessful takeover attempts of other companies, and Ting later fled to Hong Kong to avoid investigation by Canadian and US authorities, eventually serving jail time in Hong Kong for charges of false accounting.

With the benefit of hindsight, it seems clear that all was not quite right at Singer: but what exactly happened, and why did nobody realise?

- **A too good to be true news story?**
  After Ting took over Singer, the company's earnings rose consistently over the next 23 consecutive quarters. Their financial statements were fully approved by Ernst & Young auditors. But of the $98.5 million earnings reported, around $19 million actually came from asset sales, one-time investment gains and interest income, as well as fees from affiliated companies.

  Singer's earnings were almost always as expected by analysts, but looking back, this should have been a red flag to investors. How, particularly when selling across 100 countries from the US to China to India, could earnings be so completely consistent?

- **The dangers of intertwined companies**
  Ting owned a Canadian holding company called Semi-Tech Corp, and a company based in Hong Kong called Semi-Tech Global. He had purchased Singer using Semi-Tech Global.

EXHIBIT 4.11	SINGER CO.: THE BOTTOM LINE (*Continued*)

In 1993, Ting announced a scheme endorsed by the Royal Bank of Canada's Dominion Securities and Kidder, Peabody: in short, Semi-Tech Corp would (with $850 million raised in common stock and zero-coupon bonds) purchase shares of Singer from Semi-Tech Global.

Semi-Tech Global would then use the money to turn Singer not just into a sewing machine company, but one that operated across white goods.

'Almost half of Singer's stock was still owned by Semi-Tech, however, and only two of its eight directors were not linked to Semi-Tech. "It's very incestuous," said Howard Schilit, who headed the Center for Financial Research and Analysis in Rockville, Maryland.

Singer seemed to use these relationships to particular advantage. For instance, Semi-Tech Global, a company in which Semi-Tech Corp had a big stake, owned a group of lackluster businesses that used to be owned by Singer. If the businesses turned around, Singer had the right to buy them at low prices – indeed, it had already bought back seven of the original 12.'[1]

The lesson from this part of the Singer story? Investors should be extra wary when related companies have close ties with each other's business dealings.

- **Is the cash actually there?**
There were two major issues related to cash flow in the Singer Co. statements.

1. $46 million more came into the company rather than left it: but this came from a rise in borrowings, not from increased operations. An unexpectedly high cash flow should be checked to ensure where the money is coming from.
2. Singer had branched out into white goods such as refrigerators and washing machines, with half of its sales now coming from Asia and Latin America. Why was it so successful in these regions? Because it enabled customers to buy items on credit. Discrepancies between customers not paying their bills and reported sales should have been investigated.

It is, of course, easy to look back at cases such as this and wonder why nobody picked up on these signs sooner. But how many companies in recent times have gone through similar (if not quite so dramatic) stories?

Sources:
John Gorham, 'The wrecking of Singer', *Forbes* (Nov 15, 1999, accessed online)
Patricia Best, 'James Ting, boy wonder, finally has his day in court,' *The Globe and Mail* (May 12, 2005, updated April 22, 2018, accessed online)
Michael Rothfeld and Brad Reagan, 'A Maze of Paper: SEC Judgment Against Raider Paul Bilzerian: $62 Million. Collected: $3.7 Million,' *Wall Street Journal* (accessed online at https://www.wsj.com/articles/for-decades-ex-corporate-raider-holds-off-sec-effort-to-collect-62-million-judgment-1410892550)
Alison Leigh Cowan, 'How Bilzerian Scored at Singer,' *The New York Times* (Aug 24 1988, accessed online)
Reed Abelson, 'How to Spot the Seams at Singer Co,. ,The New York Times* (May 15 1995)

[1] Reed Abelson, 'How to Spot the Seams at Singer Co,. ,*The New York Times* (May 15 1995)

Obtaining the Net Cash Flow from Operating Activities Using Balance Sheet and Income Statement Accounts

Net cash flow from operating activities is defined as the difference between the cash inflow and the cash outflow from the firm's operating activities. This appendix shows how these cash flows can be estimated from the balance sheets and income statement.

MEASURING CASH INFLOW FROM SALES

As shown in the chapter, cash inflow from sales can be measured by tracing what happens to accounts receivable during the estimation period. This cash inflow is equal to sales adjusted by the change in receivables during the period:

$$\text{Cash inflow from sales} = \text{Sales} - \Delta\text{Accounts receivable} \qquad (A.4.1.1)$$

where ΔAccounts receivable is the change in accounts receivable during the period.

MEASURING CASH OUTFLOW FROM OPERATING ACTIVITIES

Cash outflow from operating activities includes payments to suppliers for purchased goods; cash expenses related to selling, general, and administrative (SG&A) expenses, *excluding* depreciation, which is not a cash item; net interest;[19] and tax payments.

We can write the following:

$$
\begin{aligned}
\text{Cash outflow from operating activities} = {} & \text{Cash outflow from purchases} \\
& + \text{Cash outflow from SG\&A and tax expenses} \\
& + \text{Cash outflow from net interest expenses}
\end{aligned}
$$

CASH OUTFLOW FROM PURCHASES

To determine cash payments to suppliers, we use the same approach as the one used to calculate cash receipts from customers. Instead of tracing what happens to receivables during the estimation period, we trace what happens to payables. Each time the firm receives an invoice from one of its suppliers, accounts payable increase by the amount of the invoice, and each time the firm pays an invoice, accounts payable decrease by the amount paid. Thus, we can write the following:

$$
\begin{aligned}
\text{Accounts payable}_{end} = {} & \text{Accounts payable}_{beginning} + \text{Purchases} \\
& - \text{Cash outflow from purchases}
\end{aligned}
$$

---

[19] We assume that interest expenses are larger than financial income, as is generally the case.

Rearranging the terms of the equation, we get the following:

$$\text{Cash outflow from purchases} = \text{Purchases} - [\text{Accounts payable}_{end} - \text{Accounts payable}_{beginning}]$$

This equation can be written as:

Cash outflow from purchases = Purchases − ΔAccounts payable (A4.1.2)

where ΔAccounts payable is the change in payables during the estimation period.

However, unlike sales, purchases are not shown in the income statement. They must be calculated indirectly from the data provided by the income statement and the balance sheets. For a distributor, inventories at the beginning of the period increase by the cost of purchases made during the period. When the firm sells the goods, these costs are released to the cost of goods sold (COGS) account. Thus, we can write the following:

$$\text{Inventories}_{beginning} + \text{Purchases} - \text{COGS} = \text{Inventories}_{end}$$

Rearranging the terms of the equation, we get the following:

Purchases = COGS + ΔInventories (A4.1.3)

where ΔInventories is the change in inventories during the period.

Equation A4.1.3 could have been obtained directly because, for a distributor, if the amount of goods purchased during the accounting period exceeds the amount of goods sold during that period, the inventories account will increase by the difference. If a distributor sells more goods than it buys during the accounting period, the inventories account will decrease by the difference.

Substituting the value of purchases given by equation A4.1.3 into equation A4.1.2 yields the following value for the firm's cash outflows from purchases:

Cash outflow from purchases = COGS + ΔInventories − ΔAccounts payable
(A.4.1.4)

CASH OUTFLOW FROM SG&A AND TAX EXPENSES

To determine the amount of cash paid for SG&A expenses and tax expense during the estimation period, we must adjust them for any change in prepaid expenses and accrued expenses. This approach is similar to adjusting purchases for changes in accounts payable to determine the cash payments to suppliers. For example, when OS Distributors' prepaid expenses decreased by $1 million in Year 0 (see Exhibit 4.1), cash paid for operating expenses (in this case, rent payments as indicated in note 2 to the balance sheet) was $1 million less than the expense reported in the income statement for Year 0. To convert operating expenses into cash payments, the decrease of $1 million must be deducted from the expenses. If the prepaid expenses had increased, the increase would have been added to the expenses. In Year −1, OS Distributors' accrued expenses increased by $2 million. This means that cash paid for operating expenses (in this case, payments for wages and tax, as indicated in note 4 to the balance sheet) was $2 million lower than the expenses recorded in the Year −1 income statement. As a result, the $2 million must be subtracted from operating expenses to arrive at the cash payment. If the accrued expenses had decreased, the decrease would have been added to the operating expenses. Therefore, if ΔAccrued expenses and ΔPrepaid expenses represent the change in the accrued and prepaid expenses accounts, respectively, we can write the following:

$$\text{Cash outflow from SG\&A and tax expenses} = \text{SG\&A expenses}$$
$$+ \text{Tax expense} + \Delta\text{Prepaid expenses} - \Delta\text{Accrued expenses} \qquad (A4.1.5)$$

Cash Outflow from Net Interest Expense

If we assume, as is often the case, that payments of interest expenses and receipts from financial income occur during the same accounting period, then when these expenses and income are recorded in the income statement, we can write:

$$\text{Cash outflow from net interest expense} = \text{Net interest expense} \qquad (A4.1.6)$$

When interest payments or receipts from financial income do not coincide with the revenues and expenses in the income statement, some adjustment to equation A4.1.6 is necessary. If, at the end of the accounting period, the firm has not totally paid the interest expenses recorded in the period's income statement, the difference is logged in the liabilities side of the balance sheet as **interest payable**.[20] Then, if we apply the same approach to interest expenses that we apply to purchases to calculate the cash outflow from purchases, the cash outflow from interest expense will be given by the following equation, similar to equation A4.1.2:

$$\text{Cash outflow from interest expense} = \text{Interest expense} - \Delta\text{Interest payable}$$

where ΔInterest payable is the change in interest payable during the accounting period.

If, at the end of the accounting period, the firm has not totally received the financial income recorded in the period's income statement, the difference is logged in the asset side of the balance sheet as **interest receivable**[21] and the cash inflow from financial income is given by the following equation, similar to equation A4.1.1:

$$\text{Cash inflow from financial income} = \text{Financial income} - \Delta\text{Interest receivable}$$

where ΔInterest receivable is the change in interest receivable during the accounting period.

In total, and assuming that interest expenses are larger than financial income, we can consolidate the two above equations as follows:

$$\text{Cash outflow from net interest expense} = \text{Net interest expense}$$
$$- [\Delta\text{Interest payable} - \Delta\text{Interest receivable}]$$

NET CASH FLOW FROM OPERATING ACTIVITIES

We can now derive a general formula for a firm's net cash flow from operating activities. Adding the cash outflow from purchases in equation A4.1.4 to the cash outflow from SG&A expenses and tax expenses in equation A4.1.5 and to the cash

---

[20] In the managerial balance sheet this short-term financial liability would be recorded as a short-term debt.

[21] In the managerial balance sheet this short-term financial asset would be recorded as cash.

outflow from net interest expense in equation A4.1.6, we get the total cash outflow from operating activities:

$$
\begin{aligned}
\text{Cash outflow from operating activities} = {} & \text{COGS} + \Delta\text{Inventories} - \Delta\text{Accounts payable} \\
& + \text{SG\&A expenses} + \text{Tax expense} \\
& + \Delta\text{Prepaid expenses} - \Delta\text{Accrued expenses} \\
& + \text{Net interest expense}
\end{aligned}
$$

Rearranging the terms of the equation, we get the following:

Cash outflow from operating activities = COGS + SG&A expenses + Tax expense + Net interest expense + [ΔInventories + ΔPrepaid expenses − ΔAccounts payable − ΔAccrued expenses]   (A4.1.7)

To obtain the net cash flow from operating activities we just have to subtract the cash outflow from operating activities in equation A4.1.7 from the cash inflow from operating activities in equation A4.1.1:

$$
\begin{aligned}
\text{Net cash flow from operating activities} = {} & [\text{Sales} - \Delta\text{Accounts receivable}] \\
& - [\text{COGS} + \text{SG\&A expenses} + \text{Tax expense} + \text{Net interest expense}] \\
& - [\Delta\text{Inventories} + \Delta\text{Prepaid expenses} - \Delta\text{Accounts payable} - \Delta\text{Accrued expenses}]
\end{aligned}
$$

The terms in this equation can be rearranged to yield:

$$
\begin{aligned}
\text{Net cash flow from operating activities} = {} & [\text{Sales} - \text{COGS} - \text{SG\&A expenses} \\
& - \text{Tax expense} - \text{Net interest expense}] - [\Delta\text{Accounts receivable} + \Delta\text{Inventories} \\
& + \Delta\text{Prepaid expenses} - \Delta\text{Accounts payable} - \Delta\text{Accrued expenses}]
\end{aligned}
$$

The expression inside the first set of brackets is EAT plus depreciation expense (see Exhibit 4.7). The expression in the second set of brackets measures the *changes* in the firm's operating assets less the *changes* in its operating liabilities, that is, the *change* in the firm's working capital requirement, or ΔWCR. Thus, the above equation can be reduced to:

$$
\text{Net cash flow from operating activities} = \text{EAT} + \text{Depreciation expense} - \Delta\text{WCR}
$$

which is equation 4.12.

SPECIMEN FINANCIAL STATEMENTS

THE GLAXOSMITHKLINE (GSK) FINANCIAL STATEMENTS

The balance sheets and income statements that we have presented so far – those of Office Supplies (OS) Distributors, a fictitious firm – have purposely been reduced to their simplest form to make it easier to grasp financial accounting's basic principles and terminology. The financial statements published by companies are more complex and more difficult to read than those of OS Distributors, even with the help of the notes that often accompany them. The first objective of this appendix is to help you decipher actual financial statements by going through the balance sheets, income statements, and statements of cash flow taken from the annual reports of GlaxoSmithKline (GSK), a global health care company. GSK is a major pharmaceutical company which sells a wide range of pharmaceutical products, vaccines, and health care products all over the world. Its financial statements are prepared according to the International Financial Reporting Standards (IFRS Standards). To avoid duplication, we review only the few accounts in the three statements that have not already been discussed in the body of the chapter. The second objective of the appendix is to show you how to transform balance sheets as reported in a company's annual report into managerial balance sheets. An analysis of GSK's financial statements is presented in the appendices of the next two chapters to complement the analysis made in these chapters on OS Distributors.

GSK'S BALANCE SHEETS AND MANAGERIAL BALANCE SHEETS

GSK's Balance Sheets

Exhibit A4.2.1 shows GSK's balance sheets on December 31 of years 2015, 2016, and 2017, taken from the company's annual reports. You will notice that assets are listed in the order of increasing liquidity: noncurrent assets first, cash last. Liabilities are listed in descending order of time to maturity: noncurrent liabilities first, short-term debt last. This presentation is typical under IFRS Standards, while under US GAAP, assets are listed in order of decreasing liquidity and liabilities in increasing order of time to maturity. Note also that new accounts appear on both sides of GSK's balance sheets. They are examined in the following sections.

Noncurrent Assets

Intangible assets represent a significant portion of GSK's noncurrent assets, as is the case with most pharmaceutical companies. They include acquired licenses, patents, brands, and computer software. These assets are amortized and subject to regular impairment tests.

Exhibit A4.2.1	GSK's Consolidated Balance Sheets.

From the company annual reports for years 2015, 2016, and 2017, ending december 31.
Figures in millions of pounds

	2015	2016	2017
Noncurrent assets			
Property, plant, and equipment	£9,668	£10,808	£10,860
Goodwill	5,162	5,965	5,734
Other intangible assets	16,672	18,776	17,562
Investments in associates and joint ventures	207	263	183
Other investments	1,255	985	918
Deferred tax assets	2,905	4,374	3,796
Derivative financial instruments	–	–	8
Other noncurrent assets	990	1,199	1,413
Total noncurrent assets	36,859	42,370	40,474
Current assets			
Inventories	4,716	5,102	5,557
Current tax recoverable	180	226	258
Trade and other receivables	5,615	6,026	6,000
Derivative financial instruments	125	156	68
Liquid investments	75	89	78
Cash and cash equivalents	5,830	4,897	3,833
Assets held for sale	46	215	113
Total current assets	16,587	16,711	15,907
Total assets	£53,446	£59,081	£56,381
Current liabilities			
Short-term borrowings	(1,308)	(4,129)	(2,825)
Contingent consideration liabilities	(306)	(561)	(1,076)
Trade and other payables	(8,885)	(10,645)	(11,060)
Put option liability	–	(1,319)	(9,910)
Derivative financial instruments	(153)	(194)	(74)
Current tax payable	(1,421)	(1,305)	(995)
Short-term provisions	(1,344)	(848)	(629)
Total current liabilities	(13,417)	(19,001)	(26,569)
Noncurrent liabilities			
Long-term borrowings	(15,324)	(14,661)	(14,264)
Deferred tax liabilities	(1,522)	(1,934)	(1,396)
Pensions and other post-employment benefits	(3,229)	(4,090)	(3,539)
Other provisions	(420)	(652)	(636)

Exhibit A4.2.1	GSK's Consolidated Balance Sheets. (*Continued*)		
	2015	2016	2017
Contingent consideration liabilities	(£3,549)	(£5,335)	(£5,096)
Other noncurrent liabilities	(7,107)	(8,445)	(1,392)
Total noncurrent liabilities	(31,151)	(35,117)	(26,323)
Total liabilities	(£44,568)	(£54,118)	(£52,892)
Net assets	£8,878	£4,963	£3,489
Equity			
Share capital	1,340	1,342	1,343
Share premium account	2,831	2,954	3,019
Retained earnings	(1,397)	(5,392)	(6,477)
Other reserves	2,340	2,220	2,047
Shareholders' equity	5,114	1,124	(68)
Non-controlling interests	3,764	3,839	3,557
Total equity	£8,878	£4,963	£3,489

Investments in associates and joint ventures represent GSK's investment in companies over which it has significant influence (associates) or joint control (joint ventures). Under IFRS Standards accounting, a company is supposed to have significant influence over another one if it holds 20 percent of the voting rights in that company.

Other investments are equity investments in other firms available for sale in the future.

Derivative financial instruments are long-term financial assets that GSK uses to hedge its interest rate and foreign-exchange risk exposure. This activity generates assets and liabilities that are recorded as derivative financial instruments, such as forward foreign currency contracts, interest rate and currency swaps, and which can be noncurrent and current assets or liabilities.[22]

Other noncurrent assets include insurance payments to be received in the future and surpluses from pension schemes.

CURRENT ASSETS

GSK holds several short-term financial assets that can be considered as cash or cash equivalents:

Assets held for sale are assets to be disposed of shortly; they are recorded at the lower of book value and fair value.

Cash equivalents are short-term bank deposits.

Liquid investments include US Treasury Notes and other government bonds. The company's other current assets include:

Trade and other receivables such as accounts receivable and receivables from debtors other than customers.

---

[22] See Chapters 16 and 17 for a definition of these instruments and their use in risk management.

Inventories which are valued according to the FIFO method, the International Financial Reporting Standard for reporting inventories.

NONCURRENT LIABILITIES

Other provisions relate mostly to legal and other disputes and major restructuring programs.

Contingent consideration is an obligation to transfer additional assets or equity interests to the owner of a business that was acquired. The consideration will only be paid if specified future events occur or conditions are met. Contingent considerations are recorded as noncurrent or current liabilities.

Other noncurrent liabilities are payables related to the acquisition of another health care company and accruals, which are payments received before delivery of products or services.

CURRENT LIABILITIES

Trade and other payables is an account which regroups a number of liabilities in addition to accounts payable such as salaries due, customer return and rebate accruals, and social security.

Put option liability is a liability resulting from agreements with other pharmaceutical companies which give them the option to sell assets to GSK over a period of time. The recorded liability represents an estimate of the payment to be made by GSK if the options are exercised in the coming year.[23]

Short-term provisions concern legal or other disputes expected to be resolved in the following year. They are estimated net of reversals and insurance recovery.

SHAREHOLDERS' EQUITY

Other reserves are reclassified retained earnings. Some are statutory reserves, others are cash-flow hedge reserves required by the firm's risk management activity, and reevaluation reserves which are the surplus generated when property, plant, and equipment are reevaluated at fair value.

GSK's MANAGERIAL BALANCE SHEETS

Exhibit A4.2.2 shows how we allocated the accounts from the GSK's balance sheets to the invested capital and capital employed accounts of the company's managerial balance sheets presented in Exhibit A4.2.3.

When in doubt, refer to the notes accompanying the financial statements to identify the transactions recorded in the particular account that has no obvious allocation. With this information, you should be able to assign the account to the relevant component of the managerial balance sheet.

For example, note that we added the "short-term provisions" and "other long-term liabilities" accounts of the actual balance sheet to the managerial balance sheet. The short-term provisions are provisions for legal and other disputes not yet resolved. They are not related to the operating cycle and thus cannot be included in the firm's working capital requirement. They cannot be considered as short-term debt either. The noncurrent liabilities account in the actual balance sheet includes both long-term borrowings and other liabilities. These liabilities are not financial debt and must be separated from the long-term debt in the managerial balance sheet.

---

[23] GSK includes this liability in the trade and other payables account.

| EXHIBIT A4.2.2 | FROM THE ACTUAL TO THE MANAGERIAL BALANCE SHEETS OF GSK. |

Actual Balance Sheet	Managerial Balance Sheet
Assets	
Assets held for sale	Cash
Cash and cash equivalents	Cash
Liquid investments	Cash
Derivative financial instruments	Cash
Trade and other receivables	Working capital requirement
Current taxes recoverable	Working capital requirement
Inventories	Working capital requirement
Property, plant, and equipment	Net fixed assets
Goodwill	Net fixed assets
Other intangible assets	Net fixed assets
Investments in associates and joint ventures	Net fixed assets
Other investments	Net fixed assets
Deferred tax assets	Net fixed assets
Derivative financial instruments	Net fixed assets
Other noncurrent assets	Net fixed assets
Liabilities and stockholders' equity	
Short-term borrowings	Short-term debt
Contingent consideration liabilities	Short-term debt
Trade and other payables	Working capital requirement
Put option liability	Short-term debt
Derivative financial instruments	Short-term debt
Current taxes payable	Working capital requirement
Short-term provisions	Short-term provisions
Long-term borrowings	Long-term debt
Deferred tax liabilities	Other long-term liabilities
Pensions and other post-employment benefits	Other long-term liabilities
Other provisions	Other long-term liabilities
Contingent consideration liabilities	Other long-term liabilities
Other noncurrent liabilities	Other long-term liabilities
Share capital	Owners' equity
Share premium	Owners' equity
Retained earnings	Owners' equity
Other reserves	Owners' equity

GSK'S INCOME STATEMENTS

The GSK income statements are shown in Exhibit A4.2.4. Their presentation does not differ much from that of OS Distributors, except that they show additional expenses, many self-explanatory, and do not show depreciation and amortization expenses as a

EXHIBIT A4.2.3	GSK's MANAGERIAL BALANCE SHEETS.

ALL DATA FROM THE BALANCE SHEETS IN EXHIBIT A4.2.1. FIGURES IN MILLIONS OF POUNDS

Year	2015		2016	2017
Invested capital				
• Cash		£6,076	£5,357	£4,092
• Working capital requirement		205	(596)	(240)
• Net fixed assets		36,859	42,370	40,474
Total invested capital		**£43,140**	**£47,131**	**£44,326**
Capital employed				
• Short-term debt		£1,767	£6,203	£13,885
• Short-term provisions		1,344	848	629
• Long-term financing		40,029	40,080	29,812
Long-term debt	£15,324		£14,661	£14,264
Other long-term liabilities	15,827		20,456	12,059
Owners' equity	8,878		4,963	3,489
Total capital employed		**£43,140**	**£47,131**	**£44,326**

EXHIBIT A4.2.4	GSK's CONSOLIDATED STATEMENTS OF INCOME.

FROM THE COMPANY 2017 ANNUAL REPORT. FIGURES IN MILLIONS OF POUNDS

	2015	2016	2017
Turnover	**£23,923**	**£27,889**	**£30,186**
Cost of goods sold	(8,853)	(9,290)	(10,342)
Gross profit	**15,070**	**18,599**	**19,844**
Selling, general, and administrative expenses	(9,232)	(9,366)	(9,672)
R&D expense	(3,560)	(3,628)	(4,476)
Royalty income	329	398	356
Other operating income (expenses)	7,715	(3,405)	(1,965)
Operating profit	**10,322**	**2,598**	**4,087**
Finance income	104	72	65
Finance expense	(757)	(736)	(734)
Profit on disposal of interest in associates	843	–	94
Share of after tax profits of associates and joint ventures	14	5	13
Profit before taxation	**10,526**	**1,939**	**3,525**
Income tax expense	(2,154)	(877)	(1,356)
Profit after taxation for the year	**£8,372**	**£1,062**	**£2,169**

separate account. Note the amount of *research and development* expenses, which shows the importance of this activity at GSK and, more generally, in the pharmaceutical industry.

Other operating income includes gains and losses from the disposal or acquisition of assets and businesses. Under US GAAP some of these items would be shown as special items.

GSK's STATEMENTS OF CASH FLOWS

Exhibit A4.2.5 presents the statements of cash flows of GSK for years 2015, 2016, and 2017 taken from the company's annual reports. GSK applies the indirect method of presenting its cash flows from operating activities. Remember that this method calculates the cash flow from operations starting with earnings after tax (profit after taxation) and makes adjustments to account for the noncash items and for the nonoperating transactions that affect EAT. GSK presents these adjustments in a note to the statement of cash flows. They are shown in Exhibit A4.2.6. Note the adjustment for net finance expense (finance expense less finance income): by doing so, and contrary to many companies also in compliance with IFRS Standards, GSK eliminates the impact of its investing and financing activities on its operating cash flows.

Cash inflows and outflows from investing and financing activities are self-explanatory and do not require any particular comment.

EXHIBIT A4.2.5	GSK's CONSOLIDATED CASH FLOW STATEMENTS.

FROM THE COMPANY 2017 ANNUAL REPORT. FIGURES IN MILLIONS OF POUNDS

	2015	2016	2017
Cash flow from operating activities			
Profit after taxation for the year	£8,372	£1,062	£2,169
Adjustments reconciling profit after tax to operating cash flows	(3,741)	7,044	6,089
Cash generated from operations	4,631	8,106	8,258
Taxation paid	(2,062)	(1,609)	(1,340)
Net cash inflow from operating activities	2,569	6,497	6,918
Cash flow from investing activities			
Purchase of property, plant, and equipment	(1,380)	(1,543)	(1,545)
Proceeds from sale of property, plant, and equipment	72	98	281
Purchase of intangible assets	(521)	(809)	(657)
Proceeds from sale of intangible assets	236	283	48
Purchase of equity investments	(82)	(96)	(80)
Proceeds from sale of equity investments	357	683	64
Contingent consideration paid	(338)	(73)	(91)
Purchase of businesses, net of cash acquired	(3,203)	17	–
Disposal of businesses	10,246	72	282
Investments in associates and joint ventures	(16)	(11)	(15)

EXHIBIT A4.2.5	GSK's CONSOLIDATED CASH FLOW STATEMENTS. (*Continued*)		
	2015	2016	2017
Proceeds from disposal of subsidiary and interest in associates	564	–	196
(Increase)/decrease in liquid investments	(2)	–	4
Interest received	99	68	64
Dividends from associates, joint ventures and equity investments	5	42	6
Net cash (outflow)/inflow from investing activities	6,037	(1,269)	(1,443)
Cash flow from financing activities			
Shares acquired by ESOP Trusts	(99)	(74)	(65)
Issue of share capital	73	89	56
Purchase of non-controlling interests	–	–	(29)
Increase in long-term loans	–	–	2,233
Increase/(decrease) in short-term loans	–	1,067	(3,200)
Repayment of short-term loans	(2,412)	(919)	–
Net repayment of obligations under finance leases	(25)	(18)	(23)
Interest paid	(762)	(732)	(781)
Dividends paid to shareholders	(3,874)	(4,850)	(3,906)
Distributions to non-controlling interests	(237)	(534)	(779)
Other financing cash flows	233	(421)	114
Net cash outflow from financing activities	(7,103)	(6,392)	(6,380)
(Decrease)/increase in cash and bank overdrafts	1,503	(1,164)	(905)
Cash and bank overdrafts at beginning of year	4,028	5,486	4,605
Exchange adjustments	(45)	283	(100)
(Decrease)/increase in cash and bank overdrafts	1,503	(1,164)	(905)
Cash and bank overdrafts at end of year	5,486	4,605	3,600
Cash and bank overdrafts at end of year comprise:			
Cash and cash equivalents	5,830	4,897	3,833
Overdrafts	(344)	(292)	(233)
	5,486	4,605	3,600

| EXHIBIT A4.2.6 | ADJUSTMENTS RECONCILING GSK's PROFIT AFTER TAX AND OPERATING CASH FLOWS. |

FROM THE COMPANY 2017 ANNUAL REPORT. FIGURES IN MILLIONS OF POUNDS

	2015	2016	2017
Profit after tax	£8,372	£1,062	£2,169
Tax on profits	2,154	877	1,356
Share of after tax profits of associates and joint ventures	(14)	(5)	(13)
Finance expense net of finance income	653	664	669
Depreciation	892	978	988
Amortization of intangible assets	738	796	934
Impairment and assets written off	822	226	1,061
Profit on sale of businesses	(9,308)	(5)	(157)
Profit on sale of intangible assets	(349)	(178)	(46)
Profit on sale of investments in associates	(843)	–	(94)
Profit on sale of equity investments	(342)	(254)	(37)
Changes in working capital	(566)	359	(663)
Contingent consideration paid	(121)	(358)	(594)
Other non-cash increase in contingent consideration liabilities	1,986	2,281	961
Increase in other payables	276	1,989	1,741
Decrease/(increase) in pension and other provisions	100	(621)	(255)
Share-based incentive plans	368	319	333
Fair value adjustments	–	(3)	
Other	(187)	(21)	(95)
Adjustments reconciling profit after tax to operating cash flows	(3,741)	7,044	6,089
Cash generated from operations	£4,631	£8,106	£8,258

FURTHER READING

1. Spiceland, David, Wayne Thomas, and Don Herrmann. *Financial Accounting*, 4th ed. McGraw Hill, 2016, chapters 1, 2, 3, 11.
2. Kieso, Donald, Jerry Weygandt, and Terry Warfield. *Intermediate Accounting*, 16th ed. John Wiley & Sons, 2016. See chapters 1 to 5.
3. Santoro, Julie, and Paul Munter. *IFRS compared to US GAAP: An Overview*, KPMG, December 2017.
4. Nissim, Doron. *"EBITDA, EBITA, or EBIT?"* Columbia Business School Research Paper, December 2017.
5. *Wiley IFRS 2018: Interpretation and Application of IFRS Standards*, PKF International Ltd, March 2018.

SELF-TEST QUESTIONS

4.1 **Accounting allocation of transactions.**

Indicate the components of the balance sheet and income statement that will change as a consequence of the following transactions:

	CA	NCA	CL	NCL	OE	REV	EXP	RE
1. Factory equipment purchased for cash								
2. Goodwill impairment loss								
3. Interest income received								
4. Dividend declared								
5. Shares repurchased								
6. Sale of merchandise on account								
7. Payment of two months' rent in advance								
8. Purchase of raw material on account								
9. Cash advance received from customer								
10. Recognition of salaries earned by employees								

CA: Current Assets   NCA: Noncurrent Assets   CL: Current Liabilities

NCL: Noncurrent Liabilities   OE: Owners' Equity   REV: Revenues

EXP: Expenses   RE: Retained Earnings

4.2 **Constructing income statements and balance sheets.**

Based on the information provided below, prepare the following financial statements for CompuStores, a company that assembles and distributes personal computers:

a. An income statement for the calendar Year 0
b. A balance sheet on December 31, Year –1
c. A balance sheet on December 31, Year 0

1. Accounts receivable increased by $6,400,000 in Year 0
2. Profits in Year 0 were taxed at 40 percent
3. At the end of Year 0, inventories equaled 10 percent of the year's sales
4. The net book value of fixed assets at the end of Year –1 was $76 million
5. Cost of goods sold, other than the direct labor expenses related to the assembling of computers, equaled 70 percent of sales in Year 0
6. The average interest rate on short- and long-term borrowing in Year 0 was 10 percent of the amount of funds borrowed at the *beginning* of the year
7. Accounts receivable at the end of Year 0 equaled 12 percent of sales
8. Accounts payable at the end of Year –1 equaled $30 million
9. Depreciation expense was $9 million in Year 0
10. The company owed its employees $4 million at the end of Year –1; a year later, it owed them $1.81 million
11. Material purchased in Year 0 amounted to $228 million
12. Selling, general, and administrative expenses for Year 0 were $18 million
13. Fees related to a technical license amount to $4 million per year

14. Taxes payable in Year –1 equaled $6 million, and the company paid in advance the same amount on December 15, Year –1
15. The balance of long-term debt was $27 million at the end of Year –1, of which $4 million was due at year-end
16. Shares of common stocks were not issued and outstanding shares were not repurchased in Year 0
17. Direct labor expenses equaled 11.25 percent of sales
18. Repayment of long-term debt is $4 million per year
19. Inventories rose from $28 million at the end of Year –1 to $32 million at the end of Year 0
20. In Year 0, one of the company's warehouses was enlarged at a cost of $14 million, which was partly financed with a $6 million long-term loan
21. Dividend payments for Year 0 were $9.36 million
22. Accounts payable at the end of Year 0 equaled 1.85 of a month of purchases
23. Equity capital at the end of Year –1 was $81 million
24. At the end of Year –1, the company had enough cash such that it could have immediately paid one-fourth of its accounts payable; at the end of Year 0, it could have paid only one-tenth
25. The company paid in advance $9.6 million of taxes on December 15, Year 0
26. The company's line of credit was $3 million at the end of Year –1. A year later it increased by two-thirds
27. In Year 0, the company had a $2 million nonrecurrent loss related to the discontinuation of an old product line
28. The company prepaid $1.5 million on rent and insurance in Year –1 and $2.085 million a year later.

4.3　Constructing managerial balance sheets.

Below are the balance sheets of Robin Ltd., a distributor of animal accessories, for Year –2, Year –1, and Year 0.

	Balance Sheets		
	December 31, Year –2	December 31, Year –1	December 31, Year 0
Cash	$600	$350	$300
Accounts receivable	2,730	3,100	4,200
Inventories	2,800	3,200	4,300
Prepaid expenses	0	0	0
Net fixed assets	1,200	1,300	1,450
Total assets	$7,330	$7,950	$10,250
Short-term debt	$300	$500	$1,900
Accounts payable	1,400	1,600	2,050
Accrued expenses	200	260	350
Long-term debt	1,300	1,200	1,100
Owners' equity	4,130	4,390	4,850
Total liabilities and owners' equity	$7,330	$7,950	$10,250

a. Compute Robin Ltd.'s working capital requirement (WCR) on December 31, Year –2, Year –1, and Year 0.

b. Prepare Robin Ltd.'s managerial balance sheets on December 31, Year –2, Year –1, and Year 0.

4.4 Transactions.

Indicate the effects of the following transactions on *net profit*, *working capital requirement (WCR)*, *earnings before interest, tax, depreciation and amortization (EBITDA)*, *and free cash flow (FCF)*. Use + to indicate an increase, – to indicate a decrease, and 0 to indicate no effect. Assume that US GAAP applies.

	NET PROFIT	WCR	EBITDA	FCF
Shares are issued for cash				
Goods from inventory are sold for cash at a profit				
Goods from inventory are sold on account at a profit				
A fixed asset is sold for cash for less than book value				
A fixed asset is sold for cash for more than book value				
Corporate income tax is paid				
Payment is made to trade creditors				
Cash is obtained through a bank loan				
A cash dividend is declared and paid				
Accounts receivable are collected				
Merchandise is purchased on account				
Cash advances are made to employees				
Minority interest in a firm is acquired for cash				
Equipment is acquired for cash				

4.5 Constructing a statement of cash flows.

The balance sheets at two consecutive year-ends and the income statement for the year in between of Allied & Consolidated Clothier (ACC), a manufacturer of coats and other garments, are shown below. All figures are in millions of dollars. Prepare a statement of cash flows for the same year as the income statement.

Balance Sheets (in millions, year-end data)					
	Year 1	Year 2		Year 1	Year 2
Cash	$100	$90	Short-term debt	$80	$90
Trade receivables	200	230	Trade payables	170	180
Inventories	160	170	Accrued expenses	40	45
Prepaid expenses	30	30	Long-term debt	140	120
Net fixed assets	390	390	Owners' equity	450	475
Total assets	**$880**	**$910**	**Total liabilities and owners' equity**	**$880**	**$910**

Income Statement Year 2 (in millions)	
Net sales	$1, 350
Cost of goods sold	970
Selling, general, and administrative expenses	165
Depreciation expense	50
Earnings before interest and tax (EBIT)	165
Net interest expense	20
Earnings before tax (EBT)	145
Income tax expense	45
Earnings after tax (EAT)	$ 100
Dividends	$75

REVIEW QUESTIONS

1. **Missing accounts.**
   Find the missing values for the following three firms. Show your computations.

	Firm 1	Firm 2	Firm 3
Assets, beginning of period	$1,000		
Assets, end of period	1,100	$500	
Owners' equity, beginning of period	500	200	
Owners' equity, end of period			$1,000
Liabilities, beginning of period		200	600
Liabilities, end of period			500
Revenues of the period	2,000		600
Expenses of the period	1,800	180	
Earnings after tax of the period		20	100
Dividends (from earnings of the period)	100	10	0
Shares issued ($ amount) during the period	0	50	0

2. **Balance sheet changes.**
   Below are incomplete balance sheets of ABC Corporation (figures in millions).

End-of-year for balance sheet items	Year 1	Year 2	Year 3	Year 4
Current assets	$16,870	$18,732	$19,950	$19,976
Noncurrent assets			29,920	
Total assets		48,050		
Current liabilities	13,466	15,284	16,574	16,080
Noncurrent liabilities	11,998		18,414	
Paid-in capital		2,298		2,798
Retained earnings	13,438	15,844		
Earnings (loss) after tax	2,014		(1,312)	5,048
Dividends	1,580	2,040	2,234	2,480
Owners' equity				
Total liabilities and owners' equity	40,936			51,070

  a. Compute the missing amounts and show the balance sheet at year-ends 1, 2, 3, and 4. Show your computations.
  b. What transactions might explain the change in total assets between years 1 and 2?
  c. What transactions might explain the change in retained earnings between years 2 and 3?
  d. What transactions might explain the change in total liabilities plus owners' equity between years 3 and 4?

3. **Balance sheet changes.**
   Below are incomplete balance sheets of OQ Corporation (figures in millions).

End-of-year for balance sheet items	Year 1	Year 2	Year 3	Year 4
Current assets	$3,092		$2,932	
Noncurrent assets		$18,160	17,996	$20,286
Total assets	21,094			
Current assets/current liabilities			1.023	1.04
Current liabilities	2,978			3,002
Noncurrent liabilities	9,286	9,830		
Owners' equity		8,868	8,058	8,084
Total liabilities and owners' equity		21,182		

  a. Compute the missing amounts, and show the balance sheet at year-ends 1, 2, 3, and 4. Show your computations.
  b. Comment on the asset and liability structure of the firm.

4. **Reconstructing an income statement.**
   Below is some income statement information on company DEF. Prepare an income statement for each of the three years. Show your computations.

	Year 1	Year 2	Year 3
Sales	$21,184		$49,308
Interest income	24	$ 132	208
Cost of goods sold	16,916	24,372	
Administrative and selling expenses	2,380	3,304	4,808
Research and development expenses	380	504	816
Income tax expense	444	864	1,696
Earnings after tax		2,124	3,776

5. **Reconstructing an income statement.**
   Below is some income statement information on company ABD. Prepare an income statement for each of the three years. Show your computations.

	Year 1	Year 2	Year 3
Sales	$21,087		$26,613
Interest expense	75	$90	81
Cost of goods sold	16,182	17,709	
Administrative and selling expenses	3,966	4,533	5,547
Income tax expense	324	252	192
Earnings after tax		408	312

6. **Reconstructing a balance sheet.**
   From the following data, reconstruct the balance sheet at the end of the year.

1. Earnings after tax	$300	At beginning of year:	
2. Increase in depreciation expense	200	13. Cash	$450
3. Sales of common stock	1,000	14. Accounts receivable	250
4. Acquisition of equipment	1,000	15. Inventories	300
5. Annual long-term debt reimbursement	100	16. Plant and equipment, net	2,000
6. Dividends	100	17. Accumulated depreciation	1,000
7. Increase in cash	50	18. Short-term debt	400
8. Increase in receivables	200	19. Accrued expenses	100
9. Increase in inventories	100	20. Long-term debt	500
10. Increase in payables	100	21. Common stock	600
11. Increase in wages payable	100	22. Retained earnings	1,100
12. Increase in taxes payable	100		

7. **Effect of transactions on working capital requirement.**
   Indicate the effect of the following transactions on the working capital requirement:

   a. More customers pay with cash instead of credit
   b. More of raw material is paid for with cash
   c. More discounts are offered to customers
   d. More finished goods are produced for order

8. **Constructing a managerial balance sheet.**
   Prepare the managerial balance sheet of the following US company balance sheet (the company applies US GAAP):

In millions	Fiscal year-end
Assets	
Current assets:	
Cash and cash equivalents	$245
Short-term investments	416
Merchandise inventories	8,209
Deferred income taxes	166
Other current assets	215
Total current assets	9,251
Property, less accumulated depreciation	22,722
Long-term investments	253
Other assets	460
Total assets	**$32,686**
Liabilities and shareholders' equity	
Current liabilities:	
Short-term borrowings	$987
Current portion of long-term debt	34
Accounts payable	4,109
Accrued compensation and employees benefits	434
Self-insurance liabilities	751
Deferred revenue	674
Other current liabilities	1,033
Total current liabilities	8,022
Long-term debt	5,039
Deferred income taxes, net	660
Other liabilities	910
Total liabilities	14,631
Shareholders' equity:	
Common stock	735
Capital-in-excess of par value	277
Retained earnings	17,049
Accumulated other comprehensive income (loss)	(6)
Total shareholders' equity	18,055
Total liabilities and shareholders' equity	**$32,686**

9. **Transactions.**

Indicate the effect of the following transactions on working capital requirement (WCR), net operating cash flow (CF$_{OPE}$), cash flow from investing activities (CF$_{INV}$), cash flow from financing activities (CF$_{FIN}$), and owners' equity. Use + to indicate an increase, − to indicate a decrease, and 0 to indicate no effect.

		WCR	CF$_{OPE}$	CF$_{INV}$	CF$_{FIN}$	Owners' Equity
1.	Shares are issued for cash					
2.	Goods from inventory are sold for cash					
3.	A fixed asset is sold for cash at a loss					
4.	Corporate income tax is paid					
5.	Cash is obtained through a bank loan					
6.	A cash dividend is paid					
7.	Accounts receivable are collected					
8.	Minority interest in a firm acquired for cash					
9.	A fixed asset is depreciated					
10.	Obsolete inventory is written off					
11.	Insurance premium is paid					
12.	Merchandise is purchased on account					

10. **Profits, losses, and cash flows.**

   a. How would you explain that a firm can generate a profit, when at the same time its cash flow from operations is negative?

   b. How would you explain that a firm showing a net loss can have a positive cash flow from operations?

ANALYZING OPERATIONAL EFFICIENCY AND LIQUIDITY

CHAPTER **5**

A firm that can no longer pay its creditors – its bankers and suppliers – is illiquid and technically bankrupt, a situation that no manager wishes to face. Managers must make decisions that do not endanger their firm's liquidity – a term that refers to the firm's ability to meet its *recurrent* cash obligations toward various creditors. A firm's liquidity is driven by the structure of its balance sheet, namely, by the nature and composition of its assets and the way they are financed.

It is easier to understand and measure a firm's liquidity if we use the *managerial balance sheet* we presented in Chapter 4 rather than the standard accounting balance sheet. The managerial balance sheet classifies the firm's investments into three categories: (1) cash and cash-equivalent assets; (2) working capital requirement, which is the difference between the assets required to support the firm's operating activities, such as inventories and trade receivables, and the firm's operating liabilities, such as trade payables; and (3) net fixed assets, such as property, plant, and equipment.

To finance these investments, the firm uses a combination of short-term and long-term sources of funds. One way a firm can manage its balance sheet and enhance its liquidity is by using the *matching strategy*. This strategy requires that long-term investments be financed with long-term funds and short-term investments with short-term funds. We show in this chapter that the matching principle helps explain how a firm's liquidity should be measured and how liquidity is affected by managerial decisions.

New concepts and terms, such as *net short-term financing* and *net long-term financing*, are introduced. We then show how they can be combined to construct a reliable measure of a firm's liquidity. Other, more traditional indicators of liquidity, such as the *current ratio* and the *acid test ratio*, are also presented and compared with our suggested measure. To illustrate these concepts, we use Office Supplies (OS) Distributors, the company whose balance sheets (standard and managerial) and income statements for the years Year –2 to Year 0 (Year 0 is this year) are examined in Chapter 4. After reading this chapter, you should understand the following:

- The structure of the managerial balance sheet
- The meaning of net long-term financing, net short-term financing, net working capital, current ratio, acid test ratio, and other ratios used to measure, analyze, and manage liquidity

- The meaning of financial cost risk and refinancing risk
- How a firm's operating decisions affect its liquidity
- How to improve a firm's liquidity through better management of the firm's operating cycle

THE STRUCTURE OF THE MANAGERIAL BALANCE SHEET

In Chapter 4 we introduced the managerial balance sheet as an alternative to the standard balance sheet in order to make it easier for operating and finance managers to evaluate their contribution to the financial performance of their firm. Exhibit 5.1 shows the standard balance sheets of OS Distributors at year-ends Year –2, Year –1, and Year 0, while Exhibit 5.2 shows the managerial version of the balance sheets at the same dates, all taken from Chapter 4.

In the upper part of the managerial balance sheet, three items are grouped under the heading **Invested capital**. These are cash and cash-equivalent holdings, working capital requirement (the firm's investment in its operating cycle), and net fixed assets.

In the bottom half of the managerial balance sheet, two items are grouped under the heading **Capital employed**. These are short-term debt and long-term financing, the latter consisting of long-term debt and owners' equity (as in previous chapters, we use the terms financing, funding, and capital interchangeably).

The managerial balance sheet provides a snapshot of the total capital the firm has available at a point in time (the capital employed shown in the lower half) and the way that capital is invested in the firm's net assets (the invested capital shown in the upper half). The following sections examine the structure of the managerial balance sheet and its relevance to the measurement of the firm's liquidity.

THE THREE COMPONENTS OF A FIRM'S INVESTED CAPITAL

A firm's capital is used to finance investments in (1) **cash and cash-equivalent** assets; (2) working capital requirement (WCR); and (3) fixed assets, such as property, plant, and equipment. We begin with a brief review of cash and fixed assets and then analyze WCR in more detail.

CASH AND CASH-EQUIVALENT ASSETS

Firms hold cash and cash-equivalent assets (also called **liquid assets**) for at least three reasons:[1] (1) to meet the cash needs of recurrent operations, (2) as a precautionary measure,[2] and (3) at the request of their banks.

Every day firms receive cash from their customers and pay their suppliers or other creditors. These recurrent cash inflows and outflows generally do not cancel out fully. Consequently, at times, firms can find themselves short of cash to pay bills on time unless they have enough cash available. The amount of cash a firm needs to meet its recurrent cash transactions is referred to as **operating cash**.

---

[1] We will use the generic word cash to refer not only to cash in hand but also to any cash-equivalent assets.

[2] The amount of cash that a company should hold as a precautionary measure is not well documented. One source indicates that it should be between 0.5 percent and 2 percent of annual sales. See Koller, Goedhart, and Wessels (2015). When the information is available, daily changes in the firm's cash account can be used to estimate the minimum amount of cash balance needed to support the firm's recurrent activities.

EXHIBIT 5.1	OS DISTRIBUTORS' BALANCE SHEETS.

FIGURES IN MILLIONS

	December 31, Year –2 (Two years ago)	December 31, Year –1 (One year ago)	December 31, Year 0 (This year)
Assets			
• **Current assets**			
Cash[1]	$ 6.0	$ 12.0	$ 8.0
Accounts receivable	44.0	48.0	56.0
Inventories	52.0	57.0	72.0
Prepaid expenses[2]	2.0	2.0	1.0
Total current assets	104.0	119.0	137.0
• **Noncurrent assets**			
Financial assets and intangibles	0.0	0.0	0.0
Property, plant, and equipment			
Gross value[3]	$90.0	$90.0	$93.0
less accumulated depreciation	(34.0) 56.0	(39.0) 51.0	(40.0) 53.0
Total noncurrent assets	56.0	51.0	53.0
Total assets	$160.0	$170.0	$190.0
Liabilities and owners' equity			
• **Current liabilities**			
Short-term debt	$ 15.0	$ 22.0	$ 23.0
Owed to banks	$7.0	$14.0	$15.0
Current portion of long-term debt	8.0	8.0	8.0
Accounts payable	37.0	40.0	48.0
Accrued expenses[4]	2.0	4.0	4.0
Total current liabilities	54.0	66.0	75.0
• **Noncurrent liabilities**			
Long-term debt[5]	42.0	34.0	38.0
Total noncurrent liabilities	42.0	34.0	38.0
• **Owners' equity[6]**	64.0	70.0	77.0
Total liabilities and owners' equity	$160.0	$170.0	$190.0

[1] Consists of cash in hand and checking accounts held to facilitate operating activities on which the firm earns no interest.
[2] Prepaid expenses comprises rent paid in advance (when recognized in the income statement, rent is included in selling, general, and administrative expenses).
[3] In Year –1, there was no disposal of existing fixed assets or acquisition of new fixed assets. However, during Year 0, a warehouse was enlarged at a cost of $12 million and existing fixed assets, bought for $9 million in the past, were sold at their net book value of $2 million.
[4] Accrued expenses consists of wages and taxes payable.
[5] Long-term debt is repaid at the rate of $8 million per year. No new long-term debt was incurred during Year –1, but during Year 0, a mortgage loan was obtained from the bank to finance the extension of a warehouse (see note 3).
[6] During the three years, no new shares were issued and none were repurchased.

| EXHIBIT 5.2 | OS DISTRIBUTORS' MANAGERIAL BALANCE SHEETS. |

ALL DATA FROM THE BALANCE SHEETS IN EXHIBIT 5.1. FIGURES IN MILLIONS

	December 31, Year –2	December 31, Year –1	December 31, Year 0
Invested capital			
• Cash	$ 6.0	$ 12.0	$ 8.0
• Working capital requirement (WCR)[1]	59.0	63.0	77.0
• Net fixed assets	56.0	51.0	53.0
Total invested capital	$121.0	$126.0	$138.0
Capital employed			
• Short-term debt	$ 15.0	$ 22.0	$ 23.0
• Long-term financing			
Long-term debt	$42.0	$34.0	$38.0
Owners' equity	64.0 106.0	70.0 104.0	77.0 115.0
Total capital employed	$121.0	$126.0	$138.0

[1] WCR = (Accounts receivable + Inventories + Prepaid expenses) – (Accounts payable + Accrued expenses).

In addition to the cash balances needed to support **operating activities** firms also may hold cash as a precautionary measure against unexpected and adverse shocks in the economic environment in which they operate. For example, during the 2008–2009 financial crisis, many firms which relied on short-term credit found themselves unable to renew their short-term debts. In such circumstances, having extra cash can help firms avoid falling into financial distress. Furthermore, and as an added precaution, firms (particularly large ones) can negotiate **credit lines** with their banks. This is an agreement in which the bank, for a fee, extends a specific amount of credit for a short period of time at the discretion of the firm. Information about the agreement is usually found in the notes to the firm's balance sheet.

Finally, banks can require their corporate clients to maintain some **compensating balances** for services they provide to the firm. OS Distributors does not hold any cash-equivalent assets such as marketable securities (securities that can be sold rapidly without a significant loss in value). It held $6 million in cash at the end of Year –2, $12 million at the end of Year –1, and $8 million at the end of Year 0.

INVESTMENT IN FIXED ASSETS

Investments in fixed assets include items such as property, plant, and equipment. Their book value is recorded in the balance sheet as net fixed assets, which is their purchase price less accumulated depreciation. Exhibit 5.2 indicates that the book value of OS Distributors' fixed assets was $56 million in Year –2, $51 million in Year –1, and $53 million in Year 0. Decisions about the acquisition and disposal of long-term assets are part of the firm's strategic activities, which are analyzed in detail in Chapters 7 through 9. In this and the next chapter, we focus on the firm's operating activities.

WORKING CAPITAL REQUIREMENT

Working capital requirement, or **operating working capital**, is the firm's investment in its **operating cycle**. As we showed in Chapter 4, it is the difference between the firm's operating assets and operating liabilities. More precisely we can write:

$$\text{Working capital requirement (WCR)} = [\text{Operating assets} - \text{Operating liabilities}]$$
$$= [\text{Accounts receivable} + \text{Inventories}$$
$$+ \text{Prepaid expenses}] - [\text{Accounts payable}$$
$$+ \text{Accrued expenses}] \qquad (5.1)$$

For most firms, operating assets exceed operating liabilities and WCR is *positive*, meaning that the firm has to finance it. When the opposite occurs, WCR is *negative* and the firm's operating cycle becomes a source *of cash* rather than a use of funds.

Firms with a negative WCR are found in the retail and service sectors of the economy. Such firms collect cash from their customers before they pay their suppliers and carry small inventories relative to their sales. Large supermarkets are a typical example. They sell mostly for cash and thus have few receivables. And because their inventories move rapidly, they are usually low relative to the sales they generate. The amount of money they owe their suppliers, however, can be very large because big supermarket chains often manage to extract generous credit terms from their suppliers. Few receivables, low inventories, and large amounts of payables is the perfect recipe for turning the firm's operating cycle into a source of cash.

Another example is mail order houses where most customers pay on order, while suppliers are paid later and inventories are tight. Consider Amazon.com. Exhibit 5.3 shows some figures taken from the company's annual reports for the years 2015, 2016, and 2017. Note the negative sign and magnitude of the WCRs at year-ends 2015, 2016, and 2017: $-\$14,872$ million, $-\$19,248$ million, and $-\$23,575$ million, respectively. Comparing these negative WCRs to the amount of cash held by the company at the same dates (last column) shows that Amazon's recurrent negative WCR is a major source of cash for the company. Other firms with a negative WCR are in industries such as publishing (customers pay for their subscription before they

EXHIBIT 5.3	**EXTRACTS FROM AMAZON.COM'S BALANCE SHEETS.**

FIGURES IN MILLIONS

Year	Accounts Receivable	Inventories	Accounts Payable	Accrued Expenses	WCR[1]	Cash
2015	$5,654	$10,243	$20,397	$10,372	–$14,872	$19,808
2016	8,339	11,461	25,309	13,739	–19,248	25,981
2017	13,164	16,047	34,616	18,170	–23,575	30,980

[1] WCR = Working capital requirement = Receivables + Inventories − Payables − Accrued expenses. Source: Yahoo! Finance.

receive their magazine) and air transportation (customers pay for their trip before their departure).[3]

OS Distributors' WCR has risen from $59 million in Year −2 to $77 million in Year 0. How can we explain this growth? We examine this issue later in the chapter.

THE TWO COMPONENTS OF A FIRM'S CAPITAL EMPLOYED

How should the firm's invested capital be financed? Two primary sources of capital are available to firms: (1) the equity capital provided by owners and (2) the debt capital provided by debt holders. Debt can be *short-term* (due to be repaid within one year) or *long-term* (due to be repaid after one year).[4] Thus, a firm's total capital employed can be classified either as equity and debt capital or as **long-term financing** (equity plus long-term debt) and **short-term financing** (short-term debt). The first approach distinguishes the *nature* of the firm's capital employed whereas the second distinguishes its *duration*.

Given these alternative sources of capital, the firm's managers must answer two questions when deciding which strategy should be adopted to fund the firm's investments:

1. What is the best combination of equity capital and debt capital?
2. What proportion of borrowed funds should be in the form of long-term debt and what proportion in the form of short-term debt?

The answer to the first question affects the firm's profitability and financial risk. It is examined in detail in Chapter 6. The answer to the second question affects primarily the firm's liquidity. It is examined later in this chapter.

THE STRUCTURE OF OS DISTRIBUTORS' MANAGERIAL BALANCE SHEET

Exhibit 5.2 indicates that OS Distributors' invested capital was $138 million at the end of Year 0 funded with $23 million of short-term debt and $115 million of long-term financing ($38 million of long-term debt plus $77 million of owners' equity). The managerial balance sheets show that the proportion of cash held by the firm fluctuated between 5 and 10 percent of total invested capital. The proportion of WCR fluctuated between 49 and 56 percent, and that of net fixed assets fluctuated between 38 and 46 percent. The relatively large amount of WCR is not surprising given that OS Distributors is a wholesale distribution company. Compared with typical manufacturing companies, firms in the wholesale distribution business have a significant amount of capital invested in their operating cycle. Turning to the structure of capital employed, notice that 83 to 88 percent of OS Distributors' investments were financed with long-term funds compared with 12 to 17 percent with short-term debt.

THE MATCHING STRATEGY

In deciding how much of the firm's investments should be financed with long-term funds and how much with short-term debt, most firms try to apply the **matching**

---

[3] Exhibit 5.6 shows a few more industries with a negative WCR.

[4] This distinction is somewhat arbitrary but is the one used in standard accounting models. In practice, there is a grey area with medium-term debt, due to be repaid after one year but less than, say, three years.

strategy. According to this strategy, *long-term investments should be financed with long-term funds and short-term investments should be financed with short-term funds*. By matching the life of an asset and the duration of its financing source, a firm can minimize the risk of *not* being able to finance the asset over its entire useful life.

Consider a piece of equipment with a useful life of five years. Its purchase price can be financed either with a five-year loan (a matched financing strategy) or with a one-year renewable loan (a mismatched financing strategy), both at the same interest rate. Which of the two strategies is riskier?

The mismatched strategy is riskier for two reasons. First, the interest rate, and thus the cost of financing the equipment, may change during the following four years. Second, the lender may be unwilling to renew the one-year loan, thus forcing the firm to repay its loan after one year. This situation may require the sale of the equipment and the early termination of the investment. These two types of risk, called **financial cost risk** and **refinancing risk**, respectively, are clearly much lower under the matching strategy.

However, matching the maturity structure of the firm's sources of financing with the maturity of its assets is not necessarily the *optimal* financing strategy for every firm at all times. Some firms, at times, may be willing to carry some financial cost and refinancing risks if they expect short-term interest rates to go down.[5] On the other hand, firms that are more risk averse may choose to carry more long-term funds than necessary under the matching strategy. Appendix 5.1 provides an illustration of matched and mismatched financing strategies for firms with growing and seasonal sales.

We can use the managerial balance sheets in Exhibit 5.2 to find out whether OS Distributors has been applying the matching strategy during the period Year −2 to Year 0. We examine each of the three investments and their financing. Cash, a short-term asset, has been fully funded with short-term debt at the end of each year and was thus matched. Similarly, net fixed assets, which are long-term investments, have been fully funded with long-term financing and also were thus matched. The matching strategy applied in both cases. Does it also apply to WCR?

Before we can answer this question, we need to know if WCR is a short-term or a long-term investment. At first glance, it may seem that it is a short-term investment because it is made up of current assets, which will become cash within a year, and current liabilities, which will decrease the firm's cash holdings within a year. But the answer is not that simple. Although these assets and liabilities are classified as current, or short-term, they will be replaced by *new* current assets and *new* current liabilities as the operating cycle repeats itself. So, as long as the firm stays in business, WCR will remain in its (managerial) balance sheet and, hence, is more *permanent* than transient in nature. In other words, WCR is essentially a long-term investment. Under a matching strategy, it should be financed with long-term funds. Exhibit 5.2 indicates that a small proportion of OS Distributors' WCR was financed with short-term funds, implying that the firm did not adhere strictly to the matching strategy. Let's examine this point further.

Some firms can adhere to the matching strategy without entirely financing their WCR with long-term funds. Consider a firm that has growing but seasonal sales. If the firm maintains a constant ratio of WCR to sales over time, then its working

---

[5] If the short-term interest rate is expected to go down, then a short-term loan that is renewable over the life of the asset would be cheaper than a long-term loan that matches the life of the asset.

capital requirement will display a seasonal growth behavior. Exhibit 5.4 illustrates this situation for WCR equal to 25 percent of sales.

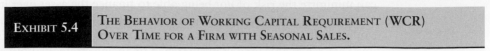

EXHIBIT 5.4	THE BEHAVIOR OF WORKING CAPITAL REQUIREMENT (WCR) OVER TIME FOR A FIRM WITH SEASONAL SALES.

WCR IS ASSUMED TO BE SET AT 25 PERCENT OF SALES

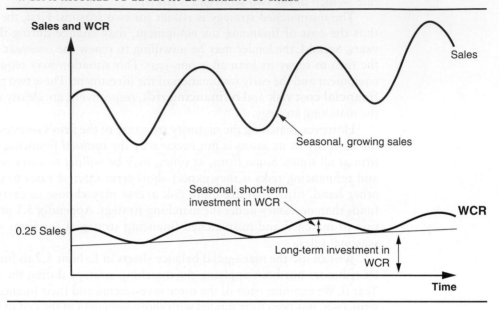

In this case, the WCR has a *long-term growth* component (called *permanent WCR*) and a *short-term seasonal* component (called *seasonal WCR*). According to the matching strategy, the long-term growth component should be financed with long-term funds and the seasonal component with short-term funds. Applying this funding strategy should reduce both financial cost and refinancing risks.

A MEASURE OF LIQUIDITY BASED ON THE FUNDING STRUCTURE OF WORKING CAPITAL REQUIREMENT

For most firms that adopt it, the matching strategy is an objective rather than a day-to-day reality. The goal of management is for long-term funds to match the firm's long-term investments (net fixed assets and permanent WCR) and for short-term funds to match the firm's short-term investments (cash, marketable securities, and seasonal WCR) *over time*. This objective may not be easily achieved in practice, and at times, the firm may find itself in a mismatched situation in which a *significant* portion of its permanent working capital is funded with short-term debt. This situation can create a liquidity problem. This section presents a measure of liquidity that managers can use to monitor their firm's liquidity position. The measure is based on the funding structure of WCR – more precisely, on the portion of WCR that is funded with long-term financing. How much long-term financing is available to fund the firm's WCR? Because net fixed assets are funded with long-term financing, any long-term financing in excess of net fixed assets can be used to fund WCR. These excess long-term funds are called **net long-term financing (NLF)**:

$$\text{Net long-term financing} = \text{Long-term financing} - \text{Net fixed assets} \qquad (5.2)$$

NLF is the portion of the firm's long-term financing available to finance the firm's other two fundamental investments, its WCR and cash. Exhibit 5.5 shows that OS Distributors' NLF at the end of Year 0 was $62 million. It is equal to the firm's $115 million of long-term financing ($38 million of long-term debt plus $77 million of equity) less the $53 million of net fixed assets.

How much short-term financing is used to fund the firm's WCR? It is simply the amount of short-term debt that is not used to finance the firm's cash. The amount of short-term debt in excess of cash is called **net short-term financing (NSF)**:

$$\text{Net short-term financing} = \text{Short-term debt} - \text{Cash} \qquad (5.3)$$

As shown at the bottom of Exhibit 5.5, OS Distributors' WCR of $77 million at the end of Year 0 was financed with $62 million of long-term funds (NLF $62 million) and $15 million of short-term funds (NSF $15 million). Thus, in Year 0, 80.5 percent of WCR was funded with long-term financing and 19.5 percent with short-term debt. We call the ratio of NLF to WCR the firm's **liquidity ratio** and use it to measure the firm's liquidity position:

$$\text{Liquidity ratio} = \frac{\text{Long-term financing} - \text{Net fixed assets}}{\text{Working capital requirement}}$$
$$= \frac{\text{Net long-term financing}}{\text{Working capital requirement}} \qquad (5.4)$$

OS Distributors' liquidity ratio dropped from 84.7 percent in Year -2 to 80.5 percent in Year 0, indicating a slight deterioration in the firm's liquidity position. In general, all else being equal, *the higher the proportion of WCR financed with long-term funds, the more liquid the firm.* This is because working capital is essentially a long-term investment; financing it with higher proportions of short-term funds creates a mismatch between investment and funding durations that could lead to a liquidity problem. In other words, *the higher the liquidity ratio, the more liquid the firm.*

If we deduct NLF from WCR, we get the portion of WCR that is financed with short-term funds, in other words, NSF:

$$\text{WCR} - \text{NLF} = \text{NSF}$$

This equation clearly shows that a firm's *net* short-term financing depends on the relative amounts of working capital and *net* long-term financing on its balance sheet. As the amount of long-term funds (NLF) used to finance WCR increases, the firm's liquidity ratio rises (see equation 5.4). Simultaneously, the amount of short-term funds (NSF) used to finance WCR decreases. In other words, when the firm increases its liquidity ratio, it is also reducing its NSF.

EXHIBIT 5.5	OS DISTRIBUTORS' NET INVESTMENTS IN ITS OPERATING CYCLE AND ITS FINANCING.

ALL DATA FROM THE BALANCE SHEETS IN EXHIBIT 5.1. FIGURES IN MILLIONS

December 31, Year –2	December 31, Year –1	December 31, Year 0

Net Investment in the Operating Cycle or WCR

WCR = [Accounts receivable + Inventories + Prepaid expenses] – [Accounts payable + Accrued expenses]

[$44 + $52 + $2] – [$37 + $2] = **$59**	[$48 + $57 + $2] – [$40 + $4] = **$63**	[$56 + $72 + $1] – [$48 + $4] = **$77**

The Financing of the Operating Cycle

Net long-term financing (NLF) = Long-term debt + Owners' equity – Net fixed assets

$42 + $64 – $56 = **$50**	$34 + $70 – $51 = **$53**	$38 + $77 – $53 = **$62**

Net short-term financing (NSF) = Short-term debt – Cash

$15 – $6 = **$9**	$22 – $12 = **$10**	$23 – $8 = **$15**

Net long-term financing / WCR

Percentage of working capital requirement financed with long-term funds

$50 / $59 = **84.7%**	$53 / $63 = **84.1%**	$62 / $77 = **80.5%**

Net short-term financing / WCR

Percentage of working capital requirement financed with short-term funds

$9 / $59 = **15.3%**	$10 / $63 = **15.9%**	$15 / $77 = **19.5%**

Working Capital Requirement and its Financing

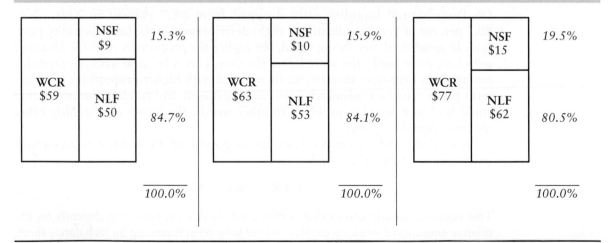

IMPROVING LIQUIDITY THROUGH BETTER MANAGEMENT OF THE OPERATING CYCLE

What drives a firm's liquidity? The answer to this question is given by the liquidity ratio in equation 5.4: a firm's liquidity position is the consequence of decisions that affect its NLF (the numerator of the liquidity ratio) and its WCR (the denominator of the liquidity ratio). A firm's liquidity position will improve if its liquidity ratio rises. According to equation 5.4, this will happen under the following circumstances:

1. Long-term financing increases, and/or
2. Net fixed assets decrease, and/or
3. WCR decreases

Decisions related to the management of long-term financing and net fixed assets are *strategic* in nature. Long-term financing will increase if the firm (1) issues long-term debt, (2) raises new equity capital (issues new shares), or (3) increases retained earnings by reducing dividend payments. Net fixed assets will decrease if the firm sells property and other fixed assets. Generally, these decisions are infrequent and involve large amounts of cash. They are also prepared well in advance so that the firm's financial manager, who actively participates in this decision-making process, can easily forecast their effect on the firm's liquidity.

Decisions affecting the firm's WCR are related to the management of the firm's *operating* cycle. They determine the amount of receivables, inventories, prepaid expenses, payables, and accrued expenses in the firm's balance sheet. Contrary to strategic decisions, operating decisions are made frequently (a company receives payments from its customers many times a day), they involve relatively small amounts of cash, and, often, they do not directly involve the firm's financial manager. They affect the firm's liquidity continually and are difficult to forecast in aggregate. Through these operating decisions, a firm's *operating* managers influence the firm's liquidity. *The lower the firm's investment in its operating cycle, the lower its WCR and the higher the firm's liquidity.* Furthermore, the lower the frequency of unexpected changes in the firm's WCR, the less volatile the firm's liquidity position and the easier it is to manage. Clearly, *control of the amount and fluctuations of a firm's WCR is the key to sound management of the firm's liquidity.*

Controlling WCR requires identifying and understanding the factors that affect its size. Five items make up a firm's WCR: receivables, inventories, prepaid expenses, payables, and accrued expenses. The size of these five items depends on the following three basic factors:

1. The nature of the *economic sector* in which the firm operates
2. The *degree of efficiency* with which the firm manages its operating cycle and
3. The *level and growth of sales.*

THE EFFECT OF THE FIRM'S ECONOMIC SECTOR ON ITS WORKING CAPITAL REQUIREMENT

The nature of a firm's business, the technology it uses, and the economic sector in which it operates affect the amount of WCR it needs to support a given level of sales. For example, an aircraft manufacturer needs more working capital than a department store to support the *same* level of sales. The business system underlying a department store allows it to operate with significantly lower amounts of receivables and inventories than those of an aircraft company with the same amount of sales. As mentioned earlier, some firms, such as large supermarket chains, may even have a *negative* WCR; in this case, the firm's operating cycle is a source of cash rather than a use of capital.

The sector effect on WCR can be measured by calculating the ratio of WCR to sales for a sample of firms in the same sector. Exhibit 5.6 reports this ratio for a number of industries in the United States. Firms in sectors with higher ratios require larger investments in their operating cycles to generate a dollar of sales. This indicates a longer operating cycle for firms in those industries.

For example, in 2017, a typical iron and steel mill needed, on average, to invest in its operating cycle an amount of capital equal to 27 percent of its sales, whereas a grocery store had, on average, *no* net investment in its operating cycle because the average WCR-to-sales ratio for the sector was zero in 2017. This difference simply reflects the fact that the operating cycle of a typical iron and steel mill is significantly longer than that of a typical grocery store. Note that very few sectors have an average WCR-to-sales ratio exceeding 25 percent and that the average ratio across all sectors is 10 percent.

Exhibit 5.7 shows that OS Distributors' ratio of WCR to sales rose from 15 percent in Year –2 to 16 percent in Year 0, indicating a slight deterioration in the management of its operating cycle during that period. Note also that OS Distributors' WCR-to-sales ratio is higher than its sector average of 13 percent reported in Exhibit 5.6 (wholesalers of durable goods), indicating a less efficient use of working capital than the average US wholesaler.

EXHIBIT 5.6	SOME BENCHMARK RATIOS OF WORKING CAPITAL REQUIREMENT TO SALES FOR A SAMPLE OF US ECONOMIC SECTORS IN 2017.[1]

WORKING CAPITAL REQUIREMENT AS PERCENTAGE OF SALES

Sector		Sector	
Iron & steel mills	27%	Merchant wholesalers: nondurable goods	10%
Textile mills	23%	Wood product manufacturing	10%
Aircraft manufacturing	21%	Drilling oil & gas wells	9%
Machinery manufacturing	18%	Computer systems design & related services	8%
Motor vehicle manufacturing	18%	Natural gas distribution	8%
Plastics & rubber products manufacturing	16%	Soap & cleaning compound manufacturing	6%
Leather & allied product manufacturing	16%	Electric power generation	5%
Computer & peripheral equipment manufacturing	15%	Grocery stores	0%
Beverage manufacturing	14%	Warehousing & storage	0%
Merchant wholesalers: durable goods	13%	Air transport	–2%
Food manufacturing	13%	Publishing industries (except Internet)	–6%
Department stores	11%	Accommodation	–6%
Average all sectors: 10%			

[1] Source: Calculated by the authors using Compustat data.

EXHIBIT 5.7	OS DISTRIBUTORS' MANAGEMENT OF ITS OPERATING CYCLE.

ALL DATA FROM THE BALANCE SHEETS IN EXHIBIT 5.1 AND THE INCOME STATEMENTS IN
EXHIBIT 4.7, CHAPTER 4. FIGURES IN MILLIONS

Ratio	Objective	December 31, Year −2	December 31, Year −1	December 31, Year 0
$\dfrac{\text{WCR}^1}{\text{Sales}}$	To evaluate the overall efficiency with which the firm's operating cycle is managed	$\dfrac{\$59}{\$390} = 15\%$	$\dfrac{\$63}{\$420} = 15\%$	$\dfrac{\$77}{\$480} = 16\%$
$\dfrac{\text{Cost of goods sold (COGS)}}{\text{Inventories}}$	To evaluate the efficiency with which inventories are managed	$\dfrac{\$328}{\$52} = 6.3$ times	$\dfrac{\$353}{\$57} = 6.2$ times	$\dfrac{\$400}{\$72} = 5.6$ times
$\dfrac{\text{Accounts receivable}}{\text{Average daily sales}^2}$	To evaluate the efficiency with which accounts receivable are managed	$\dfrac{\$44}{\$390/365} = 41$ days	$\dfrac{\$48}{\$420/365} = 42$ days	$\dfrac{\$56}{\$480/365} = 43$ days
$\dfrac{\text{Accounts payable}}{\text{Average daily purchases}^{2,3}}$	To evaluate the efficiency with which accounts payable are managed	$\dfrac{\$37}{\$332/365} = 41$ days	$\dfrac{\$40}{\$358/365} = 41$ days	$\dfrac{\$48}{\$415/365} = 42$ days

[1] WCR is found in Exhibit 5.2.
[2] We assume the year has 365 days.
[3] Purchases are equal to COGS plus the change in inventories (see equation 5.9). In Year −3, inventories were $48, thus purchases (Year −2) = $328 + ($52 − $48) = $332. Purchases (Year −1) = $353 + ($57 − $52) = $358; and purchases (Year 0) = $400 + ($72 − $57) = $415.

THE EFFECT OF MANAGERIAL EFFICIENCY ON WORKING CAPITAL REQUIREMENT

Firms in the same sector do not necessarily have the same ratio of WCR to sales. Even though they face similar constraints, some are able to manage their working capital better than others. For example, if a firm does not control its inventories and receivables as well as its sector's average, its WCR-to-sales ratio will be higher than that of its sector.

Several ratios can be used to estimate the efficiency with which a firm manages the components of its WCR. They have the advantages of being simple and of requiring data readily available in balance sheets and income statements. These ratios, discussed in the following sections, provide managers and analysts with good signals regarding both changes in a firm's managerial efficiency over time and differences across firms in the same sector.

INVENTORY TURNOVER

A firm's **inventory turnover**, or **inventory turns**, is generally defined as the ratio of its cost of goods sold (COGS) to its end-of-period inventories:

$$\text{Inventory turnover} = \frac{\text{COGS}}{\text{Ending inventory}} \tag{5.5}$$

For a distribution company, an inventory turnover of, say, six means that items in inventory turn over, on average, six times per year. Or, to put it another way, an item stays in the firm's warehouse for two months, on average. The *higher* the inventory turnover, the *lower* the firm's investment in inventories and the *higher* the efficiency with which the firm manages its inventories.

When COGS is not available, the level of sales is often used as a substitute to compute inventory turnover. Sometimes, inventories at the end of the period are replaced by average inventories during the period. Strictly speaking, the definition of inventory turnover given in equation 5.5 applies only to finished goods. To obtain the turnover for raw material inventory, the COGS in equation 5.5 is replaced by the amount of purchases.

The ratios reported in Exhibit 5.7 indicate that OS Distributors' inventory turnover deteriorated slightly, dropping from 6.3 times at the end of Year –2 to 5.6 times at the end of Year 0.

AVERAGE COLLECTION PERIOD

Also called the **average age of accounts receivable**, or **days of sales outstanding (DSO)**, the **average collection period**, expressed in days, is defined as accounts receivable at the end of the period divided by the average *daily* sales during that period:

$$\text{Average collection period} = \frac{\text{Accounts receivable}_{end}}{\text{Average daily sales}} \tag{5.6}$$

The average collection period is the number of days' worth of sales *that have not yet been collected at the date of the balance sheet*. It is an estimate of the *average* number of days the firm must wait from the time it ships its goods or delivers its services until its customers pay their bills. The faster the bills are collected, the *lower* the firm's receivables, the *higher* the efficiency with which the firm manages its receivables, and the *lower* its WCR.

This ratio is just an average; it does not represent the actual number of days a firm must wait between the time a sale is made and payment for it is collected. Not all customers settle their invoices after the same number of days. Some pay earlier than the average collection period and others pay later. If a certain group of customers is often late paying its bills, the firm should monitor that group separately.

OS Distributors' average collection periods, reported in Exhibit 5.7, indicate a slight lengthening of its collection period from 41 days at the end of Year –2 to 43 days at the end of Year 0.

AVERAGE PAYMENT PERIOD

The **average payment period** is to *purchases* what the average collection period is to sales. It is defined as the ratio of accounts payable at the end of the period to the average daily purchases during that period:

$$\text{Average payment period} = \frac{\text{Accounts payable}_{end}}{\text{Average daily purchases}} \qquad (5.7)$$

The average payment period is the number of days' worth of purchases that have not yet been paid at the date of the balance sheet. The *longer* the average payment period, the *higher* the firm's payables and the *lower* its WCR.

To compute the average daily purchases, you need to know the amount of purchases made during the accounting period ending at the date of the balance sheet. Although this information is not directly reported in the firm's financial statements, purchases made during the accounting period can be obtained indirectly from data provided in balance sheets and income statements.

First, we consider a manufacturing firm. The cost of the goods manufactured during the accounting period equals the cost of purchases plus the cost of production. We add this sum to the beginning of the period's inventories account (raw material, work in process, and finished goods inventories). As the firm sells its finished goods, inventories decrease by the COGS. The net effect of these transactions is the ending inventories:

Beginning inventories + Purchases + Production costs − COGS = Ending inventories

We can rearrange the terms in the above equation to calculate the firm's **purchases** during the accounting period as a function of COGS, production costs, and the change in inventories:

$$\text{Purchases} = \text{COGS} + \text{Change in inventories} - \text{Production costs} \qquad (5.8)$$

where the change in inventories equals the firm's ending inventories less its beginning inventories during the accounting period.

For a trading firm with no production costs, such as OS Distributors, equation 5.8 simplifies to this:

$$\text{Purchases} = \text{COGS} + \text{Change in inventories} \qquad (5.9)$$

Equation 5.9 could have been obtained directly because, for a distributor, if the amount of goods purchased during the accounting period exceeds the amount of goods sold during that period, the inventories account will increase by the difference.

If a distributor sells more goods than it buys during the accounting period, the inventories account will decrease by the difference.

The purchases of OS Distributors reported in Exhibit 5.7 are computed according to equation 5.9. These purchases are divided by 365 to obtain the average daily purchases for each year. Notice that the average payment period rose slightly from 41 to 42 days.

THE EFFECT OF SALES GROWTH ON WORKING CAPITAL REQUIREMENT

Suppose a firm's sales are expected to grow by 10 percent next year. How would the firm's WCR be affected if there is *no change in the efficiency* with which its operating cycle is managed (same inventory turnover and same collection and payment periods)? Even though efficiency remains the same, higher sales will require additional investments in the firm's operating cycle because the firm will need more receivables, more inventories, and more payables to support its additional sales. As a consequence, the firm's WCR will increase. As a first approximation, you can expect WCR to *grow at the same rate as sales*, that is, at 10 percent.

Consider the case of OS Distributors. At the end of Year 0, its WCR was equal to $77 million. If sales are expected to grow by 10 percent next year and the WCR-to-sales ratio is expected to remain the same as in Year 0, then we can expect OS Distributors' WCR also to grow by 10 percent, or $7.7 million, next year. Thus, OS Distributors will need $7.7 million of cash to finance the anticipated growth of its WCR. If OS Distributors does not have or cannot obtain $7.7 million of cash, it may face a liquidity problem. However, if management is able to improve the efficiency of the firm's operating cycle (through a combination of higher inventory turnover and faster collection of receivables), then OS Distributors will need *less* than $7.7 million of cash next year.

As this example illustrates, an *unplanned or unexpected growth in sales may create liquidity problems*. These problems can be alleviated if management maintains tight control over the firm's operating cycle and anticipates the funding needs that will result from future changes in the firm's WCR. How far can managers improve the efficiency of their firm's WCR to release the cash tied up by the firm's operating cycle? An increasing number of *manufacturing firms* have set themselves the ambitious goal of operating with close to *zero* WCR. Exhibit 5.8 explains how this can be achieved.

Inflation also puts pressure on the firm's WCR. When the price level rises, the nominal value of the firm's sales will rise even though the number of units sold may not change. Inflated sales figures require higher levels of receivables; thus, the firm's investment in its operating cycle will increase unless management becomes more efficient.

TRADITIONAL MEASURES OF LIQUIDITY

Some of the traditional measures of a firm's liquidity are reviewed in this section. We also explain why these measures are often not reliable indicators of the firm's liquidity.

NET WORKING CAPITAL

The traditional definition of a firm's **net working capital (NWC)** is the difference between its current assets and its current liabilities. The rationale for this definition is that the higher the firm's NWC, the easier it would be in the case of default to meet the firm's current liabilities by selling its current assets. However, we are interested in estimating a company's ability to meet its cash obligations on a *continual* basis as opposed to its ability to meet the same obligations only in case of default. Thus, this definition of NWC is of limited value.

There is an alternative, and in our opinion superior, way to interpret NWC. We write the balance sheet identity as follows:

Current assets + Net fixed assets = Current liabilities + Long-term financing

Rearranging the terms in this equation, we get the following:

Current assets − Current liabilities = Long-term financing − Net fixed assets

which, using the definition of NWC, can be written as:

Net working capital = Long-term financing − Net fixed assets   (5.10)

EXHIBIT 5.8	CAMPBELL REDUCES ASSETS AND GAINS MARKET SHARE.

In the 1990s, President and CEO of Campbell Soup Company David W. Johnson made some sweeping changes that required drastic restructuring, in an attempt to increase Campbell's industry share outside of the US and to pare the company down to its roots.

Johnson was appointed in January 1990, and by June 1991 he had (among other cost-cutting measures) overseen the sale or closure of 20 plants and a 15.5 percent reduction in the workforce. Overall, working capital was pared down by $80 million.

First of all, why did Johnson reduce working capital? There are two key reasons: creating one-time contributions to cash flow (in this case, to spend on expanding the company into the European Community's single market as well as South America and Asia); and saving money in the long term. If plants or factories can be closed, production expenditures rapidly decrease. In this case, Campbell expected to have an extra $50 million in profits on top of the $80 million reduction in working capital: consistent profits that would come from saving on expenses such as overtime and storage costs.

Secondly, why was working capital reduced so rapidly? Surely a decision that would affect the company so drastically should have taken years?

Well, not necessarily. In fact, generally speaking, the lower the working capital, the better run the company. In an ideal world, companies would manufacture goods as they were ordered, meaning that demand was met but nothing was wasted: no storage space needed in warehouses and no leftover stock requiring scrappage. This system is based on just-in-time inventories, and is known as demand-flow or demand-based management. Most companies are unable to realistically work on a demand-flow model, and sustain their just-in-time models by shopping from pre-manufactured large inventories, thus containing their costs. Johnson's goal was for a company that immediately eliminated unsuccessful lines while constantly manufacturing successful ones as they were ordered, thus reducing the need for plants and warehouses.

Throughout the 90s, Johnson continued to expand in Europe and Asia while selling off any assets that underperformed, to the tune of $500 million worth. Soup was sold in Mexico and Japan, and V8 vegetable juice was begun to be marketed in Europe. Acquisitions were made of companies that tied into Campbell's core brand of soup, and assets such as frozen food were divested to ensure that the leading Campbell brands were manageable. By 2000, Campbell was the largest soup seller in most of Europe and had increased its share in the European soup market by 10 percent.

References:

"Raiding a Company's Hidden Cash" by Shawn Tully and Robert A. Miller from Fortune, August 22, 1994. Copyright © 1994. Reprinted by permission of Fortune.

https://www.encyclopedia.com/social-sciences-and-law/economics-business-and-labor/businesses-and-occupations/campbell-soup-company

---

Now compare equation 5.10 with equation 5.2, which measures the net long-term funds available to finance WCR. *Net working capital* given by equation 5.10 and *net long-term financing* given by equation 5.2 are the same. In other words, NWC can be interpreted in the same way as NLF. The definition of NWC as the difference between long-term financing and net fixed assets has a clear economic meaning. It says that *net working capital is the amount of long-term financing available to fund the firm's operating cycle after the firm has funded its long-term strategic investment in fixed assets.* This definition of NWC is more useful than the traditional definition, which has no particular managerial meaning. Furthermore, using the traditional definition of NWC may lead to the conclusion that it is determined by the firm's short-term operating decisions, which we know is not the case.

Exhibit 5.9 reports OS Distributors' NWC at the end of Year –2, Year –1, and Year 0, using the two definitions presented above. NWC grew from $50 million at the end of Year –2 to $62 million at the end of Year 0, meaning that OS Distributors had, in Year 0, an additional $12 million of long-term financing to fund its operating cycle compared with what it had in Year –2.

THE CURRENT RATIO

The **current ratio** is obtained by dividing the firm's current assets by its current liabilities:

$$\text{Current ratio} = \frac{\text{Current assets}}{\text{Current liabilities}} \tag{5.11}$$

It is often said that the larger the current ratio, the more liquid the firm, and that the current ratio should be at least greater than one and preferably close to two. This reasoning, similar to the one used for the traditional definition of net working capital, is based on the notion that the higher the current ratio, the easier it would be for the firm to repay its short-term liabilities with the cash raised from the sale of its short-term assets. For this to be possible, the firm's current assets should be at least equal to its current liabilities. In other words, its current ratio should be at least equal to one.

EXHIBIT 5.9	OS DISTRIBUTORS' NET WORKING CAPITAL AND CURRENT AND QUICK RATIOS.

ALL DATA FROM THE BALANCE SHEETS IN EXHIBIT 5.1. FIGURES IN MILLIONS

	December 31, Year –2	December 31, Year –1	December 31, Year 0
• **Net working capital =** [Current assets – Current liabilities][1]	$104 – $54 = $50	$119 – $66 = $53	$137 – $75 = $62
• **Net working capital =** [Long-term financing[2] – Net fixed assets][3]	($42 + $64) – $56 = $50	($34 + $70) – $51 = $53	($38 + $77) – $53 = $62
• **Current ratio** $= \dfrac{\text{Current assets}}{\text{Current liabilities}}$	$\dfrac{\$104}{\$54} = 1.93$	$\dfrac{\$119}{\$66} = 1.80$	$\dfrac{\$137}{\$75} = 1.83$
• **Quick ratio** $= \dfrac{\text{Cash + Accounts receivable}}{\text{Current liabilities}}$	$\dfrac{\$6 + \$44}{\$54} = 0.93$	$\dfrac{\$12 + \$48}{\$66} = 0.91$	$\dfrac{\$8 + \$56}{\$75} = 0.85$

[1] This is the traditional definition of net working capital.
[2] Long-term financing = Long-term debt + Owners' equity.
[3] According to this definition, net working capital is the same as net long-term financing (see equation 5.2).

But if liquidity increases when the current ratio increases, why not have clients pay as late as possible to increase the firm's accounts receivable, why not keep as many goods as possible in stock, and why not pay the firm's suppliers as soon as possible? The first two decisions will significantly increase the firm's current assets, and the third decision will substantially reduce its current liabilities. As a result, the firm's current ratio will go sky-high. But has the firm's liquidity increased? Certainly not. The current ratio is definitely not a reliable measure of the firm's liquidity.

The value of OS Distributors' current ratio at the end of Year –2, Year –1, and Year 0 is given in Exhibit 5.9. It varied from a low of 1.80 in Year –1 to a high of 1.93 in Year –2.

THE ACID TEST OR QUICK RATIO

Sometimes, analysts modify the current ratio by eliminating the relatively illiquid inventories and prepaid expenses from the firm's current assets. What remains is simply the sum of cash and receivables, the two most liquid current assets, also called **quick assets**. The result is called the **acid test** or **quick ratio**:

$$\text{Acid test or quick ratio} = \frac{\text{Cash} + \text{Accounts receivable}}{\text{Current liabilities}} \qquad (5.12)$$

The quick ratio is an improvement over the current ratio, but it still emphasizes a *liquidation view* of the firm as opposed to a *going-concern approach to* liquidity analysis. Furthermore, a firm's inventories are not always less liquid than its accounts receivable.

The value of OS Distributors' quick ratio is reported in Exhibit 5.9. It varied from a low of 0.85 in Year 0 to a high of 0.93 in Year –2. Creditors usually prefer a ratio close to one for most manufacturing firms.

KEY POINTS

1. A firm's liquidity, which refers to its ability to meet its recurrent cash obligations, is driven by the structure of its balance sheet, that is, by the nature and composition of its assets and the way they are financed. Liquidity is easier to analyze if the standard balance sheet is restructured into the managerial balance sheet, as shown in Chapter 4.

2. Liquidity should be measured by the ratio of its net long-term financing (NLF) to working capital requirement (WCR), where NLF is the sum of equity capital and long-term debt minus net fixed assets. The higher that ratio, the higher the proportion of working capital that is financed with long-term funds and the higher the firm's liquidity.

3. The portion of working capital that is not financed with long-term funds is obviously financed with short-term debt. These short-term borrowings in *excess* of cash are called net short-term financing (NSF). To minimize the effect of both financial cost risk (unexpected changes in short-term interest rates) and refinancing risk (unexpected cuts in the availability of short-term debt), most firms should limit the short-term financing of their working capital to its seasonal short-term component while financing the permanent long-term component with long-term funds. This approach to funding is known as the matching strategy.

4. The key to good liquidity management is good management of the firm's working capital cycle; a *liquidity crisis is often the symptom of a mismanaged working capital cycle*. If a firm's WCR grows out of control and is not properly financed, liquidity problems appear immediately. Broadly speaking, good management of the working capital cycle means two things. First, accounts receivable and inventories, the two major components of working capital, must be held at their minimum levels relative to sales. This will allow the firm to save the cash it would have needed to fund a larger amount of receivables and inventories. Second, because WCR is essentially a long-term investment, a firm's liquidity will rise as higher proportions of its working capital are financed with long-term funds.

5. Finally, the ratio of NLF to WCR is a better indicator of a firm's liquidity position than the traditional benchmarks of net working capital, current ratio, or quick ratio. These last two ratios may be good indicators of a firm's ability to rapidly repay its current liabilities with the cash raised from the sale of its current assets, but they are not reliable measures of a firm's capacity to meet its cash obligations on a *recurrent basis*.

FINANCING STRATEGIES

Firms may choose different financial strategies regarding the maturity structure of the funds used to finance their invested capital. The matching strategy, examined in this chapter, is the most common one and calls for matching the duration of the sources of funds with that of the investments. Some firms, however, may adopt other financing strategies, depending on the level of risk they are willing to take. They can adopt a **conservative strategy** if they want less risk, or an **aggressive strategy** if they are prepared to accept more risk. This appendix examines the three strategies for a firm with seasonal and growing sales. The three strategies are illustrated in Exhibits A5.1.1, A5.1.2, and A5.1.3.

A firm with seasonal sales experiences changes in its working capital requirement (WCR) during the seasonal cycle. WCR increases as sales increase and decreases as sales decrease. This is shown in Exhibit 5.4, where the behavior of WCR is decomposed into a long-term permanent component and a short-term seasonal component. This short-term component of WCR is usually the only component of the firm's three fundamental investments that is directly linked to changes in sales during the seasonal cycle. The sum of cash, net fixed assets, and the long-term component of WCR makes up the firm's *permanent* investments. These investments are not significantly affected by seasonality in sales. Seasonal and permanent components of the firm's investments

| EXHIBIT A5.1.1 | FINANCING INVESTMENTS USING A MATCHING STRATEGY. |

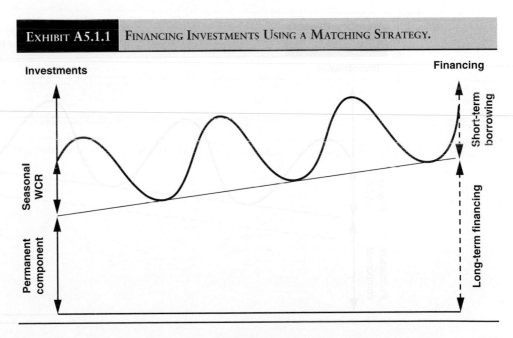

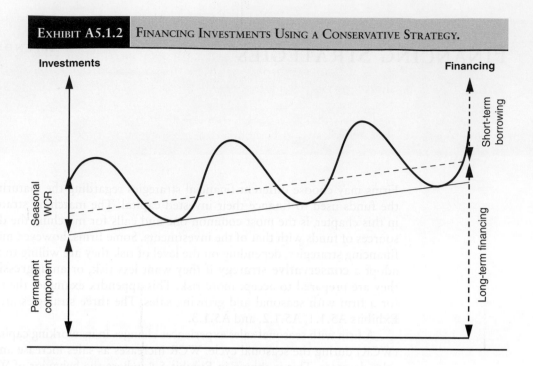

EXHIBIT A5.1.2   FINANCING INVESTMENTS USING A CONSERVATIVE STRATEGY.

are shown on the left side of Exhibits A5.1.1 to A5.1.3. The right side shows the two components of the financing policy: long-term financing (owners' equity plus long-term debt) and short-term borrowing.

Exhibit A5.1.1 illustrates the matching strategy. *Permanent investment is financed with long-term funds and seasonal investment with short-term funds.* The objective

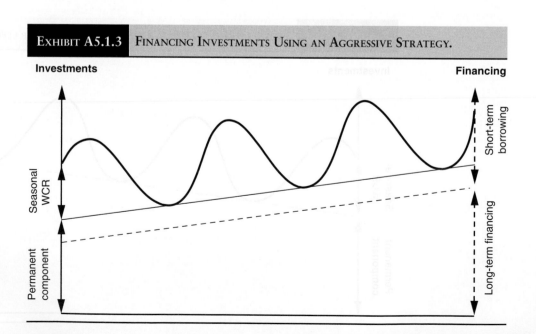

EXHIBIT A5.1.3   FINANCING INVESTMENTS USING AN AGGRESSIVE STRATEGY.

of this strategy is to minimize (but not completely eliminate) the risk resulting from having a mismatched balance sheet.

Exhibit A5.1.2 shows the effect of adopting a conservative strategy. *Permanent needs and some seasonal needs are financed with long-term funds*. In this case, short-term borrowing covers only a portion of the firm's seasonal needs. At times, near the cyclical trough, the firm would have some **excess cash** (negative short-term financing). This "margin of safety" can be used to meet unforeseen cash needs that would have to be financed by an increase in short-term borrowing under the matching strategy.

The aggressive strategy, illustrated in Exhibit A5.1.3, implies that the *firm uses short-term funds to finance a portion of the permanent component of its investments*. This strategy is riskier than either of the other two strategies because the firm would bear greater **financial cost** and **refinancing risks**. The financial cost risk originates from possible variations in the cost of debt during the useful life of the investments; the refinancing risk refers to the possibility that the firm may not be able to renew the short-term loans needed to finance a portion of the permanent component of the firm's investments.

A firm may choose to bear more financial cost and refinancing risks if it expects the short-term interest rate to decrease and, on average, to be lower than the current long-term rate over the useful life of the investment. In some instances, a firm may be forced to adopt an aggressive strategy. This situation happens when firms have limited access to long-term funds and must rely heavily on short-term financing.

THE GLAXOSMITHKLINE LIQUIDITY AND OPERATIONAL EFFICIENCY

To analyze GlaxoSmithKline (GSK) liquidity, we use the company's managerial balance sheets, which were presented in Appendix 4.2 to Chapter 4. The balance sheets cover the three-year period from 2015 to 2017.

We then apply the approach taken in the chapter to examine the company's liquidity and the management of its operating cycle. For comparison purposes, we also show the results of the same analysis applied to Sanofi, a major competitor to GSK.[6]

GSK'S LIQUIDITY POSITION

Exhibit A5.2.1 presents GSK's managerial balance sheets and two measures of the firm's liquidity at the end of years 2015, 2016, and 2017. The balance sheets were taken from Exhibit A4.2.3 of Chapter 4, while the liquidity measures are the firm's net long-term financing and the liquidity ratio as defined in equations 5.2 and 5.4.

GSK's balance sheet size slightly increased over the three-year period, from £43,140 million at year-end 2015 to £44,326 million at year-end 2017.

On the invested capital side, increases in fixed assets were counterbalanced by decreases in cash holdings and working capital requirement, the latter becoming negative.

On the capital employed side, long-term financing decreased substantially from £40,029 million at year-end 2015 to £29,812 million at year-end 2017. Note the significant decrease in owners' equity from £8,878 million at year-end 2015 to £3,489 million at year-end 2017. According to GSK's annual reports, the decrease in owners' equity is directly related to the company's decision to pay large dividends relative to profit (in 2016 and 2017 the company paid more dividends than its earnings after tax). The total amount of short-term liabilities did change significantly over the three-year period from £1,767 million at year-end 2015 to £13,885 million at year-end 2017. According to the company's balance sheets (Exhibit A4.2.1 in Chapter 4), most of the change is due to increases in contingent consideration and put option liabilities.

At year-end 2015, GSK's net long-term financing was positive and its liquidity ratio was higher than one, indicating a conservative financing strategy. Then it turned negative at the end of the next two years to reach −£10,662 million at year-end 2017, which implies a change to a riskier strategy. However, as indicated in the company's

---

[6] Both companies present their financial statements according to IFRS Standards.

EXHIBIT A5.2.1	GSK's MANAGERIAL BALANCE SHEETS.

FROM EXHIBIT A4.2.3, APPENDIX 4.2, CHAPTER 4. FIGURES IN MILLIONS OF POUNDS

Year		2015		2016		2017
Invested capital						
• Cash		£6,076		£5,357		£4,092
• Working capital requirement		205		(596)		(240)
• Net fixed assets		36,859		42,370		40,474
Total invested capital		**£43,140**		**£47,131**		**£44,326**
Capital employed						
• Short-term debt		£1,767		£6,203		£13,885
• Short-term provisions		1,344		848		629
• Long-term financing		40,029		40,080		29,812
Long-term debt	£15,324		£14,661		£14,264	
Other long-term liabilities	15,827		20,456		12,059	
Owners' equity	8,878		4,963		3,489	
Total capital employed		**£43,140**		**£47,131**		**£44,326**
Net long-term financing[1]		£3,170		−£2,290		−£10,662
$\dfrac{\text{Net long-term financing}}{\text{Working capital requirement}}$		15.5		Not meaningful[2]		Not meaningful[2]

[1] Long-term financing minus net fixed assets.
[2] As working capital requirement is negative, the ratio has no more meaning.

2017 annual report, GSK has access to nearly £12 billion of credit facility and holds more than £4 billion in cash and cash equivalents at year-end 2017, more than the deficit of £10,662 million in net long-term financing. As an indication of the GSK's liquidity position, the company's long-term credit ratings with Standard and Poor's and with Moody's Investor Services are qualified as 'stable outlook' by both agencies (A+ for Standard and Poor's, and A2 for Moody's).

Sanofi's net long-term financing over the three-year period from 2015 to 2017 has constantly been positive indicating a constant conservative strategy over that period. The company's credit rating is the second highest rating with Standard and Poor's (AA) and with Moody's (A1).

GSK'S MANAGEMENT OF THE OPERATING CYCLE

Exhibit A5.2.2 reports six ratios related to the management of the operating cycle of GSK and Sanofi, at year-ends 2015, 2016, and 2017.

GSK's working capital requirement-to-net sales ratio decreased from 0.9 percent at year-end 2015 to −0.8 percent at year-end 2017. During the same period, Sanofi's WCR-to-net sales ratio went down from 7 percent at year-end 2015 to 5.3 percent at year-end 2017. To identify the reasons for the significant difference with the Sanofi ratio, we split the two companies' working capital requirement into two components: a component we call **core working capital requirement** and another one we call **non-core working capital requirement**. The first one is equal to accounts receivable plus inventories less accounts payable while the second one is the difference between working capital requirement's other operating assets and other operating liabilities. We called the first component core working capital requirement because it is usually under the control of operating managers while the second one, which includes assets such as taxes recoverable or liabilities such as tax payables, is not.

The second and third rows of Exhibit A5.2.2 show the core and non-core working capital requirement-to-net sales ratios for both companies. Note how negative the non-core working capital requirement ratio of both companies is: it varies between −21.8 percent and −24.1 percent for GSK and between −21.5 percent and −24.1 percent for Sanofi over the three-year period. At year-end 2017, £6,943 million (23 percent of £30,186 million of sales in 2017) of GSK's investment in its operating cycle was self-financed in the form of liabilities other than accounts payable. At the

EXHIBIT A5.2.2	GSK's AND SANOFI's OPERATING CYCLE MANAGEMENT.

DATA FROM THE FIRMS' INCOME STATEMENTS, BALANCE SHEETS, AND MANAGERIAL BALANCE SHEETS

	GSK			Sanofi		
Year	2015	2016	2017	2015	2016	2017
$\dfrac{\text{Working capital requirement}}{\text{Net sales}}$	0.9%	−2.1%	−0.8%	7.0%	5.2%	5.3%
$\dfrac{\text{Core working capital requirement}^1}{\text{Net sales}}$	22.7%	21.9%	22.2%	29.6%	29.3%	25.8%
$\dfrac{\text{Non-core working capital requirement}^2}{\text{Net sales}}$	−21.8%	−24.1%	−23.0%	−22.6%	−24.1%	−21.5%
$\dfrac{\text{Accounts receivable}}{\text{Average daily sales}^3}$	58.3 days	60.4 days	56.5 days	79.2 days	78.9 days	75.2 days
$\dfrac{\text{Cost of goods sold}}{\text{Inventories}}$	1.9 times	1.8 times	1.9 times	1.7 times	1.6 times	1.7 times
$\dfrac{\text{Accounts payable}}{\text{Average daily sales}^{3,4}}$	47.6 days	47.0 days	42.7 days	40.9 days	45.2 days	46.7 days

[1] Core working capital requirement is equal to Accounts receivable + Inventories − Accounts payable. GSK does not show accounts receivable and accounts payable separately in its balance sheets. Accounts receivable are part of the *Trade and other receivables* account while accounts payable are part of the *Trade and other payables* account. However, the amount of the two accounts are provided elsewhere in notes to the balance sheets. Accounts receivable were equal to £3,824 million at year-end 2015, £4,615 million at year-end 2016, and £4,672 million at year-end 2017. At the same dates, accounts payable were equal to £3,120 million, £3,596 million, and £3,528 million, respectively.
[2] Non-core working capital requirement is equal to Other working capital requirement assets − Other working capital requirement liabilities. Data are from the companies' annual reports.
[3] Daily averages are computed on the basis of 365 days a year.
[4] Since neither GSK nor Sanofi indicates the amount of their annual purchases, we measure the payment period as days of sale.

same date, the firm's inventories and receivables amounted to £10,229 million.[7] In other words, at the end of 2017, 68 percent of the GSK's investment in inventories and receivables (£6,943 million divided by £10,229 million) was financed by liabilities generated by the operating cycle other than the suppliers' credit. At year-ends 2015 and 2016, the ratios were 61 and 69 percent, respectively. For Sanofi, the ratio was significantly lower: 55 percent, 57 percent, and 54 percent at year-ends 2015, 2016, and 2017, respectively.

The core working capital requirement-to-net sales ratio of GSK decreased slightly from 22.7 percent at year-end 2015 to 22.2 percent at year-end 2017. During the three-year period, the average collection period decreased from 58.3 days to 56.5 days, the average payment period decreased from 47.6 days to 42.7 days, while the inventory turnover remained the same (1.9 times). The continuous improvement in operating management efficiency is cited as a major objective in GSK's annual reports. However, notice that while the non-core working capital requirement-to-net sales ratio improved by 1.2 percentage points from year-end 2015 to year-end 2017 (from −21.8 percent to −23.0 percent), the core ratio improved only by 0.5 percentage points (from 22.7 percent to 22.2 percent). This means that a significant portion of the decrease in GSK's working capital requirement over the three-year period from 2015 to 2017 came from items which are usually not under the control of operating managers.

GSK's core working capital requirement-to-net sales ratio is lower than Sanofi's each year over the three-year period from 2015 to 2017. While Sanofi's core working capital requirement-to-net sales ratio has continuously improved from year-end 2015 to year-end 2017, it is still 3.6 percentage points higher than GSK's at year-end 2017 (25.8 percent minus 22.2 percent). Note that, at the end of each year, Sanofi's collection period is much longer than GSK's. According to Sanofi's 2017 annual report, this relatively high collection period is due to the economic and credit conditions in some countries where a few of the company's customers – especially governments' health care agencies – are located.

FURTHER READING

1. Hodrick, Simon Laurie. "Are US Firms Really Holding Too Much Cash?", *Stanford Institute for Economic Policy Research*, Stanford University, July 2014.
2. Berk, Jonathan, and Peter DeMarzo. *Corporate Finance*, Global Edition, 4th ed. Pearson, 2017. See chapters 2, 26, and 27.
3. Koller, Tim, Marc Goedhart, and David Wessels, *Valuation, Measuring and Managing the Value of Companies*, 6th ed. John Wiley & Sons, Inc., 2015, chapter 9.

---

[7] £5,557 million of inventories and £4,672 million of receivables (from GSK's 2017 annual report).

SELF-TEST QUESTIONS

5.1   Evaluating managerial performance.
Allied & Consolidated Clothiers (ACC), a clothing manufacturer, launched an aggressive marketing program aimed at raising the *growth rate* in sales in Year 0 by at least 50 percent compared with the *growth rate* achieved in Year –1. The company's financial statements from Year –2 to Year 0 are shown below and on the following page. The income statements span a calendar year and balance sheets are dated December 31. All figures are in millions of dollars.

a. Has ACC achieved its marketing objective?

b. Restate ACC's balance sheets in their managerial form. What does working capital requirement (WCR) measure? Is it a long-term or a short-term investment?

c. Examine the structures of invested capital and capital used in the managerial balance sheets prepared in the previous question (state each component as a percentage of the total). What do you observe?

d. Compare the Year –2 balance sheet with the Year 0 balance sheet. Are these balance sheets matched or unmatched?

e. Analyze ACC's operational efficiency from Year –2 to Year 0. Calculate and compare the following efficiency ratios for the three-year period. What can you conclude?

    1.   WCR-to-sales ratio
    2.   Average collection period
    3.   Inventory turnover
    4.   Average payment period (use cost of goods sold)

f. Analyze ACC's liquidity position from Year –2 to Year 0. Calculate and compare the following liquidity ratios over the three-year period. What can you conclude?

    1.   The liquidity ratio (net long-term financing to WCR)
    2.   The current ratio
    3.   The quick ratio

g. What general conclusion can you draw from your analysis?

Balance Sheets (in millions)							
Year End	Year –2	Year –1	Year 0		Year –2	Year –1	Year 0
Cash	$100	$ 90	$ 50	Short-term debt	$ 80	$ 90	$ 135
Trade receivables	200	230	290	Trade payables	170	180	220
Inventories	160	170	300	Accrued expenses	40	45	50
Prepaid expenses	30	30	35	Long-term debt	140	120	100
Net fixed assets	390	390	365	Owners' equity	450	475	535
Total assets	$880	$910	$1,040	Total liabilities & owners' equity	$ 880	$910	$ 1,040

Income Statements (in millions)			
	Year –2	Year –1	Year 0
Net sales	$1,200	$1,350	$1,600
Cost of goods sold	860	970	1,160
Selling, general, and administrative expenses	150	165	200
Depreciation expense	40	50	55
Earnings before interest and tax (EBIT)	150	165	185
Net interest expense	20	20	25
Earnings before tax (EBT)	130	145	160
Income tax expense	40	45	50
Earnings after tax (EAT)	$90	$100	$110
Dividends	$75	$75	$50

5.2 **Working capital management for a retailer.**
The consolidated financial statements of Carrefour, the French retailer, for the years 2016 and 2017, are shown below.

a. Calculate working capital requirement (WCR) at year-ends 2016 and 2017. Interpret your results.

b. Calculate the ratio of WCR to sales. What is the effect of faster growth on Carrefour's liquidity position?

c. What were Carrefour's average collection periods, inventory turnover, and average payment periods (based on cost of sales) in 2016 and 2017? What can you conclude about the effect of these parameters on the magnitude of Carrefour's WCR?

d. Calculate Carrefour's current ratios and quick ratios. What can you conclude about the reliability of these liquidity ratios for the case of retailers such as Carrefour?

Income Statements (in millions)		
	2016	2017
Net sales	€ 78,774	€ 80,974
Cost of goods sold	(60,789)	(62,760)
Selling, general, and administrative expenses	(14,147)	(14,641)
Depreciation, amortization, and provisions	(1,487)	(1,567)
Financial income, net of expenses	(515)	(445)
Income tax expense	(494)	(618)
Net income[1]	€ 1,342	€ 943

[1] Excluding special items.

Balance Sheets (in millions)						
End of year	2016	2017			2016	2017
Current assets			Liabilities			
Cash and securities	€ 3,305	€ 3,594	Short-term borrowings		€ 1,875	€ 1,069
Trade receivables[2]	2,682	2,750	Accounts payable		15,396	15,082
Inventories	7,039	6,690	Accrued expenses		4,413	4,094
Other current assets[3]	6,122	5,783	Other current liabilities[4]		3,411	2,828
			Noncurrent liabilities		11,742	12,581
Long-term assets	29,697	28,996	Stockholders' equity		12,008	12,159
Total assets	€ 48,845	€ 47,813	Total liabilities and owners' equity		€48,845	€47,813

[2] Mainly from the group's franchisees.
[3] Receivables from suppliers for rebates and commercial incentives plus short-term consumer credit.
[4] Mainly short-term consumer credit refinancing.

REVIEW QUESTIONS

1. **Transactions.**
   Indicate the effects of the following transactions on *net long-term financing (NLF)*, *working capital requirement (WCR)*, *net short-term financing (NSF)*, and *net profit*. Use + to indicate an increase, − to indicate a decrease, and 0 to indicate no effect.

	NLF	WCR	NSF	NET PROFIT
1. Shares are issued for cash				
2. Goods from inventory are sold for cash				
3. Goods from inventory are sold on account				
4. A fixed asset is sold for cash for less than book value				
5. A fixed asset is sold for cash for more than book value				
6. Corporate income tax is paid				
7. Payment is made to trade creditors				
8. Cash is obtained through a short-term bank loan				
9. Cash is obtained through a long-term bank loan				
10. A cash dividend is declared and paid				
11. Accounts receivable are collected				
12. Merchandise is purchased on account				
13. Cash advances are made to employees				
14. Minority interest in a firm is acquired for cash				
15. Equipment is acquired for cash				

2. **Reconstructing a balance sheet.**
    Use the following information to complete the balance sheet below.

    a. Collection period: 40 days
    b. Inventory turnover: 6 times sales
    c. Working capital requirement/sales: 20 percent
    d. Liabilities/total assets: 60 percent
    e. Cash in days of sales: 20 days
    f. Short-term debt: 10 percent of total financial debt

    Assume a 360-day year.

Balance Sheet		
Cash	$ 400,000	Short-term debt
Accounts receivable		Accounts payable
Inventory		
Total current assets		**Total current liabilities**
Net fixed assets		Long-term debt
		Owners' equity
Total assets	**$5,000,000**	**Total liabilities and owners' equity**

3. **Managing liquidity.**
    Indicate which of the following four statements are right or wrong:

    a. Because working capital requirement (WCR) = net long-term financing (NLF) + net short-term financing (NSF), I can reduce my investment in the operating cycle by either reducing my long-term financing through the repurchase of shares or by borrowing less on a short-term basis.
    b. The lower my WCR, the more liquid my business unit is. One way to reduce WCR is to reduce inventories. I can do that by writing down some of my obsolete inventories.
    c. Although I can improve my liquidity or acid test ratios by letting my customer pay later, the result would be a decrease in the liquidity of my business unit.
    d. If I decrease my WCR, I will increase my cash holdings and be able to borrow less from my bank. But my bank, which makes money by lending funds, will be unhappy.

4. **Trade credit terms.**
    It is often the case that suppliers offer their customers to either pay the full amount of the invoice within a certain number of days, for example within 30 days, or receive a discount if they pay earlier, for example within 15 days. The first option would usually be referred to as 'Net 30'. If, in the second option, the discount is 2 percent, the option would be referred to as '2/15, net 30'.

    Suppose that La Tierra Inc. has received an offer from one of its suppliers to pay invoices '1/30, net 60'. What is the effective annual cost for La Tierra Inc. if it does not take up the offer? Assume a 365-day year.

5. **Optimal credit policy.**

Algebra Ltd. is selling inventory management software for small to mid-sized firms. Currently, the computer program is sold only for cash. In order to increase its revenues, the company is considering the alternative of offering a credit for one month to all its customers. However, by providing customer credit, the company expects that it will incur the risk of attracting high risk customers that could default on their payments. The two strategies are outlined below:

	Cash-based sales	Credit sales
Unit sale price	$100	$100
Quantity sold	100	130
Cost per unit	$ 50	$ 55[1]
Probability of customer defaulting	0 percent	10 percent

[1] The $5 difference in unit cost reflects the cost of managing the credit policy.

Algebra Ltd.'s cost of capital is 1 percent per month.

a. What is the net present value (NPV) of selling the computer program for cash?
b. What is the NPV of selling the computer program on credit?
c. What should Algebra Ltd. do?

6. **The consequences of the 2008 financial crisis.**

Following the bankruptcy of Lehmann Brothers on September 15, 2008, the short-term credit market came to a halt. Many companies found themselves unable to renew their short-term debt and fell into financial distress. If, at that time, your company held a lot of cash, would you have felt immune to the financial crisis?

7. **Industry effect on the working capital requirement.**

Below are selected accounting data of four US firms:

(in millions)	Firm 1	Firm 2	Firm 3	Firm 4
Revenue	$2,796	$15,382	$56,786	$469,162
Accounts receivable	471	730	10,556	6,768
Inventories	1,481	390	8,476	43,803
Prepaid expenses	—	—	—	—
Other current assets	187	236	334	1,588
Accounts payable	650	1,977	10,425	50,952
Accrued expenses	—	3,629	—	—
Other current liabilities	—	—	—	—

a. For each of the firms, compute the following: working capital requirement (WCR), WCR-to-revenue ratio, collection period in days (using 365 days per year), and inventory turnover (using revenue rather than cost of goods sold).

b. The four firms and their industry are:

Firm	Walmart Stores, Inc.	Constellation Brands, Inc.	The Dow Chemical Company	Carnival Corporation
Industry	Retail (Nongrocery)	Beverages (Alcoholic)	Chemical Manufacturing	Recreational Activities (Cruises)

Which company is Firm 1, Firm 2, Firm 3, and Firm 4? Explain your choice.

8. **Financing strategies.**
   Which of the following three companies has a matching, a conservative, and an aggressive financing strategy? Explain why.

	Firm A	Firm B	Firm C
Cash	$ 0	$ 10	$ 0
Accounts receivable	25	20	25
Inventories	25	20	25
Net fixed assets	50	50	50
Total assets	$100	$100	$100
Short-term debt	$ 0	$ 0	$ 10
Accounts payable	25	25	25
Long-term debt	25	25	15
Owners' equity	50	50	50
Total liabilities and owners' equity	$100	$100	$100

9. **The financial effect of the management of the operating cycle.**
   Below are the last three years' financial statements for Sentec Inc., a distributor of electrical fixtures.

Income Statements (in thousands)			
	Year 1	Year 2	Year 3
Sales	$22,100	$24,300	$31,600
Cost of goods sold	17,600	19,300	25,100
Selling, general, and administrative expenses	3,750	4,000	5,000
Depreciation expense	100	100	150
Earnings before interest and tax	650	900	1,350
Net interest expense	110	130	260
Earnings before tax	540	770	1,090
Income tax expense	220	310	430
Earnings after tax	$ 320	$ 460	$ 660
Dividends	$ 180	$ 200	$ 200

Balance Sheets (in thousands)			
	Year-end 1	Year-end 2	Year-end 3
Cash	$ 600	$ 350	$ 300
Accounts receivable	2,730	3,100	4,200
Inventories	2,800	3,200	4,300
Prepaid expenses	0	0	0
Net fixed assets	1,200	1,300	1,450
Total assets	$7,330	$7,950	$10,250
Short-term debt	$ 300	$ 500	$ 1,900
Accounts payable	1,400	1,600	2,050
Accrued expenses	200	260	350
Long-term debt	1,300	1,200	1,100
Owners' equity	4,130	4,390	4,850
Total liabilities and owners' equity	$7,330	$7,950	$10,250

a. Compute Sentec Inc.'s working capital requirement (WCR) at year-end 1, year-end 2, and year-end 3.

b. Prepare Sentec Inc.'s managerial balance sheets at year-end 1, year-end 2, and year-end 3.

c. Compute Sentec Inc.'s net long-term financing (NLF) and net short-term financing (NSF) at year-end 1, year-end 2, and year-end 3. Comment on the change in Sentec Inc.'s financing policy. Has it become more conservative? Aggressive? What caused this change?

d. In year 3, firms in the same sector as Sentec Inc. had an average collection period of 30 days, average payment period of 33 days, and inventory turnover of 8 days. Suppose that Sentec Inc. had managed its operating cycle like the average firm in the sector. At year-end 3, what would its WCR have been? Its managerial balance sheet, NLF, and NSF? What would have been the effect on its financing strategy?

10. **Seasonal business.**
Mars Electronics is a distributor for the Global Electric Company (GEC), a large manufacturer of electrical and electronics products for consumer and institutional markets. Below are the semi-annual financial statements of the company for the last year and a half.

Income Statements (in thousands)			
	Six Months to June 30, Year –1	Six Months to December 31, Year –1	Six Months to June 30, Year 0
Net Sales	$10,655	$13,851	$11,720
Cost of goods sold	8,940	11,671	9,834
Selling, general, and administrative expenses	1,554	1,925	1,677
Depreciation expense	44	55	76
Interest expense	62	90	70
Tax expense	23	44	26
Earnings after tax	$ 32	$ 66	$ 37
Dividends	$ 5	$ 44	$ 1

Balance Sheets (in thousands)			
	June 30, Year –1	December 31, Year –1	June 30, Year 0
Cash	$ 160	$ 60	$ 70
Accounts receivable	1,953	2,616	2,100
Inventories	1,986	2,694	2,085
Prepaid expenses	80	42	25
Net fixed assets	733	818	830
Total assets	$4,912	$6,230	$5,110
Short-term debt	$ 50	$880	$50
Accounts payable	1,450	1,950	1,650
Accrued expenses	98	114	138
Long-term debt	800	750	700
Owners' equity	2,514	2,536	2,572
Total liabilities and owners' equity	$4,912	$6,230	$5,110

a. Compute Mars Electronics' working capital requirement on June 30, Year –1, December 31, Year –1, and June 30, Year 0. Also, compute the collection period, inventory turnover, and payment period at the same dates. (The average payment period on June 30, Year –1, was 29 days.)

b. Prepare Mars Electronics' managerial balance sheet on June 30, Year –1, December 31, Year –1, and June 30, Year 0.

c. Compute Mars Electronics' net long-term financing and net short-term financing on June 30, Year –1, December 31, Year –1, and June 30, Year 0. Comment on Mars Electronics' financing strategy. Is it a conservative one? An aggressive one? A matching one?

ANALYZING PROFITABILITY, RISK, AND GROWTH

What effect do managerial decisions have on the firm's profitability? At first glance, this may seem to be an easy question. To find the answer, all you need to do is compare this year's net profit to last year's figure. If you see an increase, you can conclude that the managers have improved profitability. If you see a decrease, you can assume that the managers did not run the firm profitably. Unfortunately, this straightforward comparison may not tell the whole story.

Suppose, for example, that higher profits came from an increase in sales that was achieved by giving customers significantly more time than usual to pay their bills and by simultaneously letting the firm's inventories rise to unusual levels to meet every customer's request promptly. In this case, looking just at profits in the firm's income statement is not enough. The rises in sales and profits have been achieved by increasing the size of the firm's balance sheet through higher accounts receivable and inventories. And a larger balance sheet means that more capital is used to finance the firm's activities. Because capital is costly, a larger balance sheet may be detrimental to the firm. You need to know, instead, whether profits *per dollar of capital employed* have increased.

Alternatively, suppose a fall in profits came from a rise in interest expenses because of additional borrowing. This does not mean that financial managers made borrowing decisions that impaired profitability. Borrowing can be advantageous under certain conditions. If this were not the case, then firms wishing to achieve higher levels of profitability would never borrow. Our point is that an increase or a decrease in profits, in and of itself, is not a good indicator of a firm's profitability.

The integrated approach to profitability analysis presented in this chapter considers the effects of managerial decisions not only on the firm's income statement but also on its balance sheet. For example, the approach is able to differentiate between an increase in profits that is accompanied by a rise in accounts receivable (a balance sheet item) from one that is accompanied by no change in receivables. We also show that an increase in borrowing does not necessarily reduce the firm's profitability. Alternative measures of profitability are discussed, and we explain how they are related to one another. We also show how financial leverage, a measure of the impact of borrowing on a firm's profitability, affects the firm's riskiness. Finally, we review the concept of self-sustainable growth and its application to the management of the firm's growth strategy. As in previous chapters, the financial statements of Office Supplies (OS) Distributors are used to illustrate our analysis. After reading this chapter, you should understand the following:

- How to measure a firm's profitability
- The key drivers of profitability
- How to analyze the structure of a firm's overall profitability
- How business risk and the use of debt financing affect profitability
- How to assess a firm's capacity to finance its expected growth in sales

MEASURES OF PROFITABILITY

Every manager has a favorite measure of profitability. It is usually a ratio calculated by dividing the firm's earnings after tax (EAT) or net profit by (1) sales to get **return on sales (ROS)**, or (2) total assets to get **return on assets (ROA)**,[1] or (3) owners' equity to get **return on equity (ROE)**. ROS measures the profit generated by one dollar of sales. It is traditionally used to measure the ability of managers to generate profits from the firm's sales. ROA measures the profit generated by one dollar of assets. It is used to assess the ability of managers to generate profits from the firm's assets. Finally, ROE measures the profit generated by one dollar of equity. It is the standard measure of the profitability to shareholders of the equity capital they invested in the firm.

The measure of profitability that is adopted depends on the manager's area of responsibility. A sales manager would look at ROS; the manager of an operating unit, with responsibility for that unit's assets, would choose ROA. The chief executive, concerned with the firm's profitability to shareholders, would pay attention to ROE. The three measures of profitability raise a number of questions. How are they related to one another? Which one is the most *comprehensive* indicator of profitability? How does risk affect profitability? What can managers do to raise the profitability of their firm? These questions are answered in this chapter.

RETURN ON EQUITY

ROE is the most comprehensive indicator of profitability because it is the final outcome of *all* the firm's activities and decisions made during the year. It considers the operating and investing decisions as well as the financing and tax-related decisions that the firm's managers have made. The following sections show how to calculate ROE and then explain in detail why it is the most comprehensive measure of profitability.

MEASURING RETURN ON EQUITY

ROE measures the firm's profitability from the perspective of the owners, those who invested equity capital in the firm. Their reward is the firm's net profit. The return on their investment is the ratio of EAT to owners' equity:

$$\text{Return on equity(ROE)} = \frac{\text{Earnings after tax (EAT)}}{\text{Owners' equity}} \tag{6.1}$$

[1] A variation of ROA is **return on investment (ROI)**, where the term *investment* refers to either the firm's total assets or a subset of its assets.

The amount of investment in the denominator of a profitability ratio – owners' equity in this case – can be measured at the beginning or the end of the period during which EAT was generated. In general, taking the average of the beginning and ending figures is usually the best alternative. The examples in this chapter use the *year-end* figures in all the profitability ratios because we compare the *three* years of data reported in OS Distributors' financial statements.

Based on the earnings and equity figures in Exhibits 6.1 and 6.2, OS Distributors' ROE rose from 10.9 percent in Year –2 (EAT of $7 million divided by $64 million of equity) to 13.2 percent in Year 0 (EAT of $10.2 million divided by $77 million of equity). What are the firm's activities and decisions that produced this rise in ROE? To answer this question, we must first find out how the firm's operating and financing activities affect its ROE.

The Effect of Operating Decisions on ROE

Operating decisions, broadly defined, involve the acquisition and disposal of fixed assets and the management of the firm's operating assets (such as inventories and trade receivables) and operating liabilities (mostly trade payables). ROS (net profit per dollar of sales) and ROA (net profit per dollar of total assets) are not appropriate measures of the profitability generated by the firm's operating activities because they are calculated with *net* profit (earnings after tax). Net profit is obtained after deducting *interest expenses* – the outcome of a *financing* decision – from the firm's pre-tax operating profit. ROS and ROA are thus affected by financing decisions and do not reflect only operating decisions. The following sections present three ratios that are commonly used as substitutes for ROS and ROA when evaluating the specific contribution of operating decisions to the firm's overall profitability.

Return on Invested Capital before Tax $(ROIC_{BT})$[2]

A relevant measure of **operating profitability** should have in its numerator the firm's pre-tax *operating* profit, or earnings before interest and tax (EBIT), and should have in its denominator the investments that were made to generate EBIT. EBIT is shown in the firm's income statement (see Exhibit 6.2), and the appropriate investments are shown in its restructured or managerial balance sheet, which was introduced in Chapter 4 (see Exhibit 6.3). The investments are listed on the upper section of the managerial balance sheet and are referred to as **invested capital**. We have the following:

Invested capital = Cash + Working capital requirement + Net fixed assets   (6.2)

Cash and net fixed assets are the same as those shown in the standard balance sheets in Exhibit 6.1. Working capital requirement (WCR), a measure of the firm's *net* investment in its operating cycle, is the difference between operating assets (receivables, inventories, and prepaid expenses) and operating liabilities (payables and accrued expenses).

---

[2] We use the following convention to distinguish *after-tax* returns from *pre-tax* returns: when returns are measured *after tax*, we do not put any subscript; when they are measured *before tax*, we indicate this with the subscript BT$(_{BT})$.

EXHIBIT 6.1	OS DISTRIBUTORS' BALANCE SHEETS.

FIGURES IN MILLIONS

	December 31, Year –2 (Two years ago)	December 31, Year –1 (One year ago)	December 31, Year 0 (This year)
Assets			
• **Current assets**			
Cash[1]	$ 6.0	$ 12.0	$ 8.0
Accounts receivable	44.0	48.0	56.0
Inventories	52.0	57.0	72.0
Prepaid expenses[2]	2.0	2.0	1.0
Total current assets	104.0	119.0	137.0
• **Noncurrent assets**			
Financial assets and intangibles	0.0	0.0	0.0
Property, plant, and equipment			
Gross value[3]	$90.0	$90.0	$93.0
less accumulated depreciation	(34.0) 56.0	(39.0) 51.0	(40.0) 53.0
Total noncurrent assets	56.0	51.0	53.0
Total assets	**$160.0**	**$170.0**	**$190.0**
Liabilities and owners' equity			
• **Current liabilities**			
Short-term debt	$ 15.0	$ 22.0	$ 23.0
Owed to banks	$7.0	$14.0	$15.0
Current portion of long-term debt	8.0	8.0	8.0
Accounts payable	37.0	40.0	48.0
Accrued expenses[4]	2.0	4.0	4.0
Total current liabilities	54.0	66.0	75.0
• **Noncurrent liabilities**			
Long-term debt[5]	42.0	34.0	38.0
Total noncurrent liabilities	42.0	34.0	38.0
• **Owners' equity[6]**	64.0	70.0	77.0
Total liabilities and owners' equity	**$160.0**	**$170.0**	**$190.0**

[1] Consists of cash in hand and checking accounts held to facilitate operating activities on which the firm earns no interest.
[2] Prepaid expenses comprises rent paid in advance (when recognized in the income statement, rent is included in selling, general, and administrative expenses).
[3] In Year –1, there was no disposal of existing fixed assets or acquisition of new fixed assets. However, during Year 0, a warehouse was enlarged at a cost of $12 million and existing fixed assets, bought for $9 million in the past, were sold at their net book value of $2 million.
[4] Accrued expenses consists of wages and taxes payable.
[5] Long-term debt is repaid at the rate of $8 million per year. No new long-term debt was incurred during Year –1, but during Year 0, a mortgage loan was obtained from the bank to finance the extension of a warehouse (see note 3).
[6] During the three years, no new shares were issued and none were repurchased.

EXHIBIT 6.2	OS DISTRIBUTORS' INCOME STATEMENTS.

FIGURES IN MILLIONS

	Year –2	Year –1	Year 0
Net sales	$390.0	$420.0	$480.0
Cost of goods sold	328.0	353.0	400.0
Gross profit	62.0	67.0	80.0
Selling, general, and administrative expenses	39.8	43.7	48.0
Depreciation expense	5.0	5.0	8.0
Operating profit	17.2	18.3	24.0
Special items	0.0	0.0	0.0
Earnings before interest and tax (EBIT)	17.2	18.3	24.0
Net interest expense[1]	5.5	5.0	7.0
Earnings before tax (EBT)	11.7	13.3	17.0
Income tax expense	4.7	5.3	6.8
Earnings after tax (EAT)	$ 7.0	$ 8.0	$ 10.2
Dividends	$ 2.0	$ 2.0	$ 3.2
Addition to retained earnings	$ 5.0	$ 6.0	$ 7.0

[1] There is no interest income, so net interest expense is equal to interest expense.

Thus, a firm's operating profitability can be measured by the ratio of its EBIT to its invested capital. This ratio is known as the firm's **return on invested capital before tax** or $ROIC_{BT}$:

$$\text{Return on invested capital before tax } (ROIC_{BT}) = \frac{\text{Earnings before interest and tax (EBIT)}}{\text{Invested capital}} \quad (6.3)$$

We can make several noteworthy observations about this definition of operating profitability. First, **ROIC** can be measured before tax, as shown above, or after tax. To get the after-tax ROIC, EBIT in equation 6.3 must be reduced by the amount of tax it generates, which is EBIT × Tax rate, so that the numerator of equation 6.3 becomes EBIT × (1 − Tax rate). We show in Chapter 17 that ROIC is an important measure of performance when estimating the value created by a business.

Second, the ratio in equation 6.3 can also be interpreted as operating profitability per dollar of **capital employed** because, according to the managerial balance sheet (see Exhibit 6.3), invested capital is equal to capital employed, the sum of all the sources of funds (both debt and equity capital) used to finance the firm's investments. Thus, $ROIC_{BT}$ is the same as **return on capital employed before tax** or $ROCE_{BT}$.

Third, because cash is included in the definition of invested capital (see Exhibit 6.3), any interest *income* earned on cash balances should be *included* in EBIT.

Fourth, to evaluate the performance of a business unit that has no control over its cash, a variation of $ROIC_{BT}$ can be constructed. This ratio would exclude cash from invested capital and exclude interest income from EBIT. This measure of operating profitability can be called pre-tax **return on business assets** or **ROBA** where **business assets** are defined as the sum of WCR and net fixed assets.

EXHIBIT 6.3	OS DISTRIBUTORS' MANAGERIAL BALANCE SHEETS.

ALL DATA FROM THE BALANCE SHEETS IN EXHIBIT 6.1. FIGURES IN MILLIONS

		December 31, Year −2		December 31, Year −1		December 31, Year 0
Invested capital						
• Cash		$ 6.0		$ 12.0		$ 8.0
• Working capital requirement (WCR)[1]		59.0		63.0		77.0
• Net fixed assets		56.0		51.0		53.0
Total invested capital		**$121.0**		**$126.0**		**$138.0**
Capital employed						
• Short-term debt		$ 15.0		$ 22.0		$ 23.0
• Long-term financing						
Long-term debt	$42.0		$34.0		$38.0	
Owners' equity	64.0	106.0	70.0	104.0	77.0	115.0
Total capital employed		**$121.0**		**$126.0**		**$138.0**

[1] WCR = (Accounts receivable + Inventories + Prepaid expenses) − (Accounts payable + Accrued expenses).

Another measure of operating profitability is **return on total assets**, or **ROTA**, the ratio of EBIT to the firm's *total* assets as reported in its standard balance sheet. Note the distinction we make between ROTA and ROA (return on assets). The former is the ratio of EBIT to total assets, whereas the latter is the ratio of EAT to total assets. In this and the remaining chapters, we measure operating profitability with ROIC. But keep in mind that $ROIC_{BT}$ is the same as $ROCE_{BT}$. Finally, note that $ROIC_{BT}$ can be replaced by either $ROBA_{BT}$ or $ROTA_{BT}$ in the following analysis without any loss of generality.

OS Distributors' $ROIC_{BT}$ is given in the last column of Exhibit 6.4. It rose from 14.2 percent in Year −2 to 17.4 percent in Year 0. To understand why this improvement occurred, we need to know what drives operating profitability.

THE DRIVERS OF OPERATING PROFITABILITY

$ROIC_{BT}$ is the ratio of pre-tax operating profit (EBIT) to invested capital, so any improvement in $ROIC_{BT}$ must be the outcome of (1) an increase in EBIT for the *same* level of invested capital, or (2) a reduction of invested capital for the *same* level of EBIT.

To find out how these two components of operating profitability affect $ROIC_{BT}$, we write equation 6.3 as follows:

$$ROIC_{BT} = \frac{EBIT}{Invested\ capital} = \frac{EBIT}{Sales} \times \frac{Sales}{Invested\ capital} \qquad (6.4)$$

The first ratio on the right side of the equation (EBIT/Sales) is called the firm's **operating profit margin,** and the second one (Sales/Invested capital) is called its **capital turnover.**

| EXHIBIT 6.4 | THE STRUCTURE OF OS DISTRIBUTORS' PRE-TAX RETURN ON INVESTED CAPITAL.[1] |

ALL DATA FROM THE INCOME STATEMENTS IN EXHIBIT 6.2 AND THE BALANCE SHEETS IN EXHIBIT 6.3. FIGURES IN MILLIONS

Year	Operating Profit Margin		Capital Turnover		Return on Invested Capital Before Tax
	$\dfrac{\text{EBIT}}{\text{Sales}}$	$\times$	$\dfrac{\text{Sales}}{\text{Invested capital}^1}$	$=$	$\dfrac{\text{EBIT}}{\text{Invested capital}}$
	$\dfrac{\$17.2}{\$390}$	$\times$	$\dfrac{\$390}{\$121}$	$=$	$\dfrac{\$17.2}{\$121}$
Year −2	4.4%	$\times$	3.2	$=$	14.2%
	$\dfrac{\$18.3}{\$420}$	$\times$	$\dfrac{\$420}{\$126}$	$=$	$\dfrac{\$18.3}{\$126}$
Year −1	4.4%	$\times$	3.3	$=$	14.5%
	$\dfrac{\$24}{\$480}$	$\times$	$\dfrac{\$480}{\$138}$	$=$	$\dfrac{\$24}{\$138}$
Year 0	5.0%	$\times$	3.5	$=$	17.4%

[1] Invested capital = Cash + Working capital requirement + Net fixed assets.

Thus, a firm's ROIC_{BT} is simply the product of its operating profit margin and its capital turnover:

Return on invested capital before tax = Operating profit margin × Capital turnover

For example, Exhibit 6.4 shows that OS Distributors had an operating profit margin of 4.4 percent in Year −2, meaning that it generated that year, on average, $4.40 of pre-tax operating profit (EBIT) per $100 of sales. Its capital turnover was 3.2, indicating that the company needed, on average, $100 of invested capital to generate $320 of sales.

Obviously, the higher a firm's operating profit margin and capital turnover, the higher its operating profitability. A higher operating profit margin is obtained by increasing operating profit (EBIT) more than sales. This can be achieved, for example, by reducing operating expenses without losing sales or by raising sales without increasing operating expenses. A higher capital turnover is obtained through a more efficient use of the assets required to support the firm's sales activities. This can be achieved, for example, through a faster inventory turnover, a shorter collection period for receivables, or fewer fixed assets per dollar of sales.

As shown in Exhibit 6.4, OS Distributors' operating profitability rose slightly from 14.2 percent in Year −2 to 14.5 percent in Year −1 because of a small rise in capital turnover from 3.2 to 3.3. In Year 0, operating profitability increased to 17.4 percent as a result of a rise in operating profit margin from 4.4 percent to 5.0 percent accompanied by an increase in capital turnover from 3.3 to 3.5.

If the key to higher operating profitability is a combination of higher operating profit margin and faster capital turnover, what are the underlying factors that would allow a firm to achieve this outcome? The relative importance of the factors that affect ROIC_{BT} can be determined empirically only by examining the historical relationships between these factors and the pre-tax operating profitability of a large sample of firms. A study of this type was conducted on a sample that included more than 3,000 business divisions that were drawn from some 500 corporations (mostly North American and European) from a wide range of industries.[3]

Three factors emerge from the study as major determinants of operating profitability: (1) the firm's competitive position as measured by its *market share* relative to that of its competitors; (2) the relative *quality of its products and services* as perceived by its customers; and (3) the firm's *cost and assets structures*, namely, the composition and concentration of its assets, the structure of its costs, and its degrees of vertical integration and capacity utilization. The evidence indicates that *high market share* and *superior product quality*, on average, *boost* operating profitability, while *high investments* and *high fixed costs*, on average, *depress* it. In the sample, those businesses with the highest market shares and superior products and services had an average pre-tax operating profitability of 39 percent, while those with the lowest market shares and inferior products or services had an average pre-tax operating profitability of only 9 percent. Businesses with low capital turnover – those with relatively higher fixed assets and fixed costs per dollar of sales – were, on average, unable to offset their lower capital turnover with higher operating profit margin and hence, in general, had lower pre-tax operating profitability than businesses with high capital turnover. Businesses with a capital turnover below 1.5 had an average pre-tax operating profitability of 8 percent, whereas those with a capital turnover above 3.3 had an average pre-tax operating profitability of 38 percent.

Why are businesses with low capital turnover usually unable to generate higher profit margins? One explanation is that investment-intensive businesses with low capital turnover usually have relatively high fixed costs and are prone to price and marketing wars that weaken their margin. When economic conditions become unfavorable, these businesses tend to cut prices to maintain high rates of capacity utilization. Furthermore, because these businesses have relatively high amounts of capital tied up in their operations, they cannot easily exit the business (they have high **exit barriers**). They usually try to ride out the unfavorable market conditions in the hope of better future days. This behavior is typical in such sectors as airlines, refining, commodity pulp and paper, shipbuilding, and base chemicals.

THE LINK BETWEEN ROE AND OPERATING PROFITABILITY

To understand the link between ROE and operating profitability (ROIC), consider the case of a firm that has not borrowed a single dollar; its investments are entirely financed with equity capital. What is the relationship between this firm's ROE and its ROIC? Because the firm has not borrowed a single dollar, it has no interest expense and thus its pre-tax profit, or earnings before tax (EBT), must be equal to its EBIT. And because the firm's investments are entirely financed with equity (recall that the firm does not borrow), its invested capital must be equal to its owners' equity. In other words, *if a firm does not borrow, its ROIC is the same as its ROE.*

---

[3] The unit of analysis was not an entire company but a business division within a corporation selling a distinct product or service to an identifiable group of customers. The data were collected by the Profit Impact of Market Strategy (PIMS) Program. For further information, refer to the article by Jagiello and Mandry (2004).

THE EFFECT OF FINANCING DECISIONS ON RETURN ON EQUITY

If ROIC and ROE are the same when a firm does not borrow, then any difference between them must be caused by the use of debt to finance the firm's investments. What are the effects of the firm's financing decisions on its ROE?

Let's consider what happens when a firm replaces some of its equity capital with an equal amount of debt. The higher proportion of debt financing resulting from this **recapitalization**[4] increases the firm's **financial leverage** (also called **gearing**). A firm without borrowed funds is said to be an **unlevered firm**. A firm with borrowed funds is said to be levered. And the higher the amount of debt relative to equity, the higher the firm's financial leverage. A higher leverage affects the firm's ROE in two ways. First, the firm's interest expense increases and its EAT decreases. This will reduce ROE because EAT is the numerator of ROE. Second, owners' equity decreases because debt has replaced equity. This will increase ROE because owners' equity is the denominator of ROE. Conclusion: you cannot predict how financial leverage affects the firm's ROE. There is a **financial cost effect** that reduces ROE (EAT goes down because of the higher interest expense) and a simultaneous **financial structure effect** that increases ROE (because of lower equity capital). The net effect depends on the strength of the former relative to the latter. If the financial cost effect is weaker than the financial structure effect, higher financial leverage will *increase* the firm's ROE. If it is stronger, higher financial leverage will *decrease* the firm's ROE. The ratios that measure these two effects are discussed in the following sections.

THE FINANCIAL COST RATIO

The financial cost effect is captured in the firm's *income statement*. It is measured using the **financial cost ratio**, which is defined as the firm's EBT divided by its EBIT:

$$\text{Financial cost ratio} = \frac{\text{Earnings before tax (EBT)}}{\text{Earnings before interest and tax (EBIT)}} \tag{6.5}$$

As the amount of debt financing *increases* (1) EBT relative to EBIT *decreases*, (2) the financial cost ratio *decreases*, and (3) the firm's ROE *decreases*, all else remaining the same. If the firm is entirely equity financed, then the ratio is equal to one because EBT and EBIT are equal in this case. This is the *maximum* value of the ratio. If the firm borrows, its financial cost ratio will be smaller than one.

OS Distributors' financial cost ratios are given in the fourth column of Exhibit 6.5. The ratio was 0.68 in Year –2, 0.73 in Year –1, and 0.71 in Year 0. The ratios indicate that OS Distributors had an interest expense during the three years (the three ratios are smaller than one), and that the interest expense relative to pre-tax operating profit (EBIT) was highest in Year –2 (the ratio is lowest that year).

A popular ratio, similar to the financial cost ratio, is the **times-interest-earned ratio** or **interest coverage ratio**. It is defined as EBIT divided by interest expenses:

$$\text{Times-interest-earned ratio} = \frac{\text{Earnings before interest and tax (EBIT)}}{\text{Interest expenses}} \tag{6.6}$$

This ratio indicates how many times the firm's pre-tax operating profit (EBIT) covers its interest expense. For example, OS Distributors' Year 0 income statement

---

[4] Recapitalization refers to the substitution of debt for equity, leaving the firm's assets unchanged. It can be carried out by using the proceeds from borrowing to buy back common stock from shareholders.

| EXHIBIT 6.5 | THE STRUCTURE OF OS DISTRIBUTORS' RETURN ON EQUITY. |

ALL DATA FROM THE INCOME STATEMENTS IN EXHIBIT 6.2 AND THE BALANCE SHEETS IN EXHIBIT 6.3. FIGURES IN MILLIONS

Year	Return on Equity	=	Operating Profitability			×	Financial Leverage Multiplier			×	Tax Effect
	ROE	=	Operating profit margin	×	Capital turnover		Financial cost ratio	×	Financial structure ratio	×	Tax effect ratio
	$\dfrac{EAT}{\text{Owners' equity}}$	=	$\dfrac{EBIT}{Sales}$	×	$\dfrac{Sales}{\text{Invested capital}}$		$\dfrac{EBT}{EBIT}$	×	$\dfrac{\text{Invested capital}}{\text{Owners' equity}}$	×	$\dfrac{EAT}{EBT}$
					Pre-tax return on invested capital ($ROIC_{BT}$)			Financial leverage multiplier			
Year −2	$\dfrac{\$7}{\$64}$ = 10.9%	=	$\dfrac{\$17.2}{\$390}$ = 4.4%	×	$\dfrac{\$390}{\$121}$ = 3.2 → 14.2%	×	$\dfrac{\$11.7}{\$17.2}$ = 0.68	×	$\dfrac{\$121}{\$64}$ = 1.89 → 1.29	×	$\dfrac{\$7}{\$11.7}$ = 0.60
Year −1	$\dfrac{\$8}{\$70}$ = 11.4%	=	$\dfrac{\$18.3}{\$420}$ = 4.4%	×	$\dfrac{\$420}{\$126}$ = 3.3 → 14.5%	×	$\dfrac{\$13.3}{\$18.3}$ = 0.73	×	$\dfrac{\$126}{\$70}$ = 1.80 → 1.31	×	$\dfrac{\$8}{\$13.3}$ = 0.60
Year 0	$\dfrac{\$10.2}{\$77}$ = 13.2%	=	$\dfrac{\$24}{\$480}$ = 5.0%	×	$\dfrac{\$480}{\$138}$ = 3.5 → 17.4%	×	$\dfrac{\$17}{\$24}$ = 0.71	×	$\dfrac{\$138}{\$77}$ = 1.79 → 1.27	×	$\dfrac{\$10.2}{\$17}$ = 0.60

in Exhibit 6.2 shows that the firm's EBIT of $24 million covered its $7 million of interest expense 3.4 times ($24 million divided by $7 million). The higher the ratio, the higher the firm's ability to meet its interest payments.

THE FINANCIAL STRUCTURE RATIO

The financial structure effect is captured in the firm's balance sheet. It is measured using the **financial structure ratio**, also known as the **equity multiplier**. It is the ratio of invested capital to owners' equity:

$$\text{Financial structure ratio} = \frac{\text{Invested capital}}{\text{Owners' equity}} \qquad (6.7)$$

For a given amount of invested capital, as the amount of debt financing *increases* (1) owners' equity *decreases*, (2) the financial structure ratio *increases*, and (3) the firm's ROE *increases*, all else remaining the same. If the firm's invested capital is entirely financed with equity, then invested capital is equal to owners' equity and the financial structure ratio is equal to one, its *minimum* value. It can reach, theoretically, very large values as more debt is used to finance the firm's investments.

OS Distributors' financial structure ratios are given in the fifth column of Exhibit 6.5. The ratio went from 1.89 in Year –2 to 1.79 in Year 0, indicating that the *proportion* of OS Distributors' investments that was financed with debt decreased during that period as can be verified in Exhibit 6.3 and discussed below.

OTHER MEASURES OF FINANCIAL LEVERAGE

The financial structure ratio is one of several **debt ratios** used to measure the firm's borrowing relative to its equity financing. Other popular ratios include the **debt-to-equity ratio** (debt divided by owners' equity) and the **debt-to-invested capital ratio** (debt divided by invested capital).

Using the data in Exhibit 6.3, we can get the debt ratios of OS Distributors in Year 0. Its debt-to-equity ratio was 79.2 percent ($61 million of total debt divided by $77 million of equity) and its debt-to-invested capital ratio was 44.2 percent ($61 million of total debt divided by $138 million of invested capital). We examine in Chapter 13 the factors that determine a firm's debt ratio.

THE INCIDENCE OF TAXATION ON RETURN ON EQUITY

The third determinant of a firm's ROE is the incidence of corporate taxation. The higher the tax rate applied to a firm's EBT, the lower its ROE. The incidence of tax is measured by the **tax-effect ratio** – that is, the ratio of EAT to EBT:

$$\text{Tax effect ratio} = \frac{\text{EAT}}{\text{EBT}} = \frac{\text{EBT}(1 - \text{Effective tax rate})}{\text{EBT}}$$
$$= 1 - \text{Effective tax rate} \qquad (6.8)$$

Note that because EAT is equal to EBT(1 − Effective tax rate), the tax-effect ratio is equal to one minus the effective corporate tax rate.

As the effective corporate tax rate increases, the tax-effect ratio decreases and the firm keeps a smaller percentage of its pre-tax earnings. Other things being equal, the firm's ROE decreases. Consider OS Distributors. Its pre-tax earnings (EBT) are taxed at the rate of 40 percent; hence, its tax-effect ratio is 60 percent, as shown in the last column of Exhibit 6.5.

The relevant corporate tax rate is the **effective tax rate** the firm pays, not the **statutory tax rate**.[5] As shown in Exhibit 6.6, the effective corporate income tax rate in some countries is significantly lower than the maximum statutory tax rate imposed by the tax authorities. The implication is that a firm can improve its ROE by locating its operations in countries with the lowest effective corporate tax rates.

EXHIBIT 6.6	STATUTORY AND EFFECTIVE CORPORATE INCOME TAX RATES IN 2014 FOR DIFFERENT COUNTRIES.[1]						
	Canada	France	Germany	India	Japan	United Kingdom	United States of America
Statutory rate	26.3%	34.4%	30.2%	30.9%	34.6%	21.0%	39.1%
Effective rate	23.2%	31.0%	27.3%	24.0%	31.9%	20.7%	34.1%

[1] Source: US Department of Treasury, Office of Tax Analysis.

PUTTING IT ALL TOGETHER: THE STRUCTURE OF A FIRM'S PROFITABILITY

The previous sections identify five ratios that affect a firm's ROE: (1) its operating profit margin (EBIT/Sales); (2) its capital turnover (Sales/Invested capital); (3) its financial cost ratio (EBT/EBIT); (4) its financial structure ratio (Invested capital/Equity); and (5) its tax-effect ratio (EAT/EBT). The relationship that ties these ratios to the firm's ROE is straightforward: *ROE is simply equal to the product of these five ratios:*

$$ROE = \frac{EAT}{Owners'equity}$$

$$= \frac{EBIT}{Sales} \times \frac{Sales}{Invested\ capital} \times \frac{EBT}{EBIT} \times \frac{Invested\ capital}{Owners'equity} \times \frac{EAT}{EBT} \quad (6.9)$$

The product of the five ratios on the right side of equation 6.9 is equal to EAT divided by owners' equity. You can check this by simply canceling EBIT, Sales, Invested capital, and EBT because they appear in both a numerator and a denominator. The only items left are EAT in the numerator and owners' equity in the denominator.

The first two ratios capture the effect of the firm's investing and operating decisions on its overall profitability. Their product is equal to the firm's operating profitability measured by the $ROIC_{BT}$ (see equation 6.4). The third and fourth ratios capture the effect of the firm's financial policy on its overall profitability. We call their product the firm's **financial leverage multiplier**:

Financial leverage multiplier =
Financial cost ratio × Financial structure ratio   (6.10)

[5] For information on the latest *statutory* tax rates prevailing in member countries of the Organisation for Economic Cooperation and Development, go to www.oecd.org/ctp/tax-policy/tax-database.htm#C_CorporateCapital.

The last ratio captures the effect of corporate taxation on return on equity and, as shown in equation 6.8, is equal to $(1 - \text{Effective tax rate})$. Thus, equation 6.9 can be written as the following:

$$\text{ROE} = \text{ROIC}_{BT} \times \text{Financial leverage multiplier} \times (1 - \text{Effective tax rate}) \quad (6.11)$$

Exhibit 6.7 provides a pictorial representation of the five ratios behind ROE and the way they are related.

EXHIBIT 6.7	THE DRIVERS OF RETURN ON EQUITY.

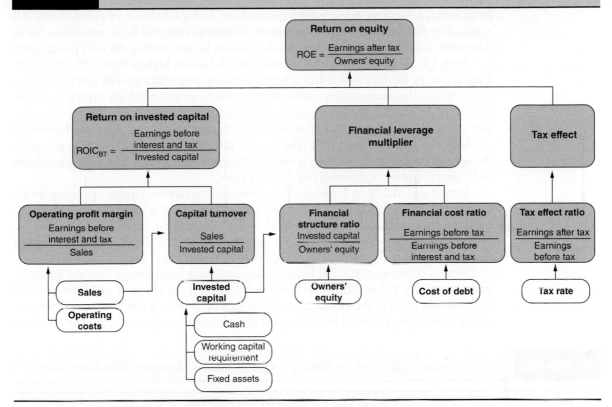

If we ignore the incidence of taxes on profitability and focus on **return on equity before tax** (ROE_{BT}), equation 6.11 can be written as follows:

$$\text{ROE}_{BT} = \text{ROIC}_{BT} \times \text{Financial leverage multiplier}$$

Obviously, if the financial leverage multiplier is greater than one, ROE_{BT} exceeds ROIC_{BT}. If it is less than one, ROE_{BT} is lower than ROIC_{BT}.

We can now examine the structure of OS Distributors' profitability, shown in Exhibit 6.5. Compare ROE in Year –2 with ROE in Year 0: it increased from 10.9 percent in Year –2 to 13.2 percent in Year 0. Is this overall performance improvement the outcome of improved operating management, a higher financial leverage multiplier, or a reduction in OS Distributors' effective tax rate? The Exhibit indicates that the improvement in ROE is caused by a better operating profit margin coupled with a higher capital turnover.[6] These two effects pushed operating profitability from 14.2 percent to

---

[6] A firm's capital turnover can increase as a result of the depreciation of fixed assets, which reduces net fixed assets. When this is the case, the improvement in turnover cannot be attributed to better management of the firm's invested capital.

17.4 percent. The financial leverage multiplier declined slightly, from 1.29 to 1.27, and the tax effect was unchanged.

THE STRUCTURE OF ROE ACROSS INDUSTRIES

The structure of a firm's return on equity depends to a large extent on the nature of the industry in which it operates and the competitive advantages it has been able to achieve over time.

To illustrate this phenomenon, refer to Exhibit 6.8, which reports the ROE structure of four firms in 2016. The companies include a US software company, a bank from India, a German manufacturing company, and a UK chain of retail stores. All are leading firms in their respective sectors. Given the reported ROE structures, try to determine which company belongs to which sector before reading the next paragraphs.

Firm 1 is Microsoft, the software company. It has the highest ROE (29.3 percent). This is due to the fact that it has a high operating profit margin (its software has a very high market share and is relatively inexpensive to produce). Its capital turnover ratio of 0.48 might appear low since software production is not a capital-intensive activity: most of the company's invested capital, however, is cash, not fixed assets or working capital requirement. Its effective tax rate of 8.4 percent (1 − 91.6 percent), the second lowest in the sample, is the result of producing and distributing products in foreign countries with relatively low tax rates.

Firm 2 is ICICI Bank Limited, the Indian bank. It has the largest operating profit margin (44.3 percent), typical of banks that have no cost of goods sold and operating expenses that are mainly selling, general, and administrative expenses. It has also the lowest capital turnover (0.11) due to high amounts of financial assets generating limited revenue in the form of interest, dividends, and fees.

Firm 3 is Siemens AG, the largest manufacturing company in Europe. Its operating margin of 9.2 percent, which is much less than the margins of Microsoft and ICICI Bank, reflects the competitive environment in which the company operates. Its capital turnover of 0.88 is also typical of a manufacturing company. The resulting

EXHIBIT 6.8	**THE STRUCTURE OF RETURN ON EQUITY FOR FOUR FIRMS IN DIFFERENT SECTORS (2016).**[1]						

Firm[2]	Operating Profit Margin[3] (1)	Capital Turnover[4] (2)	Return on Invested Capital[5] (3) = (1) × (2)	Financial Leverage Multiplier[6] (4)	Pre-Tax Return on Equity[7] (5) = (3) × (4)	Tax Effect[8] (6)	Return on Equity[9] (7) = (5) × (6)
1	25.7%	0.48	12.4%	2.58	32.0%	91.6%	29.3%
2	44.3%	0.11	4.9%	2.38	11.6%	93.0%	10.8%
3	9.2%	0.88	8.1%	2.69	21.8%	73.5%	16.0%
4	2.3%	2.17	5.0%	2.28	11.4%	69.5%	7.9%

[1] Compiled by the authors with accounting data from the firms' annual reports.
[2] See text for names of companies.
[3] Operating profit margin = Earnings before interest and tax/Sales.
[4] Capital turnover = Sales/Invested capital, where Invested capital = Cash + Working capital requirement + Net fixed assets.
[5] Return on invested capital before tax = Earnings before interest and tax/Invested capital.
[6] Financial leverage multiplier = Pre-tax return on equity/Pre-tax return on invested capital.
[7] Pre-tax return on equity = Earnings before tax/Owners' equity.
[8] Tax effect = Earnings after tax/Earnings before tax = (1 − Effective tax rate).
[9] Return on equity = Earnings after tax/Owners' equity.

return on invested capital of 8.1 percent is leveraged by the highest financial leverage multiplier in the group (2.69) to give a 21.8 percent pre-tax return on equity. The tax effect, which is significantly lower than that of Microsoft and ICICI Bank, is due to having operating activities in jurisdictions with higher effective tax rates.

Firm 4 is Tesco PLC, the largest grocery and general merchandise company in the UK. Because it competes on price, it has a low operating profit margin (2.3 percent), the lowest in the group. In contrast, it has a high capital turnover (2.17), the highest in the group, because retail firms typically use relatively little capital to generate sales (they have a very low or negative working capital requirement along with fixed assets often limited to shelf space). However, capital turnover is not high enough to compensate for the low operating margin, and the resulting operating profitability (5 percent) is the second lowest in the sample (after the bank). With the lowest financial leverage multiplier of the four companies (2.28), both its pretax and after-tax return on equity are the lowest among the companies listed in the Exhibit.

OTHER MEASURES OF PROFITABILITY

The measures of profitability discussed so far are based on the accounting data shown on a firm's income statement and balance sheet. A number of other popular profitability-related ratios combine financial *accounting data* with financial market data. These ratios include the firm's **earnings per share**, its **price-to-earnings ratio**, and its **market-to-book ratio**.

EARNINGS PER SHARE (EPS)

Earnings per share, or **EPS**, is simply the firm's earnings after tax divided by its total number of shares outstanding:

$$\text{Earnings per share (EPS)} = \frac{\text{Earnings after tax}}{\text{Number of shares outstanding}}$$

EPS, a favorite of financial analysts, is essentially a "normalized" measure of the firm's earnings after tax. OS Distributors has 10 million shares outstanding (see Exhibit 4.9 in Chapter 4) and has generated earnings after tax of $10.2 million in Year 0. Thus, its EPS in Year 0 is equal to $1.02 ($10.2 million divided by 10 million shares).

THE PRICE-TO-EARNINGS RATIO (P/E)

The **price-to-earnings ratio** (**P/E** or **PER**), also known as the firm's **earnings multiple**, is another favorite of financial analysts. It is defined as follows.

$$\text{Price-to-earnings ratio (P/E or PER)} = \frac{\text{Share price}}{\text{Earnings per share}}$$

Suppose OS Distributors had shares listed on a stock market. If the quoted price per share were $14, OS Distributors' P/E would be 13.7 ($14 divided by $1.02). In other words, OS Distributors would be trading at 13.7 times its current earnings. (This is why a firm's P/E is also known as its earnings multiple.) Higher P/Es mean that investors in the market are assigning higher values to each dollar of current earnings per share generated by the firm. Chapter 10 examines the determinants of firms' P/E and explains why these ratios vary across firms.

THE MARKET-TO-BOOK RATIO

The third ratio, the **market-to-book ratio**, is defined as follows:

$$\text{Market-to-book ratio} = \frac{\text{Share price}}{\text{Book value per share}}$$

where book value per share is equal to the firm's owners' equity, as recorded in its balance sheet, divided by the number of shares outstanding.

For OS Distributors, book value per share is $7.7 at the end of Year 0 ($77 million book value of equity divided by 10 million shares). Given a share price of $14, the market-to-book ratio is 1.8 (a share price of $14 divided by a book value per share of $7.70). In other words, OS Distributors' shares are traded in the market at a premium over book value, that is, 1.8 times their book value. The fact that OS Distributors' shares trade at a premium means the firm is creating value for its shareholders. This is explained in detail in Chapter 18.

FINANCIAL LEVERAGE AND RISK

A firm's financial structure affects its ROE through the financial leverage multiplier. How exactly does financial leverage work? Consider two firms with identical assets that are funded with $100 million of capital. The only difference between the two firms is their financing strategy. One firm finances its assets *exclusively* with equity (the unlevered firm); the other firm finances half of its assets with $50 million of equity and the balance with $50 million of borrowed funds at a cost of debt of 10 percent (the levered firm). For the sake of simplicity, assume that the firms pay no corporate taxes (this assumption does not affect the conclusion).

Let's now introduce risk into the analysis. At the beginning of the year when the two firms established their **capital structure**, they did not know what their year-end pre-tax operating profit (EBIT) would be. Thus, suppose they forecast three equally likely levels of EBIT, each based on different expectations about the economic environment during the coming year. If the economic environment was favorable, EBIT would be $14 million. If the environment was average, EBIT would be $10 million. And if it was unfavorable, EBIT would be only $8 million. Which one of these three possible levels of EBIT the firm achieved would not be known until the end of the year? This situation is what we call **business risk**. *A firm faces business risk because of its inability to know for certain the outcome of its current investing and operating decisions*. The best a firm can do is determine alternative outcomes for EBIT and their likelihood of occurrence.

The two firms have invested the same amount of capital and face the same probability distribution of EBIT, so they have the same business risk. How will the difference in their financing strategies affect their profitability? Exhibit 6.9 shows each firm's profitability ratios – return on invested capital (ROIC_{BT}) and return on equity (ROE_{BT}) – for each of the three possible levels of EBIT. Consider first the case of the unlevered firm. The firm's operating profitability (ROIC_{BT}) varies from a high of 14 percent (EBIT of $14 million divided by $100 million of invested capital) to a low of 8 percent. Its ROE_{BT} is equal to its ROIC_{BT} because it has no debt and pays no taxes. (Both its financial leverage multiplier and its tax-effect ratio are equal to one.)

What is the profitability of the levered firm? Its ROIC_{BT} is the same as that of the unlevered firm because both firms have identical assets and operating profit. The firm

| EXHIBIT 6.9 | EFFECT OF FINANCING ON PROFITABILITY FOR DIFFERENT LEVELS OF EBIT. |

Alternative Levels of Pre-Tax Operating Profit	Profitability of the Firm with 100% Equity Financing		Profitability of the Firm with 50% Equity Financing	
EBIT	$ROIC_{BT}$	ROE_{BT}	$ROIC_{BT}$	ROE_{BT}
$14 million	14%	14%	14%	18%
$10 million	10%	10%	10%	10%
$8 million	8%	8%	8%	6%

pays no taxes, its interest expense is $5 million (10 percent of $50 million of debt), and it has $50 million of equity capital. Its ROE_{BT} is thus:

$$ROE_{BT} = \frac{EBIT - Interest\ expense}{Owners'\ equity} = \frac{EBIT - \$5\ million}{\$50\ million}$$

When EBIT is $14 million, ROE_{BT} is 18 percent ($14 million minus $5 million divided by $50 million). In this case, the levered firm's ROE_{BT} is *higher* than that of the unlevered firm (18 percent versus 14 percent). Although the $5 million of interest expense for the levered firm reduced owners' profit to $9 million ($14 million of EBIT less the $5 million of interest expense), *profit per dollar of invested equity* (ROE_{BT}) rose to 18 percent because the equity base is smaller for the levered firm than it is for the unlevered firm ($50 million instead of $100 million). In this case, financial leverage is *favorable* to the owners of the levered firm because a positive financial structure effect has more than offset a negative financial cost effect.

When EBIT is equal to $10 million, the levered firm's ROE_{BT} is 10 percent. In this case, financial leverage is neutral because the levered firm's ROE_{BT} is equal to that of the unlevered firm. Finally, when EBIT is equal to $8 million, the levered firm's ROE_{BT} is 6 percent. In this case, financial leverage is *unfavorable* to the firm's owners because the levered firm's ROE_{BT} is lower than that of the unlevered firm (6 percent versus 8 percent). Notice how financial leverage (borrowing at a fixed rate of interest) affects ROE. The unlevered firm's ROE_{BT} varies from a high of 14 percent to a low of 8 percent in response to changes in EBIT, whereas the levered firm's ROE_{BT} varies from a high of 18 percent to a low of 6 percent in response to the same changes in EBIT. The two firms face the same business risk because the changes in EBIT are the same for both. However, the levered firm's ROE_{BT} varies more widely than the ROE_{BT} of the unlevered firm. In other words, *financial leverage (borrowing) magnifies a firm's business risk*. Borrowing at a fixed interest rate adds **financial risk** to the firm's existing business risk. The owners of the levered firm face *both* business risk and financial risk, whereas the owners of the unlevered firm face only business risk. The levered firm is riskier than the unlevered one, and its risk increases with rising levels of borrowing.

HOW DOES FINANCIAL LEVERAGE WORK?

Why is financial leverage favorable to the firm's owners when EBIT is $14 million (they get a *higher* ROE_{BT} than the firm that has not borrowed), neutral when EBIT is

$10 million (they get the *same* ROE_{BT} as the firm that has not borrowed), and unfavorable when EBIT is $8 million (they get a *lower* ROE_{BT} than the firm that has not borrowed)? The answer is straightforward. In the first case, the firm's owners borrow at 10 percent to finance assets that generate a pre-tax return of 14 percent ($ROIC_{BT}$ is equal to 14 percent in the first case). You do not have to be a financial wizard to realize that borrowing at 10 percent to achieve a return on investment of 14 percent is a profitable proposition. Financial leverage enhances the firm's overall profitability (its ROE_{BT}). In the second case, the firm borrows at 10 percent to achieve an $ROIC_{BT}$ of 10 percent. Financial leverage is neutral, and ROE_{BT} is the same as if the firm did not borrow. In the third case, the firm borrows at 10 percent to achieve an $ROIC_{BT}$ of only 8 percent. This is clearly a losing proposition. Borrowing, in this case, turns out to be a poor decision.

The relationship that links a firm's after-tax ROE to its pre-tax $ROIC_{BT}$ *for a given cost of debt, tax rate*, and a *debt-to-equity ratio* can be written as follows:

$$ROE = ROIC_{BT}(1 - T_C) + [ROIC_{BT} - \text{Cost of debt}](1 - T_C) \times \frac{\text{Debt}}{\text{Owners' equity}}$$

where T_C is the effective corporate tax rate. For any given debt-to-equity ratio, ROE will be higher than $ROIC_{BT}$ if $ROIC_{BT}$ is higher than the cost of debt. When $ROIC_{BT}$ is equal to the cost of debt, ROE is equal to $ROIC_{BT}$. And when $ROIC_{BT}$ is smaller than the cost of debt, ROE is smaller than $ROIC_{BT}$.

To illustrate this relationship, we return to our earlier example. The 50 percent equity-financed firm has a debt-to-equity ratio of one ($50 million of debt divided by $50 million of equity). The cost of debt is 10 percent, and the firm does not pay any tax ($T_C = 0$). Here are the three cases:

1. When $ROIC_{BT} = 14\%$, $ROE = 14\% + [14\% - 10\%] \times 1 = 14\% + 4\% = 18\%$
2. When $ROIC_{BT} = 10\%$, $ROE = 10\% + [10\% - 10\%] \times 1 = 10\% + 0\% = 10\%$
3. When $ROIC_{BT} = 8\%$, $ROE = 8\% + [8\% - 10\%] \times 1 = 8\% - 2\% = 6\%$

Although we can compute a firm's ROE for any combination of $ROIC_{BT}$ and debt-to-equity ratio, the formula will *never* provide the *optimal* or best level of debt for the firm. We return to this issue in Chapter 13 when we examine how a firm should determine its capital structure.

TWO RELATED CAVEATS: RISK AND THE ABILITY TO CREATE VALUE

One obvious conclusion from the previous discussion is that a firm seeking to enhance its ROE should borrow as long as its $ROIC_{BT}$ exceeds its cost of debt, and refrain from borrowing whenever its $ROIC_{BT}$ is lower than its cost of debt. There are, however, two important and related caveats to this conclusion.

The first is that managers do not know their firm's future $ROIC_{BT}$ at the time they borrow to fund the firm's assets. Hence, they can only compare the cost of debt with an *expected* (risky) $ROIC_{BT}$ that may or may not be the one the firm will eventually achieve. Risk cannot be ignored when applying the ROE formula. Higher levels of *expected* $ROIC_{BT}$ will produce higher levels of *expected* ROE. However, the *expectation* of achieving a higher ROE must be weighed against the risk of not achieving it. (You hope to achieve 18 percent but you may well end up with only 6 percent; you just don't know!)

The second caveat, which is related to the first, is that a high *expected* ROE does not necessarily mean that the firm is creating value for its owners. Consider again the firm with a debt-to-equity ratio of one that can borrow at 10 percent. Suppose the firm can acquire assets that are expected to generate an ROIC$_{BT}$ of 14 percent. As shown above, financial leverage will have a positive effect on the firm's ROE, which will reach 18 percent. But this does not mean that the firm should acquire the assets. What if the firm's owners expect a return of, say, 25 percent to compensate them for the business and financial risks attached to the equity they have invested in the firm? If this is the case, then the acquisition's expected ROE of 18 percent is not sufficient to remunerate the firm's owners. The acquisition should not be undertaken, because it is not a value-creating proposition. More on this point in Chapter 18.

SELF-SUSTAINABLE GROWTH

Without a sustainable level of profit, a firm will be constrained in its ability to finance its future growth. Consider OS Distributors. Sales in Year 0 grew by 14.3 percent, from $420 million to $480 million. Suppose OS Distributors expects sales to grow by, say, 15 percent next year. As sales increase, more receivables will be generated, more inventories will be needed, and eventually more fixed assets will be required to support the higher levels of sales. This growth in assets will have to be financed with debt, equity, or a combination of these two sources of funds. How can OS Distributors' management anticipate the financing implications of the expected growth in sales?

Firms can finance their anticipated growth in two ways: (1) internally, through the retention of profits (additions to retained earnings), or (2) externally, through the issuance of shares and through borrowing. Because *external* equity financing is more costly than *internal* equity financing,[7] firms often try to finance their expected growth with internally generated equity (retained earnings). For this reason, managers need to have an indicator of the *maximum* growth their firm can achieve *without raising external equity*. The firm's **self-sustainable growth rate (SGR)** is this indicator. It is the *maximum rate of growth in sales a firm can achieve without issuing new shares or changing either its operating policy (its operating profit margin and capital turnover remain the same) or its financing policy (its debt-to-equity ratio and* **dividend payout ratio** *remain the same*).

How is the self-sustainable growth rate determined? Let's begin by estimating the rate for OS Distributors at the end of Year 0. From the firm's financial data in Exhibits 6.2 and 6.3, we know that the firm's $70 million of equity at the beginning of Year 0 (the same as end of Year –1) generated $10.2 million in earnings after tax. The firm retained $7 million and distributed the balance of $3.2 million to owners in the form of dividends. As a result, owners' equity increased by 10 percent, from $70 million to $77 million. If the firm expects its equity to increase by the same percentage next year, and if it wants to maintain its current debt-to-equity ratio, then its debt must also increase by 10 percent. If both owners' equity and debt increase by 10 percent, their sum, which is equal to the firm's invested capital, will also increase by 10 percent. Furthermore, if the firm's capital turnover (sales divided by invested capital) does not change, sales will also increase by 10 percent. This 10 percent growth in sales is OS Distributors' SGR. It is equal to the 10 percent growth in the firm's equity and is *the fastest growth rate in sales the firm can achieve without changing its operating and financial policies, and without raising new equity through a share issue.*

---

[7] Raising equity through the issuance of shares involves transaction costs that can add several percentage points to the cost of equity. More on this point in Chapter 13.

From this example, we can now derive a general formula to compute the SGR of any firm. We define a firm's **profit retention rate** as the ratio of its addition to retained earnings to its earnings after tax:

$$\text{Profit retention rate} = \frac{\text{Addition to retained earnings}}{\text{Earnings after tax}}$$

Then, the SGR, which is equal to the rate of increase in owners' equity, can be written as follows:

$$\text{Self-sustainable growth rate} = \frac{\text{Retained earnings}}{\text{Owners' equity}}$$

$$= \frac{\text{Profit retention rate} \times \text{EAT}}{\text{Owners' equity}}$$

Self-sustainable growth rate = Profit retention rate × Return on equity   (6.12)

where ROE is calculated by dividing the year's net profit or EAT by the book value of the firm's equity at the *beginning* of the year.

We know that ROE can be written as the product of operating profit margin, capital turnover, financial leverage multiplier, and the tax-effect ratio (see equations 6.9 and 6.10). Thus, the firm's SGR can be written as follows:

$$
\begin{aligned}
\text{Self-sustainable growth rate} = &\ \text{Profit retention rate} \times \text{Operating margin} \\
&\times \text{Capital turnover} \\
&\times \text{Financial leverage multiplier} \\
&\times (1 - \text{Effective tax rate})
\end{aligned}
$$

This equation clearly identifies the five factors that determine the firm's capacity to grow *without* raising new equity. The second and third factors reflect the firm's operating policy (its operating profit margin and capital turnover), the first and fourth reflect its financing policy (its profit retention rate and financial leverage multiplier), and the fifth reflects the effective rate at which its pre-tax profit is taxed. The point to remember is this: *if these five factors stay fixed, a firm cannot grow its sales faster than its self-sustainable growth rate unless it issues new shares.*

Let's return to OS Distributors. Exhibit 6.10 shows the firm's SGR in Year −1 and Year 0, computed according to equation 6.12, and the growth in sales the firm experienced during these two years.

EXHIBIT 6.10	OS DISTRIBUTORS' SELF-SUSTAINABLE GROWTH RATE COMPARED WITH GROWTH IN SALES.

Year	Retention Rate	Return on Equity	Self-Sustainable Growth Rate	Growth in Sales
Year 0	$\frac{7.0}{10.2} = 0.69$	$\frac{10.2}{70.0} = 14.6\%$	$0.69 \times 14.6\% = 10\%$	14.3%
Year −1	$\frac{6.0}{8.0} = 0.75$	$\frac{8.0}{64.0} = 12.5\%$	$0.75 \times 12.5\% = 9.4\%$	7.7%

OS Distributors' SGR was 10 percent in Year 0, slightly higher than its value of 9.4 percent a year earlier. Its sales, however, grew by 14.3 percent during Year 0, a rate almost twice that achieved in the previous year (7.7 percent). How did OS Distributors grow its sales by 14.3 percent in Year 0 with roughly the same SGR as in Year –1 without issuing new shares? In other words, where did the firm get the additional capital required to grow sales beyond the SGR of 10 percent? The answer is found in OS Distributors' managerial balance sheet (see Exhibit 6.3). Cash decreased from $12 million at the beginning of Year 0 to $8 million at the end of that year, a one-year drop of 33 percent. Thus, OS Distributors used its cash holdings to finance the gap between its SGR and its growth in sales.

This example illustrates an important point: *firms with sales growing faster than their SGR will eventually experience a cash deficit; firms with sales growing slower than their SGR will eventually generate a cash surplus*. This phenomenon is illustrated in Exhibit 6.11.

Firms positioned on the line that bisects the plane are in **financial balance**. Their SGR is equal to their growth in sales. Firms with sales growth exceeding their SGR are above the line, and firms with sales growth slower than their SGR are below the line. Cash deficit firms face a *funding problem*; firms with a cash surplus have an *investment problem* – they generate more cash than they can invest.

How can management respond to unsustainable levels of growth in sales, that is, to growth rates that exceed the firm's SGR? For example, suppose OS Distributors

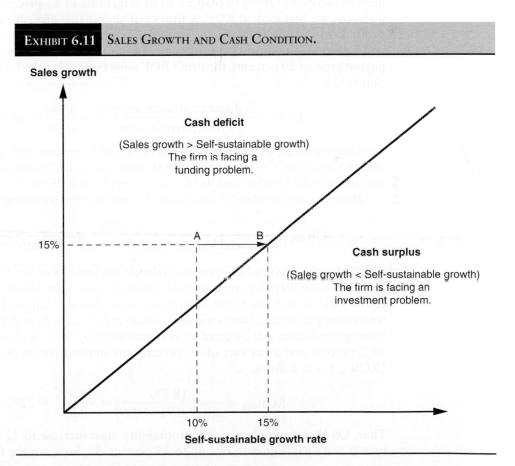

EXHIBIT 6.11   SALES GROWTH AND CASH CONDITION.

expects its sales to grow by 15 percent next year. This growth rate is clearly unsustainable if OS Distributors maintains its SGR at its current level of 10 percent (see the initial position of OS Distributors at point A in Exhibit 6.11). If raising new equity is not an option, then OS Distributors' management will have to make operating or financing decisions that will raise the firm's SGR to 15 percent (see the desired final position of OS Distributors at point B in Exhibit 6.11). Otherwise, OS Distributors will experience a continued loss of cash next year that may eventually initiate a funding and liquidity crisis.

Let's examine some of the options available to OS Distributors. If we assume that next year's ROE will be the same as this year's (14.6 percent), then one possible option is to retain 100 percent of the firm's profit. With a retention rate of one, the firm's self-sustainable growth rate will be equal to its ROE. Thus, this option, which implies an elimination of dividend payments, would raise the firm's SGR to 14.6 percent, a figure close to the firm's 15 percent expected growth in sales. But it is unlikely that the firm's owners will find this option acceptable. They will probably impose some financial constraints on the firm's management. Let's assume (1) they are unwilling to cut dividends below 20 percent of profits, and (2) their desired debt-to-equity ratio is one. *After management has met these financial constraints, the firm's self-sustainable growth rate can be increased only through an improvement in the firm's operating profitability.*

How much does OS Distributors' operating profitability, measured by its $ROIC_{BT}$, need to increase to bring its SGR up to its target rate of 15 percent? To answer this question, we first look at ROE. A firm's self-sustainable growth rate is equal to its profit retention rate multiplied by its ROE. To achieve a self-sustainable growth rate of 15 percent with a profit retention rate of 0.80 (which corresponds to a dividend payout ratio of 20 percent), the firm's ROE must be equal to the following (see equation 6.12):

$$ROE = \frac{\text{Self-sustainable growth rate}}{\text{Profit retention rate}} = \frac{15\%}{0.80} = 18.7\%$$

To achieve a target self-sustainable growth rate of 15 percent with a profit retention rate of 80 percent, OS Distributors' ROE must rise to 18.7 percent. What combination of financial leverage and $ROIC_{BT}$ will provide an ROE of 18.7 percent? Rearranging the terms in equation 6.11, we have the following:

$$ROIC_{BT} = \frac{ROE}{\text{Financial leverage multiplier} \times (1 - \text{Effective tax rate})}$$

Recall that the financial leverage multiplier is the product of the financial structure (Invested capital/Equity) ratio and the financial cost ratio. Given a target debt-to-equity ratio of one, the financial structure ratio (Invested capital/Equity) is two. If we assume the financial cost ratio will remain at 0.71 as in Year 0, then the financial leverage multiplier will be equal to two multiplied by 0.71. With a desired ROE of 18.7 percent and a tax rate of 40 percent, the implied return on invested capital ($ROIC_{BT}$) is as follows:

$$ROIC_{BT} = \frac{18.7\%}{2.0 \times 0.71 \times 0.60} = \frac{18.7\%}{0.85} = 22\%$$

Thus, OS Distributors' operating profitability must increase to 22 percent to bring its self-sustainable growth rate up to 15 percent. So, how can the firm's operations achieve an $ROIC_{BT}$ of 22 percent next year? $ROIC_{BT}$ can rise only through a combination of higher operating profit margin and faster capital turnover. Suppose in a previous meeting of OS Distributors' managers, the marketing manager said that operating profit margin is expected to rise to 5.5 percent next year. How high must capital turnover rise to achieve an $ROIC_{BT}$ of 22 percent given that operating profit margin is expected to be 5.5 percent? $ROIC_{BT}$ is the product of capital turnover and operating profit margin, so we can write the following:

$$\text{Capital turnover} = \frac{\text{Pre-tax return on invested capital}}{\text{Operating profit margin}} = \frac{22\%}{5.5\%} = 4.0$$

We now know that OS Distributors must raise its capital turnover to 4.0 next year to raise its self-sustainable growth rate to 15 percent. How can this objective be achieved? The operations manager will have to focus first on the firm's WCR; receivables will have to be collected faster and inventories will have to turn over as quickly as possible. Being in the distribution business, however, OS Distributors uses a relatively small amount of fixed assets and thus has a lower opportunity to rapidly improve its **fixed asset turnover ratio** (sales divided by fixed assets). This challenge may have to be addressed eventually if OS Distributors is to raise its self-sustainable growth rate to 15 percent without raising new equity.

The conclusion is inescapable: given OS Distributors' financial constraints, if the firm's management cannot achieve the targeted improvements in the firm's operations, the firm's owners will have to inject new equity into the business, issue new shares, or accept lower-than-expected sales.

KEY POINTS

1. A firm's profitability, risk, and growth are related to one another and must be managed in a way that allows the firm to grow smoothly without impairing its ability to create wealth for its owners. A firm's return on equity (ROE) measures the firm's overall profitability and is affected by the firm's operating, investing, and financing activities as well as its effective tax rate.

2. The effect of operating and investing activities on ROE is captured by return on invested capital before tax ($ROIC_{BT}$), which is obtained by dividing the firm's earnings before interest and tax (EBIT) by its invested capital (the sum of cash, working capital requirement, and net fixed assets). $ROIC_{BT}$ is equal to the firm's operating profit margin (EBIT/Sales) multiplied by its capital turnover (Sales/Invested capital). Empirical evidence indicates that a firm's $ROIC_{BT}$ is essentially driven by its competitive position (the size of its market share), the relative quality of its products and services, and the structure of its costs and assets.

3. A firm's financing strategy also has an effect on ROE. A firm's pre-tax ROE is equal to its operating profitability multiplied by the financial leverage multiplier, a measure of the effect of borrowing on the firm's profitability. When operating profitability *exceeds* the cost of debt, the financial leverage multiplier is *higher* than one and financial leverage is *favorable* to the firm's owners. When operating profitability is *lower* than the cost of debt, the firm's financial leverage multiplier is *lower* than one and financial leverage is *unfavorable* to the firm's owners. However, a firm cannot easily take advantage of favorable financial leverage because of business risk (the unpredictable fluctuations in the firm's EBIT and operating

profitability). In other words, the firm will generally be unable to predict its operating profitability at the time it borrows to finance its investments. Financial leverage adds another layer of risk to the firm's business risk, and this additional risk, called financial risk, affects the firm's performance.

4. Taxation also affects ROE. Firms should try to minimize the negative effect of corporate taxes on their profitability by taking advantage, whenever possible, of tax breaks and tax subsidies that are offered, for example, by countries or regions that want to attract investments.

5. Other measures of profitability, besides ROE, include the firm's earnings per share (earnings after tax divided by the number of shares outstanding), its price-to-earnings ratio (share price divided by earnings per share), and its market-to-book ratio (share price divided by book value per share).

6. The ability of a firm to finance its growth is determined by its self-sustainable growth rate (SGR). This rate is equal to the fraction of profits retained by the firm (its profit retention rate) multiplied by its ROE. A firm's SGR indicates whether the firm can finance its anticipated growth in sales without raising new equity or changing either its operating policy (its operating profit margin and capital turnover remain the same) or its financing policy (its debt-to-equity and dividend-payout ratios remain the same). A firm that grows its sales faster than its SGR will eventually experience a cash deficit. If it is unable to raise its SGR through a higher profit retention rate or a higher ROE, then its only option for eliminating its cash deficit is to issue new equity. A firm that is unable to grow its sales as fast as its SGR will eventually experience a cash surplus. A firm facing this situation must then decide how to spend its cash surplus to create value for its owners. If it is unable to find value-creating investment opportunities, it should simply return the excess cash to its shareholders through a dividend payment or a share repurchase program (see Chapter 11).

GlaxoSmithKline's Profitability APPENDIX 6.1

In this appendix, we analyze GlaxoSmithKline (GSK)'s profitability over the three years 2015, 2016, and 2017. Using the return on equity (ROE) formula in equation 6.9, we show how the company's operating activity, financial policy, and taxation have contributed to its profitability, and provide some comparison with Sanofi, a major competitor of GSK in the pharmaceutical industry.

GSK'S PROFITABILITY STRUCTURE

We apply equation 6.9 to GSK's data taken from its income statements in Exhibit A6.1.1 and managerial balance sheets in Exhibit A6.1.2.[8]

The result is presented in Exhibit A6.1.3, which shows the effect of operations, financial policy, and taxation on GSK's ROE in 2015, 2016, and 2017.

For comparison purposes, we also show, in the same Exhibit, the profitability of Sanofi during the same period.

GSK's ROE decreased from 94.3 percent in 2015 to 21.4 percent in 2016, and then increased to 62.2 percent in 2017. During the same period, Sanofi's ROE was much lower and less volatile: 6.4 percent in 2015, 7.8 percent in 2016, and 6.7 percent in 2017. What accounts for GSK's important changes in ROE and for the differences between the two companies? This question is addressed in the next sections in which we analyze the ROE structure of the two companies based on the data in Exhibit A6.1.3.

RETURN ON EQUITY

GSK's return on invested capital before tax ($ROIC_{BT}$) decreased from 23.9 percent in 2015 to 5.5 percent in 2016, and then slightly increased to 9.2 percent in 2017. During the same period, Sanofi's $ROIC_{BT}$ increased from 5.4 percent in 2015 to 7.3 percent in 2016, and then slightly decreased to 6.8 percent in 2017. Remember that $ROIC_{BT}$ is driven by operating margin (Earnings before interest and tax (EBIT) divided by net sales) and invested capital turnover. With this in mind, let's see how these two drivers of operating profitability evolved over the period 2015–2017 for GSK and Sanofi and how we can explain the difference in operating profitability between the two companies.

THE EFFECT OF OPERATING MARGIN ON GSK'S OPERATING PROFITABILITY

Note the large decrease in GSK's operating margin from 43.15 percent in 2015 to 9.32 percent in 2016 followed by an increase to 13.54 percent in 2017. During

---

[8] GSK's income statements were presented in Chapter 4, Appendix 4.2 (Exhibit A4.2.4), and its managerial balance sheets in Chapter 4, Appendix 4.2 (Exhibit A4.2.3).

EXHIBIT A6.1.1	GSK's CONSOLIDATED STATEMENTS OF INCOME.

FROM EXHIBIT A4.2.4, APPENDIX 4.2, CHAPTER 4. FIGURES IN MILLIONS OF POUNDS

	2015	2016	2017
Turnover	£23,923	£27,889	£30,186
Cost of goods sold	(8,853)	(9,290)	(10,342)
Gross profit	15,070	18,599	19,844
Selling, general, and administrative expenses	(9,232)	(9,366)	(9,672)
R&D expense	(3,560)	(3,628)	(4,476)
Royalty income	329	398	356
Other operating income (expenses)	7,715	(3,405)	(1,965)
Operating profit	10,322	2,598	4,087
Net interest expense[1]	204	(659)	(562)
Profit before taxation	10,526	1,939	3,525
Income tax expense	(2,154)	(877)	(1,356)
Profit after taxation for the year	£8,372	£1,062	£2,169

[1] Net interest expense is interest income less interest expense plus share of after tax profits of associates and joint ventures.

EXHIBIT A6.1.2	GSK's MANAGERIAL BALANCE SHEETS.

FROM EXHIBIT A4.2.3, APPENDIX 4.2, CHAPTER 4. FIGURES IN MILLIONS OF POUNDS

Year-end		2015		2016		2017
Invested capital						
• Cash		£6,076		£5,357		£4,092
• Working capital requirement		205		(596)		(240)
• Net fixed assets		36,859		42,370		40,474
Total invested capital		£43,140		£47,131		£44,326
Capital employed						
• Short-term debt		£1,767		£6,203		£13,885
• Short-term provisions		1,344		848		629
• Long-term financing		40,029		40,080		29,812
Long-term debt	£15,324		£14,661		£14,264	
Other long-term liabilities	15,827		20,456		12,059	
Owners' equity	8,878		4,963		3,489	
Total capital employed		£43,140		£47,131		£44,326

EXHIBIT A6.1.3	THE STRUCTURE OF RETURN ON EQUITY FOR GSK AND SANOFI.

ALL DATA FROM THE FIRMS' INCOME STATEMENTS AND MANAGERIAL BALANCE SHEETS

	Return on Equity	=	Operating Profitability	×	Financial Leverage Multiplier	=	Return on Equity Before Tax	×	Tax Effect
	$\dfrac{\text{EAT}}{\text{Owners' equity}}$	=	$\dfrac{\text{EBIT}}{\text{Net sales}}$ × $\dfrac{\text{Net sales}}{\text{Invested capital}}$	×	$\dfrac{\text{EBT}}{\text{EBIT}}$ × $\dfrac{\text{Invested capital}}{\text{Owners' equity}}$	=	$\dfrac{\text{EBT}}{\text{Owners' equity}}$	×	$\dfrac{\text{EAT}}{\text{EBT}}$
			Pre-tax return on invested capital (ROIC$_{BT}$)[1]		Financial leverage multiplier[2]				
GSK									
2015	94.3%	=	43.15% × 0.555 ⟹ 23.9%	×	1.019 × 4.859 ⟹ 4.95	=	118.6%	×	0.795
2016	21.4%	=	9.32% × 0.592 ⟹ 5.5%	×	0.746 × 9.496 ⟹ 7.08	=	39.1%	×	0.548
2017	62.2%	=	13.54% × 0.682 ⟹ 9.2%	×	0.862 × 12.705 ⟹ 10.95	=	101.1%	×	0.615
Sanofi									
2015	6.4%	=	14.16% × 0.383 ⟹ 5.4%	×	0.916 × 1.528 ⟹ 1.40	=	7.6%	×	0.839
2016	7.8%	=	18.82% × 0.386 ⟹ 7.3%	×	0.890 × 1.560 ⟹ 1.39	=	10.1%	×	0.772
2017	6.7%	=	16.03% × 0.423 ⟹ 6.8%	×	0.971 × 1.470 ⟹ 1.43	=	9.7%	×	0.688

[1] Rounded to the first decimal
[2] Rounded to the second decimal

the same period, Sanofi's operating margin increased from 14.16 percent in 2015 to 18.82 percent in 2016, and then decreased to 16.03 percent in 2017. Note the significant differences between GSK's and Sanofi's margins, especially in 2015 and 2016 (43.15 percent compared to 14.16 percent in 2015 and 9.32 percent compared to 18.82 percent in 2016).

Differences in operating margins result from different operating revenues and expenses associated with recurring activities such as purchasing, producing, and selling but also with unusual or infrequent events such as restructuring, divestments, discontinued operations, and lawsuits. The effect of these nonrecurring events on the operating margin of the two companies needs to be excluded from our analysis in order to identify the key trends and factors that affect each company's ability to operate profitability and explain their difference. This is done in Exhibit A6.1.4 using data provided by both companies in their annual reports.

When nonrecurring items are removed from GSK operating expenses, its operating margin changes significantly and becomes less volatile. It changes from 43.1 percent to 21.2 percent in 2015, from 9.3 percent to 24.7 percent in 2016, and from 13.5 percent to 26.0 percent in 2017. GSK's adjusted operating margin improved by nearly 5 percent from 21.2 percent in 2015 to 26.0 percent in 2017. During the same period, Sanofi's operating margin also improved by slightly more than 1 percent (from 23.4 percent in 2015 to 24.5 percent in 2017). On average, GSK's and Sanofi's margins over the three-year period are not significantly different (24.0 percent for GSK and 23.5 percent for Sanofi).

Let's now look at the components of the adjusted operating margin for both companies over the three-year period.

The adjusted gross margin of both companies increased from 2015 to 2017 (68.6 percent to 70.9 percent for GSK and 67.9 percent to 70.2 percent for Sanofi). GSK's gross margin is higher than that of Sanofi in each of the three years although the difference is not significant (less than 1 percent in 2015 and 2017).

GSK's adjusted selling, general, and administrative expenses as a percentage of sales decreased significantly from 33.1 percent in 2015 to 30.9 percent in 2017, while

EXHIBIT A6.1.4	GSK's AND SANOFI's GROSS MARGIN AND ITS COMPONENTS AS A PERCENTAGE OF NET SALES WHEN ADJUSTED FOR NONRECURRING EXPENSES.

FROM THE FIRMS' ANNUAL REPORTS

		GSK			Sanofi		
		2015	2016	2017	2015	2016	2017
Operating margin	Actual	43.1%	9.3%	13.5%			
	Adjusted	21.2%	24.7%	26.0%	23.4%	22.5%	24.5%
Gross margin	Actual	63.0%	66.7%	65.7%			
	Adjusted	68.6%	70.1%	70.9%	67.9%	68.4%	70.2%
Selling, general, and administrative expenses	Actual	38.6%	33.6%	32.0%			
	Adjusted	33.1%	32.0%	30.9%	27.5%	28.0%	28.7%
R&D expenses	Actual	14.9%	13.0%	14.8%			
	Adjusted	12.9%	12.4%	12.8%	14.9%	15.3%	15.6%
Royalty income	Actual	1.4%	1.4%	1.2%			
	Adjusted	1.4%	1.4%	1.2%	2.3%	2.6%	2.3%

that of Sanofi remained stable at around 28 percent. Over the three-year period, GSK expenses relative to sales were always higher than Sanofi's with a maximum difference of 5.6 percent arising in 2015 (33.1 percent compared to 27.5 percent).

The adjusted R&D expenses-to-sales ratio of GSK did not change much over the three-year period (12.9 percent in 2015, 12.4 percent in 2016, and 12.8 percent in 2017). During the same period, Sanofi's ratio went up from 14.9 percent to 15.6 percent, nearly 3 percent higher than GSK's ratio. Sanofi spent more in R&D as a percentage of sales than GSK in each year over the three-year period.

Adjusted royalty income of GSK represents a very small proportion of its revenues (1.4 percent in 2015 and 2016, and 1.2 percent in 2017). GSK received less royalty income relative to sales than did Sanofi in each of the three years (1 percent on average).

In summary, when exceptional items are excluded from reported operating profits, GSK's operating margins become more stable, which is not surprising, but also do not differ much from Sanofi's. In other words, both companies generated as much operating profit from their core operations per pound or euro of sales. However, when analyzing the components of the operating margin over the three-year period, important differences emerge: on average and relative to sales, GSK spent significantly more on administrative and selling activities than did Sanofi, but significantly less on R&D.

THE EFFECT OF INVESTED CAPITAL TURNOVER ON GSK'S OPERATING PROFITABILITY

Exhibit A6.1.3 shows that GSK generated £0.56 in 2015, £0.59 in 2016, and £0.68 in 2017 of sales per pound of invested capital. Furthermore, the ratio increased continuously and significantly over the three-year period.

A look at Exhibit A6.1.2 indicates that net fixed assets is the largest component of the company's invested capital, representing between 85 percent (in 2015) and 91 percent (in 2017) of total invested capital. Turning to Exhibit A6.1.5, we see that GSK's ratio of net sales to fixed assets increased from 0.65 in 2015 to 0.75 in 2017, which represents a 15 percent increase in the efficient use of the company's fixed assets over the three-year period.

Exhibit A6.1.5 also shows that GSK's net sales-to-fixed assets ratio has been consistently much higher than Sanofi's. For example, in 2017, GSK generated 0.75 pounds of sales from one pound invested in fixed assets while Sanofi generated only 0.48 euros per euro invested in the same assets. A look at Sanofi's balance sheets shows that more of its fixed assets at year-ends 2015, 2016, and 2017 is goodwill which arises from the acquisition of businesses or firms.[9] It seems that Sanofi had not been able to generate enough sales per euro spent on acquisitions to match GSK's much higher net sales-to-fixed assets ratio.

EXHIBIT A6.1.5	GSK'S AND SANOFI'S NET SALES-TO-FIXED ASSETS RATIO.					

FROM THE FIRMS' INCOME STATEMENTS AND BALANCE SHEETS

	GSK			Sanofi		
End of year	2015	2016	2017	2015	2016	2017
Net sales-to-fixed assets ratio	0.65	0.66	0.75	0.48	0.47	0.48

---

[9] By comparison, GSK's goodwill represents only 14 percent of its fixed assets over the three-year period (see Exhibit A4.2.1 in Chapter 4).

THE EFFECT OF GSK'S FINANCIAL POLICY ON ITS RETURN ON EQUITY

GSK's financial leverage multiplier in 2015 was 4.95 (see Exhibit A6.1.3). It increased to 7.08 in 2016, and again to 10.95 in 2017. During the same period, Sanofi's multiplier was always much lower than that of GSK, in the range of 1.39 (in 2016) to 1.43 (in 2017).

Changes in the financial cost ratio (EBT/EBIT), which went down from 1.02 in 2015 to 0.75 in 2016, and then increased to 0.86 in 2017, only partially explain the increase in the multiplier from 2015 to 2017: most of it is the result of changes in the financial structure ratio (invested capital/owners' equity), which went up from 4.86 at year-end 2015 to 9.50 at year-end 2016, and to 12.70 at year-end 2017. Is this increase the result of an increase in invested capital or a decrease in owners' equity, or both? A look at GSK's managerial balance sheet (Exhibit A6.1.2) shows that changes in its invested capital never exceeded 10 percent while the financial structure ratio nearly doubled between 2015 and 2016 and increased again by 34 percent between 2016 and 2017. Thus, most of the increases in GSK's financial structure ratio can be attributed to decreases in owners' equity which went down from £8,878 million, to £4,963 million, and to £3,489 million at year-end 2015, 2016, and 2017, respectively (see Exhibit A6.1.2). As mentioned in Appendix 2 of Chapter 5, when we analyzed GSK's liquidity, these decreases were the direct consequence of paying dividends that were higher than the firm's net income in 2016 and 2017. According to the firm's annual reports, GSK's dividends are determined primarily by the amount of free cash flow available for distribution after funding the firm's business investments and its debt obligations. For example, in 2016 and 2017, the firm's free cash flow was large enough to distribute an amount of dividends which happened to be larger than these years' net income. Over the three-year period from 2015 to 2017, Sanofi and GSK have comparable financial cost ratios but very different financial structure ratios: while GSK's ratio varies between 4.86 to 12.70, Sanofi's ratio is stable at around a much lower value of 1.5.

The financial structure ratio is directly related to the debt-to-invested capital ratio. Exhibit A6.1.6 shows this ratio for GSK and Sanofi from 2015 to 2017.

GSK's debt ratio was 39.6 percent at year-end 2015 and increased to 44.3 percent at year-end 2016, to reach 63.5 percent at year-end 2017. According to GSK's 2017 annual report, the company expected its future cash flows generated from operations to be large enough to support its debt service costs and, at the same time, meet the firm's future capital expenditures, restructuring expenditures, and dividends. This assertion was credible enough to have convinced the credit agencies Standard & Poor's (S&P) and Moody's Investor Service A2 to maintain GSK's credit rating over the three-year period from 2015 to 2017 (A+ and A2, respectively) despite the

EXHIBIT A6.1.6	DEBT RATIOS FOR GSK AND SANOFI.					

DATA FROM THE FIRMS' MANAGERIAL BALANCE SHEETS

	GSK			Sanofi		
	2015	2016	2017	2015	2016	2017
Total debt / Invested capital	39.6%	44.3%	63.5%	19.7%	22.0%	18.2%

significant increase in the firm's debt ratio over the three-year period.[10] Sanofi's debt ratio stayed relatively stable during the same period at around 20 percent, which is much lower than GSK's ratio. This is reflected in Sanofi's higher credit ratings from S&P (AA) and from Moody's (A1), the second highest rating for both agencies.

THE EFFECT OF TAXATION ON GSK'S RETURN ON EQUITY

GSK's pre-tax ROE dropped down from 118.6 percent in 2015 to 39.1 percent in 2016 and jumped back to 101.1 percent in 2017. The high volatility of ROE as well as its high values in 2015 and 2017 are related to exceptional events such as those mentioned above when we analyzed the firm's operating margin. During the same period, Sanofi's pre-tax ROE remained stable at around 9 percent, as the effect of nonrecurring events on the ratio was much less pronounced than for GSK.

Taxation affected GSK's profitability slightly more than Sanofi's, as shown by the EAT to EBT ratio, which ranged from 0.5 to 0.8 for GSK and from 0.7 to 0.8 for Sanofi. But the difference was not large enough to reduce significantly the huge disparity in pre-tax profitability between the two companies.

FURTHER READING

1. Jagiello, Kevin, and Gordon Mandry. "Structural Determinants of Performance: Insight from the PIMS Data Base." *The Handbook of Management*. Edited by D. F. Channon. Blackwell, 2004.
2. Rappaport, Alfred. *Creating Shareholder Value*. The Free Press, 2000. See chapter 2.

SELF-TEST QUESTIONS

6.1 **Profitability analysis.**
The financial statements of Allied & Consolidated Clothier (ACC), a manufacturer of coats and other garments, are shown below. ACC's operational efficiency and liquidity position are analyzed in Chapter 5. The income statements span a calendar year, and balance sheets are dated December 31. All figures are in millions of dollars.

Balance Sheets (in millions)							
Year End	Year −2	Year −1	Year 0		Year −2	Year −1	Year 0
Cash	$100	$90	$50	Short-term debt	$80	$90	$135
Trade receivables	200	230	290	Trade payables	170	180	220
Inventories	160	170	300	Accrued expenses	40	45	50
Prepaid expenses	30	30	35	Long-term debt	140	120	100
Net fixed assets	390	390	365	Owners' equity	450	475	535
Total assets	$880	$910	$1,040	Total liabilities & owners' equity	$880	$910	$1,040

[10] See Chapter 13 for a discussion on debt ratings.

Income Statements (in millions)			
	Year –2	Year –1	Year 0
Net sales	$1,200	$1,350	$1,600
Cost of goods sold	860	970	1,160
Selling, general, and administrative expenses	150	165	200
Depreciation expense	40	50	55
Earnings before interest and tax (EBIT)	150	165	185
Net interest expense	20	20	25
Earnings before tax (EBT)	130	145	160
Income tax expense	40	45	50
Earnings after tax (EAT)	$90	$100	$110
Dividends	$75	$75	$50

a. Restructure ACC's balance sheets in their managerial form.
b. Calculate ACC's return on equity (ROE) in Year –2, Year –1, and Year 0 both before and after tax (use year-end owners' equity).
c. Calculate ACC's pre-tax operating profitability in Year –2, Year –1, and Year 0, using year-end data and the three measures of operating profitability presented in the chapter: return on invested capital before tax ($ROIC_{BT}$), return on total assets (ROTA), and return on business assets (ROBA). Explain how these measures are different. Why do these measures of profitability differ from return on assets (ROA), which we defined as net profits over total assets?
d. What is return on capital employed before tax ($ROCE_{BT}$)?
e. What the drivers are of pre-tax ROIC? Provide a measure of these drivers in Year –2, Year –1, and Year 0. What can you conclude when you compare ACC's operating profitability in Year 0 with its Year –2 performance?
f. Why is pre-tax ROE (see question b.) higher than pre-tax ROIC (see question c.)?
g. Given your answer to the previous question, is it correct to claim that as long as ACC borrows to finance its investments, its shareholders are better off because they will have a higher ROE?
h. Provide measures of the extent of ACC's borrowing in Year –2, Year –1, and Year 0, using the ratios that follow. Briefly compare the information provided by these financial ratios:

   1. Financial cost ratio
   2. Times-interest-earned
   3. Financial structure ratio
   4. Debt-to-equity ratio
   5. Debt-to-invested capital ratio

i. Break down ROE into its five fundamental components in Year –2, Year –1, and Year 0. What can you conclude about the structure of ACC's profitability?
j. Given that ACC has 50 million shares outstanding that were worth $20 at the end of Year –2, $24 at the end of Year –1, and $30 at the end of Year 0, what were ACC's earnings per share, price-to-earnings ratio, and market-to-book ratio on those dates? What information do these measures of profitability provide?

6.2 Balance sheet and operating profitability structures across industries.

Balance sheet and operating profitability structures for three companies are shown below. The information comes from their 2016 annual reports. The companies are Alphabet Inc., the parent company of Google, the browser developer; The Boeing Company, the aircraft manufacturer; and China Southern Airlines, the airline company. Identify each company and explain your choice.

Balance Sheet Structure (in percentage)	Company A	Company B	Company C
Cash and cash equivalent	11%	2%	52%
Accounts receivable	10%	1%	8%
Inventories	48%	1%	~0%
Other current assets	0%	5%	3%
Net fixed assets	31%	91%	37%
Total assets	100%	100%	100%
Short-term debt	0%	18%	0%
Accounts payable	12%	0%	9%
Accruals and others	43%[1]	16%[1]	1%
Long-term debt	11%	36%	2%
Other long-term liabilities	33%	3%	5%
Owners' equity	1%	27%	83%
Total liabilities and owners' equity	100%	100%	100%

[1] Include significant advance payments from clients

Operating Profitability Structure	Company A	Company B	Company C
Return on total assets (ROTA)[1]	6.6%	4.3%	14.2%
Operating profit margin[2]	5.9%	7.5%	26.3%
Total asset turnover[3]	1.11	0.57	0.54

[1] Earnings before interest and tax (EBIT)/Total assets = EBIT/Sales × Sales/Total assets
[2] EBIT/Sales
[3] Sales/Total assets

6.3 Sustainable growth analysis.

Return to Allied & Consolidated Clothier (ACC), whose financial statements are reported in question 6.1.

a. Compare the company's growth rate in sales in Year 0 with its sustainable growth rate that same year. What can you conclude?

b. Suppose that ACC expects its sales to grow by 25 percent in Year +1.

1. How much equity capital will it need to finance that growth if it does not modify its financing policy and operational efficiency? How will ACC obtain this equity capital?

2. What will be the consequence of the 25 percent growth in sales on the firm's debt-to-equity ratio if ACC does not issue new equity, modify its dividend policy, or change its operational efficiency?

3. What will be the consequence of the 25 percent growth in sales on the firm's profit retention policy if ACC does not issue new equity, modify its debt-to-equity ratio, or change its operational efficiency?

4. How should ACC modify its operational efficiency if it wishes to grow its sales by 25 percent without issuing new equity or modifying its financing policy?

c. Suppose that ACC expects its sales to grow by 10 percent in Year +1.

1. What will be the consequence of the 10 percent growth in sales on the firm's cash position if ACC does not modify its financing policy or change its operational efficiency?

2. What can ACC do with the extra cash? What should it do?

REVIEW QUESTIONS

1. **Transactions.**
Indicate the effects of the following transactions on *operating margin, invested capital turnover*, and *debt ratio*. Use + to indicate an increase, – to indicate a decrease, and 0 to indicate no effect.

	Operating margin	Invested capital turnover	Debt ratio
1. Shares are issued for cash			
2. Goods from inventory are sold for cash at a profit			
3. A fixed asset is sold for cash at its book value			
4. A fixed asset is sold for more than its book value			
5. A dividend is declared and paid			
6. Cash is obtained through a bank loan			
7. Accounts receivable are collected			
8. Minority interest in a firm is acquired for cash			
9. A fixed asset is depreciated			
10. Obsolete inventory is written off			
11. Merchandise is purchased on account			
12. Shares are repurchased			

2. **ROIC$_{BT}$, ROCE$_{BT}$, ROBA, and ROTA.**

   From the balance sheets and income statements of OS Distributors in Exhibits 6.1, 6.2, and 6.3, compute the firm's return on invested capital before tax (ROIC$_{BT}$), return on capital employed before tax (ROCE$_{BT}$), return on business assets (ROBA), and return on total assets (ROTA) for Year 0. What are the differences between these different measures of return?

3. **Book versus market return on equity.**

   Return on equity (ROE) can be estimated using financial statements (book value) or financial market data (market value). The book value of ROE over an accounting period is earnings after tax divided by owners' equity. The market value of ROE is the return that an investor would have experienced during the same period. It is the difference in share price plus dividend paid during the period divided by the share price at the beginning of the period. Why are the two ratios different? If the market ROE is more relevant to an investor, what is the use of the book ROE?

4. **The structure of a firm's profitability.**

   a. If a firm has a return on equity (ROE) of 15 percent, a financial multiplier of 2, and does not pay any tax, what is its return on invested capital before tax?

   b. If a firm has an ROE of 15 percent, a financial cost effect of 0.9, and a pre-tax ROIC of 10 percent, what is its debt-to-equity ratio (total debt divided by owners' equity)? Assume that the firm does not pay any tax.

   c. Under what condition(s) can a firm have, at the same time, a negative pre-tax ROIC and a positive ROE?

5. **Misuse of the structure of return on equity.**

   Cite two cases in which a bad decision (that is, a decision that negatively affects the market value of a firm) would increase its return on equity.

6. **Financial leverage.**

   Under what intuitive condition will an increase in debt (either short-term or long-term) relative to equity always increase a firm's return on equity? Can the structure of return on equity relationship be used to determine a firm's optimal debt-to-equity ratio?

7. **Industry effect on the structure of return on equity.**

   Below are summarized balance sheets and income statements of three US companies:

Income Statements (in millions)			
	Firm 1	Firm 2	Firm 3
Revenues	$166,809	$7,132	$22,956
Earnings before interest and tax	10,105	1,419	10,937
Earnings before tax	9,083	1,114	14,275
Earnings after tax	$ 5,745	$ 714	$ 9,421

Balance Sheets (in millions)			
	Firm 1	Firm 2	Firm 3
Cash	$ 1,856	$ 485	$23,798
Accounts receivable	1,341	770	3,250
Inventories	19,793	223	0
Prepaid expenses	1,366	237	3,260
Net fixed assets	45,993	13,816	21,842
Total assets	$ 70,349	$15,531	$52,150
Short-term debt	$ 5,408	$ 890	$ 0
Accounts payable	13,105	616	1,083
Accrued expenses	7,290	158	8,672[1]
Long-term liabilities	18,712	8,205	1,027
Owners' equity	25,834	5,662	41,368
Total liabilities and owners' equity	$ 70,349	$15,531	$52,150

[1] Mostly unearned revenues.

a. Compute the working capital requirement of the three firms and prepare their managerial balance sheets.

b. Compute the three firms' operating margin, invested capital turnover, return on capital employed, financial multiplier, and the tax effect. What is the relationship between these ratios and the firms' return on equity?

c. One firm is in the retail (nongrocery) industry, another is a utility firm, and the last one is in the software industry. Which of the companies corresponds to Firm 1, Firm 2, and Firm 3?

8. **The effect of the management of the operating cycle on the firm's profitability.**
Below are the last three years' financial statements of Sentec Inc., a distributor of electrical fixtures.

Income Statements (in thousands)			
	Year 1	Year 2	Year 3
Sales	$22,100	$24,300	$31,600
Cost of goods sold	17,600	19,300	25,100
Selling, general, and administrative expenses	3,750	4,000	5,000
Depreciation expense	100	100	150
Earnings before interest and tax	650	900	1,350
Net interest expense	110	130	260
Earnings before tax	540	770	1,090
Income tax expense	220	310	430
Earnings after tax	$ 320	$ 460	$ 660
Dividends	$ 180	$ 200	$ 200

Balance Sheets (in thousands)			
	Year-end 1	Year-end 2	Year-end 3
Cash	$ 600	$ 350	$ 300
Accounts receivable	2,730	3,100	4,200
Inventories	2,800	3,200	4,300
Prepaid expenses	0	0	0
Net fixed assets[1]	1,200	1,300	1,450
Total assets	$7,330	$7,950	$10,250
Short-term debt	$300	$500	$1,900
Accounts payable	1,400	1,600	2,050
Accrued expenses	200	260	350
Long-term debt	1,300	1,200	1,100
Owners' equity	4,130	4,390	4,850
Total liabilities and owners' equity	$7,330	$7,950	$10,250

[1] The company did not sell any fixed assets in Years 2 and 3.

a. Compute Sentec Inc.'s working capital requirement (WCR) and prepare its managerial balance sheets at Year-end 1, Year-end 2, and Year-end 3.

b. Compute Sentec's operating margin, invested capital turnover, return on capital employed, financial cost ratio, financial structure ratio, and the tax effect in Year 1, Year 2, and Year 3. What is the relationship between these ratios and Sentec's return on equity (ROE) over the three-year period?

c. What accounts for the change in the firm's ROE over the three-year period?

d. In Year 3, firms in the same business sector as Sentec Inc. had an average collection period of 30 days, an average payment period of 33 days, and an inventory turnover of 8. Suppose Sentec Inc. had managed its operating cycle like the average firm in the sector. What would its WCR, managerial balance sheet, operating margin, invested capital turnover, return on capital employed, financial cost ratio, financial structure ratio, and the tax effect have been in Year 3? Its ROE? Assume a ratio of interest expense to earnings before interest and tax of 4 percent, and an effective tax rate of 40 percent.

9. **Seasonal business.**

Mars Electronics is a distributor for the Global Electric Company (GEC), a large manufacturer of electrical and electronics products for consumer and institutional markets. On the next page are the semi-annual financial statements of the company for the last year and a half.

a. Prepare Mars Electronics' managerial balance sheet on June 30, Year –1, December 31, Year –1, and June 30, Year 0.

b. What was the structure of the return on equity (ROE) of Mars Electronics for the six months ending June 30, Year –1, December 31, Year –1, and June 30, Year 0?

c. What accounts for the changes in the firm's ROE?

Income Statements (in thousands)			
	Six Months to June 30, Year −1	Six Months to December 31, Year −1	Six Months to June 30, Year 0
Net sales	$10,655	$13,851	$11,720
Cost of goods sold	8,940	11,671	9,834
Selling, general, and administrative expenses	1,554	1,925	1,677
Depreciation expense	44	55	76
Interest expense	62	90	70
Tax expense	23	44	26
Earnings after tax	$ 32	$ 66	$ 37
Dividends	$ 5	$ 44	$ 1

Balance Sheets (in thousands)			
	June 30, Year −1	December 31, Year −1	June 30, Year 0
Cash	$ 160	$ 60	$ 70
Accounts receivable	1,953	2,616	2,100
Inventories	1,986	2,694	2,085
Prepaid expenses	80	42	25
Net fixed assets[1]	733	818	830
Total assets	$4,912	$6,230	$5,110
Short-term debt	$ 50	$ 880	$ 50
Accounts payable	1,450	1,950	1,650
Accrued expenses	98	114	138
Long-term debt	800	750	700
Owners' equity	2,514	2,536	2,572
Total liabilities and owners' equity	$4,912	$6,230	$5,110

[1] The firm did not sell any fixed assets over the three-year period.

10. **Self-sustainable growth rate.**

Ambersome Inc. has decided against borrowing and to have all its assets financed by equity. Furthermore, it intends to keep its payout ratio at 40 percent. Its assets turnover ratio is 0.9, its profit margin (defined as earnings before interest and tax divided by sales) is 8 percent, and profits are taxed at 40 percent. The firm's target growth rate in sales is 5 percent.

a. Is the target growth rate consistent with the firm's financing policy?

b. If not, by how much does it need to increase the assets turnover ratio or profit margin to meet the target growth rate?

c. Suppose the firm can borrow at 10 percent. Would borrowing help it to meet the target growth rate?

Using the Net Present Value Rule to Make Value-Creating Investment Decisions

One of the most important decisions a manager can make is the capital investment decision. This key decision requires spending cash now to acquire long-lived assets that will be a source of cash flows in the future. A successful capital investment program will contribute positively to the firm's financial performance for many years. The firm's managers will be commended for their skills in identifying potentially successful projects and carrying them to fruition (we use the terms *project*, *investment*, and *proposal* interchangeably). If the capital investment program fails, the firm's performance may be affected negatively for years. Moreover, the firm's suppliers of funds – the shareholders and creditors – could lose confidence in the ability of the firm's managers to make good investment decisions and may become reluctant to provide additional funds in the future.

What is a good investment decision? From a financial management perspective, *a good investment decision is a decision that raises the current market value of the firm's equity, thereby creating value for the firm's owners*. An investment decision can have other objectives, but managers who ignore the value-creation objective may jeopardize both the future of their firms and their employment prospects. The value-creating investment decision must raise *market* value, not *book* value or accounting profit. Shareholders cash in on their investment by selling their shares for cash, not for accounting profits.

Capital budgeting involves comparing the amount of cash spent today on an investment with the cash inflows expected from it in the future. Because future cash flows are generated at different dates over a long period of time, they cannot be compared directly with cash spent today. Recall that a dollar received later is worth less than a dollar received earlier. One reason for this is that the firm can earn interest on earlier cash inflows. This preference for "early cash" is called the *time value of money*. Chapter 2 shows how to account for the time value of money by converting future *known* (or certain) cash flows into an equivalent value today. The mechanism is called *discounting*. By discounting future cash flows at a discount rate that accounts for the time value of money, we can convert these future cash flows into their *present value* (or *discounted value*).

Apart from the timing issue, the risk associated with future cash flows is also an issue. Future cash flows are risky because of the probability that the cash flows realized in the future may not be the expected ones. The discount rate used in discounting *expected* future cash flows must also take this risk into account.

Decision models that consider both the time value of money and the risk of an investment's cash flows are called *discounted cash flow (DCF) models*.[1] In this chapter we present the net present value (NPV) model, show how to use the model to make investment decisions and briefly examine a useful variation, the profitability index (PI).[2] In Chapter 8 we present and compare other DCF and non-DCF models and conclude that the NPV approach to investment appraisal is superior to alternative methods.

There are two critical elements in a DCF valuation. One is the identification and measurement of the project's expected cash flows, and the other is the estimation of the appropriate discount rate required to calculate the project's present value. Chapter 9 is devoted entirely to the first issue, and Chapter 12 deals with the second. In this chapter we assume that both the investment's expected cash-flow stream and its appropriate discount rate are known and show how to calculate the investment's NPV. We also explain what NPV measures and how it should be interpreted.

The valuation of a project is a critical element in the capital investment process, but it is not the only one. Thus, we review the major steps involved in a capital investment decision before we explain how to perform an NPV analysis. After reading this chapter, you should understand the following:

- The major steps involved in a capital budgeting decision
- How to calculate the present value of a stream of future cash flows
- The NPV rule and how to apply it to investment decisions
- Why a project's NPV is a measure of the value it creates
- How to use the NPV rule to choose among projects of different sizes or different useful lives
- How the flexibility of a project can be described with the help of managerial options

THE CAPITAL INVESTMENT PROCESS

The **capital investment decision**, also called the **capital budgeting decision** or **capital expenditure decision**, involves several steps that are summarized in Exhibit 7.1.

The process is initiated when the firm *identifies* business opportunities that can be translated into potentially valuable investment proposals. This is arguably the most important step in the process. Management must foster a climate within the firm that is conducive to the generation of ideas and the uncovering of opportunities that could lead to successful long-term investments.

Identified investment proposals must then be *evaluated* financially. The inputs required for the financial evaluation of a project include: (1) the estimation of its **useful life**; (2) the estimation of the cash flows the project is expected to generate over that useful life; and (3) the appropriate **discount rate** required to calculate the present value of the project's expected cash-flow stream. Estimating the parameters required for the financial analysis of a proposed investment is not an easy task;

---

[1] DCF models are also used to value bonds and common stocks. See Chapter 10.

[2] The NPV model is briefly described in Chapter 1 and Chapter 2.

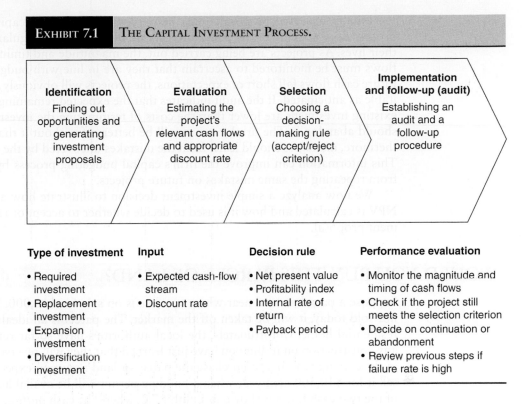

EXHIBIT 7.1	THE CAPITAL INVESTMENT PROCESS.

Identification
Finding out opportunities and generating investment proposals

Evaluation
Estimating the project's relevant cash flows and appropriate discount rate

Selection
Choosing a decision-making rule (accept/reject criterion)

Implementation and follow-up (audit)
Establishing an audit and a follow-up procedure

Type of investment	Input	Decision rule	Performance evaluation
• Required investment • Replacement investment • Expansion investment • Diversification investment	• Expected cash-flow stream • Discount rate	• Net present value • Profitability index • Internal rate of return • Payback period	• Monitor the magnitude and timing of cash flows • Check if the project still meets the selection criterion • Decide on continuation or abandonment • Review previous steps if failure rate is high

these estimation procedures are explained in detail in Chapter 9 (cash flows) and Chapter 12 (appropriate discount rate).

Proposals are usually classified by how difficult it is to estimate the key parameters needed for financial evaluation. **Required investments** are those the firm must make to comply with safety, health, and environmental regulations. In this case, managers want to know whether the present value of the cash expenses needed to comply with the regulations is greater than the cost of closing down. If it is, the project should be abandoned. Estimating such expenses should not be too complicated because, in most cases, they are already specified by the regulatory authorities. **Replacement investments** are essentially cost-saving projects that do not generate extra cash inflows. Their future cash benefits (basically cash savings) consist of reductions in anticipated costs that managers can identify with relative ease. Financial evaluation for **expansion investments** is more challenging because these projects require the firm to estimate the additional sales revenues, margins, and working capital that the expansion is expected to generate. Finally, financial evaluation for **diversification investments** is usually the most difficult. The cash flows these proposals are expected to generate are probably the hardest to forecast because the firm will enter an industry it does not know as well as its own.

After the proposal's financial parameters have been estimated, an investment criterion should be applied to *decide* whether the proposal will be accepted or rejected. This chapter examines the **net present value (NPV) rule** in detail and the **profitability index** briefly. Chapter 8 looks at other popular selection criteria, such as the **internal rate of return** and the **payback period**, and discusses the profitability index in more detail.

Finally, accepted proposals must be *implemented*. But the capital investment process does not end at this point. Projects should be *audited* regularly throughout their lives. As projects are being carried out, the magnitude and timing of their cash flows must be monitored to ascertain that they are in line with budgeted figures. If future cash flows fall short of expectations, the projects will obviously not be as profitable as anticipated. If the audit indicates that the expected remaining benefits of an existing investment are lower than the costs of terminating the investment, the firm should abandon it. The firm's owners will be better off without it than with it. Furthermore, managers should learn from the mistakes uncovered by the regular audits. This information can improve the firm's capital budgeting process by preventing it from repeating the same mistakes on future projects.

We now analyze a simple investment decision to illustrate how an investment's NPV is calculated and how it is used to decide whether to accept or reject an investment proposal.

WOULD YOU BUY THIS PARCEL OF LAND?

Suppose a parcel of land near where you live is on sale for $10,000. If the parcel is not sold today, it will be taken off the market. The parcel is an ideal location for a residential home. Unfortunately, the local authorities have so far refused to allow any construction on it. But you have just learned that they will reverse their decision in the coming year. If you purchase the parcel of land now, you expect to be able to sell it for $10,500 next year when a building permit will be available. The sequence of the two cash flows is shown in Exhibit 7.2, where the cash *outflow* is represented by a descending arrow and the cash *inflow* by an ascending arrow. Given the pattern of cash flows in Exhibit 7.2, you can easily calculate your expected return on investment. It is 5 percent, an expected gain of $500 on an investment of $10,000.

Suppose today is your lucky day and you have just received notification that you have inherited exactly $10,000, available immediately. Should you purchase the parcel of land? Before you can answer this question, you need additional information. One valuable piece of information is the highest return you can earn on a *comparable* investment. Clearly, if you can earn *more* than 5 percent on a truly comparable or **alternative investment**, you should not buy the land.

THE ALTERNATIVE INVESTMENT

The alternative investment and the one under consideration must be compared to see whether they share the same attributes. The most important attribute is **risk**.

EXHIBIT 7.2	TIMELINE FOR THE PARCEL OF LAND.

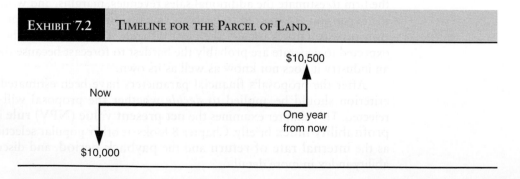

The parcel of land is a risky investment because you do not know for certain that it will sell for $10,500 next year. Some probability exists that it will sell for more or less than its expected future price. The higher the probability that actual cash flows will deviate from their expected values, the higher the risk of the expected cash-flow stream. The alternative investment must have the same risk characteristics as the parcel of land. In financial terminology, they should both belong to the same **risk class**.

Another relevant investment characteristic is the *tax treatment* of the investment's expected gains. It must be the same for the two investments because investors are interested only in their *after-tax* return on investment. For the time being and for the sake of simplicity, we assume that you live in a country that does not tax investment income. Thus, the alternative investment has the same tax treatment as the land.

The *liquidity* of the investment, that is, the ability to sell it rapidly at its current market price, is still another investment attribute that might be considered when identifying investments that are similar to the parcel of land. Risk and taxes, however, are the most important characteristics the two investments must share.

The Opportunity Cost of Capital

To estimate the rate of return on an alternative investment in the same risk class as the parcel of land, we should look at the return on comparable parcels of land in the market. To simplify the analysis at this stage, we assume that the proposed investment is *riskless* to you. If you sell the land next year for less than $10,500, we will pay you the difference; if you sell it for more than $10,500, you will give us the difference. This deal assures you that you will get $10,500 regardless of the market price of the parcel of land next year. Because the project is now riskless, the alternative investment is the deposit of the inherited $10,000 in a savings account that is government-insured, which is currently offering a 3 percent return. This is the expected return from any project that is riskless. This is also the return that you will give up if you buy the land, so it is called the **project's opportunity cost of capital**, or simply, the **project's cost of capital**.[3] You can think of a project's cost of capital as the interest rate you would pay if you borrowed the $10,000 to buy the land. The project being riskless, you should be able to borrow the $10,000 at 3 percent. In other words, the *project's discount rate is the cost of financing the project.*

Now, should you purchase the parcel of land? The answer is yes because the 5 percent you will earn on the land exceeds the 3 percent you will earn on the savings account. Put differently, you should buy the land because the 5 percent you will earn on that investment exceeds the 3 percent cost of financing it (the opportunity cost of capital).

Comparing a project's return with the return offered by an alternative investment is a simple and straightforward approach to investment analysis. Although this approach works well for one-period projects (such as the parcel of land), we show in Chapter 8 that it may sometimes fail when the project has cash flows occurring over several periods. There is, however, another approach to evaluating projects that can deal with any pattern of cash flows: it is the NPV rule explained below.

---

[3] The estimation of the cost of capital is the subject of Chapter 12.

THE NET PRESENT VALUE RULE

The approach to investment analysis in the previous section compares the rates of return for two investments – the parcel of land and the savings account. An alternative approach is to compare the $10,000 payable now to acquire the land with the dollar amount that would have to be invested *now* in the savings account to have $10,500 one year from now. This comparison is the foundation of the NPV rule. It is explained first for a one-period investment.[4]

A ONE-PERIOD INVESTMENT

How much should you invest now in a savings account with a 3 percent interest rate if you want to receive $10,500 in one year? The answer is $10,194. If you invest $10,194 now at 3 percent, in one year you will have $10,500, the sum of your initial deposit ($10,194) and the interest earned on it in one year ($306):

$$\$10,194 + [\$10,194 \times 3\%] = \$10,194 + \$306 = \$10,500$$

The left side of the above equation can be rewritten as follows:

$$\$10,194 + [\$10,194 \times 3\%] = \$10,194 \times [1 + 0.03] = \$10,500$$

The $10,500 you will receive in one year is called the **future value**, or **compounded value**, of $10,194 at 3 percent for one year. The term $(1 + 0.03)$ is called the one-year **compound factor** at 3 percent. It is equal to 1.03 (1 plus the 3 percent interest rate).

How did we find the $10,194 in the first place? We simply divided the future cash flow of $10,500 by $(1 + 0.03)$, the one-year compound factor:

$$\frac{\$10,500}{(1 + 0.03)} = \$10,194$$

The left side of the above equation can be rewritten as follows:

$$\$10,500 \times \frac{1}{(1 + 0.03)} = \$10,500 \times 0.9709 = \$10,194$$

The $10,194 you should invest now in the savings account is called the **discounted value** or **present value (PV)** of $10,500 at 3 percent for one year. The term $\dfrac{1}{(1 + 0.03)}$ is called the one-year **discount factor (DF)** at 3 percent. It is equal to 0.9709, the present value, at a 3 percent discount rate, of one dollar to be received in one year. In other words, one dollar in one year is worth approximately 97 cent today, if the discount rate is 3 percent. **Discounting** has "shrunk" the dollar by roughly 3 percent.[5]

As you may have already noticed, the discount factor is the *inverse* of the compound factor, and discounting is the *reverse* of **compounding**. Compounding provides the future cash flow ($10,500) if you know the present one ($10,194) and discounting provides the present cash flow ($10,194) if you know the future one ($10,500). In other words, at 3 percent, you should be *indifferent* whether you receive $10,194 now or $10,500 in one year. *At that rate, the two cash flows are equivalent.*

---

[4] The period could be of any duration. In this instance, we assume a period of one year, which is the typical length adopted in capital budgeting.

[5] The discounting and compounding mechanisms are also explained in Chapter 2.

Let's return to the comparison between the parcel of land and the savings account. The parcel of land costs $10,000 and generates $10,500 in one year. The savings account requires a deposit of $10,194 to generate $10,500 in one year. Which one do you prefer? Obviously, you would prefer the parcel of land because both investments generate the same cash inflows in one year, but the parcel of land requires a smaller initial investment.

The difference between $10,194 (the present value at 3 percent of the $10,500 future cash flow the land will generate in one year) and the initial cash outlay of $10,000 (the cost of the land) is called the **net present value (NPV)** of the parcel of land. It is usually presented as follows:

$$\text{NPV(land)} = -[\text{Initial cash outlay}] + [\text{Present value of the future cash flow at the cost of capital}]$$

$$\text{NPV(land at 3\%)} = -[\$10,000] + [\$10,194] = \$194$$

The NPV is positive, so you should purchase the parcel of land. The present *value* of its future cash inflow is higher than its present *cost*. If the NPV had been negative, you would have invested in the savings account. In general, *an investment should be accepted if its NPV is positive and should be rejected if its NPV is negative.* This is the **net present value rule.** If the NPV had been zero, you would be indifferent between buying the parcel of land and depositing your money in the savings account.

In Exhibit 7.3, CF_0 designates the initial cash outlay (the cash flow at time zero) and CF_1 designates the cash flow at the end of a one-period project (the cash flow at time 1). If k is the opportunity cost of capital, then the NPV of a one-period investment can be written as follows:

$$\text{NPV (investment)} = -CF_0 + \left[CF_1 \times \frac{1}{(1 + k)^1} \right] = -CF_0 + [CF_1 \times DF_1]$$

where $DF_1 = \dfrac{1}{(1 + k)^1}$ is the one-year discount factor at cost of capital k. For the land project, we have:

$$\text{NPV(land at 3\%)} = -\$10,000 + [\$10,500 \times DF_1]$$
$$= -\$10,000 + \left[\$10,500 \times \frac{1}{(1 + 0.03)^1} \right]$$
$$= -\$10,000 + [\$10,500 \times 0.9709]$$
$$= -\$10,000 + \$10,194 = \$194$$

EXHIBIT 7.3	TIMELINE FOR A ONE-PERIOD INVESTMENT.

A TWO-PERIOD INVESTMENT WITHOUT AN INTERMEDIATE CASH FLOW

Suppose you will receive the future cash flow of $10,500 for the parcel of land not in one year but in two years, all else unchanged. The sequence of cash flows now looks like the one in Exhibit 7.4.

Should you still buy the parcel of land? Before you decide, you need to consider the **time value of money:**[6] $10,500 in two years is not as valuable as $10,500 in one year. How much would you have to invest now in the 3 percent savings account to receive $10,500 two years from now? In other words, what is the present value of a parcel of land that will yield $10,500 in two years if your opportunity cost of capital is 3 percent? It is $9,897 because $9,897 invested at 3 percent per year will produce $10,500 in two years. In one year, the $9,897 will grow to $9,897 \times (1 + 0.03)$. This amount will in turn grow by $(1 + 0.03)$ during the second year. We can write the following equation:

$$[\$9,897 \times (1 + 0.03)] \times (1 + 0.03) = \$9,897 \times (1 + 0.03)^2$$
$$= \$9,897 \times 1.0609 = \$10,500$$

where, $(1 + 0.03)^2$ which is equal to 1.0609, is the two-year compound factor at 3 percent. The $9,897 present value is found by simply discounting the future value of $10,500 twice at 3 percent, which is:

$$PV(\$10,500 \text{ at } 3\%) = \$10,500 \times \frac{1}{(1 + 0.03)(1 + 0.03)}$$
$$= \$10,500 \times \frac{1}{(1 + 0.03)^2}$$
$$= \$10,500 \times 0.9426 = \$9,897$$

where 0.9426 is the two-year discount factor at 3 percent, that is:

$$DF_2 = \frac{1}{(1 + 0.03)^2} = 0.9426$$

You have to invest only $9,897 in the savings account now to receive $10,500 in two years, whereas you have to invest $10,000 in the parcel of land to receive the same amount at the same date. The savings account is clearly the better investment because it requires a smaller initial cash outlay to generate the same payoff in two years.

EXHIBIT 7.4	TIMELINE FOR THE TWO-PERIOD INVESTMENT, NO INTERMEDIATE CASH FLOW.

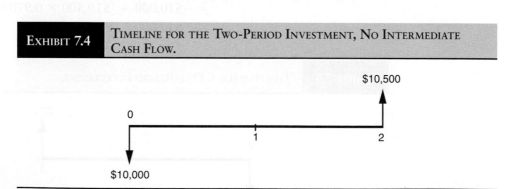

---

[6] See Chapter 2 for a detailed analysis of the time value of money.

Now, consider the NPV of the land for this case. We have the following:

$$\text{NPV(land at 3\%)} = -\text{Initial cash outlay} + \text{Present value of \$10,500 at 3\%}$$
$$= -\$10,000 + \$9,897 = -\$103$$

The NPV is negative, so the previous NPV rule is still valid: accept a project if its NPV is positive, and reject it if its NPV is negative.

A TWO-PERIOD INVESTMENT WITH AN INTERMEDIATE CASH FLOW

Given the two-year land investment in the previous section, suppose you could rent out the parcel of land during the two years. The land is fertile and you should be able to rent it to a vegetable gardener or farmer for, say, $1,000 per year, payable at the end of each year. The cash-flow profile of the investment in the parcel of land now looks like the one in Exhibit 7.5.

The investment requires an initial cash outlay (CF_0) of $10,000, yields a first-year cash flow (CF_1) of $1,000, and a terminal cash flow (CF_2) of $11,500, the sum of the second-year $1,000 rent and the $10,500 resale value of the land. Should you purchase the parcel of land in this case? The present value (PV) of the land's future cash-flow stream ($CF_1 = \$1,000$ and $CF_2 = \$11,500$) at a cost of capital of 3 percent is as follows:

$$\text{PV}(CF_1, CF_2 \text{ at } 3\%) = [CF_1 \times DF_1] + [CF_2 \times DF_2]$$
$$= [\$1,000 \times 0.9709] + [\$11,500 \times 0.9426]$$
$$= \$971 + \$10,840 = \$11,811$$

where $DF_1 = 0.9709$ is the one-year discount factor at 3 percent and $DF_2 = 0.9426$ is the two-year discount factor at 3 percent. The present value of the land's future cash-flow stream ($11,811) is greater than its cost ($10,000), so you should purchase the land. The NPV of the parcel of land is the difference between $11,811 and $10,000:

$$\text{NPV(land)} = -\$10,000 + \$11,811 = \$1,811$$

The NPV is positive, indicating that the investment should be accepted. The NPV rule continues to hold: accept a project when its NPV is positive, and reject it when its NPV is negative.

EXHIBIT 7.5	TIMELINE FOR THE TWO-PERIOD INVESTMENT WITH AN INTERMEDIATE CASH FLOW.

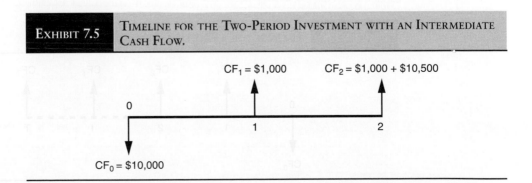

MULTIPLE-PERIOD INVESTMENTS

The analysis of the two-period investment case can be extended easily to a multiple-period investment with any number of intermediate cash flows. The longer the duration of the expected cash-flow stream, the longer the calculation, but the NPV approach still works. A business investment project can always be reduced to a stream of expected periodic cash flows, so the NPV rule can be applied directly to the analysis of any capital expenditure.

Let's call CF_t the expected cash flow at the end of year t from an investment project that requires an initial cash outlay CF_0. Assume that the investment will generate a stream of cash flows for a duration of T years. The cash-flow profile of the investment would now look like the one in Exhibit 7.6. As before, the NPV of the investment is the difference between the present value of its expected cash-flow stream and the investment's initial cash outlay. The present value, PV (CF_t), of a cash flow occurring at time t, at cost of capital k, is as follows:

$$PV(CF_t) = CF_t \times \frac{1}{(1 + k)^t} = CF_t \times DF_t$$

where $DF_t = \dfrac{1}{(1 + k)^t}$ is the t-period discount factor at cost of capital k. DF_t is the present value at cost of capital k of *one* dollar of cash flow occurring at time t. It follows that the present value of CF_t dollars of cash flow must be equal to CF_t multiplied by DF_t.

We can express the NPV of an investment with a cash-flow stream lasting for T years and a cost of capital k as follows:

$$NPV(k, T) = -CF_0 + [CF_1 \times DF_1] + [CF_2 \times DF_2] + \ldots$$
$$+ [CF_t \times DF_t] + \ldots\ldots + [CF_T \times DF_T]$$

The previous decision rule still holds: *an investment should be undertaken if its NPV is positive and should be rejected if its NPV is negative.* If the NPV is zero, you should be indifferent about accepting or rejecting the investment.

Replacing DF_1 with $\dfrac{1}{(1 + k)^1}$, DF_2 with $\dfrac{1}{(1 + k)^2}$, DF_t with $\dfrac{1}{(1 + k)^t}$, and DF_T with $\dfrac{1}{(1 + k)^T}$ in the above equation, we have another familiar expression for net present value:

$$NPV(k,T) = -CF_0 + \frac{CF_1}{(1 + k)^1} + \frac{CF_2}{(1 + k)^2} + \ldots + \frac{CF_t}{(1 + k)^t} + \ldots + \frac{CF_T}{(1 + k)^T}$$

| EXHIBIT 7.6 | TIMELINE FOR A MULTIPLE-PERIOD INVESTMENT. |

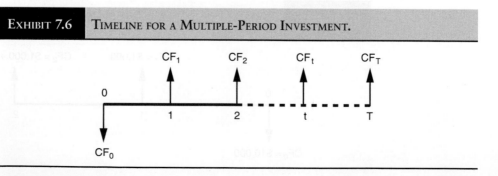

APPLYING THE NET PRESENT VALUE RULE TO A CAPITAL INVESTMENT DECISION

Applying the NPV rule to a capital investment decision is a straightforward exercise *assuming that all the relevant inputs have been estimated*. These inputs are the stream of cash flows that the project is expected to generate over its anticipated useful life and the cost of capital applicable to the investment under consideration. After these inputs are estimated, the present value of the project's stream of expected cash flows is calculated by discounting the cash flows at the project's cost of capital. Then, the project's initial cash outlay is subtracted from this present value to find the project's NPV. If the NPV is positive, the project is accepted; if the NPV is negative, the project is rejected. We use an example to explain the procedure.

Sunlight Manufacturing Company (SMC) has been successfully producing and selling various types of electrical equipment for the last 20 years and is considering adding a new product, a designer desk lamp, to its existing product line. The firm would have to spend $2,360,000 now to launch the new product, which is expected to be obsolete after five years. The investment is expected to generate an annual net cash flow of $832,000 at the end of its first year, $822,000 at the end of its second year, $692,000 at the end of its third year, $554,000 at the end of its fourth year, and a terminal net cash flow of $466,000 at the end of its fifth year. The terminal cash flow includes the estimated resale value of any equipment used to manufacture the product, net of any liquidation cost. The project's estimated cost of capital is 7.6 percent.[7] Should SMC launch the new product? To answer this question, we need to find the project's NPV.

First, the present value of each expected cash flow is calculated by multiplying it by its corresponding discount factor at the cost of capital of 7.6 percent (see Exhibit 7.7, Part I). Then, the initial cash outlay of $2,360,000 is subtracted from the total present value of the project's expected cash-flow stream to obtain the project's NPV:

$$\text{NPV(new product at } 7.6\%) = -\$2,360,000 + \$2,775,083 = \$415,083$$

The project's NPV is positive, so SMC should launch the designer desk lamp. As you may have already noticed, the computation of NPVs for multiple-period projects can be tedious. Fortunately, computer-based spreadsheets can make the task of computing NPVs quite easy. We show in Part II of Exhibit 7.7 how a spreadsheet can be used to compute the NPV of the designer desk lamp project. Note also that most electronic financial calculators have several financial functions, including an NPV function. To use this function, simply enter the cash-flow values starting with the initial cash outlay and ending with last period cash flow. Then, enter the investment's cost of capital and press the NPV key. The calculator will compute the present value of the expected cash-flow stream and provide the project's NPV. A far more complex and challenging task is the estimation of the inputs required to perform this calculation, namely the project's expected cash-flow stream and its corresponding cost of capital. These issues are addressed in Chapters 9 and 12, respectively.

---

[7] Chapter 12 shows why SMC's cost of capital is 7.6 percent.

EXHIBIT 7.7	CALCULATION OF PRESENT VALUES FOR THE SMC DESIGNER DESK LAMP PROJECT.

Part I Direct calculations

Present value of CF$_1$ $= \$832,000 \times \dfrac{1}{(1+0.076)^1} = \$832,000 \times 0.92937 = \$ 773,234$

Present value of CF$_2$ $= 822,000 \times \dfrac{1}{(1+0.076)^2} = 822,000 \times 0.86372 = 709,978$

Present value of CF$_3$ $= 692,000 \times \dfrac{1}{(1+0.076)^3} = 692,000 \times 0.80272 = 555,483$

Present value of CF$_4$ $= 554,000 \times \dfrac{1}{(1+0.076)^4} = 554,000 \times 0.74602 = 413,296$

Present value of CF$_5$ $= 466,000 \times \dfrac{1}{(1+0.076)^5} = 466,000 \times 0.69333 = 323,092$

Total present values at 7.6%   **$2,775,083**
Initial cash outlay   −$2,360,000

Net present value   **= $415,083**

Part II Using a spreadsheet

	A	B	C	D	E	F	G
	Timeline	Now			End of Year		
1		0	1	2	3	4	5
2	Cash flows	−$2,360,000	$832,000	$822,000	$692,000	$554,000	$466,000
3	Cost of capital	7.6%					
4	Present value of cash inflows	$2,775,083					
5	Net present value	**$415,083**					

- *The formula in cell B4 is = NPV(B3,C2:G2). Note that the function is identified as NPV even though the formula provides the present value of the future cash-flow stream and not its NPV*
- *The formula in cell B5 is = B2 + B4*

WHY THE NPV RULE IS A GOOD INVESTMENT RULE

The NPV rule is a desirable investment decision rule because, as discussed in this section, it has the following properties:

1. It is a measure of value creation: when the project's NPV is positive, the project creates value, and when it is negative, the project destroys value
2. It adjusts for the timing of the project's expected cash flows
3. It adjusts for the risk of the project's expected cash flows
4. It is additive

The first three properties are essential for any selection criterion used to decide whether to accept or reject a capital investment. In Chapter 8, the comparisons of the NPV rule to alternative selection criteria are based on these important properties.

The additive property of the NPV rule simply means that if one project has an NPV of $100,000 and another an NPV of $50,000, then the two projects, taken together, have a combined NPV of $150,000, assuming that the two projects are independent. This property has several useful implications.

NPV IS A MEASURE OF VALUE CREATION

At the beginning of this chapter, we define a good investment decision as one that increases the market value of the firm's equity. Would a positive NPV project be one?

Consider again the one-period real estate investment example. Recall that the initial cash outlay is $10,000 and that the present value of its expected cash inflow of $10,500 is $10,194 at 3 percent. Suppose you make the investment and, as soon as you have done so, an interested investor wants to purchase the parcel of land from you.

What *minimum* price should you quote? You should not accept any price less than $10,194. If you sell it for less, say $10,100, the best alternative investment available is to put the $10,100 in a savings account. After a year, you will have $10,403 ($10,100 plus 3 percent of $10,100 or $303). This is less than the $10,500 you will receive in a year from your parcel of land. Clearly, you would not want to sell the land for less than $10,194.

What is the *maximum* price the interested investor would be willing to pay for the parcel of land? The maximum price for the investor is also $10,194. This is the amount the investor would have to spend now on the alternative investment (the savings account) to have an amount in a year equal to the return on the land. At a higher purchase price, the investor will be "poorer" than if the money was put in the alternative investment.

If there is a price that both you and the interested investor can agree on, it is indeed $10,194. This would also be the price at which your new property would be sold to any other buyer in an active real estate market. Thus, $10,194 is the *market value* of the parcel of land. In other words, its present value is also its market value. By extension, this is also true for any capital investment. In fact, *the present value of a project's expected cash-flow stream at its cost of capital is an estimate of how much the project would sell for if a market existed for it.* In other words, the market value of any investment is determined by the present value of the cash flows that it is expected to generate in the future.

The parcel of land you bought for only $10,000 has a market value of $10,194. Thus, your wealth has increased by $194 ($10,194 less $10,000). This is exactly the same as the NPV of the investment. By extension, *the NPV of an investment project represents the immediate change in the wealth of the firm's owners if the project is accepted.* If positive, the project creates value for the firm's owners; if negative, it destroys value. From the perspective of the owners, a decision to invest in a positive NPV project is clearly a good investment decision. It increases the owner's current wealth.

Although a project with a positive NPV is expected to create value, NPV does not provide any indication about the source of value creation. Firms can generate positive NPV projects and create value for the firm's owners for many reasons. The firm may have creative managers supported by a superior workforce. It may hold a strong position in a product or service market that makes it difficult for new entrants to compete on an equal footing. More importantly, some projects cannot be easily replicated by competitors, either because they require expertise that is specific to the firm or because they are protected by patents. For these reasons, a firm may be able to generate cash flows from some of its investments that have present values higher than the cost of investing in these projects.

NPV ADJUSTS FOR THE TIMING OF THE PROJECT'S CASH FLOWS

A good investment decision must take into consideration the timing of the investment's expected cash flows. Does the NPV rule do this? A project's NPV is the difference between the present value of its expected cash flows and its current cost. The present values of these cash flows are obtained by discounting each of them at the project's opportunity cost of capital. The more distant the cash flows, the lower their contribution to the investment's present value because the discount factor, $\dfrac{1}{(1 + k)^t}$, by which the cash flows are multiplied in the net present value formula, becomes smaller as the number of years (t) increases. Thus, the NPV rule adjusts for the timing of a project's expected cash flows through the discount factors.

To illustrate, consider two five-year investments, A and B. Both require an initial cash outlay of $1 million and have a cost of capital of 10 percent. The cash flows expected from the two investments are shown in Exhibit 7.8.

Assume that the investments are **mutually exclusive**, meaning that if one is chosen, the other must be turned down. (An example is the choice between building either a bridge or a tunnel to allow traffic to cross a river.) A firm confronted with this choice should prefer to invest in project A because it would receive cash faster than if it invested in project B. Does the NPV rule lead to the same selection? To find out, compute the present values of the two investments' expected cash flows, as shown in Exhibit 7.9A. The initial cash outflow is $1 million in both cases. Thus, the NPVs of the two projects are:

$$\text{NPV (A at 10\%)} = -\$1,000,000 + \$1,722,361 = \$722,361$$
$$\text{NPV (B at 10\%)} = -\$1,000,000 + \$1,463,269 = \$463,269$$

Both investments are worth undertaking because both have a positive NPV. However, the NPV of investment A is larger than the NPV of investment B. In other words, the NPV rule favors the investment with the faster cash return. Exhibit 7.9B shows the calculations using a spreadsheet.

NPV ADJUSTS FOR THE RISK OF THE PROJECT'S CASH FLOWS

Does the NPV rule consider the risk of a project? It certainly does. The risk adjustment is made through the project's discount rate. As the risk of the stream of future cash flows expected from the investment increases, the discount rate (the opportunity

EXHIBIT 7.8	CASH FLOWS FOR TWO INVESTMENTS WITH $CF_0 = \$1$ MILLION AND $k = 10\%$.	
End of Year	**Investment A**	**Investment B**
1	$CF_1 = \$800,000$	$CF_1 = \$100,000$
2	$CF_2 = 600,000$	$CF_2 = 200,000$
3	$CF_3 = 400,000$	$CF_3 = 400,000$
4	$CF_4 = 200,000$	$CF_4 = 600,000$
5	$CF_5 = 100,000$	$CF_5 = 800,000$
Total cash flows	**$2,100,000**	**$2,100,000**

Exhibit 7.9A	Present Value of Cash Flows for Two Investments Using a Calculator.

NPV adjusts for the timing of a project's cash flows
Figures from Exhibit 7.8

End of Year	Investment A Opportunity Cost of Capital = 10%				
1	PV($800,000)	=	$800,000 × 0.9091	=	$727,273
2	PV($600,000)	=	600,000 × 0.8264	=	495,868
3	PV($400,000)	=	400,000 × 0.7513	=	300,526
4	PV($200,000)	=	200,000 × 0.6830	=	136,602
5	PV($100,000)	=	100,000 × 0.6209	=	62,092
Total present values					$1,722,361[1]
Initial cash outlay					−$1,000,000
Net present value					$722,361

End of Year	Investment B Opportunity Cost of Capital = 10%				
1	PV($100,000)	=	$100,000 × 0.9091	=	$90,909
2	PV($200,000)	=	200,000 × 0.8264	=	165,289
3	PV($400,000)	=	400,000 × 0.7513	=	300,526
4	PV($600,000)	=	600,000 × 0.6830	=	409,808
5	PV($800,000)	=	800,000 × 0.6209	=	496,737
Total present values					$1,463,269
Initial cash outlay					−$1,000,000
Net present value					$463,269

[1] The present values do not add up exactly to the amount shown because of rounding errors in the discount factors.

cost of capital) used to calculate the present value of the expected cash-flow stream should also increase. The reason is that investors are **risk averse**. They buy shares of firms with riskier projects only if they expect to earn a higher return to compensate them for the higher risk they have to bear.[8] By discounting the future stream of expected cash flows at a rate that increases with risk, the NPV rule adjusts not only for the time value of money but also for the project's risk – that is, the riskier the project, the higher the discount rate and the lower the NPV. In other words, the riskier the project the less valuable it is.

To illustrate, consider two five-year investments, C and D, both requiring the same initial cash outlay of $1 million. Investment D is riskier than investment C.

---

[8] The relationship between the returns investors will require and the risk they are willing to bear is discussed in Chapter 3 and in Chapter 12.

EXHIBIT 7.9B	PRESENT VALUE OF CASH FLOWS FOR TWO INVESTMENTS USING A SPREADSHEET.

NPV ADJUSTS FOR THE TIMING OF A PROJECT'S CASH FLOWS
FIGURES FROM EXHIBIT 7.8

	Investment A Opportunity Cost of Capital = 10%						
	A	B	C	D	E	F	G
	Timeline	Now			End of Year		
1		0	1	2	3	4	5
2	Cash flows	−$1,000,000	$800,000	$600,000	$400,000	$200,000	$100,000
3	Cost of capital	10.0%					
4	Net present value	$722,361					

• *The formula in cell B4 is = B2+NPV(B3,C2:G2)*

	Investment B Opportunity Cost of Capital = 10%						
	A	B	C	D	E	F	G
	Timeline	Now			End of Year		
1		0	1	2	3	4	5
2	Cash flows	−$1,000,000	$100,000	$200,000	$400,000	$600,000	$800,000
3	Cost of capital	10.0%					
4	Net present value	$463,269					

• *The formula in cell B4 is = B2+NPV(B3,C2:G2)*

As a result, it has an opportunity cost of capital of 12 percent, whereas C has an opportunity cost of capital of only 8 percent. The two investments have the identical expected cash-flow streams shown in Exhibit 7.10.

Assume again that the investments are mutually exclusive; the firm can choose only one of the two. A manager making investment decisions on behalf of risk-averse investors should prefer investment C. Its expected cash flows are identical to those of investment D, but they are *less risky*. Does the NPV rule favor the same investment? To find out, compute the present values of the investments' expected cash flows, as shown in Exhibit 7.11.

The initial cash outflow is $1 million in both cases. Thus, the NPVs of the two projects are:

$$NPV(C\ at\ 8\%) = -\$1,000,000 + \$1,197,813 = \$197,813$$
$$NPV(D\ at\ 12\%) = -\$1,000,000 + \$1,081,433 = \$81,433$$

EXHIBIT 7.10	CASH FLOWS FOR TWO INVESTMENTS WITH $CF_0 = \$1$ MILLION; $k = 8\%$ FOR INVESTMENT C AND $k = 12\%$ FOR INVESTMENT D.

End of Year	Investment C	Investment D
1	$CF_1 = \$300,000$	$CF_1 = \$300,000$
2	$CF_2 = 300,000$	$CF_2 = 300,000$
3	$CF_3 = 300,000$	$CF_3 = 300,000$
4	$CF_4 = 300,000$	$CF_4 = 300,000$
5	$CF_5 = 300,000$	$CF_5 = 300,000$
Total cash flows	$1,500,000	$1,500,000

EXHIBIT 7.11	PRESENT VALUE OF CASH FLOWS FOR TWO INVESTMENTS.

NPV ADJUSTS FOR THE RISK OF A PROJECT'S CASH FLOWS
FIGURES FROM EXHIBIT 7.10

Part I Calculations

End of Year			Investment C Opportunity Cost of Capital = 8%		
1	PV($300,000)	=	$300,000 \times 0.92593$	=	$277,779
2	PV($300,000)	=	$300,000 \times 0.85734$	=	257,202
3	PV($300,000)	=	$300,000 \times 0.79383$	=	238,149
4	PV($300,000)	=	$300,000 \times 0.73503$	=	220,509
5	PV($300,000)	=	$300,000 \times 0.68058$	=	204,174
Total present values					$1,197,813
Initial cash outlay					−$1,000,000
Net present value					$197,813

Part II Using a spreadsheet

	A	B	C	D	E	F	G
1	Timeline	Now			End of Year		
		0	1	2	3	4	5
2	Cash flows	−$1,000,000	$300,000	$300,000	$300,000	$300,000	$300,000
3	Cost of capital	8.0%					
4	Net present value	$197,813					

- *The formula in cell B4 is* = B2+NPV(B3,C2:G2)

EXHIBIT 7.11	PRESENT VALUE OF CASH FLOWS FOR TWO INVESTMENTS. (*Continued*)

NPV ADJUSTS FOR THE RISK OF A PROJECT'S CASH FLOWS
FIGURES FROM EXHIBIT 7.10

Part I Calculations

End of Year			Investment D Opportunity Cost of Capital = 12%		
1	PV($300,000)	=	$300,000 × 0.89286	=	$267,858
2	PV($300,000)	=	300,000 × 0.79719	=	239,157
3	PV($300,000)	=	300,000 × 0.71178	=	213,534
4	PV($300,000)	=	300,000 × 0.63552	=	190,655
5	PV($300,000)	=	300,000 × 0.56743	=	170,229
Total present values					**$1,081,433**
Initial cash outlay					−$1,000,000
Net present value					**$81,433**

Part II Using a spreadsheet

	A	B	C	D	E	F	G
1	Timeline	Now			End of Year		
		0	1	2	3	4	5
2	Cash flows	−$1,000,000	$300,000	$300,000	$300,000	$300,000	$300,000
3	Cost of capital	12%					
4	Net present value	$81,433					

• *The formula in cell B4 is* = *B2+NPV(B3,C2:G2)*

The investment with the lower risk (investment C) has the larger NPV. In other words, the NPV rule favors the same investment as the one the firm would select. The higher the risk attached to a project's stream of expected cash flows, the higher *the opportunity cost of capital required to discount those cash flows, and the lower the project's NPV.* In other words, the NPV method adjusts for the risk of a project by raising the project's cost of capital to reflect the higher risk of the project's expected cash flows. The effect of this adjustment is to reduce the project's NPV, thus making it less attractive to the firm.

NPV IS ADDITIVE

The additive property of the NPV rule has practical implications for the capital expenditure decision. Consider again investments A and B presented earlier and assume now that they are no longer mutually exclusive; the firm can choose to invest in both projects. Because the NPV rule is additive, the value created by the two investments taken together is equal to the sum of their NPVs:[9]

$$\text{NPV (A + B)} = \text{NPV (A)} + \text{NPV (B)}$$
$$\text{NPV (A + B)} = \$722,361 + \$463,269 = \$1,185,630$$

Thus, to find the NPV of investing in both projects, you do not need to calculate the sum of their combined cash flows, discount them at their cost of capital of 10 percent, and deduct the $2 million initial cash outlay required to launch the two projects. Adding their NPVs produces the same result. Together, the two projects should raise the market value of the firm's equity by an estimated $1,185,630.

The additive property has other useful implications. Suppose that the analysis of investment B overlooked a relevant and recurrent cost that would have reduced each annual cash flow by an estimated $50,000. To determine the investment's NPV with the corrected cash flows, simply calculate the present value of the future stream of "overlooked" cash outflows ($50,000 per year) and add it to the NPV of the original investment. We have the following:

$$\text{NPV } (-\$50,000 \text{ for 5 years at 10\%}) = -\$189,539$$

The corrected NPV is thus as follows:

$$\text{NPV(corrected)} = \text{NPV(original)} + \text{NPV}(-\$50,000 \text{ sequence})$$
$$= \$463,269 - \$189,539 = \$273,730$$

The NPV is still positive. The project remains attractive, but the magnitude of its NPV has been reduced by almost 41 percent to reflect the overlooked costs.

The additive property can also help the firm's managers determine the *change* in the value created by an investment if the risk of its expected cash-flow stream is suddenly revised upward or if the magnitude of its expected cash flows is revised downward. Suppose the risk of investment C, discussed earlier, is revised upward. The appropriate discount rate, which reflects the investment's higher risk, is no longer 8 percent but, say, 12 percent. The firm should expect the upward revision of the risk of investment C to reduce the market value of the firm's equity by $116,380, an amount equal to the NPV of the additional risk:

$$\text{NPV(additional risk)} = \text{NPV(C at 12\%)} - \text{NPV(C at 8\%)}$$
$$= \$81,433 - \$197,813 = -\$116,380$$

How much can the value of investment C be reduced because of overlooked future costs, initial cost overruns, or higher-than-expected levels of risk and *still earn its cost of capital?* For Investment C to still earn its 8 percent cost of capital, its value can be reduced no more than $197,813, the NPV of the original investment. The upward revision of the project's risk (which resulted in an increase in the cost of capital to 12 percent) has already reduced the project's initial NPV by $116,380. If the present value of, say, additional overlooked costs exceeds $81,433 ($197,813 less $116,380), the project's NPV will become negative and will no longer earn its *new* opportunity cost of capital of 12 percent. In other words, an investment's positive NPV is a measure of value creation to the firm's owners *only if the project proceeds according to the budgeted figures.* From the firm's managers' perspective, a project's

---

[9] The implicit assumption is that the projects' expected cash-flow streams are independent of each other. Investing in one project will have no effect on the cash-flow stream of the other.

positive NPV is the maximum present value that they can afford to "lose" on the project (because of downward revision of the project's cash flows or upward revision of the project's risk) and still earn the project's cost of capital. Further "losses" will change the project's NPV to a negative value, and the investment will become a value-destroying proposition.

SPECIAL CASES OF CAPITAL BUDGETING

We have examined how the timing and the risk of expected cash flows affect the NPVs of investments with equal sizes and equal lives. However, projects usually have different sizes or different life spans. Further, a firm's investment budget may not be large enough to allow the firm to fund all its investment proposals that have a positive NPV. When these proposals vary greatly in size (measured by their initial cash outlay), managers have to decide which positive NPV project to accept and which to reject, a process called budgeting under **capital rationing**. Managers may also have several choices for replacing an aging machine, with each possibility having a different expected useful life. The following sections show how to use the NPV method to select investments with different sizes or different life spans.

COMPARING PROJECTS OF UNEQUAL SIZE

Suppose a firm is considering the three investments described in Exhibit 7.12. According to the NPV rule, all three investments should be undertaken because they all have a positive NPV. This decision assumes that the three projects are not mutually exclusive and that the firm can raise the $2 million it needs to launch the three projects (the sum of their initial cash outlays).

What if the firm can raise only $1 million? In this case, the choice narrows down to either investing only in E or investing in both F and G. Investments F and G are clearly the superior choice because they have a value-creating potential of $272,727 (the sum of their NPVs) compared with only $140,496 for investment E. Thus, *if the total capital available for investment is limited, the firm cannot simply select the project with the highest NPV.*[10] It must first determine the combination of investments

	EXHIBIT 7.12	CASH FLOWS, PRESENT VALUES, AND NET PRESENT VALUES FOR THREE INVESTMENTS OF UNEQUAL SIZE WITH k = 10%.

	Investment E	Investment F	Investment G
(1) Initial cash outlay (CF$_0$)	$1,000,000	$500,000	$500,000
Year-one cash flow (CF$_1$)	800,000	200,000	100,000
Year-two cash flow (CF$_2$)	500,000	510,000	700,000
(2) Present value of CF$_1$ and CF$_2$ at 10%	$1,140,496	$603,306	$669,421
Net present value = (2) minus (1)	$140,496	$103,306	$169,421

[10] Note that this problem occurs only because the three projects do not have the same initial size. If they did, then the projects should be ranked by decreasing order of their NPV, and the projects with the largest NPV should be selected.

with the highest present value of future cash flows *per dollar of initial cash outlay*. This can be done by using the project's **profitability index**. An investment's profitability index is defined as the ratio of the present value of the investment's expected cash-flow stream to the investment's initial cash outlay. The profitability indexes of investments E, F, and G are shown in Exhibit 7.13.

An investment's profitability index is equivalent to a benefit-to-cost ratio. If the investment has a positive NPV, then its benefit (line 2 of Exhibit 7.13) must exceed its cost (line 1 of Exhibit 7.13), and its profitability index is greater than one. If it has a negative NPV, then its cost must exceed its benefit, and its profitability index is less than one. Investments E, F, and G all have a positive NPV, so their profitability indexes are all greater than one. Project E yields $0.14 of *net* present value per $1 of initial investment, project F yields $0.21, and project G yields $0.34.

If the firm has limited funds available for investment, it should first rank the three projects in decreasing order of their profitability indexes (first G, then F, and finally E). Then, *it should select the projects with the highest profitability index until it has allocated the total amount of funds at its disposal*. In our case, this allocation rule will select project G and then project F for a total investment of $1 million.

Allocating limited capital to a set of projects on the basis of their profitability indexes does not, unfortunately, resolve the size problem entirely because this method deals with a situation in which the limit on capital expenditures is imposed during the year the projects are under review. In our case, the $1 million limit applies to the initial year. What will happen next year?

Suppose that the $1 million limit on capital applies again the following year and that project H, costing $1.8 million and having an NPV of $400,000, becomes available. Will the firm be able to finance project H? The firm will have a maximum of $1.3 million of funds to invest: the $1 million capital budget plus the $300,000 of cash flow generated by projects F and G at the end of year one. (Recall that the firm selected projects F and G last year and that their combined first-year cash flows are equal to $300,000, as indicated in Exhibit 7.12.) Project H costs $1.8 million, so $1.3 million is not enough to fund it. It will have to be turned down. Conclusion: because the firm invested in projects F and G last year, it must now turn down a project with a $400,000 NPV.

If the firm had selected investment E last year, it would be able to fund investment H. Investment E would have generated $800,000 at the end of year one, which, added to the $1 million capital budget, would provide the funds required

| EXHIBIT 7.13 | PROFITABILITY INDEXES FOR THREE INVESTMENTS OF UNEQUAL SIZE. |

AN INVESTMENT'S PROFITABILITY INDEX IS EQUIVALENT TO A BENEFIT-TO-COST RATIO
FIGURES FROM EXHIBIT 7.12

	Investment E	Investment F	Investment G
(1) Initial cash outlay	$1,000,000	$500,000	$500,000
(2) Present value of future cash flows	$1,140,496	$603,306	$669,421
(3) Profitability index $= \dfrac{(2)}{(1)}$	$\dfrac{\$1,140,496}{\$1,000,000} = 1.14$	$\dfrac{\$603,306}{\$500,000} = 1.21$	$\dfrac{\$669,421}{\$500,000} = 1.34$

to invest in H. Investments E and H have a combined NPV of $540,496 ($140,496 plus $400,000), a higher value than the combination of F and G ($103,306 plus $169,421), even after adjusting the NPV of project H to account for the fact that it occurs a year later.[11]

Thus, *a firm operating under capital constraints should not make today's investment decisions without considering investments that may be available tomorrow.* However, this may be difficult in practice because information about tomorrow's investments may not be readily available today. If the firm does not have enough information on future potential projects, then using the profitability index to make optimal decisions on the basis of currently available information may be the *second-best* solution. The next chapter discusses the profitability index in more detail and re-examines its reliability as a rule to select alternative investments.

COMPARING PROJECTS WITH UNEQUAL LIFE SPANS

We now consider a firm that must make a choice between two investments with unequal life spans. Suppose a firm must decide whether to purchase machine A or machine B. Machine A costs $80,000, has a useful life of two years, and has annual maintenance costs of $4,000. It is assumed to be worthless after two years of operation. Machine B costs $120,000, has a useful life of four years, and has annual maintenance costs of $3,000. It will be worthless in four years. Machine B is 50 percent more expensive than machine A, but its useful life is twice as long and its annual maintenance costs are lower. The two machines are expected to generate the same annual cash flows. The firm's managers want to find out which machine the firm should buy.

If the two machines generate identical future annual cash inflows, the one with the lower present value of overall costs should be preferred because its NPV would be higher. The problem is that the two machines have unequal life spans; machine A will last two years and machine B will last four years. We cannot make a meaningful comparison unless both machines operate over the same period of time. Thus, we assume that at the end of the second year the firm will purchase a new machine A that will last two years. With this approach, we can compare a sequence of *two* machines A lasting four years to *one* machine B, also lasting four years.

Let's assume that the appropriate cost of capital applicable to this type of cost analysis is 10 percent. The relevant streams of cash outflows for two machines A and one machine B and their present values at 10 percent are shown in Exhibit 7.14 (Part I using a calculator to compute the NPV and Part II using a spreadsheet).

The present value of the total cost of a sequence of two machines A ($158,795) is higher than the present value of the total cost of a single machine B ($129,510) over the same span of useful life. The firm should buy machine B even though it is more expensive. The present value of the total cost of a *single* machine A bought today is equal only to $86,924 (not shown in the exhibit). If the firm compares that cost with the cost of machine B ($129,510), it will find machine A cheaper and will incorrectly purchase it.

In the case we have just examined, a sequence of two machines A is equivalent to one machine B. If, for example, machine B had a five-year useful life and machine A had only a three-year life, we would have compared a sequence of *five* machines A against a sequence of *three* machines B to have two sequences

---

[11] The $400,000 NPV of project H is worth only $363,636 a year earlier if discounted at the firm's cost of capital of 10 percent.

EXHIBIT 7.14	CASH OUTFLOWS AND PRESENT VALUES OF COST FOR TWO INVESTMENTS WITH UNEQUAL LIFE SPANS.

Part I Calculations

End of Year	Sequence of Two Machines A				One Machine B	
	Cash Flows			Present Value at 10%		Present Value at 10%
	Machine 1	Machine 2	Total		Cash Flows	
Now	−$80,000		−$80,000	−$80,000	−$120,000	−$120,000
1	−4,000		−4,000	−3,636	−3,000	−2,727
2	−4,000	−$80,000	−84,000	−69,422	−3,000	−2,479
3		−4,000	−4,000	−3,005	−3,000	−2,255
4		−4,000	−4,000	−2,732	−3,000	−2,049
			Present value of costs	−$158,795	Present value of costs	−$129,510

Part II Using a spreadsheet

	A	B	C	D	E	F
			Sequence of Two Machines A			
1	Timeline	Now		End of Year		
		0	1	2	3	4
2	Machine 1 cash flows	−$80,000	−$4,000	−$4,000		
3	Machine 2 cash flows			−$80,000	−$4,000	−$4,000
4	Total cash flows	−$80,000	−$4,000	−$84,000	−$4,000	−$4,000
5	Cost of capital	10%				
6	Present value of costs	−$158,795				

• *The formula in cell B6 is = B4+NPV(B5,C4:F4)*

	A	B	C	D	E	F
			One Machine B			
1	Timeline	Now		End of Year		
		0	1	2	3	4
2	Cash flows	−$120,000	−$3,000	−$3,000	−$3,000	−$3,000
3	Cost of capital	10%				
4	Present value of costs	−$129,510				

• *The formula in cell B4 is = B2+NPV(B3,C2:F2)*

with *equal lives* of 15 years. Fortunately, a shortcut exists that avoids these tedious calculations. We convert each machine's total stream of cash outflows into an equivalent stream of *equal* annual cash flows, with the same present value as the total cash-outflow stream, called **annuity-equivalent cash flow** or

constant annual-equivalent cash flow. A firm should select the machine with the *lowest* annuity-equivalent cash flow.

In Exhibit 7.15 we present the two machines' original cash flows, their annuity-equivalents and their present values. How do we calculate annual-equivalent cash flows?

The constant annual-equivalent cash-flow stream must have the same present value as the original cash-flow stream at a cost of capital of 10 percent. For example, in the case of machine B, we must have the following:

$$\$129{,}510 = [\text{Constant annual-equivalent cash flow}] \times \left[\tfrac{1}{(1+0.10)^1} + \tfrac{1}{(1+0.10)^2} + \tfrac{1}{(1+0.10)^3} + \tfrac{1}{(1+0.10)^4} \right]$$

The sum of the fractions in brackets is called the four-year **annuity discount factor (ADF)** at a cost of capital of 10 percent. We show in Chapter 2 (equation 2.11) that it is equal to:

$$\text{ADF}_{4,10\%} = \frac{1}{0.10}\left[1 - \frac{1}{(1+0.10)^4} \right] = 3.1699$$

We can now write:

$$\text{Annuity-equivalent cash flow} = \frac{\$129{,}510}{3.1699} = \$40{,}855$$

More generally, we have the following:

$$\text{Annuity-equivalent cash flow} = \frac{\text{Present value of original cash flows}}{\text{Annuity discount factor}}$$

The same computation applied to machine A will give an annuity-equivalent cash flow of $50,096.

The total stream of cash outflows generated by machine A has a two-year annuity-equivalent cash outflow of $50,096, and the total stream of cash outflows generated by machine B has a four-year annuity-equivalent cash outflow of $40,855.

| EXHIBIT 7.15 | ORIGINAL AND ANNUITY-EQUIVALENT CASH FLOWS FOR TWO INVESTMENTS WITH UNEQUAL LIFE SPANS. |

FIGURES FROM EXHIBIT 7.14

	Machine A		Machine B	
End of Year	Original Cash Flows	Annuity-Equivalent Cash Flows	Original Cash Flows	Annuity-Equivalent Cash Flows
Now	−$80,000		−$120,000	
1	−4,000	−$50,096	−3,000	−$40,855
2	−4,000	−50,096	−3,000	−40,855
3			−3,000	−40,855
4			−3,000	−40,855
Present value at 10%	−$86,942	−$86,942	−$129,510	−$129,510

Because $40,855 is less than $50,096, machine B should be selected because it can be replaced by an *infinite* sequence of machines B with an annual cost of $40,855, whereas machine A is replaceable by an *infinite* sequence of machines A with a higher annual cost of $50,096.

LIMITATIONS OF THE NET PRESENT VALUE CRITERION

Although the NPV criterion can be adjusted to deal with particular cases, such as the comparison of two projects of unequal size or unequal life spans, in other cases the required adjustments to the NPV criterion are far too complex to be easily implemented. In most cases, these situations arise because the NPV criterion is a take-it-or-leave-it rule that is based only on the information available at the time the NPV is estimated. Hence, *the NPV criterion ignores the opportunities to make changes to the project as time passes and more information becomes available.*

NPV is estimated from the stream of *expected* cash flows generated by the proposal and discounted at the project's cost of capital, which depends on the project's risk. The estimation of both the cash flows and their corresponding cost of capital depends on information available at the time NPV is calculated. This information involves factors such as the marketability of the product, its selling price, the risk of obsolescence, the technology used in manufacturing the product, and the economic, regulatory, and tax environments.

A project that can be adjusted easily and inexpensively to significant changes in these factors will contribute more to the value of the firm than indicated by its NPV. It will also be more valuable than an alternative proposal with the same NPV that cannot be altered easily and as cheaply. A project's flexibility, that is, the ability of a project to adjust to changing circumstances, is usually described by **managerial** or **real options**, which can be exercised to alter a project during its useful life.

MANAGERIAL OR REAL OPTIONS EMBEDDED IN INVESTMENT PROJECTS

The following sections present two important managerial options – the option to switch technologies and the option to abandon a project. We use the designer desk lamp project of SMC to illustrate the concepts.

THE OPTION TO SWITCH TECHNOLOGIES

Suppose SMC can use two different types of machine to manufacture the designer desk lamp during the five years the project is expected to last. One is a multi-purpose standard machine and the other is a single purpose, untested digitally driven machine which was developed by SMC's research department specifically for the project. Assume that the machine used does not significantly affect the project's NPV. Although engineers at SMC are confident the newer machine will prove to be reliable, the project's manager believes it is possible that the newer machine will not be able to meet the stringent volume and quality requirements of mass production and may have to be scrapped and replaced with the standard machine. If the standard machine is selected, it can easily be replaced with the newer one, after the new machine has successfully passed extra reliability tests, with minimal disruption and adjustment to the manufacturing process. However, the reverse is not true, because replacing the new machine with the standard one would require a complete revamping of the production line. In other words, although management will have the *option to switch* machines while the project is running, this option has more value if the standard machine is chosen.

The importance and the value of the option to switch not only technologies but also production facilities have long been recognized by firms in some industries. For example, some Japanese auto manufacturers have established manufacturing operations in the United States and Europe so that they can switch production from one continent to the other when changes occur in the relative costs of producing a car. If the yen appreciates against the US dollar or against European currencies, cars manufactured in the United States or in Europe can be exported to Japan, where they can be sold at a higher margin than locally-made cars.

THE OPTION TO ABANDON A PROJECT

Suppose SMC's designer desk lamp is a flop and does not sell. Although the decision to go ahead with the project implicitly assumed that it will last five years, SMC's management will always have the *option to abandon* the project at an earlier date. Does this option add value to the project's NPV of $415,083 (see Exhibit 7.7)?

To answer this question, we assume that within one year after the project's launch, SMC knows more about the fate of the designer desk lamps. Depending on whether the lamp is a success or a failure, the expected cash flows for the remaining years (from the second to the fifth year) will change as shown in Exhibit 7.16.

If the designer desk lamp project is a success, the present value of the remaining cash flows at the project's cost of capital of 7.6 percent is $2,382,629. If the project turns out to be a failure, the present value is $1,620,618. Assuming that the project can be abandoned at the end of the first year and that the net proceeds from its liquidation will be $1,650,000, what should SMC do one year after it launches the project?

If the designer desk lamps are a success, SMC should continue with the project because the present value of the remaining cash flows ($2,382,629) exceeds the net proceeds from liquidating the project ($1,650,000). But if the lamp is a failure, the present value of the remaining cash flows ($1,620,618) is less than the net proceeds from liquidation, and SMC should abandon the project. Thus, in one year, the investment will be worth either $2,382,629 (with the success scenario) or $1,650,000 (with the failure scenario). If there is a 30 percent chance that the project will fail and a 70 percent chance that it will succeed, the expected value of the project in

EXHIBIT 7.16	EXPECTED CASH FLOWS, YEARS 2 THROUGH 5, AND THEIR PRESENT VALUES FOR SUCCESS AND FAILURE OF THE SMC DESIGNER DESK LAMP PROJECT.

	Year 2	Year 3	Year 4	Year 5	Present Value at 7.6%
Expected cash flows according to the initial estimation	$822,000	$692,000	$554,000	$466,000	—
Expected cash flows if the project is successful	$890,000	$783,000	$612,000	$520,000	$2,382,629
Expected cash flows if the project is a failure	$662,000	$480,000	$420,000	$340,000	$1,620,618

one year's time will be $2,162,840 (30 percent of $1,650,000 plus 70 percent of $2,382,629).

We can now recalculate the project's NPV taking into account the possibility that it could be abandoned after one year. The initial cash outlay ($2,360,000) and the first year's expected cash flow ($832,000) have not changed, but the cash flows from the second to the fifth years are now replaced by the project's worth at the end of the first year, that is, $2,162,840.[12] Both the first year's cash flow and the project's worth at the end of that year need to be discounted at the project's cost of capital of 7.6 percent to obtain the NPV with the abandonment option:

$$\text{NPV}_{\text{with abandonment option}} = -\$2,360,000 + \frac{\$832,000 + \$2,162,840}{1 + 0.076} = \$423.309$$

The project's NPV without accounting for the abandonment option was $415,083. Thus, the option to abandon the project after one year adds $8,226 of value ($423,309 less $415,083). Although $8,226 represents only 2 percent of the original NPV of the designer desk lamp project and does not affect the investment decision, this may not always be the case. For example, a proposal that is rejected because its NPV is negative may turn into a positive NPV project, and consequently accepted, when the abandonment option is considered.

DEALING WITH MANAGERIAL OPTIONS

The option to switch technologies and the option to abandon a project are embedded in most investment projects. However, these are not the only managerial options. Managers have many opportunities to enhance the value of an investment during its lifetime as circumstances change. A counterpoint to the option to abandon a project is the *option to expand* the project. For example, suppose the designer desk lamp is a big winner and the project needs to be expanded to meet increased demand. Regardless of the machine used to manufacture the lamps, SMC's management will have the option to expand the production line. But, contrary to the previous cases, it is not clear that the value of this option will be different for different machines because there is no reason to believe that it will be easier to increase the production of lamps with one machine rather than with the other one. However, this is not always the case, and a project that can be expanded is worth more than a project that cannot.

An investment can usually be postponed, so another important managerial option is the *option to defer* an investment. This kind of option is particularly valuable in the mining and oil extraction industries where the output (mineral or oil) prices are particularly volatile. For example, the NPV of an oil reserve may be negative, given the current market expectations about the future price of oil. However, because the development of the reserve can be postponed, sometimes for many years, the capital expenditures needed to start the extraction of oil can be deferred until the market prices rise. And the more volatile the oil prices, the higher the chance that the NPV of the reserve will become positive, and the higher the value of the option to defer the development of the reserve.

---

[12] The expected cash flows in the original estimation of the project NPV are the same as the average of the expected cash flows under the success and the failure scenarios, weighted by the chances of success (70 percent) and failure (30 percent). For example, the original cash flow in year 3 ($692,000) is equal to 70 percent of $783,000 (cash flow if the lamp is a hit) plus 30 percent of $480,000 (cash flow if the lamp is a flop).

The designer desk lamp example explains how an option to abandon can be estimated. However, our result depended to a large extent on (1) the probability that the project will be either a failure or a success and (2) the date at which this failure or success will be recognized. Unfortunately, it is difficult to make reliable estimates based on these uncertain outcomes. An alternative approach is to use option valuation models that were initially developed to value options on financial securities. This is done in Chapter 16 in which we show how to value the option to expand an investment project. But these models require data that are usually difficult to obtain and often unreliable. Furthermore, as mentioned previously, investment projects have a large number of embedded options, and it would be almost impossible to identify and evaluate them all.

In the case when the valuation of these options becomes impractical, our advice is to remember that an investment decision should not be based on a single number – that is, its NPV. Before arriving at a decision, managers should conduct a sensitivity analysis to identify the most salient options embedded in the project, attempt to value them as we did for the abandonment option, and exercise sound judgment. Options embedded in a project are either worthless or have a positive value. Thus, the NPV of a project will always *underestimate* the value of an investment project. The larger the number of options embedded in the project and the higher the probability that the value of the project is sensitive to changing circumstances, the greater the value of these options and the higher the value of the investment project.

KEY POINTS

1. An investment proposal can be evaluated by estimating its net present value (NPV). According to the NPV rule, if the investment has a positive (negative) NPV, it creates (destroys) value and should be undertaken (rejected). The NPV rule is a good investment decision rule because it adjusts the investment's expected cash flows for both their timing and risk and has the convenient property of being additive. Most important is the capacity of the NPV method to evaluate the value-creating potential of an investment proposal. In addition, the NPV of an investment proposal is an estimate of the current value the proposal will create or destroy if undertaken.

2. The steps involved in applying the NPV rule to evaluate an investment proposal are summarized in Exhibit 7.17. Two inputs are required to calculate a project's NPV: (1) the expected cash-flow stream that the project will generate over its useful life and (2) the appropriate cost of capital that reflects the risk of the expected cash flows. The cost of capital is the rate at which the project's future cash flows need to be discounted to compare their present value with the investment cost. Chapter 9 shows how to estimate a project's expected cash-flow stream, and Chapter 12 shows how to estimate its appropriate risk-adjusted cost of capital. After these inputs have been estimated, a financial calculator or any computer equipped with a spreadsheet application can compute the project's NPV. If the NPV is positive, the project creates value and should be undertaken. The present value of its future cash-flow stream is expected to more than compensate for the investment cost. If the project's NPV is negative, the project destroys value and should be rejected. In this

EXHIBIT 7.17	STEPS INVOLVED IN APPLYING THE NET PRESENT VALUE RULE.

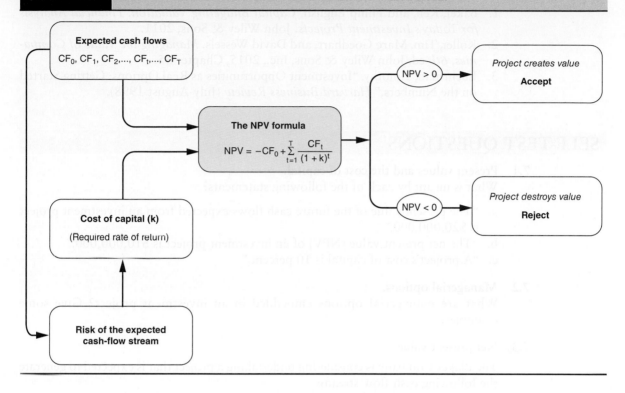

case, the present value of its future cash-flow stream is not expected to cover the investment cost.

3. The NPV rule can be used to choose among projects with different initial sizes or different life spans. If a firm has a limit on the amount of funds it can invest in new projects, it may not be able to undertake all available positive NPV projects. If the alternative projects have different initial cash outlays (different sizes), then the project's profitability index can be used to select the combination of projects that would create the most value. However, if the constraint on the availability of funds is imposed every year, rather than just during the initial year, the profitability index may lead to suboptimal investment decisions. If projects have unequal life spans, the comparison should be made between sequences of projects of the same duration. The calculations for this comparison are easier if the projects' annuity-equivalent cash flows are compared. The project with the lowest annuity-equivalent cost or the highest annuity-equivalent benefit should be selected.

4. Most projects have managerial options, options to change course after the project is launched, which are ignored in standard NPV analysis. The added value provided by these options is difficult to estimate. Although sensitivity analysis is not a perfect substitute, it can identify the most critical options embedded in a project, thus providing valuable information for the final decision to accept or reject.

FURTHER READING

1. Baker, Ken, and Philip English. *Capital Budgeting Valuation: Financial Analysis for Today's Investment Projects*. John Wiley & Sons, 2011.
2. Koller, Tim, Marc Goedhart, and David Wessels. *Managing the Value of Companies, 6th* ed. John Wiley & Sons, Inc., 2015, Chapter 35.
3. Luehrman, Timothy. "Investment Opportunities as Real Options: Getting Started on the Numbers," *Harvard Business Review* (July-August 1998).

SELF-TEST QUESTIONS

7.1   Present values and the cost of capital.

What is meant by each of the following statements?

a. "The present value of the future cash flows expected from an investment project is $20,000,000."
b. "The net present value (NPV) of an investment project is $10,000,000."
c. "A project's cost of capital is 10 percent."

7.2   Managerial options.

What are managerial options embedded in an investment project? Give some examples.

7.3   Net present value.

The Blaker Company is considering undertaking a project that is expected to generate the following cash-flow stream:

	Expected Cash Flow
Now	−$100,000
End of year 1	50,000
End of year 2	50,000
End of year 3	50,000

a. If the project's cost of capital is 12 percent, what is the present value of the project's expected cash-flow stream?
b. What is the net present value of the project?
c. What is the profitability index of the project?
d. Should the project be undertaken? Explain.

7.4   Choosing between two investments with unequal costs and life spans.

Perfect Color Company (PCC) is in the business of dyeing material. Business is booming, and PCC is considering buying a new color printer. Two printers are available on the market: printer X costs $50,000, requires $5,000 per year to operate, and has a useful life of two years; printer Y costs $60,000, requires $7,000 per year to operate, and will need to be replaced every three years. PCC's cost of capital is 10 percent.

a. What are the present values of the total costs of the two printers over their useful life?
b. Why are the two present values not comparable?

    c. What is the annual-equivalent cost for each of the printers?

    d. Which printer should PCC purchase?

7.5 Replacing an existing machine with a new one.

Pasta Uno is operating an old pasta-making machine that is not expected to last more than two years. During that time, the machine is expected to generate a cash inflow of $20,000 per year. It could be replaced by a new machine at a cost of $150,000. The new machine is more efficient than the current one and, as a result, is expected to generate a net cash flow of $75,000 per year for three years. The management of Pasta Uno is wondering whether to replace the old machine now or wait another year. Pasta Uno's cost of capital is 10 percent.

    a. Assume that the current resale value of the old machine is zero and that the new machine will also have a zero resale value in the future. What is the annual-equivalent cash flow of using the new machine?

    b. What should the management of Pasta Uno do? Explain.

REVIEW QUESTIONS

1. **Future values of an investment.**

Suppose you deposit $1,000 in one year, $2,000 in two years, and $4,000 in three years. Assume a 4 percent interest rate throughout.

    a. How much will you have in five years?

    b. Suppose you plan to withdraw $1,500 in four years and there is no penalty for early withdrawal. How much will you have in five years?

2. **Present value of a contract.**

A basketball player has just signed a $30 million contract to play for three years. She will receive $5 million as an immediate cash bonus, $5 million at the end of the first year, $8 million at the end of the second year, and the remaining $12 million at the end of the contract. Assuming a discount rate of 10 percent, what is the value of the package?

3. **Buying a machine.**

You can invest in a machine that costs $500,000. You can expect revenues net of any expense, except maintenance costs, of $150,000 at the end of each year for five years. You will subcontract the maintenance costs at a rate of $20,000 a year, to be paid at the beginning of each year. You expect to get $100,000 from selling the machine at the end of the fifth year. All these revenues and costs are after tax, as is the 10 percent cost of capital. Should you buy the machine?

4. **Buying a car.**

You are buying a car. No Better Deals will give you $500 off the list price on a $10,000 car.

    a. You can get the same car from Best Deals if you pay $4,000 down and the rest at the end of two years. If the interest rate is 12 percent, where would you buy the car?

    b. Best Deals has revised its offer. You now pay $2,000 down, $3,000 at the end of the first year, and $5,000 at the end of the second year. If the interest rate is still 12 percent, where would you buy the car?

c. No Better Deals, in turn, makes a new offer. You pay $10,000, but you can borrow the sum from the dealer at 0.5 percent per month for 36 months even though the going market rate is 1 percent per month, with the first payment made when the car is delivered. If you accept the offer, (1) What would your monthly payments be? (2) What would the cost of the car be to you?

> *Note: The objective of this exercise is not to learn how to use present value tables or set up a spreadsheet, but rather to explicitly identify the financial decisions underlying the different alternatives.*

5. **Saving for college.**
    You expect that your daughter will go to college ten years from now. Taking account of inflation, you estimate that you will need $160,000 to support her during her years in college. Assume an interest rate of 4 percent on your saving accounts. How much will you have to pay into those accounts in the next ten years to get $160,000 by then?

6. **Saving for retirement.**
    Suppose you have decided to set up a personal pension fund for your retirement. You have just turned 25. You expect to retire at age 65 and believe it is reasonable to count on living at least 20 years after retirement. Furthermore, you wish to have an annual income of $100,000 during your retirement starting when you turn 65 and that upon receipt of the 20th payment, the entire capital sum would have been distributed. You have been offered two investment plans by your financial adviser: (1) an "aggressive" portfolio of well-diversified equities that promises to yield on average a 12 percent rate and (2) a "conservative" portfolio of government bonds that promises to yield on average a 6 percent rate.

    a. How much must you invest in each of the two savings schemes each year, starting now until you retire, to ensure that you receive the $100,000 per year retirement income?
    b. What investment strategy would you recommend?

7. **Financial deals.**
    Five years ago, your favorite aunt won a $1million lottery. The prize money is paid out $50,000 per year for 20 years. Unfortunately, your aunt needs as much as $250,000 cash now to pay for medical bills that she and your uncle incurred as a result of an accident. A local finance company has proposed to provide her with the $250,000 cash in return for the $50,000 annual payments over the next nine years.

    a. What is the interest rate implicit in the local finance company proposal?
    b. What advice would you give to your aunt?

8. **Value of a firm.**
    Hellenic Vultures is expected to generate $100,000 of net cash flows next year, $120,000 the year after, and $150,000 for the following three years. It is expected that the firm could be sold for $500,000 at the end of the fifth year. The owners of Hellenic Vultures, who would like to sell their firm, strongly believe that their investment in the firm should generate a 10 percent return. What is the minimum price at which they should sell the firm?

9. **Competing investment projects.**

Lolastar Co. is evaluating two competing investment projects. They both require an investment of $25 million. The company cost of capital is 10 percent for projects of this type. The expected cash flows are as follows:

	Project I (millions)	Project II (millions)
End of year 1	$3	$12
End of year 2	5	9
End of year 3	8	7
End of year 4	10	4
End of year 5	13	3
Total cash flows	$39	$35

a. Which of the two projects would you recommend? Why?

b. Will your choice be the same whatever the cost of capital?

10. **Comparing projects with unequal economic life.**

Rollon Inc. is comparing the operating costs of two types of equipment. The standard model costs $50,000 and will have a useful life of four years. Operating costs are expected to be $4,000 per year. The superior model costs $90,000 and will have a useful life of six years. Its operating costs are expected to be $2,500 per year. Both models will be able to operate at the same level of output and quality and generate the same cash earnings. Rollon's cost of capital is 8 percent.

a. Compute the present values of the cash costs over the useful life of each model.

b. Can the two present values be compared? If not, why not?

c. What is the *annuity-equivalent cost* of each model?

d. Which model should the company purchase? Explain.

ALTERNATIVES TO THE NET PRESENT VALUE RULE

CHAPTER **8**

The net present value (NPV) rule is not the only criterion available to evaluate a capital investment proposal. You may be familiar with the payback period, the internal rate of return, or another criterion. This chapter examines and explains how to apply five alternatives to the NPV rule: the ordinary payback period rule, the discounted payback period rule, the internal rate of return (IRR) rule, the profitability index (PI) rule, and the average accounting return rule. Exhibit 8.1 shows the criteria used by a large sample of companies in different countries when making capital budgeting decisions. We analyze whether these five alternatives to the NPV rule satisfy the conditions of a good investment decision rule.

Recall that a good investment decision rule must take into account the timing of a project's expected cash flows and the project's risk. In addition, it should select projects that increase the market value of the firm's equity.

In our analysis of the alternative rules, we identify a number of cases in which these methods lead to a decision that contradicts the NPV rule. We explain why these conflicts occur and why some firms still use some of these techniques to screen investment proposals. We use six projects to illustrate how the five alternatives to the NPV rule are usually applied in making investment decisions and compare their performance with that of the NPV rule. After reading this chapter, you should understand the following:

- A project's ordinary payback period, discounted payback period, internal rate of return, profitability index, and average accounting return; and how to calculate these measures
- How to apply the alternative rules to screen investment proposals
- The major shortcomings of the alternative rules
- Why these rules are still used even though they are not as reliable as the NPV rule

THE PAYBACK PERIOD

A project's **payback period** is the number of periods (usually measured in years) required for the sum of the project's expected cash flows to equal its initial cash outlay. In other words, the payback period is the time it takes for a firm to recover its initial investment. Consider investment A, whose characteristics are reported in

| EXHIBIT 8.1 | POPULARITY OF DIFFERENT CAPITAL BUDGETING TECHNIQUES. PERCENTAGE USED BY COMPANIES. |

	France[1]	Germany[1]	Netherlands[1]	Sweden[2]	United Kingdom[1]	United States[3]
Net present value	39%	48%	70%	64%	47%	75%
Internal rate of return	44%	42%	56%	26%	53%	76%
Payback period	51%	50%	65%	57%	69%	57%
Discounted payback period	11%	31%	25%	13%	25%	30%
Average accounting return	16%	32%	25%	22%	38%	20%
Profitability index	38%	16%	8%	11%	16%	11%

[1] Brounen, D., De Jong, A. and Koedijk, K., "Corporate finance in Europe: Confronting theory with practice," *Financial Management*, Vol. 33 (4), 2004.
[2] Fredrik Hartwig, "The use of capital budgeting and cost of capital estimation methods in Swedish-listed companies," *The Journal of Applied Business Research*, Vol. 28 (6), 2012.
[3] Graham, J.R. and Harvey, C.R., "The theory and practice of corporate finance: Evidence from the field," *Journal of Financial Economics*, Vol. 60 (2–3), 2001.

Exhibit 8.2 and whose expected and cumulative cash flows are shown in Exhibit 8.3. The investment's payback period is the length of time it takes for the firm to get back its initial cash outlay of $1 million.

As indicated in Exhibit 8.3, we assume that the cash flows occur at the end of each year. Project A has a payback period of three years because it takes exactly three years for the project's *cumulative* cash flows to reach a value equal to the initial cash flow of $1 million.

Sometimes, a project's payback period includes a fraction of a year. For example, investment E requires an initial cash outlay of $1 million and generates a cumulative cash flow of $975,000 after three years and $1,300,000 after four years (see Exhibit 8.4). The project's payback period is between three and four years. It is equal to three years plus the *fraction* of the Year 4 cash flow ($325,000) required to recover the initial investment:

$$\text{Payback period (E)} = 3 + \frac{\text{Initial cash flow} - \text{Cumulative cash flow to year 3}}{\text{Year 4 cash flow}}$$

$$= 3 + \frac{\$1,000,000 - \$975,000}{\$325,000}$$

$$= 3 \text{ years} + 0.08 \text{ year} = 3.08 \text{ years}$$

Exhibit 8.4 shows how to use a spreadsheet to compute payback periods, taking investment E as an example. The payback periods for the investment proposals defined in Exhibit 8.2 are shown in Exhibit 8.5.

THE PAYBACK PERIOD RULE

According to the **payback period rule,** *a project is acceptable if its payback period is shorter than or equal to a specified number of periods called the* **cutoff period**.

EXHIBIT 8.2	EXPECTED CASH-FLOW STREAMS, COST OF CAPITAL, AND NET PRESENT VALUES OF ALTERNATIVE INVESTMENT PROPOSALS.

ALL INVESTMENTS ARE FIVE YEARS LONG AND REQUIRE AN INITIAL CASH OUTLAY OF $1 MILLION

	Investments A and B	
End of Year	Investment A	Investment B
1	$ 600,000	$ 100,000
2	300,000	300,000
3	100,000	600,000
4	200,000	200,000
5	300,000	300,000
Total cash flows	$1,500,000	$1,500,000
Cost of capital	10%	10%
NPV	$ 191,399	$ 112,511

	Investments C and D	
End of Year	Investment C	Investment D
1	$ 250,000	$ 250,000
2	250,000	250,000
3	250,000	250,000
4	250,000	250,000
5	250,000	250,000
Total cash flows	$ 1,250,000	$1,250,000
Cost of capital	5%	10%
NPV	$ 82,369	$ −52,303

	Investments E and F	
End of Year	Investment E	Investment F
1	$ 325,000	$ 325,000
2	325,000	325,000
3	325,000	325,000
4	325,000	325,000
5	325,000	975,000
Total cash flows	$ 1,625,000	$2,275,000
Cost of capital	10%	10%
NPV	$ 232,006	$ 635,605

EXHIBIT 8.3	EXPECTED AND CUMULATIVE CASH FLOWS FOR INVESTMENT A.

EXPECTED CASH FLOWS FROM EXHIBIT 8.2

End of Year	Expected Cash Flows	Cumulative Cash Flows
1	$600,000	$ 600,000
2	300,000	900,000
3	100,000	1,000,000
4	200,000	1,200,000
5	300,000	1,500,000

EXHIBIT 8.4	COMPUTING THE PAYBACK PERIOD FOR INVESTMENT E USING A SPREADSHEET.

EXPECTED CASH FLOWS FROM EXHIBIT 8.2

	A	B	C	D	E	F	G
		Now			**End of Year**		
1		0	1	2	3	4	5
2	Cash flows	−$1,000,000	$325,000	$325,000	$325,000	$ 325,000	$ 325,000
3	Cumulative cash inflows		$325,000	$650,000	$975,000	$1,300,000	$1,625,000
4	Payback period		–	–	–	3.08	–

- *0 is now; 1, 2, 3,... is end of year*
- *The formula in cell C3 is =C2. The formula in cell D3 is =C3+D2. Then copy formula in cell D3 to next cells in row 3*
- *The formula in C4 is =IF(OR(C3<=–$B$2,B3>–$B$2),"–",B1+(–$B$2–B3)/C2). Then copy formula in cell C4 to next cells in row 4*

EXHIBIT 8.5	PAYBACK PERIODS FOR THE SIX INVESTMENTS IN EXHIBIT 8.2.

Investment	A	B	C	D	E	F
Payback period (in years)	3.00	3.00	4.00	4.00	3.08	3.08

If the choice is between several mutually exclusive projects with payback periods shorter than the cutoff period, the one with the shortest payback period should be selected.

If the firm reviewing projects A–F adopts a cutoff period of four years, then all six projects are acceptable. None of their payback periods exceeds the firm's four-year cutoff period (see Exhibit 8.5). If the choice is between projects A and B, or C and

D, or E and F, then each project within a pair is as good as the other because they have the same payback period. If the choice is between projects A, C, and E, then A should be selected because it has the shortest payback period.

DOES THE PAYBACK RULE ADJUST FOR THE TIMING OF CASH FLOWS?

Consider investments A and B. They require the same initial cash outlay, have the same useful life, and carry the same risk (they have the same cost of capital). Their payback periods are also the same, but the timing of their cash flows differs. The largest cash inflow ($600,000) occurs at the end of the first year for investment A, and occurs at the end of the third year for investment B. Thus, the payback period rule does *not* take into consideration the timing of the cash flows. It simply adds them and ignores the time value of money.

DOES THE PAYBACK RULE ADJUST FOR RISK?

Now, consider investments C and D. They are both five-year projects and have the same initial cash outlay and expected annual cash flows of $250,000. Even though the expected cash-flow stream of investment D is riskier than that of investment C (the cost of capital for D is higher than the cost of capital for C), their payback periods are identical (four years). Thus, the payback period rule ignores risk.

DOES THE PAYBACK RULE MAXIMIZE THE FIRM'S EQUITY VALUE?

It is unlikely that an investment decision rule that ignores the timing and the risk of a project's expected cash flows would systematically select projects that maximize the market value of the firm's equity. Furthermore, when managers apply the payback period rule, they must have the "right" cutoff period. Unfortunately, there is no objective reason to believe that a particular cutoff period exists that is consistent with the maximization of the market value of the firm's equity. The choice of a cutoff period is always *arbitrary*.

One consequence of this shortcoming is illustrated by comparing investments E and F. The payback period rule does not discriminate between the two projects because they both have the same payback period of 3.08 years. But the firm's managers would certainly prefer to invest in F because, all else being equal, at the end of Year 5 that project is expected to generate a cash inflow that is three times larger than the one generated by project E. Clearly, the payback period rule ignores expected cash flows that occur after the cutoff period. As far as the firm is concerned, these cash flows are simply irrelevant. In other words, this decision rule is biased against long-term investments.

WHY DO MANAGERS USE THE PAYBACK PERIOD RULE?

Despite its well-known shortcomings, many managers still use the payback period rule. All the studies that survey the techniques that managers use to make investment decisions reveal a large proportion of payback period users.[1] Which redeeming qualities does the payback period rule offer that can explain its popularity among managers?

---

[1] However, most payback period users usually use this method in addition to other approaches (such as NPV or IRR). The payback period method is rarely used alone to evaluate large projects. See Exhibit 8.1.

The payback period's strongest appeal is its simplicity and ease of application. Managers in large companies make many accept/reject decisions on small and repetitive investments with typical cash-flow patterns. Over time, these managers may develop good intuition regarding the appropriate cutoff periods for which these investments have a positive NPV. Under these circumstances, it is possible that the "cost" of occasionally making wrong decisions with the payback period rule is lower than the "cost" of using more elaborate and time-consuming decision rules.

Another reason why managers use the payback period rule is that it favors projects that "pay back quickly" and thus contribute to the firm's overall cash availability. This could be an important consideration for small firms that rely primarily on internally generated funds to finance their activities because they do not have easy access to long-term funding through their banks or the financial markets.

Sometimes, two projects have the *same* NPV but have *different* payback periods. In this case, selecting the project with the shortest payback makes sense. To illustrate, we compare investment A in Exhibit 8.2 with investment G; the latter requires the same initial cash outlay as A ($1 million), has the same cost of capital (10 percent), and generates the expected cash flows shown in Exhibit 8.6.

At a cost of capital of 10 percent, the two investments have the same NPV of $191,399. However, the payback period of investment A is three years, whereas that of G is one year longer. According to the NPV rule, a firm should be indifferent in its choice between the two investments, but the payback period rule clearly favors investment A because of its shorter payback period (essentially because of its first-year cash inflow of $600,000).

Finally, because the payback period rule tends to favor short-term projects over long-term ones, it is often used when future events are difficult to quantify, such as for projects subject to political risk. Suppose a firm has a choice between two investments in a foreign country, one with a three-year payback period and one with a ten-year payback period. An election *may* take place in the foreign country in four years, and there is some chance that a new government may harden its policy toward foreign investments. It is very difficult (1) to estimate the probability of the occurrence of this type of event and (2) to quantify its implications on the magnitude of the project's expected cash flows and cost of capital. Even if the longer project has

EXHIBIT 8.6	COMPARISON OF TWO INVESTMENTS WITH THE SAME NPV AND DIFFERENT PAYBACK PERIODS.	
End of Year	Investment A	Investment G
Now	−$1,000,000	−$1,000,000
1	600,000	200,000
2	300,000	200,000
3	100,000	300,000
4	200,000	300,000
5	300,000	666,740
NPV at 10%	$ 191,399	$ 191,399
Payback period	3 years	4 years

a higher positive NPV than the shorter investment, the firm's managers may opt for the project with the three-year payback period. Many risk-averse managers believe that this type of trade-off is relevant.

THE DISCOUNTED PAYBACK PERIOD

A project's **discounted payback period**, also known as the **economic payback period**, is the number of periods—usually measured in years—required for the sum of the *present values* of the project's expected cash flows to equal its initial cash outlay. To illustrate, we calculate the discounted payback period of investment A. The cumulative sums of the present values of its expected cash flows, at a cost of capital of 10 percent, are shown in the last column of Exhibit 8.7, indicating a discounted payback period slightly less than four years (recall that investment A requires an initial cash outlay of $1 million). The discounted payback periods of the investment proposals presented in Exhibit 8.2 are shown in Exhibit 8.8, where we find that project A's discounted payback period is 3.96 years. Exhibit 8.9 shows how to calculate discounted payback periods using a spreadsheet, taking project E as an example.

The discounted payback periods are *longer* than the ordinary payback periods calculated earlier (compare the data in Exhibit 8.8 with the data in Exhibit 8.5). This is not surprising because the discounted payback periods are measured with discounted cash flows that are smaller than the undiscounted cash flows used to calculate the ordinary payback periods. Notice also that the *ranking* of the investments according to their discounted payback periods is different from the ranking according to their ordinary payback periods. Furthermore, note that investments A and B as well as C and D no longer have the same payback periods.

EXHIBIT 8.7	DISCOUNTED PAYBACK PERIOD CALCULATIONS FOR INVESTMENT A.

EXPECTED CASH FLOWS FROM EXHIBIT 8.2

End of Year	Expected Cash Flows	Discount Factor at 10%[1]	Present Value	Cumulative Present Value of Cash Flows
1	$600,000	0.9091	$545,455	$ 545,455
2	300,000	0.8264	247,934	793,389
3	100,000	0.7513	75,131	868,520
4	200,000	0.6830	136,603	1,005,123
5	300,000	0.6209	186,276	1,191,399

[1] The discount factors are four-digit approximations, but the present values are calculated on the basis of more exact approximations.

EXHIBIT 8.8	DISCOUNTED PAYBACK PERIODS FOR THE SIX INVESTMENTS IN EXHIBIT 8.2.

Investment	A	B	C	D	E	F
Discounted payback period (in years)	3.96	4.40	4.58	>5	3.86	3.86

EXHIBIT 8.9	**COMPUTING THE DISCOUNTED PAYBACK PERIOD FOR INVESTMENT E USING A SPREADSHEET.**					

EXPECTED CASH FLOWS FROM EXHIBIT 8.2

	A	B	C	D	E	F	G
		Now			End of Year		
1		0	1	2	3	4	5
2	Cash flows	−$1,000,000	$325,000	$325,000	$325,000	$ 325,000	$ 325,000
3	Cost of capital	10%					
4	Discounted cash flows		$295,455	$268,595	$244,177	$ 221,979	$ 201,799
5	Cumulative discounted cash flows		$295,455	$564,050	$808,227	$1,030,206	$1,232,005
6	Discounted payback period		–	–	–	3.86	–

- *0 is now; 1, 2, 3,... is end of year*
- *The formula in cell C4 is =C2/(1+$B$3)^C1. Then copy formula in cell C4 to next cells in row 4*
- *The formula in cell C5 is =C4. The formula in cell D5 is =C5+D4. Then copy formula in cell D5 to next cells in row 5*
- *The formula in cell C6 is = IF(OR(C5<=−$B$2,B5>−$B$2),"–",B1+(−$B$2−B5)/C4). Then copy formula in cell C6 to next cells in row 6*

THE DISCOUNTED PAYBACK PERIOD RULE

As for the ordinary payback period rule, the **discounted payback period rule** says that *a project is acceptable if its discounted payback period is shorter than or equal to a specified number of periods called the cutoff period*. If the choice is among several projects, the one with the shortest discounted payback period should be selected.

If the cutoff period is maintained at four years, only investments A, E, and F are acceptable. In the case of the ordinary payback period rule, all six investments could be undertaken.

DOES THE DISCOUNTED PAYBACK RULE ADJUST FOR THE TIMING OF CASH FLOWS?

Consider investments A and B in Exhibit 8.2. They are identical except that the first-year and third-year cash flows have been interchanged. The largest cash flow of $600,000 occurs at the end of the first year for investment A, and it occurs at the end of the third year for investment B. The discounted payback period takes this difference into account because the discounted payback period of A (3.96 years) is shorter than that of B (4.40 years). Thus, the discounted payback period rule takes the time value of money into account but *only* for the cash flows occurring up to the discounted payback period. Those following the payback period are still ignored.

DOES THE DISCOUNTED PAYBACK RULE ADJUST FOR RISK?

Consider investments C and D. They have an identical cash-flow stream, but investment C is less risky than D. The discounted payback period of C (4.58 years) is shorter than that of D (more than 5 years). Thus, the discounted payback period rule takes the risk of a project's expected cash flows into consideration but, as in the previous case, only for those cash flows occurring up to the discounted payback period. The cash flows after the discounted payback period, as well as their risk, are ignored.

DOES THE DISCOUNTED PAYBACK RULE MAXIMIZE THE FIRM'S EQUITY VALUE?

According to the discounted payback period rule, the present value of a project's expected cash flows up to their discounted payback period is equal to the project's initial cash outlay. In other words, if we calculate the project's NPV for the cash flows that occur up to the project's discounted payback period, we will find that it is equal to zero. *This means that a project's discounted payback period is equal to its "breakeven" period.* For example, investment A, which has a discounted payback period of 3.96 years, creates value only if it lasts *more* than 3.96 years. If we then include cash inflows expected to occur *after* the discounted payback period, the project's NPV will be positive. Thus, if a project's cutoff period is *longer* than its discounted payback period, the project's NPV, estimated with cash flows up to the cutoff period, is always positive.

We cannot, however, conclude that the discounted payback period will systematically select those projects that contribute the most to the wealth of the firm's owners. The "correct" cutoff period must be determined, and this is an arbitrary decision. Consider investments E and F. Their discounted payback period is the same and equal to 3.86 years. Like the ordinary payback period rule, the discounted payback period rule cannot discriminate between the two investments because it ignores the fifth year's cash flow, which is three times larger for F than it is for E. Thus, the discounted payback period rule ignores cash flows beyond the cutoff period and is biased against long-term investments.

THE DISCOUNTED PAYBACK PERIOD RULE VERSUS THE ORDINARY PAYBACK PERIOD RULE

The discounted payback period rule has two major advantages over the ordinary payback period rule: it considers the time value of money, and it considers the risk of the investment's expected cash flows. However, it considers these conditions of a good investment rule only for cash flows expected to occur up to the discounted payback period. The discounted payback period is certainly superior to the ordinary payback period as an indicator of the time necessary to recover the project's initial cash outlay because it takes into consideration the opportunity cost of capital. But it is more complicated to estimate than the ordinary payback period. Indeed, it requires the same inputs as the NPV rule, that is, the project's useful life, its expected cash-flow stream, and its cost of capital. This may explain why the discounted payback period rule is less frequently used than the ordinary payback period rule, particularly for managers making frequent accept/reject decisions.

THE INTERNAL RATE OF RETURN

A project's **internal rate of return (IRR)** is the discount rate that makes the NPV of the project equal to zero. For example, to compute the IRR of investment A, we set NPV(A) equal to zero and find the discount rate that satisfies this condition. That rate is the investment's IRR:

$$\text{NPV(A)} = 0 = -\$1{,}000{,}000 + \frac{\$6{,}00{,}000}{(1 + \text{IRR})^1} + \frac{\$300{,}000}{(1 + \text{IRR})^2} + \frac{\$100{,}000}{(1 + \text{IRR})^3}$$
$$+ \frac{\$200{,}000}{(1 + \text{IRR})^4} + \frac{\$300{,}000}{(1 + \text{IRR})^5}$$

Unfortunately, there is no simple way to compute the IRR of a cash-flow stream except for the trivial case in which the project is a one-period investment or an annuity.[2] For example, if a project requires an initial investment of $10,000 and will generate an expected cash flow of $12,000 in one year, then its IRR is simply equal to 20 percent. For investments with longer lives, we can try to find the IRR by trial and error: we first guess a rate, use it to calculate the project's NPV, and then adjust the rate until we find the one that makes the NPV equal to zero. As you can imagine, this is a tedious and time-consuming exercise, especially if we want a precise number. Fortunately, any financial calculator or computer spreadsheet application will have an IRR function. Both search for the IRR by the trial-and-error method but do so quickly and accurately. Exhibit 8.10 shows how to compute investment E's IRR using a spreadsheet, and Exhibit 8.11 presents the IRR for the investment proposals defined in Exhibit 8.2.

EXHIBIT 8.10	COMPUTING THE INTERNAL RATE OF RETURN OF INVESTMENT E USING A SPREADSHEET.

EXPECTED CASH FLOWS FROM EXHIBIT 8.2

	A	B	C	D	E	F	G
		Now			End of Year		
1		0	1	2	3	4	5
2	Cash flows	−$1,000,000	$325,000	$325,000	$325,000	$325,000	$325,000
3	Internal rate of return	18.72%					

- *0 is now; 1, 2, 3,... is end of year*
- *The formula in cell B3 is =IRR(B2:G2,.1) where .1 or 10 percent is a guess value for the IRR*

---

[2] An annuity is a cash-flow stream with equal annual cash flows. The calculation of the present value of an annuity is presented in Chapter 2.

EXHIBIT 8.11	IRR FOR THE SIX INVESTMENTS IN EXHIBIT 8.2.					
Investment	A	B	C	D	E	F
Internal rate of return	19.05%	13.92%	7.93%	7.93%	18.72%	28.52%

In general, if $CF_1, CF_2, \ldots, CF_t, \ldots, CF_T$, is the sequence of expected cash flows from an investment of T periods with an initial cash outlay of CF_0, then the investment's IRR is the solution to the following equation:

$$0 = CF_0 + \frac{CF_1}{(1 + IRR)^1} + \frac{CF_2}{(1 + IRR)^2} + \cdots + \frac{CF_t}{(1 + IRR)^t} + \cdots + \frac{CF_T}{(1 + IRR)^T}$$

All that is needed to calculate the IRR of an investment is the sequence of cash flows the investment is expected to generate. In effect, an investment's IRR summarizes its expected cash-flow stream with a single rate of return. The rate is called internal because it considers only the expected cash flows related to the investment and does not depend on rates that can be earned on alternative investments.

THE IRR RULE

Consider investment A. Its IRR is 19.05 percent, and its opportunity cost of capital is 10 percent. Recall that investment A's opportunity cost of capital is the highest return a firm can get on an alternative investment with the same risk as A.[3] Should the firm accept investment A? Yes, because the project's IRR (19.05 percent) is greater than the highest return the firm can get on another investment with the same risk (the 10 percent opportunity cost of capital).

According to the **internal rate of return rule**, *an investment should be accepted if its IRR is higher than its cost of capital and should be rejected if its IRR is lower.* If the investment's IRR is equal to the cost of capital, the firm should be indifferent about accepting or rejecting the project.

A project's IRR can be interpreted as a measure of the profitability of its expected cash flow *before* considering the project's cost of capital. Thus, if a project's IRR is *lower* than its cost of capital, the project does not earn its cost of capital and should be rejected. If it is *higher,* the project earns more than its cost of capital and should be accepted.[4]

When used in comparison with the IRR, the investment's opportunity cost of capital is usually referred to as the **hurdle rate**, the **minimum required rate of return**, or, simply, the investment's *required return*. In other words, if a project's IRR is lower than its required return, it should be rejected; if it is higher, it should be accepted.

---

[3] See Chapter 7 for a definition of an investment's opportunity cost of capital.

[4] The IRR should not be confused with the average accounting rate of return sometimes used to evaluate investment proposals. The latter is discussed in the last section of this chapter.

DOES THE IRR RULE ADJUST FOR THE TIMING OF CASH FLOWS?

Consider investments A and B in Exhibit 8.2. As pointed out earlier, investment A is preferable to investment B because its largest cash flow ($600,000) occurs earlier. The IRR rule indicates the same preference because the IRR of investment A (19.05 percent) is higher than the IRR of investment B (13.92 percent). Thus, the IRR rule takes into account the time value of money.

DOES THE IRR RULE ADJUST FOR RISK?

Compare investments C and D shown in Exhibit 8.2. They have the same expected cash-flow stream, but investment D, with a cost of capital of 10 percent, is riskier than investment C, whose cost of capital is only 5 percent. The two investments have the same IRR of 7.93 percent. Does the IRR rule take the risk of the two investments into consideration? Yes, it does, indirectly, through the comparison of the investment's IRR with its cost of capital. The IRR of investment C (7.93 percent) is greater than the minimum required return of 5 percent for this type of investment, so it should be accepted. Investment D should be rejected because its IRR of 7.93 percent is lower than the hurdle rate of 10 percent that the firm wants to earn on riskier investments similar to investment D.

The risk of an investment does not enter into the *computation* of its IRR, but the IRR *rule* does consider the risk of the investment because it compares the project's IRR with the minimum required rate of return, which is a measure of the risk of the investment.

DOES THE IRR RULE MAXIMIZE THE FIRM'S EQUITY VALUE?

A project's IRR is determined by setting its NPV equal to zero, so we would expect a project's NPV to be related to its IRR. To illustrate, we compute the NPV of investment E for various discount rates, as shown in Exhibit 8.12.

From the figures in Exhibit 8.12, we can draw a graph that shows the changes in NPV(E) as the discount rate varies. The graph, known as the project's **net present value (NPV) profile**, is shown in Exhibit 8.13. NPV(E) is on the vertical axis and the discount rate is on the horizontal axis.

The graph shows an inverse relationship between NPV(E) and the discount rate. As the discount rate increases, NPV(E) decreases because its expected cash flows are discounted at increasingly higher rates. The NPV curve intersects the horizontal axis at the point at which NPV(E) is equal to zero. At this point, the discount rate used to calculate the NPV of investment E must be equal to the IRR of investment E because the IRR is the discount rate at which the NPV is equal to zero. This discount rate is 18.72 percent (see Exhibit 8.13).

According to the IRR rule, investment E should be accepted if its cost of capital is lower than its IRR of 18.72 percent and should be rejected if its cost of capital is

EXHIBIT 8.12	NET PRESENT VALUE OF INVESTMENT E FOR VARIOUS DISCOUNT RATES.						
Discount Rate	0%	5%	10%	15%	20%	25%	30%
NPV(E)	$625,000	$407,080	$232,006	$89,450	−$28,050	−$125,984	−$208,440

EXHIBIT 8.13	THE NPV PROFILE OF INVESTMENT E.

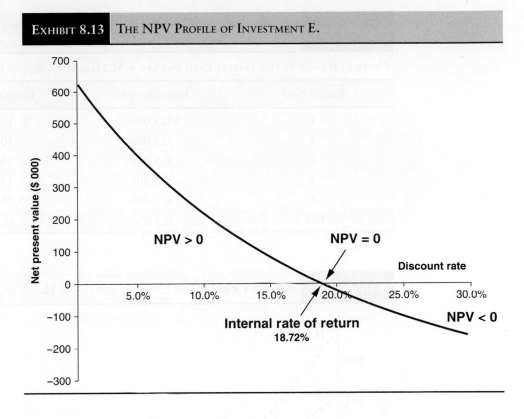

higher. The graph indicates that for discount rates (or costs of capital) lower than 18.72 percent, the project's NPV is positive, and for discount rates higher than 18.72 percent, the project's NPV is negative. In other words, the graph indicates that when the NPV is positive, the IRR is higher than the cost of capital, and when it is negative, the IRR is lower than the cost of capital. The two rules are thus equivalent. And because the NPV rule is consistent with the maximization of the firm's equity value, so is the IRR rule.

THE IRR RULE MAY BE UNRELIABLE

The IRR rule may sometimes provide the *incorrect* investment decision when (1) the firm is reviewing two mutually exclusive investments (the firm cannot invest in both; if it accepts one, it must reject the other), and/or (2) the project's cash flow stream changes signs more than once (the sequence of *future* cash flows contains at least one negative cash flow after a positive one).

THE CASE OF MUTUALLY EXCLUSIVE INVESTMENTS

When two projects are **mutually exclusive**, the IRR rule and the NPV rule may, under certain circumstances, select different investment proposals. Suppose we compare investment E in Exhibit 8.2 with investment H in Exhibit 8.14. They have the same useful life (five years), the same initial cash outlay ($1 million), and the same cost of capital (10 percent). Investment E has an IRR of 18.72 percent, and investment H has an IRR of 16.59 percent.

EXHIBIT 8.14	COMPARISON OF TWO MUTUALLY EXCLUSIVE INVESTMENTS WITH DIFFERENT CASH FLOWS AND IRR.	

USEFUL LIFE = 5 YEARS; INITIAL CASH OUTLAY = $1 MILLION; COST OF CAPITAL = 10%

End of Year	Investment E	Investment H
1	$325,000	$ 100,000
2	325,000	100,000
3	325,000	100,000
4	325,000	150,000
5	325,000	1,500,000
IRR	18.72%	16.59%

EXHIBIT 8.15	THE NPV PROFILES OF INVESTMENTS E AND H.

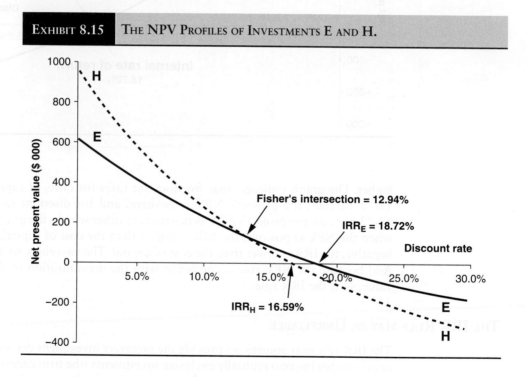

Both investments have an IRR that exceeds the cost of capital of 10 percent, so they should both be accepted according to the IRR rule. However, the investments are mutually exclusive, so the firm can accept only one. Which should it select? Intuition suggests the selection of investment E because it has a higher IRR than investment H. Unfortunately, intuition does not always lead to the correct decision. According to the NPV rule, investment H is preferable to investment E: at a cost of capital of 10 percent, the NPV of investment H is $282,519, whereas that of investment E is only $232,006 (see Exhibit 8.2).

The NPV profiles of investments E and H in Exhibit 8.15 show why the IRR and NPV rules disagree. The graph indicates that both the NPV and IRR rules favor investment E when the discount rate is higher than 12.94 percent (the rate at which the two NPV curves intersect)[5] and lower than 18.72 percent. For rates above 18.72 percent, the two projects should be rejected; both have a negative NPV and a discount rate higher than the IRR. For rates lower than 12.94 percent, the NPV rule favors investment H, but the IRR rule still favors investment E (it has a higher IRR than H).

This situation usually arises when the cash-flow patterns of two mutually exclusive investments differ widely, as in the case of investments E and H. Investment E's cash flows are evenly distributed during the project's life, whereas those of H are much higher in the last year of the project's life. At high discount rates, the discounting effect (the "shrinking" of cash flows resulting from discounting) on distant cash flows is more pronounced than when the rate is low. As a consequence, when the discount rate increases, the NPV of the investment with much higher cash flows at the end of the project's life (such as investment H) decreases more rapidly than the NPV of the investment whose cash flows are more evenly distributed (such as investment E). The two projects have the same NPV at the point at which their NPV curves intersect. After that point, the NPV ranking of the two projects changes.

With a cost of capital of 10 percent, project H is the better investment because its NPV is larger than that of project E, thus creating more value to the firm's owners. Because the IRR approach would lead to the opposite choice, it would also have the opposite effect. In general, when a firm wants to rank projects according to their contribution to the value of the firm's equity, it should use the NPV rule rather than the IRR rule.

THE CASE OF INVESTMENTS WITH SOME NEGATIVE FUTURE CASH FLOWS

The IRR rule may be unreliable when a project's stream of expected cash flows includes negative cash flows. Negative cash flows can occur when an investment requires the construction of several facilities that are built at different times in the future. During the year when a new unit is built, the cash flow generated by the previously installed unit might not be large enough to cover the cost of the new one. The result is that the project's total cash flow for that year becomes negative. A project can also have a negative future cash flow if the project's termination requires a major capital expenditure, such as for a strip-mining project. Closing the mine and restoring the area's landscape at the end of the project's useful life may make the project's terminal cash flow negative.

When negative cash flows occur, a project may have more than one IRR or none at all. We illustrate this phenomenon with a two-year project that has a cost of capital of 20 percent and the pattern of expected cash flows shown in Exhibit 8.16.

The project has an IRR of 5 percent and an IRR of 40 percent. (If you check this, you will find that the project's NPV is zero at both 5 percent and 40 percent.) If the project has a cost of capital of 20 percent, it should be rejected if its IRR is 5 percent and accepted if its IRR is 40 percent. The choice is not obvious. What should the firm's managers do in this case? They should ignore the IRR rule and use the NPV rule instead. At a cost of capital of 20 percent, the project has a positive NPV of $20,833 and should be undertaken.

---

[5] The intersection rate is often referred to as **Fisher's intersection**, named after the economist Irving Fisher, who was among the first to study this phenomenon.

EXHIBIT 8.16	EXPECTED CASH FLOWS, IRR, AND NPV OF A PROJECT WITH NEGATIVE CASH FLOWS AND A COST OF CAPITAL OF 20%.

End of Year	Cash Flow
Now	−$1,000,000
1	+2,450,000
2	−1,470,000
IRR	5% and 40%
NPV at 20%	$20,833

WHY DO MANAGERS USUALLY PREFER THE IRR RULE TO THE NPV RULE?

Despite its shortcomings, the IRR rule is popular among managers. One reason may be that the calculation of a project's IRR requires a single input, the cash-flow stream that the project is expected to generate. An estimate of the project's cost of capital is not necessary, whereas the calculation of a project's NPV requires estimates of both the expected cash-flow stream and the cost of capital. However, the application of the IRR rule requires both inputs. To decide whether to invest, managers must compare the project's IRR to its cost of capital. Thus, even though the IRR can be computed without knowing the project's cost of capital, the cost of capital is still needed to decide whether to undertake the project. If both methods require the same inputs to select projects, what is the advantage of using the IRR rule?

The advantage may be that it is easier to estimate a project's IRR than its NPV when the project's cost of capital is uncertain (the *computation* of the IRR does not require knowing the cost of capital). Then, the decision whether to accept or reject the project is made after an appropriate required return is determined.[6] Our suspicion is that managers favor the IRR rule for a simpler reason: it is easier for them to communicate a project's potential profitability using its IRR than its NPV. When "selling" an investment proposal, you will certainly be more convincing if you indicate that the proposal has a potential return of 35 percent than if you say it has an NPV of $4,531,284. Managers usually have a good understanding of what an investment should "return" (partly because they are accustomed to measuring business performance with indicators such as return on sales and return on assets). A comparison of that implicit "return" with the project's IRR is straightforward. A comparison with the project's NPV is not so obvious.

Our advice: a project's NPV can be estimated with the same information required to apply the IRR rule, so you should compute both. When both rules lead to the same recommendation, mention the project's IRR instead of its NPV. When the outcome of your analysis indicates a conflict between the two methods, you should trust the NPV rule.

---

[6] This would usually happen if the firm adopted a "bottom-up" approach to capital budgeting for some of its difficult-to-assess projects. In this approach, divisions submit projects with their IRR to a committee. The decision to invest is made by comparing the IRR of the projects with the relevant risk-adjusted required returns established by the investment committee.

THE PROFITABILITY INDEX

A project's **profitability index (PI)** is equal to the ratio of the present value of its expected cash-flow stream to its initial cash outlay (CF_0):

$$PI(project) = \frac{(CF_1 \times DF_1) + \ldots + (CF_t \times DF_t) + \ldots + (CF_T \times DF_T)}{CF_0}$$

where DF_t is the discount factor calculated with the project's cost of capital k. The PI is a benefit-to-cost ratio because it is the ratio of the benefit derived from the investment (the present value of its expected cash flows at the cost of capital) to its cost (the initial cash outlay).

Applying the definition to investment A in Exhibit 8.2 (all financial figures in thousands of dollars), we get the following:

$$PI(A) = \frac{(\$600 \times 0.9091) + (\$300 \times 0.8264) + (\$100 \times 0.7513) + (\$200 \times 0.6830) + (\$300 \times 0.6209)}{\$1,000}$$

$$PI(A) = \frac{\$1,191}{\$1,000} = 1.19$$

Exhibit 8.17 shows how to compute PIs using a spreadsheet, taking investment E as an example. Exhibit 8.18 presents the PIs of the investment proposals in Exhibit 8.2.

THE PROFITABILITY INDEX RULE

According to the **profitability index rule**, *a project should be accepted if its PI is greater than one and rejected if it is less than one.* If the investment's PI is equal to one, the firm should be indifferent about whether to accept or reject the project. According to this rule, all projects except project D should be accepted (see Exhibit 8.18).

EXHIBIT 8.17	COMPUTING THE PROFITABILITY INDEX OF INVESTMENT E USING A SPREADSHEET.

EXPECTED CASH FLOWS FROM EXHIBIT 8.2

	A	B	C	D	E	F	G
		Now			End of Year		
1		0	1	2	3	4	5
2	Cash flows	−$1,000,000	$325,000	$325,000	$325,000	$325,000	$325,000
3	Cost of capital	10%					
4	Profitability index	1.23					

- *0 is now; 1, 2, 3,… is end of year*
- *The formula in cell B4 is =NPV(B3,C2:G2)/−B2*

EXHIBIT 8.18	PROFITABILITY INDEXES FOR THE SIX INVESTMENTS IN EXHIBIT 8.2.					
Investment	A	B	C	D	E	F
Profitability index	1.19	1.11	1.08	0.95	1.23	1.64

DOES THE PROFITABILITY INDEX RULE ADJUST FOR THE TIMING OF CASH FLOWS?

The PI rule takes into account the time value of money because the projects' expected cash flows are discounted at their cost of capital. Like the NPV and IRR rules, the PI rule favors project A over project B (see Exhibit 8.18), and the only difference between these two projects is the timing of their respective expected cash flows.

DOES THE PROFITABILITY INDEX RULE ADJUST FOR RISK?

The PI rule considers the risk of an investment because it uses the cost of capital (which reflects the risk of the expected cash-flow stream) as the discount rate. Again, like the NPV and IRR rules, the PI rule chooses investment C over riskier investment D, even though the two investments have the same expected cash-flow stream.

DOES THE PROFITABILITY INDEX RULE MAXIMIZE THE FIRM'S EQUITY VALUE?

When a project has a PI greater than one, the present value of its expected cash flows is greater than the initial cash outlay, and the project's NPV is positive. Conversely, if the PI is less than one, the project's NPV is negative. It may seem to follow that the PI rule is a substitute for the NPV rule and will select projects that contribute the most to enhancing the firm's market value.

Unfortunately, the PI rule may lead to an incorrect decision when it is applied to two mutually exclusive investments with different initial cash outlays. To illustrate, we compare investment A in Exhibit 8.2 with investment K, which has the same useful life (five years) and the same cost of capital (10 percent), but investment K requires an initial cash outlay twice as large as that of investment A and has a different cash-flow stream. The cash-flow streams, the NPVs, and the PIs for the two investments are shown in Exhibit 8.19.

Investment A's PI (1.19) is higher than that of investment K (1.12). Before concluding that investment A is superior to K, we should first compare the NPV of the investments. Investment A has a lower NPV than investment K, so the PI has chosen the investment that creates the least value to the firm's owners. Conclusion: the PI rule is not consistent with the maximization of the firm's market value when used to make a choice between mutually exclusive projects with different initial cash outlays.

USE OF THE PROFITABILITY INDEX RULE

Despite the problem that occurs when the choice is between mutually exclusive projects of unequal sizes, the PI is a useful substitute for the NPV rule. Like the IRR, it is easier to communicate the potential profitability of an investment proposal with the PI than with the NPV. The reason is that both the PI and the IRR are *relative* measures of an investment's value, whereas the NPV is an *absolute* measure.

EXHIBIT 8.19	COMPARISON OF TWO MUTUALLY EXCLUSIVE INVESTMENTS WITH DIFFERENT INITIAL CASH OUTLAYS AND EXPECTED CASH FLOWS.

End of Year	Investment A	Investment K
Now	−$1,000,000	−$2,000,000
1	600,000	100,000
2	300,000	300,000
3	100,000	600,000
4	200,000	200,000
5	300,000	2,100,000
NPV at 10%	$ 191,399	$ 230,169
Profitability index	1.19	1.12

The index shows how much present benefit a project is expected to generate *per dollar* of investment, whereas the NPV provides the present value of the benefits net of the project's initial cost.[7]

THE AVERAGE ACCOUNTING RETURN

Although many measures of **average accounting returns (AAR)** are applied to investment proposals, they are always defined as the ratio of some measure of average accounting profit expected from the proposal to some average amount of assets that the investment is expected to use over its useful life. The most general measure of average accounting return is defined as follows:

$$AAR = \frac{\text{Average earnings after tax expected from the project}}{\text{Average book value of the project}}$$

As an example, let's assume that project P requires an initial cash outlay of $1 million for the purchase of a piece of equipment that is expected to last five years. The investment will be depreciated at a rate of $200,000 a year over its useful life. The project is expected to generate annual earnings after tax of $100,000, $80,000, $60,000, $40,000, and $20,000 in Years 1, 2, 3, 4, and 5, respectively. Thus, the average expected earnings after tax is as follows:

$$\frac{\$100,000 + \$80,000 + \$60,000 + \$40,000 + \$20,000}{5} = \$60,000$$

The initial book value of the investment is $1,000,000 and is zero at the end of its useful life. Thus, the average book value of the investment is $500,000 and the average accounting return of the project is as follows:

$$AAR = \frac{\$60,000}{\$500,000} = 12 \text{ percent}$$

---

[7] Chapter 7 shows how the PI rule can be used to compare investments of unequal sizes (investments with different cash outlays).

THE AVERAGE ACCOUNTING RETURN RULE

According to the **average accounting return rule**, *a project is acceptable if its average accounting return is higher than a target average return.*

DOES THE AAR RULE ADJUST FOR THE TIMING OF CASH FLOWS?

The rule relies on accounting numbers such as earnings after tax and book value of investments, which are not cash flows. Like the payback period rule, it does not account for the time value of money. But, unlike the payback period, which can be improved to account for the timing of cash flows by discounting them at the cost of capital, the average accounting return rule does not adjust for the timing of earnings.

DOES THE AAR RULE ADJUST FOR RISK?

In the discounted cash flow rules, such as the NPV or IRR rules, the risk of the project is accounted for in the cost of capital. By extension, we would expect that risk in the average accounting return rule is taken care of in the target return. This may be the case, but there is no objective way to adjust the target return to the project's risk.

DOES THE AAR RULE MAXIMIZE THE FIRM'S EQUITY VALUE?

It is unlikely that the AAR rule would always select investment proposals that maximize shareholder value because it is based on accounting data (as opposed to cash flows), ignores the time value of money, and treats risk on an ad hoc basis.

Given the rather serious shortcomings of the AAR, why do 20 percent of the US chief financial officers in the survey presented in Exhibit 8.1 use this rule? We suggest two reasons. First, the rule is easy to apply because it uses accounting numbers that are usually readily available. Second, because most measures of performance used in compensation and reward systems are still based on accounting figures, it makes sense that managers may want to check the accounting return of their investment proposals.

KEY POINTS

1. Our analysis of the alternatives to the net present value (NPV) rule has shown that the NPV rule is the best criterion for selecting desirable investment proposals (projects that are expected to raise the market value of a firm's equity and, thereby, increase the wealth of the firm's owners). This conclusion does not imply that the alternative capital budgeting techniques presented in this chapter should be discarded. A project's profitability index, internal rate of return, payback period, and average accounting return may provide useful information to managers and are often easier to interpret and communicate than the NPV.

2. As Exhibit 8.1 shows, companies rarely rely on a single method to screen investment proposals. Most firms using the NPV rule also use alternative decision criteria. But this observation should not detract from the fact that *all* the alternatives to the NPV method have some shortcomings and that some have serious weaknesses in assessing the value-creating capacity of a project.

3. Exhibit 8.20 summarizes the properties of the five alternative investment evaluation methods. Our final recommendation: when alternative methods provide conflicting signals, the value-creating manager should trust the NPV approach.

EXHIBIT 8.20	PROPERTIES OF ALTERNATIVE CAPITAL BUDGETING RULES.

Evaluation method	Inputs required		Decision rule		Does the rule adjust cash flows for		Is the rule consistent with the maximization of the firm's equity value?
	for calculator	for decision	Accept	Reject	Time?	Risk?	
Net present value (NPV)	• Cash flows • Cost of capital (k)	• NPV	NPV > 0	NPV < 0	Yes	Yes	Yes, a project's NPV is a measure of the value the project creates or destroys.
Internal rate of return (IRR)	• Cash flows	• IRR • Cost of capital (k)	IRR > k	IRR < k	Yes	Yes	Yes, but *may* fail when: • projects are mutually exclusive • cash flows change signs more than once
Payback period (PP)	• Cash flows	• PP • Cutoff period	PP < Cutoff period	PP > Cutoff period	No	No	No
Discounted payback period (DPP)	• Cash flows • Cost of capital (k)	• DPP • Cutoff period	DPP < Cutoff period	DPP > Cutoff period	Only within DPP	Only within DPP	Only when the project's discounted payback period is *shorter* than its cutoff period.
Profitability index (PI)	• Cash flows • Cost of capital (k)	• PI	PI > 1	PI < 1	Yes	Yes	Yes, but *may* fail to select the project with the highest NPV when projects are mutually exclusive.

FURTHER READING

Baker, Ken, and Philip English. *Capital Budgeting Valuation: Financial Analysis for Today's Investment Projects*. John Wiley & Sons, 2011.

SELF-TEST QUESTIONS

8.1   Shortcomings of the payback period.
What are the shortcomings of the payback period rule, and why, despite these shortcomings, do many firms still use the payback period as an important input in the investment decision?

8.2   Internal rate of return versus cost of capital.
What is the difference between a project's cost of capital and its internal rate of return?

8.3   Internal rate of return versus return on invested capital.
What is the difference between the internal rate of return and the return on invested capital?

8.4   Shortcomings of the internal rate of return and the profitability index rules.
Under which circumstances may the internal rate of return rule and the profitability index rule lead to the wrong investment decision?

8.5   Evaluating two projects using alternative decision rules.
Two projects have the expected cash flows shown below. The projects have similar risk characteristics, and their cost of capital is 10 percent.

	Project A	Project B
Now	−$2,000,000	−$2,000,000
End of year 1	200,000	1,400,000
End of year 2	1,200,000	1,000,000
End of year 3	1,700,000	400,000

a. Calculate the net present value (NPV) of each project. According to the NPV rule, which project should be accepted if they are independent? What if they are mutually exclusive?
b. Calculate the payback period and the discounted payback period of each project. If the two projects are mutually exclusive, which project should be accepted?
c. Calculate the internal rate of return of each project. Which project should be accepted if they are independent? If they are mutually exclusive?

d. Calculate the profitability index of each project. Which project should be accepted if they are independent? If they are mutually exclusive?

e. Based on your answers to questions a–d, which criterion leads to the best investment decision if the projects are independent? What if they are mutually exclusive?

REVIEW QUESTIONS

1. **Investment criteria.**
   The Global Chemical Company (GCC) uses the following criteria to make capital investment decisions:

   1. Effect on earnings per share (*must be positive*)
   2. Payback period (*must be less than six years*)
   3. Internal rate of return (*must be at least 12 percent*)
   4. Net present value (*must be positive at a 12 percent discount rate*)

   a. What are the advantages and disadvantages of each of these measures?
   b. Why do you think GCC uses all of these measures rather than just one of them?

2. **Relationship between investment criteria.**
   A project with a cash outlay now is followed by positive expected cash flows in the future and a positive net present value. What does this information tell you about the project's discounted payback period, internal rate of return, profitability index, and average accounting return?

3. **Net present value and payback period.**
   A project with a cash outlay now is followed by positive expected cash flows in the future and a payback period less than its economic life. Is its net present value positive or negative? Explain.

   Now suppose that the discounted payback period is less than the useful life of the project. Is its net present value positive or negative? Explain.

4. **The internal rate of return of mutually exclusive projects.**
   The following chart plots the net present value (NPV) of projects A and B at different discount rates. The projects have similar risk and are mutually exclusive.

   a. What is the significance of the point on the graph where the two lines intersect?
   b. What is the significance of the points on the graph where the two lines cross the zero NPV axis?
   c. What is the likely explanation for the differences in net present value at the various discount rates?
   d. Which project would you recommend? Why?

NPV versus IRR

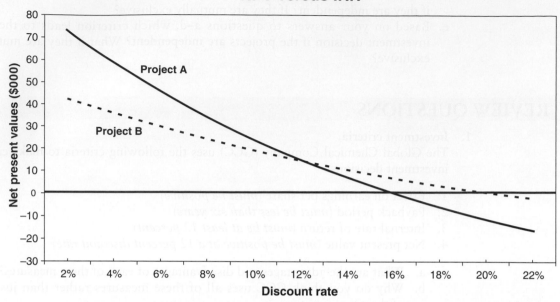

5. **The case of multiple internal rates of return.**
   The International Industrial Company has an investment project with the following cash flows:

	Cash Flow	Type of Cash Flow
Now	−$200	Purchase of equipment
End of year 1	600	Cash earnings from project
End of year 2	−400	Cash earnings from project less cleanup costs

   a. What is the net present value of these cash flows at 0, 25, 50, and 100 percent discount rates?
   b. What is the internal rate of return of this project?
   c. Under what conditions should the project be accepted?

6. **The net present value rule versus the internal rate of return rule.**
   You must choose between the two projects whose cash flows are shown below. The projects have the same risk.

	Project A	Project B
Now	−$12,000	−$2,400
End of year 1	7,900	2,500
End of year 2	6,850	950

   a. Compute the internal rate of return and the net present value for the two projects. Assume a 10 percent discount rate.
   b. Which of the projects is better according to each of the two methods?

   c. What is the explanation for the differences in rankings between the net present value and the internal rate of return?

   d. Which method is correct? Why?

   e. Compute the internal rate of return (IRR) for the incremental cash flows (project A minus project B). For discount rates below this IRR, which project is best? For discount rates above this IRR, which project is best? Is this consistent with your answer to question d?

7. **The internal rate of return rule and the net present value rule.**

Consider the three projects A, B, and C. The cost of capital is 12 percent, and the projects have the following expected cash flows:

	Project A	Project B	Project C
Now	−$150,000	−$300,000	−$150,000
End of year 1	120,000	200,000	110,000
End of year 2	80,000	180,000	90,000

   a. What is the internal rate of return of the three projects?

   b. What is the net present value of the three projects?

   c. If the three projects are independent, which projects should be accepted?

   d. If the three projects are mutually exclusive, which project should be selected?

   e. If the total budget for the three projects is limited to $450,000, which projects should be selected?

8. **The net present value rule versus the profitability index rule.**

You must choose between the two projects whose cash flows are shown below. The projects have the same risk.

	Project A	Project B
Now	−$16,000	−$3,200
End of year 1	10,500	3,300
End of year 2	9,100	1,260
End of year 3	3,000	600

   a. Compute the net present value (NPV) and the profitability index (PI) for the two projects. Assume a 10 percent discount rate.

   b. Which of the projects is better according to each of the two methods?

   c. What is the explanation for the differences in rankings between the NPV and PI methods of analysis?

   d. Which method is correct? Why?

9. **The average accounting return.**

The Alpha Printer Company is considering the purchase of a $2 million printing machine. Its economic life is estimated at five years, and it will have no resale value after that time. The machine would generate an additional $200,000 of earnings after tax for the company during the first year of operation and this will grow at a rate of 10 percent per year thereafter. The company applies straight-line depreciation to its property, plant, and equipment assets. What is the average accounting return of the investment? Should the machine be bought if the firm's target average accounting return on its investment is 20 percent? Would you feel comfortable with your decision based on this approach to capital budgeting? Why or why not?

10. **Investment criteria.**

The Great Eastern Toys Company is evaluating a new product. The cash flows that are expected from this product over its five years' expected life are shown below. Note that the final year's cash flow includes $2,000 of working capital to be recovered at the end of the project.

	Cash Flow
Now	−$18,000
End of year 1 to 4	5,200
End of year 5	7,200

a. Compute the following measures:

1. Payback period
2. Discounted payback period at a 10 percent discount rate
3. Net present value at a 10 percent discount rate
4. Internal rate of return
5. Profitability index

b. Should the project be undertaken?

IDENTIFYING AND ESTIMATING A PROJECT'S CASH FLOWS

CHAPTER 9

Chapters 7 and 8 explain rules that help managers make capital expenditure decisions. All these rules require the estimation of the cash-flow stream the investment is expected to generate in the future. This chapter shows how to identify and estimate the cash flows that are relevant to an investment decision.

Two fundamental principles provide some guidance in the determination of a project's cash flows: the *actual cash-flow principle* and the *with/without principle*. According to the first, cash flows must be measured *at the time they actually occur*, that is, during the period cash is actually received or paid out. According to the second, the cash flows relevant to an investment decision are only those that change the firm's *overall* cash position if the investment is undertaken.

First, we present and explain these principles, and then show how to apply them to the Sunlight Manufacturing Company's designer desk lamp project, whose net present value (NPV) was first computed in Chapter 7. After reading this chapter, you should understand the following:

- The actual cash-flow principle and the with/without principle, and how to apply them to make capital expenditure decisions
- How to identify a project's relevant cash flows
- Sunk costs and opportunity costs
- How to estimate a project's relevant cash flows

THE ACTUAL CASH-FLOW PRINCIPLE

According to the **actual cash-flow principle**, an investment's cash flows must be measured at the time they actually occur. For example, suppose a proposal is expected to generate a tax expense next year that will be paid the following year. The cash outflow must be taken into account the year the tax is paid, not the year the tax expense is recorded in the firm's income statement.

Investment proposals are often supported with data obtained from projected income statements that show the expected impact of the project on the firm's accounting earnings. But like tax expense, revenues and expenses reported in the income statement are generally not cash-flow figures. Thus, it is incorrect to use the investment's contribution to the firm's accounting earnings as a proxy for cash flows. This chapter shows how to convert accounting flows into cash flows for the purpose of making investment decisions.

Another implication of the actual cash-flow principle is that the dollar value of a project's future cash flows must be calculated with the prices and costs that are expected to prevail in the future, not with today's prices and costs. In other words, if the prices and costs associated with a project are expected to rise because of inflation, **nominal cash flows**, the cash flows that incorporate anticipated inflation, should be estimated. Furthermore, if the decision to invest is made on the basis of the project's NPV or its internal rate of return (IRR), then the cost of capital used to calculate the project's NPV or to compare with the project's IRR must also incorporate the anticipated rate of inflation.

If the effect of future inflation rates on the project's cash flows is too difficult to estimate, such as in countries subject to hyperinflation or a volatile inflation rate, a project's expected **real cash flows** can be estimated instead of its expected nominal cash flows. Real cash flows are the values of cash flows calculated with the assumption that prices and costs will not be affected by anticipated inflation. In this case, however, the project's cost of capital also must be estimated without the effect of anticipated inflation. Inflation must be treated consistently. If it is excluded from the cash flows, it also must be excluded from the cost of capital. If it is taken into account, it should be incorporated in both the project's expected cash flows and its cost of capital.

Finally, a project's expected cash flows must be measured in the same currency. When an investment decision involves prices or costs that are denominated in a foreign currency, these variables must be converted to their equivalent domestic values at the exchange rates that are expected to prevail in the future. This requirement necessitates forecasting future exchange rates, an issue we address in Chapter 17.

THE WITH/WITHOUT PRINCIPLE

The second guiding principle in estimating an investment's cash flows is the **with/without principle**. According to this principle, the **relevant cash flows** associated with an investment decision are only those cash flows that will *change* the firm's overall future cash position as a result of the decision to invest. In other words, relevant cash flows are **incremental**, or **differential, cash flows**.[1] They are equal to the difference between the firm's expected cash flows if the investment is made (the firm "with" the project) and its expected cash flows if the investment is rejected (the firm "without" the project). If CF_t denotes the cash flows occurring during period t,

$$\text{Project's } CF_t = \text{Firm's incremental } CF_t$$
$$= \text{Firm's } CF_t \text{ (with project)} - \text{Firm's } CF_t \text{ (without project)}$$

To illustrate, consider trying to decide whether to drive to work or take public transportation. Suppose you are currently driving to work (this is your situation *without* the project). Last month, you took the train and found it less tiring than driving. The monthly train tickets cost $140. You want to know whether commuting by train on

---

[1] A similar notion, used in economic analysis, is the concept of marginal cost. The difference between a marginal cost and an incremental cost is that the former usually refers to the additional cost of, say, producing one more unit of a product, whereas the latter refers to the total extra cost resulting from the acceptance of a project.

a regular basis (your situation *with* the project) is cheaper than driving. These are the monthly cash expenses related to your car:

1. Insurance $120
2. Rent on the garage near your apartment $150
3. Parking fees near your office $ 90
4. Gas and car service related to commuting $110

If you take the train, your *total* monthly cash expenses will include the cost of the train tickets, and the insurance and garage rental costs, which you will still have to pay (we assume you will not sell your car):

$$\text{CF(with the project)} = \text{CF(train)} = -\text{Insurance cost} - \text{Garage rental cost}$$
$$-\text{Train tickets cost}$$
$$= -\$120 - \$150 - \$140 = -\$410$$

If you drive your car, your *total* monthly cash expenses will include the office parking fees, gas and car service costs, and insurance and garage rental costs. Therefore,

$$\text{CF(without the project)} = \text{CF(car)} = -\text{Insurance cost} - \text{Garage rental cost}$$
$$-\text{Office parking fees} - \text{Gas and service cost}$$
$$= -\$120 - \$150 - \$90 - \$110 = -\$470$$

If you take the train, your total monthly cash outflow is $410. If you take the car, it is $470. The project's incremental monthly cash flow is thus $60:

$$\text{Project's CF} = \text{Incremental CF} = \text{CF(train)} - \text{CF(car)}$$
$$= [-\$410] - [-\$470] = \$60$$

The $60 incremental cash flow can be determined directly if you identify which of the four expenses are relevant to commuting by train and which are irrelevant. The **relevant costs** are those cash expenses that will increase your monthly *total* or *overall* expenses; the **irrelevant costs** are those cash expenses that will not affect them. The first two costs (insurance and garage rental) are irrelevant to your decision because they will be incurred regardless of whether or not you take the train. In other words, they are **unavoidable costs**. The third and fourth costs (office parking fees and gas and car service) are relevant costs because they can be saved if you decide to take the train. They are **avoidable costs**. They amount to $200 per month ($90 plus $110). Because the monthly train ticket costs $140, the train is the cheaper commuting alternative. Every month, you would save $60, the difference between $200 and $140, which is exactly the project's monthly incremental cash flow that we found previously. The difference from the previous approach is that we ignored the common expenses of insurance ($120) and garage rental ($150) because they are irrelevant to the decision.

The $140 you paid *last month* to take the train on a trial basis is irrelevant to your decision. That money has already been spent and will not be recovered whether or not you decide to go to work by car or by train in the future. These types of costs are called **sunk costs**.

Now, let's add a small complication to the choice between the car and the train. Suppose you drive a colleague to work twice a week with the understanding that he will fill your gas tank once a month at a cost of $35. Is this a relevant cost to your commuting decision? Yes, it is, because if you take the train, you will no longer receive the $35. In this situation, the advantage of taking the train instead of the car will drop to $25 a month ($60 less $35). The cost we have just described is called an **opportunity cost**. It is relevant because it represents a loss of income if the train alternative is adopted. Sunk costs and opportunity costs are discussed in more detail later in the chapter in the context of Sunlight Manufacturing Company's designer desk lamp project.

The assumption so far is that your car will stay in the garage. But what if your daughter decides to drive to college twice a week now that the car is available? If the monthly cost of these trips (gas and parking) exceeds $25, then commuting to work by train will be more expensive than driving your car. This example illustrates an important point. When estimating a project's incremental cash flows, *all* the side effects must be identified. This can be a challenging task for many investments. But you cannot estimate a project's expected cash flows properly if you have not considered *all* the relevant costs and benefits.

A final comment: the relevant benefits and costs associated with a project cannot all be quantified easily. For example, our analysis indicates that commuting by car is more expensive than taking the train. But you may find that driving is more convenient and less time-consuming. Although putting a dollar value on these benefits may not be simple, you must do so because they may justify taking the car.

We now turn to the analysis of a complex case – the designer desk lamp project whose NPV is computed in Chapter 7.

THE DESIGNER DESK LAMP PROJECT

Recall that Sunlight Manufacturing Company (SMC) has been successfully producing and selling electrical appliances for the past 20 years and is considering a possible extension of its existing product line. The company's general manager has recently proposed that SMC enter the relatively high-margin, high-quality designer desk lamp market. This section describes the project's characteristics, which are summarized in Exhibit 9.1.

A consulting company was hired to do a preliminary study of the potential market for this type of product. Its report indicates that SMC can sell as many as 45,000 lamps the first year of the project, 40,000 the second year, 30,000 the third year, 20,000 the fourth year, and 10,000 the fifth year, after which the project will be terminated. The lamps can be sold for $40 each the first year, and that price can be raised annually by no more than 3 percent, a rate of increase equal to the rate of inflation expected to prevail during the project's five-year life. The consulting company billed SMC $30,000 for the study and was paid a month later.

SMC's sales manager is concerned that the new product will reduce the sales of SMC's standard desk lamps. She fears that potential customers will switch from buying standard desk lamps to buying the new designer desk lamps and estimates that SMC's potential losses could reduce the firm's after-tax operating cash flows by as much as $110,000 per year.

If SMC decides to produce the designer desk lamp, it will use a building it already owns that is unoccupied. Recently, SMC received a letter from the vice president of a nearby department store who wanted to know whether SMC would be willing to rent the building to them as a storage area. SMC's accounting department indicates that, given current market rates, the building can be rented out for $10,000 a year for five years.

EXHIBIT 9.1	DATA SUMMARY OF THE DESIGNER DESK LAMP PROJECT.		

Item	Corresponding Units or Value	Type	Timing
1. Expected annual unit sales	45,000; 40,000; 30,000; 20,000; 10,000	Revenue	End of year 1 to 5
2. Price per unit	$40 the first year, then rising annually at 3%	Revenue	End of year 1 to 5
3. Consulting company's fee	$30,000	Expense	Already incurred
4. Losses on standard lamps	$110,000	Net cash loss	End of year 1 to 5
5. Rental of building to outsiders	$10,000	Revenue	End of year 1 to 5
6. Cost of the equipment	$2,000,000	Asset	Now
7. Straight-line depreciation expense	$400,000 ($2,000,000 divided by 5 years)	Expense	End of year 1 to 5
8. Resale value of equipment	$100,000	Revenue	End of year 5
9. Raw material cost per unit	$10 the first year, then rising annually at 3%	Expense	End of year 1 to 5
10. Raw material inventory	7 days of sales	Asset	Now
11. Accounts payable	4 weeks (or 28 days) of purchases	Liability	Now
12. Accounts receivable	8 weeks (or 56 days) of sales	Asset	Now
13. In-process and finished goods inventories	16 days of sales	Asset	Now
14. Direct labor cost per unit	$5 the first year, then rising annually at 3%	Expense	End of year 1 to 5
15. Energy cost per unit	$1 the first year, then rising annually at 3%	Expense	End of year 1 to 5
16. Overhead charge	1% of sales	Expense	End of year 1 to 5
17. Financing charge	12% of the net book value of assets	Expense	End of year 1 to 5
18. Tax expense on income	40% of pre-tax profits	Expense	End of year 1 to 5
19. Tax expense on capital gains	40% of pre-tax capital gains	Expense	End of year 5
20. After tax cost of capital	7.6% (see Chapter 12)	Not a cash flow	

The engineering department has determined that the equipment needed to produce the lamps will cost $2 million, shipped and installed. For tax purposes, the equipment can be depreciated using the straight-line method over the next five years, that is, at a rate of $400,000 per year ($2 million divided by five). The resale value of the equipment is estimated at $100,000 if it is sold at the end of the project's fifth year.

After consulting a few suppliers, the purchasing department says that the raw materials required to produce the designer desk lamp will cost $10 per lamp the first year of the project and will most likely rise at the annual expected rate of inflation of 3 percent. To avoid disruption in supply, SMC will need seven days of raw material inventory. The firm pays its suppliers, on average, four weeks (28 days) after the raw materials are delivered, and receives payment from its customers, on average, eight weeks (56 days) after the products are shipped.

The production department has estimated that the project's necessary amount of work in process and finished goods inventories will be worth 16 days of sales. Furthermore, SMC's direct labor costs will rise by $5 per lamp and its energy costs will rise by $1 per lamp the first year of the project. These costs will rise at the expected annual rate of inflation of 3 percent during the project's life. Because the company's existing personnel and organizational structure are expected to be able to support the sale of the new product, the firm will not have additional selling, general, and administrative expenses.

To cover SMC's overhead costs (corporate fixed costs), the accounting department charges new projects a standard fee equal to 1 percent of the projects' sales revenues. New projects are also charged an additional fee to cover the cost of financing the assets used to support the projects. This financing charge is equal to 12 percent of the book (accounting) value of the assets employed.

Tax laws allow the $2 million worth of equipment to be fully depreciated on a straight-line basis over a five-year period if the equipment has a terminal book value of zero. A terminal or residual book value greater than zero is considered a capital gain. SMC is subject to a 40 percent tax on both earnings and capital gains.

The firm's financial manager must now estimate the project's expected cash flows and find out whether the investment is a value-creating proposal. We show later that the cost of capital that SMC uses for projects similar to the designer desk lamp project is 7.6 percent.

IDENTIFYING A PROJECT'S RELEVANT CASH FLOWS

In the commuting example presented earlier in the chapter, the project's relevant cash flows were reasonably easy to determine because the alternative situation was clearly defined: it was to continue driving to work. But for many investments, the alternative scenario (the firm's *future* situation if the project is *not* undertaken) is not clearly defined. This complicates the identification of the project's relevant cash flows, as illustrated below for the designer desk lamp project.

SUNK COSTS

A sunk cost is a cost that has already been paid and that has no alternative use at the time when the decision to accept or reject the project is being made. The with/without principle *excludes* sunk costs from the analysis of an investment because they are irrelevant to the decision to invest. The firm has already paid them. For the designer desk lamp project, the $30,000 fee paid to the consulting company (item 3 in Exhibit 9.1) is a sunk cost. It should not affect the decision to produce and launch the new lamp. Most sunk costs are costs related to research and development and to market tests performed *before* the investment decision is made.

To further clarify the point, assume for a moment that the designer desk lamp project has an NPV of $10,000, *excluding the after-tax* consulting fee of $18,000 ($30,000 × (1 − 40%)). What should SMC's managers do in this case? Should they reject the project because its NPV does not cover the after-tax consulting fee (NPV *with* the fee is a *negative* $8,000), or go ahead with the project? The correct decision is to go ahead with the project because the consulting fee cannot be recovered if the project is *not* undertaken. Taking it into account means that it is counted twice: once when it was paid and again against the project's future cash flows. Accepting the project does not destroy $8,000 of value; it creates $10,000 of value.

Opportunity Costs

Based on the discussion about sunk costs, it may seem logical to ignore any costs related to the use of the unoccupied building in which the equipment will be installed because SMC has already paid for the building. However, the building can be rented out for $10,000 a year if it is not used for manufacturing the new product (item 5 in Exhibit 9.1). In other words, the decision to undertake the designer desk lamp project means that SMC must forfeit $10,000 annual rental income for the next five years. This "loss" of potential cash is the direct consequence of undertaking the project. According to the with/without principle, it represents a $10,000 annual reduction in cash flow.

Costs associated with resources that the firm could use to generate cash if it does not undertake a project are called opportunity costs. These costs do not involve any movement of cash in or out of the firm. But the fact that they are not recorded as a transaction in the firm's books does not mean they should be ignored. The cash revenues a firm can earn if it does *not* undertake a project are equivalent to a loss of cash if the project is undertaken.

Opportunity costs are not always easy to identify and quantify. In the case of the unused building, SMC has an offer to rent the building and a market price can be established for the rent. But what if the building cannot be rented because there is no practical way to allow outsiders access to the building without disturbing SMC's normal operations? In this case, an opportunity cost still exists. If the designer desk lamp project occupies the building, then other projects that arise in the future will not be able to use it and new facilities will have to be built. Estimating the dollar value of that potential displacement is not easy but should nevertheless be done. Assigning the empty building free of charge to the designer desk lamp project *understates* the real cost of the project.

Costs Implied by Potential Sales Erosion

Recall that SMC's sales manager is concerned about the potential loss of sales for standard desk lamps if the designer desk lamp project is launched (item 4 in Exhibit 9.1). In this case, the cash flows that the new lamps are expected to generate must be reduced by the estimated loss of cash flows caused by the sales erosion of standard desk lamps. This appears to be another example of an opportunity cost, similar to the potential loss of rental income if the project is launched.

Sales erosion, however, is more complicated than the loss of rental income because sales erosion can be caused by SMC or by a competing firm. Lost sales should be counted as relevant costs *only* if they are directly related to SMC's decision to produce the new lamps. What if SMC were to lose sales on its existing standard lamps even if it does *not* launch the new lamps? How could this be possible? This situation can occur if *competitors* decide to launch newly designed desk lamps that compete directly with SMC's standard desk lamps. In this case, the loss of sales will occur *anyway* and the erosion should *not* be counted as a relevant cost in the decision to launch the new product. It is an irrelevant cost because it is a part of the "SMC-without-the-project" scenario. If this occurs, sales erosion is no longer similar to an opportunity cost but, rather, is comparable to a sunk cost.

The question that SMC's managers must answer is this: what will happen to the firm's future cash flows if it does *not* launch the designer desk lamp? In other words, what is the scenario if SMC does *not* undertake the project (the "without" situation)? If SMC's managers believe that some sales erosion will take place, then the corresponding loss of cash flows should be ignored; in this case, they are similar to a sunk cost. Our point is that a firm cannot evaluate an investment properly if it does not know what will happen if *it does not invest*. We return to the issue of sales erosion when we estimate the NPV of the designer desk lamp project.

ALLOCATED COSTS

Like many firms, SMC spreads its overhead costs over a number of projects using standard allocation rules. But according to the with/without principle, these allocated costs are irrelevant because the firm will have to pay them even if the project is not undertaken. *Only increases in overhead cash expenses resulting from the project should be taken into account.* The project should not have to pay a share of the existing overhead expenses. Because no increases in overhead expenses are expected to occur for the designer desk lamp, it would be incorrect to charge this project a fee of 1 percent of sales as required by the accounting department (item 16 in Exhibit 9.1).

DEPRECIATION EXPENSE

If SMC decides to buy the $2 million piece of equipment, it will incur an initial cash outflow of $2 million. The equipment will be listed as a fixed asset on SMC's balance sheet and depreciated at a rate of $400,000 per year (item 7 in Exhibit 9.1). Recall that depreciation expense does not involve any cash outflows; it is not paid to anyone and is thus irrelevant to the investment decision.

However, firms must pay taxes. Even though depreciation does not affect *pre-tax* cash flows, it has an effect on *after-tax* cash flows. When the firm pays taxes, depreciation becomes relevant because it reduces the firm's taxable profit. With a lower taxable income, the firm pays less in taxes and saves an equivalent amount of cash. With a corporate tax rate of 40 percent (item 18 in Exhibit 9.1), SMC saves $0.40 of taxes for every $1 of depreciation expense.[2]

TAX EXPENSE

If an investment is profitable, the firm will have to pay more taxes. According to the with/without principle, the *additional* tax the firm must pay as a result of the project's acceptance is a relevant cash outflow. To compute this additional tax payment, we must first estimate the incremental earnings before interest and tax (EBIT) that the project is expected to generate if adopted. The contribution of the project to the firm's total tax bill is then found by multiplying the incremental EBIT by the corporate

---

[2] The tax savings from depreciation expenses must be computed from the amount of depreciation expenses allowed by the tax authorities. This is not necessarily the same amount the firm reports in its income statement (see Chapter 4).

tax rate applicable to the extra amount of pre-tax profit. This rate is known as the marginal corporate tax rate. We have:

$$\text{Project tax} = \text{Project EBIT} \times \text{Marginal corporate tax rate}$$

where:

$$\text{Project EBIT} = \text{Project revenues} - \text{Project operating expenses} \\ - \text{Project depreciation}$$

We use the project's EBIT to calculate the project tax so we can account for the tax savings that result from the depreciation of the project's assets. However, the project's EBIT is the incremental profit *before* the deduction of interest expense. Thus, we seem to have ignored the corporate tax reduction that results from the deduction of interest expenses on the funds borrowed to finance the project. This is not the case. We ignore it in the cash flows, but, as shown below, we account for it in the cost of capital, which is measured on an *after-tax* basis. In other words, *the tax savings from the deductibility of interest expense are not taken into account in the project's cash flows, but in the project's estimated after-tax cost of capital.*

What would happen if SMC has a loss next year and thus has no taxes to pay? Obviously, in this case, the tax savings from the deduction of depreciation and interest expenses will not be available. To get the tax savings, SMC must pay some taxes in the first place. If no taxes are paid, then none can be saved. Fortunately, the tax authorities in most countries allow companies to **carry forward** or **carry back** their tax savings. This means that companies that cannot take advantage of the tax savings during the current tax year (because they made no profit) can do so against profits generated during the previous three to five years (the carry-back method) or during the forthcoming three to five years (the carry-forward method).

FINANCING COSTS

The cost of financing an investment is certainly a relevant cost when deciding whether to invest. But financing costs are cash flows *to* the investors who fund the project, not cash flows *from* the project. If a project is analyzed using the NPV rule, the project's expected cash-flow stream is discounted at the project's cost of capital. And the project's cost of capital is the return required by the investors who will finance the project. Thus, the *cost of capital is the cost of financing the project.* If financing costs are deducted from the project's expected cash-flow stream, the present value calculations will count them twice – once in the expected cash flows and a second time when the cash flows are discounted. Hence *financing costs should be ignored when estimating a project's relevant cash flows.* They will be captured in the project's cost of capital.

To illustrate the distinction that must be made between cash flows *from* the project (investment-related cash flows) and cash flows *to* the suppliers of capital (financing-related cash flows), consider the case of a one-year investment that requires an initial cash outlay of $1,000 that will generate a future cash inflow of $1,200. Suppose that the investment is financed with a $1,000 loan at 10 percent. The firm borrows $1,000 from a bank (an initial cash inflow) to finance the project and repays $1,100 at the end of the year (a year-end cash outflow). The cash-flow streams related to the investment and financing decisions, the total cash flows, and the NPVs are shown in Exhibit 9.2.

EXHIBIT 9.2	INVESTMENT- AND FINANCING-RELATED CASH-FLOW STREAMS.		

Type of Cash-Flow Stream	Initial Cash Flow	Terminal Cash Flow	NPV at 10%
Investment-related cash flows	−$1,000	+$1,200	+$91
Financing-related cash flows	+$1,000	−$1,100	Zero
Total cash flows	Zero	+$ 100	+$91

The cash flows related to the financing decision have an NPV of zero. Hence the project's NPV is the same as the total NPV, which takes into account the cash flows from both the investment decision and the financing decision. Deducting the $100 of financing expense (10 percent of $1,000) from the project's $1,200 future cash flow, and then discounting the difference at the cost of capital of 10 percent will introduce the double counting mentioned earlier.

How can we estimate the appropriate cost of capital for the designer desk lamp project? In the previous example, the investment was financed entirely with debt, so the cost of debt is the cost of capital. Chapter 12 shows that 25 percent of the designer desk lamp project will be financed with debt borrowed at 4.5 percent and the remaining 75 percent will be financed with equity capital provided by SMC's shareholders, who expect to earn a 9.2 percent return on their equity investment. The 9.2 percent return expected by SMC's shareholders is SMC's cost of equity.

Given the financing structure and costs, what is the designer desk lamp project's overall cost of capital? It is the weighted average of the project's *after-tax cost* of debt (because interest expenses are tax deductible) and the project's cost of equity. Shareholders receive dividend payments that are *not* tax deductible at the corporate level, so the cost of equity is not measured on an after-tax basis. The weights used in the calculation are the proportions of debt and equity financing. With a pre-tax cost of debt of 4.5 percent, a tax rate of 40 percent, a proportion of debt financing of 25 percent, a cost of equity of 9.2 percent, and a proportion of equity financing of 75 percent, the project's weighted average cost of capital, k, is as follows:

$$\text{Project's cost of capital (k)} = [4.5\% \times (1 - 0.40) \times 25\%] + [9.2\% \times 75\%]$$
$$= 7.6\%$$

The project's appropriate cost of capital is 7.6 percent. It is not the 12 percent rate that SMC's accounting department applies to the book value of the project's assets (item 17 in Exhibit 9.1). The reason is twofold. First, a financing cost should not affect the project's expected cash flows; it affects the project's discount rate or cost of capital. But more to the point, the 12 percent charge is an inappropriate estimate of the project's cost of capital because it is an allocated financial expense that does not reflect the actual opportunity cost of the funds required to finance the project.

INFLATION

The 3 percent annual rate of inflation expected to prevail during the life of the project will affect several of the project's variables. The lamp's price (item 2 in Exhibit 9.1), the cost of raw material (item 9), and the labor and energy costs (items 14 and 15) are all expected to increase at the 3 percent anticipated rate of inflation. SMC's management has little or no control over the expected rise in the costs of raw material, energy, and labor unless SMC can exert pressure on its suppliers and prevent wages from rising – an unlikely outcome given competitive market forces. But management *can* decide not to raise the price of SMC's lamps by the 3 percent annual inflation rate if, for example, competitors keep the price of their products constant.

Inflation is also involved in another cost over which management has no influence. The firm's 7.6 percent cost of capital, which is entirely determined by the financial markets, is assumed to incorporate the market's 3 percent expected rate of inflation. The suppliers of capital will obviously require compensation to cover the potential erosion of their purchasing power caused by price inflation.

How will the 3 percent expected inflation rate affect the project's evaluation? If the cost of capital already incorporates the market's anticipated rate of inflation, then consistency requires that the inflation rate also be incorporated in the cash-flow stream that the project is expected to generate. In other words, the project's cash flows should be measured in nominal terms, inflation included. The only component of cash flows that does not need to incorporate the 3 percent anticipated inflation rate is the lamp's selling price.[3] For competitive reasons, management can decide to keep that price at a constant $40. In the following analysis of the designer desk lamp project, we first assume that the price of the lamp will rise by the 3 percent expected inflation rate and later examine what would happen to the project's profitability if the price remains constant at $40.

ESTIMATING A PROJECT'S RELEVANT CASH FLOWS

We let CF_t designate the project's relevant cash flow at the *end* of year t.[4] Then, CF_0 denotes the project's initial cash outflow, CF_1 to CF_{T-1} denote the project's intermediate cash flows from the end of year 1 to the end of year T–1, and CF_T denotes the **terminal cash flow**, which is the cash flow at the end of year T, the last year of the project. As shown in Chapter 7, the project's NPV can be expressed as follows:

$$NPV(project) = CF_0 + \frac{CF_1}{(1+k)^1} + \frac{CF_2}{(1+k)^2} + \dots + \frac{CF_t}{(1+k)^t} + \dots + \frac{CF_T}{(1+k)^T} \quad (9.1)$$

where k = the project's cost of capital;

$\frac{CF_t}{(1+k)^t}$ = the present value of CF_t at the project's cost of capital k, and

T = the project's **economic** or **useful life**, that is, the number of years over which the project is expected to provide benefits to the firm's owners.

---

[3] One other component of a project's cash flows that may not be affected by inflation is the tax savings from depreciation expense. In most countries, accounting conventions do not allow firms to change their depreciation expense to compensate for the effect of inflation on the value of assets.

[4] This assumption is made for computational convenience because discounting requires that the cash flow occurs at a specific point. If this assumption is not realistic for the project being analyzed, the length of the cash flow period should be shortened to six months or less.

Recall that if a project has a positive NPV, it is a value-creating proposition and should be undertaken. If it has a negative NPV, it should be rejected. As an illustration, we will estimate the NPV of the designer desk lamp project using an economic life equal to five years (T = 5), the same as its **accounting life** or number of years over which the project's fixed assets are depreciated (item 7 in Exhibit 9.1). However, the project may have an economic or useful life that is longer than five years, meaning that the project may still generate *positive* net cash flows beyond the fifth year. If this occurs, the project will be continued if its NPV at the end of year 5 is higher than the NPV of the net cash flow resulting from the project's termination at that time.

MEASURING THE CASH FLOWS GENERATED BY A PROJECT

According to the with/without principle, CF_t, the cash flow generated by a project in year t is equal to the *change* in the firm's *overall* cash flow in year t if the project is undertaken. It is given by the following general expression (see Chapter 4 for details):

$$CF_t = EBIT_t (1 - Tax_t) + Dep_t - \Delta WCR_t - Capex_t \qquad (9.2)$$

where CF_t = the incremental cash flow generated by the project in year t, which is assumed to occur at the end of the year;

$EBIT_t$ = the incremental earnings before interest and tax, or pre-tax operating profit, generated by the project in year t; it is equal to sales$_t$ *less* operating expenses$_t$ *less* depreciation expense$_t$;

Tax_t = the marginal corporate tax rate applicable to the incremental $EBIT_t$;

Dep_t = the depreciation expense in year t that is related to the fixed assets used to support the project;

ΔWCR_t = the incremental working capital required in year t to support the sales that the project is expected to generate *the following* year;[5] WCR_t is equal to the project's operating assets (mostly accounts receivable and inventories) *less* its operating liabilities (mostly accounts payable); and

$Capex_t$ = capital expenditures or incremental investment in fixed assets in year t.

CF_t, the cash flow *from* the project, excludes all cash movements related to the financing of the project, such as the cash inflows from borrowing or the cash outflows associated with interest and dividend payments made to lenders and shareholders. As discussed earlier, these financing costs are captured by the project's weighted average cost of capital.

Because we want to exclude financing costs from the project's cash flows, the first term in equation 9.2 is the after-tax profit generated from the project's *operations*. It is the earnings before interest and taxes (EBIT) adjusted by the corporate tax rate: $EBIT_t(1 - Tax_t)$.[6] This after-tax operating profit is then

---

[5] WCR builds up throughout the year. Recognizing the change in WCR at the beginning rather than the end of the year will reduce the project's NPV, because the change in WCR reduces cash flows. This is preferable to recognizing the investment later and *overstating* the project's NPV.

[6] The actual tax payment the firm must make is obtained by applying the corporate tax rate to profits after *deducting interest expenses*. However, as discussed earlier, applying the tax rate to EBIT does not ignore interest expenses and the corresponding reduction in taxes they provide; both are accounted for in the project's cost of capital.

converted into an after-tax cash flow by making three adjustments (see Self-Test Question 9.2):

1. Depreciation expense (Dep_t) is added because it is not a cash expense[7]
2. Any cash used to finance the growth of the working capital required to support the sales generated by the project (ΔWCR_t) is subtracted
3. The cash used to acquire the fixed assets needed to launch the project and keep it going over its useful life $(Capex_t)$ is subtracted.

The following sections examine the estimation of a project's initial, intermediate, and terminal cash flows using the designer desk lamp project as an illustration. A summary of the estimation procedure is presented in Exhibits 9.3A and 9.3B.

Estimating the Project's Initial Cash Outflow

The project's initial cash outflow, CF_0, includes the following items:

1. The cost of the assets acquired to launch the project
2. Any setup costs, including shipping and installation costs
3. Any additional working capital required to support the sales that the project is expected to generate the first year
4. Any tax credits provided by the government to induce firms to invest
5. Any cash inflows resulting from the sale of existing assets when the project involves a decision to replace assets, including any taxes related to that sale.

All these costs must be *cash* costs and should not include any sunk costs, such as those related to research and development or market research, if these expenses occurred before the decision to accept or reject the project.

For the designer desk lamp project, the initial cash outflow is equal to the sum of the following:

1. The $2 million cost of acquiring and installing the equipment in the existing building (item 6 in Exhibit 9.1)
2. The initial working capital required to support the first year of sales the project is expected to generate.

We can estimate the project's working capital requirement (WCR) from the information reported in Exhibit 9.1. WCR is usually expressed as a percentage of sales. In other words, if we know the expected sales in year t, we can estimate the amount of working capital that is required at the beginning of that year to support these sales. For the designer desk lamp project:

$$WCR = Receivables + Inventories - Payables$$

Receivables are equal to 56 days of sales (item 12 in Exhibit 9.1), and inventories are equal to 23 days of sales (items 10 and 13). Payables are equal to four weeks of purchases (item 11), which is equivalent to one week (7 days) of sales because the $10 cost for raw material is one-fourth of the $40 lamp price, and one-fourth of four weeks is one week. It follows that the project's WCR is equal to 72 days of

---

[7] Depreciation expense is included in EBIT. After we have calculated the tax expense by applying the tax rate to cash-flow EBIT, we must add depreciation expense to remove its effect on cash flow. We need depreciation expense in the first place only to calculate the tax liability triggered by the project.

EXHIBIT 9.3A	ESTIMATION OF THE CASH FLOWS GENERATED BY THE DESIGNER DESK LAMP PROJECT: CALCULATIONS.

FIGURES IN THOUSANDS. DATA FROM EXHIBIT 9.1

		Forecasts for				
	Now	Year 1	Year 2	Year 3	Year 4	Year 5
I. Revenues						
1. Expected unit sales in thousands		45	40	30	20	10
2. *Price per unit, rising at 3% per year*		$40.00	$41.20	$42.44	$43.71	$45.02
3. Total sales revenues (line 1 × line 2)		$1,800	$1,648	$1,273	$874	$450
II. Operating expenses						
4. *Material cost per unit, rising at 3% per year*		$10.00	$10.30	$10.61	$10.93	$11.26
5. Total material cost (line 1 × line 4)		450	412	318	219	113
6. *Labor cost per unit, rising at 3% per year*		5.00	5.15	5.30	5.46	5.63
7. Total labor cost (line 1 × line 6)		225	206	159	109	56
8. *Energy cost per unit, rising at 3% per year*		1.00	1.03	1.06	1.09	1.13
9. Total energy cost (line 1 × line 8)		45	41	32	22	11
10. Loss of rental income (opportunity cost)		10	10	10	10	10
11. Depreciation expense ($2,000/5)		400	400	400	400	400
12. Total operating expenses (lines 5+7+9+10+11)		$1,130	$1,069	$919	$760	$590
III. Operating profit						
13. Pre-tax operating profit (EBIT) (line 3 − line 12)		$670	$579	$354	$115	($140)
14. Less tax at 40% (when positive, it is a tax credit)		(268)	(232)	(142)	(46)	56
15. After-tax operating profit (line 13 + line 14)		$402	$347	$212	$69	($84)
IV. Cash flow generated by the project						
16. After-tax operating profit (line 15)		$402	$347	$212	$69	($84)
17. Depreciation expense (line 11)		400	400	400	400	400
18. *Working capital requirement at 20% of next year's sales*	360	330	255	175	90	0
19. Change in working capital requirement from previous year	360	(30)	(75)	(80)	(85)	(90)
20. Capital expenditure	2,000	0	0	0	0	0
21. Recovery of the after-tax value of equipment						60
22. Initial cash flow	($2,360)					
23. Cash flow from the project (line 22 for initial cash outlay and then lines 16+17−19−20+21)	($2,360)	$832	$822	$692	$554	$466

| | EXHIBIT 9.3B | ESTIMATION OF THE CASH FLOWS GENERATED BY THE DESIGNER DESK LAMP PROJECT: USING A SPREADSHEET. |

FIGURES IN THOUSANDS. DATA FROM EXHIBIT 9.1

	A	B	C	D	E	F	G
					Forecasts for		
1		Now	Year 1	Year 2	Year 3	Year 4	Year 5
2	I. Revenues						
3	Expected unit sales in thousands		45	40	30	20	10
4	Price increase			3.0%	3.0%	3.0%	3.0%
5	Price per unit		$40.00	$41.20	$42.44	$43.71	$45.02
6	Total sales revenues		$1,800	$1,648	$1,273	$874	$450

- *Values in rows 3 and 4 are data*
- *Value in cell C5 is data. Formula in cell D5 is =C5*(1+D4). Then copy formula in cell D5 to next cells in row 5*
- *The formula in cell C6 is =C3*C5. Then copy formula in cell C6 to next cells in row 6*

	A	B	C	D	E	F	G
7	II. Operating expenses						
8	Increase in unit of material cost			3.0%	3.0%	3.0%	3.0%
9	Per unit material cost		$10.00	$10.30	$10.61	$10.93	$11.26
10	Total material cost		$450	$412	$318	$219	$113
11	Increase in unit of labor cost			3.0%	3.0%	3.0%	3.0%
12	Per unit labor cost		$5.00	$5.15	$5.30	$5.46	$5.63
13	Total labor cost		$225	$206	$159	$109	$56
14	Increase in unit of energy cost			3.0%	3.0%	3.0%	3.0%
15	Per unit energy cost		$1.00	$1.03	$1.06	$1.09	$1.13
16	Total energy cost		$45	$41	$32	$22	$11
17	Loss of rental income		$10	$10	$10	$10	$10
18	Depreciation expense		$400	$400	$400	$400	$400
19	Total operating expenses		$1,130	$1,069	$919	$760	$590

- *Values in rows 8, 11, 14, and 17 are data*
- *Values in cells C9, C12, and C15 are data*
- *Formula in cell C18 is = SLN(2000,0,5) where 2000 is the equipment cost. Then copy formula in cell C18 to next cells in row 18*
- *Formulas in cells D9, D12, and D15 are =C9*(1+D8), =C12*(1+D11), and =C15*(1+D14), respectively. Then copy formulas in cells D9, D12, and D15 to next cells in rows 9, 12, and15, respectively*
- *Formulas in cells C10, C13, and C16 are =C3*C9, =C3*C12, and =C3*C15, respectively. Then copy formulas in cells C10, C13, and C16 to next cells in rows 10, 13, and 16, respectively*
- *Formula in cell C19 is =C10+C13+C16+C17+C18. Then copy formula in cell C19 to next cells in row 19*

| | EXHIBIT 9.3B | ESTIMATION OF THE CASH FLOWS GENERATED BY THE DESIGNER DESK LAMP PROJECT: USING A SPREADSHEET. (*Continued*) |

	A	B	C	D	E	F	G
20	**III. Operating profit**						
21	Pre-tax operating profit (EBIT)		$670	$579	$354	$115	($140)
22	Income tax rate		40.0%	40.0%	40.0%	40.0%	40.0%
23	Income tax		$268	$232	$142	$46	($56)
24	**After-tax operating profit**		$402	$347	$212	$69	($84)

- *Formula in cell C21 is =C6−C19. Then copy formula in cell C21 to next cells in row 21*
- *Values in row 22 are data*
- *Formula in cell C23 is =−C22*C21. Then copy formula in cell C23 to next cells in row 23*
- *Formula in cell C24 is =C21+C23. Then copy formula in cell C24 to next cells in row 24*

	A	B	C	D	E	F	G
25	**IV. Cash flow generated by the project**						
26	Working capital requirement/ Sales$_{t+1}$		20.0%	20.0%	20.0%	20.0%	
27	Working capital requirement	$360	$330	$255	$175	$90	$0
28	Change in working capital requirement	$360	($30)	($75)	($80)	($85)	($90)
29	Capital expenditure	$2,000	$0	$0	$0	$0	$0
30	After-tax resale of equipment						$60
31	**Cash flow from the project**	($2,360)	$832	$822	$692	$554	$466

- *Values in rows 26 and 29 are data*
- *Value in B27 is data from text*
- *Formula in cell C27 is =C26*D6. Then copy formula in cell C27 to next cells in row 27*
- *Formula in cell B28 is =B27. Formula in cell C28 is =C27−B27. Then copy formula in cell C28 to next cells in row 28*
- *Formula in cell G30 is =100*(1−G22), where 100 is the dollar resale value of the equipment*
- *Formula in cell B31 is =B28+B29*
- *Formula in cell C31 is =C24+C18−C28−C29+C30. Then copy formula in cell C31 to next cells in row 31*

sales (56 days of receivables plus 23 days of inventories less 7 days of payables). This is equivalent to 20 percent of annual sales (72 days of sales divided by 360 days of annual sales).

The next step is to estimate sales revenues at the end of the first year. From items 1 and 2 in Exhibit 9.1:

Sales revenues at the end of year 1 = 45,000 units × $40 = $1,800,000

This figure is reported in Exhibit 9.3A in line 3 of the column labeled "End of Year 1." WCR is equal to 20 percent of sales:

Initial WCR = 20% × $1,800,000 = $360,000

Thus, the total initial cash outlay required to launch the project is as follows:

$$CF_0 = \$2,000,000 + \$360,000 = \$2,360,000$$

The \$360,000 initial WCR and the total initial cash flow of \$2,360,000 are reported in the "Now" column of Exhibit 9.3A, lines 19 and 22, respectively. Note that CF_0 can be obtained as a special case of equation 9.2, the general cash-flow equation. In the case of CF_0, EBIT and depreciation expense are zero (there are no initial profit and no depreciation expense), the change in WCR is \$360,000 (more precisely, it is \$360,000 minus zero because \$360,000 is the initial investment in working capital), and capital expenditures are \$2 million.

ESTIMATING THE PROJECT'S INTERMEDIATE CASH FLOWS

The estimates of the desk lamp project's intermediate cash flows (CF_1 to CF_4) are based on the information in Exhibit 9.1 and are calculated using the project's cash-flow formula given in equation 9.2. Exhibit 9.3A shows the inputs and summarizes the cash-flow estimates.

We illustrate the procedure for CF_1, the cash flow that the project is expected to generate the first year. Sales revenues, as computed earlier, are \$1,800,000 (line 3 in Exhibit 9.3A).

Total operating expenses are \$1,130,000 (line 12). They include the total material expense (line 5), total direct labor expense (line 7), total energy expense (line 9), loss of rental income (line 10), and depreciation expense (line 11). They exclude the \$30,000 fee paid to the consulting company (a sunk cost), the overhead charge of 1 percent of sales (SMC's overhead expenses are not expected to rise if the project is adopted), and the 12 percent financing charge required by the accounting department (financing costs are captured by the project's 7.6 percent weighted average cost of capital). They also exclude the effect of sales erosion. This item will be examined later.

With \$1,800,000 of sales revenues and \$1,130,000 of total operating expenses, the project's pre-tax operating profit (EBIT) is \$670,000 (line 13). Deducting 40 percent of tax expense (line 14), we get an after-tax operating profit of \$402,000 (line 15). In section IV of Exhibit 9.3A, this figure is converted into a cash flow by adding back \$400,000 of depreciation expense (line 17) and deducting \$30,000, the *change* in WCR (line 19). (Line 18 shows that WCR *decreased* from \$360,000 to \$330,000.) Thus, the project's cash flow is \$832,000 at the end of the first year (line 23) because there is no additional capital expenditure in year one ($Capex_1 = 0$). Using equation 9.2:

$$CF_1 = (\$1,800,000 - \$1,130,000) \times (1 - 40\%) + \$400,000 - (-\$30,000) - \$0$$
$$CF_1 - \$402,000 + \$400,000 + \$30,000 = \$832,000$$

WCR declines after the first year because sales decline after the first year and WCR is based on next year's sales. Thus, SMC needs to invest a decreasing amount of cash in its operating cycle to support the project's sales. As a consequence, the changes in WCR from year one to year five are negative. Note that the sum of all the changes in WCR over a project's life must equal zero because the firm recovers its initial investment in WCR during the project's duration. For the designer desk lamp project, we have the following:

Sum of the *changes* in WCR =
$$\$360,000 - \$30,000 - \$75,000 - \$80,000 - \$85,000 - \$90,000 = 0$$

ESTIMATING THE PROJECT'S TERMINAL CASH FLOW

The incremental cash flow for the last year of any project, its terminal cash flow, should include the following items:

1. The last incremental net cash flow the project is expected to generate
2. The recovery of the project's incremental working capital requirement, if any
3. The after-tax resale value of any physical assets acquired earlier in relation to the project
4. Any capital expenditure and other costs associated with the termination of the project.

At the end of a project, inventories associated with the project are sold, accounts receivable are collected, and accounts payable are paid. In other words, the cash value of the project's contribution to the firm's WCR is recovered. For the designer desk lamp project, the WCR that will be recovered at the end of the fifth year is worth $90,000.

Some of a project's fixed assets may have a resale value when the project is terminated. The sale of these assets will generate a cash inflow that must be counted in the project's terminal cash flow after adjustments for the incidence of any taxes associated with the sale. The resale value of the assets, also known as their **residual value** or **salvage value**, affects the firm's overall tax bill *only if it is different from the assets' book value*. If the resale value is higher than the book value, the project's termination will generate a taxable capital gain (equal to the difference between the resale value and the book value) that will increase the firm's overall tax bill. If they are equal, there are no tax implications. And if the resale value is lower than the book value, then the project's termination will generate a capital loss that will reduce the firm's overall tax bill.

For the designer desk lamp project, the initial equipment has an expected residual value of $100,000 (see item 8 in Exhibit 9.1) and a book value of zero at the end of year five (see item 7 in Exhibit 9.1). The sale of that asset is thus expected to generate a capital gain of $100,000 that will be taxed at 40 percent (see item 19 in Exhibit 9.1). As a result, the project's terminal cash flow, CF_5, should increase by $60,000 ($100,000 less 40 percent of $100,000), an amount equal to the expected *after-tax* resale value of the equipment.

Combining the various items that contribute to the project's terminal cash flow, we have the following:

$$CF_T = EBIT_T(1 - Tax_T) + Dep_T - \Delta WCR_T + \text{After-tax residual value}_T$$

Applying this formula to the designer desk lamp project, as shown in the last column of Exhibit 9.3A, provides a total terminal cash flow, CF_5, of $466,000:

$$CF_5 = -\$84,000 + \$400,000 - (-\$90,000) + \$60,000 = \$466,000$$

The last operating "profit" for the project (line 13 in Exhibit 9.3A) is in fact a loss of $140,000. SMC's overall taxable income will be reduced by that amount, providing a tax saving of $56,000 (40 percent of $140,000) and yielding an *after-tax* operating loss of $84,000 for the project. Although the after-tax net income is negative, the net cash flow from the project is positive, and the decision to invest should be based on cash flows, not profits.

The same analysis we performed with a calculator in Exhibit 9.3A is reproduced in Exhibit 9.3B using a spreadsheet.

SHOULD SMC LAUNCH THE NEW PRODUCT?

We have now identified and estimated the entire cash-flow stream the designer desk lamp project is expected to generate during the next five years. It is shown in the last row of Exhibit 9.3A. The project's cost of capital is 7.6 percent (item 20 in Exhibit 9.1). The calculations for the project's NPV according to equation 9.1 are shown in Exhibit 9.4. Part I shows the calculations, and Part II shows the same using a spreadsheet.

The designer desk lamp project has a positive NPV of $415,083, so SMC should launch the new product.[8] Before concluding, however, we should perform a sensitivity analysis on the project's NPV because the $415,083 ignores two

---

EXHIBIT 9.4	CALCULATION OF NET PRESENT VALUE FOR SMC'S DESIGNER DESK LAMP PROJECT.

FIGURES FROM EXHIBIT 9.3

Part I Calculations

$$\text{Initial cash outlay } CF_0 = \qquad\qquad\qquad\qquad\qquad\qquad\qquad\qquad\qquad -\$2,360,000$$

$$\text{Present value of } CF_1 = \$832,000 \times \frac{1}{(1+0.076)^1} = \$832,000 \times 0.92937 = \$773,234$$

$$\text{Present value of } CF_2 = 822,000 \times \frac{1}{(1+0.076)^2} = 822,000 \times 0.86372 = 709,978$$

$$\text{Present value of } CF_3 = 692,000 \times \frac{1}{(1+0.076)^3} = 692,000 \times 0.80272 = 555,483$$

$$\text{Present value of } CF_4 = 554,000 \times \frac{1}{(1+0.076)^4} = 554,000 \times 0.74602 = 413,296$$

$$\text{Present value of } CF_5 = 466,000 \times \frac{1}{(1+0.076)^5} = 466,000 \times 0.69333 = 323,092$$

Net present value at 7.6%	$ 415,083

Part II Using a spreadsheet

	A	B	C	D	E	F	G
1		Now	Forecasts for				
			Year 1	Year 2	Year 3	Year 4	Year 5
2	Cash flows	−$2,360,000	$832,000	$822,000	$692,000	$554,000	$466,000
3	Cost of capital	7.6%					
4	Net present value	$415,083					

• The formula in cell B4 is =B2+NPV(B3,C2:G2)

---

[8] Alternatively, the project's internal rate of return (IRR) is equal to 14.8 percent. Because the project's IRR exceeds the 7.6 percent cost of capital, the project is a value-creating proposal.

important elements: (1) SMC may not be able to raise the price of its new lamps above $40 and (2) SMC may incur net cash losses of as much as $110,000 per year (item 4 in Exhibit 9.1) as a result of a potential reduction in the sales of SMC's standard desk lamps due to sales erosion. We did not consider the potential sales erosion in our earlier analysis because we assumed it would occur whether or not SMC launched the new lamps. However, if the sales erosion will occur *only as a result of the launch of the new lamps*, then it must be considered in the calculation of the project's NPV.

SENSITIVITY OF THE PROJECT'S NPV TO CHANGES IN THE LAMP PRICE

What will happen to the project's net present value if SMC is unable to raise the price of lamps by the 3 percent expected increase in the annual rate of inflation? If SMC keeps the price constant at $40 while costs are rising by 3 percent, the project's NPV drops from $415,083 to $304,190, a 27 percent reduction.[9] But the project is still worth undertaking because its NPV remains positive.

By using a spreadsheet like the one presented in Exhibit 9.3B, you can perform sensitivity analysis rapidly and efficiently. Just change the values of the variables that are expected to deviate significantly from their expected value. The spreadsheet will automatically be updated and show the NPV under each scenario.

SENSITIVITY OF NPV TO SALES EROSION

The present value at 7.6 percent of the loss of annual net cash flows of $110,000 for five years is equal to $443,872.[10] If we deduct this amount from the project's NPV of $415,083, we have the following:

$$\text{NPV(project with erosion)} = \text{NPV(project without erosion)} - \text{NPV(erosion)}$$
$$= \$415,083 - \$443,872 = -\$28,789$$

Thus, with $110,000 yearly sales erosion, the designer desk lamp project is no longer a value-creating proposal. However, the project can withstand some sales erosion and still have a positive NPV. The project will break even if the annual reduction in net cash flow is $102,866.[11] In other words, if sales erosion is expected to reduce SMC's net cash flows by more than $102,866 per year for the next five years, then the

---

[9] The estimation procedure is the same as the one shown in Exhibit 9.3A except that the price of a lamp remains at $40. Note, however, that in this case WCR will be *less* than 20 percent of sales. Accounts payable are going to be *higher* than one week of sales, because the cost of raw material is rising by 3 percent while the price of a lamp remains constant. We kept WCR at 20 percent of sales in our calculation. A lower ratio would have produced larger cash flows and a higher NPV.

[10] This cash-flow stream is an annuity. Chapter 2 shows that the present value of an annuity is equal to the constant cash flow multiplied by the annuity discount factor (ADF), where ADF is equal to (1 − Discount factor) divided by k. With k = 7.6% and T = 5, ADF = (1 − 0.69333)/0.076 = 4.0352 and the present value of the $110,000 annuity is $110,000 × 4.0352 = $443,872.

[11] The breakeven point is obtained when the project's NPV is equal to the present value of the annuity. We have $415,083 = Annuity × ADF. With ADF equal to 4.0352, the annuity is equal to $415,083 divided by 4.0352, that is, $102,866.

project will no longer be acceptable. If annual sales erosion is less than $102,866, the project has a positive NPV and may still be acceptable.

The preceding analysis clearly indicates that the magnitude of the potential annual reduction in sales and net cash flows due to sales erosion must be determined by SMC's managers before they decide whether to launch the designer desk lamp project. In other words, SMC's managers must have a clear understanding of their firm's competitive position in the standard desk lamp market before they evaluate the value-creating potential of the new product.

Will competitors enter the standard desk lamp market with a competing product that will erode SMC's position in that market? If the answer is yes, then the effect of erosion on the project's cash flows can be ignored. The sales erosion will happen anyway and thus is irrelevant to the decision to produce the designer desk lamps. In this case, the project's NPV is positive, and SMC should launch the new product. If the answer is that erosion will take place only if SMC launches the new lamp, then the effect of erosion on the firm's net cash flows should be carefully estimated and taken into account. If erosion is expected to reduce the firm's annual net cash flows by less than $102,866, the project is still worth undertaking because its NPV is still positive. If management believes that erosion will reduce cash flows by more than $102,866 a year, the project should be rejected.

Sensitivity analysis is a useful tool when dealing with project uncertainty. By showing how sensitive NPV is to changes in underlying assumptions, it identifies those variables that have the greatest effect on the value of the proposal and indicates where more information is needed before a decision can be made.

KEY POINTS

1. Managers can use a number of principles and rules to identify and estimate the cash flows that are relevant to an investment decision. Relevant cash flows are the ones that should be discounted at the project's estimated cost of capital to obtain the project's net present value (NPV) or used to calculate the project's internal rate of return (IRR). The decision of whether to invest should be made using only relevant cash flows.

2. Remember the two fundamental principles when estimating a project's cash flows. The first is the *actual cash-flow principle*, according to which a project's relevant cash flows must be measured at the time they occur. Relevant cash flows *exclude* any financing costs associated with the project because these costs are already taken into account in estimating the project's weighted average cost of capital. The weighted average cost of capital is the discount rate that must be used to convert a project's expected future cash-flow stream into its present-value equivalent. Deducting the project's initial investment from this present value provides an estimate of the project's NPV. If it is positive, the project is a value-creating proposition and should be undertaken.

3. The second principle is the *with/without principle*, according to which a project's relevant cash flows are those that are expected to either increase or decrease the firm's *overall* cash position if the project is adopted. Examples of cash outflows that should be ignored are those related to *sunk costs*. These are costs that are incurred *before* the project's net present value is estimated. These costs cannot be recovered, so they should be ignored. Asking the project to cover them means that the firm pays twice for these costs.

4. Examples of cash flows indirectly related to a project that should nevertheless be taken into account are those related to *opportunity costs*. These are usually cash inflows the firm will have to give up if it undertakes the project. Contrary to sunk costs that are relatively easy to determine because they have already been paid, opportunity costs are usually difficult to identify because they involve *potential future* cash flows rather than actual *past* cash flows.

5. One of the most difficult types of costs to identify is the effect that competitors may have on a firm's existing and potential products or services. For example, a firm's managers considering the launch of a new product must find out whether the new product will erode the sales of the firm's existing products. To make the proper decision to invest or not, managers must first forecast the firm's future development if the firm does *not* go ahead with the project (the firm without the project). Then, they must compare the firm's future prospect *with* the project against its future outlook *without* the project. If sales erosion is expected to occur even if the firm does not launch the new product, then the sales erosion of existing products is irrelevant to the decision of whether to launch the new product.

FURTHER READING

Baker, Ken, and Philip English. *Capital Budgeting Valuation: Financial Analysis for Today's Investment Projects*. John Wiley & Sons, 2011.

SELF-TEST QUESTIONS

9.1   Interest payments and project's cash flow.
Why is interest paid on the debt raised to finance an investment project not included in the estimation of the cash flows that are relevant to the evaluation of the project?

9.2   Understanding the structure of the cash flow formula.
The estimation of a project's cash flows is usually based on the formula Cash flow = EBIT(1 − Tax) + Depreciation − ΔWCR − Capex, where EBIT = Earnings before interest and tax, Tax = Marginal tax rate, ΔWCR = Change in working capital requirement, and Capex = Capital expenditures required to support the project. Neither EBIT nor depreciation expense is a cash-flow item. Why do they appear in the cash-flow formula?

9.3   Alternative formula to estimate a project's cash flow.
The cash-flow formula Cash flow = EBIT(1 − Tax) + Depreciation − ΔWCR − Capex is sometimes replaced by the following formula: Cash flow = EBITDA(1 − Tax) + (Tax × Depreciation) − ΔWCR − Capex, where EBIT, Tax, ΔWCR, and Capex are defined as in Self-Test Question 9.2, and EBITDA is earnings before interest and tax, depreciation, and amortization. Show that the two formulas are equivalent.

9.4   Identifying a project's relevant cash flows.
Your company, Printers Inc., is considering investing in a new plant to manufacture a new generation of printers developed by the firm's research and development

(R&D) department. Comment on the analysis of the proposal that is summarized below.

1. *Project's useful life*: The company expects the plant to operate for five years
2. *Capital expenditures*: $6 million, which includes the construction costs and the costs of machinery and installation. The plant will be built on a parking lot owned by the company
3. *Depreciation*: For tax purposes, the building and equipment will be depreciated over ten years using the straight-line method
4. *Revenue*: The company expects to sell 5,000 printers in year one, 10,000 in year two, and 20,000 thereafter. The printers will be sold at $800 each
5. *R&D costs*: $1 million spent a year ago and this year
6. *Overhead costs*: 3.75 percent of the project revenues, as stipulated by the corporate manual
7. *Operating costs*: Direct and indirect costs are expected to be $500 per unit produced
8. *Inventories*: The initial investment in raw material, work in process, and finished goods inventories is estimated at $1,500,000
9. *Financing cost*: 10 percent of capital expenditures per year, as stipulated by the corporate manual
10. *Tax rate*: 40 percent (includes federal and state taxes)
11. *Discount rate*: 8 percent. This is Printers Inc.'s current borrowing rate.
12. *Cash-flow stream and net present value (figures are in thousands of dollars; figures from year 1 to year 5 are at the year-end)*:

		Now	Year 1	Year 2	Year 3	Year 4	Year 5
1.	Capital expenditures	−$6,000					
2.	Inventories	−1,500					
3.	R&D expenses	−1,000					
4.	Revenue		$4,000	$8,000	$16,000	$16,000	$16,000
5.	Overhead costs		−150	−300	−600	−600	−600
6.	Operating costs		−2,500	−5,000	−10,000	−10,000	−10,000
7.	Depreciation		−600	−600	−600	−600	−600
8.	EBIT		750	2,100	4,800	4,800	4,800
9.	EBIT(1 − Tax rate)		450	1,260	2,880	2,880	2,880
10.	Add depreciation		1,050	1,860	3,480	3,480	3,480
11.	Net cash flow	−$8,500	$1,050	$1,860	$3,480	$3,480	$3,480
12.	Discount rate	8%					
13.	Net present value	$1,755					

9.5 Estimating a project's relevant cash flows and net present value.

Suppose you are given the following additional information on the investment proposal described in Self-Test Question 9.4. What is the net present value of the project? Should it be accepted?

1. Salvage value at the end of year five is $3 million
2. Tax rate on capital gains is 20 percent
3. Ratio of working capital requirement to sales is 30 percent

4. Because of competitive pressure, the printer's sale price is expected to decrease at the following rate: $800 in year one, $700 in year two, and $600 thereafter
5. Fixed operating costs are $800,000 per year
6. Variable operating costs are $400 per unit produced
7. Overhead costs will not be significantly affected by the project
8. Printers Inc. will have to rent parking spaces for its employees at an estimated cost of $50,000 per year
9. Expected inflation rate is 3 percent. Inflation is expected to affect only the operating costs that can be assumed to grow at the inflation rate
10. Cost of capital is 12 percent.

REVIEW QUESTIONS

1. **Pondering an investment offer.**
   Your brother-in-law offers you the opportunity to invest $15,000 in a project that he promises will return $17,000 at the end of the year. Because you have only $3,000 in cash, you will have to borrow $12,000 from your bank. The bank charges interest at 12 percent. After reflection, you decide not to accept the offer because you figure the net return would be only $15,560 ($17,000 less $1,440 of interest paid to the bank). When your brother-in-law asks why, you tell him that because the bank charges you 12 percent, it is ridiculous for him to expect you to invest in a risky project that returns less than 4 percent. Please comment. Is the offer that "ridiculous"?

2. **The effect of inflation on the investment decision.**
   The company's financial manager and accountant were arguing over how to properly take account of inflation when analyzing capital investment projects. The accountant typically included estimates of price-level changes when estimating and projecting future cash flows. For this, he took the government's gross domestic product (GDP) price deflator as the best estimate for the future inflation rate. This was 5 percent per year. He therefore believed that the company's discount rate should take into account inflation and that the standard 12 percent they used should be increased by 5 percent to avoid biasing the analysis and overestimating the net present value of the project. The financial manager disagreed, arguing that what the accountant was proposing would really underestimate the net present value. The 12 percent discount rate had been computed by taking the firm's 10 percent expected borrowing rate from its bank, its estimated cost of equity of 15 percent, and a 25 percent corporate tax rate. Who is correct in this argument? Please elaborate.

3. **Changing machines in a world without taxes.**
   The Clampton Company is considering the purchase of a new machine to perform operations currently being performed on different, less efficient equipment. The purchase price is $110,000, delivered and installed. A Clampton production engineer estimates that the new equipment will produce savings of $30,000 in labor and other direct costs annually, compared with the present equipment. He estimates the proposed equipment's economic life at five years, with zero salvage value. The present equipment is in good working order and will last, physically, for at least ten more years. The company requires a return of at least 10 percent before taxes on an investment of this type. Taxes are to be disregarded.

   a. Assuming the present equipment has zero book value and zero resale value, should the company buy the proposed piece of equipment?

b. Assuming the present equipment is being depreciated at a straight-line rate of 10 percent, that is, it has a book value of $40,000 (cost, $80,000; accumulated depreciation, $40,000) and has zero net resale value today, should the company buy the proposed equipment?

The Clampton Company decides to purchase the equipment, hereafter called Model A. Two years later, even better equipment (called Model B) is available on the market and makes the other equipment completely obsolete, with no resale value. The Model B equipment costs $150,000 delivered and installed, but it is expected to result in annual savings of $40,000 over the cost of operating the Model A equipment. The economic life of Model B is estimated to be five years. It will be depreciated at a straight-line rate of 20 percent.

c. What action should the company take?
d. The company decides to purchase the Model B equipment, but a mistake has been made somewhere, because good equipment, bought only two years previously, is being scrapped. How did this mistake come about?

4. **Changing machines in a world with taxes.**
Assume that the Clampton Company in the previous question expects to pay income taxes of 40 percent and that a loss on the sale or disposal of equipment is treated as an ordinary deduction, resulting in a tax saving of 40 percent. The Clampton Company wants to earn 8 percent on its investment after taxes. Depreciation for tax purposes is computed on the straight-line method.

a. Should the company buy the equipment if the facts are otherwise as described in the first scenario from the previous question?
b. Should the company buy the equipment if the facts are otherwise as described in the second scenario from the previous question?

5. **Investing in the production of toys.**
The Great Eastern Toy Company management is considering an investment in a new product. It would require the acquisition of a piece of equipment for $16 million with a ten-year operational life, providing regular maintenance is carried out. Salvage value of the equipment is estimated at $800,000. The product's economic life is expected to be five years, with annual revenues estimated at $10.8 million during this period. Raw material for the new product is estimated at $95 per unit produced, and an inventory equivalent to one month's production, or 3,000 units, would be needed. Direct costs of manufacture are expected to be $130,000 per month. Work-in-progress and finished goods inventories would rise by $150,000. For tax purposes, fixed assets must be depreciated according to the straight-line method. The corporate income tax rate is 40 percent and so is the capital-gain tax rate. The company's cost of capital is 12 percent.

a. Based on the above data, set out the cash flows expected from the project.
b. What is the net present value of the project?

6. **The effect of accounts receivable, accounts payable, overhead, and financial costs on the investment decision.**
Reviewing the cash-flow forecasts of a new investment project that appear in the following table, the Avon company's finance manager noted that there was no mention of any effect of the investment on the firm's accounts receivable and payable. The average collection period on the new product was expected to be 50 days, and new

raw material purchases were expected to be settled in 36 days on average. Also, he noted that the standard charges of 1 percent of sales revenues from new projects had not been made; neither had the annual financing charge of 10 percent been levied against the book value of the assets used by the project. How would the project's profitability be affected by including its effect on Avon's:

a. accounts receivable and accounts payable;
b. overhead costs; and
c. financing charges?

(in thousands)	Now	Years 1 to 4	Year 5
1. Revenues		$12,000	$12,000
2. Raw materials cost		4,000	4,000
3. Direct costs		1,000	1,000
4. Depreciation expense		4,000	4,000
5. Pre-tax operating profit		3,000	3,000
6. Tax rate		40%	40%
7. After-tax operating profit		1,800	1,800
8. Increase in inventories	$ 400	0	−400
9. Capital expenditures	20,000	0	0
10. After-tax resale value of equipment			0
11. Cash flow from the project	−20,400	5,800	6,200
12. **Project net present value at 11% cost of capital**	$ 1,274		

7. **The effect of depreciation for tax purposes.**
   According to the Modified Accelerated Cost Recovery System (MACRS) of depreciation imposed by US tax law, autos and computers must be depreciated the following way for tax purposes:

Year 1	Year 2	Year 3	Year 4	Year 5	Year 6
20.00%	32.00%	19.20%	11.52%	11.52%	5.76%

   a. What is the present value of the interest tax shield from the purchase of an automobile for $50,000, with a cost of capital of 10 percent and a tax rate of 34 percent?
   b. What would be the effect of a change in the tax law from MACRS to straight-line depreciation?

8. **The effect of cannibalization.**
   Although he was initially satisfied by the apparent profitability of the new project, the Avon company's chief executive officer (CEO) was troubled by some other aspects of the project that he thought the finance manager had left out of the analysis. First, he was concerned about whether the new project could possibly cannibalize sales of the firm's existing products. In a worst-case scenario, he believed that a negative effect on after-tax cash flows by as much as $650,000 per year was possible. Second, a building owned by the company, but unoccupied, would be used to produce the

new product. They had recently received an offer from an adjacent business to rent this property for $100,000 per year. Finally, the firm had commissioned and already paid to a consultant $500,000 for a market study of the new product. How would the project's profitability be affected by including these items in the cash-flow estimates that are shown on the table in Review Question 6?

9. **Breakeven analysis.**

Suppose Snowmobile Inc. is considering whether or not to launch a new snowmobile. It expects to sell the vehicle for $10,000 over five years at a rate of 100 per year. The variable costs of making one unit are $5,000, and the fixed costs are expected to be $125,000 per year. The investment would be $1 million and would be depreciated according to the straight-line method over five years with zero salvage value. Snowmobile Inc.'s cost of capital is 10 percent. The corporate tax rate is 40 percent. The investment would not require any significant addition to the firm's working capital requirement.

a. What is the net present value of the investment?
b. How many snowmobiles would the company need to sell to breakeven (i.e., for the project to have a zero net present value)?
c. At the breakeven level, what would be the project's discounted payback period and internal rate of return?

10. **Bid price.**

Maintainit Inc. is asked to submit a bid for watering and spraying trees in a housing development for the next five years. To provide this service, Maintainit would have to buy new equipment for $100,000 and invest $30,000 in its working capital requirement. The equipment would be depreciated straight-line to zero salvage value over the five-year period. Total labor and other costs would be $80,000 a year. The tax rate is 40 percent and Maintainit's cost of capital is 10 percent. What would Maintainit's minimum bid price need to be?

VALUING BONDS AND STOCKS

CHAPTER **10**

Firms need cash to finance their activities. Where does it usually come from? Some of it is generated by the firm's activities and some is borrowed from banks. There are times, however, when the cash from current activities and bank borrowing is not enough to finance operations and growth. When this happens, firms could raise additional cash by selling *corporate bonds* to individual investors and financial institutions (such as insurance companies and pension funds). Firms could also raise additional cash by issuing new shares of common *stocks* to its existing shareholders or to new shareholders. In this chapter we explain what bonds and common stocks are and show how to apply the *discounted cash flow* (DCF) model presented in Chapter 2 to value them. How firms issue new shares and what are all the possible sources of funding available to them are topics discussed in the next chapter.

Knowing how to value bonds and stocks is important because the cost of the capital that is needed to fund a firm's activities is determined by the price of the firm's bonds and common stocks. Specifically, a firm's cost of debt is determined by the price at which its bonds are traded in the *bond market* (and firms that do not issue bonds can use the cost of debt of similar firms that issue bonds to estimate their own cost of debt). Likewise, a firm's cost of equity is determined by the price at which its stocks are traded in public markets (and privately-held firms that do not have shares listed and traded in public markets can use the estimated cost of equity of similar firms that have publicly traded shares to estimate their own cost of equity). In Chapter 12 we show how to estimate the *cost of capital* based on the price of bonds and stocks. After reading this chapter, you should understand the following:

- What bonds and common stocks are
- How to apply the discounted cash-flow model in order to value bonds and stocks
- What *yield curves* are and how to use them to value bonds
- What the risk of holding bonds is and how to measure it
- How to value common stocks using alternative valuation models

WHAT ARE BONDS AND COMMON STOCKS?

Bonds and **common stocks (stocks)** are **financial instruments** issued by firms to investors in exchange for cash.[1] These financial instruments – also called **securities** or **financial assets** – are **certificates**[2] that state the terms and conditions under which the firm receives the cash, as described below.

BOND FEATURES AND TERMINOLOGY

A bond is a negotiable debt instrument that specifies the terms under which the firm is borrowing from investors (who are lending their money to the firm).[3] The terms indicate how much is borrowed, at what rate, and for how long. Consider, for example, a bond issued *a year ago* by the Pacific Engineering Company (PEC) to raise $100 million. Because bonds are typically issued in multiples of $1,000, the $100 million issue consists of 100,000 individual bonds. Several words are used to refer to the bond's $1,000 minimum denomination: it is called the bond's **face value, nominal value, par value, principal** or **redemption value**.[4] The PEC bonds have an **original term to maturity** of six years (this is the "life" of the bonds from the day they were issued to the day they will be redeemed or repaid). Because one year has passed, the bonds have a *remaining* maturity – called **current maturity** or **tenor** – of five years. According to the terms of the bond, the issuer (PEC) must pay the bondholders an annual interest rate of 5 percent, called the bond's **coupon rate**. This means that a holder of one bond receives an *annual* **coupon payment**[5] of $50 (5 percent of $1,000) as well as the bond's face value of $1,000 when the bond matures (when its "life" expires). The following timeline shows the sequence of cash flows a holder of a PEC bond is expected to receive:

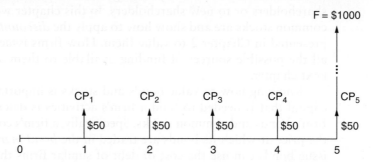

where CP_1 to CP_5 are the five coupon payments and F is the face value. Note that a bond is a package of an **annuity** (in our case a five-year annuity of $50) and a final "balloon payment" equal to the bond's face value.

---

[1] In this chapter we examine straight bonds and common stocks. In Chapter 11 we review nonstandard bonds (such as convertible bonds) and different types of stocks (such as preferred shares).

[2] Today, most bonds are **registered bonds**. They are not issued in paper form; they are digital book entries registered with a depository institution.

[3] The focus in this section is on bonds issued by firms (corporate bonds). Later in this chapter we examine bonds issued by national governments. Other types of issuers include agencies of national governments, and international institutions such as the World Bank and the International Monetary Fund.

[4] A bond's redemption value is usually 100 percent of its face value, but some bonds may have redemption values that are higher or lower than the bond's face value.

[5] Some bonds pay the coupon semi-annually; in this case the coupon payment is $25 every six months (more on this later in the chapter). The word "coupon" is used because, originally, physical bond certificates had paper coupons attached to them, which had to be detached periodically and presented to the issuer to be redeemed for cash.

PEC bonds are listed and traded in the **bond market**. As of today, one year after they were issued, these bonds have specific features which are summarized in Exhibit 10.1. Note that today's quoted price is $978.65. The questions we want to answer later are: how is that price determined, and why is it below the bond's face value of $1,000?

COMMON STOCK FEATURES AND TERMINOLOGY

A common stock is an equity instrument that represents an ownership position in a firm. It recognizes the portion of the firm's total equity value that is owned by the stockholder. Contrary to bonds, common stocks have no **maturity date** and pay no coupon because the stockholder is an owner, not a lender. However, common stocks entitle the holder to vote on matters brought up at shareholder meetings (such as the

EXHIBIT 10.1	BOND FEATURES AND TERMINOLOGY.

A 6-YEAR, 5% COUPON-PAYING BOND ISSUED BY THE PACIFIC ENGINEERING COMPANY (PEC) A YEAR AGO

Data	Symbol	Value	Definition
1. Face value	F	$1,000	• The bond's denomination
			• It is fixed at the time the bond is issued and does not change as time passes
			• It is paid to the bondholder on the day the bond matures
2. Coupon rate	c	5%	• The annual interest rate the issuer of the bond (PEC) pays per dollar of face value
			• It is fixed at the time the bond is issued and does not change as time passes
3. Coupon payment	CP = c × F	$50	• The bond's annual interest payment based on the bond's face value
			• It is fixed at the time the bond is issued and does not change as time passes
4. Original term to maturity	T	6 years	• The bond's life from the day it is issued to the day it is repaid
			• It is fixed at the time the bond is issued
5. Current maturity or tenor	T	5 years	• The bond's term to maturity one year after the bond was issued
			• Current maturity shortens as the bond's maturity date approaches
6. Market price	P	$978.65	• The bond price one year after it was issued
			• The bond price fluctuates over the life of the bond as market conditions and interest rates change
7. Current yield	CP/P	5.11%	• The return, based on today's bond price, from collecting the annual coupon payment, that is, $\frac{\$50}{\$978.65} = 5.11\%$
			• The current yield changes over time as the bond price fluctuates

selection of the firm's board of directors) and to receive a **cash dividend**. (We show in Chapter 11 how firms make these dividend-paying decisions and how dividends are paid out.)

Consider the case of PEC, which is a public company. It has 200 million shares of common stock listed on the local stock exchange. The price of a share of PEC's common stock in early January is $15.97. This share price implies a **market capitalization** (the total market value of PEC's equity) of $3,194 million (200 million shares multiplied by $15.97). Note that a firm's market capitalization is different from the book or accounting value of its equity: the PEC balance sheet at the end of December (not shown here) indicates a **book value of equity** of $2,000 million. (See Chapter 4 for details on the accounting valuation of equity.) PEC reported net profits – also called earnings after tax (EAT) or net income – of $230 million for the year ending in December and distributed to its shareholders a total annual cash dividend of $160 million. With this information we can calculate a number of ratios to describe a company's common stock and compare them to the stocks of other firms. These ratios are summarized and defined in Exhibit 10.2.

The questions we want to answer later are: how is the price of PEC's shares today ($15.97) determined in the market, and why is it above its book value of $10 (see row 7 in Exhibit 10.2)?

THE DISCOUNTED CASH FLOW (DCF) MODEL

Before examining the specific valuation of bonds and stocks, we first introduce the **discounted cash flow (DCF) model** and show how to use it to value any security. The model is based on the concept of "the time value of money" introduced in Chapter 2. If you are not familiar with that concept, you should review Chapter 2 before proceeding.

According to the DCF model, *the value of a security is determined by the stream of cash flows the security is expected to generate in the future discounted to the present at a rate that reflects the risk of the cash-flow stream.* In other words, *it is the expectation that a security will generate future cash flows that makes it valuable.* When you buy a security, you are actually buying a future cash-flow stream. For example, the buyer of a PEC bond is buying an expected stream of five future coupon payments of $50 and a **terminal value** of $1,000. And a buyer of a PEC common stock is buying an expected perpetual stream of future dividend payments. To apply the DCF model we need two inputs: (1) an estimate of the expected cash flow the security will generate at the *end of each year* in the future (CF_1, CF_2, . . .), and (2) an estimate of the discount rate (k) that is required to convert this estimated future cash-flow stream into a present value. The model is expressed as follows:

$$\text{Security Value} = \frac{CF_1}{(1 + k)} + \frac{CF_2}{(1 + k)^2} + \cdots + \frac{CF_t}{(1 + k)^t} + \cdots \quad (10.1)$$

What is the appropriate discount rate (k)? It is the rate required by the security buyers to compensate them for (1) the time value of money (they have to wait to get the full stream of cash flows), and (2) the risk of the future cash-flow stream (the issuer may not be able to pay the expected cash-flow stream). In the case of bonds, the discount rate is the return required by bondholders. In the case of common stocks, it is the return required by shareholders. Note that *the riskier the security,*

EXHIBIT 10.2	COMMON STOCK FEATURES AND TERMINOLOGY.

PUBLICLY TRADED SHARES OF THE PACIFIC ENGINEERING COMPANY (PEC)

Data	Symbol	Definition	Value
PRIMARY DATA			
1. Share price	P	The stock market price of one share	$15.97
2. Number of shares	N	The number of shares issued by the company	200 million
3. Market capitalization	V_E	The market value of the firm's equity = The market value of all issued shares ($V_E = N \times P$)	$3,194 million
4. Book value	BV	The accounting value of the firm's equity reported in its balance sheet	$2,000 million
5. Earnings after tax	EAT	Earnings after tax reported in the firm's income statement	$230 million
6. Dividend payment	Div	The amount of annual cash dividend paid out to shareholders	$160 million
PER SHARE DATA			
7. Book value per share	BVS	$\dfrac{BV}{N} = \dfrac{\$2,000m}{200m}$	$10
8. Earnings per share	EPS	$\dfrac{EAT}{N} = \dfrac{\$230m}{200m}$	$1.15
9. Dividend per share	DPS	$\dfrac{Div}{N} = \dfrac{\$160m}{200m}$	$0.80
RATIOS			
10. Price-to-book ratio	PBR	$\dfrac{P}{BVS} = \dfrac{\$15.97}{\$10}$	1.60[1]
11. Price-to-earnings ratio	PER	$\dfrac{P}{EPS} = \dfrac{\$15.97}{\$1.15}$	13.89[2]
12. Dividend yield	DPS/P	$\dfrac{DPS}{P} = \dfrac{\$0.80}{\$15.97}$	5.01%[3]
13. Profit retention rate	b	$\dfrac{EAT - Div}{EAT} = \dfrac{\$70 \text{ million}}{\$230 \text{ million}}$	30.43%[4]
14. Dividend payout ratio	1 – b	$\dfrac{Div}{EAT} = \dfrac{\$160 \text{ million}}{\$230 \text{ million}}$	69.57%[5]

[1] The market is pricing PEC's share at a 60-percent premium over PEC's book value.
[2] The market is pricing PEC's shares at $13.89 for every dollar of PEC's EPS, that is, at 13.89 times its EPS.
[3] The return to shareholders, based on today's price, from collecting the annual dividend per share.
[4] The portion of profits retained in the business and not paid out to shareholders.
[5] The portion of profits paid out to shareholders in cash dividends.

the higher the discount rate and the lower the security's present value. In other words, the riskier the security, the less desirable it is and the lower its price. How is that discount rate determined? We answer this question in this chapter for the case of bonds. For common stocks, the return required by shareholders was introduced in Chapter 3 and its estimation is described in Chapter 12.

VALUING BONDS

If T is the current maturity of a bond, CP_1 to CP_T its stream of annual coupon payments, F its face value, and y the discount rate that reflects the riskiness of the bond's expected cash-flow stream, then the **bond price**, or **bond value**, derived from equation (10.1), is:

$$\text{Bond price} = \text{Bond value} = \frac{CP_1}{(1 + y)} + \frac{CP_2}{(1 + y)^2} + \dots + \frac{CP_T + F}{(1 + y)^T} \quad (10.2)$$

The discount rate y is called the bond's yield to maturity, market yield or simply the **bond yield.** We show later how it is determined. Just think of the yield to maturity as an indicator of the annual return bondholders will earn if they held the bond to maturity and reinvested the intermediate coupon payments at that yield (we examine this reinvestment assumption later in the chapter).

In this section, we first show (1) how to calculate the price of a bond when its yield is known, and (2) how to calculate the yield of a bond when its price is known. After presenting some conventions regarding how bond prices and yields are quoted, we examine the cases of two particular types of bonds: **zero-coupon bonds** and **perpetual bonds**.

FINDING THE PRICE OF A BOND WHEN ITS YIELD IS KNOWN

Let's use the bond pricing equation 10.2 to find the price of the PEC bond described in Exhibit 10.1. The bond has a current maturity of five years. This means that its expected cash-flow stream has five future annual cash flows. The first *four* annual cash flows are equal to the bond's annual coupon payment of $50 assumed to be paid at the *end* of each year as illustrated earlier on the bond's timeline. The fifth and last cash flow, to be received when the bond matures, is equal to $1,050, the sum of the last coupon payment ($50) and the bond's face value ($1,000). We have:

$$\text{Bond Price (PEC)} = \frac{\$50}{(1 + y)} + \frac{\$50}{(1 + y)^2} + \frac{\$50}{(1 + y)^3} + \frac{\$50}{(1 + y)^4} + \frac{\$50 + \$1,000}{(1 + y)^5} \quad (10.3)$$

To calculate the price of a PEC bond with the above equation we need to know the bond yield (y). What is it? It must be equal to the yield of five-year corporate bonds with *the same risk* as the PEC bond. Suppose that five-year corporate bonds with the same risk as the PEC bond are currently priced to yield 5.5 percent (0.50 percent higher than the 5 percent coupon rate offered last year on PEC bonds). In this case, *PEC bonds must also be priced to yield 5.5 percent otherwise no investors would buy them.*[6] The yield to maturity to apply to equation 10.3 is thus 5.5 percent. With a yield of 5.5 percent, the price of a PEC bond is $978.65:

---

[6] This answer may not be satisfactory as you may rightly ask how the yield of the comparative bond (5.5 percent) is determined. We explain this later in the chapter.

$$\text{Bond Price(PEC)} = \frac{\$50}{(1+5.5\%)} + \frac{\$50}{(1+5.5\%)^2} + \frac{\$50}{(1+5.5\%)^3} + \frac{\$50}{(1+5.5\%)^4} + \frac{\$1,050}{(1+5.5\%)^5} = \$978.65$$

We show next how to use a financial calculator or a spreadsheet to quickly find the price of a bond if we know its yield.

USING A FINANCIAL CALCULATOR TO FIND THE PRICE OF A BOND

You can find the price of a bond using a financial calculator if you know the bond's yield to maturity. Refer to the section on the use of financial calculators in Chapter 2 in which the relevant calculator keys are described. In the case of a bond, the N key is the bond's term to maturity,[7] the I/YR key is the bond's yield to maturity (without the percentage sign), the PV key is the bond price, the PMT key is the bond's periodic coupon payments, and FV key is the bond's face value.

To find the price of the PEC bond enter 5 and press the N key, enter 5.50 and press the I/YR key, enter 50 and press the PMT key, enter 1000 and press the FV key. Now press the PV key and the calculator screen will display a bond price of −978.65. The negative sign means that you have to pay $978.65 today (a cash *out*flow) in order to receive the bond's future cash *in*flows.

USING A SPREADSHEET TO FIND THE PRICE OF A BOND

You can also find the price of a PEC bond using the spreadsheet function *PV* as follows:

	A	B
1	Yield to maturity	5.50%
2	Number of periods (term to maturity)	5
3	Coupon payment	$50
4	Principal repayment	$1,000
5	**Bond price**	<u>$978.65</u>

* The formula in cell B5 is = −PV (B1, B2, B3, B4)

HOW CHANGES IN YIELD AFFECT BOND PRICES

We have calculated below the price of the PEC bond with different market yields starting with a yield of zero up to a yield of 10 percent (check these prices with your financial calculator or spreadsheet):

Yield	0	2%	4%	5%	5.50%	6%	8%	10%
Price	$1,250	$1,141.40	$1,044.52	$1,000	$978.65	$957.88	$880.22	$810.46

---

[7] Recall that we use T (for time) to indicate the number of years whereas financial calculators usually use the letter N.

You can see clearly that *there is an inverse relationship between bond yields and bond prices*: when the yield goes *up* from zero to 10 percent, the price of the bond goes *down* from a high of $1,250 to a low of $810.46. At a zero yield, there are no time-related adjustments to the future cash flows and the bond price is the sum of its five cash flows, that is, $1,250 (five coupons of $50 each plus the $1,000 of face value). When the yield is not zero, the bond price is lower than $1,250 to account for the fact that a future dollar is worth less than a dollar today, and the higher the yield, the lower the price of the bond.

Bond Price versus Face Value

Refer to the previous relationship between the price of the PEC bond and its yield to maturity. As you may have noticed, when the yield is the same as the coupon rate (5 percent), the bond price is equal to its face value and the bond is said to trade *at par*. When the market yield is *above* the coupon rate, the bond price is *below* its face value and the bond is said to trade at a **discount from par value**. When the market yield is *below* the coupon rate, the bond price is *above* its face value and the bond is said to trade at a **premium from par value**.

At a yield of 5.5 percent, the PEC bond is priced at a discount from face value. If an investor holds the bond to maturity, she will realize a capital *gain* of $21.35 ($1,000 less $978.65) on the day the bond matures. She thus gets her yield to maturity of 5.5 percent through the 5 percent coupon rate and the capital gain. If the yield on PEC bonds were 5 percent, the entire bond yield would be earned through the 5 percent coupon rate. And if the yield were lower than 5 percent, say 4 percent, the bond would be priced at a premium from face value ($1,044.52) and the investor would incur a capital *loss* of $44.52 at maturity ($1,000 less $1,044.52) which reduces the bond yield below its 5 percent coupon rate (to 4 percent).

Finding the Yield of a Bond when its Price is Known

So far, we have shown how to find the price of a bond if we know its yield. We now want to do the reverse, that is, we want to find the bond yield if we know its price. Let's do it with the PEC bond. Its price is $978.65, what is its yield (y)? It is the solution to the following equation:

$$\$978.65 = \frac{\$50}{(1 + y)^1} + \frac{\$50}{(1 + y)^2} + \frac{\$50}{(1 + y)^3} + \frac{\$50}{(1 + y)^4} + \frac{\$50}{(1 + y)^5}$$

Unfortunately, we cannot solve this equation explicitly to get the yield (y). We can only find the yield through a trial-and-error search, that is, we must enter different values of "y" into the equation until we find the one that provides a price of $978.65.[8] Of course, you do not have to go through this tedious process. Financial calculators and spreadsheets will do it, as illustrated below.

---

[8] This is the same issue we encountered in Chapter 8 when we wanted to find a project's internal rate of return (IRR). We could only get it through a trial-and-error search. You may have noticed that a bond's yield to maturity is the IRR of the investment in the bond. Thus, a bond's net present value (NPV) calculated at its market yield must be zero because the IRR is the rate that makes the NPV zero. In other words, buying a bond at its market price is a zero NPV investment.

Using a Financial Calculator to Find the Yield of a Bond

To find the yield of the PEC bond given its price of $978.65, go through the following steps. Enter 5 and press the N key, enter −978.65 and press the PV key, enter 50 and press the PMT key, enter 1000 and press the FV key. Now press the I/YR key and the calculator screen will display 5.50, which is the bond's 5.50 percent yield to maturity. As mentioned earlier, you can think of the yield to maturity as an indicator of the average return you would earn if you purchased the bond at $978.65 and held it to maturity with the assumption that you would reinvest the four intermediate coupon payments at that yield.

Using a Spreadsheet to Find the Yield of a Bond

You can also find the yield of the PEC bond using the spreadsheet function *RATE* as follows:

	A	B
1	Number of periods	5
2	Coupon payment	$50
3	Bond price	$978.65
4	Principal repayment	$1,000
5	**Yield to maturity**	**5.50%**

- *The formula in cell B5 is =RATE (B1, B2, −B3, B4)*

The Market Yield of a Bond is the Cost of Debt to the Firm

PEC bonds were issued at par *last year* at 5 percent with a face value of $1,000. A year later their price is down to $978.65. What is PEC's cost of debt *today*? It is not the 5 percent coupon rate. It is not even the bond's **current yield** of 5.11 percent $\left(\dfrac{\$50}{\$978.65}\right)$ shown in Exhibit 10.1. PEC's cost of debt is the market yield of 5.50 percent *because this is the rate PEC would have to pay today if it issued five-year bonds.*

Price Quotation and Yield Conventions

There are a number of conventions regarding how bond prices and yields are quoted and calculated. We review some of them below.

Quoted Price

The price of a bond depends on the size of its face value; in the case of the PEC bond the face value is $1,000 and the price is $978.65. If the face value were $10,000 the price would be $9,786.50. In order to avoid having to specify the face value, *bond prices are usually quoted as a percentage of face value*; for example, the price of a PEC bond would be quoted as 97.8650 percent or simply 97.8650, irrespective of the size of its face value.

PRICING AND YIELD WITH SEMI-ANNUAL COUPON PAYMENTS

The PEC bond pays its coupon annually ($50 every year). Other bonds may pay their coupon every six months.[9] If the PEC bond paid its coupon semi-annually, the coupon payment would be $25 every six months (instead of $50 every 12 months). If the price of the bond is $978.65, the six-month yield, which is equal to $\frac{y}{2}$ (instead of 'y' for 12 months), must be the solution to the following pricing equation (note that there are now ten periods of six months):

$$\$978.65 = \frac{\$25}{\left(1 + \dfrac{y}{2}\right)} + \frac{\$25}{\left(1 + \dfrac{y}{2}\right)^2} + \ldots + \frac{\$25}{\left(1 + \dfrac{y}{2}\right)^9} + \frac{\$1,025}{\left(1 + \dfrac{y}{2}\right)^{10}}$$

To find the yield, enter the following information in your calculator: N = 10, PV = −978.65, PMT = 25, and FV = 1000. Press the I/YR key and you get a semi-annual yield $\left(\dfrac{y}{2}\right)$ of 2.7471 percent.[10] The annualized yield is thus 5.4942 percent, that is, 2.7471 percent multiplied by two. This annualized yield is called the **bond equivalent yield**. It is the yield reported in the financial press.

PRICE QUOTATION BETWEEN COUPON PAYMENTS

When we priced the PEC bond, we assumed that the first $50 of coupon payment would be received in precisely one year. What if we wanted to price the bond between two coupon dates, for example, exactly half-way between two coupon dates? In this case half of the next coupon payment of $50 belongs to the bond seller and the other half to the bond buyer. Because the bond buyer will collect $50 in six months she must compensate the bond seller by paying her $25 of so-called **accrued interest** (which is the part of the coupon payment she does not own). The **invoice price** (also called the **full price** or the **dirty price**) that the buyer pays the seller consists of the **clean** or **flat price** of $978.65 (which is the **quoted price** in the financial press) plus $25 of accrued interest.[11]

THE CASE OF ZERO-COUPON BONDS

As their name indicates, **zero-coupon bonds** do not pay any coupon. These bonds, also called **zeros**, are issued at an *original discount* from their face value and redeemed at maturity for their face value. Bondholders earn their return on investment entirely through capital gains (the difference between the price at which the bond was purchased and its face value).

---

[9] The frequency of coupon payments varies across countries. It is annual in Germany, France, the Netherlands, and Switzerland, and for international bonds (see Chapter 11). It is semi-annual in the US, the UK, Japan, Canada, and Australia. In some rare cases, the coupon is paid quarterly.

[10] Alternatively, you could use a spreadsheet function *RATE*, as we did earlier.

[11] This convention is not universal. For example, UK government bonds are quoted on an **ex-coupon date** basis. In this case, the bonds are traded without the next coupon payment about one month before the coupon is paid. The investor who buys the bond after the *ex-date* does not receive the coupon, which goes to the seller. In this case, the invoice price drops on the *ex-date* as the buyer loses the right to the next coupon.

FINDING THE PRICE OF A ZERO-COUPON BOND WHEN ITS YIELD IS KNOWN

Consider the zero-coupon bonds issued by the Southern Electric Company (SEC) to raise $50 million.[12] The bonds have a five-year maturity and a face value of $1,000. Their yield to maturity is 5.80 percent. What is their price? All intermediate cash flows (from CF_1 to CF_4) are zero and the terminal cash flow (CF_5) is equal to $1,000 (the face value). The bond price (P_Z) is thus equal to the present value of $1,000 to be received in five years and discounted to the present at a rate of 5.80 percent:

$$\text{Zero-Coupon Bond Price} = P_Z = \frac{\$1,000}{(1 + 0.058)^5} = \$754.35$$

You can find the price with a financial calculator by entering the following inputs: N = 5, I/YR = 5.8, PMT = 0, and FV = 1000. Press the PV key. Your calculator screen shows a bond price of −754.35. You could also get the bond price by entering the appropriate figures for a zero-coupon bond in the spreadsheet we used earlier to find the PEC bond price. How many bonds will SEC have to issue to raise the $50 million? Because each bond is worth $754.35, SEC will have to issue about 66,283 bonds (50 million divided by 754.35).

In general, the price of a zero-coupon bond (P_Z) with T years to maturity, a face value F and a yield y is given by the following formula:

$$P_Z = \frac{F}{(1 + y)^T} = F \times DF_{T,y} \tag{10.4}$$

where $DF_{T,y}$ is the discount factor at the rate y for T years. In the case of the SEC bond, the discount factor ($DF_{5,5.8\%}$) is equal to 0.75435 and the bond price is $1,000 times 0.75453, that is, $754.35. Note that *the price of a zero-coupon bond with a face value of $1 is equal to the discount factor.*

Why would an investor prefer a zero-coupon bond to a coupon-paying bond with the same maturity and issuer? For example, why would an investor prefer the SEC five-year zero-coupon bond over a PEC five-year, 5-percent coupon bond? One reason is that the five-year zero-coupon bond has no **reinvestment risk** if held to maturity. If an investor buys the coupon-paying bond and holds it for five years, he will receive a $50 coupon every year that will have to be reinvested. For example, the first $50 he will receive in one year will have to be reinvested for four years at a rate *unknown* today to the investor. This is what we call reinvestment risk; it is the risk of not knowing your return on investment when you buy a coupon-paying bond and hold it to maturity. A zero-coupon bond is not exposed to reinvestment risk *if held to maturity* because there are no coupon payments to reinvest. If the owner of a five-year SEC zero-coupon bond holds it to maturity, he will get a return equal to the bond's yield to maturity of 5.8 percent no matter what happens to future interest rates.[13]

---

[12] The first public issue of a zero-coupon bond in the US market was made in April 1981 by JC Penney (a department store). In June of the same year, PepsiCo Overseas issued a three-year zero-coupon Eurobond at 67.25 percent of face value to yield 14.14 percent.

[13] Note that if the zero-coupon bond is sold *before* its maturity date, its price will depend on the prevailing interest rate on that day. The bond is in this case exposed to reinvestment risk. In other words, the reinvestment risk of a zero-coupon bond depends on the investor's holding period. If held for five years, the five-year zero-coupon bond has no reinvestment risk. If held for less than five years it is exposed to reinvestment risk.

FINDING THE YIELD OF A ZERO-COUPON BOND WHEN ITS PRICE IS KNOWN

The yield of a zero-coupon bond is found by solving the pricing equation 10.4 for the yield y:

$$y = \left(\frac{F}{P_Z}\right)^{\frac{1}{T}} - 1 \qquad (10.5)$$

What is the yield of a six-year zero-coupon bond priced at $697.03? According to equation 10.5 we have:

$$y = \left(\frac{\$1,000}{\$697.03}\right)^{\frac{1}{6}} - 1 = (1.4347)^{\frac{1}{6}} - 1 = 0.0620 = 6.20\%$$

Given its price of $697.03, the six-year zero-coupon bond has a yield to maturity of 6.20 percent. To find the yield on a financial calculator, enter N = 6, PV = −697.03, PMT = 0, and FV = 1000. Press the I/YR key. You get a yield of 6.20 percent.[14]

THE CASE OF PERPETUAL BONDS

Perpetual bonds are bonds that never mature; the issuer continues to pay the coupon forever. This raises the immediate question of whether the issuer will be around forever. Because of this uncertainty, perpetual bonds have usually been issued by governments (for example, the British and French governments issued perpetual bonds in the 19th century) although some non-government entities, such as banks, have issued perpetual bonds in the past.

Suppose the Northern Banking Company (NBC) wishes to raise funds through an issue of perpetual bonds with a 5 percent coupon rate and a $1,000 face value. If investors require a yield of 6 percent on this type of bond, what is the issue price? The bonds are expected to pay an annual coupon of $50 (5 percent of $1,000). Their price is thus the present value of a $50 perpetual cash-flow stream. We have shown in Chapter 2 that the present value of a perpetual cash flow is equal to the annual cash flow ($50 in our case) divided by the discount rate (the 6-percent market yield in our case). The price of NBC's perpetual bond is thus:

$$P_{perp} = \frac{\text{Coupon payment}}{\text{Market yield}} = \frac{c \times F}{y} = \frac{5\% \times \$1,000}{6\%} = \frac{\$50}{0.06} = \$833.3 \qquad (10.6)$$

Although firms rarely issue perpetual bonds, some have issued so-called century bonds, that is, bonds with a 100-year maturity.[15] Because of its very long maturity, the price of a century bond is very close to the price of an equivalent perpetual bond. To see this, assume that the 5 percent NBC bond is a century bond. What would be its price at the 6 percent market yield? Using a financial calculator, enter the following inputs: N = 100, I/YR = 6, PMT = 50, and FV = 1000. You find PV = −833.82. The price of the century bond is only $0.49 higher than the price of the perpetual bond ($833.33).

---

[14] Alternatively, you could use a spreadsheet function *RATE*, as we did earlier.

[15] During the 1990s, more than 40 US companies issued century bonds, including IBM.

A CLOSER LOOK AT BOND YIELDS AND RISK

Refer to the characteristics of the PEC bond shown in Exhibit 10.1. It has a current maturity of 5 years, a coupon rate of 5 percent and a face value of $1,000. We found its price of $978.65 by discounting its expected cash-flow stream at 5.5 percent, the market yield on 5-year corporate bonds with the same risk as the PEC bond. How is that rate determined? And how is the risk of a bond measured? We answer these questions in this section.

RISK IS THE MAJOR DETERMINANT OF A BOND'S YIELD

A bond's market yield should compensate bondholders for (1) the time value of money (they have to wait to get the full stream of cash flows) and (2) the risk of the future cash-flow stream (the issuer may not be able to pay the promised cash-flow stream). We first examine the two major risks faced by a holder of a corporate bond: **credit risk** and **interest-rate risk**. We then look at how the time value of money interacts with risk to determine a bond's market yield.

Credit risk (also called **default risk**) occurs because the issuing firm may not be able to *service* its bonds (it may not be able to pay the promised coupons on their scheduled dates and/or repay the bond's face value on its maturity date). Interest-rate risk (also called **market risk**) occurs because the price of bonds fluctuates *unpredictably* in response to *unexpected* changes in the level of interest rates. In the following sections we first examine credit risk and then interest-rate risk.

CREDIT RISK, CREDIT RATINGS, AND CREDIT SPREADS

Firms that want to sell their bonds to the public are usually required to first obtain a **credit rating** from a **credit rating agency**, such as Moody's or Standard & Poor's. The **bond rating** provides an overall assessment of the bond's credit risk. For example, Standard & Poor's assigns a triple A rating (AAA) to bonds with the highest financial strength, followed by double A, single A, and triple B ratings. Bonds that have been assigned one of these four top ratings are known as **investment-grade bonds**. Bonds with lower ratings (BB, B, and CCC) are known as **speculative-grade bonds, junk bonds**, or **high-yield bonds**.[16]

Look at Exhibit 10.3. It shows the yield on 10-year corporate bonds with different credit ratings as well as the yield on 10-year government bonds[17] on the same date. Government bonds typically have the lowest yield followed by corporate bonds with the highest credit rating (AAA). As the credit rating weakens, the yield of corporate bonds rises. Exhibit 10.3 shows the additional return offered by corporate bonds over government bonds for each credit rating.

This extra return is called a **credit spread, yield spread**, or **credit risk premium**. Note that the size of credit spread increases as the credit rating weakens.

---

[16] In many countries, institutional investors such as pension funds and insurance companies are usually restricted by regulation to only buy investment-grade bonds.

[17] Because bonds are denominated in US dollars, the government in our case is the US Treasury.

| EXHIBIT 10.3 | BOND RATINGS AND MARKET YIELDS FOR 10-YEAR BONDS.[1] | |

THE YIELD AND THE CREDIT SPREAD RISE WHEN THE RATING WEAKENS

Bond Rating	Market Yield	Credit Spread over the Government Bond
Government	3.50%	—
AAA	4.54%	1.04% (104 basis points)
AA	4.88%	1.38% (138 basis points)
A	5.48%	1.98% (198 basis points)
BBB	6.06%	2.56% (256 basis points)

[1] Because we use the US dollar, the government in this case is the US Treasury. The data reported in the table do not correspond to actual figures on a particular date. They are only illustrative.

CREDIT SPREADS AND THE COST OF DEBT

Government bonds are considered the least risky of all bonds because the government is least likely to default on its debt obligations.[18] For this reason, *the yield on government bonds is typically the lowest yield in the market and, in practice, government bonds are considered to be default-free bonds.* As the credit risk rises, the yield of corporate bonds goes up because bondholders require a higher return to hold riskier bonds. Consequently, the yield of a corporate bond (y_{Corp}) can be expressed as the sum of two components: (1) the yield of government bonds (y_{gov}) with the same maturity, and (2) a credit risk premium to compensate bondholders for the credit risk of corporate bonds:

$$y_{Crop} = y_{Gov} + \text{Credit Risk Premium} \qquad (10.7)$$

As indicated by equation 10.7, *government bonds are the benchmark against which corporate bond yields are calculated.* In other words, if you want to get an estimate of the cost of debt of a particular company over a specific maturity, you must first find out the yield on government bonds with the same maturity and add to that default-free yield a credit risk premium equal to the average credit spread of corporate bonds with the same credit rating as the company. To illustrate, suppose that PEC is considering issuing a 10-year bond at a time when 10-year government bonds are offering 3.50 percent. If PEC's credit rating is BBB and the average credit spread for 10-year BBB bonds is 2.56 percent, then the estimated cost of PEC's 10-year debt is 6.06 percent, the riskless rate of 3.50 percent plus a credit risk premium of 2.56 percent. Note that the size of the credit risk premium is not fixed; it varies over time with changes in market conditions and outlook as shown in Exhibit 10.4 in the case of US credit spreads. Notice the spikes in the credit spreads during periods of financial crises such as the 2007–2009 period.

---

[18] This does not mean that governments never default on their debt obligations. But government defaults in most developed countries are very rare events that are much less likely to occur than corporate defaults.

EXHIBIT 10.4	CREDIT SPREADS BETWEEN US CORPORATE BONDS AND 10-YEAR US GOVERNMENT BONDS.

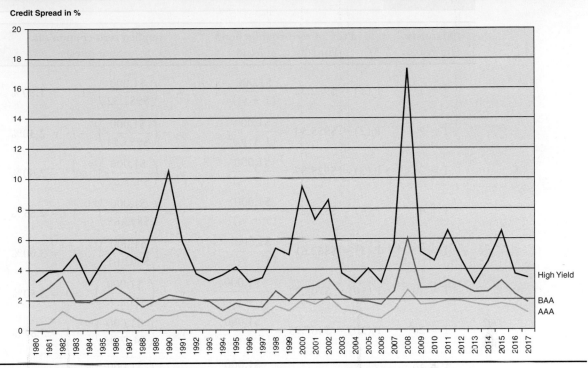

Source: Federal Reserve Bank (www.federalreserve.gov) and Federal Reserve Bank of St. Louis (www.stlouisfed.org).

THE TERM STRUCTURE OF INTEREST RATES

When zero-coupon bonds are issued by the government they are called **pure discount bonds** and their riskless yields are called **spot interest rates** or simply spot rates.

Look at Exhibit 10.5. The second column reports the price of zero-coupon government bonds for the different maturities shown in the first column. The third column reports the bonds' spot rates calculated with equation 10.5. The resulting sequence of spot rates is called the **term structure of interest rates** because it provides the spot rates for different terms to maturity (in our case from 1 year up to 30 years).

SPOT YIELD CURVES

The **spot yield curve** is a graph of the term structure of interest rates. It shows the relationship between different spot rates and their corresponding maturity on a given date (because rates change every day, one can draw a new **yield curve** every day). Exhibit 10.6 shows the spot yield curve drawn with the data in Exhibit 10.5.

The term to maturity is on the horizontal axis and the corresponding spot yields are on the vertical axis. The yield curve is rising (it is said to be upward sloping) because the spot rates increase when maturity is lengthened. If spot rates were not

EXHIBIT 10.5	SAME DATE PRICES AND RATES OF RISKLESS ZERO-COUPON GOVERNMENT BONDS WITH DIFFERENT MATURITIES.[1]

Maturity (in years)	Price of zero-coupon bond (Pure discount bonds)	Implied zero-coupon rate (Spot rates)
T = 1	$P_z(1) = \$982.32 = \dfrac{\$1,000}{(1 + y_1)}$	$y_1 = \left(\dfrac{\$1,000}{\$982.32}\right) - 1 = 1.80\%$
T = 2	$P_z(2) = \$955.54 = \dfrac{\$1,000}{(1 + y_2)^2}$	$y_2 = \left(\dfrac{\$1,000}{\$955.54}\right)^{1/2} - 1 = 2.30\%$
T = 3	$P_z(3) = \$925.87 = \dfrac{\$1,000}{(1 + y_3)^3}$	$y_3 = \left(\dfrac{\$1,000}{\$925.87}\right)^{1/3} - 1 = 2.60\%$
T = 4	$P_z(4) = \$893.68 = \dfrac{\$1,000}{(1 + y_4)^4}$	$y_4 = \left(\dfrac{\$1,000}{\$893.68}\right)^{1/4} - 1 = 2.85\%$
T = 5	$P_z(5) = \$862.61 = \dfrac{\$1,000}{(1 + y_5)^5}$	$y_5 = \left(\dfrac{\$1,000}{\$862.61}\right)^{1/5} - 1 = 3.00\%$
T = 10	$P_z(10) = \$708.92 = \dfrac{\$1,000}{(1 + y_{10})^{10}}$	$y_{10} = \left(\dfrac{\$1,000}{\$708.92}\right)^{1/10} - 1 = 3.50\%$
T = 20	$P_z(20) = \$467.95 = \dfrac{\$1,000}{(1 + y_{20})^{20}}$	$y_{20} = \left(\dfrac{\$1,000}{\$467.95}\right)^{1/20} - 1 = 3.87\%$
T = 30	$P_z(30) = \$291.05 = \dfrac{\$1,000}{(1 + y_{30})^{30}}$	$y_{30} = \left(\dfrac{\$1,000}{\$291.05}\right)^{1/30} - 1 = 4.20\%$

[1] The data reported in the table do not correspond to actual figures on a particular date. They are only illustrative.

available we could have drawn a yield curve using coupon-paying government bonds with different maturities.[19]

CORPORATE YIELD CURVES

We can also draw corporate yield curves as shown in Exhibit 10.7. Each curve is drawn for a specific credit rating, meaning that all corporate bonds on the curve have the same credit rating and thus the same credit risk. Note that the corporate yield curves are above the government yield curve, and the lower the rating the higher the yield curve. This is the case because the yield on corporate bonds is higher than the yield on default-free government bonds with the same maturity, as indicated in equation 10.7. For a given maturity and a given credit rating, the distance between the corporate yield curve and the government yield curve is the credit spread or credit risk premium for that maturity and rating. As indicated in Exhibit 10.7, the five-year credit risk premium is 1 percent for AAA corporate

[19] The yield curves reported in the financial press are usually based on coupon-paying government bonds. Note, however, that if zero-coupon yields are not available, one can always extract these yields from coupon-paying bonds. See how to do this in self-test question 10.3.

EXHIBIT 10.6	THE SPOT YIELD CURVE.

A GRAPH OF THE RELATIONSHIP BETWEEN THE ZERO-COUPON RATES AND THE MATURITIES OF RISKLESS ZERO-COUPON GOVERNMENT BONDS BASED ON THE RATES IN EXHIBIT 10.5 AND DRAWN ON THE SAME DATE

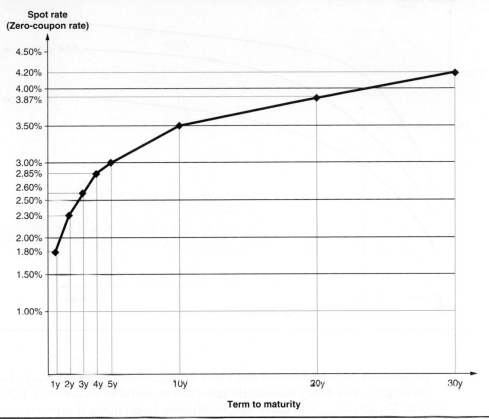

bonds (4 percent less 3 percent) and 2.50 percent for BBB corporate bonds (5.50 percent less 3 percent).

EXPLAINING THE SHAPE OF THE YIELD CURVE

The shape of the spot yield curve changes constantly over time because interest rates fluctuate. In general, the curves are rising – as shown in Exhibit 10.7 – because long-term rates are usually higher than short-term rates for the same issuer. The reason long-term rates are higher is because, as we show below, long-term bonds are exposed to higher interest-rate risk: for a given change in interest rates, their prices fluctuate more than the prices of short-term bonds. For this reason, bondholders demand, and receive, higher yield to hold bonds with longer maturities.

But yield curves can also be declining or downward sloping. This occurs when short-term rates are *higher* than long-term rates. Why would this happen? It could happen if short-term rates are currently high relative to their historical average and the market expects them to go down in the future. For example, assume that current inflation is high, which pushes short-term rates up. If the market expects the

EXHIBIT 10.7   CORPORATE YIELD CURVES.

CORPORATE YIELD CURVES ARE ABOVE THE DEFAULT-FREE GOVERNMENT BONDS

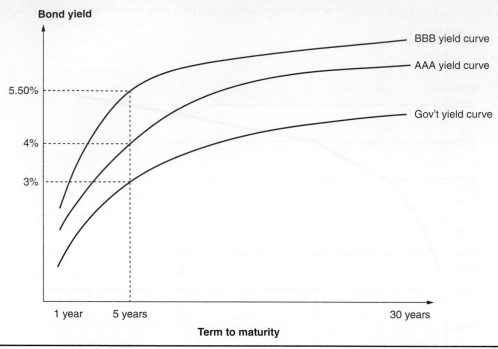

government to fight inflation and lower its rate, investors would accept lower rates on longer bonds if they believed the government would be successful in fighting inflation. The resulting yield curve will, in this case, be declining if expectations of lower future inflation rates have a more powerful downward effect on longer rates than the upward effect that interest-rate risk has on longer rates.

For example, assume that a majority of firms expect interest rates to fall in the future because they feel confident that the inflation rate will go down. In that case, many firms would prefer borrowing short-term to avoid paying high interest rates for a long time in the future. As a result, the demand for long-term bonds will decrease, which will force long-term investors to accept lower rates. This phenomenon may cause long-term rates to be lower than short-term rates for a certain period of time. During this period, the resulting yield curve will be declining.

FORWARD RATES

Refer to the yield curve in Exhibit 10.6. The 1-year spot rate (y_1) is 1.80 percent and the two-year spot rate (y_2) is 2.30 percent. Suppose you have a two-year investment horizon. You can invest one dollar for two years and earn the 2-year spot rate. At the end of the two-year period you will have $(1+y_2)^2$ dollars, that is, $(\$1.023)^2 = \$1.0465$. Alternatively, you can invest one dollar for one year, earn the 1-year spot rate and invest your earnings of $(1+y_1)$ dollars, that is, $\$1.0180$, for a second year at a rate f_1, called the 1-year **forward rate**. At the end of the two-year period you will have $(1+y_1)\times(1+f_1)$ dollars. What exactly is the forward rate? It is the rate, *known to you today*, that will make you *indifferent* between investing over two years at the 2-year spot rate and investing over one year at the 1-year spot rate and a second year at the 1-year forward rate.

If you're indifferent between the two investment strategies, the forward rate can be calculated by solving the following equation in which the left side is your return on the two-year investment strategy and the right side is your return on the sequence of two one-year investments:

$$(1 + y_2)^2 = (1 + y_1) \times (1 + f_1)$$

from which we get:

$$f_1 = \frac{(1 + y_2)^2}{(1 + y_1)} - 1 \qquad (10.8)$$

In our case, the 1-year forward rate is thus:

$$f_1 = \frac{(1.0230)^2}{1.0180} - 1 = \frac{1.0465}{1.0180} - 1 = 1.0280 - 1 = 0.0280 = 2.80\%$$

Note that the 2-year spot rate is an average of the 1-year spot rate and the 1-year forward rate (1.80 percent plus 2.80 percent divided by two is equal to 2.30 percent) and that the yield curve is rising because the 1-year forward rate is higher than the 1-year spot rate.

What is the usefulness of the forward rate? The forward rate is quite useful because *it is the rate known to you today at which you can borrow in one year*. Suppose you need $10,000 in one year's time for a period of one year. You don't want to take a chance and borrow in one year at a rate unknown to you today. *You can lock in today your borrowing rate at the forward rate* of 2.80 percent as follows: borrow $9,823 now[20] at 2.30 percent for two years (recall that 2.30 percent is the prevailing 2-year spot rate). At the end of the second year you will have to repay $10,280, that is, $9,823 × (1.023)². Deposit the $9,823 for one year at 1.80 percent (recall that 1.80 percent is the prevailing 1-year spot rate). At the end of the year you will get $10,000, that is, $9,823 × (1.018). What is your one-year borrowing rate one year from now? It is the forward rate of 2.80 percent because you will receive $10,000 in a year and repay $10,280 a year later.

FINDING THE PRICE AND THE YIELD OF A BOND IF THE SPOT RATES ARE KNOWN

If you know the yield of a bond you can get its price using equation 10.2. And if you know the bond price you can get its yield using the same equation. There is another way to get the price and the yield of a coupon-paying bond if you know the spot rates. Consider a four-year government bond with a coupon rate of 4 percent and a face value of $1,000. The prevailing spot rates are those shown in Exhibit 10.5. If you do not have the bond yield you can use the spot rates to get the bond price. How? *Just notice that the four-year, 4 percent coupon bond is in effect a portfolio of four zero-coupon bonds.* Specifically, it is a portfolio containing a one-year zero with a face value of $40 (the first coupon), a two-year zero with a face value of $40 (the second coupon), a three-year zero with a face value of $40 (the third coupon), and a four-year zero with a face value of $1,040 (the last coupon and the face value).

---

[20] This is the present value of $10,000 in one year discounted to the present at 1.80 percent.

We can therefore get the price of the coupon bond as the sum of the prices of the four zero-coupon bonds that make up the bond:

$$P_{Gov} = \frac{\$40}{1+1.80\%} + \frac{\$40}{(1+2.30\%)^2} + \frac{\$40}{(1+2.60\%)^3} + \frac{\$40}{(1+2.85\%)^4} = \$1,043.98$$

and once you have the bond price, you can get its yield using a financial calculator. You should find a bond yield of 2.8219 percent. Check on the calculator that with a yield of 2.8219 percent you get the bond price of $1,043.98. In other words, the exact same price of $1,043.98 can be found either with the four spot rates or with the yield to maturity. *Think of a bond's yield to maturity as a weighted average of the spot rates*. The yield to maturity of 2.8219 percent is close to and slightly lower than the 4-year spot rate of 2.85 percent because the price (or weight) of the four-year zero-coupon bond is much higher than the price of the other three zero-coupon bonds.

INTEREST-RATE RISK

Recall that corporate bonds are exposed to both credit risk and interest-rate risk. Government bonds, however, are assumed to be default-free (they do not have credit risk) and therefore have only interest-rate risk. In other words, *all* bonds are exposed to interest-rate risk, irrespective of their issuer, because *their prices fluctuate unexpectedly in response to unanticipated changes in interest rates*. Consider the following example: the central bank raises interest rates unexpectedly (the reason may be that the bank wants to slow down the economy's inflationary pressure). As interest rates rise, the price of *all* bonds falls immediately (recall the inverse relationship between yield and prices). Had the central bank reduced interest rates unexpectedly, the price of *all* bonds would have risen unexpectedly.

Not all bonds, however, react to changes in interest rates in the same fashion; some bonds are more sensitive to a change in interest rates than others. In other words, *different bonds have different exposures to interest-rate risk*. We will show that *the longer a bond's term to maturity and the lower its coupon rate the higher its interest-rate risk*. This phenomenon is illustrated in Exhibit 10.8 with a comparison of three different bonds from the same issuer (they have the same credit risk): bond A is a ten-year, 6-percent coupon bond, bond B is a ten-year zero-coupon bond, and bond C is a 6-percent perpetual bond.

Their respective prices are calculated first at a market yield of 5 percent (in row 6) and again, at 5.2 percent (in row 7) in order to determine the immediate percentage change in price resulting from an unanticipated rise in yield of 20 basis points (0.20 percent). Look at row 8: the price of bond A drops by 1.49 percent, the price of bond B drops by 1.88 percent, and the price of bond C drops by 3.85 percent. In other words, bond C (the one with the longest maturity) is riskier than bond A (which has a shorter maturity but the same coupon rate), and bond B (the one with the lowest coupon rate) is riskier than bond A (which has the same maturity but a higher coupon rate).

Why do bonds with shorter maturity and higher coupon rates have less interest-rate risk? *Because with shorter maturities and higher coupon payments, bondholders get their money back sooner, which dampens the impact of changes in rates on the price of the bond.*

| EXHIBIT 10.8 | THE PRICING OF DIFFERENT TYPES OF BONDS AND THEIR SENSITIVITY TO CHANGES IN THE MARKET YIELD. | | |

Type of bond	Bond A Coupon bond	Bond B Zero-coupon bond	Bond C Perpetual bond
1. Maturity (T)	10 years	10 years	Infinite
2. Coupon rate (c)	6%	0%	6%
3. Face value (F)	$1,000	$1,000	$1,000
4. Coupon payment (CP)[1]	$60	$0	$60
5. Pricing formula[2]	$P = \dfrac{CP_1}{1 + y} + \ldots + \dfrac{CP_T + F}{(1 + y)^T}$	$P_z = \dfrac{F}{(1 + y)^T}$	$P_{Perp} = \dfrac{CP}{y}$
6. Price at yield = 5%[3]	$1,077.22	$613.91	$1,200.00
7. Price at yield = 5.2%[4]	$1,061.18	$602.34	$1,153.85
8. $\dfrac{Price(5.2\%) - Price(5\%)}{Price(5\%)}$	−1.49%	−1.88%	−3.85%

[1] row 2 × row 3.
[2] See equations 10.2, 10.4 and 10.6, respectively.
[3] Based on the formulas in row 5.
[4] Based on the formulas in row 5.

Here is a summary of how the prices of bonds with different maturities and different coupon rates react to changes in interest rates:

1. *If two bonds have the same coupon rate, the one with the longer maturity has a higher interest-rate risk.* This phenomenon is referred to as the **maturity effect** of a change in interest rates.
2. *If two bonds have the same maturity, the one with the lower coupon rate has a higher interest-rate risk.* This phenomenon is referred to as the **coupon effect** of a change in interest rates.
3. *The lower the market yield (all else remaining the same), the higher the bond's interest-rate risk.* This means that, irrespective of maturity and coupon rate, a bond will be more sensitive to a rise in yield from, say, 2 percent to 2.20 percent than a rise in yield from 5 percent to 5.2 percent. To illustrate, compare the percentage change in the price of bond A under the two scenarios. When the rate rises from 2 percent to 2.20 percent, its price drops by 1.58 percent (check this out with your calculator) compared to 1.49 percent when the rate rises from 5 percent to 5.20 percent (see row 8 in Exhibit 10.8).

DURATION AS A MEASURE OF INTEREST-RATE RISK

Consider the following two bonds: bond K and bond Q. The first has an 11-year maturity and a 6 percent coupon rate. The second has a 10-year maturity and a 2 percent coupon rate. Which bond has more interest-rate risk? If you compare their maturity, bond K is riskier (it has a longer maturity). If you compare their coupon rate, bond Q is riskier (it has a lower coupon rate). There is no way to tell which of the two bonds is riskier because we do not know if the maturity effect is stronger than the coupon effect or the other way around. We need a *comprehensive* measure of interest-rate risk that takes into account *both* the maturity effect and the coupon effect. Such a measure of interest-rate risk exists: it is called **duration** and is calculated in years. We show in Appendix 10.1 how to calculate a bond's duration. You are told that the duration of bond K is 8.70 years and that of bond Q is 9.12 years. Because the duration of bond K is *shorter* than the duration of bond Q you can unambiguously conclude that bond K has *less* interest-rate risk than bond Q even though it has a longer maturity. You will find in Appendix 10.1 a summary of the properties of duration and an explanation of why bonds with shorter durations have lower interest-rate risk.

VALUING COMMON STOCKS

We can now turn to the pricing of common stocks. There are two broad types of common stock valuation models: one type is based on discounted cash flow models (known as DCF models) and the other on the value of comparable firms (known as **valuation by comparables**). There are at least three DCF models: the **dividend-discount model**, the **free-cash-flow discount model** and the **cash-flow-to-equity-holders discount model**. We review these models in this section and show how to apply them to value PEC's common stocks. There are many comparative valuation methods. We present here the methods based on the **price-to-earnings ratio** (**P/E** or **PER**), the **price-to-book ratio** (**P/B** or **PBR**), and the **enterprise value-to-EBITDA ratio** (**EV/EBITDA**) where EBITDA is earnings before interest, tax, depreciation, and amortization.

VALUATION BASED ON THE DIVIDEND-DISCOUNT MODEL (DDM)

According to the **dividend-discount model** (DDM), a firm's share price is equal to the future stream of dividend per share (DPS) the firm is expected to distribute discounted to the present at the firm's **cost of equity** capital (k_E). Why is the discount rate equal to the cost of equity capital in this case? Recall that the appropriate discount rate must reflect the risk of the particular cash-flow stream being discounted. That risk is captured by the return expected by the investors to whom the cash-flow stream belongs. In the DDM, the cash-flow stream (which is the stream of dividend payments) belongs to shareholders, and the cost of equity is the return expected by shareholders on their equity investment in the firm. We can express the DDM as follows:

$$\text{Share Price} = \frac{\text{DPS}_1}{(1 + k_E)} + \frac{\text{DPS}_2}{(1 + k_E)^2} + \dots + \frac{\text{DPS}_t}{(1 + k_E)^t} + \dots \qquad (10.9)$$

where DPS_1, DPS_2, ... is the stream of expected annual dividends per share. The stream is a **perpetuity** because the firm is assumed to be a "going concern", meaning that the firm is managed under the assumption that it will operate forever. In order to get an estimate of the firm's share price according to equation 10.9 we need two inputs: (1) an estimate of the expected future DPS stream, and (2) an estimate of the firm's cost of equity (k_E).

One question that arises with this valuation model is: what would the share price be if the firm pays no dividends? If all the DPS in equation 10.9 are zero, the share price would also be zero. The answer is that no firm is expected to operate forever without paying dividends. A high-growth firm may not pay dividends for a while but, as growth eventually slows down, the firm will begin to distribute some of its free cash flow as dividends to its shareholders. One practical implication is that the DDM is not easily applicable to high-growth firms that are expected to begin paying dividends only in the very distant future. The model applies best to mature companies that pay stable and predictable dividends.

THE CONSTANT DIVIDEND-GROWTH MODEL

A special case of the dividend-discount model is the **constant dividend-growth model**. In this case, the annual dividends are expected to grow forever at the *same* rate "g". We have shown in Chapter 2 that the present value (PV) of a perpetual cash flow that begins next year with CF_1 and grows at a constant rate g, discounted to the present at the rate k, is:

$$PV = \frac{CF_1}{k - g} \qquad (10.10a)$$

Let's apply this model to estimate PEC's share price. CF_1 is the dividend per share PEC is expected to pay in one year, k is the firm's cost of equity, and g is the constant growth rate in dividends per share. Recall that PEC has just paid a dividend per share (DPS_0) of $0.80 (see row 9 in Exhibit 10.2). If the constant growth rate is 3.50 percent and the firm's cost of equity is 9 percent (we show below how to estimate these numbers), PEC's estimated share price (P_{PEC}) according to equation 10.10a is:

$$P_{PEC} = \frac{DPS_1}{k_E - g} = \frac{DPS_0(1 + g)}{k_E - g} = \frac{\$0.80 \times 1.035}{0.09 - 0.035} = \frac{\$0.828}{0.055} = \$15.05 \qquad (10.10b)$$

How did we get the constant growth rate of 3.50 percent and the cost of equity of 9 percent? The growth rate can be estimated by examining the historical growth rate of the firm's dividends and adjusting it for future expectations. It can be also determined with the sustainable growth formula introduced in Chapter 6 (see equation 6.12). According to that formula, the growth rate is equal to the firm's profit retention rate (b) multiplied by the firm's return on equity (ROE). In the case of PEC, the retention rate is 30.43 percent (see row 13 in Exhibit 10.2) and ROE is 11.50 percent ($230 million of profits divided by a book value of equity of $2,000 million as indicated in Exhibit 10.2, rows 5 and 4, respectively). The corresponding sustainable growth rate is thus 3.50 percent:

$$g = b \times ROE = 0.3043 \times 11.50\% = 3.5\%$$

The cost of equity has been estimated with the **Capital Asset Pricing Model (CAPM)** as shown in Chapter 3 (see equation 3.13a):

$$k_E = \text{Riskless rate} + (\text{Market Risk Premium} \times \text{Beta}) \qquad (10.11a)$$

In our case the long-term riskless rate is 3.5 percent (the 10-year spot rate in Exhibit 10.5) and the market risk premium is 5 percent.[21] Assuming that PEC has an estimated beta of 1.10,[22] PEC's cost of equity according to the CAPM is:

$$k_E = 3.5\% + (5\% \times 1.10) = 9\% \qquad (10.11b)$$

---

[21] A 10-year maturity is chosen to estimate the long-term riskless rate because 10-year government bonds are usually the most liquid of all long-term government bonds. See Chapter 12 for a discussion on why we chose 5 percent as an estimate of the market risk premium.

[22] We show in Chapter 12 how to estimate a company's beta.

ESTIMATED STOCK PRICE VERSUS ACTUAL STOCK PRICE

A look at row 1 in Exhibit 10.2 indicates that PEC's share price is $15.97 whereas the estimated price found with the constant dividend-growth model is $15.05. Why is our estimated price ($15.05) lower than the actual price ($15.97)? If all investors use the constant dividend-growth model to value shares, have the same expected rate of return of 9 percent, and the same dividend growth rate of 3.50 percent, then the estimated price based on the constant dividend-growth model would be the same as the observed market price. Obviously, not all investors make the same valuation assumptions.

In our case, our assumed growth rate of 3.50 percent and/or discount rate of 9 percent must be different from those reflected in the market price (assuming all investors use the constant dividend-growth model). You can see this if you assume the price is $15.97 (the observed market price), the discount rate is 9 percent, and you use equation 10.10b to infer the growth rate. With these two numbers, you should find a growth rate of 3.80 percent (plug into equation 10.10b a growth rate of 3.80 percent instead of 3.50 percent and you will find a price of $15.97). What this means is that our estimated price of $15.05 is lower than the market price of $15.97 because we assumed a lower growth rate (3.50 percent) than the market consensus (3.80 percent). But as a rule of thumb, as long as the estimated price is not more than 10 percent higher or lower than the actual price, we can conclude that our valuation is OK (in our case, the estimated price of $15.05 is about 6 percent lower than the actual price of $15.97).

THE MULTISTAGE DIVIDEND GROWTH MODEL

Assuming a constant growth rate in dividends simplifies the valuation process, but it may not be realistic for most firms. What if the growth rate in dividends is not the same forever? We have seen in Chapter 2 how to value cash flows with two stages of growth: an above-average growth rate (g_1) during a first stage of T years followed by a lower rate (g_2) in perpetuity. The present value (PV) of the two streams of cash flows is given by the following equation (it looks complicated but it is straight-forward to understand and apply):

$$PV = \frac{CF_1}{k - g_1}\left[1 - \left(\frac{1 + g_1}{1 + k}\right)^T\right] + \frac{\left[\dfrac{CF_{T+1}}{k - g_2}\right]}{(1 + k)^T} \tag{10.12}$$

with $CF_{T+1} = CF_T(1 + g_2) = CF_0(1 + g_1)^T (1 + g_2)$.

The first term in equation 10.12 is the present value of the first-stage cash-flow stream that grows at the rate g_1 for T years (see formula 2.12 in Chapter 2). The numerator in the second term is the value, at the end of year T, of the second-stage cash-flow stream that grows at the rate g_2 in perpetuity (see formula 2.9 in Chapter 2). The denominator in the second term gives the present value of the second-stage cash-flow stream.

Let's apply equation 10.12 to value PEC's shares. If we assume that PEC's current dividend-per-share of $0.80 ($CF_0 = 0.80$) will grow at 5 percent for the next five years and then at 3 percent forever (instead of growing at 3.50 percent all the time), then PEC's estimated share price can be expressed as follows:

$$P_{PEC} = \frac{\$0.80 \times 1.05}{0.09 - 0.05}\left[1 - \left(\frac{1.05}{1.09}\right)^5\right] + \frac{\left[\dfrac{\$0.80 \times (1.05)^5 \times 1.03}{0.09 - 0.03}\right]}{(1 + 0.09)^5}$$

$$P_{PEC} = \$3.58 + \frac{\$17.53}{1.5386} = \$3.58 + \$11.39 = \$14.97$$

The present value of PEC's first-stage cash-flow stream is $3.58. The value of the second-stage cash-flow stream, at the end of the fifth year, is $17.53, and its present value is $11.39. Adding the present values of the two stages gives an estimated share price of $14.97. Note that it is lower than PEC's current share price of $15.97. Again, this means that our assumed growth rates are lower than those implicit in the market consensus (assuming the cost of equity is 9 percent). But the difference in price is within the acceptable 10 percent range (our estimated price of $14.97 is about 6 percent lower than the actual price of $15.97).

VALUATION BASED ON DISCOUNTED FREE CASH FLOWS

In the discounted free cash flow model, the estimated value of a firm's equity is determined *indirectly*. We first estimate the value of the firm's **business assets**, which is called its **enterprise value (EV)**. It is the sum of the market values of its working capital requirement (see equation 4.7 in Chapter 4) and net fixed assets. Refer to the *market-value* balance sheet shown in Exhibit 10.9 which illustrates how to get an estimate of the firm's equity value (V_E), also called its market capitalization, if you have an estimate of its enterprise value.

We have the following balance-sheet equality:[23]

$$\text{Enterprise Value (EV)} + \text{Cash} = \text{Debt (D)} + \text{Equity Value (}V_E\text{)}$$

EXHIBIT 10.9	PEC's MARKET VALUE BALANCE SHEET.

CASH + ENTERPRISE VALUE = DEBT + EQUITY VALUE

```
              ┌──────────────────────────┬──────────────────────┐
              │  Cash $250 million²      │                      │
              │                          │   Debt³              │
              │                          │   $1,067 million     │
              │                          │                      │
              │                          ├──────────────────────┤
              │                          │                      │
              │   Enterprise             │                      │
              │   Value¹                 │   Equity Value⁴      │
              │                          │                      │
              │   (WCR +NFA)             │   (Market            │
              │                          │   Capitalization)    │
              │                          │                      │
              └──────────────────────────┴──────────────────────┘
```

[1] Enterprise value is the market value of business assets, which exclude cash and other financial assets. It is the sum of working capital requirement (WCR) and net fixed assets (NFA). WCR is equal to inventories plus accounts receivable less accounts payable. See Chapter 4, equation 4.7.
[2] Cash is PEC's only financial asset.
[3] PEC's interest-bearing debt has a market value equal to its book value.
[4] PEC has 200 million shares outstanding.

[23] Note that this is the same as the managerial balance sheet introduced in Chapter 4 except that in this case we have market values instead of accounting or book values. See the section on the managerial balance sheet in Chapter 4.

Rearranging the terms of the above equation we can express equity value as a function of enterprise value:

$$\text{Equity Value } (V_E) = \text{Enterprise Value (EV)} + \text{Cash} - \text{Debt} \qquad (10.13)$$

The firm's equity value is equal to its enterprise value to which we add the firm's cash holding and any other financial assets, and from which we deduct the firm's debt (borrowed funds).

The reason we use this roundabout method to get the value of the firm's equity is that it is easier to estimate a firm's enterprise value than its equity value. The firm's enterprise value is the present value of the cash-flow stream that will be generated by the firm's business assets. These cash flows are called **free cash flows** (FCF) (see formula 4.15 in Chapter 4). They are discounted to the present at the firm's **weighted average cost of capital** (WACC) (see formula 12.12 in Chapter 12) to obtain an estimate of the firm's enterprise value.

THE WEIGHTED AVERAGE COST OF CAPITAL

Before we review below how free cash flows are calculated, let's first explain why the WACC is the relevant discount rate in this case. Recall the rule: the discount rate must reflect the risk of the cash-flow stream being discounted. And that risk is captured by the rate required by the investors who will receive the cash flows. Who are the investors in this case? The free cash flows generated by the firm's business assets go to pay back *all* the investors who provide funds to the firm: the shareholders who expect a return of k_E (which is the firm's cost of equity) and the lenders who require a return of k_D (which is the firm's cost of debt). The WACC is the weighted average of these two costs; the cost of equity (k_E) and the **after-tax cost of debt** ($k_D(1-T_c)$).[24] The weights are the percentages of equity financing and debt financing used to fund the firm's business assets. We have:

$$\text{WACC} = [\% \text{ equity financing} \times k_E] + [\% \text{ debt financing} \times k_D(1 - T_c)] \quad (10.14)$$

The firm's enterprise value (EV), which is the estimated value of the firm's business assets, can thus be written as:

$$\text{EV} = \frac{FCF_1}{(1 + \text{WACC})} + \frac{FCF_2}{(1 + \text{WACC})^2} + \dots + \frac{FCF_t}{(1 + \text{WACC})^t} + \dots \quad (10.15)$$

FREE CASH FLOW CALCULATION

We have shown in Chapter 4 that a firm's free cash flow is calculated as follows (see equation 4.15):

$$\text{FCF} = \text{EBIT} (1 - T_C) + \text{Depreciation expense} - \Delta\text{WCR} - \text{Net capital expenditure} \quad (10.16)$$

where EBIT are the firm's earnings before interest and tax, T_C is its corporate tax rate, ΔWCR is the change in working capital requirement, and **net capital expenditure** is the firm's capital expenditure net of any asset sales. The formula to estimate the free cash flows generated by the firm's business assets is the same, except that *EBIT must exclude any earnings from the firm's cash holding* because cash is not included in business assets.

---

[24] The cost of debt is taken after tax because interest payments are tax-deductible expenses which reduce the amount of taxes the firm has to pay. This adjustment is explained in detail in Chapter 12. T_C is the corporate tax rate.

VALUING PEC WITH THE DISCOUNTED FREE CASH FLOW MODEL

Let's apply the free cash flow model to estimate PEC's equity value (V_E) and share price with free cash flows estimated for the next five years.[25] In this case, PEC's enterprise value, according to equation 10.15, can be written:

$$EV = \frac{FCF_1}{(1 + WACC)} + \frac{FCF_2}{(1 + WACC)^2} + \frac{FCF_3}{(1 + WACC)^3} + \frac{FCF_4}{(1 + WACC)^4} + \frac{FCF_5 + TV_5}{(1 + WACC)^5} \quad (10.17a)$$

where the terminal value at the end of the fifth year (TV_5) is the present value of a perpetual cash flow that begins at the end of year six (FCF_6) and grows forever at the constant rate g_5 (see equation 10.10b). We thus have:

$$TV_5 = \frac{FCF_6}{WACC - g_5} = \frac{FCF_5(1 + g_5)}{WACC - g_5} \quad (10.17b)$$

Exhibit 10.10 provides the forecasting assumptions that allow us to estimate PEC's (1) free cash flows from year one to year five (shown in row 16); (2) terminal value at the end of year five (shown in cell G18); (3) enterprise value (shown in cell B20); (4) equity value (shown in cell B23); and, finally, (5) share price (shown in cell B25). Sales are expected to grow at 8 percent the first year (from the current $3,640 million), 7 percent the second year, 6 percent the third year, 4 percent the fourth year, and finally 3 percent forever starting in the fifth year (row 3). The corresponding sales forecasts are in row 4.

EBIT is expected to be 10 percent of sales the first two years, 9 percent of sales the third year, and then 8 percent of sales forever (row 5). The corresponding EBIT forecasts are in row 6. The corporate tax rate is expected to stay at 25 percent (row 7), and the corresponding after-tax EBITs are shown in row 8. Depreciation expense is expected to be 2 percent of sales (rows 9 and 10), and WCR is assumed to remain at 20 percent of sales (row 12). The corresponding changes in WCR are shown in row 13. Finally, capital expenditures are assumed to be 3 percent of sales (rows 14 and 15).

With these forecasting assumptions, the resulting expected stream of free cash flows is shown in row 16. To estimate EV (with equation 10.17a) and TV_5 (with equation 10.17b) we need an estimate of the company's WACC using equation 10.14.

PEC's average cost of debt is 6.4 percent,[26] its cost of equity is 9 percent (see equation 10.11b), the percentage of debt in PEC's capital structure is 25 percent, and the percentage of equity is thus 75 percent.[27] With these numbers, PEC's WACC, according to equation 10.14, is 7.95 percent:

$$WACC = (75\% \times 9\%) + (25\% \times 6.4\% \times (1 - 25\%)) = 7.95\%$$

With a WACC of 7.95 percent and a terminal growth rate g_5 of 3 percent,[28] the estimated terminal value at the end of the fifth year (TV_5 in equation 10.17b) is $4,390.30 million (cell G18), and PEC's enterprise value is $3,817.13 million (cell B20):

---

[25] We use five years to illustrate the valuation method. In practice, one should forecast cash flows up to the year where the growth rate finally reaches its lower, long-term constant value. This period could be longer than five years.

[26] Note that this is PEC's average cost of debt. It is different from the 5.5 percent market yield of the bond PEC issued last year because PEC has other sources of debt in its balance sheet whose rates are higher than 5.5 percent.

[27] With a debt ratio of 25 percent PEC is assumed to have an optimal (best) capital structure which does not change. How a firm designs an optimal capital structure is the topic of Chapter 13.

[28] Note that the growth rate of the terminal cash flows is the same as the growth rate in sales.

EXHIBIT 10.10	ESTIMATION OF PEC'S SHARE PRICE BASED ON FREE CASH FLOWS (FCF) DISCOUNTED AT THE WEIGHTED AVERAGE COST OF CAPITAL (WACC).

DOLLARS ARE IN MILLIONS EXCEPT FOR SHARE PRICE

	A	B	C	D	E	F	G
1		Now			Forecasts Year		
2		0	1	2	3	4	5
3	Growth in sales (input)		8%	7%	6%	4%	3%
4	Sales (based on growth rates in row 3)	$3,640.00	$3,931.20	$4,206.38	$4,458.77	$4,637.12	$4,776.23
5	Operating profit margin (OPM) (input)	10%	10%	10%	9%	8%	8%
6	EBIT = OPM × Sales = row 5 × row 4		$393.12	$420.64	$401.29	$370.97	$382.10
7	Tax rate (T) (input)	25%	25%	25%	25%	25%	25%
8	EBIT(1-T) = row 6 × (1 − row 7)		$294.84	$315.48	$300.97	$278.23	$286.57
9	Depreciation expense/Sales (input)		2%	2%	2%	2%	2%
10	Depreciation expense = row 9 × row 4		$78.62	$84.13	$89.18	$92.74	$95.52
11	WCR/Sales (input)	20%	20%	20%	20%	20%	20%
12	WCR = row 11 × row 4	$728.00	$786.24	$841.28	$891.75	$927.42	$955.25
13	Change in WCR based on row 12		$58.24	$55.04	$50.48	$35.67	$27.82
14	Capital expenditures/Sales (input)		3%	3%	3%	3%	3%
15	Capital expenditure = row 14 × row 4		$117.94	$126.19	$133.76	$139.11	$143.29
16	Free CF = row 8 + row 10 − row 13 − row 15		$197.29	$218.38	$205.90	$196.19	$210.99
17	WACC =	7.95%					
	[75% × 9%] + [25% × 6.4% × (1 − 25%)]						
18	Terminal value =						$4,390.30
	210.99 × (1 + 3%)/(7.95% − 3%)						
19	Free CF stream (FCF) = row 16 + row 18		$197.29	$218.38	$205.90	$196.19	$4,601.29
20	Enterprise value =	$3,817.13					
	Present value [FCF stream at 7.95%]						
21	Cash (input)	$250.00					
22	Debt (input)	$1,067.00					
23	Equity value =	$3,000.13					
	Enterprise value + Cash − Debt						
24	Number of shares (input)	200					
25	Estimated share price (P_{PEC}) =	$15.00					
	Equity value/200						

- *Formula in cell C4 is =B4*(1+C3). Then copy cell C4 to next cells in row 4*
- *Formula in cell C6 is =C5*C4. Then copy cell C6 to next cells in row 6*
- *Formula in cell C8 is =C6*(1−C7). Then copy cell C8 to next cells in row 8*
- *Formula in cell C10 is =C9*C4. Then copy cell C10 to next cells in row 10*
- *Formula in cell C12 is =C11*C4. Then copy cell C12 to next cells in row 12*
- *Formula in cell C13 is =C12−B12. Then copy cell C13 to next cells in row 13*
- *Formula in cell C15 is =C14*C4. Then copy cell C15 to next cells in row 15*
- *Formula in cell C16 is =C8+C10−C13−C15. Then copy cell C16 to next cells in row 16*
- *Formula in cell G18 is =G16*(1+G3)/(B17−G3)*
- *Formula in cell C19 is =C16+C18. Then copy cell C19 to next cells in row 19*
- *Formula in cell B20 is =NPV(B17,C19:G19)*
- *Formula in cell B23 is =B20+B21−B22*
- *Formula in cell B25 is =B24/200*

$$TV_5 = \frac{\$210.99m(1+3\%)}{7.95\% - 3\%} = \$4,390.30 \text{ million}$$

$$EV = \frac{\$197.29m}{(1.0795)} + \frac{\$218.38m}{(1.0795)^2} + \frac{\$205.90m}{(1.0795)^3} + \frac{\$196.19m}{(1.0795)^4} + \frac{\$4,601.29m}{(1.0795)^5} = \$3,817.13 \text{ million}$$

Adding cash holdings of $250 million (cell B21) and deducting debt of $1,067 million (cell B22), PEC's estimated equity value based on equation 10.13 is $3,000.13 million (cell B23) and its estimated share price is $15.00 (cell B25) based on 200 million shares outstanding (B24):

$$V_E = EV + Cash - Debt = \$3,817.13m + \$250m - \$1,067m = \$3,000.13 \text{ million}$$

$$P_{PEC} = \frac{\text{Estimated equity value}}{\text{Number of shares}} = \frac{\$3,000.13m}{200m} = \$15$$

VALUATION BASED ON DISCOUNTED CASH FLOWS TO EQUITY HOLDERS

According to the discounted cash flow to equity holders' model, the estimated value of a firm's equity is determined *directly* by discounting at the cost of equity (k_E) the cash flow that the firm's equity holders (the shareholders) are entitled to. Why is the cost of equity the relevant discount rate in this case? It is because the cash-flow stream belongs to equity holders and the return expected by equity holders on that cash-flow stream is the firm's cost of equity.

CALCULATION OF THE CASH FLOW TO EQUITY HOLDERS

As its name indicates, the **cash flow to equity holders** (CFE) is the cash flow that belongs to the firm's shareholders. Note that it is *not* the dividends but the cash flow available to pay dividends. It is generated by the firm's business assets, that is, the firm's free cash flow (FCF), less interest payments to lenders adjusted for taxes[29] (a cash *out*flow to equity holders) plus any increase in debt (a cash *in*flow to equity holders):

$$CEF = FCF - \text{Interest Payment} \times (1 - T_C) + \text{Increase in Debt} \qquad (10.18)$$

VALUING PEC WITH THE DISCOUNTED CASH FLOW TO EQUITY HOLDERS MODEL

Let's now apply the cash flow to equity holders' model to estimate PEC's equity value (V_E) with cash flows to equity holders (CFE) estimated for the next five years. In this case, the *direct* estimated value of PEC's equity can be written:

$$V_E = \frac{CFF_1}{(1+k_E)} + \frac{CFE_2}{(1+k_E)^2} + \frac{CFE_3}{(1+k_E)^3} + \frac{CFE_4}{(1+k_E)^4} + \frac{CFE_5 + TV_5}{(1+k_L)^5} \qquad (10.19a)$$

where the terminal value at the end of the fifth year (TV_5) is the present value of a perpetual cash flow that begins at the end of year six (CFE_6) and grows forever at the constant rate g_5 of 3 percent (see row 3 in Exhibit 10.10). We thus have:

$$TV_5 = \frac{CEF_6}{k_E - g_5} = \frac{CEF_5(1+g_5)}{k_E - g_5} \qquad (10.19b)$$

---

[29] As pointed out earlier, the cost of debt is taken after tax because interest payments are tax-deductible expenses which reduce the amount of taxes the firm has to pay. This adjustment is explained in more detail in Chapter 12.

We can now get estimates of CFE_1, CFE_2, CFE_3, CFE_4, CFE_5, and TV_5 based on the assumptions in Exhibit 10.11.

The free cash flows found in Exhibit 10.10 are reproduced in row 3. The increase in debt is in row 4 and the corresponding debt levels are in row 5. After-tax interest payments are in row 9 and the resulting cash flows to equity holders are in row 10. With a cost of equity of 9 percent (see equation 10.11b) we get the following estimated values for TV_5, V_E, and PEC's share price:

$$TV_5 = \frac{\$201m(1 + 3\%)}{9\% - 3\%} = \$3,450.50 \text{ million}$$

EXHIBIT 10.11	**ESTIMATION OF PEC'S SHARE PRICE BASED ON DISCOUNTED CASH FLOWS TO EQUITY HOLDERS (CFE) AT THE COST OF EQUITY.**

DOLLARS ARE IN MILLIONS EXCEPT FOR SHARE PRICE

	A	B	C	D	E	F	G
1		Now			Forecasts Year		
2		0	1	2	3	4	5
3	Free cash flow (row 16 in Exhibit 10.10)		$197.29	$218.38	$205.90	$196.19	$210.99
4	Increase in debt (input)		$42.68	$44.39	$46.16	$48.01	$49.93
5	$Debt_t = Debt_{t-1} +$ Increase in debt	$1,067.00	$1,109.68	$1,154.07	$1,200.23	$1,248.24	$1,298.17
6	Interest rate (input)		6.4%	6.4%	6.4%	6.4%	6.4%
7	Interest payment$_t = Debt_{t-1} \times$ row 6		$68.29	$71.02	$73.86	$76.81	$79.89
8	Tax rate (input)		25%	25%	25%	25%	25%
9	After-tax interest payment = row 7 $\times$ (1 − row 8)		$51.22	$53.26	$55.40	$57.61	$59.92
10	Cash flow to equity (CFE) = row 3 − row 9 + row 4		$188.75	$209.50	$196.67	$186.58	$201.00
11	**Cost of equity** (input)	9%					
12	Terminal value (TV_5) = 201 × (1+3%)/(9% − 3%)						$3,450.50
13	CFE stream = row 10 + row 12		$188.75	$209.50	$196.67	$186.58	$3,651.50
14	Equity value (V_E) = Present value [row 13 at 9%]	$3,006.76					
15	Number of shares (input)	200					
16	**Estimated share price** (P_{PEC}) = Equity value/200	**$15.03**					

- *Formula in cell C5 is =B5+C4. Then copy cell C5 to next cells in row 5*
- *Formula in cell C7 is =B5*C6. Then copy cell C7 to next cells in row 7*
- *Formula in cell C9 is =C7*(1-C8). Then copy cell C9 to next cells in row 9*
- *Formula in cell C10 is =C3-C9+C4. Then copy cell C10 to next cells in row 10*
- *Formula in cell G12 is =G10*(1+3%)/(B11-3%)*
- *Formula in cell C13 is =C10+C12. Then copy cell C13 to next cells in row 15*
- *Formula in cell B14 is =NPV(B11,C13:G13)*
- *Formula in cell B16 is =B14/B15*

$$V_E = \frac{\$188.75m}{(1.09)} + \frac{\$209.50m}{(1.09)^2} + \frac{\$196.67m}{(1.09)^3} + \frac{\$186.58m}{(1.09)^4} + \frac{\$3,651.50m}{(1.09)^5} = \$3,006.76 \text{ million}$$

$$P_{PEC} = \frac{V_E}{\text{Number of shares}} = \frac{\$3,006.80 \text{ million}}{200 \text{ million}} = \$15.03$$

COMPARING THE THREE DISCOUNTED CASH FLOW MODELS

PEC's estimated share price according to the cash flow to equity holders' model and the assumptions we made is $15.03. It is practically the same as the $15 share price we found with the discounted free cash flow model (see Exhibit 10.10), the two-stage dividend-discount model ($14.97), and the constant dividend-growth model ($15.05). These prices, which have been estimated through specific valuation models, are usually called **fundamental values** or **intrinsic values**. Note that the four intrinsic values we found for PEC's shares ($15.03, $15.00, $14.97, and $15.05) are below PEC's observed market price of $15.97 (see Exhibit 10.2), indicating that PEC's share price is overvalued according to our estimated prices.

The three **equity valuation models** (the dividend-discount model, the free cash flow model and the cash flow to equity holders' model) are summarized in Exhibit 10.12. Note that these DCF models allow you to perform sensitivity analysis, that is, they allow you to find out how the estimated share price varies when you change one or more inputs in the valuation formula. For example, you can recalculate the estimated share price with alternative growth rates in sales, different operating profit margins, or different ratios of WCR to sales to find out how sensitive the estimated share price is to changes in the sales growth rates, operating profit margins, or WCR to sales ratios. We examine this point in detail in Chapter 14.

VALUATION BASED ON COMPARABLE FIRMS

A quicker but *less reliable* method to value the shares of a company is to compare the company to a similar one for which you have data on share price, profits, and other accounting numbers. Three of the most popular comparative valuation methods are based on the price-to-earnings ratio (PER), the price-to-book ratio (PBR), and the enterprise value-to-EBITDA ratio (earnings before interest, tax, depreciation, and

---

EXHIBIT 10.12 SUMMARY OF EQUITY VALUATION MODELS BASED ON DISCOUNTED CASH FLOWS.

DCF Model	Cash-Flow Stream	Discount Rate	Present Value	Share Price
Dividend Discount Model	Dividend Per Share See equation 10.9	Cost of equity (k_E) See equation 10.11a	Share price (P)	P
Free Cash Flow Model	Free Cash Flows See equation 10.16	WACC See equation 10.14	Enterprise Value (EV) See equation 10.15	$P = \frac{EV + C - D}{N}$
Cash Flow to Equityholders Model	Cash Flow to Equity See equation 10.18	Cost of equity (k_E) See equation 10.11a	Equity value (V_E) See equation 10.19a	$P = \frac{V_E}{N}$

WACC = Weighted Average Cost of Capital; C = Cash; D = Debt; N = Number of shares outstanding.

amortization). The first two methods provide a *direct* estimate of a firm's share price. The third method is *indirect*: enterprise value is first estimated from which share price is then inferred.

Let's illustrate these methods with the following example. The Western Engineering Company (WEC) is a privately-held firm with no shares trading in the market. Suppose that a group of investors is considering buying it and wants to get a first and quick estimate of its equity value. They could, of course, apply the DCF models presented earlier, but they only have limited financial information on WEC for the moment. The fastest way to get a first estimate of WEC's value is to find a comparable company in the same sector. Let's assume that the Pacific Engineering Company (PEC) and WEC have comparable size and profitability and face similar market conditions. What would be WEC's equity value and share price based on PEC's price-to-earnings ratio of 13.89 (see row 11 in Exhibit 10.2), PEC's price-to- book ratio of 1.60 (see row 10 in Exhibit 10.2), and PEC's EV-to-EBITDA ratio of 8.72 (given)?

DIRECT VALUATION OF A FIRM'S EQUITY BASED ON THE PRICE-TO-EARNINGS RATIO

If PEC and WEC are similar firms, we can assume that if WEC's shares were listed they would trade at the same price-to-earnings ratio (PER) as PEC's, which is 13.89 (the price-to-earnings ratio or **PER** is also called the **earnings multiple**). Note that a firm's PER can be expressed either on a per share basis (share price divided by **earnings per share (EPS)**) or on a total value basis (value of equity divided by earnings after tax). In other words, if WEC's PER or earnings multiple is 13.89, then its estimated value will be 13.89 times its earnings. Suppose that we find out WEC's latest earnings after tax are $288 million. Based on these numbers we can write:

$$\frac{\text{Estimated Equity Value of WEC}}{\text{Earnings after tax of WEC}} = \frac{\text{Estimated Equity Value of WEC}}{\$288 \text{ million}} = \text{PER of PEC} = 13.89$$

from which we get:

$$\text{Estimated Equity Value of WEC} = \$288 \text{ million} \times 13.89 = \$4,000 \text{ million}$$

The above equation can be interpreted as follows: a PER of 13.89 means that the market is paying $13.89 for every dollar of earnings PEC generates. Applying the same multiple to WEC's $288 million of profits we find an equity value of $4,000 million.

If WEC has 120 million shares, then its estimated share price (P_{WEC}), if the firm were listed, would be:

$$P_{WEC} = \frac{\$4,000 \text{ million}}{120 \text{ million}} = \$33.33$$

WHAT FACTORS DETERMINE THE SIZE OF THE PRICE-TO-EARNINGS RATIO?[30]

The size of the PER depends essentially on two key factors: the firm's growth rate and the firm's risk. Faster growing firms have *higher* PERs because growth is a positive, value-creating factor, all else remaining the same. And riskier firms have *lower* PERs because risk is a negative, value-reducing factor, all else remaining the same.

---

[30] We examine the factors that determine the size of the price-to-book ratio in Chapter 18, Appendix 18.2.

You could see this by rewriting the pricing formula 10.10a as follows (divide both sides of the formula by CF_1):

$$\frac{PV}{CF_1} = \frac{1}{1-g}$$

The left side of the above equation is equivalent to a PER; it is equal to one over $(k-g)$. When the growth rate g goes up, $(k-g)$ becomes smaller and the PER goes up. And when risk goes up, the discount factor k goes up, $(k-g)$ becomes larger and the PER goes down.

DIRECT VALUATION OF A FIRM'S EQUITY BASED ON THE PRICE-TO-BOOK RATIO

If PEC and WEC are similar firms, we can, alternatively, assume that if WEC's shares were listed they would trade at the same price-to-book ratio as PEC's, which is 1.60 (the price-to-book ratio or **PBR** is also called the **book value multiple**). Recall that a firm's PBR can be expressed either on a per share basis (share price divided by book value per share) or on a total value basis (market value of equity divided by book value of equity). In other words, if WEC has the same PBR as PEC, its estimated equity value will be 1.60 times its book value. Suppose that we find out that WEC's latest book value is $2,380 million. Based on these numbers we can write:

$$\frac{\text{Estimated Equity Value of WEC}}{\text{Book Value of WEC}} = \frac{\text{Estimated Equity Value of WEC}}{\$2,380 \text{ million}} = \text{PBR of PEC} = 1.60$$

from which we get:

$$\text{Estimated Equity Value of WEC} = \$2,280 \text{ million} \times 1.60 = \$3,808 \text{ million}$$

If WEC has 120 million shares then its estimated share price (P_{WEC}), if the firm were listed, would be:

$$P_{WEC} = \frac{\$3,808 \text{ million}}{120 \text{ million}} = \$31.73$$

You should not be surprised that WEC's estimated price based on the PBR ($31.73) is different from the one based on the PER ($33.33). Different ratios will generate different prices. As pointed out earlier, as long as the estimated values are within a reasonable range (a range of no more than, say, 10 percent between the highest and lowest estimates) they can be considered acceptable. If the range is too wide, then some of the ratios may not be appropriate and should be discarded.

INDIRECT VALUATION OF A FIRM'S EQUITY BASED ON THE EV-TO-EBITDA RATIO

Recall that PEC has an EV-to-EBITDA ratio of 8.72 (this ratio is also called the **EBITDA multiple**). If PEC and WEC are similar firms, we can assume that WEC has the same EV-to-EBITDA ratio as PEC. Suppose we find out that WEC's latest EBITDA is $521 million. Based on these numbers we can write:

$$\frac{\text{Estimated Enterprise Value of WEC}}{\text{EBITDA of WEC}} = \frac{\text{Estimated Market Value of WEC}}{\$521 \text{ million}} = 8.72$$

from which we get:

Estimated Enterprise Value of WEC = \$521 million × 8.72 = \$4,543 million

If WEC holds \$300 million of cash and has \$1,149 million of debt, its estimated equity value is:

Estimated Equity Value of WEC = EV + Cash − Debt = \$4,543m + \$300m − \$1,149m

$$= \$3,694 \text{ million}$$

Given that WEC has 120 million shares, its estimated share price (P_{WEC}), if the firm were listed, would be:

$$P_{WEC} = \frac{\$3,694 \text{ million}}{120 \text{ million}} = \$30.78$$

WEC's estimated share price based on the three **multiples** ranges from a low of \$30.78 (based on the EBITDA multiple) to a high of \$33.33 (based on the earnings multiple).

KEY POINTS

1. When firms are short of cash they can raise funds by issuing bonds to investors and/or issuing common stocks to shareholders. In this chapter we examined the features of bonds and common stocks and showed how to value them. Knowing how to value bonds and stocks is important because the cost of the capital that is needed to finance the firm's activities is determined by the price of the firm's bonds and common stocks.

2. Bonds are tradable debt instruments that specify the terms under which the firm is borrowing from investors. The terms indicate how much is borrowed, at what rate (called the bond's coupon rate), and for how long (called the bond's term to maturity). If you know a bond's coupon rate and its term to maturity, you can calculate its price for a given market yield (also called yield to maturity). This yield is determined in the market to reflect the risk of the bond: the riskier the bond, the higher its market yield and the lower its price.

3. The holder of a corporate bond is exposed to two risks: credit risk and interest-rate risk. Credit risk occurs because the issuing corporation may not be able to pay the promised coupon payments on their scheduled dates and/or repay the bond's face value on its maturity date. A bond's exposure to credit risk is measured by its credit rating: the weaker a firm's financial conditions, the lower the credit rating of its bonds, the higher their market yield, and the lower their price. Interest-rate risk occurs because bond prices fluctuate unpredictably in response to unexpected changes in the market yield. A bond's exposure to interest-rate risk increases when the bond maturity is lengthened and its coupon rate is lowered. This exposure is measured with a statistic called duration, which is calculated in years. The longer the bond's duration, the riskier is the bond.

4. Government bonds are usually considered default-free; they are only exposed to interest-rate risk. Using the yield on default-free zero-coupon government bonds with different maturities (called spot rates), you can draw a spot yield curve and use it as a benchmark to estimate the yield of corporate bonds with the same

maturity by adding a credit risk premium to the default-free spot rate that reflects the credit risk of corporate bonds. The spot yield curve is often rising because long rates are usually higher than short rates. You can extract forward rates from the spot yield curve. These are future rates (known today) at which borrowers can lock in now the rate at which they will borrow (or invest) in the future.

5. A common stock is an equity instrument that represents an ownership in a firm. It recognizes the portion of the firm's total equity that is owned by the shareholder. Contrary to bonds, common stocks have no maturity date and pay no coupon because the shareholder is an owner, not a lender. Shareholders receive cash dividends whenever the firm's board of directors decides to pay any.

6. There are a number of alternative methods to estimate the price of a share of common stock. The two most popular valuation approaches are the discounted cash flow models (DCF models) and the valuation based on the value of comparable firms (comparative valuation models). We examined in this chapter three DCF models: the dividend-discount model, the free cash flow model, and the cash flow to equity holders' model. There are many comparative valuation models. We reviewed here the methods based on three ratios: the price-to-earnings ratio, the price-to-book ratio, and the enterprise value-to-EBITDA ratio.

7. The dividend-discount model discounts the expected future stream of dividends per share at the firm's cost of equity. The free cash flow model provides an indirect estimate of the firm's equity value. It first discounts the firm's expected free cash flow stream at the weighted average cost of capital to get an estimate of the value of the firm's business assets (called enterprise value). The firm's estimated equity value is then found by adding cash holdings (and other financial assets, if any) to the estimated enterprise value and deducting debt (borrowed funds). The third DCF model discounts the cash flow to the firm's shareholders at the firm's cost of equity to get a direct estimate of the firm's equity value.

8. A quicker but less reliable method to value shares is to compare the company we want to value to a similar one for which we have data on share price, profits, and other accounting numbers. Three of the most popular comparative valuation methods are based on the price-to-earnings ratio (PER), the price-to-book ratio (PBR), and the enterprise value-to-EBITDA (earnings before interest, tax, depreciation, and amortization) ratio. To get an estimate of equity value with the PER method, we multiply the profits of the firm we want to value by the PER of the comparable firm. To get an estimate of the equity value with the PBR method, we multiply the book value of the firm we want to value by the PBR of the comparable firm. To get an estimate of the enterprise value (EV) with the EV-to-EBITDA ratio, we multiply the EBITDA of the firm we want to value by the EV-to-EBITDA ratio of the comparable firm.

9. All else remaining the same, faster growing firms have higher PERs and riskier firms have lower PERs.

10. Although equity valuation methods based on comparable firms are straight-forward and simpler to apply than the discounted cash flow models, they do not provide the flexibility and insight one can gain by performing sensitivity analysis, an exercise that only discounted cash flow models offer.

Here is a summary of the properties of duration you should know. These properties are illustrated in Exhibit A10.1.1 with the same three bonds as in Exhibit 10.8.

1. *The duration of a zero-coupon bond is equal to its current maturity.* This is because a zero-coupon bond makes no intermediate coupon payments; all the cash is received at maturity:

$$\text{Dur (zero coupon bond)} = T \tag{A10.1.1}$$

Look at bond B in Exhibit A10.1.1. It is a zero-coupon bond with a 10-year maturity. Its duration is thus equal to ten years. *Maturity is the maximum value duration can take and this happens only when the bond is a zero-coupon bond.*

2. *The duration of a perpetual bond is equal to one plus the reciprocal of its yield.* We have:

$$\text{Dur (perpetual bond)} = 1 + \frac{1}{y} \tag{A10.1.2}$$

Look at bond C in Exhibit A10.1.1. It is a 6 percent perpetual bond. Its duration for a yield of 5 percent is equal to 21 years $\left(1 + \dfrac{1}{0.05}\right)$. Notice that the duration of a perpetual bond is independent of its coupon rate (the coupon rate does not appear in the formula of a perpetual's duration); the duration of a perpetual bond is only determined by its yield.

3. *The duration of a standard coupon bond is given by the following formula:*[31]

$$\text{Dur (coupon bond)} = \frac{c(1 + y)\text{ADF} + T(y - c)\,\text{DF}}{c + (y - c)\text{DF}} \tag{A10.1.3}$$

where c is the bond coupon rate, y is the market yield, T is the bond maturity, DF is the discount factor for T and y, and ADF is the annuity discount factor which is equal to $\dfrac{1 - \text{DF}}{y}$. Applying formula A10.1.3 to bond A, we have c = 6 percent, y = 5 percent, T = 10, DF = $(1.050)^{-10}$ = 0.6139, ADF = $\dfrac{1 - 0.6139}{0.05}$ = 7.7220. The duration of bond A is thus:

$$\text{Dur}_A = \frac{[0.06 \times 1.05 \times 7.7220] + [10 \times (0.05 - 0.06) \times 0.6139]}{0.06 + (0.05 - 0.06) \times 0.6139} = \frac{0.4251}{0.0539} = 7.89 \text{ years}$$

---

[31] For a proof, see Hawawini (1984). Note that if the bond is a perpetual, DF is zero and ADF is one over y. In this case, formula A10.1.3 becomes formula A10.1.2.

EXHIBIT A10.1.1	DURATION AS A MEASURE OF INTEREST-RATE RISK.

THE LONGER THE DURATION, THE RISKIER THE BOND

Type of bond	Bond A Coupon bond	Bond B Zero-coupon bond	Bond C Perpetual bond
1. Maturity (T)	10 years	10 years	Infinite
2. Coupon rate (c)	6%	0%	6%
3. $\dfrac{\text{Price (5.2\%)} - \text{Price (5\%)}}{\text{Price (5\%)}}$	−1.49%	−1.88%	−3.85%
4. Duration formula[1]	$\dfrac{c(1 + y)\text{ADF} + T(y - c)\text{DF}}{c + (y - c)\text{DF}}$	T	$1 + \dfrac{1}{y}$
5. Duration calculation using the formula in row 4 (y = 5%)	7.89 years	10 years	21 years
6. $\dfrac{\Delta p}{p} \approx -\left(\dfrac{\text{Dur}}{1 + y}\right)\Delta y = -\left(\dfrac{\text{Dur}}{1.05}\right)0.002$	−1.50%	−1.90%	−4.00%
7. Error = Row 3 − Row 6	0.01%	0.02%	0.15%

[1] y = market yield; DF = Discount Factor = $(1 + y)^{-T}$; ADF = Annuity Discount Factor = $\dfrac{1}{y}(1 - \text{DF})$

4. *A bond's duration is a measure of its interest-rate risk*. The percentage change in the price of a bond is related to its duration through the following *approximate* formula:[32]

$$\frac{\Delta P}{P} \approx -\left(\frac{\text{Dur}}{1 + y}\right) \times \Delta y \qquad\qquad (A10.1.4)$$

Formula A10.1.4 clearly shows that the sensitivity of a bond price $\left(\dfrac{\Delta P}{P}\right)$ to a change in yield (Δy) is directly related to its duration. The negative sign indicates that changes in prices are inversely related to changes in yields. The formula holds approximately; the smaller the change in yield (Δy) the more precise the formula is. In our case we have y = 5 percent and Δy = 0.2 percent = 0.002. Using the above formula we can calculate the approximate change in bond prices

---

[32] If you are not familiar with calculus, ignore this footnote; otherwise take the derivative of P with respect to y (where dP and dy are infinitely small changes in price and yield):

$$\frac{dp}{dy} = -\frac{1}{1 + y}\left[1 \times \left(\frac{C}{1 + y}\right) + 2 \times \left(\frac{C}{(1 + y)^2}\right) + \ldots + T \times \left(\frac{C + F}{(1 + y)^T}\right)\right]$$

divide both sides of the above equation by P and multiply them by "dy":

$$\frac{dp}{p} = -\frac{1}{1 + y}\left\{\frac{1}{P}\left[1 \times \left(\frac{C}{1 + y}\right) + 2 \times \left(\frac{C}{(1 + y)^2}\right) + \ldots + T \times \left(\frac{C + F}{(1 + y)^T}\right)\right]\right\} \times dy$$

We show in point 8 and in Exhibit A10.1.2 that duration is the expression within the curly brackets.

resulting from an increase in yield from 5 percent to 5.2 percent. For example, in the case of bond A whose duration is 7.89 years, the approximate change in price is:

$$\frac{\Delta P_A}{P_A} \approx -\left(\frac{7.89}{1.05}\right) \times 0.002 = -1.50\%$$

Compare this approximate drop of 1.50 percent to the exact drop of 1.49 percent (see row 3 in Exhibit A10.1.1). The error is equal to one basis point (0.01 percent) as shown in row 7. In the case of bond B the error is 0.02 percent. And in the case of bond C it is 0.15 percent. The error increases when the coupon goes down and the maturity goes up (see row 7 in Exhibit A10.1.1).

5. *Bonds with the same duration have the same interest-rate risk.* For example, the perpetual bond C has the same interest-rate risk as a zero-coupon bond with a 21-year maturity.

6. *Cash has a duration of zero.* This is because cash has no interest-rate risk (the "value" of cash is not affected by changes in interest rates).

7. *The duration of a bond increases the longer the bond maturity, the lower its coupon rate,[33] and the lower the market yield.* To see the maturity effect, compare bond A to bond C. They have the same coupon rate (6 percent) but the longer bond (bond C) has a longer duration than the shorter bond (bond A). To see the coupon effect, compare bond A to bond B. They have the same maturity (ten years), but the lowest-coupon bond (bond B) has a longer duration than the higher coupon bond (bond A). To see the yield effect, compare the duration of bond A calculated with a yield of 5 percent to its duration calculated with a yield of 6 percent. At a yield of 5 percent, the duration is 7.89 years. At a yield of 6 percent, the duration is 7.80 years. The duration is longer when the yield is lower.

8. *Duration is a measure of the "effective maturity" of a bond.* Duration takes into account the fact that two bonds with the same maturity but different coupon rates do not have the same "effective maturity" because the one with the highest coupon payments returns cash faster to the bondholder. *You can think of duration as measure of the "speed" with which the bond returns cash to its holder and the faster bondholders get their cash back the lower the bond's interest-rate risk and the shorter its duration.* The calculation of duration as an average maturity is illustrated in Exhibit A10.1.2 for the case of a four-year, 4 percent coupon bond with a $1,000 face value and a 5 percent yield.

As pointed out earlier, you could view this coupon-paying bond as a portfolio of four zero-coupon bonds, that is, as a portfolio containing a one-year zero with a $40 face value (the first coupon), a two-year zero with a $40 face value (the second coupon), a three-year zero with $40 face value (the third coupon), and a four-year zero with a $1,040 face value (the last coupon and the face value). Each of these four zero-coupon bonds has a duration equal to its maturity. What is the duration of the coupon bond? *It is the weighted average of the durations of the four zero-coupon bonds that make up the bond.* The calculation of the duration of the

---

[33] The duration of a coupon bond selling at a discount may reach a maximum before maturity reaches infinity, that is, for deep discount bonds there may be cases where duration would fall when maturity increases. See Hawawini (1984).

EXHIBIT A10.1.2	DURATION AS AVERAGE MATURITY.

CALCULATING THE EFFECTIVE MATURITY OF A 4-YEAR, 4% COUPON BOND AT A 5% MARKET YIELD

Time T (1)	Cash Flow CF (2)	Present value of cash flow PV(CF) at 5% yield (3)	PV(CF) as % of bond price (3)/$964.54 (4)	(1)×(4) (5)
1 year	$40	$38.10	3.95%	0.0395 year
2 years	40	36.28	3.76%	0.0752 year
3 years	40	34.55	3.58%	0.1074 year
4 years	1,040	855.61	88.71%	3.5484 years
		Bond Price = $964.54	100.00%	Dur = 3.7705 years

coupon-paying bond as a weighted average of the durations of the four zeros is shown in Exhibit A10.1.2.

The first column gives the maturity of each zero (which is also their duration), the second column gives their face value, and the third column their price at a 5 percent yield. The price of the coupon bond is the sum of the prices of the four zeros, that is, $964.54. The fourth column gives the price of each zero as a percentage of the price of the coupon bond. For example, the one-year zero is worth $38.10, which is 3.95 percent of the price of the coupon bond ($38.10/$964.54). The duration of the coupon bond is thus:

$$\text{Dur} = (3.95\% \times 1 \text{ year}) + (3.76\% \times 2 \text{ years}) + (3.58\% \times 3 \text{ years}) + (88.71\% \times 4 \text{ years})$$

$$\text{Dur} = 0.0395 \text{ years} + 0.0752 \text{ years} + 0.1074 \text{ years} + 3.5484 \text{ years} = 3.77 \text{ years}$$

The duration of the four-year, 4 percent coupon bond at a market yield of 5 percent is thus 3.77 years. This is the same duration you would have found if you had used formula A10.1.3 (check this out). Calculating a bond's duration with the formula, however, is a lot faster than going through the steps shown in Exhibit A10.1.2 if the bond has a long maturity. Note that the duration is slightly shorter than four years because the last zero-coupon bond has the highest weight since its price is the highest compared to that of the first three zero-coupon bonds.

FURTHER READING

1. Hawawini, Gabriel. "Controlling the Interest-Rate Risk of Bonds: An Introduction to Duration Analysis and Immunization Strategies." *Financial Markets and Portfolio Management* 1 (1987).
2. Hawawini, Gabriel. "On the Relationship between Macaulay's Bond Duration and the Term to Maturity." *Economics Letters* 16 (1984).
3. Koller, Tim, Marc Goedhart, and David Wessels. *Valuation, Measuring, and Managing the Value of Companies*, 6th ed. John Wiley & Sons, Inc., 2015, Chapter 13.
4. Smith, Donald. *Bond Math: The Theory behind the Formulas*. John Wiley & Sons, 2011.

SELF-TEST QUESTIONS

10.1   Pricing of PEC bonds four years after they were issued.
Refer to the PEC bond described in Exhibit 10.1 and assume that four years have passed since the bond was issued. The 1-year default-free spot rate is 2 percent and the 2-year default-free spot rate is 2.50 percent. PEC's bonds now have a credit spread of 2.60 percent for all maturities.

a.   What is the price of a PEC bond?
b.   What is the yield to maturity of a PEC bond?
c.   What is the current yield of a PEC bond?
d.   What is PEC's two-year cost of debt?
e.   Calculate the duration of a PEC bond using the duration formula.
f.   Calculate the duration of a PEC bond based on the weighted average of the zeros that make up the bond.
g.   Calculate the instantaneous percentage change in the price of a PEC bond if the market yield rises by 10 basis points.
h.   Calculate the same instantaneous percentage change in price as in the previous question using the duration formula A10.1.3. Compare your answer to that of the previous question.

10.2   Bond pricing and forward rates.
The 1-year spot rate is 3 percent and the 1-year forward rate is 5 percent.

a.   What is the price of a two-year, 4 percent coupon bond?
b.   What is the yield to maturity of the two-year, 4 percent coupon bond?
c.   Calculate the price of the two-year, 4 percent coupon bond based on the yield to maturity you found in the previous question.
d.   Suppose one year has passed and the 1-year spot rate is now 3.5 percent. What is the price of the bond? What is the holding period return for a bondholder who bought the bond one year ago?

10.3   Extracting spot rates from coupon-paying bonds.
The price of a one-year, 3 percent government bond is $1,004.88, the price of a two-year, 3.5 percent government bond is $1,009.73, and the price of a three-year, 4 percent government bond is $1,014.75.

a.   What are the 1-year, 2-year, and 3-year spot rates?
b.   What is the yield to maturity of each of the three bonds? Compare each yield to maturity to its corresponding spot rate of the same maturity.

10.4   Present value of growth opportunities.
Consider the PEC common stock described in Exhibit 10.2. PEC's cost of equity is 9 percent.

a.   What would be PEC's share price if PEC paid out all its profits in the form of dividend?
b.   What would be PEC's share price if PEC retained 30 percent of its profits and its dividends grew at the constant rate of 4.50 percent in perpetuity?
c.   How can you interpret the difference between PEC's share prices in the previous two questions?

10.5   Discounted cash flow valuation.

Calculate two DCF estimates of the share price of the General Power Company (GPC), one based on the discounted free cash flow model and the other based on the discounted cash flow to equity holders using the information provided below. The GPC's cost of debt is 8 percent and its estimated cost of equity is 12 percent. Debt outstanding is $1,200 million and cash is $150 million. The debt-to-equity ratio is one-third and the corporate tax rate is 25 percent. Capital expenditure is equal to depreciation expense, and free cash flows are expected to grow at 3 percent after the third year. Every year, new debt is equal to the annual after-tax interest payment. GPC has 300 million shares outstanding.

	Now	In one year	In two years	In three years
EBIT[1]		$500 million	$600 million	$660 million
WCR[2]	$3,000 million	$3,200 million	$3,400 million	$3,500 million

[1] EBIT = Earnings Before Interest and Taxes
[2] WCR = Working Capital Requirement

REVIEW QUESTIONS

1. **Bond pricing and risk.**

   A two-year corporate bond has a coupon rate of 4 percent. The 1 year spot rate is 3 percent and the forward rate is 5 percent. The bond's credit spread is 1 percent for both the one-year and the two-year maturities.

   a. What is the price of the bond expressed as a percentage of its face value?
   b. What is the bond's yield to maturity?
   c. What is the bond price calculated with the bond's yield to maturity?
   d. Calculate the bond duration first with the duration formula and then with duration as the weighted average maturity of the bond cash flow.
   e. What would be the maturity of a zero-coupon bond with the same interest-rate risk as the two-year corporate bond assuming that the two bonds have the same credit risk?
   f. Calculate the percentage change in the bond price if the yield rises by 20 basis points.
   g. Calculate the percentage change in the bond price if the yield rises by 20 basis points using the bond duration and compare your answer to that in the previous question.

2. **Bond quotation.**

   Consider a 6 percent coupon bond with a $1,000 face value maturing tomorrow.

   a. What would be the price at which the bond is quoted?
   b. According to bond conventions, what is the bond's flat price?
   c. What is the accrued interest if the bond pays a coupon semi-annually?
   d. What is the bond's invoice price?

3. **The cost of debt.**

Thalin Inc. has decided to extend its current product line. To finance the project, the firm is considering issuing a ten-year, 10 percent coupon bond. The firm has made public that its target debt-to-equity ratio of 30 percent is not going to change in the foreseeable future. Two years ago the firm issued a 12-year, 10 percent coupon bond to finance a similar project. The current market price of the bond is $1,065. What is Thalin's cost of debt?

4. **Reinvestment risk.**

Consider a two-year, 5 percent coupon bond selling at par. Answer the following questions.

a. What is the bond's yield to maturity? What assumption does the yield make regarding the first coupon payment?

b. Assume that in a year the one-year market rate is 7 percent (this future rate is unknown today; it is assumed to be known to illustrate the reinvestment risk). What is the return a bondholder will earn if she purchased the two-year bond today, reinvested the first coupon payment at that rate, and held the bond to maturity? Compare this return to the yield to maturity.

c. Assume that in a year the one-year market rate is 3 percent. What is the return a bondholder will earn if she purchased the two-year bond today, reinvested the first coupon payment at that rate, and held the bond to maturity? Compare this return to the yield to maturity.

5. **Bond stripping.**

Suppose there are no government zero-coupon bonds. If investors demand default-free zeros, outline the process that would create these zeros using government coupon-paying bonds. Illustrate the method with the case of a four-year, 5 percent government zero.

6. **Bond arbitrage.**

A three-year, 4 percent government bond is trading at $1,001. The spot yield curve indicates that the 1-year spot rate is 2 percent, the 2-year spot rate is 3 percent, and the 3-year spot rate is 4 percent. Is there an arbitrage opportunity, that is, is it possible to earn a riskless profit by constructing a portfolio with no net investment (assume all transaction costs are zero)? Describe this portfolio.

7. **Forward rates.**

The 1-year spot rate is 2 percent, the 2-year spot rate is 3 percent, the 3-spot rate is 4 percent, and the 4-year spot rate is 5 percent.

a. How many forward rates are there over the four-year period? Identify each forward rate with the symbol $_tf_{t+n}$ which represents the forward rate over the period from the end of year "t" to the end of year "t+n". For example, $_2f_4$ is the 2-year forward rate from the end of year 2 to the end of year 4.

b. Calculate all the forward rates you have identified in the previous question.

c. Suppose you need to borrow $10,000 in one year for three years and wish to lock in your three-year borrowing rate today. What would be that rate? Explain how you will achieve your objective.

8. **Growth stocks versus income stocks.**
    Therol Inc. has no debt. Its invested capital generates $5 of earnings per share, and all these earnings are paid out as dividends.

    a. Suppose that Therol's shareholders require a return of 10 percent on their investment in the firm. What is Therol's stock price if the firm's earnings per share stays at $5 and if its dividend policy does not change over the foreseeable future?
    b. Suppose that Therol pays out 60 percent of its earnings from existing invested capital and reinvests the remaining 40 percent in new plant and equipment, from which it expects a return of 10 percent. What would be the effect on Therol's stock price? Compare it with the stock price found in question (a) and explain.
    c. What if the return on new plant and equipment is 15 percent instead of 10 percent? What is your interpretation of the difference in the stock price?

9. **Dividend-discount model.**
    Financial analysts expect Theron Co.'s earnings and dividends to grow at a rate of 16 percent during the next three years, 12 percent in the fourth and fifth years, and at a constant rate of 6 percent thereafter. Theron's dividend, which has just been paid, was $1.20. If the expected rate of return on the stock is 12 percent, what is the price of the stock today?

10. **Valuation based on comparable firms.**
    The General Distribution Company (GDC) is a privately-held company in the wholesale food distribution sector. You collected data on a sample of five listed companies in the same sector which are similar to GDC. Get five estimates of GDC's equity value based on the following data:

Characteristics	GDC	Average of 5 comparable companies
Sales	$4,079 million	$6,615 million
EBITDA[1]	$390 million	$580 million
Cash flow to equity holders	$102 million	$180 million
net profits	$168 million	$280 million
Book value of equity	$1,288 million	$2,100 million
Market capitalization	unknown	$2,646 million
Enterprise value	unknown	$3,584 million
Net debt (debt less cash)	$856 million	Not available

[1] EBITDA = Earnings Before Interest, Taxes, Depreciation, and Amortization.

RAISING CAPITAL AND PAYING OUT CASH

CHAPTER **11**

Firms need cash to finance new investments in fixed assets and working capital. For most firms, the major source of funds is the cash they generate from their operations, net of the cash used to service existing debt (pay interest expenses and repay loans), settle taxes, pay dividends to shareholders, and repurchase their shares in the open market. When internally generated cash is not sufficient to finance all their investments, firms have to raise additional funds from *external* sources in the form of debt or equity capital.

Sources of borrowed funds include bank loans, leases, and the sale of bonds to debt holders (lenders); external sources of equity include the sale of preferred and common stocks to existing and new equity holders (shareholders). These various sources of capital are surveyed in this chapter. The valuation of debt and equity capital is the subject of Chapter 10 and the determination of their cost is found in Chapter 12. As in previous chapters, the words capital, funds, financing, and money are used interchangeably.

Although new funds are usually used to finance asset growth, a firm may borrow to restructure its capital, that is, to repay part of its existing debt or to buy back some of its outstanding common stocks. Chapter 13 explains why a firm might want to modify its capital structure. The focus here is on the description of the various forms of debt and equity capital available to firms and the methods used to raise these funds. Firms are not always short of cash; there are times when they face the opposite situation: they have a cash surplus instead of a cash deficit. In this case, they are in a position to distribute some of their excess cash to their shareholders either through dividend payments or through the repurchase of their own shares in the open market, a transaction that is the reverse of an issue of new shares. We review in the chapter why and how firms pay dividends and buy back their own shares. We also examine how a firm's payout policy (*how much* cash they typically pay out to their shareholders and *when* they pay it out) affects its share price and the wealth of its shareholders. After reading this chapter, you should understand the following:

- How to estimate the amount of external funds a firm needs to finance its growth
- How the financial system works and what functions it performs

- The differences between the various sources of debt and equity capital
- How firms issue common stocks in the financial markets
- Why and how firms distribute cash to their shareholders through dividend payments
- Why and how firms distribute cash to their shareholders through the repurchase of their own shares in the open market and how share buybacks differ from dividend payments
- How a firm's payout policy affects its share price and the wealth of its shareholders

ESTIMATING THE AMOUNT OF REQUIRED EXTERNAL FUNDS

To determine the amount of external funds a firm will need, say, next year, we must estimate (1) the amount by which its investments are expected to grow during the coming year and (2) the amount of *internal* funds the firm expects to generate next year. If **internally generated funds** are less than the amount by which the firm's assets are expected to grow, the difference is the amount of external funds the firm will need to raise.

Recall from Chapter 4 that a firm's investments include cash and cash-equivalent assets, working capital requirement or WCR (a measure of the firm's net investment in its operating cycle), and fixed assets (property, plant, and equipment or PP&E). Because the firm will need to finance any expected growth in these investments, we can write:[1]

$$\text{Funding needs} = \Delta\text{Cash} + \Delta\text{WCR} + \Delta\text{Fixed assets}$$

where (1) ΔCash is the expected change in the firm's cash holding, (2) ΔWCR is the expected change in working capital requirement (which is equal to the changes in inventories, accounts receivable, and prepaid operating expenses less the changes in accounts payable and accrued operating expenses), and (3) ΔFixed assets is the expected *new* capital expenditures and acquisitions less expected cash raised from the sale of existing fixed assets (disposals and divestitures).

The source of internally generated funds is the firm's retained earnings, that is, the portion of its net profit that is not distributed as dividends. However, depreciation expenses are charged against the firm's net profit but are not cash expenses, so they must be added to retained earnings to obtain the firm's internally generated funds. (Any other noncash expenses charged to the firm's net profit, such as provisions against bad debts, must also be added back to retained earnings.) In general, we have the following:

$$\text{Internally generated funds} = \text{Retained earnings} + \text{Depreciation expense}$$

We can now write:

$$\text{External funds need} = [\text{Funding needs}] - [\text{Internally generated funds}],$$

which can be expressed as follows:

$$\begin{aligned}\textbf{External funds need} = &[\Delta\textbf{Cash} + \Delta\textbf{WCR} + \Delta\textbf{Fixed assets}] \\ &- [\textbf{Retained earnings} + \textbf{Depreciation expense}] \quad (11.1)\end{aligned}$$

---

[1] Note that any reduction in growth would be a source of funds.

Note that any funds needed to pay interest on existing debt and distribute dividends to shareholders are already accounted for in equation 11.1 because retained earnings are calculated after deducting both interest expenses and **dividend payments** from operating profit.

To illustrate equation 11.1, we revisit Office Supplies (OS) Distributors, the firm we analyzed in Chapters 4 through 6. Let's assume it is the end of Year −1 (last year) and we want to estimate the amount of funds OS Distributors will need to raise externally in Year 0 (this year). Exhibit 11.1 shows the firm's balance sheet at the end of Year −1 in managerial form (see Chapter 4). Exhibit 11.2 shows the asset side of the firm's pro forma (projected) balance sheet at the end of Year 0 and its Year 0 pro forma income statement.

From the pro forma income statement, we see that OS Distributors expects to generate $7 million of retained earnings in Year 0. Adding the $8 million of depreciation expense reported in the income statement, we conclude that OS Distributors expects to generate internally $15 million in Year 0.

What are OS Distributors' **funding needs** for Year 0? A comparison of the balance sheets at the end of Year −1 and Year 0 (see Exhibits 11.1 and 11.2) indicates that OS Distributors' invested capital should grow from $126 million to $138 million; cash holdings should decrease by $4 million (from $12 million to $8 million); working capital requirement should increase by $14 million (from $63 million to $77 million); and net fixed assets should rise by $2 million (from $51 million to $53 million). However, the *net* fixed assets reported in the balance sheets are *net* of depreciation expense, so the $2 million increase in net fixed assets is not the expected increase in *gross* fixed assets, that is, fixed assets before depreciation.

EXHIBIT 11.1	OS DISTRIBUTORS' BALANCE SHEET ON DECEMBER 31, YEAR −1.

FIGURES IN MILLIONS

Invested capital		
• Cash		$ 12.0
• Working capital requirement[1]		63.0
• Net fixed assets		51.0
Gross value	$ 90.0	
Accumulated depreciation	(39.0)	
Total invested capital		**$126.0**

Capital employed		
• Short-term debt		$ 22.0
• Long-term debt[2]		34.0
• Owners' equity		70.0
Total capital employed		**$126.0**

[1] WCR = (Accounts receivable + Inventories + Prepaid expenses) − (Accounts payable + Accrued expenses).
[2] Long-term debt is repaid at a rate of $8 million per year.

EXHIBIT 11.2	OS DISTRIBUTORS' PRO FORMA FINANCIAL STATEMENTS FOR YEAR 0.

FIGURES IN MILLIONS

Pro Forma (Projected) Balance Sheet, Invested Capital Side		
		December 31, Year 0
Invested capital		
• Cash		$ 8.0
• Working capital requirement		77.0
• Net fixed assets		53.0
Gross value[1]	$ 93.0	
Accumulated depreciation	(40.0)	
Total invested capital		**$138.0**

Pro Forma (Projected) Income Statement	
	Year 0
• **Net sales**	$480.0
Cost of goods sold	(400.0)
• **Gross profit**	80.0
Selling, general, and administrative expenses	(48.0)
Depreciation expense	(8.0)
• **Operating profit**	24.0
Special items	0
• **Earnings before interest and tax (EBIT)**	24.0
Net interest expense[2]	(7.0)
• **Earnings before tax (EBT)**	17.0
Income tax expense	(6.8)
• **Earnings after tax (EAT)**	**$ 10.2**
Dividends	$3.2
• Addition to retained earnings	$7.0

[1] In Year 0, a warehouse will be enlarged at a cost of $12 million, and existing assets, bought for $9 million in the past, are expected to be sold at their book value of $2 million.
[2] There is no interest income, so net interest expense is equal to interest expense.

The expected amount needed to finance gross fixed assets in Year 0 is $10 million: $12 million for the enlargement of the warehouse less $2 million expected from the sale of existing assets. (See note 1 at the bottom of the balance sheet in Exhibit 11.2.) In total, OS Distributors' funding needs for Year 0 are thus $20 million: $14 million to finance the rise in WCR plus $10 million to finance the increase in fixed assets less $4 million of cash reduction.

To summarize, OS Distributors expects to generate internally $15 million in Year 0, and its funding needs are expected to amount to $20 million during that period. To bridge the gap, OS Distributors will have to raise $5 million.

If OS Distributors behaves like most firms, it will raise the $5 million it needs through borrowing. (You can check that this is indeed the case by examining OS Distributors' balance sheet at the end of Year 0 in Exhibit 4.1 in Chapter 4. You will see that the firm increased its short-term borrowing by $1 million and its long-term borrowing by $4 million.) Aggregate figures on the funding structures of nonfinancial firms in the world's largest economies show that most of the funds needed to finance new investments are generated by the firm's own activities, with the balance mostly raised through borrowing. As an illustration, we show in Exhibit 11.3 the relative weight of the sources of financing for a very large sample of nonfinancial US corporations from 1946 to 2017 (negative net equity means more equity was repurchased than issued).

Over this period of time, *nonfinancial firms have relied primarily on borrowed funds to cover their cash deficits.* Other statistics indicate that 60 to 80 percent of total funds available are used to finance capital expenditures, with the balance going to finance WCR and cash holdings.

In the following we explain how firms raise external funds through the **financial system.** We begin with a description of the structure of that system and the functions it performs.

| EXHIBIT 11.3 | SOURCES OF FUNDING FOR NONFARM, NONFINANCIAL US FIRMS, 1946–2017. |

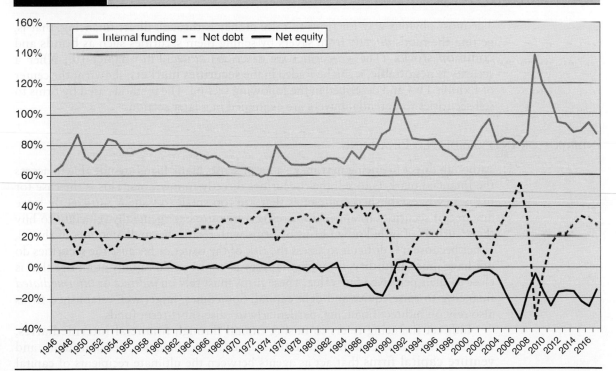

Source: Board of Governors of the Federal Reserve System, *Flow of Funds Accounts.* Net debt is the amount of long-term and short-term debt issued less debt repayments. Net equity is the amount of equity issued less the amount of equity repurchased. Negative net equity indicates that more equity was repurchased than issued during that year.

THE FINANCIAL SYSTEM: ITS STRUCTURE AND FUNCTIONS

The fundamental role of a financial system is to act as a conduit through which the cash surplus of savers is channeled to firms that need cash. Without a financial system, entrepreneurs would have to finance their activities exclusively with their own savings and their firm's internally generated funds. The financial system provides another option by allowing firms with a cash shortage to tap the sector of the economy that has a cash surplus. Most of that surplus is supplied by the **household sector**, individuals who, on aggregate, save more than they consume. In addition, firms with temporary excess cash may lend it to cash-deficit firms for *short* periods of time. The household sector's savings do not all go to cash-starved firms, however. Companies usually compete for funds with governments that need to finance their budget deficits.

The various components of the financial system and the way they interact are described in Exhibit 11.4. The cash-deficit firms that want to raise funds are on the right side. (We have excluded the cash-deficit governments because our focus is on the fund-raising activities of firms.) The suppliers of capital, mostly the household sector, are on the left side. The institutions and processes that facilitate the transfer of funds between these two groups constitute what we call the financial system. To understand how this system operates, we examine the two alternative financing channels through which the excess funds of the cash-surplus sector are transferred to firms with a cash shortage: they are referred to as **direct financing** and **indirect financing**.

DIRECT FINANCING

The most obvious way for firms to raise money is through direct financing, that is, getting the funds *directly* from savers by selling them securities such as **bonds** and **common stocks**. (These securities are described in detail in Chapter 10.) When a security is **negotiable**, it can be traded in the **securities markets**, shown at the center of Exhibit 11.4 and described in the following section. The methods used by firms to sell securities to potential buyers are examined in a later section.

INDIRECT OR INTERMEDIATED FINANCING

Although direct financing may make a lot of sense, many firms are not able to access the financial markets to sell their securities directly to investors. This is the case for many newly established companies that are too small to issue a sufficiently large amount of securities to appeal to investors. Investors are generally reluctant to buy the securities of little-known firms or firms with relatively small amounts of shares, either because it is difficult to assess the risk of the issuer or because the securities do not have much **liquidity**, meaning that they cannot be sold rapidly at a price that is close to their perceived fair value. These firms must rely on *indirect* or *intermediated* financing to raise equity and debt capital. Sometimes, large, well-established firms also rely on indirect financing, particularly to raise short-term funds.

Indirect financing refers to raising capital through **financial intermediaries**, institutions such as **commercial banks**, insurance companies, pension funds, and **venture capital firms** that act as agents between the ultimate recipients of capital (the firms with a cash shortage) and the ultimate providers of capital (the households with a cash surplus). Commercial banks typically offer short- to medium-term loans

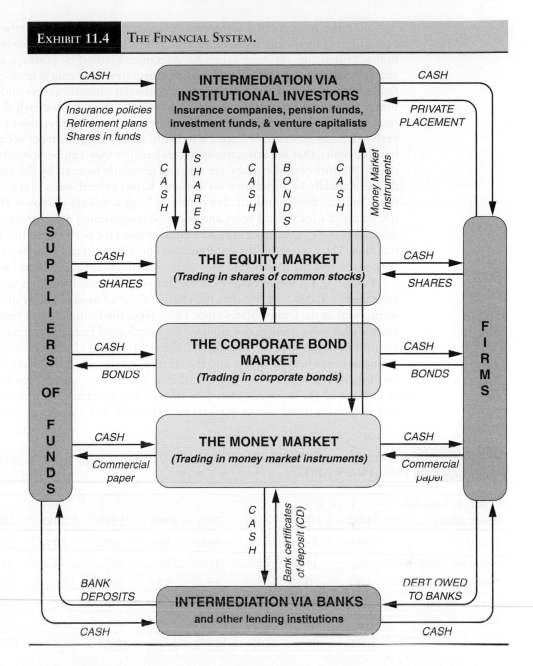

EXHIBIT 11.4   THE FINANCIAL SYSTEM.

with maturities of one day to ten years. Longer-term debt and equity capital can be obtained through the **private placement** of securities, usually with insurance companies, pension funds, or venture capital firms, the latter specializing in supplying equity to recently established firms with limited track records.

To see how financial intermediation works, consider a commercial bank. As shown at the bottom of Exhibit 11.4, a bank gets cash from depositors in the form of checking and savings accounts and from investors to whom it sells short-term securities, also called **negotiable certificates of deposit** or **CDs**. The bank then lends these funds to firms by extending short- to medium-term loans.

Note the fundamental difference between direct and indirect financing. In the case of direct financing, ultimate savers hold securities issued by *firms*. In the case of indirect financing, ultimate savers hold securities issued by *banks*, such as checking and savings accounts and CDs. Bank-intermediated financing is important because it *facilitates* and *increases* the flow of funds between ultimate savers and cash-deficient firms. Individual savers may be reluctant to lend their excess cash directly to firms (will they get their money back?), but they may find it convenient to deposit their cash in a bank that can then lend it to firms. Banks offer **indirect securities**, such as bank deposits, that are attractive to savers because they can be opened with relatively small amounts of money, they are safe and generally insured by the government, and they can usually be withdrawn on demand. Banks extend loans that are convenient to firms because these loans involve relatively large amounts of money that can be borrowed rapidly for several years and could be renegotiated if the firm encounters some difficulties. Of course, banks must be compensated for performing this intermediation function. Their reward is the difference, or spread, between the interest rate they offer depositors and the higher rate they charge on the loans they extend to firms.

Financing via intermediaries is the dominant channel through which companies raise money. Exhibit 11.5 shows the relative share of assets held by different financial institutions in the United States since 1860. Note the following two trends: (1) the rise in the dollar value, though not adjusted for inflation, of financial assets held by financial institutions (shown at the bottom of Exhibit 11.5), and (2) the decline in the share of financial assets held by banks and the corresponding rise in the share held by pension and investment funds. Since the late 1990s, nonbanking institutions have held about two-thirds of the securities issued by firms. They purchase them directly from firms or buy them in the securities markets with the cash they receive from ultimate savers.[2]

EXHIBIT 11.5	RELATIVE SHARE OF ASSETS HELD BY FINANCIAL INSTITUTIONS IN THE UNITED STATES FROM 1860 TO 2017.[1]								
Types of Financial Intermediary	1860	1900	1939	1970	1980	1990	2000	2010	2017
Banks[2]	89%	81%	65%	56%	56%	42%	29%	29%	29%
Insurance companies[3]	11	14	27	18	15	16	14	12	11
Pension funds	0	0	2	15	19	24	26	25	24
Investment funds	0	0	2	4	4	10	22	22	27
Other	0	5	4	7	6	8	9	12	9
	100%	100%	100%	100%	100%	100%	100%	100%	100%
Total (in billions of US dollars)	$1	$16	$129	$1,809	$5,061	$13,486	$32,831	$58,858	$82,426

[1] From 1860 to 1980, adapted from Kaufman and Mote, *Economic Perspectives* (pp. 2–21, May/June 1994), Federal Reserve Bank of Chicago. From 1990 to 2017, from the Board of Governors of the Federal Reserve System, *Flow of Funds Account*.
[2] Includes commercial and savings banks.
[3] Includes life, property, and casualty insurance companies.

---

[2] With the exception of the United Kingdom, the predominance of banks among financial institutions is generally more pronounced in other countries than in the United States. However, the trends observed in the United States are also at work in other industrialized countries around the world.

As shown in the upper part of Exhibit 11.4, these savers receive insurance policies, retirement plans, and shares in investment funds in exchange. Nonbanking intermediaries offer insurance and pension products to savers and, in the case of investment funds, convenient and cheap access to the securities markets, risk diversification, and investment management.

Why would a firm borrow from a bank if it can sell debt securities to nonbanking institutions or individual investors? This question brings up a subtle function performed by banks, called *monitoring*. To understand what this function achieves, think of the problem investors face when they consider buying bonds. They wonder whether the issuing firm has told them everything about its ability to service its debt. What if the firm has withheld information that would indicate some potential difficulties in repaying the borrowed funds? Investors try to protect themselves by imposing protective **covenants** in the written contract between the bond issuer and the lenders, known as **indentures**. These covenants would, for example, require the firm to maintain a minimum amount of working capital and restrict its ability to sell assets, pay dividends, or issue new debt. But covenants are not as good as an insider watching over managers' shoulders and preventing them from taking actions that are detrimental to the **debt holders**. A bank is expected to be this insider. In performing this task, the bank is playing a monitoring role that provides bond buyers with additional protection. In other words, although large firms can sell debt securities directly to investors, they are willing to borrow from banks and pay higher rates to reassure the potential buyers of their bonds. In this case, the firm's choice is not between borrowing from a bank or issuing debt securities: some bank borrowing may be needed to facilitate the firm's access to the debt market.

SECURITIES MARKETS

We now turn to the description of the markets in which **listed securities** are issued and then traded among investors. Securities markets, shown at the center of Exhibit 11.4, can be classified along several dimensions: whether they are primary or secondary markets, whether they trade equity securities or debt securities, and whether they are domestic (within one country) or international (outside the reach of domestic regulators).

PRIMARY VERSUS SECONDARY MARKETS

Primary markets are the markets in which *newly* issued securities are sold to investors for the first time. When a firm sells equity securities to the general public for the first time, the issue is called an **initial public offering (IPO)**.[3] When the firm returns to the market for another public issue of equity, usually a few years later, the process is referred to as a **seasoned issue**. A seasoned issue should not be confused with a **secondary public offering**, or a **secondary distribution**, which is the sale to the public of a relatively large block of equity held by an investor who acquired it earlier directly from the firm. An example of a secondary public offering would be

---

[3] Launching an IPO is a costly and complex process. Beyond the difficulties of going to the stock market and complying with all the IPO's rules and regulations, there is the issue of pricing. Setting the correct offer price in an IPO is not an easy task. If it is set too high, investors might be reluctant to buy the issue, which may lead to its withdrawal. If it is set too low, the company's existing shareholders would give away the difference between the true value of their shares and the offer price. Empirical studies show that IPOs are often significantly underpriced.

the public sale by the Ford Foundation of a block of shares it received initially from the Ford Motor Company.

After they are issued, securities are traded in the **secondary market** where they are bought and sold by investors. These transactions no longer provide cash to the issuing firm. The securities are exchanged among investors at a price established by the interaction of demand and supply. In the process, the market performs two important functions: it enables the quoted prices to reflect all publicly available information, and it provides the liquidity required to facilitate transactions. These functions are performed through the continuous trading of securities among investors on the basis of **fair prices**, prices that can be observed during the time the markets are open and that allow potential buyers and sellers to quickly trade securities and settle their transactions at a relatively low cost.

What exactly are fair prices? The answer to this question can easily fill an entire chapter. Suffice it to say that an extensive body of accumulated empirical evidence indicates that well-developed market economies have reasonably **efficient securities markets**, meaning that security prices in these markets reflect all available *public* information regarding the firm that has issued the securities. In other words, they are fair prices in the sense that they provide the best *estimate* of the true, but *unobservable*, value of a firm's securities. The existence of a secondary market is critical for the trading of the securities issued by corporations because investors are more inclined to purchase securities in the primary market when they know they can sell them later in an active and efficient secondary market.

EQUITY VERSUS DEBT MARKETS

Equity securities, or shares in firms' stock, are traded in the **equity markets** (also called **stock markets** or **stock exchanges**). These markets, shown in the center of Exhibit 11.4, can be either **organized stock exchanges** or **over-the-counter (OTC) markets**. The former are regulated markets and allow firms to list their securities only if the firms meet a number of stringent conditions.[4] In an organized stock exchange, shares are traded by **members of the exchange**, who may act as **dealers** or as **brokers**. Dealers trade shares that they own; brokers trade on behalf of a third party and do not own the traded shares. **Unlisted securities**, usually shares of smaller companies, trade in OTC markets. These markets do not require companies to meet the listing requirements of organized exchanges. In OTC markets, shares are traded through dealers connected by a telephone and computer network rather than on the floor of an organized exchange.

In most industrialized countries, the bulk of the trading in the stock markets is done by **institutional investors**. The activities of institutional investors provide an example of another type of financial intermediation, illustrated at the top of Exhibit 11.4: an insurance company or a pension fund issues indirect securities to ultimate savers in the form of insurance policies in the former case and pension contracts in the latter. The funds collected are then invested in securities issued by cash-deficit firms. These securities can be purchased either in the financial markets or directly from the issuing firm. The latter channel, called private placement, shown on the upper-right side of Exhibit 11.4, is discussed in the next section.

---

[4] They must have a minimum acceptable number of publicly held shares, a minimum asset size, and a history of dividend payments, and they must publish financial reports that provide relevant and timely information.

Debt securities trade in the debt or **credit markets**. Credit markets are usually identified by the **maturity** of the debt securities that are traded in them. Debt securities with an **original maturity** not exceeding one year, known as **money market instruments**, are issued and traded in the **money market**. **Corporate notes** have maturities ranging from one to five years, and **corporate bonds** have maturities exceeding five years. These securities trade in the **bond market**.[5] Two money market instruments are shown in Exhibit 11.4: (1) certificates of deposit issued by banks, which we mentioned earlier in the discussion on financial intermediation, and (2) **commercial paper (CP)**, which is issued by firms with high credit standing to raise short-term debt from the market as an alternative to borrowing short term from banks.

The volume of securities issued in the US financial markets from 1970 to 2017 is reported in Exhibit 11.6. Note the growth in the volume of securities issued after 1990 and the dominance of debt instruments over common stocks, preferred stocks, and convertible securities.[6] Exhibit 11.7 reports the largest IPOs listed on the US equity markets.

Domestic versus International Markets

Large and well-established firms can raise funds outside their domestic financial markets by selling their securities in the domestic markets of another country. These **foreign securities** can be denominated in the currency of the foreign country or in the currency of the issuer's country. For example, a US company can sell **foreign**

| Exhibit 11.6 | Securities Issued Publicly in the United States.[1] |

FIGURES IN BILLIONS

Types of Security	1970	1980	1990	2000	2010	2015	2017
Debt[2]	$23	$37	$108	$1,243	$1,395	$1,546	$1,642
Common stocks	4	13	20	168	241	226	200
Preferred stocks[3]	–	2	4	12	13	33	24
Convertible debt	3	4	5	16	16	4	20
Convertible preferred[4]	–	1	–	5	10	17	6
Total	$30	$58	$137	$1,444	$1,675	$1,826	$1,892

[1] Source: *Securities Data Corporation Platinum*.
[2] Nonconvertible debt, excluding mortgage-backed and asset-backed debt.
[3] Nonconvertible preferred stocks; less than a billion were issued in 1970.
[4] Less than a billion were issued in 1970 and 1990.

[5] The term *financial markets* usually refers to all security markets, whereas the term *capital market* usually refers to the market for long-term securities only, that is, equity and debt securities with a maturity exceeding one year. Thus, financial markets can be divided into capital and money markets, and capital markets can be divided into equity and bond markets.

[6] These securities are examined later in the chapter.

EXHIBIT 11.7	BIGGEST IPOs LISTED ON THE US EQUITY MARKET.

FIGURES IN BILLIONS

Company	Country	Year	Exchange	Amount raised	Market value at IPO
Alibaba Group	China	2014	NYSE	$21.77	$228.53
Visa	USA	2008	NYSE	$17.86	$42.53
ENEL	Italy	1999	NYSE	$16.45	$54.85
Facebook	USA	2012	NASDAQ	$16.01	$81.25
General Motors	USA	2010	NYSE	$15.77	$49.50
Deutsche Telekom	Germany	1996	NYSE	$13.03	$50.11
AT&T Wireless	USA	2000	NYSE	$10.62	$58.85
Kraft Foods	USA	2001	NYSE	$8.68	$53.79
Spotify	Sweden	2018	NYSE	$7.36	$29.50

Source: www.renaissancecapital.com/IPO-Center/Stats/Largest-US-IPOs.

bonds in the Japanese corporate bond market denominated either in Japanese yen or in US dollars.[7]

Alternatively, a firm can sell bonds in the **Euromarket**,[8] a market that is outside the direct control and jurisdiction of the issuer's country of origin. For example, a US company can simultaneously sell **Eurobonds** denominated either in US dollars (**Eurodollar bonds**) or Japanese yen (**Euroyen bonds**) to German, French, and Japanese investors. In this situation, a group of international banks act as selling agents through, for example, British investment accounts. Eurobonds, which are sold outside the holder's country of residence, are **bearer bonds** and are not subject to the laws, taxes, and regulations that affect domestic issues.[9] As a result, firms can issue Eurobonds at a lower rate than that on an equivalent taxable bond sold in their domestic market or in the domestic market of another country.

If a company issues bonds in a foreign-denominated currency, it is exposed to the risk of unexpected movements in the value of the foreign currency, a risk known as **currency risk** or **foreign-exchange risk**. This risk is examined in detail in Chapter 17.

In addition to foreign bonds and Eurobonds, other securities in international markets include foreign equity (stocks sold in a foreign country), **Euro-equity** (stocks sold in the Euromarkets), and **Euro-commercial paper (Euro-CP)**. The first two are the equity equivalent of foreign and Eurobonds, and the third is the Euromarket variation of domestic CP.

---

[7] If the bonds are denominated in yen, they are called **Samurai bonds**. They are called **Shogun bonds** if they are denominated in US dollars. Bonds issued by foreign firms in the United States (denominated in US dollars or other currencies) are called **Yankee bonds**.

[8] The prefix "Euro" in "Euro-markets" and "Euro-securities" means "external to a domestic market." It does not refer to the "euro," the currency of some European countries.

[9] The holder's name does not appear on a bearer bond. Domestic bonds are usually **registered bonds** and identify the holder's name.

HOW FIRMS ISSUE SECURITIES

Firms can sell their debt and equity securities to the public at large through a **public offering**, or they can sell them to **qualified investors** (individuals and financial institutions that meet some minimum standards set by regulatory authorities) through a private placement. Both distribution channels are usually regulated. In the United States, the regulatory agency is the **Securities and Exchange Commission (SEC)**. Most countries with developed securities markets have institutions that perform similar functions. The reasons why some firms choose private placement and the mechanisms through which securities are distributed in a public issue are discussed in this section.

PRIVATE PLACEMENT

A firm that chooses to sell securities privately can have the issue tailored to meet specific needs, such as the option to renegotiate the issue in response to unexpected events. Furthermore, unlike a public issue, a private placement does not have to be registered with a government agency, which is a costly process. Clearly, private placement provides a firm with a flexible, discreet, and speedy method of raising funds. The drawback is that the absence of organized trading in privately placed securities makes it difficult for the investors who subscribed to the issue to easily resell the securities. As a result, it is generally more expensive for a firm to place its securities privately than it is to issue them to the public at large. Even so, this may be the only way little-known companies can raise cash.

PUBLIC OFFERINGS

Relatively large firms can offer their securities to the public after they have registered them with a government agency that approves the issuance and distribution of securities and regulates their subsequent trading on public markets. To help with the public offering process, firms use the services of an **investment bank**.[10] At the earliest stage, the bank advises the firm about the type and amount of securities it should be issuing. Then, the investment bank seeks the approval of all the supervising government agencies, determines an appropriate selling price for the securities (a price that is both acceptable to the firm and attractive to buyers), and determines the best period of time for the offering. Finally, the investment bank ensures that the securities are purchased by investors by stimulating widespread interest in the offering. The last step, which involves the marketing and distribution of the securities to the public, is the most important function the investment bank plays in a public offering. We illustrate this process using a new equity issue, as shown in Exhibit 11.8.

Aside from a private placement, a firm can offer its shares to any interested buyer through a **general cash offering** or can offer its shares exclusively to its *existing* stockholders through a **rights offering**.

GENERAL CASH OFFERINGS

In a general cash offering, the investment bank can either do its best to sell the securities on behalf of the firm or buy the securities and then resell them to the public *at its own risk*. In the first case, the investment bank acts as an agent for the firm,

---

[10] Firms may also use the services of investment banks to help them place their securities privately.

EXHIBIT 11.8	ALTERNATIVE METHODS USED BY FIRMS AND THEIR INVESTMENT BANKS TO DISTRIBUTE EQUITY SECURITIES.

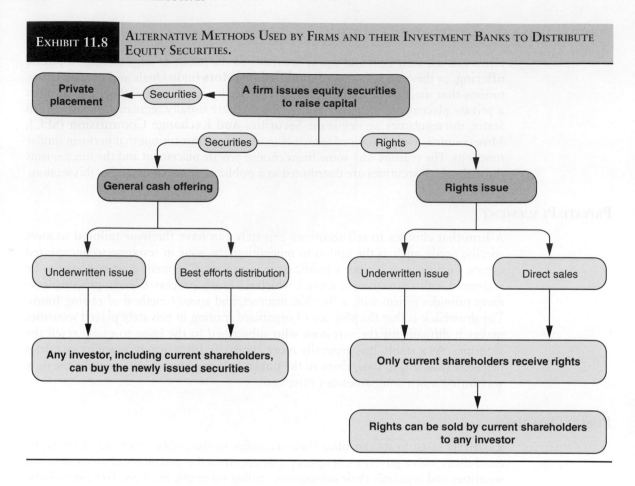

distributing securities on a **best efforts basis**. In a best efforts deal, if the investment bank fails to distribute a predetermined minimum number of shares during a specified period of time, the offering is canceled.

In the second case, the investment bank is said to act as an **underwriter**. When an issue is underwritten, the bank *buys* the securities from the firm in order to resell them to the public at a higher price. The **spread** between the price at which the issue is sold to the public and the price paid to the issuing firm is the investment bank's compensation. Studies of underwritten equity issues around the world indicate that the spread is between 2 and 8 percent of the value of the issue, depending on its size and quality, and the market conditions. To reduce the risk of being unable to sell the securities at a profit and to reach as many potential buyers as possible, the investment bank that has initiated the deal, called the **originating house**, **lead manager**, or **book runner**, forms an **underwriting syndicate** with other investment banks.[11] The originating house then sells some of the securities to the members of the syndicate, which they in turn sell to the public. To further broaden and speed distribution, a **selling group** is

[11] It is worth pointing out that the underwriting risk in the United States is not very high, because the price of the issue is usually set the day before the offering is made. Any price risk before that day is actually borne by the issuer, not the investment bank. In the United Kingdom, however, the underwriting risk is higher because the price is announced a few weeks before the issue is available for trading. See Massa et al. (2013) for the international evidence on rights offerings, trading, and regulation around the world.

formed to bring in additional investment banks that agree to sell the securities allocated to them for a fee. (Members of the selling group do not act as underwriters.) If needed, during the distribution period, the members of the underwriting group may buy the security in the open market to support its price and ensure the success of the offering. How is the spread shared among the various intermediaries? In a typical transaction, the originating house receives 15 to 20 percent of the spread, 20 to 30 percent goes to the members of the underwriting syndicate, and the balance is paid to members of the selling group as a **selling concession**.

Although new issues of equity and debt are generally underwritten, in many cases securities are distributed on a best efforts basis. Issues sold this way usually fall into two extreme categories. One category includes small and risky firms that are involved in IPOs for which investment banks are reluctant to bear the underwriting risk; the other category includes large and well-established companies whose strength and reputation allow them to issue securities that are not underwritten, thus saving the underwriting commission and related expenses.

An investment bank that underwrites a securities issue is providing more than a mechanism to sell securities. The bank is also telling the market that it believes the securities are of sufficient quality, otherwise it would not have underwritten them. In other words, the bank is playing a **certification role**. Clearly, top-quality firms may not need this seal of approval. Also, banks may be reluctant to "certify" the securities of risky firms, fearing that if the issue turns out to be a failure, their reputations may be damaged.

Rights Issues

When a firm sells common stocks exclusively to *new* investors, it obviously reduces the fraction of the firm's equity held by its *existing* shareholders. One way to prevent this **dilution** of property rights is to give existing shareholders the right to buy the portion of a new stock issue that will preserve their fractional ownership. The charters of most European companies require them to raise equity capital through rights issues only. This is not the case in the United States, where firms usually issue shares through general cash offers.

We illustrate the mechanics of a rights offering using an example that ignores **issuance costs** for the sake of simplicity. Suppose European Engines Corporation (EEC) has just announced that it will issue one million new shares of common stock through a rights issue at the **subscription price** of €80. (The subscription price is the selling price of the new shares.) Before the announcement, EEC shares were trading at €100 and there were four million shares outstanding. Next, EEC will notify its shareholders that they are granted one **right** for every share they hold and that the rights will expire at a specific future date (usually a few weeks after the offer date).[12] Before that date, the shares are usually referred to as **rights-on shares**; afterward, they are called **ex-rights shares**. Shareholders have three possibilities: (1) they can exercise their rights and subscribe to the issue; (2) they can sell their rights to interested investors if they do not want to buy new shares; or (3) they can do nothing and let the rights expire.

There are several questions to answer at this point: (1) Why is the subscription price (€80) set below the market price prevailing immediately before the announcement of the rights issue (€100)? (2) How many rights are needed to buy one new share?

---

[12] Rights are call options on the issuing firm's stock with the exercise price equal to the subscription price. See Chapter 16.

(3) What will happen to the share price when the shares become ex-rights shares, and what is the value of one right? (4) What effect does the issue have on the wealth of existing shareholders? (5) What is the role played by investment banks in a rights offer?

Setting an Appropriate Subscription Price. The subscription price (€80) is set below the market price (€100) because the rights offer is good for a few weeks. If the market price falls below the subscription price by the time the offer expires, no rational shareholder will exercise the right to buy a share for more than its prevailing market price. Thus, to ensure the success of the issue, the firm must set the subscription price at a sufficiently large discount to reduce the risk that the market price may drop *below* the subscription price during the period the offer is outstanding.

Number of Rights Required to Buy One New Share. There were four million shares outstanding before the issue was announced, so there will be four million rights granted by EEC. This represents four rights per new share issued (four million "old" shares divided by one million new shares). In other words, any investor, including the current shareholders, will need to own four rights to be able to buy one new share. Generalizing, if N_0 is the number of "old" shares and N_n is the number of new shares, the number of rights required to acquire one new share is $N = N_0/N_n$.

The Ex-Rights Price of a Share and the Value of a Right. Before the offer was announced, a shareholder who owned four shares had a holding worth €400 (four times €100). Because they hold four rights, they now have the opportunity to get a fifth share for €80. If they purchase the share, they will have five EEC shares worth €480(€400 + €80). It follows that the price of a share after the offer will no longer be €100 but €96 (€480 divided by five). The only difference between the €100 shares and the €96 shares is that the former are rights-on shares (they have a right attached to them) and the latter are ex-rights shares (they no longer carry rights). Consequently, the €4 difference between the two prices represents the price of a right.

To generalize the results, if N is the number of rights required to buy one new share, the ex-rights price is given by the following formula:

$$\text{Ex-Rights price} = \frac{N \times \text{Rights-on price} + \text{Subscription price}}{N + 1} \qquad (11.2)$$

and the value of a right is the difference between the rights-on price and the ex-rights price:[13]

$$\text{Value of one right} = \text{Rights-on price} - \text{Ex-rights price} \qquad (11.3)$$

Effect of the Rights Issue on the Wealth of Existing Shareholders. A right is an option issued by the firm to its existing shareholders, giving them the privilege, but *not* the obligation, to buy shares of the firm at a fixed price (the subscription price) over a fixed period of time (the life of the right). This is known as a **call option.** As mentioned, a shareholder who has received rights can exercise them and buy new shares at the subscription price, can sell them to other investors, or can let the rights "die."

---

[13] Using the ex-rights price given by equation 11.2, the value of one right is the following:

$$\text{Value of one right} = \frac{\text{Rights-on price} - \text{Subscription price}}{N + 1} = \frac{€100 - €80}{4 + 1} = \frac{€20}{5} = €4$$

Whether the shareholder exercises his option by tendering his rights to buy new shares or sells his option, his initial wealth will not change, as shown in Exhibit 11.9. Starting with an initial holding of €480 that consists of four EEC shares and €80 in cash, an investor will end up with the same amount of wealth. Only when the shareholder lets his rights expire (usually by ignorance or because the expiration date has passed before he could exercise or sell them) will his wealth be affected by the issue because the rights are then worthless.

The Role of Investment Banks in Rights Offerings.   In a rights offering, a firm can sell shares directly to its shareholders (and some firms do), but the possibility always exists that the market price will fall below the subscription price or that some investors may not exercise their rights to buy the new shares. To avoid this situation, the firm can arrange a **standby agreement** with an underwriting syndicate of investment banks. The syndicate agrees to buy any shares that have not been sold during the period the rights offering is outstanding at the subscription price less a **take-up fee**. In this case, investment banks underwrite only the unsold portion of the rights offering for a **standby fee**.

ISSUANCE COSTS OF PUBLIC OFFERINGS

Data indicate that issuance costs of public offerings, measured as a percentage of the gross amount raised, are higher for small issues than for large ones. Furthermore, rights offerings are less expensive than underwritten issues, and a rights offering without a standby agreement is the least expensive method for firms to raise new equity capital.

RAISING DEBT CAPITAL

In this section we review the alternative sources of debt financing available to firms. For most firms, the primary source of borrowed funds is bank loans. These loans can be supplemented by leasing contracts and, for relatively large firms with high credit standing, by the issue of commercial paper and corporate bonds.

EXHIBIT 11.9	EFFECT OF RIGHTS ISSUE ON THE WEALTH OF EXISTING SHAREHOLDER.

Initial Wealth		Decision	Ending Wealth		
		Case 1:	5 shares at €96	=	€480
		Tender 4 rights and buy 1 new share at €80	Cash	=	0
4 shares at €100	= €400		Total	=	€480
Cash	= 80				
Total	= €480	**Case 2:**			
		Sell 4 rights at €4 for €16	4 shares at €96	=	€384
			Cash (€80 + €16)	=	96
			Total	=	€480

BORROWING THROUGH BANK LOANS

Bank loans, particularly short-term loans, are the dominant source of debt. If a firm cannot access the corporate debt markets, then bank loans (short-term, medium-term, and long-term) are the only source of borrowed funds.

SHORT-TERM BANK LOANS

Firms that need to finance the seasonal buildup in their WCR usually resort to short-term bank loans. These loans are described as **self-liquidating** loans because banks expect firms to repay the loans with the cash that will be released by the subsequent reduction in WCR. For example, a company selling toys will need to borrow to finance the buildup of its inventory before the holiday season. After the goods are sold, some of the collected cash will be used to repay the bank loan. These loans can be extended for several months, after which they must be repaid or renewed for another period. How do banks ensure that firms that have borrowed short term do not use the loan to finance long-term investments? To protect themselves, banks usually impose a **cleanup clause** that requires the firm to be completely out of debt to the bank for at least one month during the year.

Short-term bank loans are often **unsecured loans**, meaning that the firm does not have to provide any assets as **collateral**, or guarantee, in case of default. When a short-term loan is a secured loan, assets such as accounts receivable and inventories are pledged as collateral. Three forms of unsecured loans are commonly used: (1) a **transaction loan**, which is a one-time loan used to finance a specific, nonrecurring need; (2) a **line of credit**, which is a nonbinding arrangement in which the bank lends the firm a stated amount of money over a fixed, but renewable, period of time, usually a year; and (3) a **revolving credit agreement**, which is the same as a line of credit except that the bank is *legally committed* to lend the money, a guarantee for which the bank charges a commitment fee on the unused portion of the **credit line**. These loans are extended at the **bank prime rate** (the **reference rate** for the pricing of loans to domestic borrowers) plus a spread over prime to reflect the specific risk of the borrowing firm. For example, if the prime rate is 5 percent, a firm that is charged a 3 percent spread over prime will borrow at 8 percent.

MEDIUM- AND LONG-TERM LOANS

Medium- and long-term loans are extended by banks and insurance companies and are known as **term loans**. Their duration is between one and ten years, and they are usually repaid in equal periodic installments that include the loan reimbursement as well as interest on the loan. This repayment schedule is known as an **annuity**. Contrary to most short-term loans, term loans are backed by collateral, meaning that the firm must provide the lender with assets to secure the loan. For example, a **mortgage loan** is backed by real estate and an **equipment financing loan** (which is often extended by the **captive finance subsidiary** of the equipment manufacturer) is backed by the piece of machinery. These types of loans are also known as **asset-based borrowing**. A popular alternative to term loans is **lease financing**.

BORROWING THROUGH LEASE AGREEMENTS

Leasing is an alternative source of debt capital that allows firms to finance the *use* of assets – such as computers, copiers, trucks, utility vehicles, or aircraft – without actually owning them. It is estimated that as much equipment is financed with leasing as through any other source of capital.

A lease is a contractual agreement between the owner of the asset, known as the **lessor**, and the user of the asset, known as the **lessee**. The agreement says the lessee has the right to use the asset in exchange for periodic payments to the lessor. The lessor can be a manufacturer, a financial institution, or an independent leasing company. When the lessor is not the manufacturer, the asset is sold by the manufacturer to the lessor, who, in turn, leases it to the lessee. When the contract expires, the asset is returned to the lessor, or, if the contract gives the lessee the option of purchasing the asset, the lessee may decide to buy it. This section describes two of the most common types of leases: **operating leases** and **financial leases**.[14] Then, after showing that a long-term lease is just another way of borrowing and using the proceeds to purchase the leased asset, we present a procedure for analyzing a leasing-versus-borrowing decision, using a long-term equipment lease as an illustration.

OPERATING LEASES

An operating lease is a short-term lease that usually, but not always, has the following characteristics. First, the length of the contract is shorter than the useful life of the asset, which means that the lessor must re-lease the asset or sell it at the expiration of the contract to recover its full cost. Second, the lessor is responsible for the maintenance and insurance costs while the asset is leased. Third, the lessee has the right to cancel the lease contract before it expires. This option is particularly valuable to the lessee when the asset leased is a piece of equipment that can quickly become obsolete because of rapid technological advances. However, to cancel the contract, the lessee may have to pay a cancellation fee.

FINANCIAL LEASES

A financial lease is a long-term lease that differs significantly from an operating lease. Contrary to an operating lease, it usually extends over most of the useful life of the asset; it is the lessee, not the lessor, that pays the maintenance and the insurance costs; and, generally, it cannot be canceled.

Most financial leases are one of the following: **direct lease, sale and leaseback**, or **leveraged lease**. A direct lease is a contract between the lessee and the owner of the asset. The owner can be the manufacturer of the asset or a leasing company that bought the asset from the manufacturer for the purpose of leasing it. Under a sale and leaseback lease, the firm owning the asset sells it to the leasing company, which immediately leases it back to the firm. Finally, in a leveraged lease, the leasing company finances the purchase of the asset with a substantial level of debt, using as collateral the lease contract and the **salvage value** of the asset – its value at the end of the lease contract.

LEASING AS AN ALTERNATIVE TO BORROWING

Suppose a firm has decided to change ten forklifts used in its plants and is considering leasing the new ones instead of purchasing them. Because the plants will be in

---

[14] The way accountants classify and record leases varies depending upon the accounting system of reference, IFRS or US GAAP. See '*Leases: Top Differences between IFRS 16 and ASC 842*'. kpmg-institutes.com.

operation for many more years, the lease must be a long-term, or financial, lease. The decision to lease or buy will not affect the way the vehicles are used, their useful life, or the cost of insuring and maintaining them. Thus, the difference between leasing and purchasing is only financial. If the firm decides to lease, it will not incur any initial large cash outlay to buy the equipment. Instead, it will have to make annual payments to the leasing company. If the firm decides to purchase the forklifts, it will incur a large initial cash outlay equal to the purchase price of the new forklifts. In this case, if the investment is financed with equity, the firm will also have to pay dividends to its shareholders, or, if it is financed by debt, make interest payments to its banks or bondholders.

Lease payments, like interest payments, are *fixed* obligations. Thus, the *relevant comparison is between lease financing and debt financing*, not equity financing. In other words, a financial lease is just an alternative to borrowing and using the proceeds of the loan to purchase the (leased) assets. This is why financial analysts count financial leases as debt in calculating a firm's debt ratios.

DECIDING WHETHER TO LEASE OR BORROW

Chapter 7 explains that the best management decisions are those with the highest net present value (NPV) because these decisions will maximize the firm's equity value. One way to apply the NPV rule to the decision of whether to lease or to borrow and buy is to compute the NPV of the *difference* in cash flows between leasing and buying. This NPV is known as the **net advantage to leasing** or **NAL**. If NAL is positive, the asset should be leased; if it is negative, it should be bought.

To illustrate, we return to the firm that needs to replace ten forklifts. The replacement decision has a positive NPV. The question is whether the firm should lease the equipment or borrow money and buy it. If purchased, the cost is $10,000 per vehicle, for a total of $100,000. This expenditure will be financed over the equipment's useful life of five years with a $100,000 loan of the same maturity. The interest rate on the loan is 5 percent. The vehicles will be depreciated for fiscal purposes over five years, according to the straight-line method. In other words, the annual depreciation expense will be $2,000 per vehicle ($10,000 divided by five) or $20,000 for the whole fleet (ten times $2,000). The *after-tax* scrap or salvage value of each vehicle is estimated at $1,000, meaning that in five years' time the firm should get $10,000 (ten times $1,000) from the sale of the forklifts. The corporate tax rate is 40 percent. If the firm leases the forklifts, the terms of the lease call for annual payments of $1,500 per vehicle or $15,000 for all of them. The lease payments are payable at the *beginning* of the year. The firm is responsible for the maintenance and insurance on the vehicles, regardless of whether it leases or buys.

Exhibit 11.10 summarizes the *difference* between the cash flows from leasing the forklifts and the cash flows from buying them. There are four differences in these cash flows.

First, we have the *after-tax* annual lease payments, the first one due *immediately* (the "now" column in the exhibit). The tax rate is 40 percent, so these annual payments, net of tax savings, will amount to $9,000 (60 percent of $15,000). Second, because the vehicles will be leased, the firm cannot depreciate them for tax purposes. It will therefore *lose* the tax savings from depreciation it would have had if it had owned the equipment. The annual tax *saving* resulting from the deductibility of annual depreciation expense amounts to $8,000 ($20,000 multiplied by a tax rate of 40 percent; it is the amount of tax the firm would have saved if it had been able to depreciate the assets). Third, the firm will not get the $10,000 after-tax scrap value of

EXHIBIT 11.10	SUMMARY OF DIFFERENCE IN CASH FLOWS WHEN FORKLIFTS ARE LEASED RATHER THAN PURCHASED.					

Lease versus Buy	Now	Year 1	Year 2	Year 3	Year 4	Year 5
After-tax lease payments	−$9,000	−$9,000	−$9,000	−$9,000	−$9,000	
Loss of tax savings on depreciation		−8,000	−8,000	−8,000	−8,000	−8,000
Loss of the after-tax scrap value						−10,000
Cash saved because the forklifts are not bought	+100,000					
Total differential cash flows	**$91,000**	**−$17,000**	**−$17,000**	**−$17,000**	**−$17,000**	**−$18,000**

the vehicles at the end of the fifth year because it will not own the forklifts. Fourth, if the vehicles are leased, the firm will not have to spend $100,000 to buy them.

The initial differential cash flow is positive, whereas those from year one to year five are negative. This reflects the fact that leasing the forklifts allows the firm to exchange the purchase price of $100,000 for cash outflows in the following five years. Because leasing is comparable to borrowing, the relevant discount rate is simply the after-tax cost of debt, that is, 3 percent [5% × (1 − 0.40)]. Discounting the total differential cash flows at 3 percent,[15] we found a positive NPV, or net advantage of leasing, of $12,282. Conclusion: leasing is "cheaper" than borrowing. The firm should lease the forklifts instead of borrowing to buy them.

BORROWING BY ISSUING SHORT-TERM SECURITIES

As mentioned earlier, large firms with high-credit standings can raise short-term funds by issuing commercial paper (CP) in their domestic money markets and Euro-CP in the Euromarkets. CP is usually unsecured; that is, the holder has no claim on the firm's income or assets if the issuing firm defaults. However, a CP issue is almost always backed by bank lines of credit, meaning that the bank agrees to lend money to the firm to repay the CP when it is due if, at the CP's maturity date, the firm is unable to issue new securities on preferential terms to repay the maturing paper.

CP is usually sold in large denominations ($5 million and higher), at a discount from face value, and with a maturity of 2 to 270 days in the US market and up to 360 days in the Euromarkets. The paper can be issued either directly to investors or through brokers specializing in the distribution of CP. In general, firms that are able to access the CP market find this debt instrument slightly cheaper and more flexible than a short-term bank loan.

BORROWING BY ISSUING CORPORATE BONDS

The alternative to borrowing medium- and long-term funds through bank loans and lease agreements is to borrow by issuing corporate bonds that can be either sold to the public at large or placed privately. Corporate bonds are long-term securities

---

[15] If the salvage value is uncertain, it should be discounted at a higher rate to adjust for the additional risk.

issued by firms to raise debt capital over periods ranging from 5 years to as many as 100 years, although most corporate bonds are issued with a maturity ranging between 5 and 30 years. As pointed out earlier, issues with a maturity longer than one year but shorter than five years are usually called corporate notes. For the sake of simplicity in the following discussion, we will not make any distinction between bonds and notes, calling any corporate debt security with a maturity longer than a year a bond.

We have seen in Chapter 10 that the bond-issuing firm has a contractual obligation to pay bondholders a fixed annual **coupon payment** over the bond's life and to repay the borrowed funds on the day the bonds reach their maturity date. (Coupons are sometimes paid semi-annually.) Corporate bonds denominated in US dollars are usually issued at a par or face value of $1,000, which is the amount of money that the firm must repay at maturity.

Suppose that Allied Equipment Corporation (AEC) issues 50,000 bonds with a par value of $1,000, a maturity date of five years, and a **coupon rate** of 5 percent. The buyer of one bond will receive a coupon payment of $50 each year (5 percent of $1,000) and will receive $1,000 at the end of the fifth year. If the bond is held to maturity, the holder earns an annual rate of return equal to the 5 percent coupon rate, because buying the bond is equivalent to depositing $1,000 in a bank account, receiving an annual interest rate of 5 percent for five years, and withdrawing the $1,000 at the end of the fifth year. If the bonds are priced at par value, AEC will receive $50 million ($1,000 multiplied by 50,000 bonds) less the cost of issuing the bonds, called **flotation costs**. If the bonds are offered at a discount, AEC will receive less than $50 million. For example, if the **original price discount** is 2 percent, the bonds will sell at $980 a piece (2 percent less than the par value) and AEC will receive $49 million less the cost of issuing the bonds. Note that bond prices are usually quoted as a percentage of par value. AEC's bond price will thus be quoted at 98 percent, which is equivalent to $980 per $1,000 of face value.

Security, Seniority, Sinking Funds, and Call Provisions

Corporate bonds are usually issued with a number of provisions attached to them that provide specific rights to either the bond buyer or the issuing firm. The buyer is protected by the bond's security, seniority, and sinking funds provisions. The issuing firm is protected against a possible drop in interest rates by a **call provision**.

Security. The issuer of a **secured bond** has provided collateral to the lender. For example, a firm issuing a **mortgage bond** offers as collateral the property it buys with the cash raised from the sale of the bond. If the firm fails to service the bond, the lenders, acting through their **trustee**, can seize and resell the property. **Unsecured bonds**, sometimes called **debentures**, are supported only by the general credit standing of the issuing firm.[16]

Seniority. A **senior bond** has a claim on the firm's assets (in the event of liquidation) that precedes the claim of **junior** or **subordinated debt**, which, in turn, takes precedence over the claims of the firm's shareholders.

---

[16] This is the terminology used in the United States. In the United Kingdom, debentures refer to secured bonds.

Sinking Fund Provision.   A sinking fund provision requires the bond issuer to set aside cash in a special **trust** account according to a regular schedule. This cash accumulates during the bond's life to allow the firm to either redeem the bonds at maturity or redeem parts of the outstanding bonds before they reach their maturity date. Because the trust is legally separated from the issuer's assets, a sinking fund provision reduces the risk that the issuer will be unable to redeem the bonds at maturity.

Call Provision.   The issuer of a **callable bond** has the option of **redeeming the bond** before it reaches its maturity date. For example, suppose AEC issues a five-year, 5.25 percent coupon bond at par ($1,000) that is callable at 2 percent over par ($1,020) any time *after* two years. (In this case, the bond has a **deferred call provision.**) The call option gives AEC the right to buy the bond from its holder at a **call value** that is 2 percent higher than its par value.

A callable bond is clearly less valuable to its *holder* than an identical bond that is not callable. The issuer will most likely call the bond when it can issue new ones at a lower coupon rate, thus forcing the holder to replace the original bond with a lower coupon one. This is why the issuer must compensate the holder with a redemption value that exceeds par value and with a higher coupon rate. (AEC's callable bond has a coupon rate of 5.25 percent, whereas the identical non-callable bond has a 5 percent coupon rate.) From the issuer's point of view, the call provision is valuable because it gives the option to retire the bond and refinance at a lower rate if market rates fall. But this option is costly to the issuer because a callable bond's coupon rate exceeds the rate of an identical, non-callable bond.

Floating Rate and Variable Rate Bonds

Some corporate bonds are called **floating rate bonds** or **floaters** because they have floating coupon rates; their coupon rates are related to another rate, called the **reference** or **benchmark rate,** which usually changes every six months. The reference rate is often the interest rate at which *international* banks lend US dollars to one another, known as the **London Interbank Offering Rate (LIBOR).** To illustrate, suppose AEC wants to issue five-year bonds but does not wish to pay a fixed coupon rate for the next five years because it expects rates to drop in the future. A floater may be the answer. The coupon rate that AEC will pay during the ten consecutive six-month periods over the next five years is the six-month LIBOR prevailing at the beginning of each period, plus a *fixed* **spread** of, say, 85 basis points (0.85 percent above LIBOR). The five-year floater allows AEC to eliminate its **refinancing risk** (the risk of not being able to renew the loan during the five-year period) while still bearing the risk of changing interest rates.

A floating rate bond should not be confused with a **variable rate bond.** The latter is a bond that has a coupon rate set at more than one level; for example, a 15-year bond may have a zero-coupon rate during its first five years and a 10 percent coupon rate during its remaining ten-year life. This pattern of coupon payments is attractive to a firm planning to invest the funds in a long-term project that is not expected to generate positive cash flows before its fifth year.

Convertible Bonds

As its name indicates, a **convertible bond** can be converted into the firm's common stock at the option of the bondholder. This **conversion option**, called a **sweetener** or an **equity kicker**, makes these bonds more attractive to investors. At the same time, firms can issue them at a lower rate than bonds without a conversion option. To illustrate, suppose General Beverage Company (GBC) issues ten-year, 5 percent bonds at $1,000 par value that are convertible into ten shares of GBC (this is the bond's **conversion ratio**). The share's **conversion price** is thus $100 ($1,000 divided by ten).[17] Shares of GBC are currently trading at $80, so the **conversion premium** is 25 percent ($100 less $80, divided by $80) and the bond's **conversion value** is $800 (ten times $80). If GBC issued ten-year *straight* bonds, it would have to pay a coupon rate of 6 percent. Thus, GBC has reduced its cost of debt by a full percentage point by giving investors the option to convert their bonds into equity.

The value of the conversion option is equal to the difference between the value of the convertible bond and the value of the bond if it were not convertible (which is called the **bond value of the convertible bond**). We know that GBC issued the convertible bond at $1,000, so this is its value. What is the bond value of the convertible bond, that is, its value if it were not convertible? It is the value of a bond with a face value of $1,000, a coupon rate of 5 percent, a term to maturity of ten years, and a yield of 6 percent (the rate it would have if it were not convertible). Entering these figures in the bond-price spreadsheet presented in Chapter 10, we get a value of $926.40:

	A	B
1	Yield to maturity	6%
2	Number of periods (term to maturity)	10
3	Coupon payment (5% of $1,000)	$50
4	Principal repayment	$1,000
5	Bond price	$926.40

- The formula in cell B5 is =PV(B1, B2, B3, B4)

Thus, the value of the conversion option is as follows:

$$\text{Option value} = \text{Value of convertible} - \text{Bond value}$$
$$= \$1,000 - \$926.40 = \$73.60$$

The convertible bond that GBC has sold to investors is equivalent to a package containing a ten-year, 5 percent *straight* bond worth $926.40 plus an *option* to buy ten shares of GBC at $100 per share (the option to buy equity) worth $73.60. Note that the option allows investors to buy shares, currently worth $80, for $100. The option is valuable because there is a chance that GBC's share price will rise above $100 during the next ten years. If it does, and if it exceeds the convertible bond value, investors will exercise their right to convert, and GBC will have to issue equity at $100 in exchange for the bonds. Does the deal make sense for GBC?

If the convertible bond is properly priced, then its option value ($73.60) is the appropriate "payment" that the firm must make to lower its cost of debt financing (from 6 percent to 5 percent). The convertible bond is, in this case, a fair deal that should neither reduce nor enhance the firm's value. Firms do not issue convertible bonds because the interest cost of a convertible bond is lower than the interest cost of

---

[17] A convertible bond can be viewed as straight bond plus a call option on the issuing firm shares. See Chapter 16.

a straight bond. The embedded option gives bondholders the right to convert the bond into the firm's common stock, and we have just shown that this option is valuable to bondholders. As a consequence, they are willing to accept a lower rate of return on the bond portion of the issue. In equilibrium, there should be a perfect trade-off, which explains why the value of the firm should not be affected by a convertible issue.

Firms may decide to issue convertible bonds for two main reasons. First, the lower coupon rate of a convertible, compared with that of a straight bond issue, can be attractive to high-growth, high-risk, cash-starved firms. For these firms, the cash flows from operations may not be high enough to fund their large capital expenditure programs. Furthermore, their level of risk may command high interest rates. By issuing convertibles that have lower coupon rates than straight bonds, the pressure on the firm's cash flows can be somewhat relieved and, to some extent, transformed instead into a pressure to generate capital gains for investors.

Second, convertible bonds may be attractive to bondholders who find it difficult to assess the risk of the firm issuing the securities or who fear that the firm's management may not act in their best interests. The straight-bond portion of the convertible package, which obliges the firm to make coupon payments and repay the principal, provides bondholders with some protection if the firm does not do well, and the option to convert the bonds into the firm's stock allows them to share in the increase in the firm's value if the firm does well.

RAISING EQUITY CAPITAL

External equity capital comes from two sources: common stock and **preferred stock**. Common stocks are described in detail in Chapter 10. In this section, we look at preferred stocks and compare them to common stocks; their comparative characteristics are summarized in Exhibit 11.11.

PREFERRED STOCKS

Preferred stockholders have priority over common stockholders in the payment of dividends and have a prior claim on the firm's assets in the event of liquidation (if there is anything left after debt holders and creditors have been paid). Preferred stockholders usually have no voting rights, but they may have **contingent voting rights**, such as the right to elect members to the board of directors *if* the company has skipped dividend payments for a specified number of quarters. Preferred shares, like bonds, may have sinking funds, can be callable, and can be converted into common equity.

Because straight preferred stocks pay a constant perpetual dividend, they are priced like perpetual bonds. To illustrate, suppose two years ago the Consolidated Motor Company (CMC) issued straight preferred stocks that pay a constant annual dividend of $6. A company in the same sector and with the same risk profile as CMC has just issued straight preferred stocks at $50 that promise to pay a constant dividend of $4. What is the current price of one share of CMC preferred stocks given that both CMC and the similar company quote their dividend payment on the basis of a face value of $100? The market yield of the similar preferred stock is 8 percent ($4 divided by $50). This is the yield that investors will require to hold CMC's preferred stocks. Again, recognizing that the value of a preferred stock is the same as the value of a perpetual bond with the annual dividend payments substituting for the coupon payments, we can apply the perpetual bond pricing formula given by equation 10.6

EXHIBIT 11.11	COMPARATIVE CHARACTERISTICS OF COMMON AND PREFERRED STOCKS.	

Characteristic	Common Stocks	Preferred Stocks
Control and voting rights		
	Common stockholders have full control and voting rights	Preferred stockholders have no control but some voting rights only if the firm skips dividend payments for a specified number of periods
Dividend payments		
Seniority	Can be paid only after payment to preferred stockholders	Paid before payment to common stockholders but after interest payments to debt holders
Are they cumulative?[1]	No	Most preferred are cumulative
Can they vary?	Yes, according to the firm's dividend payment policy	Yes, with payments often linked to money market rates
Is there a maximum payment?	No	There is usually an upper limit
Are they tax deductible for the issuing corporation?	No	No
Provisions		
Any sinking fund provision?	No	Some preferred have sinking funds
Is it callable by the firm?	Cannot be called	Some preferred are callable
Is it convertible into another type of security?	Cannot be converted	Some preferred are convertible into common stocks
Why and when they are usually issued?		
	To raise permanent equity capital to fund the firm's growth	To allow owners to raise quasi-equity without losing control. Often used as payment when buying another company
Pricing		
	See common stock valuation in Chapter 10	A straight preferred is priced like a perpetual bond (fixed dividend divided by market yield); see equation 11.4
Flexibility to issuing firm		
	The most flexible type of security a firm can issue	More flexible than bonds but less flexible than common stocks
Risk		
	Higher than preferred stocks and bonds	Higher than bonds but lower than common stocks

[1] Cumulative dividends means that if the firm skips the payment of dividends for a period of time, it will have to pay the missed dividends (called arrearage) when it resumes paying dividends.

in Chapter 10 to the valuation of CMC's preferred stocks. With a perpetual dividend payment of $6, CMC's preferred stock price is the following:

$$\text{Perpetual stock price} = \frac{\text{Annual dividend payment}}{\text{Market yield}} = \frac{\$6}{0.08} = \$75 \qquad (11.4)$$

If the preferred stocks are both callable and convertible into common stock, the $75 price will have to be *reduced* by the estimated value of the call option (which the holder has in effect *sold* to CMC) and *increased* by the estimated value of the option to convert into common stock (which the holder has in effect *purchased* from CMC).

Tracking Stock

A **tracking stock** is a special class of common stock carrying claims on the cash flows of a particular segment of a company, such as a subsidiary, division, or business unit.[18] Holders of tracking stocks receive dividends linked to the performance of the segment, but they neither legally own the assets of the segment nor have full voting rights. Diversified companies use these stocks to unlock the value of a specific activity for the benefit of investors who prefer having a direct equity claim on that activity instead of sharing it with claims on the company's other businesses.

Equity Warrants

Warrants are options sold by firms that give the holder the right to buy a specific number of shares of common stock at a fixed price (the **exercise price**) during the life of the warrant. In other words, these instruments are **call options** (an option to buy). Warrants are usually issued by firms as a sweetener attached to bonds or preferred shares, although firms have issued "plain" warrants that are not attached to any securities.

An issue of straight bonds sold with warrants is similar to a convertible bond issue. Both combine the features of a straight bond and an option on the firm's common stock and are appropriate financing instruments for high-growth, high-risk, cash-hungry companies. However, there are some differences. A convertible bond does not permit the holder to separate the bond from the option to convert, whereas warrants can be detached and sold separately from the bond. Also, when investors exchange their convertibles into equity, the firm's total capital does not change because the firm issues equity to replace debt. But when investors exercise their warrants, equity is issued (in return for cash), whereas debt is not automatically retired.

Contingent Value Rights

Contingent value rights (CVR) are options sold by companies that give the holder the right to *sell* a fixed number of shares to the issuing company at a fixed price during the life of the CVR. These option-type instruments are called **put options**.[19] They are valuable to investors who believe the share price of the issuing firm is currently *overvalued* and who expect the share price to fall *below* the exercise price of the CVR before their expiration date.

---

[18] The first notable issue of tracking stock took place in 1984 when General Motors (GM) acquired Electronic Data Systems. To finance the deal, GM issued stock that would track the performance of the new acquisition, rather than that of all GM's subsidiaries and business units. The phenomenon amplified in the late 1990s and early 2000s. For example, in 2000, AT&T Corp. issued $10.6 billion of tracking stock for its Wireless Group, one of the largest public offerings in US history.

[19] Put options are examined in Chapter 16.

Why would a firm want to issue this type of financial instrument? One reason is to raise funds; another is to signal to the market that the firm believes that its stock price is *not* overvalued. (If the firm thought its shares were overvalued, it would not issue the CVR.) A third reason is that when the CVR are sold in conjunction with a stock issue, they are an insurance given to the subscribers. The value of the shares they bought cannot be lower than the exercise price of the CVR because they can sell the shares back to the issuing firm at that price (at least until the CVR expire).

DISTRIBUTING CASH TO SHAREHOLDERS

So far in this chapter we have examined how firms *raise* the cash they need to fund their operations and grow their business. We now turn to the examination of the reverse decision, that is, the decision to *distribute* cash to shareholders either in the form of dividend payments or through the repurchase of the firm's own shares in the stock market. Why would a firm want to distribute cash to its shareholders and how does it make this decision? To answer this question we first review the actual **payout policies** of firms (*how much* cash they typically pay out and *when* they pay it out), and then look at how these policies affect the firm's share price and the wealth of its shareholders.

OBSERVED PAYOUT POLICIES

Consider the case of Apple Inc. The firm was incorporated in January 1977 and became a stock-market listed company in December 1980 with an initial public offering (IPO) of common stocks at $22 a share. On April 23, 1987, ten years after it was incorporated, and after a period of fast growth and strong profits, Apple declared its first quarterly dividend of 12 cents per share to be paid on June 15. On the same day, the firm also announced that it would split its shares two-for-one on June 15, giving shareholders one extra share for every share they already owned. As reported at the bottom of Exhibit 11.12, the 12 cent dividend for one old share became a 6 cent dividend for each new share because a **stock split** does not change the total amount of dividend shareholders receive.[20]

The stock market reacted positively to the *announcement* of the combined dividend payment and stock split: Apple's share price rose by 11 percent over the week following the announcement.[21] Why did Apple split its shares and pay a dividend, and why did the market react favorably to the announcement? One reason is that Apple's strong performance during the previous ten years allowed it to accumulate enough cash to start paying regular dividends. With the decision to pay dividends, Apple's management also sent a double signal to the market.

One signal was that Apple management was confident about the firm's future prospects and its capacity to sustain the dividend payments. The other signal was that management would rather pay dividends than waste the cash on unprofitable

---

[20] As indicated in Exhibit 11.12, as of June 2014, Apple has split its shares four times since they were first listed at $22 in December 1980 (three 2-for-1 splits followed by a 7-for-1 split). Its *split-adjusted* initial share price is thus $0.39 ($22 divided by two, three times, and then divided by seven). Thus, an investor who bought one share in the IPO in 1980 would now have 56 shares in 2014 (one share multiplied by two, three times, and then multiplied by seven). Note that a stock split is equivalent to a **stock dividend** because shareholders receive a dividend in the form of new shares instead of cash. When a company pays a stock dividend using shares of one of its subsidiaries, the stock dividend is called a **spin-off**.

[21] See Exhibit 11.12 and Apple website for its history of dividend payments, and Yahoo Finance for the history of Apple share prices.

EXHIBIT 11.12	APPLE DIVIDENDS, SHARE PRICES AND EARNINGS.

DIVIDENDS ARE MORE STABLE THAN PRICES AND EARNINGS

Date of Dividend Payment		Dividend Per Share	Share Price[1]	Earnings Quarter	Earnings Per Share
2018	February 15	$0.63	$172.99	2018-Q1	$3.89
2017	November 16	$0.63	$171.10	2017-Q4	$2.07
	August 17	$0.63	$157.86	2017-Q3	$1.68
	May 18	$0.63	$152.54	2017-Q2	$2.10
	February 16	$0.63	$135.35	2017-Q1	$3.36
2016	November 10	$0.57	$107.79	2016-Q4	$1.69
	August 11	$0.57	$107.93	2016-Q3	$1.43
	May 12	$0.57	$ 90.34	2016-Q2	$1.91
	February 11	$0.52	$ 93.70	2016-Q1	$3.28
2015	November 12	$0.52	$115.72	2015-Q4	$3.06
	August 13	$0.52	$115.15	2015-Q3	$2.33
	May 14	$0.52	$128.95	2015-Q2	$1.86
	February 12	$0.47	$126.46	2015-Q1	$1.97
2014	November 13	$0.47	$112.82	2014-Q4	$1.42
	August 14	$0.47	$97.50	2014-Q3	$1.29
	June 9	7-for-1 Stock Split	$645.75[2]	2014-Q3	$10.01
	May 15	$3.29	588.82	2014-Q2	9.03
	February 13	3.05	543.99	2014-Q1	11.79
2013	November 14	3.05	528.16	2013-Q4	14.56
	August 15	3.05	495.02	2013-Q3	8.31
	May 16	3.05	429.22	2013-Q2	7.51
	February 14	2.65	457.81	2013-Q1	10.16
2012	November 15	2.65	512.74	2012-Q4	13.93
	August 16	2.65	617.92	2012-Q3	8.76
2005	February 28	2-for-1 Stock Split	88.99[2]	2005-Q1	0.35
2000	June 21	2-for-1 Stock Split	101.25[2]	2000-Q2	0.62
1995	December 15	0.12	35.25	1995-Q4	−0.56
	September 08	0.12	44.75	1995-Q3	0.48
	June 23	0.12	48.75	1995-Q2	0.84
	March 10	0.12	39.50	1995-Q1	0.59
1994	December 16	0.12	37.25	1994-Q4	1.55
	September 9	0.12	35.25	1994-Q3	0.95

EXHIBIT 11.12	APPLE DIVIDENDS, SHARE PRICES AND EARNINGS. (*Continued*)

DIVIDENDS ARE MORE STABLE THAN PRICES AND EARNINGS

Date of Dividend Payment		Dividend Per Share	Share Price[1]	Earnings Quarter	Earnings Per Share
	June 24	0.12	25.61	1994-Q2	1.16
	March 04	0.12	34.63	1994-Q1	0.15
1993	December 17	0.12	29.50	1993-Q4	0.34
	September 10	0.12	26.25	1993-Q3	0.02
	June 25	0.12	41.75	1993-Q2	−1.63
	March 12	0.12	56.25	1993-Q1	0.92
1992	December 18	0.12	58.25	1992-Q4	1.33
	September 11	0.12	47.63	1992-Q3	0.81
	June 19	0.12	44.75	1992-Q2	1.07
	March 13	0.12	63.13	1992-Q1	1.09
1991	December 13	0.12	50.38	1991-Q4	1.36
	September 13	0.12	48.63	1991-Q3	0.67
	June 14	0.12	41.13	1991-Q2	−0.44
	March 15	0.12	66.25	1991-Q1	1.07
1990	December 14	0.12	39.50	1990-Q4	1.28
	September 14	0.11	34.00	1990-Q3	0.81
	June 15	0.11	39.50	1990-Q2	0.96
	March 15	0.11	36.50	1990-Q1	1.04
1989	December 15	0.11	33.75	1989-Q4	0.96
	September 15	$0.10	$45.00	1989-Q3	$1.24
	June 15	0.10	47.50	1989-Q2	0.74
	March 15	0.10	35.00	1989-Q1	0.44
1988	December 15	0.10	39.50	1988-Q4	1.10
	September 15	0.08	41.63	1988-Q3	0.84
	June 15	0.08	45.75	1988-Q2	0.71
	March 15	0.08	45.00	1988-Q1	0.61
1987	December 15	0.08	37.50	1987-Q4	0.92
	September 15	0.06	51.75	1987-Q3	0.54
	June 15	0.06	41.50	1987-Q2	0.40
	June 15	2-for-1 Stock Split	78.50[2]	1987-Q1	0.51

[1] Closing share price on the day the dividend was paid or the shares were split.
[2] Pre-split price.

investments that would destroy the firm's value. The signal to the market came in the form of an *implicit* commitment to pay a quarterly dividend of *at least* 6 cents per share for the foreseeable future. This is exactly what Apple did, as reported in Exhibit 11.12. Dividends per share rose to 8 cents in December 1987, 10 cents in December 1988, 11 cents in December 1989, and 12 cents in December 1990, and stayed at that level until December 1995 after which Apple stopped paying dividends because its business and financial condition began to deteriorate in the early nineties, a few years before dividend payments were discontinued.[22]

Shareholders had to wait for 17 years before seeing the resumption of dividend payments in August 2012, long after the revival and success of Apple that had begun ten years earlier. On March 19, 2012 Apple announced that it would start paying in a quarterly dividend in August of $2.65 cents and launch a $15 billion **share repurchase program** to be carried out over three years. The firm's share price rose on that day to reach an all-time high of $601.10.

A look at Exhibit 11.12 shows that Apple's quarterly earnings per share and share price have fluctuated widely while its dividends, when paid, grew in a stable, step-wise fashion. Apple's pattern of dividend payments is typical of most firms. When a newly established company is growing, it usually does not pay dividends because it needs the cash to fund its growth and has little need to signal to the market (via regular dividend payments) its confidence in the future and its commitment not to waste cash on unprofitable investments. When its growth rate levels off and its cash flow strengthens, the firm would typically begin paying dividends but keep the payments stable or increase them slightly even if it has the cash to raise them significantly. Firms adopt this prudent payout policy because they want to avoid cutting their dividend if their cash flow unexpectedly weakens. Only if their business and financial condition deteriorate significantly will firms reduce their dividend or cut it completely, as Apple did in 1996. If their business and financial situation improve, firms may resume paying dividends but would do so long after their condition has strengthened as Apple did in 2012 following its strong recovery that began ten years earlier.

These observations are confirmed by executives who were asked to describe their firm's **dividend policy**. A look at Exhibit 11.13 shows that the vast majority of executives say that they try to maintain a smooth dividend stream from year to year and are reluctant to reduce dividend per share.

One implication of this approach to dividend payments is that firms operating in sectors that generate stable and predictable cash flows tend to have *higher* average **dividend payout ratios** (dividend payments as a percentage of net profits) than firms operating in sectors that generate unstable and uncertain cash flows. This phenomenon is confirmed by the data reported in Exhibit 11.14. It shows that firms operating in sectors with stable and more predictable cash flow, such as tobacco and utilities companies, have average payout ratios exceeding 50 percent whereas firms operating in unstable and less predictable cash-flow sectors, such as software services and biotechnology, have average payout ratios not exceeding 10 percent.

To summarize: firms usually begin paying regular and stable dividends when their growth rate levels off following a period of strong earnings and cash accumulation. Dividend payments signal to the market that management is confident in the firm's future

---

[22] These stable patterns of dividend payments are referred to as **regular dividend payments** as opposed to the case of a one-time dividend payment called a **special dividend payment**. When a firm makes a special dividend payment, it signals to the market that this is an exceptional event that may not be repeated soon. The signal does not have the same strength as in the case of a regular dividend payment.

Exhibit 11.13	Survey Responses for 166 Dividend-Paying Firms.

Do these statements describe factors that affect your company's dividend decisions?	Percent of executives who agree or strongly agree
1. We try to avoid reducing dividends per share	93.8
2. We try to maintain a smooth dividend stream from year to year	89.6
3. We consider the level of dividends per share that we have paid in recent quarters	88.2
4. We are reluctant to make dividend changes that might have to be reversed in the future	77.9
5. We consider the change or growth in dividends per share	66.7

Source: A. Brav, J.R. Graham, C.R. Harvey, and R. Michaely, "Payout Policy in the 21st Century," *Journal of Financial Economics* 77, September 2005, pp. 483–527.

Exhibit 11.14	Average Dividend Payout Ratios by Sectors for a Large Sample of US Firms over the Period 2010–2017.[1,2]

FIRMS IN SECTORS GENERATING STABLE AND PREDICTABLE CASH FLOWS TEND TO HAVE HIGHER PAYOUT RATIOS THAN FIRMS IN SECTORS GENERATING UNSTABLE AND UNCERTAIN CASH FLOWS

Sectors with High-Payout Ratios		Sectors with Low-Payout Ratios	
Tobacco	88%	Research and consulting services	10%
Multi-utilities (electric, gas, and water)	75%	Systems software	9%
Oil and gas refineries	74%	Technological distributors	8%
Electric utilities	68%	Internet software	6%
Water utilities	55%	Biotechnology	4%
Average all sectors 50%			

[1] Source: Compiled by the authors with data from *Capital IQ*.

[2] For similar results for a sample of European firms, see Baker, H. Kent. *Dividends and Dividend Policy,* John Wiley & Sons, 2009.

performance and committed to avoid wasting cash on value-destroying investments. This may explain why the announcement of the initiation of a dividend-payment program usually raises the firm's share price. If the firm's subsequent performance deteriorates, management is usually reluctant to reduce or eliminate dividends unless it believes that performance will remain weak for a while. Cutting or omitting dividends would send a negative signal to the market and is usually accompanied by a drop in share price.

HOW AND WHY FIRMS PAY DIVIDENDS AND BUY BACK THEIR SHARES

How do firms pay dividends to their shareholders and repurchase their shares in the stock market? Even though both payout methods return cash to the firm's owners, the *way* the cash is distributed is not the same. We look at how the two methods differ and whether these differences matter to shareholders. Comparing the two cash-distribution methods will also provide us with further insight into why firms pay out cash to their shareholders.

How Firms Pay Dividends

Consider the case of Apple Inc. On February 1, 2018, the Apple Board of directors announced that the company will pay a quarterly dividend of $0.63 per share.[23] When will Apple shareholders receive the declared dividend? Refer to Exhibit 11.15. It illustrates the sequence of events from the day the dividend is declared (the **dividend declaration date**) to the day the dividend is paid (the **dividend payment date**). Note that 14 days separate the declaration date (February 1) from the payment date (February 15).

Because the list of a firm's shareholders changes constantly (some "old" shareholders sell their shares to "new" shareholders), the company must set a **record date** in order to know to whom it will pay the dividend. In the case of Apple, the record date was February 12, 2018. This means that Apple will pay the quarterly dividend only to the shareholders who are registered with the company as at the close of business on that date.

But there is an additional timing problem because it takes a few days for the buyers of a company's common stocks to register their shares with the firm. Let's say it takes four days. In this case, only shareholders who buy Apple shares at least four days *before the record date* will receive the dividend (they are referred to as the **shareholders of record**). This date (February 9) is known as the **ex-dividend date**. Anyone who buys the stock on or after that date will *not* receive the dividend. Before the ex-dividend date, the stock is said to trade **cum-dividend**, which means *with* the right to receive the dividend. On and after the ex-dividend date, the stock is said to trade **ex-dividend**, that is, *without* the right to receive the dividend. What is the relationship between the cum-dividend price and the ex-dividend price?

In the absence of tax payments, on the ex-dividend date, the share price should drop by an amount equal to the dividend payment so that the cum-dividend price is equal to the ex-dividend price plus the dividend payment. When dividend income is taxed at a higher rate than capital gains, the drop in share price is less than the dividend payment. This is illustrated in self-test question 11.3. Refer to the question and its answer to see how different tax rates on income and capital gains affect the relationship between the cum-dividend price and the ex-dividend price.

How Firms Repurchase their Shares

There are several methods a firm can use to return cash to its shareholders by repurchasing its own shares. The most common method is through a discretionary **open**

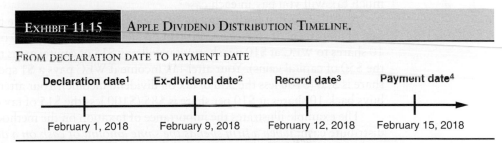

| **Exhibit 11.15** | Apple Dividend Distribution Timeline. |

From declaration date to payment date

Declaration date[1]	Ex-dividend date[2]	Record date[3]	Payment date[4]
February 1, 2018	February 9, 2018	February 12, 2018	February 15, 2018

[1] On this date the Apple board announced a quarterly dividend of $0.63 per share.
[2] On or after this date buyers of Apple shares will not receive the $0.63 dividend.
[3] Apple will pay the $0.63 dividend to the shareholders who are registered on that date.
[4] This is the date when Apple will transfer the $0.63 per share to the shareholders of record.

---

[23] Firms must comply with certain legal rules before being able to pay a dividend. In general, a dividend payment cannot exceed the firm's cumulative amount of retained earnings (past and current earnings' retentions) reported in the firm's balance sheet. Also, firms that are legally insolvent or firms that have filed for bankruptcy cannot pay a dividend even if they have the cash to make the payment.

market purchase. In this case, the firm announces that it will launch a share repurchase program stating the amount of cash it intends to spend and the expected duration of the program, as Apple did in May 2017. During that time frame, the firm will buy back its shares in the stock market at whatever price the shares trade on that day.[24]

Other, less frequent, methods a firm could use to buy back its shares are **tender offers** and **privately negotiated repurchases.** An example of the first case is when a firm wants to counter an unfriendly takeover bid: to prevent the takeover attempt, the firm announces that it will buy back its shares at a premium from the market price (typically around 20 percent above the current market price) from any shareholder ready to tender them during a specified period of time (typically about one month). If fewer shares than expected are tendered, the firm may cancel the offer.

There are situations when a firm would consider buying back shares directly from a shareholder through a privately negotiated transaction. For example, a firm may buy a large block of shares directly from a shareholder at a *discount* from the current market price to avoid a sale in the stock market that may put a downward pressure on share prices if the market for the firm's shares is not liquid enough. Another example is when a firm buys a large number of shares from an individual who is threatening to take over the firm. To avoid being taken over, the firm would offer to buy the shares at a *premium* from their current market price.

DIFFERENCES BETWEEN DIVIDEND PAYMENTS AND SHARE REPURCHASES

There are significant differences between dividend payments and share repurchases, and some shareholders may prefer one method over the other. We review below some of the most important differences and explain why some shareholders have a preference for one of the two distribution methods.

Share repurchases generally expose shareholders to lower taxes than dividend payments.   Let's say you bought 100 shares of the World Entertainment Company (WEC) a year ago at $5 dollar a share. The shares are now worth $10 each. Suppose that WEC can either pay a special dividend of $1 per share or buy back shares at $10 each. If WEC pays the $1 special dividend, you will receive $100 of dividends on your 100 shares. If, instead, WEC uses the $100 to buy back ten of your shares, you will realize a capital gain of $50 (recall that you bought the ten shares at $5 each). How much tax will you pay in each case?

Assume first that both dividend payments and capital gains are taxed at the same rate of 30 percent. If you receive $100 of dividends you will pay $30 of taxes. If you sell 10 shares to WEC at $10 per share, you will pay $15 of capital gains tax (30 percent of the $50 of capital gains). Your after-tax income if WEC pays a $1 special dividend per share is $70 ($100 less the $30 of tax on dividend income). Your after-tax gain if WEC buys back 10 shares at $10 per share is $85 ($100 less the $15 of tax on capital gains).

The example illustrates the importance of taxation on the method the firm uses to distribute cash: *when a firm spends the same amount of cash on a dividend payment and a share buyback, the after-tax gains to shareholders from the share buyback is higher than the after-tax income from the dividend payment even though both are taxed at the same rate.* This happens because in the case of dividend payments the

---

[24] Open market purchases are usually controlled by capital market regulators in order to prevent firms from manipulating their share price. Regulators generally do not allow firms to buy more than a certain percentage of their shares per day and prohibit firms from buying at the start of the trading session or close to the end of the trading session.

tax is paid on the full $100 of dividend income whereas in the case of a sale of shares the tax is paid on the smaller $50 of capital gains.

If the tax rate on capital gains is *lower* than the tax rate on dividend income (which is often the case around the world), shareholders will pay an even *lower* amount of taxes when they sell shares. The implication is clear: *a firm's optimal payout policy should be to distribute cash to its shareholders only through share buybacks and never pay a dividend if the firm wants to minimize its shareholders' tax payments.*[25] So why do firms pay dividends?

The answer is not obvious. This is why the payment of dividends is often referred to in the financial literature as the **dividend puzzle**. One answer to the puzzle is that the tax code in many countries exempts some investors from paying taxes on dividend income. These investors will demand dividend-paying stocks if they need regular income. (Note that if they raise the cash by selling shares they will incur **transactions costs**.) Who are these investors? They include (1) non-profits, tax-exempt institutions such as pension funds and endowments; and (2) corporations that are exempted from paying taxes on the dividends they receive from companies they own but must pay taxes on capital gains. All else being equal, these corporations prefer to hold the shares of firms that pay high dividends.

Another answer to the puzzle is that some institutional and individual investors demand dividend-paying stocks *despite their tax disadvantage*. Who are these investors? They include (1) investment companies that are legally restricted to only buy dividend-paying stocks; (2) endowment funds and trust companies that are legally required to only spend income (and not capital gains) and thus demand dividend-paying stocks; and (3) some individuals in lower tax brackets who prefer to receive a regular income from dividends rather than sell shares on a regular basis to raise the cash they need. They just like the self-imposed discipline of only spending their regular dividend income rather than having to rely on the regular sale of shares to get the cash they need. If they rely on share sales, they may be tempted to consume more than they should and sell more shares than they really have to. This behavioral explanation of the preference for dividend payments in the presence of taxation is known in the literature as the **self-control hypothesis**.

There is another answer to the dividend puzzle. Recall our earlier observation regarding firms' actual payout policies: some firms would pay dividends even if the distribution is not tax-efficient for their shareholders because dividend payments are not only a cash-distribution mechanism but also a way to convey information to shareholders about the confidence of management in the firm's future prospects and to signal to shareholders that management does not want to waste cash on value-destroying projects. This alternative explanation is usually referred to in the financial literature as the **dividend signaling hypothesis**.

Whether the self-control hypothesis, the presence of different types of institutional investors that are subject to different legal constraints and tax rules, or the dividend signaling hypothesis can explain why firms pay dividends is still an open question which we revisit in the next section after we look at how payout policies affect share prices.

Share repurchases do not send as strong a signal as dividend payments.   Because dividend payments are a stronger commitment to distribute cash that is not easily reversed, we would expect firms to opt for a dividend payment rather than a

---

[25] Note that share buybacks have an additional tax advantage over dividend payments: shareholders will pay the capital gains tax only if they sell their shares. In other words, they can postpone the capital gains tax as long as they don't sell their shares.

repurchase program if they want to send a credible signal of confidence in their future prospects and convince their shareholders that they would rather give them back cash than spend it on value-destroying investment.[26]

Share repurchases allow firms to neutralize the impact of dilution from granting stocks and options to employees.   They also allow firms to get the shares they need to acquire other companies. Some firms rely heavily on attracting and retaining key people by granting them shares or options to buy shares. This means that these firms have to issue new shares for distribution to employees who were granted equity as well as to employees who exercise their options to buy shares. The issuance of these additional shares reduces or dilutes *earnings per share* because the firm's earnings are divided by a larger number of shares. Firms usually offset these dilutions by buying back their shares in the open market. They may also buy back their own shares to use them to acquire other companies in exchange for shares instead of cash.

Share repurchases are more flexible than dividend payments.   A commitment to pay dividends is less flexible than a **share buyback program** because, once a dividend is announced, the firm is legally obligated to make the payment and would find it difficult to omit or cancel future payments unless it encounters serious financial problems, as discussed earlier. With a share buyback program the firm is not obligated to spend the full amount it announced. Some firms never implement their announced share repurchase program if market conditions no longer justify carrying out the program.

Share repurchases allow the firm to support its share price when shares are temporarily undervalued.   Firms often announce share buyback programs when the stock market experiences steep declines in value. Buying back the firm's shares would in this case prevent their price from falling sharply for reasons that are not directly related to the firm's performance but to the pessimism of market participants regarding the prospect for the entire economy. In this case, buying back its shares in the open market allows the firm to signal that it believes its shares are temporarily undervalued.

DOES A FIRM PAYOUT POLICY AFFECT ITS SHARE PRICE AND THE WEALTH OF ITS SHAREHOLDERS?

Let's use the case of the Atlantic Water Company (AWC) to find out if and how a firm payout policy affects its share price and the wealth of its shareholders. The board of directors of AWC is meeting to decide whether to pay a *special* **cash dividend** to its shareholders. The firm holds $250 million of cash, generates a constant annual cash flow of $100 million, and has no debt. It has 100 million shares outstanding listed on the stock market, and its shareholders expect a return of 10 percent on their equity investment. Its share price, based on that information, is $12.50, as shown in the upper part of Exhibit 11.16.

Note that AWC is a zero-growth firm: it pays out every year its entire annual cash flow of $100 million in dividends: its *regular* annual dividend per share is thus $1 ($100 million divided by 100 million shares).

---

[26] If the firm wishes to signal through share repurchases it should do it through a fixed-price tender offer rather than through discretionary open market purchases: the tender offer would send a stronger signal because it is implemented over a shorter time period with a commitment to buy the shares at a premium.

EXHIBIT 11.16	AWC SHARE PRICE AND SHAREHOLDER WEALTH WITH ALTERNATIVE PAYOUT POLICIES.

THE ALTERNATIVE PAYOUT POLICIES DO NOT AFFECT THE WEALTH OF SHAREHOLDERS

AWC initial share price

- AWC does not grow; it generates a constant annual cash flow of $100m per year forever
- AWC holds $250m in cash and has no debt (it is an all-equity financed firm)
- AWC has 100 million of shares outstanding and its shareholders expect a return of 10% on their investment
- The value of AWC non-cash assets is thus the present value of a no-growth perpetuity of $100m at 10%[1]:

$$V(\text{non-cash assets}) = \frac{\$100m}{10\%} = \$1,000m$$

- The value of all AWC assets = Cash holding + V(non-cash assets) = $250m + $1,000m = $1,250m
- The value of AWC equity = The value of all its assets (because AWC has no debt) = $1,250m
- AWC share price (P) is thus:

$$P = \frac{\text{Value of equity}}{\text{Number of shares}} = \frac{\$1,250m}{100m} = \$12.50$$

Recommendation No.1: AWC uses its cash to pay an immediate dividend of $250 million

- Immediate dividend per share = $DPS_0 = \dfrac{\text{Total dividend payment}}{\text{Number of shares}} = \dfrac{\$250m}{100m} = \$2.50$
- AWC does not grow and pays out all its future annual perpetual cash flow of $100m in dividend
- AWC perpetual annual dividend per share starting at the end of the first year: $DPS = \dfrac{\$100m}{100m} = \$1$
- AWC ex-dividend share price after the immediate dividend payment is thus:[1]

$$P_{ex} = PV(\text{perpetual DPS of \$1 at }10\%) = \frac{\$1}{10\%} = \$10$$

- Shareholder wealth per share (W_S) after the immediate dividend payment is thus:

$$W_S = DPS_0 + P_{ex} = \$2.50 + \$10 = \underline{\$12.50}$$

Recommendation No.2: AWC repurchases $250 million of its shares in the open market at $12.50

- Number of shares repurchased $= \dfrac{\$250m}{\$12.50} = 20m$
- Number of shares outstanding after the repurchase = 100m − 20m = 80m
- Dividend per share after the repurchase (starting at the end of the first year): $DPS = \dfrac{\$100m}{80m} = \$1.25$
- AWC share price after the repurchase is thus:[1]

$$P_{rep} = PV(\text{perpetual DPS of \$1.25 at }10\%) = \frac{\$1.25}{10\%} = \underline{\$12.50}$$

Recommendation No.3: AWC issues $100 million of equity and pays an immediate dividend of $350 million (using the $250 million of initial cash holding plus the $100 million from the share issuance)

- Number of new shares issued $= \dfrac{\$100m}{\$12.50} = 8m$
- Total number of shares after the share issuance = 100m + 8m = 108m
- Immediate dividend per share after the share issuance: $DPS_0 = \dfrac{\$350m}{108m} = \$3.24$
- Perpetual future dividend per share after the share issuance: $DPS = \dfrac{\$100m}{108m} = \$0.926$
- AWC ex-dividend share price after the issuance is thus:[1]

$$P_{ex} = PV(\text{perpetual DPS of \$0.926 at }10\%) = \frac{\$0.926}{10\%} = \$9.26$$

- Shareholder wealth per share (W_S) after the immediate dividend payment is thus:

$$W_S = DPS_0 + P_{ex} = \$3.24 + \$9.26 = \underline{\$12.50}$$

---

[1] Recall that the present value of a perpetual cash flow is the cash flow divided by the appropriate discount rate (see formula 2.6 in Chapter 2).

Some directors recommended that the cash holding of $250 million be used to repurchase AWC shares in the open market. Others wanted to use the cash to pay a special dividend of $250 million, arguing that shareholders would be better off with $250 million in their pocket than a share repurchase. Another group felt that the board should send a strong signal to the market about its confidence in the firm's future and pay a higher dividend of $350 million. When asked where the additional $100 million will come from, the proponents of the $350 million dividend payment said that the extra $100 million could be borrowed or raised through a new issue of stocks. Some board members felt that it would be inefficient to raise money in the market for the sole purpose of immediately giving it back to shareholders.

AWC's chief executive had an alternative proposal: he wanted to use the $250 million to upgrade AWC's water purification plants instead of paying out the cash to shareholders or buy back the company's shares. He told the board that the upgraded facilities would generate a higher future cash flow that would allow AWC to pay a higher dividend starting next year. Each group felt that their recommendation, if implemented, would lift AWC's share price above $12.50 and increase the wealth of AWC shareholders. What should the board do?

Let's first examine how each recommendation would affect AWC's share price and the wealth of its shareholders *assuming that markets are perfect*. In a perfect market environment (1) there are no taxes on income and capital gains; (2) there are no **transaction costs** (there are no costs to shareholders if they buy or sell AWC shares); (3) there are no flotation costs (there are no costs to AWC if it issues stocks or bonds); (4) there is complete **transparency** (shareholders know as much about AWC's prospects as AWC's managers) and hence there is no need for the AWC board to use dividend payments and share buybacks to signal its confidence in the firm's future performance; and (5) there are no **agency costs;** this means that AWC managers, who work as *agents* on behalf of shareholders, will not undertake activities that would destroy shareholder value (these value-destroying projects, if undertaken, are referred to as "agency costs"). In the next section we revisit these assumptions and examine how firms should adjust their payout policy when markets are not perfect. Why do we assume that markets are perfect when we know they are not? If we want to understand how a firm's payout policy affects its share price, we need first to examine the link between payout policy and share price in the absence of market frictions. We show here that *in a perfect market environment, a firm's payout policy does not affect the wealth of its shareholders*. Armed with this conclusion, we later ask ourselves how payout policies affect shareholder wealth in the presence of markets imperfections. It is easier to understand how market imperfections affect payout policies if we know that payout policies are irrelevant in a perfect market environment.

Suppose you own a share of AWC worth $12.50. What are the effects of the three payout recommendations on your wealth in a perfect market environment? The answers are summarized in Exhibit 11.16. The effect on AWC's share price if the $250 million is invested in a project is reported in Exhibit 11.17. Let's review each recommendation in turn.

PAYING AN IMMEDIATE SPECIAL DIVIDEND OF $250 MILLION

Refer to the first recommendation in Exhibit 11.16. In this case, the board of AWC declares a one-off special dividend of $250 million.

Size of the immediate special dividend per share (DPS$_0$). The immediate special dividend per share is equal to $2.50 ($250 million divided by 100 million shares).

Ex-dividend share price (P_{ex}). Recall that AWC's share price before the announcement (the cum-dividend share price) was $12.50. When the stock goes ex-dividend, the share price drops to its ex-dividend price of $10 (the present value of a perpetual stream of $1 dividend discounted at 10 percent). In other words, because of our perfect-market assumption of no tax payments, the difference between the cum-dividend and ex-dividend price ($12.50 minus $10) is equal to the dividend payment ($2.50), a relationship we reported earlier.

Effect on the wealth of shareholders (W_s). Before the announcement you owned a share worth $12.50. When the share goes ex-dividend, you own a share worth $10 and receive a $2.50 dividend, for a total of $12.50. In other words, your wealth (and the wealth of the other AWC shareholders) is not affected by the board decision to pay a special dividend.

Undoing the special dividend payment. What if you did not want to receive the special dividend? Not a problem! Suppose you own eight shares. All you have to do is sell your eight shares at $12.50 on the declaration date, collect $100, and then buy back ten shares at $10 per share after they go ex-dividend. You now own ten shares worth $100 instead of eight shares worth $80 plus a dividend of $20 (eight times $2.50): you have not collected the dividend and your wealth is still $100. (Recall that because of the perfect-market assumption you do not incur transactions costs when you sell and buy shares.)

Conclusion: *in a perfect market environment, a firm's dividend policy does not affect the wealth of its shareholders. If some shareholders do not want to receive the dividend, they can sell their shares on the declaration date at the cum-dividend price and buy more shares after the ex-dividend date at the lower ex-dividend price.*

Buying Back $250 million of Shares in the Open Market

Refer to the second recommendation in Exhibit 11.16. In this case, the board of AWC announces that AWC will immediately buy back $250 million of its own shares in the open market at $12.50 per share. AWC can buy its shares at $12.50 because of the perfect-market assumptions, that is, because there are no transactions costs and no positive signal associated with the repurchase. With a share price of $12.50, AWC can buy 20 million shares ($250 million divided by $12.50). After the purchase, there are 80 million shares left in the market, and the regular dividend per share rises to $1.25 (because the cash flow of $100 million is now divided by 80 million shares).

Share price after the repurchase (P_{rep}). What is AWC's share price after the repurchase? It is still $12.50 (it is equal to the present value of a perpetual future dividend per share of $1.25 discounted at 10 percent).

Effect on the wealth of shareholders (W_s). Before the buyback you owned a share worth $12.50. After the buyback your share is still worth $12.50. Your wealth (and the wealth of the other AWC shareholders) is thus unaffected by the share repurchase decision.

Homemade dividend. What if you wanted a cash dividend instead of a share buyback? No problem! All you have to do is sell some of your shares to create your own dividend payment. Suppose you own ten shares worth $125 (ten times $12.50). If you sell two shares you now own eight shares worth $100 (eight times $12.50) plus $25 of cash. Your wealth is the same as if AWC had paid an immediate dividend of

$2.50 (you would have collected $25 of dividends on your ten shares whose price would have dropped to $10 per share, that is, $100 for ten shares).

The possibility of creating a personal dividend payment through a sale of shares is appropriately called a **homemade dividend payment** because the shareholder made the payment, not the firm.

Conclusion: *in a perfect market environment, repurchasing shares instead of paying a dividend of the same amount does not affect the firm's share price and the wealth of its shareholders. If shareholders prefer a dividend payment to a share repurchase, they can pay themselves a homemade dividend by selling shares.*

ISSUING $100 MILLION OF NEW EQUITY TO PAY AN IMMEDIATE DIVIDEND OF $350 MILLION

Refer to the third recommendation in Exhibit 11.16. In this case, AWC issues $100 million of new shares at $12.50 per share. Note that because of our perfect-market assumptions there are no flotation costs and no change in the share price on the announcement of the new equity issue. This is why AWC issues shares at $12.50 and receives $12.50 per share. The number of new shares issued is eight million ($100 million divided by $12.50), and the total number of shares outstanding is now 108 million.

Size of the immediate special dividend per share (DPS_0).   AWC can now pay an immediate dividend of $350 million with the $250 million of cash it already has and the $100 million it has just raised. The corresponding immediate special dividend per share is $3.24 ($350 million divided by 108 million shares).

Ex-dividend share price (P_{ex}).   The perpetual regular future dividend per share after the share issuance is $0.926 (the $100 million cash flow divided by 108 million shares) and the ex-dividend share price on the announcement date is the present value of a perpetual stream of $0.926 of dividend per share worth $9.26 at 10 percent ($0.926 divided by 10 percent).

Effect on the wealth of shareholders (W_S).   Before the capital transactions you owned a share worth $12.50. After the transactions, you own a share valued $9.26 and receive a $3.24 dividend, for a total of $12.50. In other words, your wealth (and the wealth of the other AWC shareholders) is unaffected by the $100 million equity issue followed by the $350 million special dividend payment.

EXHIBIT 11.17	AWC SHARE PRICE IF IT INVESTS IMMEDIATELY ITS $250 MILLION OF CASH INTO PROJECTS WITH DIFFERENT EXPECTED RETURNS.		
1. Expected annual return from the project (r)	10%	12%	8%
2. Perpetual annual cash flow from the project = $250m \times r$	$25m	$30m	$20m
3. AWC perpetual annual cash flow with the project (CF)[1]	$125m	$130m	$120m
4. Perpetual dividend per share with the project (DPS)[2] = CF/100m	$1.25	$1.30	$1.20
5. Share price with the project[3] = DPS/10%	$12.50	$13	$12

[1] $100m without the project plus the project's cash flow in row 2.
[2] Row 3 divided by 100 million shares.
[3] Present value of the perpetual DPS in row 4 at shareholders' required return of 10 percent.

What if AWC had borrowed the $100 million instead of issuing $100 million of equity? We show in self-test question 11.4 that borrowing the $100 million instead of issuing $100 million of new shares will make no difference: your wealth remains the same (refer to the question and its answer).

Conclusion: *in a perfect market environment, raising new equity or borrowing to pay a dividend does not affect the wealth of the firm's shareholders.*

INVESTING $250 MILLION IN A PROJECT

Refer to Exhibit 11.17. In this case, AWC uses its $250 million of cash to invest in a project with the same risk profile as AWC's risk. How will this decision affect AWC's share price and the wealth of its shareholders? The answer depends on the return that the $250 million investment is expected to generate.

Let's examine the three possibilities summarized in Exhibit 11.17. In the first case, the project's expected annual return is 8 percent and the investment will generate a perpetual annual cash flow of $20 million (8 percent of $250 million) that will allow AWC to increase its annual dividend payment to $120 million (its regular $100 million cash flow plus the $20 million). Dividend per share is thus $1.20 based on AWC's 100 million shares outstanding. The corresponding share price is $12 (the present value of a perpetual dividend stream of $1.20 discounted at 10 percent). In this case, AWC's share price drops from $12.50 to $12 as a result of the decision to invest in a project whose expected return is 8 percent. Why does the share price drop? Simply because AWC is investing the $250 million at an expected return of 8 percent that is *lower* than the 10 percent return expected by shareholders. The result, we know, is value destruction. Recall, however, that when markets are perfect, management will always make decisions that increase shareholder wealth and hence will not undertake this value-destroying project.

Examine now the other two cases in Exhibit 11.17. When the project has an expected return of 10 percent, AWC's share price stays at $12.50 because the project's expected return is the *same* as the rate expected by shareholders. And when the project has an expected return of 12 percent, AWC's share price rises to $13 because the project's expected return is *higher* than the return expected by shareholders. The result, we know, is value creation.

Conclusion: *if a firm cannot invest its cash in projects whose expected returns are at least equal to the return expected by its shareholders, then the firm should distribute the cash to its shareholders if it wants to avoid destroying shareholder value.*

This type of distribution policy is known as the **residual payout policy** because the firm pays out all the cash that remains after it has invested in all available value-creating projects. It is doubtful, however, that firms adhere *strictly* to this type of policy because it would produce an unstable dividend distribution over time (value-creating projects do not occur on a regular basis). As we pointed out earlier, this is not what we observe in practice.

PAYOUT POLICY IS IRRELEVANT IN A PERFECT MARKET ENVIRONMENT AS LONG AS THE FIRM'S INVESTING AND FINANCING POLICIES DO NOT CHANGE

The general conclusion from our previous review of the alternative payout policies is that in a perfect market environment a firm's payout policy does not affect the wealth of its shareholders and that shareholders can always undo the effect of the firm's payout decision. For example, if the firm decides to pay a dividend they do not want to receive, they can sell their shares before the dividend is distributed and buy back shares after the dividend is paid; and if the firm decides not to pay a dividend, shareholders can get cash by selling some of their shares and create what we called earlier a homemade dividend payment: in both cases their wealth stays the same.

There is only one case where the payout policy matters: it is when the firm changes its investment policy, that is, when it invests in a project whose return either exceeds or falls short of the firm's cost of capital. In the former case, the investment raises the firm's share price. In the latter case it lowers it. This is why we say that payout policy is irrelevant *as long as the firm's investment policy does not change*. Likewise, financing policy must not change as a result of the firm's payout policy. If financing policy affects share price, for example if the firm's borrowing changes its capital structure, which in turn affects its share price, then clearly the change in price is triggered by the new financial structure and not the payout policy.

To summarize: *in a perfect capital market, payout policy is irrelevant as long as the firm's investment and financing policies do not change.*[27]

PAYOUT POLICY WITH MARKET IMPERFECTIONS

How do market imperfections affect a firm's payout policy? Let's now examine the payout policy that a firm should adopt in the presence of the market imperfections we identified earlier: (1) taxes, (2) transaction costs, (3) flotation costs, (4) lack of information about the firm (shareholders have less information than managers about the firm's prospects, a situation usually described as **asymmetric information**), and (5) agency costs.

TAXES AND THE CLIENTELE EFFECT

We have shown earlier that shareholders generally pay more taxes on dividend income than on capital gains and, all else remaining the same, should prefer cash distributions through share repurchases rather than dividend payments. We have also pointed out that some institutional and individual investors demand dividend-paying stocks despite their tax disadvantage. So where do these observations leave us regarding the relevance of dividend policy? *Could dividend policy be irrelevant even if dividend payments are taxed?*

One way to answer this question is to propose a market mechanism that can explain the irrelevance of dividend policy in the presence of taxation. A suggested market mechanism, called the **clientele effect**, operates as follows: shareholders who are subject to high income tax rates will buy shares of companies that pay little or no dividends, while shareholders who pay little or no taxes, and prefer income to capital gains, will buy shares of dividend-paying companies. According to the **clientele hypothesis**, firms design their payout policy to attract groups of investors (that is, clients) who have specific distribution preferences. When equilibrium is reached in the market, each type of investor is holding shares of companies that satisfy their payout preference and no single firm will be able to influence its share price by adopting a different payout policy.

TRANSACTION COSTS

All else being equal, when investors incur transaction costs to buy and sell shares they would prefer dividend payments to capital gains because they do not incur

---

[27] Look at self-test question 11.5 that compares AWC's dividend payments under alternative payout policies.

transaction costs when they receive dividends. But it is unlikely that the avoidance of transaction costs will make dividend income preferable to capital gains because the income tax shareholders will have to pay on dividends is likely to be much higher than the transactions costs they would save if they receive dividends instead of capital gains.

Flotation Costs

When a firm pays regular dividends it may find itself short of cash to finance value-creating projects. We have seen that in a perfect market environment this situation does not matter because the firm can always issue stocks and bonds without incurring flotation costs. When there are direct and indirect costs associated with the issuance of stocks and bonds, firms would prefer to first use their cash holdings to fund value-creating projects and then distribute any left-over cash: this is the residual dividend policy discussed earlier. Although this behavior makes sense from a cost-minimization perspective, we have already observed that firms do not seem to follow that policy in practice: they instead tend to pay regular, stable dividends and, if they need cash, raise capital to fund value-creating projects even if they have to incur issuance costs.

Asymmetric Information

When markets are imperfect, outsiders do not have access to all the information about firms. In this case management knows more about their firm's current condition and future prospects than do outsiders, including outside shareholders. We say that there is **asymmetric information** between outsiders and insiders. Management could resolve this situation by revealing to the market all the relevant information. But there are two issues with this approach: first, management may not want competitors to find out exactly what the firm is doing or is about to do, and, second, outsiders may doubt that management has revealed all the relevant information.

One way management can overcome these two issues is by sending to the market an *indirect* and *credible* signal about the firm's condition. As discussed earlier, the commitment to pay a regular dividend signals to the market that management is confident about the firm's future prospects without having to reveal specific strategic details. And the signal is credible because if the firm reduces or omits future dividend payments, its share price will drop, offsetting the initial price rise when the dividend was initiated. Another reason the signal is credible is that it tells the market that management is confident it can raise new equity and debt if it unexpectedly needs more cash to invest in a profitable investment that could materialize in the future. Issuing stocks and bonds will subject the firm's management to the scrutiny of investment bankers, financial analysts, and rating agencies; in other words, management is signaling its confidence by saying that it is willing to be monitored by outside professionals.

Likewise, the announcement of a share repurchase program can be used as a signal to the market that management believes the firm's shares are temporarily undervalued. We have already pointed out that, on average, share prices react positively to the announcements of dividend payments and share repurchases;[28] what this means is that cash distributions have information-content that is valued by shareholders. Note that it is the **information-content of payout policies** that affects share prices, not the dividend payment or the share repurchase by and of itself.

---

[28] See Manconi et al. (2013) for a review of the international evidence of the share price reaction to buy-back announcements.

AGENCY COSTS

When shareholders do not manage the company they own we say that there is a separation of ownership and control. This is the case of all publicly-owned companies where managers are "agents" appointed by shareholders (who are the "principals") to manage the firm on their behalf. This agent-principal relationship gives rise to potential conflicts of interest between management and shareholders because managers can make decisions that benefit them to the detriment of shareholders. For example, they might invest in negative NPV projects that increase the firm's size but do not create value. A larger firm built with negative NPV projects does not benefit shareholders but provides benefits to managers because size generates more prestige, additional perquisites, and higher compensation. These costs, borne by shareholders, are called **agency costs of equity**. Paying dividends and buying back shares are ways to reduce these agency costs because the cash is distributed to shareholders rather than wasted on negative NPV projects.

The opposite situation is the case of the tightly controlled firm where key shareholders are directly involved in the firm's management; in this case, agency costs are minimal and these firms would typically pay little or no regular dividends.

A SUMMARY OF PAYOUT POLICY WITH MARKET IMPERFECTIONS

Exhibit 11.18 provides a summary of how market imperfections affect payout policy. The first column lists the most important imperfections, including legal constraints which we discussed earlier but did not list in our review of imperfections. The second column indicates if the imperfection would affect the firm's decision to distribute cash. And the third column indicates whether a dividend payment or a share buyback should be used if the firm decides to distribute cash.

Some imperfections favor the retention of cash while others favor the distribution of cash. When all the imperfections are taken into account, it is not clear which dominate the others. But we know that large, cash-rich firms generally pay regular and stable dividends and occasionally buy back their shares, and we know that these distribution decisions, when announced, raise share prices; in other words, the net effect favors cash distribution, but the exact mechanism that would explain why this is the case remains elusive.

What should firms do? We recommend that they conform to their industry payout norms by adopting a payout policy similar to that of comparable firms in their sector and adjust these industry-wide standards to reflect any firm-specific conditions that require either higher or lower cash distributions than comparable firms.

KEY POINTS

1. Most of the funds needed to finance a firm's growth are generated by its internal activities. When firms experience a cash deficit, they must raise external funds. External funds are usually borrowed via bank loans and the issuance of debt securities; however, at times, they are supplemented with new issues of equity.
2. The source of internally generated funds is retained earnings, adjusted for non-cash expenses such as depreciation expenses. The amount of external financing the firm needs is the difference between these internally generated funds and the money required to finance the expected growth in the firm's working capital requirement and fixed assets.

EXHIBIT 11.18	SUMMARY OF PAYOUT POLICIES IN THE PRESENCE OF MARKET IMPERFECTIONS.

Market Imperfection	Should the firm distribute cash?	If cash is paid out, which of dividends or buybacks is preferred?
Taxation (1) *Capital gains and income are taxed, but gains are taxed at a lower rate than income*	Yes, but it should use a distribution method that minimizes the tax liability of its shareholders	Buybacks are preferred because shareholders will pay less taxes; also with buybacks, shareholders can postpone the tax payments if they don't sell their shares
Taxation (2) *Capital gains and income are taxed, but income is taxed at a lower rate than gains*	Yes, but it should use a distribution method that minimizes the tax liability of its shareholders	Dividend payments are preferred to buybacks because income is taxed at a lower rate than capital gains
Taxation (3) *Some institutional investors are tax-exempt*	Yes, because shareholders do not pay taxes	No difference between the two types of cash distribution, but dividend payments may be preferred because no transaction costs are incurred
Investor preference *Some investors prefer dividends even if they are taxed*	Yes, because these investors prefer to receive regular dividend payments instead of having to sell shares to get the cash they need (self-control hypothesis)	Dividend payments only (even if income is taxed at a higher rate than capital gains)
Transaction costs	Yes, if cash is paid out with dividends because shareholders do not incur transaction costs	Dividend payments only because a buyback would require the shares to be sold to get the cash and thus would incur transaction costs
Flotation costs	Yes, but only after the firm has funded all its positive NPV projects; any left-over cash should be distributed (residual dividend policy)	No difference between the two types of cash distribution
Legal constraints *Some institutional investors can only hold dividend-paying stocks or only distribute cash from income*	Yes, because these investors will demand dividend-paying stocks	Regular dividend payments should be made because share repurchases will not satisfy the demands of these investors
Asymmetric information	Yes, because dividend payments signal that the firm is confident about its future, and share repurchases signal that the firm's shares are undervalued	Regular dividend payments should be used to signal confidence and share buybacks to signal undervaluation
Agency costs	Yes, because distributed cash cannot be wasted on negative NPV projects; the distribution reduces agency costs	No difference between the two types of cash distribution; both will return cash to shareholders but buybacks will generate lower tax liabilities

3. External funds are raised through the financial system, which channels savers' excess cash to the firms that need it. Funds can be transferred directly from savers to firms or can be transferred indirectly via financial intermediaries. In the first case, the firms sell securities to savers in the form of shares or bonds. In the second case, an intermediary, such as a bank, receives funds from savers, typically in the form of deposits and lends these funds to firms in the form of loans. Firms can place their debt and equity securities privately with financial institutions, such as insurance companies and pension funds. Alternatively, they can sell them in the securities markets, where they are traded among investors.

4. The function of primary markets is to ensure the success of new issues; the function of secondary markets is to ensure that investors can buy and sell existing securities at a fair price, a price that reflects all available public information. In addition to the distinction between primary and secondary markets, securities markets can be classified according to whether they are organized exchanges or over-the-counter markets, equity or debt markets, or domestic or international markets.

5. Firms issue shares and bonds either through private placement or through public offerings. For an equity issue, firms can raise capital through a general cash offering or via a rights issue. In a rights issue, current shareholders are given subscription rights that allow them to purchase new shares; in a general cash offering, shares are offered to the public at large and no distinction is made between current shareholders and other investors. The various sources of debt financing available to firms include bank loans, lease agreements, and bond issues. A firm can issue a wide range of securities in addition to common stocks and straight bonds. These include convertible bonds, preferred shares, warrants, and contingent value rights.

6. There are times when firms have a cash surplus instead of a cash deficit. In this case, they are in a position to distribute some of their excess cash to their shareholders either through dividend payments or through the repurchase of their own shares in the open market, a transaction that is the reverse of an issue of new shares.

7. Whether a firm is facing a cash deficit or a cash surplus at a particular point in time depends on a number of factors, some of which are event-specific such as an unanticipated shortfall in cash due to an unexpected poor performance or a surplus of cash resulting from the sale of a major asset. Cash deficits and surpluses depend also on the firm's growth rate: a newly established and successful company usually experiences a higher than average growth rate and would typically abstain from paying dividends because it needs the cash to fund its growth. It would usually begin paying regular and stable dividends when its growth rate levels off following a period of strong earnings and cash accumulation.

8. Dividend payments are not only a cash-distribution mechanism. They are also a way for the company's managers to signal to the market their confidence in the firm's future performance and their commitment to avoid wasting cash on value-destroying investments (cash paid out in dividends cannot be used to fund negative NPV projects). Dividend payments are thus a way to convey good news to the market. This may explain why the announcement of the initiation of a dividend-payment program usually raises the firm's share price. If the firm's

subsequent performance deteriorates, management is usually reluctant to reduce or eliminate dividends unless it believes that performance will remain weak for a while. Cutting or omitting dividends would send a negative signal to the market and is usually accompanied by a drop in share price. Likewise, the announcement of a share repurchase program conveys information to the market: it signals that management believes the firm's shares may be temporarily undervalued. These announcements are typically accompanied by a rise in share price.

9. If markets were perfect (no taxes, no transaction and flotation costs, no asymmetric information, and no agency costs), then payout policies will not affect the wealth of the firm's shareholders as long as the firm's investment and financing policies remain unchanged. This is the case because paying dividends or buying back shares simply transfer cash (at no cost) from the firm to its shareholders with no effect on their overall wealth (the cash is theirs in both cases).

10. With market imperfections, payout policy matters. For example, if taxes on capital gains (generated by share repurchases) are lower than taxes on dividend income, then cash should be distributed via share buybacks instead of dividends. And if there is asymmetric information between managers and outside shareholders, or if there are agency costs (such as cash wasted by managers on value-destroying projects), then paying regular and stable dividends is a way to convey information to outsiders and reduce agency costs. What is the net effect when we take into consideration all market imperfections? We know that large, cash-rich firms generally pay regular and stable dividends and occasionally buy back their shares, and we know that these distribution decisions, when announced, raise share prices; in other words, when firms have excess cash the net effect favors cash distribution, but the exact mechanism that would explain why this is the case remains elusive. What should firms do? We recommend that they conform to their industry payout norms by adopting a payout policy similar to that of comparable firms in their sector and adjust these industry-wide standards to reflect any firm-specific conditions that require either higher or lower cash distributions than comparable firms.

FURTHER READING

1. Allen, Franklin, and Roni Michaely. "Dividend Policy." Chapter 25 in *Handbooks in Operations Research and Management Science*, Volume 9, Finance, edited by R.A. Jarrow, V. Maksimovic, and W.T. Ziemba, Elsevier, 2006.

2. Baker, H. Kent. *Dividends and Dividend Policy*, John Wiley & Sons, 2009.

3. Brav, Alon, John R. Graham, Campbell R. Harvey, and Roni Michaely. "Payout Policy in the 21st Century." *Journal of Financial Economics* 77 (September 2005).

4. Farre-Mensa, Joan, Roni Michaely, and Martin Schmalz. "Payout Policy." Ross School of Business, University of Michigan, Working Paper no. 1227, 2016.

5. Manconi, Alberto, Urs Peyer, and Theo Vermaelen. "Buybacks around the World." INSEAD Working Paper September 2013.

6. Massa, Massimo, Theo Vermaelen, and Moqi Xu. "Rights Offerings, Trading, and Regulation: A Global Perspective." INSEAD Working Paper October 2013.

7. Smith, Roy, Ingo Walter, and Gayle DeLong, *Global Banking*. Oxford University Press, 2012. See chapters 2, 4, and 5.

SELF-TEST QUESTIONS

11.1 **Estimating external funding needs.**

Office Supplies (OS) Distributors wants to estimate the external funds it will need in Year 0 based on the data available in Exhibit 11.2 and the following information and assumptions for Year 0:

- Cash need: same as in Year –1.
- Working capital requirement: up 10 percent
- Capital expenditure: $10 million with $1 million annual depreciation
- Depreciation on existing assets: same as in Year –1
- Net profit: up 10 percent
- Retention rate: same as in Year –1

a. What are OS Distributors' expected total funding needs for Year 0?

b. What are OS Distributors' expected internally generated funds in Year 0?

c. What are OS Distributors' expected external funding needs for Year 0?

d. What should OS Distributors do to cover its external funding needs?

11.2 **Leasing.**

Do you agree with these statements?

a. Different tax rates between lessees and lessors may affect the magnitude of lease payments.

b. A lease reduces uncertainty.

c. An operating lease will reduce the liabilities of the firm as opposed to a purchase financed by debt.

11.3 **Taxes and dividend payments.**

Consider an investor who buys a stock at the cum-dividend price (P_{cum}) of $12.50 just before it goes ex-dividend, and sells it immediately after it goes ex-dividend at the ex-dividend price (P_{ex}). The investor incurs a capital loss because the ex-dividend price is lower than the cum-dividend price, but he qualifies for the dividend payment (DPS). Answer the following questions:

a. If the tax rate on capital gains is T_G and the tax rate on dividend income is T_D, show that the following relationship must hold in order to eliminate any possible arbitrage opportunity:

$$(P_{cum} - P_{ex})(1 - T_G) = DPS(1 - T_D)$$

b. Show that, in this case, the ex-dividend price can be expressed as:

$$P_{ex} = P_{cum} - DPS\left(\frac{1 - T_D}{1 - T_G}\right)$$

c. If the dividend per share is one dollar, what is the ex-dividend price if the income tax rate is 40 percent and the tax rate on capital gains is 20 percent?

d. Under which conditions will the dividend per share be equal to the difference between the cum-dividend price and the ex-dividend price?

11.4 **Borrowing to pay dividends.**

According to recommendation no. 3 in Exhibit 11.17, AWC should pay an immediate dividend of $350 million using the $250 million of cash it already has, plus the

$100 million it has raised through the issuance of shares. Suppose that the additional $100 million is borrowed at 5 percent by issuing a perpetual bond instead of equity. Markets are perfect. Answer the following questions:

a. What is the immediate special dividend per share when AWC distributed $350 million using its $250 million of cash and the borrowed $100 million? Compare the dividend per share when the $100 million is borrowed to the dividend per share when the $100 million is raised by issuing equity.

b. What is AWC's share price after it issued the bond and paid the special dividend assuming that the value of the firm's assets is unaffected by the borrowing (we show in Chapter 13 that the value of a firm's assets is independent of its capital structure when markets are perfect)?

c. What is the wealth per share of AWC's shareholders after the $350 million dividend payment?

d. What can you conclude?

11.5   **Comparing dividend streams under alternative payout policies.**

a. Refer to the data on AWC in Exhibits 11.16 and 11.17 to complete the table below by filling in the appropriate amount of dividend per share for each dividend policy.

b. What can you conclude about alternative payout methods in perfect markets?

c. Based on your answer, explain the following sentence: *in perfect markets, dividends matter but dividend policy does not.*

	Now	In one year	In two years	In t years
Alternative payout methods	DPS_0	DPS_1	DPS_2	DPS_t
1. Immediate dividend of $250 million				
2. Share buyback of $250 million				
3. Immediate dividend of $350 million funded with a $100 million equity issue				
4. Invest the $250 million at 10 percent				
5. Invest the $250 million at 12 percent				
6. Invest the $250 million at 8 percent				

REVIEW QUESTIONS

1. **Structure and characteristics of financial markets.**
   Briefly explain the distinction between the two items that make up each of the following pairs:

   a. Direct financing versus indirect financing
   b. Primary markets versus secondary markets
   c. Organized exchanges versus over-the-counter markets
   d. Domestic securities versus international securities
   e. Domestic securities versus foreign securities

    f. Private placement versus public offering
    g. Rights issue versus general cash offering
    h. Underwritten issue versus best efforts distribution
    i. Originating house versus selling group
    j. Seasoned issue versus secondary distribution

2. **Rights issue.**

Micro-Electronics Corporation (MEC) has just announced that it will issue 10 million shares of common stock through a rights issue at a subscription price of $20. Before the announcement, MEC shares were trading at $26, and there were 50 million shares outstanding.

    a. How many rights will MEC grant to its existing shareholders?
    b. How many rights will an investor need to buy one new share?
    c. What will happen to MEC's share price when the rights issue is announced?
    d. What should be the value of one right?

3. **Leasing versus borrowing.**

Office Supplies (OS) Distributors needs a new truck. It can buy it for $24,000, depreciate it over four years at an annual rate of $6,000, and finance the purchase with a four-year loan at 10 percent. The truck could be sold for $5,000 in four years. Alternatively, it can lease the truck and make four annual lease payments of $6,500 (payments are made at the *beginning* of the year). OS Distributors is subject to a 40 percent corporate tax rate and is responsible for the maintenance and insurance of the truck, regardless of whether it leases or buys it.

    a. Should OS Distributors lease or buy the truck?
    b. What resale value of the truck in four years will make OS Distributors indifferent about buying versus leasing?

4. **Leasing.**

Thorenberg Inc. is considering the purchase of a machine from Hydraulic Engineering Company (HECO) to make hard pressed-metal sheets. The machine will cost $100,000 and would replace the currently used one. Savings are expected to be $60,000 per year, and the new machine is expected to last five years with proper maintenance. For tax purposes, the machine would be depreciated according to the straight-line method, and the tax rate is 36 percent. As an alternative to buying the machine, Thorenberg could lease it from Foster Leasing Corporation at a rate of $25,000 a year for five years, with payments made at the beginning of the year. All insurance, maintenance, and the cost of operating the machine would be the responsibility of Thorenberg. The interest rate at which Thorenberg can borrow on a medium- or long-term basis is 8 percent.

    a. What are the cash flows from leasing relative to buying for Thorenberg Inc.? Should Thorenberg Inc. lease or buy the new machine?
    b. What are the after-tax cash flows to Foster Leasing Corporation from buying and then leasing the machine to Thorenberg? Why are they the exact opposite of the cash flows to Thorenberg? (Assume that the two companies have the same effective corporate tax rate.)
    c. If the cash flows to the lessee (Thorenberg) and the cash flows to the lessor (Foster) are exactly the opposite, why would the leasing nevertheless take place?

5. **Convertible preferred.**

   The International Supplies Company (ISC) has convertible preferred stocks trading at $80 and serving an annual dividend of $2.40. The preferred is convertible into two shares of ISC common stocks. Shares of common stocks are currently trading at $32.

   a. What is the conversion ratio of the convertible preferred?
   b. What is the conversion price of a share of common stock?
   c. What is the conversion premium?
   d. What is the conversion value of the convertible preferred?
   e. What is the value of the preferred if it were not convertible?
   f. If ISC had issued its preferred without the option to convert them into common stocks, it would have offered an annual dividend of $2.72 instead of $2.40. What is the value of the option to convert the preferred shares into common stocks?

6. **Deferred dividend payment.**

   Refer to the data on AWC in Exhibit 11.16. Suppose the board of AWC decides to invest the $250 million of cash in 1-year government bills yielding 4 percent and use the proceeds from the sale of the bills to pay a higher dividend next year.

   a. What would be AWC's share price in this case?
   b. Compare the share price with the deferred dividend to the share price when the $250 million is immediately paid out in dividends. What can you conclude?

7. **Cash retention and corporate taxes.**

   Refer to the data on AWC in Exhibit 11.16. Suppose the board of AWC decides to retain $250 million of cash permanently and invest it in a perpetual government bond.

   a. What would be AWC's share price in this case? Compare it to the share price if AWC pays an immediate dividend of $250 million. What can you conclude?
   b. If AWC must pay 30 percent tax on the income earned on the perpetual bond, what would be AWC's share price in this case? Compare it to the share price with no tax. What can you conclude?

8. **Investment decision versus dividend payment.**

   Refer to the data on AWC in Exhibit 11.17 to answer the following questions:

   a. What is the net present value of the 8 percent project? Explain its sign.
   b. What is the net present value of the 10 percent project? Explain its sign.
   c. What is the net present value of the 12 percent project? Explain its sign.

9. **Investment decision versus share buyback.**

   The Rolleston Company (TRC), an all-equity financed company, generates perpetual free cash flow of $40 million. It holds $100 million of cash, has 50 million shares outstanding, and its shareholders require a 10 percent return on their investment in the firm. TRC management wants to invest the $100 million of cash in a project that would raise the firm's future free cash flow by 20 percent without changing the firm's risk. Markets are assumed to be perfect. Answer the following questions:

   a. What is TRC's share price before it invests the $100 million?
   b. What would be TRC's share price if it went ahead with the investment?
   c. What is the net present value of the investment? Should TRC make the investment?

d. Should TRC's management use the $100 million of cash to buy back its shares instead of going ahead with the investment?

10. **Payout policies of a growing firm.**

The Southern Appliance Company (SAC) has a current free cash flow of $10 million that is expected to grow in perpetuity at a constant annual rate of 5 percent. The firm has $40 million of cash and 10 million shares outstanding. SAC has no debt and its shareholders expect a return of 10 percent on their equity investment. Markets are assumed to be perfect. Answer the following questions:

a. What is SAC's share price?

b. If SAC pays an immediate dividend of $40 million, what is its ex-dividend share price and the effect on its shareholders' wealth per share immediately after the dividend is paid?

c. If SAC immediately uses its cash to buy back its shares in the open market, what is the effect on its share price and on its shareholders' wealth per share immediately after the share buyback?

d. If SAC issues two million new shares and uses the proceeds and its $40 million of cash to pay an immediate dividend, what is its ex-dividend share price and the effect on its shareholders' wealth per share immediately after the dividend is paid?

e. How much should SAC borrow and immediately add to the proceeds of its $40 million of cash in order to pay the same immediate dividend per share as in the case of the two million share issuance in the previous question? What is the ex-dividend share price and the effect on its shareholders' wealth per share immediately after the dividend is paid (recall that, in a perfect market, the value of a firm's noncash assets is independent of its capital structure)?

ESTIMATING THE COST OF CAPITAL

Firms need cash to finance their investment projects. Usually, this cash is generated internally from the firm's operations. If there is a shortage of internally generated funds, firms will ask investors (lenders and shareholders) to supply them with additional cash. Chapter 11 shows how firms can raise cash from external sources. Whatever its origin, cash is not free; it comes at a price. The price is the cost to the firm of using investors' money. When this cost is expressed as the return expected by investors for the capital they supply, it is called the *cost of capital*. Chapter 7 shows that the cost of capital is the rate at which a project's stream of future cash flows must be discounted to estimate its net present value (NPV) and to decide whether the project is worth undertaking, that is, whether it has the potential to create value. Chapter 8 shows that it is also the rate against which the project's internal rate of return (IRR) must be compared for the same purpose of deciding whether to accept or reject the project.

This chapter shows how to estimate the cost of capital to be used in the NPV, the IRR, or any other discounted cash flow method applied to the analysis of an investment project. This cost of capital is called the *project's* cost of capital, not to be confused with the *firm's* cost of capital. The latter is the return expected by investors from *all* the assets acquired and managed by the firm.

As mentioned in Chapter 7, the rate investors require from their investment in a project is the return they expect to receive from investing their cash in alternative investments that have the same risk profile as the risk profile of the project. Thus, to estimate the cost of capital for a particular project, we first need to identify similar projects available to investors. The problem is that investors usually do not invest directly in projects; they invest in the firms that undertake the projects. The challenge, then, is to identify firms that exhibit the same risk characteristics as the project under consideration. These comparable firms are called *proxies* or *pure-plays*.

After a proxy company has been identified, we must estimate the returns expected by the investors who hold the securities (bonds and shares) the proxy firm has issued. These investors have claims on the cash flows generated by the proxy's assets, which differ depending on the *type* of security held. Debt holders and shareholders of the same company have claims on the same cash flows generated by the firm's assets, but debt holders have a prior and fixed claim on these cash flows and thus bear *less* risk than shareholders. Consequently, the return expected from holding debt is *lower* than the return expected from holding shares of the same company. This chapter shows how to estimate the expected returns from the two most common financial instruments, straight bonds and common stocks, using financial market data. The theoretical foundation on which these estimations are based is the relationship between expected return and risk analyzed in Chapter 3 and the valuation models presented in Chapter 10.

The return expected from the assets acquired and managed by a firm belongs to the investors who financed these assets and to no one else. Thus, this return must be the total of the returns expected by debt holders and shareholders, weighted by their respective contribution to the funding of these assets. In other words, a firm's cost of capital must be equal to the weighted average of the costs of each of its financing sources. This cost of capital, which is first mentioned in Chapter 1 and then used in Chapter 10 to estimate a company's share price, is known as the firm's weighted average cost of capital (WACC). Although we cannot directly measure the return investors expect from the assets managed by firms, we can use the firm's WACC as a surrogate. We show how to estimate a firm's WACC and how to find a project's cost of capital based on the WACC of proxy firms.

As an illustration, we estimate the cost of capital of Sunlight Manufacturing Company's (SMC) desk lamp project that was introduced in Chapter 7 and analyzed in detail in Chapter 9. Because this project has the same risk profile as SMC's overall risk, the project's cost of capital is, in this case, the same as the firm's cost of capital. We also discuss another example that illustrates how to estimate the project's cost of capital when the project has a risk that *differs* from the risk of the firm that would undertake it.

Remember that the terms *cost of capital*, *investors' required return*, and *investors' expected return* mean the same thing and can thus be used interchangeably. A firm's cost of equity capital is the return expected by investors who hold stock in the firm; a firm's cost of debt capital is the return expected by investors who hold the loans and bonds the firm has issued. After reading this chapter, you should understand the following:

- How to estimate the cost of debt capital
- How to estimate the cost of equity capital
- How to combine the cost of different sources of financing to obtain a project's weighted average cost of capital (WACC)
- The difference between the cost of capital for a firm and the cost of capital for a project

IDENTIFYING PROXY OR PURE-PLAY FIRMS

Identifying the alternative investments that have risks similar to those of the project being considered is the first and most crucial step in the estimation of a **project's cost of capital**. Data from these investments are the inputs for the models that are used to estimate the project's cost of capital. Regardless of the degree of sophistication of the models, the reliability of the estimated cost of capital always depends on the quality of the inputs chosen to perform the estimation.

When a project is in the same line of business as the firm that would undertake it – in other words, when the project's risk profile is *similar* to the firm's risk profile – the proxy is the firm itself. This is the case for the designer desk lamp project discussed in Chapter 9, because the firm that wanted to launch the project, Sunlight Manufacturing Company, specializes in the production of small light fixtures.

When the risk of the project is *different* from the risk of the firm that would undertake it, we need to identify **proxy** or **pure-play** firms. These are firms that have a single line of business, are in the same industry as the project, and compete in the same input and output markets. Pure-plays are usually selected using industry classification codes that identify firms according to their type of business. Unfortunately, these classification systems are far from perfect. The sample of firms must be examined critically, and only those firms that replicate as closely as possible the business of the investment project should be selected. Exact duplication is unlikely, and often a choice must be made between a small sample of closely comparable companies and a larger sample of firms that are loosely comparable to the project.

In a small sample, the proxies will be more representative of the business to which the project belongs. But if some of the proxies' data have large measurement errors, the sample may be too small for these errors to wash out when the data are averaged across the proxies. In a larger sample, the proxies will be less comparable to the project, but the effect of large measurement errors may be greatly reduced in the averaging process.

Having indicated how to identify pure-plays, we show in the next sections how to estimate the return investors expect from holding debt securities (bonds) and common stocks (shares) issued by firms. These returns are, respectively, estimates of the cost of debt and the cost of equity.

ESTIMATING THE COST OF DEBT

A firm can borrow from a bank by taking out a loan. In this case, the firm's **cost of debt** is simply the interest rate the bank charges the firm. Alternatively, if the firm is large enough, it can borrow directly from investors by selling them bonds. (Bonds are debt securities described in Chapter 10.) This section shows how to use the market price of a firm's bonds to estimate the firm's cost of debt. We use SMC (the company that is considering the investment in the designer desk lamp project) as an illustration. Assume that *five* years ago SMC issued bonds with an *original* maturity of *ten* years. This means the bonds will be repaid *five* years from now. (Their *current*, or remaining, maturity is *five* years.) The bonds have a face value of $1,000 and pay an annual coupon of $60. The bonds' coupon rate is thus 6 percent ($60 divided by $1,000). The current market price of the bonds is $1,066. The bond's expected rate of return, also known as its **market yield** or **yield to maturity**, is an estimate of SMC's cost of debt. How can we calculate that rate?

An investor buying an SMC bond now and planning to keep it until maturity can expect to receive from SMC $60 every year for the next five years plus $1,000 at the end of the fifth year. As shown in Chapter 10, in a well-functioning bond market, the $1,066 bond price must be equal to the present (or discounted) value of the future stream of cash payments the bondholder is expected to receive during the next five years. We can write the following:

$$\$1,066 = \frac{\$60}{1 + k_D} + \frac{\$60}{(1 + k_D)^2} + \frac{\$60}{(1 + k_D)^3} + \frac{\$60}{(1 + k_D)^4} + \frac{\$1,060}{(1 + k_D)^5} \quad (12.1)$$

where k_D, the bondholders' expected return, is the firm's estimated cost of debt. As we show in Chapter 10, this valuation formula can be solved for k_D, using a spreadsheet as follows:

	A	B
1	Number of years	5
2	Coupon payment	$60
3	Bond price	$1,066
4	Principal repayment	$1,000
5	**Yield to maturity**	**4.50%**
	• *The formula in cell B5 is = RATE(B1,B2,–B3,B4)*	

Our calculation indicates that k_D is 4.5 percent.

To summarize, if we know the price of the bond, its coupon payments, and its face value, the valuation formula can be solved for the rate of return investors require to hold the security. *This rate is an estimate of the cost of debt for the issuer.* Why is the bond's 4.5 percent *market yield* (its expected return) the relevant cost of debt instead of the bond's 6 percent *coupon rate*, or the bond's *current yield* of 5.6 percent (a bond's current yield is found by dividing its coupon payment ($60) by its price ($1,066))? The reason is simple: SMC's cost of debt is the interest rate it will have to pay if it decided *today* to issue *new* bonds to investors. This rate is the market yield of 4.5 percent. Both the coupon rate and the current yield are based on an interest rate that was set five years ago when the bond was originally issued. If SMC issues new bonds today that have a five-year maturity, it will have to offer investors a yield of 4.5 percent, not 6 percent (the coupon rate on the previously issued bond) or 5.6 percent (the current yield of the previously issued bond).

If the firm has no bonds outstanding, its cost of debt for a given maturity can be estimated by adding to the prevailing market yield on *government* bonds with the *same* maturity, an estimate of the firm's credit-risk spread (see Chapter 10 for a discussion on how to estimate a firm's credit-risk spread):

$$\text{Cost of debt} = \text{Market yield on government bonds} + \text{Estimated credit-risk spread} \qquad (12.2)$$

To illustrate, suppose you want to estimate the ten-year cost of debt of Allied Distribution Stores (ADS). If the market yield on ten-year government bonds at the time of the analysis is 3.5 percent, and firms with a credit risk similar to ADS can borrow, on average, at 3 percent above the yield on government bonds, then ADS's estimated cost of debt is 6.5 percent (3.5 percent plus 3 percent).

Regardless of the method used to estimate the firm's cost of debt, the cost needs to be adjusted for corporate taxes. Because interest expenses are tax deductible, the effective or **after-tax cost of debt** to the firm is less than its *pre-tax* cost. For example, if SMC has a marginal tax rate of 40 percent, then every dollar of interest expense reduces the firm's tax bill by $0.40 and the after-tax interest expense is only $0.60 cent per $1 of interest expense ($1 less $0.40 of tax saved). Given SMC's pre-tax cost of debt (k_D) of 4.5 percent and a marginal corporate tax rate (T_C) of 40 percent, the after-tax cost of debt is 4.1 percent:

$$\text{After-tax cost of debt} = k_D \times (1 - T_C) = 4.5\% \times (1 - 40\%) = 2.7\% \qquad (12.3)$$

Remember that the above relationship is valid only if (1) the firm is profitable enough to take full advantage of the tax deductibility of interest expenses; or (2) the firm is not profitable enough during the current period, but the tax authority allows it to deduct current interest expenses from past or future profits, a rule known as the **carry-back** or **carry-forward** method (see Chapter 9).

ESTIMATING THE COST OF EQUITY

Equity securities are financial instruments that give their holders a proportional right to ownership of the firm's assets. The standard type of equity security is common stock, described in Chapter 10. There are two fundamental models to estimate the return expected by holders of common stocks: the dividend-discount model and the capital asset pricing model, which is based on the relationship between the risk investors bear from holding common stocks and the return they expect from these stocks.[1]

ESTIMATING THE COST OF EQUITY USING THE DIVIDEND-DISCOUNT MODEL

Owners of common stock have a *residual* claim on any cash left after the firm has paid all its obligations, including interest and principal on debt. **Cash dividends** are paid by the firm to its shareholders as a return on their investment.

We use DPS_1, DPS_2, DPS_3, ..., DPS_t, ... to represent the stream of future annual cash dividends expected from an investment in one share of a company and k_E to represent the expected return from that share. We know that the expected return k_E is the cost of equity for the firm that issued the share. According to the **dividend-discount model** (DDM, see Chapter 10), the price of a share should be equal to the present (or discounted) value of the stream of cash dividends shareholders are expected to receive:

$$\text{Share Price} = \frac{DPS_1}{(1 + k_E)} + \frac{DPS_2}{(1 + k_E)^2} + \dots + \frac{DPS_t}{(1 + k_E)^t} + \dots \qquad (12.4)$$

where k_E, the shareholders' expected return, is the firm's estimated **cost of equity**.

This formula does not explicitly take into account the future prices of the share. As explained in Chapter 10, this does not mean that future share prices are ignored. They are implicitly taken into account by the valuation formula because, for example, the share price in two years can be expressed as a function of the expected cash dividends that will be received after the second year.

We can use equation 12.4 to estimate the firm's cost of equity if we know the firm's share price and the dividends it is expected to pay. The procedure is similar to the one used to estimate the cost of debt. Unfortunately, although we know the expected coupon payments for bonds (because they are contractual), we do not know the expected dividend payments for shares. We can circumvent this difficulty if we make some simplifying assumptions about the growth of future dividends. The next section examines the particular case in which dividends are expected to grow *forever* at a *constant* rate.

---

[1] See Chapter 3 for a detailed analysis of the capital asset pricing model and Chapter 10 for the dividend-discount model.

THE CASE WHEN DIVIDENDS GROW AT A CONSTANT RATE

Suppose we assume the dividend DPS_1 that a firm is expected to pay next year will grow at a constant rate g forever. Then, the DDM reduces to the following:

$$\text{Share price} = \frac{DPS_1}{k_E - g}$$

This valuation formula, first presented in Chapter 10, is known as the constant dividend growth model. The terms of the formula can be rearranged to express the expected cost of equity k_E as a function of next year's dividend, the current share price, and the expected constant growth rate:[2]

$$k_E = \frac{DPS_1}{\text{Share price}} + g \qquad (12.5)$$

Equation 12.5 shows that the firm's estimated cost of equity is the sum of two components. The first is the firm's expected dividend yield, that is, the firm's expected dividend payment per share divided by its current share price. The second is the expected growth rate in future dividends.

To illustrate, consider the case of All Bearing Company (ABC). The company's stock is selling at $50, the company is expected to pay a dividend per share of $3 next year, and the dividend per share is anticipated to grow at 3 percent a year forever. According to equation 12.5, ABC and *all firms that have the same risk profile as that of ABC* have the following estimated cost of equity:

$$k_E = \frac{\$3}{\$50} + 3\% = 9\%$$

HOW RELIABLE IS THE DIVIDEND-DISCOUNT MODEL?

In its general form, the DDM shown in equation 12.4 is not very useful because it requires forecasting an infinite number of dividends. The model can be reduced to a more manageable form under some simplifying assumptions about the future growth of the firm's dividends. Unfortunately, these assumptions are unrealistic.[3]

Casual observation of a series of dividends paid on common stocks shows that dividends neither stay constant forever nor grow at a constant rate for very long. Furthermore, a number of firms pay no dividends at all, at least for a certain period of time. For these firms, we would have to estimate the date at which the payment of dividends will resume in addition to estimating the dividend's magnitude and its future rate of growth – quite a challenging task.

The simplified version of the DDM (equation 12.5) can be reliably applied only to the small subset of firms that pay regular dividends with a fairly stable pattern of growth, such as utility companies. For the vast majority of companies, the simplistic and unrealistic assumptions underlying the reduced version of the DDM are not acceptable. The following section presents an alternative valuation model that directly

---

[2] Multiply both sides of the price formula by $(k_E - g)$, divide both sides by the share price, and move g from the left to the right side of the equation.

[3] The exception is the dividend from *preferred* stock, which is fixed and does not have a maturity date. In this case, we can apply equation 12.5 with a growth rate equal to zero. For example, if a share of preferred stock sells for $10 and pays a dividend of $1 per share, the expected return from the stock is 10 percent ($1 divided by $10).

relates the expected return on any security to its risk. When this model, called the capital asset pricing model, is applied to common stocks, it provides a better estimate of a firm's cost of equity capital because it does not rely on forecasting future patterns of dividend payments.

Estimating the Cost of Equity Using the Capital Asset Pricing Model

We know that the return required by investors on an investment depends on that investment's risk: *the greater the risk, the higher the expected return*. But what is the nature of risk, and how is it measured? These questions are addressed in detail in Chapter 3 where we present a theoretical analysis of risk and its relation to expected return, a relationship known as the **capital asset pricing model** (**CAPM**). In this section we review these topics before applying the CAPM to estimate SMC's cost of equity capital.

Diversification Reduces Risk

Suppose there is an island in the Caribbean where the sun shines half the time and it rains the other half. There are two companies on the island: one company, Sun Cream Inc., sells suntan lotion; the other, Umbrella & Co., sells umbrellas. The shares of the two firms trade on the local stock exchange. An analysis of their historical monthly returns reveals that they have identical *average* returns of 15 per cent. As illustrated in Exhibit 12.1, the actual monthly returns for both stocks vary over time, meaning that investing in either stock is risky. Note that the amplitude and frequency of the returns on both stocks are the same. In other words, their **volatility**, and thus their risk, are identical.

Suppose you have $1,000 to invest in the two companies' stocks. What investment strategy should you use? Should you invest in only one of the two stocks because they both have the same average return and risk? If you do so, you will become a victim of "weather risk." If you buy shares of Sun Cream Inc., your investment will perform well when the sun shines but not when it rains. If you buy shares of Umbrella & Co., the opposite will occur: your investment will do well when it rains but not when the sun shines. A smarter strategy, based on the principle of "not putting all your eggs in one basket," would be to buy $500 worth of shares in each of the two firms. Any loss on one share would be offset by a gain on the other, whatever the weather turns out to be. In other words, as shown at the bottom of Exhibit 12.1, regardless of the weather conditions, the strategy locks in a *riskless* return of 15 percent, which is the expected return on an investment in either one of the two stocks.

This example is obviously unrealistic, because it is impossible to find two investments whose returns move in exactly opposite directions and in the same proportions. Nevertheless, it does illustrate an important phenomenon: *diversification helps reduce risk*. When the shares of different firms are held together in a diversified portfolio, variations in their returns tend to average out and the risk of the portfolio goes down rapidly. In Chapter 3 we mentioned a study that has analyzed the effect of diversification on portfolio risk. The study shows that portfolios made up of about 25 randomly chosen stocks have a risk that can be as low as 40 percent of the average risk of their component securities. Moreover, investing in 25 stocks is not significantly more costly than investing the same amount of money in a single stock, so portfolio diversification costs almost nothing. As a result, any rational investor who dislikes risk will choose to hold a diversified portfolio of stocks rather than invest his entire wealth in a single asset.

EXHIBIT 12.1   RISK AND RETURN FOR THE SUN CREAM AND UMBRELLA INVESTMENTS.

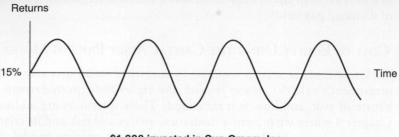

$1,000 invested in Sun Cream, Inc.

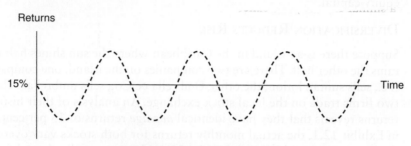

$1,000 invested in Umbrella & Co.

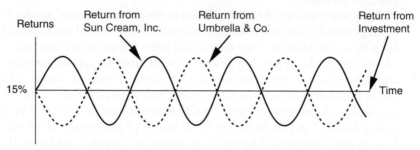

$500 invested in Sun Cream, Inc. and $500 in Umbrella & Co.

A major implication of the above analysis is that the risk of holding a single stock can be divided into two types of risks. One risk can be eliminated through portfolio diversification; the other risk remains despite the risk reduction property of diversification. The first is called **diversifiable**, or **unsystematic, risk**. The second is called **undiversifiable**, or **systematic, risk**. We can now express the total risk of a stock as follows:

$$\text{Total risk} = \text{Systematic risk} + \text{Unsystematic risk}$$

The source of unsystematic risk is firm-specific events that may have either a positive or a negative effect on share prices. Examples of positive, or favorable, events are the unanticipated win of a liability lawsuit, the discovery of a new product, or the announcement of higher-than-expected earnings. Examples of negative, or unfavorable, events include a labor strike, an accident that temporarily shuts down major production facilities, or the unanticipated loss of a liability lawsuit. Those events, taken together, are unlikely to have a significant effect on the returns of a *well-diversified* portfolio, because the positive effect of favorable events for some stocks will *cancel out* the negative effect of the unfavorable ones for the other stocks. The portfolio's unsystematic risk will approach zero.

The source of systematic (or undiversifiable) risk is events that affect the entire economy instead of only a single stock. These include changes in the economy's growth rate, inflation rate, and interest rates as well as changes in the political and social environments. These market-wide events tend to affect all share prices in the same fashion. For example, if the market expects the central bank to raise interest rates, an event that is usually interpreted as unfavorable to the stock market, the price of most shares should go down. Because this type of risk affects most shares in a similar fashion, it is called *systematic* risk. And because it cannot be eliminated or reduced through diversified portfolio holdings, it is also called *undiversifiable* risk. Note, however, that some stocks will exhibit more (or less) systematic risk than others because they are more (or less) sensitive to market-wide events.

To summarize, a stock's total risk has two components. One, called *unsystematic risk*, can be eliminated or reduced at very low cost through diversification. The other, called *systematic risk*, cannot be eliminated or reduced through diversified portfolio holdings. This separation of risk between a systematic component and an unsystematic component has an important implication for the determination of the return required by shareholders.

Because unsystematic risk can be eliminated through diversification at practically no significant cost, the financial market will not reward it. Put another way, the financial market will reward only the risk that investors cannot avoid, that is, systematic or undiversifiable risk. We have said many times that the return required from a financial asset depends on the risk of that asset. We can now say: *the only risk that matters in determining the required return on a financial asset is the asset's systematic risk*. The implication is so important that it is worth repeating: *the required rate of return on a financial asset depends only on the asset's systematic risk*. Which leads to the next question: how is systematic risk measured?

Measuring Systematic Risk with the Beta Coefficient

The systematic risk of an individual stock is usually measured relative to a benchmark portfolio called the **market portfolio**. Theoretically, the market portfolio contains all the assets in the world – not just stocks but also bonds, domestic and foreign assets, currencies, and even real estate. It is the portfolio that ensures maximum diversification and thus provides maximum risk reduction. The variations in the returns of this portfolio reflect only the effect of market-wide events, which are the source of systematic risk. In practice, building such a portfolio is a formidable, if not impossible, task. Instead, when estimating an individual stock's systematic risk, analysts use a domestic stock market index that is sufficiently broad, such as the Standard & Poor's Composite Index (S&P 500) in the United States and the Financial Times All Share Index in the United Kingdom.

Measuring the systematic risk of an individual stock relative to the market portfolio boils down to measuring the sensitivity of the stock's returns to changes in the returns of a broad stock market index. This measure of sensitivity is called the stock's **beta coefficient** or simply its **beta**. We show how to estimate a stock's beta using Sunlight Manufacturing Company (SMC) as an illustration.

The graph in Exhibit 12.2 shows the monthly returns of SMC's stocks plotted against the monthly returns of the S&P 500 during the five-year period from January of Year 1 to December of Year 5.

The sixty monthly returns to SMC stockholders, r_{SMC}, were computed as follows:

$$r_{SMC} = \frac{\text{End of month share price} + \text{Dividend (if any)} - \text{Beginning of month share price}}{\text{Beginning of month share price}}$$

The corresponding monthly returns for the stock market index were computed the same way. Each point on the graph represents a pair of monthly returns (one for SMC's stock and the other for the S&P 500). For example, as shown in Exhibit 12.2, during August of Year 4, the price of SMC's shares increased by 4 percent while the S&P 500 rose by 2.5 percent.

EXHIBIT 12.2   SMC MONTHLY RETURNS VERSUS S&P MONTHLY RETURNS.

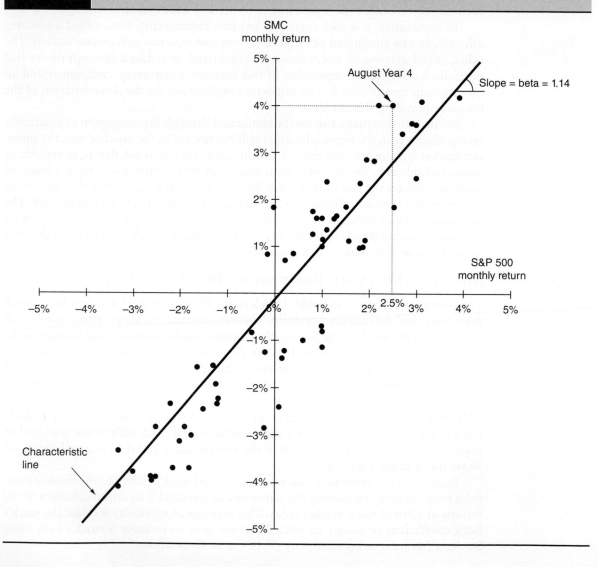

On the graph, we have also drawn the line that is closest to *all* the points. This line is called the security's **characteristic line**.[4] Its slope is 1.14, indicating that for each increase (or decrease) of 1 percent in the S&P 500, SMC's stock return increases (or decreases) by 1.14 percent, *on average*. In other words, the *slope of the characteristic line measures the sensitivity of SMC's stock returns to changes in the returns of the market index*. Therefore, it is an estimate of the beta coefficient of SMC's stock.

The return on the market index measures the reaction of the stock market to economy-wide events. For example, in August of Year 4, these events had a positive effect on the market because the index rose by 2.5 percent. During the same month, SMC's stock increased by 4 percent. The return on SMC's stock can be divided into two parts. One part reflects the impact of the economy-wide events on SMC's stock, and the other part reflects the effect of events that are specific to SMC, such as the success of a marketing campaign or the successful launch of a new product. What is the contribution of each type of event to the 4 percent return achieved in August of Year 4? The positive economy-wide events contributed 71 percent (a market return of 2.5 percent multiplied by a beta of 1.14 and divided by 4 percent) and favorable SMC-specific events contributed the remaining 29 percent. The fluctuation of the first part is the systematic risk of SMC's stock, whereas the fluctuation of the second part is its unsystematic risk, which can be eliminated through diversification.

Each stock has its own beta. Think of it as an identification number that measures the stock's systematic risk exposure to economy-wide events. A stock with a beta of 1 fluctuates, *on average*, the same as the market index against which its movement is measured because, by definition, the beta of the market index is 1. Stocks with a beta *higher* than 1 are more sensitive to economy-wide events than the market index is. And stocks with a beta *lower* than 1 are less sensitive to economy-wide events than the market index. Exhibit 12.3 shows the beta coefficients of the stocks of a number of firms listed on the stock exchanges of various countries.[5]

Managers do not have to estimate betas. The betas of most listed companies around the world are available from a number of financial information services firms. These firms estimate betas from market data, updating them regularly and often making them available online through a subscription service.

THE EFFECT OF BORROWING ON A COMPANY'S STOCK BETA

Most firms finance their activities with both debt and equity capital. Both debt holders and shareholders have claims on the cash flows generated by the firm's assets, and both are affected by the volatility, or risk, of these cash flows. This risk, which originates from the firm's assets, is called **business risk**. Debt holders, however, have a priority claim over shareholders on the firm's cash flows (they receive interest payments *before* shareholders receive dividends). As a consequence, shareholders bear *more* risk than debt holders. This additional risk, which results from the decision to borrow, is called **financial risk** (see Chapters 1 and 6 for details). As the firm increases its debt relative to its equity capital, financial risk will rise. Conclusion: *a*

---

[4] In statistics, the characteristic line would be called a regression line. Most spreadsheets contain an application, usually called *regression analysis*, which can be used to draw the characteristic line.

[5] Exhibit 12.3 is the same as Exhibit 3.14.

EXHIBIT 12.3	ESTIMATION OF THE BETA OF A SAMPLE OF COMPANIES IN DIFFERENT STOCK EXCHANGES AND INDUSTRIES[1]		
Company	**Stock Exchange**	**Industry**	**Estimated Beta**
Peugeot S.A.	Euronext Paris	Motor vehicle manufacturing	1.81
General Motors	New York Stock Exchange	Motor vehicle manufacturing	1.55
Honda Motor	Tokyo Stock Exchange	Motor vehicle manufacturing	1.28
Amazon.com Inc.	Nasdaq (New York)	Online distribution	1.71
Microsoft Corporation	Nasdaq (New York)	Software and services	1.28
Alphabet (Google)	Nasdaq (New York)	Internet information	1.27
Hewlett-Packard	New York Stock Exchange	Electronic equipment	1.72
Nokia	Helsinki Stock Exchange	Electronic equipment	1.55
Cisco Systems	Nasdaq (New York)	Electronic equipment	1.22
Morgan Stanley	New York Stock Exchange	Banking	1.49
Citigroup	New York Stock Exchange	Banking	1.49
Goldman Sachs Group	New York Stock Exchange	Banking	1.29
Groupe Casino	Euronext Paris	Distribution – discount	1.25
Costco Wholesale	Nasdaq (New York)	Distribution – discount	1.06
Carrefour	Euronext Paris	Distribution – discount	1.01
Chevron Corporation	New York Stock Exchange	Major oil and gas	1.21
Total	Euronext Paris	Major oil and gas	0.89
Exxon Mobil	New York Stock Exchange	Major oil and gas	0.82
Unilever	Euronext Amsterdam	Personal products	1.01
Nestlé	SIX-Swiss Exchange	Personal products	0.80
Delta Airlines	New York Stock Exchange	Major airlines	0.97
Air France - KLM	Euronext Paris	Major airlines	0.72
PepsiCo, Inc.	New York Stock Exchange	Beverages – soft drinks	0.64
Coca-Cola Company	New York Stock Exchange	Beverages – soft drinks	0.57
Verizon Communications	New York Stock Exchange	Telecom services	0.70
ATT	New York Stock Exchange	Telecom services	0.34

[1] Source: Datastream April 2018.

firm's beta coefficient will be affected by both business risk and financial risk, and the higher these risks, the higher the firm's beta. How can we measure the respective effect of business risk and financial risk on beta?

We use the words **asset beta** or **unlevered beta** (designated by β_{asset}) to refer to the beta of a stock *when the firm is all-equity financed*. In this case, the firm's owners face only business risk. There is no financial risk because there is no debt. Hence, the firm's asset or unlevered beta captures the firm's business risk. We use the words **equity beta, levered beta**, or **market beta** (designated by β_{equity}) to refer to the beta of a stock when the firm has borrowed. In this case, the firm's owners face both business risk and financial risk and the firm's equity, or levered, beta captures both sources of risk. The relationship between a company's unlevered, or asset, beta and its levered, or equity, beta can be expressed as follows:

$$\beta_{equity} = \beta_{asset}\left[1 + \frac{Debt}{Equity}\right] \tag{12.6}$$

where debt and equity are measured at their market value and not at their book, or accounting, value.[6] As the amount of borrowing increases relative to equity financing, the firm's debt-to-equity ratio increases, the firm's financial risk increases, and the firm's equity, or levered, beta increases.

The terms of equation 12.6 can be rearranged to express asset beta as a function of equity beta. We get the following:

$$\beta_{asset} = \frac{\beta_{equity}}{\left[1 + \dfrac{Debt}{Equity}\right]} \tag{12.7}$$

Consider SMC. We will show that the firm currently has a debt-to-equity ratio of one to three. Its levered, or equity, beta was estimated earlier at 1.14. Its unlevered, or asset, beta is thus:

$$\beta_{asset,SMC} = \frac{1.14}{\left[1 + \dfrac{1}{3}\right]} = 0.86$$

Note that slightly more than 75 percent of SMC's beta (0.86 divided by 1.14) originates from business risk, and the remaining 25 percent comes from financial risk.

THE CAPITAL ASSET PRICING MODEL

Exhibit 12.4 shows the average annual returns for three types of securities – common stocks, long-term government bonds, and short-term government bills – in the United States, the United Kingdom, and the world, for the period 1900 to 2017.

EXHIBIT 12.4	AVERAGE ANNUAL RATE OF RETURN ON COMMON STOCKS, GOVERNMENT BONDS, AND BILLS IN THE UNITED STATES, THE UNITED KINGDOM, AND THE WORLD (IN US DOLLARS).[1]		

	United States 1900 to 2017	United Kingdom 1900 to 2017	World[2] 1900 to 2017
Common stocks	11.5%	11.2%	9.6%
Government bonds	5.3%	6.2%	5.3%
Government bills	3.8%	4.8%	3.8%

[1] Source: Credit Suisse *Global Investment Returns Yearbook 2018*.
[2] World includes 23 countries (15 European plus Australia, Canada, China, Japan, New Zealand, South Africa, Russia, and the United States) with returns converted into US dollars.

[6] The formula assumes that the interest tax shield, which is the tax credit originating from the tax deductibility of interest payments (see Chapter 13), is as risky as the firm's assets. In the case when the tax shield is as risky as the firm's debt, the formula changes to $\beta_{equity} = \beta_{asset}\left[1 + (1 - \text{Tax rate})\dfrac{Debt}{Equity}\right]$. See Appendix 13.1, Chapter 13.

Not surprisingly, common stocks offered the highest returns, followed by long-term government bonds and short-term government bills. These three categories of assets have different returns because they have different risks, and, as expected, the higher the risk of a type of security, the higher its return.

Common stocks generate the highest average returns because they are the riskiest type of security: they do not promise fixed payments and shareholders receive whatever is left after all debt holders are paid. Government bonds are much less risky because they promise bondholders regular, government-guaranteed coupon payments and the repayment of the amount borrowed when the bonds mature. Finally, government bills offer, on average, a lower return than government bonds because bills, which are very short-term securities, are much less sensitive to changes in the rate of inflation than long-term bonds. All factors considered, bills are the safest investment available. This is why their rate of return is usually taken as a surrogate for the **riskless rate**, or **risk-free rate**.

In general, the difference between the *expected* return on any security, such as a bond or a share of stock, and the risk-free rate is the **security risk premium**:

Security's risk premium = Security's expected return − Risk-free rate

Rearranging the terms of the above equation, we have the following:

Security's expected return = Risk-free rate + Security's risk premium   (12.8)

When the risk premium is computed for the portfolio of *all* existing common stocks, it is called the stock market risk premium, or simply the **market risk premium**:

Market risk premium = Market portfolio expected return − Risk-free rate (12.9)

We know that the beta of a security measures its risk relative to the market portfolio. Thus, the risk premium of a *security* must be equal to the market risk premium multiplied by the security's beta coefficient:

Security's risk premium = Market risk premium × Security's beta

We can now write equation 12.8 as follows:

Security's expected return = Risk-free rate + Market risk premium × Security's beta

With symbols, we have the following:

$$E(R_i) = R_F + [E(R_M) − R_F]\beta_i \qquad (12.10)$$

where $E(R_i)$ is the expected return on security i, R_F is the risk-free rate, β_i is the security's beta, and $E(R_M)$ less R_F is the market risk premium as expressed in equation 12.9. This formula, which relates a security's expected return to its systematic risk or beta, is the capital asset pricing model (CAPM).[7] Its interpretation is straightforward. It says that the expected return on any security is the sum of two factors: (1) the risk-free rate, which measures the compensation for investing money without taking any risk, and (2) the expected reward for bearing systematic risk, which is equal to the market risk premium multiplied by the security's beta coefficient.

The CAPM is a linear relationship between expected return and risk. This relationship is shown in the graph in Exhibit 12.5.

Expected returns are plotted against betas according to the CAPM, where the risk-free rate is set equal to a government bill rate of 3.5 percent and an expected market portfolio return of 8.5 percent. The line starts at the point that represents the

---

[7] Note that the formula is the same as equation 3.13a in Chapter 3.

| EXHIBIT 12.5 | THE CAPITAL ASSET PRICING MODEL. |

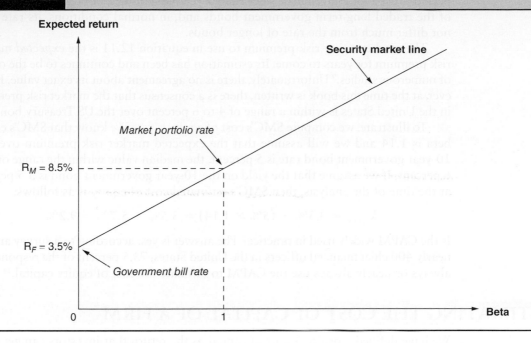

investment in government bills. That investment bears no risk, so its beta is equal to zero. The line then passes through the point that identifies the market portfolio. By definition, this portfolio has a beta of 1. Its expected return is 8.5 percent, the sum of a risk-free rate of 3.5 percent and a market risk premium of 5 percent. The line, called the **security market line (SML)**, has a positive slope. This is not surprising, because the higher the beta, the higher the systematic risk and the higher the expected return.

USING THE CAPM TO ESTIMATE SMC'S COST OF EQUITY

We have identified the relevant risk of a stock, we know how to measure this risk, and we know how to relate the risk to the stock's required return. We are now in a position to estimate the cost of equity for any firm. If $k_{E,i}$ denotes the cost of equity of firm i and $\beta_{equity,i}$ denotes the firm's equity beta, then according to the CAPM, we can write the following:

$$k_{E,i} = R_F + [E(R_M) - R_F]\beta_{equity,i} \qquad (12.11)$$

However, the CAPM expressed in equation 12.11 applies to short periods of time, because, as already mentioned, the risk-free rate is measured by the return on government bills, which mature in less than one year. Consequently, a firm's cost of equity derived from equation 12.11 is relevant only for a short period of time, say one year. Because firms' activities continue over many years, we would need, theoretically, to estimate a cost of equity for each coming year, depending on the government bill rate that is expected to prevail that year. In practice, given the difficulties of estimating future bill rates, only one cost of equity is estimated. This cost of equity is obtained using a proxy for the *average* future government bill rates. The proxy most commonly used is the 10-year government bond rate because it can be shown to be equal to the average of the short-term government bill rate over the next ten years.[8] The ten-year period is used for convenience since the 10-year government bond is the most liquid of the traded long-term government bonds and, in normal conditions, its rate does not differ much from the rate of longer bonds.

The market equity risk premium to use in equation 12.11 is the *expected* market risk premium for years to come. Its estimation has been and continues to be the object of numerous studies.[9] Unfortunately, there is no agreement about its exact value. However, at the time this book is written, there is a consensus that the market risk premium in the United States is within a range of 4 to 6 percent over the US Treasury bonds.[10]

To illustrate, we compute SMC's cost of equity $k_{E,SMC}$. We know that SMC's equity beta is 1.14 and we will assume that the expected market risk premium over the 10-year government bond rate is 5 percent, the median value within the range of 4 to 6 percent. If we assume that the yield on the 10-year government bond is 3.5 percent at the time of the analysis, then SMC's estimated cost of equity is as follows:

$$k_{E,SMC} = 3.5\% + (5\% \times 1.14) = 3.5\% + 5.7\% = 9.2\%$$

Is the CAPM widely used in practice? The answer is yes: according to a survey among nearly 400 chief financial officers in the United States, 73.5 percent of the respondents always or nearly always use the CAPM to estimate the cost of equity capital.[11]

ESTIMATING THE COST OF CAPITAL OF A FIRM

We have defined a project's cost of capital as the return that investors can get from similar investments with the same risk profile. Unfortunately, the proxy firms that have undertaken similar investments do not publish their returns. We are therefore left with the task of estimating the proxy's cost of capital using only information that is publicly available. In this section, we estimate the cost of capital of a *firm*, leaving the estimation of a *project's* cost of capital to the following section.

WHAT IS A FIRM'S COST OF CAPITAL?

Suppose that a firm is considering a one-year project that requires an initial investment of $30 million to be financed two-thirds with equity ($20 million) and one-third with debt ($10 million). If the project and the firm have the same risk profiles, the firm's debt holders will require a return on the debt portion of the investment that is equal to the firm's cost of debt. And shareholders will expect a return on the equity portion of the investment that is equal to the firm's cost of equity. If the firm's cost of debt is 6 percent and its cost of equity is 12 percent, the firm is expected, next year, to pay its debt holders $10,600,000 (the initial $10 million plus 6 percent of $10 million) and give its shareholders $22,400,000 (the initial $20 million plus 12 percent of $20 million).

---

[8] The relevant bond must be the 10-year government zero coupon bond, if available, because it does not bear any interest risk. Zero-coupon bonds are described and analyzed in detail in Chapter 10.

[9] For the different approaches to the estimation of the market risk premium, see Koller, Tim, Marc Goedhart, and David Wessels, *Valuation, Measuring and Managing the Value of Companies*, 6th ed., John Wiley & Sons, Inc., 2015, chapter 13.

[10] The market risk premium differs across countries because market conditions, attitudes toward risk, and the structure and organization of financial markets are not the same in all countries. Its estimation generally varies between 3 and 6 percent over the 10-year government bond rate.

[11] Graham, J.R. and Harvey, C.R., "The Theory and Practice of Corporate Finance: Evidence from the Field," *Journal of Financial Economics*, Vol. 60 (2–3), 2001.

The project will meet debt holders' and shareholders' expectations only if its return on the initial $30 million investment generates a net cash flow of at least $33 million ($10,600,000 plus $22,400,000). This is equivalent to a 10 percent rate of return ($30 million plus 10 percent of $30 million). This rate is the project's cost of capital or the project's **weighted average cost of capital (WACC)**. It is the *minimum* rate of return the project must generate to meet the return expectations of its suppliers of capital. And, because we assumed that the project has the *same risk* as the firm, this rate is also the **firm's cost of capital** (or its WACC).

Generalizing from our example, if a firm finances its activities with D dollars of equity and E dollars of debt, the project's WACC must be as follows:

$$(D + E) \times (1 + WACC) = D \times (1 + \text{Cost of debt}) + E \times (1 + \text{Cost of equity})$$

which can be written as follows:

$$WACC = \text{Cost of debt} \times \frac{D}{E + D} + \text{Cost of equity} \times \frac{E}{E \times D}$$

To account for the tax deductibility of interest expenses, the cost of debt must be calculated on an after-tax basis. According to equation 12.3, the after-tax cost of debt is $k_D(1 - T_C)$ where k_D is the pre-tax cost of debt and T_C is the marginal corporate tax rate. If, as before, k_E denotes the firm's cost of equity, then the WACC of any firm that finances its investment projects with debt and equity is as follows:

$$WACC = k_D(1 - T_C)\frac{D}{E + D} + k_E \frac{E}{E + D} \tag{12.12}$$

Equation 12.12,[12] which considers a firm financed with only equity and debt, can be easily extended to a firm that also uses other sources of funds such as, for example, PR dollars of preferred stocks with a cost equal to k_{PR}. In this case:

$$WACC = k_D(1 - T_C)\frac{D}{E + D + PR} + k_{PR}\frac{PR}{E + D + PR} + k_E\frac{E}{E + D + PR} \tag{12.13}$$

In the following sections, we consider only firms that are financed with a mix of debt and equity. Thus, to estimate a firm's WACC according to equation 12.12, we need four inputs:

1. The debt and equity ratios, $\dfrac{D}{E + D}$ and $\dfrac{E}{E + D}$
2. The cost of debt, k_D
3. The marginal corporate tax rate, T_C
4. The cost of capital, k_E

THE FIRM'S TARGET CAPITAL STRUCTURE

The debt-equity mix to use in the estimation of a firm's WACC must reflect the relative proportions of debt and equity that the firm intends to use in financing its investment projects. We call this mix the firm's **target capital structure**. In this chapter, these proportions are given; Chapter 13 discusses how a firm determines its target capital structure. However, there are two caveats when estimating the relevant proportions of debt and equity in the WACC formula (equation 12.12).

---

[12] Note that the formula is the same as equation 10.14 in Chapter 10.

First, the firm's current capital structure may *not* be its target capital structure. Issuing securities is costly, so firms typically do not issue debt and equity simultaneously when they raise capital. A firm may, for example, issue debt today, which will move the firm away from its target capital structure. To restore capital structure to its target values, the firm will have to issue equity at a later date. Because of this process, the firm's capital structure changes over time and the structure we observe at one particular point in time may not be the firm's target capital structure. In computing the WACC, the long-run target capital structure must be used.

Second, the proportions of debt and equity financing in the WACC should be estimated with the *market values* of debt and equity, not with their *accounting* or *book values*. Firms issue stocks and bonds at their market values, not at their book values. Thus, the firm's current book values of debt and equity are irrelevant. To illustrate this point, consider again the case of SMC. The firm's managerial balance sheet,[13] shown in Exhibit 12.6, indicates that the firm's book value of debt is $100 million and the book value of equity is $213 million. Hence the *book* values of the financing proportions in equation 12.12 are 32 percent debt ($100 million divided by $313 million, the sum of debt and equity) and 68 percent equity.

To estimate the *market values* of the debt and equity ratios, we need the market values of the firm's debt and equity. SMC's only debt consists of 100,000 bonds (see Exhibit 12.6). Recall that the market value of one bond is $1,066 (see equation 12.1), so the market value of SMC's debt is $106.6 million ($1,066 times 100,000). SMC's share price is currently $12.79 (given). With 25 million shares outstanding

EXHIBIT 12.6	SMC's MANAGERIAL BALANCE SHEET.

Invested capital	
• Cash	$ 5,000,000
• Working capital requirement[1]	48,000,000
• Net fixed assets	260,000,000
Total invested capital	**$313,000,000**

Capital employed		
• Long-term debt[2]		$100,000,000
100,000 bonds at par value $1,000		
• Owners' equity		$213,000,000
25,000,000 shares at par value[3] $2	50,000,000	
Retained earnings	163,000,000	
Total capital employed		**$313,000,000**

[1] WCR = [Accounts receivable + Inventories + Prepaid expenses] − [Accounts payable + Accrued expenses].
[2] SMC has no short-term debt.
[3] The par value of common stocks is an arbitrary fixed value assigned to shares when they are initially issued.

---

[13] The managerial balance sheet is a modified version of the standard balance sheet introduced in Chapter 5. On the upper part of the balance sheet, it reports the firm's investment in cash, operations (working capital requirement), and fixed assets. On the lower part, it shows the amount of capital (borrowed funds and owners' equity) employed to finance these investments.

(see Exhibit 12.6), the market value of SMC's equity is thus $319.8 million ($12.79 times 25 million). Based on these market values, the debt ratio is as follows:

$$\text{Debt ratio at market value} = \frac{\$106,600,000}{\$106,600,000 + \$319,800,000} = 25\%$$

The debt ratio is 25 percent when measured at *market* value and 32 percent when measured at *book* value. And the equity ratio is 75 percent at *market* value and 68 percent at *book* value. In practice, differences of this magnitude are not uncommon.

Clearly, estimating the debt and equity ratios at market value requires knowing the market values of the firm's debt and equity. When the firm's shares are publicly traded, as in the case of SMC, the market value of equity is simply the share price multiplied by the number of shares outstanding. The estimation of the market value of debt is more complicated because the debt securities of most firms are not publicly traded. One way to circumvent this difficulty is to apply the bond valuation formula (see equation 12.1) to each of the firm's debt issues and then add these values to obtain the total market value of the firm's debt.

 In practice, many analysts would simply use the book value of debt as a surrogate for its unavailable market value. When the firm's shares are not publicly traded, the book value of equity is used as a substitute for its market value. These approximations are less than satisfactory because ratios based on market values can be quite different from their book value equivalents. As an alternative, we suggest using the market value ratios of proxy firms that have publicly traded bonds and stocks.

THE FIRM'S COSTS OF DEBT AND EQUITY

The previous sections present a number of models that can be used to estimate a firm's costs of debt and equity. Let's briefly recapitulate.

1   The cost of debt k_D can be estimated using the bond valuation formula (equation 12.1) or the credit-risk spread equation (equation 12.2). Recall that if we know the bond price, its promised coupon payments, and its face value, the valuation formula (equation 12.1) can be solved for k_D. When we applied this technique to SMC, we found k_D equal to 4.5 percent.

In practice, firms do not have to perform these calculations. They either use the credit-risk spread approximation (equation 12.2) or simply call their bank. Indeed, banks and other financial institutions constantly follow changes in bond prices and market interest rates. Thus, a less time-consuming way to estimate k_D is to ask your banker, who will quote you a rate when needed. This alternative is particularly useful for firms that do not have publicly traded bonds from which they can estimate their most recent cost of debt.

2.   The cost of equity k_E can be estimated with the help of the CAPM using equation 12.11. To estimate k_E, we need three items: the prevailing market yield on 10-year government bonds, the market risk premium, and the firm's equity beta. The market yield on government bonds is regularly published in the business pages of major daily newspapers. The expected market risk premium over the 10-year government bonds is in the range of 4 to 6 percent in the United States. Most industrial countries with an active equity market have a historical market risk premium in the range of 3 to 6 percent. The betas of publicly traded stocks can easily be obtained from financial information services firms.

Using a government bond yield of 3.5 percent, an equity beta of 1.14, and an expected market risk premium of 5 per cent, we found that SMC has an estimated cost of equity of 9.2 percent. Recall that we need share prices to estimate betas. However, even when there are no available share prices, which is the case for firms whose shares are not publicly traded, the CAPM can still be applied. In this case, the betas of proxy (similar) firms are used. This approach is described later in the chapter.

SUMMARY OF THE FIRM'S WACC CALCULATIONS

Exhibit 12.7 summarizes the four steps required to estimate a firm's WACC. Each of the first three steps corresponds to a particular component of the WACC. For each, the exhibit indicates how to estimate its value and shows the results of the estimation for SMC. The last step is simply the computation of the WACC using equation 12.12. SMC's financing ratios at market value are 25 percent debt and 75 percent equity. Its pre-tax cost of debt is 4.5 percent, its cost of equity is 9.2 percent, and the tax rate is 40 percent. Applying equation 12.12, we find the following:

$$\text{WACC}_{\text{SMC}} = [4.5\% \times (1 - 0.40) \times 25\%] + [9.2\% \times 75\%] = 7.6\%$$

This is the discount rate that SMC should use when making investment decisions involving projects that have the same risk profile as that of the firm. Any proposal that has a risk profile similar to that of SMC but does not expect to generate a return in excess of 7.6 percent should be rejected. This is the discount rate we used in Chapter 9 to evaluate SMC's investment in the designer desk lamp project, a project with the same risk profile as SMC.

ESTIMATING THE COST OF CAPITAL OF A PROJECT

A project's cost of capital is primarily determined by the project's risk, which can be classified into one of two categories. The first category includes projects that have risk characteristics *similar* to those of the firm that would undertake them. SMC's designer desk lamp project belongs to this category.

The second category includes projects that have a risk profile *different* from the risk profile of the firm that would undertake them. As an illustration of this type of project, we use a fictitious food-processing company called Fine Foods. Managers at Fine Foods, convinced that their company will benefit from vertical integration into restaurants, are considering opening a chain of restaurants under the name Grady's. The Grady's restaurants project belongs to the second category because the firm that would undertake the project, Fine Foods, is in the food-processing business, not the restaurant business.

The following sections show how to estimate the cost of capital for these two types of projects.

THE PROJECT'S RISK IS SIMILAR TO THE RISK OF THE FIRM

If the project's risk is the same as the risk of the firm, then the firm is the appropriate proxy for the project, and the project's WACC is simply the firm's WACC. The estimation procedure for the firm's WACC is described in the previous section and summarized in Exhibit 12.7.

The designer desk lamp project has the same risk as SMC's risk, so the 7.6 percent WACC of SMC is the appropriate cost of capital for that project. This is the discount rate we used in Chapter 9 to estimate the net present value of the project.

| EXHIBIT 12.7 | THE ESTIMATION OF A FIRM'S WEIGHTED AVERAGE COST OF CAPITAL (WACC), INCLUDING AN APPLICATION TO SUNLIGHT MANUFACTURING COMPANY (SMC). | |

Steps to Follow	Method	SMC
Step 1: Estimate the firm's relative proportion of debt (D) and equity (E) financing: $\dfrac{D}{E + D}$ and $\dfrac{E}{E + D}$	• Use the firm's market values of debt and equity	Bond price = $1,066 Stock price = $12.79
	• The market value of debt is computed from data on outstanding bonds using the bond valuation formula (equation 12.1)	$106,600,000 ($1,066 × 100,000 bonds)
	• The market value of equity is the share price multiplied by the number of shares outstanding	$319,800,000 ($12.79 × 25,000,000 shares)
	• If the firm's securities are not publicly traded, use the market value ratio of proxy firms	$\dfrac{D}{E + D} = 0.25$ and $\dfrac{E}{E + D} = 0.75$
Step 2: Estimate the firm's after-tax cost of debt: $k_D(1 - T_C)$	• If the firm has outstanding bonds that are publicly traded, use equation 12.1 to estimate k_D	$k_D = 4.5\%$
	• Otherwise, use the credit-spread equation 12.2 or ask the bank	
	• Use the marginal corporate tax rate for T_C	$T_C = 40\%$
	• Calculate the after-tax cost of debt with equation 12.3	$k_D(1 - T_C) = 4.5\% \times (1 - 0.40)$ $= 2.7\%$
Step 3: Estimate the firm's cost of equity: k_E	• Use the capital asset pricing model	
	• The risk-free rate is the prevailing rate on government bonds	3.5%
	• The market premium is 5%	5%
	• Apply the CAPM to the firm's equity beta. If the firm's shares are not publicly traded, estimate beta from proxies	1.14
	• Calculate the cost of equity with equation 12.11	$k_E = 3.5\% + (5\% \times 1.14) = 9.2\%$
Step 4: Calculate the firm's weighted average cost of capital: WACC	• Calculate the WACC with equation 12.12	WACC = (2.7% × 0.25) + (9.2% × 0.75) = 7.6%

THE PROJECT'S RISK IS DIFFERENT FROM THE RISK OF THE FIRM

When a project has a different risk profile from the risk profile of the firm that would undertake it, such as in the case of the Grady's restaurants project, the firm is no longer the right proxy for the project because investors require the project's cost of capital to reflect the risk of the *project*, not the risk of the *firm*. As indicated at the beginning of the chapter, investors expect a return from the project that is at least equal to the return they would get from the proxy firms.

How should the project's cost of capital be estimated in this case? Should it be set equal to the average value of the proxies' WACC, where the WACC of each proxy is estimated as in the previous section? A potential problem with this approach is that the project may have different target debt and equity ratios than those of the proxy firms. A solution to this problem is to estimate the cost of capital of the proxy firms *assuming that they have no debt financing*. Then, these estimates are adjusted to reflect the project's target capital structure. This procedure is illustrated using the Grady's restaurants project.

THE PROJECT'S TARGET CAPITAL STRUCTURE

Chapter 13 explains that many factors affect a firm's capital structure, among them the type of assets owned by the firm. Because proxy firms operate in the same line of business as the project and are expected to own assets that are similar to those of the project, it is generally assumed that their capital structure is a good approximation of the proportions of debt and equity that should be used to finance the project. In other words, the project's financing ratios can be set equal to the *average* of the proxies' financing ratios.

To estimate the proxies' financing ratios, the same approach is used as in the case where the firm itself (SMC) is the proxy. The two caveats mentioned earlier are still valid. First, market values should be used instead of book values. Second, the *observed* capital structure of a particular proxy firm may not be that firm's target structure. However, taking the mean of the proxies' financing ratios should reduce the effect of most measurement errors.

Exhibit 12.8 reports the financing ratios for the Grady's restaurant proxy firms. The three proxies selected are All-Star Restaurants, McRonalds', and Best Burgers.

EXHIBIT 12.8	PROXIES FOR THE GRADY'S RESTAURANTS PROJECT.		
	Equity beta	$\dfrac{\text{Debt}}{\text{Equity}}$	Asset beta[1]
All-Star Restaurants	0.83	0.19	0.70
McRonalds'	1.26	0.75	0.72
Best Burgers	1.41	0.85	0.76
Average beta of proxies	1.17		0.73

[1] Asset betas are calculated according to equation 12.7 using the data in the exhibit.

THE PROJECT'S COSTS OF DEBT AND EQUITY

As mentioned earlier, both the cost of debt and cost of equity depend on the firm's debt ratio. The higher the debt ratio, the higher the financial risk and the greater the returns required by shareholders and debt holders. Therefore, if we want to use the proxies' costs of debt and equity to estimate the project's cost of capital, we must first adjust these costs to account for the differences in debt ratios between the proxies and the project. In practice, however, it is assumed that the cost of debt is less sensitive to changes in financial leverage than the cost of equity,[14] so only the latter is adjusted for differences in capital structure.

---

[14] At least for firms that do not exhibit an extreme degree of financial leverage.

ESTIMATING THE COST OF DEBT FOR THE GRADY'S RESTAURANTS PROJECT

To estimate the rate of interest at which the three proxy firms could borrow, we need their credit ratings and the corresponding rates.[15] All-Star Restaurants is rated a less risky borrower than the other two companies. Firms with the same ratings as All-Star Restaurants could borrow long term at 3.9 percent while those with a rating identical to that of McRonalds' and Best Burgers could borrow long term at 5.2 percent. Because Fine Foods has a credit rating closer to that of All-Star Restaurants than the other two companies, we take 3.9 percent as our estimate of the rate of interest Fine Foods would be charged to finance its project. Given that Fine Foods has a marginal tax rate of 33 percent, the project's after-tax cost of debt is:

$$k_D(1 - T_C) = 3.9\% \times (1 - 0.33) = 2.6\%$$

In practice, firms do not need to compute the required rates of interest because these rates are readily available from banks and other financial institutions. However, banks will often quote a rate for a company as a whole, not for a specific project. We can use this rate as long as the project's risk is not very different from the risk of the company. But if this is not the case, the bank should quote the rates for proxy firms, not the rate for the company.

ESTIMATING THE COST OF EQUITY FOR THE GRADY'S RESTAURANTS PROJECT

Recall that a firm's beta coefficient increases with financial leverage. Thus, if we employ the CAPM to estimate a project's cost of equity, we want to ensure that the beta coefficient we use reflects the effect of the project's target capital structure.

If proxies have different capital structures than the project's target capital structure, their betas need to be adjusted to account for the difference. The adjustment is done in two steps. First, each of the proxies' equity betas is "unlevered," meaning that its corresponding unlevered or asset beta is calculated using equation 12.7. Second, the *mean* of the "unlevered" betas is "re-levered" at the *project's* target capital structure using equation 12.6 to obtain the *project's* equity beta. This is the beta coefficient that should be used to estimate the project's cost of equity according to the CAPM.

We illustrate this procedure using the Grady's restaurants project. The unlevered, or asset, betas of the proxies are shown in Exhibit 12.8. They are calculated using equation 12.7 and the relevant data for each proxy firm is reported in Exhibit 12.8. The betas have a mean value of 0.73. Note that the estimates of asset betas are much closer to one another than the estimates of equity betas, because the three proxies have similar assets but different debt ratios. This is why we want to remove the effects of borrowing from the proxy equity betas, and re-lever the average asset beta of 0.73 at the debt-to-equity ratio and tax rate of the Grady's restaurants project.

What should Fine Foods take as a target debt-to-equity ratio for its Grady's restaurants project? Note how low the ratio of All-Star Restaurants is compared to the other two proxies (0.19 versus 0.75 and 0.85). This is because All-Star Restaurants issued recently a large amount of equity to fund new investments. As explained in Chapter 13, a firm debt-to-equity ratio typically deviates from its target ratio following an equity or a debt issue. In other words, we cannot take 0.19 as an estimate of All-Star Restaurants *target* debt-to-equity ratio. For this reason, we drop All-Star Restaurants and take the average ratio of the other two comparable companies as the target ratio for the Grady's restaurant project, which is equal to 0.80 (0.75 plus

---

[15] Credit ratings and their providers, the rating agencies, are discussed in Chapter 11.

0.85 divided by two). This is equivalent to 44 percent debt-to-total financing and 56 percent equity-to-total financing.[16]

We now need to re-lever the average asset beta of 0.73 to the target debt-to-equity ratio of 0.80. Applying equation 12.6 we get the following:

$$\beta_{equity,Grady's} = 0.73 \times (1 + 0.80) = 1.31$$

The estimated equity beta of 1.31 for the project is significantly different from the average equity beta of 1.17 shown in Exhibit 12.8. This explains why it is important to go through all the steps required to get a proper estimate of the project's equity beta. Just taking the average equity beta of the proxy companies would not produce a good estimate when the debt ratios of the proxy firms are far apart.

Applying the CAPM in equation 12.11 with an equity beta of 1.31, and using the same risk-free rate of 3.5 percent and market risk premium of 5 percent as in the case of SMC, we get the following estimate of the cost of equity for the Grady's restaurants project:

$$k_{E,Grady's} = 3.5\% + (5\% \times 1.31) = 3.5\% + 6.55\% = 10\%$$

ESTIMATING THE WACC FOR THE GRADY'S RESTAURANTS PROJECT

Exhibit 12.9 summarizes the steps required to estimate the cost of capital when the project's risk is different from the firm's risk. Each step shows the application to the Grady's restaurants project.

Recall that Grady's target debt-to-equity ratio is 80 percent, which means that its target financing ratios are 44 percent debt and 56 percent equity. Its pre-tax cost of debt is 3.9 percent, its cost of equity is 10 percent, and the tax rate is 33 percent. Applying the WACC formula in equation 12.12, we get the following:

$$WACC_{Grady's} = [3.9\% \times (1 - 0.33) \times 0.44] + [10\% \times 0.56] = 6.75\%$$

This is the appropriate rate that managers of Fine Foods should use to decide whether to open a chain of Grady's fast-food restaurants.

THREE MISTAKES TO AVOID WHEN ESTIMATING A PROJECT'S COST OF CAPITAL

We close this section by discussing three mistakes that are commonly made when estimating a project's cost of capital. These mistakes reveal some dangerous misconceptions about the precise meaning and the correct estimation of a project's cost of capital.

MISTAKE NUMBER 1

The project is going to be financed entirely with debt, so its relevant cost of capital is the interest rate on the debt.

or:

The project is going to be financed entirely with equity, so its relevant cost of capital is the cost of equity.

Suppose that SMC, being short of funds, decided to borrow $2 million to finance the entire cost of its designer desk lamp project at an interest rate of 4.5 percent (the same rate as the one used earlier) or 2.7 percent after tax [$4.5\% \times (1 - 0.40)$].

---

[16] Note that $\dfrac{D}{E + D} = \dfrac{(D/E)}{1 + (D/E))} = \dfrac{0.8}{1 + 0.8} = 44\%$.

| EXHIBIT 12.9 | THE ESTIMATION OF A PROJECT'S WEIGHTED AVERAGE COST OF CAPITAL (WACC), WHEN ITS RISK IS DIFFERENT FROM THE RISK OF THE FIRM, INCLUDING AN APPLICATION TO THE GRADY'S RESTAURANTS PROJECT. | |

Steps to Follow	Method	Grady's Restaurants
Step 1: Estimate the project's relative proportion of debt (D) and equity (E) financing: $\dfrac{D}{E+D}$ and $\dfrac{E}{E+D}$	• Use the proxies' market values of debt and equity	$\dfrac{D}{E+D} = 0.44$ and $\dfrac{E}{E+D} = 0.56$
	• The market value of debt is computed from data on outstanding bonds using the bond valuation formula (equation 12.1)	
	• The market value of equity is the share price multiplied by the number of shares outstanding	
	• Take the mean of the proxies' ratios	
Step 2: Estimate the project's after-tax cost of debt: $k_D(1 - T_C)$	• Use the proxies' credit ratings and the corresponding borrowing rates	$k_D = 3.9\%$
	• Take the mean of the proxies' borrowing	
	• Use the marginal corporate tax rate for T_C	$T_C = 33\%$
	• Calculate the after-tax cost of debt with equation 12.3	$k_D(1 - T_C) = 3.9\% \times (1 - 0.33) = 2.6\%$
Step 3: Estimate the project's cost of equity: k_E	• Use the CAPM (equation 12.11)	
	• The risk-free rate is the prevailing rate on government bonds	3.5%
	• The market premium is 5% (historical average)	5%
	• Unlever the proxies' equity beta using equation 12.7 to get their unlevered betas	0.73
	• Re-lever the mean of the proxies' asset betas at the project's target debt-to-equity ratio using equation 12.6 to get the project's equity beta	1.31
	• Calculate the cost of equity using equation 12.11	$k_E = 3.5\% + (5\% \times 1.31) = 10\%$
Step 4: Calculate the project's weighted average cost of capital: WACC	• Calculate the WACC with equation 12.12	$\begin{aligned} \text{WACC} &= (2.6\% \times 0.44) + (10\% \times 0.56) \\ &= 6.75\% \end{aligned}$

If we mechanically apply the WACC formula (equation 12.12), the project's cost of capital would be 2.7 percent because there is no equity financing in this case. If you think something is wrong with this, you are right. Let's see why.

First, the firm could borrow $2 million at 4.5 percent, not on the merit of the project but because it has enough equity and other valuable assets that serve as guarantees for the lender. Although SMC as a whole can borrow $2 million, no bank or any other potential lender would be willing to lend the full cost of the designer desk lamp project with the project's assets as sole guarantee. Second, and more fundamentally, the WACC formula was incorrectly used. Remember that the cost of capital of the desk lamp project is the rate of return that the project needs to generate to meet investors' return expectations. Because the project has the same risk as SMC's risk, the relevant cost of capital for the project must be the same as SMC's cost of capital. The latter can be estimated using the WACC formula *applied to SMC*, which, we know, is *not* 100 percent financed by debt.

MISTAKE NUMBER 2

> *Although the project does not have the same risk as the firm, its relevant cost of capital should be equal to the firm's WACC because the firm's shareholders and debt holders are paid with cash from the firm's cash flows, not from the project's cash flows.*

It is true that dividends and interest expenses are paid out of the firm's cash flows. However, this does not imply that the cost of capital of any project undertaken by the firm must be the same as the firm's cost of capital. The return that investors want to earn on a project is the same as the one they would get from an alternative investment with the same risk characteristics, irrespective of the return they are currently getting from the firm. For example, should the cost of capital of the investments to be made by Grady's (a chain of restaurants) be the same as the cost of capital of Fine Foods (a food-processing company)? The answer is no, because investors will certainly not view investments made in the restaurant sector the same way they view investments in the food-processing industry. They would rather compare them to investments made by firms that invest exclusively in restaurants. Remember: it is not the *firm's* cost of capital that determines a *project's* cost of capital; it is the *other way around*. Each project has its own cost of capital, and the firm's cost of capital is simply the weighted average of the capital costs of the various projects that the firm has undertaken.

Unfortunately, many firms still use a company-wide cost of capital, often called the **hurdle rate**, which they apply indiscriminately to all projects. Unless all these projects have the same risk, this procedure is incorrect.

To illustrate this point, we consider MultiTek, a firm that is using the company's WACC to evaluate all its projects. To simplify, suppose that MultiTek has no debt and that its beta is equal to 1. Suppose further that the rate on government bonds is 5 percent and that the market risk premium is 4 percent. According to the CAPM, expressed in equation 12.11, MultiTek's cost of equity, which is also its WACC because the firm has no debt, is equal to the following:

$$k_{E,\text{MultiTek}} = \text{WACC}_{\text{MultiTek}} = 5\% + (4\% \times 1) = 9\%$$

Note that 9 percent is also the expected return on the market portfolio because MultiTek has a beta coefficient equal to 1. Because MultiTek uses its WACC to evaluate its investment proposals, it will accept any project that has a return higher than 9 percent and reject any project that has a return lower than 9 percent. This decision rule is illustrated in Exhibit 12.10, where the 9 percent line separates the point at which projects are accepted from the point at which they are rejected.

EXHIBIT 12.10	COMPANY-WIDE COST OF CAPITAL AND PROJECTS' EXPECTED RATES OF RETURN.

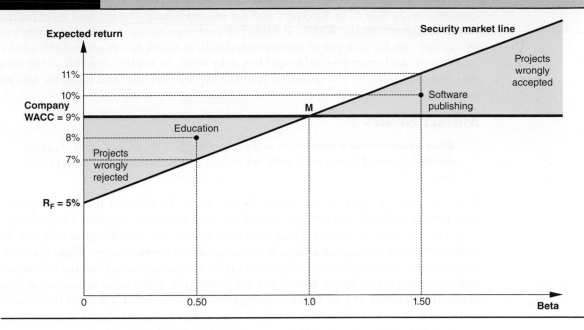

We have also drawn the security market line (SML), which provides a project's expected return given the project's beta coefficient. It starts at 5 percent, the prevailing risk-free rate at that time, and passes through point M, the market expected return of 9 percent. If MultiTek used the project's betas instead of the firm's beta to evaluate its investment projects, it would reject any project *below* the SML and accept any project *above* the SML because the SML represents the relationship between any investment's expected returns and its corresponding beta coefficient. Exhibit 12.10 shows that using a single rate for all types of projects may lead MultiTek to incorrectly accept some high-risk projects and incorrectly reject some low-risk projects.

To see why this would happen, suppose MultiTek has two divisions: a low-risk one in the education sector and a high-risk one in the software-publishing sector. Let's assume that proxy firms for the former have an average asset beta of 0.50, while the proxies for the latter have an average asset beta of 1.50. Because MultiTek does not carry any debt, the cost of capital for each of the divisions is its cost of equity. Using the CAPM to estimate each division's cost of capital, we find the following:

$$k_{E,Education} = 5\% + (4\% \times 0.50) = 7\%$$
$$k_{E,Software} = 5\% + (4\% \times 1.50) = 11\%$$

If the education division is considering an investment with an IRR of 8 percent (see Exhibit 12.10), the project should be accepted because it would provide MultiTek's shareholders with a return that is higher than the required 7 percent return. If the software-publishing division has a project with an IRR of 10 percent (see Exhibit 12.10), it should be rejected because its IRR is lower than the 11 percent return required by MultiTek's shareholders. However, under the decision rule applied by MultiTek, the first project is rejected because its expected return is less than the company-wide WACC of 9 percent and the second is accepted because its expected return is higher than the WACC. If MultiTek continues to use its WACC of 9 percent as a cutoff rate for all types of investment, it will, at times, accept unprofitable risky investments and reject profitable and less risky ones. As a result, the risk of the firm will rise over time, its risk-adjusted profitability will decline, and its value will go down.

MISTAKE NUMBER 3

When a project's risk is different from the risk of the firm, the project's cost of capital should be lowered to account for the risk reduction that diversification brings to the firm.

It is true that a project whose returns do not vary like those of the firm's existing investments will reduce the firm's overall risk through diversification. For example, you may argue that by diversifying into restaurants, Fine Foods' total risk will be reduced because earnings in its two businesses will not move in steps. When the earnings from the food-processing industry go up (or down), earnings from the restaurant industry may also go up (or down), but not necessarily in the same proportions. As a result, the volatility of Fine Foods' earnings will be smoother if it decides to invest in restaurants. You may, therefore, conclude that using restaurant chains as proxies for Grady's without accounting for this risk reduction effect is incorrect.

Although it is true that the total risk of the firm will be reduced if it invests in restaurants, the effect is irrelevant to its shareholders because they can benefit directly from the same risk reduction by buying shares in other restaurant chains. Consequently, they would certainly not accept that the return they require from the project be reduced because of the risk diversification that they can achieve in their personal portfolio without the help of Fine Foods' managers.

AVOIDING MISTAKES

Mistakes made when estimating a project's cost of capital can lead to a distorted allocation of capital among projects and eventually to value destruction, as in the case of a firm using a company-wide cost of capital irrespective of the systematic risk (beta) of the project it evaluates. When in doubt, always remember that *a project's cost of capital is determined by financial markets, not by managers.* What you can do, and must do, is use market data, such as market interest rates, betas, and the capital structure of proxies, to determine the return that the market is expecting from the project being evaluated. What you should not do is set values for the WACC that are based on internally generated data, such as accounting data. Doing so could incorrectly influence the outcome of your evaluation.

KEY POINTS

1. The *firm's* cost of capital is simply the return that investors expect to earn on the firm's invested capital. When a project has the *same* risk profile as that of the firm that would undertake it, the *project's* cost of capital is the same as the firm's cost of capital.

2. When a project's risk is different from the firm's risk, the firm's cost of capital is no longer the appropriate cost of capital of the project. In this case, proxies, or pure-plays, that have the *same* risk as the project's risk must be identified, and the proxies' cost of capital must be used to evaluate the project.

3. Unfortunately, a firm's cost of capital is not directly observable. It must be inferred from the return investors expect to earn on the capital they invest in the firm. This expected return can be estimated using data on the securities the firm has issued. The cost of debt can be inferred from the price of the firm's outstanding bonds. The cost of equity can be estimated using either the dividend-discount model (DDM) or the capital asset pricing model (CAPM). The DDM can be applied only to companies that pay regular and stable dividends. The CAPM is more general and is the standard model used to estimate the cost of equity.

4. The overall cost of capital is simply the weighted average of the cost of debt and the cost of equity, where the weights are the proportions of debt and equity the firm has raised to finance its investments. This overall cost of capital is called the weighted average cost of capital (WACC).

5. The firm's WACC is also the project's cost of capital when the project risk is similar to the risk of the firm. When the project's risk differs from that of the firm, the firm's WACC no longer represents the return that investors require from the project. In this case, the project's WACC is estimated from the cost of equity and the cost of debt of proxy firms that have the same risk as that of the project.

6. Mistakes are often made when estimating a project's cost of capital. These mistakes can be traced to some misconceptions about a project's cost of capital, and they can be easily avoided by remembering that a project's cost of capital is determined by financial markets, not by managers.

FURTHER READING

1. Berk, Jonathan, and Peter DeMarzo, *Corporate Finance*, 4th ed. Pearson, 2017. See chapter 12.
2. Credit Suisse *Global Investment Returns Yearbook*, 2018.
3. Fernandez, Pablo, Vitaly Pershin, and Isabel Fernández Acín. "Discount Rate (Risk-Free Rate and Market Risk Premium) for 41 Countries in 2017: A Survey (April 17, 2017)." Available at SSRN: https://ssrn.com/abstract=2954142.
4. Ibbotson *SBBI Valuation Yearbook*, Morningstar, 2017.
5. Koller, Tim, Marc Goedhart, and David Wessels, *Valuation, Measuring and Managing the Value of Companies*, 6th ed., John Wiley & Sons, Inc., 2015. See chapter 13.

SELF-TEST QUESTIONS

12.1 **Cost of debt versus cost of equity.**
When we say that a firm, a division, or a project has a cost of equity capital of 10 percent and a cost of debt of 8 percent, what do we mean? Why is the cost of debt lower than the cost of equity?

12.2 Cash flows from bonds and stocks.

What are the cash flows associated with a bond? With a share of common stock? How are these cash flows related to the market value of the bond? The market value of the share of common stock?

12.3 The capital asset pricing model.

What does the capital asset pricing model (CAPM) claim?

12.4 The cost of capital of a firm.

Vanhoff Line Corp. has an equity beta of 1.16 and a debt-to-equity ratio of 1. The expected market portfolio return is 10 percent. The interest rate on government bonds is 5 percent. Vanhoff Line can borrow long term at a rate of 6 percent. The corporate tax rate is 40 percent.

a. What is Vanhoff Line's cost of equity?
b. What is Vanhoff Line's cost of capital?

12.5 An estimate of the cost of capital.

Your company, PacificCom, manufactures telecommunication equipment and communication software. You have just received a copy of a consultant's report that strongly recommends that investment proposals be accepted only if their internal rate of return is higher than 8 percent. The rate of 8 percent is presented as the weighted average cost of capital (WACC) of PacificCom and was computed as follows:

$$\text{WACC} = [5.78\%(1 - 40\%) \times 40\%] + [11\% \times 60\%] = 7.99\% \text{ rounded to } 8\%$$

where k_D = 5.78 percent is the rate at which PacificCom can borrow from its banks; T_C = 40 percent is the firm's marginal corporate tax rate; $[D/(E + D)]$ = 40 percent, and $[E/(E + D)]$ = 60 percent are PacificCom financing ratios, and D and E are the amounts of debt and equity taken from the firm's most recent balance sheet; and k_E = 11 percent is PacificCom's cost of equity. The rate was calculated using the capital asset pricing model, with a risk-free rate equal to the government bond rate of 5 percent, a market risk premium of 5 percent, and a firm's beta coefficient of 1.2 $[k_E = 5\% + (1.2 \times 5\%)]$ = 11 percent.

Do you agree with the consultant's estimate of PacificCom's cost of capital?

REVIEW QUESTIONS

1. Historical returns.

The following table shows the annual realized returns on the following US securities from 1997 to 2016: the stock market (S&P 500), corporate bonds, government bonds, and Treasury bills.

Time Period	S&P 500	Corporate Bonds Rate	Government Bonds Rate	Treasury Bills Rate
1997	33.4%	12.9%	15.9%	5.3%
1998	28.6	10.8	13.1	4.9
1999	21.0	−7.4	−9.0	4.7
2000	−9.1	12.9	21.5	5.9
2001	−11.9	10.6	3.7	3.8
2002	−22.1	16.3	17.8	1.6
2003	28.7	5.3	1.4	1.0
2004	10.9	8.7	8.5	1.2
2005	4.9	5.9	7.8	3.0
2006	15.8	3.2	1.2	4.8
2007	5.5	2.6	9.9	4.7
2008	−37.0	8.8	25.9	1.6
2009	26.5	3.0	−14.9	0.1
2010	15.1	12.4	10.1	0.1
2011	2.1	17.9	27.1	0.0
2012	16.0	10.7	3.4	0.1
2013	32.4	−7.1	−12.8	0.0
2014	13.7	17.3	24.7	0.0
2015	1.4	−1.0	−0.7	0.0
2016	12.0	6.7	1.8	0.2
Annual arithmetic average				
1998–2016	9.4%	7.5%	7.8%	2.6%
1926–2016	12.0%	6.3%	6.0%	3.4%

Source: *2017 SBBI Yearbook.*

a. Theory suggests that the riskier the investment, the higher the expected return. To what extent is that illustrated by the data in the table?

b. How do you explain the relatively high volatility in the annual returns on both corporate and government long-term bonds?

c. What was the market risk premium of the S&P 500 for each of the years from 1997 to 2016? What was it over the two periods 1997–2012 and 1926–2016? What conclusions can you draw from your observations?

2. **Risk and return.**
   Do you agree or disagree with the following statements? Explain.

   a. "The best forecast of future returns on the stock market is the average over the past ten years of historical returns."

   b. "Because stocks offer a higher return over the long term than bonds, all rational investors should prefer stocks."

   c. "Because a government bond is considered risk-free, that means an investor would never suffer a loss."

3. **The cost of equity and the cost of debt.**
   Your chief operating officer argues the following:

   a. "Our stock price is currently $60, and our dividend per share is $6. It means that it costs us 10 percent to use shareholders' cash ($6 divided by $60)."
   b. "From our balance sheet our liabilities are $80 million. From our income statement our interest expenses are $5 million. Thus, our cost of debt is 6.25 percent ($5 million divided by $80 million)."

   Which statement is true and which false?

4. **The cost of debt.**
   Cordona Corp. has bonds outstanding that will mature 12 years from now. These bonds are currently quoted at 110 percent above par value. The issue makes annual payments of $80 on $1,000 bond face value. What is Cordona's cost of debt?

5. **The cost of equity.**
   The dividend of Onogo Inc. is currently $2 per share and is supposed to grow at 5 percent a year forever. Its share price is $50. Its beta is 1.08. The market risk premium is 5 percent and the risk-free rate is 4 percent. What is your best estimate of Onogo's cost of equity?

6. **Practical application of the capital asset pricing model.**
   According to the capital asset pricing model:

   $$E(R_i) = R_F + [E(R_M) - R_F]\beta_i$$

   where $E(R_i)$ – the expected return on security i – is the sum of the return on a risk-free investment and $[E(R_M) - R_F]\beta_i$, the expected extra return over the risk-free rate for taking on the risk of holding the security. β_i measures the relative sensitivity of the security's returns to changes in the return of a market index. $E(R_M)$ is the expected return on a market index, and $[E(R_M) - R_F]$ is the difference between the expected market return and the risk-free rate, otherwise known as the market risk premium.

   In recent years, there has been considerable debate about the size of the market risk premium. Most textbooks, including this one, give a range between 4 and 6 percent. However, some of the major investment banks are using a market risk premium as low as 3 percent when they are computing the cost of capital for valuing a company in mergers or other transactions.

   How could rates as low as 3 percent be justified? What are the possible arguments used by the banks? If you were buying another company, would you agree to such a low rate? What if you were the selling firm?

7. **Calculating the weighted average cost of capital.**
   Suppose that Tale Inc. has the following target capital structure: 50 percent stock, 40 percent debt, and 10 percent preferred stock. Its cost of equity is estimated at 10 percent, that of debt 6 percent, and that of preferred stock 4.5 percent. The tax rate is 35 percent.

   a. What is Tale's cost of capital?
   b. Should Tale use more preferred stock financing than debt financing since it is cheaper?

8. **Estimating the cost of capital of a firm.**

You have been asked to estimate the cost of capital for the CAT corporation. The company has 4 million shares and 125,000 bonds outstanding at par value $1,000. In addition, it has $20 million in short-term debt from its bank. The target capital structure ratio is 55 percent equity, 40 percent long-term debt, and 5 percent short-term debt. The current capital structure has temporarily moved slightly away from the target ratio.

The company's shares currently trade at $50 with a beta of 1.03. The book value of the shares is $16. The annual coupon rate of the bonds is 9 percent, they trade at 108 percent of par, and they will mature in ten years. Interest on the short-term debt is 3.5 percent. The current yield on ten-year government bonds is 5.2 percent. The market risk premium is 5 percent. The corporate tax rate applicable is expected to be 35 percent.

Based on these data, calculate the cost of capital for the CAT Corporation.

9. **Estimation of the cost of capital of a division.**
    FarWest Inc. manufactures telecommunication equipment and communication software. The equipment division is asking the finance department of FarWest for an estimate of its cost of capital. FarWest can borrow long term at 7 percent; its corporate tax rate is 40 percent. Its target debt ratio is 30 percent (debt to total financing ratio). Its beta coefficient is 1.05. The rate of interest on government bonds is currently 5.2 percent, and the market risk premium is 5 percent.

    The finance department has identified three single business companies with activities that are similar to those of the equipment division of FarWest Inc. Their beta coefficients and debt-to-equity ratios are as follows:

	Proxy A	Proxy B	Proxy C
Equity beta	0.70	1.00	1.02
Debt-to-equity ratio at market value	1.00	0.80	0.70

    How would you estimate the equipment division's weighted average cost of capital if that division's target debt-to-equity ratio is 1.20?

10. **Estimation of cost of capital for a spinoff.**
    A diversified company plans to sell a division as part of a restructuring program. The division to be sold is a regional airline that was acquired by a previous management. The finance department has been asked by the chief executive officer (CEO) to estimate what they consider an acceptable price before entering into discussion with their investment bankers. The chief financial officer (CFO) intends to value the division on the basis of the present value of its future cash flows. He agrees with the CEO on the major assumptions that will affect the cash flows. But they disagree on the appropriate discount rate. The CEO believes that they should use the company's weighted average cost of capital (WACC), which at present is 6.4 percent and calculated as follows:

    - Debt-to-equity ratio (D/E) = 0.5; cost of debt (k_D) = 6 percent; risk-free rate (R_F) = 5 percent; corporate tax rate = 30 percent; market risk premium = 5 percent; company beta = 0.5
    - Cost of equity k_E:

    $$k_E = R_F + [E(R_M) - R_F]\beta$$

where $R_F = 5$ percent is the risk-free rate, $[E(R_M) - R_F] = 5$ percent is the market risk premium, and $\beta = 0.5$ is the company's beta coefficient. Thus,

$$k_E = 5\% + 5\% \times 0.50 = 7.5\%$$

- $$WACC = k_D(1 - T_C)\frac{D}{E + D} + k_E\frac{E}{E + D}$$

$$= 6.0\% \times (1 - 0.3) \times \frac{1}{3} + 7.5\% \times \frac{2}{3} = 6.4\%$$

The CFO disagrees, arguing that the airline is a completely different type of business and that it carries much more debt than the other divisions because of very large equipment purchases. Therefore, the corporate WACC is completely inappropriate for valuing the cash flows of the airline division. They should base the valuation on a cost of capital typical for the airline industry. To do this, the CFO obtains the following data for a sample of pure-play airline companies.

	Airline A	Airline B	Airline C	Airline D	Airline E
Equity beta	1.20	0.95	1.35	1.45	1.55
Debt-to-equity ratio at market value	1.25	1.85	1.35	1.70	3.40
Average cost of debt	6%	7%	7.50%	7.25%	8.50%

a. The cost of borrowing and the debt-to-equity ratio for the division were to be set at the average for the group of airlines shown in the table. Based on the comparative data shown in the table, a risk-free rate of 5 percent, a market risk premium of 5 percent, and a tax rate of 30 percent, estimate the division's WACC.
b. If the company's WACC had been used instead of the divisional WACC you have just computed, what effect would that have on the valuation?

Designing a Capital Structure   CHAPTER 13

Broadly speaking, managers need to make two major decisions. They need to decide which investment projects create the most value, and they need to decide which mix of sources of capital is best for financing the firm's investments. Previous chapters show how managers should select value-creating projects. This chapter shows how they should design a value-creating capital structure, keeping in mind that the opportunities to create value through a change in the mix of debt and equity capital are more limited than those available through the selection of superior investment projects.

The decision to finance part of the firm's assets with borrowed funds has important managerial implications. If the firm finds it increasingly difficult to service its debt (paying interest and repaying the borrowed funds) because of excessive borrowing, its management will be under pressure to make decisions that may not be in the best interest of shareholders. For example, management may have to quickly sell *value-creating* assets for less than they are worth to the firm, to raise the cash needed to make the payments required to service the firm's debt. Conversely, a firm with too little debt may pass up the opportunity to reduce its tax payments and increase its value through tax savings (the more interest the firm pays, the less taxes it owes because interest payments reduce taxable income). By replacing equity with debt, the firm can deduct more interest expenses from its taxable income and save an equivalent amount of cash that would have been used to pay taxes. If too much debt is damaging and too little debt is fiscally inefficient, what, then, is the right amount of debt? This is the question we answer in this chapter.

Managers can choose from a variety of sources of funds to finance their businesses. Most of these are hybrids of two basic types of capital: debt, such as bank loans and bonds; and equity, which includes retained earnings and common stocks. This chapter examines how managers should combine debt and equity financing to establish a capital structure that maximizes *the value of the firm's assets and equity*. A firm's capital structure is usually identified by its *debt ratios*, either its debt-to-equity ratio (the amount of borrowing divided by the amount of equity) or its debt-to-assets ratio (the portion of the firm's assets financed with borrowed funds). These two debt ratios are often used interchangeably.

The firm's *optimal capital structure* is the debt ratio that maximizes the market value of the firm's assets. We show that this is generally the same as maximizing the market value of the firm's *equity* and minimizing its cost of capital. The optimal debt ratio depends on several factors; some are easily identifiable and measurable, others are not.

445

To find out what these factors are and how they affect the firm's profitability and value, we analyze how a change in the firm's debt ratio affects (1) its profitability, measured with earnings per share (EPS), that is, earnings after tax divided by the number of shares outstanding; (2) the market value of its assets; (3) its share price; and (4) its cost of capital.

In Chapter 12 we use unlevered (or asset) betas (β_U) to estimate the value of a firm. These unlevered betas were given by a formula that is a function of the firm's levered (or equity) betas (β_L) and the firm's capital structure (see equation 12.7). The Appendix to the current chapter explains how levered and unlevered betas are related.

After reading this chapter, you should understand the following:

- How changes in capital structure affect the firm's EPS, asset value, equity value, share price, and cost of capital
- The trade-offs that are implied in the capital structure decision
- How corporate taxes and the *costs of financial distress* affect the capital structure decision
- Why firms in different industries and countries can have different capital structures
- The factors, in addition to taxes and the costs of financial distress, which must be taken into account when establishing an optimal capital structure, including *agency costs* and the presence of *information asymmetry* between managers and outside investors
- How levered and unlevered betas are related

THE CAPITAL STRUCTURE DECISION IN A WORLD WITHOUT CORPORATE INCOME TAX AND FINANCIAL DISTRESS COSTS

This section examines how changes in **capital structure** affect the firm's profitability, the market value of its assets and equity, its share price, and its cost of capital in a world in which firms do *not* pay corporate income taxes and do *not* face **financial distress costs** – costs resulting from excessive borrowing that affect the firm's ability to perform efficiently and consequently reduce its value. These two restrictions are lifted in the following sections. Examining first the capital structure decision without the complications of taxes and financial distress costs will make it easier to understand the general model presented later.

EFFECTS OF BORROWING ON THE FIRM'S PROFITABILITY (NO CORPORATE INCOME TAX AND NO FINANCIAL DISTRESS COSTS)

In physics, leverage refers to the increase in power that comes from using a lever. In finance, **leverage**, or **gearing**, refers to the increase in profitability, usually measured with earnings per share (EPS), that can come from using debt financing.[1] To see why and how borrowing affects EPS, we examine the Jolly Bear Company (JBC). JBC is currently *all-equity* financed with two million shares outstanding worth $100 each. The firm's equity value is thus $200 million ($100 times two million shares). Because the firm has no debt, the value of its assets is the same as the value of its equity ($200 million). JBC's chief financial officer, Ms Johnson, is considering borrowing

---

[1] The effect of borrowing on another measure of profitability, the firm's return on equity, is examined in detail in Chapter 6.

$100 million at 10 percent and using the cash to repurchase one-half of the firm's shares at $100 per share (we explain later why the share price is not affected by the repurchase). She wants to know how this change in JBC's capital structure might affect the firm's EPS.

Exhibit 13.1 illustrates the effect of this **recapitalization** decision on EPS for three possible scenarios for the future performance of the economy – recession, expected performance, and expansion. The firm's profit from operations, that is, its earnings before interest and tax (EBIT), is not affected by the decision to borrow. Operating profit is $10 million under the recession scenario, $30 million under the expected performance scenario, and $40 million under the expansion scenario, irrespective of the amount of debt Ms Johnson decides to issue.

Consider first the case of the expected scenario. With no debt (upper part of Exhibit 13.1), net earnings are $30 million, the same as EBIT, because there are no interest or tax payments. With two million shares outstanding, EPS is equal to $15 ($30 million divided by two million shares). With $100 million of debt at an interest rate of 10 percent (lower part of Exhibit 13.1), the interest payment is $10 million and net earnings drop to $20 million. Before concluding that borrowing has a negative effect, we should examine its impact on EPS. Because there are only one million shares after the share repurchase, EPS is now $20 ($20 million divided by one million

EXHIBIT 13.1	JBC's EARNINGS PER SHARE UNDER THE CURRENT AND PROPOSED CAPITAL STRUCTURES AND IN THE ABSENCE OF TAXES.

Current capital structure: no debt and two million shares at $100 per share

	Recession	Expected	Expansion
Earnings before interest and tax (EBIT)	$10,000,000	$30,000,000	$40,000,000
less interest expenses	0	0	0
less tax	0	0	0
Equals net earnings	$10,000,000	$30,000,000	$40,000,000
Divided by the number of shares	2,000,000	2,000,000	2,000,000
Equals earnings per share (EPS)	$ 5	$ 15	$ 20

Proposed capital structure: borrow $100 million at 10 percent and use the cash to repurchase one million shares at $100 per share

	Recession	Expected	Expansion
Earnings before interest and tax (EBIT)	$10,000,000	$30,000,000	$40,000,000
less interest expenses	(10,000,000)	(10,000,000)	(10,000,000)
less tax	0	0	0
Equals net earnings	$ 0	$20,000,000	$30,000,000
Divided by the number of shares	1,000,000	1,000,000	1,000,000
Equals earnings per share (EPS)	$ 0	$ 20	$ 30

shares). Thus, debt financing boosts expected EPS from $15 to $20. **Financial leverage** seems to have the same effect as leverage has in the world of physics.

Leverage also works to the advantage of shareholders in the expansion scenario, with EPS rising by 50 percent, from $20 to $30 (see Exhibit 13.1). Under the recession scenario, however, EPS, which is positive in the no-debt case, is zero in the borrowing case.

We can see this phenomenon graphically by plotting EPS against EBIT for the current and proposed capital structure, as shown in Exhibit 13.2. The no-debt line starts at the origin because EPS is zero when EBIT is zero. As EBIT increases, EPS increases by $0.50 for each $1 million rise in EBIT. With $100 million of debt, the line starts with a negative $10 EPS; at this point, EBIT is zero, but JBC still has to pay $10 million of interest expenses. The result is a loss of $10 million. Divided by one million shares, this loss produces a $10 loss per share. When EBIT rises, EPS increases twice as fast as when there is no debt, that is, EPS increases by $1 for each $1 million rise in EBIT. The reason should be clear: the number of shares outstanding is reduced by half when the firm borrows $100 million to repurchase equity.

Now, consider the point at which the two lines intersect. For values of EBIT less than its value at the intersection point, EPS is higher if JBC selects an all-equity capital structure. At the point at which the lines intersect, EPS is the same for both financing alternatives. For values of EBIT greater than its value at the intersection point, EPS is higher with debt financing. We determine the values of EBIT and EPS at the intersection point by using the fact that, at this point, EPS with no debt is equal to EPS with $100 million of debt. For the no-debt line, EPS equals EBIT divided by two million shares outstanding, as shown on the left side of the equation below. With $100 million of debt financing, EPS equals EBIT less $10 million of interest expenses divided by

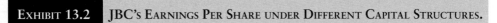

EXHIBIT 13.2   JBC's Earnings Per Share under Different Capital Structures.

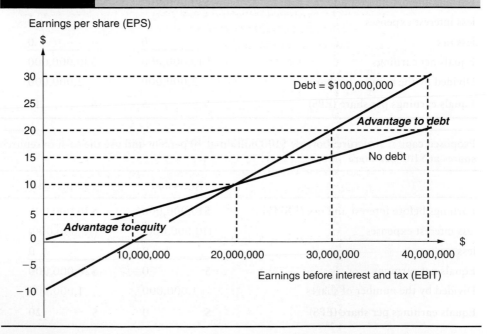

one million shares, as shown on the right side of the equation. At the intersection point, the two are the same:

$$EPS = \frac{EBIT}{2,000,000} = \frac{EBIT - \$10,000,000}{1,000,000}$$

from which we get:

$$EBIT = \$20,000,000$$

and

$$EPS = \frac{\$20,000,000}{2,000,000} = \$10$$

Thus, when EBIT equals \$20 million, EPS is \$10 for both capital structures. Note that when EBIT is \$20 million, JBC's return on assets is 10 percent (\$20 million of EBIT divided by \$200 million of assets), which is the same as the rate of interest on the debt. As long as JBC earns a return on its assets that is higher than its cost of debt, its shareholders are better off with debt financing.[2] From this analysis, Ms Johnson can draw the following tentative conclusions:

1. The capital structure decision affects the firm's profitability measured by EPS
2. Financial leverage increases EPS as long as EBIT is higher than \$20 million, which is the same as saying that return on assets exceeds the 10 percent cost of debt
3. At the \$30 million expected level of EBIT, EPS is \$15 with no debt financing and \$20 with \$100 million of debt financing.

Clearly, under the *expected scenario*, borrowing would benefit JBC's shareholders. However, Ms Johnson knows that she cannot make a decision on the basis of a single scenario. There is some probability that the economy will fall into a recession, in which case borrowing will hurt rather than benefit shareholders. Before Ms Johnson makes her decision, she must consider the *risk* that EBIT and return on assets are lower than their threshold values of \$20 million and 10 percent, respectively.

UNDERSTANDING THE TRADE-OFF BETWEEN PROFITABILITY AND RISK

The relationship between borrowing and risk is illustrated in the graph shown in Exhibit 13.3. The lines represent the changes in JBC's EPS as a function of time for the two capital structures of the previous section: no debt financing and \$100 million of debt financing. EPS is calculated for values of EBIT that vary over time between the recession and the expansion scenarios, that is, between \$10 million and \$40 million. In the absence of debt, EPS varies between \$5 and \$20, as shown in Exhibit 13.1. The variations in EPS result from changes in general economic conditions and from factors affecting the industry to which JBC belongs. (Examples of such factors include changes in input and output prices, technology, and competition.) The risk generated by these changes, which originates from the business environment in which the firm operates, is rightly called **business risk**. This type of risk is independent of JBC's

---

[2] The same result was obtained in Chapter 6. Remember, however, the two limitations we mention in that chapter. The discussion ignores risk and does not examine whether the higher leverage is accompanied by an increase in the value of the firm. These issues are discussed later in this chapter.

EXHIBIT 13.3	BORROWING AND RISK.

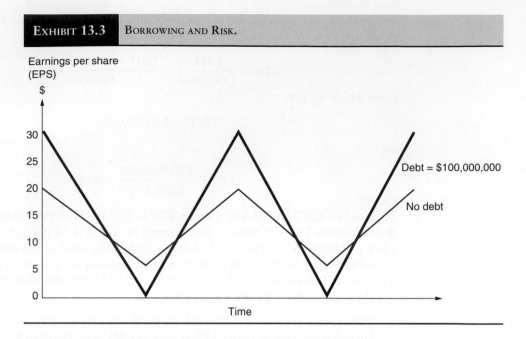

capital structure. In other words, business risk is the same for any amount of funds that Ms Johnson decides to borrow.

In the presence of debt, EPS varies between $0 and $30. The graph in Exhibit 13.3 clearly shows that debt financing amplifies the variability of EPS. The extra risk related to this magnifying effect is called **financial risk**. If Ms Johnson decides to finance a portion of JBC's assets with debt, the risk borne by JBC's shareholders will rise. Ms Johnson is thus faced with a trade-off between the following:

1. She can issue debt to increase JBC's *expected* EPS, but the firm's shareholders will have to take on more risk
2. She can maintain all-equity financing to reduce risk, but JBC's shareholders will end up with lower *expected* EPS

Unfortunately, the analysis performed so far does not tell us what to do. To find out, we must determine how debt financing affects the firm's *value*, not just EPS. *The alternative that produces the highest value for the firm would be preferred.* How, then, does debt financing affect the firm's value in the absence of taxes and financial distress costs? The so-called pizza theory of capital structure provides the answer.

EFFECT OF BORROWING ON THE VALUE OF THE FIRM'S ASSETS AND ITS SHARE PRICE (NO CORPORATE INCOME TAX AND NO FINANCIAL DISTRESS COSTS)

In its culinary version, the so-called pizza theory says that no one can increase the size of a pizza by slicing it. In its corporate finance version, we could think of the market value of the firm's assets as a gigantic pizza and the firm's shareholders and debt holders as the claimants to the slices, where the slices represent the cash flows generated by the assets (called **cash flow from business assets** or **free cash flow**). The pizza theory says that the market value of the firm's assets (the pizza) cannot be increased by changing the proportions of the cash flows (the slices) going to the firm's shareholders and debt holders *provided these cash flows are not taxed*. In other words, the market value of the firm's assets is determined only by the cash flows the assets generate and is not affected by the relative proportions of debt and equity capital used to finance the assets.

To illustrate this phenomenon, suppose that Ms Johnson decides to borrow the $100 million and buy back half of the firm's two million shares. Consider the implications of this recapitalization on the wealth of JBC's shareholders. Before the change in capital structure, their claim against JBC's assets amounted to the market value of the entire firm ($200 million) because the firm had no debt. After JBC is levered up, shareholders' claims against the $200 million of assets are reduced by $100 million, which represents the value of the debt now owned by JBC. But this reduction in value is exactly offset by the $100 million shareholders received from the one million shares they sold back to the firm. Shareholders will be as well off after the change in capital structure as they were before. (Their collective and aggregate wealth remains at $200 million.) Thus, the change should not have any effect on JBC's share price.

The formal proof of the theory that changes in the firm's capital structure do not affect its total market value or share price was provided by Nobel Prize laureates Franco Modigliani and Merton Miller (MM) in two seminal papers published in 1958 and 1961. The intuition behind the theory is straightforward: the value of a firm's assets is determined only by the ability of its managers to generate as much cash flow as possible from these assets. Simply reshuffling paper claims on these cash flows does not add value to or subtract value from the firm's assets. Furthermore, it does not affect the firm's share price. In other words, the price of a pizza is independent of the way you slice it.

Let's follow MM's reasoning as it applies to JBC's capital structure. If JBC borrows $100 million, EPS is $0 under the recession scenario, $20 under the expected scenario, and $30 under the expansion scenario. The computations are reproduced on the upper part of Exhibit 13.4, which also shows the corresponding returns on shareholders' equity investment obtained by dividing the EPS by $100, the price of one share. The return is zero percent under the recession scenario, 20 percent under the expected scenario, and 30 percent under the expansion scenario.

Suppose now that Ms Johnson decides *not* to change JBC's capital structure. (She does not borrow the $100 million and JBC remains with its initial debt-free capital structure.) You, a shareholder with one share, would have preferred that the firm borrows the $100 million because you like the higher EPS that would result if the economy expands. What can you do? You can try to persuade Ms Johnson to change her mind, but you would probably be wasting your time unless you own a substantial number of shares. Well, you do not need to bother Ms Johnson. *You can get the capital structure you want even if JBC remains debt-free.* How is this possible? The trick is to manufacture your own *personal* leverage that will replicate the returns JBC would have delivered if Ms Johnson had decided to borrow the $100 million.

All you have to do is borrow $100 at *10 percent* and use the cash to buy another share of JBC. You now own two shares, the one you already had plus the one you just bought. These transactions have created a **homemade leverage**, that is, a personal financial leverage as opposed to a corporate financial leverage. The lower part of Exhibit 13.4 shows how to calculate the returns on your investment under the three scenarios using JBC's EPS with all-equity financing (see Exhibit 13.1). Because you own two shares of JBC, you get twice the EPS in each of the three scenarios. However, your earnings are reduced in each scenario by the $10 interest payment you have to

EXHIBIT 13.4	CORPORATE LEVERAGE VERSUS HOMEMADE LEVERAGE.

Shareholder's return on a $100 investment when JBC borrows $100 million

	Recession	Expected	Expansion
JBC's net earnings with debt (from Exhibit 13.1)	$ 0	$20,000,000	$30,000,000
Divided by the number of shares	1,000,000	1,000,000	1,000,000
Equals earnings per share (EPS)	$ 0	$ 20	$ 30
Return on investment (EPS divided by $100)	0%	20%	30%

Shareholder's return on a $100 net investment when JBC maintains the all-equity capital structure. The investor buys two shares of JBC, one with his own money and the other with borrowed money

	Recession	Expected	Expansion
JBC's net earnings with no debt (from Exhibit 13.1)	$10,000,000	$30,000,000	$40,000,000
Divided by the number of shares	2,000,000	2,000,000	2,000,000
Equals earnings per share (EPS)	$ 5	$ 15	$ 20
Earnings on two shares	10	30	40
less interest payment of 10% on $100	(10)	(10)	(10)
Equals net earnings	$ 0	$ 20	$ 30
Return on investment (net earnings divided by $100)	0%	20%	30%

make on the $100 you borrowed (10 percent of $100). The last row of Exhibit 13.4 shows the net returns on your $100 investment. (Although you *own* two shares, your *personal* investment, net of borrowing, is only $100.) *These returns are exactly the same as those you would have achieved if the firm had decided to recapitalize.* In other words, it does not matter whether the firm borrows to leverage its assets or whether investors borrow to leverage their own shareholdings. What firms can do to their capital structure, investors can replicate on their own. Therefore, investors would neither reward nor penalize the firm if it changes its capital structure. Under those conditions, the firm's share price must remain the same.

You may have noticed the two critical assumptions required to reach this conclusion. The first assumption is that the changes in capital structure must occur in a world without taxes. The second assumption is that investors can borrow at the same rate as the firm (10 percent in the JBC example). Later in this chapter, we examine what happens without the first assumption, that is, when the changes in capital structure occur in a world with taxes. You may think the second assumption is unrealistic because interest rates on personal borrowing are usually higher than the rates at which firms borrow. But investors do not have to borrow directly to build up their homemade leverage. To understand why, recall that investors diversify their investments. They don't just buy the shares of a single firm; they buy shares of other firms as well (see Chapter 3). Consequently, it is the financial leverage of all the firms in the investor's portfolio that is relevant, not just that of a particular firm in the portfolio. Given the large number of publicly traded companies offering a wide range of debt ratios, investors can easily reach any degree of financial leverage *in their portfolios* by constructing them in such a way that its average debt ratio is the one they want. And they do not need to borrow to achieve this; the firms in their portfolios have already done the borrowing.

The **MM theory of capital structure** does not mention risk. But, in the previous section, we show that any increase in the firm's debt ratio increases the risk borne by its shareholders. How can JBC's share price *not* go down as a result of the increase in risk generated by the firm's decision to borrow $100 million? The answer is straightforward: the increase in risk is exactly offset by the rise in the EPS the shareholders can expect from higher financial leverage. In a world without taxes, the trade-off between risk and higher expected EPS that confronts Ms Johnson does not actually exist. Whichever debt ratio she chooses, JBC's share price will not change because shareholders are exactly compensated for the higher risk with higher expected EPS. However, the *return* expected by shareholders from their equity investment in JBC – which is JBC's cost of equity – will rise to reflect the higher risk. We explain this phenomenon in the next section.

EFFECT OF BORROWING ON THE FIRM'S COST OF CAPITAL (NO CORPORATE INCOME TAX AND NO FINANCIAL DISTRESS COSTS)

If JBC's capital structure remains debt-free, the return expected by its shareholders from their investment in the firm (which is the firm's cost of equity capital) is equal to the return expected from its assets, because in this case shareholders are the only claimants to the cash flows generated by the firm's assets. If r_A denotes the expected return from the firm's assets and k_E^U denotes the firm's cost of equity when the firm does not borrow (called the unlevered cost of equity), then, in the absence of debt and taxes, the two rates are the same ($r_A = k_E^U$).

If the firm decides to replace some equity with debt, the debt holders will also have claims on the firm's cash flows. In other words, r_A will be split into the return expected by shareholders when the firm borrows (called the levered cost of equity, k_E^L) and the rate required by its debt holders (denoted by k_D). Their claims on the firm's return on assets will be proportional to their respective contributions to the funding of the firm's assets. If E is the amount of equity funding and D the amount of debt funding, then their relative contributions to the total funding of JBC's assets are $\dfrac{E}{E + D}$ and $\dfrac{D}{E + D}$, respectively. We can write the following:

$$r_A = k_E^L \frac{E}{E + D} + k_D \frac{D}{E + D} \tag{13.1}$$

The right side of the relationship is the firm's weighted average cost of capital (the WACC), which was discussed in Chapter 12. Assuming a fixed interest rate (k_D) on the firm's debt, equation 13.1 indicates that any change in the proportions of equity and debt financing must be compensated for by a change in the cost of equity (k_E^L) because the return on assets (r_A) is not affected by the way returns are split between shareholders and debt holders. To show how the cost of equity varies when the **debt-to-equity ratio** increases, we can rearrange the terms of equation 13.1 to express k_E^L as a function of r_A, k_D, and the debt ratio. We get the following:

$$k_E^L = r_A + (r_A - k_D)\frac{D}{E} \equiv k_E^U + (k_E^U - k_D)\frac{D}{E} \tag{13.2}$$

Note the two identical versions of the levered cost of equity in equation 13.2: in the version on the right, we have simply replaced r_A by k_E^U because they are the same. To illustrate, we consider JBC under the expected scenario. JBC's expected return on assets, r_A, is 15 percent (EBIT of \$30 million divided by \$200 million of assets) and its cost of debt, k_D, is 10 percent. Exhibit 13.5 shows JBC's cost of equity and WACC for two alternative debt-to-equity ratios, 0.25 (20 percent debt and 80 percent equity) and 1.00 (50 percent debt and 50 percent equity, the capital structure Ms Johnson has proposed). With a debt-to-equity ratio of 0.25, JBC's shareholders require a return of 16.25 percent, which is JBC's cost of equity. With a debt-to-equity ratio of 1.00, they require 20 percent to compensate them for the additional financial risk generated by the increase in leverage. Note, however, that the firm's WACC, which is the expected return on assets, is a constant 15 percent irrespective of the debt-to-equity ratio.

Exhibit 13.6 illustrates how the return on assets (r_A), the WACC, the cost of equity (k_E^L), and the cost of debt (k_D) vary when the debt-to-equity ratio increases. When the firm carries no debt, its cost of equity and WACC are 15 percent, the same as the expected return on the firm's assets. As the firm replaces equity with debt, shareholders bear increasing levels of financial risk and, therefore, expect higher returns from their investment; however, the firm's WACC remains equal to 15 percent, the return expected from the firm's assets.

An increasing cost of equity is not in contradiction with a constant share price. Shareholders expect a higher return from higher risk and, as shown earlier, they get it through higher expected EPS. As a result, the firm's share price does not move. It stays at \$100 as shown in Exhibit 13.7.

When there is no debt in the capital structure, the firm does not carry any financial risk and the market value of its assets (\$200 million) is also the market value of its equity. With two million shares outstanding, the share price is \$100. As the proportion of assets financed by debt rises, financial risk increases. If the firm wants to finance 20 percent of its assets with debt, it must borrow \$40 million (20 percent of \$200 million) and repurchase 400,000 shares at \$100 each. When the recapitalization is over, the firm's equity is \$160 million (\$200 million minus \$40 million worth of repurchased shares) and the number of shares outstanding is 1,600,000 (2 million shares minus 400,000 shares repurchased), yielding a share price of \$100 (\$160 million divided by 1,600,000 shares). Applying the same reasoning to the case in which the firm finances 50 percent of its assets with debt shows that the share price remains at \$100.

To summarize, in a world without taxes and financial distress costs, the MM theory of capital structure says that *a firm's **financial structure decision** does not*

Exhibit 13.5	JBC's Cost of Equity and WACC for Two Debt-To-Equity Ratios, R_A = 15% and k_D = 10%.

Debt-to-Equity Ratio	$\dfrac{\text{Debt}}{\text{Equity}} = \dfrac{0.20}{0.80} = 0.25$	$\dfrac{\text{Debt}}{\text{Equity}} = \dfrac{0.50}{0.50} = 1.00$
Cost of equity from equation 13.2	15% + [(15% − 10%) × 0.25] = 16.25%	15% + [(15% − 10%) × 1.00] = 20%
Weighted average cost of capital from the right side of equation 13.1	(16.25% × 0.80) + (10% × 0.20) = 15%	(20% × 0.50) + (10% × 0.50) = 15%

EXHIBIT 13.6	THE COST OF CAPITAL AS A FUNCTION OF THE DEBT-TO-EQUITY RATIO ACCORDING TO THE MM THEORY IN THE ABSENCE OF TAXES.

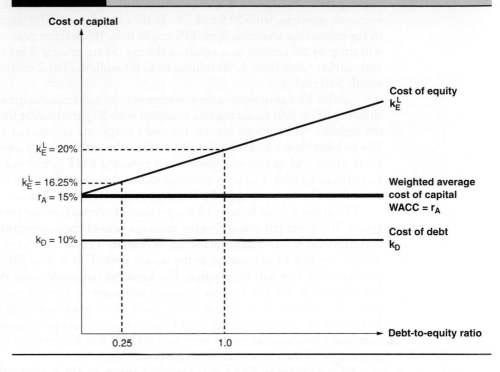

EXHIBIT 13.7	JBC's SHARE PRICE FOR DIFFERENT CAPITAL STRUCTURES.

Capital Structure	Financial Risk	Market Value of Assets (1)	Amount of Debt Financing (2)	Market Value of Equity (1) − (2) = (3)	Number of Shares (4)	Price per Share (3)/(4)
No debt	None	$200 million	None	$200 million	2,000,000	$100
20% debt	Low	$200 million	$40 million	$160 million	1,600,000	$100
50% debt	Higher	$200 million	$100 million	$100 million	1,000,000	$100

affect the market value of its assets, its share price, or its weighted average cost of capital. We show in the next section that this is no longer true when taxes are included in the analysis.

THE CAPITAL STRUCTURE DECISION IN A WORLD WITH CORPORATE INCOME TAX BUT WITHOUT FINANCIAL DISTRESS COSTS

The analysis so far has ignored corporate income taxes. What would happen to JBC's profits, market value of assets, and share price if a 50 percent tax were imposed on the firm's earnings? To answer this question, we have to refer again to the MM theory of capital structure, but this time in the presence of corporate income taxes. Consider first the case in which JBC is all-equity financed. The EPS reported in the upper part of Exhibit 13.1 will be reduced by 50 percent, from $5 to $2.50 in the recession scenario, from $15 to $7.50 in the expected scenario, and from $20 to $10 in the expansion scenario. With EPS cut in half, JBC's share price and market value will drop by 50 percent as a result of the tax. Share price will go from $100 to $50 and market value from $200 million to $100 million. (The 2 million shares are now worth $50 each.)

Exhibit 13.8 summarizes the consequences of a change in capital structure from a situation of no debt financing to a situation with 50 percent debt financing under two tax regimes: no corporate income tax and a corporate income tax rate of 50 percent. The exhibit shows how the tax affects the value of the firm's assets and equity, its share price, and its cost of capital when expected EBIT is $30 million (the expected scenario in Exhibit 13.1). As mentioned, the change in the capital structure will be carried out by borrowing and using the cash to buy back shares.

The upper part of Exhibit 13.8 reproduces the results of our previous analysis (no taxes). The lower left side shows the consequences of the imposition of the 50 percent corporate tax with no debt financing, as described earlier. The cost of equity and the WACC are still 15 percent, as in the no-tax case. This is why JBC's share price and market value lost half their value. The business risk underlying the firm's assets is not affected by the tax rate, so investors still want to earn 15 percent. With profits and EPS at half their original amount, JBC's share price and value must decrease by 50 percent for investors to still earn 15 percent on shares purchased after the tax was imposed. Obviously, investors who held JBC's shares *before* the tax was imposed lost 50 percent of the value of their investment.

We now want to find out what will happen to JBC's asset value, equity value, share price, and cost of capital if Ms Johnson decides to change JBC's capital structure by borrowing $50 million (half the value of assets) to repurchase an equal amount of equity. Will the value of JBC's assets and its share price remain the same as in the case of no taxes? The answer is no. In the presence of corporate income taxes, both the value of the firm's assets and its share price will *rise* as debt replaces equity in the firm's balance sheet, as shown in the lower-right side of Exhibit 13.8. In the next sections, we explain why this happens.

EFFECT OF BORROWING ON THE VALUE OF A FIRM'S ASSETS (WITH CORPORATE INCOME TAX AND NO FINANCIAL DISTRESS COSTS)

Corporate tax laws favor debt financing because interest paid by the company to its creditors is a tax-deductible expense, whereas dividends and retained earnings are not. Replacing equity with debt financing reduces the amount of tax JBC must pay and thus increases the after-tax cash flow generated by the firm's assets. A higher cash flow from assets raises the market value of assets.

To illustrate the tax effect on asset value, we estimate the amount of taxes JBC will save if Ms Johnson decides to borrow $50 million at 10 percent and use the cash to repurchase equity. JBC will pay $5 million of interest every year, and its taxable income will drop to $25 million ($30 million of EBIT less $5 million of interest expenses). As a result, it will pay $12.5 million in taxes (50 percent of $25 million). If the firm does not borrow, its expected annual tax payment will be $15 million (50 percent of an expected EBIT of $30 million). Thus, by borrowing $50 million at 10 percent, JBC can save $2.5 million in taxes every year ($15 million minus

EXHIBIT 13.8	EFFECTS OF CHANGES IN CAPITAL STRUCTURE ON THE FIRM'S EARNINGS PER SHARE, SHARE PRICE, MARKET VALUE, AND COST OF CAPITAL WITHOUT CORPORATE INCOME TAX AND WITH A 50 PERCENT CORPORATE INCOME TAX RATE.

CAPITAL STRUCTURE

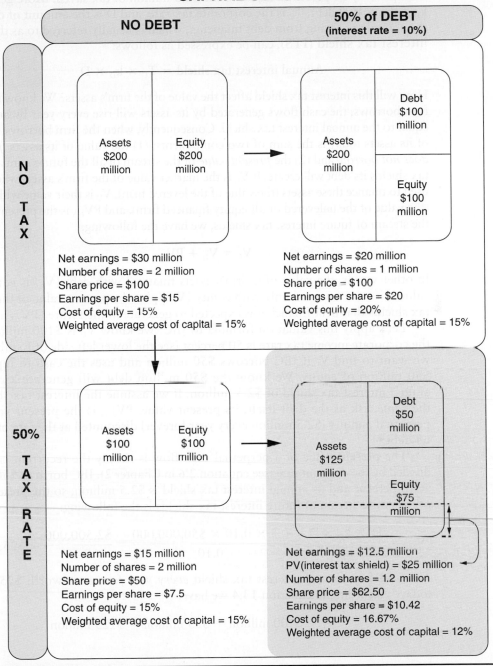

NO DEBT

50% of DEBT
(interest rate = 10%)

NO TAX

Assets
$200
million

Equity
$200
million

Assets
$200
million

Debt
$100
million

Equity
$100
million

Net earnings = $30 million
Number of shares = 2 million
Share price = $100
Earnings per share = $15
Cost of equity = 15%
Weighted average cost of capital = 15%

Net earnings = $20 million
Number of shares = 1 million
Share price = $100
Earnings per share = $20
Cost of equity = 20%
Weighted average cost of capital = 15%

50% TAX RATE

Assets
$100
million

Equity
$100
million

Assets
$125
million

Debt
$50
million

Equity
$75
million

Net earnings = $15 million
Number of shares = 2 million
Share price = $50
Earnings per share = $7.5
Cost of equity = 15%
Weighted average cost of capital = 15%

Net earnings = $12.5 million
PV(interest tax shield) = $25 million
Number of shares = 1.2 million
Share price = $62.50
Earnings per share = $10.42
Cost of equity = 16.67%
Weighted average cost of capital = 12%

$12.5 million), and the annual cash flows generated by its assets will increase by the same amount. Because taxable income is reduced by an amount equal to interest expenses, this annual tax saving can be calculated directly by simply multiplying the amount of interest expenses by the corporate income tax rate. In our case, $5 million multiplied by 50 percent is equal to the $2.5 million of tax saved. More generally, if k_D is the cost of debt, T_C is the corporate tax rate, and D is the amount of debt, then the annual tax saving from debt financing, which is usually referred to as the annual **interest tax shield (ITS)**, can be expressed as follows:

$$\text{Annual interest tax shield} = T_C \times k_D \times D \qquad (13.3)$$

How will this interest tax shield affect the value of the firm's assets? We know that if the firm borrows, the cash flows generated by its assets will rise every year by an amount equal to the annual interest tax shield. Consequently, when the firm borrows, the value of its assets today is the sum of two components: (1) the value of its assets *if the firm does not borrow* and (2) the *present value* of the stream of all the future annual interest tax shields its debt will create. If V_L is the market value of the firm's assets when debt is used to finance these assets (the value of the levered firm), V_U is their value without debt (the value of the unlevered or all-equity financed firm), and PV_{ITS} is the present value of the stream of future interest tax shields, we have the following:

$$V_L = V_U + PV_{ITS} \qquad (13.4)$$

In other words, the value of a firm's assets financed with debt (V_L) is equal to its value if it were financed only with equity (V_U), plus the present value of the interest tax shields that debt financing is expected to generate in the future (PV_{ITS}).[3]

Let's apply this valuation formula to JBC. We know V_U is $100 million when the corporate income tax rate is 50 percent (see the lower left side of Exhibit 13.8); we want to find V_L if JBC borrows $50 million and uses the cash to repurchase $50 million of equity. We know the $50 million debt will generate a recurrent annual interest tax shield of $2.5 million. If we assume the interest tax shield has the *same* risk as the debt itself, its present value, PV_{ITS}, is the present value of a perpetual annuity ($2.5 million every year forever) discounted at the rate of interest on debt.

The present value of a perpetual cash flow is simply the recurrent cash flow divided by the discount rate (see equation 2.6 in Chapter 2). JBC borrows $50 million at 10 percent and its annual interest tax shield is $2.5 million, so the present value of the entire stream of future interest tax shields is the following:

$$PV_{ITS} = \frac{T_C \times k_D \times D}{k_D} = \frac{0.5 \times 0.10 \times \$50,000,000}{0.10} = \frac{\$2,500,000}{0.10} = \$25,000,000$$

Thus, $2.5 million of interest tax shield *every year forever* is worth $25 million today.[4] According to equation 13.4 we have:

$$V_L = \$100 \text{ million} + \$25 \text{ million} = \$125 \text{ million}$$

---

[3] Our result ignores the effect of investors' personal taxes, a point we discuss later in this chapter.

[4] Note that when the tax shield is a perpetual annuity, PV_{ITS} is simply equal to T_C multiplied by debt. In our case, it is 50% × $50 million = $25 million.

By replacing $50 million worth of equity with debt, Ms Johnson can increase the value of JBC's assets by $25 million, as shown in the lower-right side of Exhibit 13.8. Note that the more JBC borrows, the larger the present value of the interest tax shield and the higher the value of the firm's assets. This phenomenon is reported in the first four columns in Exhibit 13.9 and is illustrated in the rising graph in Exhibit 13.10. As JBC increases its borrowing, the value of its assets increases. This happens because, as the amount of borrowing goes up, the firm's interest tax shield increases and its tax payment decreases. With lower tax payments, the value of the firm's assets rises.

Consider the result of JBC's proposed recapitalization: by borrowing $50 million to finance the firm's assets, Ms Johnson can increase the value of the assets by 25 percent, even *though they are exactly the same assets the firm had before borrowing*. The reason they are more valuable is that the recapitalization *reduces* the portion of cash flow from assets paid out as corporate tax. By refinancing JBC's assets with debt, Ms Johnson can make a value-creating financing decision.

There is another way to think about the effect of financial leverage. Suppose another company wants to buy JBC's assets and plans to finance the acquisition with $50 million of debt. This company would be ready to pay up to $125 million to acquire JBC's assets: $100 million for the capacity of these assets to generate operating cash flows (V_U in equation 13.4), and an additional $25 million for the present value of the taxes that will be saved through the $50 million debt financing (PV_{ITS} in equation 13.4).

EXHIBIT 13.9	EFFECT OF BORROWING ON JBC'S ASSET VALUE, EQUITY VALUE, AND SHARE PRICE WITH A 50 PERCENT CORPORATE INCOME TAX RATE.				
Amount of Borrowing (1)	Present Value of ITS (2) = 50% × (1)	Unlevered Value of Assets (3)	Levered Value of Assets (4) = (2) + (3)	Levered Value of Equity (5) = (4) − (1)	Unlevered Number of Shares (6)
Zero	Zero	$100 million	$100 million	$100 million	2,000,000
$20 million	$10 million	$100 million	$110 million	$ 90 million	2,000,000
$50 million	$25 million	$100 million	$125 million	$ 75 million	2,000,000
$100 million	$50 million	$100 million	$150 million	$ 50 million	2,000,000

Unlevered Share Price (7) = (3)/(6)	Present Value of ITS per Share (8) = (2)/(6)	Levered Share Price (9) = (7) + (8)	Number of Shares to Buy (10) = (1)/(9)	Number of Shares Left (11) = (6) − (10)	Levered Value of Equity (12) = (9) × (11)
$50.00	Zero	$50.00	Zero	2,000,000	$100 million
$50.00	$5.00	$55.00	363,636	1,636,364	$ 90 million
$50.00	$12.50	$62.50	800,000	1,200,000	$ 75 million
$50.00	$25.00	$75.00	1,333,333	666,667	$ 50 million

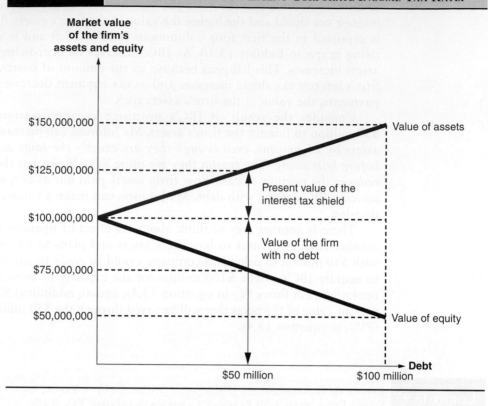

EXHIBIT 13.10 THE VALUE OF JBC'S ASSETS AND EQUITY AS A FUNCTION OF ITS BORROWING WITH A 50 PERCENT CORPORATE INCOME TAX RATE.

EFFECT OF BORROWING ON THE FIRM'S MARKET VALUE OF EQUITY (WITH CORPORATE INCOME TAX AND NO FINANCIAL DISTRESS COSTS)

As JBC increases its borrowing and uses the money to repurchase its equity, the firm's equity decreases. If we denote the value of equity (when the firm borrows) by E_L, we can write the following:

$$E_L = V_L - D \qquad (13.5)$$

where V_L is still the value of the firm's assets when the firm borrows and D is the amount of borrowing. The declining value of JBC's equity as the firm increases its borrowing is shown in the fifth column of Exhibit 13.9 and illustrated in the descending line in Exhibit 13.10.

EFFECT OF BORROWING ON THE FIRM'S SHARE PRICE (WITH CORPORATE INCOME TAX AND NO FINANCIAL DISTRESS COSTS)

You may ask at this point, why should the firm borrow if the result is a reduction in the value of its equity? Is this financing policy advantageous to its shareholders? The answer is yes, because what matters to shareholders is not the total value of equity but the price per share. When the firm borrows to buy back its shares, the number of shares obviously goes down, but as we will show, the price per share goes up.

We can illustrate this phenomenon in the case of JBC. When the firm has no debt, its share price is $50 as shown at the bottom left side of Exhibit 13.8 and column 7 in Exhibit 13.9. What will happen to JBC's share price if Ms Johnson decides to borrow $50 million to repurchase equity? As soon as this recapitalization decision is announced, JBC's share price will rise to reflect the increase in the value of the firm's assets. We know that the value of assets will go up by an amount equal to the present value of the interest tax shield, which is worth $25 million (50 percent of $50 million of borrowing as indicated in column 2 in Exhibit 13.9). Because JBC has two million shares, each share will rise by $12.50, which is equal to the present value of the interest tax shield (PV_{ITS}) of $25 million divided by the two million shares. If we use P_L to designate the share price with borrowing (the levered share price), P_U, the share price without borrowing (the unlevered share price), and N_U, the number of shares *before* recapitalization, then we can write the following:

$$P_L = P_U + \frac{PV_{ITS}}{N_U} \tag{13.6}$$

In the case of JBC, we have:

$$P_L = \$50 + \frac{\$25,000,000}{2,000,000} = \$50 + \$12.50 = \$62.50$$

as shown at the bottom right side of Exhibit 13.8 and in column 9 of Exhibit 13.9. How many shares can JBC buy with the $50 million it has borrowed? Given that each share will rise to $62.50 *when the announcement is made*, this is the price per share JBC will have to pay. The number of shares it can buy is thus equal to $50 million divided by $62.50, that is, 800,000 shares, as shown in column 10 in Exhibit 13.9. The number of shares that will remain in the hands of shareholders after the share repurchase is 1,200,000 (2 million less 800,000) as indicated in column 11 in Exhibit 13.9. We know that the total value of equity after the share buyback is $75 million (see column 5 in Exhibit 13.9). You can now check for consistency: if you multiply the number of shares after the buyback (1,200,000) by their price ($62.50), you get $75 million. This is indeed the case as shown in column 12 in Exhibit 13.9 and on the bottom right side of Exhibit 13.8.

We have shown so far that the levered value of JBC's assets (V_L) and its share price (P_L) keep rising as JBC increases its borrowing. How long can this process go on? When we carry the logic of debt financing to its extreme, a problem occurs because managers who wish to maximize the value of their firm's assets and its share price would be advised to borrow as much as possible. This advice will have to be re-examined because the excessive use of debt generates a number of problems that we have not yet considered. Before we do so, we examine how the cost of capital is affected by corporate income taxes.

EFFECT OF BORROWING ON THE COST OF CAPITAL (WITH CORPORATE INCOME TAX AND NO FINANCIAL DISTRESS COSTS)

When a firm has no debt and pays income taxes, the return expected by its shareholders from their equity investment – the firm's unlevered cost of equity (k_E^U) – is still equal to the return on the firm's assets (r_A). However, when the firm has debt in its capital structure and pays taxes, we must account for the tax reduction resulting from the deductibility of interest expenses. In this case, equation 13.1, which relates r_A

to the levered cost of equity (k_E^L) and the cost of debt (k_D), is no longer valid. It can be shown that it must be replaced with the following to reflect the tax effect:

$$r_A = k_E^L \frac{E}{E + D(1 - T_C)} + k_D(1 - T_C)\frac{D}{E + D(1 - T_C)}$$

where T_C is the corporate income tax rate. Rearranging the terms of the above equation to express the cost of equity (k_E^L) as a function of the other variables, we get the following:

$$k_E^L = r_A + (r_A - k_D)(1 - T_C)\frac{D}{E} \equiv k_E^U + (k_E^U - k_D)(1 - T_C)\frac{D}{E} \qquad (13.7)$$

Note the two *identical* versions of the levered cost of equity in equation 13.7: in the version on the right, we have simply replaced r_A by k_E^U because they are the same. Furthermore, because of the tax deductibility of interest expenses, the relevant cost of debt is now the *after-tax* cost of debt, that is, $k_D(1 - T_C)$, so that the after-tax WACC becomes as follows:

$$\text{WACC} = k_E^L \frac{E}{E + D} + k_D(1 - T_C)\frac{D}{E + D} \qquad (13.8)$$

Exhibit 13.11 shows how the cost of equity (k_E^L) in equation 13.7 and the WACC in equation 13.8 vary when the debt-to-equity ratio increases according to the MM

EXHIBIT 13.11	THE COST OF CAPITAL AS A FUNCTION OF THE DEBT-TO-EQUITY RATIO ACCORDING TO THE MM THEORY WITH A 50 PERCENT CORPORATE INCOME TAX RATE.

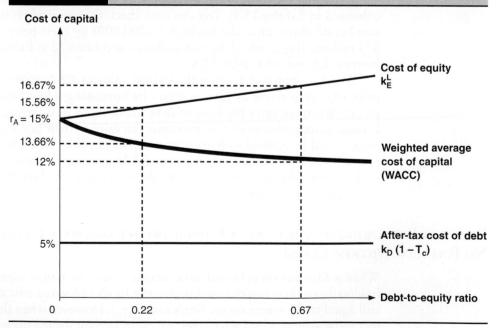

theory of capital structure in the presence of corporate income taxes. As in a world without corporate income taxes, the cost of equity (k_E) increases with debt because of the financial risk that comes with debt financing. The WACC decreases when the firm's borrowing rises because the extra return from the interest tax shield and the lower after-tax cost of debt more than offset the higher financial risk generated by higher levels of debt.

To illustrate, we again consider JBC, where the expected return on assets (which is the same as the unlevered cost of equity) is 15 percent, the cost of debt is 10 percent, and the corporate income tax rate is 50 percent. The previous analysis showed that with $20 million of debt, the market value of JBC's equity is $90 million; with $50 million of debt, it is $75 million. Exhibit 13.12 shows JBC's cost of equity and WACC in this situation. As leverage increases, the cost of equity rises but the WACC declines, as illustrated in Exhibit 13.11.

Exhibit 13.13 provides a list of valuation formulas (referred to as MM valuation formulas) with and without borrowing in the presence of corporate tax.

According to the MM theory of capital structure: *"when taxes are taken into account, the firm's financing decision affects the value of its assets, its share price, and its cost of capital. When more and more debt replaces equity in the firm's capital structure, the value of the firm's assets and its share price increase, whereas its WACC decreases."* The implication, we know, is awkward but clear: when corporate taxes are taken into account, the capital structure that maximizes the value of the firm's assets and its share price is close to 100 percent debt financing. This result, however, is inconsistent with what we observe in practice: most companies do not carry very large amounts of debt. We explain in the rest of this chapter why this is the case.

EXHIBIT 13.12	JBC's Cost of Equity and WACC for Two Debt-To-Equity Ratios; $R_A = 15\%$, $K_D = 10\%$, and $T_C = 50\%$.

VALUE OF EQUITY FROM EXHIBIT 13.9

Amount Borrowed	$20 Million	$50 Million
Value of equity	$90 million	$75 million
Debt-to-equity ratio	$\dfrac{\$20\text{ million}}{\$90\text{ million}} = 0.22$	$\dfrac{\$50\text{ million}}{\$75\text{ million}} = 0.67$
$\dfrac{\text{Debt}}{\text{Debt} + \text{Equity}}$	$\dfrac{\$20\text{ million}}{\$110\text{ million}} = 0.18$	$\dfrac{\$50\text{ million}}{\$125\text{ million}} = 0.40$
Cost of equity from equation 13.7	$15\% + [(15\% - 10\%) \times (1 - 50\%) \times 0.22]$ $= 15.56\%$	$15\% + [(15\% - 10\%) \times (1 - 50\%) \times 0.67]$ $= 16.67\%$
Weighted average cost of capital from equation 13.8	$(15.56\% \times 0.82) + (5\% \times 0.18)$ $= 13.66\%$	$(16.67\% \times 0.60) + (5\% \times 0.40)$ $= 12.00\%$

EXHIBIT 13.13	SUMMARY OF MODIGLIANI AND MILLER VALUATION FORMULAS WITHOUT AND WITH BORROWING IN THE PRESENCE OF CORPORATE INCOME TAX (T_C).

	No Borrowing[1] *The firm's assets are unlevered* *(subscript U means unlevered)*	With Borrowing (D) *The firm's assets are levered* *(subscript L means levered)*
Value of assets[2, 3] **(V)** *See equation 13.4*	(1) $V_U = P_U \times N_U$ (2) $V_U = \dfrac{EBIT(1 - T_C)}{k_U}$	$V_L = V_U + PV_{ITS}$ $V_L = V_U + (T_C \times D)$
Value of equity[4] **(E)** *See equation 13.5*	$E_U \equiv V_U$	$E_L = V_L - D$
Share price[5] **(P)** *See equation 13.6*	$P_U = \dfrac{E_U}{N_U}$	$P_L = P_U + \dfrac{PV_{ITS}}{N_U}$
Cost of debt[6] **(k_D)** *See equation 12.3*	$k_D^{BT} = 0$	$k_D^{AT} = k_D^{BT}(1 - T_C)$
Cost of equity[7] **(k_E)** *See equation 13.7*	$k_E^U \equiv r_A$	$k_E^L = k_E^U + (k_E^U - k_D^{BT})(1 - T_C)\dfrac{D}{E_L}$
Weighted average cost of capital[8] **(WACC)** *See equation 13.8*	$WACC_U = k_E^U$	$WACC_L = k_E^L\dfrac{E}{E + D} + k_D^{BT}(1 - T_C)\dfrac{D}{E + D}$

[1] "No borrowing" is a special case of "with borrowing"; to get the formulas with "no borrowing," simply set to zero the tax rate (T_C), the amount of borrowing (D), and the cost of debt (k_D) in the "with borrowing" formulas.

[2] V_U is the unlevered value of assets; referring to Exhibit 13.8, we have V_U = $100 million. We get this value by either multiplying the $50 share price (P_U) by the 2 million shares (N_U) or, assuming perpetual valuation, by dividing net earnings (EBIT) of $15 million by the 15% unlevered cost of equity (k_E^U).

[3] PV_{ITS} is the present value of interest tax shield; referring to Exhibit 13.8, we have $PV_{ITS} = T_C \times D$ = $25 million (50% of $50 million).

[4] E is the market value of the firm's equity; referring to Exhibit 13.8, we have E_U = $100 million and E_L = $75 million ($125 million less $50 million).

[5] P is the price per share; referring to Exhibit 13.8, we have P_U = $50 and P_L = $62.50 ($50 plus $25 million divided by 2 million shares).

[6] k_D^{BT} is the pre-tax cost of debt (10%), and k_D^{AT} is the after-tax cost of debt (5%).

[7] k_E^U is the unlevered cost of equity, r_A the unlevered return on assets, and k_E^L the levered cost of equity; referring to Exhibit 13.8, we have $k_E^U = r_A$ = 15% and k_E^L = 16.67% (see Exhibit 13.12).

[8] $WACC_U$ and $WACC_L$ are, respectively, the unlevered and levered weighted average cost of capital; referring to Exhibit 13.8, we have $WACC_U$ = 15% and $WACC_L$ = 12%.

THE CAPITAL STRUCTURE DECISION WHEN FINANCIAL DISTRESS IS COSTLY

Debt puts pressure on firms because interest and principal payments are contractual obligations firms must meet. If a firm finds it increasingly difficult to service its debt, it will face a situation that is referred to as **financial distress** and may ultimately go bankrupt. Financial distress generates costs, described below, that reduce the cash flows expected from the firm's assets. In the context of the pizza theory of capital structure, we can say that **financial distress costs** reduce the size of the pizza, leaving less of it for investors (both debt holders and shareholders). And as the pizza shrinks, the firm's value and its share price go down. Shareholders bear most of the financial distress costs because debt holders have a prior and fixed claim on the smaller pizza.

The **direct costs of financial distress** are the actual costs the firm incurs if it becomes legally bankrupt. **Bankruptcy** is a legal procedure through which the ownership of the firm's assets is transferred to debt holders. Associated with this transfer are legal and administrative costs as well as lawyers' and consultants' fees; these expenses are the direct costs of financial distress.

Before a firm legally declares bankruptcy, it may have already incurred significant **indirect costs of financial distress**. The increasing probability that it will have to declare bankruptcy creates a situation that prevents the firm from operating at maximum efficiency. With too much debt outstanding, the firm may have to pass up valuable investment opportunities, cut research and development activities, or reduce marketing expenses to conserve cash and avoid bankruptcy. Customers may question the firm's long-term ability to deliver reliable goods and services and decide to switch to other companies. Suppliers may be reluctant to provide trade credit. Valuable employees may leave. Conflicts of interest between managers, shareholders, debt holders, and employees may arise, with each group trying to pursue a different strategy of self-preservation. All these indirect costs, which have a negative effect on the firm's value, become increasingly significant as the firm's indebtedness rises.

The previous section shows that when the proportion of debt in the firm's capital structure increases, the firm's value rises because of larger interest tax shields. However, in the presence of costly financial distress, these tax-related gains are eventually offset by the expected costs of financial distress. The relationship between the value of the levered firm (V_L), its unlevered value (V_U), and the present value of the interest tax shield (PT_{ITS}) expressed in equation 13.4 must be modified to account for this offsetting effect. If PV_{CFD} is the present value of the expected costs of financial distress, we can adjust the valuation formula to reflect the reduction in value generated by these costs:

$$V_L = V_U + PV_{ITS} - PV_{CFD} \qquad (13.9)$$

How large is the present value of the expected costs of financial distress (PV_{CFD})? The question can be answered only empirically. The evidence indicates that these costs are not insignificant. They can reach 10 to 15 percent of the value of the firm's assets as early as several years before filing for bankruptcy.

Exhibit 13.14 shows the rising value of the firm's assets (the straight line first presented in Exhibit 13.10) from which we deducted the present value of the costs of financial distress. At low to moderate levels of debt, the probability of financial distress is negligible and the firm can capture the entire value of the interest tax shield. As more and more debt replaces equity, the probability of financial distress rises and the present value of the associated costs grows at an increasing rate. At some debt level, denoted D*, the increase in the present value of financial distress costs arising from an extra dollar of borrowing exactly offsets the increase in the present value of the interest tax shield. At that point, the firm has reached its **optimal capital structure**. This is the firm's best capital structure because it is the one that maximizes the value of its assets and share price.

Exhibit 13.15 illustrates the effect of changes in capital structure on the firm's cost of capital in the presence of financial distress costs. As shown earlier in Exhibit 13.11, where financial distress costs were nonexistent, the cost of equity first increases proportionally with a rise in the debt-to-equity ratio. When the present value of financial distress costs becomes significant, the cost of equity begins to rise at a faster

EXHIBIT 13.14	THE VALUE OF A FIRM AS A FUNCTION OF BORROWING IN THE PRESENCE OF CORPORATE INCOME TAX AND FINANCIAL DISTRESS COSTS.

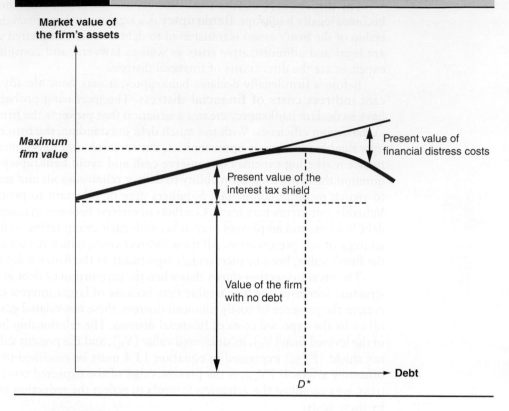

EXHIBIT 13.15	THE COST OF CAPITAL AS A FUNCTION OF THE DEBT-TO-EQUITY RATIO IN THE PRESENCE OF CORPORATE INCOME TAX AND FINANCIAL DISTRESS COSTS.

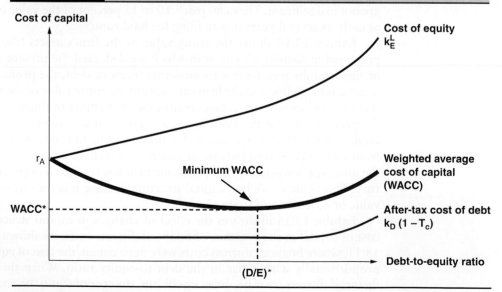

rate to reflect the increasing risk. For the same reason, the cost of debt also begins to rise at some point. The WACC declines until the benefit of the interest tax shield is offset by the negative effect of expected financial distress on the costs of equity and debt. At this point, the firm has reached its optimal capital structure: its WACC is at its minimum, its debt-to-equity ratio is at its optimal value (D/E)*, and the value of the firm's assets and its share price are maximized. This model of debt financing is known as the **trade-off model of capital structure**.

The conclusion is that an optimal capital structure exists, at least conceptually, which is the outcome of a trade-off between the benefit of the interest tax shield and the cost of financial distress arising from an increasing use of debt financing.

Unfortunately, we cannot tell you how to determine that optimal debt ratio because it is impossible to estimate financial distress costs precisely. However, this does not mean that the capital structure decision analysis done so far is not useful to managers. On the contrary, as shown next, it provides a solid conceptual framework within which the firm's managers can formulate a capital structure policy for their firm.

FORMULATING A CAPITAL STRUCTURE POLICY

The previous analysis of the trade-off model of capital structure looks at the two major determinants of a firm's borrowing decision: the value-creating effect of the tax deductibility of interest expenses and the value-destroying effect of financial distress costs. This section extends the basic trade-off model by examining additional factors that have an effect on the formulation of a capital structure policy. We first examine two questions related to the trade-off model:

1. How do personal taxes, which investors must pay on the income they receive from firms, affect the size of the interest tax shield?
2. Which types of firms are more likely to experience a state of financial distress?

We then look at a number of issues that go beyond the standard trade-off model of capital structure to shed more light on the underlying variables that shape a firm's capital structure:

1. Are there reasons for firms to borrow even *if debt does not provide tax savings*?
2. Are there reasons for firms to abstain from borrowing *even if debt financing generates little or no financial distress costs*?
3. Why do firms prefer to finance their activities with internally generated funds (retained earnings) rather than external funds?

The answers to these questions provide additional insights into the factors that affect a firm's capital structure decision and help both managers and firms' owners establish an appropriate capital structure for their companies.

A CLOSER LOOK AT THE TRADE-OFF MODEL OF CAPITAL STRUCTURE

This section examines two issues that are related to the major determinants of the trade-off model of capital structure. First, we want to determine how personal income taxes influence the value-creating effect of the tax deductibility of corporate interest expenses. Second, we want to find out which types of firms are more likely to be affected by the value-destroying effect of financial distress costs.

THE EFFECT OF PERSONAL TAXES

The interest tax shield given in equation 13.3 ignores the tax that debt holders and shareholders must pay on the income they receive from their investments in the firm. Debt holders receive interest payments. Shareholders receive cash dividends, and they receive capital gains if they sell shares at a price higher than their purchase price. If the personal tax rate on interest income is T_D and the *average* personal tax rate on equity income (dividends and capital gains) is T_E, it can be shown that the interest tax shield is in this case:

$$\text{Interest tax shield} = \left[1 - (1 - T_C) \times \frac{(1 - T_E)}{(1 - T_D)} \right] \times k_D \times D \qquad (13.10)$$

When the personal tax rates on debt and equity income are equal ($T_D = T_E$), equation 13.10 reduces to $T_C \times k_D \times D$, which is the annual interest tax shield when personal taxes are ignored (see equation 13.3). But the personal tax rate on equity income is generally *lower* than that on interest income because capital gains are usually taxed at a lower rate than interest income. In this case, the annual interest tax shield is lower than in the case in which personal taxes are not considered.

To illustrate, consider a firm with $50 million of debt, a cost of debt of 10 percent, a corporate tax rate of 50 percent, and personal tax rates of 50 percent on interest income and 25 percent on equity income. The interest tax shield according to equation 13.10 is as follows:

$$\text{Interest tax shield} = \left[1 - (1 - 0.50) \times \frac{(1 - 0.25)}{(1 - 0.50)} \right]$$
$$\times 0.10 \times \$50 \text{ million} = \$1.25 \text{ Million}$$

This is half the $2.5 million of interest tax shield when the personal tax rates on debt and equity income are equal ($T_C \times k_D \times D = 50\% \times 10\% \times \$50$ million = $2.5 million). Hence ignoring the possibility that the personal tax rate on equity income can be lower than the personal tax rate on income from debt is likely to *overestimate* the true tax benefit of debt financing.

FACTORS AFFECTING THE RISK AND COST OF FINANCIAL DISTRESS

When a firm increases its borrowing, it also increases the probability that it will experience a state of financial distress and incur (financial distress) costs that will reduce its value. But not every firm is exposed to the same **financial distress risk** or bears the same costs of financial distress. Some may reach a state of financial distress at lower debt ratios than others. In this section, we identify a number of firm-specific factors that are likely to increase the probability that a firm will experience a state of financial distress. We would expect firms with a higher risk of financial distress to have relatively lower debt ratios, which will move their optimal amount of debt financing to the left in Exhibit 13.14.

The Volatility of the Firm's Operating Profits. A firm that has highly volatile and cyclical operating cash flows (that is, a firm with high *business* risk) faces a higher probability of experiencing financial distress than a firm that has stable operating cash flows, assuming both firms have the *same* debt ratio. This is why firms with high

| EXHIBIT 13.16 | DEBT RATIOS FOR SELECTED US INDUSTRIES.[1,2] |

Industries with high ratios of debt as a percentage of debt plus equity		Industries with low ratios of debt as a percentage of debt plus equity	
Real estate investment companies	74%	Research & consulting services	23%
Department stores	63	Healthcare technology	22
Automotive retailers	58	Application software	19
Multi-utilities	57	Electronic equipment and instruments	19
Drug retail	55	Semiconductors	18
Gas utilities	53	Internet software and services	17
Household products	51	Consumer electronics	16
Automobile manufacturers	50	Biotechnology	14
Average debt ratio of all industries 31%			

[1] Debt ratios are calculated by dividing debt by the sum of debt and equity. Debt is measured at book value, and equity at market value. Industry ratios in the exhibit are the average of the ratios of the individual companies in the industry measured at the end of the fiscal year over the two-year period 2016–2017.
[2] *Source:* computed by the authors using data from *Compustat* North America.

business risk, such as internet software and services companies and biotechnology firms, have lower debt ratios than real estate investment companies and gas utilities, as shown in Exhibit 13.16. Utilities are usually able to generate a steadier and more predictable stream of operating profits and cash flows and hence have relatively low business risk. In other words, firms with low business risk can afford higher financial risk (higher debt ratios) than firms with high business risk. A simple way to find out whether a company can take full advantage of the interest tax shield is to draw an after-tax EPS-EBIT graph like the one shown in Exhibit 13.2. Simply check to see whether the probability of falling below the break-even point is negligible.

The Type of Assets the Firm Holds.   When financial distress occurs, creditors are less likely to extend credit to firms with few tangible assets (such as software and internet companies) than to firms with assets that can be valuable in case of liquidation (such as real estate and airline companies). Thus, firms that have relatively large investments in human capital, research, brands, and other intangible assets face higher costs of financial distress than firms that have the *same* debt ratio but have large investments in land, buildings, and similar tangible assets that can be sold in case of bankruptcy. Firms with relatively large proportions of intangible assets can reduce the probability of financial distress by borrowing less than firms with relatively large proportions of tangible and liquid assets. This may explain why internet services and software companies as well as biotechnology firms – which have comparatively lower amounts of tangible assets – have lower debt ratios than real estate companies and department stores, which have comparatively higher amounts of tangible assets, as reported in Exhibit 13.16.

The Type of Products or Services the Firm Sells.   When the firm sells a commodity or when the firm's service can be obtained elsewhere, customers do not usually care whether their supplier goes bankrupt, because another firm will always fill the void. When the product or service is unique, however, customers are concerned about the consequences of their supplier experiencing financial distress. Thus, a commodity supplier faces lower costs of financial distress than a supplier of unique goods or services with the *same* debt ratio. The former can afford relatively large levels of debt without making its customers nervous, but the supplier of a unique product or service would rather rely on relatively less debt to reassure its customers that its future viability will not be jeopardized by an excessive debt burden.

Even if the product is a commodity, however, customers may be concerned if the product needs future service or repair. For example, if you believe a car manufacturer will go bankrupt, you will probably not buy one of its cars. But if bankruptcy threatens a food company, you may still buy its products, because they do not need to be serviced or repaired.

The Structure of the Country's Financial System.   The risk of a firm experiencing financial distress is not related just to factors specific to the firm or its industry. It is also affected by the structure of the financial system in which the firm operates. In countries in which some of the banks are owned or controlled by the state or in countries that allow banks to own shares of companies, firms usually have higher debt ratios than in countries in which banks are in the private sector and must restrict their activities only to lending.

When banks are state owned and can be both lenders and shareholders of the same company, they are more likely to help that company avoid bankruptcy, particularly if the company is large. State-owned banks may continue to lend to a company if the state wants to keep the company afloat. Banks that are allowed to own shares in companies may accept converting excessive debt into equity. This may explain why some large companies in countries such as France, Germany, Italy, and Japan usually have higher debt ratios than their counterparts in the United States or the United Kingdom.

FACTORS OTHER THAN TAXES THAT MAY FAVOR BORROWING

The major benefit of debt financing is the tax savings that come from the deductibility of interest expenses. If the tax reductions associated with debt were no longer available (either because the tax authority denies them or because firms cannot take advantage of them), would a firm's owners still have an incentive to borrow? Yes, they would. A firm's owners may want to borrow for several reasons that are not based on the tax advantage of debt financing.

DEBT IS A DEVICE THAT HELPS REDUCE THE AGENCY COSTS ARISING FROM THE SEPARATION OF OWNERSHIP FROM CONTROL

Managers may not always act in the best interests of shareholders. They sometimes make decisions that benefit themselves but that reduce the firm's value. Suppose that a firm has generated a large cash surplus because it had an exceptionally good year. Managers may be tempted to spend this cash unwisely, such as on expensive and often useless perquisites that are not really needed, or on "empire-building" investments that allow the firm to grow in revenues and size but do not create value.

This behavior illustrates what is called an **agency problem**. It arises from the separation of ownership and control. When managers run a firm on behalf of shareholders (they act as the agents of shareholders), they may not always make decisions that benefit shareholders. They may make decisions that increase their own level of comfort and satisfaction but reduce the firm's value. An example is an executive who buys a corporate plane when such an acquisition has no identifiable benefit beyond enhancing the executive's status. This executive reduces the firm's value by an amount equal to the after-tax cost of the plane. This value reduction is referred to as an **agency cost of equity financing**.

Consider another example, directly related to the capital structure decision. The income and wealth of managers are generally not as well diversified as those of shareholders. Managers' income, their job tenure, and most of their wealth depend on the firm that employs them, whereas most shareholders invest only a small fraction of their total wealth in a single firm. Because they are poorly diversified, managers are more exposed to risk than their well-diversified shareholders. Consequently, they may adopt a more conservative debt policy than the one that maximizes the firm's value. The difference between the firm's value under the conservative debt policy and its potential maximum value with more debt financing is another example of an agency cost of equity financing.

One way to reduce agency costs is to turn managers into partial owners by giving them either shares in the firm or options to buy shares at a predetermined fixed price. However, the number of shares or options owned by the managers needs to be substantial to induce them to make the maximization of shareholder value their overriding concern. What if shareholders are reluctant to distribute large amounts of shares or options to managers?

Debt financing can be another solution to the agency problem. Issuing debt and using the cash to buy back shares reduces the agency costs of equity in two ways. First, the portion of the firm's cash flow that goes to shareholders falls because there is less equity. And the portion that goes to debt holders rises because managers must now allocate a larger part of the firm's cash flows to service debt. This means that managers have less of that cash flow to squander on things such as aeroplanes. Second, if managers already have some equity in the firm, their *percentage share* of the firm's ownership rises, because, even though they hold the same amount of equity, they now own a bigger portion of the firm's total equity. Both of these debt-related effects should motivate managers to act in the interests of shareholders. The first effect acts as the proverbial stick, the second as the carrot. Thus, debt financing becomes a device that helps reduce the agency costs associated with equity financing by aligning managers' interests with those of shareholders.

In this case, borrowing should increase the market value of the firm and its share price through two distinct channels. One is through the tax-induced gains generated by debt financing and the other is through the reduction in the agency costs of equity. The latter results from the increased focus and discipline imposed on managers by higher debt levels and the enhanced motivation provided by a higher fractional ownership of the firm for managers who held shares before the recapitalization.

DEBT IS A DEVICE THAT ALLOWS CURRENT OWNERS TO RETAIN CONTROL

The choice of debt over new equity may be dictated by the desire of current owners to retain **control** of their firm. Fresh equity, supplied by new investors, reduces the percentage of the firm's equity capital controlled by the original owners, but debt financing avoids this **dilution** effect. Thus, if the firm needs outside funding and the current owners wish to retain control, they will prefer that the firm borrow rather than issue new shares, regardless of tax considerations.

If the decision to issue debt rather than equity is motivated by control considerations, we can expect the firm's shares to trade at a discount, because that will greatly diminish the ability of outsiders to take over the company. If the present value of the tax gains generated by the debt issued to retain control is smaller than the market discount caused by a tight control, the net effect is a *lower* equity value. But this does not mean that shareholders are necessarily worse off. Control may generate *nonmonetary* benefits that are more valuable to them than the loss of market value.

DEBT IS A DEVICE THAT HELPS RESOLVE THE PROBLEM OF INFORMATION ASYMMETRY BETWEEN MANAGERS AND OUTSIDE INVESTORS

Asymmetric information is present when management knows more about the future prospects of their firm than do outside investors (shareholders and creditors). This occurs when it is expensive for a company to keep outside investors informed about the firm's current condition and future prospects. It can also arise when management does not want future plans to be public knowledge because such information might be valuable to its competitors. Let's see why the presence of asymmetric information can create a managerial preference for debt financing.

Suppose JBC has decided to invest in a new project that will require external financing. Ms Johnson could either issue shares at the current market price of, say, $70 or issue bonds. Suppose Ms Johnson is convinced that the firm's future is more promising than the financial market expects. She believes JBC's equity is *underpriced* and JBC's shares are worth at least $90. What should she do? If she issues undervalued shares, she penalizes the current shareholders by handing a gift to new shareholders who would pay only $70 for what she values at $90. Ms Johnson, who cares about the firm's existing shareholders, would rather issue bonds. Now consider the opposite case in which Ms Johnson believes JBC's shares are *overpriced* and a price of $60 would be more in line with her expectation regarding JBC's future prospects. If she issues bonds, the required interest and principal payments may create an added burden when she should focus her full attention on improving the firm's prospects. She should issue shares. If she could issue shares at a price close to their current price of $70, she would provide a windfall profit to current shareholders at the expense of new shareholders.

There is another point to consider, however. If investors are aware that firms issue shares only when managers think the firm's equity is overvalued, they will revise their expectations downward when a firm announces its intention to issue shares and bid down its share price. The evidence seems to support this view because the price of existing shares usually goes down on the day firms announce their intention to issue new shares. Managers, who typically do not like to see a drop in their firm's share price, are often reluctant to issue shares, whether or not they find their equity underpriced or overpriced. This may explain why, for most corporations, debt is the favored means of external financing, irrespective of the tax benefit it procures.

FACTORS OTHER THAN FINANCIAL DISTRESS COSTS THAT MAY DISCOURAGE BORROWING

Although debt financing provides valuable tax reductions, increasing borrowing eventually generates financial distress costs that rise with higher debt ratios. The question, then, is whether firms would increase borrowing even if financial distress costs were insignificant. Some firms may deliberately decide to refrain from borrowing even if financial distress costs are moderate or nonexistent because the debt the firm must issue to take advantage of the tax savings may create a number of constraints that owners and managers find too costly. If the expected costs generated by these constraints are higher than the potential tax benefits of debt financing, the firm may decide not to issue additional debt.

EXCESSIVE DEBT MAY PREVENT FIRMS FROM TAKING FULL ADVANTAGE OF THE INTEREST TAX SHIELD

To take advantage of the tax savings from interest expenses, a firm needs to generate relatively large operating profits to allow it to deduct the full amount of interest expenses. Firms that operate in capital-intensive industries can already reduce their tax liability through accelerated depreciation schedules. Consequently, they may not have sufficient pre-tax operating profits to benefit fully from the additional tax savings offered by the interest expenses generated by high levels of debt.

EXCESSIVE DEBT MAY CREATE COSTLY CONFLICTS OF INTEREST BETWEEN SHAREHOLDERS AND DEBT HOLDERS

Excessive debt may give rise to costly conflicts of interest between shareholders and lenders that can affect the firm's capital structure decision. We use an extreme example to illustrate the point. Suppose that management, acting on the instructions of shareholders, borrows $8 million at 10 percent to invest in a $10 million project that is risky. Furthermore, assume that the lenders do not have all the details about the riskiness of the project. In one year, the project should yield either $30 million or nothing, with an equal probability of each occurrence. If the project goes well, the shareholders repay $8.8 million to the lenders (the $8 million loan plus 10 percent interest) and keep the rest ($21.2 million). If the project fails, everyone loses, but the lenders will lose more than the shareholders, because they financed 80 percent of the project. This is rightly described as "gambling away" lenders' *money*. The lenders, of course, anticipate this type of behavior and try to protect their investment by imposing restrictions on the firm's ability to spend the borrowed funds as it wishes. In other words, the lenders make it more expensive for the shareholders to raise debt capital.

The protection the suppliers of debt demand takes the form of **restrictive covenants** in the formal agreement between the borrowing firm and its lenders. For example, these covenants may impose limits on the amount of dividends the firm is allowed to pay, the amount of additional debt it can borrow, or the type of assets it can acquire or sell. The more debt the firm already has, the more restrictive the protective covenants associated with additional borrowing become. In other words, additional debt becomes increasingly costly, not only in terms of the higher interest payments lenders may demand but also in the loss of managerial flexibility. The costs eventually reach the point at which they offset the benefit of the interest tax shield.

These **bonding** and **monitoring costs** are also referred to as **agency costs of debt financing** because they are the outcome of another type of agency problem. In this case, the shareholders are the agents of the debt holders because they decide how debt holders' funds will be spent. You could argue that agency costs of debt are actually a subset of financial distress costs. Like financial distress costs, they are expected to discourage firms from borrowing too much.

Note that the agency costs of *debt* financing and the agency costs of *equity* financing have *opposite* effects on the firm's value. When a firm increases its borrowing, its agency costs of debt *rise* and the value of the firm's assets and share price *fall* (because additional debt gets more costly). Simultaneously, its agency costs of equity *fall* and the value of the firm's assets and share price *rise*. The net effect depends on the relative magnitude of the two types of agency costs.

EXCESSIVE DEBT MAY CONSTRAIN THE FIRM'S ABILITY TO PAY STABLE DIVIDENDS

We have seen in Chapter 11 that managers generally prefer to adopt **stable dividend policies**. They try to distribute dividends regularly and to increase their amount steadily over time to keep pace with the rise in the firm's share price. The objective is usually to attain an unbroken record of dividend payments. When a firm faces a temporary liquidity problem, it will try not to cut its dividend. Cutting or skipping a dividend payment may be interpreted by the market as a signal that the firm is facing a fundamental cash-flow problem that will prevent it from paying dividends for the foreseeable future. The market reaction can be a sharp drop in the firm's share price. To avoid these negative **signaling effects**, firms try to pursue stable dividend policies unless they face a severe cash-flow problem and have no choice but to cut dividends. The implication for the capital structure decision is clear: firms with excessive debt may be unable to maintain a stable dividend policy. Consider JBC's alternative capital structures reported in Exhibit 13.1. Suppose the firm pays a $5 dividend per share. With no debt in its capital structure, JBC will be able to pay its dividend even if the worst-case scenario occurs. If recession hits, EPS will be $5, enough to cover the $5 dividend. But with $100 million of debt, JBC will be unable to pay dividends if recession occurs. No cash may be available after paying the $10 million of interest on the debt.

If a firm adopts a stable dividend policy and if the market prefers stable dividends, the value of the firm should rise. But this potential increase in value will be offset by the loss of the tax benefits of debt *not* issued. The value of the firm's assets and its share price will rise only if the gains derived from a stable dividend policy exceed the foregone tax benefits of debt financing.

EXCESSIVE DEBT MAY REDUCE THE FIRM'S FINANCIAL FLEXIBILITY AND AFFECT ITS CREDIT RATING

Some firms are tempted to build up cash during good times. This cash buildup, often referred to as **financial slack**, may be valuable because it is immediately available if a value-creating investment opportunity is found. In addition, a cash buildup contributes to increasing the firm's **debt capacity**, that is, its ability to quickly raise debt in the future if the need for funds arises unexpectedly. Clearly, a firm with excessive debt will not be able to enjoy this sort of flexibility. **Financial flexibility** may be valuable to managers, but does it create value for shareholders? This is a difficult question to answer. Holding cash and reducing debt should have a negative effect on the firm's value because cash does not earn high returns and debt reduction means that valuable tax savings are lost. The net effect on value will be positive only if the expected gains from acting rapidly to take advantage of investment opportunities exceed these negative effects.

Another illustration of how financial flexibility may lead to a capital structure with less than optimal debt is managers' desire to retain or improve the **credit rating** of their firm's debt. Companies that issue debt securities are required to obtain a rating from a **credit rating agency**. This rating reflects the agency's assessment of the quality of the firm's debt (see Chapter 11 for details). If the agency downgrades the firm's debt, the firm's cost of debt will rise and its ability to raise debt quickly may be impaired, thus reducing the firm's financial flexibility. For this reason, most managers avoid borrowing in excess of the amount that may trigger a credit downgrade, even if more debt makes sense otherwise. Again, the net effect on share price is not obvious.

IS THERE A PREFERENCE FOR RETAINED EARNINGS?

Managers seem to have a marked preference for retained earnings over external financing, whether in the form of debt or new equity. How can we explain this reticence toward external financing, and what are its implications for the capital structure decision?

CONTRARY TO SECURITIES, RETAINED EARNINGS DO NOT HAVE ISSUE COSTS

Contrary to bond and stock issues, retained earnings do not have any **flotation** or **issue costs** and are thus less expensive than a stock issue. Flotation costs include administrative costs (such as filing fees, legal fees, and printing fees), taxes, and the costs of using the services of investment banks that sell the firm's securities to the public (see Chapter 11). Most of these costs are fixed, so the total cost of selling bonds and stocks is proportionally lower for large issues than for small ones. This may explain why firms raise large amounts of external funds infrequently rather than small amounts more often. (For issues of the same size, it has been shown that the cost of raising equity is higher than the cost of raising debt.)

DO FIRMS HAVE A PREFERRED ORDER IN THEIR CHOICE OF FINANCING?

Evidence suggests that firms usually raise capital according to a **pecking order**, meaning that they rely first on retained earnings and then, if external financing is needed, issue debt before raising new equity. Some of the reasons why firms issue bonds rather than stocks were reviewed in the previous section. They include the desire of current owners to retain control, the role of debt as a mechanism to reduce the agency costs of equity, and the negative market reaction to the announcement of a new equity issue, a reaction arising from asymmetric information between managers and outside investors. Firms may prefer to issue bonds rather than stocks, but why would they prefer internal financing (retained earnings) to external financing?

One reason is that no issue costs are associated with retained earnings, whereas significant costs are associated with any form of external financing. Another reason is that firms do not have to provide as much information to outsiders to justify a retention of profits as when making a new issue of stocks or bonds. This argument, often defended by the need to prevent competitors from getting valuable information, is generally not well received by shareholders, who interpret it as an excuse for not providing them with valuable information on the use of their funds. This is the dilemma created by shareholders' demand for **transparency**. More transparency should enhance the firm's value, but it could also harm the firm if competitors use the information to their advantage.

One implication of the pecking order hypothesis is that *firms may not have a specific* **target debt ratio** or, if they have one, they do not aim for it consistently. When they have investment opportunities, they retain earnings to fund them. If an investment requires more funds than are available internally, the firm will first issue debt and then raise new equity, thus allowing its capital structure to vary over time in response to investment opportunities.

PUTTING IT ALL TOGETHER

We would have liked to provide a formula that ties together all the factors that influence a firm's capital structure and market value, and that identifies an optimal debt ratio for a firm. Unfortunately, such a formula does not exist. All we have is a basic framework that tells us an optimal capital structure is reached at the point at which the tax benefit of an additional amount of debt is offset by the present value of the expected financial distress costs created by the additional borrowing. From this point, we must make adjustments to reflect the influence of a number of factors that would justify a lower or higher debt-to-equity ratio. These factors are summarized in Exhibit 13.17.

The combined effect of all these factors on the firm's optimal capital structure and market value is practically impossible to estimate with any degree of precision. You will have to exercise a lot of judgment to determine a firm's appropriate capital structure. In making that judgment, the average debt ratio of similar firms in the sector is the best starting point for the analysis. These industry ratios, such as those shown in Exhibit 13.16, must then be adjusted upward or downward to reflect the firm's particular conditions and specific situation with respect to the factors surveyed in this section.

After a firm has established a desirable **target capital structure**, it should make financing decisions that are consistent with that target structure. This does not mean that the firm's actual debt ratio must always be equal to its target value. If a firm needs external funds, it does not necessarily need to issue debt and equity in the same proportion as dictated by the target debt ratio. Furthermore, financial market conditions may, at times, favor one type of financing over the other. This means that firms *may have to deviate temporarily from their target debt ratio*. The objective is to ensure that, *over time*, the firm's average debt ratio is close to its target value. And if the business and financial environments that led to the choice of a particular target debt ratio change, the firm should adjust its target capital structure to reflect the new environment.

As a final note, we present two exhibits on the financing of firms. Exhibit 13.18 shows the ratio of equity financing to total assets of a very large sample of US corporations from 1945 to 2017, measured at market value. Notice the steady decline in equity financing from around 75 percent in the late 1940s to between 50 to 60 percent since the early 1980s. A similar phenomenon is reported in most countries around the world. The last exhibit, Exhibit 13.19, shows the result of a survey among chief financial officers that indicates the most important factors they refer to when deciding the debt level of their companies: financial flexibility and avoidance of credit ratings downgrades seem to be a higher priority than the tax advantage of interest payments or the costs of financial distress.

EXHIBIT 13.17	FACTORS AFFECTING THE CAPITAL STRUCTURE DECISION.

Factors That Favor Borrowing

Primary Factor

Corporate income tax	Debt is a device that allows firms to reduce their corporate income tax because interest expenses are tax deductible, whereas dividends and retained earnings are not. However, the interest tax shield at the corporate level may be reduced by the impact of personal income taxes.

Important Secondary Factors

Agency costs of equity	Debt is a device that helps *reduce* the agency costs of equity arising from the tendency of managers to make decisions that are not always in the best interests of shareholders. Debt increases the firm's value because debt servicing imposes focus and discipline on managers, who will then be less likely to "waste" shareholders' funds.
Retention of control	Debt allows current owners to retain control of the firm. This factor, however, may reduce share price because of the inability of outsiders to take over the company when its ownership is not dispersed.
Information asymmetry	Issuing debt instead of equity allows the firm to avoid the drop in share price that usually accompanies a new equity issue. This drop occurs because outside shareholders think that managers issue shares only when they believe the firm's shares are overvalued.

Factors That Discourage (Excessive) Borrowing

Primary Factor

Costs of financial distress	Excessive debt increases the probability that the firm will experience financial distress. And the higher the probability of financial distress, the larger the present value of the expected costs associated with financial distress and the lower the value of the firm. Firms that face higher probability of financial distress include companies with pre-tax operating profits that are cyclical and volatile, companies with a relatively large amount of intangible and illiquid assets, and companies with unique products and services or with products that require after-sale service and repair.

Important Secondary Factors

Agency costs of debt	Additional borrowing comes with strings attached. Lenders impose increasingly constraining and costly protective covenants in new debt contracts to protect themselves against the potential misallocation of borrowed funds by managers acting on behalf of shareholders.
Dividend policy	Excessive debt may constrain the firm's ability to adopt a stable dividend policy.
Financial flexibility	Excessive debt may reduce the firm's financial flexibility, that is, its ability to quickly seize a value-creating investment opportunity.

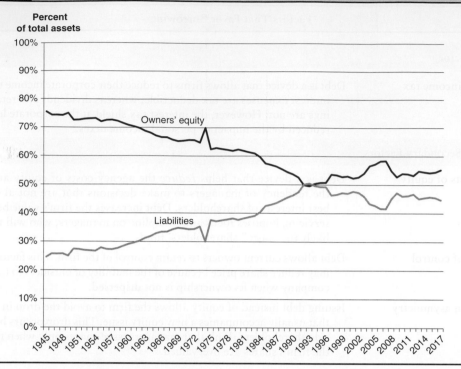

EXHIBIT 13.18	EQUITY FINANCING OF NONFINANCIAL US FIRMS (AT MARKET VALUE) AS A PERCENTAGE OF TOTAL ASSETS.

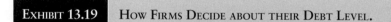

Source: FRED Economic Data, Federal Reserve Bank of St Louis.

EXHIBIT 13.19	HOW FIRMS DECIDE ABOUT THEIR DEBT LEVEL.

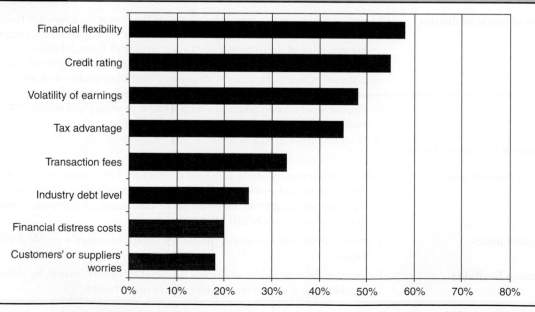

Source: Graham, John R., and Campbell R. Harvey. "How Do CFOs Make Capital Budgeting and Capital Structure Decisions?" *The Journal of Applied Corporate Finance* 14, No. 4 (2002).

KEY POINTS

1. The choice of funds used to finance a firm's investments is important, and certain factors need to be taken into account when designing an optimal capital structure, namely, a capital structure that maximizes the firm's value and share price. Our analysis of the capital structure decision begins with how changes in the firm's debt-to-equity ratio affect the firm's profitability, measured by its earnings per share (EPS). By increasing its financial leverage (higher debt ratios), a firm can increase its *expected* EPS, but it must bear the increasing financial risk (wider swings in EPS) that accompanies higher levels of debt. Unfortunately, the EPS approach to capital structure – although providing useful insights about the capital structure decision – does not identify the ideal trade-off between higher expected EPS and wider fluctuations in EPS. We need to know how debt affects the firm's value.

2. The MM theory of capital structure provides a starting point for understanding how debt financing affects the firm's value. The theory says that, like a pizza whose size cannot be increased by slicing it, the value of a firm and its share price cannot be increased by changing the proportions of debt and equity in its capital structure, *provided there are no corporate income taxes*. According to this theory, developed by Modigliani and Miller, as the firm increases its financial leverage, the extra benefits accruing to shareholders from higher expected EPS is a compensation for the extra risk brought about by that leverage. Although the cost of equity increases with leverage, the firm's weighted average cost of capital (WACC), and thus the value of the firm's assets, do not change.

3. When corporate income taxes are considered, debt financing is definitely better than equity financing because the annual interest tax shield resulting from the tax deductibility of interest expenses provides value to shareholders. Similarly, the firm's WACC falls, and the value of the firm rises, as the relative amount of debt financing increases. However, if investors' revenues from equity investment (dividends and capital gains) are taxed at a lower rate than investors' income from holding the firm's debt, then the annual interest tax shield may be lower than predicted. Nevertheless, in a world with corporate income taxes, the policy recommendation is that firms should maximize their value by financing their assets with as much debt as possible. This is an awkward policy, never observed in practice.

4. When financial distress costs are considered, high levels of debt financing become less desirable. Financial distress arises when the firm begins to encounter some difficulties in servicing its debt. When a firm is affected by financial distress, managers' ability to conduct business is impaired; acute conflicts of interest between managers, shareholders, and debt holders emerge; and customers, suppliers, and employees worry about the firm's capacity to meet its contractual obligations. All these factors generate increasing costs that reduce the firm's value as its debt ratio rises.

5. An optimal level of debt financing is reached when the marginal benefit derived from the interest tax shield is exactly compensated for by the additional costs of financial distress. At this level of debt, the firm's WACC is at its lowest and the firm's assets and share price have reached their maximum value. This should be the firm's target debt ratio. This model of optimal financing is called the trade-off model of capital structure.

6. Finally, a number of additional factors (other than taxes and financial distress costs) need to be examined when formulating a firm's capital structure policy. These factors include the volatility of the firm's operating profits (in other words, its business risk), the type of assets the firm holds, the type of products and services it sells, the presence of agency costs associated with both equity and debt financing, the constraints imposed by dividend policy, the importance of asymmetric information between managers and outside investors, and the existence of a pecking order in the choice of financing sources.

7. Unfortunately, a formula does not exist that integrates all these factors to provide managers with their firm's optimal debt ratio. Designing the right capital structure involves more than applying formulas. It is the art of combining the conceptual framework provided here with judgment, insight, and timing to establish a viable debt ratio for the firm.

CAPITAL STRUCTURE AND SYSTEMATIC RISK (BETA)

In Chapter 12 we use unlevered (or asset) betas (β_U) to estimate the value of a firm. These unlevered betas were given by a formula that is a function of the firm's levered (or equity) betas (β_L) and the firm's capital structure (see equation 12.7). The formula was presented without a proof because we had not yet explained how capital structure affects the value of a firm's assets. Now that we know the relationship between capital structure and value, we can explain how levered and unlevered betas are related.

HOW TO EXTRACT UNLEVERED BETAS FROM LEVERED BETAS

To establish the relationship between levered and unlevered betas we start with two ways to express the value of a firm's assets when these assets are financed with debt. One way is to express the firm's leveraged asset value (V_L) as the sum of the firm's equity (E) and debt (D) employed to finance these assets ($V_L = E + D$). The other way is to use equation 13.4 according to which V_L is the sum of the firm's unlevered asset value (V_U) and the present value of the future stream of interest tax savings (PV_{ITS}) that is generated by the tax-deductibility of the interest payments on the debt employed to finance the firm's assets ($V_L = V_U + PV_{ITS}$). In equilibrium the two expressions must be equal:

$$V_L = E + D = V_U + PV_{ITS} \tag{A13.1}$$

Equation A13.1 says that a firm can be viewed as either one of two different portfolios with the same value but made up of different assets. (Note that all the values in equation A13.1 are market values, not book values.) The one on the left includes the equity of the levered firm (owned by its shareholders) plus its debt (owned by the firm's debt holders), while the one on the right includes the assets of the firm plus the value of the interest tax shield (both owned by the firm's shareholders). Each of these assets carries some risk. Let's measure their risk with their beta coefficient, that is, their systematic risk:[5] β_U is the *unlevered beta* of the firm's *unlevered* asset value (V_U), β_{ITS} is the beta of the present value of the future stream of ITS (PV_{ITS}), β_L is the *levered beta* of the firm's equity value (E), and β_D is the beta of the firm's debt (D). Because the beta of a portfolio of assets is the weighted average of the beta of each asset in the portfolio where the weights are the value of each asset divided by the value of the portfolio, we can write:

$$\beta_L \left(\frac{E}{V_L} \right) + \beta_D \left(\frac{D}{V_L} \right) = \beta_U \left(\frac{V_U}{V_L} \right) + \beta_{ITS} \left(\frac{PV_{ITS}}{V_L} \right)$$

---

[5] In Chapters 3 and 12 we explain why systematic risk and betas are relevant measures of risk.

We can remove the common denominator V_L in the above equation, which becomes:

$$\beta_L E + \beta_D D = \beta_U V_U + \beta_{ITS} PV_{ITS} \qquad (A13.2)$$

To find the value of β_U as a function of β_L and β_D, we need to know β_{ITS} and PV_{ITS}. We will consider two cases. The first case assumes that the firm's capital structure, that is, its *debt-to-equity ratio (D/E), is constant over time*. This assumption implies that the amount of debt (D) will have to change over time when the value of equity (E) changes so that the ratio stays the same. The second case assumes that *the amount of debt (D) the firm uses to finance its assets is constant over time*. This assumption implies that the firm's capital structure – its debt-to-equity ratio (D/E) – will have to change over time when the value of equity (E) changes. Let's examine the implications of each case for the calculation of the firm's unlevered beta (β_U).

CASE 1: THE DEBT-TO-EQUITY RATIO (D/E) IS CONSTANT OVER TIME

In this case the value of firm's debt (D) and, as a consequence, the value of the interest tax shield (ITS)[6] will change over time in a fixed proportion to the value of the firm's equity (E) in order to keep the debt-to-equity ratio constant. As a result, the systematic risk of the ITS will be the same as the systematic risk of the firm's assets, and hence $\beta_{ITS} = \beta_U$. Noting from equation A13.1 that $V_U = V_L - PV_{ITS} = E + D - PV_{ITS}$, we can rewrite equation A13.2 as follows:

$$\beta_L E + \beta_D D = \beta_U (E + D - PV_{ITS}) + \beta_U PV_{ITS}$$

from which we get:

$$\beta_U = \frac{\beta_L + \beta_D \dfrac{D}{E}}{1 + \dfrac{D}{E}} \qquad (A13.3)$$

If we assume that debt is riskless, β_D is zero and the formula for unlevered beta becomes:

$$\beta_U = \frac{\beta_L}{1 + \dfrac{D}{E}} \qquad (A13.4)$$

which is equation 12.7.

CASE 2: THE AMOUNT OF DEBT (D) IS CONSTANT OVER TIME

In this case, the interest tax shield (ITS) is a fixed proportion of the firm's debt.[7] As a result, the systematic risk of the ITS is the *same* as the systematic risk of the debt, and, consequently, the risk-adjusted discount rate, k_{ITS}, needed to get the present value

---

[6] The interest tax shield is equal to $T_C \times D \times k_D$ where T_C is the firm's corporate tax rate and k_D is the interest rate (see equation 13.3).

[7] The proportion is $T_C \times k_D$ (see equation 13.3).

of the interest tax shield, is the same as the cost of debt, k_D. It follows that the present value of the ITS (PV_{ITS}) is:[8]

$$PV_{ITS} = \frac{T_C \times D \times k_D}{k_{ITS}} = \frac{T_C \times D \times k_D}{k_D} = T_C \times D$$

Replacing PV_{ITS} in equation A13.1 by $T \times D$, we get:

$$V_U = V_L - PV_{ITS} = E + D - (T_C \times D) = E + (1 - T_C)D$$

If the interest tax shield and the debt have the same systematic risk $\beta_{ITS} = \beta_D$, equation A13.2 can be rewritten as:

$$\beta_L E + \beta_D D = \beta_U[E + (1 - T_C)D] + \beta_D(T_C \times D)$$

from which we get:

$$\beta_U[E + (1 - T_C)D] = \beta_L E + \beta_D D - \beta_D(T_C \times D) = \beta_L E + \beta_D(1 - T_C)D$$

Dividing both sides of the above equation by E yields:

$$\beta_U = \frac{\beta_L + \beta_D(1 - T_C)\dfrac{D}{E}}{1 + (1 - T_C)\dfrac{D}{E}} \tag{A13.5}$$

If debt is riskless, β_D is zero and the formula for unlevered beta becomes:

$$\beta_U = \frac{\beta_L}{1 + (1 - T_C)\dfrac{D}{E}} \tag{A13.6}$$

WHICH FORMULA SHOULD BE USED TO GET UNLEVERED BETAS?

As you recall, when we apply the Net Present Value rule to make investment decisions (see Chapter 7) and when we value stocks (see Chapter 10), we use the *same* weighted average cost of capital (WACC) to discount all the expected future free cash flows. This means that the debt-to-equity ratio used to finance a project or a firm's assets stays the same over time. If a firm's valuation requires the calculation of unlevered betas as in Chapter 12, then these betas should be calculated with formulas A13.3 and A13.4.

---

[8] For simplification, we also assume that the ITS is a perpetuity. The present value of a perpetuity is given in Chapter 2 (equation 2.6).

FURTHER READING

1. Modigliani, Franco, and Merton Miller. "The Cost of Capital, Corporate Finance and the Theory of Investment." *American Economic Review* 53 (June 1963).
2. Modigliani, Franco, and Merton Miller. "Corporate Income Taxes and the Cost of Capital: A Correction." *American Economic Review* 48 (June 1958).
3. Merton Miller. "Debt and Taxes." *Journal of Finance* 32 (May 1977).
4. Shivdasani, Anil, and Mark Zenner. "How to Choose a Capital Structure: Navigating the Debt-Equity Decision." *Journal of Applied Corporate Finance* 17 (Winter 2005).

SELF-TEST QUESTIONS

13.1   Effect of borrowing on share price.

An increase in debt makes equity riskier because the volatility of the earnings per share increases with debt. Suppose there are no taxes and no financial distress costs. Does that necessarily mean that the share price of a firm must decrease when its indebtedness increases? Answer the same question for when there are taxes and financial distress costs.

13.2   Risk of debt and equity and risk of the firm.

Increasing debt financing makes the firm's equity riskier. It also makes the firm's debt riskier, because the probability that the firm will default increases with more debt. Because both equity and debt become riskier, the risk of the firm as a whole should increase. True or false?

13.3   Factors affecting the optimal debt-to-equity ratio.

Assume that the debt-to-equity ratio of Alternative Solutions Inc. is optimal. Under which of the following circumstances should the ratio be changed to still be optimal?

a. An increase in the corporate tax rate
b. An increase in the personal capital gains tax rate
c. The firm, which specializes in the development of software products, acquires an office building
d. Management believes strongly that their firm's shares are grossly undervalued
e. The firm's working capital requirement (the amount it invests in its operating cycle) keeps on decreasing
f. The firm is taken over by a competitor.

13.4   Earnings per share analysis.

Albine Inc. has no debt. It has 10,000 shares of equity outstanding with a market price of $100. It is considering two alternative recapitalization plans. The low-debt plan calls for issuing $200,000 of debt, whereas the high-debt plan would involve issuing $400,000 of debt. In both cases, the cost of debt would be 10 percent. The firm does not pay any tax.

a. Earnings before interest and tax (EBIT) are projected to be either $90,000 or $170,000. What would be Albine's earnings per share (EPS) in both scenarios under each of the two refinancing plans? Suppose that both scenarios are equally likely so that the expected EBIT is $130,000. What would the expected EPS be?
b. If EBIT is equal to $100,000, what would EPS be under each of the two recapitalization plans? Why are they the same?

13.5   **The value of the interest tax shield.**
Ilbane Corp. has no debt, and the market value of its equity is $100 million. It can borrow at 5 percent. If the corporate tax rate is 35 percent, what will be the value of Ilbane Corp. if it borrows the following amounts and uses the proceeds to repurchase stock?

a. $20 million
b. $80 million

REVIEW QUESTIONS

1.   **Earnings per share analysis.**
Chloroline Inc. has two million shares outstanding and no debt. Earnings before interest and tax (EBIT) are projected to be $15 million under normal conditions, $5 million for a downturn in the economic environment, and $20 million for an economic expansion. Chloroline considers a debt issue of $50 million with an 8 percent interest rate. The proceeds would be used to buy back one million shares at the current market price of $50 a share. The corporate tax rate is 40 percent.

a. Calculate Chloroline's earnings per share (EPS) and return on investment (EPS divided by share price) under the two scenarios, first before any new debt is issued and then after the recapitalization.
b. From your answers to part a, would you recommend that Chloroline goes ahead with the recapitalization?

2.   **Firm value and capital structure in the absence of tax.**
Assume a zero corporate tax rate. Because both the risk of a firm's equity and debt increase with debt financing, then the value of the firm should decrease when it uses more and more debt. True or false?

3.   **Homemade leverage.**
Alberton Inc., an all-equity-financed equipment manufacturer, has announced that it will change its capital structure to one that will have 30 percent of debt, using the proceeds from the debt issue to buy back shares. The firm has one million shares outstanding and the share price is $60. Its operating margin, or earnings before interest and tax (EBIT), is expected to stay at its current level of $4 million for the foreseeable future. The interest rate on the debt that will be issued is 10 percent, and the firm does not pay any tax. Furthermore, Alberton has a dividend payout ratio of 100 percent, that is, all its earnings are distributed as dividends.

a. Mr Robert owns 140,000 shares of stock. How much will Mr Robert receive every year from Alberton under the current capital structure?
b. What will his cash flow be under the new capital structure, assuming that Mr Robert keeps all of his shares?
c. Why will the cash flow received by Mr Robert under the new capital structure be lower than under the current one? What can he do to avoid this cash loss and keep getting the same cash flow from the amount he invested in Alberton?

4.   **Cost of debt versus cost of equity.**
Because the cost of debt is lower than the cost of equity, firms must increase their use of debt as much as possible to increase the firm's value. What is your answer to this argument?

From the capital asset pricing model presented in Chapter 12, how can you show that the cost of equity changes with the use of debt?

5. **Changes in capital structure and the cost of capital.**
Starline & Co. has no debt, and its cost of equity is 14 percent. It can borrow at 8 percent. The corporate tax rate is 40 percent.

   a. Calculate the cost of equity and the weighted average cost of capital (WACC) of Starline if it decides to borrow up to the equivalent of 25, 50, 75, or 100 percent of its current equity. The proceeds would be used to buy back shares of the firm.
   b. Draw a graph showing how Starline's cost of equity, cost of debt, and WACC vary with the debt-to-equity ratio.
   c. On the basis of your results, would you recommend that Starline change its capital structure?

6. **The cost of equity, the weighted average cost of capital, and financial leverage.**
Albarval Co. expects its return on assets to be stable at 12 percent, assuming a target capital structure of 80 percent equity and 20 percent debt. Suppose that the firm's borrowing rate is 8 percent, for a wide range of capital structures.

   a. Suppose that Albarval does not pay any tax. What is Albarval's cost of equity? Hint: refer to equation 13.2. What would Albarval's cost of equity be if the target capital structure is 50 percent equity, 50 percent debt? Show that under both capital structures the firm's weighted average cost of capital (WACC) is the same and that it is equal to 12 percent.
   b. Suppose now that the firm's tax rate is 40 percent. What is the cost of equity and the WACC under the two capital structures? Hint: refer to equations 13.7 and 13.8. Why are the cost of equity and the WACC different under the two capital structures?

7. **The value of the interest tax shield.**
Lannion Co. is a manufacturing firm with no debt outstanding. It is considering borrowing $25 million at 8 percent and using the proceeds to buy back shares. Its equity market value is $100 million, and its profits are taxed at 35 percent.

   a. What would be the present value of the interest tax shield if the debt is permanent? If it matures in five years?
   b. What would be the present value of the interest tax shield if the interest rate increases to 9 percent immediately after the debt is issued?

8. **Industry influence on the capital structure.**
How would you rank these three firms in decreasing order of expected debt ratios: a biotechnology firm, an auto-parts firm, and an electric utility firm? Explain.

9. **Board of directors and management.**
Why are companies with a weak board of directors likely to be underlevered (they would use less debt than the optimal amount they could issue)?

10. **Agency costs.**
How can shareholders expropriate wealth from bondholders?

VALUING AND ACQUIRING A BUSINESS

CHAPTER 14

Should you replace an existing piece of equipment with a newer, more efficient one? Build a plant to launch a new product? Acquire a competitor? You should go ahead with these investments only if you are sufficiently confident that undertaking them will raise your firm's market value. This occurs only if the estimated *value* of the assets purchased is higher than the *price* paid to buy them. This chapter shows how to value a business. The business can be either an entire firm or only part of a firm, such as one of its divisions. In the valuation of an entire firm, we must distinguish between the value of the firm's assets and the value of its equity, where the value of equity represents the claims of shareholders on the firm's assets. Obviously, these values are related, because the value of a firm's equity is the difference between the value of its assets and the value of its debts. The value of a division is simply the value of the division's assets.

The most common application of business valuation is the estimation of the price at which the shares of a firm can be acquired. For example, in a *takeover*, one firm (the *bidding* company) wants to acquire all or a portion of another firm's shares and needs to determine the price at which the shares of the *target* firm should be bought. The target firm may be a public firm whose shares are traded and quoted on a stock exchange, or it may be a privately held company with no quoted price. To decide if the acquisition is a value-creating proposal, the bidding firm needs to determine how much the target firm's shares are worth to it (the *bidder*). If the shares of the target firm are quoted at $20 a share and the bidder estimates their value at $30, buying them for *less* than $30 is a value-creating decision. In this case, the acquisition is a value-creating investment because the shares are worth more to the bidding firm than the price it has to pay for them. Any acquisition price *above* an average price of $30 per share is a value-destroying acquisition because the shares are worth less to the *bidder* than the price it has to pay for them.

An *initial public offering* (IPO) is another typical situation that requires the valuation of a company's equity. In an IPO, a privately held company is considering issuing shares to the public for the first time. An offer price that will ensure the success of the sale to the public must be estimated. A similar situation occurs when state-owned firms are privatized, that is, sold to the public.

After a brief introduction to the main valuation methods, this chapter focuses on the methods that are most commonly used. We begin with a review of valuation by *comparables*, which we first presented in Chapter 10: this method values a firm using stock market data on firms similar to the business or the firm we want to value. As an illustration, we apply this method to value Office Supplies (OS) Distributors, a firm we analyzed in Chapters 4 to 6. We then apply the *discounted cash flow* (DCF) approach, also presented in Chapter 10, which values a firm's assets by discounting the future cash flows expected from these assets. The estimated value of the firm's equity is the difference between the estimated value of its assets and the value of its debts. We show how the method can be implemented by estimating two different values of OS Distributors' equity: (1) its "*stand-alone*" or "*as-is*" value and (2) its value as an acquisition target (its target value). We examine in detail the sources of value creation in an acquisition and show how to estimate them. We also describe why a conglomerate merger, which is the combination of unrelated businesses, is not likely to create value. Finally, we present the *adjusted present value* (APV) method, a variation of the DCF approach. OS Distributors is again used to illustrate this method, this time as a *leveraged buyout* (LBO) target, meaning that the firm's assets will be financed with an unusually high proportion of debt. After reading this chapter, you should understand the following:

- The alternative methods used to value businesses and how to apply them in practice to estimate the value of a company
- Why some companies acquire other firms
- How to value a potential acquisition
- Why a high proportion of acquisitions usually fail to deliver value to the shareholders of the acquiring firm
- Leveraged buyout deals and how they are put together

ALTERNATIVE VALUATION METHODS

Suppose the asking price of a 2,000-square-foot house you wish to buy is $220,000. You want to find out whether $220,000 is a fair price for this property. There are two basic ways to estimate the value of the house. First, you can find the selling price of a *similar* house. A real estate agent tells you that a 1,500-square-foot house on the same street sold for $150,000 last week. What can you conclude? The comparable house was sold for $100 per square foot ($150,000 divided by 1,500 square feet). Applying that rate to the house you want to buy gives a value of $200,000 (2,000 square feet times $100 per square foot). You have just estimated the value of the house using a method called **valuation by comparables**. The reason the estimated value ($200,000) is not the *same* as the asking price ($220,000) is that the comparable house is not *identical* to the one on sale (it is clearly not possible to find an identical house in the exact same location). We can assume that the seller is asking more than $200,000 because he believes that his house is slightly more attractive than the comparable house. The same procedure we used to value a house can be used to value a company by comparing it to similar firms in its sector.

The second approach to estimating the value of the house is to determine its rental value. The real estate agent says that you could expect an annual net rental income of $21,000 for the house. This amount needs to be compared with what you could earn on your savings if you did not buy the house. An investment in long-term, high-grade corporate bonds, which you consider as risky as owning this particular house, is currently offering a 10 percent annual return. How much should you pay for the house to earn the same 10 percent return based on a $21,000 annual rental income? The answer is $210,000 (because an annual rate of 10 percent applied to $210,000 yields a perpetual annual income of $21,000). You have just estimated the value of the house using the **discounted cash flow (DCF) valuation** method. According to the DCF valuation, the asking price of the house ($220,000) is higher than its estimated DCF value ($210,000).

Recall that the valuation by comparables produced an estimated value of $200,000. Different valuation methods usually lead to different estimations, but the differences should not be too large. If different methods produce a wide spread in estimated values (say, more than 10 percent), the validity of the assumptions underlying the alternative methods and the reliability of the data used in the valuation process should be checked. As pointed out earlier, the other house on the street should be as similar as possible to the one you want to buy. With the DCF method, the annual net rental income should remain the same in the future, and the 10 percent return on long-term high-grade corporate bonds should be a good substitute for your required return on the rented house (these two investments should have similar risk characteristics). Poorly estimated input data will lead to unreliable estimated values.

To conclude, what should you offer for the house? An offer between $200,000 and $210,000 would be reasonable, based on your estimates. A higher offer would exceed your estimated values and produce an investment with a negative *net present value* (NPV), that is, an investment whose price is higher than its estimated value. Of course, it would be best to buy the house at the lowest possible price. But if the real estate market is reasonably efficient, it has few real bargains to offer.

Although valuation by comparables and DCF valuation are the most common approaches to valuing a business, they are not the only methods. Two other possible estimated values are the **liquidation value** and the **replacement value** of a firm's assets. The liquidation value of a firm's assets is the amount of cash you would receive if you sold separately the various items that make up the firm's assets (its trade receivables, inventories, equipment, land, and buildings). The replacement value of a firm's assets is what it would cost today to replace these assets with similar ones to start a new business with the same earning power as the one you wish to purchase. Clearly, the liquidation value of a business is the *minimum* price you would expect to pay for its assets. If you could buy the assets for less than their liquidation value and resell them immediately at that value, you would earn a sure profit, a situation unlikely to occur in a properly functioning market. Although the replacement value of a *tangible* asset, such as a building, is the *maximum* price you would pay for it – you would not pay more for a building than what it would cost to build a similar one – you may be ready to offer a higher price for a business if it has some *intangible* assets that are valuable to you and that cannot be replaced, such as patents or trademarks.

VALUING A FIRM'S EQUITY USING COMPARABLE FIRMS

OS Distributors is an unlisted, privately owned firm whose financial performance is analyzed in Chapters 4 to 6. The balance sheets of OS Distributors, a nationwide distributor of office equipment and supplies, are reported in Exhibit 14.1 at the end of Year –2, Year –1, and Year 0 (two years ago, one year ago, and this year). Its income

EXHIBIT 14.1	OS DISTRIBUTORS' BALANCE SHEETS.

FIGURES IN MILLIONS

	December 31, Year −2 (Two years ago)	December 31, Year −1 (One year ago)	December 31, Year 0 (This year)
Assets			
• **Current assets**			
Cash[1]	$ 6.0	$ 12.0	$ 8.0
Accounts receivable	44.0	48.0	56.0
Inventories	52.0	57.0	72.0
Prepaid expenses[2]	2.0	2.0	1.0
Total current assets	104.0	119.0	137.0
• **Noncurrent assets**			
Financial assets and intangibles	0.0	0.0	0.0
Property, plant, and equipment			
Gross value[3]	$90.0	$90.0	$93.0
less accumulated depreciation	(34.0)　56.0	(39.0)　51.0	(40.0)　53.0
Total noncurrent assets	56.0	51.0	53.0
Total assets	**$160.0**	**$170.0**	**$190.0**
Liabilities and owners' equity			
• **Current liabilities**			
Short-term debt	$ 15.0	$ 22.0	$ 23.0
Owed to banks	$ 7.0	$14.0	$15.0
Current portion of long-term debt	8.0	8.0	8.0
Accounts payable	37.0	40.0	48.0
Accrued expenses[4]	2.0	4.0	4.0
Total current liabilities	54.0	66.0	75.0
• **Noncurrent liabilities**			
Long-term debt[5]	42.0	34.0	38.0
Total noncurrent liabilities	42.0	34.0	38.0
• Owners' equity[6]	64.0	70.0	77.0
Total liabilities and owners' equity	**$160.0**	**$170.0**	**$190.0**

[1] Consists of cash in hand and checking accounts held to facilitate operating activities on which the firm earns no interest.

[2] Prepaid expenses is rent paid in advance (when recognized in the income statement, rent is included in selling, general, and administrative expenses).

[3] In Year −1, there was no disposal of existing fixed assets or acquisition of new fixed assets. However, during Year 0, a warehouse was enlarged at a cost of $12 million and existing fixed assets, bought for $9 million in the past, were sold at their net book value of $2 million.

[4] Accrued expenses consist of wages and taxes payable.

[5] Long-term debt is repaid at the rate of $8 million per year. No new long-term debt was incurred during Year −1, but during Year 0, a mortgage loan was obtained from the bank to finance the extension of a warehouse (see note 3).

[6] During the three years, no new shares were issued and none was repurchased.

statements for the same years are presented in Exhibit 14.2. We want to estimate the equity value of OS Distributors in January of Year 1 (which we assume to be the same as at the end of December of Year 0).

The balance sheet at the end of Year 0 indicates that the company's accounting, or book, value of equity is $77 million. This value, recorded as "owners' equity" at the bottom of the balance sheet, measures the *net* cumulative amount of equity capital the firm's shareholders have invested in the company since it was first established. It is a measure of the aggregate amount of net equity capital injected into the firm over time, up to the date of the balance sheet. It is *not* a measure of what shareholders would expect to receive from the sale of their shares. Neither is it a measure of what the firm's equity would be worth if it were listed on a stock market.

The firm has a recent record of steadily increasing profits and dividend payments, and it is likely this trend will continue in the future. Thus, the *market value* of OS Distributors' equity, which is the price it would sell for, should be higher than its book value of $77 million. Because the ownership of a share in a firm's equity entitles the shareholder to receive *future* dividend payments as well as a share of any *future* appreciation in the firm's value, *the equity value that matters to investors is the market value, not the book value*. The book value of equity, which reflects *past* earnings performance and *past* dividend distributions, is relevant only to the extent that it provides some useful information about the *firm's future* performance.

| **EXHIBIT 14.2** | **OS DISTRIBUTORS' INCOME STATEMENTS.** |

FIGURES IN MILLIONS

	Year −2	Year −1	Year 0
• Net sales	$390.0	$420.0	$480.0
Cost of goods sold	328.0	353.0	400.0
• Gross profit	62.0	67.0	80.0
Selling, general, and administrative expenses	39.8	43.7	48.0
Depreciation expense	5.0	5.0	8.0
• Operating profit	17.2	18.3	24.0
Special items	0.0	0.0	0.0
• Earnings before interest and tax (EBIT)	17.2	18.3	24.0
Net interest expense[1]	5.5	5.0	7.0
• Earnings before tax (EBT)	11.7	13.3	17.0
Income tax expense	4.7	5.3	6.8
• Earnings after tax (EAT)	$7.0	$8.0	$10.2
Dividends	$2.0	$2.0	$3.2
Addition to retained earnings	$5.0	$6.0	$7.0

[1] There is no interest income, so net interest expense is equal to interest expense.

DIRECT ESTIMATION OF A FIRM'S EQUITY VALUE BASED ON THE EQUITY VALUE OF COMPARABLE FIRMS[1]

What would the value of OS Distributors' equity be if the firm were listed on a stock market? One way to estimate this value is to use data from comparable firms whose shares are listed on a stock exchange. The first step is to identify these companies. One of these companies is General Equipment and Supplies (GES). GES is also a distributor of office equipment and supplies. It is larger than OS Distributors but is similar in asset and cost structures. (If we could not find a firm similar enough to OS Distributors, we could compare OS Distributors to the wholesale merchandise sector.)

Exhibit 14.3 shows comparable accounting and financial market data for the two companies. Items 1 to 8 are from the companies' financial statements. Items 9 and 10 correspond to items 7 and 3 restated on a per share basis. Item 11 is the market price of a share in January of Year 1, which is available only for GES.

Using this information, we can calculate the following two ratios for GES (these are items 14 and 15 in Exhibit 14.3):

$$\text{Price-to-earnings ratio} = \frac{\text{Share price}}{\text{Earnings per share}} = \frac{\$20}{\$0.8} = 25$$

$$\text{Price-to-book ratio} = \frac{\text{Share price}}{\text{Book value per share}} = \frac{\$20}{\$5.88} = 3.40$$

These two ratios depend on GES's share price, which is determined by the market. This is why these ratios are also referred to as **market multiples** or **equity multiples**. The **price-to-earnings ratio (PER or P/E ratio)** of 25 times is also called GES's **earnings multiple**. It indicates that GES's shares were trading in January of Year 1 at a price equal to 25 times the firm's most recent **earnings per share (EPS)** (25 times $0.80 equals $20). The **price-to-book ratio (PBR or P/B ratio)** of 3.40 is also called GES's **book-value multiple**. It indicates that GES's shares were trading in January of Year 1 at a price equal to 3.40 times GES's most recent book value per share (3.40 times $5.88 equals $20).

Could we construct another multiple by taking, for example, the ratio of share price to earnings before interest and tax (EBIT) per share? Would this make sense? Not really, because this ratio would relate only to the firm's operational contribution to its share price (recall that EBIT is a measure of earnings from operations) when we know that share price is also affected by nonoperational decisions, such as financing decisions. Note that the two multiples discussed here are consistent because they are defined as the ratio of share price to an accounting number that incorporates all the firm's decisions that affect its share price, either earnings after tax (EAT) per share (EAT is net profit to equity holders) or book value of equity per share.

These market multiples are called **historical**, or **trailing**, **multiples**. They are calculated using *past* earnings and book values. If we had a forecast of the earnings or book value for the *next* period, we could have calculated **expected**, or **prospective**, **multiples**.

[1] We can also get a direct estimation of the discounted cash flow value of a firm's equity by discounting its **cash flow to equity holders** at the cost of equity. The cash-flow-to-equity holders discount model is discussed in detail in Chapter 10. It is also reported in the summary of the valuation techniques shown in Exhibit 14.13. We do not apply this technique in this chapter because it is not usually used to value an acquisition, particularly when the buyer wishes to value the target's assets under alternative managerial assumptions.

Exhibit 14.3	Accounting and Market-Based Data for OS Distributors and GES, a Comparable Firm.

	GES	OS Distributors
Accounting data Year 0		
Balance sheet data		
1. Cash	$70 million	$8 million
2. Debt	$430 million	$61 million
3. Book value of equity	$294 million	$77 million
4. Number of shares outstanding	50 million shares	10 million shares
Income statement data		
5. EBIT[1]	$102 million	$24 million
6. Depreciation expense	$33 million	$8 million
7. EAT[2]	$40 million	$10.2 million
8. EBITDA[3] = EBIT + Depreciation expense	$135 million	$32 million
On a per-share basis		
9. Earnings per share (EPS) = [(7)/(4)]	$0.80	$1.02
10. Book value of equity per share = [(3)/(4)]	$5.88	$7.70
Market-based data (January of Year 1)		
11. Share price	$20	not available
12. Market capitalization[4] = [(11) × (4)]	$1,000 million	not available
13. Enterprise value (EV) = [(12) + (2) − (1)]	$1,360 million	not available
Multiples		
14. Price-to-earnings ratio (PER) = [(11)/(9)]	25.00	not available
15. Price-to-book ratio (PBR) = [(11)/(10)]	3.40	not available
16. EV to-EBITDA ratio = [(13)/(8)]	10.10	not available

[1] EBIT = Earnings before interest and tax.
[2] EAT = Earnings after tax (same as net income).
[3] EBITDA is an approximation of the firm's cash flow from assets (see Chapter 4).
[4] Market capitalization is the total market value of a company's equity at a given date; it is equal to its share price on that day multiplied by the total number of shares the company has issued.

We can now estimate the equity value of OS Distributors based on the comparable market multiples of GES. According to this approach, comparable *firms should trade at the same market multiples* (historical or expected). In other words, if OS Distributors is similar to GES, then GES's market multiples can be used to estimate the value that OS Distributors' equity would have if it were listed on a stock market.[2]

[2] No two firms are exactly the same. We know that GES is significantly larger than OS Distributors. Furthermore, GES is a listed company known to the market, whereas OS Distributors is not. This means that OS Distributors' (unobservable) multiples would most likely not be identical to those of GES. Applying GES multiples to OS Distributors' earnings and book value figures provides approximate values.

This is the same procedure we used to estimate the value of the house in the previous section using the price per square foot of the comparable house. For OS Distributors (OSD), we have the following two estimates of equity value:

$$\text{Estimated equity value of OSD} = [\text{OSD's EAT}] \times [\text{GES's PER}]$$
$$= [\$10.2 \text{ million}] \times [25]$$
$$= \$255 \text{ million}$$

$$\text{Estimated equity value of OSD} = [\text{OSD's Book value}] \times [\text{GES's PBR}]$$
$$= [\$77 \text{ million}] \times [3.40]$$
$$= \$262 \text{ million}$$

These two estimates of OS Distributors' equity value are based on GES's historical market multiples. The highest is $262 million and the lowest $255 million. As pointed out earlier, different valuation approaches usually produce different estimated values. Valuation is not a precise exercise, and as long as the spread is within a reasonable range, you should not be concerned. The highest estimated value for OS Distributors ($262 million) is 2.8 percent higher than the lowest estimated value ($255 million), a relatively narrow spread.

Is one multiple more appropriate than the other? Some analysts recommend the use of a particular multiple to value certain types of businesses, suggesting, for example, earnings multiples for industrial companies and book-value multiples for financial services firms, such as banks and insurance companies.[3]

Which one of these two estimated values should we take for OS Distributors' equity? We will answer this question after we estimate the equity value of OS Distributors using two other valuation methods.

INDIRECT ESTIMATION OF A FIRM'S EQUITY VALUE BASED ON THE ENTERPRISE VALUE OF COMPARABLE FIRMS

In the previous section, we presented two *direct* estimates of a firm's equity value based on two different equity multiples of a comparable firm. There is an alternative, *indirect* method to estimate a firm's equity value: we first get an estimate of the value of the firm's *assets* from which we deduct the value of the firm's *debt* to obtain an indirect value of the firm's *equity*. We first illustrate this method using the data from OS Distributors and GES, its comparable firm, in Exhibit 14.3. We then explain the logic of the indirect method and its advantages over the direct approach.

The first step is to estimate the value of the **business assets** of the comparable firm, called **enterprise value (EV)**. This is the value of the firm's invested capital *excluding* cash and other financial assets the firm may hold. A firm's invested capital is the sum of its fixed assets, working capital requirement, and cash (see Chapter 4). Equation 14.1 below and Exhibit 14.4 show how to calculate a firm's enterprise value:

Enterprise value (EV) = Equity value + Debt − Cash and other financial assets (14.1)

In the case of GES, equity value (also called **market capitalization**) is $1,000 million (item 12 in Exhibit 14.3), debt is $430 million (item 2 in Exhibit 14.3), and cash is $70 million (item 1 in Exhibit 14.3). Using equation 14.1, we find an enterprise value of $1,360 million for GES (item 13 in Exhibit 14.3).

---

[3] The factors that determine the price-to-earnings ratio are presented in Chapter 10 and those that affect the price-to-book ratio can be found in Chapter 18 (see Appendix 18.2).

EXHIBIT 14.4	GES's ENTERPRISE VALUE BASED ON DATA IN EXHIBIT 14.3.

GES MARKET VALUE BALANCE SHEET

Cash[1] $70 million	**Debt**[2] $430 million
Enterprise value[4] $1,360 million	**Equity value**[3] $1,000 million

[1] The only financial asset GES has is cash: see item 1 in Exhibit 14.3.
[2] Interest-bearing debt has a market value equal to its book value. See item 2 in Exhibit 14.3 and footnote 9.
[3] Equity value is the market capitalization of GES: see item 12 in Exhibit 14.3.
[4] Enterprise value is the value of invested capital *excluding* cash and other financial assets. We can write:
Enterprise value – Equity value + Debt – Cash = $1,360 million.

The second step is to calculate GES's **earnings before interest, tax, depreciation, and amortization (EBITDA)**. EBITDA is equal to EBIT plus depreciation and amortization expenses (see Chapter 4). In the case of GES, there is no amortization, and its EBITDA of $135 million is equal to EBIT plus depreciation expense (item 8 in Exhibit 14.3).

The third step is to calculate GES's enterprise value-to-EBITDA ratio, also called the **EBITDA multiple**:

$$\text{EBITDA multiple} = \frac{EV}{EBITDA} = \frac{\$1,360 \text{ million}}{\$135 \text{ million}} = 10.1$$

The fourth step is to apply this EBITDA multiple to the EBITDA of OS Distributors ($32 million; item 8 in Exhibit 14.3) to get an estimate of the enterprise value of OS Distributors (OSD):

Enterprise value of OSD = [OSD's EBITDA] × [GES's EBITDA multiple]
= [$32 million] × [10.1] = $323 million

The final step is to add cash and other financial assets to this enterprise value and deduct debt to obtain an *indirect* estimate of the firm's equity value:

Equity value = Enterprise value + Cash and other financial assets − Debt   (14.2)

Applying the above to the case of OS Distributors (OSD), we get the following (the data are from Exhibit 14.3):

Equity value of OSD = $323 million + $8 million − $61 million
= $270 million

This *indirect* estimate of OS Distributors' equity value is higher than those obtained with the direct method but still within an acceptable range. It is about 6 percent higher than the lowest of the two direct equity values we found earlier ($255 million, based on the book-value multiple of GES).

What are the advantages of using the EV/EBITDA ratio, over an equity multiple such as the P/E ratio? Suppose you want to compare the values of a number of telecom companies that have *different* debt ratios and *different* effective tax rates. In this case, the P/E ratio approach may not provide a good estimate of equity value because that ratio assumes the firms have similar debt ratios and tax rates (recall that earnings in the P/E ratio are measured *after* interest payments and taxes). The EV/EBITDA ratio, however, ignores debt and tax rates (because EBITDA is measured *before* interest and tax payments) and thus provides a more reliable estimate.

VALUING A FIRM'S BUSINESS ASSETS AND EQUITY USING THE DISCOUNTED CASH FLOW (DCF) METHOD

According to the discounted cash flow (DCF) method, *the value of a firm's business assets (which is its enterprise value) is determined by the capacity of those assets to generate future **free cash flows***. When a buyer purchases a firm's business assets, he acquires the entire stream of free cash flows these assets are *expected* to produce in the future. In other words, owning a firm's business assets is the same as owning the entire stream of free cash flows those assets will generate in the *future*. How are these free cash flows estimated and how are they valued?

We have shown in Chapter 4 that free cash flows (FCF) are estimated as follows (see equation 4.15 in Chapter 4):

$$FCF = EBIT(1 - T_C) + \text{Depreciation expense} - \Delta WCR - \text{Net capital expenditure} \tag{14.3}$$

where EBIT are the firm's earnings before interest and tax, T_C is its corporate tax rate, ΔWCR is the *change* in working capital requirement (see equation 4.7 in Chapter 4), and **net capital expenditure** is the firm's capital expenditure net of any asset sales. What is the present value of these future free cash flows?

We have shown in Chapter 10 that the present value of a stream of free cash flows is obtained by discounting these cash flows at the **weighted average cost of capital (WACC)**. This present value is the DCF value of the firm's business assets, which is the same as its enterprise value:

$$\text{DCF value of business assets} = \text{Enterprise Value (EV)}$$

$$= \frac{FCF_1}{1 + WACC} + \frac{FCF_2}{(1 + WACC)^2} + \dots + \frac{FCF_t}{(1 + WACC)^t} + \dots \tag{14.4a}$$

The estimation of the WACC is discussed in detail in Chapter 12; it is given by the equation below in which k_D is the estimated cost of debt and k_E is the estimated cost of equity:

$$WACC = [k_D \times (1 - T_C) \times \% \text{ debt financing}] + [k_E \times \% \text{ of equity financing}] \tag{14.5}$$

Note that the stream of cash flows in equation 14.4a goes on forever because the firm is assumed to operate as a **going concern**, meaning that it has no intention to stop operating in the future. This assumption raises the question of how many years of future cash flows should we estimate?

Typically, the length of the forecasting period is five to ten years, beyond which we assume that the cash flows will grow forever at a relatively low constant rate 'g' equal to that of the long-term growth rate of the entire economy (we show later how to estimate this rate). If the firm's sales are currently growing at a relatively high rate that is expected to last a few years, the forecasting period can be extended to ten years, otherwise a five-year forecasting period is usually adopted. In this case, we need to forecast free cash flows up to year five and then estimate the value of the firm's assets at the end of year five, called the **terminal value (TV)**. The terminal value usually assumes that cash flows will grow forever at the constant rate 'g'.

With a five-year forecasting period, the firm's enterprise value (EV) can thus be written as follows:

$$EV = \frac{FCF_1}{1 + WACC} + \frac{FCF_2}{(1 + WACC)^2} + \cdots + \frac{FCF_5 + TV_5}{(1 + WACC)^5} \qquad (14.4b)$$

where TV_5 is the terminal value at the end of year five. It is the present value of a perpetual cash-flow stream beginning at the end of year six and growing forever at the rate 'g' (see equation 2.9 in Chapter 2):

$$TV_5 = \frac{FCF_6}{WACC - g} \qquad (14.6)$$

We summarize below the six steps required to estimate a firm's enterprise value and equity value. In the next section we apply this valuation approach to estimate the enterprise and equity values of OS Distributors.

Step 1	Determine the length (T) of the forecasting period
Step 2	Estimate the stream of free cash flows (FCF) up to year (T+1) using equation 14.3 (you need to estimate FCF_{t+1} in order to get the terminal value in step 4)
Step 3	Estimate the weighted average cost of capital (WACC) using equation 14.5
Step 4	Estimate the terminal value of the firm's business assets (TV_T) at the end of year T using equation 14.6
Step 5	Calculate the firm's enterprise value (EV) by discounting its free cash-flow stream at the WACC using equation 14.4b
Step 6	Calculate the firm's equity value using equation 14.2

ESTIMATION OF OS DISTRIBUTORS' ENTERPRISE AND EQUITY VALUES

Now that we have reviewed the various steps required to estimate the DCF value of a firm's business assets and equity, we can turn to the valuation of OS Distributors on December 31, Year 0, which is the same as in January 1, Year 1. In this section, we assume that OS Distributors stays **as is**, meaning that its operating efficiency remains the same as in Year 0, the most recent year for which data are available.

In other words, we estimate the firm's **stand-alone value**. In the following sections we will assume that the firm is managed differently and re-estimate its value based on these new assumptions and compare these alternative values to OS Distributors' stand-alone value.

As you can imagine, the application of DCF models to the valuation of a firm's business assets, more specifically to the valuation of the stream of cash flows expected from these assets, requires numerous and repetitive computations. Using a spreadsheet to do these computations can save time and, as we will see later in the chapter, can allow for an easy analysis of the sensitivity of the DCF value to changes in the valuation inputs. For these reasons, the exhibits illustrating the valuation examples in the rest of the chapter will be shown as spreadsheets.

STEP 1: DETERMINATION OF THE LENGTH OF THE FORECASTING PERIOD

We do not expect OS Distributors to grow at a higher than average rate beyond the next five years. For this reason we develop a forecast of that firm's cash flows during the six-year period from Year 1 to Year 6. As mentioned earlier, the sixth year is needed to estimate the firm's terminal value at the end of Year 5 based on equation 14.6.

STEP 2: ESTIMATION OF THE FREE CASH FLOW FROM BUSINESS ASSETS

Our forecast of the free cash flows that OS Distributors' business assets are expected to generate from Year 1 to Year 6 is shown in Exhibit 14.5.

Before we show how to generate these forecasts, we review OS Distributors' past performance. The firm's historical efficiency ratios (from Year –2 to Year 0) are summarized in rows 4 through 7. Sales grew by 7.7 percent during Year –1 and by 14.3 percent during Year 0. Operating expenses, expressed as a percentage of sales, declined during the period, with the cost of goods sold (COGS) decreasing from 84.1 percent of sales in Year –2 to 83.33 percent of sales in Year 0. Similarly, selling, general, and administrative expenses (SG&A) decreased from 10.21 percent of sales to 10 percent of sales during the period. The efficiency with which the firm managed its operating cycle, measured by the ratio of working capital requirement (WCR) to sales, however, deteriorated. During Year –2, OS Distributors used $15.13 of working capital to generate $100 of sales. Two years later, that figure had risen to $16.04.

We now examine the logic behind our forecasting method with particular attention to the first year's forecast (Year 1). Row 9 gives the annual sales forecast based on the growth rates assumed in row 4. Note that we assume the growth rate will decline steadily, from its peak value of 14.3 percent achieved in Year 0 to a terminal rate of 3 percent beyond Year 5. In other words, *after* Year 5, sales are assumed to grow at a constant rate of 3 percent *forever*. The higher growth rate achieved in Year 0 is caused by particular circumstances that are not expected to occur again. These assumptions about the sales growth rate are critical because the rest of the forecast is based on these assumed growth rates. If they are unrealistic, the estimated DCF value will not be realistic.

What is a realistic assumption about growth rates? Unless you have strong evidence and a high level of confidence that the firm's sales will grow at exceptionally high rates for a number of years, you should, without being overly conservative, assume that the growth rate will eventually drop to its terminal level of *no more than a few percentage points*. Think of it this way: no company can grow forever at a rate

EXHIBIT 14.5 DISCOUNTED CASH FLOW (DCF) VALUATION OF OS DISTRIBUTORS' EQUITY AT THE BEGINNING OF YEAR 1.

FIGURES IN MILLIONS

	A	B	C	D	E	F	G	H	I	J
		Past Performance			Forecast for					
2		Year –2	Year –1	Year 0	Year 1	Year 2	Year 3	Year 4	Year 5	Year 6 and beyond
3										
4	Sales growth rate		7.70%	14.30%	10.00%	8.00%	7.00%	5.00%	4.00%	3.00%
5	COGS[1] in percent of sales	84.10%	84.05%	83.33%	83.33%	83.33%	83.33%	83.33%	83.33%	83.33%
6	SG&A as percent of sale	10.21%	10.40%	10.00%	10.00%	10.00%	10.00%	10.00%	10.00%	10.00%
7	WCR[1] in percent of sales	15.13%	15.00%	16.04%	16.04%	16.04%	16.04%	16.04%	16.04%	16.04%
8	Free cash flow from business assets									
9	Sales	$390.0	$420.0	$480.0	$528.0	$570.2	$610.2	$640.7	$666.3	$686.3
10	less COGS	(328.0)	(353.0)	(400.0)	(440.0)	(475.2)	(508.5)	(533.9)	(555.2)	(571.9)
11	less SG&A	(39.8)	(43.7)	(48.0)	(52.8)	(57.0)	(61.0)	(64.1)	(66.6)	(68.6)
12	less depreciation expense	(5.0)	(5.0)	(8.0)	(8.0)	(8.0)	(7.0)	(6.0)	(6.0)	(6.0)
13	equals EBIT[1]	17.2	18.3	24.0	27.2	30.0	33.7	36.7	38.4	39.8
14	EBIT × (1 – Tax rate of 40%)	10.3	11.0	14.4	16.3	18.0	20.2	22.0	23.1	23.9
15	plus depreciation expense	5.0	5.0	8.0	8.0	8.0	7.0	6.0	6.0	6.0
16	WCR at year-end	59.0	63.0	77.0	84.7	91.5	97.9	102.8	106.9	110.1
17	less change in WCR		(4.0)	(14.0)	(7.7)	(6.8)	(6.4)	(4.9)	(4.1)	(3.2)
18	less net capital expenditure		0.0	(10.0)	(8.0)	(8.0)	(7.0)	(6.0)	(6.0)	(6.0)
19	Equals free cash flow from business assets			$(1.6)	$8.6	$11.2	$13.8	$17.1	$19.0	$20.6
20	Terminal value year-end of Year 5								$412.9	

(Continued)

EXHIBIT 14.5   DISCOUNTED CASH FLOW (DCF) VALUATION OF OS DISTRIBUTORS' EQUITY AT THE BEGINNING OF YEAR 1.   (*Continued*)

FIGURES IN MILLIONS

	A	B	C	D	E	F	G	H	I	J
21	**Beginning Year 1**									
22	WACC[1]	8.00%								
23	**DCF value of business assets (enterprise value)**	$335.1								
24	*plus* cash	$ 8.0								
25	*less* book value of debt	$ 61.0								
26	**equals DCF value of equity**	**$282.1**								

- *Rows 4 to 7, 12, 15, 18 plus cells B22, B24, and B25 are data*
- *Formula in cell C9 is* =B9*(1+C4). *Then copy cell C9 to next cells in row 9*
- *Formula in cell B10 is* =−B5*B9. *Then copy cell B10 to next cells in row 10*
- *Formula in cell B11 is* =−B6*B9. *Then copy cell B11 to next cells in row 11*
- *Formula in cell B13 is* =SUM(B9:B12). *Then copy cell B13 to next cells in row 13*
- *Formula in cell B14 is* =B13*(1−.4). *Then copy cell B14 to next cells in row 14*
- *Formula in cell B16 is* =B7*B9. *Then copy cell B16 to next cells in row 16*
- *Formula in cell C17 is* = −(C16−B16). *Then copy cell C17 to next cells in row 17*
- *Formula in cell D19 is* =D14+D15+D17+D18. *Then copy cell D19 to next cells in row 19*
- *Formula in cell I20 is* =J19/(B22−J4)
- *Formula in cell B23 is* =NPV(B22,E19:I19)+I20/(1+B22)^5
- *Formula in cell B26 is* =D23+D24−D25

[1]COGS = Cost of goods sold; SG&A = Selling, general, and administrative expenses; EBIT = Earnings before interest and expenses; WCR = Working capital requirement; WACC = Weighted average cost of capital.

faster than the entire economy. If it did, it would eventually overtake the economy. The *long-term real* growth rate of developed economies is about 2 to 3 percent. Adding a long-term inflation rate of 2 to 3 percent (a reasonable assumption in most well-developed countries)[4] gives a *long-term nominal* growth rate of 4 to 6 percent. *Assuming a figure significantly higher than 4 to 6 percent for the terminal growth rate of a company would be unrealistic.* Some analysts take the most conservative view and assume a *zero growth rate beyond* the forecasting period. In this case, the cash flows after the forecasting period are assumed to remain the same forever, which, in effect, means that they decline in *real terms* when the expected inflation rate is taken into account. What should you do if you are dealing with the valuation of a company that is expected to sustain an above-average rate of growth beyond the forecasting period? As discussed earlier, you should in this case extend the length of the forecasting period rather than assume a higher terminal growth rate.

After the sales growth rates are estimated, expenses are calculated as a percentage of sales as shown in Exhibit 14.5. These percentages depend on the efficiency with which OS Distributors will manage its operations. Because we are valuing the company "as is," we assume that the operating efficiency ratios are equal to their latest historical values. (Later in this chapter, we revalue OS Distributors under alternative assumptions about its operating efficiency.) Thus, COGS is 83.33 percent of sales, SG&A is 10 percent of sales, and WCR is 16.04 percent of sales from Year 1 to Year 6. Based on these assumptions, the expected free cash flow from OS Distributors' assets in Year 1 can be estimated using equation 14.3.

To estimate EBIT in Year 1, we start with sales of $528 million (row 9) and deduct the COGS (row 10), the SG&A expenses (row 11), and depreciation expense (row 12, assumed to be $8 million, the same as in Year 0). Thus, EBIT is equal to $27.2 million (row 13). EBIT adjusted for taxes is $16.3 million (row 14).[5] We then add back the $8 million of depreciation expense (row 15) and deduct the *change* in WCR (row 17). The $7.7 million growth in WCR in Year 1 is the difference between WCR at the end of Year 1 and WCR at the end of Year 0. The $84.7 million of WCR at the end of Year 1 is obtained by multiplying the sales figure in row 9 by the ratio of WCR to sales in row 7; the $77 million of WCR at the end of Year 0 is computed directly from the balance sheet in Exhibit 14.1. Finally, we deduct the expected net capital expenditure of $8 million for Year 1 (row 18) to get an estimated free cash flow of $8.6 million in Year 1 (row 19).

We assume annual net capital expenditure equal to depreciation expense (compare row 18 with row 12) because we are valuing OS Distributors "as is." Thus, we do not expect any major investment beyond the *maintenance of existing assets*, and we assume that maintenance cost will be exactly the same as the annual depreciation expense. Although we assume depreciation expense in Year 1 and Year 2 is the same as its Year 0 historical value of $8 million, we expect depreciation expense to drop to $7 million in Year 3 and $6 million in Year 4 and remain at that level thereafter. Depreciation expense declines in line with the reduction in sales growth and capital expenditure. It is important to be consistent in our assumptions. If the firm's activities

---

[4] For example, between 1926 and 2017, the Consumer Price Index in the United States increased at an average annual rate of 3 percent.

[5] The corporate tax rate is assumed to be the same as the historical one. Unless you know that the rate is expected to change, taking the historical corporate tax rate is the standard assumption. As pointed out earlier, the tax is calculated on the basis of EBIT because the definition of free cash flows assumes that the firm is all-equity financed. In this case, EBIT is the same as EBT and the tax rate can be applied to EBIT.

slow down, so will its capital expenditure and depreciation expense.[6] Applying the same approach for the next five years yields the stream of free cash flows up to Year 6 shown on row 19.

STEP 3: ESTIMATION OF THE WEIGHTED AVERAGE COST OF CAPITAL

The relevant rate at which to discount the free cash flows from business assets is the WACC in equation 14.5. As indicated in that equation, to calculate the WACC we need the proportions of debt and equity employed to finance the firm's assets as well as the costs of equity and debt. We first estimate these costs and then address the issue of the appropriate proportions of debt and equity we should use to get the WACC of OS Distributors.

ESTIMATED COST OF DEBT

The cost of debt is the after-tax cost of *new* borrowing. As mentioned earlier, the relevant cost of debt must be calculated after tax because interest payments are tax-deductible expenses. Suppose that OS Distributors can borrow at an average cost of 7 percent (see Chapter 12 for details about how to estimate the cost of debt). Given a tax rate of 40 percent, OS Distributors' after-tax cost of debt is thus 4.2 percent $[7\% \times (1 - 40\%)]$.

ESTIMATED COST OF EQUITY

We estimate the cost of equity capital using the **capital asset pricing model (CAPM)** discussed in Chapters 3 and 12. According to the CAPM, the rate of return required by equity investors (which is the same as the firm's cost of equity) is equal to the rate of return they can get from investing in a *riskless* government bond (r_F) plus a risk premium that will compensate them for the risk of holding the firm's shares. That risk premium is estimated by multiplying the firm's **beta coefficient** (β)[7] by the **market risk premium** (which is the risk premium of the entire stock market). We can write:

$$k_E = R_F + (\text{Market risk premium} \times \beta) \qquad (14.7a)$$

To get an estimate of the cost of equity using equation 14.7a,[8] we need the following inputs: (1) the yield on long-term government bonds, which we assume to be 4.7 percent; (2) the market risk premium for which we use the historical average of 5 percent; and (3) OS Distributors' beta coefficient.

---

[6] There are alternative models for estimating future capital expenditure; most of these models relate capital expenditure to sales forecast. A popular one uses historical ratios between annual capital expenditure and previous years' sales and applies the ratio to future annual sales to get the desired estimate.

[7] A company's beta coefficient is a measure of the sensitivity of its stock returns to the overall market movements. By definition, the market has a beta of 1. Companies whose stock returns fluctuate *more* than the overall market movements are riskier than the market and have betas higher than 1. Those with stock returns that fluctuate less than the overall market movements are less risky than the market and have betas that are less than 1 (see Chapters 3 and 12). For example, if a company has a beta of 1.50, it means that, on *average*, when the market rises (drops) by 1 percent, the company's share price increases (decreases) by 1.5 percent.

[8] Equation 14.7a is the same as equation 12.11 in Chapter 12.

Because OS Distributors is not a listed company, we do not have its beta coefficient. However, GES, the comparable firm we used in the section on valuation by comparables, has a beta coefficient of 0.98. We can use this figure for the unobservable beta coefficient of OS Distributors. Applying equation 14.7a with a riskless rate of 4.7 percent, a market risk premium of 5 percent, and a beta of 0.98, we get the following estimate of OS Distributors' cost of equity:

$$\text{Cost of equity } (k_E) = 4.7\% + (5\% \times 0.98) = 4.7\% + 4.9\% = 9.6\% \quad (14.7b)$$

PROPORTIONS OF EQUITY AND DEBT FINANCING

The appropriate proportions of equity and debt financing must be based on the *market values* of equity and debt, not their accounting or book values (see Chapter 12). Unfortunately, we cannot observe the market values of OS Distributors' equity and debt because neither the firm's equity nor its debt is traded on a stock exchange. We have no choice but to resort to the procedure of using the data from GES, the comparable firm whose equity is listed on a stock exchange.

The market value of GES's equity in early January of Year 1 was $1,000 million (GES has 50 million shares with an average price of $20; see Exhibit 14.3). Its balance sheet at the end of Year 0 (not provided here) shows $430 million of total debt.[9] We thus have the following:

$$\text{Proportion of equity} = \frac{\text{Market value of equity}}{\text{Market value of equity} + \text{Value of debt}} \quad (14.8)$$

$$= \frac{\$1,000 \text{ million}}{\$1,000 \text{ million} + \$430 \text{ million}} = \frac{\$1,000 \text{ million}}{\$1,430 \text{ million}} = 70\%$$

and the proportion of debt is 30 percent.

ESTIMATED AVERAGE COST OF CAPITAL (WACC)

We now have all the elements we need to estimate OS Distributors' WACC according to equation 14.5:

$$\text{WACC of OS Distributors} = (4.2\% \times 30\%) + (9.6\% \times 70\%)$$
$$= 7.98\% \text{ rounded up to } 8\%$$

This is the WACC shown in cell B22 in Exhibit 14.5. It is an estimate of the required rate of return on the free cash flows generated by OS Distributors' business assets.

STEP 4: ESTIMATION OF THE TERMINAL VALUE OF BUSINESS ASSETS AT THE END OF YEAR 5

To estimate the terminal value of OS Distributors' business assets at the end of Year 5, we need two pieces of information. First, we need to know the rate at which the free cash flows will grow in perpetuity after Year 5. We argued earlier that we should assume a constant rate of growth that is close to the growth rate of the entire economy.

---

[9] We should estimate GES's debt at its market rather than book value. However, if we assume that the average rate of interest OS Distributors is paying on the funds it has borrowed in the past is close to the current market rate of interest, market and book values are not significantly different. The relationship between the market value of debt and interest rates is presented in Chapter 10.

For OS Distributors, we assume a rate of 3 percent, the same as that of sales.[10] And second, we need the firm's WACC which we estimated at 8 percent in the previous section.

We can then use equation 14.6 to estimate the terminal value of the business assets of OS Distributors at the end of Year 5:[11]

$$TV_{Year\ 5} = \frac{FCF_{Year\ 6}}{WACC - g} = \frac{\$20.645\ million}{8\% - 3\%} = \$412.9\ million$$

With a free cash flow growing in perpetuity at an annual rate of 3 percent and an estimated WACC of 8 percent, the value of OS Distributors' business assets at the end of Year 5 is $412.9 million (cell I20).

STEP 5: ESTIMATION OF THE DCF VALUE OF BUSINESS ASSETS (ENTERPRISE VALUE)

We can now estimate the value of OS Distributors' business assets using the DCF valuation formula 14.4b. For OS Distributors, the cash flows are our forecasts from Year 1 to Year 5, including the terminal value of assets at the end of Year 5 (shown in rows 19 and 20 in Exhibit 14.5). The appropriate discount rate is OS Distributors' WACC of 8 percent. OS Distributors' enterprise value (EV_{OSD}), which is shown in Exhibit 14.5 in cell B23, is thus (dollar figures are in millions):

$$EV_{OSD} = \frac{\$8.6}{(1+0.08)} + \frac{\$11.2}{(1+0.08)^2} + \frac{\$13.8}{(1+0.08)^3} + \frac{\$17.1}{(1+0.08)^4} + \frac{\$19.0}{(1+0.08)^5} + \frac{\$412.9}{(1+0.08)^5}$$

$$= \$7.96 + \$9.60 + \$10.95 + \$12.57 + \$12.93 + \$281.01 = \$335.1$$

Note the magnitude of the terminal value in comparison with the yearly cash flow estimates. Its present value at 8 percent is $281.01 million, which represents 84 percent of the $335.1 million DCF value of OS Distributors' business assets. This high percentage is not unusual, particularly in cases in which the growth rates during the forecasting period are not exceptionally high and are assumed to decline steadily toward their perpetual level. This is why we insist that great care be given to the estimation of the perpetual growth rate beyond the forecasting period.

STEP 6: ESTIMATION OF THE DCF VALUE OF EQUITY

The estimated value of OS Distributors' *equity* is found using equation 14.2. It is equal to its estimated enterprise value ($335.1 million) plus its cash holding of $8 million less the $61 million of debt in Year 0 (the sum of short-term debt and long-term debt in Exhibit 14.1):

DCF value of OS Distributors' equity = $335.1 million + $8 million − $61 million
= $282.1 million

---

[10] If the growth rate in sales is constant and capital expenditure is equal to depreciation expense, then the growth of cash flows is close to the growth in sales (even though not identical because of fixed operating costs). We nevertheless assume that, beyond Year 6, cash flows grow at the same rate as sales.

[11] Recall that we need to estimate the cash-flow stream for six years in order to get an estimate of the terminal value because the latter depends on the estimated cash flow in Year 6, which, in turn, depends on the previous five years' cash flows.

COMPARISON OF DCF VALUATION AND VALUATION BY COMPARABLES

We now have four estimates for the value of OS Distributors' equity. In increasing order, they are as follows: $255 million (based on an earnings multiple of 25), $262 million (based on a book-value multiple of 3.40), $270 million (based on an EBITDA multiple of 10.1), and $282 million (based on the DCF value). The highest estimate ($282 million) is about 10 percent higher than the lowest ($255 million), so the estimated values are within an acceptable range.

We can conclude that a figure in the range of $255 million to $280 million would be a fair estimate of OS Distributors' equity value if the company were listed and traded on a stock exchange. Given that OS Distributors has 10 million shares outstanding (see Exhibit 14.3), these estimates are equivalent to a share price of $25.50 to $28. If you owned OS Distributors and wanted to sell it, you would ask *at least* $280 million. If you were the buyer, you would obviously wish to pay *no more* than $255 million. *The price at which a transaction may take place will be the outcome of a negotiation process. That price may or may not be within the estimated price range.*

ESTIMATING THE ACQUISITION VALUE OF OS DISTRIBUTORS

The DCF equity value of $282 million for OS Distributors is an estimated value of the equity of the firm "as is." It does not take into account any potential improvement in the way the firm is managed. If you acquire OS Distributors and enhance its performance, its value to you is obviously more than $282 million. Suppose a number of improvements can raise OS Distributors' estimated DCF equity value to $340 million. This represents a *potential* value creation of $58 million ($340 million less $282 million). Acquiring the company for less than $340 million is a positive NPV investment, an investment whose price is *lower* than its estimated value. Suppose you end up paying $300 million to acquire OS Distributors. This represents a **takeover premium** of $18 million over its stand-alone value of $282 million ($300 million less $282 million). In this case, the acquisition's NPV is the difference between the potential value creation and the takeover premium:

$$\text{NPV (acquisition)} = \text{Potential value creation} - \text{Takeover premium}$$
$$= \$58 \text{ million} - \$18 \text{ million} = \$40 \text{ million}$$

You must be careful not to give OS Distributors' shareholders most of the future value *you* will create *after* you buy the company (the potential value creation) by paying too high a takeover premium. In general, the higher the potential value creation relative to the takeover premium, the larger the acquisition's NPV.

To estimate the acquisition value of OS Distributors, we must first identify the potential sources of value creation in an acquisition. We then show that when these sources are not present, such as when unrelated businesses are combined in a **conglomerate merger**, an acquisition is not likely to create value. After examining a conglomerate merger, we provide a complete analysis of the estimated acquisition value of OS Distributors.

IDENTIFYING THE POTENTIAL SOURCES OF VALUE CREATION IN AN ACQUISITION

The easiest way to identify potential sources of value creation in an acquisition is to look at how the DCF value is determined. Consider the case of a business expected to generate a perpetual free cash-flow stream growing at a constant rate. The DCF value of its business assets is equal to next year's free cash flow (FCF_1) divided by the difference between the WACC and the growth rate in the cash flows (see equation 2.9 in Chapter 2):

$$\text{DCF value of business assets} = \frac{FCF_1}{\text{WACC} - \text{Growth rate}}$$

To create value, that is, to raise the DCF value of the **target firm's** assets, an acquisition must achieve one of three things, all else being the same:[12]

1. Increase the free cash flows generated by the target firm's business assets
2. Raise the growth rate of the target firm's sales
3. Lower the WACC of the *target* firm

If the acquiring firm is unable to make one or more of the above changes in the target firm, the acquisition should not be carried out. These changes will happen if either or both of the following conditions are met:

1. The target firm is *not* currently managed at (1) its most efficient level (it has excessive costs and inefficient asset usage), (2) its highest growth rate in sales, or (3) its optimal capital structure (it has too little or too much debt financing), *and* the acquiring firm's managers believe they can do a better job of running the target firm. Those conditions are usually referred to as the **inefficient management** explanation of why acquisitions occur. Note that in this case an acquisition does not actually have to take place to enhance value. The target's current managers can, in principle, improve their firm's performance if they have the will and the required skills. This is why managers *are advised to run their firm as if it were a potential target.*
2. Combining the target firm with the acquiring company creates **economies of scale** that lead to cost and market synergies. This is known as the **synergy** explanation of why acquisitions take place. **Cost synergies** can be achieved, for example, in administration, marketing, and distribution if the target firm's costs and investments can be reduced, because these activities can be fully or partly carried out at a *lower* combined cost. Typically, this means eliminating redundancy in management, streamlining management information systems, and reducing sales forces. **Market synergies** can be achieved, for example, by distributing the target firm's products and services through the acquiring company's distribution channels for the purpose of increasing sales.

Together, inefficient management and potential synergy provide the most powerful reasons to justify an acquisition. Other, less convincing reasons include the **undervaluation hypothesis,** according to which the acquiring company has superior skills in finding undervalued target firms that can be bought cheaply, and the **market power hypothesis,** which claims that after an acquisition the acquiring firm has a larger market share that may enable it to raise the price of its products or services and thus increase its cash flow and value (assuming, of course, that the government does not block the merger for anticompetitive reasons). Although these are plausible hypotheses as to why some acquisitions take place, indirect empirical evidence (from US and other stock markets around the world) indicates that they

---

[12] Strictly speaking, an acquisition creates value if the value of the merged firms after the acquisition is higher than the *sum* of their respective values before the merger. Here, the focus is exclusively on the potential value creation the acquirer can achieve by improving the performance of the target firm.

are not the major sources of value creation behind most acquisitions.[13] We now examine the three specific sources of value creation in an acquisition, which we listed earlier.

INCREASING THE FREE CASH FLOWS GENERATED BY THE TARGET FIRM'S ASSETS

A reduction in both the COGS and SG&A expenses per dollar of sales will widen the target firm's operating margin and thus increase its operating profits (EBIT). According to the cash-flow equation 14.3, an increase in EBIT will increase a firm's cash flow. A reduction in tax expenses will have the same effect.

Tax expenses merit a special comment. Suppose the acquiring firm has a pre-tax profit of $100 million and the target firm has a pre-tax loss of $40 million. Their combined profits will be $60 million, and the acquirer will pay less tax after the merger than it would have paid on its pre-merger pre-tax profit of $100 million. However, firms seldom buy each other simply to reduce their tax liabilities, because the tax reduction is usually a one-time gain whose magnitude rarely justifies an acquisition. Furthermore, in most countries, the tax authorities do not allow the reduction in tax liability if the *only* purpose of the acquisition is to reduce taxes; a "business reason" has to support the acquisition.

Another way to increase the cash flows generated by the target firm's assets is to use its assets more efficiently. A more efficient use of assets will result in higher sales and higher cash flows per dollar of asset employed. A more efficient use of assets can be achieved in several ways. Any overinvestment, particularly in cash and in working capital requirement (WCR), should be rapidly reduced to a level that is justified by the firm's current operations and near-term developments. Any excess cash that cannot be invested in a value-creating project should be returned to shareholders through a **share repurchase program** or a special dividend payment (see Chapter 11). If the firm holds excessive WCR that is not justified by the firm's current and expected level of operations, it should be reduced to its optimal level via faster collection of receivables and higher inventory turnover (see Chapter 5). The same logic applies to long-term assets if they are currently underutilized and have no identifiable use in the near future to support the firm's value-creating activities.

RAISING THE SALES GROWTH RATE

Assuming the target firm is already creating value or will create value under the management of the acquiring firm, then, all other things being equal, faster growth in sales will create additional value. This can be achieved by increasing the volume of goods and services sold by the target firm or by raising their price (without an offsetting reduction in volume) via superior marketing skills and strategies. A more effective advertising campaign, a better mix of products, a wider or different distribution network, a closer relationship with customers, and the development of new markets,

---

[13] If the undervaluation hypothesis were valid, then target firms whose share price rises on the announcement of an acquisition (because the market becomes aware of their undervaluation) should *maintain their higher value if the acquisition fails to take place*. The empirical evidence indicates that the share prices of unsuccessful target firms usually drop back to their pre-announcement level, a behavior that is inconsistent with the undervaluation hypothesis. If the market power hypothesis were valid, then the share prices of *all firms* in a sector should rise on the announcement day of a specific acquisition, because all firms in the sector should benefit from a potential increase in the price of the product or service, not just the merging firms. The empirical evidence indicates that this is generally not the case.

both domestically and abroad, are just a few of the possibilities worth exploring to improve the growth prospects of the target firm.

LOWERING THE COST OF CAPITAL

If the target firm's capital structure is not close to its optimal level (too little or too much borrowing compared with the optimal debt ratio), then changing the firm's capital structure should lower its WACC and raise its value. As shown in Chapter 13, the major advantage of debt financing is that it allows a firm to reduce its taxes (because of the deductibility of interest expenses) and thus enhance its after-tax cash flow and value. But the excessive use of debt will expose the firm to financial distress and possibly bankruptcy, which are costly. Hence, the existence of an optimal capital structure at the point at which the marginal tax advantage of debt financing is exactly offset by the marginal costs of financial distress and bankruptcy. It follows that if the target firm has too little or too much debt in its capital structure, a change in the proportion of debt financing relative to equity will lower its WACC and raise its value.

The target firm's WACC, as well as that of the **bidder** (**bidding company**), will also decline if, after the merger, their costs of equity and debt are lower than before the merger. A merger is unlikely to lead to a reduction in the cost of equity (see later discussion), but it is often argued that if the merged firms are perceived by their creditors to be less likely to fail as a combination than as separate entities (this is usually referred to as the **coinsurance effect**), then their post-merger cost of debt should, in principle, be lower. However, a lower cost of debt should be accompanied by an increase in the cost of equity. Equity is now riskier because shareholders have, in effect, given debt holders a superior guarantee against failure. This increase in the cost of equity should balance the decrease in the cost of debt, leaving the firm's WACC unchanged.

WHY CONGLOMERATE MERGERS ARE UNLIKELY TO CREATE LASTING VALUE THROUGH ACQUISITIONS

A conglomerate merger is a combination of two or more unrelated (or independent) businesses for which no obvious synergy exists. A firm that grows through conglomerate mergers is unlikely to create lasting value for its shareholders because adding an unrelated business to its existing ones will neither raise its cash flows by more than the target's cash flows nor reduce its cost of capital. It may, under certain circumstances, increase the conglomerate's earnings per share (EPS), but the growth in EPS is unlikely to be accompanied by a permanent rise in shareholder value.

ACQUIRING UNRELATED BUSINESSES IS UNLIKELY TO CREATE LASTING VALUE

Suppose a personal computer (PC) firm buys a life insurance company because it believes the merger will provide an opportunity to reduce the business risk of the combined firms via the diversification of their activities. The regular and predictable revenues generated by the life insurance business will smooth out the cyclical revenues from the PC business. The resulting reduction in risk should, in principle, reduce the conglomerate's cost of equity and thus raise the market value of its equity beyond the sum of the market values of the two pre-merger firms' equity.

Although this diversification strategy may make sense from the perspective of the PC company's managers, it is unlikely to generate the anticipated increase in market value. The reason is that *investors can achieve the same diversification themselves by combining shares of the PC and the insurance companies in their personal portfolios*. And one could argue that this **homemade diversification** is superior to that of the PC company's diversification strategy because it is cheaper to implement and allows investors to set their own proportions of holdings. Thus, it is doubtful that investors will be willing to pay a higher price for the diversified firm. As a result, it is unlikely that the financial market will value the combination of the two firms for more than the sum of their pre-merger values.

As pointed out earlier, the only types of business combinations that are likely to create lasting value are those that result in managerial improvements or synergistic gains. An example of such a combination is a **horizontal merger** (two firms in the same sector pooling their resources). Even **vertical mergers** (the integration of, say, a car manufacturer with its major supplier or its major distributor) are not likely to achieve lasting value creation; there is no obvious reason why a vertical merger will result in sales growth or cost reductions in a competitive environment. This explains why *some of the most successful value-creating firms focus their efforts on a single activity for which they have developed over time a unique set of skills and competencies that existing and potential competitors cannot easily imitate. It is these "difficult-to-replicate" skills and competencies that are the sources of a sustained increase in their market values.*

RAISING EARNINGS PER SHARE THROUGH CONGLOMERATE MERGERS IS UNLIKELY TO CREATE LASTING VALUE

Some conglomerates grow rapidly by continually buying firms that have a *lower* price-to-earnings ratio (PER or P/E ratio) than the PER of the conglomerate firm. The premise is that the market will value the combination for more than the sum of the pre-merger firms. Consider the conglomerate merger described in Exhibit 14.6. The most recent figure for the earnings after tax (EAT) of the acquiring firm is $300 million, whereas that of the target firm is $200 million (line 1). The acquiring firm has 150 million shares outstanding and the target firm has 100 million (line 2), so their earnings per share (EPS) are the same and equal to $2 (line 3). The acquirer has a PER of 20, whereas the target has a PER of only 10 (line 4), a reflection of the market expectation of a much higher growth rate for the acquirer than for the target. The corresponding share prices and aggregate equity market values are, respectively, $40 and $6 billion for the acquirer and $20 and $2 billion for the target firm (lines 5 and 6).

Suppose the acquirer can buy the target firm at its prevailing market value of $2 billion and pay for the purchase by offering its own shares (worth $40 each) in exchange for those of the target firm (worth $20 each). The acquirer will have to issue 50 million shares ($2 billion divided by $40) to raise $2 billion. When the acquisition is complete, the shares of the target firm will no longer exist and the acquirer will have 200 million shares, the original 150 million plus the additional 50 million issued to pay for the acquisition.

If the acquisition is a simple combination that does not create any value, that is, if the merger is "value neutral," then the merged firms must have (1) an aggregate market value of $8 billion, the sum of the acquiring and target firms' pre-merger values; (2) a total profit of $500 million, the sum of the acquiring and target firms' pre-merger profits; and (3) a price per share of $40, the same price the acquirer had before the merger.

EXHIBIT 14.6	DATA FOR A CONGLOMERATE MERGER BASED ON RAISING EPS.	

	The Acquiring Firm	The Target Firm
1. Earnings after tax	$300 million	$200 million
2. Number of shares	150 million	100 million
3. Earnings per share (EPS) = (1)/(2)	$2.00	$2.00
4. Price-to-earnings ratio (PER)	20	10
5. Share price = (3) × (4)	$40	$20
6. Total value = (2) × (5)	$6,000 million	$2,000 million

	Value of the merged firms if the market assigns the combination a P/E that:	
	Is value neutral	Exceeds value neutrality
1. Earnings after tax	$500 million	$500 million
2. Number of shares	200 million	200 million
3. Earnings per share (EPS) = (1)/(2)	$2.50	$2.50
4. Price-to-earnings ratio (PER)	16	18
5. Share price = (3) × (4)	$40	$45
6. Total value = (2) × (5)	$8,000 million	$9,000 million

What is the acquirer's EPS after the acquisition is completed? With 200 million shares and $500 million of total profit, the resulting EPS is $2.50 ($500 million divided by 200 million shares). The acquirer has increased its EPS from a pre-merger value of $2 to a post-merger value of $2.50, a 25 percent rise. Not bad for a value neutral acquisition; but do not be fooled. This higher EPS does not increase the value of the combined firms to more than $8 billion because the market assigns an earnings multiple (P/E ratio) of 16 that leaves the share price unchanged ($2.50 times 16 equals $40).

What if the market is fooled and assigns an earnings multiple exceeding 16? In this case, the acquirer's share price will rise to more than $40. If, for example, the post-merger market multiple is 18, then the post-merger share price would be $45 ($2.50 multiplied by 18). The acquirer could then use its higher share price to make another acquisition and another and another until the bubble bursts. This phenomenon happened in the US market in the 1960s.

THE ACQUISITION VALUE OF OS DISTRIBUTORS' EQUITY

We now return to DCF valuation. The greatest advantage of the DCF valuation approach over the comparables, or multiples, method is its ability to provide an estimate of the potential value that a particular managerial action can create. The potential value created by increasing OS Distributors' sales, reducing its operating expenses per dollar of sales, managing its WCR more tightly, or lowering its average cost of capital, can be determined by modifying the original forecasts in Exhibit 14.5

and recalculating the DCF value of OS Distributors' equity. First, however, it must be determined that OS Distributors' current performance can be improved. If there is indeed room for improvement, a credible **restructuring plan** should be formulated. In a horizontal merger, the obvious starting point to determine whether the performance of a target company can be improved is to compare it with that of the acquirer. Clearly, if the target underperforms relative to the acquirer, there are ways to get its performance up to the level of the acquiring firm. In addition, the performance of the target can be improved beyond just better management if room exists for synergistic gains after the acquisition is completed.

Let's assume that your company, which is in the same business as OS Distributors, is considering acquiring it. After a careful analysis of OS Distributors' current performance and its comparison with that of your company, you conclude that a combination of better management and the realization of significant economies of scale in marketing, distribution, and administration, can produce the following improvements in the future performance of OS Distributors (without producing any significant changes in the performance of your firm):

1. A reduction of its COGS by a full percentage point (from 83.33 percent of sales to 82.33 percent of sales)
2. A reduction of its SG&A expenses, essentially overhead expenses, by half a percentage point (from 10 percent of sales to 9.5 percent of sales)
3. A decrease of its WCR from its current level of 16.04 percent of sales to 13 percent of sales
4. An increase in its growth rates in sales from Year 1 to Year 5 by 2 percentage points above the figures shown in line 4 in Exhibit 14.5, with no increase in the growth rate after Year 5.

How much are these changes in future performance worth today to your firm? If you can answer this question, you will know how much your company should pay to acquire OS Distributors and still have a positive NPV acquisition. The analysis required to answer this question is shown in Exhibits 14.7 and 14.8. The first exhibit shows the separate effects of a reduction in the COGS, SG&A, and WCR. The second shows the effect of a higher growth rate in sales and the cumulative effect of improved operational efficiency and faster sales growth. The DCF values are all calculated using the same spreadsheet as in Exhibit 14.5 with a WACC of 8 percent, the same as the one used to value OS Distributors' equity "as is."

The effect of the improved performance on value creation is summarized in Exhibit 14.9. The reduction in the COGS and overhead is worth $106 million ($71 million plus $35 million); the reduction of WCR relative to sales is worth $27 million; and the faster growth in sales is worth $30 million. The four separate improvements add to a potential value creation of $163 million. But taken *together*, they produce a potential aggregate value of $173 million (see Exhibit 14.9), which represents an increase of 61 percent over the DCF value of OS Distributors "as is." The extra $10 million (the difference between $173 million and $163 million) is generated by the *interaction* of more efficient operating performance on faster growth.

Depending on your confidence in achieving one or more of the changes described above, the target value of OS Distributors' equity could be as high as $455 million ($282 million "as is" plus $173 million of potential value creation). We did not consider the possibility of a reduction in OS Distributors' cost of capital if it is taken over. If its WACC can be lowered below 8 percent, then all the potential value creations mentioned above will be higher.

EXHIBIT 14.7	EFFECT OF IMPROVED OPERATIONAL EFFICIENCY ON THE ESTIMATED VALUE OF OS DISTRIBUTORS' EQUITY AT THE BEGINNING OF YEAR 1.

FIGURES IN MILLIONS

	Beginning	Forecast for					
	Year 1	Year 1	Year 2	Year 3	Year 4	Year 5	Year 6 beyond
Value of OS Distributors' Equity As Is (see Exhibit 14.5)							
Growth in sales		10%	8%	7%	5%	4%	3%
COGS[1] as % of sales		83.33%	83.33%	83.33%	83.33%	83.33%	
SG&A[1] as % of sales		10.00%	10.00%	10.00%	10.00%	10.00%	
WCR[1] as % of sales		16.04%	16.04%	16.04%	16.04%	16.04%	
Free cash flow from business assets		$8.6	$11.2	$13.8	$17.1	$ 19.0	
Terminal value of assets at the end of Year 5[2]						$412.9	
DCF value of business assets at 8%	$335						
plus cash less debt[3]	*$(53)*						
DCF value of equity	$282						
Effect of a Reduction in the Cost of Goods Sold							
COGS[1] as % of sales		82.33%	82.33%	82.33%	82.33%	82.33%	
Free cash flow from business assets		$11.8	$14.7	$17.5	$21.0	$ 23.0	
Terminal value of assets at the end of Year 5[2]						$495.5	
DCF value of business assets at 8%	$406						
plus cash less debt[3]	*$(53)*						
DCF value of equity	$353						
Potential value creation[4]	$71						
Effect of a Reduction in Selling, General, and Administrative Expenses							
SG&A[1] as % of sales		9.50%	9.50%	9.50%	9.50%	9.50%	
Free cash flow from business assets		$10.2	$13.0	$15.7	$19.1	$ 21.0	
Terminal value of assets at the end of Year 5[2]						$454.4	
DCF value of business assets at 8%	$370						
plus cash less debt[3]	*$(53)*						
DCF value of equity	$317						
Potential value creation[4]	$35						
Effect of a Decrease in the Ratio Working Capital Requirement to Sales							
WCR as % of sales		13%	13%	13%	13%	13%	
Free cash flows from business assets		$24.7	$12.5	$15.0	$18.1	$ 19.7	
Terminal value of assets the end of Year 5[2]						$425.3	
DCF value of business assets at 8%	$362						
plus cash less debt	*$(53)*						
DCF value of equity	$309						
Potential value creation	$27						

[1] COGS = Cost of goods sold; SG&A = Selling, general, and administrative expenses; WCR = Working capital requirement.
[2] Terminal value is $FCF_{Year 6}/(8\% - 3\%)$.
[3] Cash of $8 million less book value of debt of $61 million equals $53 million.
[4] Potential value creation = DCF value of equity less $282 million (the value of OS Distributors' equity as is).

EXHIBIT 14.8	EFFECT OF FASTER GROWTH IN SALES AND IMPROVED OPERATIONAL EFFICIENCY ON THE ESTIMATED VALUE OF OS DISTRIBUTORS' EQUITY AT THE BEGINNING OF YEAR 1.

FIGURES IN MILLIONS

	Beginning Year 1	Forecast for					Year 6 beyond
		Year 1	Year 2	Year 3	Year 4	Year 5	
Value of OS Distributors' Equity As Is (see Exhibit 14.5)							
Growth in sales		10%	8%	7%	5%	4%	3%
COGS[1] as % of sales		83.33%	83.33%	83.33%	83.33%	83.33%	
SG&A[1] as % of sales		10.00%	10.00%	10.00%	10.00%	10.00%	
WCR[1] as % of sales		16.04%	16.04%	16.04%	16.04%	16.04%	
Free cash flow from business assets		$8.6	$11.2	$13.8	$17.1	$ 19.0	
Terminal value of assets at the end of Year 5[2]						$412.9	
DCF value of business assets at 8%	$335						
plus cash less debt[3]	$(53)						
DCF value of equity	$282						
Effect of Faster Growth in Sales							
Growth in sales		12%	10%	9%	7%	6%	3%
COGS[1] as % of sales		83.33%	83.33%	83.33%	83.33%	83.33%	
SG&A[1] as % of sales		10.00%	10.00%	10.00%	10.00%	10.00%	
WCR[1] as % of sales		16.04%	16.04%	16.04%	16.04%	16.04%	
Free cash flow from business assets		$7.5	$10.2	$13.1	$16.8	$ 19.0	
Terminal value of assets at the end of Year 5[2]						$460.4	
DCF value of business assets at 8%	$365						
plus cash less debt[3]	$(53)						
DCF value of equity	$312						
Potential value creation[4]	$30						
Effect of Faster Growth in Sales and Improved Managerial Efficiency							
growth in sales		12%	10%	9%	7%	6%	3%
COGS[1] as % of sales		82.33%	82.33%	82.33%	82.33%	82.33%	
SG&A[1] as % of sales		9.50%	9.50%	9.50%	9.50%	9.50%	
WCR[1] as % of sales		13%	13%	13%	13%	13%	
Free cash flow from business assets		$28.7	$17.2	$20.5	$24.3	$ 26.9	
Terminal value of assets at the end of Year 5[2]						$609.2	
DCF value of business assets at 8%	$508						
plus cash less debt[3]	$(53)						
DCF value of equity	$455						
Potential value creation[4]	$173						

[1] COGS = Cost of goods sold; SG&A = Selling, general, and administrative expenses; WCR = Working capital requirement.
[2] Terminal value is $FCF_{Year\,6}/(8\% - 3\%)$.
[3] Cash of $8 million less book value of debt of $61 million equals $53 million.
[4] Potential value creation = DCF value of equity less $282 million (the value of OS Distributors' equity as is).

EXHIBIT 14.9	SUMMARY OF DATA IN EXHIBITS 14.7 AND 14.8.

Sources of Value Creation	Potential Value Creation	
1. Reduction in the cost of goods sold to 82.33% of sales	$ 71 million	(41%)
2. Reduction in overheads to 9.50% of sales	$ 35 million	(20%)
3. Reduction of working capital requirement to 13% of sales	$ 27 million	(16%)
4. Faster growth in sales (2 percentage points higher)	$ 30 million	(17%)
5. Interaction of growth and improved operations	$ 10 million	(6%)
Total potential value creation	$173 million	(100%)

An acquiring firm, however, must not become overconfident about its ability to realize (or even exceed) the full potential value of a target. This overconfidence can lead to paying too much for the target. Unfortunately, the evidence indicates that this often occurs, and the result is an acquisition with an NPV close to zero. This means that most, if not all, of the gains from the acquisition end up in the pockets of the target company's shareholders.

ESTIMATING THE LEVERAGED BUYOUT VALUE OF OS DISTRIBUTORS

In a typical **leveraged buyout (LBO)**, a group of private equity investors purchases a presumably underperforming firm by raising an unusually large amount of debt relative to equity capital (up to $4 of debt for every $1 of equity). The investors often include the firm's managers in association with private equity investors and possibly a **venture capital firm** (an investment firm specializing in the financing of small and new ventures). The strategy is to restructure the firm, rapidly improve its performance, and increase the cash flows generated by the firm's business assets to repay a large part of the initial debt within a reasonable period of time (three to five years). *The new shareholders do not normally receive any cash dividends during the restructuring period.* They anticipate cashing in on their investment at the end of that period by selling some (or all) of their shares to the general public. As an alternative to this **exit strategy**, the firm can be sold to another company or to a new group of private investors.

Suppose OS Distributors' owners wish to retire. In January of Year 1, four of the firm's most senior managers, in association with a private equity firm, agree to buy the firm's assets for $298 million, including the $8 million of cash. They believe that the owners have a conservative management policy and that significant value can be unlocked if the firm is managed more aggressively through a combination of tighter control of expenses, better use of assets, and faster growth in sales. The acquisition will be financed with $220 million of debt and $78 million of equity (the management team will invest $30 million, and the private equity firm another $48 million).

To keep the analysis as simple as possible, we assume the $220 million of debt consists of a single loan at a fixed interest rate of 8 percent. The loan must be repaid at the rate of $20 million per year for the next five years, with the first payment due at the end of Year 1. After the fifth year, any repayment on the balance of the loan can be refinanced with new borrowing. The cost of debt is one full percentage point higher than the 7 percent rate on new borrowing that OS Distributors' current owners can obtain. The higher borrowing rate reflects the higher risk borne by the lenders in a leveraged deal such as an LBO.

We can compare the financial structure of OS Distributors before and after the LBO (but before any improvement in the firm's performance) by constructing a reduced form of the balance sheet after the LBO and comparing it with its actual balance sheet at the end of Year 0, as shown in Exhibit 14.10.[14]

The acquiring team has estimated that OS Distributors' long-term assets are grossly undervalued and believes that they are worth at least $213 million, more than four times the book value of $53 million reported in the firm's balance sheet. Long-term assets are hence recorded in the post-LBO balance sheet at $213 million and will be depreciated on the basis of their higher value. The *additional* yearly depreciation expenses resulting from the revaluation of fixed assets are assumed to equal $20 million for the next eight years ($213 million less $53 million divided by 8) and are fully tax deductible.[15] Cash and WCR are reported in the post LBO balance sheet at their pre-LBO accounting values. Notice the highly leveraged capital structure in the **pro forma** balance sheet (the *expected* balance sheet after the LBO). The $298 million of assets are financed with $220 million of debt and $78 million of equity, giving the post-LBO firm a debt ratio (debt divided by total capital) of 74 percent, which is significantly higher than the pre-LBO debt ratio of 44 percent.

The structure of debt used to finance a typical LBO is far more complex than that of the single loan we assume for OS Distributors. In practice, a package of different types of loans is put together by the private equity firm and its advisors. At the top of the package is the **senior debt** secured by the firm's assets. (A secured loan is one for which the firm has pledged some of its assets – such as property, trade receivables, or inventories – as **collateral**, which the lender can seize and sell if the firm fails to service the loan.) This collateralized debt is also known as **top-floor financing**. It is senior to the **subordinated**, or **junior debt**, which is usually **unsecured** (no

EXHIBIT 14.10	COMPARISON OF OS DISTRIBUTORS' BALANCE SHEET BEFORE AND AFTER THE LBO.

BEFORE-LBO FIGURES FROM EXHIBIT 14.1. FIGURES IN MILLIONS

Balance Sheet	Before the LBO		After the LBO	
Cash	$ 8	(6%)	$ 8	(3%)
Working capital requirement	77	(56%)	77	(26%)
Net fixed assets	53	(38%)	213	(71%)
Invested capital	$138	(100%)	$298	(100%)
Total debt	$ 61	(44%)	$220	(74%)
Equity	77	(56%)	78	(26%)
Capital employed	$138	(100%)	$298	(100%)

[14] The reduced form of the balance sheet is similar to the managerial balance sheet (see Chapter 4). The current liabilities associated with the operating cycle (accounts payable and accrued expenses) are accounted for in the working capital requirement where they are deducted from the receivables, inventories, and prepaid expenses.

[15] In some countries, the tax authority may deny the tax reductions resulting from these depreciation expenses.

collateral is offered) and more expensive. This type of debt is often referred to as **mezzanine financing** because it is positioned between top-floor financing and equity capital, which is known as **ground-floor financing**.

Two key issues should be examined in relation to the LBO of OS Distributors. The first is whether the acquisition of the firm's assets for $298 million is a value creating investment, that is, an investment with a positive net present value. The second is whether these assets will generate sufficient cash to service the $220 million loan (both interest payments and debt repayment) during the next five years.

Estimating the Leveraged Buyout Value of Business Assets Using the Adjusted Present Value Method (the APV Method)

To find out whether the OS Distributors' LBO is a positive NPV acquisition, we must estimate the value of OS Distributors' business assets based on the cash flows they are expected to generate under the new and more efficient management. If this estimated assets' value exceeds $298 million (the purchase price), the acquisition is a positive NPV investment. In principle, we can estimate the LBO value of OS Distributors' assets using the standard DCF approach. However, this approach assumes that the WACC remains constant, an assumption that does not hold in the case of an LBO. Remember that the post-LBO debt ratio is 74 percent (see Exhibit 14.10). The rapid repayment of the loan during the next five years means that the firm's debt ratio will decline during that period. In other words, the firm's WACC will not remain constant during these years. If we want to use the DCF approach to value the LBO, we need to estimate a different WACC for each of the five years, quite a cumbersome task. Fortunately, a variant of the DCF valuation approach, called the **adjusted present value (APV)** method, circumvents this problem.

The Adjusted Present Value Method

According to the APV method, the valuation of a firm's business assets is carried out in two separate steps. In the first step, the DCF value of the assets is estimated *assuming they are entirely financed with equity*. This all-equity-financed value is called the **unlevered asset value**. If assets are unlevered, then the WACC used in estimating their DCF value must be constant and equal to the cost of equity for an all-equity-financed firm. (This cost is referred to as the **unlevered cost of equity**.) This procedure clearly solves the problem of a WACC changing over time. But ignoring debt means that we fail to take into account the major benefit of debt financing – the reduction in the firm's taxes resulting from the deductibility of the interest expenses related to borrowed funds.[16] The second step in the APV approach corrects for this failure. In this step, the present value of the tax savings the firm will realize in the future from the additional depreciation expenses on the revalued assets and the interest payments on the loan are added to the DCF value of the unlevered assets. Thus, according to the APV method, the DCF value of a firm's **levered assets** (the assets financed with debt and equity) can be expressed as follows:

$$\text{DCF value of } \textit{levered} \text{ assets} =$$

$$\text{DCF value of } \textit{unlevered} \text{ assets} + \text{DCF value of future tax savings} \qquad (14.9)$$

The DCF value of unlevered assets is estimated by discounting the cash flows generated by these assets at the unlevered cost of equity. The DCF value of future tax

---

[16] The effect of debt financing on the firm's value is examined in detail in Chapter 13.

savings from interest expenses is estimated by discounting the future stream of tax savings at the cost of debt.[17]

THE LEVERAGED BUYOUT VALUE OF OS DISTRIBUTORS' BUSINESS ASSETS

We can now apply the APV approach to estimate the LBO value of OS Distributors' business assets. The new management team believes that it can improve operating efficiency by (1) reducing the COGS to 82.33 percent of sales (from the current 83.33 percent level), (2) cutting the SG&A expenses to 9.5 percent of sales (from their current 10 percent level), and (3) lowering the WCR to 13 percent of sales (from the current 16.04 percent level). The team also believes it can add two percentage points to the growth in sales for the next five years. This, as you may have noticed, is the restructuring plan we analyzed earlier in the context of a potential merger. However, a major difference exists between a potential merger and an LBO. In a merger, some of the performance improvements are expected to come from synergistic gains resulting from combining the two businesses. In an LBO, there is no merger and thus there are no opportunities for synergistic gains. *All the improved performance must come from better management of the firm.*

When OS Distributors is valued as a potential target, the successful implementation of the restructuring plan has a value-creating potential of $173 million (see the bottom of Exhibit 14.9). Unfortunately, we cannot use this figure as a measure of the potential value the LBO deal can create because, as discussed previously, the WACC will change over time. We now explain how to use the APV approach to estimate the leveraged value of OS Distributors' assets under the LBO financing plan.

OS Distributors' Unlevered Cost of Equity. We can use the capital asset pricing model reported in equation 14.7a to get an estimate of the *unlevered* **cost of equity** of OS Distributors. The beta coefficient in this case must be the *unlevered* **beta** (also called **asset beta**) of OS Distributors. We show in Chapter 12 that a firm's unlevered beta can be estimated as follows (see equation 12.7):

$$\text{Unlevered beta} = \frac{\text{Levered beta}}{1 + \dfrac{\text{Debt}}{\text{Equity}}}$$

The levered beta coefficient of OS Distributors is 0.98 (estimated earlier from a comparable firm with the similar capital structure) and the ratio of debt to equity is 30 percent debt to 70 percent equity (see equation 14.8). OS Distributors' unlevered beta is thus:

$$\text{OS Distributors' unlevered beta} = \frac{0.98}{1 + \dfrac{0.30}{0.70}} = 0.69$$

Applying the capital asset pricing model shown in equation 14.7b with an unlevered beta equal to 0.69 provides an estimate of OS Distributors' unlevered cost of equity:

$$\text{OS Distributors' unlevered cost of equity} = 4.7\% + (5\% \times 0.69) = 8.2\%$$

---

[17] Each cash-flow stream should be discounted to the present at a rate that reflects its particular risk. We assume here that OS Distributors is committed to its debt repayment schedule. In this case, the tax savings are as risky as the firm's debt and should be discounted at the cost of debt. Alternatively, if the tax savings are considered as risky as the free cash flows from assets, they should be discounted at the unlevered cost of equity.

Estimated Value of OS Distributors' Unlevered Assets.   The APV valuation steps are described in Exhibit 14.11. We start with the free cash flows from business assets given at the bottom of Exhibit 14.8. We can use these cash flows because the expected improvements in performance in the case of the LBO are the same as in the case of the merger. (Because the cash flow for Year 6 is not shown in Exhibit 14.8, we calculated it using the spreadsheet in Exhibit 14.5 assuming the performance expectations of the LBO.) Next, we estimate the terminal value of the business assets at the end of Year 5 (cell G7) in the same way as we estimated the terminal value for OS Distributors in the previous sections, but this time we use the *unlevered* cost of equity of 8.2 percent instead of a WACC of 8 percent.[18] Finally, we discount the stream of free cash flows (row 4) and the terminal value at the unlevered cost of equity of 8.2 percent. The result is a DCF value of $488.8 million for the unlevered assets of OS Distributors (cell B8).

Estimated LBO Value of OS Distributors' Assets. The estimated LBO value of OS Distributors' assets is the value of its levered assets. As indicated in equation 14.9, to get this levered asset value we must add to the unlevered asset value of $488.8 million the tax savings generated by the additional depreciation expenses provided by the revaluation of fixed assets and by the interest expenses provided by the $220 million loan.[19] Let's illustrate this procedure with the data in Exhibit 14.11.

With a corporate tax rate of 40 percent, the additional depreciation expenses will generate annual tax savings of $8 million for eight years ($20 million times 40 percent). This is the amount of tax OS Distributors will *not* pay because its pre-tax profit is reduced by the $20 million of annual depreciation. The tax savings from Year 1 to Year 5 are shown in row 11. The terminal value of the additional depreciation expenses at the end of Year 5 is $20.6 million (cell G13). (This is the present value of $8 million every year for the remaining three years of depreciation discounted at the unlevered cost of equity of 8.2 percent.)[19] The total DCF value of the tax savings from depreciation is $45.6 million (cell B14).

To estimate the tax savings from interest expenses, we first need to estimate the interest expenses. Row 16 shows the amount of outstanding debt at the *beginning* of each year from Year 1 to Year 6. Because of high annual debt repayments, OS Distributors' debt is expected to decrease rapidly. Based on the initial borrowing of $220 million and annual repayments of $20 million, the amount of outstanding debt by the end of Year 5 will be reduced to $120 million. Assuming that the large debt repayments will stop after Year 6, we can expect that debt, interest expenses, and tax savings will then increase at the same rate as the growth in sales, expected to be 3 percent per year. The annual interest expenses in row 20 are obtained by multiplying the amount of debt outstanding at the beginning of the year by the interest rate of 8 percent. Row 21 shows the corresponding tax savings using a tax rate of 40 percent.[19] Row 23 gives the terminal value of the tax savings from the expected annual interest after Year 5. It is calculated as the present value of a constant growth perpetuity where the following year's cash flow is $3.8 million (the tax savings of

---

[18] Recall that when the firm is unlevered, it has no debt and its WACC is equal to its unlevered cost of equity.

[19] We assume that the firm will be profitable and will thus pay taxes which will allow it to take advantage of these reduced tax payments. We show in Exhibit 14.12 that the firm will indeed be profitable every year except in Year 1. We hence assume that the firm will carry forward to Year 2 any unused tax reduction of Year 1.

| | Exhibit 14.11 | Estimated Value of OS Distributors' Unlevered Assets at the Beginning of Year 1. | | | | | | |

Dollars in millions

	A	B	C	D	E	F	G	H
1		Beginning			Forecast for			
2		Year 1	Year 1	Year 2	Year 3	Year 4	Year 5	Year 6 and beyond
3	**Value of the unlevered assets**							
4	Free cash flow from business assets (see bottom of Exhibit 14.8)		$ 28.7	$ 17.2	$ 20.5	$ 24.3	$ 26.9	$30.5
5	Growth rate of cash flow after Year 5							3.0%
6	Unlevered cost of equity	8.2%						
7	Terminal value of unlevered assets						$586.5	
8	DCF value of unlevered assets	$488.8						
9	**Value of tax savings on additional depreciation expenses**							
10	Additional depreciation expenses for 8 years		$ 20.0	$ 20.0	$ 20.0	$ 20.0	$ 20.0	$20.0
11	Tax savings (tax rate = 40%)		8.0	8.0	8.0	8.0	8.0	8.0
12	Discount rate	8.2%						
13	Terminal value of tax savings						$ 20.5	
14	DCF value of tax savings from depreciation expenses	$45.6						
15	**Value of tax savings on interest expenses**							
16	Debt outstanding at the beginning of the year		$220.0	$200.0	$180.0	$160.0	$140.0	$120.0
17	Debt repayment		20.0	20.0	20.0	20.0	20.0	(3.6)[1]
18	Debt outstanding at the end of the year		200.0	180.0	160.0	140.0	120.0	123.6
19	Interest rate	8.0%						
20	Interest expense		17.6	16.0	14.4	12.8	11.2	9.6
21	Tax savings (tax rate = 40%)		7.0	6.4	5.8	5.1	4.5	3.8
22	Tax savings growth rate after Year 5							3.0%
23	Terminal value of tax savings discounted at 8.0%						$ 77.0	
24	DCF value of tax savings from interest payments at 8.0%	$75.8						
25	**Leverage buyout value**							
26	Unlevered asset value (B8)	$488.8						
27	Overall tax savings value (B14+B24)	$121.4						
28	Leverage buyout value (B26+B27)	$610.2						

- Rows 4,10, 17, plus cells H5, B6, B12, C16, B19, H22 are data
- Formula in cell G7 is =H4/(B6−H5)
- Formula in cell B8 is =NPV(B6,C4:G4)+G7/(1+B6)^5
- Formula in cell C11 is =0.4*C10. Then copy cell C11 to next cells in row 11
- Formula in cell G13 is =−PV(B12,3,G11), where 3 is the number of remaining tax savings periods
- Formula in cell B14 is = NPV(B12,C11:G11)+G13/(1+B12)^5
- Formula in cell D16 is =C16−C17. Then copy cell D16 to next cells in row 16
- Formula in cell C18 is =D16. Then copy cell C18 to cells D24 to G18. Formula in cell H18 is =H16*(1+.03)
- Formula in cell C20 is =$B$19*C16. Then copy cell C20 to next cells in row 20
- Formula in cell C21 is =0.4*C20. Then copy cell C21 to next cells in row 21
- Formula in cell G23 is =H21/(B19−H22)
- Formula in cell B24 is =NPV(B19,C21:G21)+G23/(1+B19)^5
- Formula in cell B26 is =B8
- Formula in cell B27 is =B14+B24
- Formula in cell B28 is =B26+B27

[1] Debt at the end of Year 6 is $120(1 + 3%) = $123.6 and the firm will thus borrow $3.6 at the end of Year 6. The figure is negative because in this case it is a borrowing and not a debt repayment.

Year 6), the required return is 8 percent (the cost of debt), and the growth rate is 3 percent. Adding the present value of the annual tax savings from Year 1 to Year 5 to that of the terminal value of the tax savings of $77.0 million in Year 5 gives a total tax saving from interest expenses of $75.8 million (cell B24).

Adding the DCF values of the tax savings from depreciation ($45.6 million) and the tax savings from interest expenses ($75.8 million) to the unlevered asset value of $488.8 million yields an estimated LBO value of $610.2 million.

Note that this value is more than double the $290 million the LBO team will have to pay for the business assets ($298 million less $8 million of cash). The LBO, if successful, has the potential to create $320 million of value ($610 million less $290 million).[20]

WILL OS DISTRIBUTORS BE ABLE TO SERVICE ITS DEBT?

We now consider the issue of whether OS Distributors will be able to service its $220 million loan. Although the LBO deal makes sense from a value-creation perspective (its NPV is positive), OS Distributors' management must still meet the challenge of servicing an inordinate amount of debt, particularly the heavy burden of early and rapid principal repayment. *The question is whether the firm's assets under new management will generate enough cash flow to service the firm's debt.* If they do *not*, the financing plan must be revised, that is, borrowing should be reduced and replaced with equity. If additional equity cannot be obtained, the deal may have to be abandoned even though it is a value-creating proposal.

The cash flow analysis from Year 1 to Year 6 is summarized in Exhibit 14.12. Part I reports the effect on cash flows of the LBO deal. The total cash flows in row 7 are the cash flows from business assets (row 4 in Exhibit 14.11) plus the tax savings from the additional depreciation expenses (row 11 in Exhibit 14.11). Are the cash flows in row 7 high enough to service the $220 million loan?

The amount of cash required to service the loan is shown in row 13 and its calculation in rows 9 to 12. The amount of debt outstanding at the beginning of each year, the annual interest expenses, and the debt repayments are from Exhibit 14.11. Interest expenses are tax deductible, and they have been adjusted using a tax rate of 40 percent. The cash flows to equity holders are given in row 14 with their cumulative values in row 15. The firm has enough cash to pay the debt holders, but Year 2 and Year 3 will be critical. An unexpected decline in free cash flows, even if relatively small, may cause a serious liquidity problem.

Part II of the exhibit presents the pro forma (i.e., future) income statements based on current expectations. EBIT is computed as in Exhibit 14.5 but with the operational efficiency ratios and the growth rates in sales expected from the LBO restructuring plan. EAT, obtained after deducting the additional depreciation expenses and the interest expenses from EBIT, shows a marginal loss the first year of the LBO followed by a steady increase in profits.

Assuming that the firm will not pay any dividends until after Year 6, the firm's equity will increase each year by the amount of EAT. Starting with a book value of equity at $77 million in Year 0, we can estimate the book values of equity at the end of each year until Year 6. These values are shown in Part III of the exhibit, along with the total capital (equity plus debt outstanding) and the debt ratios (debt-to-total

---

[20] Note that the LBO's enterprise value ($610.2 million) is significantly larger than the DCF value of $508 million reported at the bottom of Exhibit 14.8. The difference comes from the tax savings provided by the LBO deal.

EXHIBIT 14.12	FINANCING OS DISTRIBUTORS' LEVERAGED BUYOUT.

DOLLARS IN MILLIONS

A	B	C	D	E	F	G	H
1				Forecast for			
2	Year 0	Year 1	Year 2	Year 3	Year 4	Year 5	Year 6
3 I. Cash Flow Implications							
4 Total cash flow from business assets							
5 Free cash flow from business assets		$ 28.7	$ 17.2	$ 20.5	$ 24.3	$ 26.9	$ 30.5
6 Tax savings on additional depreciation expenses		8.0	8.0	8.0	8.0	8.0	8.0
7 Total cash flow from business assets		$ 36.7	$ 25.2	$ 28.5	$ 32.3	$ 34.9	$ 38.5
8 Total cash flow to debt holders							
9 Debt outstanding at the beginning of the year		$220.0	$200.0	$180.0	$160.0	$140.0	$120.0
10 Interest payment		17.6	16.0	14.4	12.8	11.2	9.6
11 After-tax interest payment (tax rate = 40%)		10.6	9.6	8.6	7.7	6.7	5.8
12 Debt repayment		20.0	20.0	20.0	20.0	20.0	(3.6)
13 After-tax cash flow to debt holders		$ 30.6	$ 29.6	$ 28.6	$ 27.7	$ 26.7	$ 2.2
14 Cash flow to equity holders		$ 6.1	$ (4.4)	$ (0.1)	$ 4.6	$ 8.2	$ 36.3
15 Cumulative cash flow to equity holders		$ 6.1	$ 1.7	$ 1.6	$ 6.2	$ 14.4	$ 50.7
16 II. Pro Forma Income Statement							
17 *Sales growth rate*		12.0%	10.0%	9.0%	7.0%	6.0%	3.0%
18 *COGS[1] as percent of sales*		82.3%	82.3%	82.3%	82.3%	82.3%	82.3%
19 *SG&A[1] as percent of sales*		9.5%	9.5%	9.5%	9.5%	9.5%	9.5%
20 Sales	$480.0	$537.6	$591.4	$644.6	$689.7	$731.1	$753.0
21 *less* COGS	(400.0)	(442.6)	(486.9)	(530.7)	(567.8)	(601.9)	(620.0)
22 *less* SG&A	(48.0)	(51.1)	(56.2)	(61.2)	(65.5)	(69.5)	(71.5)
23 *less* initial depreciation expenses	(8.0)	(8.0)	(8.0)	(7.0)	(6.0)	(6.0)	(6.0)
24 *less* additional depreciation expenses		(20.0)	(20.0)	(20.0)	(20.0)	(20.0)	(20.0)
25 Equals earnings before interest and tax (EBIT)	$ 24.0	$ 15.9	$ 20.3	$ 25.7	$ 30.3	$ 33.7	$ 35.5
26 *less* interest expenses	(7.0)	(17.6)	(16.0)	(14.4)	(12.8)	(11.2)	(9.6)
27 Equals earnings before tax	$ 17.0	$ (1.7)	$ 4.3	$ 11.3	$ 17.5	$ 22.5	$ 25.9
28 *less* tax at 40%	(6.8)	0[21]	(1.0)	(4.5)	(7.0)	(9.0)	(10.4)
29 Earnings after tax	$ 10.2	$ (1.7)	$ 3.3	$ 6.8	$ 10.5	$ 13.5	$ 15.5

(Continued)

[21] In Year 1 the negative $1.7 million of earnings before tax generates a tax credit of $0.68 million (40 percent of 1.7 million). This unused tax credit is carried forward in Year 2 to reduce that year's income tax of $1.72 million (40 percent of $4.3 million) to $1.04 million ($1.72 million − $0.68 million), rounded to $1 million.

EXHIBIT 14.12	FINANCING OS DISTRIBUTORS' LEVERAGED BUYOUT. *(Continued)*

DOLLARS IN MILLIONS

A	B	C	D	E	F	G	H
30 III. Capital and Debt Ratios							
31 Debt outstanding end-of-year	$ 61.0	$200.0	$180.0	$160.0	$140.0	$120.0	$123.6
32 Equity capital	77.0	75.3	78.7	85.5	96.1	109.5	125.1
33 Total capital	$138.0	$275.3	$258.7	$245.5	$236.1	$229.5	$248.7
34 Ratio of debt to total capital	44.2%	72.6%	69.6%	65.2%	59.3%	52.3%	49.7%

- Rows 5, 6, 10, 12, 17, 18, 19, 23, 24, 26, and 31 plus cells C9, B20, B21, B22, and B32 are data
- Formula in cell C7 is =C5+C6. Then copy formula in cell C7 to next cells in row 7
- Formula in cell D9 is =C9–C12. Then copy formula in cell D9 to next cells in row 9
- Formula in cell C11 is =C10*(1–.4). Then copy cell C11 to next cells in row 11
- Formula in cell C13 is =C11+C12. Then copy formula in cell C13 to next cells in row 13
- Formula in cell C14 is = C7–C13. Then copy formula in cell C14 to next cells in row 14
- Formula in cell C15 is =C14. Formula in cell D15 is =C15+D14. Then copy formula in cell D15 to next cells in row 15
- Formula in cell C20 is =B20*(1+C17). Then copy formula in cell C20 to next cells in row 20
- Formula in cell C21 is =–C18*C20. Then copy formula in cell C21 to next cells in row 21
- Formula in cell C22 is =–C19*C20. Then copy formula in cell C22 to next cells in row 22
- Formula in cell B25 is = SUM(B20:B24). Then copy formula in cell B25 to next cells in row 25
- Formula in cell B27 is =B25+B26. Then copy formula in cell B27 to next cells in row 27
- Formula in cell B28 is =0.4*B27. Then copy cell B28 to next cells in row 28
- Formula in cell B29 is =B27+B28. Then copy cell B29 to next cells in row 29
- Formula in cell B32 is =77. Formula in cell C32 is =B32+C29. Then copy formula in cell C32 to next cells in row 32
- Formula in cell B33 is =B31+B32. Then copy formula in cell B33 to next cells in row 33
- Formula in cell B34 is =B31/B33. Then copy formula in cell B34 to next cells in row 34

[1] COGS = Cost of goods sold; SG&A = Selling, general, and administrative expenses.

capital) at year-end. The figures show a continuous decrease in the debt ratio. However, it will take more than five years for the firm to return to the pre-LBO ratio of 44 percent and presumably to start paying dividends.

Should the management team go ahead with the deal? Only those directly involved can answer that question. The $298 million price tag is not excessive if the management team is confident that it can rapidly improve the firm's performance according to the restructuring plan. But they will have to keep a close watch on the firm's cash position to avoid any major liquidity problems.

The preceding discussion illustrates an important aspect of an LBO deal: good candidates for an LBO acquisition are generally *underperforming* firms that are expected to generate *stable* and *predictable* cash flows. An LBO involving a firm with volatile and unpredictable free cash flows from assets is not recommended because the chances of servicing its debt successfully are lower than in the case of a firm with stable cash flows. Furthermore, because private equity firms are often providers of both equity capital and junior debt financing (which are the riskiest types of financing in an LBO), they usually impose a rapid repayment of debt that is easier to achieve with stable and predictable free cash flows from assets. Why impose a rapid debt repayment schedule? Because it is the best guarantee for private equity investors that the management team will do its utmost to achieve the *restructuring* plan that will allow investors to get the returns they expect from their contribution to the financing of the LBO. Indeed, a rapid restructuring of the firm's assets is ultimately the key to a successful LBO.

KEY POINTS

1. One approach to the valuation of a firm's equity is based on the market multiples of firms comparable to the one being valued. Although this valuation technique is easy to apply, it does not allow you to test the effect on the firm's value of alternative assumptions about operational efficiency, growth in sales, and different capital structures (this exercise is called sensitivity analysis). Neither can you estimate the potential value that a particular managerial action is expected to create.

2. The second approach to valuation, the discounted cash flow (DCF) method, is more complex. First, the future free cash-flow stream expected from the firm's business assets must be estimated. Then, these cash flows must be discounted to the present at the firm's weighted average cost of capital (WACC) to obtain the DCF value of the firm's business assets, also called its enterprise value. To get an estimate of the firm's equity value, add cash and deduct current debt from the estimated enterprise value.

3. The advantage of the DCF approach is that, contrary to the valuation by comparables, it allows you to do sensitivity analysis to find out how a change in one or more of the valuation parameters under your control will ultimately affect the firm's DCF value. We show that this approach is a valuable tool to assess the potential value creation of an acquisition; it is also a powerful diagnostic technique that can be used to examine whether a change in management strategy and policies could be a source of value creation.

4. A variation of the DCF approach, the adjusted present value (APV) method, is also explained. The advantage of the APV method is in its ability to value a firm whose capital structure is expected to change over time. Therefore, it is particularly suitable for valuing a leveraged buyout (LBO) deal.

5. We illustrate in the chapter how to implement the alternative DCF valuation methods to the case of OS Distributors for which three different values are estimated: its "as-is" value, its potential acquisition or target value, and its LBO value.

6. The different valuation methods presented in this chapter are summarized in Exhibit 14.13. On the upper-left side is the equity-multiple approach (or valuation by comparables). On the lower-left side is the DCF approach based on the WACC, and on the lower-right side is the APV approach. At the bottom is the valuation based on earnings before interest, tax, depreciation, and amortization (EBITDA) multiples. For each approach, Exhibit 14.13 shows the steps and the required inputs needed to obtain an estimated value of equity.

Exhibit 14.13   Alternative Equity Valuation Models.[1]

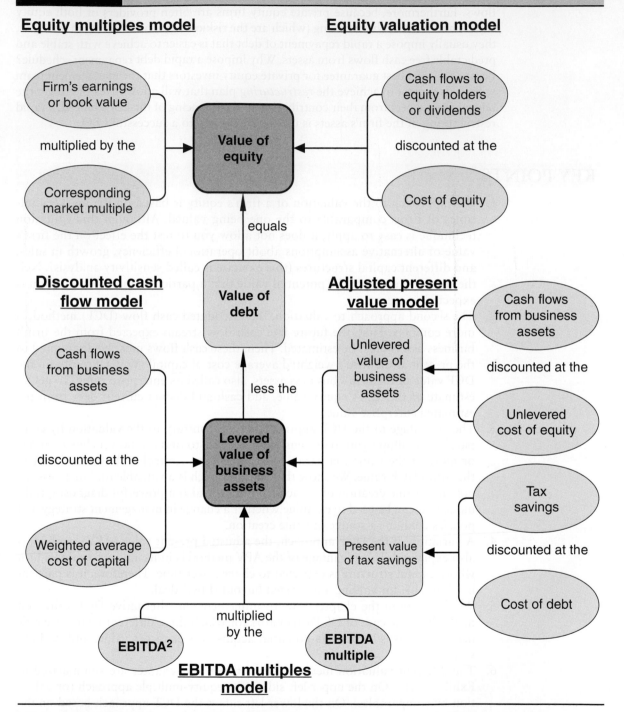

7. Exhibit 14.13 shows another valuation approach that is presented in Chapter 10. It is shown on the upper-right side of the exhibit. The equity valuation model provides a direct estimate of the firm's equity value by discounting at the *cost of equity* the stream of cash flows the firm is expected to distribute to its *shareholders*. This approach is described in detail in Chapter 10. Conceptually, the three DCF methods (the WACC, the APV, and the equity valuation model) should provide the same estimate of a firm's equity value. In practice they will not, because the assumptions made to estimate the cash flows and the discount rates used in the DCF formulas are usually not perfectly consistent across the three methods.

8. Which of the valuation methods in Exhibit 14.13 do practitioners use when they value companies? The valuation by multiples is the most commonly employed, with DCF valuation a close second. We recommend the use of both methods. Each has its own merits, and they are not mutually exclusive. The multiples approach is relatively easy to implement and, because it is based on comparables, provides a good approximation of the firm's "as-is" value. The DCF approach is more complex but is superior when the acquisition of a firm is expected to generate additional value through improved performance or synergistic gains or, in the case of an LBO, through significant tax savings.

FURTHER READING

1. Damodaran, Aswath, *Damodaran on Valuation: Security Analysis for Investment and Corporate Finance*, 2nd ed. John Wiley & Sons, 2015. See chapters 3 to 6.
2. Koller, Tim, Marc Goedhart, and David Wessels. *Valuation: Measuring and Managing the Value of Companies*, 6th ed. John Wiley & Sons, 2015.
3. Rappaport, Alfred. *Creating Shareholder Value*. The Free Press, 2000. See Chapter 8.

SELF-TEST QUESTIONS

14.1 The price-to-earnings ratio.
Explain, without using mathematical formulas, why growth and risk are the main factors that determine the price-to-earnings ratio.

14.2 Alternative valuation methods and value-creating acquisitions.
Explain why each of the following statements is generally incorrect:

a. "A company's liquidating value acts as a ceiling on its market value, whereas its replacement value acts as a floor."
b. "Because accounting rules differ across countries, price-earnings ratios are better than price-to-cash-flow ratios when making international valuation comparisons."
c. "Different valuation methods, if properly applied, will generate estimates of firm values that are practically identical."

14.3 Valuation by comparables.
The Light Motors Company (LMC) is privately held. Its owners are thinking of listing at least 45 percent of their company's equity on the local stock exchange. Thus, they wish to estimate the value of their company using financial data drawn from the Rapid Engine Corporation (REC), a company listed on the local stock market and

comparable to LMC in assets and financial structures. Based on the data given below, provide three estimates of LMC's value. Why do they differ from one other?

	LMC	REC
Earnings before interest, tax, depreciation, and amortization	$125 million	$250 million
Earnings after tax	$ 46 million	$ 90 million
Debt	$420 million	$800 million
Cash	$ 4 million	$ 10 million
Book value of equity	$270 million	$590 million
Number of shares outstanding	not available	40 million
Share price	unlisted	$ 30

14.4 Equity valuation.

Ralph Anders, single owner of Baltek Inc., a distribution company, wonders how much his equity in Baltek is worth. He expects that its cash flow from assets will be $1 million for the current year, with a growth rate of around 3 percent a year for the foreseeable future. He thinks that a return of 8 percent a year from investments in businesses as risky as Baltek is reasonable. Baltek has no debt.

a. What is the discounted cash-flow value of Baltek's assets?
b. What is the value of Baltek's equity?

14.5 Discounted cash-flow valuation.

Using the discounted cash flow method and the following assumptions, provide an estimate of Light Engines Company's (LEC) equity value.

- Sales, currently at $620 million, will grow by 8 percent for the next two years, by 6 percent during the following two years, and then by 4 percent in perpetuity
- Pre-tax operating margin will remain at 20 percent
- Capital expenditure will be equal to annual depreciation expense
- The working capital requirement will remain at 20 percent of sales
- LEC has $280 million of debt outstanding at 6 percent and is expected to pay a 40 percent corporate tax rate
- National Engines Corporation – a comparable firm that is listed on the local stock exchange – has a ratio of equity-to-total capital of 80 percent at *market* value, and an equity beta of 1.20
- Both the risk-free rate and the market risk premium are 5 percent

REVIEW QUESTIONS

1. **Valuation issues.**

Explain why each of the following statements is generally incorrect:

a. "Price-earnings ratios should increase when the yield on government securities rises."
b. "A company's discounted cash-flow value is usually dominated by the magnitude of its expected cash-flow stream during the future five to ten years, whereas its terminal value usually has a negligible effect on its DCF value."

    c. "The use of high debt ratios to finance leveraged buyouts is essentially a device to capture the tax savings generated by the deductibility of interest expenses."

2. **Some issues in mergers and acquisitions.**
   Comment on the following statements:

   a. "Only synergistic mergers have the potential to create value."
   b. "If a merger cannot generate synergistic gains through cost reductions, it will not create value."
   c. "Conglomerate mergers can create value through superior growth in earnings per share."
   d. "There is strong empirical evidence indicating that acquiring firms create value mostly through their superior ability to uncover target companies that are under-valued by the stock market."

3. **Leveraged buyout.**
   What are the potential sources of value creation and value destruction in a leveraged buyout when compared with an acquisition?

4. **Mergers and price-to-earnings ratios.**
   Maltonese Inc. has five million shares outstanding selling at $60 each, and its price-to-earnings ratio (PER) is 10. Targeton Corp. has 1.5 million shares outstanding with a market price of $30 each, and its PER is 6. Maltonese is considering the acquisition of Targeton because it expects that the merger will create $15 million of value.

   a. What is the maximum price that Maltonese should pay for one share of Targeton?
   b. What would be the PER of the merged firm if Maltonese issues new shares to finance the acquisition, with Targeton shareholders receiving one Maltonese share for two Targeton shares?

5. **Mergers and price-to-earnings ratios.**
   Mergecandor Corp. is considering the acquisition of Tenderon Inc. Mergecandor has two million shares outstanding selling at $30, or 7.5 times its earnings per share, and Tenderon has one million shares outstanding selling at $15, or five times its earnings per share. Mergecandor would offer to exchange two shares of Tenderon for one share of Mergecandor.

   a. If there would be no wealth created from the merger, what would be the earnings per share of the merged firm? Its price-to-earnings ratio (PER)? Its share price? Would there be any wealth transfer between the shareholders of the two companies?
   b. Suppose that, after the merger, the market would not adjust the PER of Merge-candor, which will stay at 7.5. What would be the new share price of the merged firm? Would there be any wealth transfer between the shareholders of the two companies?

6. **Net present value of an acquisition.**
   Motoran Inc. is contemplating the acquisition of a competitor, Tortoran Corp., for $25 million. Motoran's market value is $40 million, whereas that of Tortoran is $20 million. Motoran expects that after the merger the administrative costs of the two companies will be reduced by $1 million forever. Motoran's cost of capital is 12.5 percent.

   a. What would be the amount of wealth created by the merger?
   b. What is the net present value of the acquisition?

7. **Discounted cash flow valuation.**

Murlow Company is a privately held firm. David Murlow, its owner-manager, has been approached by Murson Inc. for a possible acquisition. The firm has no debt. What is the minimum price David Murlow should ask, given the following information about his firm?

- Sales, currently at $500 million, are expected to grow by 6 percent for the next three years, and then by 4 percent in perpetuity
- The operating margin before tax is expected to remain at 20 percent of sales
- Annual capital expenditure is expected to be equal to the depreciation expense of the year
- The working capital requirement would remain at 18 percent of sales
- The corporate tax rate is 40 percent
- David Murlow requires a return of at least 10 percent for his family investment in the firm

8. **Discounted cash-flow valuation.**

We wish to estimate the value of Portal Inc. under alternative assumptions about the firm's performance.

a. Using the discounted cash flow (DCF) approach to valuation and the following assumptions, provide an estimate of Portal's value.

- This year sales are expected to be $750 million. They are expected to grow at a rate of 5 percent per year for the next four years, and then at 3 percent per year forever
- The pre-tax operating margin currently at 15 percent will grow at a rate of 1 percent every year for four years and then stabilize at 20 percent forever
- The working capital requirement to sales ratio will remain at its current level of 18 percent forever
- Capital expenditure will be $50 million this year and will grow at the same rate as the sales
- Annual depreciation expense for the current year will be $50 million and then grow at the same rate as the capital expenditure
- Portal Inc. has $500 million of debt outstanding. It can borrow at 6 percent
- Portal's income tax rate is 40 percent
- Portal's beta is 1.05. The risk-free rate and the market risk premium are 5 percent
- The debt-to-total-capital ratio of Portal, at market value, is 50 percent

b. Assume that Portal's performance can be improved through the following:

1. A half a percentage point increase in the growth rate in sales every year
2. An improvement in operating margin after tax of 1 percent per year, every year
3. A reduction of the ratio working capital requirement to sales from 18 percent to 16 percent immediately
4. A recapitalization that could lower Portal's weighted average cost of capital by 30 basis points

Show how each of these actions will change the firm's estimated DCF value. What will the change in value be if all actions are implemented simultaneously? Why is the sum of the changes in value resulting from each action smaller than the change in value resulting from their cumulative effects?

9. **Alternatives to cash acquisition.**

   Osiris Inc. is considering the acquisition of a competitor, Polos Corp. Osiris expects that the purchase would add $800,000 to its annual cash flow from assets indefinitely. Both firms are fully equity financed and do not carry any debt. The current market value of Osiris is $50 million, and that of Polos is $30 million. Osiris's cost of capital is 8 percent. Osiris hesitates between offering $20 million in cash and offering 25 percent of its shares to Polos's shareholders.

   a. What is the value of the acquisition to Osiris?
   b. What is the cost of Polos to Osiris under each alternative?
   c. What is the net present value of the purchase to Osiris?

10. **Cash or stock offer?**

    Mirandel Inc. is considering the acquisition of Tarantel Corp. Mirandel's earnings after tax are $2 million, it has two million shares outstanding, and its price-to-earnings ratio (PER) is 20. Tarantel's earnings are $1.5 million, it has 0.5 million shares, and its PER is 15. Mirandel's earnings and dividends are expected to grow at a constant rate of 5 percent per year. With the acquisition of Tarantel, the growth rate is expected to increase to 8 percent.

    a. If Mirandel's current dividend per share is $1.50, what is Mirandel's cost of equity capital if its dividend per share grows at a constant rate of 5 percent forever? (Hint: Mirandel's share price is the present value of a dividend per share growing at a constant rate forever.)
    b. What is the value of Tarantel for Mirandel's shareholders?
    c. What will the net present value of the acquisition be if Mirandel offers $50 in cash for each outstanding share of Tarantel? What if it offers 756,000 of its shares in exchange for all the outstanding shares of Tarantel? Should Mirandel make a cash or a share exchange offer?

Managing Corporate Risk

CHAPTER 15

Firms are exposed to multiple sources of risk because they operate in an uncertain economic, political, and social environment. Risk cannot be dissociated from business activities – it is the essence of doing business. If managers did not take any risk, their firm would not earn more than the rate of return on riskless assets. Who, then, would invest in a riskless firm when a risk-free rate of return can be earned by simply holding government bonds that are safe and highly liquid?

The question a value-creating manager should ask is *not* how to eliminate risk but whether the return from the firm's investments is high enough to compensate for the risk the firm is taking. This risk is borne by the firm's owners, not the firm's managers. If management is unable to generate an adequate *risk-adjusted* return for the firm's owners, they should take immediate action to either increase the expected return to a level that properly compensates owners for the risk they bear or reduce the risk to a level commensurate with current expected return. This is a direct application of the fundamental finance principle presented in Chapter 1 that calls for managers to make decisions that create value for the firm's owners. This principle, however, assumes that managers are able to identify, measure, and control the various risks the firm faces. We present in this chapter a comprehensive risk management system that helps managers achieve this objective.

We have shown in the previous chapters that firms are exposed to at least two broad types of risk, *business risk* and *financial risk*. Business risk occurs because of the firm's inability to know for certain the outcome of its investment decisions. The best-laid plans may go wrong, and the firm's value will suffer. Financial risk occurs when the firm borrows. It is the risk that the firm may not be able to service its debt, meaning that it may not be able to pay the interest on the funds it has borrowed and repay its loans when they are due.

We review in this chapter why business and financial risks occur and show how these risks should be managed. We also examine two other sources of risk a firm faces: *financial investment risk* (the unexpected changes in the value of the *financial* investments the firm has made) and *currency risk* (the risk associated with doing business in a foreign currency). Note that some of these risks are unavoidable and must be borne by the firm and its owners (such as the business risk associated with

531

the launch of a new product), while other risks can be transferred to an insurance company (by purchasing insurance contracts against, for example, the risk of damage caused by fire) or reduced – and, in some cases, eliminated – through the use of risk management instruments. We show in the next two chapters how a firm can use forward, futures, and option contracts to reduce or eliminate some of the risks it is exposed to.

After reading this chapter, you should understand the following:

- What risk is and why it should be managed
- Why firms should manage risk centrally
- The difference between project risk and corporate risk
- The process of managing a firm's exposure to risk
- The four different sources of risk a firm faces: business risk, financial risk, financial investment risk, and currency risk
- How to measure the impact of risk on the firm's value

WHAT IS RISK?

We have encountered and discussed different types of **risk** throughout the previous chapters. In this chapter, we review the various kinds of risk presented earlier, extend the list to additional risks the firm faces, clarify *what* risk means, explain *why* it should be managed, and finally show *how* to formulate and implement a risk management program.

Risk manifests itself in various ways. It could be an **event risk** or an **ongoing risk**. An event risk is an unexpected incident (such as an earthquake or a disruption in the firm's supply chain) that reduces the firm's value if and when it occurs. An ongoing risk is the continuous, unexpected change in the firm's environment that causes the firm's value to *rise* or *fall* unpredictably. An example is the effect of continuous changes in **foreign-exchange rates**. Consider the case of a US firm that receives quarterly dividend payments from a number of subsidiaries located around the world. An unexpected *fall* in the value of the US dollar against foreign currencies will *increase* the firm's dividend receipts when measured in US dollars. (The firm will get more dollars in exchange for its dividends denominated in foreign currencies.) An unexpected *rise* in the value of the US dollar will have the opposite effect – it will *decrease* the firm's dividend receipts when measured in US dollars. If the firm is unable to control these recurrent and fluctuating cash inflows, its value will rise or fall continuously and unpredictably.

Note that an event risk is always "bad news" because it always reduces the firm's value if and when it happens, whereas an ongoing risk can be either "bad news" or "good news" because it manifests itself as a deviation from an expected outcome. Consider again the firm that receives cash dividends from abroad: "bad news" means that the firm's value declines when it receives lower-than-expected dollar-denominated dividend payments, while "good news" means that the firm's value rises when it receives higher-than-expected dollar-denominated dividend payments. In other words, ongoing risk is defined as *deviations from expectations*: it either manifests itself as an unexpected "upside gain" when the outcome exceeds expectation or an unexpected "downside loss" when the outcome falls short of expectation.

Risk, then, means *knowing* that something can happen that will affect the firm's future value but *not knowing* when it will happen and how it will affect the firm's value when it happens.[1] In the next sections, we compile a comprehensive list of the potential risks a firm faces and suggest a method to measure and manage the firm's exposure to these risks. Before we do this, we first explain *why* a firm should manage risk and then make the point that the risks a firm faces must be managed *centrally* at the corporate level.

WHY SHOULD FIRMS MANAGE RISK?

Should a firm manage the risks it faces? According to the fundamental finance principle, the answer depends on whether the firm's value will be higher with risk management than without it. Benefits as well as costs are associated with managing risks: if the benefits exceed the costs, risk management is a value-creating activity, and the firm should actively manage the risks it faces.

To better understand the conditions under which risk management is a value-creating activity, we first examine the conditions under which it is *irrelevant*, that is, the conditions under which managing risk does not change the firm's value. Understanding when risk management is irrelevant will help us identify the cases when it matters.

We show in Chapter 13 that in the ideal setting of "perfect markets" the firm's value does not change when the firm increases its financial risk through borrowing. Perfect markets are characterized by complete and costless information available to everyone (meaning that managers and investors know all about the firm's prospects) as well as by no taxes, no transaction costs, no financial distress costs,[2] no bankruptcy costs (meaning that no costs are associated with reorganizing bankrupt firms), and no agency costs (meaning that managers always make decisions that benefit the firm's owners; see Chapter 13).

When markets are perfect and risk management instruments are correctly priced, then managing a firm's risk does not change its value; this is a generalization of the irrelevance of debt financing in perfect markets to all the risks a firm faces. Firms cannot add value through risk management because investors can do it themselves. For example, an oil company could not increase its value by using risk management instruments to protect itself against fluctuations in the price of oil because the firm's investors, who know as much as the firm's managers about that risk exposure and its consequences, could protect themselves *directly* and at the *same* cost as the firm if they want to eliminate that risk.

Now that we know that risk management is irrelevant in perfect markets, we should expect it to be relevant when markets are not perfect. In other words, risk management can be a value-creating activity in a world in which there are taxes, transaction costs, financial distress costs, agency costs, and imperfect and costly information.

---

[1] Risk is thus "known-unknowns." (We know something can happen, but we do not know when and how it will affect the firm's value.) "Unknown-unknowns" (*not* knowing that something can happen and, obviously, not knowing how it will affect the firm's value) are *unidentifiable* sources of risk: there is not much a firm can do in this case except become more flexible and resilient in its operations.

[2] When a firm experiences financial difficulties resulting from excessive risk taking, it incurs **financial distress costs** (see Chapter 13). Examples of these costs include the loss of suppliers who no longer want to sell goods to the firm, the loss of customers who no longer want to buy the firm's goods, and the loss of key employees who no longer want to work for the firm because they all fear that the firm may go out of business.

We show below that when markets are imperfect, corporate risk management can add value by (1) reducing the firm's income tax payments over time; (2) protecting the firm against risks at a lower cost than if investors did it themselves; (3) lowering the firm's financial distress and agency costs; and (4) providing clearer information to investors about the firm's core activities. Furthermore, when information is imperfect, managers know more about their firm's prospects than do outside shareholders. In this case, managers can identify risk exposures and protect against them better than outside shareholders.

RISK MANAGEMENT CAN REDUCE CORPORATE INCOME TAX PAYMENTS

A firm that faces a *progressive* income tax schedule can lower its expected tax payments over time and thus raise its value by reducing the *volatility* of its taxable income through hedging, that is, through the use of risk management instruments.[3]

RISK MANAGEMENT CAN LOWER THE COST OF PROTECTION AGAINST RISK

When markets are not perfect, firms can buy protection against risk at a lower cost than the firm's shareholders because firms – particularly the larger ones that are frequent buyers of risk-protection tools – have access to the wholesale market for risk-protection instruments, an option that is not available to individual shareholders. In this case, corporate risk management creates value for the firm's shareholders.

RISK MANAGEMENT CAN LOWER FINANCIAL DISTRESS COSTS

By controlling the risks the firm faces, risk management can reduce the probability that the firm would experience **financial distress**, thus lowering the costs associated with financial distress (see footnote 2) and increasing the firm's value.

RISK MANAGEMENT CAN PROVIDE CLEARER INFORMATION TO INVESTORS ABOUT THE FIRM'S CORE ACTIVITIES

By protecting itself against risks that are unrelated to its core activities (for example, **foreign-exchange risk**), a firm can provide a clearer picture of its core activities to investors because they will be able to better distinguish between performance related to superior management (for example, the ability to effectively operate in foreign countries) and performance related to luck (for example, gains from unexpected movements in foreign-exchange rates). Clearer information about the firm's core activities should allow markets to value the firm more accurately, which should raise its value.

RISK MANAGEMENT CAN LOWER AGENCY COSTS

Following up on the previous point, to the extent that risk management allows shareholders to distinguish between superior performance resulting from managerial skill and superior performance resulting from luck, one can expect managers who are evaluated on their skill rather than luck to make investment decisions that are more

---

[3] See Graham and Smith (1999) who show that a 5 percent reduction in the volatility of taxable income can generate average tax savings of about 5.4 percent of expected tax liabilities. In extreme cases, these savings could exceed 40 percent.

aligned with shareholders' interests than their own interests. We return to this point later in the chapter.

CORPORATE RISK MANAGEMENT

Having explained *why* firms should manage the risk they face, we now turn to the issue of *how* firms should formulate and implement a risk management program. We presented in Chapter 7 the standard method to deal with risk when making an investment decision. Let's briefly review this method. To decide whether to make an investment, management should estimate the investment's net present value (NPV) by discounting to the present the cash-flow stream the investment is expected to generate in the future and deducting from that present value the investment's initial costs.[4] If the NPV is positive, the investment creates value and should be undertaken. If it is negative, the investment destroys value and should be rejected. How do we adjust the NPV formula to account for the risk of the investment? We do it by adjusting the discount rate for the risk of the investment: the riskier the investment, the higher the discount rate and the lower its NPV. In other words, the riskier the investment, the less valuable it is, reflecting the *risk aversion* of the firm's owners and lenders who financed the investment.

This method deals only with risk at the *project* level. Project-specific risks are best managed by the individuals who are directly responsible for the project. Firms, however, are exposed to multiple sources of risk that are not directly associated with specific projects. Some examples of **corporate risk** include the risk that key employees may leave the company, the risk of a company-wide labor unrest, the risk of a change in tax liability, the risk of a lawsuit, and the risk of damage to facilities caused by fire, weather, or earthquakes. These examples highlight the need to manage corporate risks centrally because otherwise some sources of risk unrelated to specific projects may be overlooked. Other reasons for wanting to manage risk centrally include: (1) risk netting, (2) cost savings, (3) risk policy, and (4) risk learning.

RISK NETTING

A **risk-netting** opportunity occurs when some project-specific risks cancel one another. For example, consider Felton, Inc., a US-based firm with two divisions that have international activities. Division A *buys* machinery parts in Germany and is thus exposed to the risk of having to purchase euros with US dollars to pay for the parts at a future date at an unknown exchange rate. Division B *sells* equipment in France and is thus exposed to the *opposite* risk of having to buy US dollars with the euros it will receive from selling the equipment at a future date at an unknown exchange rate. Each division carries a separate exposure to foreign-exchange risk, but what matters to the firm as a whole (and its owners) is the *net* exposure to the euro at the corporate level, which, in this case, is significantly lower than the individual risks borne by the two divisions.

COST SAVINGS

A cost-saving opportunity occurs when risk protection can be purchased centrally at a lower cost than if purchased at the division level. For example, buying centrally

---

[4] The discount rate is the weighted average of the costs of debt and equity used to finance the investment, called the weighted average cost of capital (WACC). See Chapter 12.

a fire insurance contract to protect all the firm's facilities around the world should be cheaper than the sum of all the individual contracts purchased locally to protect each facility separately.

RISK POLICY

A corporate-wide risk policy should be formulated because firms are exposed to multiple sources of risk with different individuals usually responsible for managing different types of risk. Typically, the treasurer buys protection against unexpected changes in foreign exchange and interest rates, the risk manager purchases insurance coverage and chooses the level of deductibles, and the procurement manager decides whether to protect against the fluctuations in the price of the commodities the firm buys as inputs to its production process. In principle, these individuals should coordinate their decisions, but in practice, often do not. Thus, it is essential to spell out how particular exposures to risk should be dealt with at the corporate as well as the divisional level.

Additionally, a governance system should be adopted that ensures that the policy is enforced. This aspect of risk management can be achieved only at the corporate level. If each division adopts its own risk policy and governance system, the aggregate impact at the corporate level is unlikely to be optimal. The risk policy should indicate which types of risk are acceptable for the company and which should be rejected and whether some protection against risk must be purchased if a risk is taken. We return to this point later in the chapter.

RISK LEARNING

One final reason for wanting to manage risk at the corporate level is to develop a central expertise in risk management. In this case, the department responsible for managing risk centrally can specialize in this function, learn from multiple experiences, develop deeper knowledge of risk management techniques, and provide better advice to each division than if they had to do it on their own. This approach, of course, does not mean that risk learning should occur only at the center. Risk learning should take place throughout the organization, from project-level all the way to headquarters, because risk is everyone's business.

THE RISK MANAGEMENT PROCESS

Firms may be exposed to risks they have not yet identified, as well as to risks they have identified but not properly assessed, that is, risks they have either underestimated or overestimated. The consequences are obvious: (1) risks as yet unidentified, against which the firm could have protected itself, can destroy value if they occur; (2) value-destroying investments are made because their risk has been underestimated; and (3) value-creating investments are turned down because their risk has been overestimated. To avoid these unfortunate consequences, firms must set up a comprehensive system to identify, measure, manage, and monitor the risks they face. The process required to set up such a system is described in Exhibit 15.1. It consists of the following five steps that are explained in the following sections:

Step 1: The identification of the potential risks the firm faces
Step 2: The measurement of these risks

Step 3: Their prioritization on a scale ranging from minor to major risks

Step 4: The formulation and enforcement of a company-wide risk policy that spells out how to deal with risk

Step 5: The continuous monitoring and improvement of the process over time

EXHIBIT 15.1	THE RISK MANAGEMENT PROCESS.

Step 1 Risk Identification	Step 2 Risk Measurement	Step 3 Risk Prioritization	Step 4 Risk Policy	Step 5 Risk Monitoring
Identifying and understanding the various sources of risk that can adversely affect the firm's cash flows and value	Measuring the impact of each risk on the firm's value by assessing the probability that the risk will occur[1] and estimating the resulting reduction in the firm's value	Classifying the risks according to their intensity by assigning them to categories ranging from minor risks to major risks	Formulating a policy to help decide which risks should be rejected and which should be accepted (either without or with protection) Stating who in the organization has the responsibility to make these decisions	Putting in place an internal audit and control system to continuously monitor the risk management process Reviewing periodically the previous four steps and modifying them in light of any learning experience

[1] The probability of occurrence is assessed within a given period of time, typically equal to the firm's planning horizon.

STEP 1: RISK IDENTIFICATION

The first step of any risk management system is to identify and understand the circumstances and events that give rise to a risk that may reduce the firm's value if it occurs. These circumstances and events are the source of risk – we say that they create a risk *exposure* for the firm. Of course, the number of such risks is large, and the purpose of the exercise is to come up with the list of those that are the most relevant to the firm. To facilitate this exercise, a checklist of potential risks is provided in Exhibit 15.2.

The first column in Exhibit 15.2 identifies the four distinct and main sources of risk faced by a typical firm. They are referred to as first-level risks or *level-1 risks*. These are (1) **business risk**; (2) **financial risk**; (3) **financial investment risk**; and (4) **currency risk**. Exhibit 15.3 shows where these four sources of risk originate on the firm's balance sheet. They are reviewed below.

BUSINESS RISK

Business risk is the most fundamental risk a firm faces. It is the direct consequence of conducting business in a constantly changing economic, political, and social environment while competing within an industry that is continuously evolving. Sources of business risk are unanticipated events and situations that can affect the firm's market value when they occur. As shown in Exhibits 15.2 and 15.4, this risk can be broken down into three non-overlapping second-level risks or *level-2 risks*, called **macro risk, strategic risk**, and **operational risk**, discussed below.

EXHIBIT 15.2	TYPES AND LEVELS OF CORPORATE RISK.

Level-1 Risks	Level-2 Risks	Level-3 Risks
1. Business risk	1.1 Macro risk	Economic risk
		Political risk
		Social risk
	1.2 Strategic risk	Competition risk
		Technological risk
		Other strategic risks
	1.3 Operational risk	Business process risk
		Commodity price risk
		Credit risk
		Fiscal risk
		Human capital risk
		Legal risk
		Property damage risk
		Reputational risk
		Other operational risks
2. Financial risk	2.1 Financial leverage risk	Financial distress risk
	2.2 Financing cost risk	
	2.3 Refinancing risk	
3. Financial investment risk	3.1 Liquidity risk	
	3.2 Price risk	
4. Currency risk	4.1 Exchange-rate risk	Country risk
	4.2 Exchange-control risk	Country risk

A large number of future events and situations can create business risk. How can the firm's management identify them? The standard method is to interview employees and consult experts. Conducting in-depth interviews with experienced employees who are familiar with the various aspects of the firm's operations quickly will reveal a multitude of business risks. Of course, some of those risks may not be important at the corporate level even if they matter to a particular area of the firm, but the exercise must first be exhaustive before the list can be eventually narrowed down.

Macro Risk.   Macro risk originates in the broad economic, political, and social environments in which the firm operates. It can thus be broken down into three separate categories based on the three "environments" that affect the firm's performance. They are listed as *level-3 risks* in the last column of Exhibit 15.2 and referred to as economic risk, political risk, and social or societal.

An example of **economic risk** is a steeper-than-expected slowdown in economic activity that would reduce the firm's future cash flow from assets and thus its current market value.

An example of **political risk** is *regulatory risk*, the risk of a change in government regulation that would restrict the firm's ability to raise the price of some of its

| EXHIBIT 15.3 | IDENTIFYING THE SOURCES OF FIRM RISK. |

RISKS ORIGINATING FROM THE FIRM'S BALANCE SHEET'

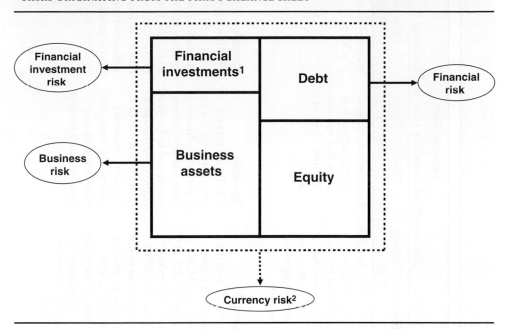

[1] Financial investments include cash, marketable securities, and long-term financial assets such as bonds and shares of other companies.

[2] Currency risk occurs when some of the firm's business assets, financial investments, or borrowing (debt) are denominated in a foreign currency. If a firm exports some of its products or services abroad, it will have accounts receivable denominated in foreign currencies; if it imports goods or services from abroad, it will have accounts payable denominated in foreign currencies.

goods and services; another example of political risk is **country risk**, the risk that a foreign government may prohibit a firm from transferring cash out of the foreign country in which it is doing business. Regulatory and country risks can be referred to as *level-4 risks* (not mentioned in Exhibit 15.2). This does not mean, however, that they are less important than higher-level risks. *For some firms, a level-4 risk, such as regulatory or country risk, may be the major source of business risk.*

Social risk or **societal risk** is generated by unanticipated changes in people's attitude toward work and consumption. Examples include changes in the behavior of a younger generation of employees that may require firms to modify the way work is organized (more freedom, more creative challenges), or changes in consumer behavior that may affect the type of products and services they want to buy. Firms may not correctly anticipate these behavioral changes. This, in turn, could adversely affect their market value because of their failure to adapt to a new type of workforce or to adjust to new consumer tastes.

Strategic Risk.   Strategic risk is associated with unanticipated changes in the dynamics of a firm's *industry* that may have a negative impact on the firm's market value. Some of these risks are listed as *level-3* risks in the last column of Exhibit 15.2 and described on the left side of Exhibit 15.4. The major sources of strategic risk are actions taken by competitors and key suppliers that would reduce the firm's market value. They include competition risk and technological risk.

EXHIBIT 15.4   SOURCES OF BUSINESS AND FINANCIAL RISKS.

Business Risk			Financial Risk		
Events that affect the firm's expected cash flow from assets			Additional risks resulting from debt financing		
Macro Risk	Strategic Risk	Operational Risk	Financial Leverage Risk	Financing Cost Risk	Refinancing Risk
Unanticipated "macro" events (over which the firm has little control) that may reduce expected revenues and/or raise expected costs	Unanticipated industry events (over which the firm has little control) that may reduce expected revenues and/or raise expected costs	Unanticipated events that occur when the firm implements its strategy that may reduce its expected revenues and/or raise its expected operating costs	When a firm borrows, the variability of its net profits increases, thus making the firm more risky to its owners	Unexpected changes in market interest rates that increase the firm's cost of debt	Inability to renew a loan
Examples: *Economic risk* A steeper-than-expected slowdown in economic activity	**Examples:** *Competition risk* More competition in the product market that lowers product prices, or less competition in the input market that raises input prices	**Examples:** *Business process risk* Disruptions in the supply chain, IT system, etc.; delays in the delivery of plant and equipment; labor unrest; and/or frauds and theft	**Example:** See the case of the Hologram Light Company (HLC) in Exhibit 15.5. If the firm does not borrow, its profits vary between minus 26 percent and plus EBIT); with	**Example:** The firm has taken out a one-year loan at 7 percent to finance a two-year investment. At the end of the year, market interest rates go up as a result of a	**Example:** The firm has taken out a one-year loan to finance a two-year investment. At the end of the year, the firm's bank refuses to renew the loan for an
Political risk Unexpected government regulations that constrain the firm's ability to generate profits	*Technological risk* New technology that makes existing products obsolete	*Commodity price risk* *Property damage risk* Damage to property due to fire, accidents, natural disasters, etc.	borrowing its profits vary between minus and plus 31 percent (see EAT)	"tighter" monetary policy. The firm can only renew its one-year loan at 9 percent	additional year. The firm is facing a major funding risk
Social risk Unanticipated changes in employees' and consumers' behavior		*Reputational risk* Withdrawal of defective products			

Examples of *competition risk* include an unexpected price reduction by a competitor on a product similar to the one offered by the firm that may force the firm to respond by cutting the price of its own product, which will reduce its future free cash-flow stream and hence its current market value; the launch by a competitor of a new product or service that would erode the sales of the firm's similar offerings; and the decision by a supplier to raise the price of a key input for which no substitute is immediately available.

Other types of strategic risk include *technological risk* – that is, the risk that the firm may not be able to adopt as rapidly as its competitors an emerging technology that will render the existing one obsolete. A classic example of this phenomenon is digital photography that eventually wiped out chemical photographic films.

Operational Risk.   The third and last source of business risk is operational risk. Operational risk occurs when the firm implements its strategy. These risks are associated with the "execution" of the firm's strategy. Examples of this type of risk include unexpected disruptions and delays in the firm's supply chain and information technology (IT) systems, possible labor unrest, unforeseen delays in the delivery of new plant and equipment, and the risk of fraud and theft. We group these sources of operational risks under the heading of *business process risk*.

Other types of operational risk include *commodity price risk* (the unexpected changes in the price of commodities the firm uses as inputs in its production processes); **credit risk** (the risk that some customers may not pay on time for the goods and services they purchased and possibly default on their payments to the firm);[5] *fiscal risk* (the risk of a change in the amount of taxes a firm has to pay, either because of a tax audit that ends up raising the amount of tax payment or because of a change in the tax laws); *human capital risk* (the inability to replace key employees who may leave the firm); *legal risk* (the risk of a lawsuit that may create a significant legal liability for the firm); *property damage risk* (the risk caused by events that damage the firm's plant, equipment, and facilities such as fire, accidents, floods, and earthquakes); and *reputational risk*. Reputational risk occurs, for example, when the firm has sold a product that is harmful to consumers or defective, causing the firm to withdraw the unsafe product from the market or recall the product with defective parts. The risk is that the firm's reputation may be damaged, which may reduce the firm's value temporarily or permanently.

Commodity price risk has been classified as operational because firms can protect against it (for example, an airline company can hedge against unexpected changes in the price of fuel). Credit risk has been classified as operational because it arises from the business practice of letting customers pay their bills at a later date, which is essentially an operating decision. Reputational risk has been classified as operational because it occurs as a consequence of poor execution, not because of a flawed strategy. In other words, the firm may have the right strategy but has failed to put in place a rigorous enough quality control system to detect unsafe or defective products. (For example, it is a sound strategy for Toyota to build cars in the United States, but its reputation was sullied when some of its US-built cars had defective parts.)

Changes in commodity prices, uncollectible accounts receivable, the departure of a key employee, supply disruptions, labor unrest, delivery delays, damages to property, higher-than-expected taxes, and defective products, are not strategic risks. They are adverse events that occur in the process of carrying out the firm's strategy.

---

[5] To account for this risk, firms make allowances for doubtful customers' accounts, that is, they reduce the reported value of their accounts receivable to reflect the potential losses (see Chapter 4).

The firm has some control over these *level-3* risks – indeed, hedging commodity prices, asking high-risk customers to pay their bills immediately in cash, introducing a more effective employee retention program, and enforcing more efficient management processes and policies can reduce these risks significantly.

Financial Risk

The second main source of risk a firm faces is financial risk. As pointed out in the introduction, this risk occurs when the firm borrows, as shown on the right side of the firm's balance sheet in Exhibit 15.3. If the firm is all-equity financed (that is, if it is 100 percent financed with equity capital), it does not carry any financial risk.

Financial risk is broken down into three nonoverlapping *level-2* risks that are the direct consequence of borrowing: **financial leverage risk**, **financing cost risk**, and **refinancing risk**. These risks are listed in the second column of Exhibit 15.2 and described in the right side of Exhibit 15.4.

Financial Leverage Risk.   We show in Chapter 13 that the risk borne by the firm's owners increases when the firm borrows. This risk, called financial leverage risk, is the most important manifestation of financial risk. When a firm borrows, it increases the *volatility* of its net profits, making the firm more risky for its shareholders. This phenomenon is illustrated in Exhibit 15.5 with the case of the Hologram Lighting Company (HLC), a firm we first encountered in Chapter 1. Its projected income statement, one year from now, shows expected sales of $1,000 million and expected operating expenses of $760 million (one half of operating expenses is variable, and the other is fixed). The resulting expected operating profit is $240 million (earnings before interest and tax, or EBIT). Deducting $40 million of *fixed* interest expenses gives a taxable profit of $200 million (earnings before tax, or EBT). Finally, deducting $100 million of tax expenses leaves an expected net profit of $100 million (earnings after tax, or EAT).

Consider now an unexpected drop or rise in sales of 10 percent. How does the variability of sales affect operating profit (EBIT) and net profit (EAT)? Look at the data in Exhibit 15.5. When sales vary between minus 10 percent and plus 10 percent,

EXHIBIT 15.5	UNDERSTANDING BUSINESS AND FINANCIAL RISKS: EFFECT ON EBIT, EBT, AND EAT OF A 10% DROP OR RISE IN SALES.

FIGURES IN MILLIONS

	Expected	Sales Down 10%		Sales Up 10%	
Sales	$1,000	$900	−10%	$1,100	+10%
less variable operating expenses	(380)	(342)	−10%	(418)	+10%
less fixed operating expenses	(380)	(380)	0%	(380)	0%
EBIT (earnings before interest and tax)	$240	$178	−26%	$302	+26%
less fixed interest expenses	(40)	(40)	0%	(40)	0%
EBT (earnings before tax)	$200	$138	−31%	$262	+31%
less variable tax expenses (50% tax rate)	(100)	(69)	−31%	(131)	+31%
EAT (earnings after tax)	$100	$69	−31%	$131	+31%

[1] Note that the expected scenario is the same as the one shown in the income statement in Exhibit 1.8 in Chapter 1.

EBIT varies between minus 26 percent and plus 26 percent and EAT between minus 31 percent and plus 31 percent. Clearly, the presence of *fixed* operating expenses has magnified the variability of EBIT. Likewise, the presence of *fixed* interest expenses has magnified the variability of EAT.

Had HLC not borrowed, its pre-tax net profit would be equal to EBIT (no interest expenses will be deducted in this case), and the risk borne by HLC's owners would be captured by the 26 percent volatility that is all business risk (there is no financial risk because there is no borrowing). With borrowing, HLC's pre-tax net profit is equal to EBT and the risk borne by HLC's owners has been magnified to 31 percent because of the financial risk created by the presence of *fixed* interest expenses. Conclusion: without borrowing, HLC's owners bear only business risk; with borrowing, they bear both business risk and financial risk.

What is the effect of financial leverage on the firm's value? We showed in Chapter 13 that in the presence of taxes and costly financial distress (see footnote 2), the firm's value is affected by financial leverage: there is an optimal level of borrowing for which the value of the firm's assets is maximized. Lower or higher levels of debt will reduce the value of the firm's assets below its optimal value.

Financing Cost Risk.   Financing cost risk, first introduced in Chapter 5, is the risk of not knowing the cost of the debt used to finance an investment. Why would a firm not know its cost of debt when it decides to make an investment? To illustrate, suppose that HLC borrows $1 million at 7 percent for *one* year to buy a new piece of equipment that it will operate over a period of two years. The firm's intention is to renew the one-year loan at the end of the first year for one more year. Assume further that HLC could have borrowed initially for two years at the same rate of 7 percent, but because it expected the one-year interest rate to *drop* below 7 percent next year, it decided to finance the investment with two consecutive one-year loans (instead of a single two-year loan at 7 percent). If next year's rate drops below 7 percent, the average cost of debt over the two-year investment will obviously be less than 7 percent. If it rises above 7 percent, the average cost of debt will be more than 7 percent. HLC is clearly taking a risk. More precisely, it is *speculating* that next year's interest rate will drop. It could have avoided that risk if it had borrowed for two years. Is that risk worth taking? Probably not, because the nature of HLC's business is not to make money speculating on the direction of interest rates. If HLC's owners wanted to speculate on the direction of interest rates, they would do it directly or invest in a financial firm that specializes in this type of activity.

Refinancing Risk.   Continuing with the same example, if HLC borrows for one year to finance the two-year investment, it is incurring an additional risk called refinancing risk, first discussed in Chapter 5. Suppose that in one year the economic outlook deteriorates and that HLC's bank responds to this new environment by restricting credit to HLC, turning down the firm's request to renew the loan for one year. What would happen in this case? HLC may have to terminate the project and sell the piece of equipment it bought last year to repay the loan. Most likely, it will sell it for less than $1 million and may thus find itself in a precarious situation if it is unable to repay the bank loan. HLC could have avoided this risk if it had borrowed for two years. Again, is that risk worth taking? Certainly not, because the consequences for the firm if it is not able to renew its loan are significantly more important than the potential gain from a possible drop in interest rates next year.

FINANCIAL INVESTMENT RISK

Although firms are generally net borrowers (their debt exceeds their cash holding), they also act as lenders to other firms and often hold shares in other companies. They thus carry risks associated with *financial* investments, which we call *financial* investment risk. This risk is shown on the left side of the firm's balance sheet in Exhibit 15.3. This risk is, in turn, broken down into two no overlapping *level-2* risks called **liquidity risk** and **price risk** (see Exhibit 15.2).

Consider HLC again. Assume it holds marketable securities such as commercial paper (see Chapter 11) as well as shares in a company called ALPAC. ALPAC was a division of HLC. Two years ago, HLC decided to list it on the stock market as a separate company through an initial public offering. HLC, however, still holds 10 percent of ALPAC shares. Both the marketable securities and the ALPAC shares that HLC holds carry a specific financial investment risk discussed below.

Liquidity Risk.   Even though the marketable securities HLC holds are liquid – meaning that HLC should be able to convert them into cash rapidly and without significant loss of value – they nevertheless carry a liquidity risk. This is the risk that HLC may have an unexpected need for cash and may end up selling some of these short-term securities at a loss if market conditions are unstable.[6]

Price Risk.   ALPAC shares carry a price risk – that is, the risk that their price may fall below the price HLC received when it listed them. The ALPAC share price moves up and down as the market updates its assessment of ALPAC's business prospects. Over time, ALPAC may underperform and its share price may drop below its original price. As a result, the value of HLC will decline to reflect the loss on the ALPAC shares it owns.

CURRENCY RISK

Broadly speaking, currency risk occurs because of unexpected changes in the exchange rate between the home currency and the currency of a foreign country in which a firm is doing business. We can distinguish between two forms of *level-2* currency risk: **exchange-rate risk** and **exchange-control risk**. The former is caused by the market fluctuations in the exchange rates between two currencies in a regime of free-floating rates. The latter is caused by unexpected changes in the *fixed* exchange rate between two currencies in a regime of managed float or exchange control.[7] A *level-3* currency risk includes country risk, such as the restrictions imposed by a foreign government on the flow of funds between the home country

---

[6] We have argued earlier that firms should manage the risk of their net exposure; in this case, their net debt position (debt net of cash and marketable securities). However, two firms with the same amount of net debt might face a different risk exposure if they hold marketable securities with different liquidity risk. Furthermore, net debt is also affected by the risk associated with maturity mismatch (debt has typically longer maturities than cash equivalents). We, therefore, recommend that firms manage the risk of their cash-equivalent position independently from their borrowing risk.

[7] In a managed float regime, a government allows its currency to fluctuate within a narrow band in relation to a foreign currency (usually the US dollar) and intervenes in the foreign-exchange market to buy or sell its currency to maintain it within the chosen band. In a fixed exchange rate regime, a government will intervene in the market to maintain a fixed rate between the home currency and a foreign currency (usually the US dollar).

and the rest of the world. Currency risk and its effect on the firm's decision to invest abroad are examined in Chapter 17.

Step 2: Risk Measurement

Having identified the potential risks the firm is facing, management must now measure these risks and rank them. Identifying them is only the first step in the risk management process. If these risks cannot be measured, the firm will not be able to manage them (you cannot manage what you cannot measure). What would then be the appropriate measure of a risk a firm is facing? Because what matters in the end is whether that risk has a negative impact on the firm's *value*, the appropriate measure of a risk is the *expected reduction in the firm's value if that risk occurs*. We call it **market value at risk (MVR)** and calculate it as follows:

$$
\text{MVR} = \begin{bmatrix} \text{Reduction in the} \\ \text{firm's value if} \\ \text{the risk occurs} \end{bmatrix} \times \begin{bmatrix} \text{Probability that} \\ \text{the risk will occur} \end{bmatrix} \qquad (15.1)
$$

To illustrate, let's consider the simplified case of the No Growth Company (NGC). It generates an annual perpetual cash flow from assets of $100 million, and its cost of capital is 10 percent. NGC's enterprise value is thus $1,000 million ($100 million of perpetual cash flow divided by a 10 percent cost of capital; see Chapter 10). Suppose that NGC is exposed to the four risks listed in the first column in Exhibit 15.6.

The first is a strategic risk (Risk A). NGC's management believes that there is a 50 percent chance that a competing firm will launch a new product within the next 12 months that will reduce NGC's annual free cash flows by $20 million forever. The present value, at the cost of capital of 10 percent, of this annual perpetual reduction in cash flow is $200 million (see the third column in Exhibit 15.6). With a 50 percent chance of occurrence, the impact of this risk on NGC's enterprise value is $100 million (50 percent of $200 million). The $100 million is the measure of NGC's strategic risk exposure that we call MVR.

Referring to Exhibit 15.6 and using the same approach, NGC's management estimates that the firm is exposed to a currency risk (Risk B) with an MVR of $20 million, a financing cost risk (Risk C) with an MVR of $10 million, and a business process risk related to potential disruptions in the supply chain (Risk D) with an MVR of $1 million (refer to the answer to Self-Test Question 15.3 that shows how these risk measures are estimated).

Note in the fifth column of Exhibit 15.6 the relative rating of the four risks. Risk A has the largest MVR ($100 million), but why is it rated "a high risk"? Recall that NGC's enterprise value is $1,000 million; thus, the MVR of Risk A is equal to 10 percent of NGC's enterprise value, which represents a significant risk exposure. The MVR of Risk B is 2 percent of enterprise value and that of Risk C is 1 percent. Both are rated "moderate." The MVR of Risk D is 0.1 percent of enterprise value and is rated "low." In general, a risk with an MVR of 10 percent or more of a firm's enterprise value would be rated high, and a risk with an MVR of 0.1 percent or less of a firm's enterprise value would be rated low. There is, of course, no rigid risk-rating rule – each firm should adjust the scale according to its owners' tolerance for risk.

EXHIBIT 15.6	RISK MEASUREMENT.

Type of Risk[1] (1)	Probability of Occurrence[2] (2)	Impact on the Firm's Market Value[3] (3)	Market Value at Risk (MVR)		Ability to Control the Risk[4] (5)
			(4) = (2) × (3)	Rating	
Strategic risk (A)	50%	$200 million	$100 million	High	Low
Currency risk (B)	10%	$200 million	$ 20 million	Moderate	High
Financing cost risk (C)	50%	$ 20 million	$ 10 million	Moderate	Moderate
Business process risk (D)	10%	$ 10 million	$ 1 million	Low	Moderate

[1] See Exhibit 15.2.

[2] Within the next 12 months.

[3] Estimation of the reduction in the firm's market value if the corresponding risk materializes.

[4] The firm's ability to take action to reduce the risk.

STEP 3: RISK PRIORITIZATION

A firm does not have to bear all the risk exposures it faces. It can protect itself against some of them. For example, the currency risk NGC faces (Risk B) can be eliminated over the next 12 months using a technique we present in Chapter 17. It is thus rated "highly controllable" in the last column of Exhibit 15.6, meaning that it is possible for NGC to eliminate this type of risk over the next 12 months at a reasonable cost.

Contrary to the case of currency risk, the ability of NGC to control Risk A is low because NGC cannot do much during the next 12 months to prevent the competitor's new product from eroding NGC's sales. NGC should have anticipated this move earlier. (Is NGC investing enough time and resources to find out what the competition is doing?) It could have launched a new product, but at this point, NGC can do little to mitigate that risk. The financing cost risk (Risk C) and the risk of disruptions in the supply chain (Risk D) are both rated "moderate." NGC could use risk-control instruments to reduce the financing cost risk it faces, but these instruments are not as reliable and inexpensive as those used to control currency risk. The supply-disruption risk was rated "moderate" because NGC has the ability to switch rapidly and inexpensively to another supplier if disruptions occur with its current supplier.

We can now put each risk in one of the nine boxes shown in the graph in Exhibit 15.7. The MVR is on the vertical axis, going from low to high MVR. The firm's ability to control risk is shown on the horizontal axis, going from high to low control. The graph has nine possible combinations: three are labeled "major risk," two are labeled "important risk," and four are labeled "minor risk." These three different labels (major, important, and minor risks) are a measure of **risk severity**. For example, Risk A (strategic risk) is a "major risk" because it has a high impact on NGC's value, but the firm's ability to control it is low. Risk C (financing cost risk) is an "important risk" because it has a moderate impact on NGC's value, and the firm's ability to control it is moderate. Both Risk B and Risk D are minor risks.

EXHIBIT 15.7	MAPPING FIRM RISKS ACCORDING TO THEIR SEVERITY.[1]

Impact of risk on the firm's market value

	High	Moderate	Low
High	Important risk	Major risk	Major risk *(Risk A in Exhibit 15.6)*
Moderate	Minor risk *(Risk B in Exhibit 15.6)*	Important risk *(Risk C in Exhibit 15.6)*	Major risk
Low	Minor risk	Minor risk *(Risk D in Exhibit 15.6)*	Minor risk

Ability to control risk

[1] There are three levels of risk severity: minor risks, important risks, and major risks.

A risk with a high MVR (meaning that its impact on the firm's value is high if it occurs) is not necessarily a major risk if it is highly controllable (see the upper-left-side box in Exhibit 15.7). Likewise, a risk with a moderate MVR can be a major risk if the firm's ability to control it is low (see the middle-right-side box in Exhibit 15.7). In other words, risk severity (major, important, or minor) depends on the impact the risk has on the firm's value *adjusted* by the firm's ability to control that risk.

STEP 4: RISK POLICY

Having identified, measured, and mapped the risks the firm is facing, management must now formulate a policy to deal with these exposures. Specifically, faced with a risk exposure, management can do one of three things:

1. *Reject the risk altogether*, that is, decide not to undertake the activity that generates the risk (or abandon an ongoing activity whose risk has increased)
2. *Accept the risk without protecting the firm against it*, that is, decide to go ahead with the activity (or maintain it if it is ongoing) and cover any losses that may occur using the firm's own resources
3. *Accept the risk and protect the firm against it*, that is, go ahead with the activity and take action to protect the firm against the risk exposure through one of three methods: *insurance, diversification,* or *hedging*

The issue then is to formulate a corporate-wide risk policy that will help managers decide which options to select when confronted with a risky decision. Before examining these options, we first review some of the most important characteristics that a firm's risk policy should display.

GOVERNANCE

Who should formulate the firm's risk policy? It is the role of senior management to design the firm's risk policy and submit it to the board of directors for approval. The firm may then appoint a chief risk officer to oversee and coordinate the implementation of the policy, reporting to the firm's chief executive. If the firm is not large enough to justify the creation of the position of chief risk officer, the firm's chief financial officer or the senior executive in charge of strategy usually takes on the responsibility. Who should make the decision to reject or accept the major and important risks the firm faces? That decision is often made by a *risk management committee* co-chaired by the firm's chief executive and the chief risk officer. In other words, risk management is the domain of the most senior executives. This does not mean, however, that the rest of the organization is not concerned; on the contrary, as we pointed out earlier, senior management should foster a culture of "risk-is-everyone's business" throughout the firm.

VALUE CREATION

The guiding principle for making risk management decisions is still the fundamental finance principle stated in Chapter 1 and reviewed earlier in this chapter: management must manage the firm's resources with the ultimate objective of creating value. This value-creation objective is achieved only when the firm accepts new risky investments (or retains existing risky investments) that have a positive NPV *after adjusting the NPV for all the risks associated with the investment.*

CORPORATE RISK

The firm is not only exposed to project-specific risks but also to sources of corporate risk that are not captured by its individual projects. The firm's risk policy must provide guidance on how to deal with these risks. For example, the risk management committee, with the help of the firm's human resources department, should formulate a personnel-retention policy to reduce the loss of key employees, an important source of corporate risk. Other examples include the formulation of policies that minimize the risks of lawsuits, fiscal audits, product recalls, IT system failures, and so on.

ALIGNING THE INTERESTS OF MANAGERS WITH THOSE OF OWNERS

Managers may have a different tolerance for risk than that of the firm's owners. In general, one would expect them to be more conservative than shareholders because their salaries, employment prospects, and retirement income may be endangered if the firm makes risky investments that could threaten its survival. Shareholders are usually more diversified than managers (because they hold shares in many companies) and are thus willing to accept more risk than managers to achieve higher expected returns.[8]

---

[8] In some cases, the firm's managers are *more* diversified than the firm's owners and thus ready to invest in riskier projects than owners would have liked. This would be the case of a firm that belongs to undiversified owners who invested all their wealth in the firm while managers' wealth is diversified. In this case, some managers, particularly those with a bonus related to a high profit, would be ready to invest in risky projects that produce high profits (they get the bonus) or high losses (they lose the bonus, but their portfolio is not affected). See Chapter 16.

The firm's risk policy must align the interests of managers with those of share-holders by encouraging managers to accept value-creating projects even if these projects have more risk than they wish to accept as individuals.

PERFORMANCE EVALUATION

Consider a US-based firm that exports some of its products to Japan. Manager A has bought protection against changes in the exchange rate between the US dollar and the Japanese yen, and his division generated a year-end operating profit of $15 million ($16 million less $1 million for foreign-exchange protection) on $100 million of invested capital, that is, a return on invested capital (ROIC) of 15 percent (16 percent less the 1 percent cost of protection). Manager B did not protect her profit against foreign-exchange risk. A year later, the US dollar weakened and her division, which also employs $100 million of capital, reported $20 million of operating profits of which $5 million were foreign-exchange gains resulting from the weakening of the US dollar relative to the Japanese yen. Manager B's ROIC is thus 20 percent, including 5 percent of foreign-exchange gains. How should we judge the performance of the two managers? If the firm's risk policy requires that foreign-exchange risk be systematically covered, then Manager A should *not* be penalized for covering his division's foreign-exchange risk and missing the opportunity to make a currency gain. His reward should be based on whether his 15 percent performance exceeds a minimum required rate of return for the division. Under the same policy, Manager B should *not* be rewarded for reporting a 5 percent extra operating profit through currency gains and *should* be blamed for not covering her division's foreign-exchange risk. Her reward should be based on whether her 15 percent performance exceeds a minimum required rate of return for the division.

COORDINATION WITH THE FIRM'S STRATEGIC MANAGEMENT PROCESS

A firm's risk management process cannot take place separately from the firm's strategic decision-making process. The two processes must be coordinated. It is not possible to formulate a sound strategy independently of the risk exposures that the strategy creates. Likewise, it is not possible to devise a corporate-wide risk policy independently of the strategies that generate those risks. Clearly, the decisions of the risk management committee must be coordinated with those of the firm's strategy committee with the single objective of making risk-adjusted value-creating decisions. Having presented a number of issues a firm's risk policy should address, we now return to the three options open to management when faced with an identified and measured risk. As you recall, there are three courses of action: (1) reject the risk and the investment that generates it; (2) accept the risk without protecting the firm against it; and (3) accept the risk and protect the firm against it. It is the role of the risk management committee to provide guidance on which alternative to choose when facing a particular risk.

THE DECISION TO REJECT THE RISK

The firm's management may decide that some major risks are not acceptable either as a matter of principle (for example, the firm does not invest in developing countries with poor human rights records) or because management has concluded that the investment could not generate an expected return high enough to justify the risk (for example, the firm does not invest in countries where it believes political risk is too high even if the expected return is also high).

THE DECISION TO ACCEPT THE RISK WITHOUT PROTECTION

In this case, the firm decides to undertake an activity that carries an important or major risk without trying to reduce that risk. Why would a firm undertake an activity without risk protection? One reason may be that the risk protection is unavailable or that it is prohibitively expensive and thus unjustified. But the most important reason to accept a risk without protection is that risk taking is the essence of business activities. As we said in the introduction, if the firm does not accept some risk, it would not be able to generate a return that would attract equity capital.

Accepting the risk without protection does not mean that the firm should not take any measure to reduce the risk. For example, if fire insurance is not available on some of the firm's facilities, strict measures should be enforced to prevent fires from occurring.

THE DECISION TO ACCEPT THE RISK AND PROTECT AGAINST IT

As pointed out earlier, a firm can use three methods to protect itself against a risk exposure: insurance, diversification, or hedging.

Insurance.   In this case, the firm buys the protection (if available) by paying an **insurance premium** to an insurance company. (The premium is the amount of money the firm must pay to be insured against a risk during a specific period of time.)[9] Only certain types of risk can be insured; they are usually event risks, that is, risks that occur infrequently and that reduce the firm's value significantly if they occur. An example of such "catastrophic" risk is the destruction of property caused by fire and natural disasters.

Firms usually do not purchase full insurance coverage; they may buy insurance for damages above a certain amount (called a deductible) to reduce the premium paid. The objective for the firm is to purchase an optimal insurance coverage at the least possible overall cost.

Diversification.   The risk-reduction property of diversification is explained in Chapters 3 and 12. As long as the firm combines investments whose expected returns are not perfectly positively correlated, the firm's owners will benefit from diversification because losses on some of the investments will be offset by gains on other investments in the firm's portfolio.

The question to ask is whether this risk management policy creates value. We show in Chapter 14 that Company A cannot create value by buying Company B for the sole purpose of reducing the risk of the combination (that is, the combined companies would *not* have a higher value than the sum of their separate values). The reason is straightforward: shareholders can achieve the same risk diversification by buying shares of the two companies, so why would they pay a premium to buy the

---

[9] The insurance company diversifies the risks it has taken by selling a large number of policies. A few facilities will be damaged by fires, and a large number will not. For the insurance company, it does not matter which firm falls into which category. To be profitable, the insurance company will set the premium so that the total money collected exceeds the expected payment to the firms whose facilities will be damaged.

merged companies? One way for a firm to create value and achieve risk diversification is to acquire assets that are *unavailable* to its shareholders and take action to increase their expected returns through better management. This could be achieved, for example, by buying assets in a foreign market that are not accessible to other firms and improving their performance.

Hedging.   Hedging is a risk management technique whose objective is to reduce or eliminate a risk exposure by taking an offsetting position. The offsetting position can be taken by buying or selling (1) a **forward contract**; (2) a **futures contract**; or (3) an **option contract**. These three types of hedging instrument are described in the next two chapters where we show how they can be used to hedge commodity price risk, financing cost risk, and currency risk.

STEP 5: RISK MONITORING

The final step in the process recognizes the dynamic nature of risk management. Once the process has been initiated, it is the responsibility of the senior executive in charge of risk management to ensure that the system in place is monitored and audited on a continuous basis. The risk management committee that was established to formulate and enforce the firm's risk policy could also be tasked with reviewing the system periodically and, if required, modifying it to make it more efficient, that is, less costly, more integrated with the firm's strategic decisions, and more focused on value creation. Over time, management learns from its experience in dealing with risk and that learning should be used to improve the firm's risk management system.

KEY POINTS

1. A firm cannot create value if it does not take on some risk. The challenge then is to manage the firm's exposure to risk with the objective of maximizing value creation.
2. When markets are imperfect, corporate risk management can add value by reducing the firm's income tax payments over time, by protecting the firm against risks at a lower cost than if investors did it themselves, by lowering the firm's financial distress and agency costs, and by providing clearer information to investors about the firm's core activities. Furthermore, when information is imperfect, managers know more about their firm's prospects than do outside shareholders. In this case, managers can identify risk exposures and protect against them better than outside shareholders.
3. Firms must set up a comprehensive system to identify, measure, manage, and monitor the risks they face. The process consists of the following five steps: (1) the identification of the potential risks the firm faces; (2) the measurement of these risks; (3) their prioritization on a scale ranging from minor to major risks; (4) the formulation and enforcement of a company-wide risk policy that spells out how to deal with risk; and (5) the continuous monitoring and improvement of the process over time.
4. We have identified four main sources of risk: (1) business risk; (2) financial risk; (3) financial investment risk; and (4) currency risk and shown how these so-called level-1 risks can be broken down into lower-level risks. This is illustrated in Exhibit 15.2.

5. A risk exposure can be measured by estimating the expected risk reduction in the firm's value if that risk occurs. This is done by calculating the market value at risk (MVR) of that risk exposure using equation 15.1.

6. After having identified and measured the risks it is facing, the firm must classify them according to their MVRs and the firm's ability to control them. This is illustrated in Exhibit 15.7.

7. Having identified, measured, and prioritized the risks the firm is facing, management must then formulate a policy to deal with these exposures by doing one of three things: (1) reject the risk altogether; (2) accept the risk without protecting the firm against it; or (3) accept the risk and protect the firm against it through one of three methods: insurance, diversification, or hedging. The final step is to monitor and review the firm's risk management system over time and improve its performance through continuous learning.

FURTHER READING

1. Graham, John, and Clifford Smith. "Tax Incentives to Hedge." *Journal of Finance* 54 (December 1999).
2. Hopkin, Paul. *Fundamentals of Risk Management*. 4th ed. Kogan Page Limited, 2017.
3. Servaes, Henri, Ane Tamayo, and Peter Tufano. "The Theory and Practice of Corporate Risk Management." *Journal of Applied Corporate Finance* 21 (Fall 2009).

SELF-TEST QUESTIONS

15.1 Risk management.

Provide five reasons that would justify why a firm should manage its risk centrally and briefly explain each reason.

15.2 Risk identification.

Consider the following situations and events that are sources of firm risk. Say whether the situation or event is a source of business risk (which type?), financial risk (which type?), financial investment risk (which type?), or currency risk (which type?), and indicate what the firm could do to protect itself against the resulting risk exposure.

1. The General Media Company holds 10 percent of the shares of Fastcom, a telecom company over which it has no control
2. A European firm receives cash dividends for a subsidiary based in the United States
3. A Japanese firm has plants located in an island that is often hit by severe storms
4. The central bank is expected to announce a more restrictive monetary policy
5. A single supplier provides the firm with an important piece of equipment
6. The firm sells on credit to a government-sponsored agency
7. The firm finances an asset with a four-year useful life using a two-year loan
8. A firm manufactures old-fashioned baby dolls

15.3 Risk measurement.

The No Growth Company (NGC) generates an expected annual perpetual cash flow from assets of $100 million and has a cost of capital of 10 percent. It is exposed to the four risks listed in the first column of Exhibit 15.6.

a. What is the market value at risk (MVR) of the strategic risk if the effect of this risk is to reduce NGC's expected cash flow from assets by $20 million if the risk occurs?
b. What is the MVR of the currency risk if the effect of this risk is to reduce NGC's expected cash flow from assets by $20 million if the risk occurs?
c. What is the MVR of the financing cost risk if the effect of this risk is to raise NGC's cost of capital to 10.2 percent if the risk occurs?
d. What is the MVR of the business process risk if the effect of this risk is to reduce NGC's expected cash flow from assets by $1 million if the risk occurs?

REVIEW QUESTIONS

1. **Various types of risk.**
   Explain the difference between the risks that make up the following pairs:

   a. Business risk versus financial risk
   b. Diversifiable risk versus undiversifiable risk
   c. Systematic risk versus unsystematic risk
   d. Insurable risk versus uninsurable risk
   e. Project risk versus corporate risk
   f. Foreign-exchange risk versus currency risk
   g. Financial investment risk versus financial risk
   h. Financial risk versus credit risk
   i. Liquidity risk versus refinancing risk
   j. Financing cost risk versus refinancing risk

2. **Systematic risk.**
   A firm has no financial investments, and all its activities are in the domestic market where it faces no foreign competition. It has a debt-to-equity ratio of 1 and is the subject of a 40 percent tax rate. Its beta coefficient is 1.20.

   a. What are the risks the firm faces? Explain your answer.
   b. What is the percentage of its systematic risk that is financial?

3. **Risk policy.**
   What are the major issues that a firm risk policy must address? Indicate what a firm could do to resolve these issues.

4. **Measuring risk exposure.**
   The General Construction Company (GCC) is expecting a cash flow from assets of €50 million next year that is expected to grow forever at 3 percent. Its cost of capital is 11 percent. The firm is exposed to the following three risks:

   • There is a 10 percent chance that its cost of capital will increase to 11.5 percent
   • There is a 60 percent chance that its growth rate will drop to 1 percent
   • There is a 40 percent chance that its cash flow will decline to €45 million

   a. What is the market value at risk of each one of the events listed above?
   b. Indicate if they are high, moderate, or low risk.

5. **Inventory value and the risk of obsolescence.**
   HDM, a computer manufacturing company, holds computer parts in its inventory whose prices fall rapidly because suppliers can produce them faster, more efficiently, and in large quantities just a few months after they are first introduced on the market. HDM also uses a standard machine to assemble its computers. Over the last five years, the company that sells this machine has come up with a new, better performing piece of equipment every two years, rendering somewhat obsolete the assembler HDM bought earlier. What are the two types of risk HDM is exposed to, and what could it do to protect itself against these two sources of risk?

UNDERSTANDING FORWARD, FUTURES, AND OPTIONS AND THEIR CONTRIBUTION TO CORPORATE FINANCE

CHAPTER **16**

In the previous chapter we identified a variety of risks a firm is exposed to. In this chapter we review a number of instruments and techniques that are used to *hedge* price risk, that is, to protect the firm against the risk of unexpected changes in the price of an asset such as a commodity or a financial asset. The commodity could be an industrial metal like copper, an agricultural product like coffee, or an energy product like crude oil. The financial asset could be a common stock, a stock market index or a government bond. Hedging against unanticipated fluctuations in the price of a foreign currency is covered in the next chapter. The basic hedging instruments are forward, futures and option contracts.

In addition to examining how a firm can hedge price risk, we also show how option contracts can be used to: (1) estimate the value of a firm's equity and debt; (2) design alternative financing instruments (for example, bonds with an option that gives the firm the right to buy them back from the bondholders under certain conditions); and (3) evaluate a project that offers the firm valuable future opportunities (for example, building today a small plant with the option to expand it later if it turns out to be successful). After reading this chapter, you should understand the following:

- What forward, futures and option contracts are and the differences between these three types of contracts
- How futures and options markets are organized and how to trade in these markets
- How to use these contracts to hedge the price risk of a commodity or a financial asset
- How to determine the price of a forward, futures and option contract
- How to design option-based investment strategies
- Why a firm's equity and debt can be viewed as options on the firm's assets
- How to identify and value the options embedded in some securities such as callable and convertible bonds
- Why some investment projects provide future opportunities to firms and how to use option models to value these opportunities

FORWARD CONTRACTS

The Wiring & Tubing Manufacturing Company (WTM) has just won a major contract to deliver copper-made electrical wires, plumbing tubes and building fixtures to a construction company that is undertaking a large housing project. WTM will begin manufacturing these products in three months and will need 100 metric tons of copper at that point in time.

PRICE RISK

The *current* price of copper – called the **cash price** or the **spot price** – is $6,000 per ton. WTM could buy 100 tons of copper now for $600,000 and store it for three months. Alternatively, it could wait and buy 100 tons of copper in three months at a price *unknown* today. In this case, WTM will have to bear some **price risk** because it may end up buying copper at a price that could be significantly higher or lower than $6,000 per ton (it is not unusual for the price of copper to rise or fall by as much as 20 percent within a three-month period).

When WTM prepared the bid for the construction job, it used a copper price of $6,000 per ton. At that price, WTM expected to make an operating profit of $200,000. What would happen if the price of copper in three months rose to $7,000 per ton? WTM will have to pay an additional $100,000 for the 100 tons of copper ($1,000 × 100 tons) and its operating profit will be cut in half. What if the price of copper *fell* in three months? WTM will have a *higher* operating profit. As the example illustrates, the price risk can either benefit or harm WTM. However, WTM's main concern will be the unfavorable scenarios in which the price of copper rises and profit falls.

One way for WTM to avoid this price risk is to ask its copper supplier to deliver 100 tons of copper in three months *at a price fixed today*. Suppose the supplier accepts and quotes a price of $6,133 per ton for delivery and payment in three months. (We show you later how prices for future delivery are determined.) By agreeing to this arrangement, WTM and its supplier have entered into a **forward contract** whereby WTM has the obligation to buy from the supplier 100 tons of copper in three months at a price of $6,133 per ton. The contractual price, which has been fixed today, is called the 3-month **forward price** of a ton of copper. Note that the forward contract does not require any payment today. On the **settlement date** of the contract (also called the contract's **maturity date** or its **expiration date**) WTM will pay, and the supplier will receive, $6,133 per ton of copper *regardless of what the spot price is on that date*, thereby eliminating the price risk for *both* parties.

The elimination of the price risk, however, does not mean that WTM and its supplier do not bear other types of risks. There are two additional risks associated with a forward contract: counterparty risk and liquidity risk.

COUNTERPARTY RISK

Counterparty risk or **credit default risk** is the risk that one of the parties defaults on its contractual obligations on the date of the settlement. In our case, either the copper supplier or WTM could default on its respective obligation. The copper supplier may not have the 100 tons of copper that must be delivered in three months, forcing WTM to buy the copper at the spot price prevailing in three months. And WTM may be short of cash and unable to pay for the copper on the settlement date.

LIQUIDITY RISK

Suppose that the housing project is delayed. In this case, WTM could take delivery of the copper in three months and pay for storage until the project begins. Alternatively, WTM could try to renegotiate the settlement date with its supplier, who may or may not accept postponing the delivery to another date. Another possibility is for WTM to try to sell the contract to a third party. In the latter case, the new counterparty will need to be approved by the copper supplier and be willing to accept buying 100 tons of copper at $6,133 a ton for delivery on the date specified in the contract. Clearly, finding a new counterparty willing to take on this particular contract is not a transaction that can be completed easily and rapidly.

The risk of not being able to rapidly and easily renegotiate the terms of a forward contract or find another party to whom the contract could be sold, is usually referred to as a **liquidity risk**: it is related to the fact that forward contracts are custom-made and therefore cannot be 'undone' before their settlement date, that is, they cannot be easily and rapidly renegotiated or passed on to a third party without incurring a significant loss.

We show in the next section how **futures markets** were created to mitigate counterparty and liquidity risks and facilitate the use of contractual agreements that settle in the future.

FUTURES CONTRACTS AND MARKETS

Our previous example illustrates how customized forward contracts between two firms can eliminate the price risk associated with the future delivery of a commodity. But these contracts carry counterparty and liquidity risks. In this section, we explain how these two risks can be practically eliminated if forward contracts are traded on **organized exchanges**, called **futures exchanges** or futures markets.[1] The forward contracts that are traded in the futures markets are called **futures contracts**. We show next how futures markets operate.

HOW FUTURES MARKETS MITIGATE COUNTERPARTY RISK

There are two structural elements of futures markets that allow them to practically eliminate counterparty risk: one is the existence of a **central clearing house**, the other is the requirement that traders settle their positions at the end of each trading day through a mechanism called **marking-to-market**.[2]

THE CENTRAL CLEARING HOUSE

Recall our earlier example of the forward contract between WTM and the copper supplier. In this privately negotiated arrangement, WTM and the copper supplier deal directly with each other and, as a result, are exposed to counterparty risk, as either one could default on its contractual obligation. Consider now the case of futures

---

[1] Note that there are so-called **over-the-counter** (OTC) **markets** in which a dealer would act as an intermediary and stand ready to buy and sell forward contracts before their settlement date. A dealer would hold the contracts until he finds a buyer. Even though OTC markets provide some liquidity, they are not easily accessible and not fully transparent. Transaction costs are also relatively high in these markets. See Chapter 11.

[2] Most futures exchanges impose a **price limit** on the trading of some futures contracts to protect them against extreme movements in futures prices. If the drop in price reaches the price limit, trading is suspended.

contracts on copper that trade on the London Metal Exchange (LME).[3] An investor who wants to buy or sell copper on a future date can enter into a futures contract with the *exchange* as counterparty rather than transacting *directly* with another investor who wants to sell or buy. By serving as counterparty to both buyers and sellers, the exchange assumes the counterparty risk of *all* the futures positions and minimizes the risk that the entire exchange fails if an individual trader defaults.[4]

Note that no money actually changes hands when contracts are 'bought' or 'sold' and thus using the terms 'buying' and 'selling' a contract is not strictly correct. The proper way to describe the buyer of a contract is to say that he has a **long position** in the contract or, simply, that he is **long**. For a seller, we say that she has a **short position** in the contract or, simply, that she is **short**.

This trading system raises the following question: how does the clearing house protect itself against potential defaults by buyers or sellers? First, as pointed out earlier, the clearing house diversifies its risk because it is unlikely that most traders will default at the same time. Second, the clearing house requires that traders who lose money at the end of the trading day pay cash for their losses after the market has closed on that day. In other words, traders are not allowed to accumulate their losses or gains until the final settlement day. They must settle their position at the end of every trading day. As mentioned earlier, this requirement is called marking-to-market.

MARKING-TO-MARKET AND MARGIN REQUIREMENT

In order to trade on a futures market, traders must first open an account with a broker in which they make an initial deposit before they can start trading. This deposit, called a **margin account**, varies between 5 to 15 percent of the value of the contract that will be traded. We say that the exchange imposes a **margin requirement** and that traders must post a margin.

Suppose WTM bought futures contracts on the LME this morning to take delivery in three months of 100 tons of copper at $6,200 per ton. (Copper contracts on the LME are denominated in US dollars.) Assume that the futures price of copper dropped to $6,190 at the close of the market. WTM has thus lost $1,000 ($10 per ton × 100 tons). Marking-to-market means that the $1,000 loss generated by WTM's long position will be deducted from its account with its broker.[5] The opposite applies to a seller of 100 tons. The $1,000 *gain* from her short position will be added to her account. (Note that a *short* position generates a *gain* when the contract price *drops*.)

HOW FUTURES MARKETS MITIGATE LIQUIDITY RISK

There are two features of futures markets that allow them to minimize liquidity risk: one is the **standardization of contracts**, the other is **secondary trading**.

STANDARDIZED CONTRACTS

To facilitate trading and provide liquidity, futures contracts are standardized. A **standardized contract** is a contract whose size and settlement date are specified

---

[3] The London Metal Exchange (www.lme.com) is the world's largest market in copper futures contracts.

[4] The clearing house acts as an 'insurance company'. It collects fees from the exchange members and uses the funds to cover potential losses.

[5] WTM has to keep a minimum amount of cash in its margin account, called a **maintenance margin**. If cash falls below the maintenance margin, WTM will receive a **margin call** requiring that it adds cash to its account.

by the exchange on which they trade. For example, all copper contracts traded on the LME require the physical delivery of 25 tons of Grade A copper (a specific quality of copper) on a specified settlement date. There are different settlement dates and a particular contract corresponds to each date. The LME offers copper contracts with daily settlement out to three months as well as contracts with weekly settlement out to six months and contracts with monthly settlement out to 123 months.

SECONDARY TRADING AND MARKET TICKS

As mentioned earlier, contracts are traded on the exchange at prices that clear the market, meaning that traders can buy or sell contracts at the latest quoted price *any time* the exchange is open. The exchange specifies the *minimum* price fluctuation of a contract, called the **tick size**. In the case of the copper contracts traded on the LME, the tick size is $0.50 per ton.

AVAILABLE FUTURES MARKETS AND CONTRACTS

There are over 100 futures markets located in more than 40 countries around the world. The types of products traded in these markets are commodities, financial instruments and currencies. Commodities include agricultural products (such as grains, coffee and sugar), energy products (such as crude oil and natural gas), industrial metals (such as aluminum and copper), precious metals (such as gold and silver), as well as rubber and wool. All major currencies (US dollar, euro, GB pound, Japanese yen) are traded in several futures exchanges around the world. Traded financial instruments include government bonds (US Treasury bonds as well as bonds issued by the governments of the largest European countries and Japan), individual common stocks, and the stock market indices of the largest stock markets around the world.

HEDGING RISK WITH FUTURES CONTRACTS

In our earlier example, WTM needed 100 tons of copper in three months and wanted to fix now the price at which it will buy the copper in three months. To achieve this objective WTM entered into a forward contract with its copper supplier whereby the supplier agreed to deliver the copper in three months and get paid $6,133 per ton on the day the copper is delivered. This contractual agreement allowed WTM to cancel the price risk of buying copper, that is, the risk of not knowing the price at which the transaction will be settled in three months. We have seen that this forward contract, however, carries counterparty and liquidity risks. The alternative is to use the futures market for copper that allows WTM to eliminate the price risk as well as the liquidity and counterparty risks. As mentioned earlier, this risk-mitigating technique is called hedging with futures contracts. It is illustrated below.

HEDGING THE PRICE RISK OF COPPER WITH COPPER FUTURES CONTRACTS

Let's say that the price of a 3-month copper futures contract is currently quoted at $6,100 per ton.[6] This is the fixed price that WTM must pay in three months to buy

---

[6] As mentioned earlier, the size of one copper contract on the LME is 25 tons. Because WTM needs 100 tons of copper it will have to buy four contracts. Futures prices on the LME, however, are not quoted per contract but per ton of copper.

one ton of copper *now*. Let's show how the purchase of this futures contract will eliminate price risk. As the futures price of a ton of copper fluctuates over the three-month period, WTM will accumulate daily gains and losses in its margin account. On the day the contract expires, WTM will hold a futures contract to buy the copper at that day's futures price *which will equal the spot price* because, on the day the contract expires, WTM can either take delivery of copper in the futures market or buy the same in the spot market.

Assume that on the day the contract expires the price of one ton of copper has risen to $6,400. This means that WTM has realized a net profit of $300 per ton ($6,400 less $6,100) from the daily marking-to-market of its long position in futures (for this reason, the hedge is referred to as a **long hedge**).[7] Therefore, the *net* price WTM has paid per ton of copper is $6,100 ($6,400 less $300), which is exactly the futures price prevailing at the beginning of the three-month period when WTM entered into the futures contract. Note also that WTM does not necessarily have to take delivery of the copper on the expiration date of the futures contracts. All it has to do is enter into a **reversing trade** on the futures exchange, that is, sell the contracts it bought three months earlier in order to cancel the delivery just before the contracts expire. It would then buy the copper at $6,400 on the spot market.

What if the price of one ton of copper had dropped to $5,800 instead of rising to $6,400? In this case, the opposite would have happened. WTM would have lost $300 per ton of copper in the futures market and the net price it would have paid to buy one ton of copper in the spot market at the expiration of the contracts would be, again, $6,100. Here is the calculation: $5,800 to buy one ton of copper in the spot market plus the loss of $300 per ton of copper. Again, this is exactly the price prevailing at the beginning of the three-month period when WTM was able to lock in its future purchase and hedge the corresponding price risk.

You can now understand what hedging with futures contracts means. It means taking a position in the futures markets that generates a gain or a loss that offsets the rise or the drop in the spot price of copper. In our case, no matter what the spot price of copper is in three months, WTM will pay a net price of $6,100 per ton, which is the futures price at the beginning of the three-month period. Had WTM not hedged, it would have paid either $6,400 or $5,800 per ton of copper.

What is the situation of a firm supplying copper that wishes to lock in today the price at which it will *sell* copper in three months' time? The supplier could hedge its exposure to price risk by *selling* futures contracts, that is, by taking a *short* position in the futures market at $6,100 a ton (for this reason, this type of hedge is usually referred to as a **short hedge**). If the price of copper rises to $6,400 in three months, the supplier loses $300 and its net selling price is $6,100. (It sells a ton of copper at $6,400 from which it must deduct the $300 loss.) If the price of copper drops to $5,800, the supplier gains $300 (recall that when you have a short position you make a profit when the price drops) and its net selling price is still $6,100. (It sells a ton of copper at $5,800 to which it adds a $300 gain.)

We now turn to hedging the price risk of financial products. As pointed out earlier, one can hedge an exposure to the price risk of a stock market index, a government bond or a foreign currency. We illustrate below how to hedge an exposure to the stock market and government bonds. Hedging currency risk is covered in detail in the next chapter.

---

[7] The $300 profit will have to be reduced by all the transaction costs WTC will incur to buy the futures contracts.

HEDGING THE STOCK MARKET PRICE RISK WITH INDEX FUTURES

Consider the case of the Atlantic Services Company (ASC). ASC has set up a pension fund for its employees. The fund invests part of the cash contributions it receives from the company and its employees in the US stock market. Suppose the fund manager expects to receive a cash contribution of $500,000 in two months that will be invested in a portfolio that mimics the Standard & Poor's 500 stock market index (the S&P 500). Let's say that the index is currently trading at 2,000 and is very volatile. What could the manager do if she wants to lock in the contribution at the *current* index value of 2,000? Put differently, how could she invest *today* money she does *not yet have*? (Recall that she will get the $500,000 in two months.) We show below that she can achieve her objective by buying futures contracts on the S&P 500 *now* because buying futures contracts now will generate a profit if the market goes up. And that profit will provide the additional cash to buy the same number of shares as when the index stood at 2,000. If the market goes down, the futures position will generate a loss, but the manager will need less than $500,000 to buy the same number of shares as when the index stood at 2,000. We illustrate this hedging strategy with the following numerical example.

Futures contracts on the S&P 500 Index trade on the Chicago Mercantile Exchange (CME). One contract is worth $250 multiplied by the value of the S&P 500 Index. Given that the S&P 500 currently stands at 2,000, one contract is thus worth $500,000 ($250 × 2,000). If the index is up one point, the contract generates a gain of $250. If it is down one point, the contract generates a loss of $250. Buying one contract allows the manager to lock in at 2,000 the $500,000 she will receive in two months. Suppose two months have passed and the market has gone up as expected. It now stands at 2,200, an increase of 10 percent. If the manager had not bought the futures contract, she would now need $550,000 to buy the same number of shares she could have bought two months earlier. With the futures contracts, the manager has the required $550,000: the $500,000 of new contributions plus the $50,000 of gains generated by the futures contract (multiply the 200 points increase in the contract by $250). Had the market gone down 200 points, the contract would have generated a loss of $50,000 but the value of the stocks would now be worth $450,000. The $500,000 of new cash contributions would cover the purchase ($450,000) and the loss ($50,000). The fund is thus hedged against stock price fluctuations: no matter what the value of the S&P 500 is in two months, the manager will buy the same number of shares as when the market stood at 2,000 two months ago.

HEDGING INTEREST-RATE RISK WITH BOND FUTURES

Next month the Eastern Electric Company (EEC) is planning to borrow $100 million for eight years. The borrowing rate is currently 7 percent and EEC's finance manager expects the rate to change significantly before the loan is secured. As a result, EEC is exposed to interest-rate risk over the coming month.[8] At the current rate of 7 percent, EEC would have to pay $7 million of annual interest for eight years and $100 million at the end of the eighth year.

To avoid paying a higher rate in one month, EEC's finance manager would like to lock in the annual interest payments at $7 million a year. (The finance manager

---

[8] Why do we refer to the **interest-rate risk** of a bond instead of its price risk? Because the two risks are the same: we have shown in Chapter 10 that the price of a bond moves in the *opposite* direction to a change in interest rates, and hence saying that a bond is exposed to interest-rate risk is the same as saying that it is exposed to price risk.

is willing to forgo paying a lower rate if rates fall instead of rising.) EEC can lock in its annual interest payment at $7 million by *selling* futures contracts on US Treasury bonds. How will this hedging strategy work?

Assume that in one month the borrowing rate rises from 7 percent to 7.50 percent. In this case, EEC will have to pay its lender the higher rate. If it does not want to pay more than $7 million in annual interest, it will have to borrow less than $100 million.[9] How much less? We showed in Chapter 10 how to calculate the value of a bond if we know the interest rate (see equation 10.3). At a rate of 7.5 percent, EEC can borrow:

$$\text{Amount to borrow at } 7.5\% = \frac{\$7m}{(1+7.5\%)} + \ldots + \frac{\$7m}{(1+7.5\%)^7} + \frac{\$7m + \$100m}{(1+7.5\%)^8} = \$97.07 \text{ million}$$

The amount EEC can now borrow has to drop to $97.07 million so that the lender earns 7.50 percent instead of 7 percent. This means that EEC will be short of slightly less than $3 million. (If the rate drops to 6.50 percent, the value of the loan will rise to $103.04 million and EEC could borrow slightly more than $3 million of additional cash.) To lock in the amount of borrowing at $100 million, EEC should take a position in the futures markets that will generate a profit of about $3 million if interest rates rise to 7.50 percent and a loss of about $3 million if interest rates drop to 6.50 percent. What type of position will generate a profit when rates go up and bond prices go down? To profit from a drop in bond prices, EEC should take a *short* position, that is, *sell* interest rate futures (same as saying selling bond futures).

The next questions are: what kind of contract and how many contracts should EEC sell to hedge its position? The answer depends on the sensitivity of the loan value to changes in interest rates compared to the sensitivity of the futures contract to changes in interest rates. Go to self-test question 16.1 to see how this hedging strategy is constructed.

THE PRICING OF FORWARD AND FUTURES CONTRACTS

In this section we show you how to calculate the forward price of a product (a commodity or a financial asset) if you know its spot price. We establish this relationship using the law of one price, according to which transactions that generate the same cash flow must have the same value. We also show you how to establish the relationship between the spot price of a product and its expected (future) spot price, that is, the spot price that is expected to prevail at the settlement date of the forward contract.

THE RELATIONSHIP BETWEEN THE SPOT PRICE AND THE FORWARD PRICE

Return to the case of WTM. The firm needs copper in three months. It can use one of two transactions to obtain one ton of copper in three months. The first is to buy one ton of copper now at the spot price S_0 ($6,000 in our case) and store it for three months.[10] The second is to enter into a forward contract to take delivery of one ton of copper in three months and pay the forward price F_0 ($6,133 in our case) when the copper is delivered. The two transactions are equivalent because

---

[9] Recall that when the rate goes up, the value of the loan goes down (see the section on valuing bonds in Chapter 10).

[10] The storage cost covers the transportation of copper to a warehouse, insuring it against possible damage or theft, and the rent paid to the storage company.

WTM will end up with one ton of copper in three months irrespective of the chosen transaction.

The relationship between the spot price (S_0) and the forward price (F_0) can be determined by applying the law of one price according to which two equivalent transactions must have the same cost. If they don't, no one would use the more expensive one and, if markets were frictionless, spot and forward prices would adjust until the cost of the two transactions is the same. Let's determine the cost of each transaction.

THE SPOT TRANSACTION: BUY COPPER IN THE SPOT MARKET AND STORE IT

Say WTM has S_0 dollars ($6,000 in our case). It can use the S_0 dollars to buy now one ton of copper and store it for a period T. (T is measured in years and hence T is 0.25 for a three-month period.) What is the storage cost that WTM will pay in three months? If we use the lower-case letter c to denote the *annual* storage cost expressed as a *percentage* of the spot price S_0, and T to denote the period during which the copper is stored, then the storage cost can be written:

$$\text{Storage cost payable at the end of period } T = -(S_0 \times c \times T)$$

The minus sign indicates a payment, which is an outflow of cash. For example, if c is 3 percent of S_0 per year, the storage cost is equal to $45 per ton of copper ($6,000 \times 0.03 \times 0.25$).

THE FORWARD TRANSACTION: BUY COPPER IN THE FORWARD MARKET

If WTM decides to enter into the forward contract, it does not incur any cost now. It can thus invest the S_0 dollars ($6,000 in our case) for three months at the annual risk-free rate (R_F), currently at 6 percent, and then pay F_0 dollars ($6,133 in our case) to buy one ton of copper on the day the forward contract settles. In this case, the net cost at the end of period T is:

$$\text{Net cost of forward at the end of period } T = -F_0 + S_0(1 + R_F)^T$$

The payment of the forward price at settlement is $-F_0$ and $S_0(1 + R_F)^T$ is the compounded value of the S_0 dollars invested at the annual rate R_F for a period of T years.[11]

THE SPOT-FORWARD PARITY RELATIONSHIP: THE COST-OF-CARRY MODEL

According to the law of one price, the costs of the two transactions must be the same because both transactions start now with the same S_0 dollars ($6,000 in our case) and end with one ton of copper at the end of period T. We can thus write:

$$-F_0 + S_0(1 + R_F)^T = -(S_0 \times c \times T)$$

from which we get:

$$F_0 = S_0[(1 + R_F)^T + (c \times T)] \tag{16.1}$$

Equation 16.1 is known as the **spot-forward parity relationship**, and the model we used to get to that equation is usually referred to as the **cost-of-carry model**. In our case S_0 is $6,000, R_F is 6 percent, T is 0.25, and c is 3 percent, thus:

$$F_0 = \$6,000[(1.06)^{0.25} + (3\% \times 0.25)] = \$6,000[1.01467 + 0.00750] = \$6,133.04$$

---

[11] See Chapter 2 for how to get the compounded value of an investment. In our case, the compounded value of $6,000 at 6 percent for three months is: $\$6,000(1.06)^{3/12} = \$6,000(1.06)^{0.25} = \$6,088.04$

As you recall, this is exactly the forward price the copper supplier quoted WTM for one ton of copper in our earlier example. Had the supplier quoted a higher forward price, WTM could have bought the copper in the spot market and stored it for three months for a lower total cost.

FORWARD PRICES VERSUS FUTURES PRICES

Equation 16.1 gives you the forward price as a function of the spot price. Could we assume that the same equation applies to the *futures* price? There is one important difference between forward and futures contracts that could push the futures price above or below the forward price given by equation 16.1. We showed earlier that in the case of futures markets, marking-to-market requires traders to realize their daily gains or losses. When changes in futures prices are highly *positively* correlated with interest rates, traders with a long position (those who 'bought' contracts) will earn significant interest on their accumulated gains and would thus be willing to pay a *higher* price for futures than the one given by equation 16.1. The opposite is true for traders with a short position: they will benefit if changes in futures prices are highly *negatively* correlated with interest rates because, when futures prices are down and rates are up, they can invest their gains at higher rates and would hence be willing to sell contracts at a *lower* price than the one given by equation 16.1. In practice, the correlation between changes in futures prices and interest rates, however, is not high enough to create a significant difference between the forward and the futures prices given by the parity relationship.[12]

THE SPOT-FORWARD PARITY RELATIONSHIP APPLIED TO FINANCIAL ASSETS

We can easily extend equation 16.1 to the case of a forward contract on a financial asset such as a stock market index or a government bond. There are two differences between holding a physical product such as copper and holding a financial asset. First, the holder of a financial asset does not incur any storage cost because carrying a financial asset is costless. Second, the holder of a financial asset may earn an income, that is, dividend payments in the case of a stock market index and coupon payments in the case of bonds. In other words, instead of incurring a cash outflow to cover storage cost, the holder of a financial asset receives a cash inflow from dividend or coupon payments. If we use the lower-case letter y to express dividend or coupon payments as a percentage of the financial asset's spot price (S_0), then the spot-forward parity relationship can be rewritten as:

$$F_0 = S_0(1 + R_F - y)^T \qquad (16.2)$$

The letter y is the yield on the financial asset and the minus sign indicates that the buyer of a contract does not collect the dividend or coupon payment because he does not own the underlying asset.

To illustrate, consider a six-month forward contract $(T = 0.50)$ on a stock market index that now stands at 2,000 $(S_0 = 2,000)$. The stocks that make up the index generate an average annual dividend yield of 2 percent $(y = 0.02)$, and the risk-free rate is currently at 5 percent $(R_F = 0.05)$. Entering these data into equation 16.2 gives a stock index forward value (F_0) of:

$$F_0 = 2,000(1 + 0.05 - 0.02)^{0.50} = 2,000 \times 1.0149 = 2,029.78$$

---

[12] There is an exception for long-term bonds where the correlation could be high enough to create a divergence between forward and futures prices.

If the risk-free rate exceeds the dividend yield, the forward value of the index will be higher than its spot value, and if the dividend yield exceeds the risk-free rate, the forward value of the index will be lower than its spot value.

THE RELATIONSHIP BETWEEN THE EXPECTED SPOT PRICE AND THE FORWARD PRICE

Consider the case of a commodity such as electricity that cannot be stored: you cannot buy electricity now and store it for future consumption. The implication is that the spot-forward parity relationship will not hold because the spot transaction (buying now and storing) is not possible. The only relevant relationship in this case is between the forward price (F_0) and the spot price that is *expected* to prevail on the settlement date of the forward contract at time T, written $E(S_T)$. This means, for example, that the 3-month forward price of electricity will be determined primarily by what the market expects the spot price of electricity to be in three months.

The relationship between the forward price fixed today (F_0) and the expected spot price $E(S_T)$ on the day the forward contract settles can be obtained using the discounted cash-flow model. The spot price today is equal to the expected spot price at time T discounted to the present at the risk-adjusted discount rate k_S, a rate that can be estimated using the Capital Asset Pricing Model (CAPM) presented in Chapter 12. But the spot price today is also equal to the present value of the forward price discounted to the present time at the risk-free rate R_F because the forward price is known today and hence is riskless. We thus have:

$$S_0 = \frac{E(S_T)}{(1 + k_S)^1} = \frac{F_0}{(1 + R_F)^T}$$

from which we get:

$$F_0 = E(S_T)\left[\frac{1 + R_F}{1 + k_S}\right]^T \tag{16.3}$$

To illustrate, assume that the spot rate for 100 bushels of corn expected to prevail six months from now (T = 0.50) is $400 and that the risk-free rate is 6 percent. We can use the CAPM to estimate the required rate of return (k_S) based on an estimated beta of 0.20 for corn and a market risk premium (MRP) of 5 percent (see Chapter 12):

$$k_S = R_F + (MRP \times \beta_C) = 6\% + (5\% \times 0.20) = 7\% \text{ and thus}$$

$$F_0 = E(S_T)\left[\frac{1 + R_F}{1 + k_S}\right]^T = \$400\left[\frac{1.06}{1.07}\right]^{0.50} = \$400 \times 0.9953 = \$398.12$$

Note that as long as the commodity has a *positive* beta – which is usually the case for most commodities – the required return k_S is *higher* than the risk-free rate and hence the forward price is *lower* than the expected spot price. In this case, we say that the forward price exhibits a **normal backwardation** behavior. For a commodity with a *negative* beta, the required return k_S is *lower* than the risk-free rate and hence the forward price is *higher* than the expected spot price and we say that the forward market exhibits a **contango** behavior in this case.

The relationships between spot prices, forward prices and expected prices can also be applied to foreign exchange rates. We show this in the next chapter.

OPTION CONTRACTS

The contractual agreement between WTM and the copper supplier we described earlier could have been structured differently. Instead of entering into a forward contract, WTM could have bought an **option contract** from its copper supplier at a price of $336 per ton. (We show you later how **option prices** are determined.) The option contract gives WTM the following choices in three months: (1) WTM could buy a ton of copper for $6,000 (this fixed contractual price is called the **exercise price** or the **strike price** of the option; in our case it is the same as the current $6,000 spot price) or (2) WTM could simply walk away from the deal without incurring any penalty, meaning that WTM can decide *not* to buy the copper from its supplier and *not* be penalized.

This option contract provides WTM with more flexibility than the forward contract discussed earlier. To illustrate, suppose that the spot price of a ton of copper in three months is $5,500 (recall that it was $6,000 three months earlier). In this case, WTM will let the option contract expire *unexercised* and buy the copper in the spot market at the lower price of $5,500 per ton, for a net cost of $5,836 ($5,500 plus the $336 price of the option purchased three months earlier). What if the spot price of a ton of copper is $6,500? In this case, WTM will *exercise* the option and buy a ton of copper at the strike price of $6,000 instead of paying $6,500 in the spot market, for a net cost of $6,336 ($6,000 plus the $336 price of the option purchased three months earlier). What if the project is postponed? If the price of a ton of copper is $5,500 in three months, WTM will not exercise the option and make a loss of $336 (the price it paid to buy the option). If the price is $6,500, WTM will exercise the option, buy a ton of copper at $6,000, sell it in the spot market for $6,500, and make a net profit of $164 per ton ($500 less the $336 price of the option).

As you may have noticed, the option contract is similar to an *insurance* contract against a rise in copper prices. To see the analogy, think of the option contract between WTM and the copper supplier as follows: WTM bought 'insurance' from its supplier that will pay out if the price of copper rises above $6,000 per ton (the contract's exercise price). Specifically, if in three months the price of a ton of copper is *above* $6,000, WTM will 'file a claim' and ask the supplier to deliver the copper at $6,000 per ton. If the price of copper in three months is *below* $6,000, WTM will not file a claim. It will simply buy the copper in the spot market for less than $6,000 per ton, thereby benefitting from the fall in copper prices. The price WTM has to pay today to buy this 'insurance policy' is the $336 option price. (This is why the option price is also called the **option premium** similarly to the premium one pays to buy a car or a home insurance policy.) Compare now the option contract to the forward contract discussed earlier that also allows WTM to protect its profits against a rise in copper prices but does not allow WTM to benefit if the copper price falls: the option contract offers more *flexibility* than the forward contract but, unlike the forward, it requires an upfront payment of $336 to purchase that flexibility.

Forward, futures and option contracts are called **derivative instruments**, or just **derivatives**, because they *derive* their values from an **underlying product** (copper in the WTM case). These derivatives are useful risk-management instruments because they allow individuals and firms to hedge their exposure to price risk, that is, to protect themselves against unexpected changes in the price of the underlying product.

In the rest of this chapter we examine option contracts in detail with a focus on options where the underlying asset is a common stock or a stock market index.

Options on foreign currencies are examined separately in the next chapter.[13] We also explore the role of options in corporate capital investment decisions where the underlying asset is a physical investment.

OPTION CONTRACTS DEFINED

The option contract described earlier is a **call option,** or simply a call. It is a financial instrument that gives the holder the right (but not the obligation) to *buy* the option's underlying asset (copper in our case) at a *fixed* price (the option's exercise price or the strike price) during a *fixed* period of time (the option's **maturity** or **time to expiration**). Note that the option's exercise price and its **expiration date** (also called its **maturity date**) are *fixed* when the option is *issued*.

There are also option contracts that give the holder the right (but not the obligation) to *sell* the option's underlying asset. These contracts are called **put options** and, like call options, they have an exercise price, a time to expiration and an expiration date.

OVER-THE-COUNTER (OTC) OPTIONS VERSUS TRADED OPTIONS

In the WTM example, the exercise price of the option, its time to expiration and its expiration date were directly negotiated between WTM and its copper supplier. This type of option is called an **over-the-counter (OTC) option**. It was designed to meet the specific needs of the two parties. In contrast, **traded options** have standardized exercise prices, expiration dates and, as their name suggests, are traded on organized exchanges, called **option exchanges**, that operate in the same manner as the futures exchanges we described earlier.[14]

EUROPEAN VERSUS AMERICAN OPTIONS

A **European option** (a call or a put) is an option that can only be exercised on its expiration date. An option that can be exercised any time up to its expiration date is called an **American option**.[15] We discuss later whether the early-exercise property of American options makes them more valuable than European options and show that – under certain conditions – American options can be more valuable than their European counterpart. Note that the words 'American' and 'European' do not refer to options that trade exclusively in the United States or Europe. There are European-style options that trade in the US options markets and American-style options that trade in European options markets.[16]

---

[13] There are options on many other underlying products such as interest rates, volatility and even futures contracts.

[14] Options are traded on exchanges around the world. The best known are the Chicago Board Options Exchange (CBOE), the Eurex Exchange in Frankfurt, the London International Financial and Futures Exchange (LIFFE) and the Singapore Mercantile Exchange (SMX). It should be noted that recent developments in the OTC market such as the introduction of marking-to-markets and initial margins are blurring the differences with the traded options markets.

[15] An option whose payoff at maturity (the difference between the price of the underlying asset and the option's exercise price) is based on the *average* price of the underlying asset over a specific set of dates during the option's life is called an **Asian option**.

[16] In the US options markets, all options on individual stocks are American-style options and most options on stock market indices are European-style options. In European options markets, options on individual stocks can be either European-style or American-style options.

Option Buyers and Option Writers

In our earlier example, WTM could hedge or insure its exposure to the copper price by entering into a contract that would give it the right to buy a ton of copper at $6,000 in three months. This is effectively a *European* call option with an exercise price of $6,000 maturing in three months. WTM is the buyer or holder of the option and pays the option premium of $336 upfront. WTM's supplier is the seller or **writer** of the option and collects the premium of $336 upfront. WTM's position is usually referred to as a **long call** and the supplier's position as a **short call**.

Call Options

Recall that a call option gives the holder the right to *buy* an underlying asset at a fixed price up to the call's expiration date. In this section, we look at the case of call options where the underlying asset is a common stock (shares of publicly traded companies) and examine how the value of a call varies when the price of the underlying stock changes. We first look at the case of European calls and then examine the case of American calls. Put options are explored in a separate section.

How does the Value of a European Call Vary when the Price of the Underlying Stock Changes?

Consider a European call to buy stocks of the International Software Corporation (ISC) at an exercise price of $50 with a 3-month maturity. Let's assume for the moment that ISC will not pay any dividends during the next three months. (A dividend payment *before* the call expires will affect the call price because the call holder is not entitled to that dividend. We show you later how dividend payments affect the value of a call.) We use the capital letter X to represent the exercise price (X = $50 in the case of the ISC call) and the capital letter T to represent the time to expiration in *years* ($T = \frac{3}{12} = 0.25$ in the case of the ISC call).

How does the value of the ISC call vary when the price of the ISC stock changes? The answer to this question is given in Exhibit 16.1. It shows the value of the ISC call on the vertical axis (represented by the capital letter C) as a function of the ISC stock price shown on the horizontal axis (represented by the capital letter S). For example, at point A on the curve, the ISC stock price is $45 and the corresponding call value is $0.81. When the stock price goes up, so does the call value: when the stock price is $50 (point B on the curve), the call is worth $2.86; when it is $55 (point E on the curve), the call is worth $6.42. In other words, keeping everything else the same, *the higher the stock price, the more valuable the call on that stock* because the call allows the holder to buy the stock at the *fixed* exercise price of $50 and the higher the stock price, the higher the profit when the call is exercised. We provide later a formula that gives the call value if we know the stock price and the option's characteristics.

The Intrinsic Value of a Call Option

Return to Exhibit 16.1. The thick line that breaks at the $50 exercise price gives the option value on its *expiration day*: if on that day the stock price is *below* the $50 exercise price (that is, located on the line's horizontal segment that goes from zero to the $50 exercise price), the call is worthless because no one will exercise a call to buy the ISC stock at $50 if that stock can be purchased directly in the stock market for less than $50. In general, when the stock price is *lower* than the option's exercise price, the call is said to be **out-of-the-money**. Note that even though the call is

EXHIBIT 16.1	**VALUE OF A EUROPEAN CALL OPTION (C) FOR DIFFERENT STOCK PRICES (S) OF THE INTERNATIONAL SOFTWARE CORPORATION (ISC).**

- EXERCISE PRICE OF THE CALL OPTION $(X) = \$50$
- CALL OPTION TIME TO EXPIRATION IN YEARS $(T) = 0.25$ YEAR (3 MONTHS)
- THE RISK-FREE RATE $(R_F) = 6\%$
- THE STOCK DOES NOT PAY DIVIDENDS DURING THE LIFE OF THE CALL

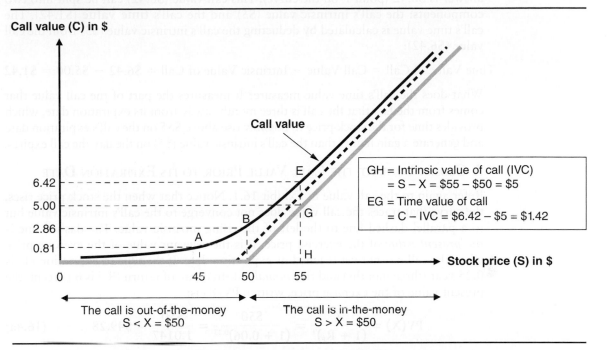

GH = Intrinsic value of call (IVC)
   = S − X = \$55 − \$50 = \$5
EG = Time value of call
   = C − IVC = \$6.42 − \$5 = \$1.42

The call is out-of-the-money
S < X = \$50

The call is in-the-money
S > X = \$50

1. The thick line is the value of the call option at expiration, called its intrinsic value. It is equal to S − X.
2. The dashed line is the present value, at the risk-free rate, of the call's intrinsic value.
3. At point B, the stock price is equal to the \$50 excercise price and the call is said to be at-the-money.

out-of-the-money, it has some value *today* because it will expire in only three months and the stock price could well rise above \$50 before the expiration date. For example, if the stock price is \$45 (point A on the curve) the call is out-of-the-money, but it is worth \$0.81. If the stock price is equal to the exercise price (S = X = \$50), the call is worth \$2.86 (point B on the curve) and is said to be **at-the-money**. If the stock price is *above* the exercise price, the call is said to be **in-the-money**.[17]

The **intrinsic value of a call** is the profit a call holder would make *if the call could be exercised immediately*. It is equal to the stock price (S) less the exercise price (X). To illustrate, if the ISC stock trade at \$55, the intrinsic value of the ISC call is \$5:

Intrinsic Value of Call = Stock Price (S) − Exercise Price (X) = \$55 − \$50 = \$5

---

[17] If the stock price is *significantly* higher than the exercise price (say more than double the exercise price), the call is said to be **deep in-the-money**; if it is *significantly* lower than the exercise price (say less than half), the call is said to be **deep out-of-the-money**.

If the stock price is equal to or *lower* than the exercise price, the call's intrinsic value is zero. (It cannot be negative because the call holder has no obligation to exercise the call; she can simply walk away.)

THE TIME VALUE OF A CALL OPTION

Look again at Exhibit 16.1. What is the call value when the stock price is $55? The answer is $6.42 (point E on the curve). This call value ($6.42) can be split into two components: the call's intrinsic value ($5) and the call's **time value** ($1.42). The call's time value is calculated by deducting the call's intrinsic value ($5) from the call value ($6.42):

Time Value of Call = Call Value − Intrinsic Value of Call = $6.42 − $5.00 = $1.42

What does the call's time value measure? It measures the part of the call value that comes from the fact that the call is three months away from its expiration date, which provides time for the stock price to possibly rise above $55 on the call's expiration date and generate a gain higher than the call's intrinsic value ($5) on the day the call expires.

A CLOSER LOOK AT THE CALL VALUE PRIOR TO ITS EXPIRATION DATE

Refer again to the call value in Exhibit 16.1. Notice that when the stock price rises, the curve that traces the call value does not converge to the call's intrinsic value but to a parallel dashed line to the left of the rising intrinsic value. The dashed line is the *present value* of the exercise price: it is the relevant value of the exercise price when the call has not yet reached its expiration date. If the time to expiration (T) is 0.25 year (three months) and the *annual* risk-free rate of return (R_F) is 6 percent, the present value of the exercise price, written PV(X) is:

$$PV(X) = \frac{X}{(1 + R_F)^T} = \frac{\$50}{(1 + 0.06)^{0.25}} = \frac{\$50}{1.0147} = \$49.28 \qquad (16.4a)$$

Alternatively, PV(X) can be calculated with interest earned *continuously*:[18]

$$PV(X) = Xe^{-R_F T} = \$50e^{-0.06 \times 0.25} = \$50 \times 0.9851 = \$49.26 \qquad (16.4b)$$

The continuous version of PV(X) is slightly lower than the discrete (or periodic) version because interest earned continuously is higher, and this higher rate lowers the present value. We present the continuous version here because we show later that the formulas that give the value of options are based on continuous compounding.

THE VALUE OF AN AMERICAN CALL COMPARED TO THE VALUE OF A EUROPEAN CALL

Look again at the call value shown on the curve in Exhibit 16.1: it is always *above* its intrinsic value. The implication of this observation is clear: it means that *it is not optimal to exercise an American call option on a non-dividend-paying stock prior to that call's expiration date.* For example, if the ISC call were an American call trading at $6.42 when its stock trades at $55 (point E on the curve), it would not make sense to exercise the call at $50 and earn $5 if you can earn $6.42 if you sold the call

---

[18] To understand the difference between the discrete and continuous versions of compounding, go to Chapter 2 and look at the table in the section entitled 'Interest Rate Quotation and Calculation'.

instead. This conclusion is obviously true for any stock price.[19] The implication is that *American calls on non-dividend-paying stocks – even though they give the holder the right to exercise early – are not worth more than their European counterparts* because they will not be exercised earlier.

THE VALUE OF A CALL ON A STOCK THAT PAYS DIVIDENDS

So far, we assumed that the call is written on a non-dividend-paying stock. If a stock pays dividends *during* the life of a call, the call (both European and American) on that stock will be *less* valuable than an identical call on the same stock that does not pay dividends. (If the stock is expected to pay a dividend *after* the call expires, this does not affect the call value.) There are two reasons dividend payments reduce the value of call. First, the call holder does not get the dividends, and second, on the day a stock goes ex-dividend its price drops,[20] which lowers the call value but does not affect its exercise price. In this case, it may be optimal to exercise an American call immediately before the underlying stock goes ex-dividend and drops in price, particularly when the dividend date is close to the call's expiration date and the dividend is large. We provide later a formula for calculating the value of a call on a stock that pays dividends during the life of the call.

SHORT POSITIONS IN CALL OPTIONS

The discussion so far has dealt with the case of call options held *long*, that is, the case where the option holder *bought* call options. We now want to examine the case of a call *writer* who *sold* calls and thus has a *short* position. The terminal **payoff** for a short position in a call on the ISC stock is given on the left side of Exhibit 16.2. It is represented by the thick line that breaks at the $50 exercise price. Also shown in the exhibit are the call writer's profits and losses when the call expires. They are represented by the dashed lines that break at the $50 exercise price.

If the stock price is equal to or lower than the $50 exercise price on the expiration date, the call is worthless, and the call writer makes a profit equal to the price at which she sold the call three months *earlier* (the call was sold at $2.86). If the stock price is higher than $50 but lower than $52.86 (the sum of the exercise price and the call value), the call writer makes a profit that is lower than the call value. When the stock price is $52.86, the call writer breaks even. Above that price the position begins to generate losses because the call writer must *sell* the ISC stock to the holder of the call who will exercise her call option to buy the stock when the stock price exceeds the exercise price.

PUT OPTIONS

Recall that a put option gives the holder the right to *sell* an underlying asset at a fixed price up to the put expiration date. As we did with calls, we look here at puts where the underlying asset is a common stock (shares of publicly traded companies) and examine how the value of a put varies when the price of the underlying stock changes. We first look at the case of European puts and then examine the case of American puts.

---

[19] This property of call options is often referred to by saying that a call is always worth more 'alive' than 'dead'. If you sell a call, you get the call price but the call is still trading, that is, it is still 'alive', but if you exercise the call, the option no longer exists, that is, it is 'dead'.

[20] See Chapter 11. On and after the so-called *ex-dividend* date, the stock owner will not receive the dividend that has been declared earlier. Because of this, the stock drops in price by the amount of the expected dividend.

EXHIBIT 16.2	VALUE AT EXPIRATION, AND PROFITS AND LOSSES, OF A SHORT POSITION IN A CALL AND A PUT FOR DIFFERENT STOCK PRICES OF THE INTERNATIONAL SOFTWARE CORPORATION (ISC).

- STOCK PRICE = S
- EXERCISE PRICE (X) OF BOTH OPTIONS = $50
- TIME TO EXPIRATION OF BOTH OPTIONS = 3 MONTHS
- CALL VALUE TODAY = $2.86
- PUT VALUE TODAY = $2.12

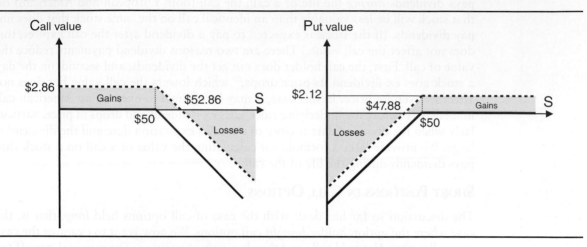

HOW DOES THE VALUE OF A EUROPEAN PUT VARY WHEN THE PRICE OF THE UNDERLYING STOCK CHANGES?

Consider an ISC European put with the same exercise price and time to expiration as the ISC European call examined earlier ($50 and three months, respectively). The put's terminal payoff, that is, its cash flow on the day it expires, is shown in Exhibit 16.3 as a thick line that breaks at $50. The curve above that thick line shows the value of the put as a function of the ISC stock price (we assume, again, that the stock will not pay any dividend during the next three months). Note the differences between the call value in Exhibit 16.1 and the put value in Exhibit 16.3: when the underlying stock price rises, the call value goes up whereas the put value goes down because the lower the stock price, the more valuable the put since it gives its holder the right to *sell* the stock at the fixed $50 exercise price. We provide later a formula that gives the put price if we know the stock price and the option's features.

THE INTRINSIC VALUE OF A PUT OPTION

The intrinsic value of the put is its exercise price less the stock price. Look at Exhibit 16.3: if the stock price is $47, the put's intrinsic value is $3 ($50 less $47). When the stock price is below the $50 exercise price, the put's intrinsic value is positive because if the holder could exercise the put, he would *sell* the stock to the put writer for $50 (the exercise price) while the stock trades at less than $50. As the stock price goes to zero, the put becomes more valuable and its value converges toward the put's intrinsic value. When the stock price is above the $50 exercise price, the put's intrinsic value is zero because the holder of a put will not exercise her option to sell the stock at the exercise price of $50 when she can sell it at a higher price in the market.

EXHIBIT 16.3	VALUE OF A EUROPEAN PUT OPTION (P) FOR DIFFERENT STOCK PRICES (S) OF THE INTERNATIONAL SOFTWARE CORPORATION (ISC).

- EXERCISE PRICE OF THE PUT OPTION (X) = $50
- PUT OPTION TIME TO EXPIRATION IN YEARS (T) = 0.25 YEAR (3 MONTHS)
- THE STOCK DOES NOT PAY DIVIDENDS DURING THE LIFE OF THE PUT

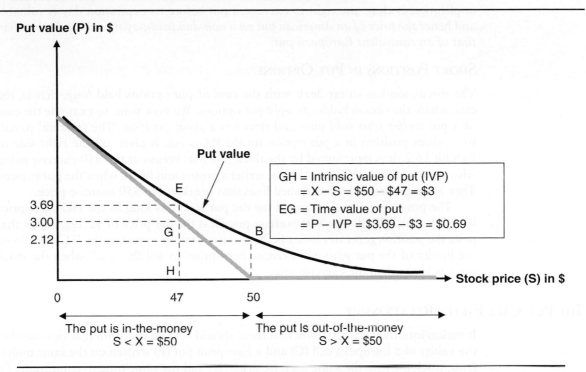

1. The thick line is the value of the put option at expiration, called its intrinsic value. It is equal to X − S.
2. At point B, the stock price is equal to the $50 excercise price and the put is said to be at-the-money.

THE TIME VALUE OF A PUT OPTION

The time value of the put option is the put value less its intrinsic value. When the stock price is $47, the put value is $3.69 (point E on the curve) and its intrinsic value is $3 ($50 exercise price minus $47 stock price). Its time value is thus $0.69, the difference between the put value of $3.69 and its intrinsic value of $3.

THE VALUE OF AN AMERICAN PUT COMPARED TO THE VALUE OF A EUROPEAN PUT

We showed earlier that the holder of a non-dividend-paying American call option – who could in principle exercise the call before its expiration date – will never exercise early and concluded that an American call on a non-dividend-paying stock must have the same price as an equivalent European call. This property does not apply to put options because there are circumstances where it may be worth exercising a put option on a non-dividend-paying stock *before* its expiration date. To see this, consider the case of a firm whose stocks are practically worthless because the company is nearly bankrupt and unlikely to be rescued. It is clear that there is no reason for the holder of a put option on that stock to wait for the expiration date of the put to exercise it because the price of a worthless stock cannot fall further and make the put even more valuable. The put holder is better off exercising now because she can invest now the exercise money she receives. Even though this example is extreme, its implication is clear: the right to exercise a put before its expiration day is valuable and hence *the price of an American put on a non-dividend-paying stock is higher than that of an equivalent European put.*

SHORT POSITIONS IN PUT OPTIONS

The discussion has so far dealt with the case of put options held *long*, that is, the case where the option holder *bought* put options. We now want to examine the case of a put *writer* who *sold* puts and thus has a *short* position. The terminal payoff for a short position in a put option on the ISC stock is given on the right side of Exhibit 16.2. It is represented by the thick line that breaks at the $50 exercise price. Also shown in the exhibit are the put writer's profits and losses when the put expires. They are represented by the dashed lines that break at the $50 exercise price.

The position generates a profit for the put writer as long as the ISC stock price is higher than $47.88 (the $50 exercise price less the put price of $2.12). Below that price the position generates losses because the put writer must *buy* the ISC stock from the holder of the put who will exercise her option to sell the *stock* when the stock price is lower than the exercise price.

THE PUT-CALL PARITY RELATIONSHIP

It makes intuitive sense to think that there should be a relationship that ties together the values of a European call (C) and a European put (P) written on the same underlying stock (S) with the same exercise price (X) and the same time to expiration (T). That relationship is given by an equation called the **put-call parity relationship**.[21] The equation can be easily established using a financial principle we have already employed in this chapter: the law of one price, which says that two investment strategies that generate the same terminal cash flows must have the same present value.

Consider the two investment strategies whose cash outflows now (at time zero) and cash inflows at time T are given in Exhibit 16.4. Assume that all options are European and that the underlying stock does not pay dividends. (We look later at the case of dividend-paying stocks.) The first investment consists of buying today a call option at a price C_0 (see row (1)) combined with the purchase of a zero-coupon bond with a face value X maturing at time T (see row (2)). The face value of the bond is set equal to the call's fixed exercise price and the bond is thus riskless. If the risk-free rate is R_F, the present value of this riskless bond is $X/(1 + R_F)^T$.[22] The present value of the combined investment is given in row (3). The cash inflow at time T is also shown in row (3) but notice that we need to consider two cases. In one case the stock price (S_T) at time T is *lower* or *equal* to the exercise price (X) and the call option expires unexercised. In this case the cash inflow from the call is zero and that from the zero-coupon

---

[21] The put-call parity relationship (see equation 16.5) holds only for European options. For American options, one can only derive upper and lower bounds for the price of these options. See Exhibit 16.6 and Hull (2017).

[22] See Chapter 10, equation 10.4.

EXHIBIT 16.4	THE PUT-CALL PARITY RELATIONSHIP.

| Investment Now | Cash Outflow Now | Cash Inflow at Time T (when options expire) | |
		$S_T \leq X$	$S_T > X$
(1) Buy a call option at C_0 with an exercise price X that expires in T years	$-C_0$	0	$S_T - X$
(2) Buy a zero-coupon bond with a face value X and a yield R_F that matures in T years	$-\dfrac{X}{(1 + R_F)^T}$	X	X
(3) Combine (1) and (2): **Buy the call and the zero-coupon bond**	$\left[-C_0 - \dfrac{X}{(1 + R_F)^T} \right]$	X	S_T
(4) Buy a put option at P_0 with an exercise price X that expires in T years	$-P_0$	$X - S_T$	0
(5) Buy a stock at S_0	$-S_0$	S_T	S_T
(6) Combine (4) and (5): **Buy the put and the stock**	$[-P_0 - S_0]$	X	S_T

bond is its face value X. The combined cash flow is equal to the exercise price (X). In the other case, the stock price (S_T) is *higher* than the exercise price (X) and the call option is exercised which generates a profit equal to S_T less X. Add to this the face value (X) of the zero-coupon bond and you get a net cash inflow of S_T.

The second investment consists of buying a put option at a price P_0 (see row (4)) combined with the purchase of the stock at a price S_0 (see row (5)). The investment's combined cash outflows and inflows are shown in row (6): if the stock price S_T at time T is *lower* or *equal* to the exercise price X, the combined cash inflow is equal to X. If the stock price S_T at time T is *higher* than the exercise price, the combined cash inflow is equal to S_T. As you can see in Exhibit 16.4, the two investments deliver the same terminal cash inflows at time T (compare row (3) to row (6)). Thus, according to the law-of-one-price, the two investments must have today the same value, that is:

$$[-P_0 - S_0] = \left[-C_0 - \frac{X}{(1 + R_F)^T} \right]$$

Rearranging the terms of the above equality provides the put-call parity relationship:

$$P_0 = C_0 + \frac{X}{(1 + R_F)^T} - S_0 \qquad (16.5a)$$

If interest is compounded continuously, the put-call parity relationship can be written (see equation 16.4b):

$$P_0 = C_0 + Xe^{-R_F T} - S_0 \qquad (16.5b)$$

GETTING THE VALUE OF A PUT IF YOU KNOW THE VALUE OF THE CALL

If you know the value of a call, you can use the put-call parity equation to get the value of an equivalent put on the same stock. To illustrate, look at Exhibit 16.1. A call option to buy one ISC stock in three months for $50 is worth $2.86 today. What is the value of a put option on the same stock with the same exercise price and the same expiration date if the stock currently trades at $50 and the risk-free rate is 6 percent? According to put-call parity equation 16.5b, the value of the put is:

$$P_0 = \$2.86 + \$50e^{-0.06 \times 0.25} - \$50 = \$2.86 + \$49.26 - \$50 = \$2.12$$

This is exactly the put value reported in Exhibit 16.3 when the stock price is $50 (point B on the curve).

CREATING SYNTHETIC OPTIONS AND SHORT POSITIONS IN STOCKS

The put-call parity relationship can also be used to help design so-called synthetic options and short positions in stocks. A synthetic option is a combination of assets that creates the same terminal cash flow as the option. To illustrate, suppose that put options on the ISC stock do not exist and you want to buy one. Specifically, you want to buy a 3-month put on the ISC stock with an exercise price equal to ISC's stock price of $50. The 3-month risk-free rate is 6 percent and 3-month call options on the ISC stock with an exercise price of $50 are currently worth $2.86. According to the put-call parity relationship, you can create a so-called **synthetic put**, that is, a *home-made* put, by buying a call for $2.86 (the first term in equation 16.5b), borrowing $49.26 at 6 percent for three months (the second term in equation 16.5b) and selling one ISC stock for $50 (the third term in equation 16.5b). The synthetic put will cost you $2.12 ($2.86 + $49.26 − $50) and generate the same terminal cash flow as a 3-month put option with an exercise price of $50.

The same method can be used to create a **synthetic call** if only puts existed, and a synthetic short position in a stock if **shorting stocks** (selling stocks you don't own) is not allowed. To create a synthetic call, buy the put at $2.12, *lend* $49.26 at 6 percent for three months and buy one share of ISC for $50: the combination creates a synthetic call worth $2.86 ($2.12 − $49.26 + $50 is equal to $2.86). To create the short position in the stock, buy the put at $2.12, sell the call (−$2.86) and lend $49.26 at 6 percent for three months ($2.12 − $2.86 − $49.26 is equal to −$50).

THE PUT-CALL PARITY RELATIONSHIP WHEN STOCKS PAY DIVIDENDS

The put-call parity relationships in equations 16.5a and 16.5b assume that the underlying stock does not pay dividends during the life of the options. If the underlying stock pays dividends during the life of the options, the put-call parity relationship must be adjusted to account for the fact that a buyer or a seller of an option is not entitled to the dividend on the underlying stock. The adjustment is straightforward: simply replace the stock price S_0 in the parity relationships with $(S_0 - PV(DPS))$. The latter term is equal to the current stock price *less* the present value (PV) of the dividend per share (DPS) that the stock is expected to pay over the life of the option.[23]

---

[23] The present value is usually calculated with the risk-free rate because the dividend is generally known when the time to expiration is relatively short.

GETTING OPTION PRICES WITH THE BLACK AND SCHOLES FORMULA

Up to now we have provided numerical examples in which the values of calls and puts were given without showing how these values were calculated. There is a formula – based on the **Black-Scholes Option Pricing Model** – that gives the price of a *European* call or put option on a *non-dividend-paying stock* if we know the following five variables or inputs (we show you later how to apply the formula to the case of American options and the case of dividend-paying stocks):

1. The current price of the stock (S_0) on which the option is written
2. The exercise or strike price of the option (X)
3. The time until the option expires (T)
4. The annual risk-free rate of return (R_F), continuously compounded
5. The volatility of the underlying stock measured by the annual standard deviation of the stock's continuous returns (σ_S).

Note that you don't have to estimate the first four variables (S_0, X, T, R_F) because they are directly observable. The only input you need to estimate is the volatility of the underlying stock returns.

The Price of a European Call on a Non-Dividend-Paying Stock

The price of a European call option on a stock that pays no dividends is given by the Black-Scholes formula 16.6 shown on the upper part of Exhibit 16.5. The formula looks complicated, but it is easy to interpret intuitively. As indicated in Exhibit 16.5, $N(d_1)$ and $N(d_2)$ are the areas under a normal distribution curve up to the value of d_1 and d_2, respectively. If there is a very high probability that the option will be exercised, then $N(d_1)$ and $N(d_2)$ are very close to one and the call price C_0 is essentially equal to $S_0 - Xe^{-R_F T}$, that is, the call price is equal to the call's intrinsic value calculated with the present value of the exercise price, which is exactly what we expect in this case. If there is a very high probability that the option will *not* be exercised, then $N(d_1)$ and $N(d_2)$ are very close to zero and the call price is essentially equal to zero, which is exactly what we expect in this case. Between these two extreme cases, there is some probability that the call will be exercised and $N(d_1)$ and $N(d_2)$ will take a value between zero and one that increases as the probability of exercising the option rises.

The Price of a European Put on a Non-Dividend-Paying Stock

We have already shown how to use the put-call parity relationship (equation 16.5b) to get the price of a European put option on a stock that pays no dividends if we know the price of the corresponding European call option on the same stock. Alternatively, you can substitute the call price formula 16.6 in Exhibit 16.5 for C_0 in the parity relationship and you will get the direct put pricing formula shown as equation 16.7 in Exhibit 16.5.

Using a Spreadsheet to Calculate the Price of European Options

Let's now use the Black-Scholes formula to calculate the price of the call on the ISC stock with the inputs given at the bottom of Exhibit 16.5. The current price of ISC stock is $50 and the call's exercise price is also $50. The time to expiration is three

| EXHIBIT 16.5 | THE BLACK-SCHOLES OPTION PRICING FORMULA. |

| Call Price Formula | $C_0 = S_0 N(d_1) - Xe^{-R_F T} N(d_2)$ | (16.6) |
| Put Price Formula | $P_0 = Xe^{-R_F T}[(1 - N(d_2))] - S_0[1 - N(d_1)]$ | (16.7) |

C_0 = Current price of the call option on stock S given by the Black-Scholes formula (to be calculated)

P_0 = Current price of the put option on stock S given by the Black-Scholes formula (to be calculated)

S_0 = Current stock price

X = Exercise price of the option

T = Time to expiration of the option measured in *years*

R_F = Annual risk-free rate of return, *continuously* compounded

σ_S = Annual standard deviation or volatility of the stock's continuous returns

$$d_1 = \frac{Ln(S_0/X) + (R_F + 0.50\sigma_S^2)T}{\sigma_S\sqrt{T}}$$

$d_2 = d_1 - \sigma_S\sqrt{T}$

Ln = Natural logarithm function. It is given by the function LN in Excel spreadsheets

N(d) = Probability that a random draw for a normal distribution will be less than 'd'. It is the area under the normal distribution curve up to 'd'. It is given by the function NORMSDIST in Excel spreadsheets

e = Base for the natural logarithm function (equal to 2.71828). It is given by the function EXP in Excel spreadsheets

USING AN EXCEL SPREADSHEET TO CALCULATE CALL AND PUT PRICES ON THE ISC STOCK

	A	B	C	D	E
1	**Inputs**	**Value**	**Outputs**	**Value**	**Formulas For Outputs In Column D**
2	S_0 (in \$)	50	d_1	0.1825	=(LN((B2–B7)/B3)+(B5+0.5*B6^2)*B4)/(B6*SQRT(B4))
3	X (in \$)	50	d_2	0.0575	=D2–B6*SQRT(B4)
4	T (in years)	0.25	$N(d_1)$	0.5724	=NORMSDIST(D2)
5	R_F (annual)	0.06	$N(d_2)$	0.5229	=NORMSDIST (D3)
6	σ_S (annual)	0.25	C_0	**2.8632**	=(B2–B7)*D4–B3*EXP(–B5*B4)*D5
7	PV(DPS)[1]	0	P_0	**2.1188**	=B3*EXP(–B5*B4)*(1–D5)–(B2–B7)*(1–D4)

[1] PV(DPS) = Present value (PV) of the stream of dividend per share (DPS) the stock is expected to pay over the life of the option

months (T = 0.25), the annual risk-free rate is 6 percent and the annual volatility of the stock returns is 25 percent. To speed up the calculation you can use the spreadsheet shown at the bottom of Exhibit 16.5 where you will find the values of d_1, d_2, $N(d_1)$ and $N(d_2)$. We have:

$$C_0 = S_0 N(d_1) - Xe^{-R_F T} N(d_2) = (\$50 \times 0.5724) - (\$50 \times 0.9851 \times 0.5229)$$

$$C_0 = \$28.62 - \$25.76 = \$2.86$$

This is the call price on the ISC stock calculated by the spreadsheet and shown in cell D6 in Exhibit 16.5. It is also the call price we used in Exhibit 16.1.

You can get the price of the ISC put that has the same characteristics as the call by applying the put price formula 16.7 in Exhibit 16.5. Using the data reported in the spreadsheet shown at the bottom the exhibit, you get:

$$P_0 - Xe^{-R_F T}[(1 - N(d_2)) - S_0[1 - N(d_1)]]$$

$$P_0 = (\$50 \times 0.9851 \times [1 - 0.5229]) - (\$50 \times [1 - 0.5724]) = \$23.50 - \$21.38 = \$2.12$$

This is the put price on the ISC stock calculated by the spreadsheet and reported in cell D7 in Exhibit 16.5. It is also the put price we used in Exhibit 16.3.

THE PRICE OF EUROPEAN OPTIONS ON DIVIDEND-PAYING STOCKS

The Black-Scholes formulas in Exhibit 16.5 can also be used to get the price of European call and put options on stocks that pay dividends. Recall that option holders are not entitled to the dividends that are paid to the owners of the underlying stock. As a consequence, the Black-Scholes formulas must be adjusted to reflect the fact that option holders do not receive dividends. This is done by simply replacing in the formulas the current stock price S_0 with S_0 *less* the present value of the stream of dividend per share PV(DPS) the option holders will not get, that is, use $[S_0 - PV(DPS)]$ instead of S_0 in the Black-Scholes formulas. The present value PV is usually calculated with the risk-free rate because the dividend is generally known when the time to expiration is relatively short. Note that the spreadsheet formulas in cells D2, D6 and D7 in Exhibit 16.5 have already been adjusted for a possible stream of dividend payments during the life of the options. All you have to do is enter the present value of the dividend stream in cell B7.

To illustrate, suppose the ISC stock in Exhibit 16.5 is expected to pay a dividend per share (DPS) of $1 in two months. The present value of the dividend, using continuous compounding, is:[24]

$$PV(DPS) = DPS \times e^{-R_F T} = \$1 \times e^{-0.06 \times \left(\frac{2}{12}\right)} = \$1 \times 0.9900 = \$0.99$$

and thus $[S_0 - PV(DPS)] = \$50 - \$0.99 = \$49.01$. Replacing the $50 stock price in cell B2 with $49.01, yields a call price of $2.33 in cell D6 and a put price of $2.57 in cell D7. Alternatively, you could have entered $0.99, the present value of the dividend per share, in cell B7 and obtained the same option prices. Note that the call price is now lower ($2.33 instead of $2.86) and the put price is higher ($2.57 instead of $2.12) because the lower stock price (due to the deduction of the present value of the dividend) makes the call options less valuable and the put options more valuable.

THE PRICE OF AMERICAN OPTIONS

We have so far used the Black-Scholes formulas to get the price of a *European* option on a stock that either pays or does not pay dividends during the life of the option. Can we use the same formulas to get the price of an *American* call or put option? We examine below the case where the underlying stock does not pay dividends and the case where it does. The different cases are summarized in Exhibit 16.6.

---

[24] If the option expired in one year and the stock was expected to pay a first dividend per share of $1 in two months and a second dividend per share of $1 in eight months (six months after the first), then PV(DPS) would be equal to the sum of the present value of the first dividend ($0.99) and the present value of the second dividend ($0.96), that is, PV(DPS) = $1.95 in this case.

EXHIBIT 16.6	APPLYING THE BLACK-SCHOLES FORMULA TO DIFFERENT TYPES OF OPTIONS.			

Does the underlying stock pay dividends during the life of the options?	European Options Cannot be exercised before maturity		American Options Can be exercised before maturity	
	Call Price	Put Price	Call Price	Put Price
No dividend payments	Use eq. 16.6 in Exhibit 16.5	Use eq. 16.7 in Exhibit 16.5	Use eq. 16.6 in Exhibit 16.5[2]	Eq. 16.7 gives only a lower bound on the put price[4]
Yes, at least one dividend payment per share (DPS)	Replace S_0 with $S_0' = S_0 - PV(DPS)$[1] and use eq. 16.6 in Exhibit 16.5	Replace S_0 with $S_0' = S_0 - PV(DPS)$[1] and use eq. 16.7 in Exhibit 16.5	Use the *highest* of: – Call price to ex-dividend dates[3] – Call price to expiration date	Eq. 16.7 in Exhibit 16.5 does not give a reliable put price in this case

[1] S_0 is the current price of the underlying stock and PV(DPS) is the present value (at the risk-free rate) of the stream of dividend per share (DPS) the stock will pay during the life of the option.
[2] Because it is never optimal to exercise an American call prior to its exercise date, an American call on a non-dividend-paying stock has the same value as an equivalent European call.
[3] When there are multiple dividend payments during the life of the option, the call price is usually calculated only for the *final* ex-dividend date.
[4] Because there are circumstances under which it is optimal to exercise an American put on a non-dividend-paying stock prior to its maturity date, the price of these puts can be higher than the value of an equivalent European put.

THE UNDERLYING STOCK DOES NOT PAY DIVIDENDS DURING THE LIFE OF THE OPTION

American call options. We have already established that an American call on a non-dividend-paying stock must have the same price as its European counterpart because it is not optimal to exercise an American call on a non-dividend-paying stock before its expiration date. This means that the Black-Scholes formula 16.6 also provides the value of an American call on a stock that does not pay dividends during the life of the call.

American put options. As pointed out earlier – and contrary to the case of an American call – there are circumstances under which it is optimal to exercise an American put on a non-dividend-paying stock before it expires. The implication is that an American put on a non-dividend-paying stock can sometimes be more valuable than its European counterpart. This means that the Black-Scholes put formula 16.7 only gives a lower bound on the value of an American put on a non-dividend-paying stock.

THE UNDERLYING STOCK PAYS A DIVIDEND DURING THE LIFE OF THE OPTION

American call options. We have shown earlier that it may be optimal to exercise an American call immediately before the underlying stock goes ex-dividend and drops in price, particularly when the dividend date is close to the call's expiration date and the dividend is large. (Note that it is never optimal to exercise an American call at times other than ex-dividend dates.) This makes the American call more valuable than its European counterpart. Can we still use the Black-Scholes formula in this case? The formula can be applied using a procedure suggested by Black.[25] The procedure

[25] See Black (1975).

consists of applying the formula assuming that the call will be exercised immediately before the ex-dividend date and comparing this value to the call value assuming that it will not be exercised, and then choose the higher of the two values as the estimated value of the American call.

Let's illustrate this procedure using the previous example of the European call on the dividend-paying stock. First, get the call price with an expiration date equal to two months ($T = 2/12 = 0.1667$) which is the date at which the dividend is expected to be paid, and then compare that call value (C_1) to the value of an equivalent European call on a dividend-paying stock (C_2). Using the spreadsheet formula in Exhibit 16.5 we get:

$$C_1[S_0 = \$50; X = \$50; T = 0.1667; R_F = 6\%; \sigma_S = 25\%] = \$2.28$$

$$C_2[S_0 - PV(DPS) = \$49.01; X = \$50; T = 0.25; R_F = 6\%; \sigma_S = 25\%] = \$2.33$$

Given that the higher of the two call values is C_2, we take \$2.33 as a lower bound estimate of the value of the American call on the dividend-paying stock.[26]

American put options. The above procedure does not apply to the valuation of American puts because it may be optimal to exercise these options at times other than dividend dates. American put options on dividend-paying stocks are thus best valued with option pricing models other than the Black-Scholes formula (such as the binomial model presented in the appendix).

RESPONSE OF OPTION PRICES TO CHANGES IN INPUT VALUES

We already know that the Black-Scholes formula gives the price of a European option on a non-dividend-paying stock as a function of five inputs: the price of the underlying stock, the option's time to expiration, the option's exercise price, the risk-free rate and the volatility of the underlying stock price. We now want to find out how the price of a European option on a non-dividend-paying stock responds to a change in the value of one of the five inputs while the other four remain the same. Here is what we observe and why it happens:

1. When the stock price *increases*, the call price *rises* because the call's intrinsic value *increases* and the put price *falls* because the put's intrinsic value *decreases*.
2. When the exercise price *increases*, the call price *falls* because the call's intrinsic value *decreases* and the put price *rises* because the put's intrinsic value *increases*.
3. When the time to expiration *lengthens*, the call price *rises* because the call holder does not pay the exercise price until the call expires, making calls with longer maturities more valuable. The price of a European put, however, *could* fall because the holder cannot exercise it early and invest the exercise money to earn additional income.
4. When the risk-free rate *increases*, the call price *rises* and the put price *falls* because the present value of the exercise price *increases*, making the call *more* valuable and the put *less* valuable.

---

[26] When there are multiple dividend payments during the life of the option, call prices should be calculated for every ex-dividend date, but in practice the call price is calculated only for the final ex-dividend date.

EXHIBIT 16.7	CHANGE IN THE PRICE OF AN OPTION IN RESPONSE TO A CHANGE IN THE VALUE OF ONE INPUT (S_0, X, T, σ_S, R_F, DPS) WHILE THE OTHER FIVE INPUTS ARE FIXED.

The value of one of the following inputs changes while the other five are fixed	European Options		American Options	
	Call price change	Put price change	Call price change	Put price change
1. Current stock price (S_0)	+[1]	−[2]	+	−
2. Exercise price of the option (X)	−	+	−	+
3. Time to expiration of the option (T)	+ or −[3]	+ or −[3]	+	+
4. Risk-free rate (R_F)	+	−	+	−
5. Volatility of the stock returns (σ_S)	+	+	+	+
6. Dividend per share paid before the option expires (DPS)	−	+	−	+

[1] A positive sign indicates that the option price changes in the *same* direction as the change in the value of the input.

[2] A negative sign indicates that the option price changes in the *opposite* direction to the change in the value of the input.

[3] When the underlying stock pays dividends during the life of the option, the change in the price of a European option can be in the opposite direction. See the numerical example in the text.

5. When the stock volatility *increases*, both the call and put prices *rise* because a higher volatility *increases* the chance that the stock price will rise above the exercise price in the case of calls or fall below the exercise price in the case of puts.

In addition to the five inputs listed here, option prices are also affected by the underlying stock's dividend payments if the dividends are paid during the life of the option; as shown earlier, dividend payments reduce call prices and raise put prices. The change in the price of European and American options in response to a change in the value of one of the six inputs while the other five are fixed is summarized in Exhibit 16.7: a *positive* sign indicates that the option price changes in the *same* direction as the change in the value of the input and a *negative* sign indicates a change in the *opposite* direction. For a numerical illustration, go to self-test question 16.2.

Note that when the underlying stock on a European option pays a dividend during the option's life, that option may be worth *less* than a *shorter-life* option on the same stock that does *not* pay dividends. To illustrate, consider a 4-week call and an 8-week call on a stock that is expected to pay a $2 dividend in six weeks. The stock price and the exercise price are both $50. The stock volatility is 25 percent and the risk-free rate is 6 percent. The 4-week call is *unaffected* by the dividend and is worth $1.50 (check this). The 8-week call is *affected* by the dividend and is worth $1.24 (check this). Conclusion: a *longer* call on a dividend-paying stock can have a *lower* value than a *shorter* call on a non-dividend-paying stock.

IMPLIED VOLATILITY

We pointed out earlier that the only input you must estimate in order to apply the Black-Scholes formula is the volatility of the stock returns. If you know the price of a call (because it is traded in the market), you can use the Black-Scholes formula backward to get an estimate of the stock volatility that is consistent with that price. The spreadsheet has a command called *Goal Seek* that will calculate volatility for a given call price (Go to self-test question 16.3 to see how to do this). For example, if the call price is $3 instead of $2.86, the corresponding **implied volatility** is 26.39 percent instead of 25 percent. As you noticed, the call with the higher price ($3) has a higher stock volatility (26.39 percent) because the more volatile the stock, the higher the chances that the stock price will end up above the exercise price, which makes the call more valuable.

HOW GOOD IS THE BLACK-SCHOLES MODEL?

We can answer this question on two levels. First, are the assumptions behind the standard Black-Scholes Model realistic in light of what we know regarding the actual behavior of stock prices? Second, irrespective of whether the model's assumptions are realistic, is the model able to predict the price of options we observe in the market? (The model may be based on some unrealistic assumptions but still able to predict option prices with a reasonable degree of accuracy.)

Let's review the key assumptions behind the model. Recall first that the model assumes options are *European* (they cannot be exercised before their expiration date) and the underlying stocks *do not pay dividends* over the life of the options. This means that the model is less accurate in predicting the price of options on stocks that pay relatively high dividends and options that can be exercised before they expire (American options). The model also assumes that the risk-free rate (R_F) and the volatility of the underlying stock (σ_S) are *constant* over the life of the option, a behavior that is often not observed in the market. All these issues mean that the model may not provide accurate estimates of option prices.

Does the Black-Scholes Model have some predictive ability? One way to check this – for European options that pay no dividends – is to examine the behavior of the implied volatility of options. If the model's predictive ability is high, options on the *same* underlying stock and the *same* expiration date but with *different* exercise prices should have the *same* implied volatility. Empirical tests have shown that this is usually not the case, that is, an option's implied volatility changes when the option's exercise price changes, an observation that is not consistent with the Black-Scholes Model. In general, the model tends to *overprice* options that are at-the-money and *underprice* options that are either deep in-the-money or deep out-of-the-money.

So where does this discussion leave us regarding the relevance and reliability of the standard Black-Scholes formula? We can conclude that the formula provides a good approximation of the price of a European option on a stock that pays no dividends and has a return distribution that is closely approximated by a log-normal distribution. When these conditions do not hold, the standard model does not perform as well. More complex models have been devised to price options on stocks that pay dividends, allow early exercise, exhibit non-constant future volatility, and have stock price movements that jump occasionally instead of displaying continuous changes. In the appendix we present one of these models, called the Binomial Option Pricing Model, which provides more accurate option prices than the Black-Scholes standard model but is more complex to apply.

DELTA: A MEASURE OF THE SENSITIVITY OF OPTION PRICES TO CHANGES IN THE UNDERLYING STOCK PRICE

We saw earlier that a rise in the price of a stock increases the price of a call on that stock, assuming that the value of all the other inputs in the Black-Scholes formula remain the same. The question we now want to answer is the following: if the stock price changes by *one dollar*, what is the corresponding change in the price of a call or a put on that stock? In other words, we want to measure the *price sensitivity* of an option to a change in the price of the underlying stock.

The Black-Scholes formula provides the answer. Let's use the symbol Δ_C (pronounced delta call) to denote the *approximate* change in the price of the call in response to a one-dollar change in the price of the underlying stock, and Δ_P (pronounced delta put) to denote the *approximate* change in the price of the put in response to a one-dollar change in the price of stock. The approximate changes in option prices are given by the Black-Scholes option pricing formulas in Exhibit 16.5:[27]

Approximate change in call price if stock price changes by one dollar = $\Delta_C = N(d_1)$ (16.8a)

Approximate change in put price if stock price changes by one dollar = $\Delta_P = N(d_1) - 1$ (16.8b)

To illustrate, consider the call and put options on the ISC stock in Exhibit 16.5: the value of $N(d_1)$ is 0.5724 and the value of $[N(d_1) - 1]$ is -0.4276. (The negative sign indicates that the put price moves in the opposite direction to the stock price.) Using these values, we can state the following: if the stock price changes by one dollar, the call price *increases* by approximately $0.5724 and the put price *decreases* by approximately $0.4276.

An option's delta, also called the option's **hedge ratio**, has several useful applications. We show below how to use it to compare the risk of an option to the risk of its underlying stock, and how to apply it to hedge the price risk of a stock you hold.

AN INVESTMENT IN AN OPTION IS ALWAYS RISKIER THAN THE SAME INVESTMENT IN THE UNDERLYING STOCK

We have just shown that if the price of the ISC stock moves by one dollar, the call on the stock moves in the same direction by approximately $0.5724 and the put on the stock moves in the opposite direction by approximately $0.4276. The change in the option price is always *smaller* than the change in the price of the underlying stock because $N(d_1)$ is smaller than one. What can we conclude from these changes in prices? Are options more or less risky than the underlying stock?

To compare the risk of options to the risk of the underlying stock we must first make sure that the amount invested in the stock is the same as the amount invested in the option. In our numerical example in Exhibit 16.5 the ISC stock is worth $50 but the call is only worth $2.8632 and the put $2.1188. Thus, the correct question to ask is: what is the change in the price of a portfolio containing $50 worth of calls or puts compared to the change in the price of the $50 underlying stock? With $50 you can buy 17.46 calls ($50 divided by $2.8632) or 23.60 puts ($50 divided by $2.1188). The next step is to find out by how much the price of the portfolio of 17.46 calls (worth $50) and the price of the portfolio of 23.60 puts (worth $50) will move when the ISC stock (worth $50) moves by one dollar.

The portfolio of calls will move up by approximately $10 (17.46 calls multiplied by $0.5724) and the portfolio of puts will move down by approximately $10 (23.60 puts multiplied by $0.4276). In other words, the options are ten times riskier than

---

[27] We focus here on *delta*, the sensitivity of the option price to a change in the underlying stock price. But we can also measure the sensitivity of the option price to a change in (1) the exercise price (called *xi*), (2) the time to expiration (called *Theta*), (3) the risk-free rate (called *Rho*), and (4) the stock volatility (called *Vega*), as well as the sensitivity of an option's *delta* to a change in the underlying stock price (called *gamma*). See Chapter 19 in Hull (2017) to get the formulas for these price sensitivities according to the Black-Scholes Model.

the underlying stock. Although this is just one numerical example, it can be generalized: *an investment in an option is always riskier than the same amount invested in the underlying stock.*

OPTION-BASED INVESTMENT STRATEGIES

Some typical option-based investment strategies are summarized in Exhibit 16.8. Their objectives are varied. The first strategy (buying **naked calls**) is used to *speculate* on an anticipated rise in a stock price, the second (buying a **protective put**) is applied to *hedge* against a possible drop in stock price, the third (**portfolio insurance**) is employed to *insure* a portfolio against a decline in the stock market, the fourth (writing **covered calls**) is adopted to *generate income* from a portfolio of stocks, the fifth (constructing a **collar** - see covered calls in Exhibit 16.8) is used to *protect* a covered call position with a put, the sixth (buying a **straddle**) is utilized to *simultaneously speculate* on a stock price rise and *hedge* against a drop in that stock, and the seventh (constructing a **spread**) is implemented to *arbitrage* a relative mispricing between two options. We briefly examine these strategies below.

SPECULATING ON A RISE IN STOCK PRICE WITH NAKED CALLS

Suppose you expect the share price of ISC, currently trading at $50, to rise. If you want to *speculate* on that expected rise in price, would you buy the stock or calls on the ISC stock priced at $2.86? If you have $5,000 to invest, you can either buy 100 ISC shares ($5,000 divided by $50) or 1,748 calls ($5,000 divided by $2.86). We showed earlier that if ISC's share price goes up by one dollar, the call will go up by about $0.5724. This means that buying 100 shares will generate a gain of $100 (100 × $1) whereas buying 1,748 calls will generate a gain of $1,000 (1,748 × $0.5724), which is ten times larger. What if the stock price goes down by one dollar? In this case, your naked call strategy will generate a *loss* of $1,000. Conclusion: if the objective is to speculate on an expected rise in the price of a stock, then buying a call on that stock will deliver significantly higher gains than buying the stock *if the risky bet turns out in favor of the speculator.*

HEDGING AGAINST A DROP IN STOCK PRICE WITH PROTECTIVE PUTS

You own 10,000 shares of ISC that are currently trading at $50 per share. You believe that this week ISC will announce an unexpected slowdown in sales, and you wish to hedge the risk of a possible drop in the price of ISC stocks. You can protect your holding against a drop in price by buying *put* options in ISC stocks: if the price of the stock takes a dip, the price of the puts will *rise* and offset the drop in the stock price. Suppose that 3-month puts on ISC stocks with a $50 exercise price are available in the market. How many puts should you buy to hedge the price risk associated with holding ISC stocks?

The delta of the put option is $[N(d_1) - 1] = -0.4276$. You want to find out the number of ISC puts, denoted n_p, that makes the change in the share price equal to the change in the put price. You know that when the share price moves by one dollar, one put moves in the opposite direction by approximately $0.4276. *The number of puts needed to get a one-dollar change is thus the inverse of the put's delta*, that is:

$$n_p = \frac{1}{\Delta_p} = \frac{\$1}{[N(d_1) - 1]} = \frac{\$1}{-\$0.4276} = -2.3386$$

EXHIBIT 16.8	SOME OPTION-BASED INVESTMENT STRATEGIES.

Strategy Name	Investment Decision	Objective and Implementation
1. Naked Calls	Buy calls on a stock instead of the stock itself. The value of the calls bought is equal to the stock price	**Speculating** on an expected rise in a stock price by holding calls on the stock instead of the stock **How does it work?** The value of the calls will increase more than the rise in the stock price because calls provide leverage
2. Protective Puts	Buy puts on a stock you own	**Hedging** against a drop in the price of a stock **How does it work?** A drop in the stock price will be offset by the rise in the price of the puts **The cost of the hedge** is the price paid to buy the puts
3. Portfolio Insurance	Buy stock-index puts to protect a diversified portfolio of stocks	**Insuring** against an unexpected drop in the value of a portfolio of stocks **How does it work?** A drop in the value of the portfolio will be offset by the rise in the price of the stock-index puts **The cost of the insurance** is the price paid to buy the puts
4. Covered Calls	Sell calls on a stock you own with an exercise price higher than the stock price (you could also buy puts with a lower exercise price than the stock price to protect the covered-call position: this strategy is called a **collar**)	**Generating income** through the sale of calls on stocks you own. If protective puts are added, the covered-call position is hedged against an unexpected sharp drop in the price of the stock
5. Long Straddles	(1) Buy a call and (2) Buy a put on the *same* stock with the *same* exercise price and the *same* expiration date (if the exercise price of the put is *lower* than the exercise price of the call, the combination is called a **strangle**)	**Speculating** on a possible rise in stock price while simultaneously **hedging** against a possible drop in the price of the same stock **How does it work?** The call will magnify a possible stock price increase while the put will protect the position against a possible decrease in price **The cost of the position** is the price paid to buy the calls and the puts
6. Spreads	(1) Buy a call (or a put) and (2) Sell a call (or a put) on the *same* stock with a *different* exercise price (this is called a **money spread**) or a *different* expiration date (this is called a **time spread**)	**Arbitraging** the relative mispricing of two options on the same underlying stock but with different exercise prices or different lives by buying the relatively cheaper one and selling the relatively expensive one **How does it work?** When prices move toward their equilibrium values, a profit is generated **The cost of the position** is the price paid for the long call less the price received from the sale of the short call

You need to buy 2.3386 puts to hedge one ISC share. Thus, to hedge 10,000 shares you need to buy 23,386 puts. You can check that the 23,386 puts will hedge the price risk of the 10,000 shares by calculating the change in the price of 23,386 puts if the shares go up by $10,000 ($1 per share): it is equal to 23,386 × $0.4276, that is, $10,000. Note that because a typical option contract is for 100 shares, you will have to buy 234 contracts.

INSURING EQUITY PORTFOLIOS

Portfolio insurance works like a protective put. The underlying asset, however, is not a single stock but a diversified portfolio of stocks. And the puts are on a stock market index and not on a particular stock. If the returns of the portfolio are not perfectly correlated with those of the market index, the position must be calibrated in order to create a quasi-perfectly hedged position in which the changes in the value of the put index options will exactly offset the corresponding changes in the value of the diversified portfolio.

WRITING COVERED CALLS TO GENERATE INCOME

Here, the holder of a stock portfolio (typically an institutional investor) wants to generate income from the portfolio – beyond the portfolio's expected return – by writing (that is, selling) call options against some of the stocks in the portfolio with *higher* exercise prices than the stock price (that is, out-of-the-money calls). The income is simply the call price multiplied by the number of calls sold. The strategy is referred to as *covered* (as opposed to *naked*) because the investor who sold the calls owns the stocks that will have to be delivered if the buyer exercises the call. If the exercise takes place, the investor will no longer own the stocks that have been delivered but the idea here is that the investor had already decided to sell the stock if its price reached the call's exercise price.

COLLARS: COVERED CALLS WITH PROTECTIVE PUTS

The risk borne by a covered call writer is an unexpected sharp drop in the price of the stock. This risk can be hedged by adding to the position a protective put with an exercise price *lower* than the stock price. The combination of the covered call (with an exercise price *higher* than the stock price) and the protective put (with an exercise price *lower* than stock price) is called a **collar**. You can also think of a collar as a protective put strategy where the put is expensive (because its exercise price is lower than the stock price), so to offset the cost of the put you sell a call at a higher exercise price, giving away some of the upside.

HEDGING STOCK PRICE VOLATILITY WITH LONG STRADDLES

Consider a construction company that submitted a bid for a major contract to build a large housing complex and assume that the company's current stock price reflects an equal chance of winning or losing the bid. If the bid is won, the stock price is expected to rise sharply on the day of the announcement. If the bid is lost, the stock price is expected to drop significantly when the announcement is made. If you own the stock, you want to benefit from a possible rise in price if the news is favorable while hedging a possible drop in price if the news is unfavorable.

What combination of options on the company's stock will deliver the profit if the price rises and provide the protection if the price falls? The answer is: a long call combined with a long put with the *same* exercise price and the *same* time to expiration. The call will deliver the profit if the bid is won and the put will provide the protection if the bid fails. This combination of options is called a long **straddle**.

ARBITRAGING OPTION PRICES WITH MONEY SPREADS OR TIME SPREADS

Consider two calls (C_1 and C_2) with different exercise prices (X_1 and X_2) but the same expiration date. Suppose you believe that C_1 is *cheap* when compared to C_2 and you expect this mispricing to correct soon. How could you profit from this situation? You should buy the cheap call C_1 and finance the purchase with the proceeds from the sale of C_2, and profit when the price of the cheap call C_1 rises. This arbitrage strategy is called a **bullish money spread** because you expect to gain when the stock price goes up (through the call C_1 you bought) while limiting your loss if it goes down (through the call C_2 you sold). A similar arbitrage strategy with two calls that have different expiration dates but the same exercise price is called a bullish **time spread**.

SECURITIES WITH OPTION FEATURES

We saw in Chapter 11 that a number of securities issued by firms have embedded option features. **Rights issues** and **warrants** are the same as *call* options because they allow the holder to *buy* shares in the future at a *pre-set* price from the firms that issued them (the pre-set price is the same as the exercise price of a call option). **Contingent value rights** are the same as *put* options because they allow the holder to *sell* shares in the future at a pre-set price to the firms that issued them. Likewise, securities such as **callable bonds** (that allow the firm to buy back its bonds in the future at a pre-set price) and **convertible bonds** (that allow the holder to convert a firm's bonds into the firm's equity at a pre-set price) can be viewed as straight bonds with embedded options. We briefly review these securities in this section. Before we do this, however, we first look at the interesting case of securities that do *not* have obvious option features – such as straight common stocks and bonds – but can nevertheless be viewed as options on the firm's assets.

EQUITY AS A CALL OPTION ON THE FIRM'S ASSETS

To see why a firm's equity can be viewed as a call option on the firm's assets, consider the case of the Allied Engineering Company (AEC), a privately-held manufacturer of small engines for motorcycles. The estimated value of the firm's assets is $100 million. These assets are funded with shareholders' equity and a 1-year zero-coupon bond with a face value of $60 million. Let's assume that neither the firm's equity value nor the bond value is known. How could we estimate these values? We could value the bond if we know its yield to maturity. Once we have the bond value, we can infer the value of equity by deducting the bond value from the $100 million value of assets. There is another way to estimate the value of equity that is based on the view that equity is like a call option on the firm's assets. One advantage of the option approach is its ability to explain the behavior of equity prices when a firm is experiencing **financial distress**.

VALUING EQUITY AS A CALL OPTION ON THE FIRM'S ASSETS

We can view AEC equity as a call option on the firm's assets because owning equity gives AEC shareholders the right to acquire AEC assets from bondholders at an exercise price of $60 million (the bond's face value) *when the bond matures in one year*. Think of it this way: on the day the bond matures, equity holders have to repay bondholders the $60 million of face value they owe them. If on that day AEC assets are worth *more* than $60 million, equity holders will repay bondholders the $60 million and keep the firm's assets. But if on the day the bond matures AEC assets are worth *less* than $60 million, equity holders have no incentive to repay bondholders the $60 million they owe them; they will be better off walking away and letting the bondholders take over AEC assets. In other words, the value of AEC equity is the same as the value of a 1-year call option on AEC assets (worth $100 million) with an exercise price equal to the bond's face value (worth $60 million):

$$\text{Value of equity } (V_E) = \text{Value of a call on the firm's assets } (C_A) \qquad (16.9)$$

What is the value of that call? We know three out of the five inputs required to value the call with the Black-Scholes formula: the value of the underlying assets ($V_A = \$100$ million), the exercise price ($X = \$60$ million) and the time to expiration ($T = 1$ year). Let's say the 1-year risk-free rate is 3 percent ($R_F = 3\%$) and that the annual volatility of AEC assets has been estimated at 30 percent ($\sigma_A = 30\%$). We can now value the call option using the spreadsheet in Exhibit 16.5. We have:

$$C_A[V_A = \$100m; X = \$60m; T = 1; R_F = 3\%; \sigma_A = 30\%] = \$42 \text{ million}$$

The value of AEC's equity is thus $42 million, and the value of its bond is $58 million ($100 million less $42 million). Given the bond value of $58 million, what is its yield? It is 3.45 percent.[28] The bond yield is very close to the 3 percent risk-free rate because the bond is quite safe given that AEC has $100 million of assets to back up a bond with a $60 million face value maturing in 12 months.

EQUITY VALUE WHEN THE FIRM IS EXPERIENCING FINANCIAL DISTRESS

Assume now that the engines AEC manufactures turn out to have a major defect forcing the firm to shut down its operations and recall its defective product, putting the firm under severe financial distress. As a result, let's say that the value of AEC assets is cut by half, dropping to $50 million from $100 million. AEC assets are now worth *less* than the bond's $60 million face value. What happens to the value of AEC equity? Is it worthless given that AEC would be unable to repay bondholders the $60 million *if it were due today*? Let's recalculate the call value assuming that all the inputs remain the same except for the value of assets. The AEC equity value is now:

$$C_A[V_A = \$50m; X = \$60m; T = 1; R_F = 3\%; \sigma_A = 30\%] = \$3.15 \text{ million}$$

The value of AEC equity drops from $42 million to $3.15 million, and the bond value drops from $58 million to $46.85 million ($50 million less $3.15 million). The equity value has dropped dramatically, but it is not worthless. This result should not surprise you because you know that equity is like a call: as long as there is one year to go before the call expires, there is still a chance that the value of AEC assets will rise

---

[28] We have: Bond value $= \$58m = \dfrac{\text{Face value}}{1+\text{yield}} = \dfrac{\$60m}{1+\text{yield}}$ from which we get a yield of 3.45%.

above the bond's $60 million face value. What is the new bond yield? It has jumped from 3.45 percent to 28.07 percent to reflect the risk of possible bankruptcy.[29]

As our example illustrates, viewing equity as a call option on the firm's assets is most illuminating when the likelihood of bankruptcy is high and equity holders are likely to let the call expire unexercised. One interesting implication of this formulation is that the value of a firm's equity *rises* when the volatility of its assets goes up, that is, when its assets are *riskier*. (Recall that a call price goes up when the volatility of the underlying asset rises.) To put it differently, when potential bankruptcy is *high*, shareholders are *better off* when the firm's assets are *riskier*.

Why Would Equity Holders Invest in a Negative Net Present Value Project?

This phenomenon leads to some interesting insights regarding managerial decision-making. It explains why a firm's owners would invest in a very risky project even if the project does not create value. The reason is that this type of project will deliver either a very *high* cash-flow stream or a very *low* cash-flow stream. If the *high* cash-flow stream occurs, the firm's equity value will rise significantly making the firm's owners better off. If the *low* cash-flow stream occurs, the firm may go bankrupt and the firm's owners can simply walk away and let bondholders take over the firm's assets.

The phenomenon can be illustrated as follows. Return to the case where AEC assets dropped to $50 million due to financial distress. Assume that shareholders decide to invest in a very risky project whose net present value (NPV) is a negative $1 million. The investment reduces the value of AEC assets to $49 million ($50 million less $1 million) and increases their volatility from 30 percent to, say, 50 percent. What is the new value of equity? We now have:

$$C_A[V_A = \$49m; X = \$60m; T = 1; R_F = 3\%; \sigma_A = 50\%] = \$6.58 \text{ million}$$

The value of equity has doubled, rising from $3.15 million to $6.58 million, and the bond value has dropped from $46.85 million to $42.42 million ($49 million less $6.58 million). Conclusion: investing in a risky, negative NPV project has made shareholders better off and left bondholders worse off.[30]

Merging Firms to Lower the Volatility of their Combined Assets Will Reduce their Merged Equity Value

Equity as a call option also explains why a merger between two firms whose *only* purpose is to *reduce* the volatility of their *combined* assets via diversification will destroy shareholder value rather than create value: the lower post-merger volatility of the combined assets (which was the purpose of the merger) means that the post-merger equity value (that is, the call option on the merged assets) will be lower than the sum of the equity values the two separate firms had before they merged their assets.

---

[29] We have: Bond value = $46.85m = $\dfrac{\text{Face value}}{1+\text{yield}} = \dfrac{\$60m}{1+\text{yield}}$ from which we get a yield of 28.07%.

[30] The opposite case is when equity holders do not invest in a positive NPV project if most of the value created goes to the bondholders. This situation is usually referred to as **debt overhang**. Check the numbers as follows: the project's NPV is $1 million and the volatility is now 20 percent. In this case the value of equity goes down from $3.15 million to $1.65 million (down $1.5 million) and the value of debt goes up from $46.85 million to $49.35 million (up $2.5 million).

CORPORATE BONDS AS RISK-FREE BONDS AND SHORT PUTS ON THE FIRM'S ASSETS

A risky corporate bond can be viewed as a risk-free bond combined with short puts on the firm's assets. This equivalence can be derived by applying the put-call parity relationship 16.5 to the case where (1) the underlying asset is the firm's assets with a value V_A; (2) P_A is the value of a put option on the firm's assets; and (3) C_A is the value of a call option on the firm's assets. Suppose that the firm's assets are financed with a single risky bond. In this case, the put-call parity relationship can be written as follows (recall that according to equation 16.9, C_A is equal to V_E, the value of the firm's equity):

$$P_A = C_A + \text{Riskless bond value} - V_A = V_E + \text{Riskless bond value} - V_A$$

The above equation can be rewritten as:

$$V_A - V_E = \text{Riskless bond value} - P_A$$

The left side of the above equation is the value of the firm's risky corporate bond (the difference between the firm's asset value V_A and its equity value V_E). It is equal to the value of the riskless bond combined with a short put on the firm's assets. In other words, *a risky bond is equivalent to a riskless bond combined with a short put*.

The relationship can be used to value risky corporate bonds using the Black-Scholes formula to price the put. It can also be used to find the value of a **Government Financial Guarantee**. For example, in many countries the government guarantees the value of savings accounts (up to a specified amount) against the default of the bank that offered the deposit, making these deposits riskless. What is the value of this financial guarantee? You can see from the above equation that the difference between the value of a riskless deposit and the value of a risky one is equal to the value of a put option. In other words, the value of the guarantee is equal to the value of the implicit put option provided by the government to depositors to protect the value of their deposit.

COLLATERALIZED LOANS

A **collateralized loan** requires that the borrowing firm assigns assets to the lender as collateral for the loan. If the borrowing firm defaults on the loan, the collateral is transferred to the lender. Pause for a moment and try to spot the option in that contract. Have you found it? Here it is: if the collateral value is *higher* than the loan value on the day the loan must be repaid, the borrowing firm will obviously repay the loan and keep the collateral. But if the collateral value is *lower* than the loan value on that day, the borrowing firm will be better off defaulting. In other words, the borrower has a call option on the collateral with an exercise price equal to the loan value: if the collateral value exceeds the loan value, the firm will exercise the option (that is, reimburse the loan and get the collateral back); if the loan value exceeds the collateral, the firm will let the option expire unexercised (that is, not reimburse the loan and surrender the collateral).

RIGHT ISSUES, WARRANTS AND CONTINGENT VALUE RIGHTS

We first described these financial instruments in Chapter 11. Companies issue rights to their *existing* shareholders to raise equity. The rights allow the holder to buy a fixed number of shares in the company at a pre-set price during a specified period of time. When rights are exercised, the company issues shares and receives cash.

Warrants are the same as rights, but they are issued to *any* investors not just the existing shareholders. Companies also issue so-called contingent value rights that give the holder the right to *sell* a fixed number of shares to the issuing company at a fixed price during a specified period of time. As pointed out earlier, all these instruments are financial options. Rights and warrants are call options. Note that when a company grants stock options to its executives and employees, it is actually issuing warrants. Contingent value rights are put options.

Can we apply the Black-Scholes formula to value these options? Yes, but with some adjustments because there is a difference between these instruments and standard options. The exercise of a standard stock option results in an exchange of cash (the exercise price) for shares between the option counterparties *with no impact on the firm*. However, when rights and warrants are exercised, the company issues new shares and receives cash. When contingent value rights are exercised, the company buys shares and pays out cash. These transactions affect the company's number of shares outstanding and its cash holding, and the Black-Scholes formula must be adjusted to account for this. Go to self-test question 16.4 where we show you how to adjust the Black-Scholes formula to value warrants.

CALLABLE AND CONVERTIBLE BONDS

These bonds were first described in Chapter 11. A callable bond gives the right to the issuing firm to buy back the bond at a fixed price during a specified period of time. In other words, a callable bond is a bond that gives the issuing firm the option to repay the bond before it reaches its maturity date. It is equivalent to a portfolio consisting of a straight non-callable bond and an implicit call option sold by the bondholder to the bond issuer. The callable bond can thus be valued as the sum of the value of the non-callable straight bond *less* the value of the implicit call option. A convertible bond is a bond that can be converted into the issuing firm's stock at the option of the bondholder. It is equivalent to a portfolio consisting of a straight bond and an option issued by the firm that gives the bondholder the right to convert the bond into a specified number of common stocks at a fixed price during a specified period of time. The value of the convertible bond is thus equal to the value of a straight, non-convertible bond *plus* the value of the call option to convert the bond into equity.

Can you use the Black-Scholes formula to get an estimate of these embedded options? The answer is yes when the options are equivalent to straight calls, but this may not always be the case. For example, some callable bonds have deferred call provisions whereby the bonds cannot be called before a specified future date. In the case of convertible bonds, the conversion ratio may change over time and the underlying stock may pay several dividends over the life of the convertible. An additional complication occurs when the convertible bond is also callable. You could still use the option pricing model, but the standard Black-Scholes formula must be modified to accommodate these special features.

REAL OPTIONS AND STRATEGIC INVESTMENT DECISIONS

A strategic investment is an investment that provides valuable future opportunities to a firm beyond the investment's *stand-alone* value, that is, its value without taking into account the future opportunities. We first discussed the future opportunities that are embedded in an investment in the last section of Chapter 7. Here we show you how to use the Black-Scholes Model to estimate the value of these opportunities.

EXPANDING ABROAD

Let's examine the case of Bellotico, an Italian fashion house that designs and produces high-quality, expensive clothing sold in exclusive stores in major cities in Italy. Its chief executive, Mario Barone, was considering expanding abroad and had asked the firm's planning staff to analyze a proposal to open one large store in Paris that will sell the entire line of Bellotico's finest clothing. The proposal – referred to as the one-stage expansion – had a negative net present value (NPV) and had to be turned down.

Before giving up on his vision to expand abroad, Barone asked his staff to look at a more flexible strategy based on a two-stage expansion strategy consisting of opening a smaller store first to test the market and then enlarging it in a year *only if the store turns out to be successful*. If the store failed, Bellotico would close it down immediately and retrench into its domestic market. Unfortunately, the two-stage expansion strategy also had a negative NPV.

Because both expansion strategies have a negative NPV, the staff recommended that Bellotico does not open a store in Paris. But Barone felt that opening a store in a major European city such as Paris would still be a good move for Bellotico. He argued that the two-stage expansion strategy merits further examination despite its negative NPV. He pointed out that the NPV calculation of the two-stage proposal had not taken into account the *flexibility* of enlarging the smaller store in one year *only if* the store turns out to be successful. He claimed that this flexibility has a value today that may be large enough to offset the negative NPV of the smaller store and asked his staff to try to value this flexibility.

How could the planning staff incorporate the value of the enlargement opportunity into the NPV of the smaller store? You may have noticed that the opportunity to enlarge the smaller store in one year can be viewed as a one-year call option that gives Bellotico the right to increase the size of that store in a year *if it turns out to be successful*. The option's underlying asset is the value *now* of enlarging the smaller store in one year and the option's exercise price is the cost of enlarging the smaller store in one year.

The major difference between an option embedded in a project and the financial options we discussed earlier is that the underlying asset in the case of a project is a physical asset (a store in our case) that does not have an observable price, whereas financial options are written on tradable financial assets that have observable prices. Options written on tangible (physical) assets are called **real options**.

In the next sections we illustrate how to value a real option embedded in a strategic investment using the Black-Scholes formula and discuss the limitations of using that formula to value real options. We conclude with an overview of other real options embedded in projects besides the option to expand in stages.

THE STANDARD VALUATION OF THE ONE-STAGE AND TWO-STAGE EXPANSIONS

Exhibit 16.9 reports the NPV calculations of the two expansion strategies under consideration by Bellotico. The row entitled 'One-stage expansion strategy' shows that the firm would have to invest €150 million now to generate a future cash-flow stream whose value today is €142 million. The NPV of that strategy is thus a *negative* €8 million (€142 million less €150 million). The following rows show the NPV of

EXHIBIT 16.9	NET PRESENT VALUE OF ALTERNATIVE EXPANSION STRATEGIES.

FIGURES IN MILLIONS

Alternative Entry Strategies		Cost of Investment		Present Value of Future Free Cash-Flow Stream		Net Present Value (NPV)	
		Now	In one year	Now	In one year	Now	In one year
One-Stage Expansion	Open a large store now	€150		€142		−€8	
Two-Stage Expansion	1. Open a small store now	€50		€45		−€5	
	2. Enlarge the store in one year		€110		€100		−€10
	3. Value now of enlargement	€105.8[1]		€89.3[2]		−€16.5[3]	

[1] This is the cost *now* of enlarging the small store in one year. It is obtained by discounting the €110 million to the present at the 1-year risk-free rate of 4 percent, that is $\left[\dfrac{€110m}{1+4\%}\right] = €105.8$ million. The risk-free rate is used because the cost of enlargement is riskless.

[2] This is the value *now* of enlarging the small store in one year. It is obtained by discounting the €100 million to the present at Bellotico's cost of capital of 12 percent, that is $\left[\dfrac{€100m}{1+12\%}\right] = €89.3$ million. Bellotico's cost of capital is used because the value of the enlargement is risky.

[3] This is the NPV *now* of the NPV of the enlargement that will take place in one year.

the two-stage expansion strategy. The NPV of opening a smaller store *now* will cost €50 million and is expected to generate a cash-flow stream with a present value of €45 million. Its NPV is thus a *negative* €5 million. The enlargement of the store *next year* would cost €110 million and the present value of the *extra* cash-flow stream that it would generate starting in one year is €100 million.

To compare the two strategies, we must convert the enlargement's NPV into its value *now*. This is done by discounting the €110 million cost of the enlargement to the present at the 1-year risk-free rate of 4 percent (because the cost of the enlargement is known for certain, it is discounted at the risk-free rate) and discounting the €100 million value of the enlargement at Bellotico's cost of capital of 12 percent (because the value of the enlargement is risky, it is discounted at a rate that reflects that risk). Both the 1-year risk-free rate of 4 percent and Bellotico's cost of capital of 12 percent are given. As shown in the last row of Exhibit 16.9, we have:

$$\text{NPV(enlargement)} = -\left[\frac{€110m}{1+4\%}\right] + \left[\frac{€100m}{1+12\%}\right] = -€105.8m + €89.3m = -€16.5m$$

We can now calculate the NPV of the two-stage expansion strategy as follows:

$$\begin{aligned}\text{NPV(two-stage strategy)} &= \text{NPV(small store)} + \text{NPV(enlargement)} \\ &= -€5m - €16.5m = -€21.5m\end{aligned}$$

The standard NPV valuation of the two-stage expansion strategy is a *negative* €21.5 million. This is why the staff recommended that Bellotico should not open the Paris store. But thinking of the two-stage expansion strategy as a sequence of two *independent*, negative NPV investments misses an important point. As Bellotico's CEO pointed out, the NPV rule applied to the two-stage investment ignores the value of the option to enlarge the store in one year if it is successful or abandon the project if the store fails to create value within one year.

CALCULATING THE VALUE OF THE OPTION TO ENLARGE THE STORE IN ONE YEAR

We can use the Black-Scholes formula 16.6 in Exhibit 16.5 to calculate the value of the call option to enlarge the smaller store in one year. The call's exercise price is the €110 million cost of enlarging the smaller store in one year, which is the price Bellotico will have to pay *in one year* to 'exercise the right to enlarge'. The call's underlying asset is valued *today* at €89.3 million: this is the value *now* of the enlargement, shown in the last row of Exhibit 16.9. The call's time to expiration is one year and the 1-year risk-free rate is 4 percent.

As you remember, we need five inputs to get the value of a call. So far, we know four: the call's exercise price ($X = €110$ million), the current value of the underlying asset ($V_A = \$89.3$ million), the call's time to expiration ($T = 1$), and the 1-year risk-free rate ($R_F = 4\%$). The last input we need is the volatility of the value of stores that sell high-quality, expensive clothing. This input must be estimated. We can use the average volatility of the asset values of a sample of listed companies with high-end clothing stores. Let's say we find this average volatility to be 45 percent ($\sigma_A = 45\%$). Given these five inputs, the call value (C_A) is €10.3 million according to the Black-Scholes formula 16.6 in Exhibit 16.5:

$$C_A[V_A = €89.3m; X = €110m; T = 1; R_F = 4\%; \sigma_A = 45\%] = €10.3 \text{ million}$$

The option to enlarge the smaller store in one year is definitely valuable and thanks to the Black-Scholes formula, we are able to estimate the value today of that future opportunity.

CALCULATING THE PROJECT'S NPV WITH THE OPTION VALUE

We know that the NPV of the smaller store is a negative €5 million (see Exhibit 16.9). We have found that the call option to enlarge the store in one year is worth €10.3 million. What is the present value of the two-stage expansion strategy based on the option pricing model and how does it compare to the negative NPV of €21.5 million the planning staff found earlier? Let's refer to the value of the project *with the option* as the project's **Adjusted Present Value** (APV).[31] We have:

$$\text{APV[project } with \text{ the option]} = \text{NPV[project } without \text{ the option]} + \text{Option value} \quad (16.10)$$

$$\text{APV} = -€5 \text{ million} + €10.3 \text{ million} = +€5.3 \text{ million}$$

As Mario Barone suspected, the option value is large enough to offset the negative NPV of opening a smaller store. As a result, the two-stage expansion strategy has a positive APV of €5.3 million. This means that this strategy is a value-creating proposal that Bellotico should undertake despite the fact that it has a *negative* NPV of €21.5 million when analyzed as the sum of two independent projects (see the previous

---

[31] Note that the term APV is usually used to refer to a project's present value as the sum of its present value if the project is financed without borrowing and the present value of any future tax savings due to borrowing (see equation 14.9 in Chapter 14). We use the term APV here in the same fashion to refer to the project's present value as the sum of its present value without the option and the present value of the option.

section on the standard valuation of a two-stage investment). Note that *a project's APV will always be higher than its standard NPV as long as the embedded option is valuable*. Another way to put it is to say the standard NPV approach *underestimates* the true value of a project that has valuable future opportunities.

DISCUSSION

1. Is it appropriate to apply the Black-Scholes formula to value real options? The major challenge is that real assets do not trade: their value must be estimated by discounting to the present the stream of free cash flows the asset is expected to generate in the future. And because the value of the underlying asset cannot be observed, its volatility must also be estimated. The other three inputs needed for applying the Black-Scholes formula are less challenging to obtain: the exercise price is generally known (the cost of the enlargement in our case) and so are the time to expiration and the risk-free rate, although the former may not be clearly defined given that it is not set contractually (in our case, the life of the enlargement option is one year, but Bellotico could still decide to enlarge the store after more than one year).

2. The estimation of the volatility of the underlying asset is a key input to the option value and the major reason the option is valuable: the riskier the project, the higher its volatility, the higher the option value, and the higher the chances that a negative stand-alone NPV will turn into a positive APV. (If the stand-alone NPV is positive, the investment should be undertaken irrespective of the value of the option.) In our case the stand-alone NPV is a negative €5 million. Thus, the option must have a high enough volatility for the option value to be worth at least €5 million in order to turn the APV positive. You can use the spreadsheet in Exhibit 16.5 to calculate the breakeven volatility: in the Bellotico case the breakeven volatility is 30 percent. A volatility lower than 30 percent will reduce the value of the option below €5 million and turn the APV negative.

3. Having acknowledged these limitations, we must nevertheless say that applying an option model to estimate the value of an investment's future opportunities, even with some margin of error, is better than accepting a negative NPV project without further analysis just because we believe that its future opportunities are large enough to justify the investment. Putting an estimated value of these opportunities beats plain intuition as our case has shown: it would have been difficult for Mario Barone, the Bellotico CEO, to overrule his staff and go ahead with the opening of the Paris store if the option value had not been estimated and shown to be large enough to offset the project's standard NPV.

4. It should be clear that valuing an investment using option models is not a substitute to using discounted cash-flow (DCF) analysis because DCF analysis is needed to estimate the value of the underlying asset and the NPV of the investment without the option.

5. The option model is particularly appropriate when one needs to estimate the value of a start-up firm or a high-risk company (such as a high-technology or a biotechnology firm) because most of the value in these cases is driven by future investment opportunities as opposed to assets already in place.

6. There is a major difference between the standard NPV approach and the option-based analysis of an investment proposal. The option approach puts a value *now* on the flexibility offered by the two-stage investment and postpones to next year the decision to enlarge the store, whereas the standard NPV rule requires that the investment decision be made *immediately*: we accept the project *now* if its NPV

is positive and reject it *now* if it is negative, regardless of what we may be able to learn from the outcome of the first stage.

7. The longer the life of the option to enlarge the Paris store, the higher the option's value (as T lengthens beyond one year, the value of the option to enlarge the store goes up), but this life extension may also give enough time to competitors to open stores in Paris that could erode the value of Bellotico's investment and jeopardize its enlargement plan. The implication of this possibility is that companies should carefully evaluate the *sustainability* of their competitive advantage and hence the value of their project's options. For example, an option to sell a product later that is protected by a license agreement or a patent will be more valuable than an unprotected option that other firms can imitate successfully.

8. There are other options embedded into the Bellotico project that we did not take into account. For example, Bellotico may have a valuable option to abandon the project in one year. It also has an option to expand beyond Paris if that store is successful (this is an option on an option, called a **compound option**). We discuss some of these additional opportunities in the next section.

DIFFERENT TYPES OF REAL OPTIONS EMBEDDED IN PROJECTS

The project we examined in the previous section provided a typical example of an option to expand. There are many other types of options, including the option to contract activities (reducing as opposed to expanding them), the option to abandon an investment, the option to delay the launch of a project, and the option to extend or shorten the life of a project. These options are described in Exhibit 16.10. For a numerical example of an option to abandon an investment, go to self-test question 16.5 where we revisit the Bellotico case and look at what the firm should do if, after one year of operation, the smaller Paris store is not successful. For a numerical example of an option to delay an investment, refer to self-test question 16.6.

KEY POINTS

1. *Price risk*. Commodities and financial assets are subject to price risk because their prices change unexpectedly in response to unpredictable changes in the market environment. But price risk can be mitigated through the use of forward, futures and option contracts.

2. *Forward contracts*. A buyer and a seller of an asset (a commodity or a security) can eliminate the price risk of the asset by entering into a forward contract that requires the delivery of the asset on a specified future date (the settlement date) at a price fixed on the day the contract is written (the forward price). The price of a forward contract depends on the type of asset. To price a forward contract on a *storable* commodity, use equation 16.1. If the commodity is *non-storable*, use equation 16.3. To price forward contract on a financial asset, use equation 16.2.

3. *Counterparty and liquidity risks*. Forward contracts can eliminate the price risk of an asset, but not its counterparty risk (the risk that the seller does not deliver the asset or the buyer does not pay for the asset on the settlement date) or its liquidity risk (the risk of not finding another party to take on the contract if one party wants to get out of the contract before the settlement date). One way to eliminate these two sources of risk is to use futures contracts.

4. *Futures contracts*. A futures contract is a standardized forward contract that is traded on a futures exchange. The exchange eliminates the counterparty risk by

EXHIBIT 16.10   ALTERNATIVE TYPES OF REAL OPTIONS.

Type of Investment Opportunity	Characteristics of the Option Held by the Firm		
	Type of Option	Underlying Asset	Exercise Price
Option to expand[1] Expanding the scale of an investment if its initial phase is successful	American call	The present value of the additional future investment	The cost of the additional investment calculated at the time of the exercise of the option
Option to contract[2] Reducing the scale of an investment if its initial size turns out to be too large	American put	The present value of the lost future cash flows due to the contraction	The saved cost of the future investment calculated at the time of the exercise of the option
Option to abandon[3] Selling or closing down an investment if it is no longer valuable	American put	The present value of the investment	The net price at which the investment can be sold, or its net liquidating value if it is closed down
Option to delay[4] Postponing the launch of a project	European call	The present value of the project	The cost of the investment calculated at the time of the exercise of the option
Option to extend[5] Extending the life of an investment by making a cash expenditure	European call	The present value of the future investment	The cash expenditure that must be made at the time of the exercise of the option to extend the life of the investment

[1] Examples include buying now the right to extract minerals or oil from a piece of land and developing the mine or the oil field only if the product price is high enough to make the investment profitable or buying farmland now and building houses on it only if the surrounding towns expand.

[2] For example, building a larger plant now and scaling it down in the future if the demand for the plant's output turns out to be weaker than expected.

[3] See self-test question 16.5 for a numerical example.

[4] See self-test question 16.6 for a numerical example.

[5] For example, renovating a hotel to extend its useful life.

requiring that traders open margin accounts, carry out their trades through a central clearing house, and have their contracts marked-to-market at the end of every trading day. Liquidity risk is mitigated through standardized contracts that can be traded any time the exchange is open.

5. *Call options.* A call option is a financial instrument that gives the holder the right, but not the obligation, to *buy* an asset at a fixed price (called the *exercise price* or the *strike price*) during a fixed period of time (called the option's maturity or *time to expiration*). The sellers of call options are known as *call writers*.

6. *Put options.* These are options that give the holder the right, but not the obligation, to *sell* an asset at a fixed price during a fixed period of time.

7. *European-style options versus American-style options.* Options that can only be exercised on their expiration date are called European options. Options

that can be exercised any time up to their expiration date are called American options.

8. *The price of European options on non-dividend-paying stocks.* The price of a European call on a non-dividend-paying stock is given by the Black-Scholes formula shown as equation 16.6 in Exhibit 16.5. The price of a put is given by equation 16.7 in Exhibit 16.5. The option prices are determined by five inputs: (1) the price of underlying asset on which the option is written; (2) the exercise price; (3) the time to expiration; (4) the volatility of the price of the underlying asset; and (5) the risk-free rate.

9. *Implied volatility.* The Black-Scholes formula can be used backward to calculate the implied volatility of a stock price if the price of the option is known. Implied volatility can then be used to estimate the Black-Scholes price of another option on the same stock whose price is not known.

10. *The price of European options on dividend-paying stocks.* The Black-Scholes formula gives the price of European options on stocks that do not pay dividends during the life of the option. The formula, however, can be used to price European options on dividend-paying stocks by replacing the stock price in the formula with the stock price less the present value of the dividends that the stock is expected to pay during the life of the option.

11. *The price of American options on non-dividend-paying stocks.* The Black-Scholes formula can be used to price American *calls* on non-dividend-paying stocks because it is not optimal to exercise an American call on non-dividend-paying stock before it expires. It may, however, be optimal under some conditions to exercise an American *put* on a non-dividend-paying stock *before* it expires. For this reason, the price of American puts on non-dividend-paying stocks could be higher than the price of their European counterparts.

12. *The price of American options on dividend-paying stocks.* The Black-Scholes formula can be used to estimate the price of an American call on a dividend-paying stock by applying the formula assuming that the call will be exercised immediately before the ex-dividend date and compare this value to the call value assuming that it will not be exercised, and then choosing the higher of the two values as a lower bound on the value of the American call.

13. *The Binomial Option Pricing Model.* The price of an option can also be determined through the Binomial Option Pricing Model presented in the chapter's appendix. Although the binomial model provides more accurate estimates of option prices when options pay dividends or when the option is an American put, it is more complex to apply than the Black-Scholes formula.

14. *The put-call parity relationship.* This relationship (shown in equation 16.5) links the price of a put to the price of a call written on the same underlying asset with the same exercise price and the same time to expiration. The relationship can be used to get the price of a put if we know the price of the corresponding call, and to create so-called synthetic calls or puts if these options do not exist.

15. *Options are riskier than their underlying asset.* An investment in an option is always riskier than the same investment in the underlying stock. The sensitivity of option prices to changes in the price of the underlying asset is given by the option *delta*, also called the *hedge ratio*, reported in equation 16.8a/b.

16. *Hedging.* Hedging is a risk management technique that is employed to eliminate price risk through the use of futures and option contracts. The idea behind hedging is to combine the risky asset with a number of futures or option contracts whose price will move in the opposite direction to the price movement of

the risky asset. The price movements will thus cancel out and the combination will be riskless. The number of option contracts that will achieve a perfect hedge is the inverse of the option delta or hedge ratio.

17. *Equity as a call option on the firm's assets*. The Black-Scholes formula can be used to estimate the value of a firm's equity and debt if we know the value of the firm's assets because equity can be viewed as a call option on the firm's underlying assets. Viewing equity as a call option explains why a firm that is technically bankrupt has a positive equity value and why its owners are better off if they invest in high-risk projects with a negative NPV. Equity as a call option also explains why a merger whose objective is to reduce the volatility of the merging firms' combined assets will most likely destroy rather than create value.

18. *Option-based investment strategies*. There are a number of investment strategies based on buying and selling options to achieve different investment objectives. *Buying naked calls* (buying calls without holding the underlying stock) is used to *speculate* on an anticipated rise in a stock price. *Buying protective puts* (buying puts and the underlying stock) is applied to *hedge* against a possible drop in stock price. *Portfolio insurance* (buying puts on a stock index to hedge a diversified portfolio of stocks) is employed to *insure* a portfolio against a decline in the stock market. Writing *covered calls* (selling calls and holding the underlying stock) is adopted by institutional investors to *generate income* from the stocks in their portfolios. A *collar* is used to *protect* a covered call position against a drop in stock price. A *straddle* (a call and a put on the same stock) is utilized to *simultaneously speculate* on a stock price rise and *hedge* against a drop in that stock price. A spread (buying calls on the same stock with different exercise prices or life) is used to *arbitrage* a relative mispricing between two options.

19. *Securities with option features*. A number of securities issued by firms have embedded option features. *Rights issues* and *warrants* are the same as call options because they allow the holder to *buy* shares from firms at a fixed price. *Contingent value rights* are the same as put options because they allow the holder to *sell* shares at a fixed price to the firm that issued them. Securities such as *callable bonds* (that allow the firm to buy back its bonds at a fixed price) and *convertible bonds* (that allow the holder to convert a firm's bonds into the firm's equity at a fixed price) can be viewed as straight bonds with embedded options. The value of these embedded options can be estimated with the Black-Scholes formula.

20. *Real options*. Some capital investments provide valuable future opportunities to a firm beyond the investment's *stand-alone* value, that is, its value without taking into account the future opportunities. These opportunities, called real options, include the opportunity to expand a project if its initial phase turns out to be successful, delay a project until more information is revealed or abandon a project if its liquidating value is higher than its expected continuing value. These future opportunities can be viewed as real options embedded into the investment. The value of these options can be estimated using the Black-Scholes formula.

The Binomial Option Pricing Model

Consider the stock and the call shown in Exhibit 16.5. They have the following characteristics: current stock price (S_0) = \$50; exercise price (X) = \$50; time to expiration (T) = 0.25 year; and the risk-free rate (R_F) = 6%. The current call price (C_0) is unknown and must be determined using the so-called **binomial option pricing model**.

Assume a *single* three-month period at the end of which the stock either goes up 2 percent (to S_u = \$51) or goes down 2 percent (to S_d = \$49). (The subscript 'u' indicates 'up' and the subscript 'd' indicates 'down'.) This very simple case is referred to as a *one-step, two-state binomial tree*. If the stock price rises to \$51 in three months, the call is worth $1(C_u = \$51 - \$50)$. If it falls to \$49, the call is worthless $(C_d = 0)$.

CREATING A RISKLESS COVERED CALL POSITION

Using the above data, we want to create a covered call position whereby we sell calls and hold the underlying stock. What is the number of shares (n) that will make the covered call position riskless? The covered call position is riskless if its terminal cash flow in three months is the same no matter what happens to the stock price. The terminal cash flows are:

Cash flow in 3 months if the stock price is up = $CF_u = nS_u - C_u = n51 - 1 = 51n - 1$

Cash flow in 3 months if stock price is down = $CF_d = nS_d - C_d = n49 - 0 = 49n$

The covered call is riskless if $CF_u = CF_d$, that is, if $(51n - 1) = 49n$, from which we get $n = \dfrac{1}{2}$. What this means is that holding half a share per call creates a riskless covered call position or perfect hedge. You can check that the position is perfectly hedged if $n = \dfrac{1}{2}$. If the stock price goes up, the cash flow is equal to $24.50 \left(CF_u = \dfrac{1}{2}\$51 - \$1 \right)$. If it goes down, the cash flow is also equal to \$24.50 $24.50 \left(CF_d = \dfrac{1}{2}\$49 \right)$. The riskless terminal cash flow is thus \$24.50.

FINDING THE CALL PRICE BASED ON THE RISKLESS COVERED CALL POSITION

How can you infer today's call price (C_0) from the above numbers? The current value of the riskless covered call position, based on the $50 stock price and a number of shares equal to one half, is:

Current value of riskless covered call position $= nS_0 - C_0 = \dfrac{1}{2} \times \$50 - C_0 = \$25 - C_0$

If the three-month covered call position is riskless with a terminal cash flow of $24.50, then the present value of $24.50 at the riskless rate of 6 percent must be equal to the current value of the riskless covered call position:

$$\$25 - C_0 = \frac{\$24.50}{(1 + 6\%)^{0.25}} = \frac{\$24.50}{1.0147} = \$24.14$$

from which we get the current call price of $0.86. This figure is a first, very rough approximation of the call price. To get better estimates, we must increase the number of steps over the three-month life of the option, which will reduce the length of time of each step. As we keep increasing the number of steps, the length of each step becomes smaller and smaller and the binomial option pricing model converges toward the Black-Scholes formula if we assume that the risk-free rate and the volatility of the stock returns are constant over the life of the option (the binomial model does not assume constant volatility and risk-free rate).

The question you may ask at this point is why bother with the binomial option pricing model if at the limit it is the same as the Black-Scholes formula? The answer is that the binomial model is more flexible and can be used to value American options and, more generally, any option where the decision can be made before maturity such as, for example, the decision by bondholders to convert a convertible bond and the decision by a company to call a callable bond. Unfortunately, the binomial model requires complex algorithms to value the option whereas the Black-Scholes Model provides a simple closed-form formula that gives the option value very rapidly with a spreadsheet (as shown in Exhibit 16.5) or a calculator. For a full exposition of the binomial model, see chapter 13 in Hull (2017).

FURTHER READING

1. Black, Fisher and Myron Scholes. "The Pricing of Options and Corporate Liabilities." *Journal of Political Economy* 81 (May/June 1973).
2. Black, Fisher. "Fact and Fantasy in the Use of Options." *Financial Analysts Journal* 31 (July/August 1975).
3. Hull, John. *Options, Futures, and Other Derivatives*, 10th ed. Pearson, 2017.

SELF-TEST QUESTIONS

16.1 **Hedging interest-rate risk with futures contracts.**
Go back to the Eastern Electric Company (EEC) case presented in the chapter in the section "Hedging Interest-Rate Risk with Bond Futures." EEC is planning to issue $100 million worth of bonds in one month with a 7 percent coupon rate and an eight-year maturity. EEC wants to lock in its borrowing rate at 7 percent, which is the current borrowing rate for firms with the same credit risk as EEC. To achieve this

objective, EEC can hedge the bond issue against a possible rise in interest rates with Treasury bond (T-bond) futures that mature in one month. The value of one T-bond futures contract is $100,000 and the deliverable T-bond has a 10-year maturity, a 5-percent coupon rate and is currently priced to yield 4 percent. Answer the following questions:

a. Should EEC buy or sell T-bond futures contracts to hedge its $100 million bond issue? Explain your answer.
b. How many T-bond futures contracts should EEC buy or sell?
c. What is the current price of the T-bond futures contract?
d. One month has passed and the rate at which EEC will issue bonds is now 7.5 percent. How much can EEC borrow now if it wants to issue bonds with a 7 percent coupon rate?
e. One month has passed and the T-bond futures contract is now yielding 4.30 percent. What is the price of the futures contract and how much has EEC lost or gained in its futures position?
f. Was EEC perfectly hedged? If not, why not?
g. How many contracts should EEC have bought to achieve a perfect hedge?

16.2   **Response of option prices to changes in the value of inputs in the Black-Scholes formula.**
Return to the options reported in Exhibit 16.5 where the stock price and the exercise price are $50, the maturity is three months, the risk-free rate is 6 percent and the stock volatility is 25 percent.

a. The underlying stock does not pay dividends during the life of the option. As shown in Exhibit 16.5, the call is worth $2.86 and the put $2.12. What are the call and put prices when one of the input values goes up by 20 percent while the others are fixed? What are the percentage changes in price compared to the original price?
b. Answer question (a) if the option is expected to pay a dividend of $2 at the end of two months.
c. Compare your answers to question (b) to your answers to question (a).
d. What is the price of the original call if maturity is five months instead of three months? Compare it to the price of the 3-month call. Assume now that the stock is expected to pay a $2 dividend in four months. What is the price of the 5-month call in this case? Compare it to the price of the 3-month call. What can you conclude?

16.3   **Valuing call and put options on a stock.**
The stock price of Universal Software Corporation (USC) is $80 and its volatility is 25 percent. The risk-free rate is 5 percent.

a. USC will not pay any dividends over the next six months. A 6-month European call on the USC stock with an exercise price of $60 is quoted on the option market at $22.85. Is the observed call price consistent with the Black-Scholes formula?
b. There are no put options on the USC stock. How can you create a synthetic put on the USC stock with the same life and exercise price as the call?
c. Assume now that USC will pay a quarterly dividend of 75 cents per share. The next dividend will be paid in two months. What is the price of the 6-month European call on the USC stock? Would the price be the same if the call was American instead of European?

d. A 6-month call on the USC stock with a $70 exercise price is quoted on the option market at $13.19. What is the call's implied volatility? Compare it to the volatility of the 6-month call with a $60 exercise price: what can you conclude?

16.4 **Valuing employee stock options and warrants.**
The Baldwin Instruments Corporation (BIC) is considering issuing 10 million of employee stock options (same as warrants) that will each give the holder the right to buy one BIC share at an exercise price of $30 in five years (employee stock options and warrants usually have a much longer time to expiration than rights issues and straight call options). BIC pays no dividends and its shares, currently trading at $20, have an annual volatility of 30 percent. BIC has 100 million shares outstanding and the 5-year risk-free rate is 4 percent.

a. What is the value of a call option to buy one BIC share?
b. What is the value of the employee stock option (ESO) or warrant? Note: because ESOs and warrants increase the number of shares outstanding when exercised, their value is calculated as follows:

$$\text{Warrant value} = \frac{N_S}{N_S + N_w} \times \text{Call value}$$

where N_S is the number of shares outstanding and N_w is the number of ESOs or warrants that will be issued.

c. What is the total cost to BIC of issuing the ESOs or warrants?
d. What should happen to the price of BIC shares when the firm announces that it will issue ESOs or warrants, assuming the market is efficient?

16.5 **Valuing an option to abandon an investment.**
Return to the Bellotico case presented in the chapter. A year has passed and the Paris store has not performed well. The estimated value of the store's future stream of free cash flows is now down to €35 million. An investment company has offered Bellotico €40 million to buy the store anytime during the next 12 months. Bellotico must now decide if it should sell the store now or give it another year to prove itself.

a. What is the immediate gain from selling the store?
b. Describe the option to abandon the investment now (Is it a call or a put? Is it a long or a short position?) and provide the option's characteristics (What are its exercise price and the value of the underlying asset?).
c. What is the value of the option in question (b)?
d. Should Bellotico sell the store now (that is, abandon the investment now) or operate the store for another year?

16.6 **Valuing an option to delay an investment.**
You have a license that gives you the right to open a fast food restaurant now or in one year at the same cost of $1.7 million. The restaurant is expected to generate a year-end free cash flow of $140,000 that will grow at an annual rate of 3 percent in perpetuity. Your required rate of return for this type of investment is 10 percent. The 1-year risk-free rate is 5 percent.

a. Would you open the restaurant now or in one year if the estimated volatility of the restaurant's value is 40 percent?
b. What is the maximum price of the license if you could sell it today?

c. Will you change your decision to open now or in one year if the volatility of the restaurant's value was 25 percent instead of 40 percent? Explain.

d. Will you open the restaurant now or in one year if waiting will cause the restaurant's free cash flow to drop by 10 percent because of competition from another fast food restaurant that is expected to open in the next few months? Explain.

REVIEW QUESTIONS

1. **Pricing forward contracts.**
   ZHU share price is $50. The risk-free rate is 2 percent. Suppose you want to enter a forward contract for delivery of ZHU shares in one year. Assuming that ZHU won't pay any dividend in the coming year:

   a. What are the forward price of the ZHU shares and the value of the forward contract when contracted?

   b. Answer the same question six months later if the ZHU share price is $60 and the risk-free rate is still equal to 2 percent.

   c. Assume now that ZHU's dividend yield is 2 percent. Repeat the same question as in part (a).

2. **Forward contracts: alternative pricing formulas.**
   Show that the forward price given by equation 16.3 is consistent with the forward price given by the spot-forward parity equation 16.2.

3. **Hedging with Eurodollar futures.**
   Jack Blair, the treasurer of the Simpson Corporation (SC) will need to borrow $1 million for three months starting December 20. He would like to hedge the borrowing rate with interest futures contracts. Searching for the right contract, he found that the Chicago Mercantile Exchange offers a 3-month Eurodollar futures contract with a settlement date on December 20, the same day he will have to borrow the $1 million. The contract currently trades at 97.00, which represents an interest rate of 3 percent per year. This rate is the London Interbank Offering Rate or LIBOR (see Chapter 11).

   a. Assuming that SC can borrow at the LIBOR rate, what hedging strategy would you recommend to Jack?

   b. Suppose that the LIBOR rate in three months is (1) 2.5 percent, (2) 3 percent, and (3) 3.5 percent. Under each of these scenarios, calculate the actual borrowing cost and borrowing rate for SC.

4. **Hedging with stock index futures.**
   You own a $1.5 million diversified portfolio of stocks that you will have to sell in three months' time to finance the purchase of a house. Fearing that the stock market might go down significantly over the next three months, you would like to hedge your portfolio against changes in stock prices using futures contracts. Assume first that your portfolio has the same volatility as the S&P index. In this case, you will hedge using S&P index futures contracts. These contracts are traded in the Chicago Mercantile Exchange (CME) and are valued at $250 times the index. Currently the 3-month index value is 3,000.

   a. Are you going short or long on the contract? How many contracts are you going to sell or buy?

Assume now that your portfolio is more volatile than the S&P index. Its beta, measured against the S&P 500 index, is 1.5, which means that when the index moves by 10 percent, the portfolio return moves by 15 percent on average (see Chapter 3).

b. How many contracts are you going to sell or buy?

c. The value of the S&P 500 is now 2,975 and the S&P 500 futures price is 3,000. What is the profit (loss) on the three-month contract?

d. Using the Capital Asset Pricing Model or CAPM (see Chapter 12), what is the expected three-month return on your portfolio when the S&P 500 is (1) 2,900, (2) 3,000, and (3) 3,100 in three months? The risk-free rate is 1 percent for three months.

e. Suppose that in three months the S&P 500 is (1) 2,900, (2) 3,000, and (3) 3,100. Under each of these scenarios calculate the expected net value of the hedged portfolio. The current index futures price is 3,000.

5. **Option premium for copper.**
   Return to the WTM case in the chapter where it is said that WTM could hedge its exposure to the price risk of copper by purchasing a call option for $336 that would give it the right to buy one ton of copper in three months for $6,000. The spot price of a ton of copper is $6,000 and the risk-free rate is 5 percent.

   a. What is the annual volatility of the price of copper?

   b. What would be the call premium to buy a ton of copper in three months at $5,900? Explain the difference with the call premium to buy a ton of copper in three months at $6,000.

   c. What should the supplier of copper do if it wants to hedge its price risk to deliver a ton of copper in three months at $6,000?

6. **Put-call parity relationship.**
   A 3-month European call option on VHQ shares trades at $5. Its exercise price is $50 and the stock price is currently $50.50.

   a. Using the put-call parity relationship, calculate the price of a put on VHQ shares with the same maturity and exercise price as the call. The risk-free interest rate is 4 percent.

   b. The put currently trades at $4.30. Is it mispriced? Is there any arbitrage opportunity to take advantage of the mispriced put? Describe your arbitrage strategy.

7. **Valuing employee stock options.**
   The board of the PQS Corporation has decided to give its employees 5 million of 4-year at-the-money call options on PQS stock. If the options are exercised, the company will issue new shares. There are 20 million PQS shares outstanding. PQS stock price is currently $75 and its volatility is 30 percent. The risk-free interest rate is 4 percent and the company does not pay dividends.

   a. What is the cost of the offer to PQS?

   b. By how much will the share price of PQS drop when the options are exercised and the PQS stock is diluted?

8. **Mergers and the value of the firm's equity and debt.**
   The American Food Corporation (AFC) and the Canadian Mining Corporation (CMC) are considering a merger whose objective is to reduce the volatility of their

combined assets. AFC assets are worth $100 million and have a 30 percent volatility; they are funded with a 10-year zero-coupon bond with a $70 million face value. CMC assets are worth $100 million and have a 40 percent volatility; they are funded with a 10-year zero-coupon bond with a $60 million face value. Because the two firms' activities are in unrelated sectors, the correlation coefficient between their asset returns is zero. The 10-year risk-free rate is 6 percent.

a. What are the equity and debt values of AFC and CMC before they merge?
b. What is the yield-to-maturity of AFC and CMC zero-coupon bonds?
c. What is the volatility of the combined assets? Recall that the variance of a portfolio combining two *uncorrelated* assets (asset A with a variance Var_A and asset B with a variance Var_B) with proportions w_A and w_B is (see equation 3.3a in Chapter 3):

$$Var_{AB} = w_A^2 Var_A + w_B^2 Var_B$$

d. What are the equity and debt values of AFC and CMC combined assets after the merger? Has the merger benefitted shareholders? Has it benefitted bondholders?

9. **Options and the valuation of a start-up firm.**
The Pacific Food Company (PFC) has created a new concept restaurant that serves low-calorie healthy pizza at competitive prices. The restaurant costs $1.2 million to launch and is expected to generate a free-cash-flow stream with a present value of $1 million and a volatility of 30 percent. Identical restaurants can be opened in one year at the same cost and with the same present value. The risk-free rate is 5 percent.

a. Should PFC open a restaurant now? Explain your answer.
b. A private equity firm has offered $2.3 million to buy the concept and the exclusive right to open health pizza restaurants across the country. How many restaurants should the private equity firm open in one year to justify the $2.3 million offer?

10. **Options and joint ventures.**
Autos for the Future (AFF) is considering a joint venture with Autos for Everyone (AFE) to build a new automobile. Each company will invest €250 million in the joint venture. The present value of the expected cash flows to AFE is €245 million. In order to induce AFE to join in the investment, AFF offers a sweetener, offering to buy AFE's stake over the next year for €230 million. Assume the project value has a standard deviation of 25 percent and the risk-free rate is 4 percent.

a. What is the value of the abandonment option for AFE?
b. Should AFE enter the joint venture?

MAKING INTERNATIONAL BUSINESS DECISIONS

CHAPTER **17**

Firms do not operate exclusively in a domestic environment. Many companies have significant foreign operations that provide managers with new opportunities and constraints that do not exist in a purely domestic environment. New factors, such as fluctuations in exchange rates, differences in interest rates, accounting rules, tax systems, and the risk of doing business abroad, have to be taken into account. Of course, the fundamental principle of corporate finance still holds: a firm's resources must be managed with the ultimate goal of increasing the firm's market value. Foreign investment projects, like domestic ones, should be undertaken only if they provide a return in excess of that required by investors. The decision criteria in previous chapters, such as the net present value (NPV) rule, are still valid, but they are usually more complicated to apply because more than one currency is involved and because specific risks are attached to cross-border investments.

This chapter analyzes the effects of (1) currency risk (the risk resulting from exchange-rate fluctuations) and (2) country risk (the risk resulting from having operations in a country with an unstable political system or regulatory environment) on management decisions in an international environment.

A firm faces two types of risk when exchange rates fluctuate. One is accounting (or translation) exposure, which is the effect of changes in exchange rates on the firm's balance sheet and income statement. The other is economic exposure, which is the effect of exchange-rate fluctuations on the firm's future cash flows. We explain in Chapter 16 how managers can use financial instruments such as forward, futures, and option contracts to reduce their firm's exposure to interest rate and commodities price risk. In this chapter we show how these instruments and currency swap contracts can be used to hedge exchange rate risk.

This chapter examines also the relationships between exchange rates, inflation rates, and interest rates that should prevail between two countries that have different currencies. Understanding these basic relationships allows you to make better international business decisions. We then show how to apply the NPV rule to two cross-border investments, one in a low-risk country and the other in a high-risk country. Finally, we propose a number of techniques and mechanisms to actively manage country risk. After reading this chapter, you should understand the following:

- The difference between accounting exposure and economic exposure to exchange-rate fluctuations
- The relationship between the inflation rates prevailing in two countries with different currencies and how it affects changes in exchange rates
- Why interest rates (the cost of debt) usually are not the same in countries with different currencies
- The relationship between the interest rates prevailing in two countries with different currencies and how it affects changes in exchange rates
- The relationship between forward rates and future spot rates
- How to use currency forward, futures, option, and swap contracts to hedge exchange rate risk
- How to apply the NPV rule to investment projects with cash flows denominated in foreign currencies and to projects in a politically or regulatory unstable environment
- How to actively manage country risk

THE FIRM'S RISK EXPOSURE FROM FOREIGN OPERATIONS

When a firm operates in a foreign environment, it is subject to a number of risks. **Foreign-exchange risk** is associated with the volatility of foreign-exchange rates. If the firm has assets and liabilities, revenues and expenses, and cash flows denominated in a foreign currency, changes in exchange rates will affect their values denominated in the domestic currency. **Accounting** (or **translation**) **exposure** is the effect of changes in exchange rates on the firm's balance sheet and income statement; **economic exposure** is the effect on the value of the firm's future cash flows. There is also the risk of operating in an environment that may not be as economically and politically stable as the domestic one. This risk, called **country risk**, takes many forms. It extends from the relatively milder risk originating from the imposition of exchange controls to the risk of expropriation of the firm's foreign assets without compensation.

ACCOUNTING, OR TRANSLATION, EXPOSURE

Accounting exposure arises from the need to translate the financial statements of the foreign business unit into the parent company's currency to prepare consolidated financial statements. A variety of approaches can be taken to translate balance sheet and income statement accounts. Most of these approaches are variations of the **monetary/nonmonetary method** and the **all current method**, which are presented in Appendix 17.1. The objective of these methods is to show how changes in exchange rates affect *reported* earnings and *book* equity values. How important are the translated accounting data to the firm's owners? The data provide some useful starting points for a financial analysis of the foreign operations, but they are of limited use for the firm's shareholders because they are not *market* values. Economic exposure is much more relevant to the firm's owners.

ECONOMIC EXPOSURE

Economic exposure focuses on the effect of unexpected changes in exchange rates on the value of the firm's future cash flows. Economic exposure is classified as

(1) **contractual** (or **transaction**) **exposure** or (2) **operating exposure**. Contractual exposure refers to the effect of exchange-rate volatility on the expected (future) cash flows from *past* transactions denominated in foreign currencies that are still outstanding. Operating exposure is also concerned with expected (future) cash flows, but from *future*, not past, transactions. In other words, although both types of exposure examine the effect of exchange-rate volatility on future cash flows, contractual exposure focuses on cash flows whose values in foreign currency are *certain*, while operating exposure is concerned with cash flows whose values are *uncertain* even when denominated in a foreign currency. The example in the following sections illustrates the distinction.

CONTRACTUAL, OR TRANSACTION, EXPOSURE

Suppose a US wine distributor has just signed a contract with a French wine-producing company for the delivery of 400 cases of champagne. The contract calls for the payment of 100,000 euros (written as EUR or €) when delivery takes place in three months. As soon as the contract is signed, the distributor is exposed to exchange-rate risk because the dollar cost of the champagne will not be known until the distributors buy €100,000 to pay the French company.[1] That purchase will be paid in dollars at the exchange rate that will prevail in three months. We say that the distributor's contractual exposure is €100,000.

In general, contractual exposure arises from the purchase or the sale of goods and services whose prices are denominated in a foreign currency. It can also arise from financial activities, such as borrowing and lending in a nondomestic currency. For most companies involved in cross-border transactions, the number of outstanding foreign contracts can be very large, typically with different maturity dates and different currency denominations. For these firms, the contractual exposure to a particular currency at a particular date is simply the *net* sum of the contractual (future) cash inflows and cash outflows in that currency measured at that date.

A firm with large and uncovered transaction exposure may find itself in a difficult financial situation resulting from adverse exchange-rate movements. The situation is similar to a firm borrowing too much debt and experiencing difficulty meeting its repayment schedule. Chapter 13 describes this situation as "financial distress" and shows that it adversely affects the value of the firm. For example, with too much exposure to exchange-rate risk, the firm may have to pass up valuable investment projects, customers may worry about the firm's ability to deliver goods and services and so switch to competitors, and suppliers may be reluctant to provide trade credit. All these indirect costs will have a negative effect on the firm's value. Fortunately, this type of exposure can be controlled using financial instruments such as currency forward, futures, and option contracts, as shown later in the chapter.

OPERATING EXPOSURE

Each time the US distributor places an order for champagne with a French company, he enters a contract to deliver euros to the French champagne exporter and is immediately exposed to foreign-exchange risk. If the distributor's business is to sell French champagne, his exposure to foreign-exchange risk is not limited to the *outstanding* contracts with his French suppliers. Future purchases of champagne (not yet made) will generate continuous exposure to the volatility of the exchange rate between the US dollar and the euro. This exposure to future exchange-rate changes is an example of an operating exposure.

It should also be pointed out that importers (or exporters) of goods and services are not the only firms subject to operating exposure. A firm that has only

---

[1] Exchange-rate risk is similar to commodity-price risk analyzed in Chapter 16.

domestic operations also can be exposed to changes in exchange rates. Consider a US distributor of US-made sparkling wine. If the value of the euro decreases relative to the US dollar (you get more euros for a dollar), the US distributor of the French-produced champagne can keep the same margin by selling his champagne at a lower price and, in the process, take a market share from the distributor of US-made sparkling wine. A similar situation occurs when domestic firms that buy, produce, and sell domestic goods are faced with competition from abroad.

Clearly, operating exposure is more difficult to manage than contractual exposure. It requires a good understanding of the economic and competitive environment in which the firm operates. Although it is nearly impossible to quantify, it needs to be controlled. The firm must anticipate future developments in the foreign-exchange market and take measures to reduce the probability of experiencing financial distress from excessive exposure to exchange-rate movements. This can be achieved by diversifying operations and financing sources. On the operations side, the firm can diversify its sources of raw materials, the locations of its production facilities, and the regions around the world where it sells. On the financing side, diversification can be achieved by raising funds in more than one currency. The firm can also use currency forward, futures, or option contracts to manage operating exposure. But the difficulty of forecasting future cash flows, far beyond those arising from outstanding contracts, makes the estimation of operating exposure less precise than the estimation of contractual exposure. As a result, using financial instruments is less efficient in controlling operating exposure than in controlling transaction exposure.

COUNTRY RISK

A firm is exposed to country risk when unforeseen economic, political, and social events in a country affect the value of the firm's investments in that country. Changes in the host country's political environment may bring about changes in government regulations or add new regulations to existing ones, resulting in restrictions or penalties for foreign operations in the country. Examples of regulations that can adversely affect a foreign subsidiary include (1) imposing ceilings or discriminatory taxation on dividends or royalties paid to the parent company; (2) imposing unfavorable exchange rates for foreign currency transactions; (3) requiring that goods produced contain a certain percentage of local content; (4) requiring that nationals hold top management positions; (5) requiring that a portion of the profits be reinvested locally; (6) allowing only joint ventures with less than 50 percent ownership by the foreign parent; (7) imposing price controls; and (8) expropriating the subsidiary without adequate compensation.

Currency forward, futures, or option contracts can considerably reduce a firm's exposure to contractual risk. They are, however, of no use to protect against country risk. How, then, could firms that invest in a politically unstable foreign country reduce their exposure to country risk? We show later in this chapter how that type of risk exposure can be reduced by following some simple rules.

MANAGING CURRENCY RISK

It is through the foreign-exchange market that a firm can carry the transactions needed to hedge its foreign-exchange exposure. The next sections describe that market and examine how firms can hedge their foreign-exchange exposure using currency forward rates, futures, options, and swap contracts.[2]

---

[2] In Chapter 16 we examine how forward, futures, and options contracts are used to hedge unexpected changes in the price of commodities and other financial assets such as stocks and bonds.

THE FOREIGN-EXCHANGE MARKET

The **foreign-exchange market** is the world's largest financial market. In a survey conducted in 2016, the Bank for International Settlement (BIS) estimated that the average daily *transactions* in that market reached $5,067 billion in April 2016. This market exists to handle the buying and selling of currencies. Any firm or individual can buy or sell a currency in this market at an **exchange rate** (or **currency rate**) that is determined by the constant interactions of those who are buying and selling currencies. The quoted exchange rate is the price that has to be paid in one country's currency to buy one unit of another country's currency. For example, if the exchange rate between the US dollar (USD) and the euro (EUR) is quoted as €0.8000 per $1 (EUR/USD 0.8000), then $1 must be paid to buy €0.8000.[3]

Unlike most stock markets, the foreign-exchange market has no central location. It is a network of banks, dealers, brokers, and multinational corporations communicating with each other via computer terminals, telephone lines, and fax machines. Major participants are large commercial banks operating through the **interbank market**. Working in rooms specially designed for currency trading, traders are surrounded by telephones and display monitors connected to trading rooms around the world. If a trader in Chicago wants to exchange US dollars for euros, up-to-date communication equipment helps her find, nearly instantly, a trader from another bank in the interbank market who is willing to trade euros for US dollars. Over the phone or directly through the computer monitors, the two traders agree on price and quantity. Each trader then enters the transaction in his or her own bank recording system. The entire procedure lasts no more than a few seconds. Later, the two banks send each other written confirmations of the trade, which may take up to two business days to settle.

A typical interbank foreign-exchange quotation mentions two rates. The **bid price** is the price at which a trader in the market is willing to buy. The **ask**, or **offer**, **price** is the price at which a trader is willing to sell. The prices are given in units of one currency per unit of the other currency with the currencies usually identified by three letters. For example, suppose the exchange rate between the euro and the US dollar is quoted at EUR/USD 0.7998–0.8002. This means that some banks are willing to buy US dollars at €0.7998 per $1 (the bid price) and sell them at €0.8002 per $1 (the ask price).

The difference between the bid price and the ask price is the bank's compensation for making the transaction, which is the reason why they do not charge commission fees. For widely traded currencies, the size of the **bid-ask spread** is usually a few **basis points** (a basis point is one-hundredth of 1 percent). Its size varies from one currency to another. For a given currency, the spread depends on the level of competition among traders in that currency, the currency's volatility, and the average volume of daily trade.

It is a common practice among traders to quote all currencies in reference to the US dollar. The exchange rate between two currencies when neither is a dollar is calculated from their respective US-dollar values. For example, if the euro is quoted at EUR/USD 0.8013 and the Japanese yen at JPY/USD 100.06,[4] then the JPY/EUR exchange rate is the JPY/USD rate divided by the EUR/USD rate:

$$\frac{\text{JPY/USD } 100.06}{\text{EUR/USD } 0.813} = \text{JPY/EUR } 124.87.$$

---

[3] The exchange rate can also be expressed as USD/EUR 1.2500 (the price of €1 in US dollars) instead of EUR/USD 0.8000 (the price of $1 in euros, which is the inverse of the price of €1 in US dollars). However, the convention is to express the exchange rate in units of foreign currency per one US dollar.

[4] These rates are bid-ask midpoints. For example, EUR/USD 0.8013 is at the midpoint between the bid price of EUR/USD 0.8011 and the ask price of EUR/USD 0.8015.

EXHIBIT 17.1	CURRENCY CROSS RATES IN APRIL 2018.

Key Currency Cross Rates: Snapshot of Foreign Exchange Cross Rates at 4 p.m. Eastern Time, April 6, 2018.					
	US Dollar (USD)	Euro (EUR)	British Pound (GBP)	Swiss Franc (CHF)	Mexican Peso (MXP)	Japanese Yen (JPY)
Japan	106.9190	131.3233	150.6382	111.5017	5.8445	–
Mexico	18.2939	22,4695	25.7743	19.0780	–	0.1711
Switzerland	0.9589	1.1778	1.3510	–	0.0524	0.0090
United Kingdom	0.7098	0.8718	–	0.7402	0.0388	0.0066
Eurozone	0.8142	–	1.1471	0.8491	0.0445	0.0076
United States	–	1.2283	1.4089	1.0429	0.0547	0.0094

Source: *The Wall Street Journal*, Market data, The Key Currency Cross Rates, April 6, 2018.

Rates between currencies computed as above are called **cross rates**. Quotations of cross rates are provided daily by financial publications and are available in real time on the Web. Exhibit 17.1 reports cross rates for six currencies.

SPOT TRANSACTIONS VERSUS FORWARD CONTRACTS

A currency **spot transaction** is a trade between two parties in which both agree to a currency exchange at a rate fixed *now* with the delivery of the currencies taking place at a **settlement date**, usually two business days later. This rate is called **spot rate**. Individuals can trade currencies for immediate delivery at the nearest bank. However, the spread is usually quite large.

A forward contract is an agreement between two parties, generally a bank and a customer, for the delivery of currencies on a specified date in the *future* but at an exchange rate fixed *today*. The contract specifies the currencies to be exchanged, the *fixed date* in the future when the delivery will actually take place, the *amount of currency* to be exchanged, and the *fixed rate* of exchange. For major currencies, contracts traded in the interbank forward market usually have a maturity of 1, 3, 6, and 12 months. However, the delivery date can be tailor-made to accommodate a customer's particular need, usually at a less favorable rate.

Spot rates and **forward rates** are provided daily by major international newspapers and in real time with currency converters on the websites.

HEDGING CONTRACTUAL EXPOSURE TO CURRENCY RISK

Consider the case of the US wine distributor who has just signed a contract with a French company for the delivery of 400 cases of champagne worth €100,000 to be paid when delivery takes place in three months. The distributor can hedge this exchange-rate risk in many ways, that is, protect himself against currency fluctuations. He can choose among several hedging techniques commonly used to reduce or eliminate the exchange-rate risk associated with the purchase of raw materials, the sale of goods, the purchase of assets, or the issuance of debt when they are denominated in a foreign currency. These techniques use instruments available in the financial markets, such as forward, futures, and option contracts as shown below.[5]

HEDGING WITH FORWARD CONTRACTS

The **currency forward hedge**, which is the currency hedging technique most widely used by corporations, can completely eliminate the exchange-rate risk associated with foreign transactions. The distributor can arrange a forward hedge simply by entering into a forward contract with a bank to buy from that bank €100,000 with US dollars in three months. In other words, the distributor can fix *today* the rate at which he will buy €100,000 from the bank in three months. The bank will most likely require the importer to establish a **foreign-exchange line of credit** to guarantee his ability to deliver US dollars in three months.

What is the *net* result of the two transactions: (1) the purchase of champagne and (2) the purchase of euros forward? If today's 3-month *forward rate* is EUR/USD 0.80, the distributor will have to pay the bank $125,000 (€100,000 divided by EUR/USD 0.80) in three months to get the €100,000. Regardless of how the USD/EUR exchange rate changes between the purchase date and the delivery date, the dollar value of the purchase will not change. It will remain equal to $125,000. The exchange-rate risk has been eliminated. By entering into a forward contract, the distributor has "locked in" an exchange rate of EUR/USD 0.80. Note that this rate is the forward rate quoted today and *not* the spot rate, which may be higher or lower than the forward rate.

What will happen if the cases of champagne are not delivered on the agreed-upon date and, consequently, the €100,000 payment to the French exporter is delayed? The distributor will still have to buy the €100,000 from his bank for $125,000 at the date fixed by the forward contract. He would then have the choice of keeping the €100,000 until the champagne is delivered or exchanging them for US dollars at the prevailing spot rate. If the distributor exchanges the euros into US dollars at the settlement of the forward contract, he will again need €100,000 to pay the French exporter when the champagne is finally delivered. In other words, he will again be exposed to exchange-rate risk. However, he can hedge this risk as before by entering into a new €100,000 forward contract with the bank. This strategy is known as **rolling over the forward contract**. An alternative to a rollover would be for the distributor to enter a **forward window contract** at the beginning. This contract is the same as a standard forward contract except that the transaction does not have to be settled on a fixed date. It can be settled on any day during an agreed-upon period of time known as the *window*. The importer would have to pay an additional fee for this flexibility, but it may be cheaper than rolling over the original contract.

What if the distributor wants to get out of the forward contract before its expiration date? In this situation, he would have to *sell* €100,000 forward by entering a forward contract that has the same expiration date as the first contract. The cash settlement for both contracts will take place at their common expiration date. The distributor would gain or lose, depending on whether the forward rate on the second contract is lower or higher than the rate on the first contract (EUR/USD 0.80). For example, suppose the forward rate on the second contract is EUR/USD 0.78. In this case, he will receive $128,205 from this contract (€100,000 divided by EUR/USD 0.78) and pay $125,000 on the first contract. His gain will be $3,205 ($128,205 less $125,000).

---

[5] The techniques of hedging currency risk using these derivative contracts are similar to the techniques used to hedge commodity and other financial assets prices as described in Chapter 16.

If the forward rate of the second contract is EUR/USD 0.82, he will lose $3,049, the difference between the $121,951 from the sale of euros (€100,000 divided by EUR/USD 0.82) and the $125,000 on the first contract.

HEDGING WITH FUTURES CONTRACTS

As an alternative to forward contracts, the US distributor of French champagne can use currency futures contracts. **Currency futures contracts**, or simply **currency futures**, are similar to forward contracts, except that they have a standard contract size and a standard delivery date. Currency futures are traded every day on organized **futures markets**, such as the Chicago Mercantile Exchange (CME) and NYSE Euronext. Currency futures markets operate in the same fashion as the futures exchanges we described in Chapter 16.

Like forward rates, futures prices are reported in the financial press and in real time on the Web.

The Currency Futures Hedge.   If our champagne distributor wants to use currency futures contracts to hedge his exposure to euros, he will have to buy 3-month futures contracts worth €100,000. Because currency futures contracts and forward contracts are similar instruments, the **futures hedge** should have the same overall effect as the forward hedge. However, as explained in Chapter 16 in the case of commodities and financial assets other than foreign exchange, there will be some differences.

First, the other party in the futures contract is not a bank but is instead the clearing corporation. The distributor, through his broker, will have to *buy* euros futures and then *sell* them later. If, in the meantime, the euro appreciates (depreciates) relative to the US dollar, the distributor will make a profit (loss) from his futures trade. But, if the euro appreciates (depreciates) relative to the dollar, he will also have to disburse more (fewer) dollars to buy, in the spot market, the €100,000 needed to pay his supplier. The profit (loss) made in the futures market will compensate for the increase (decrease) in the amount of dollars needed to buy the €100,000 in the spot market.

Second, because the size and the maturity of the futures contracts are standardized, it is not always possible to *perfectly* hedge transaction exposure using a futures contract. For example, if the distributor decides to buy euros futures contracts at the CME, he will have to buy contracts with a unit size of €125,000. If he buys one contract for €125,000, he will "overhedge" his exposure by €25,000. Moreover, the distributor will have to decide on the maturity date of the futures contract. The only four expiration dates for a futures contract are the third Wednesday of March, June, September, and December. Suppose the champagne supplier wants to be paid by the end of May. In this case, the distributor will buy June futures contracts because their expiration date is closest to the end of May. Then he will *sell* the futures contracts at the end of May. However, he will still be exposed to exchange-rate risk because he cannot know at the time the contract is bought what the price of the June futures contracts will be at the end of May. Suppose the supplier agrees to wait until July 1 to be paid and the distributor chooses to hedge with June futures. In this case, the distributor will be exposed to the USD/EUR exchange-rate volatility between the last Wednesday of June (when the June futures contracts expire) and July 1.

Finally, the distributor will have to place a margin with a broker. Also, the daily marking-to-market may trigger margin calls if the USD/EUR futures exchange rate goes down. In this situation, the distributor would have to make additional cash payments until the futures contracts expire.

A futures hedge has some disadvantages that are not present in a forward hedge. A futures hedge is more complicated, it does not completely eliminate exchange rate risk, and it requires intermediary cash payments. These drawbacks are particularly significant for the champagne distributor, who may rightly prefer to hedge his contractual exposure with forward contracts. However, there is a feature of the futures market that makes this market appealing to small firms that do not have an established reputation or to firms that do not enjoy a high credit standing: no credit check is required before trading in the futures market.

HEDGING WITH OPTION CONTRACTS

Suppose our distributor hedges his exposure to the euros by buying euros forward at EUR/USD 0.80. Regardless of whether the euro appreciates or depreciates during the hedging period, the US-dollar cost of the champagne will be $125,000 (€100,000 divided by EUR/USD 0.80). If the euro appreciates, the hedge will have accomplished its purpose, that is, it will have protected the distributor against an increase in the value of the euro. But if the euro depreciates, the distributor would have been better off if he had not hedged with forwards because he would then have benefited from the decrease in the value of the euro. Indeed, it is always the case that a forward hedge protects a firm from unfavorable exchange-rate movements but prevents it from benefiting from favorable changes in the exchange rate. Does a hedging technique exist that insulates the distributor from an appreciation of the euro but allows him to benefit from its depreciation? The answer is yes, and the technique is the **currency option hedge**.

Currency Option Contracts.   A currency option contract is available from either banks or organized exchanges which function like futures exchanges.[6] If you buy a currency **call option**, you have the right to *buy* a stated amount of currency at an agreed-upon exchange rate (the **exercise** or the **strike price**) from the seller, or **writer**, of the option. If you buy a currency **put option**, you have the right to *sell* the stated amount of currency at the exercise rate of the option to the writer of the option. The **expiration date** (also called **maturity date**) of an option is the date after which the option can no longer be exercised. For a **European option**, the exercise of the right can take place only at the maturity date; for an **American option**, the option can be exercised at any time before the maturity date.

Banks usually write over-the-counter (OTC) options. As for forward contracts, banks can tailor the currency, size, and expiration date of foreign-exchange options to the specific needs of their clients.

An option is valuable for its owner because it gives him the right, *but not the obligation*, to buy or sell a currency at a predetermined exchange rate. The price of this right, also called the **option premium**, is determined in the option market.

The Currency Option Hedge.   If the champagne distributor decides to hedge his euro exposure with options, he will buy a 3-month euro *call* option. This will give him the right to buy euros at a predetermined exchange rate (the exercise rate). He is not obligated to exercise the option, and he will not do so if the exchange rate is unfavorable. For example, if the spot rate of the euro in three months is lower than

---

[6] Today, most exchanges trade in currency options for which the underlying asset is a currency *futures* contract. When such an option is exercised, one receives a futures contract on the specified currency instead of the currency.

the exercise rate of the option, the distributor will not exercise his option and, instead, will buy the needed euros in the spot market. On the other hand, if the spot rate is higher than the exercise rate, he will exercise his option to get the euros at a lower rate. The option hedge provides a flexibility that is absent in a forward or futures hedge. However, this flexibility comes with a price, which is the price of the option.

To illustrate, suppose the distributor can buy from his bank a 3-month European call option at $0.04 per €1, with an exercise rate of $1.25 per €1. This means (1) the distributor must now pay the bank $0.04 per €1, or $4,000 for €100,000 ($0.04 multiplied by €100,000)[7] and (2) in three months, the distributor can buy €100,000 from the bank at $1.25 per €1 for a total of $125,000 ($1.25 multiplied by €100,000). Whether or not the distributor will exercise the option in three months depends on the USD/EUR spot exchange rate prevailing at that time. Exhibit 17.2 examines four cases corresponding to the following exchange rates in three months: EUR/USD 0.77, 0.79, 0.80, and 0.82.

If the exchange rate is EUR/USD 0.77 (USD/EUR 1.30), the distributor will exercise his option because he will be able to buy for $1.25 what is worth $1.30. He will get the €100,000 for $125,000 ($1.25 multiplied by €100,000) from the bank (the seller of the option) and pay his supplier of champagne. However, the option costs $4,000, so the total cost of the champagne will be $129,000 ($125,000 plus $4,000). If the exchange rate is EUR/USD 0.79 (USD/EUR 1.27), he will also exercise his option and the total cost of the champagne will remain at $129,000. If the exchange rate is EUR/USD 0.80 (USD/EUR 1.25), that is, if it is equal to the exercise rate, the distributor no longer has any incentive to exercise the option because he can get the €100,000 in the spot market at the same exchange rate. For any USD/EUR exchange rate higher than the exercise rate of $1.25 per €1 (or for any EUR/USD exchange rate lower than $0.80 per €1), the distributor will exercise his option, and the total cost of the champagne will be $129,000.

If the exchange rate is EUR/USD 0.82 (USD/EUR 1.22), the distributor will not exercise his option to buy at $1.25 what is worth only $1.22. He will buy the €100,000 in the spot market at EUR/USD 0.82 for a total cost of $121,951 (€100,000 divided by EUR/USD 0.82) and pay his supplier. However, because he paid $4,000 for the option, the total cost of the champagne will be $125,951 ($121,951 plus $4,000). For any USD/EUR spot rate lower than the exercise rate of $1.25 per €1 (or for any EUR/USD exchange rate higher than EUR/USD 0.80), the distributor will let the option expire

EXHIBIT 17.2	COMPARISON OF CURRENCY OPTION COSTS FOR FOUR EXCHANGE RATES.

| Spot Rate in Three Months' Time | | Exercise Rate | Will the Option Be Exercised? | Dollar Amount Paid for €100,000 | Cost of Option | Total Cost |
EUR/USD	USD/EUR	USD/EUR				
0.77	1.30	1.25	Yes	$125,000	$4,000	$129,000
0.79	1.27	1.25	Yes	$125,000	$4,000	$129,000
0.80	1.25	1.25	No	$125,000	$4,000	$129,000
0.82	1.22	1.25	No	$121,951	$4,000	$125,951

---

[7] The bank will set the price of the option based on the option exercise price, the spot exchange rate, the time to maturity, the volatility of the exchange rate, and the level of interest rate.

EXHIBIT 17.3	THE OPTION HEDGE FOR THE US CHAMPAGNE DISTRIBUTOR.

CONTRACTUAL EXPOSURE: €100,000 TO BE PAID IN THREE MONTHS' TIME
THREE-MONTH CALL OPTION PRICE: USD/EUR 0.04
EXERCISE PRICE: $1.25 PER EURO OR EUR/USD 0.80

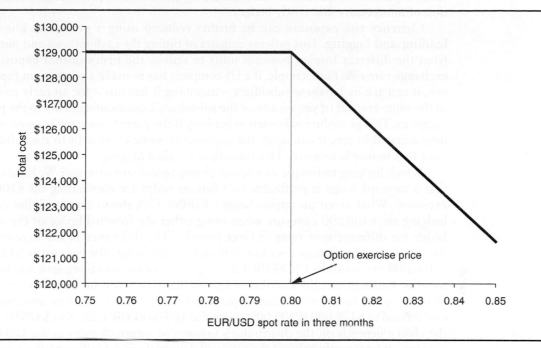

without exercising it and exchange dollars for euros at the spot rate. And the lower the USD/EUR exchange rate, the lower the dollar cost of the champagne.

Exhibit 17.3 shows the net result of the option hedge for the distributor for a wide range of spot rates in three months. The hedge accomplishes the dual goal of (1) protecting the distributor from an appreciation of the euro by setting an upper limit to the dollar amount he will have to pay for the champagne ($129,000) and (2) allowing him to benefit from a depreciation of the euro. If the euro rises above the exercise rate (the EUR/USD rate drops below 0.80), the distributor will exercise his right to buy euros at that rate, thus limiting his dollar cost of the €100,000 to $129,000 (the amount he will pay the bank ($125,000) when exercising the option plus the cost of the option ($4,000)). However, if the euro falls below the exercise rate (the EUR/USD rate rises above 0.80), the distributor will not exercise his option. The dollar cost of the €100,000 will be equal to €100,000 multiplied by the spot rate in three months plus the $4,000 cost of the option.

SELECTING A HEDGING TECHNIQUE

Before deciding which technique to use to hedge a currency exposure created by a particular transaction, a manager must first decide whether a hedge is needed at all. The hedge is not needed if another business unit belonging to the firm has a currency exposure that is the opposite of the one created by the transaction. However, a business unit manager is not usually informed of the size and timing of the currency exposure of other business units. As pointed out earlier, this is the reason why large firms engaging in foreign trade have a centralized foreign currency management group that constantly monitors the firm's *net exposure* on a currency-by-currency basis and makes the required hedging decisions. Having all the business units' currency exposures consolidated and managed by a central unit prevents the multiplication of unnecessary and costly hedges.

Currency risk exposure can be further reduced using a procedure known as **leading and lagging**. This process consists of timing the cash inflows and outflows from the different foreign business units to reduce the firm's *overall* exposure to exchange-rate risk. For example, if a US company has to make a payment in Japanese yen, it can ask its Japanese subsidiary – assuming it has one – for an early payment of the same amount of yen on any of the subsidiary's outstanding debts to the parent company. This procedure is known as *leading*. If the parent company is owed money denominated in yen, it can delay the payment of some of its debt to the subsidiary until that money is received. This procedure is called *lagging*.

Which hedging technique should our champagne distributor use? We have shown that a forward hedge is preferable to a futures hedge for eliminating his €100,000 exposure. What about an option hedge? Exhibit 17.4 shows the net dollar cost of hedging the €100,000 exposure when using either the forward hedge or the option hedge for different spot rates in three months. The difference in the outcomes of the two hedging techniques is clear. With a forward hedge, the net cost is $125,000 (€100,000 multiplied by USD/EUR 1.25) regardless of the prevailing spot rate in three months. Furthermore, the distributor knows that cost when he enters the contract. With an option hedge, the net cost depends on the spot rate in three months, with the cost limited to $129,000 (€100,000 multiplied by USD/EUR 1.25, plus $4,000). Thus, the choice depends on the distributor's opinion of future changes in the USD/EUR spot rate. If he strongly believes the euro will depreciate in the following three months, he may consider that the extra cost of the option hedge (if it turns out the euro appreciates) is not large enough to dissuade him from taking a chance. However, if he has no strong opinion about future currency movements, he may prefer the certainty of the forward hedge to the uncertain outcome of the costlier option alternative.

In practice, the currency forward contract is the favorite hedging tool, followed by the currency option and futures contracts. Exchange traded instruments, such as traded options or futures contracts, are not used very often, which may imply that corporations prefer instruments tailored to their particular needs as opposed to those that are more liquid but standardized.

HEDGING LONG-TERM CONTRACTUAL EXPOSURE TO CURRENCY RISK WITH SWAPS

Although currency forward, futures, and option contracts can be designed for any duration, in practice they are most often used to hedge short-term exposure to currency risk. A banker may be willing to offer a customized currency forward or option contract for more than a year's maturity, but the risk premium would be high because the longer the contract, the higher the risk that unanticipated events may affect the firm's ability to honor the contract. In addition, the choice for futures or traded options is limited to the contracts available in the market, which typically have less than a year's maturity.

To hedge long-term contractual exposure to currency risk, a firm may prefer to enter a **currency swap contract** with its bank. The swap contract requires that the

EXHIBIT 17.4	THE FORWARD AND OPTION HEDGES FOR THE US CHAMPAGNE DISTRIBUTOR.

CONTRACTUAL EXPOSURE: €100,000 TO BE PAID IN THREE MONTHS' TIME
THREE-MONTH FORWARD RATE: EUR/USD 0.80
THREE-MONTH CALL OPTION PRICE: USD/EUR 0.04
EXERCISE PRICE: $1.25 PER EURO OR EUR/USD 0.80

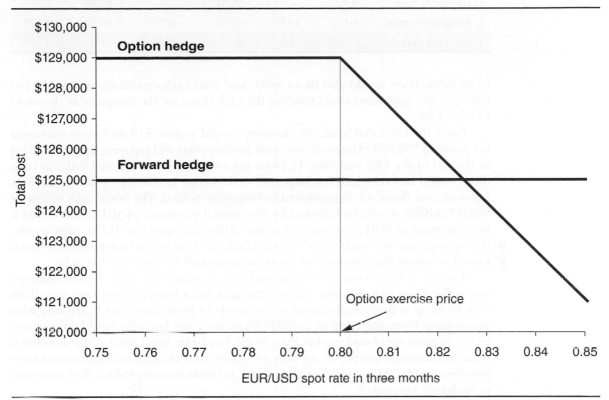

firm delivers a set of future cash flows denominated in the currency to be hedged in exchange for a set of cash flows denominated in the currency of its choice.

As an illustration, suppose a US company has arranged a five-year, $10 million loan from a US bank to finance its operations in Singapore. The coupon rate, payable annually, is 7 percent or $700,000. The firm's finance officer decided against borrowing Singapore dollars (SGD) from a Singapore bank because she could not get the same attractive credit terms in Singapore dollars as she did on US dollars borrowed in the United States. However, the firm is now exposed to exchange-rate risk because Singapore dollars (the currency of the firm's income from its operations in Singapore) will need to be exchanged for US dollars to make annual interest payments of $700,000 and repay the $10 million principal on the US-dollar loan. But the firm did not need to take this risk. The finance officer could have simply entered a US-dollar to Singapore-dollars swap agreement with a bank dealing in swaps at the same time she arranged the loan. Under this agreement, the bank would pay the company the US dollars needed to service the $10 million loan, and, in exchange, the company would make simultaneous payments in Singapore dollars to the bank.

| EXHIBIT 17.5 | CASH FLOWS FOR $10 MILLION SWAP AGREEMENT. |

FIGURES IN MILLIONS

	Initial Cash Flows		Cash Flows: Years 1–4		Cash Flows: Year 5	
	USD	SGD	USD	SGD	USD	SGD
1. US-dollar loan	+10		−0.70		−10.70	
2. Swap agreement	−10	+15	+0.70	−0.75	+10.70	−15.75
3. Net cash flow	0	15	0	−0.75	0	−15.75

In addition, there would also be an initial and final exchange of the principals. For example, the agreement could result in the cash flows for the company as shown in Exhibit 17.5.

From the US-dollar loan, the company would receive $10 million in exchange for paying $700,000 of interest every year for five years and repaying the $10 million at the end of the fifth year (line 1). From the swap agreement, these US-dollar cash flows would be exchanged for Singapore dollars (line 2). The net result would be a series of cash flows, all denominated in Singapore dollars. The initial cash inflow of SGD15 million would be followed by five annual payments of SGD750,000 and a final payment of SGD15 million at the end of the fifth year (line 3).[8] In other words, the swap agreement would transform the US-dollar loan into a Singapore dollar loan, thus eliminating the currency risk exposure generated by the US-dollar debt.

This illustration is one of the simplest forms of a currency swap. A more complex one is the swap of a floating coupon rate debt for a fixed coupon rate debt. This type of swap is particularly suited to the needs of most corporate borrowers who prefer fixed financing costs to variable financing costs but who have better access to the floating-rate bond market than to the fixed-rate bond market. By entering a fixed-for-floating currency swap, they can easily, and cheaply, transform their variable finance obligations into fixed ones and, at the same time, reduce their exposure to exchange-rate risk.

FACTORS AFFECTING CHANGES IN EXCHANGE RATES

To understand how international investment decisions should be made, we should first identify and understand the factors that determine changes in the exchange rate between the currencies of two countries. Intuition tells us that if inflation in country A is expected to be higher than inflation in country B, we can expect country A's currency to weaken relative to country's B currency. At the same time, we would expect interest rates in country A to be higher than interest rates in country because country A has a higher inflation rate. In the following sections, we examine the **parity relations** that link the spot exchange rate (the exchange rate prevailing *today*), the forward exchange rate (the exchange rate at a specified *future* date fixed *today* contractually), and the interest rates and inflation rates prevailing in the two countries.

[8] The notional principal of SGD15 million is determined by the prevailing spot rate of 1.50 Singapore dollars per US dollar. The implicit interest rate on the Singapore dollar loan is 5 percent (SGD750,000 divided by SGD15 million).

Appendix 17.2 provides a detailed analysis of each of these relationships and shows how the rates are linked to one another.

HOW DIFFERENCES IN INFLATION RATES AFFECT EXCHANGE RATES: THE PURCHASING POWER PARITY RELATION

The **purchasing power parity (PPP) relation** says that exchange rates should adjust so that the same basket of goods will cost the same in different countries.[9] It is based on the following principle: if the price of goods increases faster in one country than in another because the inflation rate is higher in the first country than in the second, then the exchange rate between the two countries should move to offset the difference in inflation rates and, consequently, the difference in prices. More formally, according to the PPP relation:

$$\text{Expected future spot rate} = \text{Current spot rate}$$
$$\times \frac{1 + \text{Expected inflation rate in the home country}}{1 + \text{Expected inflation rate in the foreign country}}$$

If $S^0_{h/f}$ is the current spot rate and $E(S^1_{h/f})$ is the expected future spot rate in one year (both expressed as the number of units of the *home* currency needed to buy one unit of the *foreign* currency), and if $E(i_h)$ and $E(i_f)$ are the expected inflation rates for next year in the home and the foreign countries, respectively, then we can write the following:

$$E(S^1_{h/f}) = S^0_{h/f} \times \frac{1 + E(i_h)}{1 + E(i_f)} \tag{17.1}$$

To illustrate this relationship, suppose that next year's expected inflation rate is 2 percent in the United States and 4 percent in the Eurozone. Furthermore, suppose that the current spot rate is USD/EUR 1.25 ($1.25 buys one euro).[10] We have $E(i_h) \equiv E(i_{US}) = 0.02$; $E(i_f) \equiv E(i_{EUR}) = 0.04$; and $S^0_{h/f} \equiv S^0_{USD/EUR} = \text{USD/EUR } 1.25$. Substituting these values in equation 17.1, we get next year's expected USD/EUR spot rate:

$$E(S^1_{USD/EUR}) = \left[\frac{USD}{EUR} 1.2500\right] \times \left[\frac{1 + 0.02}{1 + 0.04}\right] = \frac{USD}{EUR} 1.2260$$

The value of one euro expressed in US dollars is expected to *drop* from USD/EUR 1.2500 to USD/EUR 1.2260. In other words, the US dollar is expected to **appreciate** relative to the euro. (It is expected to get "stronger" in relation to the euro because it will take $1.2260, instead of $1.2500, to buy €1; it also means that the euro will be "cheaper" to buy when paying in dollars.) Conversely, the euro is expected to **depreciate** relative to the US dollar. (It is expected to get "weaker" in relation to the dollar because it will take €0.8157 [the inverse of $1.2260], instead of €0.8000 [the inverse of $1.2500], to buy one dollar; it also means that the dollar will be more "expensive" to buy when paying in euros.) In our example, the expected

[9] The PPP relation is an extension to currencies of the law of one price mentioned in Chapter 16.

[10] Note that the euro to US-dollar exchange rate is the inverse of the US dollar to euro exchange rate. If the US dollar to euro exchange rate is 1.25 ($1.25 buys €1), then the euro to US-dollar exchange rate is 1/1.25 = 0.80 (€0.80 buys $1).

appreciation of the US dollar relative to the euro, expressed as a percent, is as follows:

$$\frac{1.2500 - 1.2260}{1.2500} = 0.0192 = 1.92\%$$

Appendix 17.2 shows that when the expected inflation rate of the foreign country is small enough (less than 5 percent), equation 17.1 can be written as follows:

$$\frac{E(S_{h/f}^1) - S_{h/f}^0}{S_{h/f}^0} = E(i_h) - E(i_f) \qquad (17.2)$$

Equation 17.2 is a simpler version of the PPP relation. It says that the expected percentage change in the spot rate (in units of the home currency per unit of the foreign currency) is equal to the expected difference in the inflation rates between the home country and the foreign country. Using the expected inflation rates from the above example, the difference between the rates in the Eurozone and the United States is 2 percent (4 percent in the Eurozone minus 2 percent in the United States). Thus, according to the simpler version of the PPP relation, the expected appreciation of the US dollar relative to the euro should be 2 percent, which is close to the 1.92 percent predicted by the PPP relation given in equation 17.1.

The empirical evidence for the PPP relation is mixed. Many studies show that the relation usually does a poor job of forecasting spot rates in the near future (especially when differences in inflation rates are small). Also, the PPP relation requires a long-term forecast of inflation rates. However, if we need to forecast long-term exchange rates, such as in converting cash flows from a foreign currency to a home currency in the valuation of a cross-border long-term investment project, no other known forecast appears to be superior to the PPP relation.

THE RELATIONSHIP BETWEEN TWO COUNTRIES' INFLATION RATES AND INTEREST RATES: THE INTERNATIONAL FISHER EFFECT

Suppose that today you decide to invest $100 in a one-year bank deposit carrying an interest rate of 7.12 percent. This rate, which is the one the bank will pay you in one year, is called the **nominal interest rate**. Alternatively, with the same amount of money, you could buy 100 bottles of mineral water at your local supermarket. Suppose, too, that the inflation rate in the United States is expected to be 4 percent during the coming year and that inflation will affect all goods and services equally. In other words, you expect your local supermarket to charge you $104 for 100 bottles of water at the end of the year.

In a year, the bank deposit will be worth $107.12 [$100 × (1 + 7.12 percent)]. With this cash, you can expect to increase the amount of bottles you can buy from 100 bottles to 103 bottles ($107.12 divided by $1.04 per bottle), that is, by 3 percent. In other words, your bank deposit, which offers you a nominal rate of 7.12 percent, allows you to increase your future purchasing power by only 3 percent because of price inflation. This 3 percent rate is referred to as the **real interest rate**. It is the interest rate adjusted for the cost of living. The difference between the real interest rate and the nominal interest rate reflects, obviously, the expected rate of inflation.

We would expect lenders to be willing to make loans only if they are compensated for the effect of expected inflation. For example, suppose the real interest rate is 3 percent. If the expected inflation rate is zero, no compensation is needed and the real and nominal interest rates are both equal to 3 percent. However, if the expected inflation rate is 5 percent, the *nominal* rate of interest must be such that one dollar invested now at this rate will grow at the 3 percent *real* rate of interest to become $103 [$100 × (1 + 3 percent)] and will also grow at the 5 percent expected inflation rate to become $108.15 [$103 × (1 + 5 percent)]. To generalize, we have the following:

1 + Nominal interest rate = (1 + Real interest rate) × (1 + Expected inflation rate)

If r denotes the *nominal* rate of interest, r_r denotes the real rate of interest, and E(i) denotes the expected inflation rate, then we can write the following:

$$1 + r = (1 + r_r) \times (1 + E(i)) \tag{17.3}$$

Solving for r, we get the following:

$$r = r_r + E(i) + (r_r \times E(i)) \tag{17.4}$$

If the expected inflation rate, E(i), is small enough, the term $r_r \times E(i)$ becomes insignificant and we can write the following:

$$r = r_r + E(i) \tag{17.5}$$

In this case, the nominal interest rate is simply the sum of the real interest rate and the expected inflation rate. Equations 17.4 and 17.5 indicate that any change in the expected inflation rate is reflected in the nominal interest rate. This effect is known as the **Fisher effect**.

If real interest rates are different between two countries, we would expect capital to flow from the country with the lower rate to the country with the higher rate until the rates are equalized. Appendix 17.2 shows that the Fisher effect then implies the following relationship between interest rates and expected inflation rates in the home and foreign countries:

$$\frac{1 + r_h}{1 + r_f} = \frac{1 + E(i_h)}{1 + E(i_f)} \tag{17.6}$$

A reasonable approximation of equation 17.6 is as follows:

$$r_h - r_f = E(i_h) - E(i_f) \tag{17.7}$$

Equation 17.7 shows clearly that the difference in interest rates between two countries reflects the difference in their expected inflation rates. This effect is known as the **international Fisher effect**. Most empirical evidence supports the international Fisher effect, especially between countries with open financial markets.

HOW DIFFERENCES IN INTEREST RATES AFFECT EXCHANGE RATES: THE INTEREST-RATE PARITY RELATION

The **interest-rate parity (IRP) relation** describes how the difference in interest rates between two countries is related to the difference between their forward and spot exchange rates. Recall that the forward exchange rate defined earlier is the exchange rate agreed *today* at which two currencies will be exchanged at a specified *future* date. More precisely, if $F_{h/f}^0$ is the forward rate (in units of home currency per unit of foreign currency), $S^0_{h/f}$ is the spot rate, and r_h and r_f are the nominal rates of interest in the home country and the foreign country, respectively, we have the following:

$$\frac{F^0_{h/f} - S^0_{h/f}}{S^0_{h/f}} = \frac{r_h - r_f}{1 + r_f} \tag{17.8}$$

Appendix 17.2 shows that IRP should hold because of the actions of interbank traders who try to take advantage of any deviation from the parity relation.

The IRP relation is better known under the following simplified version, which assumes that r_f is small compared with 1:

$$\frac{F^0_{h/f} - S^0_{h/f}}{S^0_{h/f}} = r_h - r_f \tag{17.9}$$

Equation 17.9 says that the percentage difference between the forward and the spot rates is equal to the difference in interest rates between the home country and the foreign country.

Ample evidence shows that the IRP relation holds in the real world, at least for short-term interest rates. Indeed, when no active market exists for a forward rate, banks often quote their clients a rate computed from the IRP relation.

THE RELATION BETWEEN FORWARD RATES AND FUTURE SPOT RATES

Suppose the 1-year forward rate between the US dollar and the euro is USD/EUR 1.30. (This means that you have a contract that guarantees you that rate in one year.) Would anyone be willing to *buy* euros forward if the *spot* rate in one year is expected to be USD/EUR 1.20? No, because no one would enter into a contract that says that, at some future date, an asset (euros, in our case) must be bought at a *higher* price (the USD/EUR forward rate of 1.30) than the market price expected to prevail on that date (the USD/EUR future spot rate of 1.20). Would anyone be willing to *sell* euros forward at USD/EUR 1.30 if the *spot* rate in one year is expected to be USD/EUR 1.35? Again, no, because no one would enter into a contract that says that, at some future date, an asset must be sold at a *lower* price (the USD/EUR forward rate of 1.30) than the market price expected to prevail on that date (the USD/EUR future spot rate of 1.35). Thus, in equilibrium, the *expected* future spot rate must be equal to USD/EUR. In other words, the forward rate must be equal to the *expected* future spot rate.

If $E(S^1_{h/f})$ is the expected value of the spot rate one year from now and $F^0_{h/f}$ is the current 1-year forward rate (both expressed as the number of units of the home currency needed to buy one unit of foreign currency), the following relation must hold:

$$F^0_{h/f} = E(S^1_{h/f}) \tag{17.10}$$

Dividing both sides of this equation by $S^0_{h/f}$ and then subtracting 1 from both sides, we get the following:

$$\frac{F^0_{h/f} - S^0_{h/f}}{S^0_{h/f}} = \frac{E(S^1_{h/f}) - S^0_{h/f}}{S^0_{h/f}} \tag{17.11}$$

The empirical evidence for this relation is not clear-cut because risk was not taken into consideration when deriving it. The expected spot rate is only a forecast of what the spot rate will be in the future. The actual rate, which will be revealed only in one year, could be higher or lower. When you enter into a forward contract, you fix the price at which you will sell (or purchase) euros. In effect, you eliminate the currency risk. To eliminate the risk, you are willing to sell (buy) euros forward at a lower (higher) price than the expected spot price. Despite their failure to properly account for risk, equations 17.10 and 17.11 tend to hold *on average*.

PUTTING IT ALL TOGETHER

Exchange rates fluctuate constantly. The relationships we have presented show how these fluctuations are linked to changes in fundamental economic variables, such as inflation rates and interest rates. These relationships are summarized in Exhibit 17.6. The links among the parity relations are caused by the actions of **arbitrageurs,** the traders in the financial markets who try to make a riskless profit from price discrepancies, mostly in exchange rates (spot and forward) and interest rates across countries. We should expect that the lower the barriers to the free movement of capital flows, the swifter the action of arbitrageurs and the more likely that the parity relations will hold.

When a firm engages in cross-border activities, these relations have some important managerial implications. For example, the PPP relation can be used to forecast future exchange rates in the analysis of cross-border investment projects. Furthermore, these relations help to avoid classic mistakes, such as trying to increase profit from operations by buying currencies when they go down and selling them when they go up. If you borrow to accomplish these transactions, what you may gain on the foreign-exchange

EXHIBIT 17.6	THE FUNDAMENTAL RELATIONSHIPS AMONG SPOT EXCHANGE RATES, FORWARD EXCHANGE RATES, INFLATION RATES, AND INTEREST RATES.

The Relation	What Does It Say?	The Simplified Version of the Relation
Purchasing power parity (PPP)	Spot exchange rates adjust to keep the cost of living the same across countries. As a consequence, the expected percentage change in the spot rate is equal to the expected difference in the inflation rates between the two countries.	$\dfrac{E(S^1_{h/f}) - S^0_{h/f}}{S^0_{h/f}} = E(i_h) - E(i_f)$ Equation 17.2
International Fisher effect	The difference in inflation rates between two countries is reflected in the difference in their interest rates.	$r_h - r_f = E(i_h) - E(i_f)$ Equation 17.7
Interest rate parity	The percentage difference between the forward and spot exchange rates is equal to the difference in the interest rates between the two countries.	$\dfrac{F^0_{h/f} - S^0_{h/f}}{S^0_{h/f}} = r_h - r_f$ Equation 17.9
Expected spot rate and forward rate	The percentage difference between the forward and spot exchange rates is equal to the percentage difference between the expected spot rate and the current spot rate.	$\dfrac{F^0_{h/f} - S^0_{h/f}}{S^0_{h/f}} = \dfrac{E(S^1_{h/f}) - S^0_{h/f}}{S^0_{h/f}}$ Equation 17.11

$E(S^1_{h/f})$ = expected spot rate one year from now expressed in units of home currency per unit of foreign currency.
$S^0_{h/f}$ = current spot rate expressed in units of home currency per unit of foreign currency.
$E(i_h)$ = expected inflation rate in the home country during the next year.
$E(i_f)$ = expected inflation rate in the foreign country during the next year.
r_h = one-year interest rate in the home country.
r_f = one-year interest rate in the foreign country.
$F^0_{h/f}$ = forward rate now in units of home currency per unit of foreign currency.

transaction, you would lose in interest income. The only time you could gain is when the change in the rate is higher than the difference between the interest rates. Another example is the classic illusion of trying to lower the firm's cost of borrowing by taking advantage of foreign interest rates that are lower than domestic rates: on average, the net cost of borrowing abroad may not be much different from the domestic cost after accounting for the expected changes in exchange rates.

ANALYZING AN INTERNATIONAL INVESTMENT PROJECT

Chapter 7 shows how to use the net present value (NPV) rule to select investment projects that create value and reject those that destroy value. The objective of value maximization applies to any management decision, so the NPV rule is also applicable to the decision to invest in a foreign country. However, two new factors must be taken into account. First, the project's future cash flows are usually denominated in a foreign currency with an exchange rate that may fluctuate; second, the cash flows may be affected by changes in local regulations governing foreign investments, a risk we refer to as country risk. These complications make the NPV rule more difficult to apply.

After a brief review of the NPV rule, we consider the case of Surf and Zap (SAZ), a US manufacturer of a small remote-control device called Zap Scan, which can automatically show selected programs on a television set at regular and brief intervals of time. After a successful entry in the US market, the firm wants to export the device to Europe and has to decide where to locate its regional distribution center. The choice is between Switzerland and the hypothetical nation of Zaragu, two countries with significantly different country risks.

THE NET PRESENT VALUE RULE: A BRIEF REVIEW

The NPV rule is the subject of Chapter 7. Here we review the NPV rule and its implications for investment decisions. Let CF_0 be the investment's initial cash outlay, that is, the amount of cash that has to be invested today to launch the project, and CF_1, CF_2, CF_3, ..., CF_T, the sequence of future cash flows that the project is *expected* to generate over its useful life. The last cash flow, CF_T, includes the receipts from the sale of the investment. Let k be the project's cost of capital, that is, the return that investors require from investments that have the same risk characteristics as the project. The NPV of the investment is defined as follows:

$$NPV = -CF_0 + \left[\frac{CF_1}{1 + k} + \frac{CF_2}{(1 + k)^2} + \frac{CF_3}{(1 + k)^3} + \cdots + \frac{CF_T}{(1 + k)^T} \right]$$

where the sum in brackets is the present value, or the value today, of the expected future cash-flow stream. Notice that the more distant the cash flows, the lower their contribution to the project's present value because the discount factor $\frac{1}{(1 + k)^t}$ decreases with time. Note also that the higher the project's risk, the higher the rate of return (k) required by investors, the lower the discount factors, and the lower the present value of the expected cash-flow stream. In other words, everything else remaining the same, the riskier a project, the less desirable it is, and the lower its NPV.

According to the NPV rule, a project must be accepted when its NPV is positive and rejected when its NPV is negative. The rule simply means that if the present value of the benefits generated by the project (the present value of the future expected cash flows) is larger than the cost of undertaking the investment (the initial cash outlay, CF_0), then the project will create value for the firm's owners and, consequently, must be undertaken. Otherwise, it must be rejected because it will destroy value. The NPV indicates how much richer (or poorer) the firm's investors will be if they put their money in the project rather than in an alternative investment with the same risk characteristics. Note, finally, that an NPV equal to zero does not mean that the project has a zero return. It simply means that the project will not change the wealth of investors if undertaken.

SURF AND ZAP CROSS-BORDER ALTERNATIVE INVESTMENT PROJECTS

To export Zap Scan to Europe, SAZ needs to set up a European distribution center. After an extensive search for the most convenient location, the choice was reduced to two countries, Switzerland and Zaragu. Both countries are in the center of Europe and from a logistical point of view neither one appears superior to the other. However, whereas investing in Switzerland would not carry any country risk, Zaragu has recently been the subject of unfavorable articles in the press. Analysts are concerned that the country's monetary situation may deteriorate in the future and that the earnings from the subsidiaries of foreign companies in Zaragu may soon be subject to a foreign tax in addition to the regular corporate tax. The local currency is the Swiss franc (CHF) in Switzerland and the Zaragupa (ZGU) in Zaragu. Financial data on the alternative projects' cash flows are presented in Exhibit 17.7.

The cost of acquiring and refurbishing a building plus the project's startup costs are estimated at CHF 25 million for the Swiss alternative and at ZGU 230 million for the Zaragu alternative. It is expected that the investment will last five years, at which time digital television sets with incorporated zapping devices will make Zap Scan obsolete. The annual cash flows in Exhibit 17.7 are *net of all local and US taxes*. It is estimated that the Swiss building can be sold for CHF 20 million and the Zaragu building can be sold for ZGU 250 million at the end of the fifth year.

EXHIBIT 17.7	THE ZAP SCAN PROJECT.

CASH FLOWS IN MILLIONS

	Switzerland Alternative in Swiss Francs (CHF)	Zaragu Alternative in Zaragupas (ZGU)
Initial cash outlay	25.0	230
Annual cash flows		
Year 1	4.5	50
Year 2	5.0	60
Year 3	5.2	65
Year 4	5.4	70
Year 5	5.6	75
Liquidation value in Year 5	20.0	250
Current annual inflation rate	2%	10%
Current spot exchange rate	CHF/USD 1.3	ZGU/USD 10

The inflation rate in Switzerland has been remarkably stable in the past, at about 2 percent a year, and is not expected to behave differently during the next few years. In Zaragu, the inflation rate has continuously increased during the recent past. It is now at 10 percent a year and is expected to stay at this level for the foreseeable future. In the United States, the inflation rate is expected to average 3 percent a year for the next five years.

The current spot exchange rates are CHF/USD 1.3 and ZGU/USD 10. Finally, the rate of return required by SAZ from its distribution centers in the United States is 10 percent. Furthermore, SAZ requires that the NPV for all projects be estimated in US dollars.

The NPV of the Swiss Alternative

To compute the NPV of the Swiss alternative of the Zap Scan project, we need to estimate both the project's expected cash flows and its cost of capital in US dollars. This is done using the spreadsheet shown in Exhibit 17.8. The project's cash flows, taken from Exhibit 17.7, are shown in row 6. To convert these Swiss franc cash flows into their US-dollar equivalents, we need to forecast the year-end USD/CHF spot rate for the next five years. We can use the PPP relation to predict these future spot rates.

As shown in equation 17.1, the PPP relation relates the expected changes in the spot exchange rates to the expected inflation rates in the home country and the foreign country. The inflation rates in the United States and in Switzerland are expected to be 3 percent and 2 percent, respectively, in the near future, so we can use these values for the expected inflation rates $E(i_h)$ and $E(i_f)$ in equation 17.1. To find the expected value of the year-end USD/CHF spot exchange rate for years one to five, we start with the current spot exchange rate of CHF/USD 1.3000 (row 10). This rate is converted into USD/CHF 0.7692 (row 11). We then solve equation 17.1 successively for each year, using the expected future spot rate from the previous year (row 12).

The expected US-dollar value of the project's cash flows is obtained by multiplying the Swiss franc cash flows by the expected exchange rates (see row 13).

To compute the project's NPV we need to estimate the cost of capital. SAZ requires a return of 10 percent from its distribution centers in the United States. Should the firm use the same cost of capital for the Swiss alternative or should it use a higher one to account for exchange-rate risk, that is, for the probability that the future USD/CHF exchange rate may be different from the expected one? Recall from Chapters 10 and 12 that the risk that matters to investors is not the *total* risk of the investment, but rather the portion of the risk that cannot be reduced or eliminated by diversification. If we assume the portfolios of SAZ shareholders include either shares of foreign companies or shares of US firms with international business activity, we can assume the shareholders have already eliminated the portion of the Zap Scan project risk associated with USD/CHF exchange-rate volatility. In this case, no premium should be added to the domestic (US) cost of capital to account for the exchange-rate risk. What if SAZ shareholders are not diversified internationally? In this case, one can argue that the Swiss project gives them the opportunity to become diversified, albeit indirectly. As a consequence, the risk of their portfolio of assets would be *reduced*, which would imply a *lower* required rate of return for the project.

Taking a cost of capital of 10 percent (cell B14) and the project's expected cash flows in row 13 in Exhibit 17.8, we use the spreadsheet NPV formula to find the project's NPV (row 15):

$$NPV_{Switzerland} = USD\ 6.071\ million$$

EXHIBIT 17.8	THE ZAP SCAN PROJECT'S EXPECTED CASH FLOWS FROM THE SWISS ALTERNATIVE.

	A	B	C	D	E	F	G
1		Now			Forecast for		
2		0	Year 1	Year 2	Year 3	Year 4	Year 5
3	Expected cash flows in millions of Swiss francs (CHF)						
4	Cash flow	(25.0)	4.5	5.0	5.2	5.4	5.6
5	Cash flow from liquidation						20.0
6	Total cash flow	(25.0)	4.5	5.0	5.2	5.4	25.6
7	Expected USD/CHF spot rate using PPP (equation 17.1)						
8	Swiss expected inflation rate		2.0%	2.0%	2.0%	2.0%	2.0%
9	United States expected inflation rate		3.0%	3.0%	3.0%	3.0%	3.0%
10	Current spot rate CHF/USD	1.3000					
11	Current spot rate USD/CHF	0.7692					
12	Expected future spot rate USD/CHF	0.7692	0.7768	0.7844	0.7921	0.7998	0.8077
13	Expected cash flows in millions of US dollars (USD)	(19.2)	3.5	3.9	4.1	4.3	20.7
14	Cost of capital	10.0%					
15	Net present value	USD6.071	million				

- Rows 4, 5, 8, 9, 10, and cell B14 are data
- Formula in cell B6 is =B4+B5. Then copy formula in cell B6 to next cells in row 6
- Formula in cell B11 is =1/B10
- Formula in cell C12 is =B12*(1+C9)/(1+C8). Then copy formula in cell C12 to next cells in row 12
- Formula in cell B13 is =B6*B12. Then copy formula in cell B13 to next cells in row 13
- Formula in cell B15 is =B13+NPV(B14,C13:G13)

The NPV is positive, so the Swiss project would create value for SAZ investors. But one question remains: would the Zaragu project create more value?

THE NPV OF THE ZARAGU ALTERNATIVE

The procedure to estimate the expected value of the Zaragu project's cash flows is the same as the one we used for the Swiss alternative. We estimate the US-dollar value of the project's expected future cash flows and then discount these cash flows at the project's cost of capital. The PPP relation is again used to estimate the year-end USD/ZGU spot rates for the next five years, using the expected inflation rates in the United States and Zaragu. The cash flows in Zaragupas are converted into their US-dollar equivalents using the predicted spot rates. The procedure and the results of our estimation are shown in Exhibit 17.9.

If we assume for a moment that there is no country risk associated with the Zaragu alternative, there is no need to adjust the project cost of capital for exchange-rate risk. Thus, in the absence of country risk, the project cost of capital in the Zaragu alternative is 10 percent, the same as the rate used for similar projects in the United States

EXHIBIT 17.9	THE ZAP SCAN PROJECT'S EXPECTED CASH FLOWS FROM THE ZARAGU ALTERNATIVE WITHOUT COUNTRY RISK.

	A	B	C	D	E	F	G
		Now			Forecast for		
1							
2		0	Year 1	Year 2	Year 3	Year 4	Year 5
3	Expected cash flows in millions of Zaragupas (ZGU)						
4	Cash flow	(230.0)	50.0	60.0	65.0	70.0	75.0
5	Cash flow from liquidation						250.0
6	Total cash flow	(230.0)	50.0	60.0	65.0	70.0	325.0
7	Expected USD/ZGU spot rate using PPP (equation 17.1)						
8	Zaragu expected inflation rate		10.0%	10.0%	10.0%	10.0%	10.0%
9	United States expected inflation rate		3.0%	3.0%	3.0%	3.0%	3.0%
10	Current spot rate ZGU/USD	10.0000					
11	Current spot rate USD/ZGU	0.1000					
12	Expected future spot rate USD/ZGU	0.1000	0.0936	0.0877	0.0821	0.0769	0.0720
13	Expected cash flows in millions of US dollars (USD)	(23.0)	4.7	5.3	5.3	5.4	23.4
14	Cost of capital	10.0%					
15	Net present value	USD7.814	million				

• *Rows 4, 5, 8, 9, 10, and cell B14 are data*
• *Formula in cell B6 is =B4+B5. Then copy formula in cell B6 to next cells in row 6*
• *Formula in cell B11 is =1/B10*
• *Formula in cell C12 is =B12*(1+C9)/(1+C8). Then copy formula in cell C12 to next cells in row 12*
• *Formula in cell B13 is =B6*B12. Then copy formula in cell B13 to next cells in row 13*
• *Formula in cell B15 is =B13+NPV(B14,C13:G13)*

or Switzerland. Using the US-dollar denominated cash flows from Exhibit 17.9, the NPV of the Zaragu alternative is thus:

$$NPV_{Zaragu}^{No\ country\ risk} = USD\ 7.814\ million$$

However, as mentioned earlier, the project will be exposed to country risk because the authorities in Zaragu may impose a foreign tax on the project's earnings. To account for this risk, most firms systematically add a risk premium to their domestic cost of capital. We disagree with this procedure for three reasons. First, if we assume that shareholders have already eliminated the country risk by holding a well-diversified portfolio of assets, we do not need to make any adjustment at all. Second, there is no rational way to estimate the size of the risk premium for the particular risk that needs to be taken into account. For example, in the Zaragu alternative, should it be 1 percent, 2 percent, 10 percent, or another figure? No one knows. Third, simply adding an arbitrary "fudge" factor to the domestic cost of capital may lead to complacency and prevent managers from thoroughly assessing the effect of country risk on the project.

We suggest that any adjustment for country risk should be made on the project's *expected cash flows* rather than on the cost of capital. An expected cash flow is just a weighted average of the values that the cash flow can take in the future, where the weights are the probability that the cash flow will actually take these values. Thus, we can adjust these cash flows to reflect the likelihood of any form of country risk. If this is done, there is no need to adjust the cost of capital. Furthermore, the estimation of the expected cash flows forces managers to make a thorough analysis of country risk over time and its effect on the project.

Suppose that after a careful analysis of economic trends in Zaragu, we estimate a 20 percent probability that a monetary crisis will occur at some time during the project's life. Should such a crisis erupt, we can expect the project's earnings to be subjected to a foreign tax. When such a tax was imposed in the past, the tax rate was always 25 percent. There is no reason to expect that the rate will be different during the next monetary crisis, so we can apply the same rate to the project. To avoid cumbersome computations, we also assume that the project's *profits* that will be subjected to the "foreign" tax, represent, each year, 90 percent of the project's operating cash flows in the absence of the "foreign" tax.[11]

Exhibit 17.10 presents the detailed computation of the project's expected cash flows in a spreadsheet format, taking into account the risk that the "foreign" tax will be imposed on the project. The first section of Exhibit 17.10 shows the cash flows in the absence of tax taken from Exhibit 17.9. The next section presents the computation of the operating cash flows net of foreign tax if the tax is imposed. The third section shows the computation of the project's expected cash flows, taking into account the probability that the project will be subjected to the tax. If the probability of taxation is 20 percent during the life of the project, the project's expected cash flows are the cash flows net of the "foreign" tax multiplied by 20 percent plus the cash flows without the tax multiplied by 80 percent, because there is a 20 percent chance that the first outcome will occur and an 80 percent chance that the second will occur. The last part of the Exhibit shows the dollar value of the expected cash flows, using the same expected future exchange rates as in Exhibit 17.9. The NPV of the project, obtained by discounting the cash flows at the 10 percent cost of capital, is as follows:

$$NPV_{Zaragu}^{With\ country\ risk} = USD\ 6.931\ million$$

Not surprisingly, the NPV of the Zaragu alternative with country risk ($6.931 million) is lower than without country risk ($7.814 million). More to the point, however, is the finding that the NPV of the Zaragu alternative with country risk ($6.931 million) is *higher* than that of the Swiss alternative ($6.071 million). Can SAZ management therefore conclude that the distribution center should be located in Zaragu? The answer depends on how confident managers are in the assumptions they used to reach their conclusion.

In analyzing the alternatives, SAZ made two critical assumptions that could have a significant effect on the resulting NPVs. The first is that the purchasing power parity relation holds between the US dollar and the two foreign currencies. The second is that the probability assessment of the imposition of a foreign tax on the project is reliable. More generally, the second assumption refers to the probability that a portion or all of a project's cash flows accruing to the parent will be expropriated and the form this expropriation will take. The only realistic way to improve the confidence in the outcome of the NPV analysis of the Zaragu alternative is to do a *sensitivity analysis* that will show how responsive the project's NPV

---

[11] Recall that taxes are paid on profits, not cash flows. See Chapters 4 and 9 for the conversion of cash flows into profits for the purpose of estimating the amount of tax payment.

EXHIBIT 17.10	THE ZAP SCAN PROJECT'S EXPECTED CASH FLOWS FROM THE ZARAGU ALTERNATIVE WITH COUNTRY RISK.

	A	B	C	D	E	F	G
1		**Now**			Forecast for		
2		0	Year 1	Year 2	Year 3	Year 4	Year 5
3	**Expected cash flows in the absence of a foreign tax on the project's earnings in millions of Zaragupa (ZGU)**						
4	Cash flow	(230.0)	50.0	60.0	65.0	70.0	75.0
5	Cash flow from liquidation						250.0
6	**Expected operating cash flows in the presence of a foreign tax on the project's earnings in millions of Zaragupa (ZGU)**						
7	Project's earnings as percent of cash flow		90.0%	90.0%	90.0%	90.0%	90.0%
8	Project's earnings		45.0	54.0	58.5	63.0	67.5
9	Foreign tax rate		25.0%	25.0%	25.0%	25.0%	25.0%
10	Foreign tax		11.3	13.5	14.6	15.8	16.9
11	Operating cash flow net of tax		38.8	46.5	50.4	54.3	58.1
12	**Expected cash flows in millions of Zaragupas (ZGU)**						
13	Probability that the earnings will be taxed		20.0%	20.0%	20.0%	20.0%	20.0%
14	Expected operating cash flow		47.8	57.3	62.1	66.9	71.6
15	Total expected cash flow	(230.0)	47.8	57.3	62.1	66.9	321.6
16	**Expected USD/ZGU spot rate using PPP (equation 17.1)**						
17	Zaragu expected inflation rate		10.0%	10.0%	10.0%	10.0%	10.0%
18	United States expected inflation rate		3.0%	3.0%	3.0%	3.0%	3.0%
19	Current exchange rate USD/ZGU	0.1000					
20	Expected future spot rate USD/ZGU	0.1000	0.0936	0.0877	0.0821	0.0769	0.0720
21	**Expected cash flows in millions of US dollars (USD)**	(23.0)	4.5	5.0	5.1	5.1	23.2
22	**Cost of capital**	10.0%					
23	Net present value	USD6.931	million				

- *Rows 4, 5, 7, 9, 13, 17, 18 and cells B19 and B22 are data*
- *Formula in cell C8 is =C7*C4. Then copy formula in cell C8 to next cells in row 8*
- *Formula in cell C10 is =C9*C8. Then copy formula in cell C10 to next cells in row 10*
- *Formula in cell C11 is =C4-C10. Then copy formula in cell C11 to next cells in row 11*
- *Formula in cell C14 is =C13*C11+(1-C13)*C4. Then copy formula in cell C14 to next cells in row 14*
- *Formula in cell B15 is = B4. Formula in cell C15 is = C14. Then copy formula in cell C15 to cell D15, E15, and F15. Formula in cell G15 is = G14+G5*
- *Formula in cell C20 is =B20*(1+C18)/(1+C17). Then copy cell C20 to next cells in row 20*
- *Formula in cell B21 is =B15*B20. Then copy formula in cell B21 to next cells in row 21*
- *Formula in cell B23 is = B21+NPV(B22,C21:G21)*

| EXHIBIT 17.11 | THE ZAP SCAN PROJECT'S NET PRESENT VALUE (NPV) FOR THE ZARAGU ALTERNATIVE AS A FUNCTION OF THE PROBABILITY OF THE PROJECT BEING SUBJECTED TO THE "FOREIGN" TAX. |

Probability that the project will be subjected to the "foreign" tax	0%	10%	20%	30%	40%	50%
Project NPV in USD millions	7.814	7.373	6.931	6.489	6.047	5.605

is to changes in the assumptions. For example, scenarios can be developed using percentage deviations from the purchasing power parity combined with different forms of expropriation that can be expected in Zaragu. Only then can a decision be made that fully accounts for the project's risk.

In the relatively simple case of the Zap Scan project, the sensitivity analysis can be aimed at the responsiveness of the project's NPV to changes in the probability of having the project subject to a foreign tax. Repeating the same computations as in Exhibit 17.10, we estimated the project's NPV with a range of probabilities from 0 to 50 percent. The results are reported in Exhibit 17.11.

The probability for which the NPV of the Zaragu project is the same as the NPV of the Swiss project (USD6.071 million) is approximately 40 percent. This probability is twice the expected probability of 20 percent. The difference is large enough to decide that, despite the presence of some country risk, the Zap Scan project should be located in Zaragu rather than in Switzerland.

MANAGING COUNTRY RISK

The previous section analyzed the effect on a cross-border investment's NPV if a foreign tax is imposed on the cash flows expected from the investment. As indicated earlier in the chapter, the possibility of a special tax being levied on foreign investments is only one aspect of the country risk that firms confront when investing abroad. The purpose of country risk management is to limit the exposure of the parent company to these direct or indirect impediments to the transfer of funds from its foreign investments. The following sections discuss a few actions that can help a manager design a proactive strategy for managing country risk.

INVEST IN PROJECTS WITH UNIQUE FEATURES

Projects that depend on input or output markets that are controlled by the parent company are less likely to be expropriated by a local government than projects that use raw materials or sell products and services that are readily available worldwide. Projects that require an expertise unique to the parent company are also less likely to be expropriated. For example, if a plant can be operated only by foreign nationals, the local government may not impose discriminatory regulations on the foreign affiliate for fear of having the plant shut down.

USE LOCAL SOURCING

Buying goods and services locally can reduce country risk because it increases local production and local employment. However, the benefits need to be weighed against the risk of having lower-quality products or services, unreliable delivery schedules, or high local prices.

CHOOSE A LOW-RISK FINANCIAL STRATEGY

Country risk can be substantially reduced if an agency of the host-country government or a powerful international institutional investor is included as a minority shareholder or lender in the cross-border project. The host government is less likely to impose restrictions on dividends or interest payments made by a firm in which either it or an international investor such as the World Bank or the International Finance Corporation is one of the firm's shareholders or bondholders. Furthermore, because dividends to the parent are usually the first remittance from the subsidiary to be limited, blocked, or taxed, it is usually preferable to finance a cross-border investment with as little equity as possible.

DESIGN A REMITTANCE STRATEGY

Dividends or interest payments are not the only way for a parent company to be compensated for its investments in a foreign country. Royalties, management fees, transfer prices, and technical assistance fees are other forms of remittances that can complement financial transfers. Because these transfers of funds are payments for goods and services, they are usually the last on the list of transfer payments to be restricted. However, a manager should not wait for the imposition of controls on dividends or interest payments to set a new funds' transfer policy because the move will undoubtedly be seen by the host government as a means to circumvent the new regulation. Any remittance strategy must be implemented long before the imposition of restrictions on transfer payments.

CONSIDER BUYING INSURANCE AGAINST COUNTRY RISK

In many industrial countries, government-sponsored institutions provide insurance against country risk. Firms should consider buying such insurance for investments made in high-risk countries if alternative measures are difficult or costly to implement. Even if the insurance is not purchased, the insurance premium can be used to estimate the effect of country risk on the NPV of the cross-border investment. If we assume that the insurance policy eliminates the effect of any expropriation of the investment's cash flows, the present value of the insurance premium payments during the useful life of the project represents the amount by which the project's NPV should be reduced to account for country risk. This approach, contrary to sensitivity analysis, does not rely on the subjective assessment of the consequences of the country risk on the project's expected cash flows.

However, the present value of the insurance premium payments may underestimate the true cost of country risk because most insurance policies cover only the accounting value of the cross-border investment, which can be lower than the true value of the damages suffered by the parent company. Also, the insurance is provided by institutions that are generally set up by governments for the purpose of encouraging firms to invest in high-risk countries. Thus, the premium may be somewhat subsidized and be lower than the premium that would have been required by the private insurance market to cover the same level of risk.

KEY POINTS

1. The fundamental principle of financial management still holds in an international environment. Foreign operations must be managed with the objective of creating shareholder value. However, the need to deal with more than one currency raises a number of issues that are specific to the management of foreign operations.

2. A firm is confronted with several risks when operating in a foreign environment. Changes in exchange rates affect the firm's financial statements. To address this accounting, or translation, exposure, regulators have established rules that firms should use to translate the financial statements of a foreign business unit into home currency units. The two most commonly used translation methods are the monetary/nonmonetary method and the all current method.

3. Movements in the exchange rate also affect the value of the cash flows from the foreign business unit, an effect usually called economic exposure. Economic exposure is classified into two categories: (1) contractual, or transaction, exposure, which refers to the effect of exchange-rate volatility on the future cash flows from *past* transactions, and (2) operating exposure, which is also concerned with future cash flows, but from *future* transactions that have not yet occurred. Finally, firms with foreign operations may also be subject to country risk arising from an unstable economic, political, and social environment.

4. Many companies are exposed to the currency risk that arises from unexpected changes in the exchange rate between two currencies. The currencies of various countries are traded in the foreign-exchange market, the world's largest financial market, which is a network of banks, dealers, brokers, and multinational corporations communicating with each other by telephone and through computer terminals. Two basic types of transactions take place in this market, spot and forward transactions. A spot transaction is an agreement to exchange currencies at a rate fixed today, with the delivery taking place usually within two business days. A forward transaction is also an agreement to exchange currencies at a rate fixed today, with the delivery taking place at some specific date several months in the future.

5. Firms have several financial instruments they can use to hedge their exposure to currency risk. These are forward, futures, options, and swaps contracts. The currency forward contract is the most used hedging tool in managing currency risk, followed by the currency option and futures contracts.

6. Differences in expected inflation rates and interest rates between countries are the major factors governing the fluctuations in exchange rates. Three fundamental relations, known as the parity relations, link these variables. The purchasing power parity (PPP) relation links exchange rates and inflation rates. The interest-rate parity (IRP) relation links exchange rates to interest rates. Finally, the forward-spot relation provides the link between the forward exchange rate and the future spot rate.

7. A cross-border investment project, like a domestic one, creates value only if its net present value (NPV) is positive. It is, however, more complicated to estimate the NPV of a foreign investment than that of a domestic one. First, most of the cash flows from an investment in a foreign country are denominated in the foreign currency, and, second, these cash flows may be subject to country risk. To convert cash flows denominated in a foreign currency into cash flows denominated in the domestic currency, we recommend using the PPP relation. The converted cash flows will have some exchange-rate risk attached to them

because of the probability that future exchange rates may differ from those estimated by the parity relation. In principle, the cost of capital needs to be adjusted to account for this extra risk. In practice, however, no adjustment is necessary because most shareholders own diversified portfolios in which the exchange-rate risk has already been eliminated.

8. To account for the effect of country risk on the NPV of a cross-border investment, we recommend adjusting the expected cash flows for the specific actions that the host government may take to reduce the parent company's claims on the project, rather than adding a "fudge" factor to the project's cost of capital. We also recommend that a sensitivity analysis be performed to show how responsive the project's NPV is to different assumptions about the form and extent of possible expropriation measures.

9. Finally, country risk can be managed using techniques and mechanisms that can reduce the parent company's exposure to the expropriation of its foreign investments or to restrictions on the transfer of funds from its foreign subsidiaries.

TRANSLATING FINANCIAL STATEMENTS WITH THE MONETARY/ NONMONETARY METHOD AND THE ALL CURRENT METHOD

THE MONETARY/NONMONETARY METHOD

In the **monetary/nonmonetary method**, monetary assets, such as cash and accounts receivable, and monetary liabilities, such as accounts payable, accrued expenses, and short-term and long-term debts, are translated at the exchange rate prevailing on the date of the balance sheet. The nonmonetary items, such as inventories and fixed assets, are estimated using the rate prevailing at the date they were entered in the balance sheet, that is, the historic rate. The logic of this approach is that monetary assets and monetary liabilities are contracted amounts that would be redeemed at a rate that is likely to be closer to the rate prevailing on the date of the balance sheet than to the historic rate. The average exchange rate of the reporting period is used to translate the income statement accounts, except for those accounts related to the nonmonetary items, such as depreciation expenses, which are translated at the same rate as the corresponding balance sheet item. Any gain or loss from translating balance sheet accounts is reflected in the income statement and, as a result, affects reported earnings.

The top part of Exhibit A17.1.1 shows how the year-end balance sheet accounts of the French subsidiary of Uncle Sam's Bagel are translated into US dollars according to the monetary/nonmonetary method. Two possible values are shown for the exchange rate, USD/EUR 1.24 and USD/EUR 1.26. The dollar values of cash, trade receivables, trade payables, and financial debt are obtained by multiplying their euro value by the year-end exchange rate. The dollar value of inventories and fixed assets is the same regardless of the year-end exchange rate because, as nonmonetary assets, their value is determined by the exchange rate on the date when they were recorded in the balance sheet, not on the date of the balance sheet. The dollar value of the subsidiary's owners' equity, which is the difference between the dollar value of its assets and that of its liabilities, depends on the exchange rate at the end of the year. It will be $50 million if the exchange rate is USD/EUR 1.24 and $45 million if the exchange rate is USD/EUR 1.26. The difference, $5 million, is equal to the difference between the change in the value of the monetary liabilities and the change in the value of the monetary assets ($8 million less $3 million). Note, however, that owners' equity changes in the opposite direction to the change in the exchange rate: it *decreases* when the exchange rate *increases* from USD/EUR 1.24 to USD/EUR 1.26. This is not surprising because, as long as monetary liabilities are larger than monetary assets, an *appreciation* of the foreign currency (the US-dollar cost of €1 increases) will increase the dollar value of the firm's liabilities relative to that of its assets, thus reducing the dollar value of its owners' equity. For most firms, the value of monetary liabilities is greater than the value of monetary assets, so an *appreciation* of the foreign currency will usually result in a *translation loss* when using the monetary/nonmonetary method. A *depreciation* of the foreign currency will result in a *translation gain*.

EXHIBIT A17.1.1	MONETARY/NONMONETARY METHOD[1] APPLIED TO THE BALANCE SHEET OF THE FRENCH SUBSIDIARY OF UNCLE SAM'S BAGEL AT YEAR-END.

FIGURES IN THOUSANDS

		Monetary/Nonmonetary Method		
	Euros (EUR)	US dollars (USD) End-of-year exchange rate USD/EUR 1.24	US dollars (USD) End-of-year exchange rate USD/EUR 1.26	Change
Assets				
Cash	50,000	50,000 × 1.24 = 62,000	50,000 × 1.26 = 63,000	+1,000
Accounts receivable	100,000	100,000 × 1.24 = 124,000	100,000 × 1.26 = 126,000	+2,000
Total monetary assets	150,000	186,000	189,000	+3,000
Inventories	100,000	90,000	90,000	—
Property, plant, and equipment	250,000	270,000	270,000	—
Total nonmonetary assets	350,000	360,000	360,000	—
Total	500,000	546,000	549,000	+3,000
Liabilities and owners' equity				
Short-term debt	75,000	75,000 × 1.24 = 93,000	75,000 × 1.26 = 94,500	+1,500
Accounts payable	75,000	75,000 × 1.24 = 93,000	75,000 × 1.26 = 94,500	+1,500
Long-term debt	250,000	250,000 × 1.24 = 310,000	250,000 × 1.26 = 315,000	+5,000
Total monetary liabilities	400,000	496,000	504,000	+8,000
Owners' equity (Assets − Liabilities)	100,000	50,000	45,000	−5,000
Total	500,000	546,000	549,000	+3,000

[1] In the monetary/nonmonetary method, monetary assets and liabilities are translated at the exchange rate on the date of the balance sheet, and the nonmonetary assets are valued at the rate when they were entered in the balance sheet.

THE ALL CURRENT METHOD

In the **all current method**, known as FASB (Financial Accounting Standards Board) 52, *all* the balance sheet assets and liabilities are translated at the exchange rate on the balance sheet date. The income statement accounts can be translated either at the exchange rate at the date when the revenues and expenses are incurred or at the average exchange rate of the period. To avoid large variations in reported earnings, which may be caused by large fluctuations in the exchange rate, translation gains or losses are reported in a separate equity account of the parent balance sheet. The logic behind the all current method is that it does not distort the structure of the balance sheet as the monetary/nonmonetary method does because all the assets and liabilities are affected proportionally by changes in exchange rates.

Exhibit A17.1.2 shows how the balance sheet accounts of the French subsidiary of Uncle Sam's Bagel are translated according to the all current method using the same data as in Exhibit A17.1.1 in which the monetary/nonmonetary method is applied to these accounts. When the exchange rate increases from USD/EUR 1.24 to USD/EUR 1.26, the dollar value of *all* the French subsidiary's assets and liabilities increases by the same proportion as the exchange rate (1.61 percent). As a result, owners' equity also increases by the same proportion, from $124 million to $126 million. Contrary to the previous method, the all current method always shows a *translation gain* when the foreign currency *appreciates* and a *translation loss* when the foreign currency *depreciates*.

EXHIBIT A17.1.2	ALL CURRENT TRANSLATION METHOD[1] APPLIED TO THE BALANCE SHEET OF THE FRENCH SUBSIDIARY OF UNCLE SAM'S BAGEL AT YEAR-END.

FIGURES IN THOUSANDS

		All Current Method		
		US dollars (USD) End-of-year exchange rate		
	Euros (EUR)	USD/EUR 1.24	USD/EUR 1.26	Change
Assets				
Cash	50,000	50,000 × 1.24 = 62,000	50,000 × 1.26 = 63,000	+1,000
Accounts receivable	100,000	100,000 × 1.24 = 124,000	100,000 × 1.26 – 126,000	+2,000
Inventories	100,000	100,000 × 1.24 = 124,000	100,000 × 1.26 = 126,000	+2,000
Property, plant, and equipment	250,000	250,000 × 1.24 = 310,000	250,000 × 1.26 = 315,000	+5,000
Total	500,000	620,000	630,000	+10,000
Liabilities and owners' equity				
Short-term debt	75,000	75,000 × 1.24 – 93,000	75,000 × 1.26 = 94,500	+1,500
Accounts payable	75,000	75,000 × 1.24 = 93,000	75,000 × 1.26 = 94,500	+1,500
Long-term debt	250,000	250,000 × 1.24 = 310,000	250,000 × 1.26 = 315,000	+5,000
Total monetary liabilities	*400,000*	*496,000*	*504,000*	*+8,000*
Owners' equity (Assets − Liabilities)	100,000	124,000	126,000	+2,000
Total	500,000	620,000	630,000	+10,000

[1] In the all current method, all assets and all liabilities are translated at the exchange rate on the date of the balance sheet.

WHICH METHOD IS BETTER?

The difference between the monetary/nonmonetary method and the all current method comes from a different valuation of the nonmonetary assets. The first method values them at the historic exchange rate and the second at the current exchange rate. Which is the right approach? Neither approach is right because managing for value creation implies that the relevant value of a firm's assets is their *market* value, not their accounting value.

Which method do most companies use? Most companies use the all current rate method, simply because it is recommended by most accounting regulatory bodies worldwide. We believe that regulators favor the all current method because it is easier to understand and easier to apply. Most managers prefer the all current method because of the difference in the treatment of gains and losses from translation adjustments: the monetary/nonmonetary method includes them in the computation of reported income, but the all current method does not. Because managers' performance is often based on accounting figures, it may make sense to account for the effect of changes in exchange rates (over which managers have little control) separately from other sources of gain or loss.

The Parity Relations

THE LAW OF ONE PRICE

Suppose there are no transaction costs (such as transportation costs or taxes) when buying gold in one country, say the United States, and selling it in another, say France. Also, assume the following:

1. The current spot rate is USD/EUR 1.25 ($1.25 per €1)
2. Gold can be bought for $800 an ounce in New York
3. Gold can be sold at €644 an ounce in Paris

At USD/EUR 1.25, the price of gold in euros in New York is €640 ($800 divided by 1.25). Under these conditions, buying gold in New York at €640 (where it is relatively cheaper) and selling it in Paris for €644 (where it is relatively more expensive) provides a €4 riskless profit. A trader can buy one ounce of gold in New York at $800, send it to Paris, and sell it there for €644. The €644 can be exchanged for $805 (€644 multiplied by USD/EUR 1.25) for a net profit of $5 ($805 less $800).

As you have guessed, the possibility of making such a riskless arbitrage profit will not remain unnoticed for long. Arbitrageurs will act and their actions will quickly move prices and exchange rates until the price of gold in New York and Paris is the same whether the currency is denominated in the US dollar or euro.

Extending this market mechanism to any traded good, we obtain the **law of one price (LOP)**, according to which any traded good will sell for the same price regardless of the country where it is sold. The LOP can be written as follows:

$$P_h = P_f \times S_{h/f}^0$$

where P_h is the price of a good in the home country (the price of gold in the United States in our case), P_f is the price of the same good in a foreign country (the price of gold in France), and $S_{h/f}^0$ is the current exchange rate expressed in the number of units of the home currency needed to buy one unit of the foreign currency ($1.25 to buy €1 in our case). Applied to the case of gold, we have $P_h = €644 \times$ USD/EUR 1.25 = $805.

For the LOP to be true, some assumptions are necessary. For example, transaction costs must be zero, tax systems must be identical all over the world, and regulations (both real and hidden) must not prevent cross-country exchanges. The real world of international trade does not operate in such a frictionless fashion. In the case of the gold example, if these costs are at least $5, arbitrage would be a worthless activity.

THE PURCHASING POWER PARITY RELATION

The purchasing power parity (PPP) relation is a version of the LOP with less stringent assumptions. It says that the general cost of living should be the same across countries, not the cost of any individual good as the LOP requires. Suppose the USD/EUR exchange rate is 1.25 ($1.25 per €1) and the inflation rate next year is expected to be 2 percent in the United States and 4 percent in France. A basket of goods that currently costs $1.25 in the United States will cost $1.275 next year [$1.25 × (1 + 2 percent)], and a similar basket of goods that currently costs €1 in France will cost €1.04 next year. The PPP relation implies that the spot rate must change so that next year $1 exchanged into euros would still buy the same basket of goods. In other words, according to the PPP relation, the spot rate expected to prevail next year must be USD/EUR 1.275 divided by €1.04 or USD/EUR 1.226.

According to the PPP relation, we can write the following:

$$E(S^1_{h/f}) = S^0_{h/f} \times \frac{1 + E(i_h)}{1 + E(i_f)}$$

where $E(S^1_{h/f})$ is the expected exchange rate in one year's time, measured as the number of units of the home currency needed to buy one unit of the foreign currency; $S^0_{h/f}$ is the current exchange rate; and $E(i_h)$ and $E(i_f)$ are the expected inflation rates for next year at home and in the foreign country, respectively. This is equation 17.1 in the chapter.

Dividing both sides of the equation by $S^0_{h/f}$, we get the following:

$$\frac{E(S^1_{h/f})}{S^0_{h/f}} = \frac{1 + E(i_h)}{1 + E(i_f)}$$

Subtracting 1 from both sides of this equation gives the following:

$$\frac{E(S^1_{h/f})}{S^0_{h/f}} - 1 = \frac{1 + E(i_h)}{1 + E(i_f)} - 1$$

or

$$\frac{E(S^1_{h/f}) - S^0_{h/f}}{S^0_{h/f}} = \frac{E(i_h) - E(i_f)}{1 + E(i_f)}$$

When the expected inflation rate in the country is small enough, the term $1 + E(i_f)$ is not significantly different from 1, yielding the simpler version of the PPP in equation 17.2:

$$\frac{E(S^1_{h/f}) - S^0_{h/f}}{S^0_{h/f}} = E(i_h) - E(i_f)$$

THE INTERNATIONAL FISHER EFFECT

Real and nominal interest rates are related through equation 17.3 in the chapter, also known as the Fisher effect. This equation is as follows:

$$1 + r = (1 + r_r) \times (1 + E(i))$$

where r is the nominal interest rate, r_r is the real interest rate, and $E(i)$ is the expected inflation rate. We can rearrange the terms of the equation to express the real rate of interest (r_r) as a function of the nominal rate of interest (r) and the expected inflation rate, $E(i)$:

$$1 + r_r = \frac{1 + r}{1 + E(i)}$$

or

$$r_r = \frac{1 + r}{1 + E(i)} - 1$$

If real interest rates are different from one country to another, capital will flow from the countries with the lowest rate to the countries with the highest rate until rates are equalized. In equilibrium, when the real interest rates are the same in all countries, the right side of the above equation must be the same in all countries, in particular in the home country and in the foreign country. Thus, if r_h and r_f are the nominal interest rates in the home and foreign countries and $E(i_h)$ and $E(i_f)$ are the expected inflation rates in the home and foreign countries, we must have the following:

$$\frac{1 + r_h}{1 + E(i_h)} = \frac{1 + r_f}{1 + E(i_f)}$$

or

$$\frac{1 + r_h}{1 + r_f} = \frac{1 + E(i_h)}{1 + E(i_f)}$$

This is equation 17.6. As indicated earlier, a reasonable approximation of that equation is as follows:

$$r_h - r_f = E(i_h) - E(i_f)$$

which is equation 17.7. The relation between interest rates and expected inflation rates as expressed by equation 17.6 or 17.7 is known as the international Fisher effect.

THE INTEREST-RATE PARITY RELATION

Suppose you have $1 million to invest and you observe the following data for the euro and the US dollar:

- Spot exchange rate: USD/EUR 1.25
- 12-month forward rate: USD/EUR 1.27
- 1-year euro interest rate: 5 percent
- 1-year US-dollar interest rate: 6 percent

STRATEGY 1: INVESTMENT IN US DOLLARS

It appears that you will be better off next year if you invest in US dollars rather than euros because 6 percent is higher than 5 percent. Is this assumption warranted? No, because you cannot compare two interest rates expressed in different currencies. The correct comparison should be between the two investments *expressed in the same currency*. To invest in euros, you will have to change your dollars into euros and, after cashing your investment in one year, convert the euros you receive back into dollars.

EXHIBIT A17.2.1	INVESTING IN USD VERSUS INVESTING IN EUR.

Strategy 1: Invest in Dollars ($)	Strategy 2: Invest in Euros (€)
Now:	*Now:*
Invest $1,000,000 at 6 percent	1. Convert $1,000,000 at the current spot rate: $$\frac{\text{USD } 1,000,000}{\text{USD/EUR } 1.25} = €800,000$$ 2. Invest €800,000 at 5 percent. 3. Sell forward €800,000 × (1 + 0.05) = €840,000 at USD/EUR 1.27
In one year:	*In one year:*
Cash in your dollar investment. You get $1,000,000 × (1 + 0.06) = $1,060,000	1. Cash in your euro investment. You get €800,000 × (1 + 0.05) = €840,000 2. Settle your forward contract and deliver €840,000. In exchange, you receive: €840,000 × USD/EUR 1.27 = $1,066,800
$1,060,000	**$1,066,800**

By selling these euros forward, you will know precisely the dollar amount you will get in one year. If the forward rate is advantageous, it may compensate for a lower interest rate. The two investment strategies are shown in Exhibit A17.2.1.

STRATEGY 2: INVESTMENT IN EUROS

Investment in euros produces $6,800 more than investment in US dollars. The gain from buying spot euros at USD/EUR 1.25 and selling them forward at USD/EUR 1.27 is higher than the 1 percent interest rate foregone from lending at 5 percent instead of 6 percent. To earn the extra $6,800, you do not need to own $1 million. You can just borrow this amount at 6 percent, implement strategy 2, and repay your debt (interest included) in one year. You will still earn a riskless net profit of $6,800. In the competitive world of the foreign-exchange market, such "free lunches" will be short-lived. Interbank traders, acting as arbitrageurs, are quick to identify possible **arbitrage transactions** and immediately trade to benefit from them. In the above example, their actions will result in a higher interest-rate differential and a lower spread between spot and forward exchange rates. The process, which is almost instantaneous, will end when the outcomes of strategies 1 and 2 are identical. How do these arbitrage transactions affect the spot exchange rate, the forward exchange rate, and the interest rates?

Looking again at the two investment strategies, let r_h and r_f be the nominal rates of interest in the home country and the foreign country, respectively. With strategy 1, for one unit of the home currency invested, you will receive $(1 + r_h)$ in home currency a year later. With strategy 2, you will first have to exchange one unit of the home currency for $1/S_{h/f}^0$ units of the currency, where $S_{h/f}^0$ is the spot exchange rate (in units of home currency per unit of foreign currency). One year later, you will receive $(1/S_{h/f}^0) \times (1 + r_f)$ units of foreign currency that will be converted into $[(1/S_{h/f}^0) \times (1 + r_f)] \times F_{h/f}^0$ units of home currency, where $F^0_{h/f}$ is the forward rate (in units of home currency per unit of foreign currency). If the net outcomes of the two strategies are the same, we can write the following:

$$1 + r_h = \frac{1 + r_f}{S^0_{h/f}} F^0_{h/f}$$

The terms in the equation can be rearranged to obtain the following:

$$\frac{F^0_{h/f}}{S^0_{h/f}} = \frac{1 + r_h}{1 + r_f}$$

Subtracting 1 from both sides of the equation gives the following:

$$\frac{F^0_{h/f}}{S^0_{h/f}} - 1 = \frac{1 + r_h}{1 + r_f} - 1$$

or

$$\frac{F^0_{h/f} - S^0_{h/f}}{S^0_{h/f}} = \frac{r_h - r_f}{1 + r_f}$$

The above equation is equation 17.8. It is called the interest-rate parity (IRP) relation. This relation is better known under its following simplified version, which assumes that r_f is small compared with 1:

$$\frac{F^0_{h/f} - S^0_{h/f}}{S^0_{h/f}} = r_h - r_f$$

which is equation 17.9. It says that the percentage difference between the forward and the spot rates is equal to the difference in interest rates.

FURTHER READING

1. Laurent L. Jacque. *International Corporate Finance*. Wiley, 2014. See chapters 17 and 20.
2. Koller, Tim, Marc Goedhart, and David Wessels, *Valuation, Measuring and Managing the Value of Companies*, 6th ed., John Wiley & Sons, Inc., 2015, chapter 23.
3. Bekaert, Geert, Campbell Harvey, Christian Lundblad, and Stephan Siegel "Political Risk and International Valuation." *Journal of Corporate Finance*, Vol. 37, April 2016, 1–23.

SELF-TEST QUESTIONS

17.1   Accounting versus economic exposure.
What is the difference between accounting, translation, economic, transaction, contractual, and operating exposure? Why is economic exposure more relevant than accounting exposure to shareholders?

17.2   Comparing alternative hedging techniques.
Briefly describe how to hedge contractual exposure with forward, futures, option, and swap contracts. What are the main advantages and disadvantages of these four hedging techniques?

17.3   Parity relations.
Indicate in one sentence what the purchasing power parity relation says.

17.4   Country risk and the cost of capital.
The best way to account for country risk is to add a risk premium to the project cost of capital. True or false?

17.5   International capital budgeting.
A leading US sports equipment company is considering setting up a sports shoe manufacturing plant in Thailand. The investment will require an initial capital of 50 million Thai baht (THB). The investment life is five years. Based on the information provided below, should the company set up the manufacturing plant in Thailand?

1. Sales, currently at THB 20 million, will grow at the annual rate of 5 percent over the next five years
2. Earnings before interest and tax, currently at THB 18 million, will grow at the same rate as sales
3. The inflation rate in Thailand is 3 percent, and it is 4 percent in the United States. These rates are expected to remain constant during the next five years
4. The corporate tax rate in Thailand is 35 percent
5. Annual capital expenditure is equal to annual depreciation expense
6. Working capital requirement equals 10 percent of sales
7. The terminal value of the plant at the end of the fifth year is expected to be THB 15 million
8. Spot exchange rate is THB 40 per USD 1
9. The company cost of capital is 12 percent

REVIEW QUESTIONS

1. **Exposure.**
A US-based multinational corporation has a wholly owned subsidiary in the Philippines that manufactures electronics products to be sold in the North American market. The equity of the Philippines subsidiary is 2,500 million Philippine peso (PHP) (from the latest balance sheet data). Because of recent political uncertainties in the Philippines, the multinational's head office in San Jose, California, is concerned that the peso could depreciate by as much as 20 percent against the dollar from its present level of 50 pesos per $1. The chief executive officer (CEO) believes that this exposure should be hedged with a forward contract. The 3-month forward exchange rate is PHP 53 per $1. The US company uses the all current method (Financial Accounting Standards Board [FASB] 52) to translate foreign currency financial statements into dollars.

   Do you agree with the CEO? What are the arguments for and against hedging this exposure? For simplicity, assume that the subsidiary does not pay any tax.

2. **Hedging imports with forwards, futures, and options.**
MPC imports computer equipment from Japan for sale in the US market. Monthly imports have averaged ¥250 million to ¥275 million over the past year. A similar volume is expected for the coming year. Because of the volatility of the exchange rate between the Japanese yen and the US dollar, MPC's management believes that it must hedge these imports. Using the "typical" exposure of ¥250 million for a 90-day

period, how should the company manage its current position? Current market data for various instruments appear as follows:

- Spot JPY/USD = 108.09
- 90-day forward JPY/USD = 106.42
- September futures = $0.95 per ¥100 (¥12.5 million per contract); delivery date: September 17
- 90-day yen call over-the-counter (OTC) option = $0.021 per ¥100 (¥108/$1 strike price)

3. **Currency risk management.**
   Charles has a problem. His boss thinks that options are a form of gambling. The company he works for exports to European markets, which require euro invoicing. The market is cut-throat, and sales are made on the basis of competitive bidding. The average size bid is €2.5 million. Firm offers (which means that if the bid is accepted, the company must deliver) are made each month. Normally, winning bids are announced one month after the offer is made. Delivery is made one month after acceptance of the offer. Payment terms are one month after shipment. This means that payment on successful bids normally is 90 days after the bid is submitted. The company's experience has been that two out of three bids are successful.

   Charles recommended that the company buy 1-month or 3-month put options on the euro from its bank at the time a bid was made. However, his boss thought they should sell euros forward to hedge the exposure. Besides taking the view that options are speculative, Charles's boss disliked the idea of paying up front for something they might never need. Finally, he considered them much more expensive than a forward contract. The current spot rate is $0.8870 per €1. The 3-month forward rate is $0.8855 per €1. A 1-month put option on the euro with the strike price set at $0.8850 would cost $0.0095 per €1; a 3-month put option on the euro with a strike price set at $0.8850 per €1 would cost $0.0210 per €1.

   Using the average-size bid of €2.5 million to illustrate, how should Charles's company hedge its euro risk? Prepare some arguments to support his recommendation, unless you believe him to be mistaken. In the latter case, indicate why.

4. **Parity relations.**
   Indicate in one sentence what the following parity relation says:
   a. Purchasing power parity relation
   b. International Fisher effect
   c. Interest-rate parity relation
   d. The relation between forward rates and future spot rate

5. **Interest-rate parity relation.**
   As a trader, you can trade based on the following data:
   1. Spot rate: $S^0_{USD/EUR} = 1.250$
   2. Forward rate: $F^0_{USD/EUR} = 1.248$
   3. US 1-year deposit rate: $r_{USD} = 3$ percent
   4. Eurozone 1-year deposit rate: $r_{EUR} = 3.15$ percent

   a. What is the return on one US-dollar deposit?
   b. What is the return in US dollars on a dollar-covered euro lending?
   c. Can the given information provide an arbitrage opportunity?

6. **The purchasing power parity relation.**

   a. The finance manager of a US pharmaceutical company has $10 million to invest for six months. The annual interest rate in the United States is 3 percent. The annual interest rate in the United Kingdom is 1 percent. The spot rate of exchange is $1.60 per £1 and the 6-month forward rate is $1.65 per £1. In which country would the finance manager want to invest the money? (You can ignore transaction costs.)

   b. The spot rate between the US dollar and the pound sterling is $1.70 per £1. If the interest rate in the United States is 4 percent and 2 percent in the United Kingdom, what would you expect the 1-year forward rate to be if no immediate arbitrage opportunities existed?

7. **Arbitrage activity.**
   You are a currency arbitrager for a Japanese bank. The spot rate this morning is JPY/USD 111.22, and early indications are that short-term interest rates in the United States (90-day rates) are about to rise from their current level of 3.125 percent. The Federal Reserve is worried about rising inflation and has announced that it is considering increasing short-term interest rates by 25 basis points (0.25 percent). The 90-day forward rates quoted this morning to you by local banks are all about the same, JPY/USD 111.14. The current 90-day yen deposit rate of interest is 2.156 percent. You have ¥250 million to invest.

   a. How can you make a profit through an interest arbitrage transaction as described in Appendix 17.2? How much profit in yen can you hope to make in 90 days, given the above data?

   b. If future spot exchange rates are determined by interest-rate differentials (that is, if the forward rate provided a good forecast of future spot rates), what would you expect the spot rate to be in 90 days if the Federal Reserve were to increase interest rates by 25 basis points?

8. **International capital budgeting (1).**
   The Brankton Company, a US firm, considers investing in Spain. The investment will cost €125 million and is expected to generate, after taxes, €30 million a year during the next five years in real terms, that is, before inflation. The project would be liquidated at the end of the fifth year, and its terminal value is estimated at €30 million. The annual rate of inflation is expected to be 3 percent in the Eurozone and 4 percent in the United States. The cost of capital used by Brankton for its investments in the Eurozone is 7 percent above the yield on government bonds. Currently, the rate on US government bonds is 5 percent and the exchange rate is EUR/USD 0.80. Calculate the net present value of the project in US dollars.

9. **International capital budgeting (2).**
   Chateau Cheval Noir is one of the leading premium wine producers of France, with its 50-acre vineyard at St. Julien in the Bordeaux region. The owners have wanted to expand their production, but the scarcity and astronomical prices asked for vineyards adjacent to the existing property have led them to explore the possibility of buying a top winery outside of France. They identified both Australia and California as regions that could produce wines of a quality approaching those from their own vineyards. During a trip to the Barossa Valley of South Australia, the owners found an 80-acre vineyard that promised to meet all of their requirements: soil, exposure, microclimate, age and condition of the vines, condition of the wine-making facilities, and brand

image. After a preliminary study, the French owners estimate that the Australian vineyard would have the following attributes:

1. Annual sales of A$16 million, in real terms
2. Earnings before interest and tax of A$14 million, in real terms
3. Annual capital expenditure is equal to annual depreciation expense
4. Working capital requirement equal to 10 percent of sales
5. The economic life of the vineyard, for the purposes of the analysis, is five years
6. The value in Australian dollars of the vineyard at the end of five years is estimated as a growing annuity based on the level of cash flow after tax attained in the following year. No growth in real terms is expected after the end of the economic life of the project

Other available information relevant to the investment:

1. Annual expected inflation rates: Australia, 5 percent; Eurozone, 2 percent
2. Spot rate: A$1.75 per €1
3. Required rate of return on investment: 10 percent in euros and 12 percent in Australian dollars
4. Corporate tax rate in Australia: 30 percent; no additional taxes would be paid in France on repatriated income
5. Risk-free rate in euros: 5.5 percent
6. Country risk (penalty taxes imposed by Australia): very low to none

    a. What would be the maximum price in Australian dollars and in euros that the owners of Chateau Cheval Noir could pay for the Australian vineyard?
    b. Why is there a higher discount rate in Australian dollars than in euros?

10. **International capital budgeting (3).**
    A major US clothes manufacturing and distributing company plans to expand in Asia. To reduce its transportation costs, it wants to set up its own manufacturing plant in Asia. Two countries are under consideration: China and Indonesia. The expected cash flows from the manufacturing plants in the two countries are as follows:

	Now	Year 1	Year 2	Year 3	Year 4	Year 5
Plant in China (millions of yuan)	−14	3	3	5	6	6
Plant in Indonesia (millions of rupiah)	−20,000	5,000	5,000	6,000	7,000	7,000

a. In which country should the US company invest? The spot rate for Chinese yuans and Indonesian rupiahs are CNY6.82 per USD1 and IRR9,699.78 per USD1, respectively. The inflation rate in China and the United States is expected to be 4 percent and in Indonesia 6 percent during the next five years. The cost of capital of the US company is 10 percent.
b. Suppose that the net present values of both projects are positive and equal. What are other possible factors that could help the US company make a choice between the two projects?

MANAGING FOR VALUE CREATION

CHAPTER **18**

Managing for value creation is more than a business slogan. It is a comprehensive approach to management based on the principle that managers at all levels of the organization must manage their firm's resources with the ultimate objective of increasing the firm's market value. Managing with the goal of creating value provides the basis for a comprehensive and integrated *valued-based management system* that helps managers formulate relevant business plans, make sound business decisions, evaluate actual business performance, and design effective management compensation packages.

This chapter reviews the financial principles underlying a value-based management system, examines the advantages and implications of this approach to management, and explains how the system can be implemented. We first show how to measure the value that a firm has created or destroyed. We then identify the key factors that drive the process of value creation and show how firms can align the interests of managers with those of owners by tying managers' performance and reward to these drivers of value creation. Finally, we summarize the value-based management approach using a framework we call the *financial strategy matrix*. This matrix is a convenient business diagnostic tool that can be used to make value-based strategic and financing decisions and to evaluate the resulting performance.

Managing to create value for the firm's owners is not incompatible with a dedicated workforce, a loyal customer base, and a cooperative group of suppliers. Increasing a firm's market value does not mean creating wealth for the firm's owners at the expense of employees, customers, or suppliers. On the contrary, no firm can expect to generate value for its owners if it does not also provide value to its employees, customers, and suppliers. Motivated employees, satisfied customers, and efficient suppliers are an integral part of a successful recipe for enhancing the firm's value. As mentioned in Chapter 1, companies that achieve the largest increase in their stock market value are also the most admired for their ability to attract and retain better employees and loyal customers. After reading this chapter, you should understand the following:

- The meaning of managing for value creation
- How to measure value creation at the firm level using the concept of market value added (MVA)
- Why maximizing MVA is consistent with maximizing shareholder value
- When and why growth may not lead to value creation

- How to implement a management system based on a value-creation objective
- How to measure a firm's capacity to create value using the concept of economic value added (EVA)
- How to design management compensation schemes that induce managers to make value-creating decisions

MEASURING VALUE CREATION

To find out whether management has created or destroyed value at a particular point in time, we compare the *market value* of the firm's total capital (both equity and debt capital) with the amount of capital that equity holders and debt holders have invested in the firm (this is what we called the firm's **capital employed**). The difference between these amounts is the firm's **market value added** or, simply, **MVA**:

Market value added (MVA) = Market value of capital − Capital employed (18.1)

If MVA is positive, value has been created because the market value of the firm's capital (the market value of its equity and debt) is worth more than the firm's capital employed (the amount of capital that has been invested in the firm). If MVA is negative, then value has been destroyed.

Consider Infosoft, a software company created ten years ago. On December 31, last year, the firm's owners had a cumulative investment of $280 million of equity capital in the firm and debt holders had lent the firm $100 million. The total amount of capital available to Infosoft was thus $380 million. Suppose that the *market* value of that capital (equity plus debt) was $500 million on that date (we show in the next section how to calculate this value). To summarize: at the end of last year, Infosoft employed $380 million of capital whose market value was worth $500 million. Deducting the amount of capital employed ($380 million) from Infosoft's total market value ($500 million) provides a measure of the amount of value Infosoft has created as of December 31, last year:

$$\text{Infosoft's MVA}_{12/31/\text{last year}} = \$500\,\text{million} - \$380\,\text{million} = \$120\,\text{million}$$

MVA is a positive $120 million, indicating that Infosoft has created $120 million of value at the end of last year.

Suppose the market value of Infosoft's equity and debt capital was $300 million instead of $500 million. In this case, Infosoft would have *destroyed* $80 million of value at the end of last year, because the $380 million of capital would be worth only $300 million on that date.

MVA measures value creation or destruction at a *particular point in time*. To measure the value created or destroyed *during a period of time*, look at the *change* in MVA during that period. For example, if Infosoft's MVA was $140 million a year earlier (December 31, two years ago), the firm's management would have destroyed $20 million of value during last year ($120 million less $140 million).

ESTIMATING MARKET VALUE ADDED

To estimate a firm's MVA with equation 18.1, we need to know (1) the market value of the firm's equity and debt capital and (2) the amount of capital that shareholders and debt holders have invested in the firm. We now examine how these numbers can be estimated.

ESTIMATING THE MARKET VALUE OF CAPITAL

The **market value of capital** can be obtained from the financial markets, at least for firms whose equity and debt capital are publicly traded in the form of securities. If the firm is not publicly traded, its market value is unobservable and its MVA cannot be calculated. If someone makes an offer to buy the firm, however, we could then estimate the firm's MVA based on that offer price.

On December 31, last year, Infosoft had debt with a market value of $110 million: long-term bonds with a market value of $50 million and nontraded bank borrowing reported at $60 million in its balance sheet.[1] The firm had 3.9 million shares outstanding that were trading at $100 a share. The market value of its equity (its **market capitalization**) was thus $390 million ($100 multiplied by 3.9 million shares), and the total market value of its capital was $500 million ($110 million of debt plus $390 million of equity). This is the figure we used to estimate Infosoft's MVA at the end of last year.

ESTIMATING THE AMOUNT OF CAPITAL EMPLOYED

The other input needed to measure a firm's MVA is the estimate of the amount of capital employed by the firm. This figure can be extracted from the firm's balance sheet and associated notes. Debt capital includes short-term and long-term borrowings as well as sources of capital that are equivalent to debt obligations – items such as lease obligations and provisions for the retirement and pension plans of employees. Estimating the amount of equity capital is more complicated. We must add to the book value of equity reported in the balance sheet a number of items that standard accounting conventions *exclude* from the figure shown in the balance sheet.

Exhibit 18.1 presents two versions of Infosoft's balance sheets on December 31, two years ago and last year, reported in their managerial format (see Chapter 4). A managerial balance sheet shows the firm's invested capital (cash, working capital requirement,[2] and net fixed assets) and the capital the firm employs (equity plus debt) to fund these investments.

The unadjusted balance sheets report invested capital and capital employed according to standard accounting conventions; the adjusted balance sheets add to invested capital and the book value of equity a number of items that accounting conventions exclude. The amount of debt capital at the end of last year ($100 million) is the same in both types of balance sheets and is equal to the figure we used to estimate Infosoft's MVA.

What items should be added to the book value of equity to get the $280 million of adjusted owners' equity reported in last year's adjusted balance sheet in Exhibit 18.1? These are items – such as **allowance (provision) for bad debt**, the impairment of **goodwill**, and research and development (R&D) expenses – that, according to accounting conventions, are arbitrarily classified as expenses and reported in the income statement as a deduction from revenues. The effect of these deductions is to lower both reported profits and retained earnings. With less earnings retained, the equity account in the balance sheet is *understated*.

---

[1] We assume that the value of the bank debt is equal to its book value, that is, that the interest rates on these loans have not changed since Infosoft borrowed the funds.

[2] Working capital requirement is the difference between the firm's operating assets (Accounts receivable + Inventories + Prepaid expenses) and operating liabilities (Accounts payable + Accrued expenses). See Chapter 4 for details.

EXHIBIT 18.1	INFOSOFT'S MANAGERIAL BALANCE SHEETS ON DECEMBER 31, TWO YEARS AGO AND LAST YEAR.

FIGURES IN MILLIONS

Unadjusted Managerial Balance Sheet		December 31, two years ago		December 31, last year
Invested capital				
Cash			$ 5	$ 10
Working capital requirement[1] (net)			100	100
Gross value		$105		$110
Accumulated bad debt allowance		(5)		(10)
Net fixed assets			185	190
Property, plant, and equipment (net)		95		110
Goodwill[2] (net)		90		80
Total			$290	$300
Capital employed				
Short-term debt			$ 40	$ 20
Long-term financing			40	40
Lease obligations			40	40
Owners' equity			170	200
Total			$290	$300

Adjusted Managerial Balance Sheet		December 31, two years ago		December 31, last year
Invested capital				
Cash			$ 5	$ 10
Gross working capital requirement[1]			105	110
Net fixed assets			235	260
Property, plant, and equipment (net)		$ 95		$110
Gross goodwill		100		100
Capitalized R&D		40		50
Total			$345	$380
Capital employed				
Total debt capital			$120	$100
Short-term debt		$ 40		$ 20
Long-term financing		40		40
Lease obligations		40		40
Adjusted owners' equity			225	280
Book value of equity		170		200
Accumulated bad debt allowance		5		10
Accumulated goodwill impairment		10		20
Capitalized R&D		40		50
Total			$345	$380

[1] WCR = (Accounts receivable + Inventories + Prepaid expenses) − (Accounts payable + Accrued expenses).
[2] Gross value was $100 million at year-end two years ago and year-end last year.

Invested capital in last year's unadjusted balance sheet includes $10 million of accumulated bad debt allowance and $20 million of accumulated goodwill impairment. These two items, as well as $50 million of R&D expenses, are added to the $200 million of unadjusted book value of equity last year to obtain the $280 million figure shown in last year's adjusted balance sheet.

Appendix 18.1 shows why and how these adjustments are made. Notice that their effects on the magnitude of Infosoft's MVA are significant. Ignoring them would overstate Infosoft's MVA by $80 million.

Interpreting Market Value Added

We can make several noteworthy observations about the definition and interpretation of value creation given by equation 18.1. We examine the most significant ones in this section.

Maximizing MVA is Consistent with Maximizing Shareholder Value

Strictly speaking, shareholder value creation should be measured by the difference between the market value of the firm's *equity* and the amount of *equity* capital shareholders have invested in the firm. The former represents the financial market estimation of shareholders' investment in their firm, and the latter the actual amount of money they invested in it. But MVA in equation 18.1 is the difference between the market value of *total* capital (equity and debt) and *total* capital employed. We can reconcile the two definitions by noting that MVA in equation 18.1 is the sum of (1) an *equity MVA*, defined as the difference between the market value of equity and its adjusted book value, and (2) a *debt MVA*, defined as the difference between the market value of debt and its reported book value. Thus, the definition of MVA in equation 18.1 can be restated as follows:

$$\text{MVA} = \text{Equity MVA} + \text{Debt MVA} \tag{18.2}$$

For Infosoft, equity MVA is $110 million (equity market value of $390 million less adjusted equity capital of $280 million) and debt MVA is $10 million (debt market value of $110 million less debt capital of $100 million). These amounts yield a total MVA of $120 million.

If we assume that debt MVA is different from zero *only because of changes in the level of interest rates*,[3] then, *for a given level of interest rates*, maximizing MVA is equivalent to maximizing shareholder value (equity MVA). The general level of interest rates is determined by macroeconomic variables over which managers have no control, so using MVA as a measure of management performance is problematic. To isolate the change in MVA attributable to management decisions, we should first neutralize the part that is caused by broader market conditions. One corrective measure would be to deduct an estimate of the change in MVA that arises from those broader market conditions.

Maximizing the Market Value of the Firm's Capital does not Necessarily Imply Value Creation

Suppose Infosoft's management retains $15 million of profit and borrows $5 million to invest in a $20 million project. Assume that, as a consequence of the investment decision, Infosoft's market value increases by $16 million (from $500 million to

---

[3] In the case of Infosoft, interest rates have gone down and the market value of its long-term debt has gone up. See Chapter 10 for an explanation of the inverse relationship between changes in interest rates and market values.

$516 million). Can we conclude that Infosoft created $16 million of value? The answer is no. It has actually *destroyed* $4 million of value. To see why, calculate the firm's MVA after the project's announcement. It is $116 million ($516 million of market value less $400 million of capital employed – the original $380 million plus the $20 million investment). MVA is now $4 million less than it was before the project was announced ($116 million versus $120 million). This is because the company invested $20 million in a project that led to an increase in its market value of only $16 million.

Consider another example that shows why managers should maximize MVA rather than market value. Suppose we compare Infosoft's market value with the $1 billion market value of TransTech. Although TransTech's market value is twice that of Infosoft's, we cannot infer that TransTech has created twice as much value as Infosoft. Before we can draw any conclusions, we need to know how much capital TransTech is employing. Its adjusted balance sheet (not provided here) indicates that it employs $940 million of capital. Its MVA is thus $60 million ($1 billion less $940 million), half of Infosoft's $120 million MVA. Although the market value of TransTech is twice that of Infosoft, its management has created half the value of that created by Infosoft.

MVA INCREASES WHEN THE FIRM UNDERTAKES POSITIVE NET PRESENT VALUE PROJECTS

Recall the definition of a project's net present value (NPV) given in Chapter 7. It is the present value of the stream of cash flows the project is expected to generate less the amount of capital spent on it. In the MVA definition given by equation 18.1, capital employed is the same as the total amount of capital the firm has invested in its *past* and *current* investment projects. And the present value of the stream of cash flows these investments are expected to generate in the future is the market value of the firm's capital. MVA is thus the equivalent of the sum of the NPVs of all the projects the firm has undertaken. In other words, *saying that a firm has raised (or reduced) its MVA is the same as saying that it has invested in positive (or negative) NPV projects.* Later in the chapter, we show that the contribution of an investment project to a firm's MVA is indeed equal to the project's NPV.

A LOOK AT THE EVIDENCE

Consider the 500 US companies that constitute the Standard & Poor's stock market index. Exhibit 18.2 shows the ten companies that achieved the highest MVA and the ten companies that produced the lowest MVA based on a 2018 ranking compiled by ISS Corporate Solutions using 2017 data.

The second column provides the *market* value of the total capital (equity and debt) of the companies listed in the first column, and the third column shows the corresponding amount of capital employed (adjusted for accounting distortions). A company's estimated MVA, reported in the last column, is the market value of its capital less its capital employed. When MVA is positive, the company has created value. When it is negative, the company has destroyed value. We can make several noteworthy observations about the companies and their MVA.

First, the top ten companies created $3,896 billion of value in 2017, an amount that exceeds the gross domestic product (GDP) of all countries except that of the United States, China, and Japan.

Second, as pointed out earlier, when we compare two companies, the one with the highest market value of capital is not necessarily the one that has created the most

EXHIBIT 18.2	TOP VALUE CREATORS AND DESTROYERS IN THE UNITED STATES:[1] 2018 RANKING BY MARKET VALUE ADDED (MVA[2]).

THE RANKING IN 2013 IS IN PARENTHESES. VALUE CREATORS HAVE POSITIVE MVA AND VALUE DESTROYERS A NEGATIVE MVA.

FIGURES IN BILLIONS

Top Ten Companies by MVA	Market Value of Capital (1)	Capital Employed (2)	MVA (1) minus (2)
1. Apple Inc. (1)	$933.8	$213.3	$719.5
2. Alphabet Inc.[3] (3)	644.8	90.0	554.8
3. Microsoft Corp. (7)	622.1	79.3	542.8
4. Amazon.com Inc. (11)	600.7	92.2	508.5
5. Facebook Inc. (26)	480.2	46.9	433.3
6. Johnson & Johnson (15)	392.9	142.6	250.3
7. Walmart Inc. (4)	378.9	146.0	232.9
8. Home Depot Inc. (16)	265.6	36.1	229.5
9. Visa Inc. (21)	276.2	51.0	225.2
10. Verizon Communications Inc. (14)	447.1	248.0	199.1

Bottom Ten Companies by MVA	Market Value of Capital (1)	Capital Employed (2)	MVA (1) minus (2)
486. CenturyLink Inc. (324)	$65.6	$74.7	−$9.1
487. Ford Motor Co. (460)	61.5	72.8	−11.3
488. Chesapeake Energy Co. (441)	12.0	25.1	−13.1
489. Marathon Oil Co. (454)	8.8	22.4	−13.6
490. Devon Energy Co. (409)	29.3	45.0	−15.7
491. Freeport-McMoRan Inc. (409)	35.9	52.5	−16.6
492. CBS Co. (476)	34.3	55.2	−20.9
493. American International Group (480)	53.6	82.2	−28.6
494. ConocoPhillips (477)	56.4	89.6	−33.2
495. Apache Co. (468)	15.2	51.8	−36.6

[1] MVA data provided by ISS Corporate Solutions for 495 companies that are included in the Standard & Poor's Composite Index (S&P 500) based on data for fiscal year 2017.
[2] MVA = Market value of capital *less* capital employed.
[3] Alphabet Inc. is Google's parent company.

value. For example, even though Verizon Communications Inc. has a *higher* market capitalization ($447.1 billion) than the four companies listed above it (Visa, Home Depot, Walmart, and Johnson & Johnson), it has created *less* value because its MVA is *lower* than those of these four companies.

Third, MVA measures value creation and destruction in *absolute* terms (a dollar amount), not in *relative* terms (value created or destroyed per dollar of capital employed). To illustrate, compare the performance of Facebook with that of Apple. Apple is the highest absolute value creator with an MVA of $719.5 billion, whereas Facebook is ranked fifth with a lower MVA of $433.3 billion. But if value created is measured *per dollar* of capital employed, Facebook outperformed Apple. It created $9.2 of value per dollar of capital employed ($433.3 billion divided by $46.9 billion) compared to $3.4 for Apple ($719.5 billion divided by $213.3 billion). This occurs because Facebook offers internet-based services whereas Apple manufactures technology hardware: providing internet-based services requires significantly less capital than manufacturing technology hardware.

Fourth, the top ten value creators are in a variety of industries even though the technology sector dominates with Apple, Alphabet (Google), Microsoft, and Facebook. The other companies are in distribution (Amazon, Walmart, and Home Depot), drug manufacturing (Johnson & Johnson), data processing (Visa), and telecommunications (Verizon).

Fifth, although four of the top ten value creators in 2017 were also ranked among the top ten companies five years earlier (see 2013 rank in parentheses), the rankings are not immutable. Some dramatic changes can occur: Apple was ranked 274 in 2004, moving to number 5 in 2009 to finally reaching the top since 2014.

Sixth, value creators and value destroyers can be found in the same industry, no matter how well or how badly the industry is performing. For example, telecommunication companies can be found among the top value creators (Verizon) as well as the bottom value destroyers (CenturyLink). Thus, management's inability to create value cannot be blamed on industry factors alone.

What about non-US companies? The few that would have made the top ten if they were ranked with US companies in 2018 are Tencent Holdings, Alibaba Group, and Nestlé S.A. The first two are Chinese companies in the internet software and services sector, and the third is a Swiss company in the food and beverage sector.

The next section identifies the factors that drive value creation and explains why some companies are value creators and others are value destroyers.

IDENTIFYING THE DRIVERS OF VALUE CREATION

A firm's capacity to create value is essentially driven by a combination of three key factors:

1. The firm's operating profitability, measured by its after-tax **return on invested capital (ROIC)**
2. The firm's cost of capital, measured by its **weighted average cost of capital (WACC)**
3. The firm's ability to grow

The after-tax ROIC is defined here as the firm's **net operating profit after tax (NOPAT)** divided by its invested capital measured at the *beginning* of the accounting period:[4]

$$\text{ROIC} = \frac{\text{EBIT} \times (1 - \text{Tax rate})}{\text{Invested capital}} = \frac{\text{NOPAT}}{\text{Invested capital}}$$

where EBIT is earnings before interest and tax, NOPAT is after-tax EBIT, and invested capital is the sum of cash, WCR, and net fixed assets (see Exhibit 18.1).

---

[4] According to the managerial balance sheet (see Exhibit 18.1), invested capital is the same as capital employed. Thus, return on invested capital (ROIC) is the same as return on capital employed (ROCE). We can use the two ratios interchangeably.

The WACC (see Chapters 1 and 12) is as follows:

$$\text{WACC} = (\text{After-tax cost of debt} \times \text{Percentage of debt capital})$$
$$+ (\text{Cost of equity} \times \text{Percentage of equity capital})$$

To illustrate, we return to the case of Infosoft. Let's assume it earned $64.5 million before interest and tax last year. Its cost of debt is 6.7 percent, its estimated cost of equity is 12 percent (see Chapter 10 for how to estimate the cost of equity), and it is subject to a 36 percent corporate tax rate. Its adjusted invested capital at the beginning of last year (the same as at year-end two years ago) is $345 million, as shown in the adjusted balance sheet in Exhibit 18.1. Based on these figures, Infosoft's after-tax ROIC is as follows:

$$\text{ROIC} = \frac{\$64.5 \text{ million} \times (1 - 0.36)}{\$345 \text{ million}} = \frac{\$41.28 \text{ million}}{\$345 \text{ million}}$$

$$= 11.97\% \text{ rounded up to } 12\%$$

The WACC should be calculated with *market* value weights (see Chapter 12). Recall that the market value of Infosoft's equity is $390 million (3.9 million shares worth $100 a share) and that of its debt is $110 million. Thus, the WACC can be written as follows:

$$\text{WACC} = \left[6.7\% \times (1 - 0.36) \times \frac{\$110 \text{ million}}{\$500 \text{ million}} \right] + \left[12\% \times \frac{\$390 \text{ million}}{\$500 \text{ million}} \right]$$

$$\text{WACC} = [4.29\% \times 0.22] + [12\% \times 0.78] = 10.3\%$$

Let's see how we can link a firm's capacity to create value to these two rates (ROIC and WACC) and to the firm's rate of growth.

LINKING VALUE CREATION TO OPERATING PROFITABILITY, THE COST OF CAPITAL, AND GROWTH OPPORTUNITIES

To help us understand how ROIC, WACC, and the expected rate of growth interact to create value, we examine the particular case – without any loss of generality – of a firm that is expected to grow *forever* at a *constant* annual rate. Appendix 18.2 shows that in this case the firm's MVA is given by the following valuation formula:

$$\text{Market value added} = \frac{(\text{ROIC} - \text{WACC}) \times \text{Invested capital}}{\text{WACC} - \text{Growth rate}} \tag{18.3}$$

The following sections discuss two important and general conclusions that can be drawn from equation 18.3.

TO CREATE VALUE, EXPECTED ROIC MUST EXCEED THE FIRM'S WACC

The valuation formula (equation 18.3) indicates that a firm creates value only if the return it *expects* to earn on its invested capital (ROIC) is higher than the cost of financing its investments (WACC). As long as the firm's expected ROIC exceeds its estimated WACC, the numerator of the valuation formula is positive and so is its MVA, indicating that the firm creates value. Conversely, if the firm's expected ROIC is lower than its estimated WACC, MVA is negative and the firm destroys value.

As an illustration of this point, consider Infosoft. Infosoft's MVA is $120 million, the difference between its market value of $500 million and its invested capital of $380 million. What is driving Infosoft's capacity to create value? *Simply put, it is the market expectation that InfoSoft's managers will be able to earn a ROIC that exceeds the firm's estimated WACC of 10.3 percent.*[5]

Let's call the difference between **ROIC** and **WACC** the firm's **return spread**:

$$\text{Return spread} = \text{ROIC} - \text{WACC} \qquad (18.4)$$

We can now restate the condition for value creation as follows: *positive expected return spreads are the source of value creation, and negative expected return spreads are the source of value destruction.* When the return spread is zero, the firm neither creates nor destroys value. This does not mean that the firm is unable to remunerate its suppliers of capital. When the return spread is zero, ROIC is equal to the WACC, which means that the firm generates enough profit from operations to provide debt holders and equity holders with the exact return they expect and no more. To create value, the firm must deliver to its equity holders *more* than what they expect to receive, which is true only when ROIC exceeds the WACC. It is important to keep in mind that it is the entire *future* stream of *expected* return spreads, and not *past* or *historical* return spreads, that drives the process of value creation or destruction.

Thus, the objective of managers should not be the maximization of their firm's operating profitability (**ROIC**), but rather the maximization of the firm's return spread. This means that rewarding a manager's performance on the basis of ROIC may lead to a behavior that is inconsistent with value creation. For example, suppose one of Infosoft's divisions has an average ROIC of 14 percent and that its manager must decide whether to make a single-year investment whose expected ROIC is 12 percent. The investment's ROIC is expected to exceed the firm's WACC of 10.3 percent, so it should be undertaken. However, the manager whose reward is related to his division's average ROIC may *reject* the investment because accepting the investment would *lower* the division's *average* performance (it has an expected ROIC of 12 percent that is lower than the division's ROIC of 14 percent) and would reduce his remuneration. Designing a reward linked to the *return spread* should avoid this problem.

Do we have any evidence indicating that companies with a ROIC greater (lower) than their WACC are value creators (destroyers)? This question is difficult to answer because a firm's MVA is related to its *future stream* of return spreads, not to its *past* return spreads. Unfortunately, future return spreads are not observable. But we can examine the relationship between a firm's MVA and its most recent ROIC and WACC, reported in Exhibit 18.3. Note that the top ten value creators have a ROIC that exceeds their WACC, while all but one firm (Ford Motor) at the bottom of the exhibit have ROICs that are lower than their WACC. It is also interesting to note that even though Ford Motor is a value destroyer (its MVA is negative), its most recent return spread is positive, indicating that its performance has recently improved but not sufficiently to turn it into a value creator.

---

[5] If we assume that Infosoft's growth rate is constant, perpetual, and equal to 5.4 percent, then, according to equation 18.3, Infosoft's MVA is equal to the following:

$$\text{MVA} = \frac{(0.120 - 0.103) \times \$345\,\text{million}}{0.103 - 0.054} = \frac{\$5.87\,\text{million}}{0.049} = \$120\,\text{million}$$

EXHIBIT 18.3	ECONOMIC VALUE ADDED (EVA) OF TOP VALUE CREATORS AND DESTROYERS IN THE UNITED STATES: 2018 RANKING.[1]

RANKING BY MARKET VALUE ADDED (MVA) AS IN EXHIBIT 18.2. EVA RANKING IS IN PARENTHESES IN THE LAST COLUMN.[2] FIRMS WHOSE RETURN ON CAPITAL IS HIGHER (LOWER) THAN THEIR COST OF CAPITAL HAVE POSITIVE (NEGATIVE) EVAs.
FIGURES IN BILLIONS

Top Ten Companies	Return on Invested Capital	Cost of Capital	EVA[3]
1. Apple Inc.	25.7%	7.5%	+$40.1 (1)
2. Alphabet Inc.	31.1%	8.1%	+20.7 (2)
3. Microsoft Corp.	32.9%	7.4%	+20.2 (3)
4. Amazon.com Inc.	16.5%	6.9%	+6.9 (12)
5. Facebook Inc.	42.1%	8.1%	+14.8 (4)
6. Johnson & Johnson	13.4%	6.0%	+10.2 (6)
7. Walmart Inc.	9.3%	4.9%	+6.4 (15)
8. Home Depot Inc.	27.9%	4.6%	+8.2 (9)
9. Visa Inc.	17.1%	6.0%	+5.7 (24)
10. Verizon Communications Inc.	8.5%	4.4%	+10.0 (7)

Bottom Ten Companies	Return on Invested Capital	Cost of Capital	EVA[3]
486. CenturyLink Inc.	3.4%	5.2%	−$1.0 (468)
487. Ford Motor Co.	9.5%	8.3%	+0.8 (139)
488. Chesapeake Energy Co.	1.9%	6.6%	−1.1 (470)
489. Marathon Oil Co.	1.8%	7.0%	−2.0 (482)
490. Devon Energy Co.	1.7%	7.0%	−2.3 (484)
491. Freeport-McMoRan Inc.	4.4%	7.4%	−1.6 (478)
492. CBS Co.	4.1%	6.5%	−1.3 (473)
493. American International Group	1.5%	6.5%	−4.2 (491)
494. ConocoPhillips	5.7%	7.1%	−1.1 (472)
495. Apache Co.	0.7%	7.3%	−3.4 (490)

[1] EVA data provided by ISS Corporate Solutions for 495 companies that are included in the Standard & Poor's Composite Index (S&P 500) based on data for fiscal year 2017.
[2] The number in parentheses is the company's ranking according to EVA. For example, the three top companies ranked by MVA are also the three top companies ranked by EVA, whereas Amazon is ranked 4 by MVA and 12 by EVA.
[3] EVA = [(Return on invested capital) less (Cost of capital)] × [Average capital employed over the previous four quarters].

ONLY VALUE-CREATING GROWTH MATTERS

Another general implication of the valuation formula (equation 18.3) is that growth alone does not necessarily create value. It is the *sign* of the return spread that drives value creation, *irrespective* of the firm's growth rate. Some high-growth firms are value destroyers, and some low-growth firms are value creators. Only growth that is accompanied by a *positive* return spread can generate value.

EXHIBIT 18.4	COMPARISON OF VALUE CREATION FOR TWO FIRMS WITH DIFFERENT GROWTH RATES.

FIGURES IN MILLIONS

Firm	Expected Growth Rate	Expected ROIC	Estimated WACC	Expected Return Spread	Invested Capital	Market Value Added according to Equation 18.3		Is Value Created?
A	7%	10%	13%	−3%	$100	$\dfrac{-3\% \times \$100}{13\% - 7\%} =$	$\dfrac{-\$3}{0.06} = -\$50$	No
B	4%	13%	10%	+3%	$100	$\dfrac{+3\% \times \$100}{10\% - 4\%} =$	$\dfrac{+\$3}{0.06} = +\$50$	Yes

As an illustration, we compare the performance of firm A with that of firm B, whose characteristics are given in Exhibit 18.4. Both firms have $100 million of invested capital. Firm A is anticipated to grow at 7 percent, has an expected ROIC of 10 percent, and an estimated WACC of 13 percent. Its return spread is negative (−3 percent). According to equation 18.3, the firm has destroyed $50 million of value (see calculations in Exhibit 18.4). Note that it does not matter if firm A grows faster or slower than at 7 percent. It will not create value unless its managers are able to change its negative return spread to positive by raising its expected ROIC above its estimated WACC. Now, consider firm B. It is expected to grow at the slower rate of 4 percent. But its 13 percent anticipated ROIC is higher than its estimated WACC of 10 percent, so firm B has a positive return spread. According to equation 18.3, even though firm B is growing at a slower rate than firm A, it is creating $50 million of value (see calculations in Exhibit 18.4).

LINKING VALUE CREATION TO ITS FUNDAMENTAL DETERMINANTS

We can identify more basic drivers of value creation by breaking down the firm's expected ROIC into its fundamental components (see Chapter 6). Recall that pre-tax ROIC can be broken down into **operating profit margin** (the ratio of EBIT to sales) and **capital turnover** (the ratio of sales to invested capital). Taking the corporate tax into account, we can write *after-tax* ROIC as follows:

$$\text{ROIC} = \frac{\text{EBIT}}{\text{sales}} \times \frac{\text{sales}}{\text{Invested capital}} \times (1 - \text{Tax rate})$$

$$= \text{Operating profit margin} \times \text{Capital turnover} \times (1 - \text{Tax rate})$$

Thus, management can increase the firm's ROIC through a combination of the following actions:

1. *An improvement in operating profit margin*, achieved by generating higher operating profit per dollar of sales.
2. *An increase in capital turnover*, achieved by generating the same or higher sales with less capital (this can be done through faster collection of receivables, speedier inventory turns, and fewer fixed assets while keeping sales the same or, better still, while sales are increasing).
3. *A reduction of the effective tax rate*, achieved, for example, by taking advantage of various tax breaks and subsidies.

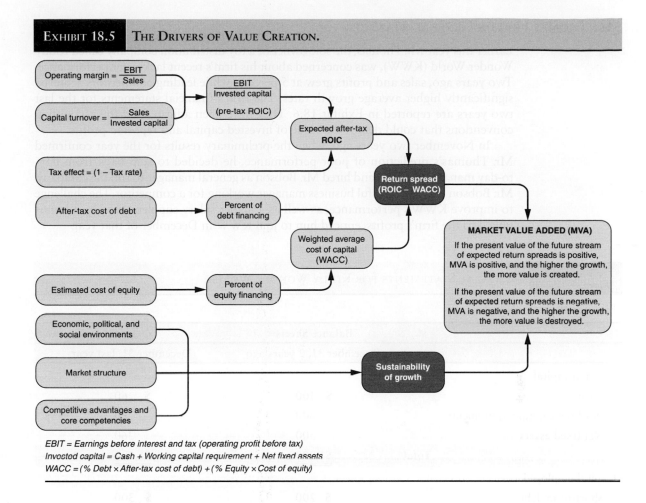

EXHIBIT 18.5   THE DRIVERS OF VALUE CREATION.

$$\text{Operating margin} = \frac{\text{EBIT}}{\text{Sales}}$$

$$\text{Capital turnover} = \frac{\text{Sales}}{\text{Invested capital}}$$

$$\frac{\text{EBIT}}{\text{Invested capital}}$$
(pre-tax ROIC)

Expected after-tax **ROIC**

Tax effect = (1 – Tax rate)

After-tax cost of debt

Percent of debt financing

Return spread (ROIC – WACC)

Weighted average cost of capital (WACC)

Estimated cost of equity

Percent of equity financing

MARKET VALUE ADDED (MVA)

If the present value of the future stream of expected return spreads is positive, MVA is positive, and the higher the growth, the more value is created.

If the present value of the future stream of expected return spreads is negative, MVA is negative, and the higher the growth, the more value is destroyed.

Economic, political, and social environments

Market structure

Competitive advantages and core competencies

Sustainability of growth

EBIT = Earnings before interest and tax (operating profit before tax)
Invested capital = Cash + Working capital requirement + Net fixed assets
WACC = (% Debt × After-tax cost of debt) + (% Equity × Cost of equity)

The various drivers of value creation are summarized in Exhibit 18.5. In addition to the two operating drivers, the exhibit also reports the components of the cost of capital.

Together, they determine the sign and size of the future stream of expected return spreads, which, in turn, determine the firm's MVA. If MVA is positive, the faster the firm grows, the more value it creates. The ability of managers to grow their business over a sustained period of time is driven by the economic, political, and social environments in which the firm evolves; the structure and dynamics of the particular sector in which it operates; and the competitive advantages and core competencies the firm has developed over time.

LINKING OPERATING PERFORMANCE AND REMUNERATION TO VALUE CREATION

In this section, we use a short case study to explain how a manager's operating performance, his remuneration package, and his ability to create value can be linked.

MR. THOMAS HIRES A GENERAL MANAGER

Earlier this year Mr. Thomas, the sole owner of a toy distribution company called Kiddy Wonder World (KWW), was concerned about his firm's recent lackluster performance. Two years ago, sales and profits grew at 5 percent, while leading competitors achieved significantly higher average growth rates. The firm's financial statements for the last two years are reported in Exhibit 18.6. They have been adjusted for the accounting conventions that could distort the value of invested capital and reported profits.

In November two years ago, when the preliminary results for the year confirmed Mr. Thomas's prediction of poor performance, he decided to step back from day-to-day managerial duties and hired Mr. Bobson as general manager to run the company. Mr. Bobson was a successful business manager working for a competitor. The challenge to improve KWW's performance, as well as a higher salary supplemented by a bonus linked to the firm's profits, enticed him to join KWW in December of that year.

EXHIBIT 18.6	FINANCIAL STATEMENTS FOR KIDDY WONDER WORLD.

FIGURES IN MILLIONS

Balance Sheets		
	December 31, 2 years ago	December 31, last year
Invested capital		
Cash	$ 100	$ 60
Working capital requirement[1]	600	780
Net fixed assets	300	360
Total	$1,000	$1,200
Capital employed		
Short-term debt	$ 200	$ 300
Long-term financing	300	300
Owners' equity	500	600
Total	$1,000	$1,200

Income Statements		
	2 years ago	Last year
Sales	$2,000	$2,200
less operating expenses	(1,850)	(2,000)
less depreciation expense	(20)	(50)
Earnings before interest and tax (EBIT)	$ 130	$ 150
less interest expense	(50)	(60)
Earnings before tax (EBT)	$ 80	$ 90
less tax expenses (40% of EBT)	(32)	(36)
Earnings after tax (net profit)	$ 48	$ 54

[1] WCR = (Accounts receivable + Inventories + Prepaid expenses) − (Accounts payable + Accrued expenses).

After getting acquainted with the company's operations, Mr. Bobson submitted his business plan for next year to Mr. Thomas. The plan was based on two major objectives: (1) increase sales by 10 percent through more aggressive marketing of existing products and the introduction of a new line of toys; and (2) tight control of operating expenses to improve operating margin and enhance the firm's profitability. Mr. Thomas approved the plan and gave Mr. Bobson full authority to implement it as he wished.

Early this year, Mr. Thomas received a copy of the company's financial statements for last year, reported in the last column of Exhibit 18.6. Using these figures, Mr. Thomas wanted to assess the effectiveness of his general manager and evaluate his firm's last year performance compared with that of the previous year and against the performance of the leading firms in the sector. He also wondered whether the equity capital he and his family had invested in the company was adequately remunerated for the business and financial risks associated with the toy manufacturing and distribution business. He was recently contacted by a friend with a proposal to invest in an enterprise whose risk profile was similar to that of the toy distribution business and from which he could expect a return of 14 percent.

To carry out his analysis, Mr. Thomas needed financial information about leading firms in the sector. This information, which was provided by a consulting company specializing in the toy manufacturing and distribution business, is reported on the last column of Exhibit 18.7. In addition to information about competitors' performance, Exhibit 18.7 provides figures for KWW's last year performance (which reflect the outcome of Mr. Bobson's decisions) compared with its performance a year earlier (before Mr. Bobson was hired). Based on all this information, Mr. Thomas had to determine whether Mr. Bobson achieved his dual objectives of faster growth in sales and earnings.

Has the General Manager Achieved His Objectives?

Exhibit 18.7 indicates that last year sales grew by 10 percent and earnings grew by 12.5 percent, both exceeding the previous year's results and the corresponding figures for the leading competitors in the sector. Operating expenses grew at a slower rate than sales (8.1 percent versus 10 percent), which explains why net profit grew faster than sales (12.5 percent versus 10 percent). It seems that Mr. Bobson has achieved his two objectives. How did he do it?

A closer look at the figures reported in Exhibit 18.7 reveals another aspect of Mr. Bobson's performance. The company's invested capital grew by 20 percent, much faster than during the previous year (4.2 percent) and much faster than the leading competitors (10 percent). This growth in invested capital was mostly the outcome of a high growth in WCR (30 percent). A consequence of the high growth in WCR is the deterioration of the company's liquidity position. As shown in Exhibit 18.6, this growth, which is largely permanent in nature, was financed through a reduction in cash holding (from $100 million to $60 million) and a 50 percent increase in short-term borrowings (from $200 million to $300 million), resulting in a higher percentage of WCR that is financed with short-term debt, as shown in Exhibit 18.7.[6] Finally, the firm's operating profitability, measured by ROIC, improved slightly from 8 percent to 8.2 percent, but is less than the average of 10 percent achieved by leading competitors. However, the reported improvement in ROIC is explained by the fact that invested capital is measured at its average value. If ROIC was measured with year-end values, it would have indicated a deterioration.

---

[6] Chapter 5 shows that reliance on short-term debt to finance a long-term commitment (such as the permanent increase in WCR) is a sign of a deteriorating liquidity position.

EXHIBIT 18.7	COMPARATIVE PERFORMANCE OF KIDDY WONDER WORLD (KWW).

FIGURES IN MILLIONS

Performance Indicator	KWW Performance Two years ago (Without Mr. Bobson)[1]	KWW Performance Last year (With Mr. Bobson)[2]	Performance of Leading Competitors
Growth in sales			
% change from previous year	5%	10%	9%
Growth in earnings (net profits)			
% change from previous year	5%	12.5%	10%
Growth in operating expenses			
% change from previous year	6%	8.1%	8.8%
Growth in invested capital			
% change from previous year	4.2%	20%	10%
Growth in WCR			
% change from previous year	8%	30%	25%
Liquidity position			
$\dfrac{\text{Short-term borrowing}}{\text{WCR}}$	$\dfrac{\$200}{\$600} = 33.3\%$	$\dfrac{\$300}{\$780} = 38.5\%$	25%
Operating profitability			
ROIC$=\dfrac{\text{After-tax EBIT}}{\text{Average invested capital}}$	$\dfrac{\$130(1-0.40)}{\$980} = 8\%$	$\dfrac{\$150(1-0.40)}{\$1,100} = 8.2\%$	10%

[1] Previous year's figures are not provided. Invested capital was $960 million three years ago.
[2] Percentage changes are calculated with data from the financial statements in Exhibit 18.6.

Mr. Bobson has increased sales and profits, but has he created value? We can find out by looking at the firm's return spread. The firm's latest ROIC is 8.2 percent. To know whether value was created, we compare this return on investment with the average cost of the capital that was required to achieve it. To estimate the firm's WACC, we need to know the proportions of equity and debt financing used to fund the firm's investments, the after-tax cost of debt, and the cost of equity.

The balance sheets in Exhibit 18.6 indicate that KWW's invested capital is financed with an equal amount of equity and debt capital.[7] The company can borrow at an average rate of 6.7 percent and the tax rate is 40 percent. Its average *after-tax* cost of debt is thus 4.02 percent. What is the estimated cost of equity? It is the 14 percent expected return that the firm's owner, Mr. Thomas, could earn if he invested his equity capital in a venture with the same risk profile as KWW.[8] We now have all the required inputs we need to estimate KWW's WACC:

$$\text{WACC} = (4.02\% \times 0.50) + (14\% \times 0.50) = 9.01\% \text{ rounded down to } 9\%$$

[7] Chapter 12 explains that the proportions of equity and debt in the WACC should be estimated from the *market* values of equity and debt. However, KWW is not a traded company, so we used book values as proxies for market values. An alternative would be to use the market value ratios of a similar company.

[8] The cost of equity is, in this case, the owner's opportunity cost of capital. For a more specific estimation of the cost of equity, see Chapter 12.

The firm's WACC of 9 percent is higher than its ROIC of 8.2 percent. The *historical* return spread is thus negative, indicating that the firm is unable to create value at a 9 percent cost of capital even though Mr. Bobson has raised both sales and earnings.[9] Mr. Bobson has invested too much capital at a cost (9 percent) that exceeds the return on that capital (8.2 percent). And, as mentioned earlier, the main reason for the growth of the firm's capital is the growth in the firm's WCR (30 percent higher than the previous year).

Economic Profits versus Accounting Profits

The conclusion from our analysis of KWW is that Mr. Bobson was successful in increasing sales and profits but grew the company's WCR much faster than sales and profits. The result was an operating profitability that fell short of the firm's WACC and an inability to create value. In a way, the growth in WCR has provided the general manager with the resources (inventories and receivables) he needed to achieve his sales and profits objectives. In other words, the growth in WCR is not accidental; it was required to increase sales and profits. One question remains: why is Mr. Bobson pushing sales and boosting profits, and neglecting the management of working capital? Perhaps we should look at the way Mr. Bobson's remuneration package was designed. Recall that Mr. Bobson's compensation includes a bonus related to *profits*. Not surprisingly, profits are up. Because the growth of working capital does not affect his bonus, Mr. Bobson may be overinvesting in working capital to raise profits and increase his bonus.

This behavior could have been prevented if Mr. Bobson had been penalized for his overinvestment in working capital and the increase in the capital required to finance it. One way to penalize Mr. Bobson for his overinvestment in working capital would have been to deduct from his NOPAT a "charge" for the capital he consumed to achieve those profits. This capital charge is determined by multiplying the firm's WACC by the amount of invested capital (cash plus WCR plus net fixed assets). We define **economic profit** or **economic value added (EVA)** as NOPAT less this capital charge:

$$\text{Economic value added (EVA)} = \text{NOPAT} - (\text{WACC} \times \text{Invested capital}) \quad (18.5)$$

where NOPAT is EBIT $\times$ (1 − Tax rate). For KWW, EBIT was $130 million two years ago and $150 million last year. The WACC is 9 percent. Average invested capital was $980 million two years ago and $1,100 million last year (see Exhibit 18.7). Thus, we can write the following:

$$\text{EVA}_{\text{Two years ago}} = [\$130\,\text{million} \times (1 - 0.40)] - [0.09 \times \$980\,\text{million}] = -\$10.2\,\text{million}$$

$$\text{EVA}_{\text{Last year}} = [\$150\,\text{million} \times (1 - 0.40)] - [0.09 \times \$1,100\,\text{million}] = -\$9\,\text{million}$$

Although KWW is "profitable" when profits are measured according to *accounting* conventions (NOPAT and net profit are positive), it is not profitable when performance is measured with *economic* profits (EVA is negative). *Linking Mr. Bobson's performance and bonus to EVA rather than accounting profits would have induced him to pay more attention to the growth of WCR.*

---

[9] We are using the historical return spread to diagnose Mr. Bobson's ability to create value. We know, however, that value creation is determined by the future expected return spreads. The implicit assumption is that future return spreads are unlikely to become positive with the current growth strategy.

There is another way to express the failure of Mr. Bobson's actions to create value. To see this, we factor out the term "invested capital" in the definition of EVA in equation 18.5:

$$EVA = \left(\frac{NOPAT}{\text{Invested capital}} - WACC \right) \times \text{Invested capital}$$

$$EVA = (ROIC - WACC) \times \text{Invested capital} \qquad (18.6)$$

Equation 18.6 clearly shows that a positive return spread implies a positive EVA, which, in turn, implies value creation. Again, Mr. Thomas, KWW's owner, should have linked Mr. Bobson's bonus to EVA rather than to accounting profits. This would have motivated his general manager to pay closer attention to invested capital and to restrict the growth of the firm's assets, particularly the growth of WCR that was used to stimulate the growth in sales. The next section outlines the key features of an EVA-related compensation plan.

Let's return to Exhibit 18.3. The last column of the exhibit shows the EVA for the top value creators and destroyers estimated according to equation 18.6. Note that companies with a positive return spread have a positive EVA, and those with a negative return spread have a negative EVA. As discussed earlier, a positive (negative) *historical* return spread or EVA does not imply that the company is necessarily a value creator (a value destroyer). Recall that it is the magnitude and the sign of the firm's *future* stream of *expected* EVA that determine whether a firm is a value creator or destroyer, not its *past* EVA.

DESIGNING COMPENSATION PLANS THAT INDUCE MANAGERS TO BEHAVE LIKE OWNERS

We have argued throughout this book that value creation should be a manager's ultimate objective. But the KWW case study clearly shows that managers do not always behave according to this principle. The challenge, then, is to create a compensation plan that induces them to make value-creating decisions rather than follow other objectives. One obvious solution is to turn managers into owners by remunerating them with equity ownership as opposed to a share of profits. Owners, however, do not always wish to transfer a significant portion of their equity investment to managers.

A possible alternative is to partly remunerate managers with a bonus linked to their ability to *increase* EVA, as mentioned in the previous section. A higher EVA is the key to value creation. Rewarding managers for their ability to improve EVA should motivate them to take actions consistent with the value-creation objective. For this type of compensation system to be effective, however, a number of conditions must be met.

First, managerial decisions made today (such as capital expenditure decisions) will most likely affect EVA for a number of subsequent years. Thus, the bonus should be related to the manager's ability to generate higher EVA for a period of several years, for example, from three to five years, not just for a single year.

Second, after the compensation plan has been established and accepted, it should not be modified and the reward should not be capped. Exceptional performance should be handsomely rewarded. But poor performance should be penalized. One way to do this is to allow managers to cash in only a *fraction* of their EVA bonus in a given year, say 25 percent, with the balance remaining on "deposit" with the firm. If EVA declines in subsequent years, the "deposit" will be reduced by an amount that is related to the magnitude of the decline in EVA. After three to five years, managers can withdraw the balance in their EVA deposit (assuming it is positive).

Third, to have a significant motivational effect on managers' behavior, the reward related to superior EVA performance must represent a relatively large portion of their total remuneration. For example, a remuneration plan in which EVA-related bonuses consist of 5 percent of total compensation, with the remaining 95 percent in the form of a guaranteed salary, is unlikely to be as effective as one in which EVA-related bonuses represent up to 50 percent of the total.

Fourth, as many managers as possible should be on the EVA-related bonus plan. The point is to focus the entire organization on generating economic profits and value. This objective is difficult to achieve if only a few senior managers are on this type of plan and the rest of the organization is on another type, such as a profit- or sales-related bonus plan, or on no bonus plan at all.

Fifth, if an EVA bonus plan is adopted, the book value of capital and the operating profit used to estimate EVA must be restated to adjust for the distortions caused by accounting conventions, as shown in Appendix 18.1. The adjustments should be limited to a few that are relevant and meaningful to managers. Too many adjustments may unnecessarily complicate a system whose major attraction is its simplicity and ease of understanding.

Finally, an EVA bonus plan must be consistent with the company's capital budgeting process, which is the key to making value-creating investment decisions (see Chapter 7). In other words, inducing managers to maximize EVA over the life of an investment must be consistent with the NPV rule we have advocated when making capital expenditure decisions. We demonstrate in the next section that this is indeed the case.

LINKING THE CAPITAL BUDGETING PROCESS TO VALUE CREATION

Chapter 7 describes how firms should make investment decisions and how they should organize their capital budgeting process. The objective is to make investment decisions that have the potential to increase the firm's market value. In this context, the NPV rule and the internal rate of return (IRR) rule both play a key role. A firm should accept only investment proposals that have a positive NPV or, equivalently, have an IRR higher than the project's WACC. Recall that we can calculate the NPV of an investment proposal by discounting to the present the cash flows the investment is expected to generate in the future and then deducting from that present value the initial cash outlay required to launch the project. Chapter 12 shows that the relevant discount rate needed to find the present value of the expected cash-flow stream is the WACC that reflects the risk of the investment. The investment's IRR is simply the discount rate for which the NPV of the investment is equal to zero.

The NPV rule, which is at the heart of the capital budgeting process, is based on cash flows, but the financial management framework described in this chapter is based on MVA and EVA. Earlier in this chapter, ROIC, WACC, and growth were linked to MVA, and operating performance and remuneration were linked to EVA. We now need to link EVA to MVA and to link the cash-flow-based NPV rule to both EVA and MVA. By connecting the measures of performance that are the concerns of the corporate finance function, we can provide a comprehensive financial management system that integrates the value-creation objective with the firm's value, its operating performance, and its remuneration and incentive plans, as well as its capital budgeting process.

THE PRESENT VALUE OF AN INVESTMENT'S FUTURE EVA IS EQUAL TO ITS MVA

We first examine the link between MVA and EVA. The previous section shows that the correct measure of a manager's ability to create value is the economic profit, or EVA, she is able to generate during a period of time, usually one year. Most managerial decisions, however, generate benefits over a number of years, not immediately. Thus, we need to measure the value *today* of the entire stream of *future* economic profits a business decision is expected to produce, rather than the economic profit generated during a single year. In other words, we need to measure the present value of the entire stream of future expected EVA. This present value is the measure of the potential value the business decision will create. The potential value created by a business decision is the MVA of the decision, which is shown in equation 18.3. The definition of EVA is given in equation 18.6. The numerator of equation 18.3 is the same as the EVA defined in equation 18.6. We can thus write equation 18.3 as follows:

$$MVA = \frac{EVA}{WACC - Growth\ rate} \tag{18.7}$$

where the stream of future EVA is, in this case, expected to grow forever at a constant annual rate. This valuation formula shows that the present value of the future stream of EVA that a business proposal is expected to generate is the MVA of that proposal. In other words, *management should maximize the entire stream of future EVA that their firm's invested capital is expected to generate to maximize their firm's MVA and create shareholder value.*

MAXIMIZING MVA IS THE SAME AS MAXIMIZING NPV

We have just shown that the value-creating manager runs her business with the goal of maximizing its MVA. In Chapter 7, we show that the value-creating manager makes decisions that maximize NPV. We now want to see whether these two decision rules are consistent with each other. We use the example reported in Exhibit 18.8 as an illustration. The exhibit is shown in a spreadsheet format.

The Investment.   A firm is considering investing in a piece of equipment. Data relevant to the investment are presented in the first part of Exhibit 18.8. The equipment, which would cost $1 million to acquire, has an expected useful life of two years and a residual value of zero. The equipment would be depreciated over the next two years, providing equal annual depreciation expense of $500,000. The investment is expected to generate sales of $2 million the first year and $4 million the second year. At the *beginning* of every year, the firm would have to increase its investment in working capital to support the sales that will be generated that year. The ratio of WCR to next year's sales is 10 percent and the ratio of operating expenses (*excluding* depreciation) to sales is 70 percent. The corporate tax rate is 40 percent, and the firm uses a cost of capital (the WACC) of 10 percent for this type of investment.

EXHIBIT 18.8	EQUIVALENCE OF NET PRESENT VALUE MEASURED WITH CASH FLOWS AND NET PRESENT VALUE MEASURED WITH ECONOMIC VALUE ADDED.

FIGURES IN THOUSANDS

	A	B	C	D
		Now	Forecast for	
1		0	Year 1	Year 2
2				
3	**Investment data**			
4	Equipment cost	$1,000		
5	Residual value of equipment			$ 0
6	Depreciation expense		$ 500	500
7	Sales		2,000	4,000
8	Working capital requirement/next year sales	10%	10%	
9	Operating expenses/sales		70%	70%
10	Corporate tax rate		40%	40%
11	Cost of capital	10%		
12	**Expected net operating profit after tax (NOPAT)**			
13	Expected operating profit		$ 100	$ 700
14	Tax on operating profit		40	280
15	Expected net operating profit after tax (NOPAT)		$ 60	$ 420
16	**Expected cash flow from the investment, net present value (NPV), and internal rate of return (IRR)**			
17	Working capital requirement	$ 200	$ 400	$ 0
18	Change in working capital requirement	200	200	–400
19	**Expected cash flow from the investment**	**–$1,200**	**$ 360**	**$1,320**
20	Net present value (NPV)	$ 218		
21	Internal rate of return (IRR)	21%		
22	**Economic value added (EVA) and market value added (MVA)**			
23	Accumulated depreciation of the equipment		$ 500	$1,000
24	Net book value of the equipment	$1,000	500	0
25	Invested capital	1,200	900	0
26	Capital charge		120	90
27	Economic value added (EVA)		–$ 60	$ 330
28	Market value added (MVA)	$ 218		

- *Rows 4 to 11 are data*
- *Formula in cell C13 is = C7*(1–C9)–C6. Then copy formula in cell C13 to next cell in row 13*
- *Formula in cell C14 is = C10*C13. Then copy formula in cell C14 to next cell in row 14*
- *Formula in cell C15 is =C13–C14. Then copy formula in cell C15 to next cells in row 15*
- *Formula in cell B17 is = B8*C7. Then copy formula in cell B17 to next cells in row 17*
- *Formula in cell B18 is = B17. Formula in cell C18 is =C17–B17. Then copy formula in cell C18 to next cell in row 18*
- *Formula in cell B19 is = –B4+B15+B6–B18. Then copy formula in cell B19 to next cells in row 19*
- *Formula in cell B20 is = B19+NPV(B11,C19:D19)*
- *Formula in cell B21 is = IRR(B19:D19)*
- *Formula in cell C23 is = C6. Formula in cell D23 is =C23+D6*
- *Formula in cell B24 is = $B$4–B23. Then copy formula in cell B24 to next cells in row 24*
- *Formula in cell B25 = B24+B17. Then copy formula in cell B25 to next cells in row 25*
- *Formula in cell C26 is = $B$11*B25. Then copy formula in cell C26 to next cell in row 26*
- *Formula in cell C27 is = C15–C26. Then copy formula in cell C27 to next cell in row 27*
- *Formula in cell B28 is = NPV(B11,C27:D27)*

Net Operating Profit After Tax (NOPAT) from the Investment.   Expected net operating profits are shown in part 2 of Exhibit 18.8. Operating profit is 30 percent of sales (because operating expenses are 70 percent of sales) minus any depreciation expense (because they are not included in operating expenses). Taxes are 40 percent of operating profit. The result is a NOPAT of $60,000 at the end of the first year and $420,000 at the end of the second year (row 15).

Cash Flows from the Investment.   Cash flows from the investment are calculated in part 3 of the exhibit. They are equal to the investment's NOPAT plus depreciation expense less net investment. Net investment includes the purchase of the piece of equipment ($1 million) and changes in the WCR over the lifetime of the investment. The firm would have to invest $200,000 of working capital at the investment date (10 percent of year one sales), and another $200,000 a year later, for a total of $400,000 at the end of year two. Note that the $400,000 would be recovered at the end of year two when the investment terminates. This calculation produces an initial cash outflow of $1.2 million to launch the project, followed by net cash inflows of $360,000 at the end of the first year and $1.32 million at the end of the second year (row 19).

Net Present Value and Internal Rate of Return.   Using a cost of capital of 10 percent, the NPV of the expected cash-flow stream from the investment is $218,200 (row 20) and its IRR is 21 percent (row 21). The investment's NPV is positive and its IRR exceeds its WACC. Thus, the investment is a value-creating proposition and should be undertaken.

Economic Value Added and Market Value Added.   The capacity of an investment to create value can also be estimated by calculating its future stream of expected EVA and discounting EVA at the cost of capital (the WACC) to provide the investment's MVA. If MVA is positive, value is created; if it is negative, value is destroyed. The procedure is shown in part 4 of Exhibit 18.8. Expected EVA is computed by deducting from NOPAT a charge for capital equal to 10 percent of the invested capital at the *beginning* of the year. For the first year, NOPAT is $60,000 (row 15), invested capital at the beginning of the year is $1.2 million (row 25), and the charge for capital is $120,000 (row 26). The expected EVA is −$60,000 (row 27). For the second year, NOPAT is $420,000, the capital charge is $90,000, and EVA is $330,000.

The MVA of the investment is equal to the present value of the expected future stream of EVA discounted at the WACC of 10 percent. This MVA, shown in row 28, is equal to $218,200. The MVA is positive, so the investment is a value-creating proposition and should be undertaken *even though the first-year EVA is negative.* Note that the investment's MVA in row 28 is *exactly the same* as its NPV in row 20.

Although the two methods are equivalent, management must be careful when using the MVA approach to value an investment decision, particularly when estimating the charge for capital consumption (invested capital multiplied by the WACC). The relevant figure is the amount of invested capital at the *beginning* of the period, not at the end of the period.

The major advantage of the NPV approach is that it takes into account any nonfinancial transactions related to the project that either reduce or add to the firm's cash holding. Thus, when using the NPV method, managers can ignore the amount of invested capital at the beginning of each period and worry only about the cash flows generated by the project. Recall that the project in Exhibit 18.8 has a *negative* first-year EVA but a *positive* first-year cash flow, an indication that although no value is created in the first year, the investment does generate cash. The major advantage of the MVA approach, of course, is its direct relation to EVA, which is based on *accounting* data with which managers are familiar.

PUTTING IT ALL TOGETHER: THE FINANCIAL STRATEGY MATRIX

Exhibit 18.9 summarizes the key elements of a firm's financial management system and shows their managerial implications within a single framework that we call the firm's **financial strategy matrix**. The firm may have one or several divisions or businesses.

The vertical axis measures the capacity of a particular business to create value. This capacity is indicated by the sign and magnitude of the firm's return spread (its expected ROIC less its WACC). When the business's return spread is positive (the upper half of the matrix), there is value creation (EVA is positive). When the return spread is negative (the lower half of the matrix), there is value destruction (EVA is negative).

EXHIBIT 18.9   THE FINANCIAL STRATEGY MATRIX.

Return spread ROIC minus WACC (vertical axis)

Value creation EVA > 0 (upper region) / **Value destruction EVA < 0** (lower region)

Cash surplus G_sales < SGR (left) — **Growth in sales minus self-sustainable growth rate** / **Cash deficit G_sales > SGR** (right)

Upper-left quadrant:
- **Use the cash surplus to grow faster**
  - Make new investments (organic growth)
  - Acquire related businesses
- **Distribute the cash surplus**
  - Increase dividend payments
  - Repurchase shares

Upper-right quadrant:
- **Raise funds**
  - Issue new equity
- **Cut dividends**
- **Reduce the growth in sales to its sustainable level**
  - Eliminate low-margin and low-capital-turnover products

Lower-left quadrant:
- **Distribute part of the cash surplus and use the rest to improve profitability**
  - Raise the efficiency with which assets are managed
  - Increase operating margin (higher volume, higher prices, and tighter control of expenses)
- **Review capital structure policy**
  - If the current capital structure is not optimal, modify the debt-to-equity ratio in order to lower the weighted average cost of capital
- **If the above fails, sell the business**

Lower-right quadrant:
- **Attempt drastic restructuring or simply exit the business**

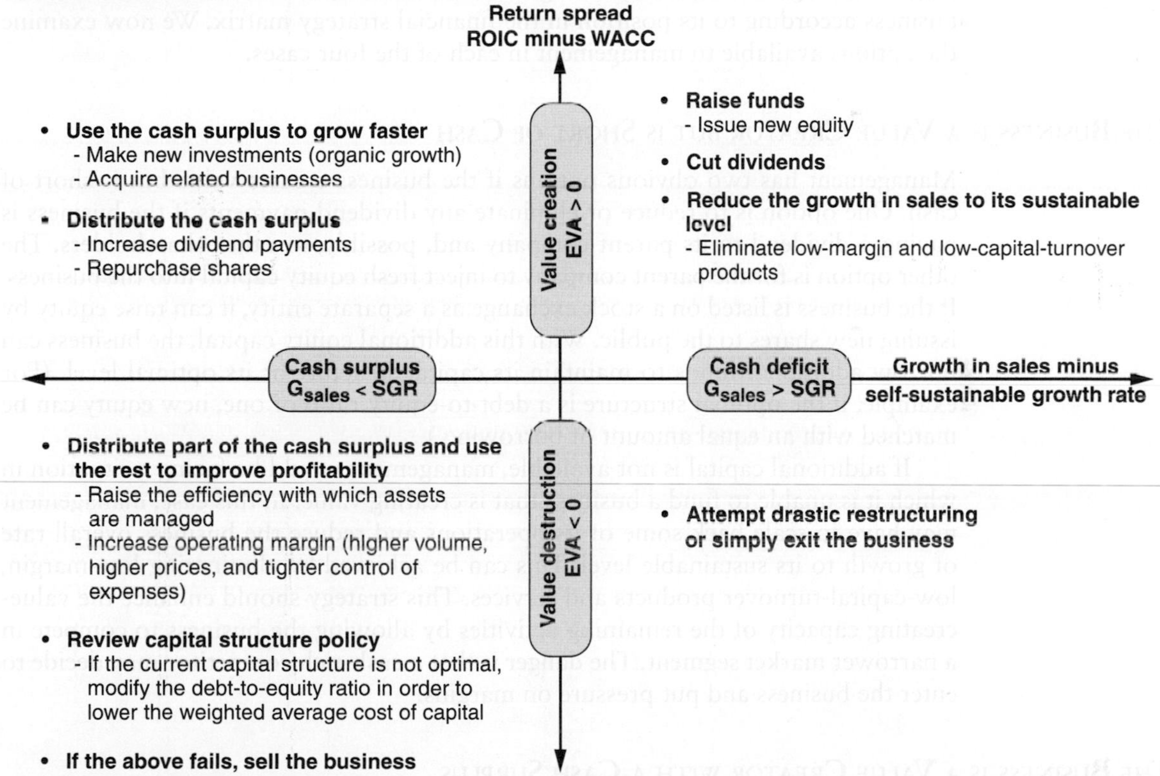

ROIC = Return on invested capital
WACC = Weighted average cost of capital
G_sales = Growth in sales
SGR = Self-sustainable growth rate

The horizontal axis measures the capacity of a business to self-finance its growth in sales. This capacity is measured by the difference between the expected growth in sales rate and the self-sustainable growth rate presented in Chapter 6. The **self-sustainable growth rate** is the maximum rate of growth in sales a business can achieve without changing its financing policy (same debt-to-equity ratio, same dividend payout ratio, and no new issue of equity or any share repurchases) or modifying its operating policy (same operating profit margin and same capital turnover). We show in Chapter 6 that the self-sustainable growth rate of a business is equal to its profit retention rate multiplied by its return on equity (ROE).

A business will experience a cash shortage if its growth rate in sales is *higher* than its self-sustainable growth rate (the right half of the matrix). It will generate a cash surplus if its growth rate in sales is *lower* than its self-sustainable growth rate (the left half of the matrix).

What are the managerial implications of the matrix in Exhibit 18.9? A business can face four possible situations: (1) the business has the capacity to create value but is short of cash (the upper-right quadrant); (2) the business has the capacity to create value and generate a cash surplus (the upper-left quadrant); (3) the business is a value destroyer but generates excess cash (the lower-left quadrant); and (4) the business is a value destroyer and suffers from a shortage of cash (lower-right quadrant). A firm with a single business will fall into one of these four quadrants. A firm with many different businesses will have to allocate them to their respective quadrant. After this diagnostic stage is completed, management will have to decide what to do with each business according to its position in the financial strategy matrix. We now examine the options available to management in each of the four cases.

THE BUSINESS IS A VALUE CREATOR BUT IS SHORT OF CASH

Management has two obvious options if the business creates value but is short of cash. One option is to reduce or eliminate any dividend payments if the business is paying a dividend to its parent company and, possibly, to other shareholders. The other option is for the parent company to inject fresh equity capital into the business. If the business is listed on a stock exchange as a separate entity, it can raise equity by issuing new shares to the public. With this additional equity capital, the business can borrow additional funds to maintain its capital structure at its optimal level. (For example, if the optimal structure is a debt-to-equity ratio of one, new equity can be matched with an equal amount of borrowing.)

If additional capital is not available, management would be facing a situation in which it is unable to fund a business that is creating value. In this case, management may have to scale back some of its operations and reduce the business overall rate of growth to its sustainable level. This can be achieved by eliminating low-margin, low-capital-turnover products and services. This strategy should enhance the value-creating capacity of the remaining activities by allowing the business to compete in a narrower market segment. The danger is that a cash-rich competitor may decide to enter the business and put pressure on margins.

THE BUSINESS IS A VALUE CREATOR WITH A CASH SURPLUS

The preferred situation is for a business to be a value creator with a cash surplus. Management can do one of two things in this case. The first is to use the cash surplus to accelerate the growth of the business. This can be accomplished by increasing investment in its business or by acquiring similar and related businesses. What if organic growth opportunities or related acquisitions are not available? The temptation, of course, would be to use the cash surplus to diversify into *unrelated* businesses that may appear profitable. As shown in Chapter 14, however, this strategy is rarely successful and generally should be avoided.

If the cash surplus cannot be invested at an expected return that exceeds the cost of capital, it should be returned to the firm's owners. They could then invest it in a value-creating venture of their choice. This cash distribution can be achieved through a special dividend payment or through a **share buyback**, or **share repurchase**, program as described in Chapter 11.

The Business is a Value Destroyer with a Cash Surplus

A value-destroying business with a cash surplus should be fixed rapidly, before the cash surplus runs out. Part of the excess cash could be returned to shareholders and the rest should be used to restructure the business as rapidly as possible, with the objective of raising its ROIC above its cost of capital.

As shown earlier in this chapter, ROIC can be increased through (1) an improved operating margin via a combination of higher volume, higher prices, and control of operating expenses and (2) a more efficient management of assets, particularly WCR, that is, with faster collection of trade receivables and higher inventory turns (see Chapters 5 and 6).

Management should also review the business's capital structure with the objective of lowering its WACC if it is not at its optimal level (see Chapters 12 and 13). The danger here is sinking too much cash into a business that has little or no chance of being turned around. The trick is to know when to seriously consider the sale of the business to someone who might manage it better.

The Business is a Value Destroyer that is Short of Cash

A value-destroying business that is short of cash is the worst situation and one that requires management's immediate attention and swift action. If the business cannot be quickly and drastically restructured, it should be sold as soon as possible. By drastic restructuring, we mean the rapid sale of some of the assets to raise cash immediately and the scaling down of remaining activities to allow short-term survival with the objective of turning these remaining activities into a value-creating business. If a quick and successful turnaround is impossible, the business must be sold immediately before it affects the long-term survival of the rest of the company. The temptation to fund the business with the cash surplus generated by other businesses that have excess cash should be resisted at all costs.

KEY POINTS

1. The greatest benefit of a management system that emphasizes value creation as opposed to earnings growth is that it induces managers throughout the organization to pay closer attention to expense control, to make a more effective use of the firm's assets, and to become more aware of the need to earn higher returns on the firm's invested capital. Good management can be many things – including superior marketing skill, great leadership, and a mastery of manufacturing. But,

essentially, good *financial* management is only one thing – that is, good *capital* management, or *the art of deploying scarce capital skillfully*.

2. How can managers make capital allocation decisions that enhance value? A firm should allocate its existing capital and, if required, raise new capital, *only* if the return it expects to earn on the capital exceeds its estimated cost. Otherwise, capital should be returned to shareholders through dividend payments or a share buyback program. And, of course, there is no point in growing a business that does not earn its cost of capital. If a business cannot be restructured to generate a return in excess of its appropriate risk-adjusted cost of capital, it should be sold. A company creates value only if its market value added (MVA) – defined as the difference between the market value of its capital and the amount of capital invested in it by shareholders and debt holders – is positive. In other words, a company creates value only when the firm's capital is worth more than its reported (adjusted) book value.

3. One way to implement a management system that is consistent with and conducive to a value-creation objective is to link the firm's operating performance, investment decisions, and remuneration system to economic profit or economic value added (EVA), defined as the difference between net operating profit after tax and the dollar cost of the capital used to generate that profit. Managers who make decisions that maximize expected future EVA will increase MVA and create value. Also, this objective is consistent with the net present value and the internal rate of return rules used in capital budgeting.

4. The key drivers of a financial management system can be summarized into a financial strategy matrix that can help managers make value-creating strategic decisions. This matrix considers businesses that show positive EVA or negative EVA and that have cash surpluses or cash shortages.

5. We conclude this book with one of the clearest and shortest statements a chief executive has made about the nature of his business and the way it is managed. This is how a former chairman of the Coca-Cola Company defined his business and management approach: "We raise capital to make concentrate [syrup], and sell it at an operating profit. Then we pay the cost of that capital. Shareholders pocket the difference."[10] If you can think of your own business in those terms, we have achieved our goal of making you a true value manager.

---

[10] Roberto Goizueta in *Fortune* (September 20, 1993), p. 24.

ADJUSTING BOOK VALUES TO ESTIMATE THE AMOUNT OF INVESTED EQUITY CAPITAL AND OPERATING PROFIT

As an illustration of the adjustments needed to correct for the distortions generated by accounting conventions, Appendix 18.1 shows how we estimated Infosoft's $380 million of invested equity capital on December 31, last year, and $80 million of earnings before interest and tax (EBIT) the same year. These are the figures we used to estimate the firm's market value added (MVA), return on invested capital (ROIC), and economic value added (EVA) for last year. Keep in mind, however, that more than 100 accounting adjustments have been identified. Obviously, the objective is to pick those few that make sense for analyzing a company's performance without adding undue complexity.

ADJUSTING THE BOOK VALUE OF EQUITY CAPITAL

Look at the asset side of Infosoft's unadjusted last-year balance sheet in Exhibit 18.1 at the beginning of the chapter: a $10 million accumulated bad debt allowance was deducted from the gross value of working capital requirement, and $20 million of accumulated goodwill impairment was removed from its net fixed assets. Accounting rules usually require that these **provisions** be charged to (deducted from) both the firm's assets and its profit. In monetary terms, the bad debt allowance represents the percentage of outstanding invoices on December 31, last year that Infosoft did not expect to collect. Goodwill results from the acquisition of a company two years ago for $100 million *above* its **fair market value** (its value under normal market conditions). The $100 million payment in excess of fair value is goodwill. After examining the value of the goodwill two years ago and last year, the company's auditors concluded that it has been impaired (has lost some value) by an amount equal to $10 million during each one of the two years.

During the two years up to December 31, last year, the bad debt allowance and the impairment of goodwill have reduced the amount of reported profit by $30 million ($10 million of bad debt allowances and $20 million of impaired goodwill). As a result, the accumulated amount of retained earnings and, consequently, the book value of Infosoft's equity capital were also reduced by $30 million. Because the capital actually invested by its shareholders was not affected by these accounting adjustments, the book value of Infosoft's equity capital on December 31, last year, must be adjusted upward by $30 million, as shown on the right side of last year's adjusted balance sheet in Exhibit 18.1.

The next section shows that on December 31, last year, Infosoft reported a net profit of $30 million and retained the entire amount (it did not pay any dividends). Thus, the book value of its equity increased by $30 million during this year. We will see that this profit figure came after the deduction of a $5 million allowance for bad debts, $10 million of goodwill impairment, and $30 million of research and development (R&D) expenses. We can adjust equity capital for the distortions caused by the way bad debt allowances and goodwill impairment are accounted for in reported profit. Is it necessary to also adjust for the way R&D expenses have been charged to last year's profit?

To answer this question, we need to know why $30 million was spent on R&D last year. If these expenses were incurred to increase profits only last year, it makes sense to account for them fully in that year. But if, as it would certainly be the case in most instances, the $30 million of R&D was disbursed to boost Infosoft's profits for several years, allocating the full $30 million only to last year does not make much sense, although accounting conventions may require doing so.

If we assume that the $30 million spent on R&D will improve profits for a five-year period, each of these five years of profits should account for a portion of the $30 million "consumed" to generate that year's profit and, consequently, that year's increase in invested equity capital. In other words, the R&D expenses, like fixed assets, must be treated as an investment made last year that needs to be amortized over a five-year period rather than fully expensed that year. For example, if the $30 million were amortized according to the straight-line method, only $6 million of R&D expenses ($30 million divided by five) should be charged to last year's profit to estimate the invested equity capital at the end of that year. Furthermore, the **capitalization of the R&D expenses** (their conversion to assets) should not be limited to last year. It should also apply to all the R&D expenses incurred by Infosoft since its inception ten years ago. How can this be done?

First, we add all the R&D annual expenses incurred since the firm was founded, including the $30 million spent last year. Then, we apply an amortization schedule to each of these annual expenses, add all the annual amortization expenses up to December 31, last year, and, finally, subtract the accumulated amortization expenses on R&D from the amount actually spent since Infosoft's inception. Assuming that the result would be a capitalized value of $50 million on December 31, last year, we can estimate that the firm's reported pre-tax profit since its inception has been underestimated by $50 million. It follows that the firm's equity capital as of December 31, last year, must be adjusted upward by the same amount, as shown on the right side of last year's adjusted balance sheet in Exhibit 18.1.

In total, Infosoft's book value of equity capital on December 31, last year, should be increased by $80 million to adjust for the accounting treatment of bad debt allowances ($10 million), goodwill impairment ($20 million), and capitalized R&D costs ($50 million). As a result, Infosoft's estimated invested capital is $380 million, the sum of its reported book value of $300 million and the $80 million of adjustments. As is often the case, Infosoft's reported invested capital ($300 million) underestimates the actual invested capital ($380 million) and, consequently, the total capital contributed by investors. In general, the extent of the underestimation depends on the number and size of the adjustments that must be made to reported profit. These adjustments, in addition to those related to bad debt allowances, goodwill impairment, and R&D expenses, include the consequences of any accounting convention that would affect reported profit without affecting the capital invested by shareholders and debt holders, such as charges associated with restructuring.

ADJUSTING EARNINGS BEFORE INTEREST AND TAX

Exhibit A18.1.1 shows last-year unadjusted and adjusted income statements for Infosoft. Infosoft reported $55 million of earnings before interest and tax that year. This figure must first be adjusted upward by the $5 million increase in the bad debt allowance, the $10 million impairment of goodwill, and the $30 million of R&D expenses. It must then be adjusted downward by the amortization of the R&D costs

EXHIBIT A18.1.1	INFOSOFT'S INCOME STATEMENT FOR LAST YEAR.

FIGURES IN MILLIONS

Income Statement last year			
Unadjusted		**Adjusted**	
Sales	$1,000	Sales	$1,000
Cost of goods sold	500	Cost of goods sold	500
SG&A expenses	382	SG&A expenses	382
Lease expense	3	Lease expense	3
Depreciation expense	15	Depreciation expense	15
R&D expenses	30	Amortization of R&D expenses	20
Bad debt provision	5		
Goodwill impairment	10		
Earnings before interest and tax	$ 55	**Earnings before interest and tax**	$ 80
Interest expense	8	Interest expense	8
Tax expense (36% of pre-tax profit)	17	Tax expense	17
Earnings after tax (net profit)	$ 30	**Earnings after tax (net profit)**	$ 55

incurred last year that result from the application of the amortization schedule used when estimating the R&D capitalized expenses. If we *assume* an R&D amortization expense of $20 million, Infosoft's EBIT should be increased by a total of $25 million (from $55 million to $80 million) – $5 million for bad debts plus $10 million of goodwill plus $30 million of R&D expenses less $20 million for the amortization of R&D costs. As a final adjustment to Infosoft's last-year income statement, we deduct the $8 million of interest expense (as given in the income statement) and the $17 million of tax expense (36 percent of the $47 million of pre-tax profit) from the adjusted EBIT to get an adjusted earnings after tax of $55 million. Because we assumed that Infosoft did not pay any dividend last year, this $55 million of adjusted net profit is also the firm's adjusted retained earnings for that year. Exhibit 18.1 shows that the firm's adjusted owners' equity went up by exactly $55 million, from $225 million two years ago to $280 million at the end of this year.

ESTIMATING MARKET VALUE ADDED (MVA) WHEN FUTURE CASH FLOWS ARE EXPECTED TO GROW AT A CONSTANT RATE IN PERPETUITY

The discounted cash flow value of assets – if we assume these assets will generate a cash-flow stream that is expected to grow at a constant annual rate forever – is given by the following (see equation 2.9 in Chapter 2):

$$\text{Value of assets} = \frac{\text{FCF}}{\text{WACC} - \text{Growth rate}} \qquad \text{(A18.2.1)}$$

where FCF is next year's free cash flow (see equation 4.15 in Chapter 4) and the discount rate is the weighted average cost of the capital (WACC) employed to finance the assets (see equation 12.12 in Chapter 12). FCF is given by:

$$\text{FCF} = \text{EBIT}(1 - T_C) + \text{Depreciation expense} - \Delta\text{WCR} - \text{Capital expenditure}$$

where EBIT is earnings before interest and tax, EBIT(1 − Tax rate) is net operating profit after tax or NOPAT, and ΔWCR is the change in working capital requirement. We can rearrange the terms of FCF to the following:

$$\text{FCF} = \text{NOPAT} - (\Delta\text{WCR} + \text{Capital expenditure} - \text{Depreciation expense})$$

Capital expenditure less depreciation expense is equal to the *change* in the firm's *net* fixed assets during the year. When added to the *change* in WCR, the sum represents the *change* in the book value of the firm's invested capital during the year (we assume no change in cash position). Thus, we can write the following:

$$\text{FCF} = \text{NOPAT} - \Delta\text{Invested capital}$$

Substituting this expression for next year's FCF in the numerator of the valuation equation (equation A18.2.1) and deducting the term "invested capital" from both sides of the equation, we get the following:

$$\text{Value of assets} - \text{Invested capital} = \frac{\text{NOPAT} - \Delta\text{Invested capital}}{\text{WACC} - \text{growth rate}} - \text{Invested capital}$$

where the left side of the equation is the market value added or MVA. This equation can be rewritten as follows:

$$\text{MVA} = \frac{\text{NOPAT} - \Delta\text{Invested capital} - (\text{Invested capital} \times [\text{WACC} - \text{Growth rate}])}{\text{WACC} - \text{Growth rate}}$$

Factoring out the term "invested capital" in the numerator, we have the following:

$$MVA = \frac{\left(\dfrac{NOPAT}{Invested\ capital} - \dfrac{\Delta Invested\ capital}{Invested\ capital} - WACC + Growth\ rate\right) \times Invested\ capital}{WACC - Growth\ rate}$$

The first term in the numerator is the ROIC, and the second term is the growth rate in invested capital, which is the same as the growth rate in cash flows because the growth rate is constant. Thus, we can write the following:

$$MVA = \frac{(ROIC - Growth\ rate - WACC + Growth\ rate) \times Invested\ capital}{WACC - Growth\ rate}$$

$$MVA = \frac{(ROIC - WACC) \times Invested\ capital}{WACC - Growth\ rate}$$

This equation is the valuation equation expressed in equation 18.3 in the chapter.

When MVA is positive, the ratio of market value to adjusted book value is greater than one. The factors that explain the sign of MVA are thus similar to those that explain the magnitude of the ratio of a firm's price per share to its book value per share. The price-to-book value ratio was presented in Chapter 10, where we said that the factors that explain its magnitude would be discussed in Chapter 18. The valuation equation (equation 18.3) indicates that these factors are as follows:

1. The return on equity (the equivalent of ROIC because we deal with equity rather than total capital)
2. The cost of equity (the equivalent of WACC because we deal with equity rather than total capital)
3. The firm's growth rate.

Thus, when return on equity is higher (lower) than the cost of equity, the price-to-book value ratio will be higher (or lower) than one.

FURTHER READING

1. Kaiser, Kevin, and David Young. *The Blue Line Imperative: What Managing for Value Really Means.* John Wiley & Sons, 2013.
2. Madden, Bartley. *Maximizing Shareholder Value and the Greater Good.* LearningWhatWorks®, 2007.
3. Rappaport, Alfred. *Creating Shareholder Value.* The Free Press, 2000.
4. Stewart, Bennett. *Best-Practice EVA: The Definitive Guide to Measuring and Maximizing Shareholder Value.* John Wiley and Sons, 2013.
5. Young, David, and Stephen F. O'Byrne. *EVA and Value-Based Management.* McGraw-Hill, 2001.

SELF-TEST QUESTIONS

18.1 **Understanding MVA and EVA.**
Explain why each of the following statements is generally incorrect:

a. "Management creates value by maximizing the market value of its firm."
b. "If a firm's market value added (MVA) is positive, then its current economic value added (EVA) must also be positive."

c. "EVA should be measured on the basis of net profits (the bottom line) and not on the basis of *operating* profit."

d. "One weakness of EVA as a performance measure is that it does not take risk into account."

e. "Giving managers a bonus related to their ability to increase the profit of their business unit is one way to enhance shareholder value."

18.2   Adjusting accounting data to estimate economic value added.
The financial statements of the Advance Devices Corporation (ADC) are shown below with balance sheets reported in their managerial form. ADC has an estimated weighted average cost of capital of 11 percent. ADC had an estimated $55 million of research and development (R&D) expenses that should have been capitalized in Year–1 and $70 million that should have been capitalized in Year 0. Amortization of R&D expenses in Year 0 is $30 million. Using this information, provide an estimate of ADC's economic value added in Year 0 based on initial invested capital and average invested capital.

Income Statement Year 0 (in millions)	
Net sales	$1,400
Cost of sales	780
Selling, general, and administrative expenses	330
Depreciation and lease expenses	45
R&D expenses	100
Bad debt provision	6
Goodwill impairment	25
Interest expense	14
Income tax expense	40
Net profit	$ 60

Managerial Balance Sheets (in millions)					
Invested capital	December 31, Year –1	December 31, Year 0	Capital employed	December 31, Year –1	December 31, Year 0
Cash	$ 10	$ 15	Short-term debt	$ 30	$ 10
Working capital (net)	140	160			
Gross value	*$147*	*$173*	Long-term debt	80	80
Accumulated bad debt allowance	*7*	*13*			
Net fixed assets	210	225	Lease obligations	50	50
Tangible (net)	110	150			
Goodwill (net)	100	75	Owners' equity	200	260
Gross value	*120*	*120*			
Accumulated impairment	*20*	*45*			
Total		$360	$400	Total	$360	$400

18.3 Market value added analysis.
The International Logistics Company (ILC) is considering buying an inventory control software program that will cost $140,000, delivered and installed (including personnel training). The program will allow the company to reduce its inventory by $100,000. The cost of the software will be expensed the year it is bought. ILC is subject to a 40 percent corporate tax rate, and its weighted average cost of capital is 10 percent. Should ILC buy the software program? Answer the question using economic value added and market value added analysis.

18.4 Market value added analysis of the designer desk lamp project.
Refer to Chapter 9 for a description of the designer desk lamp project. Exhibit 9.3 reports the cash flows the project is expected to generate. Use the information in the exhibit to estimate the project's economic value added and its market value added. The latter, if measured correctly, must be equal to the project's net present value of $415,083. The weighted average cost of capital is 7.6 percent.

18.5 The financial strategy matrix.
Amalgamated Industries (AI) has four distinct business divisions that are run as separate companies and are listed on a stock market. AI has a majority ownership in the four companies for which the following financial data have been collected:

Company	Transportation	Restaurants	Beverages	Food
Sales growth rate	8%	15%	7%	4%
Return on invested capital	8%	15%	8%	13%
Return on equity	12%	20%	12%	15%
Weighted average cost of capital	10%	12%	9%	11%
Dividend payout ratio	50%	40%	25%	60%

a. Position the four companies on the financial strategy matrix.
b. What actions should AI take regarding each of these businesses?

REVIEW QUESTIONS

1. Understanding market value added and economic value added.
Explain why each of the following statements is generally incorrect:

a. "The firm with the highest market value is the one that has created the most value for its shareholders."
b. "If a firm's market value added (MVA) is positive, then its current return on invested capital (ROIC) must exceed its weighted average cost of capital (WACC)."
c. "Growth is the key to increasing a firm's MVA."
d. "This year's economic value added (EVA) is positive, so the firm's market value added must also be positive."
e. "Giving managers a bonus related to their ability to increase the profitability (ROIC) of their business unit is one way to enhance shareholder value."

2. **Value drivers.**

Identify at least three value drivers related to the management of operations and three strategic value drivers that directly affect economic value added (EVA). Show how these drivers might increase or decrease EVA.

3. **Adjusting accounting data to estimate a firm's economic value added.**

Following are the balance sheets at the end of year–1 and Year 0 followed by the Year 0 income statement of Sactor Inc. The annual report for Year 0 provides the following supplemental information:

1. The restructuring charge of $43 million amounted to $28 million after tax
2. Accumulated goodwill impairment was $98 million at the end of Year–1 and $93 million at the end of Year 0. Goodwill impairment was $22 million in Year 0, or $14 million after tax
3. The accounts receivable are net of the bad debt allowance. At the end of Year –1, the accumulated bad debt allowance was $26 million; at the end of Year 0, it was $30 million
4. During Year–1, the firm had a nonoperating extraordinary loss of $35 million after tax

   a. Compute the unadjusted invested capital of Sactor Inc. at the end of Year–1 and the end of Year 0. Compute also the firm's net operating profit after tax (NOPAT).
   b. Adjust the amounts of invested capital and NOPAT for accounting distortions.
   c. Assuming a weighted average cost of capital of 10 percent, what was Sactor's economic value added in Year 0?

Balance Sheets (in millions)				
		December 31, Year –1		December 31, Year 0
Assets				
Cash		$ 239		$ 37
Accounts receivable, net		500		668
Inventories		416		547
Prepaid expenses		58		159
Net fixed assets		827		1,279
Property, plant, and equipment, net	$488		$634	
Goodwill, net	148		513	
Other assets	191		132	
Total		**$2,040**		**$2,690**
Liabilities and owners' equity				
Short-term debt		$ 23		$ 50
Accounts payable		264		346
Accrued expenses		437		681
Long-term liabilities		668		846
Owners' equity		648		767
Total		**$2,040**		**$2,690**

Income Statement (in millions)	
	Year 0
Net sales	$2,888
Cost of goods sold	2,167
Selling, general, and administrative expenses	434
Restructuring charge	43
Earnings before interest and tax	$ 244
Interest expense	62
Earnings before tax	$ 182
Income tax expense	64
Earnings after tax	$ 118

4. **Economic value added analysis.**

   The Southern Communication Corporation (SCC) has $1 billion of capital invested in several telecommunication projects that are expected to generate a pre-tax operating profit of $170 million next year. SCC has an estimated pre-tax cost of capital of 15 percent.

   a. What is the pre-tax economic value added (EVA) that SCC is expected to generate next year? Calculate EVA first based on pre-tax operating profit and then based on expected return on invested capital.

   b. SCC is considering five possible actions that should improve its expected pre-tax EVA. These are as follows:

      1. A $10 million reduction in operating expenses that should not affect revenues
      2. A $60 million reduction in invested capital that should not affect operating profit
      3. A re-examination of its capital structure (debt-to-equity ratio) that could lower its pre-tax cost of capital to 14 percent
      4. The sale of assets at their book value of $100 million. These assets are expected to generate a pre-tax operating profit of $10 million next year
      5. The acquisition of assets worth $100 million. These assets are expected to generate a pre-tax operating profit of $20 million next year.

   Show how each of these decisions would improve SCC's expected pre-tax economic value added.

5. **The relationship between a firm's market value, its market value added, and its economic value added.**

   a. Equation 18.7 shows that market value added (MVA) of an investment project is the present value of the stream of the future economic value added (EVA) of the project. Because a firm can be viewed as a basket of investment projects, the MVA of a firm is simply the present value of the stream of future EVA generated by the firm from these projects. Show that the market value of a firm's capital is equal to the present value (PV) of the stream of future EVA expected from the firm plus its invested capital:

   Market value of capital = PV of expected future EVA + Invested capital

b. Consider Value Inc. The firm's invested capital is $150 million, and the market value of its capital is also $150 million, so its MVA is equal to zero. Suppose that the firm announces a $50 million investment in a project from which it expects a return on invested capital of 14 percent for the next four years. Value Inc.'s weighted average cost of capital is 8 percent. By how much should the market value and the MVA of the firm increase at the announcement of the project?

6. **The effect of the management of the operating cycle on the firm's economic value added.**

   Below are the last three years' financial statements of Sentec Inc., a distributor of electrical fixtures.

Income Statements (in thousands)			
	Year 1	Year 2	Year 3
Net sales	$22,100	$24,300	$31,600
Cost of goods sold	17,600	19,300	25,100
Selling, general, and administrative expenses	3,750	4,000	5,000
Depreciation expense	100	100	150
Earnings before interest and tax	650	900	1,350
Net interest expense	110	130	260
Earnings before tax	540	770	1,090
Income tax expense	220	310	430
Earnings after tax	$ 320	$ 460	$ 660
Dividends	$ 180	$ 200	$ 200

Balance Sheets (in thousands)			
	December 31, Year 1	December 31, Year 2	December 31, Year 3
Cash	$ 600	$ 350	$ 300
Accounts receivable	2,730	3,100	4,200
Inventories	2,800	3,200	4,300
Net fixed assets	1,200	1,300	1,450
Total assets	$7,330	$7,950	$10,250
Short-term debt	$ 300	$ 500	$ 1,900
Accounts payable	1,400	1,600	2,050
Accrued expenses	200	260	350
Long-term debt	1,300	1,200	1,100
Owners' equity	4,130	4,390	4,850
Total liabilities and owners' equity	$7,330	$7,950	$10,250

a. Compute Sentec's working capital requirement (WCR) on December 31, Year 1, Year 2, and Year 3.

b. Prepare Sentec Inc.'s managerial balance sheets on December 31, Year 1, Year 2, and Year 3.

c. Sentec's weighted average cost of capital was stable at 11 percent over the three-year period from Year 1 to Year 3. How much value was created or destroyed by Sentec in each of the three years?

d. What are the likely causes of value creation and destruction at Sentec?

e. In Year 3, firms in the same business sector as Sentec Inc. have an average collection period of 30 days, an average payment period of 33 days, and an inventory turnover of eight times. Suppose that Sentec Inc. had managed its operating cycle like the average firm in the sector. On December 31, Year 3, what would its WCR have been? Its managerial balance sheet? How much more value would Sentec have created?

7. **Return on invested capital versus economic value added–based bonus systems.**
Fiona Berling's division of Mcsystems generates a net operating profit after tax, or NOPAT, of $1 million on an invested capital base of $1 million. The weighted average cost of capital of Ms Berling's division is 20 percent. The division has been asked to launch a new investment project that would return $500,000 for an investment of $1 million.

a. If bonuses at Mcsystems were based on return on invested capital achieved by its divisions, would Ms Berling find the new project acceptable?

b. What if the bonuses were based on economic value added achieved by its divisions?

c. What bonus system would you favor? Why?

8. **Economic value added-based bonus system.**
Astra Co. is considering introducing a bonus system based on economic value added (EVA) and has short-listed two bonus equations. The first one would simply compute the bonus as a percentage of EVA, such that:

$$\text{Bonus} = x \text{ percent of EVA} = x\% \times \text{EVA} \tag{1}$$

The second bonus equation will make the bonus dependent also on the improvement in EVA from one year to the next so that:

$$\begin{aligned}\text{Bonus} &= y \text{ percent of EVA} + z \text{ percent of } \Delta \\ &= y\% \times \text{EVA} + z\% \times \Delta\text{EVA}\end{aligned} \tag{2}$$

a. Suppose that the firm anticipates that its EVA will be $16 million this year, $20 million next year, and $24 million the year after. If the bonus equation (1) is chosen, x would be equal to 2 percent. If the bonus equation (2) is preferred, y would be equal to 1 percent and z to 7.5 percent. What would be the three years' cumulative bonus for each of the two equations?

b. Suppose now that the expected EVA will be −$24 million this year, −$20 million next year, and −$16 million the year after. With the same value of x, y, and z as in the previous question, what would be the three years' cumulative bonus for each of the two equations?

c. Which equations would you advise Astra to use?

9. **Economic value added, market value added, and net present value.**

Alvinstar Co. is considering investing in a new animal feed project. The product will be a soup for cats to be sold in cans. Alvinstar plans to sell 100,000 cans a year for four years at a price of $4 per can. Fixed costs will include rent on the production facility at $50,000 a year, plus annual depreciation expense of $50,000 on production equipment that will cost $200,000 installed. After taking into account the cost of removing the equipment, the net receipt of selling the equipment after four years is expected to be zero. Variable costs will amount to $2 per can. The project will require an investment in the operating cycle, or working capital requirement, of $40,000. The tax rate is 40 percent. Alvinstar's weighted average cost of capital is 10 percent.

a. Compute the project's net present value.
b. Compute the project's expected annual economic value added.
c. Compute the project's market value added.
d. What is the necessary condition for the project's net present value to be equal to the present value of its future expected economic value added and to its market value added?

10. **Comparison of investment analysis based on cash flows and economic value added.**

The Electronics Machines Corporation (EMC) is considering buying a $300,000 piece of equipment that could raise EMC's sales revenues by $1 million the first year, $2 million the second year, and $1.8 million the third year. The cost of the piece of equipment can be fully depreciated over the three-year investment according to the straight-line method with no residual value. Incremental operating expenses are estimated at 90 percent of sales, excluding depreciation expense. Working capital required to support the project's sales should be 10 percent of sales with working capital investment assumed to occur at the beginning of the year. EMC can borrow at 6 percent, is subject to a 30 percent corporate tax rate, and finances 60 percent of its activities with borrowed funds. The firm uses an estimated cost of equity of 12 percent.

a. What are the project's net present value and internal rate of return? Should the piece of equipment be purchased?
b. What is the project's market value added? Explain why the piece of equipment should be purchased even though its first-year economic value added is negative.
c. What is the key assumption used in the estimation of the project's cash flows and economic value added that makes the project's net present value equal to its market value added?

ANSWERS TO SELF-TEST QUESTIONS

1.1 Working capital requirement and managerial balance sheets.

a. $WCR_{12/31 \text{ Year } 1} = \$300$ million; $WCR_{12/31 \text{ Year } 2} = \$315$ million

b. NMC's managerial balance sheets on December 31, Year 1 and Year 2 (figures in millions):

Invested capital	12/31 Year 1	12/31 Year 2	Capital employed	12/31 Year 1	12/31 Year 2
Cash	100	105	Short-term debt	100	105
WCR	300	315	Long-term debt	300	315
Net fixed assets	600	630	Owners' equity	600	630
Total invested capital	1,000	1,050	Total capital employed	1,000	1,050

c. Dividend = EAT − Retained earnings = EAT − (change in owners' equity)
= $156 million − ($630 million − $600 million) = $126 million.

d. NMC's sustainable growth rate is 5 percent, which is the growth rate in its capital employed.

1.2 Weighted average cost of capital, profitability, and value creation.

a. After-tax cost debt = Pre-tax cost debt − tax = 8% − (25% of 8%) = 6%
Total debt to capital employed is 0.40 ($400/$1,000 or $420/$1,050)
WACC = (6% × 0.40) + (15% × 0.60) = 11.40%.

b. ROIC = [$240 × (1 − 0.25)]/$1,000 = 0.18 = 18%

c. ROE = $156/$600 = 0.26 = 26%.

d. Yes because its ROIC exceeds its WACC.

1.3 Statement of cash flows (figures in million).

	Year 2
Cash flows from operating activities	
Earnings after tax	$156
plus depreciation expense	100
less cash used to finance the growth of working capital requirement[1]	(15)
A. Net cash flow from operating activities	$241
Cash flows from investing activities	
Capital expenditures (see footnote 1 in the question)	(130)
B. Net cash flow from investing activities	($130)

Cash flows from financing activities	
New borrowings	20
less dividend payments	(126)
C. Net cash flow from financing activities	($106)
D. Total net cash flow (A + B + C)	$ 5
E. Opening cash	$100
F. Closing cash (E + D)	$105

[1] This is the difference between $WCR_{12/31 Year 2}$ and $WCR_{12/31 Year 1}$

1.4 Net present value and internal rate of return.

a. NPV = $95 million + $\dfrac{\$111.4 \text{ million}}{1 + 0.114}$ = − $95 million + $100 million = $5 million

b. IRR = ($111.4 million − $95 million)/$95 million = 17.26%.

c. Yes because its NPV is positive and its IRR is higher than its WACC.

d. NPV per share = $5 million/50 million = $0.10; the share price immediately after the announcement is thus $40.10 ($40.00 + $0.10).

1.5 The net present value of an acquisition.

a. NPV (acquisition) = − Premium + Present value of incremental cash flow
   = − ($12 million − $10 million) + ($115 million − $100 million − $10 million)
   = − $2 million + $5 million = +$3 million.

b. Yes because its NPV is positive.

2.1 Present value, future value, and discount rates.

a. $10,000, which is the amount borrowed today.

b. $15,000, which is the amount due in 5 years.

c. 8.45 percent. Using a financial calculator, enter N = 5, PV = −10,000, PMT = 0, FV = 15,000 and press I/YR. You get 8.45%.

d. Using formula 2.5, $k_{real} = \dfrac{1 + 0.0845}{1 + 0.03} - 1 = 5.29\%.$

e. Using formula 2.4, $k_{eff} = \left(1 + \dfrac{0.0845}{12}\right)^{12} - 1 = 8.78\%.$

2.2 Evaluating alternative strategies.

The firm should adopt the international strategy because it has a higher net present value:

$$\text{NPV(Domestic)} = -\$100m + \frac{\$25m}{1+8\%} + \frac{\$25m}{(1+8\%)^2} + \frac{\$30m}{(1+8\%)^3} + \frac{\$30m}{(1+8\%)^4} + \frac{\$30m}{(1+8\%)^5} = \$10.87m$$

$$\text{NPV(International)} = -\$100m + \frac{\$20m}{1+12\%} + \frac{\$30m}{(1+12\%)^2} + \frac{\$40m}{(1+12\%)^3} + \frac{\$50m}{(1+12\%)^4} + \frac{\$40m}{(1+12\%)^5} = \$24.72m$$

2.3 Making an investment decision.

a. No, the company should not purchase the machine because its net present value is negative at a discount rate of 7 percent (note that the annual savings is a 10-year, $275,000 annuity):

$$\text{NPV} = -\$2,000,000 + \frac{\$275,000}{0.07}\left[1 - \frac{1}{1.07^{10}}\right] = -\$2,000,000 + \$1,931,485 = -\$68,515$$

b. In this case the present value of the savings is $10 \times \left[\dfrac{\$275,000}{1.07} \right]$, that is, \$2,570,093 (refer to footnote 7 in the chapter). The NPV is thus positive (\$570,093) and the machine should be purchased.

c. You must find the annual reduction in costs (call it X) that makes the net present value of the investment equal to zero, that is:

$$NPV = -\$2,000,000 + \frac{X}{0.07}\left[1 - \frac{1}{1.07^{10}}\right] = 0$$

Solving for X you find that it is equal to \$284,754, which is the *minimum* reduction in annual operating costs that would justify the investment.

d. You must find the discount rate that makes the net present value of the investment equal to zero, which is the discount rate that makes the present value of the annuity equal to \$2,000,000. Using a financial calculator, enter N = 10, PV = −2,000,000, PMT = 275,000, FV = 0 and press I/YR. You find a rate of 6.25 percent, which is the highest discount rate that would justify the investment. Any rate lower than 6.25 percent would make the net present value positive.

2.4 Retirement plan.

a. There are 31 years and the discount rate is 5 percent, thus $ADF = \dfrac{1}{0.05}\left[1 - \dfrac{1}{(1.05)^{31}}\right] = 15.5928.$ Using a financial calculator, enter N = 31, I/YR = 5, PMT = 1, FV = 0 and press PV. You find 15.5928.

b. $PV(Plan) = \dfrac{\$8,000 \times ADF}{1.05^3} = \dfrac{\$124,742}{1.1576} = \$107,759$

c. $FV(Plan) = \dfrac{\$8,000}{0.05}[1.05^{31} - 1] = \$160,000 \times [4.5380 - 1] = \$566,086.32.$ Using a financial calculator, enter N = 31, I/YR = 5, PV = 0, PMT = 8,000 and press FV. You find \$566,086.32.

d. The number of years (T) is the solution to $\$566,086.32 = \dfrac{\$40,000}{0.05}\left[1 - \dfrac{1}{1.05^T}\right].$ Solving for T we get $\dfrac{1}{1.05^T} = 0.2924$ and T = 25.20 years. Using a financial calculator, enter I/YR = 5, PV = −566,086.32, PMT = 40,000, FV = 0 and press N. You find 25.20 years.

2.5 Valuing a company.

a. Using a spreadsheet. Enter the data (dollars in millions) and the formulas as follows:

	A	B	C	D	E	F	G	H	I	J	K	L	M
1	Timeline	Now	1	2	3	4	5	6	7	8	9	10	11
2	Growth rate		15%	15%	15%	15%	15%	10%	10%	10%	10%	10%	5%
3	Cash flow		\$12.00	\$13.80	\$15.87	\$18.25	\$20.99	\$24.14	\$26.55	\$29.20	\$32.13	\$35.34	\$38.87	\$40.82
4	Discount rate	10%											
5	Terminal value												\$816.31

Using a spreadsheet (*Continued*)

	A	B	C	D	E	F	G	H	I	J	K	L	M
6	PV(CF$_1$:CF$_{10}$)	$143.63											
7	PV(TV$_5$)	$314.72											
8	PV(all CFs)	**$458.35**											

- *Formula in cell C3 is =B3*(1+C2). Then copy formula in cell C3 to next cells in row 3*
- *Formula in cell L5 is =M3/(B4−M2)*
- *Formula in cell B6 is =NPV(B4,C3:L3)*
- *Formula in cell B7 is =L5/(1+B4)^10*
- *Formula in cell B8 is =B6+B7*

The value of the company is in cell B8: it is $458.35 million.
Using time-value-of-money formulas:

$$PV = \frac{13.80}{0.10-0.15}\left[1-\left(\frac{1.15}{1.10}\right)^5\right] + \frac{5\times\left(\frac{26.55}{1.10}\right)}{1.10^5} + \frac{\frac{40.82}{0.10-0.05}}{1.10^{10}} = 68.69 + 74.93 + 314.76 = 458.38$$

The first term is the present value at 10 percent of the first five cash flows whose growth rate is 15 percent, calculated with formula 2.12. It is equal to $68.69 million. The second term is the present value at 10 percent of CF$_6$ to CF$_{10}$ whose growth rate is 10 percent. Note that because the growth rate is equal to the discount rate (10 percent) the present value is equal to five times CF$_6$ discounted one period (see footnote 7 in the chapter). The present value of this second-stage growth is $74.93 million. The third term is the present value of the cash-flow stream beyond CF$_{10}$. It is equal to the value of the perpetuity at the end of year 10, that is, $\frac{CF_{11}}{k-g}$, discounted to the present at 10 percent. It is equal to $314.76 million. Note that CF$_{11}$ = CF$_0 \times (1+15\%)^5 \times (1+10\%)^5 \times (1+5\%)$ = $40.82 million.

b. With no growth the value of the company is: $\frac{\$12\text{ million}}{0.10} = \$120\text{ million}$

c. PV(future growth opportunities) = $458.38 million − $120 million = $338.38 million

$$\frac{PV\left(\text{future growth opportunities}\right)}{PV\left(\text{growth}\right)} = \frac{\$338.38\text{ million}}{\$458.38\text{ million}} = 73.82\%$$

3.1 Arithmetic versus geometric average returns.

a. One dollar invested at the beginning of January will grow to $1.0718 at the end of December because:

$$1\times(1+R_1)\times(1+R_2)\times...\times(1+R_{11})\times(1+R_{12}) = 1\times1.0226\times...\times0.0933 = 1.0718$$

b. Alto's monthly geometric average return (GR_{Alto}) is the solution to the equation $(1+GR_{Alto})^{12} = 1.0718$. Solving for GR_{Alto} you get $GR_{Alto} = (1.0718)^{1/12}-1 = 0.5798\%$.

c. The geometric average return of 0.5798 percent is lower than the arithmetic average return of 0.6667 percent. Unless the monthly returns are the same, the two averages will differ. As long as the monthly returns are independent of one another, you can use the arithmetic average return when estimating expected returns because it gives equal weighing to each of the returns (1/12 in our case) that are drawn from the return distribution. You should use the geometric average return when you need to calculate the realized, historical average return over a sequence of past returns.

3.2   **Investors' attitudes toward risk.**

a. A risk-averse investor prefers: (1) stock A to stocks E, F, and G because they have the same or lower expected returns with the same or higher risk; (2) stocks B, I, and C to stock A because they have the same or higher expected returns with the same or lower risk. We cannot tell if stock A is preferred to stock D (it has a higher expected return and a higher risk) or stock H (it has a lower expected return and a lower risk); the choice will depend on the investor's degree of risk aversion.

b. A risk-neutral investor prefers: (1) stock A to stocks H, G, and F because stock A has a higher expected return; (2) stocks B, C, and D to stock A because they have a higher expected return than stock A. The risk-neutral investor is indifferent between stocks A, I, and E.

c. A risk seeker prefers: (1) stock A to stocks I, H, and G because they have the same or lower risk with the same or lower expected returns; (2) stocks E, D, and C to stock A because they have the same or higher risk with the same or higher expected return. We cannot tell if stock A is preferred to stock B (it has a higher expected return and a lower risk) or stock F (it has a lower expected return and a higher risk); the choice will depend on the investor's degree of risk loving.

3.3   **The characteristics of a two-stock portfolio.**

a. If w_A is the proportion of funds invested in Alto we must have: $12\% = [w_A \times 8\%] + [(1 - w_A) \times 14\%]$. Solving for w_A you get: $w_A = 1/3 = 33.33\%$ and $w_B = 2/3 = 66.67\%$.

b. $\text{Var}(P_3) = [(1/3)^2 \times 0.15^2] + [(2/3)^2 \times 0.20^2] + [2 \times (1/3) \times (2/3) \times 0.40 \times 0.15 \times 0.20] = 0.0256$. Volatility is thus $\sigma(P_3) = \sqrt{0.0256} = 16\%$.

c. $E(R_{P4}) = (90\% \times 8\%) + (10\% \times 14\%) = 8.6\%$. Because the expected return of portfolio P_4 is lower than that of portfolio P_{MRP} (8.6% compared to 9.64%) it must be located on the inefficient set between the minimum-risk portfolio P_{MRP} and Alto shares. It is thus inefficient.

d. $\text{Var}(P_4) = (0.90)^2 (0.15)^2 + (0.10)^2 (0.20)^2 + 2(0.90)(0.10)(0.40)(0.15)(0.20) = 0.020785$. The proportions of funds invested in Alto and Bell with the same variance as P_4 are the solutions of the equation:

$$w_A^2 \times 0.15^2 + (1 - w_A)^2 \times 0.20^2 + 2 \times w_A \times (1 - w_A) \times 0.40 \times 0.15 \times 0.20 = 0.20785.$$

This equation has only two solutions: $w_A = 90\%$ and $w_A = 55.45\%$ (check this out). We now have two possible portfolios of Alto and Bell with the same variance: P_3, with 90 percent of the funds invested in Alto and P_5 with only with 55.45 invested in that portfolio. Since the first one is inefficient, the second must be the efficient one. Note that efficient portfolio P_5 has the same variance as the inefficient portfolio P_4 but, being efficient, it has a higher expected return (10.67%) than portfolio P_4 (8.6%):

$$E(R_{P5}) = (55.45\% \times 8\%) + (44.55\% \times 14\%) = 10.67\%.$$

3.4   The risk of a diversified portfolio when the number of stocks is very large.

a. All the proportions are equal to $\left(\dfrac{1}{N}\right)$, all the variances are equal to Var, and all the covariances are equal to Cov, thus:

$$\text{Var}_{P} = \left[\left(\frac{1}{N}\right)^2 \text{Var} + \ldots + \left(\frac{1}{N}\right)^2 \text{Var}\right] + 2\left[\left(\frac{1}{N}\right)\left(\frac{1}{N}\right)\text{Cov} + \ldots + \left(\frac{1}{N}\right)\left(\frac{1}{N}\right)\text{Cov}\right]$$

There are N variances in the first set of brackets and $\dfrac{N(N-1)}{2}$ covariances in the second set of brackets, thus:

$$\text{Var}_{P} = N\left[\left(\frac{1}{N}\right)^2 \text{Var}\right] + 2\left(\frac{N^2 - N}{2}\right)\left[\left(\frac{1}{N}\right)^2 \text{Cov}\right] = \frac{\text{Var}}{N} + \left(1 - \frac{1}{N}\right)\text{Cov}$$

b. When N becomes very large, $\dfrac{\text{Var}}{N}$ goes toward zero and $\left(1 - \dfrac{1}{N}\right)\text{Cov}$ goes toward Cov, so that $\text{Var}_{P} = \text{Cov}$. This means that the risk of the portfolio converges to the average covariance in the portfolio. In other words, the risk of a portfolio when the number of assets in it is large is close to the average covariance of the assets that make up the portfolio. This clearly shows that it is covariance that drives portfolio risk, not the volatility of the assets in the portfolio.

3.5   The capital asset pricing model.

a. No, because investing in a single share is an inefficient investment. The optimal investment decision with a target expected return of 7 percent must be on the Capital Market Line as a combination of the market portfolio and the risk-free asset. If w_M is the proportion of funds invested in the market portfolio, we have: $7\% = \left[w_M \times 10\%\right] + \left[\left(1 - w_M\right) \times 4\%\right]$. Solving for w_M you get $w_M = 50\%$ and $w_F = 50\%$. The $100,000 is thus invested as follows: $50,000 in a risk-free asset and $50,000 in the market portfolio. The $50,000 in the market portfolio are allocated among the five companies as follows: $9,000 to Atco (18% of $50,000), $6,000 to Bilco (12% of $50,000), $9,000 to Carco (18% of $50,000), $14,000 to Delco (28% of $50,000), and $12,000 to Enco (24% of $50,000). Given the share prices in the first row of Exhibit 3.12, the number of shares the investor should buy is: 900 shares of Atco, 200 shares of Bilco, 500 shares of Carco, 700 shares of Delco, and 500 shares of Enco.

b. The volatility of the optimal portfolio in the previous question is given by the CML equation. We have $E\left(R_E\right) = 7\% = 4\% + \left(0.30 \times \sigma_E\right)$. Solving for σ_E you get $\sigma_E = 10\%$. The beta of the optimal portfolio in the previous question is given by the SML equation. We have $E\left(R_E\right) = 7\% = 4\% + \left(6\% \times \beta_E\right)$. Solving for β_E you get $\beta_E = 0.50$. Alternatively, we have $\beta_E = \rho_{E,M}\left(\dfrac{\sigma_E}{\sigma_M}\right) = 1 \times \left(\dfrac{10\%}{20\%}\right) = 0.50$ because efficient portfolios are perfectly correlated with the market portfolio. Fifty percent of funds are invested in the market with a beta of 1 and 50 percent in the riskless asset with a beta of zero; the portfolio beta is thus 0.50.

c. No, because investing in a single share is an inefficient investment. The optimal investment decision with a target volatility of 40 percent must be on the Capital Market Line as a combination of the market portfolio and the risk-free asset. Its expected return is given by the CML equation. It is

$E(R_E) = 4\% + (0.30 \times \sigma_E) = 4\% + (0.30 \times 40\%) = 16\%$. If w_M is the proportion of funds invested in the market portfolio, we have: $16\% = [w_M \times 10\%] + [(1 - w_M) \times 4\%]$. Solving for w_M you get $w_M = 200\%$ and $w_F = -100\%$. The $100,000 is thus invested as follows: $100,000 is borrowed at 4 percent, added to the initial $100,000 and then the total of $200,000 is invested in the market. The $200,000 is allocated among the 5 companies as follows: $36,000 to Atco (18% of $200,000), $24,000 to Bilco (12% of $200,000), $36,000 to Carco (18% of $200,000), $56,000 to Delco (28% of $200,000), and $48,000 to Enco (24% of $200,000). Given the share prices in the first row of Exhibit 3.12, the number of shares the investor should buy is: 3,600 shares of Atco, 800 shares of Bilco, 2,000 shares of Carco, 2,800 shares of Delco, and 2,000 shares of Enco.

d. The Sharpe ratio is $\dfrac{16\% - 4\%}{40\%} = 0.30$. It is the same as that of the market portfolio because both portfolios are on the CML. We have $E(R_E) = 16\% = 4\% + (6\% \times \beta_E)$. Solving for β_E you get $\beta_E = 2$. Alternatively, we have $\beta_E = \rho_{E,M}\left(\dfrac{\sigma_E}{\sigma_M}\right) = 1 \times \left(\dfrac{40\%}{20\%}\right) = 2$ because efficient portfolios are perfectly correlated with the market portfolio. Two hundred percent of funds are invested in the market with a beta of one and 100 percent are borrowed at 4 percent with a beta of zero; the portfolio beta is thus 2.

e. The expected return of the combination is: $E(R_{BD}) = [(50\% \times 7\%) + (50\% \times 11.8\%)] = 9.4\%$. Using the SML equation we have: $E(R_{BD}) = 9.4\% = 4\% + 6\% \times \beta_{DB}$. Solving for β_{DB} you get $\beta_{DB} = 0.90$.

f. We have $E(R_{Enco}) = 13\% = 4\% + (6\% \times \beta_{Enco})$. Solving for β_{Enco} you get $\beta_{Enco} = 1.50$. We now have: $\beta_{Enco} = 1.50 - \rho_{Enco,M}\left(\dfrac{\sigma_{Enco}}{\sigma_M}\right) = \rho_{Enco,M} \times \dfrac{50\%}{20\%}$. Solving for $\rho_{Enco,M}$ you get $\rho_{Enco,M} = 0.60$. And

$$\sigma_{Enco, M} = \rho_{Enco,M} \times \sigma_{Enco} \times \sigma_M = 0.60 \times 50\% \times 20\% = 0.0600.$$

4.1   Accounting allocation of transactions.

	CA	NCA	CL	NCL	OE	REV	EXP	RE
1. Factory equipment purchased for cash	✓	✓						
2. Goodwill impairment loss		✓			✓		✓	✓
3. Interest income received	✓				✓	✓		✓
4. Dividend declared			✓		✓			✓
5. Shares repurchased	✓				✓			
6. Sell merchandise on account	✓					✓	✓	✓
7. Pay two months' rent in advance								
8. Purchase raw material on account	✓		✓					
9. Receive cash advance from customer	✓		✓					
10. Recognize salaries earned by employees			✓		✓		✓	✓

4.2   Constructing income statements and balance sheets

a.   Year 0 income statement:

In thousands		Year 0
Net sales (see items 3, 19)		$ 320,000
Cost of goods sold		(260,000)
Material cost[1] (see item 5)	$224,000	
Labor expenses (see item 17)	36,000	
Gross profit		60,000
SG&A expenses (see item 12)	18,000	
Licensing fee (see item 13)	4,000	
Depreciation expense (see item 9)	9,000	
Operating profit		29,000
Special items (see item 27)		(2,000)
Earnings before interest and tax		$ 27,000
Net interest expense (see items 6, 15, 26)		(3,000)
Earnings before tax		24,000
Income tax expense[2] (see item 2)		(9,600)
Earnings after tax		$ 14,400
Dividends (see item 21)	$ 9,360	
Addition to retained earnings	$ 5,040	

[1] You could also infer the cost of material sold during the year by noting the following:
Purchases (item 11) = Cost of material sold + Change in inventories (item 19), where the change in inventories represents the cost of the material purchased but not yet sold.
We can thus write: Cost of material sold = Purchases − Changes in inventories
= $228,000,000 − ($32,000,000 − $28,000,000) = $224,000,000.
[2] The tax paid in advance on December 15, Year 0 (item 25) was exactly equal to the tax due for Year 0. The information in item 14 is irrelevant for the construction of the Year 0 income statement

b.   Balance sheets year-end Year −1 and Year 0:

In thousands	December 31, Year −1	December 31, Year 0
Cash[1] (see item 24)	$ 7,500	$ 3,515
Accounts receivable (see items 7, 1)	32,000	38,400
Inventories (see item 19)	28,000	32,000
Prepaid expenses (see item 28)	1,500	2,085
Net fixed assets (see items 4, 9, 20)	76,000	81,000
Total assets	**$145,000**	**$157,000**

Balance sheets (*Continued*)

In thousands	December 31, Year −1	December 31, Year 0
Owed to banks (see item 26)	$3,000	$5,000
Current portion of long-term debt (see item 18)	4,000	4,000
Accounts payable (see items 8, 22, 11)	30,000	35,150
Accrued expenses[2] (see item 10)	4,000	1,810
Long-term debt[3] (see items 15, 18, 20)	23,000	25,000
Owners' equity[4] (see items 23, 16)	81,000	86,040
Total liabilities and owners' equity	**$145,000**	**$157,000**

[1] You should first identify accounts payable.
[2] Wages payable.
[3] Net long-term debt$_{12/31/Year\ -1}$ = $27 million (total amount) − $4 million (due that year; see item 15).
Net long-term debt$_{12/31/Year\ 0}$ = Long-term debt (item 15) − Debt repayment (item 18) + New debt (item 20)
= $23 million − $4 million + $6 million = $25 million:
[4] Owners' equity$_{12/31/Year\ 0}$ = Owners' equity$_{12/31/Year\ -1}$ + Addition to retained earnings ($5,040,000; see income statement).

4.3 Constructing managerial balance sheets

a. Working capital requirement (WCR) = Accounts receivable + Inventories + Prepaid expenses − Accounts payable − Accrued expenses

All figures in thousand dollars:

December 31, Year −2   WCR = $2,730 + $2,800 + $0 − $1,400 − $200 = **$3,930**

December 31, Year −1   WCR = $3,100 + $3,200 + $0 − $1,600 − $260 = **$4,440**

December 31, Year 0   WCR = $4,200 + $4,300 + $0 − $2,050 − $350 = **$6,100**

a. Managerial balance sheets

In thousands		December 31, Year −2	December 31, Year −1	December 31, Year 0
Invested capital				
Cash		$ 600	$ 350	$ 300
Working capital requirement (WCR)		3,930	4,440	6,100
Net fixed assets		1,200	1,300	1,450
Total invested capital		**$5,730**	**$6,090**	**$7,850**
Capital employed				
Short-term debt		$ 300	$500	$1,900
Long-term financing		5,430	5,590	5,950
Long-term debt	$1,300	$1,200	$1,100	
Owners' equity	4,130	4,390	4,850	
Total capital employed		**$5,730**	**$6,090**	**$ 7,850**

4.4   Transactions

	NET PROFIT	WCR	EBITDA	FCF
Shares are issued for cash	0	0	0	0
Goods from inventory are sold for cash at a profit	+	−	+	+
Goods from inventory are sold on account at a profit	+	+	+	+
A fixed asset is sold for cash for less than book value	−	0	−	+
A fixed asset is sold for cash for more than book value	+	0	+	+
Corporate income tax is paid	0	+	0	−
Payment is made to trade creditors	0	+	0	−
Cash is obtained through a bank loan	0	0	0	0
A cash dividend is declared and paid	0	0	0	0
Accounts receivable are collected	0	−	0	+
Merchandise is purchased on account	0	0	0	0
Cash advances are made to employees	0	+	0	−
Minority interest in a firm is acquired for cash	0	0	0	0
Equipment is acquired for cash	0	0	0	−

4.5   Constructing a statement of cash flows

	Year 2
Earnings after tax	**$100**
Depreciation expense	50
Change in working capital requirement	(25)
Net cash flow from operating activities	**125**
Sale of fixed assets	50
Net cash flow from investing activities	**($50)**
Increase in short-term borrowing	10
Long-term debt repaid	(20)
Dividend payments	(75)
Net cash from financing activities	**($85)**
TOTAL NET CASH FLOW	**($10)**
Cash, beginning of year	100
Cash, end of year	$90

5.1   Evaluating managerial performance.

a. Yes, in Year 0 sales grew by 18.5 percent compared to a growth rate of 12.5 percent in Year −1.

b. The restructured balance sheets in their managerial form, in millions of dollars, are as follows:

	End of year					
	Year −2		Year −1		Year 0	
Cash	$100	14.9%	$90	13.2%	$50	6.5%
Working capital requirement	180	26.9%	205	29.9%	355	46.1%
Net fixed assets	390	58.2%	390	56.9%	365	47.4%
Invested capital	$670	100.0%	$685	100.0%	$770	100.0%
Short-term debt	$80	11.9%	$90	13.2%	$135	17.5%
Long-term debt	140	20.9%	120	17.5%	100	13.0%
Owners' equity	450	67.2%	475	69.3%	535	69.5%
Capital employed	$670	100.0%	$685	100.0%	$770	100.0%

where working capital requirement or WCR is equal to trade receivables plus inventories plus prepaid expenses less trade payables less accrued expenses. WCR is a measure of the investment required to support the firm's operating activities. It is mostly a long-term investment because ACC, a clothing manufacturer, should have little seasonality in its sales, meaning that its WCR is essentially *permanent* in nature.

c. The structure of invested capital has changed between Year −2 and Year 0: the proportions of cash and net fixed assets have gone down and the proportion of working capital has gone up. The structure of capital employed has also changed, particularly the composition of debt capital: the proportion of short term debt has risen, while that of long-term debt has declined.

d. In Year −2, ACC financed its long-term investments (permanent WCR and net fixed assets) with long-term funds, and its short-term investments (cash and cash equivalents) with short-term debt, indicating a "matched," if not conservative, balance sheet. In Year 0, a significant portion of long-term investments were financed with short-term debt, indicating a "mismatched" balance sheet.

e. Operational efficiency ratios:

	End of year		
	Year −2	Year −1	Year 0
WCR/sales	15.0%	15.2%	22.2%
Average collection period	61 days	62 days	66 days
Inventory turnover	5.4 times	5.7 times	3.9 times
Average payment period	72 days	68 days	69 days

There is a significant deterioration of the efficiency with which the firm's operating cycle is managed. This is clearly indicated by the rise in the ratio of WCR over sales. It is confirmed by the lengthening of the collection period and the slow down in inventory turnover.

f. Liquidity ratios:

	End of year		
	Year −2	Year −1	Year 0
NLF/WCR	111%	100%	76%
Current ratio	1.69	1.65	1.67
Quick ratio	1.03	1.02	0.84

where NLF is net long-term financing, which is equal to long-term debt plus owners' equity less net fixed assets. The ratio of NLF to WCR, called the liquidity ratio, shows a clear deterioration: the percentage of WCR financed with long-term funds went from over 100 percent in Year −2 to 76 percent in Year 0. Note that the current ratio does not seem to pick up the deterioration in liquidity, although the quick ratio does.

g. The marketing objective was achieved in terms of growth in sales, but this accomplishment was accompanied by a deterioration in the firm's operational efficiency and the quality of its balance sheet.

5.2 Working capital management for a retailer.

a. Operating assets include trade receivables and inventories; operating liabilities include accounts payable and accrued expenses related to operations. Working capital requirement (WCR) is thus (data in millions of euros):

$$WCR = Receivables + Inventories - Payables - Accrued\ expenses$$
$$WCR_{(12/31/16)} = €2,682 + €7,039 - €15,396 - €4,413 = -€10,088$$
$$WCR_{(12/31/17)} = €2,750 + €6,990 - €15,082 - €4,093 = -€9,435$$

WCR is negative and thus represents a source of capital (cash) instead of an investment that needs to be financed.

b. Working capital requirement-to-sales ratios are as follows (data in millions of euros):

$$WCR_{(12/31/16)} = -€10,088 \quad Sales_{2016} = €78,774 \quad WCR/Sales_{(31/12/16)} = -12.8\%$$
$$WCR_{(12/31/17)} = -€9,435 \quad Sales_{2017} = €80,974 \quad WCR/Sales_{(31/12/17)} = -11.7\%$$

The negative value of WCR is due to significantly longer payment terms than average, coupled with a very short collection period (retailing is essentially a cash business) and a fast inventory turnover. The faster the company grows, the larger its (negative) WCR. Carrefour, or any other company with a negative WCR, usually has a relatively stronger liquidity position than firms with a positive WCR.

c. Operational efficiency ratios (data in millions of euros):

	End of year	
	2016	2017
Average collection period	€2,682/(€78,774/365) = 13.4 days	€2,750/(€80,974/365) = 12.4 days
Inventory turnover	€60,659/€5,658 = 10.7 times	€59,828/€5,738 = 10.4 times
Average payment period[1]		€15,082/[(€62,760 + €6,690 − €7,039)/365] = 88.2 days

---

[1] Purchases are estimated as the sum of the cost of goods sold plus the change in inventories. Because inventories at year-end 2015 were not available, we could not compute the purchases in year 2016.

d. Liquidity ratios (data in millions of euros):

	Current Ratio	Quick Ratio
December 31, 2016	€19,148/€25,095 = 0.76	€5,987/€25,095 = 0.24
December 31, 2017	€18,817/€23,073 = 0.82	€6,344/€23,073 = 0.27

The rule of thumb is for the current ratio to be close to two and the quick ratio close to one. But these standards apply to firms with positive WCR. Firms with a negative WCR can afford significantly lower ratios without experiencing a deterioration in their liquidity position.

6.1 Profitability analysis.

a. The restructured balance sheets in their managerial form are as follows:

In millions	End of year					
	Year −2		Year −1		Year 0	
Cash	$100	14.9%	$90	13.2%	$50	6.5%
Working capital requirement	180	26.9%	205	29.9%	355	46.1%
Net fixed assets	390	58.2%	390	56.9%	365	47.4%
Invested capital	$670	100.0%	$685	100.0%	$770	100.0%
Short-term debt	$80	11.9%	$90	13.2%	$135	17.5%
Long-term debt	140	20.9%	120	17.5%	100	13.0%
Owners' equity	450	67.2%	475	69.3%	535	69.5%
Capital employed	$670	100.0%	$685	100.0%	$770	100.0%

where working capital requirement is trade receivables plus inventories plus prepaid expenses less trade payables less accrued expenses.

b. Return on equity (based on year-end data):

	Year −2	Year −1	Year 0
Pre tax ROE	28.89%	30.53%	29.91%
After-tax ROE	20.00%	21.05%	20.56%

c. Alternative measures of pre-tax operating profitability (based on year-end data):

	Year −2	Year −1	Year 0
$ROIC_{BT}$ = EBIT/Invested capital	22.39%	24.09%	24.03%
ROTA = EBIT/Total assets	17.05%	18.13%	17.79%
ROBA = EBIT/Business assets	26.32%	27.73%	25.69%
ROA = EAT/Total assets	10.23%	10.99%	10.58%

where business assets are working capital requirement plus net fixed assets. The first three measures have the same numerator, and because total assets are generally larger than invested capital, which is itself usually larger than business assets, it follows that ROBA is higher than $ROIC_{BT}$ and $ROIC_{BT}$ is higher than ROTA. ROA is lower than the first three measures of profitability because net profit (EAT) is smaller than pre-tax operating profit (EBIT).

d. Return on capital employed before tax ($ROCE_{BT}$) is identical to return on invested capital before tax ($ROIC_{BT}$) because, according to the managerial balance sheet, invested capital is identical to capital employed. See the managerial balance sheets in the answer to question a.

e. Return on invested capital before tax (and generally speaking any measure of operating profitability) is driven by operating margin (EBIT/Sales) and capital turnover (Sales/Invested capital). It is equal to the product of these two ratios:

	Year −2	Year −1	Year 0
Operating margin	12.50%	12.22%	11.56%
× Capital turnover	1.79	1.97	2.08
= Return on invested capital before tax	22.39%	24.09%	24.03%

Operating profitability has improved, and the improvement is due to a higher capital turnover (more efficient use of capital), whereas operating margin has actually deteriorated.

f. Pre-tax ROE is higher than $ROIC_{BT}$ because the firm finances its investments with borrowed funds (financial debt). This is what we called financial leverage or gearing. If the firm had not used any borrowing, its ROE would have been identical to its $ROIC_{BT}$.

g. No. Financial leverage can be unfavorable to shareholders, that is, borrowing may result in an ROE that is lower rather than higher than $ROIC_{BT}$. This will happen if $ROIC_{BT}$ turns out to be lower than the cost of borrowing.

h. Measures of financial leverage:

	Year −2	Year −1	Year 0
Financial cost ratio (EBT/EBIT)	0.87	0.88	0.86
Times interest earned (EBIT/Interest)	7.50	8.25	7.40
Financial structure ratio (Invested capital/Equity)	1.49	1.44	1.44
Debt-to-equity ratio	0.49	0.44	0.44
Debt-to-invested-capital ratio	0.33	0.31	0.31

The first two ratios measure the effect of borrowing on the income statement (the effect of interest payments on profitability), and the other three ratios measure the effect of borrowing on the balance sheet (the effect of the amount borrowed on profitability). All ratios indicate a slight reduction in financial leverage over the three-year period.

i. ROE Structure

	Year −2	Year −1	Year 0
Operating margin (EBIT/Sales)	12.50%	12.22%	11.56%
× Capital turnover (Sales/Invested capital)	1.79	1.97	2.08
= $ROIC_{BT}$ (EBIT/Invested capital)	22.38%	24.08%	24.04%
× Financial structure (Invested capital/Equity)	1.49	1.44	1.44
× Financial cost (EBT/EBIT)	0.87	0.88	0.86
= Pre-tax ROE	29.00%	30.51%	29.78%
× Tax effect (EAT/EBT)	0.69	0.69	0.69
= After-tax ROE	20.00%	21.05%	20.54%

Operating profitability improves slightly, mostly because of higher capital turnover (indeed, operating margin declined over the period). ROE, however, did not reflect the slight improvement in operating profitability because of the offsetting effect of a reduction in financial leverage.

j. Valuation ratios

	Year −2	Year −1	Year 0
Earnings per share (EAT/number shares)	$ 1.80	$ 2.00	$ 2.20
Price-earnings ratio (Price/EPS)	11.1	12.0	13.6
Market-to-book ratio (Price/Equity per share)	2.2	2.5	2.8

The price-earnings ratio and the market-to-book ratio indicate a rise in the relative value of ACC over the three-year period, reflecting the growth of its earnings per share.

6.2   ROE structure across industries.

Company A is the Boeing Company: it has relatively high inventories, high advances from clients (clients make a deposit when they order planes), and high leverage.

Company B is China Southern Airlines: it has relatively very high fixed assets (the plane fleet), low inventories, high advance payments from passengers and a high level of financial debt.

Company C is Alphabet Inc.: it has strong operating profitability, high cash holdings, and very little amount of debt.

6.3   Sustainable growth analysis.

a. Using millions of dollars as units, growth in sales in Year 0 is 18.5 percent (($1,600 − $1,350)/ $1,350).

$$\text{Sustainable growth rate} = \text{SGR} = (\text{Retention rate}) \times (\text{ROE on beginning equity})$$

$$\text{SGR} = (\$60/\$110) \times (\$110/\$475) = 54.5\% \times 23.2\% = 12.6\%$$

ACC has grown faster than its capacity to finance its activities without modifying its operating and financing policies. If it continues to grow much faster than 12.6 percent and does not improve its operating profitability significantly, ACC will most likely experience an increase in financial leverage and a reduction in its capacity to pay dividends, unless it decides to issue new equity.

b.1. If ACC expects to grow its sales by 25 percent in Year 1 and does not modify its financing and operating policies, it will need 25 percent more equity in Year 1 than in Year 0, that is, $134 million (25 percent of its Year 0 equity of $535 million). This equity capital can come from two sources: addition to retained earnings or a new issue of equity.

b.2. ACC will have to rely increasingly on debt financing, and thus its debt-to-equity ratio would rise.

b.3. ACC will have to rely increasingly on retained profits, and thus its retention rate should rise. By how much? ACC's profits in Year 1 are expected to be 25 percent higher than in Year 0, that is, $137.5 million ($110 million × 1.25). We know that ACC needs $134 million of new equity. The implication is clear: ACC will have to retain most of its Year 1 profits, precisely 97.5 percent ($134 million/$137.5 million). The question, of course, is whether its shareholders will accept a reduction in dividend of this magnitude.

b.4. The sustainable growth rate will have to rise to 25 percent, only through an improvement in return on invested capital before tax ($ROIC_{BT}$). The retention rate should remain at 54.5 percent (same as in Year 0), and the financial leverage multiplier should remain at 1.24 (refer to the Year 0 ROE structure in the answer to question 6.1, where we found a financial structure ratio of 1.44 and a financial cost ratio of 0.86; multiplying these two ratios, we find a financial leverage multiplier of 1.24). Because *after-tax* ROE is equal to *after-tax* ROIC multiplied by the financial leverage multiplier, we can write

$$SGR = (54.5\%) - (\text{After-tax ROIC}) \times (1.24) = 25\%$$

from which we get an expected after-tax ROIC of 37 percent (25%/[54.5% × 1.24]). With an effective tax rate of 31 percent, this implies a $ROIC_{BT}$ of 53.6 percent, more than double the Year 0 figure of 24.03 percent (see question 6.1). It is doubtful that ACC could achieve such a dramatic improvement in operating profitability. It will then have to issue new equity unless it reduces its rate of growth in sales.

c.1. In this case ACC will grow at a slower rate than its capacity to fund its activities, because the sustainable growth rate will exceed the rate of growth in sales. As a consequence, ACC will generate extra cash.

c.2. ACC can use the extra cash to make acquisitions, repay debt, increase dividend payments, or repurchase shares. Unless acquisitions are value-creating propositions, they should be avoided. In this case, the extra cash should be returned to shareholders and debt holders through share buy-backs and debt repayment.

7.1   Present values and the cost of capital.

a. We mean that if these cash flows could be traded (bought and sold) in a market for investment projects, the estimated *value* at which they would trade is $20 million. This value takes into account the following two factors: (1) the time value of money (the further into the future the cash flows are, the less value they have) and (2) the risk attached to these cash flows, that is, the probability that they will actually differ from their expected values (the riskier they are, the less value they have). The present value of the cash flows is obtained by discounting them to the present at the project cost of capital.

b. We mean that we expect the market value of the firm's equity to increase by $10 million if the firm decides to go ahead with the project. It is the difference between the present value of the cash flows expected from the project and the initial cash outlay required to launch the project.

c. We mean that investors can get a return of 10 percent on a comparable or alternative investment. Thus, if they invest in the project under consideration they will have to give up a return of 10 percent. A comparable investment is one that exhibits the same risk characteristics as the project under consideration.

7.2   Managerial options.

Managerial options refer to project-specific features that provide managers with opportunities to make alterations in reaction to changing circumstances regarding the project. Examples include options to switch technologies and options to abandon the project, as well as options to expand, retract, or defer the project.

7.3 Net present value.

a. Present value (PV) of the projects expected cash-flow stream at 12 percent:

Part I Calculations

$$PV = \frac{\$50,000}{1 + 0.12} + \frac{\$50,000}{(1 + 0.12)^2} + \frac{\$50,000}{(1 + 0.12)^3}$$

$$= (\$50,000 \times 0.89286) + (\$50,000 \times 0.79719) + (\$50,000 \times 0.71178)$$

$$= \$120,092$$

Part II Using a spreadsheet

	A	B	C	D	E
1		Now		Forecast for	
2		0	Year 1	Year 2	Year 3
3	Cash flow	-$100,000	$50,000	$50,000	$50,000
4	Cost of capital	12.00%			
5	Present value of cash flows Year 1 to Year 3	$120,092			
6	Net present value	$ 20,092			

- Formula in cell B5 is =NPV(B4,C3:E3)
- Formula in cell B6 is =B3+B6

b. Net present value = -$100,000 + $120,092 = $20,092.

c. Profitability index $= \dfrac{\text{Present value of expected cash flows}}{\text{Initial cash outlay}} = \dfrac{\$120,095}{\$100,000} = 1.20$

d. The project should be undertaken, because it is expected to increase the value of the firm's equity by $20,095 or, equivalently, because it returns more than one dollar per dollar spent (20 percent more).

7.4 Choosing between two investments with unequal costs and life spans.

a.

Part I Calculations

Present value of printer X costs $= -\$50,000 - \dfrac{\$5,000}{1 + 0.10} - \dfrac{\$5,000}{(1 + 0.10)^2} = -\$58,678.$

Present value of printer Y costs $= -\$60,000 - \dfrac{\$7,000}{1 + 0.10} - \dfrac{\$7,000}{(1 + 0.10)^2} - \dfrac{\$7,000}{(1 + 0.10)^3} = -\$77,408.$

Part II Using a spreadsheet

	A	B	C	D	E
1		Now		Forecast for	
2		0	Year 1	Year 2	Year 3
3	**Printer X**				
4	Cash flow	−$50,000	−$5,000	−$5,000	
5	Cost of capital	10.00%			
6	Present value of cash flows	−$58,678			
7	**Printer Y**				
8	Cash flow	−$60,000	−$7,000	−$7,000	−$7,000
9	Cost of capital	10.00%			
10	**Present value of cash flows**	**−$77,408**			

- Formula in cell B6 is =B4+NPV(B5,C4:D4)
- Formula in cell B10 is =B8+NPV(B9,C8:E8)

b. The two present values are not comparable because printer X will provide two years of service, whereas printer Y could be used one more year.

c. The annual-equivalent cost of a printer is the cost per year of operating the printer that has the *same* present value as the present value of the total cost. In the case of printer X, we have to find a two-year annuity (that is, two *equal* annual payments) with a present value of $58,678. And in the case of printer Y, we have to find a three-year annuity (that is, three *equal* annual payments) with a present value of $77,408.

To compute these annuities, we use the formula presented in the chapter:

$$\text{Annuity} - \text{equivalent cash flow} = \frac{\text{Present value of original cash flow}}{\text{Annuity discount factor}}$$

For Printer X, the two-year discount factor is $\dfrac{1}{(1+0.10)^2} = 0.8264$, the annuity discount factor is $\dfrac{1-0.8264}{0.10} = 1.7355$, and the annuity-equivalent cost is thus $\dfrac{-\$58,678}{1.7355} = -\$33,810$.

For Printer Y, the three-year discount factor is $\dfrac{1}{(1+0.10)^3} = 0.7513$, the annuity discount factor is $\dfrac{1-0.7513}{0.10} = 2.4870$, and the annuity-equivalent cost is thus $\dfrac{-\$77,408}{2.4870} = -\$31,125$.

d. PCC should purchase printer Y because its effective annual cost of $31,125 is lower than the $33,810 equivalent cost of printer X. Although printer Y is more expensive than printer X to buy and operate, its longer useful life more than offsets the difference in costs.

7.5   **Replacing an existing machine with a new one.**

a. The present value of the expected cash flows from the new machine is as follows:

Part I Calculations

$$-\$150{,}000 + \frac{\$75{,}000}{1+0.10} + \frac{\$75{,}000}{(1+0.10)^2} + \frac{\$75{,}000}{(1+0.10)^3} = \$36{,}514$$

Part II Using a spreadsheet				
	A	B	C	D	E
1		Now		Forecast for	
2		0	Year 1	Year 2	Year 3
3	Cash flow	−$150,000	$75,000	$75,000	$75,000
4	Cost of capital	10.00%			
5	Present value of cash flows	$ 36,514			
• *Formula in cell B5 is =B3+NPV(B4,C3:E3)*				

From the same formula used in the answer to question 7.4 to calculate an annuity cash flow we found that the three-year discount factor is $\dfrac{1}{(1+0.10)^3} = 0.7513$, the annuity discount factor is

$\dfrac{1-0.7513}{0.10} = 2.4870$, and the annuity-equivalent cash flow is thus $\dfrac{\$36{,}514}{2.4870} = \$14{,}682$.

b. Why replace a machine that produces an annual cash flow of $20,000 with a new one that will generate only $14,682 a year? The management of Pasta Uno should keep the old machine.

8.1   **Shortcomings of the payback period.**

The payback period rule ignores the time value of money and the risk of the project (unless you use the discounted payback period); it also ignores the cash flows beyond the cutoff period and, more generally, tends to favor short-term investments. Firms still compute the payback period because it is simple to calculate and easy to interpret: it provides an indication of the speed of the recovery of the initial investment.

8.2   **Internal rate of return versus cost of capital.**

The cost of capital is the rate of return that investors require from investments with the same risk as the project, whereas the project's internal rate of return is the discount rate for which the net present value of the project is equal to zero. Put another way, the project's cost of capital is what the firm *should* earn from the project, whereas the project's internal rate of return is what the firm *can expect to earn* from it.

8.3   **Internal rate of return versus return on invested capital.**

Both the return on invested capital and the internal rate of return are measures of operating profitability, but there are several important differences between them:

	Return on Invested Capital	Internal Rate of Return
Measured with	*Accounting* data	*Cash-flow* data
Measurement period	*Single* period	*Multiple* periods
Typically used for analyzing	*Historical* profitability of *firms*	*Expected* profitability of *projects*

8.4   Shortcomings of the internal rate of return and profitability index rules.

Internal rate of return: when the choice is between two mutually exclusive investments. In the case where the cash-flow streams of the two investments differ widely, the project with the cash flows concentrated mostly in the earliest years may have a higher internal rate of return than the project with the cash flows concentrated mostly in later years, although the second project may have a higher net present value, meaning that it will contribute the most to the firm's value.

Profitability index: when the sizes of the two investments are very different. In this case, the profitability index of the smaller project may be higher than that of the *bigger* project, although its net present value may be *smaller*.

8.5   Evaluating two projects using alternative decision rules.

In what follows, all figures are in thousands of dollars.

a. Net present values

Part I Calculations

Net present value (project A) = −$2,000 + $2,451 = $451

Net present value (project B) = −$2,000 + $2,400 = $400

Part II Using a spreadsheet

	A	B	C	D	E
		Now		Forecast for	
1					
2		0	Year 1	Year 2	Year 3
3	**Project A**				
4	Cash flow	−$2,000	$ 200	$1,200	$1,700
5	Cost of capital	10%			
6	Present value of cash flows	$450.79			
7	**Project B**				
8	Cash flow	−$2,000	$1,400	$1,000	$ 400
9	Cost of capital	10%			
10	**Present value of cash flows**	$ 400			

- *Formula in cell B6 is =B4+NPV(B5,C4:E4)*
- *Formula in cell B10 is =B8+NPV(B9,C8:E8)*

If the projects are independent, *both* should be accepted, because they both create value ($451 for project A and $400 for project B). If they are mutually exclusive, project A should be preferred because it creates *more* value.

b. Payback periods

To get the payback periods of the two projects, you need first to compute their cumulative cash flows:

	Project A		Project B	
Year	Cash Flows	Cumulative Cash Flows	Cash Flows	Cumulative Cash Flows
Now	−$2,000	−$2,000	−$2,000	−$2,000
1	200	−1,800	1,400	−600
2	1,200	−600	1,000	400
3	1,700	1,100	400	800

The payback period of project A is between two and three years, because the cumulative cash flows become positive between these years. The payback period of project B is between one and two years. We can write the following:

$$\text{Payback period project A} = 2 + \frac{\$600}{\$1,700} = 2.35 \text{ years}$$

$$\text{Payback period project B} = 1 + \frac{\$600}{\$1,000} = 1.60 \text{ years}$$

	A	B	C	D	E
1		Now		Forecast for	
2		0	Year 1	Year 2	Year 3
3	Project A				
4	Cash flow	−$2,000	$200	$1,200	$1,700
5	Accumulated cash inflow		$200	$1,400	$3,100
6	Payback period		−	−	2.35

- Formula in cell C5 is = C4. Formula in cell D5 is = C5 + D4. Then copy formula in cell D5 to next cell in row 5
- Formula in cell C6 is = IF(OR(C5<=−$B$4,B5>−$B$4,"−",B2 + (−$B$4−B5)/C4). Then copy formula in cell C6 to next cells in row 6

7	Project B				
8	Cash flow	−$2,000	$1,400	$1,000	$ 400
9	Accumulated cash inflow		$1,400	$2,400	$2,800
10	Payback period		−	1.60	−

- Formula in cell C9 is =C8. Formula in cell D9 is =C9 + D8. Then copy formula in cell D9 to next cell in row 9
- Formula in cell C10 is = IF(OR(C9<=−$B$8,B9>−$B$8),"−", B2 + (−$B$8−B9)/C8). Then copy formula in cell C10 to next cells in row 10

Discounted payback period

Part I Calculations

To get the discounted payback period, you need to compute the cumulative present value of the two projects' cash-flow streams. Using a discount rate of 10 percent, we have the following:

		Project A			Project B	
Year	Cash Flows	Present Value of Cash Flows	Cumulative Present Value of Cash Flows	Cash Flows	Present Value of Cash Flows	Cumulative Present Value of Cash Flows
Now	−$2,000	−$2,000.00	−$2,000.00	−$2,000	−$2,000.00	−$2,000.00
1	200	181.82	−1,800.00	1,400	1,272.73	−727.27
2	1,200	991.74	−826.44	1,000	826.45	99.18
3	1,700	1,277.23	450.79	400	300.53	399.71

The discounted payback period is between two and three years for project A and between one and two years for project B. However, because discounting reduces the value of the cash flows, the discounted payback periods are longer than the straight payback periods. We have:

$$\text{Payback period project A} = 2 + \frac{\$826.44}{\$1,277.23} = 2.65 \text{ years}$$

$$\text{Payback period project B} = 1 + \frac{\$727.27}{\$826.45} = 1.88 \text{ years}$$

Part II Using a spreadsheet

	A	B	C	D	E
		Now		Forecast for	
1					
2		0	Year 1	Year 2	Year 3
3	**Project A**				
4	Cash flow	−$2,000	$ 200	$1,200	$1,700
5	Cost of capital	10%			
6	Discounted cash inflow		$ 181.82	$ 991.74	$1,277.24
7	Accumulated discounted cash inflow		$ 181.82	$1,173.55	$2,450.79
8	Discounted payback period		-	-	**2.65**

- *Formula in cell C6 is = C4/(1 + B5)^C2. Then copy formula C6 to next cells in row 6*
- *Formula in cell C7 is = C6. Formula in cell D7 is =C7+D6. Then copy formula in cell D7 to next cell in row 7*
- *Formula in cell C8 is =IF(OR(C7<=−$B$4,B7>−$B$4),"−",B2+(−$B$4−B7)/C6). Then copy formula in cell C8 to next cells in row 8*

	A	B	C	D	E
9	**Project B**				
10	Cash flow	−$2,000	$1,400	$1,000	$ 400
11	Cost of capital	10%			
12	Discounted cash inflow		$1,272.73	$ 826.45	$ 300.53
13	Accumulated discounted cash inflow		$1,272.73	$2,099.17	$2,399.70
14	Discounted payback period		−	**1.88**	−

Part II Using a spreadsheet (*Continued*)

- *Formula in cell C12 is = C10/(1 + B11)^C2. Then copy formula C12 to next cells in row 12*
- *Formula in cell C13 is = C12. Formula in cell D13 is =C13+D12. Then copy formula in cell D13 to next cells in row 13*
- *Formula in cell C14 is = IF(OR(C14<=-$B$10,B13>-$B$10),"–", B2+(-$B$10–B13)/B12). Then copy formula in cell C9 to next cells in row 9*

If the two projects are mutually exclusive, the initial investment of $2,000 (which is the same for both projects) will be recovered earlier from project B than from project A. However, this does not mean that you should choose project B, because the payback period does not tell you which project will create more value. We know from the answer to the previous question that project A creates more value than project B. Thus, project A should be chosen over project B.

c. The internal rate of return (IRR) of the projects is the discount rates for which the net present value of the projects is equal to zero:

$$\text{Net present value (project A)} = 0 = -\$2,000 + \frac{\$200}{1 + \text{IRR}} + \frac{\$1,200}{(1 + \text{IRR})^2} + \frac{\$1,700}{(1 + \text{IRR})^3}$$

$$\text{Net present value (project B)} = 0 = -\$2,000 + \frac{\$1,400}{1 + \text{IRR}} + \frac{\$1,000}{(1 + \text{IRR})^2} + \frac{\$400}{(1 + \text{IRR})^3}$$

Part II Using a spreadsheet

	A	B	C	D	E
1		Now		Forecast for	
2		0	Year 1	Year 2	Year 3
3	Project A				
4	Cash flow	−$2,000	$ 200	$1,200	$1,700
5	Internal rate of return	19.60%			

- *Formula in cell B5 is =IRR(B4,E4,.1) where .1 or 10 percent is a guess value for IRR*

6	Project B				
7	Cash flow	−$2,000	$1,400	$1,000	$ 400
8	Internal rate of return	23.56%			

- *Formula in cell B8 is =IRR(B7,E7,.1) where .1 or 10 percent is a guess value for IRR*

If the projects are independent, both should be accepted because their internal rate of return is higher than the 10 percent cost of capital. If the projects are mutually exclusive, intuition would suggest that project B, which has the higher internal rate of return, should be preferred to project A. However, this would be true only if project B was creating more value than project A, which we know is not the case. Thus, project A should be preferred, although it has a lower internal rate of return. This will always be true as long as the projects' cost of capital is lower than the break-even discount rate of 12.9 percent. It is only when the cost of capital is higher than 12.9 percent that the ranking of the two projects is the same, using the net present value or the internal rate of return.

d.

Part I Calculations

Present value of project A future cash flows at 10% = $2,451

Present value of project B future cash flows at 10% = $2,400

$$\text{Profitability Index A} = \frac{\text{Present value cash flows (A)}}{\text{Initial cash outlay (A)}} = \frac{\$2,451}{\$2,000} = 1.23$$

$$\text{Profitability Index B} = \frac{\text{Present value cash flows (B)}}{\text{Initial cash outlay (B)}} = \frac{\$2,400}{\$2,000} = 1.20$$

Part II Using a spreadsheet

	A	B	C	D	E
		Now		Forecast for	
2		0	Year 1	Year 2	Year 3
3	**Project A**				
4	Cash flow	−$2,000	$ 200	$1,200	$1,700
5	Cost of capital	10%			
6	Profitability index	1.23			
	• *Formula in cell B6 is = NPV(B5,C4:E4)/−B4*				
7	**Project B**				
8	Cash flow	−$2,000	$1,400	$1,000	$ 400
9	Cost of capital	10%			
10	Profitability index	1.20			
	• *Formula in cell B10 is = NPV(B9,C8:E8)/−B8*				

Both projects have a profitability index greater than one, which means that they both return more than one dollar for one dollar invested ($1.23 for project A and $1.20 for project B). Thus, both projects would create value. They should both be accepted if they are independent. If they are mutually exclusive, project A should be accepted, because it generates more dollars for each dollar invested. Note that both the net present value rule and the profitability index rule lead to the same decisions: accept both projects if they are independent and choose project A over project B if the two projects are mutually exclusive. As shown in the chapter, however, this may not always be the case, especially when both projects differ widely in size.

e. As long as the objective is to accept projects that create value, the only criterion that will always work is the net present value rule. Thus, because both projects have a positive net present value, they should be both accepted if they are independent. If they are mutually exclusive, project A is preferred to project B because it has a higher net present value.

9.1   Interest payments and project's cash flow.

Interest payments are cash flows to creditors, not cash flows *from* the project. They are claims on the cash flows generated by the project and do not affect these cash flows. Interest payments and, more generally, the costs of financing a project are taken into account in the project's cost of capital.

9.2 Understanding the structure of the cash-flow formula.

The term EBIT $(1 - \text{Tax})$ is equal to $(\text{EBIT} - \text{EBIT} \times \text{Tax})$, so that the formula can be rewritten as follows:

$$\text{Cash flow} = \text{EBIT} + \text{Depreciation} - (\text{EBIT} \times \text{Tax}) - \Delta\text{WCR} - \text{Capex}$$

Note that by adding depreciation to EBIT, the effect of depreciation on the cash flow is washed out because EBIT includes depreciation as an expense. Furthermore, because EBIT $\times$ Tax is the amount of tax to be paid on the operating profit generated by the project, it clearly needs to be accounted for in the cash flow from the project. Finally, by deducting the increase in working capital requirement, the formula takes into account any lead or lag between the accounting revenues and expenses in EBIT and their corresponding cash inflows or cash outflows (see Chapter 4).

9.3 Alternative formula to estimate a project's cash flow.

We can write EBIT = EBITDA $-$ Depreciation, so that the first formula can be rewritten as follows:

$$\begin{aligned}\text{Cash flow} &= (\text{EBITDA} - \text{Depreciation})(1 - \text{Tax}) + \text{Depreciation} - \Delta\text{WCR} - \text{Capex} \\ &= \text{EBITDA}(1 - \text{Tax}) - \text{Depreciation} + (\text{Tax} \times \text{Depreciation}) + \text{Depreciation} - \Delta\text{WCR} - \text{Capex} \\ &= \text{EBITDA}(1 - \text{Tax}) + (\text{Tax} \times \text{Depreciation}) - \Delta\text{WCR} - \text{Capex}\end{aligned}$$

which is the second formula. Note that in the second formula, the term EBITDA $(1 - \text{Tax})$ over-estimates the tax bill because it ignores the deduction of the allowable depreciation expenses. To compensate for this, the tax that would be shielded by the depreciation expense, which is captured by the term (Tax $\times$ Depreciation), is added back.

9.4 Identifying a project's relevant cash flows.

Capital expenditures:

1. Is there any opportunity cost associated with the use of the parking lot? Where will company employees park their cars? Will Printers Inc. need to rent parking spaces? If this is the case, the project should be charged for the rent.
2. A residual value should be included at the end of Year 5.

Depreciation: Would the tax office accept an accelerated depreciation scheme that will save taxes earlier?

Revenue: The sale price is assumed to be constant, that is, unaffected by competition, which is unreasonable.

Research and development costs: These are sunk costs (they were spent earlier). They should therefore be ignored.

Overhead costs: The overhead costs charged to the project are not incremental costs-they are accounting allocations. The relevant amount of overhead costs is the increase in the company overhead charges that would result from the adoption of the project, if any.

Operating costs: The direct and indirect costs are assumed to be only variable costs, which is unreasonable.

Inventories:

1. Investment in inventories is supposed to stay constant, although sales are multiplied by a factor of 4 during the life of the project. This is also unreasonable.
2. The recovery of the investment in the inventories at the end of the project is ignored.
3. What about receivables? Payables? Working capital requirement?

Financing costs:
1. Financing costs are cash flows *to* those who invested in the project and not cash flows *from* the project. Therefore, they are irrelevant.
2. Furthermore, they are accounting allocations, not incremental costs, which is incorrect.

Discount rate: The discount rate is the project's cost of capital. It should reflect the risk characteristics of the project as well as the proportion of debt capital and equity capital that is relevant for the project. It is *not* Printers Inc.'s borrowing rate.

Other: Inflation is ignored.

9.5   Estimating a project's relevant cash flows and net present value.

Part I Calculations						
	Now			Forecast for		
Dollars in thousands except for variable costs per unit	0	Year 1	Year 2	Year 3	Year 4	Year 5
I. Revenues						
1. Expected unit sales		5,000	10,000	20,000	20,000	20,000
2. Price per unit		$ .80	$ .70	$ .60	$ .60	$ .60
3. Sales revenues (line 1 × line 2)		$4,000.00	$7,000.00	$12,000.00	$12,000.00	$12,000.00
II. Operating expenses						
4. Inflation rate		3%	3%	3%	3%	3%
5. Compounded inflation rate		1.030	1.061	1.093	1.126	1.159
6. Fixed costs (now)		$ 800.00	$ 800.00	$ 800.00	$ 800.00	$ 800.00
7. Fixed costs (line 6 × line 5)		$ 824.00	$ 848.72	$ 874.18	$ 900.41	$ 927.42
8. Variable costs per unit (now)		$ 400.00	$ 400.00	$ 400.00	$ 400.00	$ 400.00
9. Variable costs per unit (line 12 × line 5)		$ 412.00	$ 424.36	$ 437.09	$ 450.20	$ 463.71
10. Total variable costs (line 1 × line 9)/1,000		$2,060.00	$4,243.60	$ 8,741.82	$ 9,004.07	$ 9,274.19
11. Depreciation expense ($6,000,000/10)		$ 600.00	$ 600.00	$ 600.00	$ 600.00	$ 600.00
12. Rental of parking spaces		$ 50.00	$ 50.00	$ 50.00	$ 50.00	$ 50.00
13. Total operating expenses (lines 7 + 10 + 11 + 12)		$3,534.00	$ 5,742.32	$10,266.00	$ 10,554.48	$ 10,851.61
III. Operating profit						
14. EBIT (line 3 − line 13)		$ 466.00	$1,257.68	$ 1,734.00	$ 1,445.52	$ 1,148.39
15. *less* tax at 40%		−$ 186.40	−$ 503.07	−$ 639.60	−$ 578.21	−$ 459.36
16. After-tax operating profit (line 14 + line 15)		$ 279.60	$ 754.61	$ 1,040.40	$ 867.31	$ 689.03

Part I Calculations (*Continued*)

Dollars in thousands except for prices and variable costs per unit	Now 0	Year 1	Year 2	Year 3	Year 4	Year 5
				Forecast for		

IV. Cash flow generated by the project

	Now 0	Year 1	Year 2	Year 3	Year 4	Year 5
17. After-tax operating profit (line 16)		$ 279.60	$ 754.61	$1,040.40	$ 867.31	$ 689.03
18. *plus* Depreciation expense (line 11)		$ 600.00	$ 600.00	$ 600.00	$ 600.00	$ 600.00
19. Year-end working capital requirement	$1,200.00	$2,100.00	$3,600.00	$3,600.00	$3,600.00	$ 0.00
20. *less* change in working capital requirement	−$1,200.00	−$ 900.00	−$1,500.00	$ 0.00	$ 0.00	$3,600.00
21. *less* capital expenditures	−$6,000.00					
22. *plus* resale of equipment (after-tax)[1]						$3,000.00
23. *equal* Cash flow from the project (lines 17 + 18 + 19 + 20 + 21 + 22)	−$7,200.00	−$ 20.40	−$ 145.39	$1,640.40	$ 1,467.31	$ 7,889.03

V. Net present value

24. Cost of capital	12%	
25. Net present value	−$ 757.56	

[1]Book value (original cost less accumulated depreciation)   = $6 million − $3 million = $3 million
Capital gain   = $0
Tax on capital gain   = $0
After-tax cash receipt from selling the equipment   = $3 million

Part II Using a spreadsheet[1]

	A	B	C	D	E	F	G
1	*Dollars in thousands except for prices and variable costs per unit*	Now			Forecast for		
2		0	Year 1	Year 2	Year 3	Year 4	Year 5
3	**I. Revenues**						
4	Expected unit sales		5,000	10,000	20,000	20,000	20,000
5	Price per unit		$ 800.00	$ 700.00	$ 600.00	$ 600.00	$ 600.00
6	Sales revenues		$4,000.00	$7,000.00	$12,000.00	$12,000.00	$12,000.00

• *Rows 4 and 5 are data*
• *Formula in cell C6 is =C4*C5/1000. Then copy cell C6 to next cells in row 6*

Part II Using a spreadsheet[1] (*Continued*)

	A	B	C	D	E	F	G
7	**II. Operating expenses**						
8	Inflation rate		3%	3%	3%	3%	3%
9	Compounded inflation rate		1.030	1.061	1.093	1.126	1.159
10	Fixed costs (now)		($ 800.00)	($ 800.00)	($ 800.00)	($ 800.00)	($ 800.00)
11	Fixed costs		($ 824.00)	($ 848.72)	($ 874.18)	($ 900.41)	($ 927.42)
12	Variable costs per unit (now)		($ 400.00)	($ 400.00)	($ 400.00)	($ 400.00)	($ 400.00)
13	Variable costs per unit		($ 412.00)	($ 424.36)	($ 437.09)	($ 450.20)	($ 463.71)
14	Total variable costs		($2,060.00)	($4,243.60)	($ 8,741.82)	($9,004.07)	($9,274.19)
15	Depreciation expense		($ 600.00)	($ 600.00)	($ 600.00)	($ 600.00)	($ 600.00)
16	Rental of parking spaces		$ 50.00	$ 50.00	$ 50.00	$ 50.00	$ 50.00
17	**Total operating expenses**		($ 3,534.00)	($ 5,742.32)	($10,266.00)	($10,554.48)	($10,851.61)

- *Rows 8, 10, 12, and 16 are data*
- *Formula in cell C9 is =1*(1+C8). Formula in cell D9 is =C9*(1+D8). Then copy formula in cell D9 to next cells in row 9*
- *Formula in cell C11 is =C10*C9. Then copy formula in cell C11 to next cells in row 11*
- *Formula in cell C13 is =C12*C9. Then copy formula in cell C13 to next cells in row 13*
- *Formula in cell C14 is =C4*C13/1000. Then copy formula in cell C14 to next cells in row 14*
- *Formula in cell C15 to G15 is = SLN(6000,10) where 6,000 is the investment and 10 the depreciation period*
- *Formula in cell C17 is =C11+C14+15−C16. Then copy formula in cell C17 to next cells in row 17*

	A	B	C	D	E	F	G
18	**III. Operating profit**						
19	EBIT		$ 466.00	$1,257.68	$1,734.00	$1,445.52	$1,148.39
20	Tax at 40%		($ 186.40)	($ 503.07)	($ 693.60)	($ 578.21)	($ 459.36)
21	**After-tax operating profit**		$ 279.60	$ 754.61	$1,040.40	$ 867.31	$ 689.03

- *Formula in cell C19 is =C6+C17. Then copy formula in cell C19 to next cells in row 19*
- *Formula in cell C20 is =C19*0.40. Then copy formula in cell C20 to next cells in row 20*
- *Formula in cell C21 is =C19+C20. Then copy formula in cell C21 to next cells in row 21*

	A	B	C	D	E	F	G
22	**IV. Cash flow generated by the project**						
23	Working capital requirement/ Sales		30%	30%	30%	30%	30%
24	Working capital requirement	$1,200.00	$2,100.00	$3,600.00	$3,600.00	$3,600.00	$ 0.00
25	Change in working capital requirement	$1,200.00	$ 900.00	$1,500.00	$ 0.00	$ 0.00	−$3,600.00

Part II Using a spreadsheet[1] (*Continued*)

	A	B	C	D	E	F	G
26	Capital expenditure	$6,000.00					
27	After-tax resale value of equipment						$3,000.00
28	Cash flow from the project	−$7,200.00	−$ 20.40	−$ 145.39	$1,640.40	$1,467.31	$ 7,889.03

- *Rows 23, 26, and 27 are data*
- *Formula in cell B24 is =C23*C6. Then copy formula in cell B24 to next cells in row 24*
- *Formula in cell B25 is =B24. Formula in cell C25 is =C24 − B24. Then copy formula in cell C25 to next cells in row 25*
- *Formula in cell B28 is =B21−B15−B25−B26+B27. Then copy formula in cell B28 to next cells in row 28*

29	**V. Net present value**						
30	Cost of capital	12%					
31	Net present value	−$ 757.56					

- *Cell B30 is data*
- *Formula in cell B31 is =B28+NPV(B30,C28:G28)*

The project's net present value is negative after taking into account the relevant cash flows from the project and discounting them at the cost of capital of 12 percent. The proposal would destroy value if undertaken, and should therefore be rejected.

10.1 Pricing and risk of PEC bonds four years after they were issued.

a. $P_1 = \dfrac{\$50}{(1+2\%+2.60\%)} + \dfrac{\$1,050}{(1+2.50\%+2.60\%)^2} = \$998.37$

b. Yield to maturity = 5.0878% (financial calculator: N = 2, PV = −998.37, PMT = 50, FV = 1,000, I/YR = 5.0878)

c. Current yield = $\dfrac{\$50}{\$998.37} = 5.01\%$

d. Cost of debt = yield to maturity = 5.0878%

e. $\text{Dur} = \dfrac{0.050 \times (1.050878) \times 1.8570 + 2 \times (0.050878 - 0.050) \times 0.905515}{0.050 + (0.050878 - 0.050) \times 0.905515} = 1.9523 \text{ years}$

f.

Cash Flow	PV(CF) at 5.0878%	PV(CF)/Bond Price
$ 50	$ 47.5793	$ 47.5793/$998.3695 = 4.7657%
$1,050	$950.7902	$950.7902/$998.3695 = 95.2343%
	$998.3695	100%

Dur = (4.7657% × 1 year) + (95.2343% × 2 years) = 1.9523 years

g. $\dfrac{\Delta P}{P} = \dfrac{P(5.1878\%) - P(5.0878\%)}{P(5.0878\%)} = \dfrac{\$996.5173 - \$998.3695}{\$998.3695} = -0.1855\%$

h. $\dfrac{\Delta P}{P} \approx -\dfrac{Dur}{1+y} \times 0.0010 = -\dfrac{1.9523}{1+5.0878\%} \times 0.0010 = -0.1858\%$

Because the change in yield is very small, the change in price based on the duration formula is very close to the actual change in price.

10.2 Bond pricing and forward rates.

a. $P_1 = \dfrac{\$40}{1+y_1} + \dfrac{\$1,040}{(1+y_2)^2} = \dfrac{\$40}{1+y_1} + \dfrac{\$1,040}{(1+y_1)(1+f_1)} = \dfrac{\$40}{1+3\%} + \dfrac{\$1,040}{(1+3\%)(1+5\%)} = \$1,000.46$

b. Using a financial calculator: Enter N=2, PV=−1000.46, PMT=40, FV=1,000 and you get I/YR = 3.9756%

c. $P_1 = \dfrac{\$40}{1.039756} + \dfrac{\$1,040}{(1.039756)^2} = \$1,000.46$

d. $P_2 = \dfrac{\$1,040}{1.035} = \$1,004.83$ and the holding-period return is $= \dfrac{(\$1,004.83 + \$40) - \$1,000.46}{\$1,000.46} = 4.43\%$

10.3 Extracting spot rates from coupon-paying bonds.

a. $P_1 = \$1,004.88 = \dfrac{\$1,030}{1+y_1}$ from which we get $y_1 = 2.50\%$

$P_2 = \$1,009.73 = \dfrac{\$35}{1.025} + \dfrac{\$1,035}{(1+y_2)^2}$ from which we get $y_2 = 3.00\%$

$P_3 = \$1,014.75 = \dfrac{\$40}{1.025} + \dfrac{\$40}{(1.03)^2} + \dfrac{\$1,040}{(1+y_3)^3}$ from which we get $y_3 = 3.50\%$

b. For the 1-year bond, the yield to maturity is the same as the spot rate, that is, 2.50 percent. For the 2-year bond and the 3-year bond, we have to use a financial calculator to search for the yield to maturity. For the 2-year bond, the yield to maturity is 2.99 percent. It is lower than the 2-year spot rate because the 1-year spot rate is lower than the 2-year spot rate. For the 3-year bond, the yield to maturity is 3.47 percent. It is lower than the 3-year spot rate because the 1-year spot rate and the 2-year spot rate are lower than the 3-year spot rate.

10.4 Present value of growth opportunities.

a. If all profits are paid out as dividends, PEC will not grow because it will not be re-investing part of its profits in new projects. In this case the dividend payout ratio is 100 percent and dividend per share is equal earnings per share. Given that the growth rate g is zero, PEC's no-growth share price is:

$$P(\text{no growth}) = \dfrac{EPS}{k} = \dfrac{\$1.15}{9\%} = \$12.78$$

b. In this case $P = \dfrac{DPS_1}{k_E - g} = \dfrac{DPS_0(1+g)}{k_E - g} = \dfrac{\$1.15 \times 70\% \times 1.045}{9\% - 4.5\%} = \dfrac{\$0.8412}{0.045} = \$18.69$

c. The share price with a growth rate of 4.5 percent is $5.91 higher than the share price with no growth. The difference represents the present value of future growth opportunities, that is, the value today of the growth that will take place in the future as a result of the retention and investment policy.

10.5 Discounted cash flow valuation.

1. Share price based on discounted free cash flow at the weighted average cost of capital (WACC)

	A	B	C	D	E
1		Now		Forecast for	
2	$ million except share price	0	Year 1	Year 2	Year 3
3	EBIT		$ 500.00	$ 600.00	$ 660.00
4	WCR	$3,000.00	$3,200.00	$3,400.00	$3,500.00
5	ΔWCR		$ 200.00	$ 200.00	$ 100.00
6	Cash flow		$ 175.00	$ 250.00	$ 395.00
7	WACC	10.50%			
8	Terminal value				$5,424.67
9	Free cash flow		$ 175.00	$ 250.00	$5,819.67
10	Asset value	$4,676.43			
11	Equity value	$3,626.43			
12	Share price	$ 12.09			

- Data in rows 3 and 4 is given
- Formula in cell C5 is =C4–B4. Then copy cell C5 to next cells in row 5
- Formula in cell C6 is =C3*.75–C5. Then copy cell C6 to next cells in row 6
- Formula in cell B7 is = 08*(1 – 0.25)*0.25+.12*0.75
- Formula in cell E8 is =E6*1.03/(B7–.03)
- Formula in cell C9 is =C6+C8. Then copy cell C9 to next cells in row 9
- Formula in cell B10 is =NPV(B7,C9:E9)
- Formula in cell B11 is =B10+150–1200
- Formula in cell B12 is =B11/300

2. Share price based on discounted cash flow from equity at the cost of equity

	A	B	C	D	E
1		Now		Forecast For	
2	$ million except share price	0	Year 1	Year 2	Year 3
3	Cash flow		$175.00	$250.00	$ 395.00
4	Cost of equity	12.00%			
5	Terminal value				$4,520.56
6	Cash flow from equity		$175.00	$250.00	$4,915.56
7	Equity value	$3,854.34			
8	Share price	$ 12.85			

- Cash flows in row 3 are from row 6 of the previous spreadsheet
- Formula in cell E5 is =E3*1.03/(B4–.03)
- Formula in cell C6 is =C3+E5. Then copy cell C6 to next cells in row 6
- Formula in cell B7 is =NPV(B4,C6:E6)
- Formula in cell B8 is =B7/300

11.1 Estimating external funding needs.

a. Total funding needs in Year 0 = ΔCash + ΔWCR + Capex
= zero + $7.7 million + $10 million = $17.7 million
b. Internally generated funds = Addition to retained earnings + Depreciation
= $7.7 million + ($8 million + $1 million) = $16.7 million
c. External funding needs = $17.7 million − $16.7 million = $1 million
d. The million-dollar gap should be borrowed. It is too small to justify an issue of new equity.

11.2 Leasing.

a. **True**
A buyer with a low effective tax rate would receive little tax credit from interest and deprecia-tion deductions. A lessor with a high tax bracket will benefit more from the same deductions. Thus, a market for leasing can emerge, with some of the tax benefit received by the lessor trans-ferred to the lessee through lower lease payments.

b. **True**
The lessee does not own the leased equipment when the lease expires. It is given back to the lessor. In fixing the lease payments, the lessor must estimate what the residual value of the equipment at expiration of the lease will be. Thus, the uncertainty in the valuation of the residual value is entirely borne by the lessor. The lessee would have to bear this uncertainty if the equipment were purchased.

c. **True**
Leased assets do not appear in the balance sheet for an operating lease, nor the correspond-ing liability to the lessor. However, it is unlikely that financial analysts would be fooled by the accounting treatment of operating leases. The balance sheet is typically adjusted by the amount of the lease liability.

11.3 Taxes and dividend payments.

a. The left side of the equation is the after-tax capital loss, at the capital gains tax rate, resulting from the drop in share price. The right side of the equation is the after-tax dividend income at the income tax rate. In equilibrium the two must be equal to eliminate any arbitrage opportu-nity.
b. Rearrange the term of the equation in the previous question to express P_{ex} as a function of all the other terms.
c. $P_{ex} = \$12.50 - \$1\left(\dfrac{1-40\%}{1-20\%}\right) = \$12.50 - \$0.75 = \$11.75.$

d. If the tax rates are zero or equal to each other.

11.4 Borrowing to pay dividends.

a. If AWC borrows $100 million it can pay $350 million of dividends on 100 million shares: the dividend per share is in this case equal to $3.50. It is higher than in case when the $100 million is raised by issuing equity because in the latter case there are more shares outstanding.
b. AWC asset value after the $350 immediate dividend payment is $1,000 million ($100 million of annual perpetual cash flow divided by an expected return of 10 percent) and its equity value is $900 million (asset value less $100 million of debt). AWC ex-dividend share price is thus $9 ($900 million divided by 100 million shares).
c. The wealth per share of AWC shareholders = $3.50 + $9 = $12.50.
d. Borrowing to pay dividends does not affect the wealth of shareholders and dividend policy is thus irrelevant.

11.5 Comparing dividend streams under alternative payout policies.

a. Dividend streams under the six payout policies:

Alternative payout methods	Now DPS$_0$	In one year DPS$_1$	In two years DPS$_2$	In three years DPS$_t$
1. Immediate dividend of $250 million	$2.50	$ 1.00	$ 1.00	$ 1.00
2. Share buyback of $250 million	$ 0	$ 1.25	$ 1.25	$ 1.25
3. Immediate dividend of $350 million funded with a $100 million equity issue	$3.24	$ 0.926	$ 0.926	$ 0.926
4. Invest the $250 million at 10 percent	$ 0	$ 1.25	$ 1.25	$ 1.25
5. Invest the $250 million at 12 percent	$ 0	$ 1.30	$ 1.30	$ 1.30
6. Invest the $250 million at 8 percent	$ 0	$ 1.20	$ 1.20	$ 1.20

b. The present values of the first four dividend streams at 10 percent are equal to $12.50, which indicates that the wealth of AWC shareholders is unaffected by the alternative payout policies. In the last two cases there is a change in investment policy and thus a change in the wealth of AWC shareholders, which means that dividend policy matters in these two cases.

c. In perfect markets, dividend *policy* does not matter because the *distribution of dividends over time* does not affect the wealth of shareholders (a lower dividend today is followed by higher dividends in the future). But dividends matter because a higher dividend in a given year, *without a change in dividends the other years*, will raise share price and the wealth of shareholders.

12.1 Cost of debt versus cost of equity.

We mean that the amount of equity capital invested in the firm, the division, or the project is *expected* to return 10 percent to the equity holders, whereas the amount invested as debt capital is *expected* to return 8 percent to the debt holders. These returns are those that the investors can get from investing in firms having the same risk as that of the firm, the division, or the project. The cost of debt is lower than the cost of equity because debt holders have a priority claim over the equity holders on the cash flows generated by the firm, the division, or the project. As a consequence, debt is less risky than equity and the cost of debt is thus lower than the cost of equity.

12.2 Cash flows from bonds and stocks.

The cash flows associated with a bond are the coupon payments and the principal repayment, whereas the cash flows associated with a share of stock are the dividends paid to the shareholders. The market value of a bond or a stock is the present value of their respective expected cash-flow streams (see equations 12.1 and 12.4). In the case of a bond, the coupon payments and principal repayment are discounted at the bondholders' expected return, whereas in the case of a share of stock, the dividends are discounted at the shareholders' expected return. Both returns depend on the risk associated with holding the securities.

12.3 The capital asset pricing model.

1. The higher the risk of a security or an asset, the higher its expected return.

2. The only relevant risk of a security is that portion of the security risk that cannot be diversified away. This risk, called systematic, undiversifiable, or market risk, is measured by the security beta coefficient. A beta coefficient of one indicates that the security has the same risk as that of a well-diversified portfolio, also called the market portfolio. A beta coefficient higher (lower) than one indicates a higher (lower) risk than that of the market portfolio.

3. The expected return on a security is the sum of the risk-free rate (the rate of return of the safest security, for example the yield on government bonds held to maturity) plus a risk premium. This risk premium is the reward for bearing the systematic risk of the security. It is equal to the security beta coefficient multiplied by the market risk premium (the difference between the return expected from holding the market portfolio and the risk-free rate).

12.4 The cost of capital of a firm.

a. From equation 12.11, Van Hoff's cost of equity, k , is

$$k_{E,Vanhoff} = R_F + [E(R_M) - R_F]\beta_{equity}$$

where R_F = 5 percent is the risk-free rate, $E(R_M)$ = 10 percent is the market portfolio expected rate of return, and β_{equity} = 1.16 is Vanhoff's equity beta coefficient. As a result,

$$k_{E,Vanhoff} = 5\% + (10\% - 5\%) \times 1.16 = 10.8\%$$

b. The relevant cost of capital of Vanhoff is the weighted average cost of its various sources of capital, that is, the weighted average cost of capital or WACC. To determine that cost, we apply equation 12.12:

$$WACC = k_D(1 - T_C)\frac{D}{E+D} + k_E\frac{E}{E+D}$$

where k_E = 10.8 percent is Vanhoff's cost of equity, $\frac{E}{E+D}$ the proportion of equity financing, k_D = 6 percent is Vanhoff's before-tax cost of debt, T_C = 40 percent is the corporate tax rate, and $\frac{D}{E+D}$ the proportion of debt financing.

Because Vanhoff Line finances its activities with as much debt as equity, $\frac{E}{E+D}$ = 0.5 and $\frac{D}{E+D}$ = 0.5.

Putting all together, we get the following:

$$WACC = (6\% \times (1 - 0.40) \times 0.5) + (10.8\% \times 0.50) = 7.20\%$$

12.5 An estimate of the cost of capital.

There are two observations to make:

1. The weighted average cost of capital of 8 percent is the cost of capital of PacificCom, that is, the average of the costs of capital of its two divisions. If the risk, and more precisely the betas, of the two divisions are different, the cost of capital that is needed to evaluate each division's investment proposals cannot be equal to 8 percent.

2. The amounts of equity capital and debt that the consultant has used to compute the financing ratios D/(E + D) and E/(E + D) are taken from PacificCom's balance sheet. In other words, they are accounting values, whereas a proper WACC should be calculated with market values.

13.1 Effect of borrowing on share price.

1. In the absence of tax and financial distress costs, the share price should not necessarily decrease, because, as the firm's debt goes up, the increase of the expected earnings per share will offset the negative effect of the increase in its volatility. Indeed, according to Modigliani and Miller, the compensation will be perfect, and the share price should not be affected at all.

2. In the presence of tax, the firm's tax bill decreases in proportion to its indebtedness because interest payments are tax deductible. The firm's share price will go up to reflect the present value of the tax savings that goes to the shareholders.

3. As the firm borrows more and more to take advantage of the interest tax shield, the probability of financial distress increases. If there are costs associated with financial distress, at some point the present value of these costs will be higher than the present value of the interest tax shield and the firm's share price will begin to decrease.

13.2 Risk of debt and equity and risk of the firm.

False.

When debt is increased, more of the cash flows generated by the firm's assets are simply going to the debt holders than to the shareholders. The volatility of the cash flows from the firm's assets is not affected. Therefore, the risk of the firm as a whole will not increase.

13.3 Factors affecting the optimal debt-to-equity ratio.

a. *Increase* the debt-to-equity ratio to take advantage of the increase in the interest tax shield.

b. *Increase* the debt-to-equity ratio because a higher personal capital gain tax will increase the spread between the tax rate on equity income and the tax rate on interest income. See equation 13.8.

c. *Increase* the debt-to-equity ratio because acquiring the building will increase the firm's tangible assets, and, as a result, the probability of financial distress should decrease.

d. If the ratio is optimal when measured on the basis of the current market value of the firm's equity, it is too high when measured on the basis of the fair value of its equity, because the firm's shares are undervalued. The firm should issue debt and buy shares with the proceeds, thus providing a strong signal that its shares are undervalued. The process should last until the share price reaches its fair value and the debt-to-equity ratio reverts to its current value.

e. *Do not change* the debt-to-equity ratio, because a decrease in the working capital requirement does not usually affect the probability of financial distress.

f. As long as Alternative Solutions Inc. and the acquirer are publicly held firms with well diversified shareholders, the ratio should not change, because, in that case, the optimal debt-to-equity ratio is not determined by the identity of the owners of the firm's assets. Note that if Alternative Solutions Inc. were a private company and its new owners were not well-diversified investors, the ratio may have to change to reflect the new owners' optimal debt-to-equity ratio.

13.4 Earnings per share analysis.

a.

	Low Debt Plan			High Debt Plan		
1. EBIT	$ 90,000	$130,000	$170,000	$ 90,000	$130,000	$170,000
2. Number of shares before recapitalization						
	10,000	10,000	10,000	10,000	10,000	10,000
3. Share price before recapitalization						
	$ 100	$ 100	$ 100	$ 100	$ 100	$ 100
4. Amount borrowed	$200,000	$200,000	$200,000	$400,000	$400,000	$400,000
5. Interest rate	10%	10%	10%	10%	10%	10%
6. Number of shares after recapitalization						
[(2) − (4)/(3)]	8,000	8,000	8,000	6,000	6,000	6,000
7. Net earnings [(1) − (4) × (5)]						
	$ 70,000	$110,000	$150,000	$ 50,000	$ 90,000	$130,000
8. EPS [(7)/(6)]	$ 8.75	$ 13.75	$ 18.75	$ 8.33	$ 15.00	$ 21.67

b.

	Low Debt Plan	High Debt Plan
1. EBIT	$100,000	$100,000
2. Number of shares before recapitalization	10,000	10,000
3. Share price before recapitalization	$ 100	$ 100
4. Amount borrowed	$200,000	$400,000
5. Interest rate	10%	10%
6. Number of shares after recapitalization [(2) − (4)/(3)]	8,000	6,000
7. Net earnings [(1) − (4) × (5)]	$ 80,000	$ 60,000
8. EPS [(7)/(6)]	$ 10.00	$ 10.00

First, note that the value of the firm's assets is $1,000,000, because Albine does not have any debt and its equity value is $1,000,000 (10,000 shares at $100 a share).

EPS is the same under the two plans, or any other recapitalization plan, because at that level of EBIT, the return on assets is 10 percent ($100,000 divided by $1,000,000 of assets), the same as the interest rate. At $100,000 of EBIT, the cost of borrowing will exactly offset the benefit of distributing the net earnings to more (less) shares, when the amount of debt relative to the amount of equity increases (decreases).

13.5 The value of the interest tax shield.

a. After the debt issue, the value of Ilbane Corp. will increase by the present value of the interest tax shield. As shown in the text, if we assume that the tax shield is forever, its present value, PV_{ITS}, is as follows:

$$PV_{ITS} = \frac{\text{Annual interest tax shield}}{\text{Cost of debt}}$$

$$PV_{ITS} = \frac{\text{Tax rate} \times \text{Interest rate} \times \text{Debt issue}}{\text{Interest rate}} = \text{Tax rate} \times \text{Debt issue}$$

$$= 0.35 \times \$20 \text{ million} = \textbf{\$7 million}$$

The value of Ilbane should increase by $7 million after the debt issue.

b. The same formula would give a value of $28 million for the interest tax shield (0.35 × $80 million). However, with a debt-to-equity ratio of 4, the financial risk of Ilbane would increase significantly. Investors will have lower expectations regarding the value of the interest tax shield, a sentiment that will be reflected in Ilbane's share price. The share price will increase less than it would have if the financial risk does not increase significantly. As a result, the value of Ilbane Corp. will increase less than $28 million.

14.1 The price-to-earnings ratio.

Companies A and B are identical, including having the same current earnings per share and the same share price volatility. However, the earnings after tax of A are expected to grow faster than that of B, making A's shares more valuable than B's shares. Therefore, the financial market will price A's current earnings more than B's earnings.

Companies A and B are identical, including having the same current earnings per share and the same earnings growth expectations. However, the share price of A is more volatile than the share price of B, making A's shares less valuable than B's shares. Thus, the financial market will price A's current earnings less than B's.

14.2 Alternative valuation methods and value-creating acquisitions.

a. A firm's liquidating value should be its *minimum* value and thus its floor (not ceiling) value. And its replacement value should be its *maximum* value and thus its ceiling (not floor) value.
b. No, price-to-cash-flow ratios should be better, because firms' cash flows are significantly less sensitive to accounting rules and conventions than are firms' reported earnings (profits).
c. Different valuation methods are expected to generate different estimated values because of conceptual differences among alternative valuation models. Furthermore, different models use different inputs (data) that do not have the same quality or reliability.

14.3 Valuation by comparables.

* Apply the following three-step method for the equity multiples:

    Step 1: Convert the comparable firm's (REC) data on a per-share basis.

1. Earnings per share ($90 million divided by 40 million shares)	$2.25
2. Book value per share ($590 million divided by 40 million shares)	$14.75

    Step 2: Calculate the comparable firm's (REC) corresponding multiples.

1. Price-to-earnings ratio ($30 divided by $2.25)	13.33
2. Price-to-book ratio ($30 divided by $14.75)	2.03

    Step 3: Estimate LMC's equity value using REC's multiples.

1. Price-to-earnings ratio:	$46 million × 13.33 = $613 million
2. Price-to-book value ratio:	$270 million × 2.03 = $548 million

- Apply the following four-step method for the asset multiple:

Step 1: Calculate REC's enterprise value (EV).

EV(REC) = Market value of equity + Debt − Cash
= ($40 × 40 million) + $800 million − $10 million = $1,990 million

Step 2: Calculate REC's ratio of EV to EBITDA.

EV-to-EBITDA ratio ($1,990 million divided by $250 million) = 7.96

Step 3: Estimate LEC's enterprise value using REC's multiple.

$125 million × 7.96 = $995 million

Step 4: Add LMC's cash and deduct its debt to get LMC's equity value.

$995 million + $4 million − $420 million = $579 million

The estimated values of LMC's equity are not expected to be the same because they are based on different multiples drawn from the Rapid Engine Corporation. As long as the highest estimate is about 20 percent higher than the lowest estimate, the range of estimated values is acceptable. In our case, the highest estimate ($613 million) is 12 percent higher than the lowest estimate ($548 million).

14.4 Equity valuation.

a. From equation 14.6, and also from equation 2.9 in Chapter 9, we can write the following:

$$\text{DCF}_{\text{Baltek}} = \frac{\text{Next year free cash flow}}{0.08 - 0.03} = \frac{\$1 \text{ million} \times (1 + 0.03)}{0.05} = \frac{\$1.03 \text{ million}}{0.05} = \$20.6 \text{ million}$$

b. The value of Baltek's equity is the same as the value of its assets since the company has no debt.

14.5 Discounted cash-flow valuation.

Apply the following three-step method:

Step 1: Provide a formula to estimate the free cash flows (FCF) that LEC is expected to generate in the next five years.
From equation 14.3, we can write

FCF = EBIT (1 − Tax rate) + Depreciation − ΔWCR − Capital expenditures

where EBIT is earnings before interest and tax, or pre-tax operating profit, and ΔWCR is the change in working capital requirement. But because annual capital expenditures will be equal to annual depreciation expenses,

$$\text{FCF}_{\text{LEC}} = \text{EBIT}(1 - \text{Tax rate}) - \Delta\text{WCR}$$

Step 2: Estimate LEC's weighted average cost of capital (WACC).

1. Cost of equity according to the capital asset pricing model (CAPM) = 5% + (1.2 × 5%) = 11%
2. Percentage of equity financing = 80%
3. After-tax cost of debt = 6% × (1 − 0.40) = 3.6%
4. Percentage of debt financing = 100% − 80% = 20%

$$\text{WACC} = (3.6\% \times 0.20) + (11\% \times 0.80) = 9.52\%$$

Step 3: Using a spreadsheet, estimate the DCF value of LEC's equity as in Exhibit 14.5 from the forecasting assumptions:

	A	B	C	D	E	F	G
					Forecast for		
1							
2	*Millions of dollars*	Current	Year 1	Year 2	Year 3	Year 4	Year 5
3	**Data**						
4	Sales growth rate		8.00%	8.00%	6.00%	6.00%	4.00%
5	Operating margin as percent of sales		20.00%	20.00%	20.00%	20.00%	20.00%
6	WCR in percent of sales	20.00%	20.00%	20.00%	20.00%	20.00%	20.00%
7	**Free cash flow from business assets**						
8	Sales	$620.0	$669.6	$723.2	$766.6	$812.6	$845.1
9	EBIT		133.9	144.6	153.3	162.5	169.0
10	EBIT × (1 - Tax rate of 40%)		80.4	86.8	92.0	97.5	101.4
11	WCR at year-end	124.0	133.92	144.63	153.31	162.51	169.01
12	less ΔWCR		(9.9)	(10.7)	(8.7)	(9.2)	(6.5)
13	**Equals free cash flow**		$70.4	$76.1	$83.3	$88.3	$94.9
14	Residual value year-end 4[1]					$1,719.31	
15	**Beginning Year 1**						
16	WACC	9.52%					
17	DCF value of assets	$1,447.6					
18	*less book value of debt*	280.0					
19	**equals DCF value of equity**	**$1,167.6**					

- Rows 4 to 6 plus cells B16 and B18 are data
- Formula in cell C8 is =B8*(1+C4). Then copy formula in cell C8 to next cells in row 8
- Formula in cell C9 is =C5*C8. Then copy formula in cell C9 to next cells in row 9
- Formula in cell C10 is =C9*(1−.4). Then copy formula in cell C10 to next cells in row 10
- Formula in cell C12 is =B11−C11. Then copy formula in cell C12 to next cells in row 12
- Formula in cell C13 is =C10+C12. Then copy formula in cell C13 to next cells in row 13
- Formula in cell F14 is =G13/(B16−G4)
- Formula in cell B17 is =NPV(B16,C13:F13)+F14/(1+B16)^4
- Formula in cell B19 is =B17−B18

[1] The residual value in Year 4 is given by the perpetual, constant-growth, valuation formula (see valuation formula 14.6). In step 2 we show that LEC's weighted average cost of capital (WACC) is 9.52 percent. The residual value is thus

$$\text{Residual value} = \frac{\text{Cash flow from assets}_{year\ 5}}{\text{WACC} - \text{Growth rate}} = \frac{\$94.9}{0.0952 - 0.04} = \frac{\$94}{0.052} = \$1719.3$$

15.1 Risk management.

A firm should manage risk centrally because (1) there are risks at the corporate level that projects do not capture; (2) different risk exposures can be netted out at the corporate level; (3) the cost of risk protection can be reduced if managed centrally; (4) a consistent risk policy can be formulated and implemented across all the firm's divisions; and (5) the firm could learn to better manage risk if a dedicated staff oversees the process centrally.

15.2 Risk identification.

Situation Event	Level-1 Risk	Level-2 Risk	Possible Protection
1	Financial investment risk	Price risk	Buy an option to protect against the drop in Fastcom's share price
2	Currency risk	Exchange rate risk	Hedge against changes in currency rates
3	Business risk	Operational risk	Buy insurance against weather storms
4	Financial risk	Financial cost risk	Hedge against changes in interest rate
5	Business risk	Operational risk	Diversify the firm's sources of supply
6	Business risk	Operational risk	Require compensation if payment is not received after an agreed upon time period
7	Financial risk	Financing cost and refinancing risks	Finance the asset with a matching loan of 4-year maturity
8	Business risk	Strategic risk	Launch a new, more modern line of dolls

15.3 Risk measurement.

a. Because the expected cash flow is a "perpetuity," the value of NGC is equal to its expected cash flow divided by its cost of capital (10 percent). If its expected cash flow is reduced by $20 million, its value will be reduced by $200 million ($20 million divided by 10 percent). If the probability that this event occurs is 50 percent, then MVR is $100 million.

b. As in the previous case, the value of NGC is reduced by $200 million. If the probability that this event occurs is 10 percent, then MVR is $20 million.

c. With a cost of capital of 10.2 percent, NGC's value is $980 million ($100 million divided by 0.102) and the reduction in value is $20 million ($1,000 million less $980 million). If the probability that this event occurs is 50 percent, then MVR is $10 million.

d. If the expected cash flow is reduced by $1 million, NGC's value will be reduced by $10 million ($1 million divided by 10 percent). If the probability that this event occurs is 10 percent, then MVR is $1 million.

16.1 Hedging interest-rate risk with futures contracts.

a. Sell futures contracts to generate a profit if rates go up and bond prices go down.

b. Number of contracts to sell $= \dfrac{100m}{100,000} = 1,000$

c. Price of contract at 4% $= \dfrac{\$5,000}{(1+4\%)} + \cdots + \dfrac{\$5,000}{(1+4\%)^9} + \dfrac{\$5,000 + \$100,000}{(1+4\%)^{10}} = \$108,110.90$

d. Value of bonds at 7.5% $= \dfrac{\$7m}{(1+7.5\%)} + \cdots + \dfrac{\$7m}{(1+7.5\%)^7} = \dfrac{\$7m + \$100m}{(1+4\%)^8} = \$97,071,348$

e. Price of contract at 4.3% $= \dfrac{\$5,000}{(1+4.3\%)} + \cdots + \dfrac{\$5,000}{(1+4.3\%)^9} + \dfrac{\$5,000 + \$100,000}{(1+4.3\%)^{10}} = \$105,593.78$

Gain from 1,000 contracts $= [\$108,110.90 - \$105,593.78] \times 1,000 = \$2,517,120$

f. The hedge is not perfect because the net change in value is:
Loss from bond issue = $97,071,348 − $100,000,000 = −$2,928,652
Net change = Loss from bond − Gain from futures = −$2,928,652 + $2,517,120 = −$411,532
The hedge is not perfect because the EEC bond is more sensitive to changes in interest rates than the T-bond futures (that is, it has a higher interest-rate risk).

g. $2,517.12 is the gain per contract – see answer (e). If n is the number of contracts needed to have a perfect hedge, we must have: $2,517.12 × n = $2,928,652 from which we get n = 1,164 contracts. In other words, to have a perfect hedge, EEC should have set the hedge ratio at 1.164 (instead of setting it at 1) and bought 1,164 contracts instead of 1,000 contracts.

16.2 Response of option prices to changes in the value of inputs in the Black-Scholes formula.

a. and b. The prices of the original options are:

$$C\ [S_0 - \$50; X = \$50; T = 0.25; R_F = 6\%; \sigma_S = 25\%] = \$2.86$$

$$P\ [S_0 = \$50; X = \$50; T = 0.25; R_F = 6\%; \sigma_S = 25\%] = \$2.12$$

The table below provides the option prices if the value of one input goes up by 20 percent while the other four remain the same under two scenarios: on the left, the underlying stock does not pay dividends; on the right, the stock is expected to pay a $2 dividend in 2 months:

	No dividend payment $PV(D) = 0$				$2 dividend payment in 2 months $PV(D) = \$2 \times c^{-0.06 \times \left(\frac{2}{12}\right)} = \$1.98$			
	Call price		Put price		Call price		Put price	
	$ price	% change	$ price	% change	$ price	% change	$ price	% change
Original option	2.86		2.12		1.86		3.09	
$S_0 = \$60$	10.91	+281%	0.17	−92%	9.06	+388%	0.30	−90%
$X = \$60$	0.28	−90%	9.39	+343%	0.13	−93%	11.22	+263%
$T = 0.30$	3.17	+11%	2.18	+8%	2.14	+16%	3.23	+5%
$R_F = 7.2\%$	2.94	+3%	2.05	−3%	1.92	+3%	3.00	−3%
$\sigma_S = 30\%$	3.35	+17%	2.61	+13%	2.33	+25%	3.57	+15%

c. When the stock pays a dividend, the call prices are lower and the put prices are higher because a dividend payment reduces the stock price.

d.
$$C\left[S_0 = \$50 \,;\, X = \$50 \,;\, T = \frac{5}{12} \,;\, R_F = 6\% \,;\, \sigma_S = 25\%; PV(D) = 0\right] = \$3.83$$

$$C\left[S_0 = \$50 \,;\, X = \$50 \,;\, T = \frac{3}{12} \,;\, R_F = 6\% \,;\, \sigma_S = 25\%; PV(D) = 0\right] = \$2.86$$

The 5-month call is *more* valuable than the 3-month call when the stock does not pay dividends during the life of the call. If the stock is expected to pay a \$2-dividend in four months, the present value of that dividend at the risk-free rate of 6 percent is:

$$PV(\$2) = D \times e^{-R_F T} = \$2 \times e^{-0.06 \times \left(\frac{4}{12}\right)} = \$2 \times 0.9802 = \$1.96$$

and the 5-month call is now *less* valuable than the 3-month call (\$2.76 instead of \$2.86):

$$C\left[S_0 = \$50 \,;\, X = \$50 \,;\, T = \frac{5}{12} \,;\, R_F = 6\% \,;\, \sigma_S = 25\%; PV(\$2) = \$1.96\right] = \$2.76$$

16.3 Valuing call and put options on a stock.

a. $C[S_0 = \$80 \,;\, X = \$60 \,;\, T = 0.50 \,;\, R_F = 5\% \,;\, \sigma_S = 25\%] = \$21.67$

The call is overvalued according to the Black-Scholes formula (the formula underestimates the \$22.85 market price).

b. Use the put-call parity equation: $P = \$21.67 + Xe^{-0.05 \times 0.50} - \$80 = \$0.19$

c. $PV(D) = 0.75\left[e^{-0.05\left(\frac{2}{12}\right)} + e^{-0.05\left(\frac{5}{12}\right)}\right] = \$1.4783$ and $[S - PV(D)] = \$78.5217$. The call price is thus

$C[S_0 = \$78.5217 \,;\, X = \$60 \,;\, T = 0.50 \,;\, R_F = 5\% \,;\, \sigma_S = 25\%] = \$20.24$. An equivalent American call would be worth at *least* \$20.24 (it could be worth more).

d. To find implied volatility on an Excel spreadsheet, go to Data/Data Tools/What If Analysis/ Goal Seek and enter 13.19 for the call price. The resulting implied volatility is 26.0276%. However, because the two options are identical except for the exercise price, they should have the same volatility, which implies that the Black-Scholes formula is not always accurate.

16.4 Valuing employee stock options and warrants.

a. $C[S_0 = \$20 \,;\, X = \$30 \,;\, T = 5 \,;\, R_F = 4\% \,;\, \sigma_S = 30\%] = \$3.8331$

b. ESO or warrant value $\dfrac{100m}{100m + 10m} \times \$3.8331 = \$3.4846$

c. Total cost to BIC of issuing ESO or warrant = 10m × \$3.4846 = \$34,846,000

d. Share price should drop by $\dfrac{\$34,846,000}{100,000,000} = \$0.35$ from \$20 to \$19.65

16.5 Valuing an option to abandon an investment.

a. Immediate gain from selling store = \$40m − \$35m = \$5m
b. It is a long put with a \$40m exercise price and a one-year life on a \$35m underlying asset.
c. $P[V_A = \$35m \,;\, X = \$40m \,;\, T = 1 \,;\, R_F = 4\% \,;\, \sigma_S = 30\%] = \$6.30m$
d. Bellotico should continue to operate the store for one year because this decision is worth \$41.30m (\$35m + \$6.30m), which is higher than selling the store now for \$40m.

16.6 Valuing an option to delay an investment.

a. Open in one year because the value of the option to open in one year ($384,273) is higher than the NPV of opening now ($300,000). Here are the calculations:

NPV (opening now) = $-\$1,700,000 + $ PV($140,000 growing at 3%, discounted at 10%)

$$= -\$1,700,000 + \frac{\$140,000}{10\% - 3\%} = -\$1,700,000 + \$2,000,000 = \$300,000$$

Value of the call option to open in 1 year is $384,273:

$$C[V_A = \frac{\$2,000,000}{1 + 10\%} \, ; X = \$1,700,000 \, ; T = 1 \, ; R_F = 5\% \, ; \sigma_S = 40\%] = \$384,273.$$

b. Maximum value of the license = Value of the call option = $384,273

c. You will open now because the value of a call option with a volatility of 25% is $289,743, which is lower than the NPV of opening now ($300,000).

d. You will open now because the value of the underlying asset is $1,636,364 and the corresponding value of the call option is $267,616, which is lower than $300,000:

$$V_A = \frac{\dfrac{\$140,000 \times 90\%}{10\% - 3\%}}{1 + 10\%} = \frac{\dfrac{\$126,000}{7\%}}{1.10\%} = \frac{\$1,800,000}{1.10} = \$1,636,364$$

$$C[V_A = \$1,636,364m \, ; X = \$1,700,000 \, ; T = 1 \, ; R_F = 5\% \, ; \sigma_S = 40\%] = \$267,616$$

17.1 Accounting versus economic exposure.

Accounting and translation exposures are the same thing. Both refer to the effect of exchange rate changes on the value of the firm's financial statements. Economic exposure refers to the effect of exchange-rate changes on the value of the firm's *future* cash flows. Transaction, contractual, and operating exposures are subsets of economic exposure. Transaction and contractual exposures are synonymous. Both have to do with the effect of the exchange-rate volatility on the future cash flows expected from past transactions denominated in foreign currencies, and operating exposure is concerned with the effect on future uncertain transactions. In the following table, we indicate why economic exposure is more relevant than accounting exposure to shareholders:

Economic Exposure	Accounting Exposure
1. It is forward looking because it is concerned with *future cash* flows	1. It is backward looking because it is concerned with *past* transactions
2. It focuses on *cash flows* that are directly related to value creation	2. It focuses on *accounting values* that are only remotely related to value creation
3. It affects firms with foreign subsidiaries, export/ import firms, as well as those that are subject to foreign competition in the input and output markets	3. It affects only a subset of firms that are subject to accounting exposure, that is, those firms that *record* transactions denominated in a foreign currency
4. Because it focuses on cash flows, it does not depend on the firm's accounting rules	4. It is affected by the accounting rules chosen by the firm

17.2 Comparing alternative hedging strategies.

	What Is It?	Advantages	Disadvantages
Forward hedging	Buying (selling) forward an amount of foreign currency equal to the value of the underlying exposed cash outflow (inflow) denominated in the same currency and for the same delivery date.	It is a tailor-made hedge that provides a perfect hedge for transactions of a known amount and known delivery dates.	1. It requires a credit check 2. It often happens that the effective delivery date is not exactly the anticipated date 3. The bid-ask spread on forward contracts can be large for infrequently traded currencies 4. Getting out of a forward contract requires entering into an offsetting forward contract with the same delivery date as the original one
Futures hedging	Buying (selling) futures contracts in the same currency as the underlying exposed cash outflow (inflow). The number of contracts to buy (sell) and the delivery date should match those of the amount of cash flow exposed and its delivery date.	1. No credit check is needed 2. Transaction costs are low 3. Default risk is low because of marking-to-market 4. It is easy to get out of a position, and the cash settlement is immediate	1. One can trade only standard-size contracts with fixed maturity dates 2. Margin must be deposited 3. Trades are marked-to-market daily
Options hedging	Buying options on the same currency as the underlying exposed cash outflow (inflow). The holder of the option has the right, but not the obligation, to buy (sell) foreign currencies over a specified period. In the case of over-the-counter options, the exercise price and the expiration date are contractually defined. In the case of traded options, the number of contracts to buy (sell) and the delivery date should match those of the amount of cash flow exposed and its delivery date.	1. It is an insurance against unfavorable exchange rate movements 2. Contrary to other hedging techniques, there is no obligation to buy (sell) the foreign currency 3. Transaction costs and default risk of traded options are lower than over-the-counter options 4. Options can be sold any time before the expiration date	1. The firm has to pay a premium to get an option (the price of the option) 2. In the case of a traded option, one can trade only standard-size contracts with fixed maturity dates 3. Margin must be deposited
Swap hedging	Exchanging interest and principal payments in one currency for interest and principal payments in another currency.	1. It is a low-cost exchange of cash flows denominated in different currencies 2. The swap market is dominated by banks, which reduces the counterparty risk	1. Its use is most often limited to long-term exposures 2. There is potentially some counterparty risk

17.3 **Parity relations.**

Purchasing power parity says that changes in the exchange rate between two countries' currencies are determined by the difference in the expected inflation rates between the two countries.

17.4 **Country risk and the cost of capital.**

False.

Although it is often the case that firms mark up their domestic cost of capital when analyzing a foreign investment, the practice fails to properly account for country risk. A better way is to reduce the *expected* cash flows of the cross-border project according to the expected consequences of the country risk associated with the country in which the investment would be made. An added advantage of adjusting the cash flows instead of the cost of capital is that it forces management to clearly identify the risks taken. It also allows for sensitivity analysis.

17.5 **International capital budgeting.**

Answer: Since the project's NPV is positive, the company would invest in the project.

	A	B	C	D	E	F	G
		Now			Forecast For		
1		0	Year 1	Year 2	Year 3	Year 4	Year 5
2							
3	Expected cash flows in millions of bhats (THB)						
4	Initial investment	−50.0					
5	Terminal value						15
6	Sales growth rate		5.0%	5.0%	5.0%	5.0%	5.0%
7	Sales	20.00	21.00	22.05	23.15	24.31	25.53
8	EBIT	18.00	18.90	19.85	20.84	21.88	22.97
9	Tax rate		35.0%	35.0%	35.0%	35.0%	35.0%
10	EBIT (1 − Tax rate)		12.29	12.90	13.54	14.22	14.93
11	WCR as a percentage of sales	10.0%	10.0%	10.0%	10.0%	10.0%	10.0%
12	WCR	2.00	2.10	2.21	2.32	2.43	2.55
13	Change in WCR		0.10	0.11	0.11	0.12	0.12
14	Cash flow	−50.00	12.19	12.79	13.43	14.11	29.81
15	Expected USD/BHT spot rate using PPP (equation 16.1)						
16	Thailand expected inflation rate		3.0%	3.0%	3.0%	3.0%	3.0%
17	United States expected inflation rate		4.0%	4.0%	4.0%	4.0%	4.0%
18	Current spot rate THB/USD	40					
19	Expected future spot rate USD/THB	0.0250	0.0252	0.0255	0.0257	0.0260	0.0262
20	Expected cash flows in millions of US dollars (USD)	−1.25	0.31	0.33	0.35	0.37	0.78
21	Cost of capital	12.0%					
22	Net present value in USD	$207,431					

- *Rows 4, 5, 6, 9, 11, 16,17 and cells B7, B8, B18 and B22 are data*
- *Formula in cell C7 is =B7*(1+C6). Then copy formula in cell C7 to next cells in row 7*
- *Formula in cell C8 is =B8*(1+C6). Then copy formula in cell C8 to next cells in row 8*
- *Formula in cell C10 is =C8*(1–C9). Then copy formula in cell C10 to next cells in row 10*
- *Formula in cell B13 is =B6*B12. Then copy formula in cell B13 to next cells in row 13*
- *Formula in cell B12 is =B11*B7. Then copy formula in cell B12 to next cells in row 12*
- *Formula in cell C13 is =C12–B12. Then copy formula in cell C13 to next cells in row 13*
- *Formula in cell B14 is =B4+B5+B10–B13. Then copy formula in cell B14 to next cells in row 14*
- *Formula in cell C19 is =B19*(1+B17)/(1+B16). Then copy formula in cell C19 to next cells in row 19*
- *Formula in cell B20 is =B14*B19. Then copy formula in cell B20 to next cells in row 20*
- *Formula in cell B22 is =B20+NPV(B21,C20:G20)*

18.1 Understanding MVA and EVA.

a. Value is created by maximizing the difference between the market value of capital and the amount of capital employed to produce that value, that is, the firm's market value added, not its absolute market value.

b. Market value added is determined by the stream of EVAs the firm is expected to generate in the *future*. If the present value of that future stream is positive, MVA is positive, even though *current* EVA can be negative.

c. Net profit is calculated by deducting interest expenses from operating profit, which means that net profit is adjusted for the cost of debt. If we then deduct a capital charge based on the WACC, we would be counting the cost of debt twice, once in net profit and again in the WACC.

d. EVA takes risk into account via the WACC. The riskier an entity's operating profit, the higher its WACC and the lower it's EVA.

e. Higher profits are only half the story. If the charge for capital employed exceeds (operating) profit, value is destroyed.

18.2 Adjusting accounting data to estimate economic value added.

$$\text{EVA} = \text{NOPAT} - \text{Charge for capital employed}$$

where: NOPAT = Net operating profit after tax = EBIT × (1 − Tax rate)

Charge for capital employed = WACC × Capital employed (same as invested capital)

To estimate EVA, apply the following procedure:

Step 1: Estimate earnings before interest and tax (EBIT).

Sales	$1,400 million
Cost of sales	(780 million)
Selling, general, and administrative expenses	(330 million)
Depreciation and lease expenses	(45 million)
Amortization of R&D expenses	(30 million)
EBIT	$ 215 million

Step 2: Estimate the tax rate (data in millions of dollars).

Tax rate = Tax expenses divided by *pre-tax* profit = $40/ ($60 + $40) = $40/$100 = 40%

Step 3: Calculate NOPAT.

NOPAT = EBIT × (1 − Tax rate) = ($215 million) × (1 − 0.40) = $129 million

Step 4: Estimate the amount of capital employed (in millions of dollars).

Capital Employed	December 31, Year−1	December 31, Year 0
Total debt capital	$160	$140
Adjusted equity capital	282	388
Book value of equity	$200	$260
Accumulated bad debt allowance	7	13
Accumulated goodwill impairment	20	45
Capitalized R&D	55	70
Total capital employed	$442	$528

Step 5: Calculate EVA given that ADC has an estimated weighted average cost of capital (WACC) of 11 percent (data in millions of dollars).

EVA(Beginning capital employed) = $129 − 11% × [$442] = $129 − $48.6 = $80.4

EVA(Average capital employed) = $129 − 11% × [($442 + $528)/2] = $129 − $53.4 = $75.6

18.3 Market value added analysis.

Acquiring the inventory-control software program costing $140,000 will immediately cut *after-tax* operating profit by $140,000 × (1 − 40%), that is, $84,000, and reduce EVA by the same amount. But *all* future EVAs will rise by $10,000 because invested capital will decrease permanently by $100,000 × 10%, that is, $10,000, because of the permanent reduction in inventories.

To determine the net effect on ILC's value, we must get the present value of the entire stream of EVAs. This present value is a measure of the effect of the decision to buy the software program on ILC's market value. In other words, it is the decision's market value added (MVA). Because that MVA is positive (+$16,000), the software acquisition is a value-creating proposition:

$$\text{MVA(Software)} = -\$84,000 + \frac{\$10,000}{0.10} = -\$84,000 + \$100,000 = +\$16,000$$

Note: Because the future stream of EVAs is a constant perpetuity, its present value is that constant amount divided by the cost of capital (see the valuation formula 18.7; the growth rate in EVAs is zero in our case).

18.4 Market value added analysis of the designer desk-lamp project.

The estimation of the future stream of economic value added (EVAs) that the designer desk lamp project is expected to generate is given below. It is based on data taken from Exhibit 9.3A in Chapter 9. The project's market value added (MVA) is found by discounting the stream of EVAs at 7.6 percent, the project's WACC. The solution is presented in a spreadsheet format (the lines referred to are from Exhibit 9.3A)

	A	B	C	D	E	F	G
1		Now			Forecast Year		
2	*In thousands of dollars*	0	1	2	3	4	5
3	**I. Net operating profit after tax (NOPAT)**						
4	After-tax operating profit (line 15)		$ 402	$ 347	$212	$ 69	($ 84)
5	Exceptional gain (line 21)						60
6	NOPAT		$ 402	$ 347	$212	$ 69	($ 24)
7	**II. Invested capital at the beginning of the year**						
8	Working capital requirement (line 18)	$ 360	$ 330	$ 255	$ 175	$ 90	$ 0
9	Net book value of fixed assets	2000	1600	1200	800	400	0
10	Total invested capital	$ 2,360	$1,930	$1,455	$ 975	$ 490	$ 0
11	**III. Capital charge**						
12	Cost of capital	7.6%					
13	Capital charge		$ 179	$ 147	$ 111	$ 74	$ 37
14	**IV. Economic value added (EVA) and market value added (MVA)**						
15	EVA		$ 223	$ 200	$ 101	($ 5)	($ 61)
16	MVA	$415.083					

- *Rows 4, 5, 9 plus cell B12 are data*
- *Formula in cell C6 is =C4+C5. Then copy formula in cell C6 to next cells in row 6*
- *Formulas in cells of row 9 are initial investment less accumulated depreciation at a rate of $400 a year*
- *Formula in cell B10 is =B8+B9. Then copy formula in cell B10 to next cells in row 10*
- *Formula in cell C13 is =$B$12*B10. Then copy formula in cell C13 to next cells in row 13*
- *Formula in cell C15 is =C6–C13. Then copy formula in cell C15 to next cells in row 15*
- *Formula in cell B16 is =NPV(B12,C15:G15)*

The project's MVA of $415,083 is exactly equal to its NPV as computed in Chapter 9.

18.5 The financial strategy matrix.

a. To position the four companies in the financial strategy matrix, apply the following two-step procedure.

Step 1: Estimate each company's return spread to determine its capacity to create value.
The return spread is the difference between a company's return on invested capital (ROIC) and its weighted average cost of capital (WACC). If the return spread is positive, so is the economic value added (EVA), and the company has created value during the period under analysis. If the return spread and EVA are negative, value has been destroyed over the diagnostic period.

Step 2: Estimate each company's self-sustainable growth rate to determine its capacity to finance its growth through earnings retention.

The self-sustainable growth rate (SGR) is equal to the retention rate (b) multiplied by return on equity (ROE). Compare each company's SGR with its growth in sales. If the growth rate in sales is higher than the SGR, the company is experiencing a cash shortage or deficit. If the growth rate in sales is lower than the SGR, the company is experiencing a cash surplus.

We have the following:

Company	ROIC − WACC	b × ROE = SGR	Growth in sales − SGR
A. Transportation	8% − 10% = −2%	0.50 × 12% = 6%	8% − 6% = +2%
B. Restaurants	15% − 12% = +3%	0.60 × 20% = 12%	15% − 12% = +3%
C. Beverages	8% − 9% = −1%	0.75 × 12% = 9%	7% − 9% = −2%
D. Food	13% − 11% = +2%	0.40 × 15% = 6%	4% − 6% = −2%

The transportation company destroys value and is short of cash (point A). The restaurant company creates value and is short of cash (point B). The beverages company is destroying value but generating a cash surplus (point C). The food company is creating value and generating a cash surplus (point D).

b. Refer to Exhibit 18.9 and the corresponding text in the chapter, where you will find a summary of the decisions/actions that Amalgamated Industries should take regarding each one of the four companies.

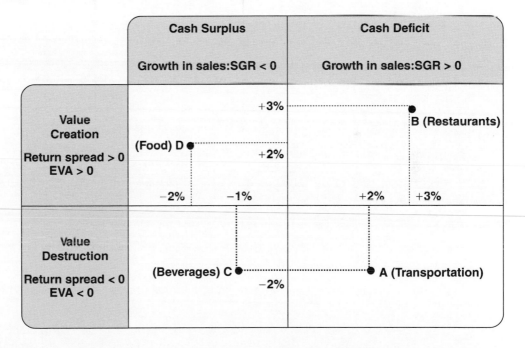

GLOSSARY

Terms are followed by the chapter number in which they appear.
Bold terms in a definition are defined elsewhere in the glossary.

AAR (8) *See* **average accounting return.**

Abnormal return (3) **Realized return** minus **expected return.** Same as **alpha coefficient.** *See* equation 3.14.

Accelerated depreciation method (4) **Depreciation** method according to which annual **depreciation expenses** are higher in the early years of an **asset's** life and lower in the later years. *See* **straight-line depreciation method.**

Accounting exposure (17) Effect of changes in **exchange rates** on **balance sheet** and **income statement** accounts. Same as **translation exposure.**

Accounting life (9) Number of years over which an **asset** is depreciated. *See* **economic life.**

Accounting period (4) Time period covered by a **financial statement,** usually one year but sometimes shorter.

Accounting principles (4) Rules governing the systematic collection, organization, and presentation of financial information. Same as accounting standards.

Accounting standards (4) *See* **accounting principles.**

Accounts payable (1, 4) Cash owed by a firm to its suppliers for purchases made on credit and not yet paid; reported in the firm's **balance sheet** as a **current liability.** Same as **payables, trade payables,** and **trade creditors.**

Accounts receivable (1, 4) Cash owed to a firm by its customers for sales made on credit and not yet paid; reported in the firm's **balance sheet** as a **current asset.** Same as **receivables, trade receivables,** and **trade debtors.**

Accrual accounting (4) Accounting system with reporting based on the **realization principle** and the **matching principle.**

Accrued expenses (4) **Liabilities** other than **accounts payable** that arise from the lag between the date at which these expenses have been incurred and the date at which they are paid.

Accrued interest (of a bond) (10) Amount of **coupon payment** that has been earned since the last coupon payment but not yet received by the **bondholder.**

Accumulated depreciation (1, 4) The sum of the periodic **depreciation expenses** deducted from the **gross value** of a **fixed asset** to obtain its **net book value.** *See* Exhibit 4.2 and acquisition cost principle.

Acid test ratio (5) *See* **quick ratio.**

Acquisition cost principle (4) **Asset** valuation principle according to which the **net book value** of a **fixed asset** is equal to its purchase price less the **accumulated depreciation** since that **asset** was bought. Same as **historical cost principle.**

Actual cash-flow principle (9) A capital budgeting principle according to which the **cash outflows** and **cash inflows** associated with an investment decision must be estimated at the time they actually occur.

ADF (2, 7) *See* **annuity discount factor.**

Adjusted present value (APV) (14, 16) A valuation method according to which the value of a firm's **assets,** is equal to the sum of (1) their value assuming that they are financed only with **equity capital** (unlevered **asset value**), and (2) the **present value** of the tax savings provided by the portion of the **assets** financed with debt. APV can also include the option value of future opportunities opened to the firm (*See* Chapter 16).

After-tax cost of debt (1, 10, 12) (Pretax **cost of debt**) times (1 minus the marginal corporate tax rate). *See* equation 12.3.

Agency costs (11, 13) *See* **agency costs of equity financing** and **agency costs of debt financing.**

Agency costs of debt financing (13) Costs associated with debt financing (and borne by **shareholders**) arising when lenders impose **restrictive covenants** that limit the firm's flexibility (for example, the **dividend** the firm can pay or the **assets** it can sell). *See* **bonding costs** and **monitoring costs.**

Agency costs of equity financing (11, 13) Costs associated with **equity capital** (and borne by **shareholders**) arising when a firm's managers (acting as agents of **shareholders**) make decisions that benefit them at the expense of **shareholders.**

Agency problem (13) Problem arising from the separation of ownership and **control** of a firm.

Aggressive (financing) strategy (5) A firm's financing strategy that uses short-term funds to finance a portion of the firm's long-term investments. *See* **matching strategy** and **conservative strategy.**

All-current method (of translation) (17) A method of translating the financial statements of a foreign business unit. Balance sheets accounts are translated at the **exchange rate** prevailing at the date of the balance sheet. Revenues and expenses in the income statement are translated at the rate when they occur or at the average rate during the period covered by the statement. *See* Appendix 17.1.

Allowance for bad debts (18) Provision for the possible uncollectibility of **accounts receivable.**

Allowance for doubtful accounts (4) Accounts arising when it is expected that some customers will not meet their payment obligations toward the firm. *See* **allowance for bad debts.**

Alpha coefficient (3) *See* **abnormal return.**

Alternative investment (7) An investment used as a benchmark for evaluating a project. The **alternative investment** must have the same **risk**, **tax**, **liquidity**, and other characteristics as the project. *See* **proxies** and **pure-plays.**

American option (16) An **option** that can be exercised at any time before the option's **maturity date**. *See* **European option.**

Amortization (4) The process of converting the cost of an **intangible** asset, such as goodwill, into periodic expenses reported in the firm's **income statement**. When the **asset** is **tangible**, the same process is called **depreciation.**

Annual percentage rate (APR) (2) The simple one-year rate of interest *without* the effect of compounding over shorter periods within one year. *See* equation 2.4.

Annual report (4) Public report that is prepared by a firm annually and that contains the year's **financial statements.**

Annuity (2, 10, 11) A cash-flow stream that is composed of a sequence of equal and uninterrupted periodic cash flows. *See* equation 2.11 and 2.13.

Annuity discount factor (ADF) (2, 7) A **discount factor** that gives the **present value** of an **annuity**. *See* equation 2.11.

Annuity-equivalent-cash flow (7) *See* constant annual-equivalent cash flow.

Appreciation (currency) (17) Increase in the value of one currency expressed in terms of another currency.

APR (2) *See* **annual percentage rate.**

APV (14) *See* **adjusted present value.**

Arbitrage transaction (17) Transaction that attempts to take advantage of discrepancies between **asset** prices.

Arbitrageurs (17) Parties involved in an **arbitrage transaction.**

As-is (value) (1, 14) *See* **stand-alone value.**

Asian option (16) An option whose payoff at maturity is based on the *average* price of the underlying asset over a specific set of dates during the option's life.

Ask price (17) The price at which a trader in the market is willing to sell. Same as **offer price**. *See* **bid price.**

Asset (1, 4) An economic resource that is expected to generate a profit in the future. In financial accounting, assets refer to what **shareholders** collectively own on the date of the **balance sheet.**

Asset-based borrowing (11) Loans extended with **tangible assets** pledged as **collateral** or guarantee.

Asset beta (12, 13, 14) The **beta** of a firm's stock if the firm is all-equity financed. Same as **unlevered beta**. *See* equation 12.7 and **equity beta.**

Asymmetric information (11, 13) A situation that arises when managers (as insiders to the firm) know more about the firm's current performance and future prospects than do outsiders.

At-the-money option (16) Describes a situation when the exercise price of the option is equal to the market price of the underlying asset.

Average accounting return (AAR) (of a project) (8) Average **earnings after tax** expected from a project divided by the project's average **book value.**

Average accounting return rule (8) According to the average accounting return rule, a project is acceptable if its average accounting return is higher than a target average return.

Average age of accounts receivable (5) *See* **average collection period.**

Average arithmetic return (3) The sum of a series of realized returns divided by the number of returns.

Average collection period (5) **Accounts receivable** at the end of the period divided by the average daily sales during that period. A measure of operating efficiency. *See* equation 5.6.

Average cost method (4) **Inventory** valuation method that assigns to all units in **inventory** the average cost of the units purchased. *See* **first-in, first-out (FIFO)** and **last-in, first-out (LIFO)** methods.

Average payment period (5) **Accounts payable** at the end of the period divided by the average daily **purchases** during that period. *See* equation 5.7.

Avoidable costs (9) Costs that can be saved if an investment is not undertaken.

β *See* **beta coefficient.**

Balance sheet (1, 4) **Financial statement** reporting, at a given date, the total amount of **assets** held by a firm and the **liabilities** and **owners' equity** that finance these **assets**. *See* equations 4.1 and 4.2, Exhibit 4.1, and **managerial balance sheet.**

Bank prime rate (11) The rate **banks** charge their most creditworthy customers.

Bankruptcy (13) A legal procedure through which the ownership of a firm's **assets** is transferred to **debt holders.**

Basis point (2, 17) One-hundredth of 1 percent. For example, 0.12 percent is equal to 12 basis points.

Bearer bonds/securities (11) **Bonds/securities** that do not indicate the holder's name. *See* **registered securities.**

Benchmark rate (11) Rate to which the coupon rate of a **floating rate bond** is linked. Same as reference rate.

Best efforts basis (11) A method of distributing **securities** whereby an **investment bank** undertakes to do its best to sell on behalf of the firm the securities the firm has issued.

Beta coefficient (β) (3, 12,13, 14) A measure of risk based on the sensitivity of an individual stock's returns to changes in the returns of a broad **stock market** index. Same as **systematic risk, market risk,** and **undiversifiable risk.**

Bid-ask spread (17) The difference between the **bid price** and the **ask price.**

Bidder (14) A firm that wants to acquire all or a portion of another firm's shares. *See* **takeover premium.**

Bidding (firm) company (3, 14) *See* **Bidder.**

Bid price (17) Price at which a trader in a market is willing to buy. *See* **ask price.**

Binomial option pricing model (16) A technique to value an option over several intermediary periods when the underlying asset can take only two values at the end of each period.

Bips (2) Denotes **basis points** and pronounced 'beeps'. *See* **basis point.**

Black-Scholes option pricing model (16) An approach to valuing an option when the underlying asset is traded continuously.

Black-Scholes formula (16) A formula to estimate the value of an option derived from the Black-Scholes option pricing model. It relates the option value to the price of the underlying stock, the interest rate, the option exercise price, its volatility, and its time to expiration.

Bond (1, 10, 11) A debt **security** acknowledging a **creditor** relationship with the issuing firm and stipulating the conditions and terms under which the money is borrowed and repaid. *See* **century-, convertible-, Eurodollar-, floating-rate-, foreign-, perpetual-, Samurai-, Shogun-, Yankee-, zero- coupon bonds** and **Eurobonds**.

Bond call value (11, 16) The price at which the issuer can buy a **callable bond** from its holder.

Bond equivalent yield (10) The annualized yield on a bond whose coupon payments are semi-annual or quarterly. It is the yield reported in the press.

Bonding costs (13) Costs (borne by **shareholders**) resulting from lenders placing restrictions on managerial flexibility. *See* **covenants** and **monitoring costs**.

Bond market (10, 11) Market where bonds are issued and traded.

Bond price (10) *See* **bond value**

Bond rating (10) Rating assigned by an agency (such as Standard & Poor's or Moody's Investors Service) that provides an assessment of the **bond's credit risk**.

Bond value (10) **Present value** of a bond's expected cash-flow stream discounted at a rate that reflects the risk of that cash-flow stream. *See* equations 10.2 and 10.3.

Bond value of a convertible bond (11) Value of a **convertible bond** if it did not have a **conversion option**.

Bond yield (10) Same as **yield to maturity** and **market yield**.

Book runner (11) *See* **originating house** and **lead manager**.

Book value multiple (10, 14) Share price divided by **book-value-of-equity** per share. Same as **price-to-book** ratio. Used to value a firm. *See* **valuation by comparables**.

Book value (of an asset) (4) Value at which the **asset** is shown in the firm's **balance sheet**. Same as accounting value.

Book value of equity (1, 4, 10) *See* **owners' equity**.

Bottom line (1, 4) *See* **earnings after tax**.

Brokers (11) Individuals or institutions that trade **securities** on behalf of a third party and do not own the **securities**.

Bullish money spread (16) An arbitrage strategy to make a profit when the stock price goes up while limiting the loss if it goes down.

Business assets (6, 10, 14) **Working capital** requirement plus **net fixed assets**. *See* **enterprise value**.

Business cycle (of a firm) (1) Sequence of events starting with the acquisition of **assets** to generate sales, produce profits, pay **dividends**, retain earnings, build up **equity capital**, raise new debt, and grow the business via asset acquisition, which starts the cycle again. *See* Exhibit 1.4.

Business risk (1, 6, 12, 13, 15) The cumulative effect of **macro risk**, **strategic risk**, and **operational risk**, stemming from the firm's inability to know for certain the outcome of its current investing and operating activities and decisions. *See* Exhibits 1.10, 15.2 and 15.4.

Callable bond (11, 16) A **bond** that gives the issuer the **option** to redeem (repay) the **bond** before it reaches its **maturity date**.

Call option (11, 16, 17) A call option gives the holder the right to *buy* an underlying asset at a fixed price up to the call's expiration date. *See* **put option**.

Call provision (11, 16) **Option** available to a bond issuer to repay the **bond** before it reaches its **maturity date**. This provision can be immediate or **deferred**. *See* **call value** and **callable bond**.

Call value (11) The price at which the issuer can buy a **callable bond** from its holder.

Capex (1) *See* **capital expenditure**.

Capital asset(s) (4) *See* **noncurrent assets**.

Capital asset pricing model (CAPM) (3, 12, 14) A formula according to which a **security's** expected return is equal to the **risk-free rate** plus a **risk premium**. It can be used to estimate the **cost of equity** of a firm or a project. *See* equations 3.13 and 12.10.

Capital budgeting decision (1, 7) *See* **capital investment decision**.

Capital employed (1, 4, 5, 6, 18) The sum of **owners' equity** and all

borrowed funds (short and long term). Equal to **invested capital**. *See* **managerial balance sheet** and Exhibit 4.6.

Capital expenditure (Capex) (1) New investment in **fixed assets**.

Capital expenditure decision (1, 7) *See* **capital investment decision**.

Capital gain (3) Positive change in the price of an asset.

Capital investment decision (7) The decision to spend cash now to acquire long-lived **assets** that will be a source of cash flows in the future. *See* **diversification, expansion, replacement**, and **required investments**.

Capital market line (CML) (3) The straight line that gives the relationship between the expected returns and the risk (measured by volatility) of efficient portfolios when there is a (unique) **market portfolio**. *See* equation 3.9.

Capitalization of the research and development (R&D) expenses (18) Conversion of R&D expenses into **assets** reported in the **balance sheet**.

Capital rationing (7) Limit on the amount of capital that can be used to finance investment projects.

Capital structure (1, 6, 13) The amount of debt relative to **equity capital** a firm should adopt to finance its assets. Same as **financial structure**. *See* **target capital structure** and **optimal capital structure**.

Capital turnover (6, 18) Sales divided by **invested capital**. A measure of the efficiency with which invested capital is managed. *See* equation 6.4.

CAPM (3, 12, 14) *See* **capital asset pricing model**.

Captive finance subsidiary (11) A finance subsidiary owned by a firm.

Carry back (9, 12) Tax rule that allows a firm to deduct current expenses from *past* profits.

Carry forward (9, 12) Tax rule that allows a firm to deduct current expenses from *future* profits.

Cash (and cash equivalents) (1, 4, 5) Cash in hand, cash on deposit with banks, and short-term liquid investments with less than a year's maturity (**marketable securities**).

Cash conversion period or cycle (4) *See* **cash-to-cash period**.

Cash dividend (1, 4, 10, 11, 12) The portion of a firm's **net profit** distributed to **shareholders** in cash. *See* **dividend**.

Cash flow from (business) assets (CFA) (4, 13) **Net cash flow** generated by a firm's **business assets**. Same as **free cash flow**. *See* equation 4.15.

Cash flow from financing activities (4) **Cash inflow** or cash outflow related to the firm's financing activity such as cash received from issuing debt (cash inflow) or cash paid to reimburse a debt (cash outflow).

Cash flow from investing activities (4) **Cash inflow** or cash outflow related to the firm's investing activity such as cash received from selling a fixed asset (cash inflow) or cash paid for acquiring fixed assets (cash outflow).

Cash flow from operating activities (4) **Cash inflow** or cash outflow related to the firm's operating activities such as cash received from a customer (cash inflow) or cash paid to a supplier (cash outflow).

Cash-flow statement (4) **Financial Statement** reporting how a firm's cash position has changed during a particular period of time. *See* **statement of cash flows**.

Cash-flow timeline (2) A line that shows the year, the size and the sign of each cash flow of a cash-flow stream.

Cash flow to equity holders (CFE) (10, 14) The portion of **free cash flow** that belongs to shareholders. *See* equation 10.18.

Cash flow to equity holders discount model (10) A direct **DCF** valuation of equity that discounts **cash flow to equity holders** at the cost of equity.

Cash inflow (4) Amount of cash or money that comes into a firm during a given period of time.

Cash outflow (4) Amount of cash or money that goes out of a firm during a given period of time.

Cash price (16) Current price of a product or an asset. Same as **spot price**.

Cash-to-cash period or **cycle** (4) Period between the dates a firm pays its suppliers and the date it collects its invoices from customers. Same as **cash conversion period** or **cycle**.

CD (4, 11) *See* **certificate of deposit**.

Central clearing house (16) A financial institution that manages the

transactions between buyers and sellers of futures, options, and other securities. The purpose is to reduce the consequences of one party failing to meet its obligations.

Certificate (10) A certificate that states the terms and conditions under which the firm receives cash from the securities it issued.

Century bonds (10) **Bonds** with a 100-year maturity.

Certificates of deposit (CD) (4, 11) Short-term **securities** sold by banks in the **money markets** to raise cash.

Certification role (11) Role played by **underwriters** with respect to guaranteeing the quality of the underwritten securities.

CFA (4) *See* **cash flow from assets**.

CFE (10) See **cash flow to equity holders**.

Characteristic line (12) A line whose slope measures the sensitivity of a stock's returns to changes in the returns of a market index. *See* **beta coefficient**.

Clean price (of a bond) (10) The price without the **accrued interest**. Same as **flat price** and **quoted price**.

Cleanup clause (11) Loan clause that requires the firm to be completely out of debt to the bank for at least one month during the year.

Clientele effect/hypothesis (11) A hypothesis according to which firms design their dividend payout policies to attract groups of investors who have specific distribution preferences.

CML (3) *See* **capital market line**.

COGS (4) *See* **cost of goods sold**.

Coinsurance effect (14) Describes a situation in which merged firms are perceived by their **creditors** to be less likely to fail as a combination than as separate entities.

Collar (16) The combination of a **covered call** (with an **exercise price** *higher* than the stock price) and a **protective put** (with an exercise price *lower* than stock price). Often used by a call writer to provide protection from an unexpected sharp drop in the price of the stock.

Collateral (11, 14) Any **assets** pledged as guarantee to a lender in case the borrower defaults.

Collateralized loan (16) A loan that requires the borrowing firm to assigns assets to the lender as collateral to the loan.

Commercial bank(s) (1, 11) **Financial intermediaries** that take deposits, make payments, and extend loans.

Commercial paper (CP) (1, 4, 11) **Unsecured security** issued by firms to raise short-term funds in the money market.

Common stock (4, 10, 11) Certificate issued by a firm to raise **equity capital** that represents a specified share of total equity funds. *See* **stock certificate** and Exhibits 10.2 and 11.11.

Common stock (account) (4) **Balance sheet** account indicating the number of shares the firm has issued since its creation multiplied by the **par** or **stated value** of the shares. *See* Exhibit 4.9.

Comparables (10, 14) *See* **valuation by comparables**.

Compensating balances (5) Deposits that banks may require their corporate clients to maintain with them in exchange for services they provide to the firm.

Compound factor (2, 7) **Future value** of one dollar growing at a particular compound (or growth) rate for a given number of years.

Compound option (16) An **option** on an option.

Compound rate (2) The rate of interest used to calculate the **future value**.

Compounded value (2, 7) **Future value** of an amount of money growing at a particular compound (or growth) rate for a given number of years.

Compounding (2, 7) The process of finding the **future value** given the **present value**. The reverse of **discounting**.

Conglomerate merger (1, 14) Combination of unrelated businesses for which there are no obvious synergies.

Conservatism principle (4) States that **assets** and **liabilities** should be reported in **financial statements** at a value that would be least likely to overstate assets or to understate **liabilities**.

Conservative (financing) strategy (5) The use of long-term funds to finance both long-term investments and a portion of short-term investments. *See* **aggressive strategy** and **matching strategy**.

Constant annual-equivalent cash flow (annuity-equivalent cash flow) (7) An equivalent stream of equal annual cash flows with the same **present value** as another stream with variable annual cash flows.

Constant dividend-growth model   (10) Formula that gives the value of a firm's equity as the **present value** of its expected future **dividend** stream discounted at a rate that reflects the risk of that **dividend** stream, when the **dividends** are assumed to grow forever at a constant rate. *See* equation 10.10.

Contango   (16) Describes a situation when the forward price is higher than the expected spot price.

Contingent value rights (CVR)   (11, 16) Put **options** sold by a firm that give the holder the right to sell a fixed number of shares to the issuing firm at a fixed priced during the life of the right.

Contingent voting rights   (11) **Right** given to holders of **preferred stock** to elect members to the board of directors if the company has skipped **dividend** payments for a specified number of quarters.

Contractual exposure   (17) Effect of changes in **exchange rates** on the firm's cash flows generated by past (contractual) transactions denominated in foreign currency and still outstanding. Same as **transaction exposure.** *See* economic exposure.

Control (retention of)   (13) Refers to the policies adopted by current owners or management to prevent any outsiders from sharing or influencing the firm's operation and strategy. *See* Exhibit 13.17.

Conversion option   (11) The right, but not the obligation, to convert a firm's **bond** or a **preferred share** into the firm's **common stocks.**

Conversion premium   (11) Difference between the **conversion price** of a **convertible bond** and the current price of the **stock**, if the former is higher, divided by the current stock price.

Conversion price   (11) Price at which the holder of a **convertible bond** has the right to buy one share of the firm's **common stock.**

Conversion ratio   (11) The number of shares into which each **convertible bond** can be converted.

Conversion value   (11) The current price of the **stock** multiplied by the number of shares to which the **convertible bond** can be converted.

Convertible bond   (11, 16) A **bond** that the holder can convert into the firm's **common stock.** *See* conversion premium, conversion price, conversion ratio, and conversion value.

Core working capital requirement   (5) Accounts receivables plus inventories less accounts payable.

Corporate bond   (11) Debt **securities** issued by firms that usually have a maturity exceeding ten years and trade in the **bond market.** *See* **primary** and **secondary markets.**

Corporate note   (11) Debt **securities** issued by firms that usually have a **maturity** between one and ten years.

Corporate risk   (15) A risk not captured by a project, but that affects the firm.

Correlation coefficient   (3) A statistical measure of the direction and the strength of the co-movements between the returns of two securities. *See* **covariance.**

Cost of capital   (1, 10) The return expected by investors for the **capital** they supply to firms. Also, the highest return on an **alternative investment** with the same risk as the investment under consideration. *See* **firm's cost of capital** and **project's cost of capital.**

Cost-of-carry model   (16) Model used to express the relationship between **spot** and **forward prices.** *See* equation 16.1.

Cost of debt   (1, 12) The cost of borrowing new funds. *See* equations 12.2 and 12.3.

Cost of equity (capital)   (1, 10, 12) Rate of return required by the firm's owners on their **equity capital** used to finance the firm's **assets** or a particular project. Can be estimated with the **constant growth dividend-discount model** *(see* equation 10.10a) or the **capital asset pricing model** *(See* equation 10.11).

Cost of goods sold (COGS)   (4) The cost of the goods the firm has sold during the accounting period; reported in the **income statement** as expenses.

Cost of sales   (4) *See* **cost of goods sold.**

Cost synergy   (14) Cost reductions resulting from combining the operations of two or more firms. *See* **market synergies.**

Counterparty risk   (16) The risk that the seller of an asset does not deliver

the asset or the buyer does not pay for the asset on the settlement date.

Country risk   (1, 15, 17) The risk that the cash flows from a project may be affected by changes in local regulations governing foreign investments. A form of **political risk.**

Coupon effect   (10) If two bonds have the same maturity, the one with the lower coupon rate has a higher interest-rate risk.

Coupon payment   (10, 11) The periodic (contractual) interest payment paid to bondholders over the life of a **bond.**

Coupon rate   (10, 11) **Coupon payment** divided by the **face value** of a **bond.**

Covariance   (3) A statistical measure of the direction and the strength of the co-movements between the returns of two securities. *See* **correlation coefficient** and equation 3.4.

Covenants (restrictive)   (11, 13) Conditions imposed by lenders and stipulated in a bond **indenture** that require managers to achieve certain financial targets or refrain from certain actions that may be detrimental to lenders' interests.

Covered calls   (16) Selling calls and holding the underlying stock to hedge an unexpected sharp drop in the price of the stock.

CP   (1, 4, 11) *See* **commercial paper.**

Credit default risk   (16) Same as **counterparty risk.**

Credit line (line of credit)   (4, 5, 11) A nonbinding arrangement in which a **bank** lends a firm a stated maximum amount of money over a fixed but renewable period of time, usually one year. In general, no fee is charged but a **compensating balance** is required. Same as **line of credit.**

Credit market   (11) Market in which debt **securities** are issued and traded.

Creditors   (1) Parties to whom a firm owes money, including lenders and suppliers.

Credit rating   (10, 13) Rating that provides an overall assessment of a borrower's **credit risk.** *See* **credit rating agency.**

Credit rating agency   (10, 13) An agency, such as Standard & Poor's or Moody's Investment Service, that provides **credit ratings.**

Credit risk   (10, 15) The risk that a borrower will be unable to service its debt. *See* **debt service.**

Credit risk premium (10) *See* **yield spread**.

Credit spread (10) *See* **yield spread** and **credit risk premium**.

Cross rates (17) **Foreign exchange rates** between two currencies computed from their exchange rate with a third currency.

Cum-dividend (11) With the right to receive the dividend.

Currency forward contract (17) An agreement between two parties for the delivery of currencies on a specific date in the future at an exchange rate fixed today.

Currency futures (contracts) (17) Standardized **forward currency contracts** traded in **futures markets**.

Currency forward hedge (17) **Hedging** with **currency forward contracts**.

Currency option hedge (17) **Hedging** with **currency options**.

Currency rate (17) *See* **foreign-exchange rate**.

Currency risk (1, 11, 15, 17) **Risk** arising from unexpected changes in the **exchange rate** between two currencies. *See* **foreign-exchange risk**.

Currency swap contract (17) Agreement with a bank to exchange a set of future cash flows denominated in one currency for another set denominated in another currency.

Current assets (4) **Assets** that are expected to be turned into cash within one year. Same as **short-term assets**. Reported in the **balance sheet**.

Current liabilities (4) Obligations of a firm that must be paid within one year. Same as **short-term liabilities**. Reported in the **balance sheet**.

Current maturity (tenor) (10) At any point in time, the time remaining until a **bond** is redeemed (repaid).

Current ratio (5) **Current assets** divided by **current liabilities**. A measure of **liquidity**. *See* equation 5.11 and **quick ratio**.

Current yield (10) A bond's **coupon payment** divided by its price.

Cutoff period (8) In **capital budgeting**, the period (usually in years) below which a project's **payback period** must fall in order to accept the project.

CVR (11) *See* **contingent value rights**.

Days of sales outstanding (DSO) (5) *See* **average collection period**.

DCF (10, 14) *See* **discounted cash flow**.

DDM (10, 12) *See* **dividend-discount model**.

Dealers (11) Individuals or institutions that trade securities that they own. *See* **brokers**.

Debentures (11) **Bonds** supported by the general credit standing of the issuing firm (US definition).

Debt capacity (13) The ability to quickly raise debt in the future if a need for funds arises unexpectedly.

Debt capital (1) **Capital** provided by borrowed funds.

Debt holders (1, 11) Holders of loans, leasing agreements, **corporate bonds**, and similar **liabilities** issued by firms to raise **debt capital**.

Debt overhang (16) Describe a situation when equity holders do not invest in a positive NPV project if most of the value created goes to the bondholders.

Debt ratio (6) A measure of financial leverage. Usually identified as the **debt-to-invested capital ratio** or the **debt-to-equity ratio**.

Debt-to-equity ratio (1, 6, 13) Total interest-bearing debt divided by **owners' equity**. A measure of **financial leverage**.

Debt-to-invested capital ratio (6) Debt divided by the sum of debt and equity.

Default risk (10) *See* **credit risk**.

Deferred call provision (11) Provision that allows the issuer of a **callable bond** to repay (or call) the bond only after a specified date (first date of call).

Deferred tax (liability) (4) Taxes owed to the tax authority originating from the difference between the amount of tax due on the firm's reported pre-tax profit and the amount of tax claimed by the tax authorities.

Degree of risk aversion (3) **Risk-averse** investors have different appetite for risk; some are more risk-averse than others.

Delta (of an option) (16) The approximate change in the price of an **option** in response to a one-dollar change in the price of the underlying stock.

Depreciation (accounting) (4) The process of periodic and systematic value-reduction of the **gross value of fixed assets** over their **accounting life**.

Depreciation (currency) (17) Reduction in the value of one

currency expressed in terms of another currency.

Depreciation charge (4) *See* **depreciation expense**.

Depreciation expense(s) (1, 4) The portion of the cost of a **fixed asset** that is expensed during the accounting period and reported in the **income statement**. Same as **depreciation charge**.

Derivatives (instruments) (16) Financial instruments such as **forwards, futures**, and **options** that derive their value from an underlying security such as a share.

DF (2, 7) *See* **discount factor**.

Differential cash flows (9) *See* **incremental cash flows**.

Dilution (11, 13) Reduction in the fraction of a firm's equity held by its existing **shareholders** after the firm sells **common stock** to new investors or grants shares to its employees.

Direct costs of financial distress (13) The actual costs the firm will incur if it becomes legally bankrupt, such as payments to lawyers and other third parties. *See* **indirect costs** of **financial distress**.

Direct financing (11) When firms raise funds by issuing **securities** that are held by ultimate savers (**household sector**) instead of **financial intermediaries**. *See* **indirect financing**.

Direct lease (11) A **financial lease** involving a straight contract between the owner of an **asset** (the **lessor**) and the user of that **asset** (the **lessee**).

Dirty price (of a bond) (10) *See* **invoice price**.

Discount (from face or par value) (10, 11) The difference between the price of a **bond** and its **face value**, if the former is lower.

Discount bond (10) Same as **zero-coupon bond**. *See* **pure discount bond**.

Discount factor (DF) (2, 7) Present value, at a particular **discount rate**, of one dollar to be received after a specified number of years.

Discount rate (1, 2, 7) Rate at which future cash flows are discounted to the present. *See* **discounting**.

Discounted cash flow (DCF) model (10) Asset valuation model based on the concept of the time value of money and risk.

Discounted cash flow (DCF) value/ model/valuation   (10, 14) The value today of an expected future cash-flow stream discounted at a rate that reflects its **risk**. The **DCF value** of a firm's equity equals the **DCF value** of its **business assets** minus the value of its debt. Same as **present value**. *See* **discounting** and exhibit 10.12.

Discounted payback period   (8) Capital budgeting method that measures a project's **payback period** with cash flows that have been discounted to the present at the project's **cost of capital**. *See* **discounted payback period rule**.

Discounted payback period rule   (8) Accept (reject) the project if its **discounted payback period** is shorter (longer) than a given **cutoff period**.

Discounted value   (2, 7) Same *as* **present value**.

Discounting   (1, 2, 7) The process used to convert future cash flows into their equivalent value today.

Diversifiable risk   (3, 12) Risk that can be eliminated through portfolio diversification. Same as **unsystematic risk** and **firm-specific risk**.

Diversification investments   (7) Investments in areas unrelated to the existing activities of the firm.

Dividend   (3, 4, 11) The portion of a firm's net profit paid out to its owners in cash. *See* Exhibit 4.11 and **cash dividend, dividend payout ratio, dividend policy,** and **dividend yield**.

Dividend declaration date   (11) The date the company's board of directors announces the dividend.

Dividend-discount model (DDM)   (10, 12) **A formula that values a firm's equity as the present value of the entire stream of cash dividends the firm is expected to generate in the future.** *See* equation 10.9 and **constant dividend-growth model**.

Dividend payment   (11) The distribution of a firm's cash to its shareholders either through a *regular* quarterly or annual payments and/ or through a *special, one-time* distribution.

Dividend payment date   (11) The date when the declared dividend is actually paid.

Dividend payout ratio   (1, 6, 11) Dividends divided by **net profit**. *See* **dividend policy**.

Dividend per share (DPS)   (3) The amount of dividend paid per share of stock.

Dividend policy   (11, 13) The decision regarding the portion of a year's profit that should be paid out in the form of cash dividends to the firm's shareholders. *See* **stable dividend policy**.

Dividend puzzle   (11) Refers to why firms pay dividends instead of using cash to buy back their shares given that dividend payments are usually taxed at a higher rate than capital gains.

Dividend signaling hypothesis   (11) Hypothesis according to which dividend announcements affect share prices because they signal good or bad prospects for the firm. See **signaling effects**.

Dividend yield   (3) **Dividend** per share divided by share price. *See* Exhibit 10.2.

Doubtful accounts   (4) *See* **allowance for doubtful accounts**.

DPS   (3) *See* **dividend per share**.

DSO   (5) *See* **days of sales outstanding**.

Duration (of a bond)   (10) A measure (in years) of a bond's **interest-rate risk**.

Earnings after tax (EAT)   (1, 4) Revenues minus all expenses, including interest and tax expenses. Same as **net income, net profit,** and **bottom line**.

Earnings before interest and tax (EBIT)   (1, 4) Difference between the firm's **operating profit** and any extraordinary items reported in its income statement.

Earnings before interest, tax, depreciation, and amortization (EBITDA)   (4, 14) Revenues minus all operating expenses excluding depreciation and amortization.

Earnings before tax (EBT)   (1, 4) Earnings before interest and tax minus net interest expenses.

Earnings multiple   (6, 10, 14) Share price divided by the firm's **earnings per share**. Same as **price-to-earnings ratio (PER)**. Used to value a firm. *See* **valuation by comparables**.

Earnings per share (EPS)   (6, 10, 14) **Earnings after tax** divided by the total number of shares outstanding.

EAT   (1, 4) *See* **earnings after tax**;

EBIT   (1, 4) *See* **earnings before interest and tax**

EBITDA   (4, 10, 14) *See* **earnings before interest, tax, depreciation, and amortization**.

EBITDA multiple   (10, 14) **Enterprise value** divided by **EBITDA**; used to estimate a firm's enterprise value. *See* **valuation by comparables**.

EBT   (1, 4) *See* **earnings before tax**.

Economic exposure   (17) Effect of changes in **exchange rates** on the value of the firm's *future* cash flows generated either by *past* and *known* transactions (**contractual or transaction exposure**) or by *future* and *uncertain* transactions (**operating exposure**).

Economic life   (9) Number of years over which a project adds value to a firm, as opposed to the number of years over which it is depreciated (**accounting life**). Same as **useful life**.

Economic payback period   (8) *See* **discounted payback period**.

Economic profit   (18) *See* **economic value added**.

Economic risk   (15) Risk arising from unexpected sales fluctuations because of the uncertain economic environment in which firms operate. *See* **business risk** and Exhibit 15.4.

Economic value added (EVA)   (18) Net **operating profit after tax (NOPAT)** minus a charge for the capital consumed to achieve that **profit**. *See* equations 18.5 and 18.6. Same as economic profit. *See* **market value added**.

Economies of scale   (14) The ability of a firm to reduce its average costs of production and distribution because of size. A motivation to acquire other companies. *See* **cost** and **market synergies**.

Effective annual interest return   (2) The annual rate of interest when compounding occurs over a shorter periods within one year. *See* **annual percentage rate** and equation 2.4.

Effective (corporate) tax rate   (6) The tax rate at which a firm actually pays its taxes, which may differ from the **statutory corporate tax rate** if some of the firm's earnings are taxed at a different rate.

Efficient investment line (EIL)   (3) The straight line that gives the relationship between the expected returns of **efficient portfolios** in the presence of a **riskless asset** and their risk (measured by volatility) in the absence of a (unique) **market portfolio**. *See* equation 3.7.

Efficient investment set (3) The set that contains all available **efficient portfolios**.

Efficient (securities) markets (1, 11) Markets in which security (share) prices adjust to new and relevant information as soon as it becomes available to market participants.

Efficient portfolio (3) Portfolios that offer the highest expected returns for any given level of risk and the lowest risk for any given level of expected return.

EIL (3) *See* **efficient investment line**.

Empirical return distribution (3) Same as **histogram**.

Enterprise value (EV) (10, 14) A firm's market value of equity plus its market value of debt less its holding of cash and other financial assets. It is the value of the firm's **business assets**. *See* equation 10.15, Exhibit 10.9, and **EBITDA multiple**.

Enterprise value-to-EBITDA ratio (EV/EBITDA) (10, 14) Same as **EBITDA multiple**.

Entry barriers (1) Barriers that are costly enough to discourage potential competitors from entering a particular market.

EPS (6, 10, 14) *See* **earnings per share**

Equipment financing loan (11) A medium- to long-term loan backed by a piece of machinery. *See* **collateral**.

Equity beta (12, 13) The beta of a firm's common stock. Same as **levered beta** and **market beta**.

Equity capital (1,4) Funds contributed by **shareholders** that are equal to the difference, at a particular date, between what a firm's **shareholders** collectively own, called **assets**, and what they owe, called **liabilities**. Same as **equity funding, owners' equity, shareholders' equity** or **funds, or net asset value**.

Equity funding (1) *See* **equity capital**.

Equity kicker (11) The **conversion option** of a **convertible bond**.

Equity market (11) *See* **stock exchange**

Equity multiples (14) Ratios used to value a firm based on **valuation by comparables**. Same as **market multiples**.

Equity multiplier (6) **Invested capital** divided by **owners' equity**. A measure of **financial leverage**.

Equity valuation models (10) Valuation models that provide a direct estimation of a firm's equity value. *See* Exhibit 10.12.

Eurobonds (11) Bonds issued in the **Euromarket**.

Euro-commercial paper (Euro-CP) (11) **Commercial paper** issued in the **Euromarket**.

Eurodollar bonds (11) **Bonds** denominated in US dollars that are sold simultaneously to investors in several countries via the **Euromarket**.

Euro-equity (11) Equity issued in the **Euromarket**.

Euromarket (11) A market that is outside the direct control and jurisdiction of the issuer's country of origin.

European option (16) An **option** that can be only exercised on the maturity date of the option. *See* **American option**.

Euroyen bonds (11) **Eurobonds** sold by firms denominated in Japanese yen.

EV (10, 14) *See* **enterprise value**.

EVA (18) *See* **economic value added**.

Event risk (15) Unexpected incident that reduces the firm's value if and when it occurs.

Excess cash (5) Amount of cash held by a firm in excess of the cash needed to support its operating activities.

Exchange-control risk (15) Unexpected changes in the *fixed* exchange rate between two currencies. *See* Exhibit 15.2.

Exchange rate (17) The price one has to pay in one country's currency to buy one unit of another country's currency. Same as **foreign-exchange rate** or **currency rate**.

Exchange-rate risk (15) **Risk** borne by firms with foreign operations that originates from unexpected changes in the **exchange rate** between two currencies.

Ex-coupon date (of a bond) (10) A bond purchased after its ex-coupon date does not entitle its owner to receive the next coupon which goes to the seller.

Ex-dividend (11) Without the right to receive the dividend.

Ex-dividend date (11) Buyers of shares on or after this date do not receive the dividend.

Exercise price (11) The fixed price at which the holder of a **warrant** or an **option** has the right to buy the underlying asset. Same as **strike price**.

Exercise price (of an option or warrant) (16, 17) The fixed price or rate at which the underlying asset can be bought or sold. Same as **strike price**.

Exit barriers (6) Barriers, such as high capital investment, that significantly reduce a firm's ability to leave an industry by selling its **assets** rapidly and easily.

Exit strategy (14) The way leveraged buyout (**LBO**) investors cash in on their investment by selling some (or all) of their shares after a period of time to other investors or through an **initial price offering (IPO)**.

Expansion investments (7) Projects that result in additional sales revenues, margins, and **working capital requirement**.

Expected (prospective) multiple (14) **Multiples** calculated using a forecast of future financial data; used to value a firm. *See* **historical multiples** and **valuation by comparables**.

Expected return (3) The return of an asset drawn from its probability distribution.

Expense (1, 4) A firm's activity that results in a decrease in the value of **owners' equity**.

Expiration date (option) (16, 17) The fixed **settlement date** of an **option** contract. Same as **maturity date**.

Ex-rights shares (11) Shares for which **rights** were issued but that are no longer traded with their **rights** attached. *See* right, **rights-on shares**, and equations 11.2 and 11.3.

External funds need (11) **Internally generated funds** less **funding needs**. *See* equation 11.1.

Face value (10) The fixed amount that has to be paid back to bondholders at the **maturity date** of a **bond**. Same as **principal, par value, nominal value**, or **redemption value**.

Fair market value (4, 18) An estimate of the amount that could be received on the sale of an **asset** under normal market conditions (as opposed to an emergency or liquidating sale).

Fair price (11) Best estimate of the unobservable value of a firm's **assets** and **securities**.

FASB (4) *See* Financial Accounting Standards Board.

Fat tails (3) Refer to the shape of the **histogram** of investment returns that shows higher returns than would be expected by a **normal distribution** at both ends of the distribution.

FCF (4, 10) *See* **free cash flows**.

FIFO (4) *See* **first-in, first-out method**.

Financial Accounting Standards Board (FASB) (4) The accounting body responsible for setting accounting standards in the United States.

Financial asset (10) *See* **securities**.

Financial balance (6) Achieved when the firm can finance its growth without modifying its operating and financing policies and without issuing new equity. *See* **self-sustainable growth rate**.

Financial (financing) cost effect (6) The negative effect of an increase in debt financing on **return on equity (ROE)**—more debt means larger interest payments, which reduces **earnings after tax (EAT)** and lowers ROE. *See* **financial structure effect**.

Financial cost ratio (6) **Earnings before tax (EBT)** divided by **earnings before interest and tax (EBIT)**. A measure of **financial leverage** based on **income statement** data. *See* **financial structure ratio** and **financial leverage multiplier**.

Financial cost risk (5, 15) **Risk** arising from unexpected changes in the level of interest rates that affect the firm's future cost of debt financing. *See* **refinancing risk** and Exhibit 15.4.

Financial distress (13, 15, 16) Situation arising when a firm finds it increasingly difficult to service its debt. *See* **debt service** and **financial distress costs**.

Financial distress costs (1, 13, 15) Direct and indirect costs borne by a firm, which has excessive borrowing and difficulties servicing its debt, and that reduce the firm's value. *See* **debt service** and **direct and indirect costs of financial distress**.

Financial distress risk (13, 15) The risk that the firm will experience **financial distress costs** as its use of debt financing rises. *See* Exhibit 15.2.

Financial flexibility (13) having a buildup of cash that allows for immediate investment and that increases the firm's **debt capacity**. *See* Exhibit 13.17.

Financial instruments (10) *See* **securities, financial assets**.

Financial intermediaries (11) Institutions that act as middlemen between the ultimate recipients of **capital** (firms) and the ultimate suppliers of **capital** (household sector). *See* Exhibit 11.4.

Financial investment risk (15) The risks associated with the firm's holding of financial investments such as shares and bonds of other companies as well as **cash** and **marketable securities**. *See* Exhibit 15.4 as well as **price risk** and **liquidity risk**.

Financial lease (11) A long-term lease that extends over most of the **useful life** of the **asset**.

Financial leverage (6, 13) The use of debt financing to complement equity financing. Same as **gearing**.

Financial leverage multiplier (6) The **financial cost ratio** multiplied by the **financial structure ratio**. *See* equation 6.10.

Financial leverage risk (15) Increase in the volatility of operating earnings because of borrowing and fixed interest payments. *See* Exhibit 15.4.

Financial markets (1) Markets in which financial assets are traded. Same as **securities markets**. *See* **financial system**.

Financial risk (1, 6, 12, 13, 15) All the risks that result from borrowing: **financial leverage risk, financial cost risk,** and **refinancing risk**. *See* Exhibits 1.10, 15.2, 15.4.

Financial slack (13) Cash surplus that firms may build up during good times. *See* **financial flexibility**.

Financial statements (1, 4) Formal documents issued by firms to provide financial information about their business and financial transactions. *See* **income statement** and **balance sheet**.

Financial strategy matrix (18) A diagnostic and managerial tool that compares the capacity of a particular business to create value versus its capacity to finance the growth of its sales. *See* Exhibit 18.9.

Financial structure decision (13) *See* **capital structure decision** and **target capital structure**.

Financial structure effect (6) The positive effect of an increase in debt financing on **return on equity**

(ROE)—more debt means less **equity capital** and thus higher **ROE**. *See* **financial cost effect**.

Financial structure ratio (6) **Invested capital** divided by **owners' equity**. A measure of **financial leverage** based on **balance sheet data**. *See* **financial cost ratio** and **financial leverage multiplier**.

Financial system (11) The institutions and practices that allow the cash surplus of savers to be channeled to firms with a cash shortage.

Finished goods inventory (4) The cost of completed units not yet sold at the date of the balance sheet.

Firm's cost of capital (12) The return expected by investors for the **capital** they supply to fund all the **assets** acquired and managed by the firm.

Firm-specific risk (3) **Risk** that can be eliminated through portfolio diversification. Same as **diversifiable risk** and **unsystematic risk**. Also called **company-specific risk**.

First-in, first-out (FIFO) method (4) **Inventory** valuation method that assigns to all units in inventory the cost of the unit purchased first. *See* **last-in, first-out (LIFO)** method and **average cost method**.

Fisher effect (17) States that the **nominal interest rate** is the sum of the **real interest rate** and the expected inflation rate.

Fisher's intersection (8) The point at which the **net present value (NPV)** profiles of two investments intersect. *See* Exhibit 8.15.

Fixed asset (4) *See* **noncurrent asset**.

Fixed asset turnover ratio (6) **Sales** divided by **fixed assets**. A measure of the efficiency of **fixed assets** management. Same as **fixed asset rotation**.

Flat price (of a bond) (10) *See* **clean price**.

Floating rate bond or floater (11) A **bond** whose rate is linked to another rate that is revised periodically.

Flotation costs (11, 13) Costs incurred when issuing **securities**. Same as **issuance** or **issue costs**.

Foreign bonds (11) **Bonds** issued in the domestic **bond market** of another country.

Foreign-exchange line of credit (17) A **credit line** demanded by a bank to guarantee a firm's ability to deliver on its **foreign-exchange obligations**.

Foreign-exchange market   (17) Market in which currencies are bought and sold. Same as currency market.

Foreign-exchange rate   (17) *See* exchange rate.

Foreign-exchange risk   (11, 15, 17) Risk arising from unexpected changes in the exchange rate between two currencies. *See* currency risk.

Foreign securities   (11) Securities issued in the domestic market of another country.

Forward (contract)   (16, 17) Agreement between two parties for delivery of an asset at an agreed-upon price and at a specified future date (settlement date).

Forward price   (16) The contractual price in a forward contract.

Forward hedge   (17) Hedging with forward contracts.

Forward rate   (10, 17) The fixed rate at which a forward contract is settled.

Forward window contract   (17) Similar to a standard forward contract except that the transaction can be settled over a period of time (the window) instead of on a fixed date.

Free cash flow   (4, 10, 13, 14) The cash flow generated by a firm's business assets. *See* equation 4.15. Same as cash flow from (business) assets.

Free cash flow discount model   (10) *See* equation 10.17a.

Full price (of a bond)   (10) *See* invoice price.

Fundamental finance principle   (1) States that a business proposal will raise the firm's value only if the present value of the future stream of net cash benefits the proposal is expected to generate exceeds the initial cash outlay required to undertake the proposal. Same as the net present value (NPV) rule.

Fundamental value   (1, 10) *See* intrinsic value.

Funding needs   (11) Funds needed to finance the growth of the firm's invested capital. *See* internally-generated funds and external funds need.

Future value (FV)   (2, 7) The value at a future date of an amount deposited today that grows at a given compound, or growth, rate.

Futures (contract)   (16, 17) A forward contract that has a standardized contract size and a standardized

delivery date; traded on futures markets.

Futures exchanges   (16) Same as futures markets.

Futures hedge   (17) Hedging with a futures contract.

Futures markets   (16, 17) Organized exchanges in which futures contracts are traded.

Futures price   (16) Price of a futures contract traded in a futures market.

FV   (2) *See* future value.

GAAP (US GAAP)   (4) *See* Generally Accepted Accounting Principles.

Gearing   (6, 13) Same as financial leverage.

General cash offering   (11) The issuance and sale of a firm's securities to any investor, including current shareholders. Same as public offering. *See* Exhibit 11.8 and rights offering.

Generally Accepted Accounting Principles (GAAP)   (4) Accounting standards and rules that firms use to prepare their financial statements.

Going concern   (14) An assumption according to which a firm will operate forever.

Goodwill   (4, 18) The difference between the (higher) price at which a firm has been acquired and either its reported net book value or its estimated fair value.

Government bills   (4) Short-term marketable securities issued by governments.

Government financial guarantee   (16) Value of deposit accounts guaranteed by the government against the default of the bank that offered the deposit, making these deposits riskless.

Gross profit   (4) The difference between the firm's net sales and its cost of goods sold.

Gross value (of fixed assets)   (4) The purchase price of fixed assets reported in the balance sheet. Same as historical price. *See* net fixed assets.

Ground-floor financing   (14) Equity capital financing in a leveraged buyout (LBO).

Hedge currency risk   (17) The process of protecting the value of an asset or a liability from currency fluctuations.

Hedge ratio   (16) The change in the price of an option when the

underlying asset price changes by one unit of currency (dollar).

Hedging   (16) A risk management technique that is employed to eliminate price risk through the use of forward, futures, and option contracts.

High-yield bond   (10) Same as junk bond and speculative-grade bond

Histogram   (3) The graphical representation of the distribution of an asset's realized returns.

Historical cost (principle)   (4) *See* acquisition cost principle.

Historical multiples   (14) Multiples calculated using past financial data. Same as trailing multiples. *See* expected or prospective multiples. Used to value a firm. *See* valuation by comparables.

Holding period return   (3) Actual return realized over a specified time horizon. *See* equation 3.1.

Homemade diversification   (14) The diversification investors can achieve themselves by combining shares of different companies in their personal portfolios.

Homemade dividend   (11) The ability of shareholders to pay themselves the equivalent of a dividend by selling shares they own instead of receiving a dividend payment.

Homemade leverage   (13) Personal financial leverage as opposed to corporate financial leverage.

Homogeneous expectations   (3) An assumption that all investors have the same forecasts of the expected return and risk of all the securities available in the market.

Horizontal merger   (14) Two firms in the same sector pooling their resources.

Household sector   (11) The sector of the economy composed of individuals and families.

Hurdle rate   (8, 12) An investment's cost of capital (*See* weighted average cost of capital) when used in comparison with the investment's internal rate of return. Same as minimum required rate of return.

IASB   (4) *See* International Accounting Standards Board.

IFRS   (4) *See* International Financial Reporting Standards.

Impairment loss   (4) The difference between the carrying amount of an asset in a balance sheet and its recoverable amount if the latter is smaller.

Impairment test   (4) A check to find whether the carrying amount of an asset in a balance sheet exceeds its recoverable amount.

Implied volatility   (16) The volatility of the price of an option's underlying asset calculated from the **Black-Scholes formula**.

Income statement   (1, 4) **Financial statement** reporting information about the firm's activities that resulted in changes in the value of **owners' equity** during a period of time, obtained by deducting from **revenues** the corresponding **expenses** incurred during that period of time.

Incremental cash flows   (9) The difference between the firm's expected cash flows if the investment is made and its expected cash flows if the investment is not undertaken. Same as **differential cash flows**.

Indenture (bonds)   (11) Formal contract between a **bond** issuing firm and its lenders.

Index model   (3) *See* equation 3.10.

Indifference curve   (3) A curve in the **risk-return plane** along which all the investment opportunities are equally preferred by an investor. *See* Exhibit 3.2.

Indirect costs of financial distress (13) Costs created by the increasing probability that a firm may become bankrupt, thus preventing it from operating at maximum efficiency. Includes loss of customers, departure of key employees, and the inability to obtain credit from suppliers. *See* **direct costs of financial distress**.

Indirect financing   (11) When firms raise funds by issuing **securities** that are held by **financial intermediaries** instead of ultimate "savers." *See* **direct financing**.

Indirect securities   (11) **Securities** issued by banks (checking and savings accounts) and other **financial intermediaries** (such as insurance policies and retirement plans).

Inefficient investment set   (3) The portion of the **opportunity set** that contains all the **inefficient portfolios**.

Inefficient management (hypothesis)   (14) Refers to a rationale for takeover whereby the target firm is not currently managed at its optimal level and the acquiring firm's managers believe that they can do a better job if they buy the target firm and run it themselves.

Inefficient portfolio   (3) A portfolio that does not offer the highest expected return for a given level of risk.

Information-content of payout policy   (11) refers to the hypothesis according to which a firm's **payout policy** conveys information to the market beyond the cash distribution itself.

Initial public offering (IPO)   (11) When a firm sells equity to the public for the first time. *See* **seasoned new issue**.

Institutional investors   (11) Any **financial intermediaries** that invest in the **financial markets**.

Insurance premium   (15) The amount of money that must be paid to an insurance company to insure against a risk during a specific period of time.

Intangible assets   (4) **Assets** such as **goodwill**, patents, trademarks, and copyrights.

Interbank (currency) market   (17) The **foreign exchange market** whose major participants are large banks.

Interest coverage ratio   (6) *See* **times-interest-earned ratio**.

Interest payable   (4) The amount of interest expenses due by the end of the accounting period.

Interest-rate parity (IRP) relation   (17) States that the percentage difference between the **forward** and **spot rates** is equal to the difference in interest rates between the home and foreign markets. *See* Exhibit 17.1, equation 17.9, and Appendix 17.2.

Interest-rate risk   (10, 16) **Risk** arising from unexpected changes in the level of interest rates that affect bond prices. *See* **market risk** and **price risk**.

Interest receivable   (4) Financial income not yet received by the end of the accounting period.

Interest tax shield (ITS)   (4, 13) The annual and recurrent tax saving resulting from debt financing. *See* equations 13.3 and 13.10.

Internal equity financing   (1) Refers to **retained earnings**, the part of a firm's profit that the firm's owners decide to invest back into their company.

Internal rate of return (IRR)   (1, 2, 7, 8) The **discount rate** that makes the **net present value** of a project equal to zero.

Internal rate of return (IRR) rule   (1, 8) Accept (reject) a proposal if its **internal rate of return (IRR)** is higher (lower) than its **weighted average cost of capital (WACC)**.

Internally generated funds   (11) The sum of **retained earnings** and **depreciation expenses**. *See* equation 11.1.

International Accounting Standards Board (IASB)   (4) An international accounting body responsible for setting accounting standards.

International Financial Reporting Standards (IFRS)   (4) **Accounting standards** and rules formulated by the **International Accounting Standards Board**.

International Fisher effect   (17) States that the difference in interest rates between two countries reflects the difference in their expected inflation rates. *See* equation 17.7, Exhibit 17.1, and Appendix 17.2.

In the black   (4) A firm with positive **earnings after tax**. *See* **in the red**.

In-the-money option   (16) Describes a situation when the exercise price of a call option is lower than the market price of the underlying asset.

In the red   (4) A firm with negative **earnings after tax**. *See* **in the black**.

Intrinsic value   (10) The estimated value of a security or an asset derived from a financial model and a set of assumptions. It may or may not be the same as the current market value.

Intrinsic (call) option value   (16) The profit a call holder would make if the call could be exercised immediately.

Inventory (ies)   (1, 4) Raw materials, work in process, and finished goods not yet sold, reported in the **balance sheet** as **current assets**. *See* **first-in, first-out (FIFO)**; **last-in, first-out (LIFO)**; and **average cost method**.

Inventory turn or **turnover**   (5) **Cost of goods sold** divided by ending inventories. *See* equation 5.5 and Exhibit 5.7. A measure of the efficiency of inventory management.

Invested capital   (1, 4, 5, 6) The sum of **cash** and **marketable securities**, **working capital requirement**, and **net fixed assets**. Equal to **capital employed**. *See* equation 4.5 and the **managerial balance sheet**.

Investment banks (bankers)   (1, 11)
Financial intermediaries that act as
"middlemen" between firms wanting
to issue **securities** to raise funds and
the suppliers of **capital**. *See* **book
runner, lead manager, originating
house, merchant bankers,** and
underwriters.

Investment-grade bonds   (10) Highly
rated **bonds** (BBB and above) that
can be purchased by pension funds
and other **institutional investors.** *See*
speculative grade bonds and **bond
ratings.**

Invoice price (of a bond)   (10) The
price without the **accrued interest.**
Same *as* **full price** and **dirty price.**

IPO   (11) *See* **initial public offering.**

IRP relation   (17) *See* **interest-rate
parity.**

IRR   (1, 8) *See* **internal rate of return.**

Irrelevant costs   (9) Costs (past or
future) that the firm must bear
even if the investment project is not
undertaken. *See* **unavoidable costs**
and **sunk costs.**

Issuance or issue costs   (11, 13) Costs
incurred when issuing **securities.**
Same as **issue costs** or **flotation
costs.**

Issue costs   (11, 13) *See* **issuance costs.**

ITS   (13) *See* **interest tax shield.**

Junior bond/debt/loan   (11, 14) *See*
subordinated bond/debt/loan.

Junk bond/debt   (10) *See* **speculative
grade bond/debt.**

Last-in, first-out (LIFO) method   (4)
Inventory valuation method that
assigns to all units in inventory the
cost of the unit purchased last. *See*
first-in, first-out (FIFO) method and
average cost method.

Law of one price (LOP)   (16, 17)
LOP states that transactions which
generate the same cash flows must
have the same value. Applied to
international transactions it states
that any traded good must sell for
the same price (when expressed in
the same currency) regardless of
the country in which it is sold. *See*
Appendix 17.2.

LBO   (14) *See* **leveraged buyout.**

Leading and lagging   (17) Timing the
cash inflows and **cash outflows** from
different foreign business units to
reduce the firm's overall exposure **to**
exchange-rate risk.

Lead manager   (11) Same as
originating house and **book runner.**

Lease financing   (11) *See* **direct lease,
financial lease, leveraged lease,
operating lease,** and **sale and
leaseback lease.**

Lessee   (11) The user of the asset that
is leased.

Lessor   (11) The owner of the asset
that is leased.

Leverage   (13) *See* **financial leverage.**

Leveraged buyout (LBO)   (14)
Transaction in which a group
of investors purchase a firm by
borrowing an unusually large amount
of debt relative to **equity capital.**

Leveraged lease   (11) A **financial
lease** in which the leasing company
finances the purchase of the **asset**
with a substantial level of debt,
using the lease contract as **collateral.**

Levered assets   (14) **Assets** financed
with some **debt capital.**

Levered beta   (12, 13) The **beta** of a
stock when the firm is indebted.
Same as **equity** or **market beta.**

Liabilities   (1, 4) What a firm's **shareholders** collectively owe on the date
of the **balance sheet.**

LIBOR   (11) *See* **London Interbank
Offering Rate.**

LIFO   (4) *See* **last-in, first-out method.**

Line of credit   (4, 11, 17) Same as
credit line.

Liquid assets   (5) *See* **cash and cash
equivalents.**

Liquidation value   (14) Amount of
cash that can be raised if the various
items that make up a firm's **assets**
are sold separately. Usually the
minimum value of **assets.**

Liquidity (of a firm)   (5) The ability of
a firm to meet short-term recurrent
cash obligations. *See* **solvency.**

Liquidity (of a market)   (11)
Characterizes a market in which
buyers and sellers can quickly trade
their securities at the quoted price
and settle their transactions at a
relatively low cost.

Liquidity (of an asset/a security)   (4, 11)
The speed with which an asset or a
security can be turned into cash without significant loss of value.

Liquidity ratio   (5) **Net long-term
financing (NLF)** divided by **working
capital requirement (WCR).**
A measure of a firm's **liquidity**
position. *See* equation 5.4.

Liquidity risk   (15) A deterioration
in **money market** conditions that

would prevent a firm from selling
rapidly and without loss of value the
marketable securities it holds. *See*
Exhibit 15.2.

**Liquidity risk of a forward
contract**   (16) The risk of not
finding another party to take on a
contract if one party wants to get
out of it before the settlement date.

Listed securities   (11) Securities
of firms that meet a number of
stringent conditions that allow them
to be traded in **organized stock
exchanges.** *See* **over-the-counter
(OTC) market.**

**London Interbank Offering Rate
(LIBOR)**   (11) The interest rate at
which international banks lend US
dollars to one another.

(be) Long   (16) Same as **long position.**

Long hedge   (16) Hedging with a **long
position** in **futures contracts.**

Long position   (16) The position of the
buyer of a contract (same as saying
that the buyer is long).

Long-term debt/liabilities   (4) **Debt/
liabilities** due after a period longer
than one year.

Long-term financing   (5) **Equity** plus
long-term debt.

LOP   (16, 17) *See* **law of one price.**

Lower-of-cost-or-market   (4) Reporting
method according to which
inventories are shown in the **balance
sheet** at their lowest value (their cost
or their **liquidation value** if the latter
is the lowest).

Macro risk   (15) Economic, political,
and social risk; it is a component of
business risk. *See* Exhibit 15.2.

Maintenance margin   (16) Minimum
amount of cash to keep in the
margin account.

Managerial balance sheet   (1, 4)
Restructured **balance sheet** that
shows **invested capital (Cash +
Working capital requirement + Net
fixed assets)** on one side and **capital
employed (Debt + Equity capital)** on
the other side. *See* Exhibit 4.3.

Managerial options   (7) Same as **real
options.**

Margin (buying shares on margin)   (3)
Buying shares by borrowing some
of the money from a broker with
which an investor has an account.

Margin account   (16, 17) Account
opened by traders with brokers in
which they must make an initial
deposit before they can start trading.

Margin call (16, 17) Call for additional deposit when the **margin account** has dropped below a preset level. *See* **margin account**.

Margin requirement (16) The amount of cash that an investor must pay into the **margin account**. It varies depending on the value of the contract that will be traded. *See* **margin account**.

Marking (Marked)-to-market (16, 17) Requirement to settle a position in the **futures market** at the end of each trading day.

Market beta (12) **Beta coefficient** of a stock when the firm is indebted. Same as equity or levered beta.

Market capitalization (1, 3, 10, 14, 18) Market value of a firm's equity. Equal to its quoted price per share multiplied by the total number of shares the company has issued. Also referred to as market cap.

Market model (3) *See* equation 3.10.

Market multiples (14) Ratios used to value a firm. Same as equity multiples. *See* **valuation by comparables**.

Market portfolio (3, 12) A benchmark portfolio containing all the assets in a particular market.

Market power hypothesis (14) Takeover rationale according to which the acquiring firm has a larger market share after the acquisition that may enable it to raise the price of its products.

Market price-to-book ratio (6) Share price divided by **book-value-of-equity** per share. Used to value firms. *See* **valuation by comparables**.

Market risk (of a bond) (10) Sensitivity of a bond price to changes in interest rates. *See* **interest rate risk** and **price risk**.

Market risk (of a common stock) (3) **Risk** that cannot be eliminated through portfolio diversification. Same as **undiversifiable risk** and **systematic risk**.

Market risk premium (3, 12, 14) The difference between the expected return on a portfolio of all existing securities and the **risk-free rate**. *See* **capital asset pricing model**.

Market synergies (14) Increased revenues, beyond pre-merger levels, resulting from combining the operations of two or more firms.

Market value added (MVA) of a firm (18) The difference between the market value of a firm's capital (equity and debt) and the amount of capital that shareholders and debt holders have invested in the firm.

Market value added (MVA) of an investment (18) The **present value** (at the **project's cost of capital**) of the future stream of annual **economic value added** that the project is expected to generate in the future.

Market value at risk (MVR) (15) The expected reduction in a firm's market value if a **risk** occurs. *See* equation 15.1.

Market value of capital (18) The market value of the firm's total capital, that is, the sum of its **market capitalization** and the market value of its **debt capital**.

Market yield (of a bond) (10, 12) The rate that makes the **bond price** equal to the **present value** of the **bond's** future cash-flow stream. Same as **yield to maturity**.

Marketable securities (4) Short-term **liquid assets investments** with less than one year's **maturity** held by a firm as a cash equivalent **asset**.

Matching principle (4) Accounting principle according to which expenses are recognized in the **income statement** not when they are paid but during the period when they effectively contribute to the firm's **revenues**. *See* **accrual accounting**.

Matching strategy (5) The financing of long-term investments with long-term funds, and short-term investments with short-term funds to minimize **financing cost risk** and re-financing risk. *See* **aggressive strategy** and **conservative strategy**.

Maturity (4, 11) A measure of the time before a **liability** is due.

Maturity date (10, 16, 17) The date on which the **face value** of a **bond** must be repaid. The date on which an **option contract** must be settled. For an **option contract**, the **maturity date** is the same as the **expiration date**.

Maturity effect (10) If two bonds have the same **coupon rate**, the one with the longer **maturity** has a higher **interest-rate risk**.

Mean-variance analysis (3) The analysis of the risk and return of alternative investments based on the average (mean) return and their risk measured by the **variance** or the **standard deviation** of their return distribution.

Members of the exchange (11) Dealers and **brokers** who have the right to trade in a **stock exchange**.

Mezzanine financing (14) **Junior unsecured debt** in a **leveraged buyout** (LBO).

Minimum required rate of return (8) An investment's **cost of capital** (*See* **weighted average cost of capital**) when used in comparison with the investment's **internal rate of return**. Same as **hurdle rate**.

Minimum-risk portfolio (MRP) (3) The portfolio on the **opportunity set** that has the least amount of **risk**.

MM theory of capital structure (13) The Modigliani and Miller theory of how changes in debt financing affect the value of a firm and its cost of capital.

Monetary/nonmonetary (translation) method (17) A method of translating the **financial statements** of a foreign business unit. Monetary assets (**cash** and **receivables**) and monetary **liabilities** (**payables**, **short-term**, and **long-term debt**) are translated at the exchange rate prevailing at the date of the financial statements, and nonmonetary **assets** (**inventories** and **fixed assets**) are translated at the rate that prevailed when they were purchased. *See* Appendix 17.1.

Money market (1, 11) Market in which firms raise short-term funds and where **money market instruments** are issued and traded.

Money market funds (4) financial intermediaries that invest in the **money market**.

Money market instruments (11) Debt securities with **maturity** not exceeding one year.

Money spread (16) An arbitrage strategy involving the sale of an **option** and the purchase of another one with the same features except for the **exercise price**.

Monitoring costs (13) Costs resulting from lenders placing restrictions on the use of the funds they lend to companies. These costs are borne by **shareholders**.

Mortgage bond/loan (11) A medium to long-term **bond/loan** backed by real estate. *See* **collateral**.

MRP (3) See minimum-risk portfolio.

Multiples (10, 14) Ratios used to value firms. See historical multiples, expected multiples, equity multiples, market multiples, and valuation by comparables.

Mutually exclusive (investments) (7, 8) If one is chosen, the other(s) must be turned down.

MVA (18) See market value added.

MVR (15) See market value at risk.

Naked call (option) (16) An investment strategy in which an investor sells call options on the open market without owning the underlying asset.

NAL (11) See net advantage to leasing.

Negotiable (certificates of deposit) (11) Short-term securities sold by banks in the money markets to raise capital.

Negotiable (security) (11) A security that can be traded (exchanged among investors) in the securities markets.

Net advantage to leasing (NAL) (11) The net present value of the difference in cash flows between leasing and buying an asset. If NAL is positive, the asset should be leased.

Net asset value (4) The difference, at a particular date, between what a firm's shareholders collectively own, called assets, and what they owe, called liabilities. Same as net worth, owners' equity, shareholders' equity, and shareholders' funds.

Net book value (of a fixed asset) (4) The value at which a fixed asset is reported in the balance sheet.

Net capital expenditure (10, 14) Capital expenditure less cash raised from the sales of existing assets.

Net cash flow (4) The difference between cash inflows and outflows during an accounting period.

Net cash flow from financing activities (4) The net cash flow from the firm's financing activities during an accounting period.

Net cash flow from investing activities (4) The difference between the cash inflows and cash outflows from investing activities.

Net cash flow from operating activities (4) The difference between the cash inflows and cash outflows from operating activities.

Net earnings (4) Same as earnings after tax, net profit, and net income. Also called the bottom line.

Net fixed assets (1, 4) Long-term assets, such as equipment, machinery, and buildings, from which accumulated depreciation expenses have been deducted. See Exhibit 1.6, fixed assets and gross value of fixed assets.

Net income (4) See earnings after tax.

Net interest expense (4) The difference between the interest expenses and interest income during an accounting period.

Net long-term financing (NLF) (5) Long-term financing less net fixed assets. See equation 5.2 and liquidity ratio.

Net loss (1) A negative change in the book value of equity over a period of time.

Net operating profit after tax (NOPAT) (4, 18) Earnings before interest and tax × (1 – Tax rate). See economic value added.

Net operating profit less adjusted taxes (4) (NOPLAT). Same as NOPAT.

Net present value (NPV) (1, 2, 7) The discounted value (at the weighted average cost of capital) of an investment's future stream of free cash flows less the initial cash outlay required to launch the investment. See fundamental finance principle and net present value (NPV) rule.

Net present value (NPV) profile (8) A graphical representation of the changes in the net present value of an investment as the discount rate varies.

Net present value (NPV) rule (1, 2, 7) If a business proposal has a positive net present value (NPV), it should be carried out because it will increase the firm's value by an amount equal to the proposal's NPV. If a proposal's NPV is negative, it should be rejected.

Net profit (1, 4) A positive change in the book value of equity over a period of time. See earnings after tax.

Net sales (4) The revenues of the accounting period net of any discounts and allowances for defective merchandise and returned items.

Net short-term financing (NSF) (5) Short-term debt less cash. Equals working capital requirement (WCR) less net long-term financing. Same as

the portion of WCR financed with short-term debt. See equation 5.3.

Net working capital (NWC) (5) Current assets less current liabilities. See equation 5.10.

Net worth (4) See owners' equity.

NLF (5) See net long-term financing.

NOCF (4) See net operating cash flow.

Nominal cash flows (9) Cash flows measured in nominal terms, that is, including inflation.

Nominal (interest) rate (2, 17) The interest rate that a borrower will actually pay, including a premium for the rate of inflation. See equation 2.5 and 17.4.

Nominal value (of a bond) (10) See face value.

Noncurrent assets (4) Long-lived assets that are not expected to be turned into cash within a year. Same as long-term financial assets, fixed assets, or capital assets. Can be tangible or intangible assets as well as financial assets.

Noncurrent (long-term) liabilities (4) Obligations of a firm that are payable after more than one year.

Non-core working capital requirement (5) Working capital requirement less core working capital requirement.

NOPAT (4, 18) See net operating profit after tax. Same as EBIT $(1 - T_C)$.

NOPLAT (4) See net operating profit less adjusted taxes. Same as NOPAT.

Normal backwardation (16) A situation when the forward price is less than the expected spot price.

Normal distribution (3) A bell-shaped distribution that is completely described by its mean and standard deviation. See Exhibit 3.1.

Notes payable (4) Bank overdrafts, drawings on lines of credit, short-term promissory notes, and the portion of long-term debt due within a year.

NPV (1, 2, 7) See net present value.

NPV rule (1, 2, 7, 8) See net present value rule.

NSF (5) See net short-term financing.

NWC (5) See net working capital.

Offer price (17) See ask price.

Ongoing risk (15) The continuous, unexpected change in the firm's environment that causes its value to rise or fall unpredictably.

Open market purchase (11) A firm's buying of its own shares in the stock market at whatever price they trade on that day.

Operating activities (4, 5) The activities related to the management of a firm's existing investments to generate sales, profit, and cash.

Operating assets (4) **Assets** related to a firm's **operating cycle**, that is, **trade receivables, inventories**, and the portion of **prepaid expenses** associated with **operating activities**.

Operating cash (5) Amount of cash held by a firm and needed to support its ongoing operations.

Operating cycle (4, 5) The sequence of **operating activities** that begins with the acquisition of raw materials and ends with the collection of cash for the sale of final goods. *See* Exhibit 4.4.

Operating expenses (1) Expenses related to **operating activities**, that is, **cost of goods sold, selling, general, and administrative expenses**, and **depreciation expenses**. **Operating expenses** exclude interest expenses, which are related to financing activities.

Operating exposure (17) Effect of changes in **exchange rates** on the firm's cash flows generated by *future* and *uncertain* transactions. *See* **economic exposure**.

Operating lease (11) A short-term lease for which the length of the contract is shorter than the **useful life** of the **asset** leased.

Operating liabilities (4) **Liabilities** related to a firm's **operating cycle**, that is, **trade payables** and the portion of **accrued expenses** associated with **operating activities**.

Operating profit (4) **Net sales** less operating expenses. Same as **EBIT**.

Operating profitability (6) The profitability of a firm's operations, which excludes all costs related to financing the firm's activities. *See* **return on invested capital**.

Operating profit margin (6, 18) **Earnings before interest and tax (EBIT)** divided by sales. A measure of profitability.

Operating working capital (1, 4, 5) Same as **working capital requirement**.

Operational risk(s) (15) The risks that arise in the course of implementing a firm's strategy; includes business process risk, commodity price risk, credit risk, legal risk, fiscal risk, and reputational risk. *See* Exhibit 15.2.

Opportunity cost (9) Loss of **revenues** that results from giving up an activity to carry out an alternative one.

Opportunity set (3) The expected return/standard deviation pairs of all portfolios that can be constructed from a given set of stocks.

Optimal capital structure (1, 13) The **debt-to-equity ratio** that maximizes the market value of the firm's **assets**. *See* **target capital structure**.

Option (contract) (16, 17) A contract that gives the holder the right (with no obligation) to buy (**call option**) or sell (**put option**) a fixed number of **securities** or a stated amount of currency, at a specified price before (**American option**) or on the **expiration date** (**European option**) of the option.

Option exchange (16) A place where options are traded.

Option premium (16, 17) The market price of an **option**.

Option price (16) Same as **option premium**.

Option writer (16) The seller of an option.

Original price discount (11) The difference between the issuing price of a **bond** and its **face value** when the former is lower.

Original term to maturity (10, 11) The time between the day a **bond** is issued and the day it is **redeemed** (repaid).

Organized exchanges (11, 16) Regulated markets in which **securities** must meet a number of stringent conditions to be listed and traded. *See* **over-the-counter (OTC) markets**.

Originating house (11) The **investment bank** that has initiated and carried out the issuance of **securities** for a firm. Same as **lead manager** or **book runner**. *See* **underwriting syndicate**.

OTC (11) *See* **over the counter market**.

Out-of-the-money option (16) Describes a situation when the **exercise price** of a **call option** is higher than the market price of the underlying asset.

Outstanding securities (1) Securities that have been issued already.

Overdraft (4) A drawing of money against a previously established **line of credit**.

Overhead (expenses) (4) *See* **selling, general, and administrative expenses**.

Over-the-counter (OTC) markets (11, 16) Markets that do not require companies to meet the listing requirements of **organized exchanges**. Stocks are traded through dealers connected by a network of telephones and computers.

Owners' equity (1, 4) The difference, at a particular date, between what a firm's shareholders collectively own, called **assets**, and what they owe, called **liabilities**. Same as **net asset value, net worth, shareholders' equity, equity capital,** and **shareholders' funds**.

P&L (1, 4) *See* **profit and loss statement**.

P/B ratio (10, 14) Same as **PBR**.

Paid-in capital in excess of par (4) The difference between the cumulative amount of cash that the firm received from shares issued up to the date of the **balance sheet** and the cash it would have received if those shares had been issued at **par value**.

Parity relations (17) Relationships linking the **spot exchange rates**, the **forward exchange rates**, the interest rates, and the inflation rates prevailing in two countries. *See* Exhibit 17.1 and Appendix 17.2.

Par value (4, 10) for a share of **stock**, an arbitrary fixed value set when shares are issued. For a **bond**, the fixed amount (**face value**) that has to be paid back to bondholders at the **maturity date** of the **bond**.

Payables (4) *See* **accounts payable**.

Payback period (7, 8) The number of periods (usually years) required for the sum of the project's expected cash flows to equal its initial cash outlay. *See* **payback period rule, cut-off period**, and **discounted payback period**.

Payback period rule (8) Accept (reject) the project if its **payback period** is shorter (longer) than a given **cutoff period**. *See* **discounted payback rule**.

Payout policy (1, 11) The amount and the timing of a firm's cash distribution in the form of **dividends** or **share buybacks**.

Payoff (from option) (16) What the option value is at the **expiration date**.

PBR (P/B ratio) (10, 14) See **price-to-book ratio**.

Pecking order (13) Refers to the order in which firms raise **capital**, relying first on **retaining earnings** then issuing debt before finally raising new equity.

Pension liabilities (4) **Liabilities** owed to employees and paid to them when they retire.

PER (P/E ratio) (6, 10, 14) *See* **price-to-earnings ratio.**

Perpetual bond (10) A **bond** that never matures. *See* equation 10.6.

Perpetual cash-flow stream (2) A cash-flow stream with an infinite life.

Perpetuity (2, 10) An **annuity** with an infinite life. *See* equation 2.6.

PI (7, 8) *See* **profitability index.**

Political risk (15, 17) Unexpected government regulations and decisions that constrain the firm's ability to generate profits. *See* Exhibit 15.4.

Portfolio insurance (16) Hedging an entire portfolio against market **volatility** using **put options**. *See* **protective put.**

PPP relation (17) *See* **purchasing power parity relation.**

Preferred stocks (11) A security that has a priority over **common stock** in the payment of **dividends** and a prior claim on the firm's **assets** in the event of liquidation, but that has no voting rights. *See* equation 11.4 and Exhibit 11.11.

Premium (from par value) (10) The difference between the price of a **bond** and its **face value**, if the former is higher.

Prepaid expenses (4) Payments made by a firm for goods or services it will receive after the date of the **balance sheet.**

Present value (PV) (1, 2, 7) The value today of an expected future cash flow stream discounted at a rate that reflects its **risk**. Same as **discounted value.** *See* **discounting** and equation 2.2.

Pre-tax operating profit (1) *See* **earnings before interest and tax (EBIT)** and **pre-tax trading profit.**

Pre-tax trading profit (1) *See* **earnings before interest and tax (EBIT)** and **pre-tax operating profit.**

Price limit (16) Limit imposed on the price of some **futures contracts** to protect them against extreme movements in **futures prices.** If the drop in price reaches the price limit, trading is suspended.

Price risk (15, 16) The risk of unexpected changes in the price of an asset such as a commodity or a financial asset.

Price-to-book ratio (PBR or P/B ratio) (10, 14) Share price divided by **book value of equity** per share. Same as **market-to-book ratio** and **book value multiple**; used to value a firm. *See* **valuation by comparables.**

Price-to-earnings ratio (PER or P/E ratio) (6, 10, 14) Share price divided by the firm's **earnings per share.** Same as **earnings multiple.** Used to value a firm. *See* **valuation by comparables.**

Primary markets (1, 11) **Financial markets** in which newly issued **securities** are sold to the public. *See* **secondary markets** and **underwriting.**

Principal value (10) *See* **face value.**

Private equity investors (14) Investors who acquire firms privately to improve their performance and resell them at a profit. *See* **leveraged buyouts.**

Private placement (11) The issuance and sale of a firm's **securities** directly to financial institutions and **qualified investors**, thus bypassing the financial markets. *See* **public offering.**

Privately negotiated repurchase (11) When a firm buys back its shares directly from one of its shareholders.

Profitability index (PI) (7, 8) The present value of an investment's expected cash-flow stream divided by the investment's initial cash outlay. *See* **profitability index rule.**

Profitability index (PI) rule (7, 8) Accept (reject) the project if its **profitability index** is higher (lower) than one.

Profit and loss (P&L) statement (1, 4) *See* **income statement.**

Profit retention rate (1, 6) **Retained earnings** divided by **net profit.**

Pro forma (statements) (14) **Financial statements** based on estimated, or projected, data.

Project's cost of capital (7, 12) The return expected by investors for the capital they supply to fund a specific project. Same as **project's opportunity cost of capital.**

Project's opportunity cost of capital (7) The highest return on an **alternative investment** that must be given up to undertake another investment with the same risk. *See* **project's cost of capital.**

Promissory note (4) A debt **security** acknowledging a **creditor** relationship with the issuing firm and stipulating the conditions and terms under which the money was borrowed.

Property, plant, and equipment (4) **Tangible assets** such as land, buildings, machines, and furniture reported in the firm's **balance sheet** as **fixed assets.**

Prospective multiples (14) *See* **expected multiples.**

Protective put (16) A **put option** bought to protect against a drop in the price of the underlying asset.

Provision for bad debt (18) Provision for possible uncollectibility of **accounts receivable.** Same as **allowance for bad debts.**

Proxies/proxy firms (12) Firms that exhibit the same risk characteristics as a project and that are used to estimate the **project's cost of capital.** Same as **pure-plays/pure-play firms.**

Public offering (11) The issuance and sale of a firm's **securities** not only to its existing **shareholders**, but also to the public at large. Same as **general cash offering.** *See* Exhibit 11.8 and **rights offering.**

Purchases (5) **Cost of goods sold** plus change in **inventories** minus production costs. *See* equations 5.8 and 5.9.

Purchasing power parity (PPP) relation (17) States that the general cost of living should be the same across countries. *See* equation 17.2, Exhibit 17.1, and Appendix 17.2.

Pure discount bond (10) A default-free zero-coupon bond.

Pure-plays/pure-play firms (12) *See* **proxies/proxy firms.**

Put-Call parity (16) The relationship between the price of a **European call option** and a **European put option** on the same underlying asset, both with the same **strike price** and **expiration date.** *See* equations 16.5a and 16.5b.

Put option (11, 16, 17) A contract that gives the holder the right (with no obligation) to sell a fixed number of shares or a certain amount of currency at a fixed price during the life of the **option** (**American option**) or at the **expiration date** of the option (**European option**). *See* **call option.**

PV (1, 2, 7) *See* **present value.**

Qualified investors   (11) Investors who meet some minimum standards set by regulatory authorities that allow them to buy securities directly from firms. *See* **private placement**.

Quick assets   (5) The sum of cash and **accounts receivable**.

Quick ratio   (5) **Cash plus accounts receivable** divided by **current liabilities**. Same as **acid test**. A measure of **liquidity**. *See* equation 5.12 and **current ratio**.

Quoted price (of a bond)   (10) *See* **clean price**.

Raw materials inventory   (4) The cost assigned to materials that have not yet entered the production process at the date of the **balance sheet**.

Real cash flows   (9) Cash flows from which the effect of inflation has been removed.

Real options   (16) **Options** written on tangible (physical) assets. Same as **managerial options**.

Real (interest) rate   (2, 17) The interest rate adjusted for changes in the cost of living. *See* **nominal interest rate**.

Realization principle   (4) The recognition of **revenue** (in an **income statement**) during the period when the transaction generating the **revenue** has taken place, not when the cash generated by the transaction is received.

Realized return   (3) Actual return over a specified time horizon. *See* equation 3.1. Same as **holding period return**.

Recapitalization   (1, 6, 13) The substitution of **debt** for **equity**, leaving **assets** unchanged.

Receivables   (4) *See* **accounts receivable**.

Record date   (11) The firm pays a dividend to the shareholders who are registered with the firm on that date.

Redeeming the bond   (11) Repaying a bond's **face value** or **call value**.

Redemption value (of a bond)   (10) The price at which the bond is redeemed by the issuer at maturity; it is usually the bond's **face value** but could be at a premium from face value. *See* **face value** and **principal value**.

Reference rate   (11) The rate to which the **coupon rate** of a **floating rate bond** is linked. Same as **benchmark rate**.

Refinancing risk   (5, 11, 15) **Risk** arising from the unwillingness of a lender to renew the loans made to finance assets, thus forcing the firm to sell part or all of these assets to repay the loan. *See* **financial cost risk** and Exhibit 15.2.

Registered bonds/securities   (10, 11) **Bonds/ securities** that identify the holder's name. *See* **bearer securities**.

Regular dividend payment   (11) When dividends follow a regular pattern.

Reinvestment risk   (10) The risk of not knowing the rate at which a bond's **coupon payment** will be reinvested.

Relevant cash flows   (9) Cash flows that are affected by an investment decision.

Relevant costs   (9) Costs incurred only if the investment project is undertaken.

Replacement investments   (7) Cost saving projects that do not generate extra **cash inflows**.

Replacement value (of an asset)   (14) What it would cost today to replace a firm's assets with similar ones to start a new business with the same earning power.

Required investments   (7) Investments a firm must make to comply with safety, health, and environmental regulations. *See* **replacement** and **expansion investments**.

Reserves   (4) The accumulation of **retained earnings** since the creation of the firm.

Residual payout policy   (11) The payment of dividend with whatever cash is left over after the firm has funded all its positive **NPV** projects.

Residual value (of an asset)   (4, 9) The resale, or scrap, value of an asset. Same as **salvage value**.

Restrictive covenants   (13) *See* **covenants**.

Restructuring plan   (14) Changes in a firm's **assets** or **financial structure** to improve its performance.

Retained earnings   (1, 4) The part of a firm's profit that owners decide to invest back into their company. *See* **retention rate**.

Retention rate   (1) **Retained earnings** divided by **earnings after tax (EAT)**.

Return on assets (ROA)   (6) **Earnings after tax (EAT)** divided by **total assets**. A measure of profitability.

Return on business assets (ROBA)   (6) **Earnings before interest and tax (EBIT)** divided by **business assets** (**working capital requirement** plus **net fixed assets**). A measure of operating profitability.

Return on capital employed (ROCE)   (1) **Net operating profit after tax (NOPAT)** or (**earnings before interest and tax (EBIT)** × (1 – Tax rate)) divided by **capital employed** (**equity** plus **debt capital**). Equal to **return on invested capital (ROIC)**.

Return on capital employed before tax (ROCE$_{BT}$)   (6) Same as **return on capital employed** with **earnings before interest and tax (EBIT)** replacing **net operating profit after tax**. Equal to **return on invested capital before tax (ROIC$_{BT}$)**.

Return on equity (ROE)   (1, 6) **Earnings after tax (EAT)** divided by **owners' equity**. A measure of the firm's profitability to **shareholders**.

Return on equity before tax (ROE$_{BT}$)   (6) **Earnings before tax (EBT)** divided by **owner's equity**.

Return on invested capital (ROIC)   (1, 6, 18) **Net operating profit after tax (NOPAT)** or (**earnings before interest and tax (EBIT)** × (1 – Tax rate)) divided by **invested capital** (**cash** plus **working capital requirement** plus **net fixed assets**). Equal to **return on capital employed (ROCE)**. **Return on invested capital before tax**.

Return on investment (ROI)   (6) A general measure of profitability that refers to the ratio of a measure of profit to a measure of the investment required to generate that profit.

Return on sales (ROS)   (6) **Earnings after tax (EAT)** divided by sales. Same as **net profit margin**. A measure of profitability.

Return on total assets (ROTA)   (6) **Earnings before interest and tax (EBIT)** divided by **total assets**. A measure of profitability.

Return spread   (18) The difference between a firm's, or a project's, after tax **return on invested capital (ROIC)** and its **weighted average cost of capital (WACC)**. *See* **economic value added**.

Revenues   (1, 4) A firm's activities that result in increases in the value of **owners' equity**.

Reverse trade   (16) Sell **futures contracts** bought earlier in order to cancel the delivery just before the contracts expire.

Revolving credit agreement (11) A legal agreement that a bank will lend a stated maximum amount of money over a fixed but renewable period of time. *See* **line of credit**.

RF (3) *See* **risk-free rate** and **riskless rate**.

Right (11, 16) The privilege given to existing **shareholders** to buy shares of their firm at a fixed price during a specified period of time. *See* equation 11.3.

Rights issue (offering) (11) Offering of a firm's **common stocks** exclusively to its existing stockholders. *See* **subscription price, standby agreement, public offering,** and Exhibit 11.8.

Rights-on shares (11) Shares for which **rights** were issued and which are traded with their rights attached. *See* **ex-rights shares** and equations 11.2 and 11.3.

Risk (1, 3, 7, 15) A term used to describe a situation in which a firm only knows the *expected value* of its future cash-flow stream. *See* **business risk, financial risk,** and Exhibits 15.2 and 15.4.

Risk-adjusted return (3) Return adjusted for risk according to the **CAPM**.

Risk-averse (investors) (1, 3, 7) Investors who would buy shares of riskier firms only if they expect to earn a higher return to compensate them for the higher **risk** they have to bear.

Risk class (7) A group of investments that exhibit the same risk characteristics.

Risk-free rate (RF) (3, 12) The rate of return of a risk-free **asset**, usually government securities. Same as **risk-less rate**.

Riskless (risk-free) asset (3) An asset with zero volatility and zero correlation with risky stocks.

Riskless rate (12) Same as **risk-free rate**.

Risk-netting (15) A situation when some project-specific risks cancel each other.

Risk-neutral (individual) (3) An investor who is indifferent to **risk**.

Risk premium (3) Return in excess of the **risk-free rate**.

Risk-return plane (3) A surface defined by **expected returns** on a vertical axis and risk (**volatility**) on a horizontal axis. *See* Exhibit 3.4.

Risk-seeker (3) An investor who prefers the riskier of two investments that have the same **expected returns**.

Risk severity (15) A measure of how intense a risk is: minor, important, or major. *See* Exhibit 15.7.

ROA (6) *See* **return on assets**.

ROBA (6) *See* **return on business assets**.

ROCE (1) *See* **return on capital employed**.

ROCEBT (6) *See* **return on capital employed before tax**.

ROE (1, 6) *See* **return on equity**.

ROEBT (6) *See* **return on equity before tax**.

ROI (6) *See* **return on investment**.

ROIC (1, 6, 18) *See* **return on invested capital**.

ROICBT *See* **return on invested capital before tax**.

Rolling over the forward contract (17) Entering into a new **forward contract** after the first contract expires.

ROS (6) *See* **return on sales**.

ROTA (6) *See* **return on total assets**.

Sale and leaseback (lease) (11) A **financial lease** under which the lessee sells the **asset** to the leasing company which immediately leases it back to the **lessee**.

Salvage value (9, 11) The resale, or scrap, value of an **asset**. Same as **residual value** and **terminal value**.

Samurai bonds (11) Yen-denominated bonds issued by non-Japanese firms to Japanese investors. *See* **Shogun bonds**.

Seasoned issue (11) When a firm returns to the market after an **initial public offering** for another issue of equity.

SEC (11) *See* **Securities and Exchange Commission**.

Secondary distribution, (11) *See* **secondary public offering**.

Secondary trading (16) Trading in a **secondary market**.

Secondary market (1, 11) **Financial market in which outstanding securities** are traded. *See* **primary market**.

Secondary public offering (11) The first-time sale to the public of a relatively large block of equity held by an outside investor who acquired

it earlier directly from the firm. Not to be confused with a **seasoned issue**.

Secured bond (11) A **bond** for which the issuer has provided **collateral** to the lender.

Security (ies) (1, 3, 10, 11) Certificate (or a book entry in the security holder's account) issued by a firm that specifies the conditions under which the firm has received the money. *See* **financial asset, bond, common** and **preferred stock**.

Securities and Exchange Commission (SEC) (11) US government agency that approves the issuance and distribution of **securities** and regulates their subsequent trading on public markets.

Securities markets (11) Markets in which **securities** can be traded.

Security market line (SML) (3, 12) A straight line that relates the expected returns of risky investments to their corresponding risk measured by the **beta coefficient**. *See* equation 3.13, Exhibits 12.5 and 12.10, and the **capital asset pricing model**.

Security risk premium (12) The difference between the *expected* return of a **security** and the **risk-free rate**.

Self-control hypothesis (11) A hypothesis according to which some investors prefer cash dividends (even if they are taxed are a higher rate than capital gains) because they provide the self-imposed discipline of only spending dividend income and thus preserving capital.

Self-liquidating (loans) (11) Short-term bank loans to firms that need to finance the seasonal buildup in their **working capital investment** and that bankers expect the firm to repay with the cash that will be released by the subsequent reduction in working capital.

Self-sustainable growth rate (SGR) (1, 6, 18) The fastest growth rate a firm can achieve by retaining a constant percentage of its profit, keeping both its operating and financing policies unchanged, and not issuing new equity. Equal to the profit **retention rate** multiplied by **return on equity**. Same as **sustainable growth rate**. *See* equation 6.12.

Selling concession (11) The fee received by the **selling group** for its efforts to sell the **securities** allocated to them by the **underwriter** of an issue. *See* **selling group**.

Selling, general, and administrative expenses (SG&As) (4) Expenses incurred by the firm that relate to the sale of its products and the running of its operations during the **accounting period**.

Selling group (11) A group of **investment banks** that agree to sell for a fee the **securities** allocated to them by the **underwriter** of an issue. *See* **selling concession**.

Senior bond/debt/loan (11, 14) A **bond**/ debt/loan that has a claim on the firm's **assets** (in the event of liquidation) that precedes the claim of **junior** or **subordinated debt**.

Separation principle (3) An investment principle according to which all investors should hold the **market portfolio** irrespective of their **degree of risk aversion** and then adjust for their degree of risk aversion by allocating their investible funds between a **riskless asset** and the **market portfolio**.

Settlement date (16, 17) The date at which the promise to deliver a product or an asset and pay for it takes place.

Settlement price (for currency futures contracts) (17) The quote of the last trade of the day for a **currency futures** that is **marked-to-market**.

SG&A (4) *See* **selling, general, and administrative expenses**.

SGR (1, 6, 18) *See* **self-sustainable growth rate**.

Share buyback (program) (1, 11, 18) The buying by a firm of its own shares for the purpose of reducing the number of shares outstanding. Same as **share repurchase program**. The opposite of a new issue of shares.

Share premium (4) *See* **Paid-in capital in excess of par**.

Share repurchase (program) (1, 11, 14, 18) *See* **share buyback**.

Shareholders (1, 4) Investors who have bought **common stocks** issued by a firm to raise **equity capital**.

Shareholders are the owners of the firm.

Shareholders' equity (4) *See* **owners' equity**.

Shareholders' funds (4) *See* **owners' equity**.

Shareholders of record (11) The list of shareholders who are registered with the firm.

Sharpe ratio (3) The **excess return** of a security or portfolio divided by its

volatility. A measure of **excess return** per unit of risk. *See* equation 3.8.

Shogun bonds (11) **Bonds** issued by non-Japanese firms to Japanese investors and denominated in any currency other than yen. *See* **Samurai bonds**.

(be) Short (16) Same **as short position**.

Short hedge (16) Hedging by selling **futures contracts**.

Short position (16) The position of the seller of a contract (same as saying that the seller is short).

Shorting stocks (16) Selling stocks you don't own.

Short-term assets (4) *See* **current assets**.

Short-term borrowing/debt/ financing (4,5) Short-term interest-bearing debt that includes bank **overdrafts**, drawings on **lines of credit**, short-term **promissory notes**, and the portion of any long-term debt due within a year.

Short-term liabilities (4) *See* **current liabilities**.

Signaling effects (13) Market reactions to a firm's actions, such as a drop in the firm's share price when the firm skips a dividend payment—an action interpreted by the market as a signal of weakening corporate cash flow.

Sinking fund provision (11) Requires that a **bond** issuing firm set aside cash in a special account according to a regular schedule to allow the firm to redeem the **bond** at **maturity**.

SML (3, 12) *See* **security market line**.

Social (or societal) risk (15) Unanticipated changes in the behavior and attitudes of employees and consumers that can affect the firm's value.

Special dividend payment (11) A one-time dividend payment.

Special items (4) Extraordinary, exceptional, and nonrecurring losses or gains reported in the firm's **income statement**.

Speculative-grade bonds (10) Corporate bonds with ratings below BBB. Same as **junk bonds** or **high-yield bonds**. *See* **bond ratings**.

Speculating (16) Making an investment decision by betting on the direction of changes in the price of an asset.

Spin-off (11) A **stock dividend** using shares of one of a firm's subsidiaries.

Spot-forward parity (16) The relationship between **spot** and **forward prices**. *See* equation (16.1).

Spot interest rate (10) The yield of a **pure discount bond**.

Spot price (16) The price at which a **spot transaction** is executed.

Spot rate (17) The rate at which a **spot transaction** is executed.

Spot transaction (16, 17) A trade between two parties in which both agree to exchange a product or a security at a rate fixed now for immediate delivery. *See* **currency forward contract**.

Spot yield curve (10) *See* **yield curve**.

Spread (in floating rate bonds) (11) The difference between the floating **coupon rate** and the **benchmark rate**.

Spread (in underwriting) (11) The difference between the price at which an issue is sold to the public and the price paid by the **underwriter** to the issuing firm.

Spread (options) (16) Arbitrage strategy to take advantage of mispricing between two **options**.

Stable dividend policy (13) A dividend distribution policy that attempts to maintain a stable **dividend yield** over time.

Stakeholders approach (1) Managing a firm with the objective of balancing out the interests of all its stakeholders: its employees, customers, suppliers, owners, and the community where it is located.

Stand-alone value (1, 14) Estimated value of a **takeover target firm** before the acquiring firm factors in any performance improvements. Same as **as-is value**.

Standard deviation (of returns) (3) The square root of the **variance** of returns. A measure of risk also called **volatility**. *See* **variance**.

Standardized futures contract (16) A **futures contract** whose size and **settlement date** are specified by the exchange on which it trades.

Standby agreement (11) An agreement between a firm and an **underwriting syndicate** of **investment banks** such that the syndicate agrees to buy any shares that have not been sold during the period that a **rights offering** is outstanding.

Standby fee (11) Fee received by **investment banks** for **underwriting** the unsold portion of a **rights issue**.

Stated value   (4) An arbitrary fixed value attached to each share of **common stock** when it is issued.

Statement of cash flows   (4) **Financial statement**, that provides information about the cash transactions between the firm and the outside world by separating these transactions into cash flows related to operating, investing, and financing activities. *See* **cash flow statement.**

Statement of shareholders' equity   (4) The statement that reports changes in owners' equity other than retained earnings, such as cash dividends, stock issued, and stock repurchased over the accounting period.

Statutory (corporate) tax rate   (6) Tax rate on earnings imposed by the tax authority. *See* **effective corporate tax rate.**

Stock (certificate)   (3, 10) An equity security that recognizes an ownership position in the issuing firm, that provides holders with a claim on the firm's earnings and **assets**, and that entitles holders to vote at shareholder meetings.

Stock dividend   (11) A dividend distribution in the form of shares as opposed to cash.

Stock exchange   (11) An **organized market** in which shares of companies are traded.

Stock markets   (11) *See* **stock exchange.**

Stock split   (11) The dividing of existing shares into multiple shares without changing the total value of equity, for example, splitting one share worth $20 into two shares worth $10 each.

Straddle   (16) A combination of a **long call option** with a **long put option** both with the *same* exercise price and the *same* **time to expiration.** Used to make a profit if the price of the **underlying asset** rises and to be protected if the price falls.

Straight-line depreciation method   (4) **Depreciation** method according to which the firm's **tangible fixed assets** are depreciated by an equal amount each year. *See* **accelerated depreciation method.**

Strategic risk   (15) **Risk** associated with unanticipated changes in the dynamics of a firm's industry that may have a negative impact on the firm's market value. *See* Exhibit 15.4.

Strike price   (16, 17) *See* **exercise price.**

Subordinated bond/debt/loan   (11, 14) **Bond**/debt/loan that has a claim on the firm's **assets** (in the event of liquidation) that follows the claim of **senior debt holders.** Same as **junior bond/debt/loan.**

Subscription price   (11) The price at which shares will be sold to existing **shareholders** during a **rights issue.**

Sunk costs   (9) Money already spent that cannot be recovered irrespective of future decisions. Same as **irrelevant costs** and **unavoidable costs.**

Sustainable growth rate   (1, 6, 18) *See* **self-sustainable growth rate.**

Swap (agreement or contract)   (17) See **currency swap contract.**

Sweetener (in a convertible bond)   (11) The **conversion option** of a **convertible bond.**

Synergy (ies)   (1, 14) *See* **cost synergies** and **market synergies.**

Synthetic call   (16) The combination of purchasing an asset, borrowing, and purchasing a **put option** on the asset.

Synthetic put   (16) The combination of a **short** sell of an asset with a **long position** on a call on the same asset.

Systematic risk   (3, 12) **Risk** that cannot be eliminated through portfolio diversification. Measured with the **beta coefficient.** Same as **market risk** or **undiversifiable risk.** *See* **capital asset pricing model.**

Takeover premium   (14) The difference between the acquisition price paid by the **bidder** and the current market value of the **target firm.**

Take-up fee   (11) The discount on the price of the shares offered to the investment bankers engaged in a **standby agreement.**

Tangent portfolio   (3) The only **efficient portfolio** when there is a **riskless asset.**

Tangible assets   (4) **Assets** such as land, buildings, machines, and furniture (collectively called property, plant, and equipment) and long-term financial **assets.**

Target capital structure   (12, 13) The **debt-to-equity ratio** that maximizes the market value of the firm's **assets.** *See* **optimal capital structure.**

Target debt ratio   (13) Same as **target capital structure.**

Target firm (company)   (3, 14) The firm whose shares the bidder is trying to acquire in a **takeover.**

Tax-effect ratio   (6) **Earnings after tax (EAT)** divided by **earnings before tax (EBT).**

Taxes payable   (4) The amount of taxes owed on the date of the **balance sheet.**

Tax shield   (13) *See* **interest tax shield.**

Tender offer   (11) When a firm announces that it will buy back its shares at a premium from the market price. Usually done when a firm wants to counter an unfriendly over bid.

Tenor   (10) Same *as* **current maturity.**

Term loan(s)   (11) Medium- to long-term loans extended by banks and insurance companies.

Term structure of interest rates   (10) The relationship between interest rates (bond **yields**) and different **terms to maturity.** *See* **yield curve.**

Term to maturity   (10) *See* **maturity.**

Terminal cash flow   (9) Cash flow that occurs in the last year of a project.

Terminal value (of a bond)   (10) The value of a bond at maturity.

Terminal value (of a firm)   (2, 14) The estimated value that the firm will have at the end of a forecasting period, which is determined by the expected cash flows beyond the forecasting period.

Tick size   (16) The minimum price fluctuation of a contract.

Time value of money (TV)   (2, 7) Time has value because a dollar received earlier is worth more than a dollar received later.

Timeline   (2) *See* **cash flow timeline.**

Times-interest-earned ratio   (6) The ratio of **earnings before interest and tax (EBIT)** divided by interest expenses. Same as **interest coverage ratio.** A measure of financial leverage based on **income statement data.**

Time spread   (16) An arbitrage strategy built with two **call options** that have different **expiration dates** but the same **exercise price.**

Time to expiration   (16) Same **as expiration date, maturity date,** and **settlement date.**

Time value of option   (16) The **option** value minus its **intrinsic value.**

Top-floor financing   (14) **Senior collateralized debt** in a **leverage buyout (LBO).**

Total net cash flow (4) The difference between the total amount of dollars received (**cash inflows**) and the total amount of dollars paid out (**cash outflows**) over a period of time.

Tracking stock (11) A special class of **common stock** carrying claims on the cash flows of a particular segment of a company, such as a subsidiary, division, or business unit.

Trade creditors (1, 4) *See* **accounts payable**.

Trade debtors (1, 4) *See* **accounts receivable**.

Traded options (16) **Options** traded in an **option exchange**.

Trade-off model of capital structure (1, 13) **Optimal capital structure** reached by means of a trade-off between the **present value** of the **interest tax shield** and the present value of **financial distress costs**.

Trade payables (1, 4) *See* **accounts payable**.

Trade receivables (1, 4) *See* **accounts receivable**.

Trading profit (1) *See* pre-tax operating profit.

Trailing multiples (14) *See* historical multiples.

Transaction exposure (17) *See* contractual exposure.

Transaction loan (11) A one-time loan used to finance a specific, nonrecurrent need.

Transactions cost (11) Cost incurred when buying or selling an **asset** or a security.

Translation exposure (17) *See* accounting exposure.

Transparency (11, 13) Providing complete information about a firm's operations and future prospects to its (outside) **shareholders**.

Treasury stock (4) The amount that a firm has spent to repurchase its own shares up to the date of the **balance sheet**.

Trust/trustee (11) A third party (usually a financial institution) that ensures that the issuer of a **bond** meets all the conditions and **provisions** reported in the bond's **indenture**.

Turnover (4) same as **net sales**.

TV (14) *See* **terminal value**.

Unavoidable costs (9) Costs incurred regardless of whether the investment is undertaken. Same as **irrelevant costs** or **sunk costs**.

Underlying asset (product) (16) The asset (product) on which an **option price** is set.

Undervaluation hypothesis (14) **Takeover** rationale according to which the acquiring company has superior skills in finding undervalued target firms that can be bought cheaply.

Underwriter (11) **Investment bank** that buys the **securities** a firm wants to issue and then resells them to the public at a higher price.

Underwriting syndicate (11) A group of **investment banks** jointly **underwriting** an issue.

Undiversifiable risk (3, 12) **Risk** that cannot be eliminated through portfolio diversification. *See* **systematic risk** and **market risk**.

Unlevered asset value (14) The estimated value of assets assuming they are financed only with **equity capital**. *See* **adjusted present value**.

Unlevered beta (12, 13, 14) *Same as* asset beta.

Unlevered cost of equity (14) The cost of **equity** of an all-equity financed firm. Can be estimated with the **capital asset pricing model** using the firm's **unlevered beta**.

Unlevered firm (6) A firm without borrowed funds. Same as an **all-equity-financed firm**.

Unlisted securities (11) **Securities** of firms that do not meet the listing requirements of **organized exchanges**.

Unsecured bond/debt/loan (11, 14) Bond/debt/loan supported only by the general credit standing of the issuing firm.

Unsystematic risk (3, 12) Risk that can be eliminated through portfolio diversification. Same as **diversifiable risk** and **firm-specific risk**.

US GAAP (4) *See* **Generally Accepted Accounting Principles**

Useful life (7, 9) *See* **economic life**.

Valuation by comparables (10, 14) A valuation method that uses financial data for firms similar to the business or firm to be valued to estimate the market value of its **equity** or its **enterprise value**. For example, the estimated equity value of a firm is equal to its **earnings after tax (EAT)** multiplied by the **earnings multiple** (or **price-to-earnings [P/E] ratio**) of the comparable firm.

Value-based management (system) (1, 18) Managing a firm's resources with the goal of increasing the firm's market value.

Variability (of returns) (3) Same as the **variance of returns**.

Variable rate bond (11) A **bond** with a **coupon rate** that takes different (known) values during the **bond's** life.

Variance (of returns) (3) A statistical measure of the dispersion of a distribution of returns around their average value. A measure of risk also called **variability**. *See* **standard deviation**.

Venture capital firm (11, 14) An investment firm specializing in the financing of small and new ventures.

Vertical merger (14) For example, the integration of a car manufacturer with its major supplier or its major distributor.

Volatility (of an asset) (3, 12) Unpredictable fluctuations in the market price of an asset. Same as the **standard deviation of return**.

Volatility (of returns) (3) Same as the **standard deviation of returns**.

WACC (1, 10, 12, 14, 18) *See* **weighted average cost of capital**.

Wages payable (4) The amount of wages owed and not yet paid at the date of the **balance sheet**.

Warrants (11, 16) **Call options** sold by a firm that give the holder the right (with no obligation) to buy a specific number of the firm's shares of **common stock** at a fixed price during the life of the **warrant**. *See* **contingent value rights**.

WCR (1, 4, 5) *See* **working capital requirement**.

Weighted average cost of capital (WACC) (1, 10, 12, 14, 18) The weighted average of the after-tax **cost of debt** and **cost of equity**. The minimum rate of return a project must generate in order to meet the return expectations of its suppliers of **capital** (lenders and **shareholders**). *See* equation 10.14 and **hurdle rate**.

With/without principle (9) States that the **cash flows** that are relevant to an investment decision are only those that increase or decrease the firm's overall cash position if the investment is undertaken.

Working capital requirement (WCR) (1, 4, 5) The difference between **operating assets** (trade receivables, inventories, and prepaid expenses) and **operating liabilities** (trade payables and accrued expenses). WCR measures the firm's net investment in its **operating cycle**.

Work in process inventory (4) The cost of the raw materials that were used in the production of unfinished units plus labor costs and other costs allocated to these units.

Writer (of an option) (16) The party who sells the underlying **asset** in an **option contract**. Same as the seller of an **option**.

Yankee bonds (11) **Bonds** issued by foreign firms in the United States, denominated in US dollars or other currencies.

Yield curve (10) A graphical representation of the **term structure of interest rates**.

Yield spread (10) The difference between the **market yield** on a non- government bond and the yield on a government bond with

the same **maturity** and currency denomination. *See* **credit spread**.

Yield to maturity (10, 12) The rate that makes the **bond** price equal to the present value of the **bond's** future cash-flow stream. Same as **market yield**.

Zero (10) *See* **zero-coupon bond**.

Zero-coupon bond (10) A **bond** with no **coupon payments** that is sold at an original discount from face value. *See* equation 10.4.

CREDITS

Any items not listed below are author created.

Ch.	Exhibit number	Sourceline
4	4.11	References:
		John Gorham, 'The wrecking of Singer', *Forbes* (Nov 15, 1999, accessed online)
		Patricia Best, 'James Ting, boy wonder, finally has his day in court,' *The Globe and Mail* (May 12, 2005, updated April 22, 2018, accessed online)
		Michael Rothfeld and Brad Reagan, 'A Maze of Paper: SEC Judgment Against Raider Paul Bilzerian: $62 Million. Collected: $3.7 Million,' *Wall Street Journal* (accessed online at https://www.wsj.com/articles/for-decades-ex-corporate-raider-holds-off-sec-effort-to-collect-62-million-judgment-1410892550)
		Alison Leigh Cowan, 'How Bilzerian Scored at Singer,' *The New York Times* (Aug 24 1988, accessed online)
		Reed Abelsons, 'How to Spot the Seams at Singer Co,. ,*The New York Times* (May 15 1995)
5	5.6	Source: Calculated by the authors using Compustat data.
5	5.8	References:
		"Raiding a Company's Hidden Cash" by Shawn Tully and Robert A. Miller from Fortune, August 22, 1994.
		https://www.encyclopedia.com/social-sciences-and-law/economics-business-and-labor/businesses-and-occupations/campbell-soup-company
6	6.6	1. From a sample of 316 global industrial products and automotive companies.
6	6.8	Compiled by the authors with accounting data from the firms' annual reports
8	8.1	Multiple footnotes, all fair use
		1. Brounen, D., De Jong, A. and Koedijk, K., "Corporate finance in Europe: Confronting theory with practice", *Financial Management*, Vol. 33 (4), No.4, 2004.
		2. Fredrik Hartwig, "The use of capital budgeting and cost of capital estimation methods in Swedish-listed companies", *The Journal of Applied Business Research*, Volume 28, No.6, 2012.
		3. Graham, J.R. and Harvey, C.R. (2001), "The theory and practice of corporate finance: Evidence from the field", *Journal of Financial Economics*, Vol. 60 (2–3), pp. 187–243.
10	10.4	Source: Federal Reserve Bank (www.federalreserve.gov) and Federal Reserve Bank of St. Louis (www.stlouisfed.org).

12	12.3	Source: Datastream April 2018.
12	12.4	Credit Suisse Global Investment Returns Sourcebook 2018.
13	13.1	Source: Computed by the authors using data from *Compustat* North America.
13	13.18	Source: FRED Economic Data, Federal Reserve Bank of St Louis.
13	13.19	Source: Graham, John R., and Campbell R. Harvey. "How do CFOs make capital budgeting and capital structure decisions?" *The Journal of Applied Corporate Finance* 14, No. 4 (2002).
17	17.8	Source: *The Wall Street Journal*, Market data, The key Currency Cross Rates, April 6, 2018.

Some Useful Formulas

11. **Working capital requirement (Chapter 4, equation 4.7)**

$$\text{WCR} = [\text{Accounts receivable} + \text{Inventories} + \text{Prepaid expenses}]$$
$$- [\text{Accounts payable} + \text{Net accruals}]$$

12. **Earnings before interest, tax, depreciation, and amortization (Chapter 4, equation 4.10)**

$$\text{EBITDA} = \text{EBIT} + \text{Depreciation expense} + \text{Amortization expense}$$

13. **Free cash flow (Chapter 4, equation 4.15)**

$$\text{FCF} = \text{EBIT}(1 - T_c) + \text{Depreciation expense}$$
$$- \Delta\text{WCR} - \text{Capital expenditures (net of disposals)}$$

14. **Return on equity (Chapter 6, equation 6.1)**

$$\text{ROE} = \frac{\text{Earnings after tax}}{\text{Owners' equity}}$$

15. **Return on invested capital before tax (Chapter 6, equation 6.4)**

$$\text{ROIC}_{BT} = \frac{\text{EBIT}}{\text{Invested capital}} = \frac{\text{EBIT}}{\text{Sales}} \times \frac{\text{Sales}}{\text{Invested capital}}$$

16. **The structure of a firm's return on equity (Chapter 6, equation 6.9)**

$$\text{ROE} = \frac{\text{EBIT}}{\text{Sales}} \times \frac{\text{Sales}}{\text{Invested capital}} \times \frac{\text{EBT}}{\text{EBIT}} \times \frac{\text{Invested capital}}{\text{Owners' equity}} \times \frac{\text{EAT}}{\text{EBT}}$$

17. **Self-sustainable growth rate (Chapter 6, equation 6.12)**

$$\text{SGR} = \text{Profit retention rate} \times \text{Return on equity}$$

18. **Net present value (Chapter 7)**

$$\text{NPV}(k,T) = -\text{CF}_0 + \frac{\text{CF}_1}{(1+k)^1} + \frac{\text{CF}_2}{(1+k)^2} + \dots + \frac{\text{CF}_t}{(1+k)^t} + \dots + \frac{\text{CF}_T}{(1+k)^T}$$
$$= -\text{CF}_0 + \sum_{t=1}^{T} \frac{\text{CF}_t}{(1+k)^t}$$

19. **Bond price (Chapter 10, equation 10.2)**

$$P = \frac{\text{CP}_1}{(1+y)} + \frac{\text{CP}_2}{(1+y)^2} + \dots + \frac{\text{CP}_T + F}{(1+y)^T}$$

20. **Share price (Chapter 10, equation 10.9)**

$$P = \frac{\text{DPS}_1}{(1+k_E)} + \frac{\text{DPS}_2}{(1+k_E)^2} + \dots + \frac{\text{DPS}_t}{(1+k_E)^t} + \dots$$

21. **Constant dividend growth model (Chapter 10, equation 10.10)**

$$P = \frac{\text{DPS}_1}{k_E - g}$$